Criminal Law

First published 1965
Reprinted 1966, 1967
Second edition 1969
Third edition 1973
Reprinted 1974, 1976, 1977
Fourth edition 1978
Reprinted 1979, 1982
Fifth edition 1983
Reprinted 1984
Reprinted 1986
Sixth edition 1988

Criminal Law

by J C Smith CBE, QC, LLD, FBA
of Lincoln's Inn, Honorary Bencher,
Honorary Fellow of Downing College,
Cambridge,
Emeritus Professor of Law,
University of Nottingham

and Brian Hogan LLB
of Gray's Inn, Barrister
Professor of Common Law and Head of Department of Law,
University of Leeds

Sixth Edition

London, Edinburgh
BUTTERWORTHS
1988

United Kingdom	Butterworth & Co (Publishers) Ltd, 88 Kingsway, LONDON WC2B 6AB and 61A North Castle Street, EDINBURGH EH2 3LJ
Australia	Butterworths Pty Ltd, SYDNEY, MELBOURNE, BRISBANE, ADELAIDE, PERTH, CANBERRA and HOBART
Canada	Butterworths. A division of Reed Inc., TORONTO and VANCOUVER
New Zealand	Butterworths of New Zealand Ltd, WELLINGTON and AUCKLAND
Singapore	Butterworth & Co (Asia) Pte Ltd, SINGAPORE
USA	Butterworths Legal Publishers, ST PAUL, Minnesota, SEATTLE, Washington, BOSTON, Massachusetts, AUSTIN, Texas and D & S Publishers, CLEARWATER, Florida

British Library Cataloguing in Publication Data

Smith, J. C. (John Cyril)
 Criminal law.—6th ed.
 1. England. Criminal law
 I. Title   II. Hogan, Brian, *1932*–
344.205

 ISBN Hardcover 0 406 65811 0
 ISBN Softcover 0 406 65812 9

Printed and bound in Great Britain by Mackays of Chatham Ltd, Kent
Typeset by Latimer Trend & Company Ltd, Plymouth

Preface to the Sixth Edition

Many important changes in the criminal law, including some of its basic concepts, have taken place since our fifth edition. The meaning of "intention" in the criminal law, which Lord Diplock thought to be "well-settled" in 1979 (*Whitehouse v Lemon* [1979] AC 617 at 638), has (if his Lordship was right) changed significantly as a result of *Maloney* [1985] AC 905 and *Hancock and Shankland* [1986] AC 455. But it is doubtful if, even now, it is well-settled. The leading case on murder, *Hyam v DPP* [1975] AC 55, has been silently overruled. Speculation continues as to the limits of recklessness after *Caldwell* and *Lawrence* [1982] AC 341 and 510. When we last wrote it appeared settled that duress could be a defence for an alleged secondary party to murder (*DPP for Northern Ireland v Lynch* [1975] AC 653) but that is no longer so (*Howe* [1987] AC 417). In conspiracy, since our last edition, *Ayres* [1984] AC 447 has come and, through the Criminal Justice Act 1987, gone. The law of impossibility in attempts to commit crime revealed a most remarkable judicial readiness to correct what was now perceived to be a recent error when *Shivpuri* [1987] AC 1 overruled *Anderton v Ryan* [1985] AC 560.

Opinions will naturally differ as to whether these developments are good or bad, but few, if any, will mourn *DPP v Smith* [1961] AC 290 which has surely been relegated to legal history by the Privy Council in *Frankland v R* [1987] AC 576. The Privy Council will also have cheered all "subjectivists" by its decision in *Beckford v R* [1988] AC 130, recognising the general significance of *Morgan v DPP* [1976] AC 182 and giving its blessing to one of the most important decisions of recent years, *Williams (Gladstone)* (1983) 78 Cr App Rep 276, where the Court of Appeal boldly ignored a long line of dicta to hold that a person acting in self-defence or the prevention of crime is to be judged on the facts as he believes them to be.

These and other developments in the law and the literature have required the substantial re-writing of the sections dealing with omissions, intention, recklessness, large parts of the law of accomplices, duress and conspiracy. Self-defence and the prevention of crime, heavily revised, now has a more logical place in general defences. We have brought together the principles governing impossibility in incitement, conspiracy and attempt in a new section. The problems of the mens rea of murder have become virtually synonymous with those of the meaning of intention, enabling the chapter on homicide to be somewhat shortened in this respect. Manslaughter by recklessness or gross negligence is in a state of greater flux than ever, following *Seymour* [1983] 2 AC 493 and *Kong Cheuk Kwan v R* (1985) 82 Cr App Rep 18, and the revised account of the law reflects this. In the law of theft, we took account at a late stage in the preparation of the fifth edition of the decision of the Court of Appeal in the important case of *Morris* and the significant modifications made to that decision by the House of Lords, [1984] AC 320, have now been incorporated. Since then, the law of theft and of criminal damage seems to have settled down and there have been no decisions on matter of basic principle of comparable importance. There has, however, been a steady stream of case law on matters of detail and this has been incorporated. Like murder, the law of forgery has seen an example of silent overruling (by *More* [1987] 3 All ER 825 of *Hassard* [1970] 2 All ER 647 and *Donnelly* (1984) 79 Cr App Rep 76), setting the law back on its true course. Otherwise, the Forgery and Counterfeiting Act 1981, to judge by the law reports, has presented few problems and our analysis of its provisions is substantially unaltered.

The most important statutory development has been the Public Order Act 1986 and we have incorporated a concise account of the offences created by that Act in the chapter on Offences against Public Order. No attempt could be made within the confines of this book to compete with the detailed analysis of the provisions to be found in the excellent monographs which have been published on that Act. Account has also been taken of the Child Abduction Act 1984, the Sexual Offences Act 1985 and those provisions of the Police and Criminal Evidence Act 1984 (universally known as "PACE") which have an impact on the substantive law.

Once again our warm thanks are due to Michael Gunn for his careful proofreading and his many perceptive and well-informed comments on matters of substance. We would like to thank all those who have written to us over the past five years with comments and criticisms. These have all been carefully considered and, where we thought appropriate, acted on. Our publishers have been as tolerant and helpful as ever.

We have endeavoured to state the law as at February 1, 1988, but reference is made to a few later decisions of the courts.

J. C. SMITH

BRIAN HOGAN

The scale of fines for summary offences
The "statutory maximum"

	Amount of fine
The statutory maximum fine on summary conviction of an offence triable either way, being the sum prescribed under the Magistrates' Courts Act 1980, s.32:	£2,000

The standard scale

The standard scale of maximum fines on an adult on conviction of a summary offence, being the sum prescribed under the Criminal Justice Act 1982, s.37:

Level on the scale	Amount of fine
1	£50
2	£100
3	£400
4	£1,000
5	£2,000

Where there is a change in the value of money, the Secretary of State is empowered by s.48 of the Criminal Justice Act 1982 to vary the maximum amount of fines, including the amounts specified in the standard scale, as appears to him to be justified by the change.

Preface to the First Edition

It is thought that university teachers and undergraduates will require no explanation or apology for the production of a new text-book on the substantive law of crime. Criminal Law has not received the same detailed and critical examination in university text-books as have other fields of the common law, for example, Contract and Tort. In the university law schools Kenny's *Outlines of Criminal Law* has long held almost unchallenged sway but it is now sixty-three years since the first edition of that classic work appeared. An immense amount of work has been done on the Criminal Law in the meantime, not least by the present learned editor of Kenny, Dr. J. W. C. Turner. There may now be something to be said for a book which makes a completely fresh start. Cross and Jones's *Introduction to Criminal Law*, on the other hand, may be thought too brief for the needs of the undergraduate—though we are full of admiration for the amount of information and learning which those authors have packed into so small a space. Moreover, both of these books deal in a single volume not only with the substantive law but also with Criminal Procedure and Evidence. Dr. Glanville Williams's great work, *Criminal Law: The General Part*, covers only general principles, while other books covering the whole field do not face up to the problems with which the undergraduate is expected to grapple.

We have endeavoured to provide the undergraduate with as complete an exposition of the substantive Criminal Law as he has to guide him in other fields of study. We have excluded Procedure and Evidence from consideration except in so far as these are necessary for an understanding of the law. Only by so doing could we give our subject the kind of treatment we think it demands. Moreover, Evidence is now commonly regarded as a worthy subject of academic study in its own right; and Criminal Procedure is by no means always part of a Criminal Law course.

All the important crimes are examined. Few courses, in or out of universities, perhaps cover so much ground; but the book allows scope for selection. In making the book reasonably comprehensive, we have not been unmindful of the fact that the practitioner commonly, and increasingly, finds assistance in the solution of problems in books designed primarily for students; and the citation of authorities is, therefore, more extensive than the needs of the undergraduate alone would have required. We have drawn freely on the published researches of scholars in the Criminal Law, not only in Britain but also in the Commonwealth and United States. In particular, we would acknowledge our debt, which will be apparent in almost every chapter, to the writings of Dr. Glanville Williams.

We have derived great assistance from many discussions with our colleagues and students at Nottingham and elsewhere; and our thanks are particularly due to Mr. P. R. H. Webb who read the whole of the manuscript. Tribute is also due to the helpfulness and, particularly, the patience of our publishers who waited a long time, without complaint, for the manuscript. Even their tolerance, however, is hardly in the same class as that of our wives, particularly throughout a recent long vacation during which we almost lived in the law library.

The book began as the work of only the first-named author, but the task proved greater than expected and a large proportion of the text has been contributed by the second. It has been revised in common and we each accept responsibility for the whole. We have endeavoured to state the law as at April 30, 1965.

J C SMITH

BRIAN HOGAN

Contents

Preface to Sixth Edition   iii

Preface to First Edition   vii

Abbreviations   xxvii

Table of Statutes   xxxi

Table of Cases   xliii

PART I.   GENERAL PRINCIPLES

Chapter 1   Crime and Sentence   3

1 RETRIBUTION AND MORAL BLAMEWORTHINESS   4

2 RETRIBUTION AND THE HARM DONE   8

3 THE SENTENCE TO FIT THE CRIME   10

4 JUSTICE AND EQUALITY   11

5 THE PROTECTION OF THE PUBLIC   12

6 THE REFORM OF THE OFFENDER   15

Chapter 2   The Definition of a Crime   17

1 CHARACTERISTICS OF A CRIME   18
1 *A public wrong*   18
2 *A moral wrong*   19

2 CRIMINAL PROCEEDINGS   20

3 THE PRACTICAL TEST   22

Chapter 3   The Classification of Offences   25

1 TREASONS, FELONIES AND MISDEMEANOURS: ARRESTABLE OFFENCES   25

2 INDICTABLE AND SUMMARY OFFENCES   27
1 *Offences triable summarily only*   28
2 *Offences triable only on indictment*   28
3 *Offences triable either way*   28

Chapter 4   The Elements of a Crime   31

1 THE ACTUS REUS   33
1 *The nature of an actus reus*   33
2 *An actus reus must be proved*   36
3 *Analysis of an actus reus*   39
4 *The conduct must be willed*   39
5 *Causation*   45
6 *A "state of affairs" as an actus reus*   46
7 *Omissions*   48

2 MENS REA   55
1 *Definition of terms*   55
   a) Intention   55
   b) Recklessness   61
   c) Negligence   68
   d) Blameless inadvertence   69
2 *Basic mens rea*   70
3 *The requirement of an ulterior intent*   70
4 *The extent to which mens rea is required varies from crime to crime*   71
5 *Transferred malice*   73
6 *Coincidence of actus reus and mens rea*   76
7 *Motive usually does not affect liability*   78
8 *Ignorance of the law is no defence*   80
9 *Mistake of law may negative mens rea*   83
10 *Absence of a "claim of right" as an element in mens rea*   84
11 *Proof of intention and foresight*   85
   Morgan and defences   87

Chapter 5   Crimes of Negligence   91

1 NEGLIGENCE AS FAILURE TO COMPLY WITH AN OBJECTIVE STANDARD   91

2 NEGLIGENCE AS THE BASIS OF LIABILITY   92

3 DEGREES OF NEGLIGENCE   94

4 SHOULD NEGLIGENCE BE A GROUND OF LIABILITY?   94

Chapter 6   Crimes of Strict Liability   98

1 THE POSITION AT COMMON LAW AND BY STATUTE   98

2 RECOGNITION OF OFFENCES OF STRICT LIABILITY   102
1 *The offence in its statutory context*   103
2 *The offence in its social context*   104
   a) Inflation   106
   b) Dangerous drugs   106
   c) Pollution   110
3 *The severity of the punishment*   111

3 LIABILITY IS STRICT, NOT "ABSOLUTE"   111

4 ARGUMENTS FOR AND AGAINST STRICT LIABILITY   112

5 STATUTORY DEFENCES   117

6 PROPOSALS FOR REFORM   119

Chapter 7   The Effect of Particular Words   120

1 *Knowingly*   120
2 *Maliciously*   122
3 *Wilfully*   122
4 *"Permitting", "suffering", or "allowing"*   124
5 *Causing*   126
6 *Fraudulently*   127
7 *Corruptly*   128
8 *Possession*   128

Chapter 8   Modes of Participation in Crime   130

1 ACCOMPLICES   130
1 *The principal*   131
2 *Secondary participation*   133
3 *Secondary parties: causation and consensus*   134
4 *The time factor*   135
5 *Presence at the crime*   136
6 *Participation by inactivity*   137
7 *Mens rea*   138
      i) Intention to aid etc   138
      ii) Knowledge of circumstances   142
      iii) Knowledge of type of crime   143
      iv) Liability of secondary party for unforeseen consequences   148
8 *Secondary participation and inchoate offences*   150
9 *Conviction of secondary party and acquittal of principal*
   offender   151
10 *Conviction of secondary party where there is no principal*   152
11 *Withdrawal by secondary party*   156
12 *Victims as parties to crime*   158
13 *Instigation for the purpose of entrapment*   160

2 VICARIOUS LIABILITY   162
1 *Strict liability and vicarious liability distinguished*   163
2 *The delegation principle*   164
3 *Where the servant's act is his master's act in law*   167
4 *Mode of participation of master and servant*   168
5 *No vicarious liability for abetting or attempting crimes*   169
6 *The special position of corporations*   170

Chapter 9   General Defences   177

1 INFANCY   178
1 *Children under ten years*   178

2 *Children over ten and under fourteen years* 179
3 *Persons over fourteen years* 181

2 INSANITY 182
1 *Insanity before the trial* 182
2 *Insanity at the trial* 185
   i) Disease of the mind 186
   ii) Disease of the mind in combination with other factors 190
   iii) Defect of reason 191
   iv) The nature and quality of his act 192
   v) Knowledge that the act is wrong 192
   vi) Insane delusions 194
   vii) Irresistible impulse 195
   viii) Burden of proof 195
   ix) The special verdict of insanity and the right of appeal 197
   x) Function of the jury 197
   xi) Proposals for reform 198

3 DIMINISHED RESPONSIBILITY 201
1 *Nature of the defence* 203
2 *The effect of the introduction of diminished responsibility* 205
3 *Hospital orders* 206

4 MISTAKE 207

5 INTOXICATION 209
1 *Intoxication by alcohol and "dangerous" drugs* 210
   i) Intoxication and "specific intention" 211
   ii) Majewski and defences 215
2 *Intoxication otherwise than by alcohol or dangerous drugs* 216
3 *Intoxication causing insanity or abnormality of mind* 217
4 *Involuntary intoxication* 218
5 *Intoxication induced with the intention of committing crime* 219
6 *Alternatives to Majewski* 220

6 NECESSITY 222

7 DURESS (OR COMPULSION) AND COERCION 229
1 *Duress* 230
   Duress and voluntariness 230
   The facts and the standard—objective or subjective 235
   Duress by an association voluntarily joined 237
2 *Coercion* 238

8 PUBLIC AND PRIVATE DEFENCE 240
   Force used in the course of preventing crime or arresting offenders 242
   Use of force, excessive in the known circumstances 247

9 SUPERIOR ORDERS 249

10 IMPOSSIBILITY 250

11 NON-COMPLIANCE WITH COMMUNITY LAW 251

Chapter 10 Incitement, Conspiracy and Attempt 252

1 INCITEMENT 252
1 *The crime incited* 254
  i) *Offences generally* 254
  ii) *Other inchoate offences* 254
  iii) *Counselling and abetting* 255

2 *Mens rea* 255

2 CONSPIRACY 256
1) Common law and statutory conspiracies 257
2) The mens rea of conspiracy 258
1 *Statutory conspiracies* 258
  i) *Intention to carry out the agreement* 259
  ii) *Intention to play some part in carrying out the agreement* 260
  iii) *The meaning of course of conduct* 260
  iv) *Conspiracy to commit strict liability offences* 262
  v) *Existence of circumstances not known, intended or believed in* 263
  vi) *Unforeseen but inevitable consequences* 264
  vii) *Where only one party has mens rea* 264
  viii) *Agreement to do acts of secondary participation* 265
2 *Conditional intention* 266
  i) *Statutory conspiracies* 266
  ii) *Common law conspiracies* 267
3 *The object of the conspiracy* 267
  a) Statutory conspiracies 267
  i) *Agreement in England to commit an offence abroad* 268
  ii) *Agreement abroad to commit an offence in England* 269
  iii) *Agreement abroad to commit an offence abroad* 269
  b) Common law conspiracies 269
  i) *Conspiracy to defraud* 269
  ii) *Conspiracy to corrupt public morals* 276
  iii) *Conspiracy to outrage public decency* 277
3) The actus reus of conspiracy 278
  1) *The agreement* 278
  2) *Proof of the agreement* 279
  3) *Conspiracy where the contemplated offence is committed* 280
  4) *Two or more parties* 281
  5) *Acquittal of the other alleged conspirators* 284
4) Sentence 285
5) Powers of arrest 285
6) Periods of limitation 286
7) Rationale of conspiracy 286

3 ATTEMPT 287
1 *Mens rea in attempts* 287
2 *Actus reus in attempt* 291
3 *Attempt by omission* 296

4 *Successful attempts* 296
5 *Offences which may be attempted* 297
   a) Attempt in England to commit an offence abroad 298
   b) Attempt abroad to commit an offence in England 299
   c) Attempt abroad to commit an offence abroad 299
6 *Withdrawal* 299

4 IMPOSSIBILITY 300

PART II.   PARTICULAR CRIMES

Chapter 11   Homicide   309

1 MURDER 309
1) Who can commit murder 309
2) Where murder can be committed 309
3) Who can be the victim 310
4) Death within a year and a day 312
5) The problem of causation 312
  1 A question of fact and law 313
  2 The "But For" principle 314
  3 Contributory causes 314
  4 A substantial cause 316
  5 Intervening acts or events 316
  6 Death caused by medical treatment of an injury 321
  7 The effect of neglect by the injured person 324
  8 Intended consequences 324
  9 Special instances of causation 325
    i) Killing by mental suffering or shock 325
    ii) Killing by frightening P into taking his own life 326
    iii) Killing by perjury 327
6) The mens rea of murder 327
7) The sentence for murder 330
8) Proposals for reform 330

2 MANSLAUGHTER 331
1) Voluntary and involuntary 331
2) Provocation 331
  1 Provocation by things done or said 332
  2 Provocation and third parties 333
    i) By whom the provocation may be given 333
    ii) Acts directed against third parties 334
  3 The subjective condition 334
  4 The objective condition 336
  5 The relationship between the provocation and the mode of resentment 340
  6 Provocation arising from a mistake of fact 342
  7 Self-induced provocation 343
  8 Provocation by a lawful act 344
3) Involuntary manslaughter 344

1 Intention to do an unlawful and dangerous act   345
  Constructive manslaughter   345
  i) The unlawful act   347
  ii) Unlawfulness arising otherwise than through negligence   349
  iii) Likely to cause harm   350
  iv) Causing harm "directly"   351
2 Reckless manslaughter   352

3 OFFENCES ANCILLARY TO MURDER   355
1) Solicitation   355
2) Threats to kill   356
3) Concealment of birth   357
4) Other offences   358

4 COMPLICITY IN SUICIDE AND SUICIDE PACTS   358
1) Complicity in another's suicide   359
2) Suicide pacts   360

5 INFANTICIDE   361

6 CHILD DESTRUCTION AND ABORTION   363
1) Child destruction   363
2) Attempting to procure miscarriage   366
3) Knowingly supplying or procuring poison, etc.   368
4) The Abortion Act 1967   369

7 GENOCIDE   374

Chapter 12   Non-Fatal Offences Against the Person   375

1 ASSAULT AND BATTERY   375
1) Elements of assault   376
  1 Actus reus   376
  2 Mens rea   379
  3 Attempt to assault   379
2) Battery   379
  1 Actus reus   379
  2 Mens rea   381
3) Defences to assault and battery   382
  1 Consent   382
    i) Effect of consent   382
    ii) Limitations on consent   383
  2 Lawful correction   386

2 AGGRAVATED ASSAULTS   387
1) Assault on, resistance to, or obstruction of constables   387
  1 A constable acting in the execution of his duty   388
  2 Mens rea in cases of assault and resistance   391
  3 Wilful obstruction   392
    i) The meaning of obstruction   392
    ii) Mens rea   395
2) Assault occasioning actual bodily harm   396

3 WOUNDING AND GRIEVOUS BODILY HARM   397
1) The actus reus   397
   1 To wound   397
   2 To cause or inflict grievous bodily harm   398
2) The mens rea   400
   1 Malice   400
   2 The ulterior intent   402

4 ADMINISTERING POISON   403
1) The actus reus   403
2) The mens rea   404

5 FALSE IMPRISONMENT   405
1) The actus reus   406
   1 Imprisonment   406
   2 Unlawful restraint   409
2) Mens rea   412
3) Kidnapping   413
4) Taking of hostages   414
5) Abduction of children   415

6 FIREARMS AND OFFENSIVE WEAPONS   416
1) The Firearms Act 1968   416
   1 Prohibited weapons   417
   2 Use of firearms or imitation firearms to resist arrest: and possession of them in relation to certain offences   418
   3 Possessing firearms with intent   420
   4 Carrying and trespassing with firearms   421
2) The Prevention of Crime Act 1953   422
   1 Offensive weapons   422
   2 Lawful authority or reasonable excuse   425
   3 A public place   426
   4 Mens rea   427
3) The Customs and Excise Management Act 1979   427
4) The Night Poaching Act 1828   427
5) Bomb hoaxes: Criminal Law Act 1977   427

Chapter 13   Sexual Offences   429

1 RAPE   429
   1 The actus reus   430
      i) Unlawful sexual intercourse   430
      ii) Sexual intercourse   432
      iii) The absence of consent   433
      iv) Fundamental mistake not arising from fraud   436
   2 The mens rea   437
   3 Boys under fourteen; and women   438

2 OTHER OFFENCES INVOLVING SEXUAL INTERCOURSE   438
   1 Procurement of women by threats or by false pretences   439
   2 Administering drugs to obtain or facilitate intercourse   440

3 *Intercourse with a girl under thirteen* 441
4 *Intercourse with a girl under sixteen* 441
5 *Procuration of girl under twenty-one* 442
6 *Intercourse with a defective* 442
7 *Procurement of a defective* 443
8 *Sexual intercourse with mentally disordered patients* 444
9 *Permitting use of premises for intercourse* 444
10 *Incest* 445

3 INDECENT ASSAULT AND INDECENCY WITH CHILDREN 446
1 *The requirement of an assault* 448
2 *Circumstances of indecency* 449
3 *Assaults by women* 451

4 ABDUCTION OF WOMEN 452
1 *Classification of abduction offences* 452
    i) *Girls under sixteen* 452
    ii) *Girls under eighteen* 453
    iii) *Defective women of any age* 453
    iv) *Abduction of woman by force or for the sake of her
        property* 453
2 *The "taking"* 453
3 *The mens rea* 454

5 OFFENCES RELATING TO PROSTITUTION 455
1 *Causing or encouraging women to become prostitutes* 456
2 *The use of premises for prostitution* 457
    i) *Brothel keeping* 457
    ii) *Tenant permitting premises to be used for prostitution* 459
3 *A man living on the earnings of prostitution* 460
4 *A woman exercising control over a prostitute* 464
5 *Loitering or soliciting in public places* 464
    i) *Common prostitute* 465
    ii) *Loiter* 465
    iii) *Solicit* 466
    iv) *In a street or public place* 466
6 *Soliciting of women by men* 467

6 INDECENT EXPOSURE 468
1 *Indecent exposure at common law* 468
    i) *The actus reus* 468
    ii) *The mens rea* 469
2 *Indecent exposure under the Vagrancy Act 1824* 470

7 UNNATURAL OFFENCES 471
1 *Buggery* 471
2 *Procuring others to commit lawful homosexual acts* 473
3 *Assault with intent to commit buggery; and attempts* 473
4 *Indecency between men* 474
5 *Penalties for buggery and gross indecency* 475
6 *Solicitation by men* 476

Chapter 14   Road Traffic Offences   478

1 CARELESS DRIVING   479

2 RECKLESS DRIVING   482

3 CAUSING DEATH BY RECKLESS DRIVING   485

Chapter 15   Theft and Related Offences   488

1 THEFT   490
1) The actus reus   491
  1 Appropriation   491
    a) Appropriation as an unauthorised act   491
    b) Appropriation by keeping and dealing   494
    c) Appropriation and the rights of an owner   495
    d) Appropriation and conversion   496
    e) Appropriation and possession   497
    f) Appropriation and consent   499
    g) Appropriation, consent and intimidation   502
    h) The exception in favour of bona fide purchasers   503
    i) Appropriation as a continuing act   504
  2 Property   504
    a) Limitations on the theft of land   506
    b) Limitations on the theft of things growing wild   507
    c) Limitations on the theft of wild creatures   508
  3 Belonging to another   509
    a) Property belonging to another: the general rule   510
    b) Trust property   513
    c) Property received for a particular purpose   513
    d) Property got by mistake   518
    e) Property of corporations   522
    f) Ownerless property   524
2) Mens rea   525
  1 Dishonesty   525
    a) Belief in legal right   526
    b) Belief in the other's consent   527
    c) Belief that property has been lost   527
    d) Other cases   527
  2 Intention permanently to deprive   532
    a) Disposal regardless of the other's right   534
    b) Conditional intention   536
    c) Borrowing or lending   537
    d) The thing   538
    e) Parting with property under a condition as to its return   538
    f) Deprivation of the owner's interest   539

2 ABSTRACTING ELECTRICITY   539

3 ROBBERY   540
  1 Use of threat of force in order to steal   541

2 On any person 542
3 Immediately before or at the time of stealing 542
4 Mens rea 543

4 OFFENCES INVOLVING DECEPTION 543
1) The deception 544
1 Deliberate or reckless deception 545
2 Words or conduct 545
3 Fact or law 547
4 Statements of intention 549
2) The obtaining 544
3) Dishonesty 555
4) Obtaining property by deception: section 15 557
1 Property belonging to another 557
2 Ownership, possession or control 557
3 Mens rea 558

5 OBTAINING A PECUNIARY ADVANTAGE BY DECEPTION: SECTION
16 558
1 Overdrafts and insurance policies 559
2 Opportunity to earn by employment or win by betting 560
3 Mens rea 558

6 OBTAINING SERVICES BY DECEPTION 561
1) Deception 561
2) Services 562
3) The benefit 563
4) The understanding 563
5) Payment 564
6) Dishonesty 564

7 EVASION OF LIABILITY BY DECEPTION 564
1) Securing remission of a liability 565
2) Inducing creditor to wait for or forgo payment 566
3) Obtaining an exemption from or an abatement of liability 567
4) Legally enforceable liability 568

8 CHEATING 568

9 MAKING OFF WITHOUT PAYMENT 569
1) Makes off 570
2) Goods supplied or service done 571
3) Unenforceable debts 572
4) Without having paid 573
5) Mens rea 573
1 Dishonestly 573
2 Knowing that payment on the spot is required or expected 573
3 Intention to avoid payment 574

10 FALSE ACCOUNTING AND OTHER FRAUDS 574
1) False accounting 574
1 Actus reus 575

    2 Mens rea 575
2) False statements by company directors 576
3) Suppression of documents 577

11 TEMPORARY DEPRIVATION 578
1) Removal of articles from places open to the public 578
    1 Actus reus 579
        a) Public access to a building in order to view 579
        b) Articles displayed or kept for display 580
        c) Removal 580
        d) Commercial exhibitions 580
    2 Mens rea 581
2) Taking conveyances 581
    1 Taking for own or another's use 582
    2 Without owner's consent or lawful authority 584
    3 Conveyance 586
    4 Driving or being carried 587
    5 Pedal cycles 587
    6 Mens rea 587

12 BLACKMAIL 588
    1 The demand 588
    2 Menaces 589
    3 Unwarranted demand 590
    4 View to gain or intent to cause loss 592
    5 Unlawful harassment of debtors 594

13 BURGLARY AND AGGRAVATED BURGLARY 595
1) Burglary 595
    1 The actus reus 595
        a) Enters 595
        b) As a trespasser 597
    2 Mens rea 607
        a) Intention to enter as a trespasser 607
        b) The ulterior offence 607
2) Aggravated burglary 609
    1 The articles of aggravation 609
    2 "At the time" of commission of burglary 610
    3 "Has with him" 610

14 POSSESSION OF ARTICLES FOR HOUSEBREAKING, ETC. 611
1) The actus reus 612
2) Mens rea 613

15 HANDLING STOLEN GOODS 615
1) The actus reus 615
    1 Stolen goods 615
        a) Things in action 615
        b) Land 616
        c) Meaning of "stolen" 616
        d) The "thief" must be guilty 617
    2 When goods cease to be stolen 617

3 Goods representing those originally stolen may be stolen goods 620
4 Forms of handling 621
  a) Receiving 621
  b) Arranging to receive 623
  c) Undertaking and assisting 623
  d) Arranging to undertake or assist 625
5 Otherwise than in the course of stealing 626
6 For the benefit of another person 629
7 Innocent receipt and subsequent retention with mens rea 630
8 Handling by the thief 631
9 Advertising for the return of stolen goods 631
2) The mens rea 632
  1 Knowledge or belief 632
  2 Dishonesty 635
  3 Proof of mens rea 635

16 MISCELLANEOUS MATTERS 636
1) Husband and wife 636
2) Corporations and their officers 637
3) Restitution 639
  i) Circumstances in which an order may be made 641
  ii) Contents of an order 641
  iii) Effect of an order 642
  iv) Police (Property) Act 1897 642
  v) Powers of Criminal Courts Act 1973, s. 35 644

Chapter 16   Forgery and Counterfeiting   645

1 FORGERY 645
1) The subject matter of forgery 646
2) The forgery 649
  1 Falsity in general 650
  2 Falsity and non-existing persons 652
  3 Falsity by omission 654
3) Mens rea: intent to prejudice 655
  1 Economic loss 656
  2 Performance of duty 657
  3 Claim or right 658
  4 Forgery and machines 661
  5 Causation 662
4) The offences 663
  1 Forgery 663
  2 Copying a false instrument 664
  3 Using false instruments and copies 664
  4 Possession offences 666

2 COUNTERFEITING 669
1) The meaning of counterfeiting 669
2) Mens rea 671
3) Passing and tendering 671

4) The offences   672
  1 Counterfeiting   672
  2 Passing counterfeit currency   672
  3 Possession of counterfeit currency   673
  4 Possession of counterfeiting implements   673
  5 Reproducing British currency   674
  6 Penalties   676
5) Codification   676

Chapter 17   Offences of Damage to Property   677

1 DESTROYING OR DAMAGING PROPERTY OF ANOTHER   677
1) Destroy or damage   677
2) Property   680
3) Belonging to another   681
4) Mens rea   683
  1 Intention and recklessness   683
  2 Lawful excuse   687
    a) Belief in consent   689
    b) Defence of property   689
    c) Cases not falling within the Act   693
    d) Self-defence and necessity   693
    e) Claim of right   695
    f) Other cases   695

2 DESTROYING OR DAMAGING PROPERTY WITH INTENT TO
  ENDANGER LIFE   696
  1 Intention and recklessness   698
  2 Lawful excuse   698

3 ARSON   699

4 THREATS TO DESTROY OR DAMAGE PROPERTY   700
  1 The conduct threatened   700
  2 The threat   701

5 POSSESSION OFFENCES   701
  1 Custody or control   702
  2 The things used   702
  3 Mens rea   703

6 KINDRED OFFENCES   703

7 MISCELLANEOUS MATTERS   704

Chapter 18   Offences Against Public Morals   705

1 BIGAMY   705
1) "Being married"   705
  1 Void and voidable marriages   707
  2 A polygamous first marriage   708
  3 Subsistence of the first marriage   708
2) The second ceremony   709
  1 Proviso (1): the place of the second marriage   710

2 *Proviso (2): continual absence for seven years* 711
3 *Proviso (3): divorce* 712
4 *Proviso (4): marriage declared void* 713
3) Mens rea 714
4) The rationale of bigamy 716

2 OTHER OFFENCES RELATING TO MARRIAGE 717
1) Offences relating to solemnisation of marriages 717
  1 *A marriage* 718
  2 *Knowingly and wilfully* 718
2) Offences relating to the registration of marriages 719

3 OBSCENE PUBLICATIONS 719
1) What is obscenity? 719
2) Offences 723
  1 *Publication* 724
  2 *Having an obscene article for publication for gain* 725
3) Defences 726
  1 *No reasonable cause to believe article obscene* 726
  2 *Public good* 727
4) Mens rea 729
  1 *At common law* 729
  2 *Under the Obscene Publications Act* 730
5) Forfeiture of obscene articles 732
6) The common law of obscene libel 733
7) What is an article? 734
8) Posting indecent or obscene matter 734
9) Obscenity in the theatre 736
10) Indecent displays 736
11) Other statutes 737

4 BLASPHEMY 737
1) Actus reus 737
2) Mens rea 738
3) Reform of the law 739

Chapter 19 Offences Relating to the Administration of Justice 740

1 PERJURY 740
  1 *Lawfully sworn as a witness* 740
  2 *A judicial proceeding* 742
  3 *"A statement material in that proceeding"* 743
  4 *The statement may be true* 746
  5 *The statement may be an opinion* 747
  6 *Mens rea* 748
  7 *Subornation of perjury* 748

2 OFFENCES AKIN TO PERJURY 749
  1 *Statements on oath not in judicial proceedings and false statements with reference to marriage* 749
  2 *False statements as to births or deaths* 750

  *3 False statutory declarations and other false statements without
  oath* 750
  *4 False declarations to obtain registration for carrying on a
  vocation* 751

3 PERVERTING THE COURSE OF JUSTICE   751
  1 The general offence 751
  2 Personating a juryman 756
  3 Disposal of corpse with intent to prevent an inquest 756
  4 Embracery 756
  5 Prison breaking, escape and rescue 756
  6 Wasteful employment of police 758

4 IMPEDING THE APPREHENSION OR PROSECUTION OF ARRESTABLE
  OFFENDERS 758
1) The actus reus   759
2) The mens rea   760
3) The sentence   763

5 COMPOUNDING AN ARRESTABLE OFFENCE   763
1) Actus reus   764
2) Mens rea   765

6 REFUSAL TO AID A CONSTABLE   767

7 CONTEMPT OF COURT   767
1) The actus reus of contempt   769
2) Contempt in court   770
3) Contempt out of court in relation to particular
   proceedings   772
   1 Unintentional interference 772
      a) The "strict liability" rule 772
      b) Innocent publication or distribution 775
      c) Further limitations on the strict liability rule 776
   2 Intentional interference 779
4) Acts tending to interfere with the course of justice in
   general   780
   1 Scandalising the court 780
   2 Intimidation of a juror or witness 781
   *3 Disclosure of information in breach of an undertaking to the
   court* 783
   *4 Publication of information relating to court sitting
   in private* 783
   5 Confidentiality of jury's deliberations 784
   6 Use of tape recorders 784
   7 Obstructing an officer of the court 784

Chapter 20   Offences Against Public Order   785

1 OFFENCES UNDER THE PUBLIC ORDER ACT 1986   785
1) Riot   786
   The Riot (Damages) Act 1886   788
2) Violent disorder   788

3) Affray   789
4) Fear or provocation of violence   790
5) Harassment, alarm or distress   791
6) Acts intended or likely to stir up racial hatred   792
7) Mens rea and proof of "threatening, abusive or insulting"   793

2 PUBLIC NUISANCE AND OBSTRUCTION OF THE HIGHWAY   794
1) Public nuisance   794
 1 *Nature of the nuisance*   794
 2 *The public*   796
 3 *Mens rea*   797
 4 *Vicarious liability*   798
2) Obstruction of the highway   798
 1 *By public nuisance*   798
 2 *Statutes relating to obstruction of the highway*   799

3 OFFENCES OF ENTERING AND REMAINING ON PROPERTY   801
1) Entering premises by violence   802
 1 *The entry*   802
 2 *Use or threat of violence*   803
 3 *The premises*   804
 4 *Presence of person opposed to entry*   804
 5 *Mens rea*   805
 6 *Without lawful authority*   806
 7 *The displaced residential occupier*   807
 8 *Other defences*   808
2) Adverse occupation of premises   809
 1 *Entry as a trespasser*   809
 2 *Requirement by displaced residential occupier or by protected intending occupier*   809
 3 *Defences*   810
3) Trespassing with a weapon of offence   811
4) Trespassing on foreign missions   811
5) Obstructing court officers etc.   812

4 CRIMINAL EVICTION AND HARASSMENT   813

5 PIRACY AND HIJACKING   815
1) Piracy   815
 1 *Piracy iure gentium*   815
   a) *The elements of piracy*   817
   b) *Mens rea*   819
 2 *Piracy by statute*   819
 3 *Punishment of piracy*   819
2) Hijacking and related offences   820
 1 *Hijacking*   821
 2 *Endangering the safety of aircraft*   821

6 LIBEL   822
1) Actus reus   822
2) Vicarious liability   825

3) Mens rea 825
4) Publication of libel known to be false 826

Chapter 21   Offences Against the Security of the State 827

1 TREASON 827
1 *Compassing the king's death* 827
2 *Levying war against the king in his realm* 828
3 *Being adherent to the king's enemies* 828
4 *Who may commit treason* 829
5 *Procedure in treason trials* 831

2 OFFENCES AKIN TO TREASON 832
1 *Under the Treason Felony Act 1848* 832
2 *Misprision of treason* 833
3 *Seditious words and libels* 833
   a) Real or presumed intention? 835
   b) Intention to cause violence 835
   c) Actus reus 836
   d) Sedition and freedom of speech 837
4 *Incitement to mutiny and disaffection* 837

3 OFFICIAL SECRETS 838
1 *Spying and sabotage* 838
   a) Scope of the section 839
   b) Mens rea 839
2 *Wrongful communication of information* 841
3 *False pretences to gain admission to prohibited places* 842
4 *Obstruction of guards in prohibited places* 842
5 *Acts preparatory, incitement and attempt* 842

4 OFFENCES CONNECTED WITH TERRORISM 842
1) Proscribed organisations 843
1 *Belonging or professing to belong* 844
2 *Solicits or invites* 844
3 *Support and contributions* 844
4 *Arranging meetings* 845
5 *Mens rea* 846
2) Displaying public support for proscribed organisations 846
3) Contributions to terrorism 847
1 *Actus reus* 847
2 *Mens rea* 848
4) Disclosing information about terrorism 848
1 *Actus reus* 849
2 *Mens rea* 849
3 *Reasonable excuse* 850
5) Exclusion orders 851
6) Arrest and detention 851
7) Suppression of terrorism, etc. 852

Index 853

Abbreviations

The following are the abbreviations used for the principal text-books and legal journals cited in this book. References are to the latest editions, as shown below, unless it is specifically stated otherwise. The particulars of other works referred to in the text are set out in the relevant footnotes.

Andenaes, GPCL	*The General Part of the Criminal Law of Norway* (1965) by Johannes Andenaes.
Archbold	*Criminal Pleading, Evidence and Practice*, by John Frederick Archbold 42nd ed (1985) by Stephen Mitchell, P J Richardson and J H Buzzard.
Blackstone, *Commentaries*, i	*Commentaries on the Laws of England*, by Sir William Blackstone, Vol i [4 vols] 17th ed (1830) by E Christian.
Burchell and Hunt, SACLP	*South African Criminal Law and Procedure*, Vol 1, *General Principles* (1983) by E M Burchell, J R L Milton and J M Burchell.
Butler	Report of the Committee on Mentally Abnormal Offenders, 1975, Cmnd 6244.
CLJ	Cambridge Law Journal.
Cal Law Rev	California Law Review.
Can Bar Rev	Canadian Bar Review.
Co 1 Inst	*Institutes of the Laws of England*, by Sir Edward Coke, Vol 1 [4 vols] (1797).
Col LR	Columbia Law Review.
Crime, Proof and Punishment	*Crime, Proof and Punishment*, Essays in honour of Sir Rupert Cross. Edited by C F H Tapper (1981).
Criminal Law Essays	Criminal Law: Essays in honour of J C Smith. Edited by P F Smith (1987).
Crim LR	Criminal Law Review.
CLP	Current Legal Problems.
CLRC/OAP/R	Criminal Law Revision Committee, Fourteenth Report, Offences against the Person, 1980, Cmnd 7844.

CLRC/OAP/WP	Criminal Law Revision Committee, Working Paper on Offences against the Person, 1976.
CLRC/SO/WP	Criminal Law Revision Committee, Working Paper on Sexual Offences, 1980.
East, 1 PC	*A Treatise of the Pleas of the Crown*, by Edward Hyde East, Vol 1 [2 vols] (1803).
Edwards, *Mens Rea*	*Mens Rea in Statutory Offences*, by J Ll J Edwards (1955).
Foster	*A Report on Crown Cases and Discourses on the Crown Law*, by Sir Michael Foster 3rd ed (1792) by M Dodson.
Gordon	*Criminal Law of Scotland* 2nd ed (1978) by G H Gordon.
Griew, *Theft*	*The Theft Acts 1968 and 1978* 5th ed (1986) by Edward Griew.
Hale, 1 PC	*The History of the Pleas of the Crown*, by Sir Matthew Hale, Vol 1 [2 vols] (1736).
Hall, *General Principles*	*General Principles of Criminal Law*, by Jerome Hall (2nd ed, 1960).
Halsbury	*The Laws of England*, by the Earl of Halsbury and other lawyers 4th ed (1973—) by Lord Hailsham of St Marylebone.
Harv LR	Harvard Law Review.
Hawkins, 1 PC	*A Treatise of the Pleas of the Crown*, by W Hawkins, Vol 1 [2 vols] 8th ed (1795) by J Curwood.
Holdsworth, 1 HEL	*A History of English Law*, by Sir William Holdsworth, Vol 1 [14 vols] (1923–64).
Howard, SR	*Strict Responsibility*, by Colin Howard (1963).
J Cr L	Journal of Criminal Law (English).
J Cr L & Cr	Journal of Criminal Law and Criminology (USA).
JSPTL	Journal of the Society of Public Teachers of Law.
Kenny, *Outlines*	*Outlines of Criminal Law*, by C S Kenny 19th ed (1965) by J W C Turner.
LQR	Law Quarterly Review.
MACL	*The Modern Approach to Criminal Law*, ed by L Radzinowicz and J W C Turner (1948).
Med Sci & L	Medicine, Science and the Law.
MLR	Modern Law Review.
NZ Essays	*Essays on Criminal Law in New Zealand*, edited by R S Clark (1971).

Phillimore	Report of the Committee on Contempt of Court, 1974, Cmnd 5794.
Pollock and Maitland, I HEL	*The History of English Law before the Time of Edward I*, by Sir Frederick Pollock and F W Maitland, Vol I [2 vols] 2nd ed.
RCCP	Report of the Royal Commission on Capital Punishment, 1953, Cmd 8932.
Reshaping the Criminal Law	*Reshaping the Criminal Law*. Essays in honour of Glanville Williams. Edited by P R Glazebrook (1978).
Russell	*Crime*, by Sir W O Russell 12th ed (1964) by J W C Turner [2 vols].
Smith, *Theft*	*The Law of Theft* 5th ed (1984) by J C Smith.
SHC	*Criminal Law: Cases and Materials* 3rd ed (1986) by J C Smith and Brian Hogan.
SALJ	South African Law Journal.
Stephen, *Digest*	*A Digest of the Criminal Law*, by Sir James Fitzjames Stephen 9th ed (1950) by L F Sturge.
Stephen, I HCL	*A History of the Criminal Law of England*, by Sir James Fitzjames Stephen, Vol I [3 vols] (1883).
Street, *Torts*	*The Law of Torts*, by M. Brazier (8th ed, 1988).
U Pa Law Rev	University of Pennsylvania Law Review.
Williams, CLGP	*Criminal Law: The General Part*, by Glanville L Williams (2nd ed, 1961).
Williams, TBCL	*Textbook of Criminal Law*, by Glanville L Williams 2nd ed (1983).
YLJ	Yale Law Journal.

Table of Statutes

References in this Table to *Statutes* are to Halsbury's Statutes of England (Fourth Edition) showing the volume and page at which the annotated text of the Act will be found.
Page references printed in **bold** type indicate where the section of an Act is printed in part or in full.

	PAGE
Abortion Act 1967 (12 *Statutes* 414) .	223, 364, 369
s 1	**369**, 373
(1)(a)	371
(b)	372
(3)	370
(4)	370, 372
2	370
4(1), (2)	373
5(1)	364
(2)	372
Accessories and Abettors Act 1861 (12 *Statutes* 91) . . .	143
s 2	359
8 . . . . 130, 133, 359	
Administration of Justice Act 1960 (11 *Statutes* 174)	
s 11	775
(1)	783
12(1)	783
(4)	783
13	769
Administration of Justice Act 1970 (12 *Statutes* 553)	
s 40	594
Age of Marriage Act 1929 . .	442
s 1	441
Age of Marriage Act 1949	
s 2	442
Air Force Act 1955 (3 *Statutes* 247)	
s 66	472
Animals Act 1971 (2 *Statutes* 345)	690
s 1	692
5(2)	692
(3)(b)	692
7	692
9(3)(a), (b)	691
Army Act 1955 (3 *Statutes* 49)	
s 66	472
Auctions (Bidding Agreements) Act 1927 (4 *Statutes* 5) . .	268
Auctions (Bidding Agreements) Act 1969 (4 *Statutes* 10)	
s 1(1)	268
Aviation Security Act 1982 (4 *Statutes* 269) . . .	821, 852
s 1	821
(1)–(3)	821

	PAGE
Aviation Security Act 1982—*contd.*	
s 2	821
(1)(a),(b)	821
(2)	822
3	822
6(1)	821
Badgers Act 1973 (2 *Statutes* 358) .	680
Banking Act 1987 (4 *Statutes* 527)	
s 98(1)	176
Bigamy (1603)	705
Bills of Exchange Act 1882 (5 *Statutes* 346)	488
Bills of Sale Act 1878 (5 *Statutes* 406)	749
Births and Deaths Registration Act 1953 (37 *Statutes* 722)	
s 36	358
British Nationality Act 1948 (31 *Statutes* 10)	
s 3	309, 830
(1)	710
British Nationality Act 1981 (31 *Statutes* 112)	
s 51(3)(a)	710
Sch 3	710, 830
Cable and Broadcasting Act 1984	
s 4	726
Caravan Sites Act 1968 (32 *Statutes* 498)	
s 3	813
Child Abduction Act 1984 (12 *Statutes* 933) . . .	415
s 2, 4	283
Children and Young Persons Act 1933 (32 *Statutes* 498) .	179
s 1	123, 386
(1)	350
(2)(a)	54
38	741
44(1)	180
50	178, 282
Children and Young Persons Act 1963 (6 *Statutes* 158) .	179
s 16	178
Children and Young Persons Act 1969 (6 *Statutes* 227) .	179
s 1	179, 180
4	181

PAGE

**Children and Young Persons Act
1969** —*contd.*
s 5 181
6(1) 30
(b) 30
(2) 30
**Children and Young Persons (Harm-
ful Publications) Act 1955 (12
Statutes 266)** . . . 4, 737
Cinemas Act 1985
Sch 2 726
Cinematograph Act 1952 . . 736
Civil Aviation Act 1949
s 62 309
**Civil Aviation Act 1982 (4 Statutes
114)**
s 92(1) 820
**Civil Evidence Act 1968 (17 Statutes
155)** 617
Coinage Offences Act 1936 . . 645, 669
**Commissioners for Oaths Act 1889
(17 Statutes 108)** . . . 743
**Common Informers Act 1951 (12
Statutes 261)** . . . 21, 766
Companies Act 1985 . . . 250
**Concealment of birth of bastards
(1623)** 357
**Conservation of Wild Creatures and
Wild Plants Act 1975** . . 508
**Conspiracy and Protection of
property Act 1875 (12 Statutes 155)**
s 3 267
**Constables Protection Act 1750 (18
Statutes 540)** . . . 409
**Contempt of Court Act 1981 (11 Stat-
utes 181)** . . 99, 767, 769
s 1(1) 773, 779
2(1) 773
(2) 773, 777
(3) 773
3 . . . 775, 776, 777, 783
4 776
(1) 777
(2) 777
5 . . . 776, 778, 779
6 773
(b) 777
8(2) 784
9 784
12 770
14 768
(1) 768
17 768
19 784
**Continental Shelf Act 1964 (29 Stat-
utes 435)**
s 3 309
**Control of Pollution Act 1974 (35
Statutes 481)**
s 31 110
Copyright Act 1956 (11 Statutes 236)
Sch 6
Pt I, IB 54

PAGE

**Corrupt Practices Prevention Act
1854**
s 2 128
**County Courts Act 1959 (11 Statutes
399)**
s 157 770
Courts Act 1971
s 4(5) 27
**Criminal Appeal Act 1968 (12 Stat-
utes 419)** 23
s 2 . . . . 293, 731
(1) 477
12 197
30, 42 640
**Criminal Attempts Act 1981 (12 Stat-
utes 845)** . 34, 38, 256, 260, 261,
265, 355, 438, 474, 724
s 1 . . . . 28, 288
(1) . 287, 288, 292, 293, 296,
298, 304
(2) 301, 302
(3) . . . 301, 302, 304
(4) 297
(b) . . 150, 265, 297, 748
(c) . . . 759, 761, 764
3 28
(1) 298
4 8
(3) 293
5 . . . . 258, 303
Schedule
Pt I 748
**Criminal Damage Act 1971 (12 Stat-
utes 557)** . 50, 63, 209, 223, 240,
246, 418, 490, 497, 609,
677
s 1 . . . . 677, 700
(1) . 53, 213, 215, 681, 683,
684, 685, 686, 688, 695,
697, 699, 704
(2) . 64, 213, 404, 683, 685, 686,
691, **696**, 697, 698, 699
(b) 64
(3) . 53, 685, 699, 702
2 . . 356, 428, **700**, 701, 704
(a) 685, 701
(b) 685, 701
3 . . . . **701**, 704
4 677
(2) 700, 701
5 . . 241, **688**, 695, 696, 698,
700
(1) 700
(2) 215, 698
(a) 689, 701
(b) 696
(3) 689, 693
(4) 692
(5) 693
6 703
10 . . . . **680**, 681, 682
(1) 681
**Criminal Evidence Act 1898 (17 Stat-
utes 116)** 22

PAGE

Criminal Justice Act 1925 (27 *Statutes* 27)
s 33 170
42 470
47 238
Criminal Justice Act 1961 (34 *Statutes* 671)
s 22(2) 758
Criminal Justice Act 1967 (12 *Statutes* 389) 15
s 8 . . 85, 86, 217, 328, 347, 401, 402, 614, 729, 730, 834
10 402
37 14
Criminal Justice Act 1972 (12 *Statutes* 567) 644
s 6(3) 639
64(1) 639
Sch 5 639
Criminal Justice Act 1982 (12 *Statutes* 868) 180, 181
Criminal Justice Act 1987 . 257, 286
s 12 . . . . . 257, 285
(3) 285
Criminal Justice Administration Act 1914 (27 *Statutes* 24)
s 28(3) 706
Criminal Law Act 1967 (12 *Statutes* 358) . . 26, 152, 296, 355, 763, 849
s 1 . . . . 25, 130, 413
2 . . . 25, 26, 38, 246, 581
(7) 115
3 . . 38, 240, 242, 243, 245, 246, 693, 694
4 . . . 759, 762, 765
(1) 26, 297
(3) 8, 763
5 765
(1) . 26, 297, 755, 764, 766
(2) 758
(3) 765
(5) 764
6(3) . . 399, 401, 759
(4) . . . 296, 466
12(4) 831
(6) 26
Sch 2 357
Criminal Law Act 1977 (12 *Statutes* 742) . 26, 27, 28, 130, 151, 246, 256, 296, 355, 397, 427, 727, 801
s 1 . . . . . 268, 726
(1) . 257, 258, 263, 265, 266, 268, 283, 287, 301, 302, 303
(a) 274
(b) . . 260, 261, 262
(2) . 258, 259, 262, 263, 264, 814
(3) 267, 814
(4) 268, 269
2 268

Criminal Law Act 1977—*contd.*
s 2(2) 281
(3) 282
3 . . . . . 25, 28
(1)–(3) 285
4(1),(2) 267
(4) 286
5(1) 257
(2) 257
(6) 268
(7) 254, 255
(8), (9) 284
(11) 267
6 . . 802, 804, 806, 808, 810, 811
(1) 802, 804
(2) 806
(3) 807
(b) 808
(4)(a) 803
(b) 802
(5),(6) 802
7 811
(1) 809
(2) 810
(a), (b) 810
(3) 810
(4)(a) 810
(5) 810
(6) 810, 812
(8) 810
8 811
(1),(3) 811
9(1),(2) 811
(3) 811, 812
(5) 811
(6) 812
(7) 802
10(1)–(3) 812
(5) 802
11 802
12(1)(a) 804
(b) 808
(2) 804
(a) 804
(b) 804
(3) 807
(4), (6) 807
(7) 809
15(4) 427
16 . . . . . 705, 794
28(1) 254
30(3) 427
(4) 254, 255
50(1) 482, 485
(2) 482
51(1)(a), (b) . . . 428
(2) 428, 796
53 726
54 . . . . . 253, 446
60 704
(1) 644
65(4) 639
Sch 2 . . . 356, 748, 794

PAGE

Criminal Law Act 1979—*contd.*
Sch 3 . . . . 704, 705
Sch 6 479
Sch 12 . . . 356, 639, 732
Criminal Law Amendment Act 1885: 439
s 4 . . . . . 435, 441
5 159
(1) 441
s 13 459
Criminal Law Amendment Act 1912
s 7 460
Criminal Lunatics Act 1800 . . 183
s 2 182
Criminal Lunatics Act 1884 . . 182
Criminal Procedure Act 1851 (12 *Statutes* 88)
s 12 296
29 751
Criminal Procedure (Insanity) Act 1964 (12 *Statutes* 347)
s 1 197
4 . . . . 182, 183, 184
(2), (3) 185
(4) 183
(5)(1)(c) 183
6 201
Sch 1 183
Customs and Excise Management Act 1979 (13 *Statutes* 273)
s 86 427
170(1)(b) 304
Dangerous Drugs Act 1964
s 9(1)(b) 111
Dangerous Drugs Act 1965 . 110
Debtors Act 1869 (4 *Statutes* 660) . 544
Defamation Act 1952 (24 *Statutes* 117)
s 1, 6 822
Diplomatic and Consular Premises Act 1987 811
Disorderly Houses Act 1751 (12 *Statutes* 26) 459
Dockyards, &c., Protection Act 1772: 703
Dogs Act 1906 (2 *Statutes* 208)
s 3 696
Domicile and Matrimonial Proceedings Act 1973 (27 *Statutes* 777)
s 15(2) 713
16 713
Drugs (Prevention of Misuse) Act 1964
s 1(1) 107
Ecclesiastical Courts Jurisdiction Act 1860 (14 *Statutes* 272)
s 2 735
Education Act 1944 (15 *Statutes* 106)
s 39(1) 47
Education (No 2) Act 1986
s 47(5), (10) 386
Evidence Act 1851 (17 *Statutes* 82) . 22
Evidence (Proceedings in Other Jurisdictions) Act 1975 (17 *Statutes* 190) 742, 743
Sch 1 743

PAGE

Explosive Substances Act 1883 (12 *Statutes* 165) . . . 821
s 1(6) 821
2 . . . . 696, 697, 703
3 703
4(1) 247
Explosives Act 1875 (17 *Statutes* 392) . 247
s 3(1) 610
Family Allowances Act 1945 . 255
Family Law Reform Act 1969 (6 *Statutes* 213)
s 9(1) 178
Fertilisers and Feeding Stuffs Act 1926
s 7(1) 119
Finance (No 2) Act 1940
s 35 173
Finance Act 1972
s 38(1) 569
Firearms Act 1968 (12 *Statutes* 458): 422, 427, 610
s 1 . . . . . 73, 416
2 416
3 417
5(1) 417
7–12 417
16 . . . 420, 421, 696, 697
17 420
(1) 418, 419
(2) . . 387, 418, 419, 425
18 421
(1) 421
19 . . . . 421, 422, 690
20 421
(1), (2) 421
21–39 417
57(1) . . . 418, 420, 422
58(2) 111, 419
Sch 1 . . . . 418, 419
Sch 3 419
Firearms Act 1982 (12 *Statutes* 858) . 416
Food Act 1984 (27 *Statutes* 401)
s 27 54
100 117
Food and Drugs Act 1955 . . 166
Forcible Entry Act 1381 . . 801
Forcible Entry Act 1429 . . 801
Forgery Act 1861 (12 *Statutes* 95) . 676
Forgery Act 1913 . 128, 645, 646, 676
s 6 665
7 663
Forgery and Counterfeiting Act 1981 (12 *Statutes* 818) . . 645, 669
s 1 . . . . 655, **663**, 665
(1), (2) 672
2 . . . . 655, **664**, 665
3 . . . . 655, **664**, 665
4 . . . . . 655, **665**
5 . . . 655, **666**, 668, 674
(1)–(4) . . . 667, 668
(5) 667
6 663
8 . . . . . . **646**
9 . . . **649**, 650, 651, 659
(1) 652, 655

PAGE

Forgery and Counterfeiting Act 1981 —
   contd.
s 9(1)(a) 650, 660
   (b) 650, 653
   (c),(d)   .   .   .   650, 655
   (e),(f)   .   .   .   650, 651
   (g) 651, 652
   (h) .   .   .   652, 653, 654
   (2) 652
10 .   .   .   .   . **655**, 657
   (1) 659, 662
     (a) .   .   . 656, 657, 658
     (b) 657
     (c) .   .   .   657, 658
   (2) 659
   (3),(4)   .   .   . 661, 662
14 .   .   .   .   . **672**, 673
   (1),(2)   676
15 .   .   .   .   . **672**, 673
   (1) 676
   (2) 676
16 .   .   .   .   . 670, **673**
   (1),(2)   676
17 .   .   .   .   . 670, **673**
   (1) 676
   (2) 674, 676
   (3) 676
   (4) 674
18 .   .   .   . 671, **674**, 676
19 .   .   .   . 671, **675**, 676
21 672
27 670
28(1)   673
   (2)(a), (b)   .   .   . 670
   (3) 670
Genocide Act 1969 (12 *Statutes* 550) . 374
Guard Dogs Act 1975 (2 *Statutes*
     385) 692
Guardianship Act 1973 (6 *Statutes*
     338)
s 1(3)   415
Guardianship of Minors Act 1971 (6
     Statutes 305)
s 7 415
Habeas Corpus Act 1679 (6 *Statutes*
     678)
s 11   21
Highway Act 1835 (20 *Statutes*
     9) 126, 800
s 72 .   .   .   .   478, 796
Highways Act 1959
s 127 801
Highways Act 1980 (20 *Statutes* 135)
s 137 .   .   .   .   799, 800
Hijacking Act 1971 .   .   . 820
Homicide Act 1957 (12 *Statutes*
     310) .   .   .   197, 345
s 1 329
2 .   .   . 201, 203, 218, 309
   (2) 201, 202
   (4) .   .   . 153, 154, 284
3 .   . 332, 333, 337, 338, 342, 344
4 360
   (1) 360

PAGE

Homicide Act 1957—*contd.*
   s 4(2), (3)   361
     (4) 154
     5 330
     (1)(a) 628
Housing Act 1936 (16 *Statutes* 46)
   s 11(1), (4)   .   .   . 604
   12 604
Human Tissue Act 1961 (28 *Statutes*
     106) 524
Incitement to Dissaffection Act 1934
     (12 *Statutes* 229)
   s 1 .   .   .   . 837, 838
   2 838
Incitement to Mutiny Act 1797 (12
     Statutes 35) .   .   . 837
Indecency With Children Act 1960
     (12 *Statutes* 329) .   . 449
Indecent Displays (Control) Act 1981
     (12 *Statutes* 811) .   . 736
Infant Life (Preservation) Act 1929
     (12 *Statutes* 222) .   310, 365
   s 1 364
     (1),(2) 364
Infanticide Act 1938 (12 *Statutes* 245)
   s 1(1)   .   .   .   361, 362
     (2) 362
Insolvency Act 1986 (4 *Statutes* 717)
   s 207 522,
     339, 341   .   .   . 524
Internationally Protected Persons Act
     1978 (10 *Statutes* 636) .   852
Interpretation Act 1978
   Sch 1   .   .   .   28, 176
   Sch 2   176
Juries Act 1974 (22 *Statutes* 409)
   s 20(5)(d) 83
Larceny (1827)
   s 39 37
Larceny Act 1861 .   .   . 488
   s 23, 24   123
   102 766
Larceny Act 1916 .   .   440, 488
   s 20 298
     (i),(iv)   .   .   . 496
   28 614
   32 36
   33(1)   621
Law of Libel Amendment Act 1888
     (24 *Statutes* 113)
   s 3 777
   8 823
Libel Act 1792 (24 *Statutes* 18) .   835
Libel Act 1843 (24 *Statutes* 95) .   99
   s 4 826
   5 823
   6 824
   7 825
Licensing Act 1872 (24 *Statutes* 298)
   s 12 46
   13 .   .   .   . 101, 165
   16 163
     (1),(2)   .   .   . 103
Licensing Act 1921
   s 4 169

PAGE

Licensing Act 1953 . . . 393
Licensing Act 1964 (24 *Statutes* 310)
  s 186(1) 393
Licensing (Consolidation) Act 1910 . 126
Local Government (Miscellaneous Provisions) Act 1982 (15 *Statutes* 326)
  s 40 795
London Hackney Carriage Act 1831 (28 *Statutes* 19)
  s 41 678
Magistrates' Courts Act 1952
  s 19(8) 254
Magistrates' Courts Act 1980 (27 *Statutes* 157) 27
  s 17 . . . . . 28, 254
  19 28
  (4) 29
  20, 21 28
  22(1) 29
  (2), (4)–(7) . . . 29
  25(2) 29
  (3) 29
  (4) 29
  29 30
  32 . . . . . 174, 482
  33 . . . . . 26, 29
  38 29
  44 130
  45 254
  (1) 28
  63(3) 768
  Sch 1 . . . . 28, 254
  Sch 2 704
  Sch 4 29
Malicious Damage Act 1861 (12 *Statutes* 92) . . 62, 490, 677, 683, 703
  s 6 603
  35,36,47 704
  48,58,72 704
Malicious Shooting or Stabbing (1803) . . 329, 357, 366
Marine &c., Broadcasting (Offences) Act 1967
  s 4 819
Marriage Act 1949 (27 *Statutes* 470)
  s 2 441
  3 718
  16(1A), (2) . . . 750
  27B(2), (4) . . . 750
  30 718
  43 717
  53,57,69 719
  75(1) 717
  (2) 717, 718
  (3) 718
  76 719
  (1)–(3) 719
  Sch 1 445
Marriage (Prohibited Degrees of Relationship) Act 1986 (27 *Statutes* 562)
  s 4 750

PAGE

Marriage (Registrar General's Licence) Act 1970 (27 *Statutes* 546)
  s 16 717
Matrimonial Causes Act 1973 (27 *Statutes* 700)
  s 11 707
  (d) 708
  12 707
  16 713
Matrimonial Homes Act 1967 . 599
Medicines Act 1968 (28 *Statutes* 344)
  s 58(2) 98
Mental Deficiency Act 1913 . . 443
Mental Health Act 1959 (28 *Statutes* 616) 442
  s 4(2) 199
  128 444
  129, 139 758
Mental Health Act 1983 (28 *Statutes* 632)
  s 1(1) 199
  23 183
  36 185
  37 206
  41 . . . . . 183, 206
  47, 48 182
Mental Health (Amendment) Act 1982 (28 *Statutes* 626) . 183, 443
Merchandise Marks Act 1887
  s 2 127
  (2) 167
Metropolitan Police Act 1839 (24 *Statutes* 294)
  s 44 164
  54 737
Midwives Act 1951
  s 9 229
Misuse of Drugs Act 1971 (28 *Statutes* 500) 96
  s 5(2) 108
  (4) 174
  (8) 124
  19 253
  20 120
  28 108
  (2), (4) 108
Motor Car Act 1903 . . . 103
Murder (Abolition of Death Penalty) Act 1965 (12 *Statutes* 357) . 330
  s 1(1) 25
National Health Service (Family Planning) Amendment Act 1972: 385
Naval Discipline Act 1957 (3 *Statutes* 442)
  s 37 472
Night Poaching Act 1828 (2 *Statutes* 152)
  s 9 427
Nullity of Marriage Act 1971 . 713
Oaths Act 1978 (17 *Statutes* 200)
  s 5 . . . . . 741, 742
Obscene Publications Act 1857 . 720, 732
Obscene Publications Act 1959 (12 *Statutes* 320) . . . 730

PAGE

Obscene Publications Act 1959—*contd.*
s 1 727
  (1) . . . 719, 724, 731, 736
  (2) 734
  (3) 724
    (b) 734
2 . . . . . 726, 727, 733
  (1) 276, 723
  (3A) 726
  (4) 733
  (4A) 726
  (5) . . . 119, 726, 731
  (6) 724
3 . . . . . 732, 734
  (1) 734
  (3A) 733
4 . . . . . 727, 736
  (1) 729, 733
  (1A) 727, 729
  (3) 729
Obscene Publications Act 1964 (12
  Statutes 344)
s 1(1) 723
  (2) 725
  (3)(a) 726
    (b) 725, 726
2(1), (2) 734
Offences against the Person Act 1828 . 358
s 13 311
22 705
Offences against the Person Act 1837 . 366
s 4 398
Offences against the Person Act 1861
  (12 *Statutes* 98) . . 355, 365,
          394, 418, 821
s 4 . . . . . 253, 355
9 309
15 359
16 356
18 . . . 50, 71, 152, 216, 264,
    373, 397, 398, 399, 400, 608
20 . . . 67, 152, 216, 397,
    398, 399, 400, 401, 608
23 . . . 62, 147, 348, 403, 404,
       405, 608, 697
24 . . . 150, 403, 404, 405
25 405
30 71
31 . . . . . 691, 696
34 348
35 478
36 . . . . . 387, 391
37 387
38 391
42, 43 375
44, 45 21
47 . . . 8, 375, 396, 397, 401
55 452
56 283
57 . . . 705, 707, 713, 714
58 . . . 159, 310, 364, 365, 366,
             368
59 368
60 357

PAGE

Offences against the Person Act
  1861—*contd.*
s 61 451
62 . . . . . 451, 473
63 451
Offences at Sea Act 1799 (12 *Statutes* 36)
s 1 . . . . . 819, 820
Official Secrets Act 1911 (12 *Statutes*
  194) 490
s 1 . . . . . 839, 842
  (1) 838
2 841
  (2) 841
3 838
Official Secrets Act 1920 (12 *Statutes*
  210)
s 1, 3, 7 842
Oil in Navigable Waters Act 1955 . 47
Perjury (1562) 743
Perjury Act 1911 (12 *Statutes* 183) . 358
s 1(1) 740, 746
  (2) 742
  (3)–(6) 743
  1A 743, 747
2 . . . . . . **749**
3 . . . . . . **749**
4(1) 750
5 . . . . . . **750**
6 751
7 . . . . . **748**, 754
13 747
15 . . . . . . **741**
  (2) 750
Schedule 740
Piracy Act 1698 (12 *Statutes* 20)
s 8 819
Piracy Act 1721 (12 *Statutes* 24)
s 1, 6 819
Piracy Act 1837 (12 *Statutes* 64)
s 2 . . . . . 25, 820
3 820
Police Act 1964 (33 *Statutes* 597) . 418
s 51 . . 387, 389, 395, 419, 812, 813
  (1)–(3) 387
53 838
Police and Criminal Evidence Act
  1984 (12 *Statutes* 941; 33 *Stat-*
  utes 676) . . . 38, 389, 695
s 2 26
17(5) 224
24 . . . 25, 246, **410**, 411
  (2) 581
  (4) 38
    (a), (b) 178
25 26
  (1) 411
26, 28 412
74 . . . . 151, 617, 760
80 706
117 802
Sch 2 . . . . . 26, 412
Police (Property) Act 1897 (33 *Stat-*
  utes 567)
s 1(1) 642, 643

PAGE

Police (Property) Act 1897—*contd.*
s 1(2)   643
2   643
Post Office Act 1953 (34 *Statutes* 395)
s 11   734
59(c)   704
60   704
63(1)   119
65   540
Post Office Act 1969
s 78   735
Post Office (Protection) Act 1884
s 7   668
Powers of Criminal Courts Act 1973
   (12 *Statutes* 597)
s 18(2) 8, 476
28   14
30 .   .   .   .   .   174, 663
   (1)   285
35 .   .   .   .   641, 644, 704
Prevention of Crime Act 1953 (12 *Statutes* 263)   .   .   .   421, 611
s 1   811
   (1), (2)   422
   (4)   .   .   422, 426, 610, 846
Prevention of Crimes Act 1871 (12
   Statutes 146)   .   .   .   418
Prevention of Fraud (Investments)
   Act 1958 (30 *Statutes* 126)
s 13   545
Prevention of Terrorism (Temporary
   Provisions) Act 1974   .   .   842
Prevention of Terrorism (Temporary
   Provisions) Act 1976   .   .   843
s 10   843
11   843
Prevention of Terrorism (Temporary
   Provisions) Act 1984 (12 *Statutes* 908)   851
s 1   852
   (1) 843, 846
      (b)   .   .   844, 845, 847
      (c)   845
   (2)   843
   (3) 844, 846
   (4), (6), (10)   844
2(1)   846
   (2)   852
3–7   851
9 .   .   .   .   .   851, 852
10 .   .   .   847, 348, 850, 852
   (1), (2)   848
   (3), (4)   847
   (5) 847, 849
   (6)   848
11 .   .   .   .   .   849, 850
   (1)   848
      (a)   850
12 .   .   .   .   .   851, 852
   (4), (6)   852
14(10), (11) .   .   .   843, 844
17   843
Sch 1   844

PAGE

Prevention of Terrorism (Temporary
   Provisions) Act 1984—*contd.*
Sch 3
   Pt II 843, 852
Prevention of Violence (Temporary
   Provisions) Act 1939 .   .   .   843
Prison Act 1952 (34 *Statutes* 643)
s 8   387
39   757
Prisoners of War (Escape) Act 1812
s 1   758
Prosecution of Offences Act 1985 (12
   Statutes 1047)   .   .   .   468
s 6(2)   18
10(1)   258
23, 24   18
Protection from Eviction Act 1977
   (23 *Statutes* 293)
s 1(1)   814
   (2)   813
   (3) 49, 813
Protection of Aircraft Act 1973   .   820
Protection of Animals Act 1911 (2 *Statutes* 212)
s 1   683
Protection of Children Act 1978 (12
   Statutes 785)   .   .   .   449
Protection of Depositors Act 1963
s 21(1)   545
Public Bodies Corrupt Practices Act
   1889 (12 *Statutes* 173)   .   128
Public Health Act 1875 (35 *Statutes* 29): 101
s 4   604
Public Meeting Act 1908 (12 *Statutes*
   182)   799
Public Order Act 1936 (12 *Statutes*
   235) 426, 467
s 1   846
5   790
Public Order Act 1986 .   .   422, 785
s 1   .   .   .   .   .   **786**, 788
   (3), (4)   785
2   .   .   .   .   .   .   **788**
   (3), (4)   785
3 .   .   .   .   .   .   **789**
   (3), (4)   785
4   .   .   .   394, 790, 792, 793
   (1)   790
   (2)   791
5   793
   (1) 790, 791
   (3) 791, 792
6   788
   (1)   787
   (2)   789
   (3)   .   .   790, 791, 792, 793
   (4) 790, 793
   (5), (6)   .   787, 789, 790, 791, 792
7(2)   791
8   .   .   .   .   .   **787**, 791
10(1)   788
17   792
18   793
   (1)   790

PAGE

Public Order Act 1986—contd.

s 19 . . . . 790, 793, 794
  (1) 790
20 . . . . 790, 793, 794
  (1) 790
21 . . . . 790, 793, 794
  (1) 790
22 . . . . . 790, 793
  (1) 790
23 . . . . 790, 793, 794
  (1) 790
Race Relations Act 1965 . . . 792
Race Relations Act 1976 (6 Statutes
  765) 792
Recognition of Divorces and Legal
  Separations Act 1971 (27 Statutes 899)
s 1 713
2–5 713
Regulation of Railways Act 1889 (36
  Statutes 177)
s 5(3) 550
Rehabilitation of Offenders Act 1974
  (12 Statutes 680) . . 545, 745
Representation of the People Act 1949
s 179 176
Revenue Act 1869
s 27 168
Riot (Damages) Act 1886 (33 Statutes
  560) 788
Rivers (Prevention of Pollution) Act
  1951
s 2(1)(a) 110
Road Traffic Act 1930 . . . 103
s 11 349
28 578
Road Traffic Act 1956
s 8 485
9(1) 46
Road Traffic Act 1960
s 2(2) 487
217 584
Road Traffic Act 1972 . . . 478
s 1 . . . . . 9, 485
2 . . . . 9, 94, 482
3 . . . 93, 94, 479, 480, 482
5(2), (3) 46
6 . . . . . 751, 752
  (1) 134, 150
  (2) 46
8 395
17 482
25 54
93(6) 130
143 54
159 390
178 800
196 426
Sch 4 . . . 479, 482, 485
Road Traffic Act 1974
s 6 388
Sch 5 479
Road Traffic Regulation Act 1967
s 42(4) 550

PAGE

Roads Act 1920 154
Sale of Food and Drugs Act 1875
s 2, 3, 6 118
Sale of Goods Act 1979
s 1 166
Sexual Offences Act 1956 (12 Statutes
  271) . . . 418, 430, 446
s 1 429
  (1) 429
  (2) 429, 435
2 . . . . 434, 442, 443
  (1) 439
3 . . . 436, 437, 442, 443
  (1) 439, 717
4(1) 437, 440
5 . . . 441, 442, 444, 458
6 . . 119, 139, 159, 441, 442,
                    444, 457
  (1) 441
  (2) 442, 447
  (3) 442, 447
7 . . . . 442, 442, 444
  (1), (2) 443
9 . . . . 442, 443, 444
  (1), (2) 443
10 445
  (1), (2) 445
11 445
  (1), (2) 445
12(1) 35, 471, 472
13 . . . . 449, 471, 474
14 . . . 447, 451, 452, 457
  (1) 66
  (3), (4) 447
15 . . 446, 447, 451, 452, 474
  (4) 447
16(1) 473, 474
17 453
  (1) 430
19 . . . . 92, 453, 454
  (1) 430
20 . . 39, 41, 72, 263, 452, 453,
                       454
21 . . . . 453, 454, 457
22 . . . . . 26, 442
  (1) 456
23 . . . . 442, 443, 456
  (1) 269, 442
24 456
25, 26 . . . . 120, 444
27 444
28 456
  (1) 456
  (2) 456, 457
  (3)–(5) 456
29(1), (2) 457
30 . . . . 460, 464
  (1) 460
  (2) 460, 461
31 464
32 . . . 466, 467, 476, 477
33 . . . . 457, 458, 459
34 . . . . 457, 458, 459
35 . . . . 458, 459

PAGE

Sexual Offences Act 1956 —contd.
s 35(1) 458
36 459
37 429
44 . . . . . 432, 433
45 . . . . . 443, 472
46 . . . . . 435, 474
47 . . . . . 442, 454
Sch 2 . . . . 429, 473
Sexual Offences Act 1967 (12 Statutes
383) . . . 17, 20, 35, 277, 471
s 1 . . . . 471, 473, 474
2 472
3 475
(1) 476
4 . . . . . 297, 473
(3) 474
5 464
6 458
Sexual Offences Act 1985 . . 446
s 1(1) 468
2(1) 468
4(4) 468
5(6) 468
Sexual Offences (Amendment) Act
1976 (12 Statutes 732): 66, 90, 263
s 1(1) 66, 429
(2) . . . 213, 236, 429
7(2) 151, 432
Smoke Nuisance (Metropolis) Act 1853: 798
Stamp Duties Management Act 1891
s 27 646
Statutory Declarations Act 1835 (17
Statutes 72) 750
Street Betting Act 1906 . . . 465
Street Offences Act 1959 (12 Statutes
317) 476
s 1(1),(2) 464
(3) 464
(4) 466, 468
4 460
Suicide Act 1961 (12 Statutes 341): 17, 131,
359
s 2 . . . . . 359, 360
(1) 297
(2) 361
Suppression of Terrorism Act 1978
(17 Statutes 537) . . . 852
Supreme Court Act 1981 (11 Statutes
756)
s 8(3) 27
46 27
Supreme Court of Judicature Act 1873
s 47 23
Supreme Court of Judicature (Consolidation) Act 1925
s 31(1)(a) 23
Taking of Hostages Act 1982 (12 Statutes 856) 414
Territorial Waters Jurisdiction Act
1878 (12 Statutes 161)
s 2 309
Theatres Act 1843
s 15 . . . . . 126, 168

PAGE

Theatres Act 1968 . . . 168, 736
s 2 736
(3), (4) 736
3 . . . . . 729, 736
4 822
6 822
7, 8 736
Theft Act 1968 (12 Statutes 514) . 5, 28,
418, 488, 515
s 1 . . . 85, 298, 521, 522, 607,
611, 616, 617
(1) . 490, 505, 522, 532, 534, 615
(2) 528
2 . . . . 526, 532, 555
(1) 527, 556
(a) . . . 496, 526, 556
(b) . 523, 526, 527, 531, 689
(c) . . . 526, 527
(2) 528
3(1) . 491, 492, 495, 496, 498
(2) . . . 496, 503, 630
4 . . . . . 504, 557
(1) . . 504, 505, 557, 615
(2) 506
(a)–(c) . . . 506, 616
(3) 507, 528
(4) 508
5 . . . . 509, 524, 682
(1) . 510, 512, 513, 514, 519,
557
(2) 513
(3) . 514, 516, 517, 518, 519
(4) . 500, 518, 519, 520, 521,
522, 620, 682
(5) 522
6 . . . . 534, 536, 558
(1) . 535, 537, 538, 539
(2) . . . 538, 539
7 490
8 . . . 540, 541, 542, 697
9 . . 595, 602, 611, 681, 697
(1)(a) 602, 608
(b) . . 602, 608, 611, 809
10 . . . . 609, 697, 811
(1)(b) . . . 422, 612
11 . . . . 145, 578, 580
(2) 580
12 . . 145, 539, 540, 578, 581,
583, 612
(1) . . . 583, 587, 612
(5) . . . 582, 587
(6) 587
(7) . . . 584, 587
(a) 586
13 . . . . . 505, 539
15 . . 36, 491, 499, 501, 521,
522, 538, 540, 544, 545,
548, 549, 550, 555, 556,
557, 558, 560, 561, 562,
577, 607, 612, 619, 638
(1) . 522, 544, 556, 557, 616,
617
(2), (3) . . . 557, 558
(4) 544, 547

PAGE

Theft Act 1968—*contd.*

16 . . . 544, 549, 555, 558, **559,**
560, 562, 565, 607, 638
  (1) 544
  (2)(a) . . . 544, 558, 565
    (b) 544
    (c) 544, 560
  (3) 544
17 . . . . . **574,** 638
  (1)(a), (b) 575
18 . . . . . 175, **638**
19 . . . . . . **576**
20 577
21 . . . 79, 356, 489, 502, 542,
588, 616, 617
  (1) 356, 591, 592
    (a), (b) 594
  (2) 589, 592
22 . . . . **615,** 621, 746
  (1) 628, 630
23 . . . . . 631, 766
24(1) 616, 640
  (2) **620**
    (a) 616
  (3) . . . 617, 619, 621
  (4) . . 616, 640, 641, 767
25 . . . . 26, 46, 553
  (1), (2) **611**
  (3) 614
  (5) 612
26 703
27(3) 635
28 . . . **639,** 640, 642, 644
  (1)(a) 642
    (c) 641
  (2) 641
  (4) 640
  (6) 641
30(1) 637
  (2) 637
  (4) 637
    (a) 637
31(2) 642
32(1) 568
34 589
  (1) 557
  (2) 528
    (a) . . 576, 592, 593, 615
    (b) . . . 615, 641
Sch 2 . . . . 123, 540
Theft Act 1978 (12 *Statutes* 780) . 488
s 1 . . 544, 549, 556, 558, **561,**
565
  (2) 556, 563
2 . . 265, 544, 549, 550, 556,
558, **564,** 565, 575
  (1) 564, 568
    (a) 565, 567
    (b) . . 566, 567, 574
    (c) 567
  (2) 556, 568
  (3) 566
  (4) 564
3 . . 500, 551, **569,** 571, 572

PAGE

Theft Act 1978—*contd.*
s 3(1) 573
  (2)–(4) 570
4 . . . . 561, 570
5(1) 544, 561
Tokyo Convention Act 1967 (4 *Statutes* 55)
s 4 816
Schedule 816
Torts (Interference with Goods) Act
1977
s 3 619
  (3)(b) 619
Town Police Clauses Act 1847
s 28 . . . . 478, 799
Trade Descriptions Act 1968 . 172, 548
s 14(a), (b) 54
24 . . . . 96, 119
Trade Disputes Act 1906 . . 390
Trade Union and Labour Relations
Act 1974 (16 *Statutes* 248)
s 12 176
15 . . . . 390, 800
Transport Act 1981
Sch 8 . 46, 134, 150, 222, 395,
751, 752
Transport Act 1982
s 31 163
Treason Act 1351 (12 *Statutes* 13) . 669,
827, 832
s 6 832
7 833
Treason Act 1702 (10 *Statutes* 55)
s 3 827
Treason Act 1795 (12 *Statutes* 34)
s 1 827
Treason Act 1800 . . . 831
Treason Act 1814 (12 *Statutes* 45)
s 1 25
Treason Act 1945 . . . 831
Treason Felony Act 1848 (12 *Statutes*
78) . . . 828, 832
Tribunals of Inquiry (Evidence) Act
1921 (10 *Statutes* 364) . 742
Unsolicited Goods and Services Act
1971 (12 *Statutes* 555)
s 4 736
Vagrancy Act 1824 (12 *Statutes* 51) . 418,
449, 460, 465
s 4 470
Vagrancy Act 1898 . . . 460
s 1(1) 466
Vessels Protection Act 1967
s 1 578
Weights and Measures Act 1963
s 26, 27 119
Wildlife and Countryside Act 1981
(32 *Statutes* 186) . . 680
s 1(1)(a) 110
Wildlife and Countryside Amendment
Act 1985 680
Wireless Telegraphy Act 1949
s 1(1) **252**

PAGE

NEW ZEALAND
Crimes Act 1908 594

PAGE

Crimes Act 1961
s 169(2)(a),(b) 338

Table of Cases

Cases are listed under the name of the accused whenever the usual method of citation would cause them to be preceded by the abbreviation "R v" signifying that the prosecution was undertaken by the Crown.

PAGE

A

A v Hayden (1984) 156 CLR 532 249
A (a juvenile) v R [1978] Crim LR 689 679
Abbott v R [1977] AC 755, [1976] 3 All ER 140, [1976] 3 WLR 462, 140 JP 567, 128
    Sol Jo 538, 63 Cr App Rep 241, [1976] Crim LR 563, PC 232, 234
Abbott v Smith [1965] 2 QB 662n, [1964] 3 All ER 762, [1965] 3 WLR 362n, 129 JP 3 . 458
Abrahams v Cavey [1968] 1 QB 479, [1967] 3 All ER 179, [1967] 3 WLR 1229, 111 Sol
    Jo 654, DC 735
Abramovitch (1914) 84 LJKB 396, [1914-15] All ER Rep 204, 112 LT 480, 79 JP 184,
    31 TLR 88, 59 Sol Jo 288, 24 Cox CC 591, 11 Cr App Rep 45, CCA . . 614, 635
Abrol (1972) 116 Sol Jo 177, CA 814
Absalom v Martin [1974] RTR 145, DC 800
Achterdam 1911 EDL 336 47
Ackers v Taylor [1974] 1 All ER 771, [1974] 1 WLR 405, 138 JP 269, 118 Sol Jo 185,
    DC 417
Ackroyds Air Travel Ltd v DPP [1950] 1 All ER 933, 114 JP 251, 48 LGR 398, 83 Ll L
    Rep 431, DC 142
Adams (1888) 22 QBD 66, 58 LJMC 1, 59 LT 903, 53 JP 377, 5 TLR 85, 16 Cox CC
    544, CCR 824
Adams [1957] Crim LR 365 313
Adams [1980] QB 575, [1980] 1 All ER 473, [1980] 3 WLR 275, 124 Sol Jo 527, 70 Cr
    App Rep 149, [1980] Crim LR 53, CA 732
Adams v Camfoni [1929] 1 KB 95, [1928] All ER Rep 53, 98 LJKB 40, 139 LT 608, 92
    JP 186, 44 TLR 822, 28 Cox CC 538, 26 LGR 542, DC 167
Advocate (HM) v Braithwaite 1945 JC 55, 1944 SN 70, 1945 SLT 209 . . . 205
Advocate (HM) v Cunningham 1963 JC 80 42
Advocate (HM) v Dingwall (1867) 5 Irv 466, 4 SLR 249 201
Advocate (HM) v Graham 1958 SLT 167 628
Advocate (HM) v Johnstone 1926 JC 89, 1926 SN 47, 1926 SLT 428 . . . 144
Advocate (HM) v MacLeod 1956 JC 20 218
Ahlers [1915] 1 KB 616, 84 LJKB 901, 112 LT 558, 79 JP 255, 31 TLR 141, 24 Cox CC
    623, 11 Cr App Rep 63, CCA 58
Ahmad (1986) 130 Sol Jo 554, 52 P & CR 346, 84 Cr App Rep 64, [1986] LS Gaz R
    2569, [1986] Crim LR 739, CA 49, 53, 814
Ahmed Din [1962] 2 All ER 123, [1962] 1 WLR 680, 106 Sol Jo 329, 46 Cr App Rep
    239, CCA 201
Alabaster (1912) 47 LJN 397 350
Albert v Lavin (1980) 125 Sol Jo 114, 72 Cr App Rep 178; on appeal [1981] 1 All ER
    628, [1981] 2 WLR 1070, 145 JP 184, 125 Sol Jo 860, [1981] CLR 238, CA; affd
    [1982] AC 546, [1981] 3 All ER 878, [1981] 3 WLR 955, 146 JP 78, 125 Sol Jo 860,
    74 Cr App Rep 150, HL 88, 245, 383

PAGE

Alderson v Booth [1969] 2 QB 216, [1969] 2 All ER 271, [1969] 2 WLR 1252, 133 JP
346, 113 Sol Jo 268, 53 Cr App Rep 301, DC 406

Aldred (1909) 74 JP 55, 22 Cox CC 1 . . . . 835, 836, 837

Alexander (1912) 107 LT 240, 76 JP 215, 28 TLR 200, 23 Cox CC 138, 7 Cr App Rep
110, CCA 453

Alexander (1913) 109 LT 745, 77 JP 483, 23 Cox CC 604, 9 Cr App Rep 139, CCA . 337

Alexander [1981] Crim LR 183, CA 559

Alexander v Rayson [1936] 1 KB 169, [1935] All ER Rep 185, 105 LJKB 148, 154 LT
205, 52 TLR 131, 80 Sol Jo 15, CA 463

Algar [1954] 1 QB 279, [1953] 2 All ER 1381, [1953] 3 WLR 1007, 118 JP 56, 97 Sol Jo
833, 37 Cr App Rep 200, CCA 707

Alhaji Mohamed v Knott [1969] 1 QB 1, [1968] 2 All ER 563, [1968] 2 WLR 1446, 132
JP 349, 121 Sol Jo 332 . . . . 39, 442

Ali Mohamed (1943) [1964] 2 QB 350n, sub nom R v Ali Mohammed (1943) [1964] 1
All ER 653n 709

Allamby [1974] 3 All ER 126, [1974] 1 WLR 1494, 138 JP 659, 118 Sol Jo 830, 59 Cr
App Rep 189, CA 424

Allan (1841) Car & M 295, 5 Jur 296 756

Allan (1963) [1965] 1 QB 130, [1963] 2 All ER 897, [1963] 3 WLR 677, 127 JP 511, 107
Sol Jo 596, 47 Cr App Rep 243, CCA 136

Allchorn v Hopkins (1905) 69 JP 355 . . . . 165, 167

Allen (1849) 1 Den 364, 2 Car & Kir 869, T & M 55, 18 LJMC 72, 12 LTOS 409, 13
JP 53, 13 Jur 108, 3 Cox CC 270, CCR 473

Allen (1872) LR 1 CCR 367, [1861-73] All ER Rep Ext 1249, 41 LJMC 97, 26 LT 664,
36 JP 820, 20 WR 756, 12 Cox CC 193, CCR 709, 716

Allen [1985] AC 1029, [1985] 2 All ER 641, [1985] 3 WLR 107, 149 JP 587, 129 Sol Jo
447, 81 Cr App Rep 200, [1985] NLJ Rep 603, [1985] LS Gaz R 2740, [1985] Crim
LR 739, HL 574

Allen v Westley (1629) Het 97 746

Allen v Whitehead [1930] 1 KB 211, [1929] All ER Rep 13, 99 LJKB 146, 142 LT 141,
94 JP 17, 45 TLR 655, 27 LGR 652, 29 Cox CC 8, DC 163, 164

Allison (alias Wilkinson) (1806) Russ & Ry 109, CCR 706

Allsop (1976) 120 Sol Jo 635, 64 Cr App Rep 29, [1976] Crim LR 738, CA . . 270

Alphacell Ltd v Woodward [1972] AC 824, [1972] 2 All ER 475, [1972] 2 WLR 1320,
136 JP 505, 116 Sol Jo 431, 70 LGR 455, 223 Estates Gazette 1271, HL . 100, 110,
114, 117, 126, 127

Amand v Home Secretary and Minister of Defence of Royal Netherlands Government
[1943] AC 147, sub nom Amand v Secretary of State for Home Affairs [1942] 2 All
ER 381, 58 TLR 382, 86 Sol Jo 384, sub nom R v Secretary of State for Home
Affairs and Minister of Defence of Royal Netherlands Government, ex p Amand
111 LJKB 657, 167 LT 177, HL 23

Ambard v A-G for Trinidad and Tobago [1936] AC 322, [1936] 1 All ER 704, 105
LJPC 72, 154 LT 616, 52 TLR 335, 80 Sol Jo 344, PC 780

Ambler [1976] Crim LR 266, CA 5

Ambler [1979] RTR 217, CA 587

Anderson (1868) LR 1 CCR 161, [1861-73] All ER Rep 999, 38 LJMC 12, 19 LT 400,
33 JP 100, 17 WR 208, 11 Cox CC 198, CCR 309

Anderson [1966] 2 QB 110, [1966] 2 WLR 1195, 110 Sol Jo 369, sub nom R v Anderson
and Morris [1966] 2 All ER 644, 130 JP 318, 50 Cr App Rep 216, CCA . . 149

Anderson [1972] 1 QB 304, [1971] 3 All ER 1152, [1971] 3 WLR 939, 136 JP 97, 115
Sol Jo 847, 56 Cr App Rep 115, CA 720, 721, 723, 735

Anderson [1978] Crim LR 223 635

Anderson (1984) [1986] AC 27, [1985] 2 All ER 961, [1985] 3 WLR 268, 129 Sol Jo
522, 81 Cr App Rep 253, [1985] Crim LR 651, [1985] NLJ Rep 727, [1985] LS Gaz
R 3172, HL 259, 260

Anderson v Miller (1976) 120 Sol Jo 735, [1976] Crim LR 743, DC 421

Anderton v Cooper (1980) 145 JP 128, 72 Cr App Rep 232, [1981] Crim LR 177 . . 457

Anderton v Ryan [1985] AC 560, [1985] 2 All ER 355, [1985] 2 WLR 968, 149 JP 433,
129 Sol Jo 362, 81 Cr App Rep 166, [1985] NLJ Rep 485, [1985] LS Gaz R 2241,
[1985] Crim LR 503, HL 304, 617

Anderton v Wish (1980) 72 Cr App Rep 23, [1980] Crim LR 319 492

Andrews [1962] 3 All ER 961n, [1962] 1 WLR 1474, 127 JP 64, 106 Sol Jo 1013, 47 Cr
App Rep 32, CCA 762

PAGE

Andrews [1973] QB 422, [1973] 1 All ER 857, [1973] 2 WLR 116, 137 JP 325, 117 Sol
Jo 86, 57 Cr App Rep 254, [1973] RTR 508n, [1973] Crim LR 117, CA . 751, 752
Andrews v DPP [1937] AC 576, [1937] 2 All ER 552, 106 LJKB 370, 101 JP 386, 53
TLR 663, 81 Sol Jo 497, 35 LGR 429, 26 Cr App Rep 34, sub nom R v Andrews
156 LT 464, 30 Cox CC 576, HL 344, 349, 485, 486
Angel [1968] 2 All ER 607n, [1968] 1 WLR 669, 112 Sol Jo 310, 52 Cr App Rep 280,
CA 472
Anglim and Cooke v Thomas [1974] VR 363 510
Anon (1704) 6 Mod Rep 105. See R v Jones
Ansell [1975] QB 215, [1974] 3 All ER 568, [1974] 3 WLR 430, 138 JP 781, 118 Sol Jo
715, 60 Cr App Rep 45, CA 463
Ansell v Swift [1987] Crim LR 194 245
Ansell v Thomas (1973) Times, 23 May, [1974] Crim LR 31, CA . . . 378
Anthony [1965] 2 QB 189, [1965] 1 All ER 440, [1965] 2 WLR 748, 129 JP 168, 49 Cr
App Rep 104, CCA 151
Antonelli and Barberi (1905) 70 JP 4 356
Appleby [1960] Crim LR 712, CCA 11
Appleyard (1985) 81 Cr App Rep 319, [1985] Crim LR 723 684
Aramah (1982) 147 JP 217, 127 Sol Jo 85, 76 Cr App Rep 190, 4 Cr App Rep (S) 407,
[1983] Crim LR 271, CA 10
Ardalan [1972] 2 All ER 257, [1972] 1 WLR 463, 136 JP 453, 116 Sol Jo 237, 56 Cr App
Rep 320, CA 279, 281
Armitage Ltd v Nicholson (1913) 108 LT 993, 77 JP 239, 29 TLR 425, 11 LGR 547, 23
Cox CC 416, DC 798
Armstrong (1885) 49 JP 745 . . . . 451, 452
Arrowsmith [1975] QB 678, [1975] 1 All ER 463, [1975] 2 WLR 484, 139 JP 221, 119
Sol Jo 165, 60 Cr App Rep 211, CA 81, 122, 837
Arthur (1980) unreported 52
Asbury [1986] Crim LR 258, CA 242
Ashman (1858) 1 F & F 88 398
Ashton-Rickardt [1978] 1 All ER 173, [1978] 1 WLR 37, 142 JP 90, 121 Sol Jo 774, 65
Cr App Rep 67, CA 108
Askey v Golden Wine Co Ltd [1948] 2 All ER 35, 64 TLR 379, 92 Sol Jo 411 . . 101
Assistant Recorder of Kingston-upon-Hull, ex p Morgan [1969] 2 QB 58, [1969] 1 All
ER 416, [1969] 2 WLR 246, 133 JP 165, 112 Sol Jo 1005, 53 Cr App Rep 96, DC . 131,
253, 472
Aston [1970] 3 All ER 1045, [1970] 1 WLR 1584, 135 JP 89, 114 Sol Jo 906, 55 Cr App
Rep 48, CA 549, 559
Atcherdam [1911] EDL 336 112
Atkinson (1869) 11 Cox CC 330 136
Atkinson [1985] Crim LR 314, CA 205
Atkinson v Sir Alfred McAlpine & Son Ltd (1974) 118 Sol Jo 564, DC . . 110, 111
A-G v Able [1984] QB 795, [1984] 1 All ER 277, [1983] 3 WLR 845, 127 Sol Jo 731, 78
Cr App Rep 197, [1984] Crim LR 35 . . . . 134, 140, 176, 359, 360
A-G v BBC [1981] AC 303, [1980] 3 All ER 161, [1980] 3 WLR 109, 124 Sol Jo 444, 78
LGR 529, HL 769
A-G v Butterworth. See A-G's Application, Re
A-G v Cozens (1934) 50 TLR 320, 78 Sol Jo 298 120
A-G v English [1982] 2 WLR 959, 126 Sol Jo 206, [1982] Crim LR 429; revsd [1983] 1
AC 116, [1982] 2 All ER 903, [1982] 3 WLR 278, 126 Sol Jo 511, 75 Cr App Rep
302, [1982] Crim LR 743, [1982] LS Gaz R 1175, HL . . . 776, 778
A-G v News Group Newspapers Ltd [1987] QB 1, [1986] 2 All ER 833, [1986] 3 WLR
365, 130 Sol Jo 408, [1986] NLJ Rep 584, [1986] LS Gaz R 1719, CA . 774
A-G v Newspaper Publishing plc [1987] 3 All ER 276, [1987] 3 WLR 942, [1987] NLJ
Rep 543; revsd [1987] 3 All ER 276, [1987] 3 WLR 942, 131 Sol Jo 1454, [1987]
NLJ Rep 686, CA 768, 769, 770, 779
A-G (on the relation of Glamorgan County Council and Pontardawe RDC) v PYA
Quarries Ltd [1957] 2 QE 169, [1957] 1 All ER 894, [1957] 2 WLR 770, 121 JP
323, 101 Sol Jo 338, 55 LGR 208, CA 795, 796
A-G v Times Newspapers (1983) Times, 12 February, DC . . . 774, 778
A-G v Times Newspapers Ltd [1974] AC 273, [1973] 3 All ER 54, [1973] 3 WLR 298,
117 Sol Jo 617, HL 774, 779

PAGE

A-G v Tod Heatley [1897] 1 Ch 560, [1895-9] All ER Rep 636, 66 LJ Ch 275, 76 LT
174, 45 WR 394, 13 TLR 220, 41 Sol Jo 311, CA   795
A-G v Whelan [1934] IR 518   231
A-G (Hong Kong) v Yeung Sun-shun [1987] HKLR 987   269
A-G for Colony of Hong Kong v Kwok-a-Sing (1873) LR 5 PC 179, 42 LJPC 64, 29
LT 114, 37 JP 772, 21 WR 825, 12 Cox CC 565, PC   818
A-G for Northern Ireland v Gallagher [1963] AC 349, [1961] 3 All ER 299, [1961] 3
WLR 619, 105 Sol Jo 646, 45 Cr App Rep 316, HL .   .   . 191, 210, 213, 219
A-G for State of South Australia v Brown [1960] AC 432, [1960] 1 All ER 734, [1960] 2
WLR 588, 104 Sol Jo 268, 44 Cr App Rep 100, [1960] ALR 395, PC   .   . 195
A-G of Ceylon v Perera [1953] AC 200, [1953] 2 WLR 238, 97 Sol Jo 78, PC   .   . 331
A-G of Ceylon v Reid [1965] AC 720, [1965] 1 All ER 812, [1965] 2 WLR 671, 109 Sol
Jo 196, PC 709, 710
A-G of Hong Kong v Nai-Keung [1988] Crim LR 125, PC   494
A-G of Hong Kong v Tse Hung-Lit [1986] AC 876, [1986] 3 All ER 173, [1986] 3
WLR 320, 130 Sol Jo 554, [1986] LS Gaz R 1995, PC   126
A-G of Hong Kong v Yip Kai-foon [1988] 1 All ER 153, PC   628
A-G's Application, Re, A-G v Butterworth [1963] 1 QB 696, LR 3 RP 327, [1962] 3
WLR 819; sub nom A-G v Butterworth [1962] 3 All ER 326, 106 Sol Jo 610, CA   . 79,
769, 782
A-G's Ref (No 5 of 1980) [1980] 3 All ER 816, [1981] 1 WLR 88, 124 Sol Jo 827,
[1981] Crim LR 45, CA   734
A-G's Reference (No 3 of 1980). See R v Hucklebridge, A-G's Reference (No 3 of
1980)
A-G's Reference (No 1 of 1975) [1975] QB 773, [1975] 2 All ER 684, [1975] 3 WLR 11,
139 JP 569, 119 Sol Jo 373, 61 Cr App Rep 118 , [1975] RTR 473, CA   .   133, 134,
135, 150
A-G's Reference (No 4 of 1979) [1981] 1 All ER 1193, [1981] 1 WLR 667, 145 JP 281,
125 Sol Jo 355, 71 Cr App Rep 341, [1981] Crim LR 51, CA   .   616, 617, 619, 621
A-G's Reference (No 1 of 1980) [1981] 1 All ER 366, [1981] 1 WLR 34, 145 JP 165,
124 Sol Jo 881, 72 Cr App Rep 60, [1981] Crim LR 41, CA   .   .   . 575
A-G's Reference (No 2 of 1980) [1981] 1 All ER 493, [1981] 1 WLR 148, 145 JP 169,
125 Sol Jo 16, 72 Cr App Rep 64, [1981] Crim LR 43, CA   .   .   . 665
A-G's Reference (No 4 of 1980) [1981] 2 All ER 617, [1981] 1 WLR 705, 145 JP 394,
125 Sol Jo 374, 73 Cr App Rep 40, [1981] Crim LR 492, CA   .   .   77, 78
A-G's Reference (No 6 of 1980) [1981] QB 715, [1981] 2 All ER 1057, [1981] 3 WLR
125, 145 JP 429, 125 Sol Jo 426, 73 Cr App Rep 63, CA   .   .   . 382, 384
A-G's Reference (No 1 of 1982) [1983] QB 751, [1983] 2 All ER 721, [1983] 3 WLR 72,
148 JP 115, 127 Sol Jo 377, [1983] Crim LR 534, CA   .   .   . 269, 271
A-G's Reference (No 2 of 1983) [1984] QB 456, [1984] 1 All ER 988, [1984] 2 WLR
465, 149 JP 104, 128 Sol Jo 203, 78 Cr App Rep 183, [1984] LS Gaz R 773, [1984]
Crim LR 289, CA   247
A-G's Reference (No 2 of 1982) [1984] QB 624, [1984] 2 All ER 216, [1984] 2 WLR
447, 128 Sol Jo 221, [1984] BCLC 60, 78 Cr App Rep 131, [1984] LS Gaz R 279,
[1984] Crim LR 241, CA   523
A-G's Reference (No 1 of 1983) [1985] QB 182, [1984] 3 All ER 369, [1984] 3 WLR
686, 128 Sol Jo 596, 79 Cr App Rep 288, [1984] Crim LR 570, [1984] LS Gaz R
2458, CA 492, 495, 519
A-G's Reference (No 1 of 1985) [1986] QB 491, [1986] 2 All ER 219, [1986] 2 WLR
733, 150 JP 242, 130 Sol Jo 299, 83 Cr App Rep 70, [1986] BSMD 75, [1986] LS
Gaz R 1226, [1986] Crim LR 476, CA   516
A-G's Reference (No 1 of 1974), Re [1974] QB 744, [1974] 2 All ER 899, [1974] 2
WLR 891, 138 JP 570, 118 Sol Jo 345, 59 Cr App Rep 203, CA   .   .   . 618
A-G's References (Nos 1 and 2 of 1979), Re [1980] QB 180, [1979] 3 All ER 143, [1979]
3 WLR 577, 143 JP 708, 123 Sol Jo 472, 69 Cr App Rep 266, [1979] Crim LR 585,
CA 290, 536, 607
A-G's reference for Northern Ireland (No 1 of 1975) [1977] AC 105, [1976] 2 All ER
937, [1976] 3 WLR 235, 120 Sol Jo 524, [1976] NI 169, HL   .   .   . 243, 248
Atwal v Massey [1971] 3 All ER 881, 136 JP 35, 56 Cr App Rep 6, DC   .   . 633
Atwell and O'Donnell (1801) 2 East PC 768   628
Audley's (Lord) Case (1631-2) Hut 115, 3 State Tr 401, sub nom Castlehaven's (Earl)
Case 1 Hale PC 629, HL   431
Austin [1961] Crim LR 416, CCA   5

PAGE

Austin (1973) 58 Cr App Rep 163, CA 398
Austin v Dowling (1870) LR 5 CP 534, 39 LJCP 260, 22 LT 721, 18 WR 1003 . . 408
Aves [1950] 2 All ER 330, 114 JP 402, 94 Sol Jo 475, 48 LGR 495, 34 Cr App Rep 159;
    sub nom Practice Note 66 (pt 2) TLR 156, CCA 635

B

B (J A) (an infant), Re [1965] Ch 1112, [1965] 2 All ER 168, [1965] 3 WLR 253, 109
    Sol Jo 556 770
B (a minor), Re (1981) [1981] 1 WLR 1421, 3 FLR 117, 12 Fam Law 25, 125 Sol Jo
    608, 80 LGR 107, CA 52
B and S v Leathley [1979] Crim LR 314 603
Bacon (1870) 22 LT 627, 11 Cox CC 540 742
Badry v DPP of Mauritius [1983] 2 AC 297, [1982] 3 All ER 973, [1983] 2 WLR 161,
    126 Sol Jo 819, PC 769, 781
Bailey (1800) Russ & Ry 1, CCR 80
Bailey [1961] Crim LR 828, CCA 198
Bailey [1983] 2 All ER 503, [1983] 1 WLR 760, 147 JP 558, 127 Sol Jo 425, 77 Cr App
    Rep 76, [1983] Crim LR 533, CA 40, 42, 209, 216, 217, 218
Baille-Smith (1977) 64 Cr App Rep 76, CA 446
Baillie (1859) 8 Cox CC 238 454
Bainbridge [1960] 1 QB 129, [1959] 3 All ER 200, [1959] 3 WLR 656, 123 JP 499, 43 Cr
    App Rep 194, CCA 144, 145
Baindail (otherwise Lawson) v Baindail [1946] P 122, [1946] 1 All ER 342, 115 LJP 65,
    174 LT 320, 62 TLR 263, 90 Sol Jo 151, CA 708
Baker (1883) 47 JP 666 375
Baker [1895] 1 QB 797, 64 LJMC 177, 72 LT 631, 43 WR 654, 11 TLR 342, 39 Sol Jo
    416, 15 R 346, CCR 745
Baker (1909) 28 NZLR 536, 11 GLR 575 144
Baker [1962] 2 QB 530, [1961] 3 All ER 703, [1961] 3 WLR 1205, 125 JP 650, 46 Cr
    App Rep 47, CCA 419
Balcombe v Desimoni [1972] ALR 513 . . . . 556, 558
Baldessare (1930) 144 LT 185, 29 Cox CC 193, 22 Cr App Rep 70, CCA . 138, 147, 148
Bale v Rosier [1977] 2 All ER 160, [1977] 1 WLR 263, 141 JP 292, 121 Sol Jo 187,
    [1977] Crim LR 224 . . . . 559, 565
Balfour v Balfour [1919] 2 KB 571, [1918-19] All ER Rep 860, 88 LJKB 1054, 121 LT
    346, 35 TLR 609, 63 Sol Jo 661, CA 514
Ball (1966) 110 Sol Jo 510, 50 Cr App Rep 266, CCA 114
Ball v Ward (1875) 33 LT 170, 40 JP 213 800
Balogh v Crown Court at St Albans [1975] QB 73, [1974] 3 All ER 283, [1974] 3 WLR
    314, 138 JP 703, 118 Sol Jo 582, CA 769, 771
Bank of England v Vagliano Bros [1891] AC 107, [1891-4] All ER Rep 93, 60 LJQB
    145, 64 LT 353, 55 JP 676, 39 WR 657, 7 TLR 333, HL 488
Banks (1794) 1 Esp 144, 5 RR 726 116
Banks (1873) 12 Cox CC 393 . . . . 253, 356
Banks [1916] 2 KB 621, [1916-17] All ER Rep 356, 85 LJKB 1657, 115 LT 457, 80 JP
    432, 25 Cox CC 535, 12 Cr App Rep 74, CCA 441
Barker [1962] 1 All ER 748, [1962] 1 WLR 349, 126 JP 274, 106 Sol Jo 289, 46 Cr App
    Rep 227, CCA 724
Barker [1983] 57 ALJR 426 601
Barker v Barker [1949] P 219, [1949] 1 All ER 247, [1949] LJR 464, 113 JP 91, 65 TLR
    49, 93 Sol Jo 88, 47 LGR 143, DC 476
Barker v Levinson [1951] 1 KB 342, [1950] 2 All ER 825, 114 JP 545, 66 (pt 2) TLR
    717, 94 Sol Jo 688, 49 LGR 110, DC 163
Barnard (1837) 7 C & P 784 545
Barnard (1980) 123 Sol Jo 803, 70 Cr App Rep 28, [1980] Crim LR 235, CA . 260
Barnet London Borough Council v Eastern Electricity Board [1973] 2 All ER 319,
    [1973] 1 WLR 430, 137 JP 486, 117 Sol Jo 245, 71 LGR 254, 25 P & CR 261, 226
    Estates Gazette 460 680
Barnett [1951] 2 KB 425, [1951] 1 All ER 917, 115 JP 305, [1951] 1 TLR 899, 95 Sol Jo
    337, 49 LGR 401, 35 Cr App Rep 37, CCA 268
Barr [1978] Crim LR 244 580
Barraclough [1906] 1 KB 201, 75 LJKB 77, 94 LT 111, 70 JP 14, 54 WR 147, 22 TLR
    41, 50 Sol Jo 44, 21 Cox CC 91, CCR 730

PAGE

Barratt (1873) LR 2 CCR 81, [1861-73] All ER Rep 792, 43 LJMC 7, 29 LT 409, 22
    WR 136, 12 Cox CC 498, CCR   435
Barrett and Barrett (1980) 124 Sol Jo 543, 72 Cr App Rep 212, CA .   .   83, 84, 88
Barronet and Allain (1852) Dears CC 51   80
Barrow (1868) LR 1 CCR 156, 38 LJMC 20, 19 LT 293, 17 WR 102, 11 Cox CC 191,
    CCR   435
Bartholomew [1908] 1 KB 554, 77 LJKB 275, 98 LT 284, 72 JP 79, 24 TLR 238, 52 Sol
    Jo 208, 6 LGR 262, 21 Cox CC 556, CCR   799
Barton [1976] Crim LR 514, CA   723
Barton v Armstrong [1976] AC 104, [1975] 2 All ER 465, [1975] 2 WLR 1050, 119 Sol
    Jo 286, 3 ALR 355, [1973] 2 NSWLR 598, PC   502
Bashir (1982) 77 Cr App Rep 59, [1982] Crim LR 687, CA .   .   .   66, 438
Bassett (1966) 111 Sol Jo 53, 51 Cr App Rep 28, CA   548
Bassey (1931) 47 TLR 222, 75 Sol Jo 121, 22 Cr App Rep 160, CCA .   271, 658
Bassi [1985] Crim LR 671, CA   752
Bastable v Little [1907] 1 KB 59, [1904-7] All ER Rep Ext 1147, 76 LJKB 77, 96 LT
    115, 71 JP 52, 23 TLR 38, 51 Sol Jo 49, 5 LGR 279, 21 Cox CC 354, DC .   392
Bastian [1958] 1 All ER 568n, [1958] 1 WLR 413, 102 Sol Jo 272, 42 Cr App Rep 75 . 201,
    202
Bateman (1925) 94 LJKB 791, [1925] All ER Rep 45, 133 LT 730, 89 JP 162, 41 TLR
    557, 69 Sol Jo 622, 28 Cox CC 33, 19 Cr App Rep 8, CCA .   .   .   353
Bateman v Evans (1964) 108 Sol Jo 522, [1964] Crim LR 601, DC .   .   .   142
Bater v Bater (otherwise Lowe) [1906] P 209, 75 LJP 60, 94 LT 835, 22 TLR 408, 50
    Sol Jo 389, CA   712
Baugh v Crago [1976] 1 Lloyd's Rep 563, [1975] RTR 453, [1976] Crim LR 72 .   124
Baxter (1970) [1972] 1 QB 1, [1971] 2 All ER 359, [1971] 2 WLR 1138, 135 JP 345, 115
    Sol Jo 246, 55 Cr App Rep 214, CA 299, 489
Bayley and Easterbrook [1980] Crim LR 503, CA 290, 536
Beach [1957] Crim LR 687, CCA   279
Beach and Owens [1957] Crim LR 687   279
Beal v Kelley [1951] 2 All ER 763, 115 JP 566, [1951] 2 TLR 865, 95 Sol Jo 685, 35 Cr
    App Rep 128, 49 LGR 833, DC   449
Beard v A-G for Northern Ireland [1963] AC 349, [1961] 3 All ER 299, [1961] 3 WLR
    619, 105 Sol Jo 646, 45 Cr App Rep 316, HL .   .   .   191, 213
Beard. See DPP v Beard
Beasley (1981) 73 Cr App Rep 44, [1981] Crim LR 635, CA .   .   .   375
Beatty v Gillbanks (1882) 9 QBD 308, [1881-5] All ER Rep 559, 51 LJMC 117, 47 LT
    194, 46 JP 789, 15 Cox CC 138   245
Becerra (1975) 62 Cr App Rep 212, CA 157, 158
Beck [1985] 1 All ER 571, [1985] 1 WLR 22, 149 JP 260, 128 Sol Jo 871, 80 Cr App
    Rep 355, [1985] LS Gaz R 762, CA .   .   .   275, 456, 577
Beckett (1836) 1 Mood & R 526   398
Beckford v R [1987] 3 All ER 425, [1987] 3 WLR 611, 131 Sol Jo 1122, [1987] NLJ Rep
    591, [1987] LS Gaz R 2192, PC .   .   86, 87, 88, 89, 93, 207, 241, 242
Bedder v DPP [1954] 2 All ER 801, [1954] 1 WLR 1119, 98 Sol Jo 556, 38 Cr App Rep
    133, HL   337
Behrendt v Burridge [1976] 3 All ER 285, [1977] 1 WLR 29, 140 JP 613, 120 Sol Jo
    538, 63 Cr App Rep 202, DC   467
Belfon [1976] 3 All ER 46, [1976] 1 WLR 741, 140 JP 523, 120 Sol Jo 329, 63 Cr App
    Rep 59, CA 71, 402
Bell [1978] Crim LR 233, CA   460
Bellamy v Wells (1890) 60 LJ Ch 156, 63 LT 635, 39 WR 158, 7 TLR 135 .   797
Bellenie [1980] Crim LR 437, CA   633
Bellerby v Carle [1983] 2 AC 101, [1983] 1 All ER 1031, [1983] 2 WLR 687, 127 Sol Jo
    272, 81 LGR 425, [1983] BSMD 78, HL   129
Bembridge (1783) 22 State Tr 1, 3 Doug KB 327   569
Benge (1865) 4 F & F 504   315
Bennett v Bale [1986] Crim LR 404, CA   392
Benstead and Taylor (1982) 126 Sol Jo 308, 75 Cr App Rep 276, CA .   .   577
Bentham [1973] QB 357, [1972] 3 All ER 271, [1972] 3 WLR 398, 136 JP 761, 116 Sol
    Jo 598, 56 Cr App Rep 618, CA 420, 703
Bentley (1850) 14 JP 671, 4 Cox CC 406   403

PAGE

Bentley [1923] 1 KB 403, 92 LJKB 366, 87 JP 55, 39 TLR 105, 67 Sol Jo 279, CCA   .   474, 475

Bentley v Brudzinski (1982) 75 Cr App Rep 217, [1982] Crim LR 825, DC   .   .   390

Bergmann and Ferguson (1948) unreported 365, 366

Bernhard [1938] 2 KB 264, [1938] 2 All ER 140, 107 LJKB 449, 159 LT 22, 102 JP 282, 54 TLR 615, 82 Sol Jo 257, 36 LGR 333, 31 Cox CC 61, 26 Cr App Rep 137, CCA   591

Berriman (1854) 6 Cox CC 388   358

Berry (1986) 83 Cr App Rep 7, [1986] Crim LR 394, CA   79

Bettaney [1985] Crim LR 104, CA   840

Betts v Stevens [1910] 1 KB 1, [1908-10] All ER Rep Ext 1245, 79 LJKB 17, 101 LT 564, 73 JP 486, 26 TLR 5, 7 LGR 1052, 22 Cox CC 187, DC   .   .   388, 392

Betts and Ridley (1930) 144 LT 526, 22 Cr App Rep 148, 29 Cox CC 259, CCA   .   .   148

Betty (1963) 48 Cr App Rep 6, CCA 149, 152

Bevan (1986) 84 Cr App Rep 143, [1987] Crim LR 129, CA   .   .   .   546, 559, 577

Beynon [1957] 2 QB 111, [1957] 2 All ER 513, [1957] 2 WLR 956, 121 JP 366, 101 Sol Jo 409, 41 Cr App Rep 123   184

Bhachu (1977) 65 Cr App Rep 261, CA   494

Bham [1966] 1 QB 159, [1965] 3 All ER 124, [1965] 3 WLR 696, 109 Sol Jo 573, 49 Cr App Rep 355, CCA   718

Bibi [1980] 1 WLR 1193, 124 Sol Jo 628, 71 Cr App Rep 360, 2 Cr App Rep (S) 177, [1980] Crim LR 732, CA   10

Bickley (1909) 73 JP 239, 53 Sol Jo 402, 2 Cr App Rep 53, CCA   .   .   .   161

Bierton [1983] Crim LR 392, CA   800

Bikram [1974] Crim LR 55, CA   428

Billinghurst [1978] Crim LR 553   384

Bingham [1973] QB 870, [1973] 2 All ER 89, [1973] 2 WLR 520, 137 JP 481, 117 Sol Jo 265, 57 Cr App Rep 439, CA   842

Bingley's Case (1821) Russ & Ry 446, CCR   132

Birch v Wigan Corpn [1953] 1 QB 136, [1952] 2 All ER 893, 116 JP 610, [1952] 2 TLR 840, 96 Sol Jo 783, 51 LGR 33, CA   604

Bird [1985] 2 All ER 513, [1985] 1 WLR 816, 129 Sol Jo 362, 81 Cr App Rep 110, [1985] LS Gaz R 1709, [1985] Crim LR 388, CA   244

Bird v Jones (1845) 7 QB 742, 15 LJQB 82, 5 LTOS 406, 10 JP 4, 9 Jur 870   .   .   407

Birmingham and Gloucester Rly Co (1842) 3 QB 223, 3 Ry & Can Cas 148, 2 Gal & Dav 236, 11 LJMC 134, 6 Jur 804   .   .   .   .   .   .   170, 171

Birtles (1911) 75 JP 288, 27 TLR 402, 6 Cr App Rep 177, CCA   .   .   .   706

Birtles [1969] 2 All ER 1131n, [1969] 1 WLR 1047, 133 JP 573, 113 Sol Jo 424, 53 Cr App Rep 469, CA   160

Biswell (1847) 9 LTOS 394, 11 JP 582, 2 Cox CC 279   453

Blake v Barnard (1840) 9 C & P 626   378

Blamires Transport Services Ltd [1964] 1 QB 278, [1963] 3 All ER 170, [1963] 3 WLR 496, 127 JP 519, 107 Sol Jo 598, 61 LGR 594, 47 Cr App Rep 272, CCA   .   .   267

Bland [1988] Crim LR 41, CA   138

Blaue [1975] 3 All ER 446, [1975] 1 WLR 1411, 139 JP 841, 119 Sol Jo 589, 61 Cr App Rep 271, CA 314, 319, 320, 322

Blayney v Knight (1975) 60 Cr App Rep 269, [1975] RTR 279, [1975] Crim LR 237   .   44

Blazina [1925] NZLR 407   594

Bliss v Lilley (1862) 32 LJQB 105, 32 LJMC 3, 3 B & S 128, 9 Jur NS 410, 7 LT 319 .   610

Bloxham (1943) 29 Cr App Rep 37, CCA   536

Bloxham [1983] 1 AC 109, [1982] 1 All ER 582, [1982] 2 WLR 392, 146 JP 201, 126 Sol Jo 154, 74 Cr App Rep 279, [1982] RTR 129, HL 621, 630

Boaler v R (1888) 21 QBD 284, 57 LJMC 85, 59 LT 554, 52 JP 791, 37 WR 29, 4 TLR 565, 16 Cox CC 488   826

Board of Trade v Owen [1957] AC 602, [1957] 1 All ER 411, [1957] 2 WLR 351, 121 JP 177, 101 Sol Jo 186, 41 Cr App Rep 11, HL 268, 271, 355

Boardman [1958] Crim LR 626, CCA   10

Bochin and Bodin [1979] Crim LR 176   255

Bogacki [1973] QB 832, [1973] 2 All ER 864, [1973] 2 WLR 937, 137 JP 676, 117 Sol Jo 355, 57 Cr App Rep 593, [1973] RTR 384, [1973] Crim LR 385, CA   .   .   582

Boggeln v Williams [1978] 2 All ER 1061, [1978] 1 WLR 873, 142 JP 503, 122 Sol Jo 94, 67 Cr App Rep 50   .   .   .   .   529, 532, 539

Bold [1962] Crim LR 58, CCA   11

PAGE

Boldizsar v Knight [1980] Crim LR 653 587
Bolduc and Bird [1967] SCR 677, [1967] 3 CCC 294, 60 WWR 665, 63 DLR (2d) 82 . 382
Bolidzsar v Knight [1980] Crim LR 653 138
Bolton v Crawley [1972] Crim LR 222, DC 213
Bolton (HL) (Engineering) Co Ltd v TJ Graham & Sons Ltd [1957] 1 QB 159, [1956]
    3 All ER 624, [1956] 3 WLR 804, 100 Sol Jo 816, 168 Estates Gazette 424, CA . 171
Bond v Evans (1888) 21 QBD 249, [1886-90] All ER Rep 1035, 57 LJMC 105, 59 LT
    411, 52 JP 613, 36 WR 767, 4 TLR 614, 16 Cox CC 461, DC . . . 125, 163
Boniface (No 2) [1967] Crim LR 186, CA 818
Bonner [1970] 2 All ER 97n, [1970] 1 WLR 838, 134 JP 429, 114 Sol Jo 188, 54 Cr App
    Rep 257, CA 488, 497, 509, 522, 523, 682
Bonnor [1957] VLR 227, ALR 187 . . . . 711, 716
Border Television Ltd, ex p A-G (1978) 122 Sol Jo 162, 68 Cr App Rep 375, [1978]
    Crim LR 221, DC 772
Boshears (1961) Times, 8 February 40
Bosley v Davies (1875) 1 QBD 84, [1874-80] All ER Rep 1284, 45 LJMC 27, 33 LT
    528, 40 JP 550, 24 WR 140, DC 125, 163
Boss v Kingston [1963] 1 All ER 177, [1963] 1 WLR 99, 106 Sol Jo 1053, 61 LGR 109,
    DC 124, 125
Boswell [1973] Crim LR 307 . . . . 326, 399
Bottrill, ex p Kuechenmeister [1947] KB 41, [1946] 2 All ER 434, 175 LT 232, 62 TLR
    570, sub nom R v Kuechenmeister, ex p Bottrill 115 LJKB 500, CA . . 829
Bouch [1983] QB 246, [1982] 3 All ER 918, [1982] 3 WLR 673, 126 Sol Jo 511, 76 Cr
    App Rep 11, CA 610
Boulter (1908) 72 JP 188 739
Boulton (1871) 12 Cox CC 87 281
Bourne [1939] 1 KB 687, [1938] 3 All ER 615, 108 LJKB 471, CCA . . 223, 365
Bourne (1952) 36 Cr App Rep 125, CCA . . 155, 156, 177, 231, 253, 256, 471
Bow (1976) 64 Cr App Rep 54, [1977] RTR 6, [1977] Crim LR 176, CA . . 583, 586
Bowker v Premier Drug Co Ltd [1928] 1 KB 217, [1927] All ER Rep 415, 96 LJKB
    750, 137 LT 347, 91 JP 118, 43 TLR 516, 25 LGR 306, 28 Cox CC 397, DC . 133,
                                                                      143
Bowman (1912) 76 JP 271, 22 Cox CC 729 837
Bowman v Secular Society Ltd [1917] AC 406, [1916-17] All ER Rep 1, 86 LJ Ch 568,
    117 LT 161, 33 TLR 376, 61 Sol Jo 478, HL 737, 738
Bowsher [1973] RTR 202, CA 81
Boxer (1944) 8 J Cr L 168-70 448
Boyce (1824) 1 Mood CC 29, CCR 402
Boyesen [1982] AC 768, [1982] 2 All ER 161, [1982] 2 WLR 882, 146 JP 217, 126 Sol Jo
    308, 75 Cr App Rep 51, HL 107, 108
Boyle (1986) 84 Cr App Rep 270, [1987] Crim LR 111, CA 294
Boyle and Merchant [1914] 3 KB 339, [1914-15] All ER Rep 553, 83 LJKB 1801, 111
    LT 638, 78 JP 390, 30 TLR 521, 58 Sol Jo 673, 24 Cox CC 406, 10 Cr App Rep
    180, CCA 503
Bracegirdle v Oxley [1947] KB 349, [1947] 1 All ER 126, [1947] LJR 815, 176 LT 187,
    111 JP 131, 63 TLR 98, 91 Sol Jo 27, 45 LGR 69, DC 481
Bradley (1979) 70 Cr App Rep 200, [1980] Crim LR 173, CA 635
Bradley v Moss [1974] Crim LR 430 426
Bradshaw (1878) 14 Cox CC 83 . . . . 347, 384
Bradshaw (1985) 82 Cr App Rep 79, [1985] Crim LR 733, CA 201
Bradshaw v Ewart-James [1983] QB 671, [1983] 1 All ER 12, [1982] 3 WLR 1000, 126
    Sol Jo 641, sub nom Bradshaw v Ewart-James, The NF Tiger [1982] 2 Lloyd's Rep
    564, DC 163, 166
Brain (1834) 6 C & P 349 310
Brambles Holdings Ltd v Carey (1976) 15 SASR 270, 2 ACLR 176 . . . 174
Bramblevale Ltd, Re [1970] Ch 128, [1969] 3 All ER 1062, [1969] 3 WLR 699, [1971] 3
    WLR 821n, 113 Sol Jo 775, CA 768
Brannan v Peek [1948] 1 KB 68, [1947] 2 All ER 572, [1948] LJR 405, 112 JP 10, 63
    TLR 592, 91 Sol Jo 654, 45 LGR 654, DC 161
Bratty v A-G for Northern Ireland [1963] AC 386, [1961] 3 All ER 523, [1961] 3 WLR
    965, 105 Sol Jo 865, 46 Cr App Rep 1, HL . . 31, 42, 43, 186, 188, 189, 196, 213
Bravery v Bravery [1954] 3 All ER 59, [1954] 1 WLR 1169, 98 Sol Jo 573, CA . . 385

PAGE

Brawn (1843) 1 Car & Kir 144, sub nom R v Bawm 1 LTOS 528, 7 JP 530, 1 Cox CC
   33   709
Brazil v Chief Constable of Surrey [1983] 3 All ER 537, [1983] 1 WLR 1155, 148 JP 22,
   127 Sol Jo 712, 77 Cr App Rep 237, [1983] Crim LR 483, DC   .   .   .   389
Brewin [1976] Crim LR 742   411
Brewster (1979) 69 Cr App Rep 375, [1979] Crim LR 798, CA   .   .   .   516
Bridge v Campbell [1947] WN 223, 177 LT 444, 63 TLR 470, 91 Sol Jo 459, 45 LGR
   556, DC   465
Bridges v Hawkesworth (1851) 21 LJQB 75, [1843-60] All ER Rep 122, 18 LTOS 154,
   15 Jur 1079   512
Bridgewater Case (prior to 1880) cited in 57 LJQB 543   257
Brien (1903) 3 SRNSW 410, 20 WNNSW 154   36
Briggs (1856) Dears & B 98, 26 LJMC 7, 28 LTOS 108, 20 JP 741, 2 Jur NS 1195, 5
   WR 53, 7 Cox CC 175, CCR   711
Brindley [1971] 2 QB 300, [1971] 2 All ER 698, [1971] 2 WLR 895, 135 JP 357, 115 Sol
   Jo 285, 55 Cr App Rep 258, CA 761, 762
Brisson v R (1983) 139 DLR 685   248
Brittain [1972] 1 QB 357, [1972] 1 All ER 353, [1972] 2 WLR 450, 136 JP 198, 116 Sol
   Jo 140, 56 Cr App Rep 235, CA   803
Britton [1973] RTR 502, [1973] Crim LR 375, CA   .   .   395, 751, 753
Broad v Broad (1898) 78 LT 687, DC   .   .   476
Broadfoot [1976] 3 All ER 753, 141 JP 40, 64 Cr App Rep 71, CA   .   442, 456
Broadhurst v R [1964] AC 441, [1964] 1 All ER 111, [1964] 2 WLR 38, 107 Sol Jo 1037,
   PC   183
Brook v Ashton [1974] Crim LR 105, 231 Estates Gazette 615   .   .   .   81
Brooks v Mason [1902] 2 KB 743, 72 LJKB 19, 88 LT 24, 67 JP 47, 51 WR 224, 19
   TLR 4, 47 Sol Jo 13, 20 Cox CC 464   120
Brooks and Brooks (1982) 126 Sol Jo 855, 76 Cr App Rep 66, CA   .   571, 574
Broome v DPP [1974] AC 587, [1974] 1 All ER 314, [1974] 2 WLR 58, 118 Sol Jo 50,
   [1974] IRLR 26   .   .   .   .   .   .   391, 800
Broome v Perkins [1987] RTR 321, [1987] Crim LR 271   .   .   43, 481
Broughton [1953] VLR 572, [1953] ALR 866   .   .   711
Broughton v Wilkerson (1880) 44 JP 781, DC   .   .   802
Brown (1776) 1 Leach 148, 1 East PC 245   .   .   .   342
Brown (1841) Car & M 314, 4 State Tr NS App A 1369   .   .   136, 250, 767
Brown (1870) LR 1 CCR 244, 39 LJMC 94, 22 LT 484, 34 JP 436, 18 WR 792, 11 Cox
   CC 517, CCR   .   357
Brown (1889) 24 QBD 357, 59 LJMC 47, 61 LT 594, 54 JP 408, 38 WR 95, 16 Cox CC
   715, CCR   471
Brown [1970] 1 QB 105, [1969] 3 All ER 198, [1969] 3 WLR 370, 133 JP 592, 113 Sol
   Jo 639, 53 Cr App Rep 527, CA   .   .   .   54, 129, 626
Brown [1972] 2 QB 229, [1972] 2 All ER 1328, [1972] 3 WLR 11, 116 Sol Jo 431, 56 Cr
   App Rep 564, CA 334, 341
Brown (1976) 64 Cr App Rep 231, [1977] RTR 160, [1977] Crim LR 291, CA   .   405
Brown [1985] Crim LR 212, CA   596
Brown [1985] Crim LR 398, CA   414
Brown v Dyerson [1969] 1 QB 45, [1968] 3 All ER 39, [1968] 3 WLR 615, 132 JP 495,
   112 Sol Jo 805, 52 Cr App Rep 630, DC   226
Browne [1973] NI 96   .   .   .   .   244, 245, 344
Brutus v Cozens [1973] AC 854, [1972] 2 All ER 1297, [1972] 3 WLR 521, 136 JP 636,
   116 Sol Jo 647, 56 Cr App Rep 799, HL   81, 120, 490, 530, 532, 790
Bruzas [1972] Crim LR 367   .   .   298, 331
Bryan (1857) Dears & B 265, 26 LJMC 84, 21 JP 372, 3 Jur NS 620, 5 WR 598, 7 Cox
   CC 312, CCR   548
Bryan v Mott (1975) 119 Sol Jo 743, 62 Cr App Rep 71, [1976] Crim LR 64, DC   .   423
Bryson [1985] Crim LR 669   402
Buckingham (1976) 63 Cr App Rep 159, CA   .   420, 703
Buckoke v Greater London Council [1971] 1 Ch 655, [1971] 2 All ER 254, [1971] 2
   WLR 760, 115 Sol Jo 174, [1971] RTR 131, 69 LGR 210, CA   .   225, 692
Budd [1962] Crim LR 49, CCA   112
Bufalo [1958] VR 363, [1958] ALR 746   248
Bull and Schmidt (1845) 7 LTOS 7, 1 Cox CC 281   132

PAGE

Bullard v R [1957] AC 635, [1961] 3 All ER 470n, [1957] 3 WLR 656, 121 JP 576, 101
  Sol Jo 797, 42 Cr App Rep 1, PC 334
Bullock v Turnbull [1952] 2 Lloyd's Rep 303 122
Bundy [1977] 2 All ER 382, [1977] 1 WLR 914, 141 JP 345, 121 Sol Jo 252, 65 Cr App
  Rep 239, [1977] RTR 357, CA 606, 613
Bunyan and Morgan (1844) 3 LTOS 453, 1 Cox CC 74 . . . . . 469, 470
Burden v Rigler [1911] 1 KB 337, 80 LJKB 100, 103 LT 758, 75 JP 36, 27 TLR 140, 9
  LGR 71, DC 799
Burdett (1820) 4 B & Ald 95, 1 State Tr 1 836
Burford (1669) 1 Vent 16 824
Burge v DPP [1962] 1 All ER 666n, [1962] 1 WLR 265, 106 Sol Jo 198, DC . . 476
Burgess (1862) Le & Ca 258, 1 New Rep 130, 32 LJMC 55, 7 LT 472, 27 JP 55, 9 Jur
  NS 28, 11 WR 96, 9 Cox CC 247, CCR 359
Burke [1987] Crim LR 336, CA 339
Burke, Howe, Bannister and Clarkson [1987] Crim LR 480, HL 76
Burles [1970] 2 QB 191, [1970] 1 All ER 642, [1970] 2 WLR 597, 134 JP 258, 114 Sol Jo
  86, 54 Cr App Rep 196, CA 185
Burns (1886) 2 TLR 510, 16 Cox CC 355 . . . . . . 834, 836, 837
Burns (1973) 58 Cr App Rep 364, CA 191, 213
Burns v Bidder [1967] 2 QB 227, [1966] 3 All ER 29, [1966] 3 WLR 99, 130 JP 342, 110
  Sol Jo 430 44
Burns v Nowell (1880) 5 QBD 444, 49 LJQB 468, 43 LT 342, 44 JP 828, 29 WR 39, 4
  Asp MLC 323, CA 47, 48, 80, 225
Burrell v Harmer [1967] Crim LR 169, 116 NLJ 1658 . . . . 382, 396
Burridge (1735) 3 P Wms 439, Sess Cas KB 200 757
Burrows [1952] 1 All ER 58n, 116 JP 47, [1952] 1 TLR 51, 96 Sol Jo 122, 35 Cr App
  Rep 180, CCA 448
Burt v Burt (1860) 2 Sw & Tr 88, 29 LJPM & A 133, 2 LT 439, 8 WR 552 . . 709
Burton v Davies [1953] QSR 26 406
Bush v Commonwealth 78 Ky 268 (1880) (Kentucky Court of Appeals) . . 319, 324
Bustler v State 184 SE 2d 24 (Tenn SC) (1944) 512
Buswell [1972] 1 All ER 75, [1972] 1 WLR 64, 136 JP 141, 116 Sol Jo 36, CA . 47, 128
Butler (1954) 38 Cr App Rep 57, CCA 646
Butt (1884) 51 LT 607, 49 JP 233, 1 TLR 103, 15 Cox CC 564, CCR . . . 132
Button (1848) 11 QB 929, 18 LJMC 19, 12 LTOS 309, 13 JP 20, 12 Jur 1017, 3 Cox
  CC 229 270
Button [1900] 2 QB 597, [1900-3] All ER Rep Ext 1648, 69 LJQB 901, 83 LT 288, 64
  JP 600, 48 WR 703, 16 TLR 525, 44 Sol Jo 659, 19 Cox CC 568, CCR . 295, 555
Byrne [1960] 2 QB 396, [1960] 3 All ER 1, [1960] 3 WLR 440, 104 Sol Jo 645, 44 Cr
  App Rep 246, CCA 202, 203, 204
Byrne [1968] 3 CCC 179, 63 WWR 385, Br Col CA 377
Byrne v Kinematograph Renters Society Ltd [1958] 2 All ER 579, [1958] 1 WLR 762,
  102 Sol Jo 509 601

C

C (a minor) v Eisenhower [1984] QB 331, [1983] 3 WLR 537, 129 Sol Jo 425, 78 Cr
  App Rep 48, sub nom JJC (a minor) v Eisenhower [1983] 3 All ER 230, [1983]
  Crim LR 567 398
C v S [1987] 1 All ER 1230, [1987] 2 WLR 1108, [1987] 2 FLR 505, [1987] Fam Law
  269, 131 Sol Jo 624, [1987] LS Gaz R 1410, CA 364
Cabbage (1815) Russ & Ry 292, CCR 528
Cade [1914] 2 KB 209, 83 LJKB 796, 110 LT 624, 78 JP 240, 30 TLR 289, 58 Sol Jo
  288, 24 Cox CC 131, 10 Cr App Rep 23, CCA 646
Cadman (1825) 1 Mood CC 114 403
Cafferata v Wilson [1936] 3 All ER 149, 155 LT 510, 100 JP 489, 53 TLR 34, 80 Sol Jo
  856, 34 LGR 546, 30 Cox CC 475, DC 140, 420
Caine [1963] Crim LR 63, CCA 14
Calder and Boyars Ltd [1969] 1 QB 151, [1968] 3 All ER 644, [1968] 3 WLR 974, 133
  JP 20, 112 Sol Jo 688, 52 Cr App Rep 706, CA . . 720, 721, 722, 723, 727, 728
Calder (John) (Publications) Ltd v Powell [1965] 1 QB 509, [1965] 1 All ER 159, [1965]
  2 WLR 138, 129 JP 136, 109 Sol Jo 71, DC 720, 728

PAGE

Caldwell (1980) 71 Cr App Rep 237, CA; affd sub nom Metropolitan Police Comr v
Caldwell [1982] AC 341, [1981] 2 WLR 509, sub nom R v Caldwell [1981] 1 All ER
961, 145 JP 211, 125 Sol Jo 239, 73 Cr App Rep 13, HL   .   62, 63, 64, 65, 66, 67, 68, 69,
70, 73, 87, 91, 92, 95, 96, 123, 207, 212, 213,
214, 215, 217, 352, 483, 685, 686, 693
Caldwell v Leech [1911-13] All ER Rep 703, 109 LT 188, 77 JP 254, 29 TLR 457, 23
Cox CC 510, DC   458
Calf and Sun Insurance Office, Re [1920] 2 KB 366, 89 LJKB 691, 123 LT 128, 84 JP
153, 36 TLR 347, 2 Ll L Rep 304, CA   803
Calhaem [1985] QB 808, [1985] 2 All ER 266, [1985] 2 WLR 826, 129 Sol Jo 331, 81 Cr
App Rep 131, [1985] LS Gaz R 1485, [1985] Crim LR 303, CA .   .   .   135
Callow v Tillstone (1900) 83 LT 411, 64 JP 823, 19 Cox CC 576, DC   .   .   143, 776
Calvert v Mayes [1954] 1 QB 342, [1954] 1 All ER 41, [1954] 2 WLR 18, 118 JP 76, 98
Sol Jo 13, DC   461
Cambridgeshire and Isle of Ely County Council v Rust [1972] 2 QB 426, [1972] 3 All
ER 232, [1972] 3 WLR 226, 136 JP 702, 116 Sol Jo 564, 70 LGR 444, DC   .   81, 83, 801
Cameron v HM Advocate 1971 JC 50, 1971 SLT 333   819
Campbell (1985) 80 Cr App Rep 47, CA   660
Campbell (1986) 84 Cr App Rep 255, [1987] Crim LR 257, CA   .   .   202, 205
Campbell v Tormey [1969] 1 All ER 961, [1969] 1 WLR 189, 133 JP 267, 112 Sol Jo
1023, 53 Cr App Rep 99   406
Camplin (1845) 1 Car & Kir 746, 1 Den 89, 5 LTOS 266, 9 JP 424, 743, 1 Cox CC
220   433
Canestra 1952 (2) SA 317 (AD)   251
Cant v Parsons (1834) 6 C & P 504   406
Cargill [1913] 2 KB 271, 82 LJKB 655, 108 LT 816, 77 JP 347, 29 TLR 382, 23 Cox
CC 382, 8 Cr App Rep 224, CCA 11, 13
Carlgarth, The [1927] P 93, 96 LJP 162, 136 LT 518, 17 Asp MLC 195, CA   .   601
Carmichael (1930) 22 Cr App Rep 142, CCA   8
Carmichael [1940] 1 KB 630, [1940] 2 All ER 165, 109 LJKB 505, 163 LT 247, 56 TLR
517, 84 Sol Jo 551, 31 Cox CC 409, 27 Cr App Rep 183, CCA   .   .   446
Carmichael & Sons (Worcester) Ltd v Cottle (1971) 114 Sol Jo 867, [1971] RTR 11   .   131
Carpenter (1911) 76 JP 158, 22 Cox CC 618   .   .   .   .   270, 549
Carpenter [1960] Crim LR 633, CCA   427
Carpenter (30 July 1979, unreported), cited in [1983] 1 All ER 1004, CA   .   .   398
Carr-Briant [1943] KB 607, [1943] 2 All ER 156, 112 LJKB 581, 169 LT 175, 107 JP
167, 59 TLR 300, 41 LGR 183, 29 Cr App Rep 76, CCA   .   .   .   32, 196
Carraher v HM Advocate 1946 JC 108   218
Carter v Mace [1949] 2 All ER 714, 113 JP 527, DC   143
Carter v Richardson [1974] RTR 314, [1974] Crim LR 190   .   .   .   142
Cartledge v Allen [1973] Crim LR 530   399
Case (1850) 1 Den 580, T & M 318, 4 New Sess Cas 347, 19 LJMC 174, 15 LTOS 306,
14 JP 339, 14 Jur 489, 4 Cox CC 220, CCR   447
Case de Libellis Famosis (1605) 5 Co Rep 125a   824
Casement [1917] 1 KB 98, [1916-17] All ER Rep 214, 86 LJKB 467, 115 LT 267, 277,
32 TLR 601, 667, 60 Sol Jo 656, 25 Cox CC 480, 503, 12 Cr App Rep 99, 80 JP Jo
316, CCA 829, 830
Casey (1947) 63 TLR 487, 91 Sol Jo 693, 32 Cr App Rep 91, CCA   .   .   .   202
Cash [1985] QB 801, [1985] 2 All ER 128, [1985] 2 WLR 735, 129 Sol Jo 268, 80 Cr
App Rep 314, [1985] LS Gaz R 1330, [1985] Crim LR 311   .   .   .   628
Cassell & Co Ltd v Broome [1972] AC 1027, [1972] 1 All ER 801, [1972] 2 WLR 645,
116 Sol Jo 199, HL   23
Cassidy v Daily Mirror Newspapers Ltd [1929] 2 KB 331, [1929] All ER Rep 117, 98
LJKB 595, 141 LT 404, 45 TLR 485, 73 Sol Jo 348, CA   .   .   .   825
Castiglione and Porteous (1912) 106 LT 1023, 76 JP 351, 28 TLR 403, 23 Cox CC 46, 7
Cr App Rep 233, CCA   743
Castlehaven's (Earl) Case. See Audley's (Lord) Case
Caswell [1984] Crim LR 111   432
Cato [1976] 1 All ER 260, 270n, [1976] 1 WLR 110, 121n, 140 JP 169, 119 Sol Jo 775,
62 Cr App Rep 41, CA 314, 316, 352, 384, 404
Caton (1874) 12 Cox CC 624   148
Cattell v Ireson (1858) EB & E 91, 27 LJMC 167, 31 LTOS 80, 22 JP 672, 4 Jur NS
560, 6 WR 469   23

PAGE

Cavendish [1961] 2 All ER 856, [1961] 1 WLR 1083, 125 JP 460, 105 Sol Jo 709, 45 Cr
App Rep 374, CCA 623
Chadbund (1982) 4 Cr App Rep (S) 334, [1983] Crim LR 48 14
Champ (1981) 73 Cr App Rep 367, [1982] Crim LR 108, CA 109
Chan Kau (alias Chan Kai) v R [1955] AC 206, [1955] 1 All ER 266, [1955] 2 WLR
192, 99 Sol Jo 72, PC 31
Chan Man-sin v A-G of Hong Kong [1988] 1 All ER 1, [1988] 1 WLR 196, PC . 495, 498,
505, 535
Chan Wing-Siu v R [1985] AC 168, [1984] 3 All ER 877, [1984] 3 WLR 677, 128 Sol Jo
685, 80 Cr App Rep 117, [1984] LS Gaz R 216, [1984] Crim LR 549, PC . 149
Chandler v DPP [1964] AC 763, [1962] 3 All ER 142, [1962] 3 WLR 694, 106 Sol Jo
588, 46 Cr App Rep 347, HL 79, 273, 451, 490, 839
Chandler v Horne (1842) 2 Mood & R 423, [1835-42] All ER Rep 621 . . . 771
Chapman [1959] 1 QB 100, [1958] 3 All ER 143, [1958] 3 WLR 401, 122 JP 462, 102
Sol Jo 621, 42 Cr App Rep 257, CCA 430
Chapman [1974] Crim LR 488, CA 503
Chapman v Honig [1963] 2 QB 502, [1963] 2 All ER 513, [1963] 3 WLR 19, 107 Sol Jo
374, 186 Estates Gazette 713, CA 782
Chappell (1985) 80 Cr App Rep 31 644
Chard (1971) 56 Cr App Rep 268, CA 90
Charlson [1955] 1 All ER 859, [1955] 1 WLR 317, 119 JP 283, 99 Sol Jo 221, 39 Cr App
Rep 37, CCA 42, 188
Chelmsford Justices, ex p Amos [1973] Crim LR 437 253
Chief Constable of Avon and Somerset Constabulary v Shimmen (1986) 84 Cr App Rep
7, [1986] Crim LR 800 . . . . 65, 686
Chief Constable of Devon and Cornwall, ex p Central Electricity Generating Board
[1982] QB 458, [1981] 3 All ER 826, [1981] 3 WLR 967, 146 JP 91, 125 Sol Jo 745,
CA 388, 411
Chief Constable of Hampshire v Mace (1986) 150 JP 470, 84 Cr App Rep 40 . . 150
Chief Constable of Kent v V [1983] QB 34, [1982] 3 All ER 36, [1982] 3 WLR 462, 126
Sol Jo 536, CA 641
Chisholm v Doulton (1889) 22 QBD 736, [1886-90] All ER Rep Ext 1406, 58 LJMC
133, 60 LT 966, 53 JP 550, 37 WR 749, 5 TLR 437, 16 Cox CC 675, DC . . 798
Chiswibo 1960 (2) SA 714 77
Chow Sik Wah and Quon Hong [1964] 1 OR 401, [1964] 1 CCC 313, 42 CR 87 . . 664
Christian (1913) 78 JP 112, 23 Cox CC 541 . . . . . . 439, 456
Christie v Leachinsky [1947] AC 573, [1947] 1 All ER 567, [1947] LJR 757, 176 LT
443, 111 JP 224, 63 TLR 231, 45 LGR 201, HL 412
Christopherson v Bare (1848) 11 QB 473, 17 LJQB 109, 10 LTOS 393, 12 JP 153, 12
Jur 374 382
Church [1966] 1 QB 59, [1965] 2 All ER 72, [1965] 2 WLR 1220, 129 JP 366, 109 Sol Jo
371, 49 Cr App Rep 206, CCA 77, 78, 346
Church (1970) 114 Sol Jo 907, 55 Cr App Rep 65, CA 640
City of Sault Ste Marie (1978) 85 DLR (3d) 161, 40 CCC (2) 353, Can SC . . 96
Clarence (1888) 22 QBD 23, [1886-90] All ER Rep 133, 58 LJMC 10, 59 LT 780, 53 JP
149, 37 WR 166, 5 TLR 61, 16 Cox CC 511, CCR . . 382, 398, 408, 431, 436
Clark (1918) 82 JP 295, 26 Cox CC 138 756
Clark (No 2) [1964] 2 QB 315, [1963] 3 WLR 1067, 62 LGR 99, sub nom R v Clark
[1963] 3 All ER 884, 107 Sol Jo 983, 48 Cr App Rep 69, CCA . . . 799
Clark and Bagg (1842) 6 JP 508 321
Clarke (1854) Dears CC 397, 24 LJMC 25, 24 LTOS 136, 18 JP 743, 18 Jur 1059, 3
WR 20, 3 CLR 86, 6 Cox CC 412, CCR 435
Clarke [1949] 2 All ER 448, 33 Cr App Rep 216 430
Clarke [1956] cited in Crim LR 369-370 513
Clarke [1962] Crim LR 836, CCA 218
Clarke [1972] 1 All ER 219, 136 JP 184, 116 Sol Jo 56, 56 Cr App Rep 225, CA . 192
Clarke (1975) 61 Cr App Rep 320, [1975] Crim LR 595, CA 14
Clarke [1976] 2 All ER 696, 140 JP 469, 63 Cr App Rep 16, CA . . . 460
Clarke (1984) 80 Cr App Rep 344, [1985] LS Gaz R 682, [1985] Crim LR 209, CA . 162
Clarkson [1971] 3 All ER 344, [1971] 1 WLR 1402, 135 JP 533, 115 Sol Jo 654, 55 Cr
App Rep 445, C-MAC 134, 136, 213
Clatworthy [1981] Crim LR 501, [1981] RTR 477, CA 587
Clayton (1980) 72 Cr App Rep 135, [1981] Crim LR 186, CA 647

PAGE

Clayton and Halsey [1963] 1 QB 163, [1962] 3 WLR 815, sub nom R v Clayton, R v
    Halsey [1962] 3 All ER 500, 127 JP 7, 106 Sol Jo 652, 46 Cr App Rep 450, CCA .   724
Clear [1968] 1 QB 670, [1968] 1 All ER 74, [1968] 2 WLR 122, 132 JP 103, 112 Sol Jo
    67, 52 Cr App Rep 58, CA 503, 590, 779
Cleary v Booth [1893] 1 QB 465, 62 LJMC 87, 68 LT 349, 57 JP 375, 41 WR 391, 9
    TLR 260, 37 Sol Jo 270, 17 Cox CC 611, 5 R 263, DC   .   .   .   347, 386
Clegg (1868) 19 LT 47   741
Clemens [1898] 1 QB 556, 67 LJQB 482, 78 LT 204, 46 WR 416, 14 TLR 273, 42 Sol
    Jo 326, 19 Cox CC 18, CCR   689
Clifford (1845) 2 Car & Kir 202   660
Clifford v Bloom (1977) 121 Sol Jo 559, [1977] RTR 351, [1977] Crim LR 485 .   .   647
Clifford and O'Sullivan, Re [1921] 2 AC 570, 90 LJPC 244, 126 LT 97, 37 TLR 988, 65
    Sol Jo 792, 27 Cox CC 120, HL   23
Close [1977] Crim LR 107, CA   617
Closs (1857) Dears & B 460, 27 LJMC 54, 30 LTOS 235, 21 JP 805, 3 Jur NS 1309, 6
    WR 109, 7 Cox CC 494, CCR   647
Clouden [1987] Crim LR 56, CA   541
Clucas [1949] 2 KB 226, [1949] 2 All ER 40, [1949] LJR 1571, 113 JP 355, 65 TLR 346,
    93 Sol Jo 407, 47 LGR 563, 33 Cr App Rep 136, CCA .   .   .   554, 560
Cobb v Williams [1973] RTR 113, [1973] Crim LR 243   168
Cobbett (1804) 29 State Tr 1   834
Cobbett v Grey (1849) 4 Exch 729, 8 State Tr NS 1075, 19 LJ Ex 137, 14 LTOS 182,
    14 JP 56   406
Cocks (1976) 63 Cr App Rep 79   534
Codere (1916) 12 Cr App Rep 21, CCA   192
Coelho (1914) 30 TLR 535, 18 Cr App Rep 210, CCA .   .   .   196
Coffey [1987] Crim LR 498, CA   537
Coffin v Smith (1980) 71 Cr App Rep 221   388
Cogan [1976] QB 217, [1975] 2 All ER 1059, [1975] 3 WLR 316, 139 JP 608, 119 Sol Jo
    473, 61 Cr App Rep 217, CA   .   .   156, 177, 213, 253, 370, 430, 431
Coggins (1873) 29 LT 469, 38 JP 38, 12 Cox CC 517, CCR .   .   627
Cohen (1916) 34 WLR 210, 10 WWR 333   836
Coleman (1920) 84 JP 112   398
Coleman (1985) 150 JP 175, [1986] Crim LR 56 .   .   .   625
Coles (G J) & Co Ltd v Goldsworthy [1985] WAR 183 .   .   173
Collins (1839) 9 C & P 456, 3 State Tr NS 1149 .   .   .   835
Collins (1864) Le & Ca 471, 4 New Rep 299, 33 LJMC 177, 10 LT 581, 28 JP 436, 10
    Jur NS 686, 12 WR 886, 9 Cox CC 497, CCR   .   .   .   304
Collins (1957) 41 Cr App Rep 231, CCA   .   .   .   650, 655
Collins [1973] QB 100, [1972] 2 All ER 1105, [1972] 3 WLR 243, 136 JP 605, 116 Sol Jo
    432, 56 Cr App Rep 554, CA   .   .   436, 598, 606, 607
Collins v Wilcock [1984] 3 All ER 374, [1984] 1 WLR 1172, 148 JP 692, 128 Sol Jo 660,
    79 Cr App Rep 229, [1984] LS Gaz R 2140, [1984] Crim LR 481 .   376, 380, 390
Collinson (1931) 75 Sol Jo 491, 23 Cr App Rep 49, CCA   .   .   466
Collis-Smith [1971] Crim LR 716, CA   554
Collister (1955) 39 Cr App Rep 100, CCA   588
Colmer (1864) 9 Cox CC 506   358
Comer v Bloomfield (1970) 55 Cr App Rep 305, [1971] RTR 49, DC   .   295
Comet Products UK Ltd v Hawkex Plastics Ltd [1971] 2 QB 67, [1971] 1 All ER 1141,
    [1971] 2 WLR 361, 114 Sol Jo 975, CA   768
Commonwealth v Crow 303 Pa 91 (1931)   296
Commonwealth v Kennedy 170 Mass 18 (1897) .   .   .   292
Conegate Ltd v Customs and Excise Comrs: 121/85 [1987] QB 254, [1986] 2 All ER
    688, [1987] 2 WLR 39, 130 Sol Jo 75, [1986] Crim LR 562, [1987] LS Gaz R 743,
    ECJ; apld [1987] QB 254, [1986] 2 All ER 688, [1987] 2 WLR 39, 131 Sol Jo 75,
    [1987] LS Gaz R 743   734
Coney (1882) 8 QBD 534, 51 LJMC 66, 46 LT 307, 46 JP 404, 30 WR 678, 15 Cox CC
    46, CCR 136, 383
Conn v David Spencer Ltd [1930] 1 DLR 805, [1930] 1 WWR 26, 42 BCR 128 .   .   406
Connatty (1919) 83 JP 292   715
Conner (1835) 7 C & P 438   350
Consolidated Co v Curtis & Son [1892] 1 QB 495, 61 LJQB 325, 56 JP 565, 40 WR 426,
    8 TLR 403, 36 Sol Jo 328   498

PAGE

Cook [1954] 1 All ER 60, [1954] 1 WLR 125, 118 JP 71, 98 Sol Jo 30 . . 439, 443
Cook v Atchison (1968) 112 Sol Jo 235, DC 43
Cook v Stockwell (1915) 84 LJKB 2187, 113 LT 426, 79 JP 394, 31 TLR 426, 15 Cox
CC 49, DC 140
Cooke [1986] AC 909, [1986] 2 All ER 985, [1986] 3 WLR 327, 150 JP 498, 130 Sol Jo
572, 83 Cr App Rep 339, [1986] NLJ Rep 730, [1987] Crim LR 114, HL . 257, 575
Cooper v Metropolitan Police Comr (1985) 82 Cr App Rep 238 800
Cooper v Rowlands [1971] RTR 291, DC 802
Cooper v Simmons (1862) 7 H & N 707, 31 LJMC 138, 5 LT 712, 26 JP 486, 8 Jur NS
81, 10 WR 270 . . . . 81, 82
Cooper v Slade (1858) 6 HL Cas 746, 27 LJQB 449, 31 LTOS 334, 22 JP 511, 4 Jur NS
791, 6 WR 461 128
Cooper and Compton [1947] 2 All ER 701, 112 JP 38, 63 TLR 561, 46 LGR 83, 32 Cr
App Rep 102, CCA 279
Coppen v Moore (No 2) [1898] 2 QB 306, [1895-9] All ER Rep 926, 67 LJQB 689, 78
LT 520, 62 JP 453, 46 WR 620, 14 TLR 414, 42 Sol Jo 539, 19 Cox CC 45 . 163, 167
Corbett v Corbett (otherwise Ashley) [1971] P 83, [1970] 2 All ER 33, [1970] 2 WLR
1306, 114 Sol Jo 131 384
Corbyn v Saunders [1978] 2 All ER 697, [1978] 1 WLR 400, 142 JP 458, 122 Sol Jo 15,
67 Cr App Rep 7 540
Corcoran v Anderton (1980) 71 Cr App Rep 104, [1980] Crim LR 385 . . 540, 541
Corcoran v Whent [1977] Crim LR 52 500
Cory Bros & Co [1927] 1 KB 810, 96 LJKB 761, 136 LT 735, 28 Cox CC 346 . . 174
Costelloe v London Borough of Camden [1986] Crim LR 249 814
Cotterill v Penn [1936] 1 KB 53, [1935] All ER Rep 204, 105 LJKB 1, 153 LT 377, 99
JP 276, 51 TLR 459, 79 Sol Jo 383, 33 LGR 307, 30 Cox CC 258, DC . . 123
Cottle [1958] NZLR 999 196
Coughlan (1976) 63 Cr App Rep 33, CA 31, 280
Court (1912) 7 Cr App Rep 127, CCA 240
Court (1960) 44 Cr App Rep 242, CCA 623
Court [1987] QB 156, [1987] 1 All ER 120, [1986] 3 WLR 1029, 130 Sol Jo 859, 84 Cr
App Rep 210, [1986] LS Gaz R 3591, [1987] Crim LR 134, CA 450
Courtie [1984] AC 463, [1984] 1 All ER 740, [1984] 2 WLR 330, 148 JP 502, 128 Sol Jo
188, 78 Cr App Rep 292, HL 35, 121, 375, 471, 474
Cousins [1982] QB 526, [1982] 2 All ER 115, [1982] 2 WLR 621, 146 JP 264, 126 Sol Jo
154, 74 Cr App Rep 363, [1982] Crim LR 444, CA 357
Cowan v Milbourn (1867) LR 2 Exch 230, 36 LJ Ex 124, 16 LT 290, 31 JP 423, 15 WR
750 737
Coward v Baddeley (1859) 4 H & N 478, 28 LJ Ex 260, 33 LTOS 125, 23 JP 296, 5 Jur
NS 414, 7 WR 466 . . . . 379, 380
Cowburn [1959] Crim LR 590, CCA 385
Cox (1818) Russ & Ry 362, CCR 402
Cox v Riley (1986) 83 Cr App Rep 54, [1986] Crim LR 460 . . . 678, 679, 681
Cox and Hodges (1982) 75 Cr App Rep 291, [1983] BCLC 169, [1983] Crim LR 167,
CA 127, 274
Coxhead (1845) 1 Car & Kir 623 358
Coxhead [1986] RTR 411, CA 753
Cozins (1834) 6 C & P 351 471
Crabtree v Hole (1879) 43 JP 799, DC 165
Craig [1962] 3 All ER 961n, [1962] 1 WLR 1474, 127 JP 64, 106 Sol Jo 1013, 47 Cr App
Rep 32, CCA 762
Craig and Bentley (1952) Times, 10-13 December 158
Cramp (1880) 14 Cox CC 390; affd 5 QBD 307, 39 LJMC 44, 42 LT 442, 44 JP 411, 28
WR 701, 14 Cox CC 401, CCR 367, 403
Cratchley (1913) 9 Cr App Rep 232, CCA 438, 473
Crawford v Haughton [1972] 1 All ER 535, [1972] 1 WLR 572, 116 Sol Jo 125, [1972]
RTR 125, [1972] Crim LR 788 168
Crawley (1862) 3 F & F 109 795
Creamer [1966] 1 QB 72, [1965] 3 All ER 257, [1965] 3 WLR 583, 129 JP 586, 109 Sol
Jo 648, 49 Cr App Rep 368, CCA 346
Creevey (1813) 1 M & S 273 825
Creighton (1909) 14 CCC 349 195
Crespigny (1795) 1 Esp 280 747

PAGE

Cresswell (1876) 1 QBD 446, 45 LJMC 77, 33 LT 760, 40 JP 536, 24 WR 281, 13 Cox
    CC 126, CCR   706
Cribben (1980) 72 Cr App Rep 121, [1981] Crim LR 38, CA   .   .   151, 285
Crichton v Victorian Dairies Ltd [1965] VR 49   81
Crimmins [1959] VR 270, [1959] ALR 674   .   .   .   849
Crisp and Homewood (1919) 83 JP 121, CCA   .   .   .   841
Croft [1944] 1 KB 295, [1944] 2 All ER 483, 113 LJKB 308, 170 LT 312, 60 TLR 226,
    88 Sol Jo 152, 29 Cr App Rep 169, CCA   .   .   .   157
Cromack [1978] Crim LR 217, CA   253
Crook v Edmondson [1966] 2 QB 81, [1966] 1 All ER 833, [1966] 2 WLR 672, 130 JP
    191, 110 Sol Jo 147, 66 Cr App Rep 90n, DC .   .   .   467, 477
Cross (1812) 3 Camp 224   796
Crossman (1986) 130 Sol Jo 89, [1986] RTR 49, 82 Cr App Rep 333, [1986] LS Gaz R
    441, [1986] Crim LR 406, CA   .   .   .   65, 485
Crumley (1986) 7 NIJB 1   845
Crump v Gilmore (1969) 113 Sol Jo 998, 68 LGR 56, DC   .   .   43
Crunden (1809) 2 Camp 89   470
Crutchley (1831) 5 C & P 133, 1 Nev & MMC 282   .   .   231, 234
Cugullere [1961] 2 All ER 343, [1961] 1 WLR 858, 125 JP 414, 105 Sol Jo 386, 45 Cr
    App Rep 108, CCA   .   .   .   47, 419, 423, 427, 611
Cullen (1840) 9 C & P 681   711
Cullen (1974) unreported, (No 968/C/74)   .   .   .   514
Cummerson [1968] 2 QB 534, [1968] 2 All ER 863, [1968] 2 WLR 1486, 112 Sol Jo 424,
    52 Cr App Rep 519, CA   100
Cummings v Granger [1977] QB 397, [1977] 1 All ER 104, [1976] 2 WLR 842, 141 JP
    95, 120 Sol Jo 453, CA   692
Cundy v Le Cocq (1884) 13 QBD 207, 53 LJMC 125, 51 LT 265, 48 JP 599, 32 WR
    769   .   .   .   .   .   101, 125, 165
Cundy v Lindsay (1878) 3 App Cas 459, [1874-80] All ER Rep 1149, 38 LT 573, 42 JP
    483, 26 WR 406, 14 Cox CC 93, sub nom Lindsay & Co v Cundy 47 LJQB 481,
    HL   520
Cunliffe v Bleasdale (1972) 116 Sol Jo 746, [1972] Crim LR 567, [1973] RTR 90 .   395
Cunningham [1957] 2 QB 396, [1957] 2 All ER 412, [1957] 3 WLR 76, 121 JP 451, 101
    Sol Jo 503, 41 Cr App Rep 155, CCA   .   62, 122, 147, 400, 404, 683, 697
Cunningham [1959] 1 QB 288, [1958] 3 All ER 711, [1959] 2 WLR 63, 123 JP 134, 103
    Sol Jo 56, 43 Cr App Rep 79, CCA   331
Cunningham [1981] Crim LR 180, CA; affd [1982] AC 566, [1981] 2 All ER 863, [1981]
    3 WLR 223, 145 JP 411, 125 Sol Jo 512, 73 Cr App Rep 253, HL   . 86, 217, 329, 330
Curgerwen (1865) LR 1 CCR 1, [1861-73] All ER Rep Ext 1368, 35 LJMC 58, 13 LT
    383, 29 JP 820, 11 Jur NS 984, 14 WR 55, 10 Cox CC 152, CCR   .   .   711
Curl (or Curll) (1727) 2 Stra 788, 1 Barn KB 29, 17 State Tr 153   .   .   719
Curlett v M'Kechnie 1938 JC 176   394
Curley (1909) 2 Cr App Rep 96, 109, CCA   326
Curphey (1957) 41 Cr App Rep 78   487
Curr [1968] 2 QB 944, [1967] 1 All ER 478, [1967] 2 WLR 595, 131 JP 245, 111 Sol Jo
    152, 51 Cr App Rep 113, CA   .   .   .   80, 253, 254, 255

D

D [1984] AC 778, [1984] 1 All ER 574, [1984] 2 WLR 112, [1984] FLR 300, 128 Sol Jo
    63, 78 Cr App Rep 219, [1984] Crim LR 103, [1983] LS Gaz R 2998, CA; revsd
    [1984] AC 778, [1984] 2 All ER 449, [1984] 3 WLR 186, [1984] FLR 847, [1984]
    Fam Law 311, 128 Sol Jo 469, 79 Cr App Rep 313, [1984] Crim LR 558, [1984] LS
    Gaz R 2458, HL 409, 413
D (infant) v Parsons [1960] 2 All ER 493, [1960] 1 WLR 797, 124 JP 375, 104 Sol Jo
    605, 58 LGR 325, DC   138
Da Silva [1964] Crim LR 68, CA   5
Dabek [1973] Crim LR 527, CA   617
Dadson (1850) 3 Car & Kir 148, 2 Den 35, T & M 385, 4 New Sess Cas 431, 20 LJMC
    57, 16 LTOS 514, 14 JP 754, 14 Jur 1051, 4 Cox CC 358, CCR   .   37
Daily Mirror, ex p Smith [1927] 1 KB 845, [1927] All ER Rep 503, 96 LJKB 352, 136
    LT 539, 43 TLR 254, 28 Cox CC 324   .   .   .   772
Dalas (1966) Times, 28 September   114

PAGE

Dalby [1982] 1 All ER 916, [1982] 1 WLR 425, 146 JP 392, 126 Sol Jo 97, 74 Cr App
    Rep 348, CA 51, 319, 345, 351
Dale (1852) 6 Cox CC 14   403
Dale v Smith [1967] 2 All ER 1133, [1967] 1 WLR 700, 131 JP 378, 111 Sol Jo 330,
    DC 476, 814
Dallaway (1847) 3 Cox CC 273   487
Dallison v Caffery [1965] 1 QB 348, [1964] 2 All ER 610, [1964] 3 WLR 385, 128 JP
    379, 108 Sol Jo 560, CA   411
Dalloway (1847) 2 Cox CC 273   315
Dammaree (1710) 15 State Tr 521   828
Daniel v Morrison (1979) 70 Cr App Rep 142, 70 LGR 142, [1980] Crim LR 181, DC .   389
Dash v Police [1970] NZLR 273   393
Davenport [1954] 1 All ER 602, [1954] 1 WLR 569, 118 JP 241, 98 Sol Jo 217, 38 Cr
    App Rep 37, CCA   505
Davey v Towle [1973] RTR 328, DC 43, 250
Davidge v Bunnett [1984] Crim LR 297   514
Davidson [1969] VR 667   372
Davidson-Acres [1980] Crim LR 50, CA   814
Davies [1965] Crim LR 251, CCA   7
Davies [1975] QB 691, [1975] 1 All ER 890, [1975] 2 WLR 586, 139 JP 381, 119 Sol Jo
    202, 60 Cr App Rep 253, CA   338
Davies (1978) 68 Cr App Rep 319, CA   10
Davies [1983] Crim LR 741   218
Davies v DPP [1954] AC 378, [1954] 1 All ER 507, [1954] 2 WLR 343, 118 JP 222, 98
    Sol Jo 161, 38 Cr App Rep 11, HL   148
Davies v Flackett (1972) 116 Sol Jo 526, [1973] RTR 8, DC .   .   .   550
Davies v Harvey (1874) LR 9 QB 433, 43 LJMC 121, 30 LT 629, 38 JP 661, 22 WR
    733   167
Davies, Turner & Co Ltd v Brodie [1954] 3 All ER 283, [1954] 1 WLR 1364, 118 JP
    532, 98 Sol Jo 770, 52 LGR 558, DC   143
Davis (1881) 14 Cox CC 563   217
Davis [1977] Crim LR 542, CA   152
Davis v Alexander (1970) 54 Cr App Rep 398, DC   423
Davis v Lisle [1936] 2 KB 434, [1936] 2 All ER 213, 105 LJKB 593, 155 LT 23, 100 JP
    280, 52 TLR 475, 80 Sol Jo 409, 34 LGR 253, 30 Cox CC 412, DC .   .   389
Davis and Wagstaffe (1883) 15 Cox CC 174   321
Davison (1821) 4 B & Ald 329, 1 State Tr NS App 1366 .   .   .   770
Davison v Birmingham Industrial Co-operative Society Ltd (1920) 90 LJKB 206, 37
    TLR 50, 18 LGR 833   423
Dawson (1696) 13 State Tr 451   815
Dawson (1976) 64 Cr App Rep 170, CA   541
Dawson [1978] VR 536   230
Day (1841) 9 C & P 722   434
Day (1844) 8 JP 186   695
Day (1845) 4 LTOS 493, 9 JP 212, 1 Cox CC 207 .   .   .   381, 398
Dayle [1973] 3 All ER 1151, [1974] 1 WLR 181, 138 JP 65, 117 Sol Jo 852, 58 Cr App
    Rep 100, CA 424, 611
Deakin [1972] 3 All ER 803, [1972] 1 WLR 1618, 137 JP 19, 116 Sol Jo 944, 56 Cr App
    Rep 841, CA 621, 623
Dearlove (1988) Times, 28 January   251
De Beauvoir (1835) 7 C & P 17   740
Debreli (1964) 107 Sol Jo 894, [1964] Crim LR 53, CCA .   .   .   419
De Castro. See Skipworth's Case
De Costa Small v Kirkpatrick (1978) 68 Cr App Rep 186 .   .   .   409
Dee (1884) 15 Cox CC 579 .   .   .   .   .   433, 435
Defiant Cycle Co Ltd v Newell [1953] 2 All ER 38, 117 JP 324, sub nom Simmonds v
    Newell [1953] 1 WLR 826, 97 Sol Jo 438, DC .   .   .   82
de Haan [1968] 2 QB 108, [1967] 3 All ER 618n, [1968] 2 WLR 626, 112 Sol Jo 189, 52
    Cr App Rep 25, sub nom R v Haan 132 JP 75, CA .   .   .   10
De Jager v A-G of Natal [1907] AC 326, [1904-7] All ER Rep 1008, 76 LJPC 62, 96 LT
    857, 23 TLR 516, PC   830
Delaney v State 164 Tenn 432 (1932)   284
Deller (1952) 36 Cr App Rep 184, CCA 36, 37, 545

PAGE

De Montalk (1932) 23 Cr App Rep 182, CCA 730
De Munck [1918] 1 KB 635, [1918-19] All ER Rep 499, 87 LJKB 682, 119 LT 88, 82
JP 100, 34 TLR 305, 62 Sol Jo 405, 26 Cox CC 302, CCA . . . 455
Denham v Scott (1983) 147 JP 521, 77 Cr App Rep 210, [1983] Crim LR 558 . 631, 767
Dennis [1982] Crim LR 7 296
Dennis v Pight (1968) 11 FLR 458 138
Dent [1955] 2 QB 590, [1955] 2 All ER 806, [1955] 3 WLR 297, 119 JP 512, 99 Sol Jo
511, 39 Cr App Rep 131, CCA 549
Denton [1982] 1 All ER 65, [1981] 1 WLR 1446, 146 JP 138, 125 Sol Jo 746, 74 Cr App
Rep 81, CA 682, 688
Dermody [1959] Crim LR 63, CCA 11
Derrick v Customs and Excise Comrs [1972] 2 QB 28, [1972] 1 All ER 993, [1972] 2
WLR 359, 136 JP 294, 116 Sol Jo 97, [1972] Crim LR 112, CA . . . 734
Derriviere (1969) 53 Cr App Rep 637, CA 386
Derry v Peek (1889) 14 App Cas 337, [1886-90] All ER Rep 1, 58 LJ Ch 864, 61 LT
265, 54 JP 148, 38 WR 33, 5 TLR 625, 1 Meg 292, HL 545
Dervish (1967) 117 NLJ 1218, CA 43
Desmond v Thorne [1982] 3 All ER 268, [1983] 1 WLR 163, 126 Sol Jo 783 . 823
Devereux [1970] 2 All ER 647, [1970] 1 WLR 1109, 134 JP 510, 114 Sol Jo 106, 54 Cr
App Rep 295, CA 652
Devito and Devito [1975] Crim LR 175, CA 753
Dial Contracts Ltd v Vickers [1971] RTR 386 142
Diamond (1920) 84 JP 211 356
Dibble v Ingleton [1972] 1 QB 480, [1972] 2 WLR 163, 116 Sol Jo 97, [1972] RTR 161,
sub nom Ingleton v Dibble [1972] 1 All ER 275, 136 JP 155, DC . . 394
Dickins v Gill [1896] 2 QB 310, [1895-9] All ER Rep Ext 1880, 65 LJMC 187, 75 LT
32, 60 JP 488, 44 WR 686, 12 TLR 427, 40 Sol Jo 517, 18 Cox CC 384, DC . 668
Dickinson v Del Solar [1930] 1 KB 376, [1929] All ER Rep 139, 99 LJKB 162, 142 LT
66, 45 TLR 637, 34 Ll L Rep 445 617
Di Duca (1959) 43 Cr App Rep 167, CCA 218
Diggin (1980) 72 Cr App Rep 204, [1981] RTR 83, [1980] Crim LR 656, CA . 213, 582,
587
Dilks v Bowman-Shaw [1981] RTR 4 481
Dillon v R [1982] AC 484, [1982] 1 All ER 1017, [1982] 2 WLR 538, 126 Sol Jo 117, 74
Cr App Rep 274, [1982] Crim LR 438, PC 757
Dimes (1911) 76 JP 47, 7 Cr App Rep 43, CCA 446
Dip Kaur v Chief Constable for Hampshire [1981] 2 All ER 430, [1981] 1 WLR 578,
145 JP 313, 125 Sol Jo 323, 72 Cr App Rep 359, [1981] Crim LR 259 . . 494
DPP v A and BC Chewing Gum Ltd [1968] 1 QB 159, [1967] 2 All ER 504, [1967] 3
WLR 493, 131 JP 373, 111 Sol Jo 331, DC 721
DPP v Beard [1920] AC 479, [1920] All ER Rep 21, 36 TLR 379, 64 Sol Jo 340, 14 Cr
App Rep 159, sub nom R v Beard 89 LJKB 437, 122 LT 625, 84 JP 129, 26 Cox
CC 573, 57 SLR 743, HL 71, 210, 211, 217, 218
DPP v Beate Uhse (UK) Ltd [1974] QB 158, [1974] 1 All ER 753, [1974] 2 WLR 50,
138 JP 247, 118 Sol Jo 34, DC 736
DPP v Bhagwan (1970) [1972] AC 60, [1970] 3 All ER 97, [1970] 3 WLR 501, 134 JP
622, 114 Sol Jo 683, 54 Cr App Rep 460, HL 279
DPP v Camplin [1978] AC 705, [1978] 2 All ER 168, [1978] 2 WLR 679, 142 JP 320,
122 Sol Jo 280, 67 Cr App Rep 14, HL 236, 335, 337
DPP v Carey [1970] AC 1072, [1969] 3 All ER 1662, [1969] 3 WLR 1169, 134 JP 59,
113 Sol Jo 962, 54 Cr App Rep 119, HL 395
DPP v Doot. See R v Doot
DPP v Humphrys [1977] AC 1, [1976] 2 All ER 497, [1976] 2 WLR 857, 140 JP 386,
120 Sol Jo 420, 63 Cr App Rep 95, [1976] RTR 339, HL 742
DPP v Jordan [1977] AC 699, [1976] 3 All ER 775, [1976] 3 WLR 887, 141 JP 13, 120
Sol Jo 817, 64 Cr App Rep 33, HL 721, 727
DPP v Kent and Sussex Contractors Ltd [1944] KB 146, [1944] 1 All ER 119, 113
LJKB 88, 170 LT 41, 108 JP 1, 60 TLR 175, 88 Sol Jo 59, 42 LGR 10, DC . 173
DPP v McDonald [1976] AC 182, [1975] 2 WLR 913, sub nom R v Morgan [1975] 1
All ER 8, 118 Sol Jo 809, CA; affd sub nom DPP v McDonald [1976] AC 182,
[1975] 2 WLR 913, 119 Sol Jo 319, 61 Cr App Rep 136, sub nom DPP v Morgan
[1975] 2 All ER 347, 139 JP 476, HL . 66, 68, 69, 86, 87, 93, 156, 207, 208, 213, 383,
429, 714, 715

PAGE

DPP v Majewski [1977] AC 443, [1976] 2 All ER 142, [1976] 2 WLR 623, 140 JP 315,
   120 Sol Jo 299, 62 Cr App Rep 262, [1976] Crim LR 374, HL   .   40, 85, 89, 211, 212,
                                                        213, 214, 215, 217, 218, 220, 221, 381
DPP v Merriman [1973] AC 584, [1972] 3 All ER 42, [1972] 3 WLR 545, 136 JP 659,
   116 Sol Jo 745, 56 Cr App Rep 766, HL   152
DPP v Morgan. See DPP v McDonald
DPP v Newbury [1977] AC 500, [1976] 2 All ER 365, [1976] 2 WLR 918, 140 JP 370,
   120 Sol Jo 402, 62 Cr App Rep 291, HL 86, 346
DPP v Nock [1978] AC 979, [1978] 2 All ER 654, [1978] 3 WLR 57, 142 JP 414, 122
   Sol Jo 417, 67 Cr App Rep 116, HL 260, 301
DPP v Ottewell [1970] AC 642, [1968] 3 All ER 153, [1968] 3 WLR 621, 132 JP 499,
   112 Sol Jo 687, 52 Cr App Rep 679, HL 10, 14
DPP v Ray [1974] AC 370, [1973] 3 All ER 131, [1973] 3 WLR 359, 137 JP 744, 117
   Sol Jo 663, 58 Cr App Rep 130, HL   .   .   .   547, 549, 551, 570
DPP v Rogers [1953] 2 All ER 644, [1953] 1 WLR 1017, 117 JP 424, 97 Sol Jo 541, 37
   Cr App Rep 137, DC 379, 448
DPP v Shannon (1974) [1975] AC 717, [1974] 3 WLR 155, 138 JP 587, 118 Sol Jo 15,
   59 Cr App Rep 250, sub nom R v Shannon [1974] 2 All ER 1009, HL .   151, 284, 760
DPP v Smith [1961] AC 290, sub nom R v Smith [1960] 2 All ER 450, [1960] 3 WLR
   92, 104 Sol Jo 510, CCA; revsd sub nom DPP v Smith [1961] AC 290, [1960] 3 All
   ER 161, [1960] 3 WLR 546, 124 JP 473, 104 Sol Jo 683, 44 Cr App Rep 261, HL . 85,
                                                   328, 396, 398
DPP v Stonehouse [1978] AC 55, [1977] 2 All ER 909, [1977] 3 WLR 143, 141 JP 473,
   121 Sol Jo 491, 65 Cr App Rep 192, [1977] Crim LR 544, HL   .   151, 292, 293, 299, 314
DPP v Turner [1974] AC 357, [1973] 3 All ER 124, [1973] 3 WLR 352, 137 JP 736, 117
   Sol Jo 664, 57 Cr App Rep 932, HL 559, 566
DPP v Whyte [1972] AC 849, [1972] 3 All ER 12, [1972] 3 WLR 410, 136 JP 686, 116
   Sol Jo 583, 57 Cr App Rep 74, HL 720, 722, 724
DPP v Withers [1975] AC 842, [1974] 3 All ER 984, [1974] 3 WLR 751, 139 JP 94, 118
   Sol Jo 862, 60 Cr App Rep 85, HL   .   .   .   256, 271, 276, 637, 758
DPP for Northern Ireland v Lynch [1975] AC 653, [1975] 2 WLR 641, 119 Sol Jo 233,
   61 Cr App Rep 6, sub nom Lynch v DPP for Northern Ireland [1975] 1 All ER
   913, 139 JP 312, [1975] NI 35, [1975] Crim LR 707, HL .   32, 133, 139, 155, 213, 226,
                                                227, 230, 232, 233, 237
DPP for Northern Ireland v Maxwell [1978] 3 All ER 1140, [1978] 1 WLR 1350, 143 JP
   63, 122 Sol Jo 758, 68 Cr App Rep 128, [1978] NI 42, HL   .   .   144, 145
Dix (1982) 74 Cr App Rep 306, [1982] Crim LR 302, CA   .   .   .   202
Dixon [1961] 3 All ER 460n, [1961] 1 WLR 337, 105 Sol Jo 208   .   .   202
Dixon v Atfield [1975] 3 All ER 265, [1975] 1 WLR 1171, 139 JP 799, 119 Sol Jo 542,
   73 LGR 357, DC   800
Dobinson [1977] QB 354, [1977] 2 All ER 341, [1977] 2 WLR 169, 141 JP 354, 121 Sol
   Jo 83, 64 Cr App Rep 186, CA 50, 345, 352
Dodd (1974) 7 SASR 151   43
Dodd (1977) 66 Cr App Rep 87, CA   477
Dodge [1972] 1 QB 416, [1971] 3 WLR 366, 55 Cr App Rep 440, sub nom R v Dodge
   and Harris [1971] 2 All ER 1523, 135 JP 523, 115 Sol Jo 623, CA   .   .   651
Dodge and Harris (1971). See R v Dodge, R v Harris (1972)
Doe d Knight v Nepean (1833) 5 B & Ad 86   711
Doherty (1887) 16 Cox CC 306   328
Dolan (1855) Dears CC 436, 24 LJMC 59, 24 LTOS 279, 19 JP 55, 1 Jur NS 72, 3 WR
   177, 3 CLR 295, 6 Cox CC 449, CCR   .   .   .   618, 619
Dolan (1975) 62 Cr App Rep 36, CA   631
Dolman [1949] 1 All ER 813, 33 Cr App Rep 128   715
Dominion Trust Co v New York Life Insurance Co [1919] AC 254, 88 LJPC 30, 119
   LT 748, PC   680
Donaghy and Marshall [1981] Crim LR 644   541
Donald (1986) 130 Sol Jo 284, 83 Cr App Rep 49, [1986] LS Gaz R 1225, [1986] Crim
   LR 535, CA   760
Donaldson v Police [1968] NZLR 32   393
Dones [1987] Crim LR 682   403
Donnelly (1984) 79 Cr App Rep 76, CA   .   .   .   651, 652
Donnelly v Jackman [1970] 1 All ER 987, [1970] 1 WLR 562, 134 JP 352, 114 Sol Jo
   130, 54 Cr App Rep 229, DC 380, 389

PAGE

Donnelly unreported 845

Donoghue (or McAlister) v Stevenson. See M'Alister (or Donoghue) v Stevenson

Donovan [1934] 2 KB 498, [1934] All ER Rep 207, 103 LJKB 683, 152 LT 46, 98 JP 409, 50 TLR 566, 78 Sol Jo 601, 32 LGR 439, 30 Cox CC 187, 25 Cr App Rep 1, CCA 382, 385, 447

Donovan v Gavin [1965] 2 QB 648, [1965] 2 All ER 611, [1965] 3 WLR 352, 129 JP 404, 109 Sol Jo 373, DC 458

Doodeward v Spence (1908) 6 CLR 406, 15 ALR 105, 95 R (NSW) 107 . . . 524

Doot [1973] QB 73, [1972] 2 All ER 1046, [1972] 3 WLR 33, 136 JP 597, 116 Sol Jo 445, 57 Cr App Rep 13, CA; revsd sub nom DPP v Doot [1973] AC 807, [1973] 1 All ER 940, [1973] 2 WLR 532, 137 JP 375, 117 Sol Jo 266, 57 Cr App Rep 600, HL 269

Douce [1972] Crim LR 105 647

Doughty (1986) 83 Cr App Rep 319, [1986] Crim LR 625, CA . . . 333, 344

Douglas [1966] NZLR 45 367

Doukas [1978] 1 All ER 1061, [1978] 1 WLR 372, 122 Sol Jo 30, 66 Cr App Rep 228, CA 553, 612

Dowdall (1960) Times, 22 January 218

Downes (1983) 147 JP 729, 57 TC 681, 77 Cr App Rep 260, [1983] Crim LR 819, CA . 538

Downes v Fell (1969) 113 Sol Jo 387, [1969] Crim LR 376 482

Druker (1988) Times, 28 January 251

Drury (1974) 60 Cr App Rep 195, CA 457

Du Cros v Lambourne [1907] 1 KB 40, 76 LJKB 50, 95 LT 782, 70 JP 525, 23 TLR 3, 21 Cox CC 311, 5 LGR 120, DC 135, 137

Duck v Peacock [1949] 1 All ER 318, 113 JP 135, 65 TLR 87, 93 Sol Jo 165, 47 LGR 271, DC 46

Dudley and Stephens (1884) 14 QBD 273, [1881-5] All ER Rep 61, 54 LJMC 32, 52 LT 107, 49 JP 69, 33 WR 347, 1 TLR 118, 15 Cox CC 624, CCR . 226, 227, 228, 318

Duffin and Marshall (1818) Russ & Ry 365, CCR 402

Duffy [1949] 1 All ER 932n, CCA 332, 335, 341

Duffy [1967] 1 QB 63, [1966] 1 All ER 62, [1966] 2 WLR 229, 130 JP 137, 110 Sol Jo 70, 50 Cr App Rep 68, CCA 244

Dugdale v R (1853) 1 E & B 435, Dears CC 64, 22 LJMC 50, 17 JP 182, 17 Jur 546, 1 CLR 549, sub nom R v Dugdale 20 LTOS 219, CCR 47

Duguid (1906) 75 LJKB 470, 94 LT 887, 70 JP 294, 22 TLR 506, 50 Sol Jo 465, 21 Cox CC 200, CCR 283

Duke [1963] 1 QB 120, [1961] 3 All ER 737, [1961] 3 WLR 1194, 105 Sol Jo 891, 46 Cr App Rep 42, CCA 197

Dume (1986) Times, 16 October, CA 381, 400

Dunbar [1958] 1 QB 1, [1957] 2 All ER 737, [1957] 3 WLR 330, 121 JP 506, 101 Sol Jo 594, 41 Cr App Rep 182, CCA 201

Dunbar [1982] 1 All ER 188, [1981] 1 WLR 1536, 125 Sol Jo 746, 74 Cr App Rep 88, [1982] Crim LR 45, CA 109

Duncan v Jones [1936] 1 KB 218, [1935] All ER Rep 710, 105 LJKB 71, 154 LT 110, 99 JP 399, 52 TLR 26, 79 Sol Jo 903, 33 LGR 491, 30 Cox CC 279, DC . . 390

Dunn v Holt (1904) 73 LJKB 341, 90 LT 577, 68 JP 271, 20 TLR 297, 48 Sol Jo 299, 2 LGR 502, 20 Cox CC 625 800

Dunning and Graham (December 1985, unreported) 146

Dunnington [1984] QB 472, [1984] 1 All ER 676, [1984] 2 WLR 125, 148 JP 316, 127 Sol Jo 822, 78 Cr App Rep 171, [1984] LS Gaz R 38, [1984] Crim LR 98, CA . 150, 297

Durante [1972] 3 All ER 962, [1972] 1 WLR 1612, 116 Sol Jo 663, 56 Cr App Rep 708, CA 213

Durkin [1973] QB 786, [1973] 2 All ER 872, [1973] 2 WLR 741, 117 Sol Jo 355, 57 Cr App Rep 637, CA 580

Durose v Wilson (1907) 96 LT 645, 71 JP 263, 21 Cox CC 421, DC . . . 458

Duru [1973] 3 All ER 715, [1974] 1 WLR 2, 118 Sol Jo 7, 58 Cr App Rep 151, CA . 538

Dwyer v Mansfield [1946] KB 437, [1946] 2 All ER 247, [1947] LJR 894, 175 LT 61, 62 TLR 401, 90 Sol Jo 443 796

Dwyer (JW) Ltd v Metropolitan Police District Receiver [1967] 2 QB 970, [1967] 2 All ER 1051, [1967] 3 WLR 731, 131 JP 416, 111 Sol Jo 372, [1967] 2 Lloyd's Rep 29 . 788

Dyce Sombre, Re (1849) 1 Mac & G 116, 1 H & Tw 285, 13 Jur 857 . . . 772

PAGE

Dyson [1908] 2 KB 454, [1908-10] All ER Rep 736, 77 LJKB 813, 99 LT 201, 72 JP
   303, 24 TLR 653, 52 Sol Jo 535, 21 Cox CC 669, 1 Cr App Rep 13, CCA   .   36, 312
Dytham [1979] QB 722, [1979] 3 All ER 641, [1979] 3 WLR 467, 123 Sol Jo 621, 69 Cr
   App Rep 387, [1979] Crim LR 666, CA   49

E

Eagle (1862) 2 F & F 827   335
Eagleton (1855) Dears CC 376, 515, [1843-60] All ER Rep 363, 24 LJMC 158, 26
   LTOS 7, 19 JP 546, 1 Jur NS 940, 4 WR 17, 3 CLR 1145, 6 Cox CC 559, CCR   .   294
Earl Russell [1901] AC 446, 70 LJKB 998, 85 LT 253, 17 TLR 685, 20 Cox CC 51,
   HL 710, 712
Easom [1971] 2 QB 315, [1971] 2 All ER 945, [1971] 3 WLR 82, 135 JP 477, 115 Sol Jo
   485, 55 Cr App Rep 410, CA 291, 496, 536
Easson v London and North Eastern Rly Co [1944] KB 421, [1944] 2 All ER 425, 113
   LJKB 449, 170 LT 234, 60 TLR 280, 88 Sol Jo 143, CA   .   .   .   481
Eaton v Cobb [1950] 1 All ER 1016, 114 JP 271, 48 LGR 528   .   .   .   122, 800
Eddy v Niman (1981) 73 Cr App Rep 237, [1981] Crim LR 502   .   .   .   492
Eden (1971) 55 Cr App Rep 193, CA   576
Edgington v Fitzmaurice (1885) 29 Ch D 459, [1881-5] All ER Rep 59, 55 LJ Ch 650,
   53 LT 369, 50 JP 52, 33 WR 911, 1 TLR 326, CA   .   .   .   549, 556
Edmonds [1963] 2 QB 142, [1963] 1 All ER 828, [1963] 2 WLR 715, 127 JP 283, 107
   Sol Jo 196, 47 Cr App Rep 114, CCA 351, 424
Edwards (1843) 1 LTOS 528, 7 JP 532, 1 Cox CC 32   543
Edwards (1910) 4 Cr App Rep 280, CCA   5
Edwards [1978] Crim LR 49, CA   554
Edwards v Ddin [1976] 3 All ER 705, [1976] 1 WLR 942, 141 JP 27, 120 Sol Jo 587, 63
   Cr App Rep 218, [1976] RTR 508, DC 500, 570
Edwards (alias Murray) v R [1973] AC 648, [1973] 1 All ER 152, [1972] 3 WLR 893,
   137 JP 119, 116 Sol Jo 822, 57 Cr App Rep 157, PC .   .   .   333, 343
Edwards v Toombs [1983] Crim LR 43, [1983] LS Gaz R 93   .   .   .   575
Edwards and Roberts (1978) 67 Cr App Rep 228, 122 Sol Jo 177, [1978] Crim LR 564,
   CA   426
Edwards and Stacey (1877) 36 LT 30, 41 JP 212, 13 Cox CC 384, CCR   .   512, 525
Egginton (1801) 2 Bos & P 508, 2 Leach 913, CCR   533
El Ghazal [1986] Crim LR 52, CA   260
El-Hakkaoui [1975] 2 All ER 146, [1975] 1 WLR 396, 139 JP 467, 119 Sol Jo 186, 60 Cr
   App Rep 281, CA   420
Eldershaw (1828) 3 C & P 396   .   .   .   .   .   .   155, 438
Eley v Lytle (1885) 50 JP 308, 2 TLR 44, DC   678
Elkins v Cartlidge [1947] 1 All ER 829, 177 LT 519, 91 Sol Jo 573, 45 LGR 329, DC   .   466,
   467
Ellames [1974] 3 All ER 130, [1974] 1 WLR 1391, 138 JP 682, 118 Sol Jo 578, 60 Cr
   App Rep 7, CA 424, 612, 613, 614
Elliot (1861) Le & Ca 103, CCR 469, 470
Elliott v C (a minor) [1983] 2 All ER 1005, [1983] 1 WLR 939, 147 JP 425, 127 Sol Jo
   442, 77 Cr App Rep 103, [1983] Crim LR 616   .   .   .   64, 96, 685
Ellis v Smith [1962] 3 All ER 954, [1962] 1 WLR 1486, 127 JP 51, 106 Sol Jo 1069, 61
   LGR 64, DC   796
Ellis and Street (1986) 130 Sol Jo 649, 84 Cr App Rep 235, [1986] LS Gaz R 2996,
   [1987] Crim LR 44, CA 35, 73, 121
Else [1964] 2 QB 341, [1964] 1 All ER 649, [1964] 2 WLR 648, 108 Sol Jo 139, 48 Cr
   App Rep 131, CCA 155, 709, 718
Elvin [1976] Crim LR 204, CA   13
Elwes v Brigg Gas Co (1886) 33 Ch D 562, [1886-90] All ER Rep 559, 55 LJ Ch 734,
   55 LT 831, 35 WR 192, 2 TLR 782   129
Eminson [1963] Crim LR 560, 584, CCA   13
Emmens v Pottle (1885) 16 QBD 354, 55 LJQB 51, 53 LT 808, 50 JP 228, 34 WR 116,
   2 TLR 115, CA   773
Ensor (1887) 3 TLR 366   824
Entick v Carrington (1765) 2 Wils 275, [1558-1774] All ER Rep 41, 19 State Tr 1029,
   1066   831
Esop (1836) 7 C & P 456   80
Essendon Engineering Co Ltd v Maile [1982] RTR 260, [1982] Crim LR 510, DC   .   171

PAGE

Etim v Hatfield [1975] Crim LR 234 550
Evans (1821) 3 Stark 35 825
Evans [1986] Crim LR 470, CA 254
Evans v Barker [1971] RTR 453 801
Evans v Dell [1937] 1 All ER 349, 156 LT 240, 101 JP 149, 53 TLR 310, 81 Sol Jo 100,
    35 LGR 105, 30 Cox CC 558 121
Evans v Ewels [1972] 2 All ER 22, [1972] 1 WLR 671, 136 JP 394, 116 Sol Jo 274, 56
    Cr App Rep 377, DC 470
Evans v Hughes [1972] 3 All ER 412, [1972] 1 WLR 1452, 136 JP 725, 116 Sol Jo 842,
    56 Cr App Rep 813, DC 425
Evans v Wright [1964] Crim LR 466 425
Evans and Gardiner [1976] VR 517 231
Evans and Gardiner (No 2) [1976] VR 523 322
Evening Standard Co Ltd [1954] 1 QB 578, [1954] 1 All ER 1026, [1954] 2 WLR 861,
    98 Sol Jo 287, DC 99, 776

F

F (a minor), Re [1977] Fam 58, [1977] 1 All ER 114, [1976] 3 WLR 813, 120 Sol Jo
    753, CA 769, 783
Fabbri v Morris [1947] 1 All ER 315, 176 LT 172, 111 JP 97, 63 TLR 34, 91 Sol Jo
    161, 45 LGR 182, DC 796
Fagan v Metropolitan Police Comr [1969] 1 QB 439, [1968] 3 All ER 442, [1968] 3
    WLR 1120, 133 JP 16, 112 Sol Jo 800, 52 Cr App Rep 700, DC . 49, 54, 76, 376, 378,
                                        379, 380
Fairclough v Whipp [1951] 2 All ER 834, 115 JP 612, [1951] 2 TLR 909, 95 Sol Jo 699,
    35 Cr App Rep 138, 49 LGR 836, DC 379, 448
Fancy [1980] Crim LR 171 . . . . 680, 702
Farr [1982] Crim LR 745, [1982] LS Gaz R 1257, CA 131
Farrant [1973] Crim LR 240 735
Farrell (1862) 9 Cox CC 446 469
Farrell [1976] Crim LR 318, CA 428
Farrington v Thomson and Bridgland [1959] VR 286, [1959] ALR 695 . . . 601
Faulkes (1903) 19 TLR 250 711
Faulkner v Talbot [1981] 3 All ER 468, [1981] 1 WLR 1528, 125 Sol Jo 859, 74 Cr App
    Rep 1, DC 376, 448, 451
Feely [1973] QB 530, [1973] 1 All ER 341, [1973] 2 WLR 201, 137 JP 157, 117 Sol Jo
    54, 57 Cr App Rep 312, CA 529, 530
Fegan [1972] NI 80 247
Fell (1963) 107 Sol Jo 97, [1963] Crim LR 207, CCA 841
Felstead v R [1914] AC 534, [1914-15] All ER Rep 41, 8 LJKB 1132, 111 LT 218, 78 JP
    313, 30 TLR 469, 58 Sol Jo 534, 24 Cox CC 243, 10 Cr App Rep 129, HL . . 197
Fennell [1971] 1 QB 428, [1970] 3 All ER 215, [1970] 3 WLR 513, 134 JP 678, 114 Sol
    Jo 651, 54 Cr App Rep 451, [1970] Crim LR 581, CA 245, 391
Fenton (1830) 1 Lew CC 179 346
Fenton (1975) 119 Sol Jo 695, 61 Cr App Rep 261, CA 218
Ferguson [1970] 2 All ER 820, [1970] 1 WLR 1246, 134 JP 608, 114 Sol Jo 472, 54 Cr
    App Rep 410, CA 640, 642
Ferguson v Weaving [1951] 1 KB 814, [1951] 1 All ER 412, 115 JP 142, [1951] 1 TLR
    465, 95 Sol Jo 90, 49 LGR 339, DC 133, 142, 169
Fernandez, ex p (1861) 10 CBNS 3, 30 LJCP 321, 4 LT 324, 7 Jur NS 571, 9 WR 832 . 771
Fernandez [1970] Crim LR 277, CA 109, 145
Ferrymasters Ltd v Adams [1980] RTR 139, [1980] Crim LR 187 124
Field [1965] 1 QB 402, [1964] 3 All ER 269, [1964] 3 WLR 593, 128 JP 573, 108 Sol Jo
    641, 48 Cr App Rep 335, CCA 753
Field [1972] Crim LR 435, CA 245
Field v Chapman [1953] CLY 787, Times, 9 October 476
Figures [1976] Crim LR 744 627
Finau v Department of Labour [1984] 2 NZLR 396 . . . . . 47, 250
Fisher (1837) 8 C & P 182 . . . . 334, 336
Fisher (1865) LR 1 CCR 7, 35 LJMC 57, 13 LT 380, 29 JP 804, 11 Jur NS 983, 14 WR
    58, 10 Cox CC 146, CCR 678
Fisher [1987] Crim LR 334, CA 242

PAGE

Fisher v Bell [1961] 1 QB 394, [1960] 3 All ER 731, [1960] 3 WLR 919, 125 JP 101, 104
Sol Jo 981, DC   725
Fisherman's Case (1584) 2 East PC 661   528
Fitzmaurice [1983] QB 1083, [1983] 1 All ER 189, [1983] 2 WLR 227, 126 Sol Jo 656,
76 Cr App Rep 17, [1982] Crim LR 677, [1982] LS Gaz R 142, CA   .   .   301
Flack v Hunt (1979) 123 Sol Jo 751, 70 Cr App Rep 51, [1980] Crim LR 44   .   400
Flattery (1877) 2 QBD 410, 46 LJMC 130, 36 LT 32, 25 WR 398, 13 Cox CC 388,
CCR 435, 436
Fletcher (1841) Russell 417   313
Fletcher (1859) Bell CC 63, 28 LJMC 85, 32 LTOS 338, 23 JP 70, 5 Jur NS 179, 7 WR
204, 8 Cox CC 131, CCR 433, 435, 436
Fletcher (1866) LR 1 CCR 39, 35 LJMC 172, 14 LT 573, 12 Jur NS 505, 14 WR 774,
10 Cox CC 248, CCR   435
Fletcher [1962] 106 Sol Jo 554, [1962] Crim LR 551, CCA   157
Flower Freight Co Ltd v Hammond [1963] 1 QB 275, [1962] 3 All ER 950, [1962] 3
WLR 1331, 127 JP 42, 106 Sol Jo 919, 61 LGR 67, DC   423
Flynn (1985) 150 JP 112, 82 Cr App Rep 319, [1986] Crim LR 239, CA   .   .   424
Foo [1976] Crim LR 456, CA   114
Forbes (1835) 7 C & P 224   660
Forbes and Webb (1865) 10 Cox CC 362   391
Ford [1978] 1 All ER 1129, [1977] 1 WLR 1083, 142 JP 264, 121 Sol Jo 528, 66 Cr App
Rep 46, [1977] Crim LR 688, CA   477
Ford v Falcone [1971] 2 All ER 1138, [1971] 1 WLR 809, 135 JP 451, 115 Sol Jo 365,
55 Cr App Rep 372, DC   470
Forde [1923] 2 KB 400, [1923] All ER Rep 477, 92 LJKB 501, 128 LT 798, 87 JP 76, 39
TLR 322, 67 Sol Jo 539, 27 Cox CC 406, 17 Cr App Rep 99, CCA   .   .   447
Fordham (1839) 4 JP 397   122
Foster (1821) Russ & Ry 459   740
Foster (1852) 6 Cox CC 25   678
Foster v Foster [1921] P 438, [1921] All ER Rep 490, 90 LJP 363, 126 LT 50, 37 TLR
942, 66 Sol Jo (WR) 1, CA   431
Fothergill v Monarch Airlines Ltd [1981] AC 251, [1980] 2 All ER 696, [1980] 3 WLR
209, 124 Sol Jo 512, [1980] 2 Lloyd's Rep 295, HL   63
Fowler [1987] Crim LR 769, CA   636
Francis [1982] Crim LR 363, CA   610
Frankland v R [1987] AC 576, [1987] 2 WLR 1251, 131 Sol Jo 541, [1987] LS Gaz R
1491, PC 85, 328
Franklin (1883) 15 Cox CC 163   346
Fransman v Sexton [1965] Crim LR 556   124
Fraser (1982) 4 Cr App Rep (S) 254, [1982] Crim LR 841, CA   .   .   .   10, 14
Frazer (1861) 8 Cox CC 446   .   .   .   .   453, 454
Freedman (1930) 22 Cr App Rep 133, CCA   623
Freeman [1970] 2 All ER 413, [1970] 1 WLR 788, 134 JP 462, 114 Sol Jo 336, 54 Cr
App Rep 251, CA   420
Freestone [1913] TPD 758   369
French (1955) 39 Cr App Rep 192, CCA   359
Fretwell (1862) Le & Ca 161, 31 LJMC 145, 6 LT 333, 26 JP 499, 8 Jur NS 466, 10
WR 545, 9 Cox CC 152, CCR 139, 140
Fretwell (1864) Le & Ca 443, 4 New Rep 156, 33 LJMC 128, 10 LT 428, 28 JP 344, 10
Jur NS 595, 12 WR 751, 9 Cox CC 471, CCR   137
Frickey and Frickey [1956] Crim LR 421   749
Fritschy [1985] Crim LR 745, CA   492
Frost (1964) 108 Sol Jo 321, 48 Cr App Rep 284, CCA   622
Fuller (1797) 1 Bos & P 180, 2 Leach 790, 1 East PC 92   837
Fuller [1974] Crim LR 134, CA   698

G

Galvin [1961] VR 733   391
Galvin (No 2) [1961] VR 740   391
Galvin (1987) 88 Cr App Rep 85, [1987] Crim LR 700, CA   841
Gambling [1975] QB 207, [1974] 3 All ER 479, [1974] 3 WLR 558, 138 JP 749, 118 Sol
Jo 735, 60 Cr App Rep 25, CA   654

PAGE

Gammon (Hong Kong) Ltd v A-G of Hong Kong [1985] AC 1, [1984] 2 All ER 503,
[1984] 3 WLR 437, 128 Sol Jo 549, 80 Cr App Rep 194, 26 BLR 159, [1984] LS
Gaz R 1993, [1984] Crim LR 479, PC 97, 99, 105, 111

Garcia [1988] Crim LR 115, CA 655

Gardner v Akeroyd [1952] 2 QB 743, [1952] 2 All ER 306, 116 JP 460, [1952] 2 TLR
169, 96 Sol Jo 483, DC 169

Garforth [1954] Crim LR 936, CCA 316, 350

Garrett v Arthur Churchill (Glass) Ltd [1970] 1 QB 92, [1969] 2 All ER 1141, [1969] 3
WLR 6, 133 JP 509, 113 Sol Jo 381, DC 141

Garrett v Hooper [1973] RTR 1, [1973] Crim LR 61 168

Garwood [1987] 1 All ER 1032, [1987] 1 WLR 319, 131 Sol Jo 357, 85 Cr App Rep 85,
[1987] LS Gaz R 819, [1987] Crim LR 476, CA 590

Gathercole (1838) 2 Lew CC 237 738

Gaumont British Distributors Ltd v Henry [1939] 2 KB 711, [1939] 2 All ER 808, 108
LJKB 675, 160 LT 646, 103 JP 256, 55 TLR 750, 83 Sol Jo 525, 37 LGR 514,
DC 120, 122

Gayford v Chouler [1898] 1 QB 316, 67 LJQB 404, 78 LT 42, 62 JP 165, 14 TLR 166,
18 Cox CC 702, DC 678

Gaynor v Allen [1959] 2 QB 403, [1959] 2 All ER 644, [1959] 3 WLR 221, 123 JP 413,
103 Sol Jo 677 479

Geach (1840) 9 C & P 499 659

Gee (1983) 139 DLR 587 248

Gelberg v Miller [1961] 1 All ER 291, [1961] 1 WLR 153, 125 JP 123, 105 Sol Jo 89,
DC 393

George (1868) 11 Cox CC 41 358

George [1956] Crim LR 52 450

Getty v Antrim County Council [1950] NI 114 678

Ghani v Jones [1970] 1 QB 693, [1969] 3 All ER 720, [1969] 3 WLR 1158, 113 Sol Jo
775; affd [1970] 1 QB 693, [1969] 3 All ER 1700, [1969] 3 WLR 1158, 134 JP 166,
113 Sol Jo 854, CA 390

Ghosh [1982] QB 1053, [1982] 2 All ER 689, [1982] 3 WLR 110, 146 JP 376, 126 Sol Jo
429, 75 Cr App Rep 154, CA 128, 274, 529, 530, 531, 532, 556, 635

Gibbins and Proctor (1918) 82 JP 287, 13 Cr App Rep 134, CCA . . . 49, 296

Gibbon (1862) Le & Ca 109, 31 LJMC 98, 5 LT 805, 26 JP 149, 8 Jur NS 159, 10 WR
350, 9 Cox CC 105, CCR 745

Gibbon v Pepper (1692) 2 Salk 638 . . . . 380, 381

Gibbons v Kahl [1956] 1 QB 59, [1955] 3 All ER 345, [1955] 3 WLR 596, 120 JP 1, 99
Sol Jo 782, 54 LGR 35, DC 481

Gibson v Wales [1983] 1 All ER 869, [1983] 1 WLR 393, 147 JP 143, 127 Sol Jo 222 . 423

Gibson and Gibson (1984) 80 Cr App Rep 24, [1984] LS Gaz R 2375, [1984] Crim LR
615, CA 138

Giles (1865) Le & Ca 502, 5 New Rep 319, 34 LJMC 50, 11 LT 643, 29 JP 165, 11 Jur
NS 119, 13 WR 327, 10 Cox CC 44, CCR 555

Giles [1976] Crim LR 253 425

Gilks [1972] 3 All ER 280, [1972] 1 WLR 1341, 136 JP 777, 116 Sol Jo 632, 56 Cr App
Rep 734, CA 514, 520

Gill [1963] 2 All ER 688, [1963] 1 WLR 841, 127 JP 429, 107 Sol Jo 417, 47 Cr App
Rep 166, CCA 31, 231, 238

Gill v Carson and Nield [1917] 2 KB 674, 86 LJKB 1290, 117 LT 285, 81 JP 250, 15
LGR 567, 25 Cox CC 774 800

Gillick v West Norfolk and Wisbech Area Health Authority [1984] QB 581, [1984] 1 All
ER 365, [1983] 3 WLR 859, 147 JP 888, [1984] FLR 249, [1984] Fam Law 207, 127
Sol Jo 696, 133 NLJ 888, [1983] LS Gaz R 2678, CA; revsd [1986] AC 112, [1985]
3 All ER 402, [1985] 3 WLR 830, [1986] 1 FLR 224, 129 Sol Jo 738, [1986] Crim
LR 113, [1985] NLJ Rep 1055, [1985] LS Gaz R 3551, HL . . . 58, 139

Gillow (1825) 1 Mood CC 85, 1 Lew CC 57, CCR 402

Gilmartin [1983] QB 953, [1983] 1 All ER 829, [1983] 2 WLR 547, 147 JP 183, 127 Sol
Jo 119, 76 Cr App Rep 238, [1983] Crim LR 330, CA 545

Giorgianni (1984) 156 CLR 473 142

Gipson [1956] Crim LR 281, CCA 423

Gittens [1984] QB 698, [1984] 3 All ER 252, [1984] 3 WLR 327, 128 Sol Jo 515, 79 Cr
App Rep 272, [1984] Crim LR 553, [1984] LS Gaz R 2376, CA . . . 205

Glanville Williams [1983] Crim LR 365, [1982] CLJ 252 . . . . 33, 64

PAGE

Gleed (1916) 12 Cr App Rep 32, CCA 624
Gnosil (1824) 1 C & P 304 541
Gold [1987] 3 All ER 618, [1987] 3 WLR 803, 131 Sol Jo 1247, [1987] LS Gaz R 2529,
CA 649, 662
Gold Star Publications Ltd v DPP (1980) [1981] 2 All ER 257, [1981] 1 WLR 732, 145
JP 289, 125 Sol Jo 376, 73 Cr App Rep 141, [1981] Crim LR 634, HL . . . 732
Goldsmith v Pressdram Ltd [1977] QB 83, [1977] 2 All ER 557, [1976] 3 WLR 191, 120
Sol Jo 502 . . . . . . 822, 823
Goodfellow (1986) 83 Cr App Rep 23, [1986] Crim LR 468, CA . . 319, 351, 352
Goodfellow v Johnson [1966] 1 QB 83, [1965] 1 All ER 941, [1965] 2 WLR 1235, 129 JP
283, [1965] Brewing Tr Rev 247, DC 166, 167, 168, 776
Gordon [1982] Crim LR 240 14
Gorman (1978) 68 Cr App Rep 319, CA 10
Gorman v Standen [1964] 1 QB 294, [1963] 3 All ER 627, [1963] 3 WLR 917, 128 JP
28, 107 Sol Jo 811, 48 Cr App Rep 30, DC 458
Gosden v Elphick and Bennet (1849) 4 Exch 445, 7 Dow & L 194, 19 LJ Ex 9, 14
LTOS 157, 14 JP 38, 13 Jur 989 408
Gosney [1971] 2 QB 674, [1971] 3 All ER 220, [1971] 3 WLR 343, 115 Sol Jo 608, 55
Cr App Rep 502, [1971] RTR 321, CA 111, 113
Gott (1922) 16 Cr App Rep 87, CCA 739
Gott v Measures [1948] 1 KB 234, [1947] 2 All ER 609, 112 JP 18, 63 TLR 555, 91 Sol
Jo 678, 45 LGR 661, DC 693
Gould [1968] 2 QB 65, [1968] 1 All ER 849, [1968] 2 WLR 643, 132 JP 209, 112 Sol Jo
69, 52 Cr App Rep 152, CA 102, 711, 712, 714, 716
Goult (1982) 76 Cr App Rep 140, 4 Cr App Rep (S) 355, [1983] Crim LR 103, CA . 770
Gouws [1982] Crim LR 187 14
Governor of Pentonville Prison, ex p Tarling (1977) 70 Cr App Rep 77; revsd sub nom
Tarling v Government of Singapore (1978) 70 Cr App Rep 77, HL . 270, 274, 276
Grade v DPP [1942] 2 All ER 118, 167 LT 252, 106 JP 228, 58 TLR 327, 86 Sol Jo 321,
40 LGR 230, DC 168, 736
Graham [1964] Crim LR 486, CCA 12
Graham [1982] 1 All ER 801, [1982] 1 WLR 294, 146 JP 206, 126 Sol Jo 117, 74 Cr
App Rep 235, CA 232, 235
Grainge [1974] 1 All ER 928, [1974] 1 WLR 619, 138 JP 275, 118 Sol Jo 116, 59 Cr App
Rep 3, CA 633, 761
Grainger v Hill (1838) 4 Bing NC 212, 1 Arn 42, 5 Scott 561, 7 LJCP 85, 2 Jur 235 . 406
Grant (1848) 7 State Tr NS 507 834
Grant [1960] Crim LR 424 202
Grant [1985] Crim LR 387, CA 460
Grant v Borg [1982] 2 All ER 257, [1982] 1 WLR 638, 126 Sol Jo 311, HL . 47, 80, 84,
121
Grantham [1984] QB 675, [1984] 3 All ER 166, [1984] 2 WLR 815, 128 Sol Jo 331, 79
Cr App Rep 86, [1984] BCLC 270, [1984] LS Gaz R 1437, [1984] Crim LR 492,
CA 128
Gray [1900] 2 QB 36, [1900-3] All ER Rep 59, 69 LJQB 502, 82 LT 534, 64 JP 484, 48
WR 474, 16 TLR 305, 44 Sol Jo 362, DC 780
Gray v Barr [1971] 2 QB 554, [1971] 2 All ER 949, [1971] 2 WLR 1334, 115 Sol Jo 364,
[1971] 2 Lloyd's Rep 1, CA 44, 346
Gray's Haulage Co Ltd v Arnold [1966] 1 All ER 896, [1966] 1 WLR 534, 130 JP 196,
110 Sol Jo 112, DC 124
Great North of England Rly Co (1846) 9 QB 315, 16 LJMC 16, 7 LTOS 468, 11 JP 21,
10 Jur 755, 2 Cox CC 70 . . . . . 170, 171
Greater London Council, ex p Blackburn (1976) [1976] 3 All ER 184, [1976] 1 WLR
550, 120 Sol Jo 421, 74 LGR 464, CA 726
Greater London Metropolitan Police Comr v Streeter (1980) 71 Cr App Rep 113 . . 618
Greedy [1964] Crim LR 669, CCA 15
Green (1862) 3 F & F 274 455
Green v Burnett [1955] 1 QB 78, [1954] 3 All ER 273, [1954] 3 WLR 631, 118 JP 536,
98 Sol Jo 771, 52 LGR 545, DC 125, 168, 169
Green v Cross (1910) 103 LT 279, 74 JP 357, 26 TLR 507 . . . 54
Green v Goddard (1702) 2 Salk 641 802
Green v Moore [1982] QB 1044, [1982] 1 All ER 428, [1982] 2 WLR 671, 146 JP 142,
126 Sol Jo 79, 74 Cr App Rep 250, [1982] Crim LR 233, DC . . . 392

PAGE

Greenberg [1972] Crim LR 331 500
Greenfield [1973] 3 All ER 1050, [1973] 1 WLR 1151, 138 JP 58, 117 Sol Jo 679, 57 Cr
 App Rep 849, CA 280
Greenstein [1976] 1 All ER 1, [1975] 1 WLR 1353, 119 Sol Jo 742, 61 Cr App Rep 296,
 CA 545
Greep (1697). See R v Gripe
Gregory [1972] 2 All ER 861, [1972] 1 WLR 991, 136 JP 569, 116 Sol Jo 506, 56 Cr
 App Rep 441, CA 510
Gregory (1981) 74 Cr App Rep 154, [1982] Crim LR 229, CA . . 504, 542, 607, 627
Grey [1982] Crim LR 176, CA 477
Griepe. See R v Gripe (1697)
Grieve v MacLeod 1967 JC 32, 1967 SLT 70 426
Griffiths, ex p A-G [1957] 2 QB 192, [1957] 2 All ER 379, [1957] 2 WLR 1064, 101 Sol
 Jo 447 . . . . 773, 776
Griffiths [1966] 1 QB 589, [1965] 2 All ER 448, [1965] 3 WLR 405, 129 JP 380, 109 Sol
 Jo 312, 49 Cr App Rep 279, CCA 279, 280
Griffiths (1974) 60 Cr App Rep 14, CA 633, 761
Griffiths v Freeman [1970] 1 All ER 1117, [1970] 1 WLR 659, 134 JP 394, 114 Sol Jo
 263, DC 621
Griffiths v Studebakers Ltd [1924] 1 KB 102, 93 LJKB 50, 130 LT 215, 87 JP 199, 40
 TLR 26, 68 Sol Jo 118, 21 LGR 796, 27 Cox CC 565 . . . 168, 170, 171
Grimes [1968] 3 All ER 179n 751
Grimshaw [1983] LS Gaz R 2998, [1984] Crim LR 109, CA 67
Grimshaw (1985) 7 Cr App Rep (S) 137, [1984] Crim LR 108, CA . . . 400
Grinham v Willey (1859) 4 H & N 496, 28 LJ Ex 242, 33 LTOS 110, 23 JP 280, 5 Jur
 NS 444, 7 WR 463 408
Gripe (1697) 1 Com 43, sub nom R v Griepe 1 Ld Raym 256, 12 Mod Rep 139, sub
 nom R v Greep Carth 421, Comb 459, Holt KB 535, 5 Mod Rep 342, 2 Salk 513 . 745,
  746
Groombridge (1836) 7 C & P 582 . . . . 181, 438
Gross (1913) 77 JP 352, 23 Cox CC 455 . . . . 75, 333
Gross v Wright [1923] 2 DLR 171, [1923] SCR 214, [1923] 1 WWR 882 . . . 601
Grubb [1915] 2 KB 683, [1914-15] All ER Rep 667, 84 LJKB 1744, 113 LT 510, 79 JP
 430, 31 TLR 429, 59 Sol Jo 547, 25 Cox CC 77, 11 Cr App Rep 153, CCA . 174, 517
Gruncell and Hopkinson (1839) 9 C & P 365 628
Grundy [1977] Crim LR 543, CA 157, 158
Gullefer [1987] Crim LR 195, CA 294
Gully v Smith (1883) 12 QBD 121, 53 LJMC 35, 48 JP 309 49
Gutch, Fisher and Alexander (1829) Mood & M 433 825

H

Hadley [1970] 3 All ER 1045, [1970] 1 WLR 1584, 135 JP 89, 114 Sol Jo 906, 55 Cr
 App Rep 48, CA 549, 559
Hagan [1985] Crim LR 598, CA 659
Halai [1983] Crim LR 624, CA 562
Hale (1964) 108 Sol Jo 321, 48 Cr App Rep 284, CCA 622
Hale (1978) 68 Cr App Rep 415, CA 504, 542, 543, 627
Haley (1959) 76 WNNSW 550 248
Hall (1849) 2 Car & Kir 947n, 1 Den 381, T & M 47, 3 New Sess Cas 407, 18 LJMC
 62, 12 LTOS 383, 13 JP 55, 13 Jur 87, 3 Cox CC 245, CCR . . 534, 535
Hall (1928) 140 LT 142, 28 Cox CC 567, 21 Cr App Rep 48, CCA . . . 335
Hall (1964). See Smith v Desmond (1965)
Hall [1968] 2 QB 788, [1968] 2 All ER 1009, [1968] 3 WLR 359, 132 JP 417, 112 Sol Jo
 621, 52 Cr App Rep 528, CA 515
Hall (1985) 129 Sol Jo 283, 81 Cr App Rep 260, [1985] NLJ Rep 604, [1985] LS Gaz R
 1485, [1985] Crim LR 377, CA 634
Hall v Cotton [1987] QB 504, [1986] 3 All ER 332, [1986] 3 WLR 681, 130 Sol Jo 785,
 83 Cr App Rep 257, [1986] LS Gaz R 3340 416
Hallam [1957] 1 QB 569, [1957] 1 All ER 665, [1957] 2 WLR 521, 121 JP 254, 101 Sol
 Jo 268, 41 Cr App Rep 111, CCA 120
Hallett [1969] SASR 141 318
Halliday (1889) 61 LT 701, [1886-90] All ER Rep 1028, 54 JP 312, 38 WR 256, 6 TLR
 109, CCR 326, 399

PAGE

Halstead v Patel [1972] 2 All ER 147, [1972] 1 WLR 661, 136 JP 465, 116 Sol Jo 218, 56
    Cr App Rep 334, DC 545
Hamand (1985) 82 Cr App Rep 65, [1985] LS Gaz R 1561, [1985] Crim LR 375, CA . 31
Hamid Shadrokh-Cigaei (1988) Times, 23 February 519
Hamilton (1845) 1 Cox CC 244 . . . . 270, 554
Hammersley (1958) 42 Cr App Rep 207, CCA 279
Hammond [1982] Crim LR 611 . . . . 571, 573
Hampshire v Mace [1986] Crim LR 752, CA 474
Hancock and Shankland [1986] AC 455, [1986] 1 All ER 641, [1986] 3 WLR 1014, 150
    JP 33, 129 Sol Jo 793, 82 Cr App Rep 264, [1985] NLJ Rep 1208, [1986] Crim LR
    180, CA; affd [1986] AC 455, [1986] 1 All ER 641, [1986] 2 WLR 357, 150 JP 203,
    130 Sol Jo 184, 82 Cr App Rep 264, [1986] NLJ Rep 214, [1986] LS Gaz R 967,
    [1986] Crim LR 400, HL 56, 60, 328, 779
Handley (1859) 1 F & F 648 . . . . 453, 454
Handley (1874) 13 Cox CC 79 310
Hands (1887) 56 LT 370, 52 JP 24, 3 TLR 442, 16 Cox CC 188, CCR . . 550, 661
Hanson (1849) 2 Car & Kir 912, 4 Cox CC 138 381
Hapgood and Wyatt (1870) LR 1 CCR 221, 21 LT 678, 34 JP 181, 18 WR 356, 11 Cox
    CC 471, sub nom R v Wyatt 39 LJMC 83, CCR 151
Hardcastle v Bielby [1892] 1 QB 709, 61 LJMC 101, 66 LT 343, 56 JP 549, DC . . 126
Hardie [1984] 3 All ER 848, [1985] 1 WLR 64, 128 Sol Jo 851, 80 Cr App Rep 157,
    [1984] LS Gaz R 3419, CA 40, 209, 217, 685, 686, 698
Harding v Price [1948] 1 KB 695, [1948] 1 All ER 283, [1948] LJR 1624, 112 JP 189, 64
    TLR 111, 92 Sol Jo 112, 46 LGR 142, DC . . . 103, 110, 116, 125, 250
Hardman v Chief Constable of Avon and Somerset Constabulary [1986] Crim LR 330 . 679
Hare [1934] 1 KB 354, [1933] All ER Rep 550, 103 LJKB 96, 150 LT 279, 98 JP 49, 50
    TLR 103, 24 Cr App Rep 108, 32 LGR 14, 30 Cox CC 64, CCA . . . 451
Hargreaves [1985] Crim LR 243, CA 614
Hargreaves v Bretherton [1959] 1 QB 45, [1958] 3 All ER 122, [1958] 3 WLR 463, 102
    Sol Jo 637 327
Harley (1830) 4 C & P 369, 2 Man & Ry MC 486 403
Harling [1938] 1 All ER 307, 26 Cr App Rep 127, CCA 435
Harman v Secretary of State for the Home Department. See Home Office v Harman
Harman's Case (1620) 2 Roll Rep 154, 1 Hale PC 534 . . . . 541, 542
Harnett v Bond [1925] AC 669, [1925] All ER Rep 110, 94 LJKB 569, 133 LT 482, 89
    JP 182, 41 TLR 509, 69 Sol Jo 575, HL 408
Harper [1968] 2 QB 108, [1967] 3 All ER 619n, [1968] 2 WLR 626, 112 Sol Jo 189, 52
    Cr App Rep 21, CA 10
Harrington (1866) 10 Cox CC 370 334
Harris (1833) 1 Mood CC 393, 6 C & P 129, 2 Nev & MMC 151, CCR . . 658
Harris [1927] NPD 347 284
Harris [1964] Crim LR 54, CCA 137
Harris [1966] 1 QB 184, [1965] 3 All ER 206n, [1965] 3 WLR 1040, 129 JP 542, 109 Sol
    Jo 572, 49 Cr App Rep 330, CCA 664, 665
Harris (1971) 115 Sol Jo 247, 55 Cr App Rep 290, CA 472
Harris (1975) 62 Cr App Rep 28, CA 545
Harris (1987) 84 Cr App Rep 75, CA 633
Harris and Cocks (1871) LR 1 CCR 282, [1861-73] All ER Rep Ext 1308, 40 LJMC 67,
    24 LT 74, 35 JP 185, 19 WR 360, 11 Cox CC 659, CCR 469
Harrison [1938] 3 All ER 134, 159 LT 95, 82 Sol Jo 436, 31 Cox CC 98, 26 Cr App Rep
    166, CCA 93, 441
Harrison v Duke of Rutland [1893] 1 QB 142, [1891-4] All ER Rep 514, 62 LJQB 117,
    68 LT 35, 57 JP 278, 41 WR 322, 9 TLR 115, 4 R 155, CA . . . 798
Harrison v Leaper (1862) 5 LT 640, 26 JP 373 126
Harrison v Thornton (1966) 110 Sol Jo 444, [1966] Crim LR 388 . . 423, 425
Harrow Justices, ex p Osaseri [1986] QB 589, [1985] 3 All ER 185, [1985] 3 WLR 819,
    149 JP 689, 129 Sol Jo 669, 81 Cr App Rep 306, [1985] NLJ Rep 799, [1985] LS
    Gaz R 3171 375
Harry [1974] Crim LR 32 . . . . 589, 590
Harvey v Farnie (1880) 5 PD 153; revsd 6 PD 35, CA; on appeal (1882) 8 App Cas 43,
    [1881-5] All ER Rep 52, 52 LJP 33, 48 LT 273, 47 JP 308, 31 WR 433, HL . 708
Harvey and Chapman (1823) 2 B & C 257, [1814-23] All ER Rep 658, 2 State Tr NS 1,
    3 Dow & Ry KB 464, 2 LJOSKB 4 834

PAGE

Harvey, Uylett and Plummer (1981) 72 Cr App Rep 139, [1981] Crim LR 104, CA . 591, 592

Hassall (1861) Le & Ca 56, 30 LJMC 175, 4 LT 561, 25 JP 613, 7 Jur NS 1064, 9 WR 708, 8 Cox CC 491, CCR 509, 513

Hassard [1970] 2 All ER 647, [1970] 1 WLR 1109, 134 JP 510, 114 Sol Jo 106, 54 Cr App Rep 295, CA 652

Hastings and Meharg (1825) 1 Mood CC 82, CCR 819

Haughian (1985) 80 Cr App Rep 334, CA 437

Haughton v Smith [1975] AC 476, sub nom R v Smith [1973] 2 All ER 896, [1973] 2 WLR 942, 137 JP 598, 117 Sol Jo 429, 57 Cr App Rep 666, CA; affd sub nom Haughton v Smith [1975] AC 476, [1973] 3 All ER 1109, [1974] 2 WLR 1, 138 JP 31, 118 Sol Jo 7, 58 Cr App Rep 198, HL . 32, 290, 301, 536, 617, 618, 623, 746

Hawkesley [1959] Crim LR 211 278

Hawkins (1985) 150 JP 65, 82 Cr App Rep 141, [1986] BTLC 142, [1985] LS Gaz R 3696, [1986] Crim LR 168, CA 273

Hayat (1976) 120 Sol Jo 434, 63 Cr App Rep 181, [1976] Crim LR 508, CA . . 551

Hayes (1976) 64 Cr App Rep 82, [1977] Crim LR 691, CA . . . 515, 517

Hayford [1921] 2 WWR 990, 62 DLR 90, 35 CCC 293, 14 SCR 375, 15 Sask LR 375 . 747

Haynes v Swain [1975] RTR 40, [1974] Crim LR 483 . . . . 482, 484

Hayward (1833) 6 C & P 157 335

Hayward (1908) 21 Cox CC 692 326

Haywood [1971] VR 755 348

Hazelton (1874) LR 2 CCR 134, 44 LJMC 11, 31 LT 451, 39 JP 37, 23 WR 139, 13 Cox CC 1, CCR 545

Heath (1810) Russ & Ry 184, CCR 47

Heatons Transport (St Helens) Ltd v Transport and General Workers' Union [1972] 2 All ER 1214, [1972] 3 WLR 73, 116 Sol Jo 484, 14 KIR 1, CA . . . 768

Hedley v Webb [1901] 2 Ch 126, 84 LT 526, 65 JP 425, 17 TLR 393, sub nom Webb v Knight, Hedley v Webb 70 LJ Ch 663 604

Heffey [1981] Crim LR 111 426

Hehl (1976) 65 Cr App Rep 45, [1977] Crim LR 285, CA . . 497, 504, 536, 627

Henderson and Battley (1984) unreported 678, 679

Hendrickson and Tichner [1977] Crim LR 356, CA 255

Henman [1987] Crim LR 333, CA 414

Hennah (1877) 13 Cox CC 547 403

Hennigan [1971] 3 All ER 133, 135 JP 504, 115 Sol Jo 268, 55 Cr App Rep 262, [1971] RTR 305, CA 314, 487

Henshall (John) (Quarries) Ltd v Harvey [1965] 2 QB 233, [1965] 1 All ER 725, [1965] 2 WLR 758, 29 JP 224, 109 Sol Jo 152, DC 169, 172

Hensler (1870) 22 LT 691, [1861-73] All ER Rep Ext 1806, 34 JP 533, 19 WR 108, 11 Cox CC 570, CCR 45, 550

Henson (1852) Dears CC 24, 20 LTOS 63, 16 JP 711 795

Hepworth and Fearnley [1955] 2 QB 600, [1955] 3 WLR 331, 99 Sol Jo 544, sub nom R v Hepworth, R v Fearnley [1955] 2 All ER 918, 119 JP 516, 39 Cr App Rep 152, CCA 635

Herd v Weardale Steel Coal and Coke Co Ltd [1913] 3 KB 771, 82 LJKB 1354, 109 LT 457, CA; affd [1915] AC 67, 84 LJKB 121, 111 LT 660, 30 TLR 620, HL . 406, 408, 409

Heron [1981] 3 All ER 641, [1981] 1 WLR 1480, 125 Sol Jo 638, 74 Cr App Rep 327, CA; affd [1982] 1 All ER 993, sub nom R v Heron, R v Storey, R v Thomas [1982] 1 WLR 451, 126 Sol Jo 242, 75 Cr App Rep 7, HL 100, 672

Herring v Boyle (1834) 1 Cr M & R 377, 6 C & P 496, 4 Tyr 801, 3 LJ Ex 344 . . 407

Herrmann v Metropolitan Leather Co Ltd [1942] Ch 248, [1942] 1 All ER 294, 111 LJ Ch 141, 166 LT 155, 58 TLR 145, 86 Sol Jo 49 423

Hetherington (1841) 5634 State Tr NS 563, 5 JP 496, 5 Jur 529 . . . 737

Hewitt (1913) 9 Cr App Rep 192, CCA 744

Hewlett (1858) 1 F & F 91 402

Hibbert (1869) LR 1 CCR 184, 38 LJMC 61, 19 LT 799, 33 JP 243, 17 WR 384, 11 Cox CC 246, CCR 72, 263, 455

Hibbert v McKiernan [1948] 2 KB 142, [1948] 1 All ER 860, [1948] LJR 1521, 112 JP 287, 64 TLR 256, 92 Sol Jo 259, 46 LGR 238, DC 129, 511

PAGE

Hicklin (1868) LR 3 QB 360, 37 LJMC 89, 16 WR 801, 11 Cox CC 19, sub nom R v
Wolverhampton Recorder, Re Scott v Wolverhampton Justices 18 LT 395, 32 JP
533   .   .   .   .   720, 729, 730, 732
Hickman v Maisey [1900] 1 QB 752, 69 LJQB 511, 82 LT 321, 48 WR 385, 16 TLR
274, 44 Sol Jo 326, CA   798
Higgins (1801) 2 East 5   252
Higgins v Richards (1912) 28 TLR 202, DC   772
Hill (1986) 83 Cr App Rep 386, [1986] Crim LR 815   405
Hill v Baxter [1958] 1 QB 277, [1958] 1 All ER 193, [1958] 2 WLR 76, 122 JP 134, 102
Sol Jo 53, 56 LGR 117, 42 Cr App Rep 51, DC 40, 44, 112
Hill & Sons (Botley & Denmead) Ltd v Hampshire Chief Constable (1971) 115 Sol Jo
675, [1972] RTR 29   124
Hillen and Pettigrew v I C I (Alkali) Ltd [1936] AC 65, [1935] All ER Rep 555, 104
LJKB 473, 153 LT 403, 51 TLR 532, 41 Com Cas 29, HL   601
Hillman (1863) Le & Ca 343, [1861-73] All ER Rep Ext 1538, 3 New Rep 176, 33
LJMC 60, 9 LT 518, 27 JP 805, 12 WR 111, 9 Cox CC 386, CCR   .   .   . 369
Hills v Ellis [1983] QB 680, [1983] 1 All ER 667, [1983] 2 WLR 234, 148 JP 379, 126
Sol Jo 768, 76 Cr App Rep 217, [1983] Crim LR 182, 133 NLJ 280, [1983] LS Gaz
R 153   395
Hinchcliffe v Sheldon [1955] 3 All ER 406, [1955] 1 WLR 1207, 120 JP 13, 99 Sol Jo
797, DC 393
Hinds (1957) 41 Cr App Rep 143, CCA   757
Hirachand Punamchand v Temple [1911] 2 KB 330, [1911-13] All ER Rep Ext 1597, 80
LJKB 1155, 105 LT 277, 27 TLR 430, 55 Sol Jo 519, CA 755
Hircock (1978) 67 Cr App Rep 278, CA   494
Hobbs v Winchester Corpn [1910] 2 KB 471, 79 LJKB 1123, 102 LT 841, 74 JP 413, 26
TLR 557, 8 LGR 1072, CA   101
Hobson v Gledhill [1978] 1 All ER 945, [1978] 1 WLR 215, 142 JP 250, 121 Sol Jo 757,
DC   692
Hobson v Impett (1957) 41 Cr App Rep 138, DC 624
Hodgson [1954] Crim LR 379   423
Hoffman v Thomas [1974] 2 All ER 233, [1974] 1 WLR 374, 138 JP 414, 118 Sol Jo
186, [1974] RTR 182, DC   388
Hogan [1960] 2 QB 513, [1960] 3 All ER 149, [1960] 3 WLR 426, 124 JP 457, 104 Sol
Jo 645, 44 Cr App Rep 255, CCA   757
Hogben v Chandler [1940] VLR 285, 46 ALR 181   394
Holbrook (1877) 3 QBD 60, 47 LJQB 35, 37 LT 530, 42 JP 53, 26 WR 144, 13 Cox CC
650   825
Holbrook (1878) 4 QBD 42, 48 LJQB 113, 39 LT 536, 43 JP 38, 27 WR 313, 14 Cox
CC 185, DC   824
Holland (1841) 2 Mood & R 351   324
Hollington v F Hewthorn & Co Ltd [1943] KB 587, [1943] 2 All ER 35, 112 LJKB 463,
169 LT 21, 59 TLR 321, 87 Sol Jo 247, CA   617
Hollinshead [1985] AC 975, [1985] 1 All ER 850, [1985] 2 WLR 761, 129 Sol Jo 219, 80
Cr App Rep 285, CA; revsd [1985] AC 975, [1985] 2 All ER 769, [1985] 3 WLR
159, 129 Sol Jo 447, 81 Cr App Rep 365, HL   .   .   .   150, 265, 266, 274
Holloway (1849) 2 Car & Kir 942, 1 Den 370, 3 New Sess Cas 410, T & M 40, 18
LJMC 60, 12 LTOS 382, 13 JP 54, 13 Jur 86, 3 Cox CC 241, CCR   .   .   . 535
Holmes (1853) 3 Car & Kir 360, Dears CC 207, 1 CLR 487, 22 LJMC 122, 21 LTOS
160, 17 JP 390, 17 Jur 562, 1 WR 416, 6 Cox CC 216, CCR   467
Holmes v DPP [1946] AC 588, [1946] 2 All ER 124, 115 LJKB 417, 175 LT 327, 62
TLR 466, 90 Sol Jo 441, HL 331, 336, 337
Holroyd (1841) 2 Mood & R 339   124
Holt [1981] 2 All ER 854, [1981] 1 WLR 1000, 145 JP 377, 125 Sol Jo 373, 73 Cr App
Rep 96, [1981] Crim LR 499, CA 565, 566
Home Office v Harman [1981] QB 534, [1981] 2 All ER 349, [1981] 2 WLR 310, QB;
on appeal [1981] QB 534, [1981] 2 All ER 349, [1981] 2 WLR 310, 125 Sol Jo 149,
CA; affd sub nom Harman v Secretary of State for the Home Department [1983] 1
AC 280, [1982] 1 All ER 532, [1982] 2 WLR 338, 126 Sol Jo 136, HL .   .   . 783
Homer v Cadman (1886) 16 Cox CC 51, DC   800
Honig (1963) 54 J Cr L & Cr 258   84
Hood-Barrs [1943] 1 KB 455, [1943] 1 All ER 665, 112 LJKB 420, 168 LT 408, 59
TLR 246, 87 Sol Jo 220, 29 Cr App Rep 55, CCA   742

PAGE

Hoof (1980) 72 Cr App Rep 126, [1980] Crim LR 719, CA 699
Hooper v Eaglestone (1977) 76 LGR 308, 34 P & CR 311, 245 Estates Gazette 572 . 813
Hopkins (1957) 41 Cr App Rep 231, CCA 650, 655
Hopley (1860) 2 F & F 202 . . . . 348, 386
Hopwood (1913) 8 Cr App Rep 143, CCA 359
Hornby and Peaple [1946] 2 All ER 487, 175 LT 518, 110 JP 391, 62 TLR 629, 44 LGR
    406, 32 Cr App Rep 1, CCA 475
Horsham Justices, ex p Farquharson [1982] QB 762, [1982] 2 All ER 269, [1982] 2
    WLR 430, 126 Sol Jo 49, DC; affd [1982] QB 762, [1982] 2 All ER 269, [1982] 2
    WLR 430, 126 Sol Jo 98, 76 Cr App Rep 87, CA 777
Horton v Gwynne [1921] 2 KB 661, [1921] All ER Rep 497, 90 LJKB 1151, 125 LT
    309, 85 JP 210, 19 LGR 351, 26 Cox CC 744, CCA 123
Horton v Mead [1913] 1 KB 154, [1911-13] All ER Rep 954, 82 LJKB 200, 108 LT
    156, 77 JP 129, 23 Cox CC 279, DC 253, 466
Hotchin v Hindmarsh [1891] 2 QB 181, 60 LJMC 146, 65 LT 149, 55 JP 775, 39 WR
    607, 7 TLR 513, DC 168
Houghton [1982] Crim LR 112, CA 421
Howard [1965] 3 All ER 684, [1966] 1 WLR 13, 130 JP 61, 109 Sol Jo 920, 50 Cr App
    Rep 56, CCA 435
Howe [1958] SASR 95, 100 CLR 448, 32 ALJR 212, [1958] ALR 753 . . 248
Howe [1987] AC 417, [1987] 1 All ER 771, [1987] 2 WLR 568, 151 JP 265, 131 Sol Jo
    258, 85 Cr App Rep 32, [1987] NLJ Rep 197, [1987] LS Gaz R 900, HL . 227, 230,
                                                                232, 233, 236, 318
Howell [1982] QB 416, [1981] 3 All ER 383, [1981] 3 WLR 501, 146 JP 13, 125 Sol Jo
    462, 73 Cr App Rep 31, CA 411
Howells [1977] QB 614, [1977] 3 All ER 417, [1977] 2 WLR 716, 141 JP 641, 121 Sol Jo
    154, 65 Cr App Rep 86, CA 100, 111, 419
Howker v Robinson [1973] QB 178, [1972] 2 All ER 786, [1972] 3 WLR 234, 136 JP
    562, 116 Sol Jo 354, DC 164, 165, 166
Huckerby v Elliott [1970] 1 All ER 189, 134 JP 175, 113 Sol Jo 1001, DC . . 175
Hucklebridge, A-G's Reference (No 3 of 1980) [1980] 3 All ER 273, [1980] 1 WLR
    1284, 145 JP 13, 124 Sol Jo 592, 71 Cr App Rep 171, CA 416
Hudson [1956] 2 QB 252, [1956] 1 All ER 814, [1956] 2 WLR 914, 120 JP 216, 100 Sol
    Jo 284, 40 Cr App Rep 55, 36 TC 561, [1956] TR 93, 35 ATC 63, CCA . . 569
Hudson [1966] 1 QB 448, [1965] 1 All ER 721, [1965] 2 WLR 604, 129 JP 193, 109 Sol
    Jo 49, 49 Cr App Rep 69, CCA 96, 236, 444, 454, 457
Hudson [1971] 2 QB 202, [1971] 2 All ER 244, [1971] 2 WLR 1047, 135 JP 407, 115 Sol
    Jo 303, 56 Cr App Rep 1, CA 234
Hudson v MacRae (1863) 4 B & S 585, 3 New Rep 76, 33 LJMC 65, 9 LT 678, 28 JP
    436, 12 WR 80 123
Huggins (1730) 2 Stra 883, 17 State Tr 309, 2 Ld Raym 1574, 1 Barn KB 396, Fitz-G
    177 162
Hughes (1841) 9 C & P 752, 2 Mood CC 190, CCR 433
Hughes (1860) Bell CC 242, 29 LJMC 71, 1 LT 450, 24 JP 101, 6 Jur NS 177, 8 WR
    195, 8 Cox CC 278, CCR 151
Hughes v Hall [1960] 2 All ER 504, [1960] 1 WLR 733, 124 JP 411, 104 Sol Jo 566,
    DC 44
Hughes v Holley (1986) 86 Cr App Rep 130 477
Hulbert (1979) 69 Cr App Rep 243, CA 617
Hulton (E) & Co v Jones [1910] AC 20, [1908-10] All ER Rep 29, 79 LJKB 198, 101
    LT 831, 26 TLR 128, 54 Sol Jo 116, HL 825
Hume v Ingleby [1975] RTR 502, [1975] Crim LR 396 . . . . 479, 481
Humphreys [1977] Crim LR 225, CA 424
Humphreys and Turner [1965] 3 All ER 689, 130 JP 45 152
Hunt (1825) 1 Mood CC 93, CCR 402
Hunt [1950] 2 All ER 291, 114 JP 382, 34 Cr App Rep 135, 48 LGR 493, CCA . 475
Hunt (1958) Times, 26 November, CCA 13
Hunt (1977) 66 Cr App Rep 105, CA 690, 694
Hunt [1987] AC 352, [1987] 1 All ER 1, [1986] 3 WLR 1115, 130 Sol Jo 984, 84 Cr App
    Rep 163, [1986] NLJ Rep 1183, [1987] LS Gaz R 417, [1987] Crim LR 263, HL . 31
Hunter [1972] Crim LR 369; affd [1974] QB 95, [1973] 3 All ER 286, [1973] 3 WLR
    374, 137 JP 774, 117 Sol Jo 430, 57 Cr App Rep 772, [1973] Crim LR 514, CA . 358,
                                                                                756

PAGE

Hurford [1963] 2 QB 398, [1963] 2 All ER 254, [1963] 2 WLR 1038, 127 JP 374, 107
   Sol Jo 275, 47 Cr App Rep 141, CCA 663
Hurley and Murray [1967] VR 526 234
Hussain [1969] 2 QB 567, [1969] 2 All ER 1117, [1969] 3 WLR 134, 113 Sol Jo 424, 53
   Cr App Rep 448, CA 73, 121, 129
Hussain [1981] 2 All ER 287, [1981] 1 WLR 416, 146 JP 23, 125 Sol Jo 166, 72 Cr App
   Rep 143, CA 100, 416
Hussey (1924) 89 JP 28, 41 TLR 205, 18 Cr App Rep 160, CCA . . 246, 802
Husseyn (or Hussein) (1977) 67 Cr App Rep 131n, [1978] Crim LR 219, CA . 267, 289,
   536
Hutchison, ex p McMahon [1936] 2 All ER 1514, 155 LT 455, 80 Sol Jo 723 . . 772
Hyam v DPP [1975] AC 55, [1974] 2 All ER 41, [1974] 2 WLR 607, 138 JP 374, 118
   Sol Jo 311, 59 Cr App Rep 91, HL 56, 59, 86, 273, 318, 328
Hyland (1898) 24 VLR 101 369

I

ICR Haulage Ltd [1944] KB 551, [1944] 1 All ER 691, 113 LJKB 492, 171 LT 180, 108
   JP 181, 60 TLR 399, 42 LGR 226, 30 Cr App Rep 31, CCA . . . 173, 174
IPH v Chief Constable of South Wales [1987] Crim LR 42 179
Iannella v French (1968) 119 CLR 84 . . . . 84, 122
Ibrams (1981) 74 Cr App Rep 154, CA 335
Ikpong [1972] Crim LR 432, CA 621
Ilyas (1983) 78 Cr App Rep 17, 147 JPN 829, CA 295
Incledon v Watson (1862) 2 F & F 841 547
Ingram [1956] 2 QB 424, [1956] 2 All ER 639, [1956] 3 WLR 309, 120 JP 397, 100 Sol
   Jo 491, 40 Cr App Rep 115, CCA 549
Ingrams, ex p Goldsmith (1976) 120 Sol Jo 835, [1977] Crim LR 40, DC . . 769, 770
Innes v Wylie (1844) 1 Car & Kir 257, 8 JP 280 380
Instan [1893] 1 QB 450, [1891-4] All ER Rep 1213, 62 LJMC 86, 68 LT 420, 57 JP 282,
   41 WR 368, 9 TLR 248, 37 Sol Jo 251, 17 Cox CC 602, 5 R 248, CCR . . 50
Invicta Plastics Ltd v Clare (1975) 120 Sol Jo 62, [1976] RTR 251, [1976] Crim LR
   131, DC 252
Inwood [1973] 2 All ER 645, [1973] 1 WLR 647, 137 JP 559, 117 Sol Jo 303, 57 Cr App
   Rep 529, [1973] Crim LR 290, CA 389
Iremonger v Wynne [1957] Crim LR 624 137
Irving [1970] Crim LR 642, CA 108, 109
Irwin v R [1968] 68 DLR (2d) 485 369
Isitt [1978] RTR 211, 67 Cr App Rep 44, [1978] Crim LR 159, CA . . . 43
Ismail [1977] Crim LR 557, CA 633, 761
Ives [1970] 1 QB 208, [1969] 3 All ER 470, [1969] 3 WLR 266, 113 Sol Jo 467, 53 Cr
   App Rep 474, CA 331
Izod (1904) 20 Cox CC 690 311

J

JBH and JH (minors) v O'Connell [1981] Crim LR 632 179
JM (a minor) v Runeckles (1984) 79 Cr App Rep 255 . . . . 179, 180
Jackson (1673) 1 Hale PC 464 158
Jackson (1822) Russ & Ry 487, CCR 435
Jackson (1864) 9 Cox CC 505 497
Jackson [1891] 1 QB 671, [1891-4] All ER Rep 61, 60 LJQB 346, 64 LT 679, 55 JP 246,
   39 WR 407, 7 TLR 382, CA 386
Jackson (1983) 147 JP 715, [1983] Crim LR 617, CA 565
Jackson [1985] RTR 257, [1985] Crim LR 674, CA 242
Jackson, Golding and Jackson [1985] Crim LR 442, CA 266
Jackson (Peter) Pty Ltd v Consolidated Insurance of Australia Ltd [1975] VR 480 . 493
Jacobs (1817) Russ & Ry 331, CCR 471
Jaggard v Dickinson [1981] QB 527, [1980] 3 All ER 716, [1981] 2 WLR 118, 124 Sol Jo
   847, 72 Cr App Rep 33, [1980] Crim LR 717 215
Jakeman (1983) 76 Cr App Rep 223, [1983] Crim LR 104, CA . . . 76
James (1837) 8 C & P 131 . . . . 249, 689
James (1913) 9 Cr App Rep 142, CCA 10
James (1976) 64 Cr App Rep 170, CA 541

PAGE

James & Son Ltd v Smee [1955] 1 QB 78, [1954] 3 All ER 273, [1954] 3 WLR 631, 118
    JP 536, 98 Sol Jo 771, 52 LGR 545, DC 125, 163
James and Ashford (1985) 82 Cr App Rep 226 .   .   .   .   .   252, 255
Jamieson (1975) 60 Cr App Rep 318, [1975] Crim LR 248, CA .   .   .   10
Jarmain [1946] KB 74, [1945] 2 All ER 613, 115 LJKB 205, 174 LT 85, 62 TLR 33, 89
    Sol Jo 497, 31 Cr App Rep 39, CCA   44
Jarvis (1903) 20 Cox CC 249   453
Jarvis v Fuller [1974] Crim LR 116, [1974] RTR 160   481
Jarvis, Langdon and Stear (1837) 2 Mood & R 40   402
Jeff (1966) 111 Sol Jo 53, 51 Cr App Rep 28, CA   548
Jellyman (1838) 8 C & P 604   471
Jennings v United States Government [1982] 3 All ER 104, sub nom R v Governor of
    Holloway Prison, ex p Jennings [1982] 1 WLR 949, 126 Sol Jo 413, [1982] Crim
    LR 590; revsd sub nom Government of the United States of America v Jennings
    [1983] 1 AC 624, [1982] 3 WLR 450, 126 Sol Jo 659, [1983] RTR 1, 75 Cr App
    Rep 367, [1982] Crim LR 748, [1982] LS Gaz R 1413, sub nom Jennings v United
    States Government [1982] 3 All ER 104, HL .   .   .   354, 485, 486
John Lewis & Co Ltd v Tims [1952] AC 676, [1952] 1 All ER 1203, [1952] 1 WLR
    1132, 116 JP 275, [1952] 1 TLR 1132, 96 Sol Jo 342, HL .   .   .   411
Johnson (1827) 1 Lew CC 164   315
Johnson [1964] 2 QB 404, [1963] 3 All ER 577, [1963] 3 WLR 1031, 127 JP 556, 107 Sol
    Jo 1042, 48 Cr App Rep 25, CCA 439, 442
Johnson [1968] SASR 132   450
Johnson, Re (1887) 20 QBD 68, 57 LJQB 1, 58 LT 160, 52 JP 230, 36 WR 51, 4 TLR
    40, CA   784
Johnson v Phillips [1975] 3 All ER 682, [1976] 1 WLR 65, 140 JP 37, 119 Sol Jo 645,
    [1976] RTR 170, DC 223, 388
Johnson v Youden [1950] 1 KB 544, [1950] 1 All ER 300, 114 JP 136, 66 (pt 1) TLR
    395, 94 Sol Jo 115, 48 LGR 276, DC 80, 142
Johnson and Jones (1841) Car & M 218   158
Johnston (1940) 5 JCL 185   715
Johnstone, Comerford and Jalil [1982] Crim LR 454   535
Jones, ex p (1806) 13 Ves 237   773
Jones (1704) 1 Salk 379, 2 Ld Raym 1013, sub nom Anon 6 Mod Rep 105 .   .   544
Jones (1812) 3 Camp 230   796
Jones (1832) 4 B & Ad 345   256
Jones (1849) 13 JP 583, 3 Cox CC 441   398
Jones (1883) 11 QBD 118, 52 LJMC 96, 48 LT 768, 47 JP 535, 31 WR 800, 15 Cox CC
    284, CCR   711
Jones [1898] 1 QB 4, 65 LJMC 28, 73 LT 584, 60 JP 89, 44 WR 110, 40 Sol Jo 85, 18
    Cox CC 207, CCR   475
Jones [1949] 1 KB 194, [1948] 2 All ER 964, 113 JP 18, 64 TLR 616, 92 Sol Jo 648, 33
    Cr App Rep 33, 47 LGR 135, CCA   762
Jones [1959] 1 QB 291, [1959] 1 All ER 411, [1959] 2 WLR 190, 123 JP 164, 103 Sol Jo
    133, 43 Cr App Rep 94, CCA   628
Jones [1973] Crim LR 621   454
Jones [1973] Crim LR 710, CA   430
Jones [1974] ICR 310, [1974] IRLR 117, 118 Sol Jo 277, 59 Cr App Rep 120, [1974]
    Crim LR 663, CA   786
Jones [1976] 3 All ER 54, [1976] 1 WLR 672, 140 JP 515, 120 Sol Jo 299, 63 Cr App
    Rep 47, CA   600
Jones [1977] RTR 385, 65 Cr App Rep 250, CA   136
Jones [1987] Crim LR 123, CA   401
Jones v Crown Court at Bristol (1985) 150 JP 93, [1986] RTR 259, 83 Cr App Rep 109 .   480
Jones v Sherwood [1942] 1 KB 127, 111 LJKB 95, 166 LT 169, 106 JP 65, 85 Sol Jo
    425, 40 LGR 4, DC   375
Jones and Jones v Lloyd [1981] Crim LR 340, DC   389
Jordan (1956) 40 Cr App Rep 152, CCA 321, 324
Jory (1985) 150 JP 65, 82 Cr App Rep 141, [1986] BTLC 142, [1985] LS Gaz R 3696,
    [1986] Crim LR 168, CA   273
Joyce v DPP [1946] AC 347, [1946] 1 All ER 186, 115 LJKB 146, 174 LT 206, 62 TLR
    208, 31 Cr App Rep 57, HL 830, 838
Jubb [1984] Crim LR 616, CA   148

PAGE

Jupiter (No 3), The [1927] P 122 606
Jura [1954] 1 QB 503, [1954] 1 All ER 696, 118 JP 260, 98 Sol Jo 198, 38 Cr App Rep
53, CCA 421, 424

K

K (1983) 78 Cr App Rep 82, [1983] Crim LR 736, CA 231, 235
K A Smith [1983] Crim LR 739 . . . . 298, 363
Kaitamaki v R [1985] AC 147, [1984] 2 All ER 435, [1984] 3 WLR 137, 128 Sol Jo 331,
79 Cr App Rep 251, [1984] LS Gaz R 1915, [1984] Crim LR 564, PC . . 136, 433
Kallides (11 November 1976, unreported) 448
Kamara v DPP [1974] AC 104, [1973] 2 All ER 1242, [1973] 3 WLR 198, 137 JP 714,
117 Sol Jo 581, 57 Cr App Rep 880, HL 801
Kamipeli [1975] 1 NZLR 610 211
Kanwar [1982] 2 All ER 528, [1982] 1 WLR 845, 146 JP 283, 126 Sol Jo 276, 75 Cr App
Rep 87, CA 624, 625
Kapigian v Der Minassian 212 Mass 412, 99 NE 264 (1962) 714
Kara [1988] Crim LR 42, CA 240
Kat v Diment [1951] 1 KB 34, [1950] 2 All ER 657, 114 JP 472, 66 (pt 2) TLR 474, 94
Sol Jo 596, 49 LGR 450, 67 RPC 158, DC 127
Kavanagh v Hiscock [1974] QB 600, [1974] 2 All ER 177, [1974] 2 WLR 421, 118 Sol
Jo 98, 16 KIR 31, [1974] IRLR 121, [1974] Crim LR 255, DC . . . 391, 800
Kay (1887) 16 Cox CC 292 706
Kay v Butterworth (1945) 173 LT 191, 110 JP 75, 61 TLR 452, 89 Sol Jo 381 . 41, 44
Kay v Hibbert [1977] Crim LR 226, 141 JP Jo 157 389
Keat. See R v Keite
Keech (1929) 21 Cr App Rep 125, CCA 447
Keite (1696-7) 1 Ld Raym 138, sub nom R v Keat 5 Mod Rep 288, Skin 666, Holt KB
481, 1 Salk 47, sub nom R v Keate Comb 406, 1 Com 13 345
Kell [1985] Crim LR 239, CA 526
Kellett [1976] QB 372, [1975] 3 All ER 468, [1975] 3 WLR 713, 140 JP 1, 119 Sol Jo
542, 61 Cr App Rep 240, CA 751, 753, 755
Kelly (1820) Russ & Ry 421 . . . . 135, 628
Kelly v Purvis [1983] QB 663, [1983] 1 All ER 525, [1983] 2 WLR 299, 147 JP 135, 127
Sol Jo 52, 76 Cr App Rep 165, [1983] Crim LR 185 458
Kelt [1977] 3 All ER 1099, [1977] 1 WLR 1365, 142 JP 60, 121 Sol Jo 423, 65 Cr App
Rep 74, CA 421
Kemp [1957] 1 QB 399, [1956] 3 All ER 249, [1956] 3 WLR 724, 120 JP 457, 100 Sol Jo
768, 40 Cr App Rep 121 . . . . 42, 186, 187, 188, 202
Kemp [1964] 2 QB 341, [1964] 1 All ER 649, [1964] 2 WLR 648, 108 Sol Jo 139, 48 Cr
App Rep 131, [1964] Crim LR 312, CCA 155, 709, 718
Kemp (1986) Times, 3 May 40
Kenlin v Gardiner [1967] 2 QB 510, [1966] 3 All ER 931, [1967] 2 WLR 129, 131 JP
91, 110 Sol Jo 848, DC 245, 380, 389
Kenny (1962) Times, 23 January 14
Kensington Borough Council v Walters [1960] 1 QB 361, [1959] 3 All ER 652, [1959] 3
WLR 945, 124 JP 54, 103 Sol Jo 921, 57 LGR 361 44
Kent [1959] Crim LR 468, CCA 13
Kewal (1983) 78 Cr App Rep 149, [1985] Crim LR 236, CA 66
Khandu (1890) ILR 15 Bom 194 76
Kidd v Reeves [1972] VR 563 116
Kilbourne [1972] 3 All ER 545, [1972] 1 WLR 1365, 116 Sol Jo 800, 56 Cr App Rep
828, CA 450
Kilbride v Lake [1962] NZLR 590 98
Killingback's (A W) Application [1976] CLY 426 347
Kimber [1983] 3 All ER 316, [1983] 1 WLR 1118, 127 Sol Jo 578, 77 Cr App Rep 225,
[1983] Crim LR 630, CA 66, 68
King [1962] Crim LR 836, CA 218
King [1964] 1 QB 285, [1963] 3 All ER 561, [1963] 3 WLR 892, 107 Sol Jo 832, 48 Cr
App Rep 17, CCA 715, 717
King [1965] 1 All ER 1053, [1965] 1 WLR 706, 129 JP 276, 109 Sol Jo 150, 391, 49 Cr
App Rep 140, CCA 850
King [1976] Crim LR 200, CA 428

PAGE

King [1987] QB 547, [1987] 1 All ER 547, [1987] 2 WLR 746, 151 JP 559, 131 Sol Jo
    325, 84 Cr App Rep 357, [1987] LS Gaz R 339, [1987] Crim LR 398, CA   .   555, 560
King v Hodges (1974) 138 JP Jo 348, [1974] Crim LR 424, DC   .   .   .   390
King v Lees (1948) 65 TLR 21, 92 Sol Jo 732, 47 LGR 42, DC   .   .   .   678
King's Case (1817) Russ & Ry 332, CCR 135, 628
King's Norton Metal Co Ltd v Edridge, Merrett & Co Ltd (1897) 14 TLR 98, CA   .   521
Kircaldy (1928) 167 LT Jo 46   .   .   .   .   706, 715
Kirkland v Robinson (1986) 151 JP 377, [1987] Crim LR 643   .   .   .   110
Kitson (1955) 39 Cr App Rep 66, CCA   226
Knight and Roffey (1781) 2 East PC 510, CCR   526
Knight's Appeal, Re (1968) FLR 81   402
Knights (1860) 2 F & F 46   311
Knowles Transport Ltd v Russell [1975] RTR 87, [1974] Crim LR 717   .   .   124
Knox v Anderton (1982) 147 JP 340, 76 Cr App Rep 156, [1983] Crim LR 114, DC   .   426
Knuller (Publishing, Printing and Promotions) Ltd v DPP [1973] AC 435, [1972] 2 All
    ER 898, [1972] 3 WLR 143, 136 JP 728, 116 Sol Jo 545, 56 Cr App Rep 633, HL   .   20,
                                              277, 279, 472, 721, 728
Knupffer v London Express Newspaper Ltd [1944] AC 116, [1944] 1 All ER 495, 113
    LJKB 251, 170 LT 362, 60 TLR 310, 88 Sol Jo 143, HL   .   .   .   824
Kohn (1979) 69 Cr App Rep 395, [1979] Crim LR 675, CA   .   .   .   505
Komaroni (1953) 103 L Jo 97   295
Kong Cheuk Kwan v R (1985) 129 Sol Jo 504, 82 Cr App Rep 18, [1985] Crim LR 787,
    [1985] NLJ Rep 753, PC   352
Kooken (1982) 74 Cr App Rep 30   202
Kopsch (1925) 19 Cr App Rep 50, CCA   195
Korniak (1983) 76 Cr App Rep 145, CA   617
Kosmos Publications v DPP [1975] Crim LR 345, DC   .   .   .   735
Kowalski [1988] Crim LR 124   432
Krause (1902) 66 JP 121, 18 TLR 238   .   .   .   .   355, 844
Kray [1970] 1 QB 125, [1969] 3 All ER 941, [1969] 3 WLR 831, 133 JP 719, 113 Sol Jo
    793, 53 Cr App Rep 569, CA   232
Kuchenmeister v Home Office [1958] 1 QB 496, [1958] 1 All ER 485, [1958] 2 WLR
    453, 122 JP 160, 102 Sol Jo 196   407
Kuechenmeister, ex p Bottrill. See R v Bottrill, ex p Kuechenmeister
Kundeus (1976) 24 CCC (2d) 276   73
Kwok Chak Ming [1963] Crim LR 748   310

L

L v K [1985] Fam 144, [1985] 1 All ER 961, [1985] 3 WLR 202, 129 Sol Jo 483   .   .   438
Lamb [1967] 2 QB 981, [1967] 2 All ER 1282, [1967] 3 WLR 888, 131 JP 456, 111 Sol
    Jo 541, 51 Cr App Rep 417, CA 65, 66, 69, 92, 348
Lambert [1972] Crim LR 422   591
Lambert v Hodgson (1823) 1 Bing 317, 8 Moore CP 326, 1 LJOSCP 114   .   .   409
Lambie [1981] 1 All ER 332, [1981] 1 WLR 78, 124 Sol Jo 808, 71 Cr App Rep 350,
    [1980] Crim LR 725, CA; revsd [1982] AC 449, [1981] 2 All ER 776, [1981] 3
    WLR 88, 145 JP 364, 125 Sol Jo 480, 73 Cr App Rep 294, [1981] Crim LR 712,
    HL   552
Lancashire Waggon Co v Fitzhugh (1861) 6 H & N 502, 30 LJ Ex 231, 3 LT 703   .   498
Landy [1981] 1 All ER 1172, [1981] 1 WLR 355, 125 Sol Jo 80, 72 Cr App Rep 237,
    [1981] Crim LR 326, CA 274, 529
Lane and Lane (1985) 82 Cr App Rep 5, [1985] Crim LR 789, CA   .   .   138
Lang (1975) 62 Cr App Rep 50, CA   437
Langford. See R v Phillips (1842)
Langham v Crisp [1975] Crim LR 652   800
Langley (1704) 6 Mod Rep 124, Holt KB 654, 2 Ld Raym 1029, 3 Salk 190   .   824
Lankford [1959] Crim LR 209, CCA 299, 473
Lapier (1784) 1 Leach 320   541
Larkin [1943] KB 174, [1943] 1 All ER 217, 112 LJKB 163, 168 LT 298, 59 TLR 105,
    87 Sol Jo 140, 29 Cr App Rep 18, CCA 346, 350
Larsonneur (1933) 149 LT 542, 97 JP 206, 77 Sol Jo 486, 31 LGR 253, 29 Cox CC 673,
    24 Cr App Rep 74, CCA 46, 98, 112, 222
Latham (1965) 109 Sol Jo 371, CCA   197

PAGE

Latimer (1886) 17 QBD 359, [1886-90] All ER Rep 386, 55 LJMC 135, 54 LT 768, 51
    JP 184, 2 TLR 626, 16 Cox CC 70, CCR 74, 75
Laverty [1970] 3 All ER 432, 134 JP 699, 54 Cr App Rep 495, [1971] RTR 124, CA   .   550
Lavey (1850) 3 Car & Kir 26, 16 LTOS 266   745
Lawrence [1971] 1 QB 373, [1970] 3 All ER 933, [1970] 3 WLR 1103, 114 Sol Jo 864,
    55 Cr App Rep 73, CA; affd sub nom Lawrence v Metropolitan Police Comr [1972]
    AC 626, [1971] 2 All ER 1253, [1971] 3 WLR 225, 135 JP 481, 115 Sol Jo 565, 55
    Cr App Rep 471, HL 498, 500, 501, 521
Lawrence (1971) 57 Cr App Rep 64, CA 589, 594
Lawrence [1980] 1 NSWLR 122   235
Lawrence [1982] AC 510, [1981] 1 All ER 974, [1981] 2 WLR 524, 145 JP 227, 125 Sol
    Jo 241, 73 Cr App Rep 1, [1981] RTR 217, [1981] Crim LR 409, HL   .   63, 64, 65, 68,
                                                                94, 96, 480, 483, 485
Laws (1928) 21 Cr App Rep 45, CCA   447
Laws v Eltringham (1881) 8 QBD 283, 51 LJMC 13, 46 LT 64, 46 JP 230, 30 WR 245,
    15 Cox CC 22, DC 678, 681
Lawson and Forsythe [1986] VR 515   245
Layton (1849) 4 Cox CC 149   196
Leak [1976] QB 217, [1975] 2 All ER 1059, [1975] 3 WLR 316, 139 JP 608, 119 Sol Jo
    473, 61 Cr App Rep 217, CA   .   .   156, 177, 213, 253, 370, 430, 431
Leary [1978] 1 SCR 29, 33 CCC (2d) 473   220
Leary v R (1977) 74 DLR (3d) 103, SCC   213
Ledger (1862) 2 F & F 857   315
Lee [1962] Crim LR 500, CA   11
Lee Chun-Chuen (alias Lee Wing-Cheuk) v R [1963] AC 220, [1963] 1 All ER 73,
    [1962] 3 WLR 1461, 106 Sol Jo 1008, PC 331, 334
Lee Shek Ching v R (1985) No 53 CA (Hong Kong)   763
Leeming (1985) 81 Cr App Rep 125, [1985] LS Gaz R 1409, [1985] Crim LR 368, CA   .   224
Leer [1982] Crim LR 310, CA   425
Lees v Parr [1967] 3 All ER 181n, DC   735
Leeson (1968) 112 Sol Jo 151, 52 Cr App Rep 185, CA   .   .   .   450
Leigh (1775) 1 Car & Kir 28n, sub nom Macklin's Case 2 Camp 372n   .   .   278
Leigh v Gladstone (1909) 26 TLR 139   223
Lesbini [1914] 3 KB 1116, 84 LJKB 1102, 112 LT 175, 24 Cox CC 516, 11 Cr App Rep
    7, CCA   336
Lesley (or Leslie) (1860) Bell CC 220, 29 LJMC 97, 1 LT 452, 24 JP 115, 6 Jur NS
    202, 8 WR 220, 8 Cox CC 269, CCR   409
Lester (1975) 63 Cr App Rep 144, [1976] Crim LR 389, CA   .   .   .   114
Leung Ping-Fat (1973) HKLJ 342   344
Levine [1927] 1 DLR 740   48
Lewis [1970] Crim LR 647, CA 326, 376, 399
Lewis v Cox [1985] QB 509, [1984] 3 All ER 672, [1984] 3 WLR 875, 148 JP 601, 128
    Sol Jo 596, [1984] LS Gaz R 2538, 80 Cr App Rep 1, [1984] Crim LR 756   .   .   395
Lewis v Dickson [1976] RTR 431, DC   249
Lewis v Lethbridge [1987] Crim LR 59   516
Lidstone [1978] Crim LR 332   405
Liepens v Spearman [1986] RTR 24, [1985] Crim LR 229   .   .   .   388
Light (1857) Dears & B 332, [1843-60] All ER Rep 934, 27 LJMC 1, 30 LTOS 137, 21
    JP 758, 3 Jur NS 1130, 6 WR 42, 7 Cox CC 389, CCR   .   .   .   378
Lim Chin Aik v R [1963] AC 160, [1963] 1 All ER 223, [1963] 2 WLR 42, 106 Sol Jo
    1028, PC 47, 82, 105, 114, 116, 250
Lindley v George W Horner & Co Ltd [1950] 1 All ER 234, 114 JP 124, 66 (pt 1) TLR
    296, 94 Sol Jo 147, 48 LGR 174, DC   117
Lines (1844) 1 Car & Kir 393   433
Linneker [1906] 2 KB 99, [1904-7] All ER Rep 797, 75 LJKB 385, 94 LT 856, 70 JP
    293, 54 WR 494, 22 TLR 495, 50 Sol Jo 440, 21 Cox CC 196, CCR   .   .   292
Linnett v Metropolitan Police Comr [1946] KB 290, [1946] 1 All ER 380, 115 LJKB
    513, 174 LT 178, 110 JP 153, 62 TLR 203, 90 Sol Jo 211, 44 LGR 95, DC   .   .   164
Linsberg and Leies (1905) 69 JP 107   406
Lipman [1970] 1 QB 152, [1969] 3 All ER 410, [1969] 3 WLR 819, 133 JP 712, 113 Sol
    Jo 670, 53 Cr App Rep 600, CA   .   .   33, 40, 209, 211, 213, 214, 348
Lloyd (1802) 4 Esp 200   796

PAGE

Lloyd (1887) 19 QBD 213, 56 LJMC 119, 56 LT 750, 52 JP 86, 35 WR 653, 3 TLR
   701, 16 Cox CC 235, CCR 742
Lloyd (1965) [1967] 1 QB 175, [1966] 1 All ER 107n, [1966] 2 WLR 13, 130 JP 118,
   109 Sol Jo 955, 50 Cr App Rep 61, CCA 204
Lloyd [1985] QB 829, [1985] 2 All ER 661, [1985] 3 WLR 30, [1986] ECC 64, 149 JP
   634, 129 Sol Jo 431, 81 Cr App Rep 182, [1986] FSR 138, [1985] NLJ Rep 605,
   [1985] LS Gaz R 1938, [1985] Crim LR 518, CA 537
Lloyd v Grace Smith & Co [1912] AC 716, [1911-13] All ER Rep 51, 81 LJKB 1140,
   107 LT 531, 28 TLR 547, 56 Sol Jo 723, HL 162
Lloyd v Johnson (1798) 1 Bos & P 340 461
Loat [1985] Crim LR 154 841
Loat v Andrews (or James) [1986] ICR 679, 150 JP 652, 130 Sol Jo 697, [1986] LS Gaz
   R 2567, [1986] Crim LR 744 841
Lobell [1957] 1 QB 547, [1957] 1 All ER 734, [1957] 2 WLR 524, 121 JP 282, 101 Sol Jo
   268, 41 Cr App Rep 100, CCA 31
Lock v Ashton (1848) 12 QB 871, 3 New Mag Cas 70, 18 LJQB 76, 12 LTOS 241, 13
   Jur 167, 12 JP 788 408
Lockyer v Gibb [1967] 2 QB 243, [1966] 2 All ER 653, [1966] 3 WLR 84, 130 JP 306,
   110 Sol Jo 507, DC 107, 114
Lodwick v Sanders [1985] 1 All ER 577, [1985] 1 WLR 382, 129 Sol Jo 69, 80 Cr App
   Rep 305, [1985] RTR 385, [1985] Crim LR 210, [1985] LS Gaz R 444 . . 390
Logdon v DPP [1976] Crim LR 121 . . . . . . 376, 377, 379
Lolley (1812) Russ & Ry 237, sub nom Sugden v Lolley 2 Cl & Fin 567n, CCR . 712
Lomas v Peek [1947] 2 All ER 574, 112 JP 13, 63 TLR 593, 40 LGR 15, DC . 126
London (1871) 24 LT 232, 35 JP 340, CCR 748
London and Globe Finance Corpn Ltd, Re [1903] 1 Ch 728, [1900-3] All ER Rep 891,
   72 LJ Ch 368, 88 LT 194, 51 WR 651, 19 TLR 314, 10 Mans 198 . . 270
Long (1888) 59 LT 33, 52 JP 630, 4 TLR 584, 16 Cox CC 442 . . . 800
Longman (1980) 72 Cr App Rep 121, [1981] Crim LR 38, CA . . 151, 285
Lord Abingdon (1794) 1 Esp 226, Peake 236 825
Loughnan [1981] VR 443 225
Lovelace v DPP [1954] 3 All ER 481, [1954] 1 WLR 1468, 119 JP 21, 98 Sol Jo 852,
   DC 126, 127, 168
Lovell (1881) 8 QBD 185, 50 LJMC 91, 44 LT 319, 45 JP 406, 30 WR 416, CCR . 503
Lovesey [1970] 1 QB 352, [1969] 2 All ER 1077, [1969] 3 WLR 213, 133 JP 571, 113 Sol
   Jo 445, 53 Cr App Rep 461, CA 149, 153
Lovett (1839) 9 C & P 462, 3 State Tr NS 1177 834
Low v Blease [1975] 119 Sol Jo 695, [1975] Crim LR 513, DC . . . 505, 539
Lowe [1973] QB 702, [1973] 1 All ER 805, [1973] 2 WLR 481, 137 JP 334, 117 Sol Jo
   144, 57 Cr App Rep 365, CA 350
Lowery (P) & Sons v Wark [1975] RTR 45 124
Lucena v Craufurd (1806) 2 Bos & PNR 269, HL 682
Ludlow v Burgess (1971) 75 Cr App Rep 227n, [1971] Crim LR 238 . . 389, 406
Ludlow Charities, Re, Lechmere Charlton's Case (1837) 2 My & Cr 316, 6 LJ Ch 185 . 770,
   772
Luganda v Service Hotels Ltd [1969] 2 Ch 209, [1969] 2 All ER 692, [1969] 2 WLR
   1056, 113 Sol Jo 206, 20 P & CR 337, 210 Estates Gazette 113, CA . . 814
Lumley (1869) LR 1 CCR 196, 38 LJMC 86, 20 LT 454, 33 JP 597, 17 WR 685, 11
   Cox CC 274, CCR 709
Lund (1921) 16 Cr App Rep 31, CCA 711
Lynch (1832) 5 C & P 324 335
Lynch [1903] 1 KB 444, [1900-3] All ER Rep 688, 72 LJKB 167, 88 LT 26, 67 JP 41,
   51 WR 619, 19 TLR 163, 20 Cox CC 468 829
Lynch v DPP for Northern Ireland. See DPP for Northern Ireland v Lynch
Lyons v May [1948] 2 All ER 1062, 113 JP 42, [1948] WN 483, 65 TLR 51, 93 Sol Jo
   59, 47 LGR 125, DC 124
Lyons (Raymond) & Co Ltd v Metropolitan Police Comr [1975] QB 321, [1975] 1 All
   ER 335, [1975] 2 WLR 197, 139 JP 213, 119 Sol Jo 82, DC . . 643, 644
Lyons, Sons & Co v Gulliver [1914] 1 Ch 631, [1911-13] All ER Rep 537, 83 LJ Ch
   281, 110 LT 284, 78 JP 98, 30 TLR 75, 58 Sol Jo 97, 12 LGR 194, CA . . 797

M

Mabley (1965) 109 Sol Jo 296, [1965] Crim LR 377, CCA 479

PAGE

M'Alister (or Donoghue) v Stevenson [1932] AC 562, 101 LJPC 119, 48 TLR 494, 37
Com Cas 350, 1932 SC (HL) 31; sub nom McAlister (or Donoghue) v Stevenson
147 LT 281, 76 Sol Jo 396; sub nom Donoghue (or McAlister) v Stevenson [1932]
All ER Rep 1, 1932 SLT 317, HL 404
McArdle v Wallace (1964) 108 Sol Jo 483, [1964] Crim LR 467, DC . . . 389
McBean v Parker (1983) 147 JP 205, [1983] Crim LR 399, DC . . . 389
McBride [1962] 2 QB 167, [1961] 3 All ER 6, [1961] 3 WLR 549, 125 JP 544, 105 Sol
Jo 572, 45 Cr App Rep 262, CCA 44
McBride v Turnock (1964) 108 Sol Jo 336, [1964] Crim LR 456 . . . 391
McCall v Abelesz [1976] QB 585, [1976] 1 All ER 727, [1976] 2 WLR 151, 120 Sol Jo
81, 31 P & CR 256, 238 Estates Gazette 335, CA 815
McCallister (1985) 80 Cr App Rep 361, CA 583
McCann (1971) 56 Cr App Rep 359, [1972] Crim LR 196, CA . . . 160
McCarthy [1954] 2 QB 105, [1954] 2 All ER 262, [1954] 2 WLR 1044, 98 Sol Jo 356, 38
Cr App Rep 74, CCA 339, 343
McCarthy [1955] 2 All ER 927, [1955] 1 WLR 856, 119 JP 504, 99 Sol Jo 511, 39 Cr
App Rep 118, CCA 15
McCarthy [1964] 1 All ER 95, [1964] 1 WLR 196, 128 JP 191, 108 Sol Jo 17, 48 Cr App
Rep 111, CCA 143
McCarthy [1967] 1 QB 68, [1966] 1 All ER 447, [1966] 2 WLR 555, 130 JP 157, 110 Sol
Jo 211, 50 Cr App Rep 109, CCA 183
McCormack [1969] 2 QB 442, [1969] 3 All ER 371, [1969] 3 WLR 175, 133 JP 630, 113
Sol Jo 507, 53 Cr App Rep 514, CA 448
McCoy 1953 (2) SA 4 (AD) 382
McCrone v Riding [1938] 1 All ER 157, 158 LT 253, 102 JP 109, 54 TLR 328, 82 Sol
Jo 175, 36 LGR 160, 30 Cox CC 670, DC 93, 479
McCullum (1973) 117 Sol Jo 525, 57 Cr App Rep 645, [1973] Crim LR 582, CA . 121, 635
McDaniel v State 15 Tex Crim 115 (1942) 406
M'Daniel's Case (1755-6) 19 State Tr 745, Fost 121, 131, 364, 1 Leach 44, 1 East PC
333 327
McDonald (1980) 70 Cr App Rep 288, [1980] Crim LR 242, CA . . . 617
McDonnell [1966] 1 QB 233, [1966] 1 All ER 193, [1965] 3 WLR 1138, 109 Sol Jo 919,
50 Cr App Rep 5 . . . . 173, 281
McEvilly (1973) 60 Cr App Rep 150, CA 160
McGill (1970) 54 Cr App Rep 300, [1970] RTR 209, [1970] Crim LR 290, CA . 584
McGowan v Chief Constable of Kingston-upon-Hull (1967) 117 NLJ 1138, [1967]
Crim LR 34, DC 389
McGrath (1869) LR 1 CCR 205, 39 LJMC 7, 21 LT 543, 34 JP 86, 18 WR 119, 11 Cox
CC 347, CCR 503
McGregor [1962] NZLR 1069 338
M'Gregor and Lambert (1844) 1 Car & Kir 429, 2 LTOS 501, 8 JP 415, 1 Cox CC
346 819
M'Growther's Case (1746) Fost 13, 18 State Tr 391, 1 East PC 71 . . 231, 235
McGuire and Page (1963) 107 Sol Jo 516, [1963] Crim LR 572 . . . 419
Machin [1961] Crim LR 844, CCA 13, 751
Machin [1980] 3 All ER 151, [1980] 1 WLR 763, 145 JP 21, 124 Sol Jo 359, 71 Cr App
Rep 166, CA 751
McHugh (1977) 64 Cr App Rep 92, CA 551
McInnes [1971] 3 All ER 295, [1971] 1 WLR 1600, 115 Sol Jo 655, 55 Cr App Rep 551,
CA 244, 248
McIntyre (1847) 2 Cox CC 379 321
McIvor [1982] 1 All ER 491, [1982] 1 WLR 409, 146 JP 193, 126 Sol Jo 48, 74 Cr App
Rep 74, CA 274, 529, 530
McKay [1957] VR 560, [1957] ALR 648 248
McKenna v Harding (1905) 69 JP 354 167
Mackenzie and Higginson (1910) 75 JP 159, 27 TLR 152, 6 Cr App Rep 64, CCA . 442
Mackie [1973] Crim LR 54; affd (1973) 57 Cr App Rep 453, [1973] Crim LR 438, CA . 326,
399
Macklin and Murphy's Case (1838) 2 Lew CC 225 132
McKnight v Davies (1973) 117 Sol Jo 940, [1974] RTR 4, [1974] Crim LR 62 . 584
McLeod (1915) 34 NZLR 430 384
McLeod (1954) 20 CR 281, 14 WWRNS 97, 111 CCC 106 391

PAGE

McLeod v St Aubyn [1899] AC 549, 68 LJPC 137, 81 LT 158, 48 WR 173, 15 TLR
   487, PC 781
McLeod and Georgia Straight Publishing Co Ltd (1970) 75 WWR 161 . . . 144
McLorie v Oxford [1982] QB 1290, [1982] 3 All ER 480, [1982] 3 WLR 423, 126 Sol Jo
   536, 75 Cr App Rep 137, [1983] RTR 265, DC 389
M'Loughlin (1838) 8 C & P 635 398
McMahon (1894) 15 NSWLR 131, 10 WNNSW 204 672
McNaghten's Case (1843) 10 Cl & Fin 200, sub nom R v McNaughton 4 St Tr NS
   847, 1 Town St Tr 314, 1 Car & Kir 130n, sub nom Insane Criminals 8 Scott NR
   595, HL 190, 192, 193, 194
McNamara (1988) Times, 16 February, CA 108
McNaughton. See McNaghten's Case
McNiff [1986] Crim LR 57 560
McPhail v Persons (names unknown) [1973] Ch 447, [1973] 3 All ER 393, [1973] 3
   WLR 71, 117 Sol Jo 448, 227 Estates Gazette 985, CA 806
McPherson (1972) 117 Sol Jo 13, [1973] Crim LR 191, CA 492
MacPherson [1973] RTR 157, CA 213, 588
McPherson [1980] Crim LR 654 445
McPherson and Watts [1985] Crim LR 508, CA 272, 275
Macro [1969] Crim LR 205 161
McShane (1977) 121 Sol Jo 632, 66 Cr App Rep 97, CA 297, 360, 404
Madan [1961] 2 QB 1, [1961] 1 All ER 588, [1961] 2 WLR 231, 125 JP 246, 105 Sol Jo
   160, 45 Cr App Rep 80, CCA 617
Madden [1975] 3 All ER 155, [1975] 1 WLR 1379, 139 JP 685, 119 Sol Jo 657, 61 Cr
   App Rep 254, CA 428
Maddox v Storer [1963] 1 QB 451, [1962] 1 All ER 831, [1962] 2 WLR 958, 126 JP 263,
   106 Sol Jo 372, 61 LGR 41, DC 423
Maddy (1671) 2 Keb 829, 1 Vent 158, sub nom R v Manning T Raym 212 . . 335
Madigan (1982) 75 Cr App Rep 145, [1982] Crim LR 692, CA . . . 484
Magellan Pirates, The (1853) 1 Ecc & Ad 81, 22 LTOS 319, 18 Jur 18 . . 816
Maginnis [1987] AC 303, [1987] 1 All ER 907, [1987] 2 WLR 765, 151 JP 537, 131 Sol
   Jo 357, 85 Cr App Rep 127, [1987] NLJ Rep 244, [1987] LS Gaz R 1141, [1987]
   Crim LR 564, HL 120
Magna Plant v Mitchell (1966) 110 Sol Jo 349, [1966] Crim LR 394, 116 NLJ 780 172
Maher v Musson (1934) 52 CLR 100, 8 ALJ 341, 41 ALR 80 96
Maidstone Borough Council v Mortimer [1980] 3 All ER 552, 144 JP 45, 79 LGR 81, 43
   P & CR 67, 256 Estates Gazette 1013, DC 100, 110, 123
Mailey [1957] Crim LR 328 751
Mainwaring (1981) 74 Cr App Rep 99, CA 514, 517
Malcherek [1981] 2 All ER 422, [1981] 1 WLR 690, 125 Sol Jo 305, 73 Cr App Rep 173,
   CA 311, 317, 319, 323
Malcolm v Cheek [1948] 1 KB 400, [1947] 2 All ER 881, [1948] LJR 388, 112 JP 94, 64
   TLR 28, 92 Sol Jo 41, 46 LGR 26, DC 118
Mallett [1978] 3 All ER 10, [1978] 1 WLR 820, 142 JP 528, 122 Sol Jo 295, 67 Cr App
   Rep 239, CA 575
Malone v Metropolitan Police Comr [1980] QB 49, [1979] 1 All ER 256, [1978] 3 WLR
   936, 122 Sol Jo 433, 69 Cr App Rep 4, [1978] Crim LR 555, CA . . 641
Manchester Guardian, ex p DPP (1924) 40 TLR 833, DC 772
Mancini v DPP [1942] AC 1, [1941] 3 All ER 272, 111 LJKB 84, 165 LT 353, 58 TLR
   25, 28 Cr App Rep 65, HL 31, 332, 337, 340
Mandla v Dowell Lee [1983] 2 AC 548, [1983] 1 All ER 1062, [1983] 2 WLR 620,
   [1983] ICR 385, [1983] IRLR 209, 127 Sol Jo 242, HL 793
Mankletow (1853) Dears CC 159, 22 LJMC 115, 21 LTOS 80, 17 JP 281, 17 Jur 352, 1
   WR 312, 1 CLR 59, 6 Cox CC 143, CCR 453, 454
Manley (1844) 3 LTOS 22, 1 Cox CC 104 132
Manley [1933] 1 KB 529, [1932] All ER Rep 565, 102 LJKB 323, 148 LT 335, 97 JP 6,
   49 TLR 130, 77 Sol Jo 65, 31 LGR 81, 24 Cr App Rep 25, 29 Cox CC 574, CCA . 758
Mann [1914] 2 KB 107, 83 LJKB 648, 110 LT 781, 78 JP 200, 30 TLR 310, 58 Sol Jo
   303, 24 Cox CC 140, 10 Cr App Rep 31, CCA 359
Manning (1671). See R v Maddy
Manning and Rogers (1871) LR 1 CCR 338, 41 LJMC 11, 25 LT 573, 36 JP 228, 20
   WR 102, 12 Cox CC 106, CCR 602, 603
Mansell v Griffin [1908] 1 KB 160 386

PAGE

Mansfield [1975] Crim LR 101, CA 614
Mansfield Justices, ex p Sharkey [1985] 1 All ER 193, 149 JP 129, [1984] IRLR 496 . 375
Manwaring (1856) Dears & B 132, 20 JP 804, 5 WR 119; sub nom R v Mainwaring 26
    LJMC 10, 28 LTOS 189, 2 Jur NS 1236, 7 Cox CC 192, CCR 706
Mapstone [1963] 3 All ER 930n, [1964] 1 WLR 439n, 128 JP 94 467
Marchant (1985) 80 Cr App Rep 361, CA 583
Marcus [1981] 2 All ER 833, [1981] 1 WLR 774, 145 JP 380, 125 Sol Jo 396, 73 Cr App
    Rep 49, CA 367, 403
Mark [1961] Crim LR 173 391
Marlow (1964) 49 Cr App Rep 49 . . . . 367, 403
Marrinan v Vibart [1963] 1 QB 528, [1962] 3 All ER 380, [1962] 3 WLR 912, 106 Sol
    Jo 649, CA 327, 408
Marriott (1838) 8 C & P 425 50
Marriott [1971] 1 All ER 595, [1971] 1 WLR 187, 135 JP 165, 115 Sol Jo 11, 55 Cr App
    Rep 82, CA 107, 109
Marsh v Johnston [1959] Crim LR 444 161
Marsh v Loader (1863) 14 CBNS 535, 2 New Rep 280, 11 WR 784 . . . 179
Marsh v Police Comr [1945] KB 43, [1944] 2 All ER 392, 171 LT 331, 109 JP 45, 61
    TLR 15, 88 Sol Jo 391, 42 LGR 305, [1944] Brewing Tr Rev 410, sub nom Marsh
    v McGee 114 LJKB 168, CA 643
Marshall v Osmond [1982] QB 857, [1982] 2 All ER 610, [1982] 3 WLR 120, 126 Sol Jo
    210 479
Martin (1832) 5 C & P 128 313
Martin (1848) 5 Cox CC 356 781
Martin (1879) 6 QBD 34, 49 LJMC 11, 41 LT 531, 44 JP 74, 28 WR 232, 14 Cox CC
    375, CCR 653
Martin (1881) 8 QBD 54, [1881-5] All ER Rep 699, 51 LJMC 36, 45 LT 444, 46 JP
    228, 30 WR 106, 14 Cox CC 633, CCR 399
Martin v Marsh [1955] Crim LR 781 511
Martin Secker Warburg Ltd [1954] 2 All ER 683, [1954] 1 WLR 1138, 118 JP 438, 98
    Sol Jo 577, 38 Cr App Rep 124 . . . . 722, 723
Martindale [1986] 3 All ER 25, [1986] 1 WLR 1042, 150 JP 548, 130 Sol Jo 613, 84 Cr
    App Rep 31, [1986] LS Gaz R 2412, [1986] Crim LR 736, CA . 121, 128, 427
Mason (1756) 1 East PC 239, Fost 132 244
Mason v Mason [1944] NI 134 713
Masterson v Holden [1986] 3 All ER 39, [1986] 1 WLR 1017, 130 Sol Jo 592, 83 Cr
    App Rep 302, [1986] LS Gaz R 2326, [1986] Crim LR 688 . . . 791
Matheson [1958] 2 All ER 87, [1958] 1 WLR 474, 102 Sol Jo 309, 42 Cr App Rep 145,
    CCA 198
Mathews v Dwan [1949] NZLR 1037 394
Matthews [1950] 1 All ER 137, 114 JP 73, 66 (pt 1) TLR 153, 48 LGR 190, 34 Cr App
    Rep 55, CCA 635
Matthews and Twigg (1876) 14 Cox CC 5 122
Mattison v Johnson (1916) 85 LJKB 741, [1916-17] All ER Rep 727, 114 LT 951, 80 JP
    243, 25 Cox CC 373, 14 LGR 457, DC 459
Matusevich v R (1977) 137 CLR 633, 51 ALJR 657, 15 ALR 117, (Aust HC) . 155, 283
Maughan (1934) 24 Cr App Rep 130, CCA 447
Mavji [1987] 2 All ER 758, [1987] 1 WLR 1388, 131 Sol Jo 1121, [1986] STC 508, 84
    Cr App Rep 34, [1987] LS Gaz R 2449, [1987] Crim LR 39, CA . 49, 569
Maxwell and Clanchy (1909) 73 JP 176, 2 Cr App Rep 26, CCA . . . 391
May (1867) 16 LT 362, 31 JP 356, 15 WR 751, 10 Cox CC 448, CCR . . 358
May [1912] 3 KB 572, 82 LJKB 1, 108 LT 351, 77 JP 31, 29 TLR 24, 23 Cox CC 327,
    8 Cr App Rep 63, CCA 382
May and Butcher Ltd v R [1934] 2 KB 17n, 103 LJKB 556n, 151 LT 246n, HL . 278
Mayberry [1973] Qd R 229 . . . . 136, 433
Mayer v Marchant (1973) 5 SASR 567 116
Mayers (1872) 12 Cox CC 311 433
Mayhew v Suttle (1854) 4 E & B 347, 3 CLR 59, 24 LJQB 54, 24 LTOS 159, 19 JP 38,
    1 Jur NS 303, 3 WR 108, Ex Ch 599
Mayling [1963] 2 QB 717, [1963] 1 All ER 687, [1963] 2 WLR 709, 127 JP 269, 107 Sol
    Jo 177, 47 Cr App Rep 102, CCA 277, 469
Mazeau (1840) 9 C & P 676 132
Meade and Belt (1823) 1 Lew CC 184 377

PAGE

Mears [1975] Crim LR 155 454
Medley (1834) 6 C & P 292, [1824-34] All ER Rep 123 . . . . 794, 798
Mee v Cruikshank (1902) 86 LT 708, 66 JP 89, 18 TLR 271, 20 Cox CC 210 . . 409
Meech [1974] QB 549, [1973] 3 All ER 939, [1973] 3 WLR 507, 138 JP 6, 117 Sol Jo
    713, 58 Cr App Rep 74, [1973] Crim LR 711, CA 493, 513, 514
Meering v Grahame-White Aviation Co Ltd (1919) 122 LT 44, [1918-19] All ER Rep
    Ext 1490, CA 407
Mehmed [1963] Crim LR 780, CCA 426
Meli v R [1954] 1 All ER 373, [1954] 1 WLR 228, 98 Sol Jo 77, PC . . 76, 77, 78
Melias Ltd v Preston [1957] 2 QB 380, [1957] 2 All ER 449, [1957] 3 WLR 42, 121 JP
    444, 101 Sol Jo 481, 55 LGR 366 . . . . 168, 169
Mella v Monahan [1961] Crim LR 175, DC 725
Mellor v Denham (1880) 5 QBD 467, 49 LJMC 89, 42 LT 493, 44 JP 472, CA . . 23
Menniss [1973] 2 NSWLR 113 211
Meredith [1973] Crim LR 253 . . . . 510, 511
Metharam [1961] 3 All ER 200, 125 JP 578, 105 Sol Jo 632, 45 Cr App Rep 304, CCA . 398
Metropolitan Music Hall Co v Lake (1889) 58 LJ Ch 513, 60 LT 749, 5 TLR 329 . 773
Metropolitan Police Comr, ex p Blackburn [1968] 2 QB 118, [1968] 1 All ER 763,
    [1968] 2 WLR 893, 112 Sol Jo 112, CA 388
Metropolitan Police Comr, ex p Blackburn (No 2) [1968] 2 QB 150, [1968] 2 All ER
    319, [1968] 2 WLR 1204, 112 Sol Jo 191, CA 781
Metropolitan Police Comr v Charles [1977] AC 177, [1976] 3 All ER 112, [1976] 3
    WLR 431, 140 JP 531, 120 Sol Jo 588, 63 Cr App Rep 252, HL . . 545, 546, 551
Metropolitan Police Comr v Wilson (1984). See R v Wilson (1983)
Meyrick (1929) 45 TLR 421, 21 Cr App Rep 94, CCA 279
Michael (1840) 9 C & P 356, 2 Mood CC 120, CCR 131, 325
Middleton (1873) LR 2 CCR 38, [1861-73] All ER Rep Ext 1120, 42 LJMC 73, 28 LT
    777, 37 JP 629, 12 Cox CC 260, 417, CCR 520
Midland Bank Trust Co Ltd v Green (No 3) [1979] Ch 496, [1979] 2 All ER 193,
    [1979] 2 WLR 594, 123 Sol Jo 306 282
Millard and Vernon [1987] Crim LR 393, CA 288
Miller (1854) 6 Cox CC 353 622
Miller [1954] 2 QB 282, [1954] 2 All ER 529, [1954] 2 WLR 138, 118 JP 340, 98 Sol Jo
    62, 38 Cr App Rep 1 . . . . 396, 431, 432
Miller [1976] Crim LR 147, CA 582, 587
Miller [1983] 2 AC 161, [1983] 1 All ER 978, [1983] 2 WLR 539, 127 Sol Jo 223, 77 Cr
    App Rep 17, [1983] Crim LR 466, HL 32, 53, 54, 76, 687, 698
Mills [1963] 1 QB 522, [1963] 1 All ER 202, [1963] 2 WLR 137, 127 JP 176, 107 Sol Jo
    38, 47 Cr App Rep 49, CCA 267, 368
Millward [1985] QB 519, [1985] 1 All ER 859, [1985] 2 WLR 532, 149 JP 545, 129 Sol
    Jo 187, 80 Cr App Rep 280, [1985] Crim LR 321, [1985] LS Gaz R 923, CA . . 748
Mirrless (1977) 65 Cr App Rep 250, CA 136
Mitchel (1848) 6 State Tr NS 599 832
Mitchell [1965] Crim LR 319, CCA 7
Mitchell [1983] QB 741, [1983] 2 All ER 427, [1983] 2 WLR 938, 127 Sol Jo 305, CA . 73,
    74, 352
Moah (1858) Dears & B 550, 27 LJMC 204, 31 LTOS 121, 22 JP 273, 4 Jur NS 464, 6
    WR 470, 7 Cox CC 503, CCR 658
Mogul SS Co v McGregor Gow & Co (1888) 21 QBD 544; on appeal (1889) 23 QBD
    598, 58 LJQB 465, 61 LT 820, 53 JP 709, 37 WR 756, 5 TLR 658, 6 Asp MLC
    455, CA; affd [1892] AC 25, [1891-4] All ER Rep 263, 61 LJQB 295, 66 LT 1, 56
    JP 101, 40 WR 337, 8 TLR 182, 7 Asp MLC 120, HL 257
Mohan [1976] QB 1, [1975] 2 All ER 193, [1975] 2 WLR 859, 139 JP 523, 119 Sol Jo
    219, 60 Cr App Rep 272, [1975] RTR 337, CA 288, 478
Mohan v R [1967] 2 AC 187, [1967] 2 All ER 58, [1967] 2 WLR 676, 111 Sol Jo 95, 11
    WIR 29, PC 136, 278
Moir v Williams [1892] 1 QB 264, 61 LJMC 33, 66 LT 215, 56 JP 197, 40 WR 69, 8
    TLR 44, 36 Sol Jo 40, CA 603
Moloney [1985] AC 905, [1985] 1 All ER 1025, [1985] 2 WLR 648, 149 JP 369, 129 Sol
    Jo 220, 81 Cr App Rep 93, [1985] NLJ Rep 315, [1985] LS Gaz R 1637, [1985]
    Crim LR 378, HL 56, 57, 59, 60, 328, 779
Moloney v Mercer [1971] 2 NSWLR 207 469
Monaghan [1979] Crim LR 673, CA 494

PAGE

Monger [1973] Crim LR 301 402
Moone v Rose (1869) LR 4 QB 486, 10 B & S 421, 38 LJQB 236, 20 LT 606, 17 WR
729 409
Moore (1832) 3 B & Ad 184, 1 LJMC 30 797
Moore (1898) 14 TLR 229 . . . . 347, 384
Moore v Branton (1974) 118 Sol Jo 405, [1974] Crim LR 439 547
Moore v Clerk of Assize, Bristol (1970) [1972] 1 All ER 58, [1971] 1 WLR 1669, 136 JP
91, 115 Sol Jo 78, CA 771, 782
Moore v Gooderham [1960] 3 All ER 575, [1960] 1 WLR 1308, 124 JP 513, 104 Sol Jo
1036, DC 418
Moore v Green [1983] 1 All ER 663, DC 392
Moore v I Bresler Ltd [1944] 2 All ER 515, DC 173
Moore v R [1987] AC 576, [1987] 2 WLR 1251, 131 Sol Jo 541, [1987] LS Gaz R 1491,
PC 328
Moore v Ray [1951] 1 KB 98, [1950] 2 All ER 561, 114 JP 486, 66 (pt 2) TLR 721, 94
Sol Jo 596, 49 LGR 187, DC 117
Moore and Dorn [1975] Crim LR 229 76
Moran [1952] 1 All ER 803n, 116 JP 216, 36 Cr App Rep 10, CCA . . . 590, 593
More [1987] 3 All ER 825, [1987] 1 WLR 1578, 131 Sol Jo 1550, HL . . 652, 653
Morgan [1972] 1 QB 436, [1972] 1 All ER 348, [1972] 2 WLR 123, 136 JP 160, 116 Sol
Jo 76, 56 Cr App Rep 181, CA 759
Morgan. See DPP v McDonald
Morgentaler [1976] 1 SCR 616, 20 CCC (2d) 449 . . . . . 223, 372
Moriarty v Brooks (1834) 6 C & P 684, 2 Nev & MMC 624, Ex Ch . . . 397
Morris [1951] 1 KB 394, [1950] 2 All ER 965, 115 JP 5, 66 (pt 2) TLR 1050, 94 Sol Jo
708, 49 LGR 95, 34 Cr App Rep 210, CCA 8
Morris (1963) 47 Cr App Rep 202 467
Morris [1983] QB 587, [1983] 2 All ER 448, [1983] 2 WLR 768, 127 Sol Jo 205, 77 Cr
App Rep 164, [1983] Crim LR 559, CA; affd [1984] AC 320, [1983] 3 All ER 288,
[1983] 3 WLR 697, 148 JP 1, 127 Sol Jo 713, 77 Cr App Rep 309, [1983] Crim LR
813, HL 489, 491, 494, 496, 501, 523, 535
Morris v Crown Office [1970] 2 QB 114, [1970] 1 All ER 1079, [1970] 2 WLR 792, 114
Sol Jo 151, CA 771
Morris v Edmonds (1897) 77 LT 56, [1895-99] All ER Rep 1089, 41 Sol Jo 698, 18 Cox
CC 627 122
Morris v Miller (1767) 1 Wm Bl 632, 4 Burr 2057, Bull NP 27b . . . 705
Morris v Tolman [1923] 1 KB 166, [1922] All ER Rep 182, 92 LJKB 215, 128 LT 118,
86 JP 221, 39 TLR 39, 67 Sol Jo 169, 20 LGR 803, 27 Cox CC 345, DC . 154
Morris and King (1984) 149 JP 60, [1984] LS Gaz R 1518, 79 Cr App Rep 104, [1984]
Crim LR 442, CA 418
Morris-Lowe [1985] 1 All ER 400, [1985] 1 WLR 29, 128 Sol Jo 872, 80 Cr App Rep
114, [1984] LS Gaz R 3336, [1984] Crim LR 50, CA 455, 465
Morrison [1938] 3 All ER 787, 27 Cr App Rep 1, CCA 706
Moseley, Re (1893). See Special Reference from Bahama Islands, Re
Moss and Harte (1985) 150 JP 26, 82 Cr App Rep 116, [1985] LS Gaz R 2905, [1985]
Crim LR 659, CA 758
Most (1881) 7 QBD 244, 50 LJMC 113, 44 LT 823, 45 JP 696, 29 WR 758, 14 Cox CC
583, CCR 355
Moule [1964] Crim LR 303, CCA 799
Mouse's Case (1608) 12 Co Rep 63, cited in 2 Bulst 280, sub nom Gravesend Barge
Case 1 Roll Rep 79 223
Mousell Bros Ltd v London and North-Western Rly Co [1917] 2 KB 836, [1916-17] All
ER Rep 1101, 87 LJKB 82, 118 LT 25, 81 JP 305, 15 LGR 706, DC . 170, 171
Mousir [1987] LS Gaz R 1328, [1987] Crim LR 561, CA . . . 73, 289, 415
Moussa Membar [1983] Crim LR 618, CA 821
Mowatt [1968] 1 QB 421, [1967] 3 All ER 47, [1967] 3 WLR 1192, 131 JP 463, 111 Sol
Jo 716, 51 Cr App Rep 402, CA 67, 122, 400, 683
Moynes v Coopper [1956] 1 QB 439, [1956] 1 All ER 450, [1956] 2 WLR 562, 120 JP
147, 100 Sol Jo 171, 40 Cr App Rep 20, DC 518
Moys (1984) 128 Sol Jo 548, 79 Cr App Rep 72, [1984] Crim LR 495, CA . . 633
Mubila 1956 (1) SA 31 324
Muir v Cassidy 1953 SLT 4 420
Mulcahy v R (1867) 15 WR 446; affd (1868) LR 3 HL 306 . . 259, 278, 832, 833

PAGE

Mullany (1865) Le & Ca 593, 6 New Rep 183, 34 LJMC 111, 12 LT 549, 29 JP 421, 11
  Jur NS 492, 13 WR 726, 10 Cox CC 97, CCR   744
Mullins (1848) 12 JP 776, 3 Cox CC 526 .   .   .   .   .   160, 162
Mullins v Collins (1874) LR 9 QB 292, [1874-80] All ER Rep 857, 43 LJMC 67, 29 LT
  838, 38 JP 629, 22 WR 297   163
Munslow [1895] 1 QB 758, 64 LJMC 138, 72 LT 301, 43 WR 495, 11 TLR 213, 39 Sol
  Jo 264, 18 Cox CC 112, 15 R 192, CCR   825
Murphy [1971] NI 193, CCA   421
Murray (1858) 1 F & F 80   745
Murray [1982] 2 All ER 225, [1982] 1 WLR 475, 126 Sol Jo 227, 75 Cr App Rep 58,
  [1982] RTR 289, CA   752
Murtagh and Kennedy (1955) 39 Cr App Rep 72, [1955] Crim LR 315, CCA   148, 152
Murton (1862) 3 F & F 492   315
Musk and Reynolds [1963] Crim LR 63, CCA   13
Mutters (1864) Le & Ca 491, 34 LJMC 22, 11 LT 387, 28 JP 804, 13 WR 100, 10 Cox
  CC 6, CCR   795
Mwenya, Re [1960] 1 QB 241, [1959] 3 All ER 525, [1959] 3 WLR 509, 103 Sol Jo 583,
  DC; revsd [1960] 1 QB 241, [1959] 3 All ER 525, [1959] 3 WLR 767, 103 Sol Jo
  898, CA 407, 831
Mycock (1871) 12 Cox CC 28   454

N

NF Tiger, The (1982). See Bradshaw v Ewart-James (1983)
Naguib [1917] 1 KB 359, 86 LJKB 709, 116 LT 640, 81 JP 116, 25 Cox CC 712, 12 Cr
  App Rep 187, CCA 706, 708, 710
Nagy v Weston [1965] 1 All ER 78, [1965] 1 WLR 280, 129 JP 104, 109 Sol Jo 215,
  DC   801
Naismith [1961] 2 All ER 735, [1961] 1 WLR 952, 105 Sol Jo 727   .   402
National Coal Board v Gamble [1959] 1 QB 11, [1958] 3 All ER 203, [1958] 3 WLR
  434, 122 JP 453, 102 Sol Jo 621, 42 Cr App Rep 240, DC .   83, 133, 137, 140, 141
National Provincial Bank Ltd v Ainsworth [1965] AC 1175, [1965] 2 All ER 472, [1965]
  3 WLR 1, 109 Sol Jo 415, HL   599
Navvabi [1986] 3 All ER 102, [1986] 1 WLR 1311, 150 JP 474, 130 Sol Jo 681, 83 Cr
  App Rep 271, [1986] NLJ Rep 893, [1986] LS Gaz R 2919, [1987] Crim LR 57,
  CA   505
Neal v Evans [1976] RTR 333, [1976] Crim LR 384, DC   .   .   395
Neal v Gribble (1978) 68 Cr App Rep 9, [1978] RTR 409   .   .   586
Neal v Reynolds (1966) 110 Sol Jo 353, [1966] Crim LR 393   .   .   44
Nedrick [1986] 3 All ER 1, [1986] 1 WLR 1025, 150 JP 589, 130 Sol Jo 572, 83 Cr App
  Rep 267, [1986] LS Gaz R 2755, [1986] Crim LR 792, CA   .   56, 328
Neil [1909] St R Qd 225   369
Nelmes v Rhys Howells Transport Ltd [1977] RTR 266, [1977] Crim LR 227   .   801
Newbury v Davis (1974) 118 Sol Jo 222, [1974] RTR 367, [1974] Crim LR 262   .   124
Newell (1980) 71 Cr App Rep 331, [1980] Crim LR 576, CA   .   .   339
Newland [1954] 1 QB 158, [1953] 2 All ER 1067, [1953] 3 WLR 826, 117 JP 573, 97 Sol
  Jo 782, 37 Cr App Rep 154, CCA   271
Newport (Salop) Justices, ex p Wright [1929] 2 KB 416, 98 LJKB 555, 141 LT 563, 93
  JP 179, 45 TLR 477, 73 Sol Jo 384, 27 LGR 518, 28 Cox CC 658, DC .   .   386
Newstead v London Express Newspaper Ltd [1940] 1 KB 377, [1939] 4 All ER 319, 109
  LJKB 166, 162 LT 17, 56 TLR 130, 83 Sol Jo 942, CA   .   .   825
Newton and Stungo [1958] Crim LR 469   365
Nichol (1807) Russ & Ry 130, CCR   382
Nicholls (1874) 13 Cox CC 75   50
Nicklin [1977] 2 All ER 444, [1977] 1 WLR 403, 141 JP 391, 121 Sol Jo 286, 64 Cr App
  Rep 205, CA   621
Nicoll v Catron (1985) 149 JP 424, 81 Cr App Rep 339, [1985] Crim LR 223   .   758
Nkosiyana 1966 (4) SA 655   252
Nolan (1960) Times, 30 March, CCA   11
Norfolk Constabulary v Seekings and Gould [1986] Crim LR 167   .   .   603
Norreys v Zeffert [1939] 2 All ER 187, 83 Sol Jo 456 .   .   .   590
Norris (1840) 9 C & P 241   678
Northern Star Mining Construction Co Ltd (1 February 1965, unreported)   .   174
Norton [1977] Crim LR 478   420

PAGE

Norton v Knowles [1969] 1 QB 572, [1967] 3 All ER 1061, [1968] 3 WLR 183, 132 JP
   100, 111 Sol Jo 890, 19 P & CR 57, 203 Estates Gazette 1026, [1968] RA 1, DC   .   814
Norton v Rowlands [1971] CLY 2384 470
Norwich Union Fire Insurance Society Ltd v William H Price Ltd [1934] AC 455,
   [1934] All ER Rep 352, 103 LJPC 115, 151 LT 309, 50 TLR 454, 78 Sol Jo 412, 40
   Com Cas 132, 49 Ll L Rep 55, PC   519
Nosworthy (1907) 26 NZLR 536 369
Nott (1958) 43 Cr App Rep 8 202

O

Oakes [1959] 2 QB 350, [1959] 2 All ER 92, [1959] 2 WLR 694, 123 JP 290, 103 Sol Jo
   373, 43 Cr App Rep 114, CCA 842
Oakley (1986) 24 CCC (3d) 351 189
O'Brien [1954] SCR 666 284
O'Brien [1974] 3 All ER 663, 138 JP 798 430
Ockley and Whitlesbyes Case (1622) Palm 294 746
O'Connor (1980) 54 ALJR 349 220
Odhams Press Ltd, ex p A-G [1957] 1 QB 73, [1956] 3 All ER 494, [1956] 3 WLR 796,
   100 Sol Jo 819, DC 772
O'Donoghue (1927) 97 LJKB 303, 138 LT 240, 91 JP 199, 44 TLR 51, 71 Sol Jo 897,
   28 Cox CC 461, 20 Cr App Rep 132, CCA 362
O'Driscoll (1977) 65 Cr App Rep 50, CA 686, 693
O'Grady [1987] QB 995, [1987] 3 All ER 420, [1987] 3 WLR 321, 131 Sol Jo 887,
   [1987] NLJ Rep 565, [1987] LS Gaz R 2044, CA 216
Ohlson v Hylton [1975] 2 All ER 490, [1975] 1 WLR 724, 139 JP 531, 119 Sol Jo 255,
   DC 424, 611
Oldcastle's Case (1419) 1 Hale PC 50 . . . . 231, 232
O'Leary (1986) 82 Cr App Rep 341 611
Olifier (1866) 10 Cox CC 402 453
Olugboja [1982] QB 320, [1981] 3 All ER 443, [1981] 3 WLR 585, 146 JP 82, 125 Sol Jo
   587, 73 Cr App Rep 344, CA 433
Olympia Press Ltd v Hollis [1974] 1 All ER 108, [1973] 1 WLR 1520, 138 JP 100, 117
   Sol Jo 813, DC 732
Omealy v Newell (1807) 8 East 364 743
O'Moran v DPP [1975] QB 864, [1975] 1 All ER 473, [1975] 2 WLR 413, 139 JP 245,
   119 Sol Jo 165, DC 846
Omychund v Barker (1744) 1 Atk 21, Willes 538, 2 Eq Cas Abr 397 pl 15, Ridg temp H
   285, 1 Wils 84 741
Ortiz (1986) 83 Cr App Rep 173, CA 231
Orton (1878) 39 LT 293, 43 JP 72, 14 Cox CC 226, CCR 383
Osborn (1919) 84 JP 63 293
Osborn v Veitch (1858) 1 F & F 317 378
Ostler v Elliott [1980] Crim LR 584, DC 396
O'Sullivan [1981] Crim LR 406, CA 432
O'Sullivan v Fisher [1954] SASR 33 . . . . 47, 112
O'Toole [1987] Crim LR 759, CA 288, 289
Overton (1843) 4 QB 83, Car & M 655, 2 Mood CC 263, 12 LJMC 61, 7 JP 513, sub
   nom Overton v R 3 Gal & Dav 133, 7 Jur 196 745
Owen [1976] 3 All ER 239, [1976] 1 WLR 840, 140 JP 609, 120 Sol Jo 470, 63 Cr App
   Rep 199, CA 753, 756
Owen [1988] 1 WLR 134, 131 Sol Jo 1696, [1988] LS Gaz R 34, CA . . . 449
Oxford v Moss (1978) 68 Cr App Rep 183, [1979] Crim LR 119 . . . 505
Oxford v Peers (1980) 72 Cr App Rep 19 495

P

P (GE) (an infant), Re [1965] Ch 568, [1964] 3 All ER 977, [1965] 2 WLR 1, 108 Sol
   Jo 916, CA 830, 831
Page [1954] 1 QB 170, [1953] 2 All ER 1355, [1953] 3 WLR 895, 97 Sol Jo 799, 37 Cr
   App Rep 189 311
Paget and Pemberton [1983] Crim LR 274 8
Pagett (1983) 76 Cr App Rep 279, [1983] Crim LR 394 . . . . 314, 318, 352

PAGE

Pain (1985) 150 JP 65, 82 Cr App Rep 141, [1986] BTLC 142, [1985] LS Gaz R 3696,
  [1986] Crim LR 168, CA   273
Pallante v Stadium Pty Ltd [1976] VR 331   383
Palmer v R [1971] AC 814, [1971] 1 All ER 1077, [1971] 2 WLR 831, 115 Sol Jo 264, 55
  Cr App Rep 223, 243n, 16 WIR 499, 511, PC 31, 241, 248
Palmer-Brown v Police [1985] 1 NZLR 365, CA   46
Panayiotou [1973] 3 All ER 112, [1973] 1 WLR 1032, 137 JP 699, 117 Sol Jo 464, 57 Cr
  App Rep 762, CA   755
Pankotai [1961] Crim LR 546   316
Pannell (1982) 76 Cr App Rep 53, CA   417
Papadimitropoulos v R (1957) 98 CLR 249 .   .   .   .   436, 437
Pappajohn v R (1980) 111 DLR (3d) 1   207
Parashuram Detaram Shamdasani v King-Emperor [1945] AC 264, 114 LJPC 95, 173
  LT 400, 61 TLR 448, PC   770
Park (1987) Times, 14 December, CA   623
Parker (1839) 9 C & P 45   700
Parker (1910) 74 JP 208 .   .   .   .   .   556, 658
Parker [1970] 2 All ER 458, [1970] 1 WLR 1003, 134 JP 497, 114 Sol Jo 396, 54 Cr App
  Rep 339, CA   642
Parker (1985) 83 Cr App Rep 69, [1985] Crim LR 589, CA .   .   128
Parker v Alder [1899] 1 QB 20, 68 LJQB 7, 79 LT 381, 62 JP 772, 47 WR 142, 15 TLR
  3, 43 Sol Jo 15, 19 Cox CC 191, DC 98, 118
Parker v British Airways Board [1982] QB 1004, [1982] 1 All ER 834, [1982] 2 WLR
  503, 126 Sol Jo 119, CA 129, 512
Parker v Green (1862) 2 B & S 299, 31 LJMC 133, 6 LT 46, 26 JP 247, 8 Jur NS 409,
  10 WR 316, 9 Cox CC 169.   23
Parker v R [1964] AC 1369, [1964] 2 All ER 641, [1964] 3 WLR 70, 108 Sol Jo 459,
  PC   331
Parkes [1973] Crim LR 358   594
Parkin v Norman [1983] QB 92, [1982] 2 All ER 583, [1982] 3 WLR 523, 126 Sol Jo
  359, [1982] Crim LR 528, DC   791
Parnerkar [1974] SCR 449, 10 CCC (2d) 253 .   .   .   188, 189
Parsons v Barnes [1973] Crim LR 537   167
Partridge v Crittenden [1968] 2 All ER 421, [1968] 1 WLR 1204, 132 JP 367, 112 Sol Jo
  582, DC   725
Patel [1970] Crim LR 274, CA   145
Patel v Comptroller of Customs [1966] AC 356, [1965] 3 All ER 593, [1965] 3 WLR
  1222, 109 Sol Jo 832.   100
Pater, ex p (1864) 5 B & S 299, 4 New Rep 147, 33 LJMC 142, 10 LT 376, 28 JP 612,
  10 Jur NS 972, 12 WR 823, 9 Cox CC 544   770
Patterson [1962] 2 QB 429, [1962] 1 All ER 340, [1962] 2 WLR 496, 126 JP 126, 106 Sol
  Jo 156, 46 Cr App Rep 106, CCA   614
Pawley v Wharldall [1966] 1 QB 373, [1965] 2 All ER 757, [1965] 3 WLR 496, 129 JP
  444, 109 Sol Jo 614   482
Peacock [1973] Crim LR 639   425
Peacock and Hoskyn v Musgrave and Porter [1956] Crim LR 414 .   .   409
Peake (1932) 97 JPN 353.   368
Pearce [1951] 1 All ER 493, 115 JP 157, [1951] 1 TLR 412, 95 Sol Jo 239, 35 Cr App
  Rep 17, 49 LGR 398, CCA   475
Pearce [1953] 1 QB 30, [1952] 2 All ER 718, 116 JP 575, [1952] 2 TLR 618, 96 Sol Jo
  712, 36 Cr App Rep 149, CCA   8
Pearce v Brooks (1866) LR 1 Exch 213, [1861-73] All ER Rep 102, 4 H & C 358, 35 LJ
  Ex 134, 14 LT 288, 30 JP 295, 12 Jur NS 342, 14 WR 614 .   .   461
Pearman [1985] RTR 39, 80 Cr App Rep 259, [1984] Crim LR 675, [1984] LS Gaz R
  2850, CA   288
Peart [1970] 2 QB 672, [1970] 2 All ER 823, [1970] 3 WLR 63, 114 Sol Jo 418, 54 Cr
  App Rep 374, CA   585
Peart v Stewart [1983] 2 AC 109, [1983] 1 All ER 859, [1983] 2 WLR 451, 4 FLR 723,
  [1984] Fam Law 54, 127 Sol Jo 206   768
Peaston (1978) 69 Cr App Rep 203, CA   109
Peck (1839) 9 Ad & El 686, sub nom Peck v R 1 Per & Dav 508, 8 LJMC 22 .   256
Pedro v Diss [1981] 2 All ER 59, 145 JP 445, 72 Cr App Rep 193, DC .   .   389

PAGE

Pembliton (1874) LR 2 CCR 119, [1874-80] All ER Rep 1163, 43 LJMC 91, 30 LT 405,
   38 JP 454, 22 WR 553, 12 Cox CC 607, CCR 74, 683, 687
Penn [1966] Crim LR 681   748
Pennington [1958] Crim LR 690, CCA   348
People v Beardsley (1967) 113 NW 1128   51
People v Lewis 124 Cal 551 (1899) (Sup Ct of California)   317
People, The v McCalla 220 Pac 436 (1923)   81
Perka v R (1984) 13 DLR (4th) 1   225
Perkins (1852) 2 Den 459, 21 LJMC 152, 16 JP 406, 16 Jur 481, 5 Cox CC 554, CCR   .   627
Perry (1883) 15 Cox CC 169   824
Peters [1955] Crim LR 712   749
Peters v Stanway (1835) 6 C & P 737   406
Peterson [1970] 1 QB 352, [1969] 2 All ER 1077, [1969] 3 WLR 213, 133 JP 571, 113
   Sol Jo 445, 53 Cr App Rep 461, CA 149, 153
Pethick [1980] Crim LR 242, CA   633
Petrie [1961] 1 All ER 466, [1961] 1 WLR 358, 125 JP 198, 105 Sol Jo 131, 45 Cr App
   Rep 72, CCA 423, 424
Pharmaceutical Society of Great Britain v Boots Cash Chemists (Southern) Ltd [1953]
   1 QB 401, [1953] 1 All ER 482, [1953] 2 WLR 427, 117 JP 132, 97 Sol Jo 149, CA .   726
Pharmaceutical Society of Great Britain v Storkwain Ltd [1985] 3 All ER 4, 149 JP 625,
   affd [1986] 2 All ER 635, [1986] 1 WLR 903, 150 JP 385, 130 Sol Jo 481, [1986]
   BTLC 135, 83 Cr App Rep 359, [1986] LS Gaz R 2238, [1986] Crim LR 813, HL .   98,
                                                                                     105
Phekoo [1981] 3 All ER 84, [1981] 1 WLR 1117, 125 Sol Jo 239, 73 Cr App Rep 107,
   sub nom R v Pheekoo 146 JP 58, CA 87, 814
Philips (1839) 8 C & P 736   .   .   .   .   181, 438
Phillips (1842) 2 Mood CC 252, sub nom R v Langford Car & M 602, CCR   .   .   684
Phillips (1987) 86 Cr App Rep 18, CA   281
Phillips v Brooks Ltd [1919] 2 KB 243, [1918-19] All ER Rep 246, 88 LJKB 953, 121
   LT 249, 35 TLR 470, 24 Com Cas 263   554
Phillips v Pringle [1973] 1 NSWLR 275, CCA   690
Phillips v R [1969] 2 AC 130, [1969] 2 WLR 581, 113 Sol Jo 14, 53 Cr App Rep 132, 13
   WIR 356, PC   342
Phillpotts (1851) 3 Car & Kir 135, 2 Den 302, T & M 607, 21 LJMC 18, 18 LTOS 173,
   15 JP 800, 16 Jur 67, 5 Cox CC 363, CCR 744, 746
Phipoe (1795) 2 Leach 673   589
Phipps (1970) 54 Cr App Rep 300, [1970] RTR 209, [1970] Crim LR 290, CA   .   584
Pick [1982] Crim LR 238   535
Pickstone [1954] Crim LR 565   184
Piddington v Bates [1960] 3 All ER 660, [1961] 1 WLR 162, 105 Sol Jo 110, DC .   .   390
Pierce (1941) 5 JCL 124   239
Pierre [1963] Crim LR 513   419
Pigg [1982] 2 All ER 591, [1982] 1 WLR 762, 146 JP 298, 126 Sol Jo 344, 74 Cr App
   Rep 352, [1983] Crim LR 446, [1982] LS Gaz R 953, CA .   66, 68, 69, 73, 289, 437
Pigney v Pointers Transport Services Ltd [1957] 2 All ER 807, [1957] 1 WLR 1121, 101
   Sol Jo 851   320
Pike v Waldrum and Peninsular and Oriental Steam Navigation Co [1952] 1 Lloyd's
   Rep 431   408
Pilgram v Dean [1974] 2 All ER 751, [1974] 1 WLR 601, 138 JP 502, 118 Sol Jo 149,
   [1974] RTR 299, DC   250
Pilgram v Rice-Smith [1977] 2 All ER 658, [1977] 1 WLR 671, 141 JP 427, 121 Sol Jo
   333, 65 Cr App Rep 142, DC   494
Pinkerton v United States 328 US 640 (1946)   133
Piracy Jure Gentium, Re [1934] AC 586, [1934] All ER Rep 506, 103 LJPC 153, 152
   LT 73, 51 TLR 12, 78 Sol Jo 585, 18 Asp MLC 528, PC   .   .   .   815
Pitchley (1972) 57 Cr App Rep 30, [1972] Crim LR 705, CA   .   .   54, 626
Pitham (1976) 65 Cr App Rep 45, [1977] Crim LR 285, CA   .   497, 504, 536, 627
Pittard v Mahoney [1977] Crim LR 169, DC   426
Pitts (1842) Car & M 284   326
Po Koon-tai [1980] HKLR 492   .   .   .   .   150, 266
Pocock v Moore (1825) Ry & M 321   406
Podola [1960] 1 QB 325, [1959] 3 All ER 418, [1959] 3 WLR 718, 103 Sol Jo 856, 43 Cr
   App Rep 220, CCA 182, 183, 184

PAGE

Police v Greaves [1964] NZLR 295 378
Police v Leaming [1975] 1 NZLR 471 514
Police v Marchant (1938) 2 JCL 324 448
Police v Smith [1974] 2 NZLR 32 424
Police Comr v Cartman [1896] 1 QB 655, 65 LJMC 113, 74 LT 726, 60 JP 357, 44 WR
  637, 12 TLR 334, 40 Sol Jo 439, 18 Cox CC 341 164
Pomroy (1971) 57 Cr App Rep 64, CA 589, 594
Ponting [1985] Crim LR 318 841
Pooley (1857) 8 State Tr NS 1089 739
Pope [1978] Crim LR 303 640
Pordage [1975] Crim LR 575, CA 211, 213
Porritt [1961] 3 All ER 463, [1961] 1 WLR 1372, 125 JP 605, 105 Sol Jo 991, 45 Cr App
  Rep 348, CCA 333
Potger (1970) 114 Sol Jo 906, 55 Cr App Rep 42, CA . . . 271, 556, 561
Potter [1958] 2 All ER 51, [1958] 1 WLR 638, 122 JP 234, 102 Sol Jo 438, 42 Cr App
  Rep 168 646
Poulton (1832) 5 C & P 329 310
Pounder v Police [1971] NZLR 1080 389
Powell [1963] Crim LR 511, CCA 425, 467
Powell v MacRae [1977] Crim LR 571, 141 JP Jo 432 516
Poynton (1862) Le & Ca 247, 32 LJMC 29, 7 LT 434, 26 JP 804, 8 Jur NS 1218, 11
  WR 73, 9 Cox CC 249, CCR 495
Practice Direction (1988) 86 Cr App Rep 142 27
Pratt [1984] Crim LR 41 450
Prebble (1858) 1 F & F 325 388
Preece and Howells [1976] Crim LR 392, CA 475
Prestney (1849) 3 Cox CC 505 122
Preston [1962] Tas SR 141 159
Preston Justices, ex p Lyons [1982] RTR 173, [1982] Crim LR 451 . . 93, 479, 481
Price (1884) 12 QBD 247, 53 LJMC 51, 33 WR 45n, 15 Cox CC 389 . . 795
Price [1963] 2 QB 1, [1962] 3 All ER 957, [1962] 3 WLR 1308, 47 Cr App Rep 21 . 201
Price v Cromack [1975] 2 All ER 113, [1975] 1 WLR 988, 139 JP 423, 119 Sol Jo 458 . 110, 126
Primelt (1858) 1 F & F 50 454
Prince (1875) LR 2 CCR 154, [1874-80] All ER Rep 881, 44 LJMC 122, 32 LT 700, 39
  JP 676, 24 WR 76, 13 Cox CC 138, CCR . 41, 70, 72, 73, 86, 93, 102, 113, 116, 391, 441, 447, 454, 472
Pritam Singh [1958] 1 All ER 199, [1958] 1 WLR 143, 122 JP 85, 102 Sol Jo 88, 42 Cr
  App Rep 44 741
Proprietary Articles Trade Association v A-G for Canada [1931] AC 310, [1931] All ER
  Rep 277, 100 LJPC 84, 144 LT 577, 47 TLR 250, PC 21
Proudman v Dayman (1941) 67 CLR 536 . . . . . . 96, 116
Provincial Motor Cab Co Ltd v Dunning [1909] 2 KB 599, 78 LJKB 822, 101 LT 231,
  73 JP 387, 25 TLR 646, 7 LGR 765, 22 Cox CC 159, DC 169
Pryse-Hughes (1958) Times, 14 May 647
Purcy [1933] All ER Rep 630, 149 LT 432, 97 JP 153, 24 Cr App Rep 70, 29 Cox CC
  657, CCA 756
Purdy (1946) 10 JCL 182 231
Purdy [1982] 2 NSWLR 964 202
Pym (1846) 6 LTOS 500, 1 Cox CC 339 321

Q

Quality Dairies (York) Ltd v Pedley [1952] 1 KB 275, [1952] 1 All ER 380, 116 JP 123,
  [1952] 1 TLR 376, 96 Sol Jo 151, 50 LGR 244, DC 166
Queen [1982] Crim LR 56 10
Quick [1973] QB 910, [1973] 3 All ER 347, [1973] 3 WLR 26, 137 JP 763, 117 Sol Jo
  371, 57 Cr App Rep 722, CA . . . 42, 187, 188, 198, 199, 211, 218
Quinn v Scott [1965] 2 All ER 588, [1965] 1 WLR 1004, 109 Sol Jo 498 . . 481
Qureshi v Qureshi [1972] Fam 173, [1971] 1 All ER 325, [1971] 2 WLR 518, 114 Sol Jo
  908 713

PAGE

R

R (1984) 149 JP 89, 79 Cr App Rep 334, CA 64, 96, 685
Rabey (1977) 37 CCC (2d) 461; affd [1980] SCR 513, 54 CCC (2d) 461 . . 188, 191
Rabey (1978) 79 DLR (3d) 414 40
Rabey v R (1981) 114 DLR (3d) 193 189
Race Relations Board v Applin [1973] QB 815, [1973] 2 All ER 1190, [1973] 2 WLR
  895, 117 Sol Jo 417, CA 253
Racimore (1976) 25 CCC (2d) 143 43
Rahman (1985) 129 Sol Jo 431, 81 Cr App Rep 349, [1985] LS Gaz R 2500, CA . 405, 409,
  412
Ram and Ram (1893) 17 Cox CC 609 . . . . 155, 438
Ramsay [1967] NZLR 1005 . . . . 77, 78
Ramsey and Foote (1883) Cab & El 126, 48 LT 733, 15 Cox CC 231 . . . 737, 739
Rankin (1960) Times, 30 March 8
Ransford (1874) 31 LT 488, 13 Cox CC 9, CCR 253
Rapier (1979) 70 Cr App Rep 17, [1980] Crim LR 48, CA 424
Rashid [1977] 2 All ER 237, [1977] 1 WLR 298, 141 JP 305, 120 Sol Jo 856, 64 Cr App
  Rep 201, [1977] Crim LR 237, CA 553, 612
Raven [1982] Crim LR 51 340
Raymond v A-G [1982] QB 839, [1982] 2 All ER 487, [1982] 2 WLR 849, 126 Sol Jo
  207, 75 Cr App Rep 34, CA 18
Raymond v Honey [1983] 1 AC 1, [1982] 1 All ER 756, [1982] 2 WLR 465, 126 Sol Jo
  188, HL 772
Read v Coker (1853) 13 CB 850, 22 LJCP 201, 21 LTOS 156, 17 Jur 990, 1 WR 413, 1
  CLR 746 378
Read v Donovan [1947] KB 326, [1947] 1 All ER 37, [1947] LJR 849, 176 LT 124, 111
  JP 46, 63 TLR 89, 91 Sol Jo 101, 45 LGR 28, DC 418
Read and Huggonson, Re (1742) 2 Atk 469, sub nom Roach v Garvan 2 Dick 794 . 773
Reader (1977) 66 Cr App Rep 33, CA 633
Reading v A-G [1951] AC 507, [1951] 1 All ER 617, [1951] 1 TLR 480, 95 Sol Jo 155,
  HL 275
Reakes [1974] Crim LR 615, CA 472
Reane (1794) 2 Leach 616, 2 East PC 734 542
Redgate v Haynes (1876) 1 QBD 89, 45 LJMC 65, 33 LT 779, 41 JP 86, DC . 125
Reed (1871) 12 Cox CC 1 470
Reed [1982] Crim LR 819, CA 134, 266, 359
Reed v Wastie [1972] Crim LR 221 243
Reekspear (1832) 1 Mood CC 342, CCR 471
Reeves (1839) 9 C & P 25 310
Regan [1959] Crim LR 529, CCA 10
Reid (Philip) [1973] 3 All ER 1020, [1973] 1 WLR 1283, 138 JP 51, 117 Sol Jo 681, 137
  JP Jo 697, 57 Cr App Rep 807, CA 80
Reid [1973] QB 299, [1972] 2 All ER 1350, [1972] 3 WLR 395, 136 JP 624, 116 Sol Jo
  565, 56 Cr App Rep 703, CA 413
Reid (1975) 62 Cr App Rep 109, CA 149, 150, 152, 351
Reiter [1954] 2 QB 16, [1954] 1 All ER 741, [1954] 2 WLR 638, 118 JP 262, 98 Sol Jo
  235, 38 Cr App Rep 62, CA 728
Reniger v Forgossa (1552) 1 Plowd 1 225
Renouf [1986] 2 All ER 449, [1986] 1 WLR 522, 130 Sol Jo 265, [1986] RTR 191, 82 Cr
  App Rep 344, [1986] LS Gaz R 870, [1986] Crim LR 408, CA . . 61, 246
Reubegard (1830) cited in 1 Den 344, cited in T & M 25 469
Reynhoudt [1962] ALR 483, 36 ALJR 26, 107 CLR 381 391
Reynolds v G H Austin & Sons Ltd [1951] 2 KB 135, [1951] 1 All ER 606, 115 JP 192,
  [1951] 1 TLR 614, 95 Sol Jo 173, 49 LGR 377, DC . . . 105, 115, 116
Rhodes [1959] Crim LR 138, CCA 13
Rhuddlan Justices, ex p HTV Ltd [1986] Crim LR 329 777
Rice v Connolly [1966] 2 QB 414, [1966] 2 All ER 649, [1966] 3 WLR 17, 130 JP 322,
  110 Sol Jo 371, DC 122, 394
Richards (No 2) [1956] Crim LR 127, CCA 11
Richards [1974] QB 776, [1973] 3 All ER 1088, [1973] 3 WLR 888, 138 JP 69, 117 Sol
  Jo 852, 58 Cr App Rep 60, CA 153, 154
Richards (1985) 81 Cr App Rep 125, [1985] LS Gaz R 1409, [1985] Crim LR 1782,
  CA 224

PAGE

Richardson (1785) 1 Leach 387 138
Richardson (1834) 6 C & P 335 622
Richman [1982] Crim LR 507 239
Ricketts v Cox (1981) 74 Cr App Rep 298, [1982] Crim LR 184, DC . . . 394
Rider [1954] 1 All ER 5, [1954] 1 WLR 463, 118 JP 73, 98 Sol Jo 146, 37 Cr App Rep
  209 441
Rider (1986) 83 Cr App Rep 207, [1986] Crim LR 626, CA 746
Rigby [1984] Crim LR 616, CA 148
Riley [1896] 1 QB 309, 65 LJMC 74, 74 LT 254, 60 JP 519, 44 WR 318, 12 TLR 178,
  40 Sol Jo 240, 18 Cox CC 285, CCR 646
Riley [1967] Crim LR 656 90
Rivett (1950) 34 Cr App Rep 87, CCA 197
Roach v Garvan. See Read and Huggonson, Re
Robert Millar (Contractors) Ltd [1970] 2 QB 54, [1970] 2 WLR 541, [1970] RTR 155n,
  sub nom R v Hart, Millar and Robert Millar (Contractors) Ltd [1969] 3 All ER
  247, 133 JP 554; affd sub nom R v Robert Millar (Contractors) Ltd, R v Millar
  [1970] 2 QB 54, [1970] 1 All ER 577, [1970] 2 WLR 541, 134 JP 240, 114 Sol Jo 16,
  54 Cr App Rep 158, [1970] RTR 147, CA 131, 148, 171, 174
Roberts [1954] 2 QB 329, [1953] 2 All ER 340, [1953] 3 WLR 178, 117 JP 341, 97 Sol
  Jo 455, 37 Cr App Rep 86 184
Roberts (1971) 115 Sol Jo 809, 56 Cr App Rep 95, CA 397
Roberts [1982] 1 All ER 609, [1982] 1 WLR 133, 146 JP 213, 126 Sol Jo 64, 74 Cr App
  Rep 242, 4 Cr App R (S) 8, CA 7
Roberts (1983) 148 JP 14, 78 Cr App Rep 41, [1985] Crim LR 218, CA . . 285
Roberts [1986] Crim LR 188, CA 431
Roberts v Inverness Local Authority 1889 17 R 19, 27 SLR 198 . . . 83
Roberts v Warne [1973] RTR 217, DC 124
Robertson [1968] 3 All ER 557, [1968] 1 WLR 1767, 133 JP 5, 112 Sol Jo 799, 52 Cr
  App Rep 690, CA 182, 184
Robertson [1977] Crim LR 629 516
Robertson v Balmain New Ferry Co. See Robinson v Balmain New Ferry Co Ltd
Robins (1844) 1 Car & Kir 456 453
Robinson (1796) 2 Leach 749, 2 East PC 1110 589
Robinson [1915] 2 KB 342, [1916-17] All ER Rep Ext 1299, 84 LJKB 1149, 113 LT
  379, 79 JP 303, 31 TLR 313, 59 Sol Jo 366, 24 Cox CC 726, 11 Cr App Rep 124,
  CCA 151, 295, 614
Robinson [1938] 1 All ER 301, 26 Cr App Rep 129, CCA 709
Robinson [1977] Crim LR 173, CA 540, 594
Robinson v Balmain New Ferry Co Ltd [1910] AC 295, sub nom Robertson v Balmain
  New Ferry Co 79 LJPC 84, 26 TLR 143, PC 408
Robinson v California 370 US 660, 8 L Ed 2d 758 (1962) 47
Robinson's Case (1746) 1 Leach 37, 2 East PC 1010 282
Robson v Biggar [1908] 1 KB 672, 77 LJKB 203, 97 LT 859, 24 TLR 125, 52 Sol Jo 76,
  CA 23
Robson v Hallett [1967] 2 QB 939, [1967] 2 All ER 407, [1967] 3 WLR 28, 131 JP 333,
  111 Sol Jo 254, 51 Cr App Rep 307, DC 389
Robson and East [1970] Crim LR 354 11
Rochford RDC v Port of London Authority [1914] 2 KB 916, 83 LJKB 1066, 111 LT
  207, 78 JP 329, 12 LGR 979, DC 125
Roe v Kingerlee [1986] Crim LR 735 679
Roffel [1985] VR 511 523
Rogers v Arnott [1960] 2 QB 244, [1960] 2 All ER 417, [1960] 3 WLR 73, 124 JP 349,
  104 Sol Jo 508, 44 Cr App Rep 195, DC 298, 497
Rogerson (1953) 103 L Jo 97 295
Rolfe (1952) 36 Cr App Rep 4, CCA 376, 448
Rolle v R [1965] 3 All ER 582, [1965] 1 WLR 1341, 109 Sol Jo 813, PC . . 334
Rolph [1962] Qd R 262 203
Ronald Evans (1987) Times, 1 December 592
Rookes v Barnard [1964] AC 1129, [1964] 1 All ER 367, [1964] 2 WLR 269, 108 Sol Jo
  93, [1964] 1 Lloyd's Rep 28, HL 23
Rooney v Snaresbrook Crown Court (1978) 68 Cr App Rep 78, [1979] Crim LR 109 . 79
Roote [1981] Crim LR 189 15

PAGE

Roper v Knott [1898] 1 QB 868, 67 LJQB 574, 78 LT 594, 62 JP 375, 46 WR 636, 14
    TLR 383, 42 Sol Jo 469, 19 Cox CC 69, DC 122, 678
Roper v Taylor's Central Garages (Exeter) Ltd [1951] 2 TLR 284, DC   .   103, 116, 121,
    427
Rose v Matt [1951] 1 KB 810, [1951] 1 All ER 361, 115 JP 122, [1951] 1 TLR 474, 95
    Sol Jo 62, 35 Cr App Rep 1, 49 LGR 199, DC 510, 512
Rose v R [1961] AC 496, [1961] 1 All ER 859, [1961] 2 WLR 506, 105 Sol Jo 253, 45 Cr
    App Rep 102, PC   205
Rosenberg (1906) 70 JP 264   358
Rosinski (1824) 1 Lew CC 11, 1 Mood CC 19, CCR   382
Ross v Moss [1965] 2 QB 396, [1965] 3 All ER 145, [1965] 3 WLR 416, 129 JP 537, 109
    Sol Jo 475, 63 LGR 321, DC 166, 168
Ross v Rivenall [1959] 2 All ER 376n, [1959] 1 WLR 713, 123 JP 352, 103 Sol Jo 491,
    DC   138
Ross Hillman Ltd v Bond [1974] QB 435, [1974] 2 All ER 287, [1974] 2 WLR 436, 138
    JP 428, 118 Sol Jo 243, 59 Cr App Rep 42, [1974] RTR 279, DC   .   .   127
Rossiter v Conway (1893) 58 JP 350, DC   802
Rothery [1976] RTR 550, CA   524
Rowe (1859) Bell CC 93, 28 LJMC 128, 32 LTOS 339, 23 JP 117, 5 Jur NS 274, 7 WR
    236, 8 Cox CC 139, CCR   512
Rowell [1978] 1 All ER 665, [1978] 1 WLR 132, 142 JP 181, 121 Sol Jo 790, 65 Cr App
    Rep 174, CA 751, 755
Rowley [1948] 1 All ER 570, 112 JP 207, 92 Sol Jo 299, 32 Cr App Rep 147, 46 LGR
    244, CCA   151
Roxburgh (1871) 12 Cox CC 8   388
Royal College of Nursing of United Kingdom v Department of Health and Social
    Security (1981) [1981] AC 800, [1981] 1 All ER 545, [1981] 2 WLR 279, 125 Sol Jo
    149, HL   371
Royle [1971] 3 All ER 1359, [1971] 1 WLR 1764, 136 JP 106, 115 Sol Jo 910, 56 Cr App
    Rep 131, CA   544
Rozsa v Samuels [1969] SASR 205   378
Rubie v Faulkner [1940] 1 KB 571, [1940] 1 All ER 285, 109 LJKB 241, 163 LT 212,
    104 JP 161, 56 TLR 303, 84 Sol Jo 257, 38 LGR 119, 31 Cox CC 385, DC   .   137
Rule [1937] 2 KB 375, [1937] 2 All ER 772, 106 LJKB 807, 157 LT 48, 53 TLR 720, 26
    Cr App Rep 87, 30 Cox CC 598, CCA   824
Rupert Griffiths [1984] Crim LR 628, CA   485
Ruse v Read [1949] 1 KB 377, [1949] 1 All ER 398, 65 TLR 124, 93 Sol Jo 184, 47
    LGR 273, 33 Cr App Rep 67, DC   213
Russell (1854) 3 E & B 942, 23 LJMC 173, 18 JP 807, 18 Jur 1022, 2 WR 555   .   798
Russell [1933] VLR 59, Argus LR 76   137
Russell (1984) 81 Cr App Rep 315, [1985] Crim LR 231, CA   .   .   .   121, 427
Russell and Russell [1987] Crim LR 494, CA   138
Russen (1777) 9 C & P 753n, 1 East PC 438, CCR   433
Russen v Lucas (1824) 1 C & P 153, Ry & M 26   406
Ryan (1839) 2 Mood & R 213   402
Ryan v R (1967) 40 ALJR 488, [1967] ALR 577, 121 CLR 205   .   .   .   43
Rymer (Grace) Investments Ltd v Waite [1958] Ch 831, [1958] 2 All ER 777, [1958] 3
    WLR 337, 102 Sol Jo 600, 172 Estates Gazette 43, CA   160

S

S v Chretien 1981 (1) SA 1097, 98 SALJ 177   220
S v De blom 1977 (3d) SA 513   82
S v Masilela 1968 (2) SA 558   77
S v Robinson 1968 (1) SA 666   .   .   .   .   146, 151
S v Thomo 1969 (1) SA 385   136
S v Van Niekerk [1970] 3 SA 655   781
Sagoo [1975] QB 885, [1975] 2 All ER 926, [1975] 3 WLR 267, 139 JP 604, 119 Sol Jo
    543, 61 Cr App Rep 191, CA   708
St Margaret's Trusts Ltd [1958] 2 All ER 289, [1958] 1 WLR 522, 122 JP 312, 102 Sol
    Jo 348, 42 Cr App Rep 183, CCA   106
Salford Health Authority, ex p Janaway (1988) Times, 5 January, CA   .   .   58, 373
Salisbury [1976] VR 452   399

PAGE

Salmon (1880) 6 QBD 79, 50 LJMC 25, 43 LT 573, 45 JP 270, 29 WR 246, 14 Cox CC
494, CCR   137
Salter [1968] 2 QB 793, [1968] 2 All ER 951, [1968] 3 WLR 39, 112 Sol Jo 480, 52 Cr
App Rep 549, CA   100
Salvo [1980] VR 401   529
Samuels v Stubbs [1972] 4 SASR 200   679
Sancoff v Halford [1973] Qd R 25   .   .   .   .   81, 731
Sanders (1867) LR 1 CCR 75, 36 LJMC 87, 16 LT 331, 15 WR 752, 10 Cox CC 445,
CCR   403
Sanders (1982) 75 Cr App Rep 84, [1982] Crim LR 695, CA   624
Sandon v Jervis (1858); affd (1859) EB & E 942, 28 LJ Ex 156, 32 LTOS 375, 5 Jur
NS 860, 7 WR 290, Ex Ch   407
Sang [1980] AC 402, [1979] 2 All ER 1222, [1979] 3 WLR 263, 143 JP 606, 123 Sol Jo
552, 69 Cr App Rep 282, HL 160, 161
Sangha (1988) Times, 2 February, CA   64
Sarwan Singh [1962] 3 All ER 612   708
Satnam (1983) 78 Cr App Rep 149, [1985] Crim LR 236, CA .   .   .   66, 68, 437
Saunders (1838) 8 C & P 265   435
Saunders [1978] Crim LR 98   388
Saunders [1985] LS Gaz R 1005, [1985] Crim LR 230, CA   328
Saunders and Archer (1573) 2 Plowd 473, Fost 371   .   .   .   .   147, 157
Scarfe v Wood (1969) 113 Sol Jo 143, [1969] Crim LR 265   800
Schifreen [1987] 3 All ER 618, [1987] 3 WLR 803, 131 Sol Jo 1247, [1985] LS Gaz R
2529, CA 649, 662
Schlesinger (1847) 10 QB 670, 17 LJMC 29, 9 LTOS 170, 12 JP 196, 12 Jur 283, 2 Cox
CC 200   747
Schmidt (1866) LR 1 CCR 15, 35 LJMC 94, 13 LT 679, 30 JP 100, 12 Jur NS 149, 14
WR 286, 10 Cox CC 172, CCR   618
Schneider v Heath (1813) 3 Camp 506   547
Scott [1967] VR 276   .   .   .   .   40, 42, 76, 757
Scott v Metropolitan Police Comr [1975] AC 819, [1974] 3 All ER 1032, [1974] 3 WLR
741, 139 JP 121, 118 Sol Jo 863, 60 Cr App Rep 124, HL .   .   .   128, 269, 273
Scott (otherwise Morgan) v Scott [1912] P 4, 81 LJP 14, 105 LT 912, 28 TLR 127, 56
Sol Jo 206; affd [1912] P 241, 81 LJP 113, 107 LT 211, 28 TLR 526, 56 Sol Jo 666,
CA; revsd [1913] AC 417, [1911-13] All ER Rep 1, 82 LJP 74, 109 LT 1, 29 TLR
520, 57 Sol Jo 498, HL   769
Scott v Shepherd (1773) 2 Wm Bl 892, [1558-1774] All ER Rep 295, 3 Wils 403 .   .   381
Scott v Warren (1973) 117 Sol Jo 916, [1974] RTR 104, [1974] Crim LR 117   .   .   481
Scott v Wolverhampton Justices, Re. See R v Hicklin
Scully (1903) 23 NZLR 380   .   .   .   .   368, 369
Seaman v Burley [1896] 2 QB 344, 65 LJMC 208, 75 LT 91, 60 JP 772, 45 WR 1, 12
TLR 599, 40 Sol Jo 684, 18 Cox CC 403, CA   23
Searle [1971] Crim LR 592, CA 129, 136
Searle v Randolph [1972] Crim LR 779, DC 108, 109
Sears v Broome [1986] Crim LR 461 .   .   .   .   .   61, 246, 693, 699
Seaward v Paterson [1897] 1 Ch 545, [1895-9] All ER Rep 1127, 66 LJ Ch 267, 76 LT
215, 45 WR 610, 13 TLR 211, CA   768
Secretary of State for Trade and Industry v Hart [1982] 1 All ER 817, [1982] 1 WLR
481, 126 Sol Jo 172, DC   83
Seers (1984) 149 JP 124, 79 Cr App Rep 261, [1985] Crim LR 315, CA   .   .   205
Selby v DPP [1972] AC 515, [1971] 3 WLR 647, 135 JP 619, 115 Sol Jo 948, 56 Cr App
Rep 72, HL 669, 671
Sellis (1837) 7 C & P 850   310
Selvage [1982] QB 372, [1982] 1 All ER 96, [1981] 3 WLR 811, 146 JP 115, 125 Sol Jo
708, 73 Cr App Rep 333, [1981] RTR 481, CA 753, 755
Senat (1968) 112 Sol Jo 252, 52 Cr App Rep 282, [1968] Crim LR 269, CA   .   754
Senior (1832) 1 Mood CC 346, CCR   311
Senior [1899] 1 QB 283, 68 LJQB 175, 79 LT 562, 63 JP 8, 47 WR 367, 15 TLR 102,
43 Sol Jo 114, 19 Cox CC 219, CCR   350
Seymour (1983) [1983] 2 AC 493, [1983] 2 All ER 1058, [1983] 3 WLR 349, 127 Sol Jo
522, 77 Cr App Rep 215, [1983] Crim LR 742, HL   352
Seymour (1983) 76 Cr App Rep 211, [1983] RTR 202, [1983] Crim LR 260, CA .   .   352

PAGE

Seymour (1983) 76 Cr App Rep 211, [1983] RTR 202, [1983] Crim LR 260, CA; affd
  [1983] 2 AC 493, [1983] 2 All ER 1058, [1983] 3 WLR 349, 127 Sol Jo 522, 77 Cr
  App Rep 215, [1983] Crim LR 742, HL   486
Shannon [1974] 2 All ER 1009, HL   151
Shannon (1980) 124 Sol Jo 374, 71 Cr App Rep 192, [1980] Crim LR 438, CA   .   .   241
Sharman (1913) 9 Cr App Rep 142, CCA   10
Sharmpal Singh [1962] AC 188, [1962] 2 WLR 238, 106 Sol Jo 56, PC   .   .   347, 432
Sharp [1987] QB 853, [1987] 3 All ER 103, [1987] 3 WLR 1, 151 JP 832, 131 Sol Jo
  624, 85 Cr App Rep 207, [1987] LS Gaz R 1491, [1987] Crim LR 566, CA   .   .   237
Sharpe [1938] 1 All ER 48, 159 LT 96, 102 JP 113, 82 Sol Jo 158, 36 LGR 254, 31 Cox
  CC 24, 26 Cr App Rep 122, CCA   753
Shaw (1911) 104 LT 112, 75 JP 191, 27 TLR 181, 22 Cox CC 376, 6 Cr App Rep 103,
  CCA   742
Shaw (1943) 60 TLR 344, CCA   706
Shaw v DPP [1962] AC 220, [1961] 2 WLR 897, sub nom R v Shaw [1961] 1 All ER
  330, CCA, affd sub nom Shaw v DPP [1962] AC 220, [1961] 2 All ER 446, [1961] 2
  WLR 897, 125 JP 437, 105 Sol Jo 421, 45 Cr App Rep 113, HL   .   20, 81, 460, 461, 730,
                                                                                            733
Sheard (1837) 7 C & P 846, 2 Mood CC 13, CCR   398
Sheehan [1975] 2 All ER 960, [1975] 1 WLR 739, 139 JP 636, 119 Sol Jo 271, 60 Cr
  App Rep 308, CA 211, 213
Sheen [1979] Crim LR 189   15
Sheldon Deliveries Ltd v Willis [1972] RTR 217, [1972] Crim LR 241   .   .   .   124
Shepherd [1987] Crim LR 686, CA   237
Sheppard (1980) 70 Cr App Rep 210, CA; revsd [1981] AC 394, [1980] 3 All ER 899,
  [1980] 3 WLR 960, 145 JP 65, 124 Sol Jo 864, 72 Cr App Rep 82, [1981] Crim LR
  171, HL 100, 114, 123, 350
Sheriff [1969] Crim LR 260, CA 376, 387
Sherlock (1866) LR 1 CCR 20, 5 LJMC 92, 13 LT 643, 30 JP 85, 12 Jur NS 126, 14
  WR 288, 10 Cox CC 170, CCR   767
Sherras v De Rutzen [1895] 1 QB 918, [1895-9] All ER Rep 1167, 64 LJMC 218, 72 LT
  839, 59 JP 440, 43 WR 526, 11 TLR 369, 39 Sol Jo 451, 18 Cox CC 157, 15 R 388 .   102,
                                                               103, 104, 116, 121, 122, 125, 163
Shiartos (19 September 1961, unreported)   231
Shickle (1868) LR 1 CCR 158, 38 LJMC 21, 19 LT 327, 32 JP 790, 17 WR 144, 11 Cox
  CC 189, CCR   512
Shillingford [1968] 2 All ER 200, [1968] 1 WLR 566, 132 JP 264, 112 Sol Jo 170, 52 Cr
  App Rep 188, CA   440
Shivpuri [1987] AC 1, [1986] 2 All ER 334, [1986] 2 WLR 988, 150 JP 353, 130 Sol Jo
  392, 83 Cr App Rep 178, [1986] NLJ Rep 488, [1986] LS Gaz R 1896, [1986] Crim
  LR 536, HL 34, 35, 121, 302, 304, 617
Shorty [1950] SR 280   76
Shukard (1811) Russ & Ry 200, CCR   672
Sibartie [1983] Crim LR 470, CA   567
Sidney (1663). See Sydlyes' Case
Silver [1956] 1 All ER 716, [1956] 1 WLR 281, 120 JP 233, 100 Sol Jo 228, 40 Cr App
  Rep 32   462
Silverman (1987) 151 JP 657, [1987] LS Gaz R 1651, [1987] Crim LR 574, CA   .   .   547
Sim v Stretch [1936] 2 All ER 1237, 52 TLR 669, 80 Sol Jo 703, HL   .   .   .   822
Simcox [1964] Crim LR 402   204
Simpson [1982] 3 All ER 789, [1983] 1 WLR 1494, 148 JP 33, 127 Sol Jo 748, 78 Cr
  App Rep 115, [1984] Crim LR 39, CA   423
Simpson v Hill (1795) 1 Esp 431   407
Simpson v Peat [1952] 2 QB 24, [1952] 1 All ER 447, 116 JP 151, [1952] 1 TLR 469, 96
  Sol Jo 132, DC 93, 479
Sinclair [1968] 3 All ER 241, [1968] 1 WLR 1246, 132 JP 527, 112 Sol Jo 703, 52 Cr
  App Rep 618, CA   274
Sinclair v Neighbour [1967] 2 QB 279, [1966] 3 All ER 988, [1967] 2 WLR 1, 110 Sol
  Jo 808, CA   530
Singh (Gurdev) v R [1974] 1 All ER 26, [1973] 1 WLR 1444, 138 JP 85, 117 Sol Jo
  776, DC   76
Singleton v Ellison [1895] 1 QB 607, [1895-9] All ER Rep Ext 2181, 64 LJMC 123, 72
  LT 236, 59 JP 119, 43 WR 426, 18 Cox CC 79, 15 R 201, DC   .   .   .   458

PAGE

Sinnasamy Selvanayagam v R [1951] AC 83, PC   58
Sirat (1985) 83 Cr App Rep 41, [1986] Crim LR 245, CA   .   .   254, 301, 474
Siviour v Napolitano [1931] 1 KB 636, [1930] All ER Rep 626, 100 LJKB 151, 144 LT
    408, 95 JP 72, 47 TLR 202, 75 Sol Jo 80, 29 LGR 195, 29 Cox CC 236, DC   .   .   459
Skipworth's Case (1873) LR 9 QB 230, 28 LT 227, sub nom R v Skipworth, R v De
    Castro 12 Cox CC 371, DC   770
Skipworth. See Skipworth's Case
Skirving [1985] QB 819, [1985] 2 All ER 705, [1985] 2 WLR 1001, 129 Sol Jo 299, 81
    Cr App Rep 9, [1985] LS Gaz R 1409, [1985] Crim LR 317, CA   .   .   .   721
Skivington [1968] 1 QB 166, [1967] 1 All ER 483, [1967] 2 WLR 665, 131 JP 265, 111
    Sol Jo 72, 51 Cr App Rep 167, CA 540, 594
Slater (1979) 1 Cr App Rep (S) 349   14
Sleep (1864) 9 Cox CC 559   358
Sloan (1974) 19 CCC 190   418
Small [1987] Crim LR 778   526
Small v Warr (1882) 47 JP 20   126
Smedleys Ltd v Breed [1974] AC 839, [1974] 2 All ER 21, [1974] 2 WLR 575, 138 JP
    439, 118 Sol Jo 363, 72 LGR 563, HL 113, 115, 118
Smith (1845) 5 LTOS 393, 9 JP 682, 1 Cox CC 260   181
Smith (1855) Dears CC 494, 24 LJMC 135, 26 LTOS 6, 19 JP 358, 1 Jur NS 575, 3
    WR 484, 3 CLR 1154, 6 Cox CC 554, CCA   622
Smith (1855) Dears CC 559, 25 LJMC 29, 26 LTOS 109, 19 JP 758, 1 Jur NS 1116, 4
    WR 128, 7 Cox CC 51, CCR   402
Smith (1858) Dears & B 566, 27 LJMC 225, 31 LTOS 135, 22 JP 274, 4 Jur NS 1003, 6
    WR 495, 8 Cox CC 32, CCR   648
Smith (1869) 11 Cox CC 210   51
Smith (1900) 17 SCR 561, 17 CGH 561   249
Smith (1910) 6 Cr App Rep 19, CCA   196
Smith (1915) 11 Cr App Rep 81, CCA   337
Smith [1959] 2 QB 35, [1959] 2 All ER 193, [1959] 2 WLR 623, 123 JP 295, 103 Sol Jo
    353, 43 Cr App Rep 121   .   .   .   .   .   .   316, 321, 322
Smith [1960] 2 QB 423, [1960] 1 All ER 256, [1960] 2 WLR 164, 124 JP 137, 104 Sol Jo
    69, 44 Cr App Rep 55, CCA 128, 161
Smith (1960). See DPP v Smith (1961)
Smith (1961) [1963] 3 All ER 597, [1963] 1 WLR 1200, 128 JP 13, 107 Sol Jo 873,
    CCA   149
Smith [1963] Crim LR 526   13
Smith [1973] 2 All ER 896. See Haughton v Smith
Smith [1974] 1 All ER 376, [1973] 1 WLR 1510, 138 JP 175, 117 Sol Jo 774, 58 Cr App
    Rep 106, CA   370
Smith [1974] QB 354, [1974] 1 All ER 632, [1974] 2 WLR 20, 138 JP 236, 117 Sol Jo
    938, 58 Cr App Rep 320, CA 83, 209, 215, 684
Smith [1975] Crim LR 468, CA   5
Smith [1976] 3 All ER 54, [1976] 1 WLR 672, 140 JP 515, 120 Sol Jo 299, 63 Cr App
    Rep 47, CA   600
Smith (1977) 64 Cr App Rep 217, CA   633
Smith [1985] LS Gaz R 198, [1985] Crim LR 42, CA   386
Smith (1986) 130 Sol Jo 649, 84 Cr App Rep 235, [1986] LS Gaz R 2996, [1987] Crim
    LR 44, CA   35
Smith, Re (1858) 3 H & N 227, 27 LJMC 186, 31 LTOS 87, 22 JP 450, 6 WR 440   .   133
Smith v Baker [1971] RTR 350   136
Smith v Chief Superintendent, Woking Police Station (1983) 76 Cr App Rep 234,
    [1983] Crim LR 323, DC   377
Smith v Desmond [1965] AC 960, sub nom R v Desmond, R v Hall [1964] 3 All ER
    587, [1964] 3 WLR 1148, 128 JP 591, 108 Sol Jo 677, 49 Cr App Rep 1, CCA; on
    appeal sub nom Smith v Desmond [1965] AC 960, [1965] 1 All ER 976, [1965] 2
    WLR 894, 129 JP 331, 109 Sol Jo 269, 49 Cr App Rep 246, HL   .   .   .   542
Smith v Hughes [1960] 2 All ER 859, [1960] 1 WLR 830, 124 JP 430, 104 Sol Jo 606,
    DC   467
Smith v Jenner (1967) 112 Sol Jo 52, DC   142
Smith v Land and House Property Corpn (1884) 28 Ch D 7, 51 LT 718, 49 JP 182,
    CA   548
Smith v Mellors and Soar [1987] RTR 210, 84 Cr App Rep 279, [1987] Crim LR 421   .   137

PAGE

Smith and Smith [1986] Crim LR 166, CA 290
Smithers (1976) 34 CCC (2d) 427 319
Snaresbrook Crown Court, ex p Metropolitan Police Commissioner (1984) 79 Cr App
   Rep 184, [1986] Crim LR 139 732
Snewing [1972] Crim LR 267 398
Socialist Worker Printers and Publishers Ltd, ex p A-G [1975] QB 637, [1975] 1 All ER
   142, [1974] 3 WLR 801, 118 Sol Jo 791, DC 783
Sockett (1908) 72 JP 428, 24 TLR 893, 52 Sol Jo 729, 1 Cr App Rep 101, CCA . 159, 283
Sodeman v R [1936] 2 All ER 1138, 80 Sol Jo 532, PC 195, 196
Solanke [1969] 3 All ER 1383, [1970] 1 WLR 1, 134 JP 80, 113 Sol Jo 834, 54 Cr App
   Rep 30, CA 122
Solomons [1909] 2 KB 980, 79 LJKB 8, 101 LT 496, 73 JP 467, 25 TLR 747, 22 Cox
   CC 178, 2 Cr App Rep 288, CCA 575
Somerset v Hart (1884) 12 QBD 360, 53 LJMC 77, 48 JP 327, 32 WR 594, DC . . 125
Somerset v Wade [1894] 1 QB 574, [1891-4] All ER Rep 1228, 63 LJMC 126, 70 LT
   452, 58 JP 231, 42 WR 399, 10 TLR 313, 10 R 105, DC 125
Sopp v Long [1970] 1 QB 518, [1969] 1 All ER 855, [1969] 2 WLR 587, 133 JP 261, 113
   Sol Jo 123, 67 LGR 389, DC 126, 127, 129, 165
Soul (1980) 70 Cr App Rep 295, [1980] Crim LR 233, CA 256
Souter [1971] 2 All ER 1151, [1971] 1 WLR 1187, 135 JP 458, 115 Sol Jo 548, 55 Cr
   App Rep 403, CA 124
South Staffordshire Water Co v Sharman [1896] 2 QB 44, [1895-9] All ER Rep 259, 65
   LJQB 460, 74 LT 761, 44 WR 653, 12 TLR 402, 40 Sol Jo 532 . . . 129
Southgate (Practice Note) [1963] 2 All ER 833, [1963] 1 WLR 809, 127 JP 538, 107 Sol
   Jo 516, 47 Cr App Rep 252, CCA 343
Southport Corpn v Esso Petroleum Co Ltd [1953] 2 All ER 1204, [1953] 3 WLR 773;
   on appeal [1954] 2 QB 182, [1954] 2 All ER 561, [1954] 3 WLR 200, 118 JP 411, 99
   Sol Jo 472, 52 LGR 404, [1954] 1 Lloyd's Rep 446, CA; revsd in part sub nom
   Esso Petroleum Co Ltd v Southport Corpn [1956] AC 218, [1955] 3 All ER 864,
   [1956] 2 WLR 81, 120 JP 54, 100 Sol Jo 32, 54 LGR 91, [1955] 2 Lloyd's Rep 655,
   HL 795, 797
Southwark London Borough Council v Williams [1971] Ch 734, [1971] 2 All ER 175,
   [1971] 2 WLR 467, 69 LGR 145, CA 224, 229
Spanner [1973] Crim LR 704, CA 426
Special Reference from Bahama Islands, Re [1893] AC 138, sub nom Re Moseley 62
   LJPC 79, 68 LT 105, 57 JP 277, PC 768, 781
Speck [1977] 2 All ER 859, 141 JP 459, 121 Sol Jo 221, 65 Cr App Rep 161, CA . 49, 449
Spence (1957) 41 Cr App Rep 80, CCA 359
Spencer [1985] QB 771, [1985] 1 All ER 673, [1985] 2 WLR 197, 129 Sol Jo 64, 80 Cr
   App Rep 264, [1985] LS Gaz R 117, [1985] Crim LR 101, CA . . . 633
Spicer [1955] Crim LR 772 367
Spicer (1970) 114 Sol Jo 824, [1970] Crim LR 695, CA 285
Spight [1986] Crim LR 817, CA 472
Spooner, ex p (1987) Times, 10 October 174
Spooner (1853) 6 Cox CC 392 398
Sporle [1971] Crim LR 706, CA 172
Spriggs [1958] 1 QB 270, [1958] 1 All ER 300, [1958] 2 WLR 162, 102 Sol Jo 89, 42 Cr
   App Rep 69, CCA 203, 205
Squires v Botwright [1972] RTR 462, DC 389
Staines (1974) 60 Cr App Rep 160, CA 545
Stamford [1972] 2 QB 391, [1972] 2 All ER 427, [1972] 2 WLR 1055, 136 JP 522, 116
   Sol Jo 313, 56 Cr App Rep 398, CA 735
Stamp v United Dominions Trust (Commercial) Ltd [1967] 1 QB 418, [1967] 1 All ER
   251, [1967] 2 WLR 541, 131 JP 177, 110 Sol Jo 906, DC 640
Staniforth, R v Jordan [1976] 2 All ER 714, [1976] 2 WLR 849, 140 JP 483, 120 Sol Jo
   266, 64 Cr App Rep 33, CA 727, 728
Stanley [1965] 2 QB 327, [1965] 1 All ER 1035, [1965] 2 WLR 917, 129 JP 279, 109 Sol
   Jo 193, 49 Cr App Rep 175, CCA 735
Stanton & Sons Ltd v Webber (1972) 116 Sol Jo 667, [1973] RTR 86, [1972] Crim LR
   544, DC 142
Stapleton v R (1952) 86 CLR 358 . . . . 193, 194
Stapylton v O'Callaghan [1973] 2 All ER 782, 137 JP 579, DC 631
State v Hamilton and Lawrie 13 Nev 386 (1878) 130

PAGE

State v Kinchen (1910) 52 So 185 157
State v Otu [1964] NNLR 113 284
State v Tally (1894) 102 Ala 25 278
State v Volschenk 1968 (2) PH H283 382
State v Wilson (1955) 218 Ore 575, 346 P (2d) 115 379
Steane [1947] KB 997, [1947] 1 All ER 813, [1947] LJR 969, 177 LT 122, 111 JP 337,
    63 TLR 403, 91 Sol Jo 279, 45 LGR 484, 32 Cr App Rep 61, CCA . 57, 71, 230, 231,
    234
Steele (1976) 65 Cr App Rep 22, CA 430
Steele v Kingsbeer [1957] NZLR 552 393
Steer [1987] 2 All ER 833, [1987] 3 WLR 205, 131 Sol Jo 939, [1987] NLJ Rep 640,
    [1987] LS Gaz R 2359, [1987] Crim LR 684, HL 698
Stein v Henshall [1976] VR 612 493
Steiner v Toronto Star Ltd [1956] OR 14, 1 DLR (2d) 297, [1950] OWN 32, 114 CCC
    117 776
Stephens (1866) LR 1 QB 702, [1861-73] All ER Rep Ext 2059, 7 B & S 710, 35 LJQB
    251, 14 LT 593, 30 JP 822, 12 Jur NS 961, 14 WR 859, 10 Cox CC 340 . 797, 798
Stephens v Myers (1830) 4 C & P 349 377
Stephenson (1884) 13 QBD 331, 53 LJMC 176, 52 LT 267, 49 JP 486, 33 WR 44, 15
    Cox CC 679, CCR 756
Stephenson [1979] QB 695, [1979] 2 All ER 1198, [1979] 3 WLR 193, 143 JP 592, 123
    Sol Jo 403, 69 Cr App Rep 213, [1979] Crim LR 590, CA 64
Stevens v Gourley (1859) 7 CBNS 99, 29 LJCP 1, 1 LT 33, 6 Jur NS 147, 8 WR 85 . 603
Stevenson (1862) 3 F & F 106, CCR 795
Stockdale v Coulson [1974] 3 All ER 154, [1974] 1 WLR 1192, 118 Sol Jo 627, DC . 250
Stokes (1848) 3 Car & Kir 185 196
Stokes (1925) 134 LT 479, 28 Cox CC 140, 19 Cr App Rep 71, CCA . . 405
Stokes [1982] Crim LR 695, [1983] RTR 59, CA 583
Stokes [1988] Crim LR 110 746
Stolady (1859) 1 F & F 518 748
Stone [1977] QB 354, [1977] 2 All ER 341, [1977] 2 WLR 169, 141 JP 354, 121 Sol Jo
    83, 64 Cr App Rep 186, CA 50, 345, 352
Stopford (1870) 11 Cox CC 643 402
Storrow and Poole [1983] Crim LR 332 505
Straker [1965] Crim LR 239, CCA 735
Straker v DPP [1963] 1 QB 926, [1963] 1 All ER 697, [1963] 2 WLR 598, 127 JP 260,
    107 Sol Jo 156, DC 734
Strath v Foxon [1956] 1 QB 67, [1955] 3 All ER 398, [1955] 3 WLR 659, 119 JP 581, 99
    Sol Jo 799, 39 Cr App Rep 162, DC 458
Stratton (1779) 1 Doug KB 239, 21 State Tr 1045 231
Strawbridge [1970] NZLR 909 116
Stripp (1978) 69 Cr App Rep 318, CA 43, 190, 218
Strowger v John (1973) 118 Sol Jo 101, [1974] RTR 124, [1974] Crim LR 123 . 98, 250
Strutt v Clift [1911] 1 KB 1, 80 LJKB 114, 103 LT 722, 74 JP 471, 27 TLR 14, 8 LGR
    989, DC 168
Stunt v Bolton (1972) 116 Sol Jo 803, [1972] RTR 435, DC . . 49, 395
Sullivan (1841) Car & M 209 402
Sullivan (1945) 30 Cr App Rep 132, CCA 550
Sullivan [1981] Crim LR 46, CA 400, 401
Sullivan [1984] AC 156, [1983] 1 All ER 577, [1983] 2 WLR 392, 127 Sol Jo 120, CA;
    on appeal [1984] AC 156, [1983] 2 All ER 673, [1983] 3 WLR 123, 148 JP 207, 127
    Sol Jo 460, HL 42, 44, 185, 186, 188, 192, 198
Sumner [1977] Crim LR 362 727
Surrey County Council v Battersby [1965] 2 QB 194, [1965] 1 All ER 273, [1965] 2
    WLR 378, 129 JP 116, 109 Sol Jo 30, 63 LGR 152, DC . . . 81
Surujpaul (called Dick) v R [1958] 3 All ER 300, [1958] 1 WLR 1050, 102 Sol Jo 757,
    42 Cr App Rep 266, PC 151, 152
Sutton [1977] 3 All ER 476, [1977] 1 WLR 1086, 141 JP 683, 121 Sol Jo 676, 66 Cr App
    Rep 21, CA 449
Sweet v Parsley [1970] AC 132, [1969] 1 All ER 347, [1969] 2 WLR 470, 133 JP 188,
    113 Sol Jo 86, 209 Estates Gazette 703, 53 Cr App Rep 221, HL . 97, 100, 102, 103, 104,
    109, 112, 114, 116
Sweet-Escott (1971) 55 Cr App Rep 316 745

PAGE

Sweetland (1957) 42 Cr App Rep 62, CCA 279
Sweetman v Industries and Commerce Department [1970] NZLR 139 . . 152
Swindall and Osborne (1846) 2 Car & Kir 230, 2 Cox CC 141 . . . 137, 315
Syce v Harrison [1980] Crim LR 649, [1981] Crim LR 110n . . . 393, 394
Sydlyes' Case (1663) 1 Keb 620, sub nom R v Sidney 1 Sid 168 . . . 468, 719
Sykes v DPP [1962] AC 528, [1961] 3 All ER 33, [1961] 3 WLR 371, 125 JP 523, 105
   Sol Jo 566, 45 Cr App Rep 230, HL 761, 849, 850, 851
Sykes v Holmes (1985) 84 LGR 355, [1985] Crim LR 791 795

T

T v T [1988] 2 WLR 189 223
Taafe [1984] AC 539, [1984] 1 All ER 747, [1984] 2 WLR 326, 148 JP 510, 128 Sol Jo
   203, 78 Cr App Rep 301, [1984] Crim LR 356, [1984] LS Gaz R 1051, HL . 121, 300
Taaffe (1983) Times, 16 April 120
Tacey (1821) Russ & Ry 452, CCR 678
Tait [1968] 2 NZLR 126 (NZCA) 664
Tamm [1973] Crim LR 115 . . . . 626, 639
Tan [1983] QB 1053, [1983] 2 All ER 12, [1983] 3 WLR 361, 147 JP 257, 127 Sol Jo
   390, 76 Cr App Rep 300, [1983] Crim LR 404, CA 459
Tandy (1987) Times, 23 December, CA 202, 205
Tansley v Painter (1968) 112 Sol Jo 1005, DC 136
Tao [1977] QB 141, [1976] 3 All ER 65, [1976] 3 WLR 25, 140 JP 596, 120 Sol Jo 420,
   63 Cr App Rep 163, [1976] Crim LR 516, CA 110
Tapsell v Maslen (1966) 110 Sol Jo 853, [1967] Crim LR 53 . . . 124
Tarling v Government of Singapore. See R v Governor of Pentonville Prison, ex p
   Tarling
Tatam (1921) 15 Cr App Rep 132, CCA 181, 438, 473
Tate (1871) 12 Cox CC 7 744
Taylor (1676) 1 Vent 293, 3 Keb 607, 621 737
Taylor (1859) 1 F & F 511 299
Taylor (1869) LR 1 CCR 194, 38 LJMC 106, 20 LT 402, 33 JP 358, 17 WR 623, 11
   Cox CC 261, CCR 398
Taylor (1875) LR 2 CCR 147, 44 LJMC 67, 32 LT 409, 39 JP 484, 23 WR 616, 13 Cox
   CC 68 138
Taylor [1950] 2 KB 368, [1950] 2 All ER 170, 66 (pt 1) TLR 1182, 94 Sol Jo 458, 34 Cr
   App Rep 138, CCA 712
Taylor (1984) 80 Cr App Rep 327, CA 437
Taylor v Jackson (1898) 78 LT 555, 62 JP 424, 19 Cox CC 62, DC . . 601
Taylor v Mucklow (1973) 117 Sol Jo 792, [1973] Crim LR 750, DC . 246, 422, 690
Taylor v Rogers (1960) 124 JP 217, [1960] Crim LR 271, DC . . . 482
Tegerdine (1982) 75 Cr App Rep 298, [1983] Crim LR 163, CA . . 452
Tennant [1976] Crim LR 133, CA 541
Terry [1961] 2 QB 314, [1961] 2 All ER 569, [1961] 2 WLR 961, 105 Sol Jo 445, 45 Cr
   App Rep 180, CCA 203
Terry [1964] VR 248 334
Terry [1984] AC 374, [1984] 1 All ER 65, [1984] 2 WLR 23, 128 Sol Jo 34, 78 Cr App
   Rep 101, [1984] RTR 129, [1984] LS Gaz R 510, HL . . . 128, 271
Tesco Supermarkets Ltd v Nattrass [1972] AC 153, [1971] 2 All ER 127, [1971] 2 WLR
   1166, 135 JP 289, 115 Sol Jo 285, 69 LGR 403, HL . 92, 171, 172, 173, 175, 480
Thain [1985] NILR Bulletin No 11 31, CA 246
Thallman (1863) Le & Ca 326, 3 New Rep 141, 33 LJMC 58, 9 LT 425, 27 JP 790, 12
   WR 88, 9 Cox CC 388, CCR 469
Thambiah v R [1966] AC 37, [1965] 3 All ER 661, [1966] 2 WLR 81, 109 Sol Jo 832,
   PC 144
Theodolou [1963] Crim LR 573, CCA 426
Thibeault [1983] RTR 318, 76 Cr App Rep 201, 4 Cr App Rep (S) 375, [1983] Crim
   LR 102, CA 639, 641
Thistlewood (1820) 33 State Tr 681, 921 827
Thomas (1816) Turner and Armitage Case on Criminal Law 67 . . . 250
Thomas [1957] 2 All ER 181, [1957] 1 WLR 747, 41 Cr App Rep 117; affd on appeal
   [1957] 2 All ER 342n, [1957] 1 WLR 747, 121 JP 338, 101 Sol Jo 430, 41 Cr App
   Rep 121, CCA 462
Thomas (1976) 63 Cr App Rep 65, CA 110, 124

PAGE

Thomas (1985) 81 Cr App Rep 331, [1985] Crim LR 677, CA . . . 376, 381, 450
Thomas v Lindop [1950] 1 All ER 966, 114 JP 290, 66 (pt 1) TLR 1241, 94 Sol Jo 371,
    48 LGR 353, DC 142, 169
Thomas v R (1937) 59 CLR 279, 44 ALR 37, 11 ALJ 343, [1938] VLR 32 . . 90, 715
Thompson (1862) Le & Ca 225, 1 New Rep 67, 32 LJMC 53, 7 LT 432, 26 JP 823, 8
    Jur NS 1184, 11 WR 40, 9 Cox CC 244, CCR 510
Thompson [1984] 3 All ER 565, [1984] 1 WLR 962, 128 Sol Jo 447, 79 Cr App Rep
    191, [1984] LS Gaz R 1438, [1984] Crim LR 427, CA 505
Thompson, Re (1860) 6 H & N 193, 30 LJMC 19, 3 LT 294, 409, 25 JP 166, 7 Jur NS
    48, 9 WR 203, 9 Cox CC 70 375
Thompson v Lodwick [1983] RTR 76, CA 124
Thompson-Schwab v Costaki [1956] 1 All ER 652, [1956] 1 WLR 335, 100 Sol Jo 246,
    CA 460
Thomson (1900) 64 JP 456 730
Thomson (1905) 70 JP 6 . . . . 706, 715
Thomson (1965) 50 Cr App Rep 1 284
Thomson v Chain Libraries Ltd [1954] 2 All ER 616, [1954] 1 WLR 999, 118 JP 395,
    98 Sol Jo 473, DC 732
Thomson Newspapers Ltd, ex p A-G [1968] 1 All ER 268, [1968] 1 WLR 1, 111 Sol Jo
    943, DC 776
Thorley v Lord Kerry (1812) 4 Taunt 355, 3 Camp 214n 822
Thorne v Motor Trade Association [1937] AC 797, [1937] 3 All ER 157, 106 LJKB 495,
    157 LT 399, 53 TLR 810, 81 Sol Jo 476, 26 Cr App Rep 51, HL . . . 589
Thornton v Mitchell [1940] 1 All ER 339, 162 LT 296, 104 JP 108, 56 TLR 296, 84 Sol
    Jo 257, 38 LGR 168, DC 154
Thurrock UDC v Shina (1972) 70 LGR 301, 23 P & CR 205, DC 813
Tibbits and Windust [1902] 1 KB 77, [1900-3] All ER Rep 896, 71 LJKB 4, 85 LT 521,
    66 JP 5, 50 WR 125, 18 TLR 49, 46 Sol Jo 51, 20 Cox CC 70, CCR . . 278, 768
Tikos [1963] VR 285 248
Tikos (No 2) [1963] VR 306 248
Timbu Kolian v R (1968) 119 CLR 47 . . . . 39, 74
Timmins (1860) Bell CC 276, 30 LJMC 45, 3 LT 337, 25 JP 453, 6 Jur NS 1309, 9 WR
    36, 8 Cox CC 401, CCR 454
Timmis [1976] Crim LR 129 757
Titley (1880) 14 Cox CC 502 369
Titus Oates (1685) 10 State Tr 1227 327
Tobierre [1986] 1 All ER 346, [1986] 1 WLR 125, 130 Sol Jo 35, 82 Cr App Rep 212,
    [1986] LS Gaz R 116, [1986] Crim LR 243, CA 655
Tolley v Giddings [1964] 2 QB 354, [1964] 1 All ER 201, [1964] 2 WLR 471, 128 JP
    182, 108 Sol Jo 36, 62 LGR 158, 48 Cr App Rep 105, DC . . . 587, 588
Tolson (1889) 23 QBD 168, [1886-90] All ER Rep 26, 58 LJMC 97, 60 LT 899, 54 JP
    4, 20, 37 WR 716, 5 TLR 465, 16 Cox CC 629, CCR . . 89, 112, 208, 711, 714, 715
Tomblin [1964] Crim LR 780 623
Tompkins [1960] 2 QB 513, [1960] 3 All ER 149, [1960] 3 WLR 426, 124 JP 457, 104
    Sol Jo 645, 44 Cr App Rep 255, CCA 757
Tomsett [1985] Crim LR 369, CA 276
Tooley (1709) 2 Ld Raym 1296, 11 Mod Rep 242, Fost 312, Fost 315, sub nom
    Reforming Constables Case Holt KB 485 37
Topham (1791) 4 Term Rep 126 824
Topping (1856) Dears CC 647, 25 LJMC 72, 27 LTOS 128, 20 JP 293, 2 Jur NS 428, 4
    WR 482, 7 Cox CC 103, CCR 707, 711
Toshack (1849) 1 Den 492, T & M 207, 13 JP 794, 13 Jur 1011, 4 Cox CC 38, CCR . 658
Tottenham Justices, ex p Arthur's Transport Services [1981] Crim LR 180 . . 28
Towers (1874) 12 Cox CC 530 326
Townsend (1866) 4 F & F 1089, 10 Cox CC 356 743
Townshend (Marquis), Re (1906) 22 TLR 341, CA 773
Trainer (1864) 4 F & F 105 249
Treacy v DPP [1971] AC 537, [1971] 1 All ER 110, [1971] 2 WLR 112, 115 Sol Jo 12,
    55 Cr App Rep 113, HL 33, 356, 589, 805
Treanor (or McAvoy) [1939] 1 All ER 330, 160 LT 286, 55 TLR 348, 83 Sol Jo 219, 31
    Cox CC 235, 27 Cr App Rep 35, CCA 712
Trendtex Trading Corpn v Central Bank of Nigeria [1977] QB 529, [1977] 1 All ER
    881, [1977] 2 WLR 356, 121 Sol Jo 85, [1977] 1 Lloyd's Rep 581, CA . . . 817

PAGE

Trilloe (1842) Car & M 650, 2 Mood CC 260, CCR 310
True (1922) 127 LT 561, 27 Cox CC 287, 16 Cr App Rep 164, CCA . . . 195
Tsang Ping-Nam v R [1981] 1 WLR 1462, 125 Sol Jo 709, 74 Cr App Rep 139, [1982]
    Crim LR 46 747
Tuberville v Savage (1669) 1 Mod Rep 3, sub nom Turbervell v Savadge 2 Keb 545 . 378
Tuck v Robson [1970] 1 All ER 1171, [1970] 1 WLR 741, 134 JP 389, 114 Sol Jo 191,
    [1970] Brewing Tr Rev 364, DC 137
Turner (No 2) [1971] 2 All ER 441, [1971] 1 WLR 901, 135 JP 419, 115 Sol Jo 405, 55
    Cr App Rep 336, [1971] RTR 396, CA 510, 511
Turner [1975] QB 834, [1975] 1 All ER 70, [1975] 2 WLR 56, 139 JP 136, 118 Sol Jo
    848, 60 Cr App Rep 80, CA 90
Turner v DPP (1978) 68 Cr App Rep 70, [1978] Crim LR 754 18
Turvey [1946] 2 All ER 60, 175 LT 308, 110 JP 270, 62 TLR 511, 90 Sol Jo 395, 44
    LGR 227, 31 Cr App Rep 154, CCA 499
Twine [1967] Crim LR 710 333
Tyler and Price (1838) 8 C & P 616 132
Tynan v Balmer [1967] 1 QB 91, [1966] 2 All ER 133, [1966] 2 WLR 1181, 110 Sol Jo
    129, DC 393
Tyrrell [1894] 1 QB 710, [1891-4] All ER Rep 1215, sub nom R v Tyrell 63 LJMC 58,
    70 LT 41, 42 WR 255, 10 TLR 167, 38 Sol Jo 130, 17 Cox CC 716, 10 R 82, CCR . 159,
    160
Tysoe v Davis [1984] RTR 88, [1983] Crim LR 684 794
Tyson (1867) LR 1 CCR 107, 37 LJMC 7, 17 LT 292, 32 JP 53, 16 WR 317, 11 Cox
    CC 1, CCR 744

U

US v Holmes 26 Fed Cas 360 (1842) 228
Umanski [1961] VLR 242 706
Upfill v Wright [1911] 1 KB 506, 80 LJKB 254, 103 LT 834, 27 TLR 160, 55 Sol Jo
    189, DC 463
Utting [1987] Crim LR 636 658
Uxbridge Permanent Benefit Building Society v Pickard [1939] 2 KB 248, [1939] 2 All
    ER 344, 108 LJKB 757, 160 LT 407, 55 TLR 579, 83 Sol Jo 297, CA . . . 162

V

Valderrama-Vega [1985] Crim LR 220, CA 230, 231
Vale of Glamorgan Borough Council v Palmer and Bowles (1982) 81 LGR 678, [1982]
    JPL 334 123
Valentine v Jackson [1972] 1 All ER 90, [1972] 1 WLR 528, 116 Sol Jo 334, DC . 393
Vane v Yiannopoullos [1965] AC 486, [1964] 3 All ER 820, [1964] 3 WLR 1218, 129 JP
    50, 108 Sol Jo 937, 63 LGR 91, HL 165, 166, 167
Vantandillo (1815) 4 M & S 73 . . . . 223, 729, 794
Vaughan v McKenzie [1969] 1 QB 557, [1968] 1 All ER 1154, [1968] 2 WLR 1133, 112
    Sol Jo 212, 206 Estates Gazette 129 802
Venna [1976] QB 421, [1975] 3 All ER 788, [1975] 3 WLR 737, 140 JP 31, 119 Sol Jo
    679, 61 Cr App Rep 310, CA 376, 379, 381
Verrier v DPP [1967] 2 AC 195, [1966] 3 All ER 568, [1966] 3 WLR 924, 131 JP 36,
    110 Sol Jo 806, 50 Cr App Rep 315, HL 8
Vickers [1957] 2 QB 664, [1957] 2 All ER 741, [1957] 3 WLR 326, 121 JP 510, 101 Sol
    Jo 593, 41 Cr App Rep 189, CCA 329
Vickers [1975] 2 All ER 945, [1975] 1 WLR 811, 139 JP 623, 119 Sol Jo 300, 61 Cr App
    Rep 48, CA 120
Villensky [1892] 2 QB 597, 61 LJMC 218, 56 JP 824, 41 WR 160, 8 TLR 780, 36 Sol Jo
    745, 5 R 16, CCR 618
Vivian [1979] 1 All ER 48, [1979] 1 WLR 291, 143 JP 102, 122 Sol Jo 680, 68 Cr App
    Rep 53, [1979] RTR 106, CA 644
Vreones [1891] 1 QB 360, [1891-4] All ER Rep Ext 2058, 60 LJMC 62, 64 LT 389, 55
    JP 536, 39 WR 365, 7 TLR 223, 17 Cox CC 267, CCR . . . 751, 752, 753

W

W (a minor) v Dolbey [1983] Crim LR 681 . . . . 67, 400
Wade (1844) 1 Car & Kir 739 622

PAGE

Waite [1892] 2 QB 600, 61 LJMC 187, 67 LT 300, 41 WR 80, 8 TLR 782, 36 Sol Jo
    745, 17 Cox CC 554, CCR 181, 438, 447
Waites [1982] Crim LR 369, CA   559
Wakeman (1912) 8 Cr App Rep 18, CCA   495
Wakeman v Farrar [1974] Crim LR 136   518
Walford (1899) 34 L Jo 116   403
Walker (1824) 1 C & P 320   315
Walker (1854) Dears CC 358, 23 LJMC 123, 23 LTOS 99, 18 JP 281, 18 Jur 409, 2 WR
    416, 6 Cox CC 371, 2 CLR 485, CCR .   .   .·   .   .   .   403
Walker [1962] Crim LR 458   278
Walker [1983] LS Gaz R 3238, [1984] Crim LR 112, CA .   .   .   489
Walkington [1979] 2 All ER 716, [1979] 1 WLR 1169, 123 Sol Jo 704, 68 Cr App Rep
    427, [1979] Crim LR 526, CA .   .   .   290, 536, 604, 605
Wall (1802) 28 State Tr 51   324
Wallace-Johnson v R [1940] AC 231, [1940] 1 All ER 241, 109 LJPC 33, 56 TLR 215,
    84 Sol Jo 149, PC   836
Wallwork v Giles [1970] RTR 117, 114 Sol Jo 36, DC   802
Walter (1799) 3 Esp 21   825
Walters [1969] 1 QB 255, [1968] 3 All ER 863, [1968] 3 WLR 987, 133 JP 73, 112 Sol
    Jo 801, 53 Cr App Rep 9, CA   46
Walters v Lunt [1951] 2 All ER 645, 115 JP 512, 95 Sol Jo 625, 49 LGR 809, 35 Cr App
    Rep 94, DC 179, 495, 617
Walters v W H Smith & Son Ltd [1914] 1 KB 595, [1911-13] All ER Rep 170, 83
    LJKB 335, 110 LT 345, 78 JP 118, 30 TLR 158, 58 Sol Jo 186 .   .   410
Waltham (1849) 13 JP 183, 3 Cox CC 442   398
Walton v R [1977] AC 788, [1978] 1 All ER 542, [1977] 3 WLR 902, 121 Sol Jo 728, 66
    Cr App Rep 25, [1977] Crim LR 747, PC 197, 204
Ward (1836) 4 Ad & El 384, 1 Har & W 703, 6 Nev & MKB 38, [1835-42] All ER Rep
    664, 5 LJKB 221   799
Ward (1872) LR 1 CCR 356, 41 LJMC 69, 26 LT 43, 36 JP 453, 20 WR 392, 12 Cox
    CC 123, CCR   400
Ward (1986) 85 Cr App Rep 71, [1987] Crim LR 338, CA .   .   .   149
Ward v Holman [1964] 2 QB 580, [1964] 2 All ER 729, [1964] 2 WLR 1313, 128 JP
    397, 108 Sol Jo 380, 62 LGR 357, DC   467
Warhurst (1955) 39 Cr App Rep 100, CCA   588
Warner [1967] 3 All ER 93, [1967] 1 WLR 1209, 131 JP 485, 111 Sol Jo 559, 51 Cr App
    Rep 437, CA   114
Warner (1970) 135 JP 199, 114 Sol Jo 971, 55 Cr App Rep 93, [1971] Crim LR 114,
    CA 534, 537
Warner v Metropolitan Police Comr [1969] 2 AC 256, [1968] 2 All ER 356, [1968] 2
    WLR 1303, 132 JP 378, 112 Sol Jo 378, 52 Cr App Rep 373, HL .   47, 100, 102,
                    104, 107, 109, 114, 116, 128, 129, 427, 618
Warner v Riddiford (1858) 4 CBNS 180, Saund & M 225 .   .   .   406
Waterfield [1964] 1 QB 164, [1963] 3 All ER 659, [1963] 3 WLR 946, 128 JP 48, 107
    Sol Jo 833, 48 Cr App Rep 42, CCA 388, 390
Waters (1963) 107 Sol Jo 275, 47 Cr App Rep 149, CCA .   .   .   467
Watkins [1976] 1 All ER 578, 140 JP 197   559
Watmore v Jenkins [1962] 2 QB 572, [1962] 2 All ER 868, [1962] 3 WLR 463, 126 JP
    432, 106 Sol Jo 492, 60 LGR 325, DC .   .   40, 42, 43, 112, 481
Watson (1847) 10 LTOS 204, 2 Cox CC 376   469
Watson (1916) 2 KB 385, [1916-17] All ER Rep 815, 85 LJKB 1142, 115 LT 159, 80 JP
    391, 32 TLR 580, 25 Cox CC 470, 12 Cr App Rep 62, CCA .   .   624
Watson v Coupland [1945] 1 All ER 217, 175 LT 92n, 109 JP 90, 43 LGR 60, DC . 167
Watson v M'Ewan [1905] AC 480, [1904-7] All ER Rep 1, 74 LJPC 151, 93 LT 489, 7
    F (HL) 109, 42 SLR 837, 13 SLT 340, HL   327
Watts (1703) 1 Salk 357, sub nom R v Watson 2 Ld Raym 856 .   .   795
Waugh (1976) Times, 1 October   767
Weatherall [1968] Crim LR 115 .   .   .   .   .   367, 405
Webb (1848) 2 Car & Kir 933, 1 Den 338, T & M 23, 18 LJMC 39, 12 LTOS 250, 12
    JP 820, 13 Jur 42, 3 Cox CC 183, CCR   469
Webb [1964] 1 QB 357, [1963] 3 All ER 177, [1963] 3 WLR 638, 127 JP 516, 107 Sol Jo
    597, 47 Cr App Rep 265, CCA   455

PAGE

Webb [1969] 2 QB 278, [1969] 2 All ER 626, [1969] 2 WLR 1088, 133 JP 437, 113 Sol
    Jo 304, 53 Cr App Rep 360, CA   185

Webley v Buxton [1977] QB 481, [1977] 2 All ER 595, [1977] 2 WLR 766, 141 JP 407,
    121 Sol Jo 153, 65 Cr App Rep 136, [1977] RTR 193   .   .   296, 297

Webster v Bakewell RDC [1916] 1 Ch 300, 85 LJ Ch 326, 114 LT 545, 80 JP 251, 32
    TLR 306, 60 Sol Jo 307, 14 LGR 547   755

Weight v Long [1986] Crim LR 746   389

Weise (1969) VR 953   193

Weisz v Monahan [1962] 1 All ER 664, [1962] 1 WLR 262, 126 JP 184, 106 Sol Jo 114,
    DC   466

Welham v DPP [1961] AC 103, [1960] 1 All ER 805, [1960] 2 WLR 669, 124 JP 280,
    104 Sol Jo 308, 44 Cr App Rep 124, HL   .   128, 268, 271, 276, 549, 577, 657

Wellard (1884) 14 QBD 63, [1881-5] All ER Rep 1018, 54 LJMC 14, 51 LT 604, 49 JP
    296, 33 WR 156, 15 Cox CC 559, CCR .   .   .   468, 469

Wellard [1978] 3 All ER 161, [1978] 1 WLR 921, 142 JP 641, 122 Sol Jo 433, 67 Cr App
    Rep 364, CA 414, 434

Wellburn (1979) 69 Cr App Rep 254   128

Wells [1939] 2 All ER 169, 83 Sol Jo 441, 27 Cr App Rep 72, CCA .   .   652

Wells v Hardy [1964] 2 QB 447, [1964] 1 All ER 953, [1964] 2 WLR 958, 128 JP 328,
    108 Sol Jo 238, DC   123

Wells Street Stipendiary Magistrate, ex p Deakin [1978] 3 All ER 252, [1978] 1 WLR
    1008, 142 JP 614, 122 Sol Jo 347, 69 Cr App Rep 59; affd sub nom Gleaves v
    Deakin [1980] AC 477, [1979] 2 All ER 497, [1979] 2 WLR 665, 123 Sol Jo 320, 69
    Cr App Rep 59, HL   822

Welsh (1869) 11 Cox CC 336   336

Welsh [1974] RTR 478, CA 524, 753

Wershof v Metropolitan Police Comr [1978] 3 All ER 540, 122 Sol Jo 279, 68 Cr App
    Rep 82, [1982] Crim LR 424   393

West (1848) 2 Car & Kir 784, 11 LTOS 49, 2 Cox CC 500 .   .   310

West [1948] 1 KB 709, [1948] 1 All ER 718, [1948] LJR 1377, 112 JP 222, 64 TLR 241,
    92 Sol Jo 232, 32 Cr App Rep 152, 46 LGR 325, DC .   .   268, 281

Westminster City Council v Croyalgrange Ltd [1985] 1 All ER 740, 149 JP 161, 84
    LGR 68; affd [1986] 2 All ER 353, [1986] 1 WLR 674, 150 JP 449, 130 Sol Jo 409,
    84 LGR 801, 83 Cr App Rep 155, [1986] NLJ Rep 491, [1986] LS Gaz R 2089,
    [1986] Crim LR 693, HL 121, 208, 209

Westminster City Council v Peart (1968) 112 Sol Jo 543, 66 LGR 561, 19 P & CR 736,
    207 Estates Gazette 140, DC   814

Wheat [1921] 2 KB 119, [1921] All ER Rep 602, 90 LJKB 583, 124 LT 830, 85 JP 203,
    47 TLR 417, 65 Sol Jo 554, 26 Cox CC 717, 15 Cr App Rep 134, CCA .   102, 715

Wheeler [1917] 1 KB 283, [1916-17] All ER Rep 1111, 86 LJKB 40, 116 LT 161, 81 JP
    75, 33 TLR 21, 61 Sol Jo 100, 25 Cox CC 603, 12 Cr App Rep 159, CCA .   741, 744

Wheeler [1967] 3 All ER 829, [1967] 1 WLR 1531, 132 JP 41, 111 Sol Jo 850, 52 Cr
    App Rep 28, CA   31

Whelpdale's Case (1604) 5 Co Rep 119a   502

Whitchurch (1890) 24 QBD 420, [1886-90] All ER Rep 1001, 59 LJMC 77, 62 LT 124,
    54 JP 472, 6 TLR 177, 16 Cox CC 743, CCR .   .   283, 367

White [1910] 2 KB 124, [1908-10] All ER Rep 340, 79 LJKB 854, 102 LT 784, 74 JP
    318, 26 TLR 466, 54 Sol Jo 523, 4 Cr App Rep 257, 22 Cox CC 325, CCA .   45, 58,
    292, 294

White v Bayley (1861) 10 CBNS 227, 30 LJ Ch 253, 7 Jur NS 948 .   .   599

White v Elmdene Estates Ltd [1960] 1 QB 1, [1959] 2 All ER 605, [1959] 3 WLR 185,
    103 Sol Jo 656, CA   564

White and Ward (1757) 1 Burr 333   794

Whitefield (1984) 79 Cr App Rep 36, [1983] LS Gaz R 3077, [1984] Crim LR 97, CA .   157

Whitehouse [1941] 1 DLR 683, [1941] 1 WWR 112, 75 CCC 65, 55 BCR 420 .   157

Whitehouse [1977] QB 868, [1977] 3 All ER 737, [1977] 2 WLR 925, 121 Sol Jo 171, 65
    Cr App Rep 33, CA   446

Whitehouse v Gay News Ltd [1979] AC 617, [1979] 2 WLR 281, 68 Cr App Rep 381,
    sub nom R v Gay News Ltd [1979] 1 All ER 898, 143 JP 315, 123 Sol Jo 163, HL .   98,
    99, 738

Whitehouse v Lemon [1979] AC 617, [1979] 1 All ER 898, [1979] 2 WLR 281, 143 JP
    315, 123 Sol Jo 163, 68 Cr App Rep 381, [1979] Crim LR 311, HL   .   .   825

Whitfield (1976) 63 Cr App Rep 39, [1976] Crim LR 443, CA .   .   .   43

PAGE

Whittaker v Campbell [1984] QB 318, [1983] 3 All ER 582, [1983] 3 WLR 676, 127 Sol
Jo 714, 77 Cr App Rep 267, [1984] RTR 220, [1983] Crim LR 812 . . . 585
Whitter v Peters [1982] 2 All ER 369, [1982] 1 WLR 389, 4 FLR 8, 12 Fam Law 84,
126 Sol Jo 100, CA 768
Whybrow (1951) 95 Sol Jo 745, 35 Cr App Rep 141, CCA . . . 255, 287, 288
Whyte [1987] 3 All ER 416, CA 241, 244
Wibberley [1966] 2 QB 214, [1965] 3 All ER 718, [1966] 2 WLR 1, 130 JP 58, 109 Sol
Jo 877, 50 Cr App Rep 51, CCA 584
Wicks [1936] 1 All ER 384, 154 LT 471, 52 TLR 253, 80 Sol Jo 289, 30 Cox CC 370, 25
Cr App Rep 168, CCA 823, 825
Widdowson (1985) 130 Sol Jo 88, [1986] BTLC 158, [1986] RTR 124, 82 Cr App Rep
314, [1986] LS Gaz R 288, [1986] Crim LR 233 . . . . . 294, 562
Wiffin v Kincard (1807) 2 Bos & PNR 471 380
Wiggins v Wiggins (otherwise Brooks) and Ingram [1958] 2 All ER 555, [1958] 1 WLR
1013, 102 Sol Jo 656 713
Wilcox v Jeffery [1951] 1 All ER 464, 115 JP 151, [1951] 1 TLR 706, 95 Sol Jo 157, 49
LGR 363, DC 135, 137
Wiley (1850) 2 Den 37, T & M 367, 4 New Sess Cas 363, 20 LJMC 4, 16 LTOS 514,
14 JP 770, 15 Jur 134, 4 Cox CC 412, CCR 622, 624
Wilkinson (1806). See R v Allison (alias Wilkinson)
Willer [1987] RTR 22, 83 Cr App Rep 225, CA 224, 246
Williams (1822) 5 B & Ald 595, 1 State Tr NS 1291, 1 Dow & Ry KB 197 . . . 824
Williams (1836) 7 C & P 354 556
Williams (1838) 8 C & P 286 435
Williams (1891) 55 JP 406 800
Williams [1893] 1 QB 320, 62 LJMC 69, 41 WR 332, 9 TLR 198, 5 R 186, CCR . 447
Williams (1898) 62 JP 310 439
Williams [1923] 1 KB 340, [1922] All ER Rep 433, 92 LJKB 230, 128 LT 128, 87 JP 67,
39 TLR 131, 67 Sol Jo 263, 27 Cox CC 350, 17 Cr App Rep 56, CCA . 436, 439, 440
Williams [1953] 1 QB 660, [1953] 1 All ER 1068, [1953] 2 WLR 937, 117 JP 251, 97 Sol
Jo 318, 37 Cr App Rep 71, CCA 712
Williams (1968) 112 Sol Jo 760, CA 331
Williams [1985] 1 NZLR 294 529
Williams (1986) 84 Cr App Rep 299, CA 79
Williams [1987] 3 All ER 411, 78 Cr App Rep 276, [1984] LS Gaz R 278, [1984] Crim
LR 163, CA 88, 216, 236, 241, 391, 396, 403, 412
Williams v Boyle (1962) 106 Sol Jo 939, DC 466
Williams v Gibbs [1958] Crim LR 127 448
Williams v Johns (1773) 1 Mer 303n, 2 Dick 477 784
Williams v Phillips (1957) 121 JP 163, 41 Cr App Rep 5, DC . . . 511, 525
Williams and Blackwood (1973) WIR 329 149
Williamson (1977) 121 Sol Jo 812, 67 Cr App Rep 35, CA 423
Williamson v Wright 1924 JC 57 465
Willmott v Atack [1977] QB 498, [1976] 3 All ER 794, [1976] 3 WLR 753, 141 JP 35,
120 Sol Jo 587, 63 Cr App Rep 207, DC 124, 395
Willshire (1881) 6 QBD 366, 50 LJMC 57, 44 LT 222, 45 JP 375, 29 WR 473, 14 Cox
CC 541, CCR 706
Wilson (1862) 3 F & F 119 706
Wilson [1955] 1 All ER 744, [1955] 1 WLR 493, 119 JP 216, 99 Sol Jo 321, 39 Cr App
Rep 12, CCA 377
Wilson [1965] 1 QB 402, [1964] 3 All ER 269, [1964] 3 WLR 593, 128 JP 573, 108 Sol
Jo 584, 48 Cr App Rep 329, CCA 9
Wilson (1973) 58 Cr App Rep 304, CA 439
Wilson [1983] 1 All ER 993, [1983] 1 WLR 356, 147 JP 344, 127 Sol Jo 187, CA; revsd
sub nom Metropolitan Police Comr v Wilson [1984] AC 242, [1983] 3 All ER 448,
[1983] 3 WLR 686, 148 JP 435, 127 Sol Jo 712, HL 377, 399, 608
Wilson (1983) 78 Cr App Rep 247 461
Wilson v Inyang [1951] 2 KB 799, [1951] 2 All ER 237, 115 JP 411, [1951] 2 TLR 553,
95 Sol Jo 562, 49 LGR 654, DC 122
Wilson v Pringle [1987] QB 237, [1986] 2 All ER 440, [1986] 1 WLR 1, 130 Sol Jo 468,
[1986] NLJ Rep 416, [1986] LS Gaz R 2160, CA 376, 379, 398
Wilson v Skeock (1949) 113 JP 294, 65 TLR 418, 93 Sol Jo 389, 47 LGR 499 . . 467
Winch [1974] Crim LR 487, CA 445

PAGE

Windle [1952] 2 QB 826, [1952] 2 All ER 1, 116 JP 365, [1952] 1 TLR 1344, 96 Sol Jo
   379, 36 Cr App Rep 85, CCA   193
Windsor, Re (1856) 6 B & S 522, 6 New Rep 96, 34 LJMC 163, 12 LTOS 307, 29 JP
   327, 11 Jur NS 807, 13 WR 655, 10 Cox CC 118   649
Wines [1953] 2 All ER 1497, [1954] 1 WLR 64, 118 JP 49, 98 Sol Jo 14, 37 Cr App Rep
   197, CCA   576
Wings Ltd v Ellis [1984] 1 All ER 1046, [1984] 1 WLR 731, 148 JP 183, 128 Sol Jo 260,
   82 LGR 544, [1984] LS Gaz R 1292, DC   53
Winson [1969] 1 QB 371, [1968] 1 All ER 197, [1968] 2 WLR 113, 112 Sol Jo 71, CA   .   165,
   166
Winter v Woolfe [1931] 1 KB 549, [1930] All ER Rep 623, 100 LJKB 92, 144 LT 311,
   95 JP 20, 47 TLR 145, 29 LGR 89, 29 Cox CC 214, CCA   .   .   .   458
Winzar v Chief Constable of Kent (1983) Times, 28 March   .   .   .   46, 112
Wiseman (1718) Fortes Rep 91   471
Woby v B and O (Juveniles) (1985) 149 JP 767, [1986] Crim LR 183   .   .   132
Wollaston (1872) 26 LT 403, 12 Cox CC 180, CCR   474
Wood (1830) 4 C & P 381, 1 Mood CC 278, CCR   398
Wood (1832) 3 B & Ad 657, 1 LJMC 93   18
Wood (or Woods) v Richards [1977] RTR 201, 65 Cr App Rep 300, [1977] Crim LR
   295   .   .   .   .   223, 479
Woodage v Moss [1974] 1 All ER 584, [1974] 1 WLR 411, 138 JP 253, 118 Sol Jo 204,
   DC   417
Woodburne and Coke (1722) 16 State Tr 53   402
Woodman [1974] QB 754, [1974] 2 All ER 955, [1974] 2 WLR 821, 138 JP 567, 118 Sol
   Jo 346, 59 Cr App Rep 200, CA 129, 511
Woodrow (1846) 15 M & W 404   100
Woodrow (1959) 43 Cr App Rep 105, CCA   786
Woods (1921) 85 JP 272   350
Woods [1969] 1 QB 447, [1968] 3 All ER 709, [1968] 3 WLR 1192, 133 JP 51, 112 Sol
   Jo 839, 53 Cr App Rep 30, CA   632
Woods (1981) 74 Cr App Rep 312, [1982] Crim LR 42, CA   .   .   213
Woodward v Koessler [1958] 3 All ER 557, [1958] 1 WLR 1255, 123 JP 14, 102 Sol Jo
   879, DC 423, 424
Woolcock [1977] Crim LR 104   678
Woolmington v DPP [1935] AC 462, [1935] All ER Rep 1, 104 LJKB 433, 153 LT 232,
   51 TLR 446, 79 Sol Jo 401, 30 Cox CC 234, 25 Cr App Rep 72, HL   31, 116, 196,
   711, 716, 797
Woolven (1983) 77 Cr App Rep 231, CA   556
Workman v Cowper [1961] 2 QB 143, [1961] 1 All ER 683, [1961] 2 WLR 386, 125 JP
   254, 105 Sol Jo 130, DC 691, 695
Worley (1849) 3 Cox CC 535   745
Wright [1968] VR 164   782
Wright (1975) 119 Sol Jo 825, 62 Cr App Rep 169, CA   .   .   108
Wrigley [1957] Crim LR 57   .   .   .   .   74, 603, 604
Wuyts [1969] 2 QB 474, [1969] 2 All ER 799, [1969] 3 WLR 1, 133 JP 492, 113 Sol Jo
   324, 53 Cr App Rep 417, CA   668
Wylie, Howe and McGuire (1919) 83 JP 295   18

X

X v X (1958) 123 JP 61, 44 Cr App Rep 1, [1958] Crim LR 805   .   .   .   180

Y

Yeadon and Birch (1861) Le & Ca 81, 31 LJMC 70, 5 LT 329, 26 JP 148, 7 Jur NS
   1128, 10 WR 64, 9 Cox CC 91, CCR   398
Yeandel v Fisher [1966] 1 QB 440, [1965] 3 All ER 158, [1965] 3 WLR 1002, 129 JP
   546, 109 Sol Jo 593, DC   106
York (1748) Fost 70, CCR   180
Young (1878) 38 LT 540, 14 Cox CC 114, CCR   433
Younghusband v Luftig [1949] 2 KB 354, [1949] 2 All ER 72, [1949] LJR 1513, 113 JP
   366, 65 TLR 397, 93 Sol Jo 375, 47 LGR 438, DC   .   .   122
Yuthiwattana (1984) 128 Sol Jo 661, 80 Cr App Rep 55, [1984] Crim LR 562, [1984]
   LS Gaz R 2537, CA 49, 814

PAGE

Z

Zamora, The [1916] 2 AC 77, 85 LJP 89, 114 LT 626, 32 TLR 436, 60 Sol Jo 416, 13
    Asp MLC 330, PC 840
Zecevic v DPP (1987) 61 ALJ 375 249

Part I

General Principles

1 Crime and Sentence

This book is about the substantive law of crime. That is, it attempts to state and to discuss the law which determines whether any act is a crime or not. The book is not about the procedure by which the law is enforced or the evidence by which criminal offences are proved, except in so far as these matters are inseparable from the discussion of the substantive law. Procedure and evidence are subjects of equal importance which are admirably discussed in other books.[1]

The criminal law is no more an end in itself than the law of procedure and evidence through which it is enforced. Our criminal law has grown up over many centuries and the purposes of those who have framed it, and of those who have enforced it, have undoubtedly been many and various. Consequently, it is not easy to state confidently what are the aims of the criminal law at the present day. The authors of a completely new code of criminal law are, however, in a position to state their objectives at the outset. "The general purposes of the provisions governing the definition of offences" in the American Law Institute's Model Penal Code[2] might be taken as a statement of the proper objectives of the substantive law of crime in a modern legal system. The purposes are:

"a) to forbid and prevent conduct that unjustifiably and inexcusably inflicts or threatens substantial harm to individual or public interests;

b) to subject to public control persons whose conduct indicates that they are disposed to commit crimes;

c) to safeguard conduct that is without fault from condemnation as criminal;

d) to give fair warning of the nature of the conduct declared to be an offense;

e) to differentiate on reasonable grounds between serious and minor offenses."

The reader will judge for himself how far these purposes are fulfilled by English criminal law as he studies the general principles and particular offences discussed in the succeeding chapters. For example, whether our law is confined to forbidding conduct that is "inexcusable", whether it adequately safeguards conduct that is without fault from condemnation as

---

1. Barnard, *The Criminal Court in Action* (3rd ed.); Iller and Goodwin, *Criminal Litigation*; Cross, *Evidence* (6th ed.); McClean and Wood, *Criminal Justice and the Treatment of Offenders*; Hall Williams, *The English Penal System in Transition*.
2. Proposed Official Draft, Art. 1 1.02 (1). Cf. Walker, *The Aims of a Penal System*.

criminal, are matters which are particularly considered in the chapter on "strict liability",[3] but which constantly arise elsewhere.

While the definition of offences can adequately *forbid* unjustifiable and inexcusable conduct, it can rarely prevent it. The Children and Young Persons (Harmful Publications) Act 1955 was said to have been "completely successful" at a time when no prosecution had been brought under it.[4] But this is unusual. The fact that an act is known to be forbidden by the criminal law may, for many persons, be sufficient to ensure that they will not commit such an act but for others this will not be enough. Hence our need for a law of criminal procedure, of evidence – and of sentencing.[5] The mere fact of conviction, being a public condemnation[6] of the conduct in question, has some value in the prevention of crime, but it is far from being sufficient. Some, at least, of the purposes for which the criminal law exists can be fulfilled only through the imposition of sentences. It is therefore desirable at the outset to enquire to what ends sentences are directed – or professedly directed – by those who impose them.[7] When a sentence is to be imposed, the first decision to be made should be as to the object to be achieved by it.[8] Is the aim simply to mete out an appropriate punishment to a wrongdoer? Or is it to deter the wrongdoer and others from committing such offences in the future? Or to protect the public by shutting the offender away? Or is it the reform of the offender? Or a combination of these objects? When this first decision has been made, a second decision – what measure is most appropriate to achieve the desired objective? – must follow. It is only with the first decision that we are concerned in this chapter.

1 Retribution and Moral Blameworthiness

The traditional attitude of the common lawyers is that a crime is essentially a moral wrong.[9] The doctrine of *mens rea* is based on the assumption that some kind of blameworthy intention is required.[10] Thus Denning LJ wrote that, ever since the time of Henry I –

---

3. Below, p. 98.
4. 299 HL Deb. col., 451, 12 Feb. 1969, quoted by Zellick [1970] Crim LR 192.
5. On sentencing generally, see Ashworth, *Sentencing and Penal Policy* (1983); D. A. Thomas, *Principles of Sentencing* (2nd ed.); N. D. Walker, *Sentencing in a Rational Society*.
6. Below, p.23.
7. Judges, unlike juries, are generally required to give reasons for their decisions; but generally they need give no reasons when imposing sentence. For a cogent argument that judges ought to be required to give reasons, see D. A. Thomas [1963] Crim LR 243. In fact, judges often do give reasons; and, of course, the Court of Appeal does so when dealing with appeals against the sentence.
8. See D. A. Thomas, "Sentencing, The Basic Principles" [1967] Crim LR 455 and 503.
9. Below, p. 20.
10. Though, as will appear below, in the modern law *mens rea* does not necessarily imply an intention which is blameworthy in any moral sense; and *mens rea* is sometimes dispensed with.

"in order that an act should be punishable it must be morally blame-worthy. It must be a sin."[11]

The criminal law assumes, in the absence of evidence to the contrary, that people have it in their power to choose whether to do criminal acts or not, and that he who chooses to do such an act is responsible for the resulting evil. The law further assumes that the evil which might result from particular crimes can be nicely measured and graded, so that we have an elaborate scale of permissible punishments, varying from life imprison-ment[12] to a mere fine. But it is also recognised that the imperfections of definition are such that an act which is within the definition of the crime may be morally blameless and deserving of no punishment. Thus it is the almost invariable practice of Parliament to fix a maximum but no minimum punishment and to leave it to the judge or magistrate to fix a sentence, varying from absolute discharge to the statutory maximum. The only significant exception to this rule is murder, where the court is required to impose a sentence of life imprisonment.

The traditional attitude of the common law and of Parliament to crime has, not unnaturally, been reflected in the sentencing practice of the courts. A scale of punishment being provided, varying with the potential moral wickedness of the offence and its danger to society, the court has generally seen its task as one of fitting the penalty to the particular degree of iniquity and dangerousness evinced by the particular defendant. Where there is a statutory maximum,[13] it should be reserved for the worst type of offence which comes before the court and a sentence which does not allow for this is wrong in principle.[14] Judges should not, however, use their imagination to conjure up unlikely worst possible kinds of case.[15] The statutory maximum is a useful guide only when it is not altogether out of proportion to contemporary attitudes to the crime in question. Many maxima have been revised recently but others remain unchanged since the nineteenth century. Their origins can be traced to the terms of transportation which took the place of capital punishment in the 1820's and 1830's. Even in the case of modern revisions, the practice of fixing the maximum to cover the worst case[16] results in maxima far above normal sentences. Such maxima afford little guidance to a court in an ordinary case. The maximum of 10 years for theft, for instance, gives no guidance whatever to a magistrates' court, or even the Crown Court, except in a quite extraordinary case. A recent interesting proposal by the Advisory Council on the Penal System[17] to provide more realistic maxima, based on the actual practice of the courts, found little support and has not been accepted.

11. *The Changing Law*, 112. Cf. Blackstone, *Commentaries*, iv, 20.
12. The death penalty may still be imposed for treason and piracy with violence; but it has, in effect, been eliminated as a penalty in peace-time.
13. In the case of common law misdemeanours, there is no maximum.
14. *Edwards* (1910) 4 Cr App Rep 280; *Austin* [1961] Crim LR 416; *Da Silva* [1964] Crim LR 68; *Smith* [1975] Crim LR 468.
15. *Ambler* [1976] Crim LR 266.
16. For example, the 10 year maximum for stealing under the Theft Act 1968.
17. "Sentences of Imprisonment: A Review of Maximum Penalties", 1978.

If punishment is assessed in accordance with the degree of moral blameworthiness, it seems to follow that it is imposed *because* of the moral blameworthiness. No further justification is needed:

"... there is a mystic bond between wrong and punishment ... Hegel ... puts it, in his quasi-mathematical form, that wrong being the negation of right, punishment is the negation of that negation, or retribution. Thus the punishment must be equal, in the sense of proportionate to the crime, because its only function is to destroy it. Others, without this logical apparatus, are content to rely upon a felt necessity that suffering should follow wrongdoing."[18]

The most forceful judicial statement of the retributive attitude to punishment is that of Stephen J:

"I am ... of opinion that this close alliance between criminal law and moral sentiment is in all ways healthy and advantageous to the community. I think it highly desirable that criminals should be hated, that the punishments inflicted upon them should be so contrived as to give expression to that hatred, and to justify it so far as the provision of means for expressing and gratifying a healthy and natural sentiment can justify and encourage it."[19]

It is unlikely that any judge would put forward views in these terms today. But it would be a mistake to assume that the attitude is dead. It is often argued today that retribution is a relic of barbarism and has no proper place in the assessment of punishment. It is clear that this is not the view of the judges. Such a theory, said Asquith LJ

"runs counter to one of the cardinal principles of justice – that punishment should be proportioned to guilt."[20]

The judge's task, after all, is to do justice; and how is punishment to be related to justice, except by asking whether it is deserved or not?[1] If punishment were to be based purely on theories of deterrence and reformation and the question of what the accused deserved were to be eliminated, would not the concept of justice be eliminated too?[2] Certainly, as a matter of fact, the courts constantly act on the assumption that the punishment must be proportioned to moral guilt; and the Court of Appeal will interfere where it is satisfied that there is a disproportion.

The question then arises, by what standards is the judge to estimate what punishment is deserved? The judicial answer seems to be, by the degree of revulsion felt by the law-abiding members of the community for the particular criminal act in question. Thus Denning LJ said:

"The punishment inflicted for grave crimes should adequately reflect the revulsion felt by the great majority of citizens for them. It is a mistake to

---

18. Holmes, *The Common Law*, 42. For Holmes's criticisms of this theory, see pp. 45–46.
19. HCL 81–82.
20. "Problems of Punishment", *The Listener*, XLIII at 821 (May 11, 1950).
  1. See C. S. Lewis (1953) 6 *Res Judicatae*, 224 at 225.
  2. See Morris and Howard, *Studies in Criminal Law*, 147 at 174. An interesting variation on the theme of punishment as justice is advanced by D. J. Galligan, "The Return to Retribution in Legal Theory," in *Crime, Proof and Punishment*, 144, 156. An individual gains an advantage over law-abiding members of society every time he commits an offence. It would be unfair if he were allowed to retain this advantage. He must pay for it through punishment so as to restore the balance.

consider the objects of punishment as being deterrent or reformative or preventive and nothing else. ... The ultimate justification of any punishment is not that it is a deterrent, but that it is the emphatic denunciation by the community of a crime. ..."[3]

Severe sentences are commonly upheld expressly on the ground that the sentence must mark public revulsion.[4] It is in fact a constant theme in judicial pronouncements about punishment that, while the judge must not be influenced by public hysteria, he must take into account the general attitude of responsible members of the public, if respect for the law is to be upheld. The criminal law, said Birkett J

"must represent a remarkably high average of the population's views with regard to penalties; and the law abiding citizen must feel that the law is effective in protecting him from infractions of his liberty by wrongdoers."[5]

Closely associated with the notion of proportioning the punishment to the public's view of the moral culpability of the offender is another idea: that it is necessary to satisfy, by a sufficient punishment, a public desire for vengeance against the wrongdoer.[6] Thus Sir John Barry of the Supreme Court of Victoria wrote:

"It is ... true beyond question that in the reality of the social process an important end of the criminal law is to reinforce and uphold the moral sentiments of the community that favour the promotion of virtue and discourage the pursuit of evildoing, and in practical affairs this is done by gratifying the desire for retaliation which a crime arouses, and by way of deterrent example."[7]

There is evidence in judicial pronouncements that this is a factor which weighs with English courts in fixing sentences, at least in some types of case, particularly sexual offences.[8]

The retributive approach to sentencing was for many years out of favour with criminologists who thought it anachronistic and, indeed, barbarous. Recently there has been a change of thought and a "Return to retribution in penal theory."[9] This is at least partly because experience has shown that we simply do not know how to reform offenders and because sentences imposed purely on the basis of prevention of crime may be unfair and oppressive. The attitude of the English judges has changed little, if at all, having always been generally retributivist.

3. RCCP (1953) Cmd 8932, p. 18.
4. *Roberts* [1982] 1 All ER 609, [1982] 1 WLR 133; *Davies* [1965] Crim LR 251; *Mitchell* [1965] Crim LR 319.
5. Eighth Clarke Hall Lecture, "The Problems of Punishment", 10; Cf. Lummus, *The Trial Judge*, 56; Hawkins J *Reminiscences*, 2, 228; Sir John Barry, op cit., footnote 7, infra, at xxiv.
6. "The thirst for vengeance is a very real, even if it be a hideous thing; and states may not ignore it till humanity has been raised to greater heights than any that has yet been scaled in all the long ages of struggle and ascent": Cardozo J, *Selected Writings*, 378.
7. Introduction to Morris and Howard, *Studies in Criminal Law* at xxv. The learned judge adds that the objective should be "to confine the elements of vindictive retribution within the narrowest possible limits ...".
8. See *Sexual Offences* (Report of the Cambridge Department of Criminal Science), 186, n.1.
9. Galligan in *Crime, Proof and Punishment*, 144; Tonry and Morris "Sentencing Reform in America" in *Reshaping the Criminal Law*, 434, 437. But cf. Wootton, *Crime and the Criminal Law* (2nd ed., 1982).

2 Retribution and the Harm Done

So far it has been assumed that retribution means that the convicted person should receive punishment proportioned to his moral guilt. It must now be noticed that there is another measure of retribution which is very much alive: that the punishment should be proportionate to the harm done. This may be illustrated by the attitude of the courts to attempts to commit crimes.[10]

An attempt to commit a crime was a common law misdemeanour and, as such, until 1967 was punishable with fine and imprisonment at the discretion of the court and without limit, provided only that the sentence was not an inordinate one.[11] Thus, it was theoretically possible to punish an attempt to commit any crime which was not punishable with life imprisonment more severely than the same crime when completed. It was, however, held to be improper to pass a sentence greater than that which could be imposed for the completed offence;[12] and this principle is now embodied in s. 4 of the Criminal Attempts Act 1981.[13] But the point of present interest is that it is the usual practice of the courts to punish an attempt to commit a crime *less* severely than if the attempt were successful.[14] Yet the moral guilt of him who attempts and fails is just as great as that of him who attempts and succeeds. Indeed, as will appear,[15] by a curious anomaly it is frequently necessary to prove a more blameworthy state of mind in order to procure a conviction for an attempt than for the corresponding complete crime. Failure to complete the offence by no means necessarily shows that the offender is the less dangerous; he may have been merely unlucky. Yet failure appears to be a mitigating factor. Nor is this attitude confined to attempts. According to the Departmental Committee on Persistent Offenders:

"... if a persistent office-breaker breaks into a railway booking office with intent to steal large sums of money and for some reason or other only manages to obtain a few trifling articles, the court will probably consider appropriate a very much lighter sentence than if he had succeeded in his object."[16]

In such cases it seems that the punishment is being proportioned to the harm done. A similar theory seems to be implicit in some rules of the substantive law. If D assaults P, occasioning him actual bodily harm, D is liable to five years' imprisonment.[17] Now suppose P dies. D is guilty of manslaughter[18] and liable to life imprisonment. Yet his act and his moral

---

10. Below, p. 287. Cf. Criminal Law Act 1967, s. 4 (3), below, p. 759.
11. *Morris* [1951] 1 KB 394, [1950] 2 All ER 965.
12. *Pearce* [1953] 1 QB 30, [1952] 2 All ER 718; *Verrier v Director of Public Prosecutions* [1966] 3 All ER 568 at 575.
13. Re-enacting s. 18 (2) of the Powers of Criminal Courts Act 1973.
14. See, e.g. *Carmichael* (1930) 22 Cr App Rep 142; *Rankin* (1960) Times, 30th March.
15. Below, p. 288.
16. Report (Cmd 4090, 1932) 9. See the discussion of this example by Cross, "Paradoxes in Prison Sentences" (1965) 81 LQR 205.
17. Offences against the Person Act 1861, s. 47; below, p. 396.
18. Below, p. 345. *Cf. Paget and Pemberton* [1983] Crim LR 274.

blameworthiness are the same in both cases. Here too the judicial attitude reflects that of the legislature – and perhaps of us all? If D drives his car recklessly, he is liable to two years' imprisonment whether he injures anyone or not;[19] but if he drives in exactly the same way with exactly the same degree of fault and kills P he is liable to five years' imprisonment.[20]

These examples seem, on the face of them, to show that there is at work "a crude retaliation theory"[1]. Professors Wechsler and Michael,[2] however, discussing the particular case of homicide, offer two reasons to justify a more severe punishment in the case where death is caused than in an otherwise exactly similar case where death is not caused:

"In the first place, popular indignation is inevitably aroused by the actual occurrence of a wrong, with the result that death and other very severe penalties are more likely to be tolerated when homicidal behaviour has resulted fatally than when it has not. In the second place, the deterrent efficacy of a body of criminal law is not greatly lessened by making the discrimination. Men who may act in order to kill will hope for and contemplate success rather than failure. Consequently if the prospect of being punished severely if they succeed will not deter them from acting, the prospect of being punished just as severely as if they fail is unlikely to do so."

The theory is (i) that the judge (and the legislator) may properly take account of public sentiment without necessarily approving of it. Thus he may, for example, impose a greater sentence in the case of the consummated crime than the attempt, not because he thinks it worse, but because he thinks public opinion either demands or will tolerate a severe sentence, which it would not demand or tolerate in the case of an attempt. The same reasoning presumably applies to the case of the thief who only gets away with a small fraction of what he hopes to get away with. And (ii) the potential offender, weighing up the pros and cons of committing the offence, will have the punishment for the complete offence in mind.

Professor Cross,[3] on the other hand, finds the best justification for sentencing more severely where the offender has succeeded than where he has not in the words used by Edmund Davies J in sentencing one of the main participants in "The Great Train Robbery":

"It would be an affront to the public weal that any of you should be at liberty in anything like the near future to enjoy any of those ill-gotten gains. Accordingly, it is in no spirit of mere retribution that I propose to secure that such an opportunity will be denied all of you for an extremely long time."[4]

---

19. Road Traffic Act 1972, s. 2; below, pp. 482–485.
20. Road Traffic Act 1972, s. 1; below, p. 485.
  1. Williams, CLGP 136.
  2. (1937) 37 Col L Rev 1294–1295. See also Smith, "The Element of Chance in Criminal Liability," [1971] Crim LR 63.
  3. (1965) 81 LQR at 218.
  4. Quoted in Cross, Sentencing, 198, from a transcript kindly supplied by Lord Edmund-Davies. See also (1964) Times, 18th April; Wilson [1965] 1 QB 402, [1964] 2 All ER 269.

Such "deterrence by deprivation of fruits" is in point where the offender has made a profit by his crime; but it has no application when the harm done does not bring a benefit to him.

3 The Sentence to Fit the Crime

In *Director of Public Prosecutions v Ottewell*[5] Lord Reid said:
"It was rather tentatively suggested by the learned Attorney General that there is a 'tariff' for each kind of offence which is varied upwards or downwards according to the circumstances of the offence and the character of the accused. Offences of a particular kind vary so vastly, however, in gravity that there cannot and should not be any 'normal' sentence, and there is no workable standard by which to judge whether any particular standard is extended beyond what is 'normal'."

While it is clear that there is no single sentence which is normal for a particular category of crime[6] – for example, rape – there is certainly a "tariff" in the sense of a range within which a sentence will be regarded as normal for that category and outside of which it will be regarded as abnormal.[7] The Court of Appeal sometimes lays down guidelines, not to impose uniformity of sentence, but to try to achieve uniformity of approach.[8] Moreover, many of the principles of sentencing are explicable only on the assumption that there is a punishment appropriate to the circumstances of the particular offence before the court. Thus it is wrong to increase the sentence because the accused has insisted on his right to jury trial[9] or on pleading not guilty or has conducted his defence in a particular way;[10] but the sentence may be reduced on the ground that he pleaded guilty.[11] The sentence may be reduced because D informed against his co-prisoner; it should not be increased because D did not inform.[12] D's good record may be a ground for mitigating the sentence; but his bad record must not be allowed to aggravate it.[13] A fine may be diminished because of D's poverty; but it may not be increased because of his wealth.[14] These rules are meaningful only if there is an appropriate sentence for the offence, from which the appropriate subtractions can be made. This appropriate

---

5. [1970] AC 642, [1968] 3 All ER 153 at 155.
6. But cf. the "Judges' Memorandum of 1901 on Normal Punishments", Appendix V, p. 391 of Jackson, *Enforcing the Law*. Professor Cross's view was that there can and should be a statement of the normal punishment for offences: (1965) 81 LQR at 213.
7. Cross, *Sentencing*, Ch. IV; Thomas, *Sentencing*, Ch. 2.
8. *Bibi* (1980) 2 Cr App Rep (S) 177.
9. *Jamieson* (1975) 60 Cr App Rep 318.
10. *Regan* [1959] Crim LR 529; *Harper* [1967] Crim LR 714.
11. *De haan* [1968] 2 QB 108, [1967] 3 All ER 618; *Fraser* [1982] Crim LR 841.
12. *James and Sharman* (1913) 9 Cr App Rep 142; *Davies and Gorman* (1978) 68 Cr App Rep 319; *Aramah* (1983) 4 Cr App Rep (S) 407.
13. *Boardman* [1958] Crim LR 626; *Queen* [1982] Crim LR 56. But Jackson says, "The reality is that courts commonly regard previous convictions as a very good reason for imposing heavier penalties": *Enforcing the Law*, 239. See also Cross, *Sentencing*, 24.
14. Thomas [1967] Crim LR 523. See Cross, *Sentencing*, 23–25.

sentence is based on notions of retribution and deterrence and the principles discussed in this paragraph do not necessarily apply where the court is thinking in terms of a preventive or reformative sentence.

4 Justice and Equality[15]

The judge seeks to do justice by imposing the sentence the criminal deserves. But he also strives to be just in another and sometimes conflicting way – that is, by treating the criminal before him equally with others who have an equal degree of moral guilt. Equality of treatment is commonly and rightly seen as fundamental to justice; and the judges are anxious to avoid the strong sense of grievance which arises from inequality. "Sentencing without conformity is a social injustice."[16] The judge may impose a sentence greater or less than he thinks the criminal deserves in order to comply with the norm. Thus an American judge writes:

"If in the district in which a judge sits his fellow judges have established and insist on following, a pattern for dealing with offenders of a particular type, it is his responsibility either to get them to change or to come close to their standard."[17]

The Court of Appeal sometimes interferes with sentences in order to implement the principle of equality of treatment. Even the principle that sentences should be proportionate to guilt may give way to the principle that they should be proportionate to one another.[18] Thus the court declared that D deserved the sentence of four years imposed on her but they reduced it to three because her co-prisoner, who was not appealing, had received only two years and the disparity was too great.[19] Where the degree of responsibility of two accused is different the principle of equality requires that they should receive different sentences.[20] But it is recognised that the severity of the sentence may vary with the locality in which the offence is committed. Thus two persons with the same moral guilt but acting in different places may properly receive different sentences; the principle of equality gives way to the necessity for protecting the public. So severe penalties have been upheld for sexual offences against young girls[1] and for using a knife to wound,[2] where the court knew, or was advised, that offences of the type in question were prevalent in the locality. Local conditions other than the prevalence of offences may cause an offence to be regarded as more serious than if it were committed elsewhere. If there is, for example, a group of goods depots in the area, dishonesty by employees

15. D. A. Thomas, "Sentencing Co-Defendants. When is Uniform Treatment Necessary?" [1964] Crim LR 22.
16. Devlin, *The Judge*, 40.
17. Judge Wyzanski, US District Judge (1952) 65 Harv L Rev 1281 at 1292.
18. *Robson and East* [1970] Crim LR 354.
19. *Richards (No. 2)* [1956] Crim LR 127. See also *Dermody* [1959] Crim LR 63; *Appleby* [1960] Crim LR 712. See Thomas, 71–73.
20. *Bold* [1962] Crim LR 58.
 1. *Cargill* (1913) 8 Cr App Rep 224; *Nolan* (1960) Times, 30th March.
 2. *Lee* [1962] Crim LR 500.

may be regarded as particularly detrimental to the public interest. Sheep-stealing in Westmorland, though not a prevalent offence, is very serious because it strikes at the root of trust necessary between neighbouring farmers in an area where sheep graze unfenced.[3]

5 The Protection of the Public

The considerations so far examined all give way in judicial thought to what, as Edmund Davies J has said, is the prime object of the criminal law – protection of the public by the maintenance of law and order. Addressing the Magistrates' Association, the judge said:

"It seems to me that accordingly every court sentence should primarily be surveyed in the light of one test: is that the best thing to do in the interest of the community? – always remembering, of course, that the convicted person, despite his wrongdoing remains a member of the community."[4]

There can be little doubt that this is the predominant judicial view.[5]

It is the deterrent aspect of punishment which is prominent here; and there is no doubt that judges do believe in the value of punishment both as a deterrent to the person sentenced and to others. From time to time examples are quoted to illustrate the effect of severe sentences: a wave of post office frauds, which subsided after the Court of Criminal Appeal had laid down that the minimum sentence should be three years' penal servitude; and an epidemic of lead stealing, which declined after the judges began to impose stiff sentences.[6] But it is impossible to be certain that the crimes stopped *because* of the sentences.

"... in concrete terms we are almost totally ignorant of the deterrent effect on potential offenders attributable to particular sentences".[7]

But, even if the judge is himself sceptical of the deterrent effect of punishment, the general belief in it is so strong that it is a factor he may not ignore. An American judge[8] points out that:

"So far as is known, nobody has devised nor even attempted to devise any method of testing its validity, certainly not in any measurable or quantitative manner. It is so subjective a factor that it is almost impossible to conceive of any method by which to test it. Yet it would seem to be one of those social realities which is real because the 'common sense' of society tells us that it is real; and the sentencing judge cannot afford to overlook it."

There may be a conflict here with the principle that sentences should be proportionate to one another; and, when this happens, it is very probable

---

3. *Graham* [1964] Crim LR 486.
4. (1963) 19 *The Magistrate*, 183.
5. Cf. Birkett J, 8th Clarke Hall Lecture at 27; Salmon J, [1960] CLJ at 45; Lord Goddard CJ, below, p. 15.
6. Lord Goddard CJ: see (1956) 120 JPN 691.
7. Wootton, *Crime and the Criminal Law*, 101.
8. Judge Joseph N. Ulman of the Supreme Bench, Maryland, "The Trial Judge's Dilemma: A Judge's View", in *Probation and Criminal Justice* (edited by S. Glueck) at 115.

that the principle will have to give way. Asquith LJ makes the point very clearly:[9]

"Everyone has heard of an 'exemplary' sentence: and nearly everyone agrees that at times such sentences are justified. But it is not always observed that an exemplary sentence is unjust; and unjust to the precise extent that it is exemplary. Assume a particular crime is becoming dangerously frequent. In normal times the appropriate sentence would be, say, two years. The judge awards three; he awards the third year entirely to deter others. This may be expedient; it may even be imperative. But one thing it is not; it is not just. The guilt of the man who commits a crime when it happens to be on the increase is no greater than that of another man who commits the same crime when it is on the wane. The truth is that in such cases the judge is not administering strict justice but choosing the lesser of two practical evils. He decides that a moderate injustice to the criminal is a lesser evil than the consequences to the public of a further rise in the crime-wave."

It is common for the courts to do "injustice" of this sort for exemplary sentences are regularly upheld by the Court of Appeal.[10] Even an exemplary sentence, however, must not exceed what is merited by the offence; but the judge may disregard some or all of the mitigating factors.

In 1958 Salmon J sentenced to four years' imprisonment each of nine youths convicted of assaults and wounding offences on coloured men; their appeal was dismissed by the Court of Criminal Appeal.[11] These young men had no previous convictions, and it is probable that, if their offence had not been committed in a period of race riots which greatly disturbed the public, they would have been much more leniently dealt with. As it was, the Court of Criminal Appeal thought "the time had certainly come for the courts to put down offences such as these with a heavy hand".[12] Subsequently Salmon J extra-judicially expressed his views on the right treatment of crimes of violence:

"Nothing is more effective to stamp out crime than a long term of imprisonment. That may sound harsh, but we have to remember the twelve thousand or so of ordinary people who last year were the victims of crimes of violence. They, and their like, must be protected. And in these circumstances it does not wring my withers at all to be told how awful it is that a comparatively young man should be shut up for a long time."[13]

When the court speaks of protecting society, it generally means protection by the deterrence of others. Society may also be protected by incarcerating the individual offender for a long period. Here, however, the principle of the just punishment comes into its own again. The courts are generally unwilling to increase a sentence beyond what is "deserved"

9. *The Listener*, XLIII at 821.
10. E.g., *Cargill* (1913) 8 Cr App Rep 224; *Rhodes* [1959] Crim LR 138; *Kent* [1959] Crim LR 468; *Machin* [1961] Crim LR 844; *Musk and Reynalds* [1963] Crim LR 63; *Eminson* [1963] Crim LR 584; *Smith* [1963] Crim LR 526; *Elvin* [1976] Crim LR 204.
11. *Hunt* (1958) Times, 26th November.
12. Ibid.
13. [1960] CLJ 45, 48. Whether the sentences in fact had any deterrent effect is questionable. See R. M. Jackson, *Enforcing the Law*, 209.

simply to protect the public from the particular offender. Thus, while a blameless record may induce the court to impose a lower sentence than the crime "merits", a bad record will not usually be considered grounds for imposing a higher.[14] This would savour of punishing the offender for his past crimes for which he has already paid. In sentencing to preventive detention[15] the courts adopted a different principle on the basis that preventive detention was not a punishment. Paradoxically, the Court of Criminal Appeal has quashed sentences of imprisonment as being too severe and then substituted a longer sentence of preventive detention.[16]

Preventive detention has now been abolished, but the court has been given instead a power to impose an "extended term of imprisonment", where the conditions specified in the Act are fulfilled and the court is satisfied, by reason of the offender's previous conduct and the likelihood of his committing further offences, that it is expedient to protect the public from him for a substantial time.[17] The extended term may exceed the statutory maximum for the offence of which D has been convicted; but the sentence may be an "extended term" within the meaning of the Act, though it is less than the statutory maximum. The expression means extended beyond the term which would have been imposed if the new power had not been given.[18] The significance of the term being certified to be an extended one is that, instead of being granted remission, the person so sentenced may be released at any time on or after the day on which he could have been discharged from prison if remission had been granted.

This emphasises the importance of the judge's decision as to his purpose in imposing sentence. If a man, convicted of an offence for which the appropriate *punishment* is one year's imprisonment, is sentenced to five years, the sentence will clearly be excessive, unless it is intended to protect the public and not simply intended to punish. The judge now declares his purpose by issuing a certificate that the sentence is an extended term.

Where the court is not exercising the statutory power to impose an extended term, the principle generally applied has been that, even where the sentence is imposed for the protection of the public, it should not exceed the maximum merited by the gravity of the current offence.[19] In some recent cases, the court appears to have departed from this principle in order to protect the public from a dangerous offender.[20]

---

14. Above, p. 10.
15. See Williams, "The Courts and Persistent Offenders" [1963] Crim LR at 730.
16. *Kenny* (1962) Times, 23rd January; four years an "excessive sentence" for larceny of a wallet; five years' P.D. substituted (39 previous convictions); *Caine* [1963] Crim LR 63; sentence of five years' imprisonment for embezzlement of £21 on one day quashed. Two years would have been the maximum appropriate sentence of imprisonment. Seven years' P.D. substituted.
17. Powers of Criminal Courts Act 1973, s. 28, re-enacting Criminal Justice Act 1967, s. 37.
18. *Director of Public Prosecutions v Ottewell* [1970] AC 642, [1968] 3 All ER 153.
19. *Clarke* (1975) 61 Cr App Rep 320; *Slater* (1979) 1 Cr App Rep (S) 349; *Fraser* [1982] Crim LR 841. Life sentences, being to an extent indeterminate, are treated differently.
20. *Gouws* [1982] Crim LR 187; *Gordon* [1982] Crim LR 240; *Chadbund* [1983] Crim LR 48 and commentary. See also Radzinowicz and Hood, "Dangerousness and Criminal Justice" [1981] Crim LR 756.

6 The Reform of the Offender

Much modern penal legislation is directed to the rehabilitation of the offender. There are still writers who maintain that reformation should be the main,[1] if not the only object of sentencing. This is not the general view of the judges. Lord Goddard CJ is reported to have said that:

"The function of the criminal law is deterrence, not reform. As law, it was not concerned with the reform of the criminal. That was a matter for those persons and societies who, to their honour, were trying to do something about it."[2]

The pre-eminence given by the courts to their duty to protect the public necessarily implies that, whenever there is a conflict – as there frequently must be – between deterrence and reform, it is probably reform that will have to give way.

Just as the principle that the punishment should fit the crime might conflict with the objective of prevention, so too it might conflict with the objective of reformation. Corrective training (abolished by the Criminal Justice Act 1967) was a sentence which was intended to be reformatory; but the courts were unwilling to impose it unless the offence which brought the accused before the court merited the period of detention involved.[3] The courts remain reluctant to extend a sentence of imprisonment beyond what they think to be deserved, so that the offender may be reformed.[4]

All this is not to say that the courts are not interested in the reform of the criminal. As the Streatfeild Committee said:

". . . the courts have always had in mind the need to protect society from the persistent offender, to deter potential offenders and to deter or reform the individual offender. But in general it was thought that the 'tariff system'[5] took these other objectives in its stride. Giving an offender the punishment he deserved was thought to be the best way of deterring him and others and of protecting society.

Over the last few decades, these other objectives have received increased attention. The development has been most obvious in the increased weight which the courts give to the needs of the offender as a person. It is realised that whatever punishment is imposed, he will eventually return to society, and sentences are increasingly passed with the deterrence or reform of the offender as the principal objective; and in assessing the offender's culpability his social and domestic background is more closely examined."[6]

But, while the judges are not entirely consistent, it would seem that, generally, the reformation of the offender is still only something they aim at in so far as it is compatible with what they regard as their main functions of

---

1. See especially Wootton, *Crime and the Criminal Law* (2nd ed.), Ch. 4.
2. (1958) 122 JPN at 479.
3. *McCarthy* [1955] 2 All ER 927, [1955] 1 WLR 856.
4. *Sheen* [1979] Crim LR 189; *Roote* [1981] Crim LR 189, but cf. *Greedy* [1964] Crim LR 669. Cf. Morris and Howard, *Studies in Criminal Law* at 175: ". . . power over a criminal's life should not be taken in excess of that which would be taken were his reform not considered as one of our purposes."
5. I.e., giving a sentence proportionate to the offender's culpability.
6. (1961) Cmnd 1289, at 76.

protecting the public and doing justice. What is probably the prevalent judicial attitude is well described by Lord Devlin:

> "When the period has been fixed as justice demands, the law authorises and indeed encourages the penologist to use it for the work of reformation. . . . The sentence must not be longer than is justified by the gravity of the crime and must not fall below the least that justice demands . . . The penologist's objective is to send the prisoner back into the world changed for the better. He may not always hope for complete reformation, but at least he does not want him to leave while there is still a reasonable chance that further treatment may improve his prospects. When these objectives clash, it is the just sentence which must prevail . . ."[7]

7. *The Judge*, 29–30.

2 The Definition of a Crime[1]

It is now rather unfashionable to begin law books with definitions. One reason for this is the difficulty frequently encountered in defining the subject-matter of a particular branch of the law; and nowhere has this been more greatly felt than in the criminal law. But a book about crimes which does not tell the reader what a crime is allows him to proceed with his own preconceived notions in the matter; and it is well recognised that there is a popular meaning of crime which is different from, and narrower than, the legal meaning. A law book must be concerned with the legal meaning of crime; and the reader is entitled to know what it is, or at least why it is so difficult to tell him.

An attempt to define *a crime* at once encounters a serious difficulty. If the definition is a true one, it should enable us to recognise any *act* (or *omission*) as a crime, or not a crime, by seeing whether it contains all the ingredients of the definition. But a moment's reflection will suffice to show that this is impossible. When Parliament enacts that a particular act shall become a crime or that an act which is now criminal shall cease to be so, the act does not change in nature in any respect other than that of legal classification. All its observable characteristics are precisely the same before as after the statute comes into force. Any attempt at definition of a crime will thus either include the act at a time when it is not a crime, or exclude it when it is. Suicide was a crime until 3 August 1961, when, by the Suicide Act 1961,[2] it became perfectly lawful to kill oneself. Homosexual acts committed in private by male persons who have attained the age of twenty-one were offences until 27 July 1967, when by the Sexual Offences Act 1967,[3] such acts became permissible. The nature of the acts in question, their morality or immorality and their consequences do not change overnight; but their legal nature does.

---

1. Kenny, *Outlines of Criminal Law* (15th ed.) Ch. 1; C. K. Allen, "The Nature of a Crime", *Journal of Society of Comparative Legislation*, February, 1931, reprinted in *Legal Duties*, 221; Winfield, *Province of the Law of Tort*, Ch. VIII; Williams, "The Definition of Crime" (1955) 8 CLP 107; Hughes, "The Concept of Crime: An American View" [1959] Crim LR 239 and 331.
2. Below, pp. 358–361
3. Below, p. 471.

1 Characteristics of a Crime

1 A Public Wrong

It is, of course, possible to point to certain characteristics which are generally found in acts which are crimes. They are generally acts which have a particularly harmful effect on the public and do more than interfere with merely private rights. Sir Carleton Allen writes:

"Crime is crime because it consists in wrongdoing which directly and in serious degree threatens the security or well-being of society, and because it is not safe to leave it redressable only by compensation of the party injured."[4]

This explains why acts have been made crimes either by judicial decision or by legislation, and it does not necessarily accurately represent the present state of affairs. A crime may remain a crime long after it has ceased to be a threat to the security or well-being of society.[5] Thus Allen's proposition tells us what – as he thinks – ought to be criminal rather than what is criminal.

The public nature of crimes is evidenced by the contrast between the rules of civil and criminal procedure. Any citizen can, as a general rule and in the absence of some provision to the contrary, bring a criminal prosecution, whether or not he has suffered any special harm over and above other members of the public. As a member of the public he has an interest in the enforcement of the criminal law. D steals P's watch. P may prosecute him – so may Q, R, S, T or any other citizen.[6] In practice, of course, the vast majority of prosecutions are carried on by the Crown Prosecution Service or other public officers who have no personal interest in the outcome. The individual who starts a prosecution may not discontinue it at will,[7] for it is not only his concern but that of every citizen. The Crown, however, through the entry of a *nolle prosequi* by the Attorney-General, may stay the proceedings at any time[8] without the consent of the prosecutor. If the prosecution succeeds and a sentence is imposed by the court, the instigator of the prosecution has no power to pardon the offender. This belongs to the Crown, representing the public interest in the matter.

All this contrasts sharply with civil wrongs – torts and breaches of contract. There, only the person injured may sue. He (and only he) may freely discontinue the proceedings at any time and, if he succeeds and an award of damages is made in his favour, he may, at his entire discretion, forgive the defendant and terminate his liability.

---

4. *Legal Duties*, at 233–234.
5. Williams, 8 CLP at 126–127.
6. The right of private prosecution is unaffected by the Prosecution of Offences Act 1985; but s. 24 empowers the High Court, on the application of the Attorney-General, to restrain a vexatious prosecutor. The DPP may take over a private prosecution at any stage (s. 6 (2)) and may discontinue a prosecution during its "preliminary stage": s. 23.
7. *Wood* (1832) 3 B & Ad 657.
8. After the indictment has been signed: *Wylie* (1919) 83 JP 295. But the Director of Public Prosecutions may intervene and offer no evidence: *Turner v Director of Public Prosecutions* (1978) 68 Cr App Rep 70 (Mars Jones J), [1978] Crim LR 754; *Raymond v A-G* [1982] QB 839, [1982] 2 All ER 487, CA, [1982] Crim LR 826 and commentary.

Crimes, then, are wrongs which the judges have held, or Parliament has from time to time laid down, are sufficiently injurious to the public to warrant the application of criminal procedure to deal with them. Of course this does not enable us to recognise an act as a crime when we see one. Some acts are so obviously harmful to the public that *anyone* would say they should be criminal – and such acts almost certainly are – but there are many others about which opinions may differ widely. When a citizen is heard urging that, "There ought to be a law against it . . .", he is expressing his personal conviction that some variety of act is so harmful to society that it ought to be discouraged by being made the subject of criminal proceedings. There will almost invariably be a body of opinion which disagrees. But even if *everyone* agreed with him, the act in question would not thereby become a crime. Public condemnation is ineffective without the endorsement of an Act of Parliament or a decision of the court.

2 A Moral Wrong

The second characteristic of crimes which is usually emphasised is that they are acts which are morally wrong. As seen above, the traditional attitude of the common law has been that crimes are essentially immoral acts deserving of punishment. In the early days of the law, when the number of crimes was relatively few and only the most outrageous acts were prohibited – murder, robbery, rape, etc. – this was, no doubt, true. But now many acts are prohibited on the grounds of social expediency and not because of their immoral nature. Especially is this so in the field of summary offences – and summary offences are crimes.[9] Moreover many acts which are regarded as immoral – for example, adultery – are not crimes. Thus the test of immorality is not a very helpful one.

Whether an act ought to be a crime simply on the ground of its immoral nature has been the subject of vigorous debate in recent years. This sprang from the view of the Wolfenden Committee on Homosexual Offences and Prostitution that the enforcement of morality is not a proper object of the criminal law. The function of the criminal law, as they saw it is:

". . . to preserve public order and decency, to protect the citizen from what is offensive or injurious, and to provide sufficient safeguards against exploitation and corruption of others, particularly those who are specially vulnerable . . .

"It is not . . . the function of the law to intervene in the private lives of citizens, or to seek to enforce any particular pattern of behaviour, further than is necessary to carry out the purposes we have outlined."[10]

This view was challenged by Lord Devlin,[11] who argued that there is a public morality which is an essential part of the bondage which keeps society together; and that society may use the criminal law to preserve morality in the same way that it uses it to preserve anything else that is essential to its existence. The standard of morality is that of "the man in the

---

9. Williams (1955) 8 CLP at 110.
10. (1957) Cmnd. 247, para. 13.
11. The Maccabaean Lecture, "The Enforcement of Morals" (1959) 45 *Proc. of British Academy*, 129 reprinted in *The Enforcement of Morals* (1965) p. 1.

jury box", based on the "mass of continuous experience half-consciously or unconsciously accumulated and embodied in the morality of common sense".

To this it has been answered[12] that it is not proper for the state to enforce the general morality without asking whether it is based on ignorance, superstition or misunderstanding; that it is not a sufficient ground for prohibiting an act that "the thought of it makes the man on the Clapham omnibus sick". But if we are not to base criminal law on the general morality, does not this imply that "our law making is or should be controlled by independent Gods of Pure Reason, installed somewhere in our political systems and endowed with power to determine such questions for society, free of the prejudices to which lesser men are subject?"[13] "A free society is as much offended by the dictates of an intellectual oligarchy as by those of an autocrat."[14]

In the midst of this controversy was decided the case of *Shaw v Director of Public Prosecutions*,[15] in which Lord Simonds asserted that

"there remains in the courts of law a residual power to enforce the supreme and fundamental purpose of the law, to conserve not only the safety and order *but also the moral welfare of the state*";

and that the King's Bench was the custos morum of the people and had the superintendency of offences contra bonos mores.

"*Shaw's* case", concludes Lord Devlin, "settles for the purpose of the law that morality in England means what twelve men and women think it means – in other words it is to be ascertained as a question of fact."[16]

Subsequently, however, the particular rule of law that caused the Wolfenden Committee to formulate its general principle[17] – that homosexual conduct between consenting male adults is an offence – has been repealed by the Sexual Offences Act 1967. The House of Lords has repudiated the suggestion that it has power to extend the criminal law to enforce good morals.[18] The enforcement of morality, as such, by the criminal law is losing ground.

2 Criminal Proceedings

Because of the impossibility of defining the criminal quality of an act, most writers – and the courts – have been driven to turn to the nature of the proceedings which may follow from its commission.

---

12. H. L. A. Hart, *The Listener* 30 July 1959, p. 162.
13. Rostow, "The Enforcement of Morals" [1960] CLJ 174 at 189.
14. Devlin, "Law, Democracy and Morality" (1962) 110 U Pa Law Rev 635 at 642 reprinted in *The Enforcement of Morals* (1965) p. 86.
15. [1962] AC 220, [1961] 2 All ER 446; below, p. 276.
16. 110 U Pa Law Rev at 648. See also H. L. A. Hart, *Law, Liberty and Morality*; Hughes, "Morals and the Criminal Law" (1962) 71 YLJ 662. For an excellent discussion of the whole controversy, see Basil Mitchell, *Law, Morality and Religion in a Secular Society* (1967).
17. Above, p. 19.
18. *Knuller (Publishing, Printing and Promotions) Ltd v Director of Public Prosecutions* [1973] AC 435, [1972] 2 All ER 898, below, p. 277.

"The criminal quality of an act cannot be discerned by intuition; nor can it be discovered by reference to any standard but one: is the act prohibited with penal consequences?"[19]

The problem then becomes one of distinguishing criminal proceedings from civil proceedings. Any attempt to distinguish between crimes and torts comes up against the same kind of difficulty encountered in defining crimes generally: that most torts are crimes as well, though some torts are not crimes and some crimes are not torts. It is not in the nature of the act, but in the nature of the proceedings that the distinction consists; and generally[20] both types of proceeding may follow where an act is both a crime and a tort.

Kenny,[1] in the most celebrated of all attempts to define a crime, directed his attention to ascertaining the essential distinction between civil and criminal procedure. He rejected any distinction based on (i) the degree of activity manifested by the State in the two types of proceeding; for though the "contrast is a genuine and vivid one", it was incapable of being applied with precision;[2] (ii) the tribunals; for both civil and criminal cases may be heard in the magistrates' courts and the House of Lords; (iii) the object of the proceedings; for, while "the object of criminal procedure is always *Punishment*", the award of exemplary damages in civil actions is also punitive; (iv) the nature of the sanctions; for, while criminal sanctions never enrich any individual, it was not true to say that all civil actions do, since some civil actions for penalties could be brought only by the Crown.

Kenny finally seized upon the degree of control exercised over the two types of proceedings by the Crown[3] as the criterion, and defined "crimes" as

"wrongs whose sanction is punitive and is in no way remissible by any private person, but is remissible by the Crown alone, *if remissible at all*."[4]

He thought it necessary to bring in the elements of punishment only to exclude action for the recovery of the Crown's debts or other civil rights; and the italicised words were included so as not to exclude certain crimes which cannot be pardoned.[5]

Kenny's definition has been much criticised. Winfield[6] thought it led to a vicious circle:

19. *Proprietary Articles Trade Association v A-G for Canada* [1931] AC 310 at 324, per Lord Atkin.
20. Assault is an exception: Offences against the Person Act 1861, ss. 44 and 45; and see Howard [1958] Crim LR 33.
  1. *Outlines of Criminal Law* (15th ed.), Ch. 1.
  2. Kenny was greatly troubled at several points in his analysis by the anomalous form of proceeding known as a penal action. This was a civil action which might be brought by any member of the public – a common informer – but its object was the punishment of the defendant; and the successful plaintiff was enriched by the penalty imposed. By the Common Informers Act 1951 such procedure is abolished and any offence formerly punishable by common informer procedure is made punishable on summary conviction by a fine not exceeding £100.
  The penal action was in no case the *sole* objection Kenny found to any of the rejected definitions; so he would presumably have reached the same result, even if these proceedings had already been abolished.
  3. Above, p. 18.
  4. Op. cit., at 16.
  5. A public nuisance while still unabated and offences under Habeas Corpus Act 1679, s. 11.
  6. *Province of the Law of Tort*, Ch. VIII.

"What is a crime? Something that the Crown alone can pardon. What is it that the Crown alone can pardon? A crime."[7]

Winfield thought it advisable not to accept this part of Kenny's definition; and he concentrated on the question, what is punishment? The answer he arrived at is that: "The essence of punishment is its inevitability . . . no option is left to the offender as to whether he shall endure it or not"; whereas, in a civil case, "he can always compromise or get rid of his liability with the assent of the injured party".[8] Thus we seem to arrive back at the just rejected test of who can remit the sanction.

More substantial is the point made by Williams.[9] If we are going to define crime by reference to procedure, we ought to make use of the whole law of procedure, not just one item of it – the power to remit the sanction. If a court has to decide whether a particular act which has been prohibited by Parliament is a crime, it may be guided by a reference in the statute to any element which exists only in civil, or only in criminal, procedure as the case may be. A crime is:

"an act that is capable of being followed by criminal proceedings, having one of the types of outcome (punishment, etc.) known to follow these proceedings."[10]

This definition is by no means so unhelpful as at first sight may appear; for there are many points of distinction between civil and criminal procedure, and the specification in a statute of any one procedural feature which is peculiar either to the civil or the criminal law will therefore point to the nature of the wrong. The question in issue may well be whether a rule of criminal, or a rule of civil, procedure should be followed.[11] While it may be that no statute or decision gives guidance on this precise point, the procedure test may yet supply the answer if a statute or decision indicates, as the appropriate procedure, some other rule which is peculiar either to civil or to criminal proceedings. Of course, the definition tells us nothing about what acts *ought* to be crimes, but that is not its purpose. Writers who set out to define a crime by reference to the nature of the act, on the other hand, inevitably end by telling us, not what a crime is, but what the writer thinks it ought to be; and that is not a definition of a crime.

3 The Practical Test

From time to time the courts have found it necessary to determine whether a proceeding is criminal or not. Before the Criminal Evidence Act 1898, the defendant could not give evidence on oath on his own behalf in a criminal case whereas (since the Evidence Act 1851) he had been able to do so in a civil action. If he wished to give evidence the nature of the proceeding had

7. Ibid., at 197.
8. Ibid., at 200.
9. 8 CLP 107 at 128.
10. Ibid., at 123.
11. Cf. P. J. Fitzgerald, "A Concept of Crime" [1960] Crim LR 257 at 259–260.

to be ascertained.[12] The same problem could arise today if it were sought to *compel* the defendant to give evidence.[13] But much the most fruitful source of this problem has been the Judicature Act 1873, s. 47, and its successor, the Judicature Act 1925, s. 31 (1) (a), which, until 1968,[14] provided that no appeal should lie to the Court of Appeal "in any criminal cause or matter". The question whether a particular proceeding is a criminal cause or matter has frequently come before the Court of Appeal and the House of Lords. In these cases the test which has regularly been applied is whether the proceedings may result in the punishment of the offender. If it may, then it is a criminal proceeding.[15] As a practical test, this seems to work well enough; but it must always be remembered that it is a rule with exceptions; for some actions for penalties are undoubtedly civil actions, and yet they have the punishment of the offender as their objective; for this reason the test of punishment is jurisprudentially unsatisfactory.[16]

The meaning of punishment itself is not easy to ascertain; for the defendant in a civil case, who is ordered to pay damages by way of compensation, may well feel that he has been punished. It has been suggested[17] that:

"What distinguishes a criminal from a civil sanction and all that distinguishes it ... is the judgment of community condemnation which accompanies and justifies its imposition."

According to this view it is the condemnation, plus the consequences of the sentence – fine or imprisonment, etc. – which together constitute the punishment; but the condemnation is the essential feature. From this, it is argued that "we can say readily enough what a 'crime' is":

"It is not simply anything which the legislature chooses to call a 'crime'. It is not simply anti-social conduct which public officers are given a responsibility to suppress. It is not simply any conduct to which a legislature chooses to attach a 'criminal' penalty. It is conduct which, if duly shown to have taken place, will incur a formal and solemn pronouncement of the moral condemnation of the community."[18]

But if "the formal and solemn pronouncement" means the judgment of a criminal court (and what else can it mean?) we are driven back to ascertaining whether the proceeding is criminal or not. How is the judge to know whether to make "solemn and formal pronouncement of condemnation" or to give judgment as in a civil action? Surely, only by ascertaining

---

12. *Cattell v Ireson* (1858) EB & E 91; *Parker v Green* (1862) 2 B & S 299.

13. He is compellable in a civil but not in a criminal case.

14. Appeal now lies to the Court of Appeal (Criminal Division) as provided by the Criminal Appeal Act 1968.

15. E.g., *Mellor v Denham* (1880) 5 QBD 467; *Seaman v Burley* [1896] 2 QB 344; *Robson v Biggar* [1908] 1 KB 672; *Re Clifford and O'Sullivan* [1921] 2 AC 570; *Amand v Home Secretary and Minister of Defence of the Royal Netherlands Government* [1943] AC 147, [1942] 2 All ER 381.

16. It is thought not to be a substantial objection that exemplary damages may be awarded in some civil cases; for this is merely ancillary to the main object and the occasions for their award are now much restricted: *Rookes v Barnard* [1964] AC 1129 at 1221, [1964] 1 All ER 367 at 407, HL; *Cassell & Co Ltd v Broome* [1972] AC 1027, [1972] 1 All ER 801, HL.

17. By H. M. Hart, "The Aims of the Criminal Law" (1958) 23 *Law and Contemporary Problems*, 401, 404.

18. H. M. Hart, "The Aims of the Criminal Law" (1958) 23 *Law and Contemporary Problems*, 405.

whether the legislature (or the courts in the case of a common law crime) have prescribed that the proceedings shall be criminal; and this must depend, primarily, upon whether it is intended to be punitive.

3 The Classification of Offences

1 Treasons, Felonies and Misdemeanours: Arrestable Offences

At common law a crime might be classified either as treason, felony or misdemeanour. Originally the distinction between felony and misdemeanour was a distinction between serious and minor offences (the former involving penalties of a different order from the latter)[1] but over the years this distinction, though always broadly discernible, became blurred. The practical importance of the distinction came to lie in certain consequences which turned upon whether the offence was felony or misdemeanour. For example, the general power of arrest without warrant was available only in respect of felonies; only in felonies was the distinction drawn between principals and accessories to the crime; and it was an offence to conceal (misprision), or to agree not to prosecute (compound), a felony, though it was not an offence to conceal a misdemeanour and probably not an offence to compound one.

But now, by s. 1 of the Criminal Law Act 1967, all distinctions between felony and misdemeanour are abolished and, on all matters on which a distinction has previously been drawn, the law is assimilated to that applicable to misdemeanour at the commencement of the Act. Consequently there is no distinction of substance between the former felonies, whether created at common law or by statute, and misdemeanours, and all may be conveniently called "offences".

It will be appreciated, however, that for some purposes, and especially for the purposes of the law of arrest without warrant, it is necessary to maintain a distinction between those (serious) offences in respect of which it is necessary that there should be a power of arrest without warrant and those (minor) offences in respect of which there is no general need for such a power. The Criminal Law Act 1967, s. 2, accordingly introduced the new concept of the arrestable offence. The definition in that Act has now been replaced and modified[3] by s. 24 of the Police and Criminal Evidence Act (PACE) 1984 where an arrestable offence is defined as any offence "for which the sentence is fixed by law[2] or for which a person (not previously

---

1. See generally, Pollock and Maitland, 2 HEL, Cap. VIII, s. 2.
2. These are murder (Murder (Abolition of Death Penalty) Act 1965, s. 1 (1)); treason (Treason Act 1814, s. 1); piracy with violence (Piracy Act 1837, s. 2).
3. The modification is that common law misdemeanours (see above, p. 5, footnote 13) are now included in the definition of arrestable offences. Statutory conspiracy to commit an arrestable offence was made an arrestable offence by s. 3 of the Criminal Law Act 1977.

convicted) may be sentenced for a term of five years (or might be so sentenced but for the restrictions imposed by s. 33 of the Magistrates' Courts Act 1980[4]), and to attempts to commit any such offence." Included in the definition of arrestable offences are certain offences (for example, indecent assault on a woman contrary to s. 22 of the Sexual Offences Act 1956, going equipped for stealing contrary to s. 25 of the Theft Act 1968) which, not carrying five years' imprisonment, would not be arrestable offences in their own right but where a power of arrest without warrant was thought necessary for the proper enforcement of the law. In other respects PACE re-states the law relating to arrest but does not provide a comprehensive code.[5]

Moreover, the Criminal Law Act 1967 created offences in relation to arrestable offences which cannot be committed in respect of other offences. Under s. 4 (1) it is an offence to assist a person guilty of an arrestable offence,[6] and s. 5 (1) creates an offence of agreeing for gain to conceal information relating to an arrestable offence.[7] These offences had their counterparts in the earlier law; the first closely resembles the former offence of being an accessory after the fact to felony, and the latter has features – though very emaciated features – of the former offences of misprision and compounding.

The modern classification of arrestable and "non-arrestable" offences has broadly and with much modification superseded the former classification of felonies and misdemeanours. No doubt it would simplify things if it were possible to dispense altogether with any mention of felony and misdemeanour, but this is not possible. The terms appear regularly in pre-1968 cases and the student must know to what they refer. Most of these cases remain unaffected by the abolition of the distinctions between felony and misdemeanour since the law is, in the main, the same for both. And even cases which raise the peculiarities of felony may remain authoritative in other respects. For example, although it is no longer necessary to draw the elaborate distinctions relating to degrees of participation in felony, the cases may remain authoritative as showing the limits of criminal participation in an offence.[8]

The Criminal Law Act 1967 does not affect the substantive law of treason,[9] and consequently the law of accessories, misprision and compounding in relation to treason remains unaltered. These topics do not

---

4. This qualification, introduced by the Criminal Law Act 1977 and continued in PACE, is to make it clear that the power of arrest remains unaffected by the fact that in certain circumstances (as to which see below, p. 29) an indictable offence may be triable only summarily.

5. Apart from retaining the arrestable offence, PACE retains a small number of statutory powers of arrest without warrant (see Sch. 2). There is no power under PACE to arrest without warrant for any other *offence* though an *offender* may be arrested without warrant if the arrest conditions specified in s. 25 are met. PACE leaves unaffected the common law power to arrest for breach of the peace. Below, pp. 409–412.

6. See further below, p. 758.

7. See further below, p. 763.

8. See further below, pp. 130–134.

9. Section 12 (6).

receive extended treatment in this book[10] since they are not of any great significance. Curiously, cases on misprision and compounding of felony may remain relevant in determining the scope of these offences in relation to treason.

2 Indictable and Summary Offences

For procedural purposes crimes are classified as indictable and summary offences. Summary offences are offences which may be tried by courts having summary jurisdiction and the trial is conducted by magistrates without a jury; all proceedings on indictment, which always take place with a jury, are now brought before the Crown Court.[11] For practical purposes it is the question of trial with or without a jury which is the important distinction between trial on indictment and summary trial.[12] In other respects the course and conduct of the trial is very much the same.

The classification of offences as indictable and summary broadly reflects a distinction between serious and minor crimes. Some offences are so obviously serious that they are triable only on indictment,[13] and some offences are so obviously minor that they can be tried only summarily. But there are very many crimes the gravity of which turns upon the particular circumstances of the case. Recognising this Parliament has from time to time provided for the summary trial of indictable offences and vice versa. Since this was done as occasion demanded without any coherent overall plan it is not surprising that the classification which eventually emerged was found by the James Committee to be "confusing, complicated and anomalous."[14] The Committee had two objectives in mind. One was to simplify the existing classification and the other was to get a better distribution of criminal business between the Crown Court and magistrates' courts with a view to relieving the pressure of work on the former. To these ends the Committee made a number of recommendations which were first given effect by the Criminal Law Act 1977 but are now for the most part to be found in the Magistrates' Courts Act 1980.

In particular the Committee recommended a three fold classification of offences and now the only classes of offence are: (a) offences triable only on indictment; (b) offences triable only summarily; and (c) offences triable either way.

---

10. But as to misprision of treason, see below, p. 833.
11. Supreme Court Act 1981, s. 46. When the Crown Court sits in the City of London it is known as the Central Criminal Court: s. 8 (3).
12. See Jackson, *Machinery of Justice*, 7th ed. (1976) Ch. 4.
13. And some serious offences are more serious than others; consequently provision is made in s. 4 (5) of the Courts Act 1971 for the allocation of cases as between High Court judges, Circuit judges and Recorders. See Practice Direction (1988) 86 Cr App Rep 142.
14. *The Distribution of Criminal Business between the Crown Court and Magistrates' Courts* (1975) Cmnd. 6323, para. 9. See also D. A. Thomas, "Committals for Trial & Sentence, the Case for Simplification" [1972] Crim LR 477; Scott & Latham, "A Comment on the Report of the James Committee" [1976] Crim LR 159.

1 Offences Triable Summarily only

A summary offence is one which, if committed by an adult, is triable only summarily.[15] Such offences are entirely the creation of statute. It is of course open to Parliament to review the appropriate class for a particular offence and the opportunity was taken in the Criminal Law Act 1977, with a view to easing the workload of the Crown Court, of making certain offences summary only, though they had formerly been triable either on indictment or summarily. These include offences concerned with drink and driving, assaulting constables in the execution of their duty and certain public order offences.

2 Offences Triable only on Indictment

An indictable offence means an offence which, if committed by an adult, is triable on indictment, whether it is exclusively so triable or triable either way.[16] Offences triable only on indictment include any offence punishable by death or imprisonment for life on first conviction, causing death by reckless driving and the more serious offences under the Theft Act 1968. Generally offences are made indictable only, either because they are of such exceptional gravity or because other reasons, such as anticipated complexity of issues, make them unsuitable for summary trial.

3 Offences Triable Either Way

An offence triable either way means an offence which, if committed by an adult, is triable either on indictment or summarily.[17] The class extended to (i) the offences listed in the Magistrates' Courts Act 1980, Sched. 1; and (ii) offences made triable either way by virtue of any other enactment.[18]

For offences falling under this head the procedure is regulated by the Magistrates' Courts Act 1980. It is for the court to decide, having regard to representations made by the prosecutor and the accused and all the circumstances of the case, which is the more suitable form of trial (s. 19). If the court decides that trial on indictment is more suitable it proceeds to consider the case as examining justices (s. 21). But if the court decides that summary trial is more suitable it cannot so proceed unless (i) having first informed the accused of his right to be tried by jury, the accused consents to be tried summarily; and (ii) the accused is informed that if he is tried summarily and convicted he may be committed to the Crown Court for sentence if, on hearing information about his character and antecedents, the court is of the opinion that a greater punishment should be inflicted than it has power to impose (s. 20).[19]

---

15. Interpretation Act 1978, Sched. 1. To incite the commission of a summary offence is itself a summary offence (Magistrates' Courts Act 1980, s. 45 (1)); to conspire to commit a summary offence is an indictable offence (Criminal Law Act 1977, s. 3); it is not generally an offence to attempt to commit an offence which is summary only, unless the statute so provides: Criminal Attempts Act 1981, ss. 1 and 3, below, p. 297.
16. Interpretation Act 1978, Sched. 1.
17. Interpretation Act 1978, Sched. 1.
18. Magistrates' Courts Act 1980, s. 17.
19. The provisions governing this procedure are mandatory; if, therefore, the court proceeds without compliance with them, the proceedings are a nullity: R v Tottenham Justices, ex parte Arthur's Transport Services [1981] Crim LR 180, DC.

If the court then proceeds to summary trial it may at any time before the conclusion of the prosecution's case discontinue summary trial and proceed to inquire into the charge as examining justices (s. 25 (2)). Conversely if the court has begun to inquire into the charge as examining justices it may at any time decide, having regard to representations made, that the case is after all more suitable for summary trial. If it does so the court may proceed to try the case summarily provided the accused, having first been informed of his right to jury trial, consents to be tried summarily (s. 25 (3) and (4)).

This is, in outline, the normal procedure for dealing with offences triable either way but there are three exceptional cases.

The first is where the prosecution is being conducted by or on behalf of the Attorney General, the Solicitor General or the Director of Public Prosecutions. If any of these officers apply for trial on indictment the court has no say in the matter and must proceed as examining justices (s. 19 (4)).

The second is where the accused is charged with a "scheduled offence" (s. 22 (1)). A scheduled offence is one specified in Schedule 2 which concerns offences of committing (or aiding and abetting the commission of, or attempting or inciting to commit) criminal damage by any means, other than fire, of property not exceeding the relevant sum (viz. £400) in value at the time of the commission of the offence. In such a case the court *must* proceed as if the offence was triable only summarily (s. 22 (2)). This procedure originates in a proposal of the James Committee,[20] again aimed at relieving pressure on the Crown Court, that minor offences of theft and criminal damage should be tried only summarily. Because of the serious consequences of a conviction for theft Parliament would not accept any limitation on the right to trial by jury, but the proposal was accepted for minor offences of criminal damage which were not thought to carry the same stigma.

The accused is thus deprived of the right to jury trial but the procedure does have advantages from his point of view because (i) the maximum penalty is limited to three months' imprisonment or a fine of £500 (s. 33 (a)); (ii) the accused cannot be committed to the Crown Court for sentence (s. 38); and (iii) the court cannot revert to proceeding with the charge as examining justices (s. 25 (2)).

Where it is not clear to the court whether the value does or does not exceed the relevant sum, the court must tell the accused that he will be tried summarily if he consents (s. 22 (4) and (5)). In this situation the accused can insist on trial by jury but if he consents to summary trial he gets the same "bonuses" mentioned in the last paragraph (s. 22 (6)).

But neither of these procedures apply where the offence charged is one of two or more offences constituting part of a series of offences of a similar character, or where the offence consists in the incitement to commit two or more offences (s. 22 (7)). In either of these eventualities, and in any case where the value involved exceeds the relevant sum, the offence becomes an offence triable either way subject to the normal procedure governing such offences which has been outlined above.

20. Cmnd. 6323, paras. 74–105.

The third exception concerns children and young persons. Where such a person is charged with any offence, other than homicide, he must be tried summarily unless (a) he is a young person (i.e. between fourteen and seventeen) charged with an offence punishable by fourteen years' imprisonment and the court considers that if convicted he should be sentenced to a long period of detention;[1] or (b) he is charged jointly with a person over seventeen in which case the court may, if it considers it necessary in the interests of justice, commit both for trial.[2]

1. Children and Young Persons Act 1969, s. 6 (1), (2).
2. Children and Young Persons Act 1969, s. 6 (1) (b). This provision was amended by the Criminal Law Act 1977 (now Magistrates' Courts Act 1980, s. 29) to allow a magistrates' court in a case falling within s. 6 (1) (b), to commit him for trial for any other indictable offences with which he is charged at the same time if they arise out of the same circumstances.

4 The Elements of a Crime

It is a general principle of criminal law that a person may not be convicted of a crime unless the prosecution have proved beyond reasonable doubt both (a) that he has caused a certain event or that responsibility is to be attributed to him for the existence of a certain state of affairs, which is forbidden by criminal law, and (b) that he had a defined state of mind in relation to the causing of the event or the existence of the state of affairs. The event, or state of affairs, is called the *actus reus* and the state of mind the *mens rea* of the crime. Though it is absolutely clear that D killed P – that is, he has caused an *actus reus* – he must be acquitted of murder if there is a reasonable possibility that the killing was accidental; for, if that is the case, it has not been proved beyond reasonable doubt that he had the requisite mental element. It was so laid down by the House of Lords in *Woolmington v Director of Public Prosecutions*[1] where it was held, overruling earlier authorities, that it is a misdirection to tell a jury that D must *satisfy* them that the killing was an accident. The true rule is that the jury must acquit even though they are not satisfied that D's story is true, if they think it might reasonably be true. They should convict only if satisfied beyond reasonable doubt that it is *not* true. This rule is of general application[2] and there is only one exception to it at common law – the defence of insanity.[3] To raise other defences at common law – for example, provocation, self-defence, automatism or duress – the accused need do no more than introduce some evidence of all the constituents of the defence; whereupon it is for the Crown to satisfy the jury that those constituents did not exist. If there is evidence of a defence, though it has not been specifically raised by the accused, the judge must direct the jury to acquit unless they are satisfied that the defence has been disproved.[4] A statute may, however, expressly or impliedly[5] impose a burden of proof on the defendant and

---

1. [1935] AC 462; **SHC 39**.
2. *Mancini v Director of Public Prosecutions* [1942] AC 1, [1941] 3 All ER 272; *Chan Kau v R* [1955] AC 206, [1955] 1 All ER 266; *Lobell* [1957] 1 QB 547, [1957] 1 All ER 734 (self-defence); *Bratty v A-G for Northern Ireland* [1963] AC 386, [1961] 3 All ER 523; **SHC 196** (automatism); *Gill* [1963] 2 All ER 688, [1963] 1 WLR 841 (duress). But the onus of proving procedural bars to trial, such as *autrefois convict* or *acquit*, may be on the defendant: *Coughlan* (1976) 63 Cr App Rep 33 at 36.
3. Below, p. 195.
4. *Palmer v R* [1971] AC 814, [1971] 1 All ER 1077 at 1080; **SHC 238**; *Wheeler* (1968) 52 Cr App Rep 28 at 30–31; *Hamand* (1985) 82 Cr App Rep 65.
5. *Hunt* [1987] 1 All ER 1 at 10, 15, HL.

frequently does so. Where an onus of proof is put upon D, he satisfies it if he proves his case on a balance of probabilities – the same standard as that on the plaintiff in a civil action – and he need not prove it beyond reasonable doubt.[6]

The principle that a man is not criminally liable for his conduct unless the prescribed state of mind is also present is frequently stated in the form of a Latin maxim: *actus non facit reum nisi mens sit rea*[7]. It is convenient, for purposes of exposition, to consider the mental element separately from the other elements of the crime. The mental element is traditionally described as the *mens rea* and the other elements as the *actus reus*. The *actus reus* amounts to a crime only when it is accompanied by the appropriate *mens rea*. To cause an *actus reus* without the requisite *mens rea* is not a crime and may be an ordinary, innocent act. For example, the offence of perjury[8] consists in making a statement, whether true or not, on oath in a judicial proceeding, knowing it to be false or not believing it to be true. Thus, every statement on oath in a judicial proceeding is the *actus reus* of perjury. When we say then that a certain event is the *actus reus* of a crime what we mean is that the event would be a crime if it were caused by a person with *mens rea*. The description of it as an *actus reus* implies no judgment whatever as to its moral or legal quality. The analysis into *actus reus* and *mens rea* is for convenience of exposition only. The only concept known to the law is the crime; and the crime exists only when *actus reus* and *mens rea* coincide.

It is not always possible to separate *actus reus* from *mens rea*.[9] Sometimes a word which describes the *actus reus*, or part of it, implies a mental element. Without that mental element the *actus reus* simply cannot exist. There are many offences of possession of proscribed objects and it has always been recognised that possession consists in a mental as well as physical element.[10] The same is true of words like "permits",[11] "appropriates",[12] "cultivates"[13] and many more. Having an offensive weapon in a public place is the *actus reus* of an offence; but whether an article is an offensive weapon depends, in some circumstances, on the intention with which it is carried. In the absence of that intention, the thing is not an offensive weapon and there is no *actus reus*.[14] The significance of this is that any mental element which is part of the *actus reus* is necessarily an element

---

6. *Carr-Briant* [1943] KB 607, [1943] 2 All ER 156. The Criminal Law Revision Committee has proposed that the law should be so amended that D would, in these cases, merely have to introduce sufficient evidence to raise the issue (an "evidential burden") whereupon the onus of proof would be on the Crown: Eleventh Report, Cmnd. 4991, paras. 137–142.

7. "Properly translated, this means 'An act does not make a man guilty of a crime, uniess his mind be also guilty.' It is thus not the *actus* which is '*reus*' but the man and his mind respectively:" per Lord Hailsham in *Haughton v Smith* [1975] AC 467 at 491–492, [1973] 3 All ER 1109 at 1113–1114. It is, however, convenient to follow the established usage of "*actus reus*". Cf. Lord Simon in *Director of Public Prosecutions for Northern Ireland v Lynch* [1975] AC 653 at 690, [1975] 1 All ER 913 at 934 and Lord Diplock in *Miller* [1983] 2 AC 161, [1983] 1 All ER 978, 979, HL.

8. Below, p. 740.

9. See A. C. E. Lynch, "The Mental Element in the Actus Reus" (1982) 98 LQR 109.

10. Below, p. 107.

11. Below, p. 124.

12. Below, p. 491.

13. Below, p. 109, footnote 9.

14. Below, p. 422.

of the offence. It is possible for the courts to dispense with *mens rea* in whole or in part, but, except in the anomalous case of an intoxicated offender,[15] they can never dispense with the *actus reus*. If an offence consists in possessing or permitting, it cannot be proved if D cannot be shown to have possessed or permitted. The court may of course give effect to the word without requiring full *mens rea*, as where it held that D was guilty of permitting the use of an uninsured vehicle where he intended to permit only the use of the vehicle (which was in fact uninsured) or cultivating a cannabis plant where he intended only to cultivate that plant (which was in fact a cannabis plant).

1 The Actus Reus

1 The Nature of an Actus Reus

Since the *actus reus* includes all the elements in the definition of the crime except the accused's mental element,[16] it follows that the *actus reus* is not merely an act. It may indeed consist in a "state of affairs", not including an act at all.[17] Much more often, the *actus reus* requires proof of an act or an omission (conduct). Usually, it must be proved that the conduct had a particular result. In murder, for example, it must be shown that the accused's conduct caused the death. Some crimes do not require evidence of any result. Perjury is committed as soon as D makes a statement on oath which he does not believe to be true. It is irrelevant whether he is believed or not. These different types of offence have been designated[18] "result crimes" and "conduct crimes" respectively. It has been said[19] that in "result crimes" the law is interested only in the result and not in the conduct bringing about the result. Similarly, a well-known definition of *actus reus* is "such result of human conduct as the law seeks to prevent".[20] But a dead man with a knife in his back is not the *actus reus* of a murder. It is putting the knife in the back thereby causing the death which is the *actus reus*. The law is no less interested in the conduct which brings about the result in a "result crime" than in a "conduct crime".[1]

True conduct crimes, such as perjury, are rare. The term has been widely interpreted by Glanville Williams to include rape and abduction – in these crimes, "you do not have to wait to see if anything happens as a result of what the defendant does."[2] So, wounding would be a conduct crime if committed with a knife but a result crime if committed with a gun,

---

15. See *Lipman* [1970] 1 QB 152, [1969] 3 All ER 410, below, p. 348.
16. It should be said that this is not the only possible definition of an *actus reus*, and that a more limited view is taken of it by some writers. It is thought, however, that it is the most useful conception of the *actus reus* and is adopted throughout this book. Cf. Williams, CLGP, 16 and [1958] Crim LR at 830.
17. Below, p. 46.
18. By Gordon, 61.
19. Ibid.
20. Kenny, 17.
1. See Lord Diplock in *Treacy v Director of Public Prosecutions* [1971] AC 537 at 560, [1971] 1 All ER 110 at 120.
2. "The Problem of Reckless Attempts", [1983] Crim LR 365 at 366, 368.

crossbow or catapult. If the distinction is to be made at all (and, while interesting, it is not clear that it has, or should have, any practical consequences) these offences are better regarded as result crimes. A result has to flow from D's physical movements, whether you have to wait for it or not.

Since the Criminal Attempts Act 1981,[3] all indictable offences are now, in a sense, potentially conduct crimes because any act, done with intent thereby[4] to commit an indictable offence may be an indictable attempt to commit it. The *actus reus* of the offence attempted need never happen and may, indeed, be impossible. Its definition serves only to define the *mens rea* of the attempt. A case can be made that the law should always have regard only to the conduct and not to the result. Whether the conduct results in harm is generally a matter of chance and does not alter the blameworthiness and dangerousness of the actor. But the law has not gone so far. If D hurls a stone, being reckless whether he injures anyone, he is guilty of an offence if the stone strikes P but of no offence – not even an attempt – if no one is injured. From a retributive point of view, it might be argued that D should be equally liable in either event. On utilitarian grounds, however, it is probably undesirable to turn the whole criminal law into "conduct crimes". The needs of deterrence are probably adequately served in most cases by "result crimes"; and the criminal law should be extended only where a clear need is established.

The *actus reus* then is made up, generally but not invariably, of conduct and sometimes its consequences and also of the circumstances in which the conduct takes place (or which constitute the state of affairs) in so far as they are relevant. Circumstances, like consequences, are relevant in so far as they are included in the definition of the crime. The definition of theft, for example, requires that it be proved that D dishonestly appropriated property *belonging to another*. If the property belonged to no-one (because it had been abandoned) D's appropriation could not constitute the *actus reus* of theft. However dishonest he might be, he could not be convicted of theft because an essential constituent of the crime is missing.[5]

Sometimes a particular state of mind on the part of the *victim* is required by the definition of the crime. If so, that state of mind is part of the *actus reus* and, if the prosecution are unable to prove its existence, they must fail. If D is prosecuted for rape, it must be proved that P did not consent to the act of intercourse. The absence of consent by P is an essential constituent of the *actus reus*. But in some crimes the consent of the victim is entirely irrelevant. If D is charged with the murder of P, it is no defence for him to show that P asked to be killed.

It is apparent from these examples that it is only by looking at the definition of the particular crime that we can see what circumstances are material to the *actus reus*. We find this definition, in the case of common law crimes, in the decisions of the courts and, in the case of statutory crimes, in

---

3. As interpreted in *Shivpuri*, below, p. 304.

4. i.e., D intends to cause the result by that act; it is the last act D intends, and needs, to do, not a merely preparatory act. An earlier act is sufficient, if "more than merely preparatory": below, p. 287.

5. He might, however, be convicted of an attempt to steal. Below, p. 300.

the words of the statute, as construed by the courts. Many factors may be relevant; for example, in bigamy, the fact that D is validly married; in treason committed abroad, that D is a British national (or under the protection of the Crown for some other reason); in handling stolen goods, that the goods have, in fact, been stolen; and so on.

The effect of penalty provisions in determining the elements of the actus reus. When, in relation to an offence, statute provides that, where a particular fact, say X, is present, a greater maximum punishment may be imposed than where X is not present, X is an element in the *actus reus* of a greater offence. It is a fact to be proved by the prosecution to the satisfaction of the jury, and not merely a fact to be proved to the judge after conviction.[6] It follows that there are now two offences: the original offence (i) with X and (ii) without X. Buggery was a single offence at common law, whether committed with or without consent, with a person of any age or sex, or with an animal. The Sexual Offences Act 1956, s. 12 (1), merely provided that this offence was punishable with life imprisonment. The Sexual Offences Act 1967, however, provided for a new scale of penalties[7] ranging from two years to imprisonment for life, depending on the age and sex of the other person and whether he consented. Until 1984 it was thought that there was a single offence and that it was for the judge to determine, e.g., whether there was consent or not. In *Courtie*[8] the House of Lords laid down the principle stated above and held that buggery with a male aged nineteen with his consent was a different offence from buggery with the same person without his consent, the second offence carrying a higher maximum. Since the indictment had not alleged absence of consent and that issue had not been decided by the jury, D could be convicted of the lesser offence only. Where Parliament provides an elaborate structure of maximum penalties, as in the case of drug offences, the substantive law is correspondingly complex.[9] But the principle is sound. Where proof of fact X entails liability to a higher penalty, the requirements of proof of X should be no less stringent than in the case of the other facts of the offence.

Actus reus *and justification or excuse.* In the terminology used by Glanville Williams:[10]
  "*Actus reus* includes ... the absence of any ground of justification or excuse, whether such justification or excuse be stated in any statute creating the crime or implied by the courts in accordance with general principle ...."
An alternative view is that of D.J. Lanham:[11]
  "As a matter of analysis we can think of a crime as being made up of three ingredients, *actus reus*, *mens rea* and (a negative element) absence of a valid defence."

6. *Courtie* [1984] AC 463, [1984] 1 All ER 740, HL.
7. Below, p. 471.
8. Above, fn. 6.
9. *Shivpuri* [1987] AC 1 [1986] 2 All ER 334, [1986] Crim LR 536 and commentary; *Ellis, Street and Smith* (1986) 84 Cr App Rep 235, [1987] Crim LR 44, CA, and commentary.
10. CLGP, 19. See also TBCL, Ch. 2.
11. [1976] Crim LR 276.

If the public executioner carries out his duty to hang a convicted traitor or D shoots to kill in reasonable defence, no offence is committed – according to Williams because there is no *actus reus* (or, indeed, *mens rea*) and, according to Lanham, because, though there is both *actus reus* and *mens rea* (the intentional killing of a human being) there is a valid defence. Williams's opinion is attractive both because it seems strange to describe an act which is required or permitted by the law as an *actus reus*[12] and because there are practical difficulties in distinguishing (as Lanham's analysis requires) between the definitional elements of an offence and defence elements. On the other hand, the enumeration of the elements of an offence becomes impossibly cumbersome if it has to include all conceivable defences – as the authors of the draft criminal code put it, "the inapplicability of every exception admitted by the definition of an offence must be treated as an element of it."[13] Moreover, defences may also require mental as well as external elements. Duress is a defence but only, of course, if D is aware of the threatening facts.[14] If the object of the Latin terminology is convenience of exposition, there is much to be said for the Lanham usage and it is generally (but not invariably) followed in this book.[15]

2 An Actus Reus must be Proved

Mens rea may exist without an *actus reus* but, if the *actus reus* of a particular crime does not exist or occur, that crime is not committed. Although D believes that he is appropriating P's property he cannot in any circumstances be guilty of theft if the property belongs to no-one. D has the *mens rea* but the *actus reus*, the other fundamental element of the crime, is lacking. D may assault P with intent to ravish her against her will but, if in fact she consents, his act cannot amount to rape. D may intend to marry during the lifetime of his wife but if, unknown to him, she is dead, he cannot commit bigamy. If D makes a statement, which he believes to be false, for the purpose of obtaining money, he cannot be convicted of obtaining by deception if the statement is, in fact, true. In each case, D may now be convicted of attempting to commit the crime in question.[16]

In *Deller*,[17] D induced P to purchase his car by representing (*inter alia*) that it was free from encumbrances. D had previously executed a document which purported to mortgage the car to a finance company and, no doubt, he thought he was telling a lie. He was charged with obtaining by false pretences.[18] It then appeared that the document by which the transaction had been effected was probably void in law as an unregistered bill of sale. If it was void the car *was* free from encumbrances – ". . . quite accidentally and, strange as it may sound, dishonestly, the appellant had told the

---

12. But, as noted above, *actus reus* implies no moral judgment, the only point of the analysis being convenience in exposition.
13. Law Com. No. 143, 7.2.
14. Below, p. 229.
15. See below, p. 75. The Latin terms are frequently used by the courts but no detailed analysis has been made by them and it cannot be said that there is a standard judicial usage.
16. Below, p. 300.
17. (1952) 36 Cr App Rep 184; **SHC** 4. Cf. *Brien* (1903) 3 SRNSW 410; *Dyson* [1908] 2 KB 454; below, p. 312.
18. Under s. 32 of the Larceny Act 1916, now replaced by s. 15 of the Theft Act 1968, below, p. 544. The same principles are applicable.

In Dadson - it was decided that the external facts ie, P was a felon required a state of mind also
Actus Reus = unlawful killing.

THE ACTUS REUS   37

truth".[19] D's conviction was, therefore, quashed by the Court of Criminal Appeal, for, though he had *mens rea*, no *actus reus* had been established. D could now be convicted of an attempt to obtain by deception.[20]

A case which is sometimes said to be inconsistent with this fundamental principle, but which is worth discussing because it illustrates the difficulties which may arise in connection with its application, is *Dadson*.[1]

D was a constable, employed to watch a copse from which wood had been stolen. He carried a loaded gun. P emerged from the copse carrying wood which he had stolen, and, ignoring D's calls to stop, ran away. D, having no other means of bringing him to justice, fired and wounded him in the leg. He was convicted of shooting at P with intent to cause him grievous bodily harm. It was assumed in this case that it was perfectly lawful to wound an escaping felon if this was the only way of arresting him;[2] but stealing growing wood was not, under s. 39 of the Larceny Act 1827, a felony unless P had two previous convictions for the same offence. In fact P had been repeatedly convicted of stealing wood, but D did not know this. Erle J told the jury that the alleged felony, *being unknown to the prisoner*, constituted no justification. On a case reserved the judges thought the conviction right: D was not justified in firing at P because the fact that P was committing a felony was not known to D at the time.

The argument runs that this case is wrong because, if we ignore D's state of mind and look at the actual facts, what he did was perfectly lawful; that there was no *actus reus*. It is submitted that this is going too far. It is important to distinguish between two types of defence which may be raised. In the first type, D merely denies the existence of an element (other than the *mens rea*) in the definition of the crime. If D makes out the defence he certainly cannot be convicted, whatever his state of mind. This is what happened in *Deller*.[3] In the second type, D admits that all the elements in the definition of the crime have been established and goes on to assert other facts which afford him a defence in law. As appears above, the establishment of this type of defence may require D to assert the existence of a mental element as well as external facts.

In *Dadson*[4] D did not deny that he shot at P or that he intended to cause him grievous bodily harm. He admitted the necessary constituents of the crime (other than "unlawfulness") but went on to assert other facts which, he alleged, made his act lawful. Whether his act was lawful depended on what were the constituents of the defence which he raised; and the case decides that the defence, like duress and self-defence, required the assertion not merely of external facts but also of a state of mind. A doctrine of *actus reus* which says that such a course *must* be wrong, as contravening a fundamental principle, is much too constricting. Whether the defence should consist simply in the external facts, or in the facts plus the state of

19. (1952) 36 Cr App Rep 184 at 191.
20 Below, p. 304.
   1. (1850) 2 Den 35; *cf. Tooley* (1709) 11 Mod Rep 242 at 251, per Holt CJ; and see Williams, CLGP, 23 et seq., and Burchell and Hunt 115.
   2. On this point, see below, p. 242.
   3. Supra.
   4. Supra.

mind, is a matter of policy; and it was a not unreasonable decision of policy to say that a man who deliberately shot another should be guilty of an offence unless he knew of circumstances justifying his conduct.

Dadson then, is perfectly reconcilable with *Deller*. It does not decide that a man can be convicted where there is no *actus reus*: there was an *actus reus* for D did unlawfully wound P. All that the case decided was that the defence to wounding, "I was arresting an escaping felon", was a defence which required a mental as well as a physical element and, the mental element lacking, the wounding was unlawful.[5]

The actual decision in *Dadson* appears to have been reversed by ss. 2 and 3 of the Criminal Law Act 1967. This is emphasised by the form of s. 24 (4) of the Police and Criminal Evidence Act 1984 ("PACE") which has now replaced s. 2 of the 1967 Act.[6] This subsection makes it clear that D may arrest P if P is in fact committing an arrestable offence, whether or not he has reasonable grounds for suspecting that P is doing so. Having reasonable grounds for suspecting that P is committing an offence is a separate and distinct justification. If D may arrest, he may use reasonable force to do so.[7]

Self-defence, however, is still governed by the common law. Suppose that D shoots at P with intent to murder him and kills him. It turns out that D did so in the nick of time because, quite unknown to D, P was about to shoot D dead. According to *Dadson*, D is guilty of murder and this seems entirely right. If he were not guilty of murder, it may be that he would be guilty of attempted murder under the Criminal Attempts Act 1981 (since, for this purpose he is to be treated as if the facts were as he believed them to be);[8] but what would a jury make of a direction that a man who has shot at another with intent to murder him and killed him is not guilty of murder but guilty of attempted murder? It would be absurd. It is, however, equally absurd to distinguish between force used in making an arrest or in the prevention of crime from force used in private defence for, frequently, the force is used for all these purposes simultaneously. The codification team thought there was much to be said in favour of the *Dadson* principle but considered themselves bound to codify the provisions of ss. 2 (then about to be confirmed and emphasised by the Police and Criminal Evidence Act 1984) and 3 of the 1967 Act. In the interests of consistency it was thought necessary to exclude the *Dadson* principle generally.[9] It is submitted, however, that a better provision would be one which made *Dadson* generally applicable.

5. Below, p. 245. For a defence of *Dadson*, see Hall, *General Principles*, 228 and Perkins, *Criminal Law*, 39. And cf. the crime of perjury, below, p. 740, where D may be convicted if he makes a statement on oath which he believes to be false though it is in fact true.

6. Below, p. 245.

7. The codification team accepted, reluctantly, that *Dadson* has been reversed: Law Com. No. 143, 13.35–13.36.

8. See Williams, CLGP, s. 12, (1982) 2 LS 233, 252. This does not apply to force used to effect an arrest. If s. 24 (4) of PACE authorises the arrest and s. 3 of the Criminal Law Act 1967 the use of force to effect it, that statutory authority would seem to rule out a conviction for an attempt, no less than a conviction for a completed offence.

9. See cl. 47.

3 Analysis of an Actus Reus

Some writers have suggested that "an act" is nothing more than a willed muscular movement – for example, the deliberate crooking of a finger. But if D crooked his finger around the trigger of a loaded pistol which was pointing at P, with the result that P was killed, to say "D crooked his finger" would be a most misleading way of describing D's "act". "Again, suppose a person orally demands money by threats of injury. Can the action of his vocal chords be separated from the resulting sound issuing from his mouth and its intended meaning to the hearer?"[10] We naturally say, "D shot P" or "D demanded money from P". This way of describing the act takes account of the circumstances surrounding the actual movement of the body (in so far as they are relevant) and its consequences (again, in so far as they are relevant), and, for ordinary purposes, it is obviously the sensible way of describing it. But for the purposes of the criminal law it is sometimes necessary to break down an "act", so comprehensively described, into the constituents of (i) the conduct which is the central feature of the crime, (ii) the surrounding material circumstances, and (iii) the consequences. One reason for so doing will soon appear. When we consider *mens rea* we will see that the law's requirements as to the mental state which must be proved are not necessarily the same for each of the different elements in the *actus reus*. To take a crime where the cases show this to be so,[11] s. 20 of the Sexual Offences Act 1956, provides:

"It is an offence for a person acting without lawful authority or excuse to take an unmarried girl under the age of sixteen out of the possession of her parent or guardian against his will."

Here the conduct which is the central feature of the crime is the physical act of taking away the girl. The material circumstances are:

a) the absence of lawful authority or excuse;
b) that the girl was unmarried and under sixteen;
c) that she was in the possession of her parent or guardian.

The material consequence is the removal of the girl from the possession of the parent.[12]

If any one of the circumstances is not present or the consequence does not occur the crime is not committed. Thus if D was acting under the order of a competent court; or if P was married,[13] or seventeen; or if she was not in the possession of any parent or guardian, in none of these cases would there be an *actus reus*.

4 The Conduct must be Willed

If the *actus reus* of the crime includes an act, it must of course be proved that D did that act. Suppose the act is "wounding" and the evidence shows that, while D was holding a knife in his hand, E seized D's hand and,

---

10. *Timbu Kolian v R* (1968) 119 CLR 47 at 69, per Windeyer J. D's act was demanding with menaces.
11. See below, pp. 41, 454.
12. Williams argues that this is not a consequence and that the offence is not a "result crime" but a "conduct crime" (above, p. 33) ([1983] Crim LR "The Problem of Reckless Attempts") but is not the removal of the girl from the father's possession as much a result as killing or wounding? See above, p. 33.
13. If under sixteen, she could be validly married if domiciled abroad at the time of the marriage. See *Mohamed v Knott* [1969] 1 QB 1, [1968] 2 All ER 563.

against D's will, plunged the knife still held by D's hand into P. Plainly D is not guilty of wounding because it was not his act. Similarly D would not be guilty of a battery if he was afflicted by St. Vitus' dance and his fist shot out in an uncontrolled spasm and struck P; or if D, startled by an unexpected explosion, dropped a weight, which he was carrying carefully, on to P's foot. If D, while driving, is attacked by a swarm of bees and disabled from controlling the vehicle, he may be held to be no longer "driving".[14] In each of these cases the movement of D's limbs was involuntary in that it did not flow from an exercise by D of his will. The event happened either against or at least without his will. In these examples, D was conscious. If he is unconscious, he cannot exercise his will, so any movements of his body are involuntary. So D was acquitted of murder where he killed a girl, according to his story (which the jury must have found might reasonably be true), in his sleep;[15] and again where he killed his wife while experiencing a condition known as "night terror".[16] Similarly D would not be liable for any "acts" done while unconscious through concussion[17] or a hypoglycaemic episode.[18]

There is one exception to the rule requiring proof that a relevant act was voluntary. Where the "act" was done while in a state of intoxication self-induced by taking alcohol or a drug (other than a merely soporific or sedative drug[19]) it will, apparently, be no defence to crimes not requiring a "specific intent", that D was unconscious or otherwise "acting" involuntarily.[20] It has been argued[1] that this is part of a wider rule that automatism induced by D's "fault" is no defence in these cases. "Fault" means doing or omitting to do something which could reasonably be foreseen to be likely to bring about such a state. There is, however, no case which does not involve the use or misuse of drink or drugs and it is thought that this anomalous rule is properly confined to such cases, the basis for it being the grave social danger seen to be presented by intoxicated persons. A diabetic who fails to take sufficient food after a normal dose of insulin may rely on consequent automatism as a defence to a charge of a crime of basic intent, unless he was actually aware of the risk of becoming aggressive, unpredictable and uncontrolled.[2] So too may a person whose condition was due to taking valium (a soporific or sedative drug) even though not on medical prescription.[3] Of course, if the "fault" is in itself sufficient to found liability for the offence charged, then the defendant is properly convicted of it under ordinary principles.[4] An elementary example is where a driver, feeling

---

14. *Hill v Baxter* [1958] 1 QB 277 at 286.
15. *Boshears* (1961) Times, 8 February. Cf. *Cogdon*, discussed in Morris and Howard, 62–64; *Fraser* (1878) 4 Coup 70 discussed by Gordon, 67.
16. *Kemp* (1986) The Times, 3 May.
17. *Scott* [1967] VR 276.
18. *Watmore v Jenkins* [1962] 2 QB 572, [1962] 2 All ER 868. The defence failed on the facts.
19. *Hardie* [1984] 3 All ER 848, [1985] 1 WLR 64, **SHC 98**, CA.
20. *Lipman* [1970] 1 QB 152, [1969] 3 All ER 410; **SHC 95**; approved in *Director of Public Prosecutions v Majewski* [1977] AC 443, [1976] 2 All ER 142. See below, p. 211.
1. McKay, "Intoxication as a Factor in Automatism", [1982] Crim LR 146, 147.
2. *Bailey* [1983] 2 All ER 503; [1983] 1 WLR 760 below, p. 216.
3. *Hardie*, supra.
4. The dictum of Martin JA in *Rabey* (1978) 79 DLR (3d) 414, 425 quoted by Mackay as a "typical example of a dictum in support of 'fault liability' ", op. cit. 147, fn. 11 seems to be saying no more than this.

sleepy, continues to drive until he falls asleep and has an accident. His failure to stop may constitute the fault necessary to convict him of careless, or even reckless, driving.[5]

Writers dispute whether the voluntariness of D's conduct should be regarded as part of the *actus reus* or as part of the *mens rea*.[6] On the one hand, it is a mental element; on the other, it is said that it is an essential constituent of the act, which is part of the *actus reus*. It has been argued that the classification is important. The argument runs: some offences, known as offences of strict liability, do not require *mens rea*; so that, if voluntariness is part of the *mens rea*, a man charged with an offence of strict liability might be convicted for an involuntary act. But an *actus reus* must be proved, even for an offence of strict liability; so if voluntariness is part of the *actus reus*, no one can be convicted of any crime if his act was involuntary. As the latter result is thought to be not only desirable but to represent the law, voluntariness can only properly be regarded as an element in the *actus reus*. The fallacy in this argument lies in the proposition that offences of strict liability require "no *mens rea*" and the assumption that this means that the whole of the mental element involved in *mens rea* may be lacking.[7] This is not so. If the mental element is part of the *actus reus*, there is certainly no way of dispensing with it;[8] but it does not follow that it must be dispensed with where an offence is held to be one of strict liability.

The leading case on strict liability, *Prince*,[9] decides that D may be convicted of the offence under s. 20 of the Sexual Offences Act 1956 although he believes in good faith and on reasonable grounds that the girl he is taking is over sixteen. We commonly say that no *mens rea* need be proved because the act which D *intends* – to take an eighteen year old girl out of the possession of her parents – is not prohibited by law – it is not an *actus reus*. But although this is an offence "requiring no *mens rea*" it is quite clear that it involves a substantial mental element, apart from the element of voluntariness. D must be proved to have intended to take a girl out of the possession of her parents. If he thought the girl was in no one's possession, he is not guilty. If he thought the girl was a boy, he is probably not guilty. No one suggests, however, that we should say that his knowledge that the girl is in the possession of her parents is part of the *actus reus*. The fact is that even in offences of strict liability, a limited degree of *mens rea* must be proved; and a jurist may, if he chooses, classify the voluntariness of the accused's act as part of the limited degree of *mens rea*. It is a matter of convenience only.

What is clear is that the voluntariness of an act is a more fundamental element of criminal liability than the intention to cause, or foresight of, results of the act which we normally think of as *mens rea*. It is a defence,

---

5. *Kay v Butterworth* (1945) 173 LT 191, below, p. 44.
6. Turner (MACL 195 and 199 and Kenny, *Outlines*, 23) thought "voluntariness" an element of *mens rea*. Williams, CLGP, s. 8 and I. Patient, [1968] Crim LR 23 think it part of the *actus reus*.
7. Cf. Howard, SR 1; R. S. Clark, *NZ Essays* at 49; Packer, 126.
8. Above, p. 36.
9. (1875) LR 2 CCR 154; **SHC 102**.

known as "automatism", that this element has not been proved by the Crown.

"What is missing in these cases appears to most people as a vital link between mind and body; and both the ordinary man and the lawyer might well insist on this by saying that in these cases there is not 'really' a human action at all and certainly nothing for which anyone should be made criminally responsible however 'strict' legal responsibility might be."[10]

Where the alleged automatism arises from a "disease of the mind", the defence is one of insanity and the onus of proof is on the accused. Where it arises from some cause other than a disease of the mind, the onus of proof is on the Crown.[11] What is a disease of the mind is a question of law. So in *Kemp*[12] where D alleged that he acted involuntarily because he suffered from arteriosclerosis which cut off the supply of blood to his brain, Devlin J held that he had set up the defence of insanity. But in *Charlson*,[13] Barry J treated an allegation of automatism arising from a cerebral tumour as a defence to be disproved beyond reasonable doubt by the Crown. The cases appear irreconcilable and it seems that *Kemp* is to be preferred. Automatism arising from psychomotor epilepsy is insanity.[14] On the other hand, acts done while sleeping, sleepwalking, in a hypoglycaemic episode[15] or under concussion[16] have been regarded as non-insane automatism. In *Quick*[17] Lawton LJ said of "disease of the mind":

". . . the fundamental concept is a malfunctioning of the mind caused by disease. A malfunctioning of the mind of transitory effect caused by the application to the body of some external factor such as violence, drugs, including anaesthetics, alcohol and hypnotic influences cannot fairly be said to be due to disease."

In that case the condition of D, a diabetic, was due to excess of insulin in the bloodstream. The taking of the insulin was "an external factor", so he was not suffering from a disease of the mind. It would apparently have been otherwise if his condition had arisen, not from the insulin, but from his diabetes.

Where the incapacity alleged by D is, in law, non-insane automatism, he bears only an evidential burden. He must lay a proper foundation for the defence by introducing evidence from which it may reasonably be inferred that the act was involuntary. Whether such a foundation has been laid is a

---

10. Hart, *Jubilee Lectures*, at 137. Note that Turner, while regarding voluntariness as *mens rea*, thought it a different and more fundamental element than foresight of consequences; MACL 195–205.

11. It appears that in Scotland the courts have now rejected a separate defence of non-insane automatism: *HM Advocate v Cunningham* 1963 JC 80, discussed by Gordon, 71, 80–81. "Any mental or pathological condition short of insanity . . . is relevant only to the question of mitigating circumstances": per Lord Clyde at 83–84.

12. [1957] 1 QB 399, [1956] 3 All ER 249, below, p. 187.

13. [1955] 1 All ER 859, [1955] 1 WLR 317.

14. *Bratty v A–G for Northern Ireland* [1963] AC 386, [1961] 3 All ER 523; **SHC 196**; *Sullivan* [1984] AC 156, [1983] 2 All ER 673, **SHC 199**, HL.

15. *Watmore v Jenkins* [1962] 2 QB 572, [1962] 2 All ER 868. *Quick* (infra). *Bailey* [1983] 2 All ER 503, [1983] 1 WLR 760.

16. *Scott* [1967] VR 276.

17. [1973] QB 910 at 922, [1973] 3 All ER 347 at 356; **SHC 193**.

question of law. Lord Denning has said that the accused's own word will rarely be sufficient,[18] unless it is supported by medical evidence. Once a proper foundation has been laid, the jury must be directed not to convict unless satisfied beyond reasonable doubt that the act was voluntary. The difficult questions which arise where there is evidence that the automatism was caused partly by disease of the mind and partly by other factors are considered below.[19]

Automatism has narrow limits as a defence. It is to be confined, according to Lord Denning,[20] to acts done while unconscious and to spasms, reflex actions and convulsions. In *Broome v Perkins*[1] D was held guilty of driving without due care and attention, though in a hypoglycaemic state, because from time to time he apparently exercised conscious control over his car, veering away from other vehicles so as to avoid a collision, braking violently, and so on. The common law never recognised "irresistible impulse" as a defence even where it arose from insanity. A fortiori, it would not be recognised in the case of a sane person. The fact that, as a result of hysterical amnesia or hysterical fugue, D was unaware of "legal restrictions or moral concern", is no defence if he knew the facts which constitute the offence charged.[2] An irresistible craving for drink is not a defence to a charge of stealing alcohol.[3] If D has punched P it is no defence (though it may mitigate the sentence) to say that this was an immediate and irresistible reaction to provocation by P. But the borderline between this and a "reflex action" must be a fine one. The nature and effect of a reflex action is itself uncertain. In *Ryan v R*,[4] D with one hand pointed a loaded shotgun at P whom he had robbed, while with the other hand he attempted to tie P up. P moved. D was startled and, he said, "involuntarily" pressed the trigger because of a "reflex action". Barwick CJ thought that, if this story had been true, D would not have been responsible in law for the "act" of pressing the trigger; but Windeyer J held that, while that act may have been "involuntary" in a dictionary sense, it was one for which he was responsible in law and not properly analogous to an act done in convulsions or an epileptic seizure. With respect, however, it seems closer to these than to "the sudden movement of a tennis player retrieving a difficult shot; not accompanied by conscious planning but certainly not involuntary".[5]

It is of course very important to identify the precise act for which D is to be held responsible. In *Ryan v R* the pointing of the loaded gun and the

---

18. In *Dervish* [1968] Crim LR 37, *Cook v Atchison* [1968] Crim LR 266 and *Stripp* (1978) 69 Cr App Rep 318, CA it was held that D's evidence that he had a "blackout" was insufficient to raise the defence; but D's own evidence is enough to raise the defence of provocation: *Whitfield* (1976) 63 Cr App Rep 39, CA.
19. P. 190.
20. In *Bratty* [1963] AC 386, [1961] 3 All ER 523 at 532. It is confined to "involuntary movement of the body or limbs of a person": *Watmore v Jenkins*, above, at 586, per Winn J. In a Canadian case, *Racimore* (1976) 25 CCC (2d) 143 a "failure to remain" after an accident was held to be involuntary because D did not know there had been an accident. This seems to be an unsatisfactory device for introducing a requirement of *mens rea* into an offence of strict liability. Cf. *Davey v Towle* [1973] RTR 328.
1. [1987] Crim LR 271, DC.
2. *Isitt* [1978] Crim LR 159, CA.
3. *Dodd* (1974) 7 SASR 151 at 157.
4. (1967) 40 ALJR 488, discussed by I. D. Elliott 41 ALJ 497.
5. Elliott, loc. cit.

placing of the finger on the trigger were clearly voluntary acts and, provided that it could be said that these acts caused death, the accused would be liable for homicide, whether the pressing of the trigger was an act for which he was responsible or not. Similarly in the English civil case of *Gray v Barr*[6] D approached P with a loaded gun and fired a shot to frighten P. D and P grappled together and P fell on the gun and was shot and killed. The trial judge and Salmon LJ thought that the real cause of P's death was the accident of his falling on the gun; whereas Denning MR and Phillimore LJ thought that the cause was D's deliberate act in approaching P with the gun. All the judges agreed, however, that D could properly have been convicted of manslaughter on these facts. The act for which D would be held responsible was not the firing of the fatal shot which was not his act but deliberately approaching P in that threatening way. Again, a man may be immune from liability for an offence involving "driving", though he is sitting at the controls of a moving vehicle, if he is unconscious through an epileptic fit; but, depending on the degree and frequency of epilepsy and the probability that he might have an attack, he might be liable through the conscious act of starting or continuing to drive.[7]

Involuntariness not arising from Automatism
A person may have full control over his body but no control over events in which it is involved. A driver's brakes fail without his fault and, consequently, he inevitably fails to accord precedence to a pedestrian on a pedestrian crossing.[8] Although it is said that this offence is absolute[9] requiring no evidence of negligence, it was held in *Burns v Bidder*[10] that such a driver has a defence. The court equated the driver's situation with that of one stunned by a swarm of bees, disabled by epilepsy,[11] or propelled by a vehicle hitting his car from behind.[12] "Voluntariness" is essential even in so-called crimes of "absolute liability".[13] On the other hand, it seems to have been held that it is no defence that the failure to accord precedence arises inevitably from the unforeseeable behaviour of the pedestrian,[14] but the driver in such a case has no more power to avert the failure than where his brakes fail. It is submitted that D should never be held criminally liable for an "act" or result of an act over which he has no control.

---

6. [1971] 2 QB 554, [1971] 2 All ER 949; below, p. 346. Cf. *Jarmain* [1946] KB 74, [1945] 2 All ER 613; *Blayney v Knight* (1975) 60 Cr App Rep 269, DC.
7. *Hill v Baxter* [1958] 1 QB 277 at 286, [1958] 1 All ER 193 at 197, per Pearson LJ; *McBride* [1962] 2 QB 167, [1961] 3 All ER 6. Similarly where D goes to sleep: *Kay v Butterworth* (1945) 173 LT 191.
8. Contrary to Reg. 4 of the Pedestrian Crossing Regulations 1954.
9. *Hughes v Hall* [1960] 2 All ER 504, [1960] 1 WLR 733.
10. [1967] 2 QB 227, [1966] 3 All ER 29. See the valuable discussion by Patient, loc. cit., above, p. 41, footnote 6.
11. But see now *Sullivan* [1984] AC 156, [1983] 1 All ER 577.
12. Cf. *Kensington Borough Council v Walters*, [1960] 1 QB 361, [1959] 3 All ER 652.
13. An alternative explanation is the existence of a general defence of "impossibility", below, p. 250.
14. *Neal v Reynolds* [1966] Crim LR 393. The case is only briefly reported and may be explained on another ground.

5 Causation

When the definition of an *actus reus* requires the occurrence of certain consequences it is necessary to prove that it was the conduct of the accused which caused those consequences to occur. In murder or manslaughter, for example, it is necessary to prove that the act of the accused caused the death. If the death came about solely through some other cause then the crime is not committed, even though all the other elements of the *actus reus* and the *mens rea* are present.

In *White*[15] it appeared that D put potassium cyanide into a drink called "nectar" with intent to murder his mother. She was found dead shortly afterwards with the glass, three parts filled, beside her. The medical evidence showed that she had died, not of poison, but of heart failure. D was acquitted of murder and convicted of an attempt to murder. Although the consequence which D intended occurred, he did not cause it to occur and there was no *actus reus* of murder. A less obvious example is *Hensler*.[16] There D wrote a begging letter to P, declaring that he was "a poor shipwrecked widow" and telling other lies. P, because he remembered something which had been told him previously, was not deceived but, nevertheless, sent five shillings. D was convicted of an *attempt* to obtain five shillings by false pretences. Once again the consequence which D intended (and which was[17] part of the *actus reus* of obtaining by false pretences) occurred but it was not D's false pretence which caused it to occur. It was as if a rogue, having tried unsuccessfully to break into a safe with an inadequate implement, were to be presented by the owner with the contents. The rogue would have got what he wanted, yet failed to bring about the *actus reus* of the crime.

Problems of causation have given rise to much difficulty and controversy in the law of tort and contract. These difficulties have been less commonly encountered in criminal cases. The reason probably is that a man will usually be held criminally liable only for such consequences of his conduct as he foresaw (or, in crimes of negligence, *ought* to have foreseen) to be likely to occur. The problem, in the criminal law, more usually takes the form of an investigation into what the accused foresaw (or ought to have foreseen) than an enquiry into problems of causation. If he foresaw (or ought to have foreseen) the harm as likely to occur, it is usually obvious that it is not too remote a consequence; if he did not foresee it (or, in crimes of negligence, there is no reason why he should have foreseen it), the problem of causation does not arise, for he has no *mens rea* (or is not negligent).

The problems of D's foresight, on the one hand, and of causation on the other are, however, distinct questions and both may have to be answered in a criminal case. The cases of *White* and *Hensler*, considered above, are both cases where D foresaw a consequence, and that consequence occurred, yet he did not cause it.

Since, however, the problem almost invariably arises in connection with cases of murder and manslaughter, detailed discussion of it is postponed to

15. [1910] 2 KB 124; **SHC 278**.
16. (1870) 11 Cox CC 570; below, p. 550.
17. As it now is of obtaining by deception: below, p. 549.

the chapters on homicide.[18] For the present it is sufficient to note the rule, which is almost invariable, that D should have caused the *actus reus*.[19]

6 A "State of Affairs" as an Actus Reus[20]

A crime may be so defined that it can be committed although there is no "act" in the sense considered above. There may be no necessity for any "willed muscular movement". Instead it may be enough if a specified "state of affairs" is proved to exist. These offences are sometimes called "status"[1] or "situation"[2] offences. Under the Road Traffic Act 1972, s. 5 (2), for example, any person who, when in charge of a motor vehicle on a road or other public place is unfit to drive through drink or drugs, commits an offence. One cannot take charge without consciously doing so, but it is not *taking* charge of the vehicle, or *becoming* unfit which is the offence, but simply *being* in charge and *being* unfit. So long as this state of affairs continues, the *actus reus* of the crime is committed. The *actus reus* may even be in process of being committed while D is sleeping peacefully,[3] for he may still be "in charge". A person commits an offence if, when not at his place of abode, he *has with him* any article for use in the course of or in connection with burglary, etc.[4] So long as he has the article with him, he is committing the offence. Of course, in both of these examples the accused will, almost invariably, have done the acts of taking charge, getting drunk, or taking up the article, but such acts seem, technically, to be no part of the crime.

This has led to extraordinary results in offences of "being found" in a particular situation. In *Larsonneur*[5] D was convicted under the Aliens Order 1920 in that she, "being an alien to whom leave to land in the United Kingdom has been refused" was found in the United Kingdom. She had been brought from Ireland into the United Kingdom against her will in the custody of the police. Notwithstanding the wide condemnation of that decision,[6] a similar result has been reached in respect of the offence under s. 12 of the Licensing Act 1872 of being found drunk in a highway. In *Winzar v Chief Constable of Kent*[7] D was taken to hospital on a stretcher but was found to be drunk and told to leave. When he was seen slumped on a seat in the corridor, the police were called and they took him to a police car stationed in the highway outside the hospital. He was convicted of being found drunk in the highway. The words, "found drunk", were held

18. See below, pp. 312 et seq.
19. For exceptions, see *Larsonneur* and *Winzar v Chief Constable of Kent*, below.
20. See Glazebrook, "Situational Liability" in *Reshaping the Criminal Law*, 108.
  1. Howard, SR Chapter 3.
  2. M. D. Cohen, 7 Israel Law Rev 186.
  3. *Duck v Peacock* [1949] 1 All ER 318; but see the defence provided by Road Traffic Act 1956, s. 9 (1) proviso, now re-enacted in Road Traffic Act 1972, s. 5 (3) and s. 6 (2), substituted by Transport Act 1981, Sch 8.
  4. Theft Act 1968, s. 25, below, p. 611.
  5. (1933) 24 Cr App Rep 74; **SHC 125**. Cf. *Walters* [1969] 1 QB 255, [1968] 3 All ER 863 (being an incorrigible rogue). See the criticism of *Larsonneur* by Howard, *Strict Responsibility*, 47. For a spirited but unconvincing defence of the case, see Lanham [1976] Crim LR 276.
  6. "The acme of strict injustice", Hall, GPCL 329, n. 14; Williams CLGP 11; Howard, *Strict Responsibility*, 47; Gordon, 287; Burchell & Hunt, 114.
  7. (1983) The Times, 28 March. Cf. *Palmer-Brown v Police* [1985] 1 NZLR 365, CA (D not "found" behaving in a particular way when behaviour occurred some time after encounter with constable).

to mean "perceived to be drunk". But "perceive" means "to become aware of" and it seems that the police became aware of D's condition in the hospital and not in the highway. Larsonneur and Winzar were convicted of offences the commission of which was in fact procured by the police; and this seems peculiarly offensive. These offences of "being found" are unusual[8] in that they require an act on the part of the finder but no act or *mens rea* of the defendant. Even "state of affairs" offences ought to require proof that D either caused the state of affairs or failed to terminate it when it was possible to do so.[9] Physical impossibility of compliance with the law should be a defence, at least where it is not proved that the impossibility arose through D's own fault.[10]

It has been held by the Privy Council that the offence of "remaining" in Singapore, having been prohibited from entering that republic, could not be committed by one who was ignorant of the prohibition.[10] It is implicit in the case that to "remain" because detained would not be an offence. It is true that "remaining" may be said to be D's act while "being found" is the act of another; but the substance of the two offences is the same. It was held[11] at common law that "being in possession" was an insufficient act to constitute the *actus reus* of a crime, but there are many cases where, by statute, mere possession is enough. Thus possession of dangerous drugs, explosive substances, firearms and forged bank-notes all constitute the *actus reus* of various crimes. "Being in possession" does not involve an act in the sense of a muscular movement at all, for a man may possess goods merely by knowingly[12] keeping them in his house. Possession which is initially lawful may become criminal because of a change of circumstances without any act by D,[13] but only after he has failed to divest himself of

8. But not unique. Being the parent of a child of compulsory school age is an offence under s. 39 (1) of the Education Act 1944 if the child fails to attend school regularly. It is unnecessary to prove any knowledge or neglect on the part of the parent: *Crump v Gilmore* [1970] Crim LR 28. See also the Oil in Navigable Waters Act 1955 which provides that the owner or master of a ship is liable if oil is discharged from a British ship in a prohibited sea area. Glazebrook, "Situational Liability" in *Reshaping the Criminal Law*, 108, contends that *Larsonneur* type liability is by no means unusual, pointing, inter alia, to the similarity, from the defendant's point of view, of vicarious liability (on which see below, p. 162).

9. Cf. *Burns v Nowell* (1880) 5 QBD 444 at 454 "... before a continuous act or proceeding, not originally unlawful, can be treated as unlawful by reason of the passing of an Act of Parliament, by which it is in terms made so, a reasonable time must be allowed for its discontinuance ..." Other jurisdictions have avoided the result in *Larsonneur*: *Achterdam* 1911 EDL 336 (Burchell & Hunt 105); *O'Sullivan v Fisher* [1954] SASR 33. In the United States, similar offences have been held unconstitutional; *Robinson v California*, 370 US 660, 8 L Ed 2d 758 (1962) (being addicted to the use of narcotics).

10. *Lim Chin Aik v R* [1963] AC 160, [1963] 1 All ER 223. See also *Finau v Department of Labour* [1984] 2 NZLR 396 (failure to leave New Zealand after revocation of permit not an offence where impossible to leave because of pregnancy). But cf. *Grant v Borg* [1982] 2 All ER 257, [1982] 1 WLR 638, HL, where an immigrant was held guilty of knowingly remaining beyond the time limited although, because of a mistake of law, he may have believed the time had been extended.

11. *Heath* (1810) Russ & Ry 184; *Dugdale v R* (1853) 1 E & B 435.

12. A man may possess a thing in the civil law although he does not know of its existence; but knowledge will usually be required in criminal law: cf. *Warner v Metropolitan Police Commissioner*, below, p. 107; *Cugullere* [1961] 2 All ER 343, [1972] 1 WLR 64; below, p. 427.

13. Cf. *Buswell* [1972] 1 All ER 75, [1961] 1 WLR 858.

possession within a reasonable time.[14] "Being in possession" is simply a state of affairs, which, in certain circumstances, involves criminal liability.

7 Omissions[15]

Liability for omissions is exceptional in English law. Stephen stated the general rule for offences against the person as follows:

"It is not a crime to cause death or bodily injury, even intentionally, by any omission. . . ."[16]

He gave the following famous illustration:

"A sees B drowning and is able to save him by holding out his hand. A abstains from doing so in order that B may be drowned, and B is drowned. A has committed no offence."

If this is the general rule for offences against the person, including murder, it must also, *a fortiori*, be the general rule for offences against property and the vast majority of offences. Of course, as Stephen went on to make clear, there are exceptional cases where the law imposes a duty to act.[17] If A, in the example, were B's parent, A would have a duty to act and would be guilty of murder. He would be regarded as having intentionally killed B. This is so even though he was in no sense responsible for B's being in the water in the first place. It is clear that this involves some extension of the notion of causation. Since *ex hypothesi*, A does nothing, B's death would have occurred in just the same way had A died or not come on the scene for any other reason. The cause of B's death was falling into the water in the first place. If A, the parent, and C, a stranger, had walked by together, it is impossible to say as a matter of fact that A has caused the death but C has not. In law, however, as the draft criminal code puts it: "A person causes a result when . . . in breach of duty, he fails to do what he might do to prevent it occurring."[18]

There are two difficulties. The first is to decide whether the offence is capable of being committed by an omission. If it is, the second question is whether the particular defendant had a duty to act. Glanville Williams has written:

"In my opinion the courts should not create liability for omissions without statutory authority. Verbs used in defining offences and prima facie implying active conduct should not be stretched by interpretation to include omissions. In general the courts follow this principle. They do not say, for instance, that a person 'wounds' another by failing to save him from being wounded, or 'damages' a building by failing to stop a fire. At least, this has never been decided."[19]

Yet many of the cases involving liability for omissions concern homicide – usually manslaughter – so the law has had no difficulty in holding that a

14. *Burns v Nowell*, above, footnote 9. *Levine* [1927] 1 DLR 740 is contrary but *Burns v Nowell* is followed in South Africa: Burchell & Hunt 264.
15. Glazebrook (1960) 76 LQR 386; Graham Hughes (1958) 67 YLJ 590.
16. *Digest of the Criminal Law* (4th ed., 1887), Art. 212.
17. For a different view, see Hogan, "Omission and the Duty Myth" in *Criminal Law Essays*, 85.
18. Law Com. No. 143, cl. 21. See Glanville Williams, "What should the Code do about Omissions ?", (1987) 7 LS 92.
19. [1982] Crim LR 773.

person may "kill" by omission. Since murder and manslaughter are common law offences, this has not required the interpretation of a particular verb in a section of a statute. Homicide can equally well be described as "causing death" – but, as we have seen, the imposition of liability for omission involves giving an extended meaning to "causing" no less than "killing". Assault, like homicide, is a concept of the common law, yet it has been assumed that assault requires an act.[20] But this assumption has been challenged.[1]

In a statutory offence, the question is one of construction. Under s. 1 (3) of the Protection from Eviction Act 1977,[2] a person commits an offence if he "does acts" calculated to interfere with the peace or comfort of a residential occupier with intent to cause him to give up occupation of the premises. In *Ahmad*[3] it was held that a landlord who, without any such intent, had done acts calculated (i.e. likely) to interfere with the peace and comfort of his tenant was not guilty of the offences when he omitted to rectify the situation with intent to cause P to give up occupation. A statute creating a new offence was to be strictly construed and "does acts" was not satisfied by an omission.[4] But "does acts" is a strong expression and it does not follow that words like "destroy" or "damage" should not be construed to include destruction or damage by omission in breach of duty.

Under the Highways Act it has been held that D is guilty of wilfully obstructing the highway when his wall falls into the highway, creating an obstruction, and, after being given notice to do so, he wilfully omits to remove it.[5] Similarly, omission to obey instructions from the police may, in certain circumstances, amount to obstructing a constable in the execution of his duty.[6] Totally passive submission to an act done by a child has been held to amount to the commission of "an act of gross indecency with or towards a child ...".[7] Common law offences are still more flexible. The offence of misconduct in a public office may be committed by a police officer's failure to take reasonable steps to assist the victim of a serious assault.[8] The common law offence of cheating the revenue may be committed by a mere omission in breach of a statutory duty.[9]

Most cases of homicide by omission have resulted in convictions for manslaughter but there is one case of murder. In *Gibbins and Proctor*[10] a man and the woman with whom he was living were convicted of murder of the man's child by withholding food. By living with the man and receiving money from him for food the woman had assumed a duty towards the child.

20. *Fagan v Metropolitan Police Commissioner* [1969] 1 QB 439, [1968] 3 All ER 442.
1. Smith (1984) 4 LS 88, 97.
2. Below, p. 813.
3. (1986) 84 Cr App Rep 64, [1986] Crim LR 739, CA.
4. Yet in *Yuthiwattana* (1984) 80 Cr App Rep 55 at 61 it was held that the landlord's refusal to replace the tenant's lost key was capable of being "an act 'calculated to interfere ...' ". The argument, however, was about whether "the act" had to be a breach of contract and the question whether it was an "act" at all may have been lost sight of.
5. *Gully v Smith* (1883) 12 QBD 121.
6. See particularly *Stunt v Bolton* [1972] RTR 435 and cases discussed below, p. 394.
7. *Speck* [1977] 2 All ER 859.
8. *Dytham* [1979] QB 722, [1979] 3 All ER 641.
9. *Mavji* [1987] 2 All ER 758, [1987] 1 WLR 1388, 84 Cr App Rep 34.
10. (1918) 13 Cr App Rep 134, CCA.

The judge was held to have rightly directed that they were guilty of murder if they withheld food with intent to cause her grievous bodily harm, as a result of which she died. If the child had sustained grievous bodily harm but not died, it is difficult to suppose that the court would not have held the defendants guilty of an offence under s. 18 of the Offences against the Person Act 1861.[11] The commission of this offence seems to have been an essential constituent of the defendant's liability, as the case was left to the jury. It would seem strange that causing death should be capable of commission by omission and causing grievous bodily harm not. It would mean that D was not in breach of a duty to act until death occurred when the duty was retrospectively imposed. That is surely unacceptable.

The CLRC recommended that liability for omissions in offences against the person should be confined to murder, manslaughter, and their proposed offences of causing serious injury with intent, unlawful detention, kidnapping, abduction and aggravated abduction.[12] It is not certain how far this is the actual law in relation to the corresponding offences as they now exist. If it is the law, causing injury which is not serious, wounding, and assault are offences incapable of commission by omission. The codification team, being obliged to accept the CLRC's recommendations, concluded that, if injury to the person was to be incapable of commission by omission, so, a fortiori, should be damage to property. This leads to the following illustration:

"20(v) D is employed as a night watchman at a factory. His duties are to take all reasonable steps to ensure the safety of the building. D sees that a small fire has broken out. There is an adjacent bucket of sand with which, as he knows, he could easily put out the fire. Having a grievance against his employer, he walks away and lets the fire burn. The factory is destroyed. He is not guilty of arson."

Such a conclusion may be unacceptable to the courts. If so, the remedy is in their hands. "Destroy" and "damage" in the Criminal Damage Act 1971[13] are capable of being construed to include omissions.

Who owes a duty? Given that the offence is capable of being committed by omission, the next question is, who may be under a duty to act? Since most cases of omission have concerned homicide, the duties so far recognised[14] are duties to preserve life. Parents owe such a duty to their children. Presumably children above the age of responsibility owe a corresponding duty to their parents.[15] Other close relationships, whether of a family, domestic, business, or other nature, possibly impose similar duties. A person who has undertaken to care for a helpless and infirm relative[16] who has become dependent on him may be held to owe a duty, particularly where he is to receive some reward for caring for the other.[17] This category

11. Below, p. 397.
12. Fourteenth Report, paras 252–255.
13. Below, p. 677.
14. Other than in cases of "supervening fault", below, p. 53.
15. E.g., a muscular fourteen year old leaves his fainting mother to drown in the notorious shallow pool.
16. *Marriott* (1838) 8 C & P 425; *Nicholls* (1874) 13 Cox CC 75 (D was P's grandmother).
17. *Instan* [1893] 1 QB 450 (D was P's niece, living in P's house, consuming food provided at P's expense and not supplying any to P); *Stone and Dobinson* [1977] QB 354, [1977] 2 All ER 341; **SHC 343**, below, p. 345.

might well be extended to an unrelated person. Persons who jointly engage in a hazardous activity whether lawful – like mountaineering – or unlawful – like drug abuse[18] – may also owe duties to one another, though there is no authority to that effect. The holder of a public office requiring him to care for others may incur criminal liability by failing to do so.

A contractual duty may found a duty under criminal law to persons not party to the contract but likely to be injured by failure to perform it.

In *Pittwood*[19] a railway crossing gate-keeper opened the gate to let a cart pass and went off to his lunch, forgetting to shut it again. Ten minutes later a haycart while crossing the line was struck by a train. D was convicted of manslaughter. It was argued on his behalf that he owed a duty of care only to his employers, the railway company, with whom he contracted. Wright J held, however, that

"there was gross and criminal negligence, as the man was paid to keep the gate shut and protect the public ... A man might incur criminal liability from a duty arising out of contract".[20]

It is not always easy to distinguish between an act and an omission. If a doctor is keeping a patient alive by cranking the handle of a machine and he stops, this looks like a clear case of omission. So too if the machine is electrically operated but switches itself off every 24 hours and the doctor deliberately does not re-start it. Switching off a functioning machine looks like an act; but is it any different in substance from the first two cases?[1] On the other hand, is it any different from cutting the high-wire on which a tight-rope walker is balancing?[2] – which is an act, if ever there was one. Is the ending of a programme of dialysis an omission, while switching off a ventilator is an act? Is the discontinuance of a drip feed, which is keeping a patient alive, by withdrawing the tube from his body an act?[3] and failure to replace an emptied bag an omission? It seems offensive if liability for homicide depends on distinctions of this kind; but it appears to be so.

The doctor is, no doubt, under a duty to make reasonable efforts, in the light of customary medical practice and all other relevant factors, to keep the patient alive.[4] Unfortunately, this does not solve the problem because the content of any duty there may be to keep alive is different from that of the duty not to kill. There is no doubt that parents have a duty to their children; yet, where parents refuse their consent to an operation on a new-born baby, suffering from Down's Syndrome, knowing that without the

---

18. The point was not decided in *Dalby* [1982] 1 All ER 916 [1982] 1 WLR 425. Cf. *People v Beardsley* (1967) 113 NW 1128.
19. (1902) 19 TLR 37.
20. Wright J said that this was not a mere case of nonfeasance, but of misfeasance. However D's breach of duty was not in opening the gate, but in omitting to close it again. Cf., however, *Smith* (1869) 11 Cox CC 210, where on similar facts Lush J ruled that there was no duty. Beynon [1982] Crim LR at 22 suggests that opening and not shutting might be regarded as one "act"; but would it really have been different if the gate had been opened by D's colleague who had just gone off duty? One hopes not.
1. Examples put by Williams [1977] Crim LR 443–452. See also TBCL, 236–237.
2. Kennedy [1977] Crim LR 443 at 452. See the discussion by Helen Beynon [1982] Crim LR 17.
3. Beynon, op. cit.
4. Williams, TBCL, 236.

operation it will die, they are not necessarily guilty of a criminal homicide if death ensues. If it were an offence, it would (in the absence of diminished responsibility) be murder because the parents intend the death of the child. In *Re B (A minor)*,[5] when the parents refused their consent, the child was made a ward of court, and the court gave consent as being in the interests of the child. Dunn LJ said that the decision of the parents to allow the child to die was one which everyone accepted as "entirely responsible". It was a decision, it seems, that the parents could lawfully take, so that the death of the child, if it had followed, would not have been an *actus reus*. Indeed, Templeman LJ thought there might possibly be cases "where the future is so certain and where the life of the child is bound to be full of pain and suffering that the court might be driven to a different conclusion" – i.e., to allow the child to die. Yet there is no doubt that if the parents – or anyone – did any positive act to kill the child, they would be guilty of murder. The undoubted duty of parents to preserve the life of their child is different from, and more restricted than, their duty not to kill it.

In *Arthur*,[6] a doctor, having noted that the parents of a Down's Syndrome child did not wish the child to survive, ordered "Nursing care only" and the administration of a drug, allegedly to stop the child seeking sustenance. At the trial of the doctor for attempted murder, Farquharson J directed the jury that it was for them to decide whether "there was an act properly so-called on the part of Dr Arthur, as distinct from simply allowing the child to die". Simply allowing the child to die would apparently have been lawful,[7] and withholding food was, according to the medical evidence put by the judge to the jury, "a negative act" – a mere omission. It is submitted that a better view is that an omission to provide such a child with food and the ordinary necessities of life ought to be equated with an act causing death rather than with an omission to perform an operation or to take some other extraordinary action. The position seems to be the same with a helpless, elderly person, incapable of taking decisions. It may be lawful for his family and the doctor to decide that an operation which would prolong a useless and painful life should not be performed; but it surely cannot be lawful to starve him to death, whether with the assistance of drugs or not.

Termination of a duty. When the duty arises out of a particular relationship, it will terminate when the relationship ends, as when an employee leaves the service of his employer. It is less clear, when, if ever, the duty of a parent to a child ends. In the case of a normal child it may well be on the attainment of the child's majority, but this could hardly be so in the case of a handicapped and dependent child. In the case of dependent persons generally, one who has undertaken the duty can probably divest himself of it only by passing it on to some responsible authority or other person.

---

5. [1981] 1 WLR 1421, CA.
6. (1981) Unreported, discussed by Gunn and Smith [1985] Crim LR 705.
7. It is submitted that nothing turned on the fact that the charge had been reduced from murder to attempted murder – see [1986] Crim LR 760–762 and Poole and Brahams [1986] Crim LR 383.

Supervening fault. Where D does an act which puts in peril P's person, his property, his liberty or any other interest protected by the criminal law and D is aware that he has created the peril, he has a duty to take reasonable steps to prevent the harm in question resulting. The act may be done without any kind of fault but, if D fails to intervene, it is undoubtedly his act which is the cause of the harm. For this reason the principle may apply to a wider range of offences than can be committed by simple omission. In *Miller,*[8] D, a squatter in P's house, went to sleep holding a lighted cigarette. He awoke to find the mattress smouldering. He did nothing to put it out but moved into an adjoining room and went to sleep there. The house caught fire. D was convicted of arson contrary to S. 1 (1) and (3) of the Criminal Damage Act 1971. The House of Lords held that the recorder had rightly directed the jury that, when D woke up, he was under a duty to take some action to put the fire out. Lord Diplock said:[9]

"I see no rational ground for excluding from conduct capable of giving rise to criminal liability conduct which consists of failing to take measures that lie within one's power to counteract a danger that one has oneself created, if at the time of such conduct one's state of mind is such as constitutes a necessary ingredient of the offence."

The Court of Appeal had upheld the conviction on a different basis:

"We would only say that an unintentional act followed by an intentional omission to rectify it or its consequences, or a reckless omission to do so when recklessness is a sufficient mens rea for the particular case, should only be regarded in toto as an intentional or reckless act when reality and common sense so require; this may well be a matter to be left to the jury. Further, in the relevant analysis we think that whether or not there is on the facts an element of adoption on the part of the alleged offender of what he has done earlier by what he deliberately or recklessly fails to do later is an important consideration."

The application of this "continuous act" theory would apparently have produced a different result in *Ahmad.*[10] If the appellant could be deemed to have acted intentionally (i.e., with intent to cause the residential occupier to give up occupation) when he rendered the flat uninhabitable, the difficulty of convicting him would have disappeared. This theory, however, involves an undesirable legal fiction. Fictions should have no place in the criminal law. Lord Diplock preferred the "duty" to the "continuous act" theory but only on the ground that the former is easier to explain to a jury. It is submitted, however, that they are different in substance as the example based on *Ahmad* shows.[11]

The *Miller* principle applies only to a result crime requiring fault where the act causing the result is done without that fault. Where the offence requires no fault, there is no room for its application. In *Wings Ltd v Ellis*[12] D Ltd, a tour operator, published a brochure which, unknown to D, contained misrepresentations. On discovering the truth, D did all they could to correct the errors but, subsequently, P read an uncorrected

8. [1983] 2 AC 161, [1983] 1 All ER 978. See [1982] Crim LR 527 and 773–774.
9. At p. 176, p. 981.
10. Above, p. 49.
11. See commentary [1982] Crim LR 527 and 773–774 and (1984) 4 LS 88 at 91.
12. [1984] 1 All ER 1046, [1984] 1 WLR 731. [1985] AC 272, [1984] 3 All ER 577, HL, revsd.

brochure and booked a holiday in reliance on it. D was convicted under the Trade Descriptions Act 1968, s. 14 (a), making a statement which they knew to be false and, s. 14 (b), recklessly making a false statement. The statement was "made" when it was read by P and, by then, D knew it was false. The Divisional Court, applying *Miller*, quashed both convictions. D had done all that could reasonably be expected to correct the false trade descriptions. The prosecutor appealed in respect of the offence under s. 14 (a) only. The appeal was allowed. Subject to a statutory defence which was not pleaded, the House held that s. 14 (a) created an "absolute" offence.[13] D knew the statement was false and no other fault was required. There was no room for the application of *Miller*. Though any reader would suppose that s. 14 (a) is the more serious offence, 14 (b) requires some element of fault, however "reckless" is interpreted, and Lord Hailsham thought that *Miller* might have been properly held applicable to that.[14]

Where the offence is one requiring fault, whether *mens rea* strictly so-called or negligence, it is submitted that the *Miller* principle is of general application.[15] If D, sitting alone in the passenger seat of a car, were accidentally to knock off the handbrake, so that the car ran away, it is submitted that he could be convicted of murder if he wilfully omitted to put the brake on again, intending the car to run over and kill P. D locks the door of a room, not knowing that P is inside. Having learned that P is within, he omits to unlock the door. Should he not be liable for false imprisonment?[16]

Statute has made omissions criminal in many cases. If, for example, owing to the presence of a motor vehicle on a road, an accident occurs, causing damage or injury to any person, vehicle, or animal, the driver of the vehicle is required to give his name and address to any person having reasonable grounds for requiring him to do so, or to report the accident to the police within twenty-four hours.[17] A person legally liable to maintain a child commits a crime if he fails to provide him with adequate food, clothing, medical aid or lodging.[18] Even handling stolen goods may be committed by omission.[19]

There are many provisions which make it illegal to do one thing unless some other thing is also done. Broadcasting a dramatic or musical performance without the consent of the performers,[20] driving a car without third-party insurance,[1] selling ice-cream in a public place without conspicuously displaying a notice of the vendor's name and address,[2] are examples. Such

13. See below, pp. 98, 120.
14. Lord Scarman thought the analogy with *Miller* "ingenious, if far-fetched" and (it is submitted unfairly) an "unhelpful and over-elaborate approach to the interpretation of an act intended to protect the public . . ."; pp. 590–591.
15. *Green v Cross* (1910) 103 LT 279 – D innocently caught a dog in a trap. Instead of releasing it he left it until it was freed two hours later by the police. Held, Channell J dissenting, that there was evidence on which he could be convicted of "cruelly ill-treating" the dog.
16. Andenaes, *GPCL of Norway*, 135; and see *Fagan v Metropolitan Police Commissioner* [1969] 1 QB 439, [1968] 3 All ER 442; below, p. 380.
17. Road Traffic Act 1972, s. 25.
18. Children and Young Persons Act 1933, s. 1 (2) (a).
19. *Brown* [1970] 1 QB 105, [1969] 3 All ER 198; *Pitchley* [1972] Crim LR 705.
20. Copyright Act 1956, Sixth Schedule, Part I, IB.
 1. Road Traffic Act 1972, s. 143.
 2. Food Act 1984, s. 27.

crimes are not purely offences of omission, for a positive act is part of the *actus reus*. The omission is an equally essential part, but the emphasis is obviously placed mainly on the positive element. The omission tends to be regarded as one of the surrounding circumstances: that is, not having obtained the performers' consent, it is criminal to broadcast the performance. Crimes with elements of both omission and commission do not then involve any special problem; it is those of mere omission which occasion difficulty.

2 Mens Rea[3]

It is a widely held view of legal historians that until the twelfth century a man might be held liable for many harms, simply because his conduct caused them, without proof of any blameworthy state of mind whatsoever on his part. Under the influence of Canon law and the Roman law, a change gradually took place and the courts began to require proof of an element of moral blameworthiness – "a guilty mind" of some kind. In the developed common law of crime, some such mental element is always necessary, and is known as *mens rea*.

1 Definition of Terms
Mens rea is a technical term. It is often loosely translated as "a guilty mind", but this translation is frequently misleading. A man may have *mens rea*, as it is generally understood today, without any feeling of guilt on his part. He may, indeed, be acting with a perfectly clear conscience, believing his act to be morally, and even legally, right, and yet be held to have *mens rea*. In order properly to appreciate the meaning of the term it is necessary to distinguish between a number of different possible mental attitudes which a man may have with respect to the *actus reus* of the crime in question. These are: (a) intention, (b) recklessness, (c) negligence and (d) blameless inadvertence.

a) *Intention*[4]
Numerous offences are defined so as to require proof of "intention" to cause specified results. It might be expected that the meaning of such a fundamental term would have been settled long ago but this is not so. The cases are inconsistent, judicial opinion has recently changed and there is still some measure of uncertainty. We may begin, however, with one well-settled proposition. Everyone agrees that a person intends to cause a result

3. Turner, "The Mental Element in Crimes at Common Law", MACL 195; Williams, *The Mental Element in Crime* and CLGP, in Ch. 2; Hart, "Negligence, *Mens rea* and Criminal Responsibility", in *Oxford Essays in Jurisprudence*, 29; Smith, "The Guilty Mind in the Criminal Law" (1960) 76 LQR 78; Ashworth, "Reason, Logic and Criminal Liability" (1975) 91 LQR 102. R. A. Duff, "Certifying Criminal Fault" in *Criminal Law and Justice*, 93; Williams, "Oblique Intention", (1987) CLJ 417.
4. Smith, "Intention in Criminal Law" (1974) 27 CLP 93; J. H. Buzzard, "Intent" [1978] Crim LR 5 and Smith, "A Reply" [1978] Crim LR 14.

if he acts with the purpose of doing so. If D has resolved to kill P and he fires a loaded gun at him with the object of doing so, he intends to kill. It is immaterial that he is aware that he is a poor shot, that P is nearly out of range, and that his chances of success are small. It is sufficient that killing is his object or purpose, that he wants to kill, that he acts in order to kill.

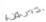

One view is that "intention" should be limited to that case – that a result should never be regarded as intended unless it was the actor's purpose, i.e. unless he acted in order to bring about the result. This is often considered to be the ordinary meaning given to the word by people generally. The courts have consistently given the word a wider meaning, sometimes described as "oblique" as distinct from "direct" intention.[5] Until recently, the predominant judicial view was that an actor intended a result if he knew that it was a highly probable (or perhaps merely probable) result of his act, although it was not his purpose or object to cause that result. In 1979 Lord Diplock said that the matter had been finally settled in this sense by the decision of the House of Lords in *Hyam v Director of Public Prosecutions*.[6] A majority of the House in *Hyam* was certainly of the opinion that this was the law but the actual decision was that foresight of high probability of serious bodily harm was a sufficient *mens rea* for murder, not that such a state of mind necessarily amounted to an intention to cause serious bodily harm. In *Moloney*,[7] however, the House held that the *mens rea* of murder is intention to cause death or serious bodily harm so it was essential to determine the meaning of "intention". *Moloney* must be read in the light of the explanation of it by the House in *Hancock and Shankland*[8] and by the Court of Appeal in *Nedrick*.[9] When it is so read it appears that:

1) A result is intended when it is the actor's purpose.
2) A court or jury may also infer that a result is intended, though it is not desired, when –
   (a) the result is a virtually certain consequence of the act, and
   (b) the actor knows that it is a virtually certain consequence.

Two criticisms. (i) The fact that the result was a virtually certain consequence of D's act is very good evidence that he knew that it was a virtually certain consequence; but it is difficult to see why it should be regarded as a necessary condition. If D thinks he knows that the result is virtually inevitable because he is making a mistake, why should he be held not to have intended it because it was not, in fact, inevitable? His state of mind is the same in either case. If D fires a gun pointed at P's heart, his intention can hardly be affected by the fact, unknown to D, that P is wearing a bullet-proof vest. The state of mind of a person who thinks he knows is the same as that of a person who actually knows. The difference is in the external circumstances.

5. Cf. Bentham, *Principles of Morals and Legislation* (Harrison ed., 207).
6. [1975] AC 55, [1974] 2 All ER 41, below, p. 59. See [1979] AC at 638.
7. [1985] AC 905, [1985] 1 All ER 1025.
8. [1986] AC 455. [1986] 1 All ER 641.
9. [1986] 3 All ER 1. [1986] 1 WLR 1025.

(ii) It is emphasised that D's knowledge that the act he is doing is virtually certain to cause the result is not intention to cause that result, but only evidence from which the court or jury may infer intention. "Intention" is, in the end, left undefined. What is this further state of mind which must be inferred? It is not desire that the result be caused because that is expressly ruled out; and that seems to leave nothing. Faced with such a direction, the jury can do no more than decide to call the defendant's awareness of virtual certainty "intention" if they think that, in all the circumstances of the case, he ought to be convicted of the offence charged; and not to call it intention if they think he ought to be acquitted. They are not instructed to *characterise* the state of mind as intention or not, as they think fit, but that appears to be all that they can do. If they ask the judge for further directions, what can he do but tell them this? – though he would, no doubt, wrap it up in the usual patter about intention being an ordinary word of the English language and its meaning a question for them.

Results known to be conditions of achievement of purpose. It may be said that no one can ever know that a result is certain to follow from an act. This is why courts and writers are driven to speak of "virtually" or "morally" or "almost" certain results. But a person may know that he cannot achieve his purpose, A, without bringing about some other result, B. If he is to bring about A, he knows he must also, at the same time or earlier, bring about B. It may be that, in any other circumstances, he would much rather B did not happen, indeed its occurrence may be abhorrent to him. But, the choice being between going without A and having A and B, he decides to have A and B. It seems fair to say that he intends to cause B as well as A. Suppose that P has made a will, leaving the whole of his large estate to D. D loves P but he has an overwhelming desire to enjoy his inheritance immediately. If he gives P what he knows to be a fatal dose of poison, he intends to kill P, though he says truthfully that it causes him anguish. D wishes to injure his enemy, Q, who is standing inside the window of the house of D's friend, P. If, knowing the window to be closed, he throws the stone through it at Q, can it be doubted that he intends to break his friend's window?

Since result A is the actor's purpose, it is immaterial that he is not certain that it will happen. He is not a good shot and he knows the stone may miss – but he intends to strike Q. And, since he knows that, if he strikes Q, it will be because he has broken P's window, he intends to break the window. It seems from these examples that we might safely say that a result known to be a condition of the achievement of the actor's purpose is intended.

Yet even this modest conclusion is not beyond doubt. In *Moloney*[10] Lord Bridge referred with approval to *Steane*[11] where D, who, during the second world war, gave broadcasts which would assist the enemy in order to save himself and his family from the horrors of the concentration camp, was held not to have had an "intent to assist the enemy". Steane may have been a loyal citizen who, in other circumstances, would have wished to do nothing to assist the enemy; but, being faced with the choice, "Assist us –

10. [1985] AC 905 at 929.
11. [1947] KB 997, [1947] 1 All ER 813.

or back to the concentration camp", he chose to assist the enemy. Of course, his purpose was to stay out of the camp; but it seems plain that he knew that his purpose could only be achieved by assisting the enemy. Reading the script was assisting the enemy.[12] In *Ahlers*,[13] a German consul who assisted German nationals to return home after the declaration of war in 1914 was held to have intended only to do his duty as consul. In *Sinnasamy Selvanayagam*[14] the Privy Council said, *obiter*, that if D remained in occupation of his home in defiance of a lawful order to quit, knowing that the owner of the property would be annoyed, his "dominant intention" was simply to retain his home and he was not guilty under the Ceylon Penal Code of remaining in occupation with intent to annoy the owner. In *Gillick*'s case[15] some of the judges seem to have been of the opinion that a doctor, who knew that his provision of contraceptive advice to a girl under sixteen would encourage a man to have sexual intercourse with her, would not be guilty of abetting the offence, because his intention was to protect the girl, not to encourage unlawful sexual intercourse with her.

In some of these cases, it seems that the concept of intention is strained to do a job for which it is not fitted. Steane's acquittal would more properly have been based on duress and the case envisaged in *Gillick* seems to have been, in substance, one of necessity – a minor encouragement of sexual intercourse was a lesser evil than an unwanted pregnancy in the young girl. In each of these cases, D had an honourable purpose. Where D's purpose is disreputable, the court is most unlikely to interpret intention so narrowly. If Steane, being a chain smoker deprived of cigarettes, had read the script in order to get a packet of Players, it is probable that Lord Goddard CJ would have had no hesitation in holding that, of course, he intended to assist the enemy. Yet, from the point of view of intention, there seems to be no difference between the cases.[16] If this is so, it produces an undesirable distortion of the concept of intention and it would be better if the true reason for the decision were articulated. *Moloney*, however, encourages such decisions – the jury appears to be left a measure of discretion to say whether they think the state of mind should be categorised as intention or not.

It is arguable that intention, in law, should extend to results known or believed by the actor to be conditions of the achievement of his purpose but should go no further. This would give effect to the constantly reiterated opinion of the courts that intention is different from desire. Result B is not

12. It might be argued that, even in these circumstances, B is not necessarily a condition of A. Someone might open the window while the stone is in flight towards it. The microphone into which Steane spoke might have been disconnected or the transmitter broken down. Lord Bridge's man who boards the plane for Manchester (the last place he wishes to go to) to escape arrest intends (as Lord Bridge says [1985] AC at 926) to go to Manchester although it is possible that the plane will be diverted to Luton. Even in the case of D who gives P the fatal dose of poison to accelerate his inheritance, it is possible that P will die of natural causes before the poison takes effect: cf. *White* [1910] 2 KB 124, CCA.
13. [1915] 1 KB 616.
14. [1951] AC 83.
15. *Gillick v West Norfolk and Wisbech Area Health Authority* [1986] AC 112, [1983] 3 All ER 402, [1986] Crim LR 113 HL and commentary. See also *Salford Health Authority, ex p Janaway* (1988) Times, 5 January, CA (Civ. Div.).
16. Glanville Williams, *The Mental Element in Crime*, 21.

desired, at least it is not desired for its own sake; but it is intended. And any overlap with recklessness is avoided. D is not merely taking a risk of causing B; he *knows* or thinks he knows that, if he achieves his aim of causing A, B will happen or have already happened.

Results known to be virtually certain to accompany achievement of purpose. Result B may also be intended, according to *Moloney*, where B is not a condition of A. It is possible for A (D's purpose) to occur without B also happening, but as D knows, causing A is virtually certain to cause B as well. D, wishing to collect the insurance on a cargo (result A), puts a time bomb in a plane to blow up in mid-Atlantic. He has no wish to kill the crew. It is *possible* for the plane and cargo to be destroyed and the crew to escape – people do occasionally fall from aircraft at great heights and survive – but the possibility is so remote as to be negligible; and D knows that. There is certainly a strong argument for saying that he intends to kill. This is so even if, as D knows, this type of bomb has a 50% failure rate. There is an even chance that nothing will happen. But he wants the explosion (result A) to happen and, if it does, killing (result B) is, as he knows, a virtual certainty. So a jury may (not must) find that there is an intention to kill.

The difficulty is that once we depart from absolute certainty, there is a question of degree and an uncertain boundary between intention and recklessness. In *Hyam*,[17] D, in order to frighten Mrs Booth, her rival for the affections of X, put blazing newspaper through the letter box of Booth's house and caused the death of two of her children. Ackner J directed the jury that D was guilty if she knew that it was highly probable that her act would cause at least serious bodily harm; and by their verdict of guilty the jury must be taken to have found that she did know that. In the light of *Moloney*, that direction was wrong but Lord Bridge[18] thought that, on a proper direction, no reasonable jury could have failed to convict Hyam. Is that really so? Might not a jury have been satisfied that D knew this was a highly probable result without being satisfied that she knew it was virtually certain? In *Moloney*,[19] Lord Hailsham and Lord Bridge put the case of a terrorist who plants a time bomb in a public building and gives a warning to enable the public to be evacuated. He knows that it is virtually certain that a bomb disposal squad will attempt to defuse the bomb. The squad does so, the bomb explodes and a member of the squad is killed. It is assumed that this is murder. The bomber intends to endanger the squad's lives (because he knows that it is virtually certain they will attempt to defuse the bomb) but he does not, surely, know that it is virtually certain that one of them will be killed or even seriously injured. It is doubtful if this would be murder even under the "highly probable" formula of *Hyam*. It looks like reckless-ness which is not enough for murder. The example might be justified if it could be proved that the terrorist wants the bomb to go off *at a time* when he knows it is virtually certain that the squad will be attempting to defuse it. That would be indistinguishable from the "bomb-in-the-plane" case, above, where the bomber wants the bomb to go off in mid-Atlantic.

17. [1975] AC 55, [1974] 2 All ER 41.
18. [1985] AC at 926, [1985] 1 All ER at 1037.
19. [1985] AC at 913, 927.

In *Moloney*, D shot his stepfather, whom he loved, when, in the course of a drunken game to establish who was quicker "on the draw" with loaded shotguns, he pulled the trigger in response to a challenge, "if you have [the guts] pull the trigger." He may not have realised that the gun was aimed at point-blank range, at P's head. His conviction was quashed because the judge misdirected the jury that D intended serious bodily harm if he foresaw that it would "probably" happen. Lord Bridge insisted on the need for "a moral certainty", a probability which is "little short of overwhelming" and an act that "will lead to a certain event unless something unexpected supervenes to prevent it".[20] Unfortunately, in summing up his opinion in the form of guidelines for trial judges, he used the term, "natural consequence", to mean a consequence that is virtually certain to ensue.

In *Hancock v Shankland*[21] two striking miners pushed from the parapet of a bridge heavy concrete blocks which struck a taxi taking a working miner to work and killed the taxi-driver. They said they intended to push the blocks on to the middle lane, not the inside lane in which the taxi was travelling, and that they intended to frighten the working miner and prevent him going to work, but not to hurt anyone. At their trial for murder, the judge closely followed the *Moloney* "guidelines". The Court of Appeal held that the conviction must be quashed. The guidelines were defective. The jury might well have understood "natural consequence" to mean "direct consequence" and not to convey the notion of moral certainty or overwhelming probability of which Lord Bridge spoke. The House of Lords agreed. Both courts stressed that even awareness that the consequence is virtually certain is not intention, but only evidence from which a jury may infer intention, if they are satisfied beyond reasonable doubt that this is the right inference. The difficulty of applying this rule is considered above.

Although the House in *Moloney* said that they were laying down the law not only for murder but for offences requiring "specific intent" generally (which, here, seems to mean merely offences requiring intent), their approval of *Steane* and the difficulty of reconciling the illustration of the bomber suggests that the word may well be held to bear different shades of meaning in different contexts.

An act may be intentional with respect to circumstances as well as consequences. Intention here means either hope that the circumstance exists – which corresponds to purpose in relation to consequences – or knowledge that the circumstance exists – which corresponds to foresight of certainty in relation to consequences.

"He who steals a letter containing a cheque, intentionally steals the cheque also if he hopes that the letter may contain one, even though he well knows that the odds against the existence of such a circumstance are very great."[1]

If D receives a car which he knows to be stolen, that is an intentional handling of stolen goods even though D would, perhaps, much prefer that

20. [1985] AC at 925, 926, 929.
21. [1986] AC 455, [1986] 1 All ER 641.
 1. Salmond, *Jurisprudence* 11th ed. (1957), 411.

the car was not stolen. If, however, D believed merely that it was probable, or highly probable, that the car was stolen, this would not be an intentional handling.

b) *Recklessness*[2]

For many crimes, either intention to cause the proscribed result or recklessness whether it be caused is sufficient to impose liability. A person who does not intend to cause a harmful result may take an unjustifiable risk of causing it. If he does so, he may be held to be reckless. Not all risk-taking constitutes recklessness. Sometimes it is justifiable to take a risk of causing harm to another's property or his person or even of causing his death. The operator of an aircraft, the surgeon performing an operation and the promoter of a tightrope act in a circus must all know that their acts might cause death but none of them would properly be described as reckless unless the risk he took was an unreasonable one. The law allows the use of reasonable force in the lawful arrest of an offender or in private defence. If D forces P's car off the road, that cannot be reckless driving if it was reasonable to use that degree of force lawfully to arrest P.[3] If D, doing an act of reasonable self-defence, damages P's window, he is not guilty of reckless criminal damage.[4] Whether it is justifiable to take a risk depends on the social value of the activity involved relative to the probability and the gravity of the harm which might be caused. The question is whether the risk was one which a reasonable and prudent man might have taken. It might be reasonable for D to shoot P's ferocious dog which is attacking his sheep, but it does not follow that it would be reasonable to take a risk of causing injury or death to P – still less a bystander, Q. The test is objective – that is to say, the court or jury lays down the required standard of care. It is impossible to say in general terms that recklessness requires any particular degree of probability of the occurrence of the harm in question. If the act is one with no social utility – for example, a game of "Russian roulette" or an armed robbery – the slightest possibility of any harm should be enough. If the act has a high degree of social utility – for example, the performance of a surgical operation – then only such a very high degree of probability of grave harm as outweighs that utility will suffice to condemn it as a reckless act.

To establish recklessness it is necessary in all cases to show that D took an unjustifiable risk; but the prosecution, in some cases at least, must go further. How much further varies because it is now established that there are two varieties of recklessness recognised by English criminal law.

Let it be assumed that D has done an act which, objectively considered, involves an unjustifiable risk of causing the harm in question. When he acted, D must have had one of three possible states of mind regarding the risk. (1) He may have known of the risk. (2) He may not have considered whether there was a risk or not. (3) He may have considered whether there was a risk and decided there was none. The first variety of recklessness, which will be called "*Cunningham* recklessness" after the leading case,

---

2. See D. J. Birch, "The Foresight Saga", [1988] Crim LR 4 and articles referred to therein.
3. *Renouf* [1986] 2 All ER 449, [1986] 1 WLR 522, 82 Cr App Rep 344.
4. *Sears v Broome* [1986] Crim LR 461, DC.

requires proof of the first state of mind.[5] The second variety, *"Caldwell* recklessness", requires proof of either the first or, where the risk would have been obvious to a reasonable person who gave thought to the matter, the second state of mind. A person with the third state of mind is not reckless in either sense. *Cunningham* recklessness is the *mens rea* required for crimes which, by their statutory definition, must be committed "maliciously". *Caldwell* recklessness is sufficient for the statutory offences of criminal damage and reckless driving and the common law offence of manslaughter. Lord Roskill has said that "reckless" should be given the *Caldwell* meaning in all offences unless Parliament has otherwise ordained;[6] but this does not seem to be accepted by the Court of Appeal which has applied a different test in rape and indecent assault,[7] both of which may be committed recklessly. Probably every usage of the term must be considered in its own context.

This strange state of affairs came about in the following way. In *Cunningham*[8] D tore a gas meter from the wall of the cellar of an unoccupied house to steal the money in it. He left the gas gushing out. It seeped into a neighbouring house and was inhaled by P whose life was endangered. D was convicted, under s. 23 of the Offences against the Person Act 1861[9] of maliciously administering a noxious thing so as to endanger life. Because the judge directed the jury that "malicious" meant simply "wicked", D's conviction was quashed. The Court of Criminal Appeal quoted with approval the principle first propounded by Kenny in 1902.[10]

"... in any statutory definition of a crime 'malice' must be taken not in the old vague sense of 'wickedness' in general, but as requiring either (i) an actual intention to do the particular *kind* of harm that in fact was done, or (ii) recklessness as to whether such harm should occur or not (i.e. the accused has foreseen that the particular kind of harm might be done, and yet has gone on to take the risk of it). It is neither limited to, nor does it indeed require, any ill-will towards the person injured."

The court reiterated: "In our opinion, the word 'maliciously' in a statutory crime postulates foresight of consequence." Cunningham was not guilty unless he knew, when he broke off the gas meter, or left the broken pipe with the gas gushing out,[11] that it might be inhaled by someone. In cases requiring "malice" it is not sufficient that, if D had stopped to think, it would have been obvious to him that there was a risk. He must actually know of the existence of the risk and deliberately take it.

This was the law applicable to the offence of damage to property under the Malicious Damage Act 1861. The Law Commission in their Report on

---

5. Cf. the proposals of the Law Commission in Law Com. No. 89: "(1) The standard test of recklessness as to result is – Did the person whose conduct is in issue foresee that his conduct might produce the result and, if so, was it unreasonable for him to take the risk of producing it? (2) The standard test of recklessness as to circumstances is – Did the person whose conduct is in issue realise that the circumstances might exist and, if so, was it unreasonable for him to take the risk of their existence?"

6. [1983] 2 All ER at 1064. Presumably the use of "maliciously" ordains the contrary.

7. Below, p. 446.

8. [1957] 2 QB 396, [1957] 2 All ER 412.

9. Below, p. 403.

10. *Outlines of Criminal Law* (16th ed., 1952) at 186.

11. See omissions, above, p. 48.

Criminal Damage[12] made many proposals for the reform of the law but they considered that the mental element, as interpreted in *Cunningham*, was satisfactory. They proposed only that it be "expressed with greater simplicity and clarity" and that this should be achieved by using "intentionally or recklessly" in place of the archaic and misleading "maliciously". Parliament adopted their proposals in the Criminal Damage Act 1971. Unfortunately, the Commission proposed no definition of recklessness and the Act contains none. Before 1981, the Court of Appeal held, though after some hesitation, that "reckless" in the 1971 Act bore the *Cunningham* meaning but in that year, the House of Lords decided in *R v Caldwell*[13] (Lords Wilberforce and Edmund-Davies dissenting) and in *Lawrence*[14] that, where the statute uses the word "reckless", a different test applies. In *Caldwell* Lord Diplock said that a person is reckless whether any property would be destroyed or damaged–

"... if (1) he does an act which in fact creates an obvious risk that property would be destroyed or damaged and (2) when he does the act he either has not given any thought to the possibility of there being any such risk or has recognised that there was some risk involved and has nonetheless gone on to do it."[15]

In *Lawrence*, a decision given on the same day by a differently constituted House, it was held that the same test is applicable to reckless driving though what is risked – injury to the person or substantial damage to property – is different. Furthermore, Lord Diplock formulated the test in slightly different terms. An "obvious" risk becomes an "obvious and serious" risk.[16] What, if anything, his Lordship meant by the addition of "serious" is highly speculative.[17] While, of course, his words have to be construed, it would be a mistake to read them as if they were in a statute. Perhaps "serious" does no more than emphasise the fundamental point that the risk must be one which it is unreasonable to take. Lord Diplock recognised that there are some risks which the ordinary prudent person would treat as negligible and "serious" may mean "not negligible". If so, it is as applicable to criminal damage and other crimes governed by *Caldwell* recklessness as it is to reckless driving.

Obvious to whom? The risk must be obvious – but obvious to whom? The individual defendant or the reasonably prudent person? There are passages

12. Law Com. No. 29 (1970), confirming proposals in Working Paper No. 23 (1969): "Where the Act has been preceded by a report of some official commission or committee that has been laid before Parliament and the legislation is introduced in consequence of that report, the report itself may be looked at by the court for the limited purpose of identifying the 'mischief' that the Act was intended to remedy, and for such assistance as is derivable from this knowledge in giving the right purposive construction to the Act." – *Fothergill v Monarch Airlines Ltd* [1980] 2 All ER 696 at 706, per Lord Diplock. The principle has been applied in numerous cases referred to in this book. The text-book writer is not limited in this way and a wider use of legislative history is made in attempting to discover the true legislative intent.
13. [1982] AC 341, [1981] 1 All ER 961. For facts, see below, p. 685.
14. [1982] AC 510, [1981] 1 All ER 974. For discussion of these decisions see commentaries at [1981] Crim LR 393 and 410; Syrota [1982] Crim LR 97; Glanville Williams [1982] CLJ 252.
15. [1981] 1 All ER at 967.
16. At one point, "some risk" which, in *Caldwell*, seems to be contrasted with "obvious risk", becomes "such risk" i.e., an obvious and serious risk. But later Lord Diplock reverts to "some risk".
17. See R. M. Lynn (1986) 37 NILQ 237.

in *Caldwell* which suggest that the individual defendant is meant and powerful arguments have been advanced in favour of this view;[18] but in *Lawrence* the House was plainly looking to the "ordinary prudent motorist" as represented by the jury. It is this test which prevails. The Divisional Court in *Elliott v C*[19] reluctantly felt themselves bound so to hold. D, a backward fourteen-year-old girl who had been out all night without food or sleep, entered a garden shed, poured white spirit on to the carpet and threw two lighted matches on it. Fire flared up and the shed was destroyed. She was charged with arson of the shed, contrary to s. 1 (2) of the Criminal Damage Act 1971. The magistrates found that she had given no thought to the possibility that the shed might be destroyed by fire and that, in the circumstances, the risk would not have been obvious to her if she had given thought to the matter. The magistrates who had acquitted were directed to convict: the risk would have been obvious to a reasonably prudent man who stopped to think. The same view was taken by the Court of Appeal with equal reluctance in *Stephen Malcolm R.*[20] A fifteen-year-old boy who had thrown petrol bombs close to a girl's bedroom window was convicted of arson contrary to s. 1 (2) (b) of the Criminal Damage Act 1971. He claimed that he was not reckless whether life would be endangered because he did not realise that, if the bomb had gone through the window, it might have killed the girl. The court held that the judge had correctly applied the test of the ordinary prudent man rejecting the argument that D was reckless only if he did an act which created a risk obvious to someone of his age and with such of his characteristics as would affect his appreciation of the risk.

The test works harshly in these cases of young people. In the case of adults, it will do so in the case of those who lack the capacities of the ordinary prudent person. In *Stephenson*[1] a tramp sheltered in a hollow in a haystack. Feeling cold, he lit a fire in the hollow. The haystack was destroyed. Any reasonable person would have been aware of the risk but Stephenson was suffering from schizophrenia and may not have been aware of it. Because this was not clearly left to the jury, the court – pre-*Caldwell* – quashed his conviction. Even if he had stopped to think it is possible that, because of his condition, he might not have realised that there was a risk of damage. *Stephenson* appears to be overruled by *Caldwell*. How far are we to go in ignoring abnormalities? Is a blind man to be held to have recklessly damaged property because he was unaware of a risk which would have been obvious to a sighted person? And what about temporary handicaps – the person who strikes a match, being unaware because of his heavy cold, that the premises reek with petrol fumes? *Caldwell*, as interpreted in *Elliott v C* and *R*, appears to be a slippery slope to intolerable injustice with no obvious exit.

Caldwell recklessness as a state of mind. Lord Diplock considered it axiomatic that *mens rea*, including recklessness, requires proof of the state of the defendant's mind. D must have been aware of the risk or not have

18. Glanville Williams [1983] Crim LR 365, Syrota [1982] Crim LR 97.
19. [1983] 2 All ER 1005, [1983] 1 WLR 939.
20. (1984) 79 Cr App Rep 334. Cf. *Sangha* (1988) Times, 2 February, CA.
 1. [1979] QB 695, [1979] 2 All ER 1198.

given thought to the possibility of its existence – "not giving thought" is a state of mind. Once the obvious (and serious) risk is proved, there seems to be only one way out for the defendant. He can escape only if he considered the matter and decided that there was no risk, or a "negligible" risk. It appears that, if D wishes the court or jury to consider this possibility, he must introduce some evidence of it. In *Lawrence* Lord Diplock said:

"If satisfied that an obvious and serious risk was created by the manner of the defendant's driving, the jury are entitled to infer that he was in one or other of the states of mind required to constitute the offence and will probably do so; but regard must be given to any explanation he gives as to his state of mind which may displace the inference."

The case where D has considered the matter and decided that there is no risk is sometimes referred to as the "lacuna" or "loophole" in the *Caldwell/Lawrence* principle. But it is an essential element in the theory for, if the lacuna were filled and D held liable where he has given thought, it would no longer be possible to maintain that a state of mind must be proved. Then the prosecution would prove their case by satisfying the jury that D's conduct involved an obvious (and serious) risk. If it matters not whether the defendant was aware of the risk, or never gave thought to the possibility of it, or decided there was no risk, his state of mind is immaterial. Consider *Lamb*.[2] D pointed a loaded revolver at his friend, P, in jest. D and P knew that there were two bullets in the revolver but they believed it was safe to pull the trigger because neither bullet was opposite the barrel. D shot P dead. Neither of them knew that, when the trigger is pulled, the cylinder containing the chambers rotates clockwise before the firing-pin strikes. D's conviction was quashed because of a misdirection by the trial judge but Sachs LJ said, obiter, that "it would, of course, have been fully open to a jury, if properly directed, to find the accused guilty, because they considered his view as to there being no danger was formed in a criminally negligent way". Lamb may well have been guilty of gross negligence but a person who has formed the view that there is no danger is not reckless in the *Caldwell/Lawrence* sense. He is not aware of the risk; and he has not failed to give thought to whether there is a risk or not. There seems to be a tendency to overlook or avoid the lacuna. In *Crossman*,[3] D, a lorry driver rejected the advice of the loaders of a piece of heavy machinery on to his lorry that it was unsafe unless chained and sheeted. It was, he said, "as safe as houses." The load fell off and killed a pedestrian. When his argument that reckless driving must have something to do with the handling or control of the vehicle was rejected, he pleaded guilty to reckless driving and his conviction was upheld. Yet, if, after his attention had been drawn to the possibility of risk, he really believed that the load was "as safe as houses", he was not reckless in the *Lawrence* sense. In *Chief Constable of Avon and Somerset Constabulary v Shimmen*[4] a self-defence expert on his way from the pub was demonstrating his skill to his friends at narrowly missing a shop window with a kick. He smashed the window. It was unsuccessfully

---

2. [1967] 2 QB 981, [1967] 2 All ER 1282, CA.
3. [1986] Crim LR 406.
4. (1986) 84 Cr App Rep 7, [1986] Crim LR 800.

argued that this was a "lacuna" case. D thought he had minimised the risk but he knew there was some risk – so he falls squarely within the second limb of the *Caldwell* test. He said he thought he had "eliminated as much risk as possible by missing by two inches instead of two millimetres". Taking even the slightest risk with the property of another can be justified only if there is some acceptable reason for taking the risk. Probably there was none in this case. D may have considered the known risk "negligible" but that was a question for the court or jury, not for him. If, however, D believes that he has eliminated all risk by some, in fact, inadequate, precaution, he cannot be held reckless. Suppose that *Lamb*[5] had observed that one of the bullets was opposite the barrel and had rotated the chamber anti-clockwise, so the bullet was at "11 o'clock" and then, believing that there was no danger, had pressed the trigger. There is no distinction between that and the actual case. It can make no difference whether D's conclusion that there was no risk arose from his initial contemplation of the circumstances or from steps taken by him to change those circumstances. Nor should D be regarded as reckless if the proportions to which he, mistakenly, believes he has reduced the risk are indeed negligible i.e., the risk which he believes he is taking is one which a reasonable and prudent person might take.

Recklessness in rape and indecent assault. Rape and indecent assault are offences which may be committed recklessly in so far as a man may be guilty of either offence if he is reckless as to whether the woman consents to the sexual intercourse, or indecent act.[6] After *Caldwell* the courts were at first disposed to hold that *Caldwell* recklessness with an additional requirement of "indifference" was enough.[7] This was found to create immense difficulties for juries and in *Kimber*[8] the Court of Appeal held that, for indecent assault, the law was that recklessness was proved only if D did not believe that P was consenting and "couldn't care less" whether she was consenting or not. This was followed in a rape case, *Satnam S, Kewal S*[9] where it was held that the common law, as stated by the House of Lords in *Morgan*[10] was, following the recommendations of the Heilbron report,[11] intended by Parliament to be incorporated in the Sexual Offences (Amendment) Act 1976. Accordingly, *Caldwell* did not apply. *Caldwell* and *Lawrence* were distinguished as cases where the question was as to the foreseeability of the consequences of the criminal act, whereas in rape the question is "foreseeability ... as to the state of mind of the victim. "Couldn't care less" seems to imply that, at least, the possibility that the woman may not be consenting has crossed the man's mind. If he then

5. Above, p. 65.
6. For rape, the requirement of recklessness is expressed in the Sexual Offences (Amendment) Act 1976, s. 1 (1) and, for indecent assault, it is implied in the Sexual Offences Act 1956, s. 14 (1).
7. *Pigg* [1982] 2 All ER 591, [1982] 1 WLR 762. CA, a case of an alleged common law attempt to rape. Cf. *Bashir* (1982) 77 Cr App Rep 59 [1982] Crim LR 687, CA.
8. [1983] 3 All ER 316, [1983] 1 WLR 1118.
9. (1983) 78 Cr App Rep 149, [1985] Crim LR 236.
10. [1976] AC 182.
11. Cmnd 6352, 1975.

proceeds to have intercourse and she is not in fact consenting he is guilty of reckless rape. "Couldn't care less" seems, in one respect, to be too narrow. D may fervently hope that the woman is consenting – he does care, but, it is submitted, not enough.

Recklessness in offences requiring "malice". Although the concept of recklessness applied in *Cunningham*[12] was subjected to criticism in *Caldwell*,[13] the former case was distinguished and not overruled. Subsequent cases have confirmed that this is so. In *W (a minor) v Dolbey*,[14] D, a fifteen-year-old boy, who had been using an air rifle to shoot at bottles, pointed it at P who told him not to. D replied, "There is nothing in the gun, I have got no pellets." D pulled the trigger. There was a pellet in the rifle and it wounded P's forehead. The Divisional Court held that D's conviction for malicious wounding, contrary to s. 20 of the Offences against the Person Act 1861, must be quashed. D did not foresee that any physical harm might come to P and he was not therefore reckless within the principle of *Cunningham*. Since he had considered whether there was a risk and decided there was none, he was probably not *Caldwell*-reckless either. If so, the result would have been the same if he had broken P's spectacles and been charged with criminal damage. *W v Dolbey* is confirmed by *Grimshaw*.[15] On a charge under s. 20, the judge, misled by Diplock LJ's use of the phrase, "should have foreseen", in *Mowatt*,[16] directed the jury that D was "malicious" if she ought to have foreseen that some physical harm might result from her act. The Court of Appeal held that it was the jury's view of what a defendant foresaw, not their view of what he ought, as a reasonable man, to have foreseen, that was material.

Recklessness of the intoxicated – "general recklessness". The word "reckless" is used in yet another sense, different from those so far considered, in the case of intoxicated offenders. This usage is discussed below.[17]

The future of recklessness. The existing variation in the meaning of recklessness is indefensible. To take an example based on *W (a minor) v Dolbey*,[18] if D takes an air rifle and, not even considering the possibility that it might be loaded (as is the fact), aims and fires it at P, breaking P's spectacles and destroying his eye, D will be liable for causing criminal damage to the spectacles but will not be criminally liable at all for the destruction of the eye. The law appears to give greater protection to spectacles than to eyes. Yet, although D has committed no crime by destroying P's eye, it appears that he will be guilty of manslaughter if P dies of the injury within a year and a day.

The *Caldwell* test fails to make a distinction which should be made between the person who knowingly takes a risk and the person who gives no

12. Above, p. 62.
13. Above, p. 63.
14. [1983] Crim LR 681, DC.
15. [1984] Crim LR 109, CA.
16. [1968] 1 QB 421 at 426.
17. P. 217.
18. [1983] Crim LR 681.

thought to whether there is a risk or not. And, on the other hand, it makes a distinction which has no moral basis. The person who, with gross negligence, fails to consider whether there is a risk is liable; but the person who considers whether there is a risk and, with gross negligence, decides there is none, is not liable.[19] The right solution, it is submitted, is to go back to the *Cunningham* test which appears to have been entirely trouble-free in practice.

"Indifference" as an element in recklessness. The notion of "indifference" has featured prominently in discussions of recklessness. It was much used by the House of Lords in *Morgan*,[20] and is the "couldn't care less" concept of *Kimber* and *Satnam S.*[1] It is submitted, however, that it is not an essential element in recklessness. A person who knowingly takes an unreasonable risk of causing a forbidden result may hope, sincerely and fervently, that it will never happen; but he is, surely, reckless. Where *Caldwell* recklessness applies, there is no room for an additional requirement of indifference, as *Pigg*[2] clearly demonstrated. But it might be otherwise if the *Cunningham* test were restored to general favour.

The problem is that of the person who is unaware that there is a risk, but would not care if he knew there was. He would carry on just the same. He is indifferent. It never crosses his mind that the woman with whom he is about to have sexual intercourse might not be consenting; but it would not make any difference if it did. It never crosses his mind that the statement he is about to make might be false, but he would say it anyway. He may well be thought to be no less reprehensible than one who is aware of the risk and takes it. His case is caught by *Caldwell* but not by *Cunningham* recklessness. There are two difficulties about extending *Cunningham* recklessness to cover this particular case. First, it requires the court or jury to answer a hypothetical question and, second, there is a problem of evidence. How is it to be proved that, if D had given thought, he would not have cared? This seems to call for an inquiry into his general character and habits which our law of evidence does not allow. To do so would savour of convicting him because he is that sort of person, not because of what he has done.

c) *Negligence*
Before the decisions in *Caldwell* and *Lawrence* it was possible to draw a clear distinction between recklessness and negligence. Recklessness was the conscious taking of an unjustifiable risk, negligence the inadvertent taking of an unjustifiable risk. If D was aware of the risk and decided to take it, he was reckless; if he was unaware of the risk, but ought to have been aware of it, he was negligent. This distinction still holds good in a crime where *Cunningham* recklessness is required; the inadvertent taking of the risk, mere negligence, does not entail liability. Where, however, we are concerned with *Caldwell* recklessness, the inadvertent risk-taker may be held

19. See the discussion of "the lacuna", above, p. 65.
20. [1976] AC 182, below, p. 86.
 1. Above, p. 66.
 2. Above, p. 66.

liable – his failure to direct his mind to the possibility of a risk, which would have been obvious to him had he done so, is reckless.

There are, however, still crimes where D may be held liable even if he did consider whether or not there was a risk and concluded, wrongly and unreasonably, that there was no risk, or so small a risk that it would have been justifiable to take it. This is now the hallmark of a crime of negligence. In such a case, D is, of course, a fortiori liable where he unreasonably failed to consider whether there was any risk and the risk was "obvious". There is thus a substantial overlap between recklessness and gross negligence.[3] Indeed the number of instances of gross negligence which do not amount to *Caldwell* recklessness will be very small. An example might be found in the facts of *Lamb*.[4]

Intention, Recklessness and Negligence as to Circumstances

Intention, recklessness and negligence may all exist with respect to circumstances as well as consequences. Sometimes the law may require intention as to one or more elements of a crime yet be satisfied with recklessness or negligence as to another or others. In obtaining by deception[5] D must intend to obtain, but he may be merely reckless whether the statement he makes is true or false. In rape, D must intend to have sexual intercourse but may be merely reckless whether P consents to his doing so.[6] It would seem that, in determining whether D's fault amounted to intention, recklessness or negligence, the same criteria should be applied to circumstances as to consequences. So an act is intentional as to a circumstance[7] when D wants the circumstance to exist (where he hopes, perhaps faintly, that the letter he steals contains money, he intends to steal money)[8] or knows that it exists; or, if the broader view of intention[9] is accepted, he is virtually certain that it exists. He is reckless whether a circumstance exists or will exist when it is obvious that it may do so and either he knows that, or (in the case of *Caldwell* recklessness)[10] does not give his mind to it. He is negligent with respect to a circumstance when, as a reasonable man, he ought to know that it exists or will exist and fails to do so, whether he has given thought to the question or not.

d) Blameless Inadvertence

Finally, a man may reasonably fail to foresee a consequence that follows from his act – as when a slight slap causes the death of an apparently healthy person; or reasonably fail to consider the possibility of the existence of a circumstance – as when goods, which are in fact stolen, are bought in the normal course of business from a trader of high repute.

3. Below, p. 353.
4. [1967] 2 QB 981, [1967] 2 All ER 1282, discussed above, p. 65.
5. Below, p. 545.
6. Below, p. 437.
7. This is not the same as saying that the circumstance is intended, because that implies a belief by D that he may be able to influence the existence of the circumstance; below, p. 262.
8. Salmond, *Jurisprudence* (11th ed.) 411.
9. Above, p. 62.
10. In *Pigg* (1982) 74 Cr App Rep 352 at 358 the Court of Appeal rejected an argument that *Caldwell* applied only to consequences and not to circumstances.

2 Basic Mens Rea

Mens rea is a term which has no single meaning. Every crime has its own *mens rea* which can be ascertained only by reference to its statutory definition or the case law. The most we can do is to state a general principle, or presumption, which governs its definition. Before *Caldwell* it could be said that this principle was that, in crimes requiring *mens rea*, as distinct from negligence, the defendant should be liable only for that which he had *chosen* to bring about, or to take the risk of bringing about, i.e., that he intended, or was reckless (in the *Cunningham* sense) whether all the elements of the offence, both results and circumstances, should occur. Because he had so chosen, he could fairly be held responsible for the occurrence of the *actus reus*. His intention or recklessness as to all the elements of the offence was *mens rea* or the basic constituent of it. Since *Caldwell*, the principle can no longer always be said to be based on the idea of choice. The person who gives no thought to the question whether there is a risk cannot be said to have chosen to take that risk.

The general principle is expressed in the draft Code as follows:

"24 (1) Unless a contrary intention appears, a person does not commit a Code offence unless he acts intentionally, knowingly or recklessly in respect of each of its elements. . . ."

Some offences are so defined that only intention with respect to one or more elements is sufficient. Others are defined so as to require only negligence, or no fault at all, with respect to particular elements; limiting, or qualifying the basic *mens rea* which cl. 24 (1) would require.

A concept similar to that embodied in cl. 24 (1) has been designated "basic intent" by Lord Simon in *Director of Public Prosecutions v Morgan*[11]:

"By 'crimes of basic intent' I mean those crimes whose definition expresses (or, more often implies) a *mens rea* which does not go beyond the *actus reus*."

Lord Simon's "basic intent" does not go beyond but (it seems) does not necessarily go as far as the *actus reus* – it may not extend to every element of it. The intent required in *Prince*[12] might thus be a "basic intent" for Lord Simon, but it would not satisfy the words italicised above. For this reason, and because it involves recklessness as well as intention, the term "basic *mens rea*" is preferred.

3 The Requirement of an Ulterior Intent

The principle stated in cl. 24 (1), by itself, would amount to a definition of the *mens rea* of many crimes, but it does not meet all cases. A crime is frequently so defined that the *mens rea* includes an intention to produce some further consequence beyond the *actus reus* of the crime in question. Burglary will serve as an example. It is not enough that D intended to enter a building as a trespasser, that is, to achieve the *actus reus* of burglary. It is necessary to go further and to show that D had the intention of committing one of a number of specified offences in the building. The actual commission of one of those offences is no part of the *actus reus* of burglary which is

11. [1975] 2 All ER 347 at 363; **SHC 102**; contrasting the term with "ulterior intent" as used in the third edition of this work and infra.
12. Below, p. 454.

complete as soon as D enters. Causing grievous bodily harm with intent to resist the lawful apprehension of any person,[13] placing gunpowder near a building with intent to do bodily injury to any person,[14] are instances of similar crimes. Where such an ulterior intent must be proved, it is sometimes referred to as a "specific intent".[15] This term, however, is one which should be regarded with caution.[16] It is variously used to mean (i) whatever intention has to be proved to establish guilt of the particular crime before the court;[17] (ii) a "direct" as distinct from an "oblique" intention;[18] or (iii) an intention ulterior to the *actus reus* or (iv) a crime where D may successfully plead lack of the prescribed *mens rea* notwithstanding the fact that he relies on evidence that he was intoxicated at the time.[19] The phrase "ulterior intent" is therefore preferred to describe the third concept. The nature of the ulterior intent required varies widely from crime to crime – an intent to commit one of a number of specified offences in burglary, an intent to cause P to act to his prejudice in forgery, an intent permanently to deprive the owner in theft and so on.

Where an ulterior intent is required, it is obvious that recklessness is not enough. On a charge of wounding with intent to cause grievous bodily harm, proof that D was reckless whether he caused grievous bodily harm will not suffice.[20]

It should again be emphasised that most crimes require only basic *mens rea* and no ulterior intent. In rape, for example, it is enough that the accused intentionally or recklessly perpetrated the *actus reus* – intercourse with a woman without her consent – and no ulterior intention need be proved. The result is that the best we can do by way of a general definition of *mens rea* is as follows: "Intention, knowledge or recklessness with respect to all the elements of the offence *together with any ulterior intent which the definition of the crime requires.*"

4 The Extent to which Mens Rea is required varies from Crime to Crime

Mens rea, as so defined, is not required for all crimes, for (a) even at common law there were many exceptions to it and (b) statutory crimes are frequently interpreted so as to exclude the necessity for either intention or recklessness with respect to some one or more elements in the *actus reus*.

Sometimes the common law is satisfied by proof of the basic *mens rea* of a lesser offence than that charged. So on a charge of murder it is enough that D intended to cause serious bodily harm.[1] Statutes are sometimes similarly interpreted and on a charge of maliciously inflicting grievous (that is, serious) bodily harm, it is enough that D intended to cause or was reckless

---

13. Offences against the Person Act 1861, s. 18.
14. Ibid., s. 30.
15. See Perkins, "A Rationale of *Mens Rea*" (1939) 52 Harv L Rev 905, 924.
16. See Cross, [1961] Crim LR 510.
17. *Director of Public Prosecutions v Beard* [1920] AC 479 at 501–502; below, p. 210.
18. Above, p. 56. *Steane* [1947] KB 997 at 1004, [1947] 1 All ER 813 at 816.
19. Below, p. 211.
20. *Belfon* [1976] 3 All ER 46, where this passage was cited at 49, [1976] 1 WLR 741.
 1. Below, p. 210.

whether he caused actual (that is, not serious) bodily harm.[2] Sometimes it is enough to prove only negligence; sometimes even this is not necessary and D may be convicted although he was blamelessly inadvertent as to a circumstance of the *actus reus*. In the latter case we shall say that the crime imposes "strict liability" as to that circumstance.

The offence under s. 20 of the Sexual Offences Act 1956 discussed above[3] will serve as an illustration. It has been held that, as to the circumstance that the girl is under sixteen, the accused may be blamelessly inadvertent and yet may be convicted. In *Prince*,[4] D took a girl out of the possession and against the will of her father and mother. He knew he was doing this; but, as the jury found, he believed her statement that she was eighteen and his belief was reasonable, for she looked very much older than sixteen. In fact, she was under sixteen and D therefore brought about the *actus reus* of the crime. He was not even negligent, let alone reckless or intentional as to the girl's age. In spite of his blameless inadvertence as to this important circumstance in the *actus reus*, D was convicted. Yet in *Hibbert*[5] D took away and seduced a young girl but was acquitted because it was not proved that he knew, or had any reason to believe, that she was in the possession of her parents. Bramwell B, though upholding the conviction in *Prince*, thought D would have a good defence if he believed he had the father's consent. That the girl is (a) under sixteen, (b) in the possession of her parents,[6] and (c) that they do not consent, are circumstances which are equally essential to the existence of an *actus reus*, yet *mens rea*, as the law stands,[7] is required as to (b) and (c) but not as to (a).

This seems illogical and unjust. An ideal rule would seem to be that stated at the beginning of this section, requiring intention or recklessness as to *all* the elements in the *actus reus*. Presumably no element is included in the definition of an *actus reus* unless it contributes to the heinousness of the offence. If the accused is blamelessly inadvertent with respect to *any* one element in the offence, and does not, therefore, appreciate the full heinousness of his conduct, is it then proper to hold him responsible for it?

That the law should impose strict liability to one circumstance and yet require *mens rea* as to another in the same crime may be partly a result of historical development for the courts' attitude to the problem of *mens rea*, and especially to how far a requirement of *mens rea* should be imported into statutory offences, has varied from time to time. One element may have fallen to be construed by a court devoted to strict liability, another by a court which adhered to the principles of *mens rea*. This may explain how the law came to be in the state it is, but it certainly does not justify it.

There is a particular difficulty in requiring *mens rea* as to an element in the *actus reus* of a morally indifferent nature. The definition of a crime

2. Below, p. 400.
3. See p. 39; and below, pp. 452–455.
4. (1875) LR 2 CCR 154; **SHC 102**. See Cross, "Centenary Reflections on Prince's Case" (1975) 91 LQR 540.
5. (1869) LR 1 CCR 184.
6. So a belief that she was eighteen might now be a defence amounting, since the reduction in the age of majority, to a belief that she was not in anyone's custody: Cross, loc. cit. 553, n. 24.
7. It is arguable that *Hibbert* is inconsistent with *Prince* but it was not overruled in this latter case.

sometimes draws an arbitrary line as to a person's age, or as to time, weight, size and other matters of degree. Ignorance of the law is no defence and a person who is unaware of the law is unlikely to direct his mind to the question whether the arbitrary line has been crossed in the particular case. There is no reason for the possessor of a shotgun to consider whether the barrel is less than twenty-four inches in length unless he knows that, if it is, possession without a firearms certificate is an offence.[8] Similarly, a person taking a girl out of the possession of her parents may give no thought to the question whether she is under or over sixteen, if he is unaware of the legal significance of that age. The case is different in a material respect from that of the person who has a positive but mistaken belief that the girl is over sixteen. Williams[9] sought to resolve the difficulty by distinguishing between cases of "mistaken belief" (where there is a positive belief) which will negative recklessness and "simple ignorance" (where there is no advertence to the question) which will not. This distinction gains some support from *Caldwell*.[10] D can truly be said to be indifferent as to the circumstance – he does not care whether the barrel of the gun is more or less than twenty-four inches or the girl under or over 16, because he is unaware that it matters. This principle, however, could only be properly applicable in respect of age, time, weight, size and other circumstances which everyone knows to exist in some degree. D knows that the barrel has length or that the girl has an age and, ex hypothesi, he does not care what it is. Where the circumstance is not simply a matter of degree but of kind, it is no longer possible to say that D was indifferent. D may buy and deliver to P a book with an attractive cover without looking at the contents and without considering whether it might contain blasphemous and obscene material, but to infer that he was indifferent would be quite unwarranted. When he learnt the facts, he might be quite horrified.[11] Under *Caldwell*, it would seem that the fact that it should have been obvious to him that the book was blasphemous and obscene would be enough to fix him with recklessness, for the references to "indifference" seem to have no substance.[12]

These problems do not arise if the court holds that the crime is one of strict liability with respect to the circumstance in question, as they did in *Prince*.[13]

5 Transferred Malice[14]

If D, with the *mens rea* of a particular crime, does an act which causes the *actus reus* of the same crime,[15] he is guilty, even though the result, in some

8. Firearms Act 1968, s. 1, below, p. 416.
9. Williams CLGP (1st ed.) 122, (2nd ed.) 151.
10. Above, p. 62; cf. *Pigg* (1982) 74 Cr App Rep 352 at 358–359.
11. The taker of the girl and the possessor of the shotgun might be equally horrified when they learnt *the law*, but that is not the same thing. We are considering recklessness as to facts, not law. Cf. *Mousir* [1987] Crim LR 561 and commentary.
12. Above, p. 68.
13. Above, p. 41.
14. See Ashworth in *Reshaping the Criminal Law*, 77–94 and in *Crime, Proof and Punishment*, 45–70; Williams "Convictions and Fair Labelling" [1983] CLJ 85.
15. See *Hussain* [1969] 2 QB 567, [1969] 2 All ER 1117, [1969] Crim LR 433 and commentary; *Ellis, Street and Smith* [1987] Crim LR 44 and commentary; cf. *Kundeus* (1976) 24 CCC (2d) 276 at 282–283.

respects, is an unintended one. D intends to murder O and, in the dusk, shoots at a man whom he believes to be O. He hits and kills the man at whom he aims, who is in fact P. In one sense this is obviously an unintended result; but D did intend to cause the *actus reus* which he has caused and he is guilty of murder. Again, D intends to enter a house, No. 6 King Street, and steal therein. In the dark he mistakenly enters No. 7. He is guilty of burglary.[16]

The law, however, carries this principle still farther. Suppose, now, that D, intending to murder O, shoots at a man who is in fact O, but *misses* and kills P who, unknown to D, was standing close by. This is an unintended result in a different – and more fundamental – respect than the example considered above.[17] Yet, once again, D, with the *mens rea* of a particular crime, has caused the *actus reus* of the same crime; and, once again, he is guilty of murder. So, where D struck O, who fell against P, who also fell and sustained a fatal injury, D was guilty of manslaughter: "The criminality of the doer of the act is precisely the same whether it is [O] or [P] who dies."[18] The application of the principle to cases of this second type is known as the doctrine of "transferred malice".

In *Latimer*,[19] D had a quarrel in a public house with O. He took off his belt and aimed a blow at O which struck him lightly, but the belt bounded off and struck P who was standing close by and wounded her severely. The jury found that the blow was unlawfully aimed at O, but that the striking of P "was purely accidental and not such a consequence of the blow as the prisoner ought to have expected" – that is, he was not even negligent with respect to this result. It was held, on a case reserved, that D was properly convicted of unlawfully and maliciously wounding P.

It is important to notice the limitations of this doctrine. It operates only when the *actus reus* and the *mens rea* of the *same* crime coincide. If D, with the *mens rea* of one crime, does an act which causes the *actus reus* of a different crime, he cannot, as a general rule, be convicted of either offence. D shoots at P's dog with intent to kill it but misses and kills P who, unknown to D, was standing close by. Obviously he cannot be criminally liable for killing the dog, for he has not done so; nor can he be convicted of murder,[20] for he has not the *mens rea* for that crime. A similar result follows where D shoots at P with intent to kill him and, quite accidentally, kills P's dog: D is guilty of neither crime. In *Pembliton*[21] D was involved in a fight outside a public house, and, as a result, was charged with maliciously breaking a window. The jury found:

---

16. See *Wrigley* [1957] Crim LR 57.
17. In *Timbu Kolian v R* (1968) 119 CLR 47, D, in the dark, aimed a blow with a stick at his wife, W. W was carrying their baby, P, in her arms. The blow which would have been only moderate, though unlawful, chastisement of W, killed P. D did not know of and had no reason to suspect the child's presence. Under the Queensland Criminal Code, transferred malice is inapplicable. The High Court of Australia quashed D's conviction for manslaughter. Two judges held that the *striking of the child* occurred "independently of the exercise of D's will" under the Code; three judges held that it was an "accident" under the Code, and one that it was an act excusable at common law, as well as being both "unwilled" and an accident.
18. *Mitchell* [1983] QB 741, [1983] 2 All ER 427, CA.
19. (1886) 17 QBD 359; **SHC 82**.
20. As to whether it could be manslaughter, see below, pp. 345 et seq. and 352.
21. (1874) LR 2 CCR 119; **SHC 81**.

"that the prisoner threw the stone which broke the window, but that he threw it at the people he had been fighting with, intending to strike one or more of them with it, but not intending to break the window."[1]

His conviction was quashed by the Court for Crown Cases Reserved, for there was no finding that he had the *mens rea* of the crime, the *actus reus* of which he had caused. Lord Coleridge pointed out that it would have been different if there had been a finding that he was reckless as to the consequence which had occurred – but there was no such finding. The intent which is transferred must be a *mens rea*, whether intention or recklessness. If D shoots at O with intent to kill, because O is making a murderous attack on him and this is the only way in which he can preserve his own life, he does not intend an *actus reus* (in the broader sense, p. 35, above), for to kill in these circumstances is justified. If, however, D misses O and inadvertently kills P, an innocent bystander, he does cause an *actus reus* but he is not guilty of murder for there is no *mens rea* (in the broader sense) to transfer; the result which he intended was a perfectly lawful one.[2]

It has been suggested by Williams[3] that the doctrine of transferred malice should be applied only where the actual consequence was brought about negligently: that is, where D, when shooting at O, *ought* to have appreciated that there was a risk of killing P. There is, however, no suggestion in the cases that the rule is to be thus limited and it will be noted that the doctrine was applied in *Latimer* even though there was an express finding that D was not negligent with respect to the consequence which actually occurred. It would, moreover, be illogical to make the commission of a crime requiring *mens rea* depend on the presence or absence of negligence.

Williams regards the doctrine of transferred malice as a "rather arbitrary exception to normal principles". He rejects the argument that "the result is *not* unintended, for the intention was to kill, and the result is a killing." He writes:[4]

"This argument ... sounds plausible only because part of the real intention is omitted. Although the result in the sense of a killing was intended, the result in the sense of a killing of P was not intended. After all the accused is not indicted for killing in the abstract; he is indicted for killing P; and it should therefore, on a strict view, be necessary to establish *mens rea* in relation to the killing of P."

The answer to this, it is submitted, is that D's act is unintentional only in a respect which is immaterial. The test of materiality in a difference of result is whether it affects the existence of the *actus reus* which D intended. Thus it would be immaterial that D intended to shoot P in the heart but, because of a quite unexpected movement by P, shot him (unintentionally) in the head. The *actus reus* of murder is the killing of a human being – *any* human being – under the Queen's Peace, and his identity is irrelevant.

---

1. Ibid., at p. 120.
2. Below, p. 240; and cf. *Gross* (1913) 23 Cox CC 455, below, p. 333.
3. CLGP 48. He would now abolish the doctrine for criminal damage. It results in "unfair labelling" where the property damaged is more valuable than the property D intended to damage. He would retain it for offences against the person: [1983] CLJ 85. Injury to one person is (presumably) as bad as the same injury to any other person.
4. CLGP at 135; and see 9 JSPTL at 170–171. S. R. L. Milton (1968) 85 SALS 115.

6 Coincidence of Actus Reus and Mens Rea[5]

The *mens rea* must coincide in point of time with the act which causes the *actus reus*.[6] "If I happen to kill my neighbour accidentally, I do not become a murderer by thereafter expressing joy over his death. My happiness over the result is not the same as a willingness to commit the illegal act."[7] *Mens rea* implies an intention to do a present act, not a future act.[8] Suppose that D is driving to P's house, bent on killing P. A person steps under the wheels of D's car, giving D no chance to avoid him, and is killed. It is P. Clearly, D is not guilty of murder. One who walks out of gaol while in a state of automatism does not commit the offence of escape[9] by deliberately remaining at large.[10] Suppose that D, having resolved to kill his wife, P, prepares and conceals a poisoned apple with the intention of giving it to her tomorrow. She finds the apple today, eats it and dies. D is not guilty of murder. He might be guilty of manslaughter on the ground that the act of leaving the apple where it might be found was reckless or grossly negligent.[11] If D does an act with intent thereby to cause the *actus reus*, and does so, it is immaterial that he has repented before the *actus reus* occurs. Where D dispatched suitcases which she knew to contain cannabis from Ghana to London, her repentance before the importation took place was no defence.[12]

Where however D has, with *mens rea*, gone beyond mere preparation and is in the course of committing an offence, it should be no answer that the final step was involuntary or accidental – as where D is on the point of pulling the trigger with intent to murder and, being startled by an explosion, does so involuntarily.[13]

Where the *actus reus* is a continuing act, it is sufficient that D has *mens rea* during its continuance.[14] Where the *actus reus* is part of a larger transaction, it may be sufficient that D has *mens rea* during the transaction, though not at the moment the *actus reus* is accomplished. D inflicts a wound upon P with intent to kill him. Then, believing that he has killed P he disposes, as he thinks, of the "corpse." In fact P was not killed by the wound but dies as a result of the act of disposal. D has undoubtedly caused the *actus reus* of murder by the act of disposal but he did not, at that time have *mens rea*. In an Indian and a Rhodesian[15] case it has been held, accordingly, that D must be acquitted of murder and convicted only of attempted murder. But in *Thabo Meli*[16] the Privy Council held that it was:

5. Marston, "Contemporaneity of Act and Intention" (1970) 86 LQR 208; A. R. White, "The Identity and Time of the Actus Reus" [1977] Crim LR 148.
6. *Jakeman* (1983) 76 Cr App Rep 223, [1983] Crim LR 104 and commentary thereon.
7. Andanaes, *CLGP of Norway*, 194.
8. "There is no law against a man's intending to commit a murder the day after tomorrow. The law only deals with conduct": Holmes, *The Criminal Law* (John Harvard ed.) 54.
9. Below, p. 756.
10. *Scott* [1967] VR 276; discussed by Howard in [1967] Crim LR at 406.
11. Below, p. 352. Cf. *Burke* [1987] Crim LR 480 and commentary.
12. *Jakeman*, supra. Cf. *Wings Ltd v Ellis*, above, p. 53.
13. See commentary on *Burke* [1987] Crim LR 480.
14. *Fagan v Metropolitan Police Comr* [1969] 1 QB 439, [1968] 3 All ER 442; below, p. 380. Cf. *Miller* [1983] 2 AC 161, [1983] 1 All ER 978, HL; *Singh (Gurdev) v R* [1974] 1 All ER 26, [1973] 1 WLR 1444, CA.
15. *Khandu* (1890) ILR 15 Bomb 194; *Shorty* [1950] SR 280.
16. [1954] 1 All ER 373; **SHC 12**. Followed in *Moore and Dorn* [1975] Crim LR 229.

"impossible to divide up what was really one series of acts in this way. There is no doubt that the accused set out to do all these acts in order to achieve their plan, and as parts of their plan: and it is much too refined a ground of judgment to say that, because they were at a misapprehension at one stage and thought that their guilty purpose was achieved before it was achieved, therefore they are to escape the penalties of the law."

This suggests that the answer might be different where there was no antecedent plan to dispose of the body and *Thabo Meli* was distinguished on this ground in New Zealand[17] and, at first, in South Africa.[18] But in *Church*[19] the Court of Criminal Appeal applied *Thabo Meli* on a manslaughter charge[20] where D, in a sudden fight, knocked P unconscious and, wrongly believing her to be dead, threw her into the river where she drowned. Here there was no antecedent plan. The point was not considered by the court, but it was apparently thought to be enough that the accused's conduct constituted "a series of acts which culminated in [P's] death." In *S v Masilela*[1] the South African court expressly extended *Thabo Meli* to a case where there was no pre-conceived plan. To hold otherwise would be "wholly unrealistic." The court pointed out that the act done with *mens rea* was a contributory cause of death – as, it would seem, it was in all the earlier cases. It has been cogently argued[2] that this is the better basis, since it requires no stretching, on grounds of expediency, of the contemporaneity principle. But, unless the principles of causation[3] are also to be stretched on "policy" grounds, it would exempt D where the act of concealment was a completely independent cause of death. For example, D administers poison to P who is bedridden and alone. Believing P to be dead, D burns down the house. P would have died in the same way even if he had not been previously poisoned. If *Church* is rightly decided perhaps the principle is that D is liable if he kills during the continuance of the "transaction" in which he acted with *mens rea*; and that transaction is continuing so long as D is covering up the homicide he believes he has committed. So that if he leaves the "body" in his attic and P dies of starvation a month later, he is guilty; but if he is carrying the "body" from the scene of the crime to hand it over to the police and accidentally drops it and kills P, he is not.

The problem is not confined to cases where D supposes P to be dead. D stuns P and gags him. P dies from suffocation, because of the gag. If the blow was struck with intent to do grievous bodily harm, D would have been guilty of murder if P had died from it. The gag was inserted with no intention to cause any harm whatever; but it was this act which killed. If this was all part of a prearranged plan, it would seem to be indistinguishable from *Thabo Meli*. Where there was no such plan, the New Zealand

17. *Ramsay* [1967] NZLR 1005.
18. *Chiswibo* 1960 (2) SA 714.
19. [1966] 1 QB 59, [1965] 2 All ER 72.
20. In *A-G's Reference (No. 4 of 1980)* [1981] 2 All ER 617 at 620, below, p. 78, the Court of Appeal left open the question whether the *Thabo Meli* principle applies to manslaughter and whether it was part of the ratio decidendi of *Church* that it does. It is submitted that the answer to the first part of the question should be in the affirmative, whatever the answer to the second.

1. 1968 (2) SA 558 (AD); **SHC 12**.
2. By Hunt (1968) 85 SALJ 383, and see Marston, loc. cit. p. 64, footnote 5, above.
3. Below, p. 312 et seq., especially p. 316.

Court of Appeal held *Thabo Meli* inapplicable.[4] The principle tentatively suggested in the previous paragraph would have led to a different result; but the Court held that, in any event, the terms of the relevant legislation excluded the application of the doctrine.

In all these cases the second act was a cause of the death. Where it is impossible to say which act caused death, it has been held that D may be convicted only if it can be proved that he acted with *mens rea* (or other appropriate degree of fault) on both occasions. Where D knocked P downstairs and then, believing that he had killed her, cut her throat in order to dispose of the body, and it was impossible to say which act caused death, it was held that the jury should have been directed that they should convict of manslaughter if they were satisfied *both* (i) that knocking P downstairs was an intentional act which was unlawful and dangerous;[5] *and* (ii) that the act of cutting the throat was one of gross criminal negligence.[6] If manslaughter was committed, it was immaterial that it was impossible to prove on which of these two closely related occasions it occurred.[7] If the jury were not satisfied on both points, there was a 50 per cent chance that this was a case of accidental death, in which case acquittal must follow. But if *Thabo Meli* applies to manslaughter,[8] the direction is too favourable. Assuming it was all one "transaction", it should have been enough to prove that D had the required *mens rea* on the first occasion.

7 Motive usually does not affect Liability

If D causes an *actus reus* with *mens rea*, he is guilty of the crime and it is entirely irrelevant to his guilt that he had a good motive. The mother who kills her imbecile and suffering child out of motives of compassion is just as guilty of murder as is the man who kills for gain. On the other hand, if either the *actus reus* or the *mens rea* of any crime is lacking, no motive, however evil, will make a man guilty of a crime.

A contrary view, it is true, has been put by an American writer:[9]

"Suppose a grave felony is about to be committed under such circumstances that the killing of the offender to prevent the crime would be justified by law, and at that very moment he is shot and killed. If the slayer was prompted by the impulse to promote the social security by preventing the felony he is guilty of no offence; if he had no such impulse but merely acted upon the urge to satisfy an old grudge by killing a personal enemy, he is guilty of murder. The intent is the same in either case – to kill the person; the difference between innocence and guilt lies in the motive which prompted this intent."

It is submitted, however, that (assuming that D knew of the facts which justified the killing) this view is contrary to principle. If it were correct, it would seem to follow that D, the public executioner, would be guilty of

---

4. *Ramsay* [1967] NZLR 1005.
5. This is manslaughter. Below, p. 345.
6. This may be and, it was assumed in the case, was manslaughter. Below, p. 352.
7. *A-G's Reference (No. 4 of 1980)* [1981] 2 All ER 617, [1981] 1 WLR 705, CA, [1981] Crim LR 493 and commentary.
8. This question was left open. *Church* suggests that it does; and that seems right in principle.
9. Perkins and Boyce, *Criminal Law* (3rd ed.), 930.

murder in hanging X, who had been condemned to death by a competent court, if it were shown that D had postponed his retirement to carry out this particular execution because he had a grudge against X and derived particular pleasure from hanging him. This can hardly be the law. If a surgical operation, though dangerous to life, is clearly justifiable on medical grounds, a surgeon who performs it with all proper skill cannot be said to be guilty of attempted murder, or, if the patient dies, murder, because he hopes the patient will die so that he can marry his wife, or inherit his property, or so that the patient will avoid the thoroughly miserable life he will face if he survives.[10]

Sometimes, when we speak of motive, we mean an emotion such as jealousy or greed, and sometimes we mean a species of intention. For example, D intends (a) to put poison in his uncle's tea, (b) to cause his uncle's death and (c) to inherit his money. We would normally say that (c) is his motive. Applying our test of "desired consequence" (c) is certainly also intended. The reason why it is considered merely a motive is that it is a consequence ulterior to the *mens rea* and the *actus reus*; it is no part of the crime. If this criterion as to the nature of motive be adopted then it follows that motive, by definition, is irrelevant to criminal responsibility – that is, a man may be lawfully convicted of a crime whatever his motive may be, or even if he has no motive. The courts are not always consistent in their terminology. If D dismisses E, an employee, who has given evidence against him, in accordance with the terms of E's contract, D will be guilty of contempt of court, it is said, if his "motive" was to punish E for his evidence but not if it was for any other reason – e.g. incompetence or redundancy.[11] Consistency in terminology would suggest that in such a case we should speak of intent or purpose rather than motive. For example, if this variety of contempt were to be defined, the definition might say, "with intent to punish the witness".

In some exceptional cases motive is an element of an offence. In a prosecution for libel, if the civil law defences of fair comment or qualified privilege are available at all,[12] they may, no doubt, be defeated by proof of motive in the sense of spite or ill-will, while in blackmail, contrary to the Theft Act 1968, s. 21,[13] the accused's motive may be relevant in ascertaining whether his demand was unwarranted.[14]

As *evidence*, motive is always relevant.[15] This means simply that, if the prosecution can prove that D had a motive for committing the crime, they may do so since the existence of a motive makes it more likely that D in fact did commit it. Men do not usually act without a motive.

Motive is important again when the question of punishment is in issue. When the law allows the judge a discretion in sentencing, he will obviously be more leniently disposed towards the convicted person who acted with a

---

10. See A. T. H. Smith in *Reshaping the Criminal Law*, 95.
11. *A-G v Butterworth* [1963] 1 QB 696, [1962] 3 All ER 326, CA, below, p. 782. Cf. *Rooney v Snaresbrook Crown Court* (1978) 68 Cr App Rep 78, [1979] Crim LR 109.
12. See below, p. 824.
13. See below, pp. 590–592.
14. Cf. *Adams*, below, p. 313; *Chandler v Director of Public Prosecutions*, below, p. 839.
15. *Williams* (1986) 84 Cr App Rep 299, CA, not following *Berry* (1986) 83 Cr App Rep 7.

good motive. When the judge has no discretion (as in murder) a good motive may similarly be a factor in inducing the Home Secretary to grant an early release on licence.

8 Ignorance of the Law is no Defence[16]

In our discussion of the general principles of *mens rea* nothing has been said about whether the accused knows his act is against the law, for, in the great majority of cases, it is irrelevant whether he knows it or not: "... the principle that ignorance of the law is no defence in crime" said Lord Bridge, "is so fundamental that to construe the word 'knowingly' in a criminal statute as requiring not merely knowledge of facts material to the offender's guilt, but also knowledge of the relevant law, would be revolutionary and, to my mind, wholly unacceptable."[17] It must usually be proved that D intended to cause, or was reckless whether he caused, the event or state of affairs which, as a matter of fact, is forbidden by law; but it is quite immaterial to his conviction (though it may affect his punishment) whether he *knew* that the event or state of affairs was forbidden by law. This is so even though it also appears that D's ignorance of the law was quite reasonable and even, apparently, if it was quite impossible[18] for him to know of the prohibition in question. It was no defence for a native of Baghdad, charged with an unnatural offence on board a ship lying in an English port, to show that the act was lawful in his own country and that he did not know English law.[19] It was held that a Frenchman might be guilty of murder in the course of duelling in England, even if he did not know that duelling was against English law.[20] In *Bailey*,[1] D was convicted of an offence created by a statute which was passed while he was on the high seas although he committed the act before the end of the voyage when he could not possibly have known of the statute.[2] In each of these cases it might be argued that D at least intended something immoral; but that makes no difference. A motorist's mistaken belief that a constable has no right in the particular circumstances to require a specimen of breath is not a reasonable excuse for not providing the specimen.[3] So, if a statute forbids the sale of a house for a price above a stated figure, D, who helps to negotiate a sale at a price of which he is aware, and which is in excess of the stated figure, has *mens rea* even though he affirmatively believes a sale at the particular price to be lawful.[4] He intends the occurrence of that event which the law

16. See Ashworth, "Excusable Mistake of Law", [1974] Crim LR 652.
17. *Grant v Borg* [1982] 2 All ER 257 at 263, HL but cf. *Curr* [1968] 2 QB 944, [1967] 1 All ER 478 below, p. 255, where the court thought that a woman improperly receiving a family allowance payment was guilty only if she knew that what she was doing "amounted to an offence". But the section required only that she should know that the allowance was not "properly payable".
18. *Bailey*, infra.
19. *Esop* (1836) 7 C & P 456.
20. *Barronet and Allain* (1852) Dears CC 51.
  1. (1800) Russ & Ry 1.
  2. But the judges recommended a pardon. Where a continuing act was made unlawful it was held that a reasonable time must be allowed for its discontinuance and that ignorance of the law was relevant to determine this question: *Burns v Nowell* (1880) 5 QBD 444. Cf. above, p. 47, footnote 9.
  3. *Reid* [1973] 3 All ER 1020, [1973] 1 WLR 1283, CA. "... if you choose at the street side to act out the part of Hampden, you have got to be right:" per Scarman, LJ.
  4. *Johnson v Youden* [1950] 1 KB 544, [1950] 1 All ER 300.

forbids. If, on the other hand, D is misled as to the price and believes it to be a figure which is, in fact, below the statutory maximum, then he has no *mens rea*.[5] The event which he now intends is not forbidden by the law. It probably makes no difference that D had received competent legal advice that his conduct would be lawful.[6] The contrary view, it has been said,[7] would result in "the advice of an attorney being paramount to the law." It is no defence that D acted in reliance on an assurance by a competent official that no prosecution would be brought;[8] but that is a most material fact when it comes to sentence. Arguably it might be different where the official advice is that the proposed act is lawful,[9] but the authorities at present are against this view.[10]

Few distinctions have given more difficulty than that between mistake of fact and mistake of law but the point has been little discussed in the present context. The decision in *Brutus v Cozens*[11] that the meaning of an ordinary word in a statute is not a question of law opens up exciting possibilities. If D studies the Public Order Act and concludes that the conduct in which he proposes to indulge is not "insulting", but the court takes a different view, why cannot D rely on his mistake "of fact"? It is thought that such a defence would be unsympathetically received by the courts and, indeed, regarded as subversive of the criminal law;[12] but, accepting (as we must) *Brutus v Cozens*, it is difficult to see that it is bad in principle.

In the case of the most serious crimes the problem does not arise; everyone knows it is against the law to murder, rob or rape. In the case of many less serious crimes, however, a person may very easily, and without negligence, be ignorant that a particular act is a crime. In such cases there will usually be nothing immoral about the act; and the conviction of a morally innocent person requires justification. Various justifications for the rule have been advanced. Blackstone[13] thought that "every person of discretion" may know the law – a proposition which is manifestly untrue today. Austin[14] based the rule upon the difficulty of disproving ignorance of the law, while Holmes,[15] who considered this no more difficult a question than many which are investigated in the courts, thought that to admit the plea would be to encourage ignorance of the law. A modern writer[16] argues

---

5. Ibid.

6. *Cooper v Simmons* (1862) 7 H & N 707; *Crichton v Victorian Dairies Ltd* [1965] VR 49. In *Shaw v Director of Public Prosecutions* [1962] AC 220, [1961] 2 All ER 446, below, p. 276, D had sought advice as to the legality of the publication and evidently believed it to be legal. See also Hall, GPCL 387; Burchell & Hunt, 262; Perkins 926; and *Cambridgeshire and Isle of Ely County Council v Rust* [1972] 2 QB 426, [1972] 3 All ER 232, DC, below, p. 801.

7. *People v McCalla*, 220 Pac 436 (1923).

8. *Arrowsmith* [1975] QB 678, [1975] 1 All ER 463.

9. Williams CLGP, s. 106; Ashworth [1974] Crim LR at 657 "A Criminal Estoppel?".

10. *Surrey County Council v Battersby* [1965] 2 QB 194 at 203, [1965] 1 All ER 273; *Cambridgeshire and Isle of Ely County Council v Rust* [1972] 2 QB 426, [1972] 3 All ER 232; *Brook v Ashton* [1974] Crim LR 105; *Bowsher* [1973] RTR 202.

11. [1973] AC 854, [1972] 2 All ER 1297, HL; below, p. 120.

12. Cf. *Sancoff v Halford* [1973] Qd R 25. (Belief that books were not obscene is a mistake of law.)

13. *Commentaries*, iv, 27.

14. *Lectures on Jurisprudence*, 497.

15. *The Common Law*, 48.

16. Jerome Hall, "Ignorance and Mistake in Criminal Law" (1957) 33 Ind LJ 1. Cf. *General Principles*, 382–383.

that to allow the defence would be to contradict one of the fundamental postulates of a legal order: that rules of law enforce objective meanings, to be ascertained by the courts:

"If that plea [*sc.* ignorance of the law] were valid, the consequence would be: whenever a defendant in a criminal case thought the law was thus and so, he is to be treated as though the law were thus and so, that is, *the law actually is thus and so.*"[17]

As this writer points out, the criminal law represents an objective code of ethics which must prevail over individual convictions and he therefore argues:[18]

"Thus, while a person who acts in accordance with his honest convictions is certainly not as culpable as one who commits a harm knowing it is wrong, it is also true that conscience sometimes leads one astray. *Mens rea* underlines the essential difference. Penal liability based on it implies the objective wrongness of the harm proscribed – regardless of motive or conviction. This may fall short of perfect justice but the ethics of a legal order must be objective."

Unfortunately, however, much modern legislation is devoid of moral content, apart from the moral obligation to obey the law. One who, being ignorant of the law, sells goods at a price in excess of the maximum fixed by statute could hardly be said to have been led astray by his conscience while the "harm proscribed" lacks "objective wrongness".

The common law rule is not universally followed and the arguments by which it is supported have been found "not very convincing to those used to another system".[19] In Scandinavian criminal law, ignorance of the law is, in varying degrees, a defence. Thus, in Norway, a man will not be excused for ignorance of "the general rules of society which apply to everybody" or "the special rules governing the business or activity in which the individual is engaged". But "a fisherman need not study the legislation on industry"; a servant may be excused for *bona fide* and reasonable obedience to illegal orders of his master; or a stranger for breaking a rule which he could not be expected to know about; or liability may be negatived because the legislation is very new, or its interpretation doubtful. Such rules seem to have much to commend them, compared with the rigid and uncompromising attitude of English law. They seek to relate guilt to moral responsibility in a way in which our rule does not.[20]

---

17. 33 Ind LJ at 19. In *Cooper v Simmons* (1862) 7 H & N 707 at 717 Martin B thought that to allow the defence would be "to substitute the opinion of a person charged with a breach of the law for the law itself."
18. Ibid., at 22.
19. Andenaes. "*Ignorantia Juris* in Scandinavian Law" in *Essays in Criminal Science* (ed Mueller), 217 at 222. For South African Law see *S v De Blom* 1977 (3) SA 513 (AD) discussed by Turpin, [1978] CLJ 8.
20. An exception to the general rule is created by the Statutory Instruments Act 1946, s. 3. See Lanham, "Delegated Legislation and Publication" (1974) 37 MLR 510. On a charge brought under a statutory instrument it is a defence for D to prove that the instrument had not been issued at the time of the alleged offence; unless the Crown then proves that reasonable steps had been taken to bring it to the notice of the public, or persons likely to be affected by it, or D. See *Defiant Cycle Co Ltd v Newell* [1953] 2 All ER 38. The Privy Council has held that, in a jurisdiction where there is no similar provision, a person who is unaware that a ministerial order applying a prohibition to him has been made may set up his ignorance as a lack of *mens rea*: *Lim Chin Aik v R* [1963] AC 160, [1963] 1 All ER 223; above, p. 47.

9 Mistake of Law may Negative Mens Rea

If D, with *mens rea*, causes the *actus reus*, he is guilty and it will not avail him to say that he did not know the *actus reus* was forbidden by the criminal law. But the *actus reus* may be so defined that a mistake of law may result in D's not being intentional or reckless with respect to some element in it and so in his not having *mens rea*. In such a case, his mistake, whether reasonable or not, is a defence. "... an honest belief in a certain state of things does afford a defence, including an honest though mistaken belief about legal rights."[1] Unless the prosecution can prove that the mistake was not made, they have not established the requisite *mens rea*. If D is charged with intentionally or recklessly damaging property belonging to another, his honest belief, arising from a mistake of law, that the property is his own, is a defence. The Court so held, in *Smith*,[2] not because of any special provision in the Criminal Damage Act but by "applying the ordinary principles of *mens rea*". In *Roberts v Inverness Local Authority*[3] D was acquitted of moving a cow from one district to another without a licence because he believed the two districts had been amalgamated into one. Likewise in *National Coal Board v Gamble*[4] it was accepted that a mistake by the weighbridge operator about his right to withhold the ticket (a question of civil law) might be "a genuine belief in the existence of circumstances which, if true, would negative an intention to aid." A person does not "act as auditor of a company at a time when he knows that he is disqualified for appointment to that office" if, through ignorance of the statutory provisions, he does not know he is disqualified.[5]

The crucial question will be, what is the *mens rea* required by the crime? A mistake negativing *mens rea* as to some element in the *actus reus* is no defence if the law does not require *mens rea* as to that element. Bigamy provides a good illustration. The *actus reus* is committed by one who "being married, marries". If D, knowing that he was already married to X, were to marry P, it would certainly be no defence for him to say that he thought the law allowed him more than one wife. He intends, being married, to marry – the *actus reus* – and would simply be saying that he did not know that the *actus reus* was forbidden by the criminal law. If, misunderstanding the law of divorce, he wrongly supposed that his first marriage had been dissolved, he would not intend the *actus reus*. His mistake as to the law of divorce would negative basic *mens rea*; and, if bigamy required basic *mens rea*, it would be a defence. The law, however, is that bigamy does not require *mens rea* as to the element, "being married". The Crown need prove only that D intended to go through the alleged second ceremony; whereupon it is a defence if it appears that D may have believed, on reasonable grounds, that he was not married.[6] So here,

1. *Barrett and Barrett* (1980) 72 Cr App Rep 212 at 216, CA, below, p. 88.
2. [1974] QB 354, [1974] 1 All ER 632, CA; **SHC 634**, below, p. 684.
3. 1889, 27 S LR 198, discussed by Widgery LCJ in *Cambridgeshire and Isle of Ely CC v Rust* [1972] 3 WLR 226 at 231. The LCJ treats the mistake as one of fact; but surely the boundaries of districts is a question of civil law.
4. [1959] 1 QB 11 at 25, per Devlin J. The facts are set out below, p. 140.
5. *Secretary of State for Trade and Industry v Hart* [1982] 1 All ER 817, [1982] 1 WLR 481. Cf. Juries Act 1974, s. 20 (5) (d).
6. Below, p. 714.

exceptionally, the mistake of law is a defence only if it is reasonable. In an Australian case[7] D, a landlord, was charged with wilfully demanding as rent a sum which was irrecoverable under the relevant statute. D wrongly believed that he was entitled to charge any rent he pleased. Three judges thought the belief no defence: it was sufficient that D wilfully demanded that sum of money. But two judges thought that D's belief precluded the *mens rea* required; that a man cannot wilfully demand an *irrecoverable* rent unless he knows it is irrecoverable. "The defendant who is not shown in such a case to know that the act is unlawful needs no excuse. The offence has not been proved against him."[8]

This principle will operate only when the definition of the *actus reus* contains some legal concept like "property belonging to another". It has no application where the law fixes a standard which is different from that in which D believes. If he kills a trespasser it is no defence for him to assert that he believed the law allows deadly force to be used to expel trespassers.[9] It does not apply where D refuses, however honestly, to accept the judgment of a court,[10] just as it would be hopeless for him to argue that he did not accept the validity of an Act of Parliament. The principle is probably also confined to the case where the legal concept belongs to the civil law – as the notion of property ownership does – and not to the criminal law.[11] Suppose that X obtains goods from P by deception and gives them to D, who knows all the facts. We have already seen that it will not avail D to say he does not know handling stolen goods is a crime. Equally, it is thought it will not avail him to say that he did not know that it is against the criminal law to obtain goods by deception and that goods so obtained are "stolen" for this purpose. "Stolen" is a concept of the criminal, not the civil law, and ignorance of it is no defence.

On the other hand, the "leave" granted to a visitor to remain in the United Kingdom looks like a civil law concept, but the House of Lords has held that a mistake of law is no answer to a charge of knowingly remaining without leave.[12]

10 Absence of a "Claim of Right" as an Element in Mens Rea

Sometimes the *mens rea* of an offence is so defined as to require the absence of a claim of right. In other words, if D believed he had a right to do the act in question, he had no *mens rea* and therefore was not guilty of the crime. This defence will prevail even if D's belief is mistaken and is based upon an entirely wrong view of the law. It is available in a number of important crimes, including theft,[13] criminal damage to property,[14] and a number of other offences requiring wilfulness or fraud. This is in accordance with the

7. *Iannella v French* (1968) 119 CLR 84.
8. At p. 97, per Barwick CJ.
9. Cf. *Barrett and Barrett* (1980) 72 Cr App Rep 212; below, pp. 88 and 246.
10. Ibid.
11. It seems that a distinction between mistakes of civil and mistakes of criminal law was found to be untenable in German law: *Honig* (1963) 54 J Cr L & Cr at 285. But the distinction taken in the text seems to be a necessary consequence of the concept of *mens rea*.
12. *Grant v Borg* [1982] 2 All ER 257, [1982] 1 WLR 638.
13. Below, p. 525.
14. Below, p. 695.

ordinary principle that a mistake of law may, indirectly, operate as a defence by preventing the accused from having *mens rea* in acting as he did. It is important to notice the limits within which this defence operates. The mistake must be one which leads the accused to believe he has a right to act as he does; it is not enough that he simply believes his act is not a crime. Here too, the distinction between mistake as to the criminal and as to the civil law seems to be important. Thus if D, having read in an out-of-date book on criminal law that it is not stealing to take another's title deeds to land,[15] were to take P's deeds, thinking that this was a way in which he could injure P without any risk of being punished, he could, no doubt, be convicted of theft under s. 1 of the Theft Act 1968. He had no claim of right. It would be otherwise if D, owing to a misunderstanding of the law of property, thought that the title deeds were his, and that P was wrongfully withholding them from him. Here, clearly, he had a claim of right. Thus, while a mistake as to the criminal law only will not give rise to a claim of right, an error as to the civil law may do so.

It certainly cannot be asserted with confidence that the absence of a claim of right is a *general* requirement of *mens rea*, as it is in the case of theft and the other crimes referred to above. The question will therefore be considered in relation to specific crimes discussed below.

11 Proof of Intention and Foresight

There was formerly high authority[16] for the view that there is an irrebuttable presumption of law that a person foresees and intends the natural consequences of his acts. Proof that he did an act the natural consequence of which was death, was conclusive proof that he intended to kill, in the absence of evidence of insanity or incapacity to form an intent. To what extent, if at all, this actually represented the law was disputed: but it is now clear beyond all doubt that it is not the law. The question in every case is as to the actual intention of the person charged at the time when he did the act. Section 8 of the Criminal Justice Act 1967 provides:

"A court or jury in determining whether a person has committed an offence,

a) shall not be bound in law to infer that he intended or foresaw a result of his actions by reason only of its being a natural and probable consequence of those actions; but

b) shall decide whether he did intend or foresee that result by reference to all the evidence drawing such inferences from the evidence as appear proper in the circumstances."

To what extent intention or foresight need be proved in any particular case depends on the law relating to the crime which is in issue. Section 8 is concerned with *how* intention or foresight must be proved, not *when* it must be proved.[17] On a charge of manslaughter, for example, it remains unnecessary to prove that D intended or foresaw that death was likely to result from

15. This was the rule at common law.
16. *Director of Public Prosecutions v Smith* [1961] AC 290, [1960] 3 All ER 161; **SHC 305**, below, p. 328. The decision cannot be technically overruled by the Privy Council but five judges, all members of the House of Lords, declared that it was wrongly decided in *Frankland* [1987] AC 576, PC.
17. *Director of Public Prosecutions v Majewski* [1976] 2 All ER 142 at 151, 170.

his act.[18] The section was once construed so as to affect the substantive law of murder[19] but this was exceptional and it is now clear that it applies only to proof and never affects the substantive law.

Section 8 is confined to the *result* of D's actions. But no satisfactory distinction can be made between the results of an action and the relevant surrounding circumstances. In this connection at least, no attempt need be made to draw such a distinction because the decision of the House of Lords in *Director of Public Prosecutions v Morgan*[20] establishes that, as a matter of common law, the same principle applies to circumstances. It used to be said that a mistake of fact could be a defence only if it was reasonable but that is refuted by *Morgan*. It may now be taken to be settled that, once it is established that the definition of a crime requires a state of mind – intention, knowledge or *Cunningham* recklessness – with respect to particular elements of an offence, a mistake of fact or of law which is inconsistent with that state of mind is also incompatible with guilt and must lead to an acquittal. In *Morgan* the trial judge stressed to the jury that the *mens rea* of rape was an intention to have intercourse with a woman *without her consent*. Yet he went on to tell them that they could convict if they found that D believed, without reasonable grounds, that P was consenting. This, as Lord Cross pointed out,[1] was to present the jury with "two incompatible alternatives." Lord Hailsham said:[2]

"Once one has accepted, what seems to me abundantly clear, that the prohibited act in rape is non-consensual sexual intercourse, and that the guilty state of mind is an intention to commit it, it seems to me to follow as a matter of inexorable logic that there is no room either for a 'defence' of honest belief or mistake, or of a defence of honest and reasonable mistake. Either the prosecution proves its case or it does not."

The significance of *Morgan*, as the courts have now[3] belatedly recognised, goes far beyond the law of rape. The requirements of "inexorable logic" extend to the criminal law generally. In no case can the judge properly present the jury with "two incompatible alternatives."

The first question in every case is, what *mens rea* does the definition of the crime in question require? Neither section 8 nor *Morgan* (except in the case of rape at common law[4]) affect the answer to this question. What s. 8 and *Morgan* do establish is that a failure to foresee consequences, whether reasonable or not (s. 8), or a failure to know of circumstances, whether reasonable or not (*Morgan*) which negatives the *mens rea* of the offence requires acquittal. Where, on the other hand, the law does not require *mens rea*, s. 8 and *Morgan* have no application. *Prince*[5] and other cases of strict liability are unaffected.[6] So are the bigamy cases[7] which lay down that a

---

18. *Director of Public Prosecutions v Newbury* [1977] AC 500, [1976] 2 All ER 365, HL; **SHC 336**.
19. *Hyam v Director of Public Prosecutions* [1975] AC 55, [1974] 2 All ER 41; **SHC 307**; above, p. 59.
20. [1976] AC 182, [1975] 2 All ER 347; **SHC 45**; below, p. 429.
1. At 352.
2. At 361.
3. *Beckford v R* [1987] 3 All ER 425, [1987] 3 WLR 611 PC.
4. Rape is now defined by statute. See below, p. 429.
5. Above, pp. 41, 72.
6. Per Lord Hailsham at 362.
7. Below, p. 714.

mistake as to the existence of the first marriage must be reasonable.[8] These cases establish as a matter of substantive law that neither intention nor recklessness is required with respect to the element, "being married", in the definition of bigamy.

It is most important to notice that *Caldwell*[9] is not inconsistent with the law as stated. By broadening the concept of recklessness it establishes that a failure to think about consequences, which would formerly have been inconsistent with recklessness, is sometimes[10] no longer inconsistent with it. *Caldwell*[11] is concerned with the definition of *mens rea* in crimes where the word "reckless" appears. *Morgan* has nothing to say about the definition of the *mens rea* in any crime, except rape at common law. The two cases are about different things. The fundamental principle of *Morgan* is in no way inconsistent with the existence of crimes of negligence, where unreasonable mistakes will be no defence. That is a matter of policy and one which, ideally, should be decided in Parliament when the statutory definitions of crimes are approved.

It was said, with some justification, in 1982 that there had been a "Retreat from *Morgan*".[12] There was a tendency for the courts to say that *Morgan* was concerned only with the law of rape and laid down no general principle. In one case,[13] the Court of Appeal said, obiter, that D might have been convicted of doing an act with intent to evict a residential occupier although he believed that the person he intended to evict was not a residential occupier but a squatter, because there was no reasonable basis for his belief. So to hold would be to defy the "inexorable logic" which Lord Hailsham found compelling in *Morgan*. Happily, the "retreat" has now been stemmed and in *Beckford v R* the Privy Council has said:

"Looking back, *Morgan* can now be seen as a landmark decision in the development of the common law, returning the law to the path upon which it might have developed but for the inability of an accused to give evidence on his own behalf."[14]

It may now perhaps be safely assumed that the courts will give full effect to the principle of the case as described above.

Morgan and Defences

Beckford v R is of great importance in that it takes the principle of *Morgan* even further than the majority of the House were at that time prepared to go. In *Morgan* the defence was a simple denial of the prosecution's case. By charging rape, the prosecution alleged that D had intercourse with a woman who did not consent and that he either knew that she did not consent or was reckless whether she did so. D denied that he knew or was reckless, as alleged. There is another type of plea, more accurately described as a defence, where D admits the allegations made by the

---

8. Lord Hailsham, loc. cit.
9. Above, p. 62.
10. That is, when *Caldwell* as distinct from *Cunningham* recklessness is in issue.
11. [1982] AC 341, [1981] 1 All ER 961, above, p. 62.
12. D. Cowley [1982] Crim LR 198.
13. *Phekoo* [1981] 3 All ER 84, [1981] 1 WLR 1117.
14. [1987] 3 All ER 425 at 431.

prosecution but asserts further facts which, in law, justify or excuse his action. Self-defence is an example. D admits that he intentionally killed or wounded P but asserts that he did so because P was making a deadly attack on him and this was the only way he could save his own life. It may transpire that D was mistaken. P was not in fact making a deadly attack. The law has long recognised that D's defence is still good if his mistaken belief of fact was based on reasonable grounds. Directions to juries and dicta in higher courts were consistent in asserting that the defence failed if there were no reasonable grounds for his belief. The majority of the House of Lords in *Morgan* did not intend to interfere with this rule. They were concerned with a mistake as to an element of the offence, this question related to a mistake as to an element of a defence. In *Beckford* the Privy Council rejected this distinction. They approved the ruling of Lane LCJ in *Gladstone Williams*.[15] Discussing the offence of assault, he said:

"The mental element necessary to constitute guilt is the intent to apply unlawful force to the victim. We do not believe that the mental element can be substantiated by simply showing an intent to apply force and no more."

If D believed, reasonably or not, in the existence of facts which would justify the force used in self-defence, he did not intend to use *unlawful* force. *Beckford* clearly applies to all instances of private defence.[16] The principle would seem to apply to defences generally but it is perhaps premature to assert that it will be so applied. In duress, for example, the courts continue to state (though obiter) that D's belief in the alleged compelling facts must be based on reasonable grounds. If, however, D is to be judged on the facts as he believed them to be when he sets up self-defence it is difficult to see why it is different in principle or in policy when he sets up duress. In both cases he is saying that, on the facts as he believed them to be, his act was not an offence. It is submitted that the principle of *Beckford* should be applicable to defences generally.

Of earlier cases, that of the Divisional Court in *Albert v Lavin*[17] must, since *Beckford*, be taken to be wrong in making a distinction in relation to assault between the definitional elements of an offence and the definitional elements of a defence. The same subjective test applies to both. *Barrett and Barrett*[18] is more complex.

D was convicted of assault occasioning actual bodily harm to bailiffs who were executing a warrant to take possession of his house. D intended to assault the bailiffs but claimed that he was justified because he believed the court order had been obtained by fraud, though his application to have it set aside had been unsuccessful. Not surprisingly, this refusal to accept the judgment of the courts was held to be no defence. If D was making a mistake, it was one of law, admittedly the civil law,[19] but of a rather special kind. It does not necessarily follow that the result would have been the same if D had believed the men were not bailiffs at all but imposters, or that

15. [1987] 3 All ER 411, (1983) 78 Cr App 276, CA; **SHC 236**.
16. Below, p. 240.
17. [1982] AC 546, [1981] 1 All ER 628, DC.
18. (1980) 72 Cr App Rep 212.
19. (1980) 72 Cr App Rep 212.

the court had made no order. He was entitled to use force to repel a trespasser. An honest and reasonable belief that the men were trespassers should certainly have been an answer; and so, it is submitted (and *Beckford* confirms this), should an honest and unreasonable belief arising from a mistake of fact. *Morgan* was discussed, in relation not to this, but to a second point. It was argued that D was justified because he honestly believed that the force the bailiffs were using was excessive. But a mistake as to the amount of force which the law permits is certainly a mistake of law which is incapable of founding a defence. If it were otherwise, every man would, in effect, fix his own standards, whereas standards are fixed by law. *Morgan,* properly understood, had nothing to do with either of these points and the court's remark that it was inapplicable because it related to rape was inapt. Indeed, the court spoke with approval of the *Tolson*[20] principle but, as they phrased it, it was the *Morgan*[1] principle: – "an honest belief in a certain state of things does afford a defence, including an honest though mistaken belief about legal rights" – not, be it noted, an honest *and reasonable* belief. The subjectivist could not ask for more; but the principle was inapplicable here because (i) refusal to accept the validity of a court order, if it is properly called a mistake at all, is not the sort of mistake that a court can, as a matter of policy, admit as a defence; and (ii) standards are conclusively settled by the law.

Although s. 8 requires the court to have regard to *all* the evidence, that is, all the evidence relevant to the question whether D did intend or foresee, the courts have consistently held that evidence that D did not intend or foresee because he had taken drink or drugs is no defence, except in the case of crimes requiring "specific intent". This practice has been reconciled with the words of s. 8 by holding that there is a rule of substantive law that the prosecution need prove no *mens rea* where D relies on evidence that he had taken drink or drugs for the purpose of showing that he lacked any *mens rea*, not being a "specific intent", which the definition of the crime requires in all other circumstances.[2]

It might be thought, at first sight, that proof of intention, foresight and knowledge presents almost insuperable difficulties. Direct evidence of a man's state of mind, except through his own confession, is not available. But the difficulties, in practice, are not so great. If D points a loaded gun at P's head, pulls the trigger and shoots him dead, it is reasonable to infer that D intended and foresaw P's death. A jury might well be convinced by such evidence that D intended to kill. If D offered an explanation of any kind – he thought the gun was unloaded, or he intended to fire above P's head – and the jury thought that it might reasonably be true, then they should acquit him of an intention to kill. If he offered no explanation, as s. 8 makes clear, the jury would not be bound to convict him of having such an intention; they would have to ask themselves whether, in the light of all the evidence, they were satisfied beyond reasonable doubt. Sometimes D's acts may afford apparently overwhelming evidence of his intention to produce a

20. See below, p. 715.
 1. Above, p. 86.
 2. *Director of Public Prosecutions v Majewski* [1977] AC 433, [1976] 2 All ER 142, HL.

particular result but evidence to the contrary is always admissible and the question must be left to the jury.[3] Similarly, the fact that any reasonable man would, in the circumstances, have known of a fact is cogent evidence that D knew of it.[4]

The difficulty of distinguishing between "he foresaw" and "he ought to have foreseen", "he knew" and "he ought to have known," is not a good reason for not drawing the line at this point. It is an inescapable difficulty when we have a law which requires us to look into men's minds; and such a requirement is essential to a civilised system of criminal law.

"... a lack of confidence in the ability of a tribunal correctly to estimate evidence of states of mind and the like can never be sufficient ground for excluding from enquiry the most fundamental element in a rational and humane criminal code."[5]

3. *Riley* [1967] Crim LR 656, is a striking instance of the rebuttal of apparently conclusive evidence of an intent. Expert evidence was admitted that D was suffering from psychoneurosis; but in the case of a normal person expert evidence as to the operation of the mind is not admissible. It is a question for the jury: *Chard* (1971) 56 Cr App Rep 268, CA. Cf. *Turner* [1975] QB 834; [1975] 1 All ER 70.
4. Sexual Offences (Amendment) Act 1976, below, p. 429.
5. *Thomas v R* (1937) 59 CLR 279 at 309, per Dixon J.

5 Crimes of Negligence[1]

1 Negligence as Failure to Comply with an Objective Standard

Intention, recklessness and negligence all involve a failure to comply with an objective standard of conduct. Where intention or *Cunningham* recklessness[2] is required a state of mind must also be proved. *Caldwell* recklessness too was said by the House of Lords to involve proof of a state of mind; but this is so only in the sense that *not* giving thought is a state of mind.[3] *Caldwell* recklessness may however be negatived by evidence of a state of mind – i.e., that D had given thought to the matter and wrongly concluded that there was no risk.[4] In a crime of negligence such evidence is no answer. Negligence may be conclusively proved by simply showing that D's conduct failed to measure up to an objective standard. It is no answer for him to say, "I considered whether there was a risk and decided there was none." Where the risk is one that he ought to have foreseen, that is an admission of negligence. It is not necessary to prove that D did not foresee the risk.[5] It could never be a defence to a charge of negligence to show that the dangerous act was done recklessly or intentionally. If D were charged with manslaughter and the prosecution's case was that he killed P by gross negligence it is inconceivable that it could be a defence for him to say, convincingly, "I wasn't negligent; I *intended* to kill him" – or "I took a quite deliberate risk of killing him." The more blameworthy state of mind must include the less; so, if D failed to comply with the objective standard, he is liable whatever his state of mind. Negligence is *conduct* which departs from the standard to be expected of a reasonable man. This is not to say that a person's state of mind is always irrelevant when negligence is in issue. He may, for example, have special knowledge which an ordinary person would not possess. The question then is, whether a reasonable man, with that knowledge, would have acted as he did. Behaviour with a revolver which is possibly not negligent in the case of an ordinary person with no

---

1. See Hart, "Negligence, *Mens Rea* and Criminal Responsibility" in *Oxford Essays in Jurisprudence*, 29. The question of liability for negligence in manslaughter and under the Road Traffic Acts is considered in detail below, pp. 352; and 479.
2. Above, p. 62.
3. See Williams [1981] CLJ 252 at 256–258.
4. Above, p. 64.
5. As it might be, theoretically, on a charge of *Caldwell* recklessness.

special knowledge might be grossly negligent if committed by a firearms expert.[6] If D has less knowledge or capacity for foresight than the reasonable man this, it seems, will not generally help him; but if he has more knowledge or capacity for foresight, a higher standard will be expected of him.

Writers differ as to whether negligence can properly be described as *mens rea*.[7] If that term is used simply as a compendious expression for the varieties of fault which may give rise to criminal liability, then it does of course include negligence. If it is taken in its more literal sense of "guilty mind", the usage is inappropriate. It is sometimes argued that the absence of foresight or knowledge is just as much a state of mind as its presence;[8] but, since negligence may be proved without establishing anything as to what was going on in D's mind, it seems more appropriate and convenient to restrict the term to intention and recklessness and that is the sense in which it is used in this book. Crimes requiring *mens rea* are contrasted with crimes of negligence.

2 Negligence as the Basis of Liability

There are very few crimes in English law in which negligence is the gist of the offence. Manslaughter has long been the most conspicuous example and, indeed, the only serious crime in this category but there is now some doubt whether even this crime can be committed with less than *Caldwell* recklessness.[9] Generally, in serious crimes, intention or recklessness is required as to the central features of the offence, but negligence with respect to some subsidiary element in the *actus reus* is sometimes enough.

So under s. 19 of the Sexual Offences Act 1956,[10] it is an offence to take an unmarried girl under the age of eighteen out of the possession of her parent or guardian against his will with the intent that she shall have unlawful sexual intercourse with men or with a particular man. It is expressly provided, however, that it is a defence "If he believes her to be of the age of eighteen or over and *has reasonable cause for the belief*". It follows that an honest but unreasonable belief that the girl is over eighteen is no defence. Negligence with respect to that element will suffice, though, of course, it must be shown that D intended[11] to take the girl out of the possession of her parent, and had the ulterior intent as to unlawful sexual intercourse.

---

6. Cf. *Lamb* [1967] 2 QB 981, [1967] 2 All ER 1282; **SHC 334** above p. 65.
7. Edwards *Mens Rea*, 206.
8. Salmond on *Jurisprudence* (11th ed.) 429. Cf. *Tesco Supermarkets v Nattrass* [1972] AC 153 at 159, per Lord Diplock. *Caldwell, supra*.
9. Below, p. 352.
10. Below, p. 452.
11. Cf. *Hibbert*, above, p. 72 and *Hudson*, below, p. 96, footnote 13.

If there had been a similar provision in the section in issue in *Prince's* case,[12] he would, of course, have been acquitted. But such a provision, as well as catching the negligent person, disposes of another difficult case. It deals satisfactorily with the case of the man who does not advert to the girl's age at all (simple ignorance), for he cannot say that "he believed her to be of the age of eighteen or over". Such a person will have no defence even though he had reasonable ground for believing the girl to be over eighteen[13] and was therefore not negligent.

The rule, once supposed to exist, that a mistake was never a defence unless it was reasonable was capable of turning almost any crime into a crime of negligence; but *Morgan*[14] and *Beckford*[15] have established that there is no such rule. Those decisions do not affect cases where it has been ruled that *mens rea* as to some element of the offence is not required and that only a reasonable mistake will excuse. For example, it has been held that if D goes through a ceremony of marriage, believing wrongly but without reasonable grounds that he is not married because his wife is dead, or his marriage has been dissolved or annulled, he is guilty of bigamy.[16] This, in effect, is to turn bigamy into a crime of negligence so far as this element of the offence is concerned. D is to be held liable because he did not take sufficient care to ascertain that his first marriage was at an end, before going through the second ceremony.

In the examples just considered, the negligence is as to a subsidiary element only. Occasionally, negligence is the central feature of the crime. Under the Road Traffic Act 1972, s. 3, for example, it is an offence to drive a motor vehicle on a road without due care and attention or without reasonable consideration for other persons using the road. On a charge of driving without due care, it is clear that negligence is the gist of the offence. This section, it has been held, establishes

"an objective standard, impersonal and universal, fixed in relation to the safety of other users of the highway. It is in no way related to the degree of proficiency or degree of experience to be attained by the individual driver."[17]

So a learner driver, who was "exercising all the skill and attention to be expected from a person with his short experience" but who failed to attain the required standard, was held guilty.[17] The offence may be committed by making an error of judgment of a kind which a reasonably prudent and skilful driver would not make.[18] It will be noted that it is not necessary to prove that any harmful consequence ensued; it is enough to show that D drove in a manner in which a reasonable man would not have driven because he would have realised it involved an unjustifiable risk.

---

12. Above, p. 41.
13. Cf. *Harrison* [1938] 3 All ER 134.
14. Above, p. 86.
15. [1987] 3 All ER 425, PC.
16. Below, p. 714 and cf., above, p. 86.
17. *McCrone v Riding* [1938] 1 All ER 157; below, p. 479; *Preston JJ ex p Lyons* [1982] RTR 173, DC, discussed by Wasik, [1982] Crim LR 411.
18. *Simpson v Peat* [1952] 2 QB 24, [1952] 1 All ER 447.

3 Degrees of Negligence

It has been said that there can be no

"degrees of inadvertence when that word is used to denote a state of mind, since it means that in the man's mind there has been a complete absence of a particular thought, a nullity; and of nullity there can be no degrees."[19]

However this may be, if negligence is considered as a failure to comply with a standard of conduct, then it is clear that there are degrees of it. It may be negligent to drive a car at 40 m.p.h. on a particular piece of road. If so, it is more negligent to do so with defective brakes, more still if there is a fog or ice on the road and so on. English law does, in fact, recognise different degrees of negligence. It has been stated repeatedly by the courts that negligence which will found civil liability is not necessarily enough on a charge of manslaughter, though that crime could then be committed negligently, whatever the position today.[20] The departure from the standard of the reasonable driver which is sufficient to constitute driving without due care and attention, contrary to s. 3 of the Road Traffic Act 1972, is not enough to found a charge of reckless driving, contrary to s. 2 of the Act. For s. 2, the driving need only create "a risk of causing inconvenience or annoyance to other road users" but for reckless driving it must be such as to create "a real risk of causing physical injury to someone else who happens to be using the road or damage to property more substantial than the kind of minor damage that may be caused by an error of judgment in the course of parking one's car".[1] Whether the negligence required for reckless driving is sufficient to found a charge of manslaughter if death is caused is considered below.[2]

Of course these different degrees of negligence are incapable of precise definition and much must necessarily depend upon the judgment of the particular jury (or bench of magistrates) and their own standard in the matter in question. The fact that the line is difficult to draw is not a good reason for not attempting to draw it, if there are practical reasons for making the distinction.[3]

4 Should Negligence be a Ground of Liability?

Distinguished academic writers have strongly contended that negligence should have no place in criminal liability. Their arguments for the most part assumed the clear-cut distinction between conscious and inadvertent risk-taking which formerly distinguished recklessness from negligence.

19. Kenny, *Outlines*, 39, criticised by Hart in *Oxford Essays in Jurisprudence* at 41.
20. Below, p. 352.
  1. *Lawrence* [1981] 1 All ER 974 at 982, per Lord Diplock. What is the difference (if any) between "a risk" and "a real risk"?
  2. Below, p. 354
  3. See Hart in *Oxford Essays in Jurisprudence*, at 42: "Negligence is gross if the precautions to be taken against harm are very simple, such as persons who are but poorly endowed with physical and mental capacities can easily take."

Since the advent of *Caldwell* recklessness much inadvertent risk-taking has been brought within the criminal law. Turner acknowledges that negligence connotes that D was

"in some measure blameworthy, and that we should expect an ordinary reasonable man to foresee the possibility of the consequences and to regulate his conduct so as to avoid them;"[4]

but contends that the moral test, on which criminal liability should be (and, indeed, is) based, is that of foresight of the consequences of one's conduct. Hall goes further and finds it difficult to accept that negligently caused harm reflects a moral fault.[5] He rejects the view that punishment stimulates care, arguing that the deterrent theory postulates a man who weighs the possibility of punishment in the balance before acting; but the inadvertent harm-doer, by definition, does not do this. Hall appears to suggest[5] that the courts themselves do not really believe that punishment deters negligence, pointing out that sentences, even for negligent homicides, are relatively light. He rejects the thesis that negligent persons may be ethically blameworthy in so far as they are insensitive to the rights of others. In the case of negligently caused motor-car accidents, for example, he argues that

"it seems much more probable that a dull mind, slow reactions, awkwardness and other ethically irrelevant factors were the underlying cause."[6]

Williams[7] acknowledges that "it is possible for punishment to bring about greater foresight, by causing the subject to stop and think before committing himself to a course of conduct;" but thinks that this justification does not go very far and that the law is wise in penalising negligence only exceptionally.

Hart[8] challenges the commonly accepted criterion of foresight. The reason why it is thought proper to punish (in most cases) the man who foresees the forbidden harm is that he can choose to cause it or not; but in some cases of negligence, at least, it may be said,

" 'he could have thought about what he was doing' with just as much rational confidence as one can say of an intentional wrong-doing, 'he could have done otherwise'."

Hart's approach to negligence, however, differs from that so far generally adopted by the courts. He would not enforce an objective, external and impersonal standard which took no account of the individual's lack of capacity. He would recognise that punishment might[9] be proper only if two questions are answered in the affirmative:[10]

"i) Did the accused fail to take those precautions which any reasonable man with normal capacities would in the circumstances have taken?

---

4. MACL 207.
5. *General Principles*, 136.
6. Ibid., at p. 138. And cf. Keedy in 22 Harv L Rev at p. 84: ". . . a man should not be held criminal because of lack of intelligence."
7. CLGP 123.
8. *Oxford Essays in Jurisprudence*, 29.
9. Hart is not concerned to *advocate* the punishment of negligence, but only to dispel the belief that liability for negligence is a form of strict or absolute liability.
10. Ibid., at p. 46.

ii) Could the accused, given his mental and physical capacities, have taken those precautions?"

Until the decisions in 1981 in *Caldwell*[11] and *Lawrence*[12] there was only one English case[13] where this line was taken. One interpretation of those decisions, now rejected at the level of the Divisional Court[14] and the Court of Appeal,[15] would have incorporated this concept of negligence into recklessness. The prevailing interpretation of *Caldwell* and *Lawrence* incorporates the broader, traditional, concept of gross negligence into recklessness, subject only to the "lacuna", and allows it a much wider rule than it had hitherto played.[16]

Hall argues[17] that negligence should be controlled in other ways – by re-examining whether negligent persons should be able to escape completely from the consequences of civil liability by insurance; by more vigorous control of licences to operate dangerous instrumentalities; and by more education and instruction.

The negligent handling of certain instruments – notably motor-vehicles – can have such drastic consequences that society is almost bound to adopt any measures which seem to have a reasonable prospect of inducing greater care; and it seems reasonable to suppose that the threat of punishment does have an effect on the care used in the handling of such instruments. There is a trend towards replacing strict liability by liability for negligence.[18] Courts in the Commonwealth have moved ahead of those in England. The lead came from Australia.[19] In Canada, the Supreme Court, in a notable judgment delivered by Dickson J, held that public welfare offences prima facie fall into an intermediate class between offences requiring *mens rea* and offences "of absolute liability". The prosecution need prove only that D caused the *actus reus* but he may escape liability by proving that he took all reasonable care to avoid the commission of the offence.[20] Without going so far as to establish any general principle, in England Parliament has recently shown an inclination to move in this direction. The Trade Descriptions Act 1968 creates a number of offences, some of which replace earlier offences of strict liability, and provides by s. 24 that it is a defence to prove (i) that the commission of the offence was due (inter alia) to a mistake or accident and (ii) that D "took all reasonable precautions and exercised all due diligence to avoid the commission of such an offence by himself or any person under his control". Thus, though the prosecution do not have to prove negligence, it is a defence for D to show that he was not negligent. Similar steps have been taken in the Misuse of Drugs Act 1971.[1]

---

11. Above, p. 62.
12. Above, p. 63.
13. *Hudson* [1966] 1 QB 448, [1965] 1 All ER 721.
14. *Elliott v C (a minor)* [1983] 2 All ER 1005, [1983] 1 WLR 939 DC; **SHC 73.**
15. *R, Stephen Malcolm* (1984) 79 Cr App Rep 334 CA; **SHC 76.**
16. Above, p. 65.
17. "Negligent Behaviour should be excluded from Penal Liability", 63 Col LR 632.
18. Below, p. 117.
19. *Maher v Musson* (1934) 52 CLR 100; *Proudman v Dayman* (1941) 67 CLR 536.
20. *City of Sault Ste Marie* (1978) 40 CCC (2d) 353, **SHC 127.**
 1. Below, p. 108.

Where there is no such express provision in a statute, it is unlikely that the courts will hold it to be implied. It is true that the House of Lords in *Sweet v Parsley*[2] looked favourably on a doctrine developed in Australia:[3]

"When a statutory prohibition is cast in terms which at first sight appear to impose strict responsibility, they should be understood merely as imposing responsibility for negligence but emphasising that the burden of rebutting negligence by affirmative proof of reasonable mistake rests upon the defendant."[4]

– but the courts have shown no inclination to put such a principle into practice. In *Gammon (Hong Kong) Ltd v. A–G of Hong Kong*,[5] the Privy Council, while stressing the need for very high standards of care, regarded the choice as a straight one between *mens rea* and strict liability.

2. [1969] 1 All ER 347 at 351, per Lord Reid, at 357, per Lord Pearce and at 362, per Lord Diplock; **SHC 115.**
3. Footnote 19, above.
4. Orchard, "The Defence of Absence of Fault in Australasia and Canada", *Criminal Law Essays*, 114.
5. [1985] AC 1, [1984] 2 All ER 503 at 509.

6 Crimes of Strict Liability

1 The Position at Common Law and by Statute

Crimes which do not require intention, recklessness or even negligence as to one or more elements in the *actus reus* are known as offences of strict liability or, sometimes, "of absolute prohibition".[1] An example is the Medicines Act 1968, s. 58 (2) which provides that no person shall sell by retail specified medicinal products except in accordance with a prescription given by an appropriate medical practitioner. In *Pharmaceutical Society of Great Britain v. Storkwain Ltd*[2] D supplied specified drugs on prescriptions purporting to be signed by a Dr Irani. The prescriptions were forged. There was no finding that D acted dishonestly, improperly or even negligently. So far as appeared, the forgery was sufficient to deceive the pharmacists without any shortcoming on their part. Yet the House of Lords held that the Divisional Court was right to direct the magistrate to convict.

The term "absolute prohibition" is somewhat misleading in so far as it suggests that an accused whose conduct has caused[3] an *actus reus* will necessarily be held liable. It is common to say that "no *mens rea*" need be proved in the case of these offences: "D can be convicted on proof by P of *actus reus* only."[4] It is only in an extreme case[5] that this is true.[6] The fact is that an offence is regarded – and properly regarded – as one of strict liability if no *mens rea* need be proved as to a single element in the *actus reus*,[7] The single element will usually be one of great significance; but it by

---

1. For discussions of these offences, see L. H. Leigh, *Strict and Vicarious Liability*; Edwards, *Mens Rea*; Sayre, "Public Welfare Offences" (1933) 33 Col LR 55; Howard, SR; Smith and Pearson, "The Value of Strict Liability" [1969] Crim LR 516; Carson, "Some Sociological Aspects of Strict Liability and the Enforcement of Factory Legislation" (1970) 33 MLR 396; Hogan, "Criminal Liability without Fault" (1969, Leeds Univ. Press); Brett, "Strict Responsibility: Possible solutions" (1974), 37 MLR 417.

2. [1986] 2 All ER 635, [1986] 1 WLR 903, HL.

3. In *Kilbride v Lake* [1962] NZLR 590, discussed by Budd and Lynch, [1978] Crim LR 74, D was acquitted of permitting a vehicle not displaying a current warrant of fitness to be on the highway, when the warrant was detached during his absence. The court took the view that there was an *actus reas* (*sed quaere?*) but that D had not caused it and he was not liable even if the offence was one of strict liability. Cf. *Parker v Alder* [1899] 1 QB 20; below, p. 118; *Strowger v John* [1974] RTR 124.

4. Howard, SR 1.

5. *Larsonneur*, above, p. 46.

6. Above, p. 41.

7. Passage approved by Lord Edmund-Davies in *Whitehouse v Gay News Ltd* [1979] AC 617 at 656, [1979] 1 All ER 898 at 920.

no means follows that *mens rea* should not be required as to the remaining constituents of the offence. In construing the Hong Kong Building Ordinance, Lord Scarman said, "Each provision clearly requires a degree of *mens rea*, but each is silent whether it is required in respect of all the facts which together constitute the offence created." The Privy Council held that D was liable for deviating in a material way from the approved plan, even though there was no evidence that he knew that his act constituted a material deviation from the plan – liability as to that element was strict.[8] Liability is thus not "absolute" and the term "strict liability" will be preferred throughout this book.

Crimes of strict liability are almost invariably the creation of statute. It is usually said[9] that there were only two exceptions at common law to the rule requiring *mens rea*. These were public nuisance and criminal libel. In the former any employer might be held liable for the act of his employee even though he himself did not know it had taken place; while in the latter a newspaper proprietor was liable for libels published by his employees without his authority or consent. Public nuisance, however, is an anomalous crime and is treated in several respects rather as if it were a civil action than an indictable offence; while in criminal libel the rule has been modified by the Libel Act 1843 which makes it a defence for the defendant to prove that the publication was without his authority, consent or knowledge and did not arise from want of due care or caution on his part. It will be noted, moreover, that both cases are instances of vicarious liability.[10] To these two instances, we must add a third – contempt of court.[11] It is an offence to publish inaccurate reports of the evidence at a trial in such a manner that the jurors might be influenced in their decision, even though the publisher believes in good faith and on reasonable grounds that the reports are accurate.[12] Parliament has expressly recognised the existence of strict liability in this offence by the Contempt of Court Act 1981.[13] "The Strict Liability Rule", as the Act calls it, continues to be a rule of the common law, though it is to some extent qualified by the Act. According to one view, there is now a fourth common law offence of strict liability – blasphemy. A minority of the House of Lords in *Lemon and Gay News Ltd*[14] thought that was the effect of the decision of the majority. The majority denied that this was so. A writing is blasphemous when it has a tendency to shock and outrage Christians. *Lemon* decides that it is unnecessary to prove that D was aware of this tendency. It is sufficient that he intentionally used words which, in fact, are likely to shock and outrage. It is submitted that the minority were right to regard this as the imposition of strict liability. D may be convicted although he is quite unaware that his act has the quality which makes it criminal. No one would deny that strict liability is imposed when a butcher is convicted of selling meat which is unfit for human

8. *Gammon (Hong Kong) Ltd v A–G of Hong Kong* [1985] AC 1, [1984] 2 All ER 503, PC.
9. But the matter is by no means so clear as is sometimes thought. See below, pp. 797 and 825.
10. See below, p. 162.
11. *Evening Standard Co Ltd* [1954] 1 QB 578, [1954] 1 All ER 1026; below, p. 776.
12. This too is sometimes said to be an instance of vicarious liability; but see below, p. 776.
13. Below, p. 772.
14. [1979] AC 617, [1979] 1 All ER 898, [1979] Crim LR 311 and commentary.

consumption although he is unaware of the dangerous character of the meat. The case of the blasphemous libel seems to be the same in principle.[15]

Apart from these instances, the common law always required *mens rea*, at least as to the more important elements in the *actus reus*, subject to the qualifications in respect of murder and manslaughter considered below.[16] It is very different with statutory offences. In a great many cases, the courts have held that Parliament intended to impose strict liability and have convicted defendants who lacked *mens rea*, not merely as to some subsidiary matter, but as to the central feature of the *actus reus*.

The validity of the imposition of strict liability was recognised by the House of Lords in *Warner v Metropolitan Police Comr* (1968),[17] the first case on the point to reach the highest tribunal. Only the next year, however, in *Sweet v Parsley*[18] the attitude of the House changed remarkably in favour of a presumption requiring *mens rea* and in 1980 in *Sheppard*[19] Lord Diplock noted that "The climate of both parliamentary and judicial opinion has been growing less favourable to the recognition of absolute offences over the last few decades ...".[20] Any expansion of strict liability should therefore be strictly scrutinised. Many offences of strict liability are, however, firmly established and recent experience confirms that it would be unrealistic to suppose that the courts will not, from time to time, discover new ones.[1]

The case which has been said[2] to be the first to impose strict liability is *Woodrow*.[3] D was found guilty of having in his possession adulterated tobacco, although he did not know it was adulterated. The prosecution emphasised the purpose of the statute – it was for the protection of the revenue – and the absence of "knowingly" or any similar word. The court relied on a section of the Act which empowered the commissioners of excise to forbear to prosecute where there was no "intention of fraud or of offending against this Act" – the implication being that the crime was still committed even when there was no fraud or intention of offending against the Act. Parke B thought that the prosecution would very rarely be able to prove knowledge; and that the public inconvenience which would follow if they were required to do so would be greater than the injustice to the

---

15. See [1979] Crim LR at 312.
16. See pp. 327–329, and 345–355.
17. [1969] 2 AC 256, [1968] 2 All ER 356, **SCH 110**, Lord Reid (whose speech deserves careful study) dissenting on this issue. The case is more fully considered below, p. 107.
18. [1970] AC 132, [1969] 1 All ER 347, HL; **SHC 75**; but the House again imposed liability in *Alphacell Ltd v Woodward* [1972] AC 824, [1972] 2 All ER 475; **SHC 89**, below, p. 110.
19. [1980] 3 All ER 899 at 906.
20. [1969] 2 AC 256, [1968] 2 All ER 356. Cases before *Sweet v Parsley* suggested an extension of strict liability; see *Patel v Comptroller of Customs* [1966] AC 356, [1965] 3 All ER 593, PC; *Salter* [1968] 2 QB 793, [1968] 2 All ER 951; *Cummerson* [1968] 2 QB 534, [1968] 2 All ER 863.
1. A recent example is *Maidstone Borough Council v Mortimer* [1980] 3 All ER 552, DC, below, p. 123. See also *Howells* [1977] QB 614, [1977], 3 All ER 417 and *Hussain* [1981] 2 All ER 287, [1981] 1 WLR 416. In the latter case the court declared the offence to be "absolute" but it is perhaps better regarded as a case of ignorance of the law; see commentary at [1981] Crim LR 251. Cf. *Heron* [1981] 3 All ER 641, [1981] 1 WLR 1480; affd. [1982] 1 All ER 993, [1982] 1 WLR 451, a decision requiring basic *mens rea* rather than one imposing "absolute liability".
2. By Sayre, op. cit.
3. (1846) 15 M & W 404.

individual if they were not. Even the exercise of reasonable care would not have saved D; according to Parke B, he was liable even if the adulteration was discoverable only by a "nice chemical analysis".[4] Notwithstanding the subsequent mass of case-law, the considerations taken into account in this early case are very much the same as those which influence the decisions of the courts today.

A number of other well-known cases may be taken as examples. In *Hobbs v Winchester Corporation*,[5] the plaintiff, a butcher, was suing for compensation for certain unsound meat which had been destroyed under the Public Health Act 1875. That Act provided that, where any person sustained damage in relation to any matter as to which he was not himself in default, full compensation should be paid. The question was: was the plaintiff in default? He was unaware, and he could not have discovered by any examination which he could reasonably be expected to make, that the meat was unsound. It was held by the Court of Appeal, reversing Channell J, that the plaintiff was in default because he was guilty of the crime of selling unsound meat. Kennedy LJ said:[6]

"the clear object, the important object [of the statute] ... is as far as possible to protect the buyer of that which, in the opinion at all events of most people, is a necessity of human life, from buying and consuming meat that is unwholesome and unfit for the food of man; and I should say that the natural inference from the statute and its object is that the peril to the butcher from innocently selling unsound meat is deemed by the legislature to be much less than the peril to the public which would follow from the necessity of proving in each case a *mens rea*.

I think that the policy of the Act is this: that if a man chooses for profit to engage in a business which involves the offering for sale of that which may be deadly or injurious to health he must take that risk, and that it is not a sufficient defence for anyone who chooses to embark on such a business to say 'I could not have discovered the disease unless I had an analyst on the premises.'"

In *Cundy v Le Cocq*[7] D was convicted of selling intoxicating liquor to a drunken person contrary to s. 13 of the Licensing Act 1872. It was proved that D did not know the person was drunk and nothing had occurred to show that he was drunk. While some sections of the Act contained the word "knowingly", s. 13 did not do so. The Divisional Court held that it was not necessary to consider whether D knew, or had means of knowing, or could with ordinary care have detected, that the person served was drunk. If he served a drink to a person who was in fact drunk, he was guilty.

It will be noted that it was established in each of these cases that D was not even negligent. The convictions were upheld notwithstanding D's

---

4. The judges suggested that D might have taken a warranty from the person from whom he bought the tobacco, indemnifying him against the consequences of a prosecution (fine and forefeiture). But there are difficulties about this. In *Askey v Golden Wine Co* [1948] 2 All ER 35 at 38, Denning J said: 'It is ... a principle of our law that the punishment inflicted by a criminal court is personal to the offender and that the civil courts will not entertain an action by the offender to recover an indemnity against consequences of that punishment."
5. [1910] 2 KB 471, CA.
6. Ibid., at 483.
7. (1884) 13 QBD 207.

blameless inadvertence as to the crucial factor in the *actus reus*. This is a very remarkable and, on the face of it, unjust result, and certainly requires explanation.

2 Recognition of Offences of Strict Liability

Since these offences are almost always the creation of statute, the courts, in enforcing them, profess merely to be implementing the expressed intention of Parliament. This is mere lip-service.

"The fact is that Parliament has no intention whatever of troubling itself about *mens rea*. If it had, the thing would have been settled long ago. All that Parliament would have to do would be to use express words that left no room for implication. One is driven to the conclusion that the reason why Parliament has never done that is that it prefers to leave the point to the judges and does not want to legislate about it."[8]

The courts then have a fairly free hand in this matter. How do they exercise their power? They usually begin with a ritual incantation of the presumption in favour of *mens rea*, commonly the well-known statement by Wright J in *Sherras v De Rutzen*:[9]

"There is a presumption that *mens rea*, or evil intention, or knowledge of the wrongfulness of the act, is an essential ingredient in every offence; but that presumption is liable to be displaced either by the words of the statute creating the offence or by the subject-matter with which it deals, and both must be considered."

This presumption seems to have been generally followed by the courts until the latter part of the nineteenth century. After the case of *Prince*[10] (1875) the courts showed a greater readiness to interpret statutory offences to impose strict liability. It has been said[11] that the doctrine of *mens rea* reached its nadir when even bigamy was held to be a crime of strict liability in *Wheat* (1921),[12] now happily overruled. The trend in the years before *Warner*[13] seems to have been in favour of strict liability; but in *Sweet v Parsley*[14] the House of Lords reaffirmed principles which were beginning to look old-fashioned: ". . . whenever a section is silent as to *mens rea* there is a presumption that, in order to give effect to the will of Parliament, we must read in words appropriate to require *mens rea*;" and ": . . it is a universal principle that if a penal provision is reasonably capable of two interpretations, that interpretation which is most favourable to the accused must be adopted."[15] According to Lord Diplock,[16] the implication of *mens rea*

---

8. Devlin, *Samples of Lawmaking*, at 71. Cf. Thornton, *Legislative Drafting* 264. Lord Reid in *Sweet v Parsley* [1969] 1 All ER 347 at 351 and the proposals of the Law Commission, below, p. 119.

9. [1895] 1 QB 918 at 921, below, p. 103.

10. See above, p. 41.

11. Williams, CLGP, 178.

12. [1921] 2 KB 119, overruled by *Gould* [1968] 2 QB 65, [1968] 1 All ER 849, considered below, p. 715.

13. *Warner v Metropolitan Police Comr* above, p. 100.

14. Below, p. 109.

15. Per Lord Reid at pp. 349–350.

16. At p. 362.

". . . stems from the principle that it is contrary to a rational and civilised criminal code, such as Parliament must be presumed to have intended, to penalise one who has performed his duty as a citizen to ascertain what acts are prohibited by law (*ignorantia juris non excusat*) and has taken all proper care to inform himself of any facts which would make his conduct unlawful."

It is difficult to say what effect the recital by the courts of the presumption has on their actual decisions. More important in practice appears to be the weight which they give to the two matters which Wright J said might displace it: (i) the words of the statute, and (ii) the subject-matter.

1 The Offence in its Statutory Context

The presence in or absence from the definition of the offence of the word "knowingly", or a similar word apt to require *mens rea*, is of great importance but it is not conclusive. *Mens rea* has often been required where no such word is used, for according to Devlin J: "All that the word 'knowingly' does is to say expressly what is normally implied."[17]

Indeed, it is only where no such word is used that there is any room for the application of the presumption in favour of *mens rea*. Even where the word "knowingly" is used, *mens rea* will not necessarily be required as to all the elements in the *actus reus* – though it ought to be unless there is some strong indication to the contrary. Where a *mens rea* word is used in one section of a statute but not in another that may suggest that the second creates an offence of strict liability; but Lord Reid has said:

"It is also firmly established that the fact that other sections of the Act expressly require *mens rea*, for example because they contain the word 'knowingly', is not itself sufficient to justify a decision that a section which is silent as to *mens rea* creates an absolute offence."[18]

In *Sherras v De Rutzen*,[19] D was charged with supplying liquor to a constable on duty, contrary to s. 16 (2) of the Licensing Act 1872. The policeman was not wearing his armlet which, it was admitted, was an indication that he was off duty. D, who was in the habit – quite lawfully – of serving constables in uniform but without their armlets, made no enquiry and took it for granted that the policeman was off duty. Section 16 (1) of the Act made it an offence for a licensee *knowingly* to harbour or suffer to remain on his premises any constable on duty. Section 16 (2) did not include the word "knowingly". Yet D's conviction was quashed. Day J said that the only inference to be drawn was that under s. 16 (1) the prosecution had to prove knowledge, while under s. 16 (2) the defendant had to prove he had no knowledge.[20] Wright J made no attempt to reconcile the two sub-sections, contenting himself with pointing out that:[1]

17. *Roper v Taylor's Central Garage* [1951] 2 TLR 284 at 288.
18. *Sweet v Parsley* [1970] AC 132 at 149, [1969] 1 All ER 347.
19. [1895] 1 QB 918. Cf. *Harding v Price* [1948] 1 KB 695, [1948] 1 All ER 283, DC (A defence to failure to report an accident to show that D did not know accident had occurred, even though word "knowingly" in the Motor Car Act 1903 was omitted when the section was repealed and replaced by the Road Traffic Act 1930).
20. This view was doubted by Devlin J in *Roper v Taylor's Central Garage* (above). If Day J intended to refer to the *evidential* burden only, the *dictum* is unobjectionable. See Edwards, *Mens Rea*, 90–97.
1. [1895] 1 QB 918 at 923.

"if guilty knowledge is not necessary, no care on the part of the publican could save him from conviction ... since it would be as easy for the constable to deny that he was on duty when asked, or to produce a forged permission from his superior officer as to remove his armlet before entering the public house."

2 The Offence in its Social Context

1) "Real" or "quasi" crime? Here an important matter is whether the court considers the offence to be "a real crime" or a "quasi-crime". Parliament makes no such distinction. An act either is, or it is not, declared by Parliament to be a crime.[2] It is the courts which decide whether it is "real" or "quasi" crime. They do so on the basis that an offence which, in the public eye, carries little or no stigma and does not involve "the disgrace of criminality",[3] is only a quasi-crime. Then, strict liability may be imposed because "it does not offend the ordinary man's sense of justice that moral guilt is not of the essence of the offence".[4] In *Sherras v De Rutzen* Wright J distinguished "a class of acts ... which are not criminal in any real sense, but are acts which in the public interest are prohibited under a penalty".[5] Since we are assuming a defendant who is morally blameless, no stigma ought to attach to him anyway. In determining whether the offence involves "stigma", it is necessary to consider the case where the offence is committed intentionally. If Parliament prohibits the causing of results because it deems them in some measure harmful, the intentional causing of the harm in question probably deserves some measure of moral condemnation. Some stigma attaches to, or should attach to, the motorist who deliberately leaves his car in a parking space for longer than is permitted by law – it is an anti-social act, likely to cause inconvenience to others. But few people, even "right-thinking" people, would consider such an act so iniquitous, even when done intentionally, that the actor ought to be locked up or even shunned and avoided. Since offences of strict liability do not distinguish between degrees of fault and no fault at all, the conviction fixes the offender with whatever stigma might attach to an intentional offender.[6]

2) A general or special prohibition? A second factor which may be of great significance is whether the provision is of general application or relates only to those following a particular trade, profession or special activity. In the latter type of case, the court may be much more ready to hold such a "regulatory offence" to impose strict liability. Lord Diplock put it as follows:[7]

"Where penal provisions are of general application to the conduct of ordinary citizens in the course of their everyday life, the presumption is

2. See Ch. 2 above.
3. Per Lord Reid in *Warner v Metropolitan Police Comr* [1969] 2 AC 256 at 272.
4. Ibid. Cf. *Wings Ltd v Ellis*, above, p. 53.
5. [1895] 1 QB 918 at 922.
6. See J. C. Smith, "Responsibility in Criminal Law", in *Barbara Wootton, Essays in Her Honour* (ed. Bean and Whynes, 1986) 141.
7. In *Sweet v Parsley* [1970] AC 132 at 163.

that the standard of care required of them in informing themselves of facts which would make their conduct unlawful is that of the familiar common law duty of care. But where the subject-matter of a statute is the regulation of a particular activity involving potential danger to public health, safety or morals, in which citizens have a choice whether they participate or not, the court may feel driven to infer an intention of Parliament to impose, by penal sanctions, a higher duty of care on those who choose to participate and to place on them an obligation to take whatever measures may be necessary to prevent the prohibited act, without regard to those considerations of cost or business practicability which play a part in the determination of what would be required of them in order to fulfil the ordinary common law duty of care."

So we find most instances of strict liability in statutes regulating the sale of food, and drugs, the management of industrial activities, the conduct of licensed premises and the like. But the "particular activity" may be one in which citizens generally engage, like driving a car. However, this is something which we choose to do and, as it involves potential danger to others, it is not inconsistent with this statement of principle that some offences regulating the conduct of motorists should be strict.

3) Possibility of amendment. According to Devlin J, it is:
"a safe general principle to follow ... that where the punishment of an individual will not promote the observance of the law either by that individual or by others whose conduct he may reasonably be expected to influence, then, in the absence of clear and express words, such punishment is not intended."[8]

This principle has been re-stated many times, for example by the Privy Council in both *Lim Chin Aik*[9] and *Gammon (Hong Kong) Ltd v A–G of Hong Kong*[10] and by the Divisional Court in *Pharmaceutical Society of Great Britain v Storkwain Ltd.*[11] But, if implemented, it would seem to require negligence, though perhaps of a high degree, rather than impose strict liability. D, it appears, must be shown to have fallen short in some respect of the standard to be expected of him. But was the principle applied in *Storkwain*? Are pharmacists expected to keep a handwriting expert on the premises to scrutinise the prescriptions? Or to telephone the doctor each time they receive a prescription for confirmation that he wrote it? Obviously the courts do not expect such wholly unreasonable precautions to be taken – but how then can the principle be satisfied in such cases?

4) Social danger. Fourthly, and by no means least, the courts are influenced by the degree of social danger which, in their opinion, will follow from breach of the particular prohibition. They take judicial notice of the problems with which the country is confronted. The greater the degree of social danger, the more likely is the offence to be interpreted as one of strict liability. Inflation, drugs, road accidents and pollution are

---

8. *Reynolds v Austin & Sons Ltd* [1951] 2 KB 135, [1951] 1 All ER 606, DC.
9. [1963] AC 160 at 174, [1963] All ER 223 at 228.
10. [1985] AC 1 at 14–15, [1984] 2 All ER 503 at 508–509.
11. [1985] 3 All ER 4, approved by the House of Lords, [1986] 2 All ER 635 at 640.

constantly brought to our attention as pressing evils; and in each case the judges have at times invoked strict liability as a protection for society.

a) *Inflation.* The economic dangers through which the country was passing were the basis of the decision in *St Margaret's Trust Ltd.*[12] In this case D Limited, a finance company, was charged with disposing of a car on hire purchase without a deposit of at least 50 per cent of the purchase price having been paid as required by the Hire Purchase Order[13] then in force. A car dealer and his customers had fraudulently misled D Limited into advancing more than 50 per cent by stating a falsely inflated price for the cars which were the subjects of the transactions. It was admitted that D Limited had acted innocently throughout and supposed that a deposit of at least 50 per cent had been paid. The company was, nevertheless, convicted.

The reasons given by the court had very little to do with the words of the statute. It is true Donovan J said:

"The words of the order themselves are an express and unqualified prohibition of the acts done in this case by St. Margaret's Trust Ltd."

But this means no more than that no such word as "knowingly" was used. He went on:

"The object of the order was to help to defend the currency against the peril of inflation which, if unchecked, would bring disaster on the country. There is no need to elaborate this. The present generation has witnessed the collapse of the currency in other countries and the consequent chaos, misery and widespread ruin. It would not be at all surprising if Parliament, determined to prevent similar calamities here, enacted measures which it intended to be absolute prohibitions of acts which might increase the risk in however small a degree. Indeed that would be the natural expectation. There would be little point in enacting that no one should breach the defences against a flood, and at the same time excusing anyone who did it innocently."[14]

b) *Dangerous drugs.* Legislation concerning dangerous drugs has had a chequered recent history. Lord Parker declared in 1966[15] that he took judicial notice of the fact that drugs are a great danger today and the Divisional Court imposed strict liability of a most draconian character in a number of cases about that time. D was held to be guilty of being "concerned in the management of premises used for the purpose of smoking cannabis" though he did not know and had no means of knowing that such smoking was taking place.[16] Being concerned in the management of premises – college, hospital, hotel, boarding house, cinema – was a dangerous activity because, if someone used those premises for smoking cannabis, those concerned in the management were guilty of an offence. It was quite irrelevant what precautions they may have taken. The only way

12. [1958] 2 All ER 289, [1958] 1 WLR 522.
13. SI 1956 No. 180. Revoked – no corresponding order in force.
14. [1958] 2 All ER 289 at 293. Would the floodgates really have opened in this way, if the case had been decided differently?
15. In *Yeandel v Fisher* [1966] 1 QB 440 at 446, [1965] 3 All ER 158 at 161.
16. *Yeandel v Fisher,* above.

to avoid the risk of being held liable was to give up being concerned in the management of premises. In other cases, it was held that D was guilty of being in unauthorised possession of a drug contrary to s. 1 (1) of the Drugs (Prevention of Misuse) Act 1964 if he knew he had control of a thing which was in fact a dangerous drug, even though he did not know, and had no reason to know, that it was either dangerous or a drug.[17] He might have reasonably believed that he had a bottle of sweets, but that would have been no defence.

Both these questions were considered by the House of Lords in the first cases on strict liability to reach the highest court. In *Warner v Metropolitan Police Commissioner*[18] the House confirmed (Lord Reid dissenting) that s. 1 (1) of the Drugs (Prevention of Misuse) Act 1964 did not require *mens rea*, as such. However, a mental element was required to establish the *actus reus* – possession of a dangerous drug. Even the court below had recognised that –

"If something were slipped into your basket and you had not the vaguest notion it was there at all you could not possibly be said to be in possession of it."[19]

The House agreed[20] with that, but the majority went further in the type of case with which they were concerned – that is, where the drug is in a container of some kind. In such a case, they held that D may possess a box and know that the box has contents and yet not possess the contents. It seems that this will be the case (though the exact *ratio decidendi* is obscure) where he (i) is "completely mistaken" as to the nature – and not merely the quality – of the contents, (ii) has had no opportunity to ascertain the nature of the contents and (iii) does not suspect that there is "anything wrong" with them. D's case was that he believed the two boxes in his possession to contain scent; and the majority held that if he had really so believed on reasonable grounds, he would have had a good defence because – if scent and drugs are different in nature – he would not have been in possession of the drugs which the boxes in fact contained. Two of their lordships were unwilling to distinguish between the box and its contents in this way. Only Lord Reid thought that *mens rea* in the sense of knowledge that the thing possessed was a prohibited drug was required. Lord Guest thought that to require *mens rea* would be to create "a drug pedlar's charter."[1] *Warner* does not affect the law where the drug was not in a container. D must know he has the thing, but it is not necessary that he should know or comprehend its nature.[2] In *Marriott*[3] D was convicted of being in possession of 0.03 grains of cannabis adhering to a penknife. It was held that the jury had been wrongly directed that he was guilty if he knew he was in possession of the

17. E.g. *Lockyer v Gibb* [1967] 2 QB 243, [1966] 2 All ER 653.
18. [1969] 2 AC 256, [1968] 2 All ER 356; **SHC 110**.
19. *Lockyer v Gibb* [1967] 2 QB 243 at 248, per Parker LCJ.
20. [1969] 2 AC at 282, 286, 300, 303 and 311.
   1. At 301.
   2. *Boyesen* [1982] AC 768, [1982] 2 All ER 161. (It is immaterial how minute the quantity is provided only that it amounts to something and D knows he has it.)
   3. [1971] 1 All ER 595, [1971] 1 WLR 187.

penknife. It was necessary to prove at least that he knew that there was some foreign matter adhering to the knife. The court thought that no further *mens rea* was necessary – so that the accused would be guilty if he thought the matter was tobacco or toffee – though "perhaps the law does not go as far as that". It now appears that it does go as far as that. In *Searle v Randolph*[4] it was held that D was guilty where he knew he had a cigarette end on him and it in fact contained cannabis. It was irrelevant that D neither knew nor had reason to believe that the end contained any foreign substance. The court did not treat the cigarette as a container – it was the same as if D had had a heroin tablet, believing it to be an aspirin tablet.

The law on the "container" cases is also fraught with difficulty. The distinction between "nature" and "quality" is one of extreme subtlety and the distinction between the container and its contents a highly technical one. In *Irving*[5] D was in possession of a bottle containing stomach pills and one amphetamine tablet. He said that the tablet had been prescribed for his wife and she must have put it in the bottle by accident when refilling it with stomach pills and that he did not know it was there. It was held that the jury had been wrongly directed that if D was knowingly in possession of the bottle he was also in possession of its contents. It seems strange to say that D was in possession of the pills and not of the tablet. From a common sense point of view, and for most legal purposes, he was equally in possession of both.

The law has been modified by the Misuse of Drugs Act 1971.[6] It is an offence under s. 5 (2) for a person to have a controlled drug in his possession, subject to s. 28 which provides:

2) "... it shall be a defence for the accused to prove that he neither knew of nor suspected nor had reason to suspect the existence of some fact alleged by the prosecution which it is necessary for the prosecution to prove if he is to be convicted of the offence charged."

The section goes on to make it clear that it is not a defence for D to prove that he did not know or believe the substance to be the particular controlled drug it in fact was, if he knew or suspected that it was a controlled drug which he was not entitled to have; and concludes –

4) "Nothing in this section shall prejudice any defence which it is open to a person charged with an offence to which this section applies to raise apart from this section."

It is only when the Crown has proved possession that D must rely on s. 28 and incur an onus of proof.[7] Though *Warner* remains the highest authority on the meaning of possession, it was held in *McNamara*[8] that a simpler concept applies for the purpose of determining the onus of proof. It is for the prosecution to prove that D was knowingly in control of the thing, or a container which he knows to contain something. The onus is then on D to prove, if he can, that he believed the contents to be different in kind or that he had no right or opportunity to open the box or reason to doubt the legitimacy of the contents. So, if D says the drug was slipped into his basket

4. [1972] Crim LR 779.
5. [1970] Crim LR 642, CA.
6. See Card, [1972] Crim LR 744.
7. *Ashton-Rickardt* [1978] 1 All ER 173, [1978] 1 WLR 37, CA; *Wright* (1975) 62 Cr App Rep 169 at 173; [1976] Crim LR 248, CA, and commentary.
8. (1988) Times, 16 February, CA, holding that *Ashton-Rickardt*, above, went further than

without his knowledge,[9] it seems that s. 28 does not apply and the onus is on the prosecution to disprove this story. But if, as in *Warner*, D admits he knew there was something in the box but says he thought it was scent, it is for him to satisfy the jury that he did so believe – even though such a belief would negative possession in the *Warner* sense. It is not clear whether *Irving*[10] would be equated with *Warner* or with the "basket case". If, in a case like *Marriott*,[11] he admits that he knew there was something adhering to the blade but thought it was toffee, he will be acquitted if, and only if, he satisfies the jury on a balance of probabilities that he did not suspect and had no reason to suspect that the thing was a controlled drug.[12] Similarly in *Searle v Randolph*,[13] D has sufficient knowledge if he has ordered a drug by post and it arrives through the letter box. He is then in possession of it, even though he is out or asleep.[14]

The second case concerning strict liability to reach the House of Lords was *Sweet v Parsley*.[15] On this occasion, the House overruled the cases which decided that being "concerned in the management of premises used for the purpose of smoking cannabis" is an offence of strict liability. D, a schoolmistress, was the subtenant of a farmhouse in the country. She let the rooms, retaining one room for her own use and visiting the farm occasionally to collect rent and see that all was well. Cannabis was smoked in the farmhouse but it was found as a fact that she had no knowledge whatever of this. The Divisional Court nevertheless dismissed her appeal. She was "concerned in the management" and that was enough. The House quashed her conviction. The "purpose" referred to in the section must be that of the person concerned in the management; and D had no such purpose. Only Lord Wilberforce was content to stop with this "prosaic interpretation of the paragraph". The remainder relied, in varying degrees, on a presumption in favour of *mens rea*. The actual decision in *Warner* was not affected,[16] but the attitude of the House, with the exception of Lord Reid, who saw no reason to alter what he had said in the earlier case, is very different. The judges are no less sensitive to the public's view of injustice than to their need for protection; and, for once, a case of strict liability had excited public interest. The public outcry and sense of injustice may not have been without influence.[17]

was necessary in holding that the Crown must prove *Warner*-type possession. That view seems to have been accepted by the House of Lords in *Boyesen* [1982] 2 All ER 161 at 166, E-G. It was criticised by Ribeiro and Perry, [1979] Crim LR 90.

9. Above, p. 107.
10. Above, p. 108.
11. Above, p. 107.
12. The position is similar where the Crown alleges "cultivation" of a drug. "Cultivation" clearly requires a mental element. In *Champ* (1981) 73 Cr App Rep 367, [1982] Crim LR 109, CA and commentary, the judge correctly directed that the prosecution need prove only deliberate cultivation of a plant which was in fact cannabis, whereupon it was for D to prove that she did not know it was cannabis. See also the exemptions provided for in Misuse of Drugs Regulations 1973 (S.I. 1973 No. 797) and *Dunbar* (1982) 74 Cr App Rep 88, [1982] Crim LR 45 (doctor in possession of controlled drugs for the purpose of treating himself in possession "as doctor" and so exempt).
13. Above, p. 108.
14. *Peaston* (1978) 69 Cr App Rep 203, CA.
15. [1970] AC 132, [1969] 1 All ER 347; **SHC 115**.
16. *Fernandez* [1970] Crim LR 277 where it was held to be enough that D knew a package might contain some prohibited article and was prepared to take it, whatever the contents were.
17. ". . . fortunately the press in this country are vigilant to expose injustice . . ." per Lord Reid, at p. 150.

The corresponding provisions of the Misuse of Drugs Act require *mens rea* and leave the onus of proof, where it belongs, with the Crown. It is an offence if an occupier[18] or person concerned in the management of premises "knowingly permits or suffers" the smoking of cannabis and other specified activities in connection with drugs. The word "knowingly" is introduced for the first time; but it does not alter the rule under the Dangerous Drugs Act 1965 that knowledge or wilful blindness is enough, but reasonable grounds for suspicion are not.[19]

c) *Pollution*. In view of the current concern about pollution it is scarcely surprising that a modern example should come from that area. In *Alphacell Ltd v Woodward*[20] the House of Lords held that D Ltd was guilty of causing polluted matter to enter a river, contrary to s. 2 (1) (*a*) of the Rivers (Prevention of Pollution) Act 1951.[21] They had built and operated settling tanks with an overflow channel into the river and provided pumps designed to prevent any overflow taking place. Because the pumps became obstructed with vegetation, an overflow of polluted water occurred. There was no evidence that D knew that pollution was taking place or that they had been in any way negligent. Lord Salmon stressed the public importance of preventing pollution and the risk of pollution from the vast and increasing number of riparian industries and said:[1]

"If ... it were held to be the law that no conviction could be obtained under the 1951 Act unless the prosecution could discharge the often impossible onus of proving that the pollution was caused intentionally or negligently, a great deal of pollution would go unpunished and undeterred to the relief of many riparian factory owners. As a result, many rivers which are now filthy would become filthier still and many rivers which are now clean would lose their cleanliness."

In *Atkinson v Sir Alfred McAlpine & Son Ltd*[2] it was held that the company was guilty of failing to give written notice, as required by the Asbestos Regulations 1969, that they were going to undertake work involving crocidolite though they neither knew nor had reason to know that the work involved crocidolite. The court distinguished *Harding v Price*[3] where Lord Goddard CJ, holding that D was not guilty of failing to report an accident, the happening of which he was unaware, said:

"If a statute contains an absolute prohibition against the doing of some act, as a general rule *mens rea* is not a constituent of the offence, but there is all the difference between prohibiting an act and imposing a duty to do

18. The occupier is a person whose degree of control is sufficient to enable him to exclude anyone likely to commit an offence under the Act. It is not limited to persons in legal possession and includes a student with rooms in college: *Tao* [1977] QB 141, [1976] 3 All ER 65.
19. *Thomas* (1976) 63 Cr App Rep 65, [1976] Crim LR 517.
20. [1972] AC 824, [1972] 2 All ER 475; **SHC 89**; Cf. *Price v Cromack* [1975] 2 All ER 113, [1975] 1 WLR 988, DC; *Maidstone Borough Council v Mortimer* [1980] 3 All ER 552, below, p. 123; *Kirkland v Robinson* [1987] Crim LR 643, DC (possession of live wild birds an offence of strict liability under the Wildlife and Countryside Act 1981, s. 1 (1) (a), taking into account the outstanding social importance of an Act designed to protect the environment).
21. See now Control of Pollution Act 1974, s. 31.
1. [1972] AC at 848.
2. (1974) 16 KIR 220, [1974] Crim LR 668, DC.
3. [1948] 1 KB 695, [1948] 1 All ER 283, DC, above, p. 103, and below, p. 250.

something on the happening of a certain event. Unless a man knows that the event has happened, how can he carry out the duty imposed? . . . Any other view would lead to calling on a man to do the impossible."

In *McAlpine*, the court said that, unlike the accident, it was "probably possible" to ascertain whether crocidolite was involved; but since they held that the mischief would not be met if "knows or ought to know" were read into the regulation, it is clear that impossibility would not be regarded as a defence.

3 The Severity of the Punishment

It is often argued that the provision for a severe maximum punishment shows that strict liability could not have been intended by Parliament. To some extent, this is in conflict with the principle previously discussed, since the provision for only a slight punishment would suggest that Parliament thought the social danger involved to be slight. Certainly, the courts do not seem to have been deterred in recent years from imposing strict liability in the case of offences carrying heavy maximum sentences – an offence under section 9 (1) (b) of the Dangerous Drugs Act 1964 was punishable with ten years' imprisonment and causing death by dangerous driving was punishable with five. The fact that an offence under s. 58 (2) of the Firearms Act 1968 is punishable with three years' imprisonment did not deter the court from holding that an honest and reasonable belief that the firearm was an antique was no defence.[4] In *Gammon (Hong Kong) Ltd v A–G of Hong Kong*[5] the Privy Council admitted that the fact the offence was punishable with a fine of $250,000 and imprisonment for three years was "a formidable point"; but found "there is nothing inconsistent with the purpose of the ordinance in imposing severe penalties for offences of strict liability".

3 Liability is Strict, not "Absolute"

It was observed at the beginning of this chapter that the need for a mental element is not ruled out completely by the fact that an offence is one of strict liability. It may be necessary to prove that D was aware of all the circumstances of the offence save that in respect of which strict liability was imposed. When the court holds that it is an offence of strict liability to sell meat which is unfit for human consumption, it decides that a reasonable mistake as to that particular fact is not a defence. It does not decide that any other defence is unavailable to D; and indeed, we have seen that a mistake as to other circumstances of the *actus reus* may afford a defence.[6] There is no reason why all other defences should not be available as they are in the case of offences requiring full *mens rea*. Even when dangerous driving was an offence of strict liability[7], it was held to be a defence if D was in a state of

---

4. *Howells* [1977] QB 614, [1977] 2 All ER 417, below, p. 419.
5. [1985] AC 1 at 17, [1984] 2 All ER 503 at 511.
6. Above, p. 41.
7. Cf. *Gosney*, below, p. 113.

automatism when he "drove" the vehicle.[8] It is perfectly clear that a child under the age of ten could in no circumstances be convicted of an offence of strict liability[9] and it is submitted that a child between ten and fourteen could be convicted only if it were proved that he knew his act was "wrong".[10] It is submitted, therefore, that other general defences – insanity, necessity, duress and coercion – should be available equally on a charge of an offence of strict liability as in the case of any other offence.[11]

Larsonneur[12] and *Winzar v Chief Constable of Kent*[13] establish that lawful compulsion is not a defence to offences of "being found". It does not follow that unlawful duress would not be a defence. If D, being drunk, were forced at gunpoint into the highway he should not be guilty of being found drunk there. Nor does it follow that even lawful compulsion may not found a defence to other, less extreme, cases of strict liability than those of "being found".

4 Arguments for and against Strict Liability

The proliferation of offences of strict liability, while generally deplored by legal writers, has been welcomed by the distinguished social scientist, Lady Wootton, on the ground that "nothing has dealt so devastating a blow at the punitive concept of the criminal process . . ."[14]

> "If, however, the primary function of the courts is conceived as the prevention of forbidden acts, there is little cause to be disturbed by the multiplication of offences of strict liability. If the law says that certain things are not to be done, it is illogical to confine this prohibition to occasions on which they are done from malice aforethought; for at least the material consequences of an action, and the reasons for prohibiting it are the same whether it is the result of sinister malicious plotting, of negligence or of sheer accident."[15]

Accepting that the primary function of the courts is the prevention of forbidden acts, there remains the question, what acts should be regarded as forbidden? Surely only such acts as we can assert ought not to have been done. Suppose that a butcher, who has taken all reasonable precautions, has the misfortune to sell some meat which is unfit for human consumption.

---

8. *Hill v Baxter* [1958] 1 QB 277, [1958] 1 All ER 193; *Budd* [1962] Crim LR 49; *Watmore v Jenkins* [1962] 2 QB 572, [1962] 2 All ER 868. See Patient, "Some Remarks about the Element of Voluntariness in Absolute Offences" [1968] Crim LR 23.

9. Below, p. 178.

10. Below, p. 179. Cf. Cave J in *Tolson* (1889) 23 QBD 168 at 182 and Lord Diplock in *Sweet v Parsley* [1969] 1 All ER 347 at 361.

11. For discussion of this question see Sayre, "Public Welfare Offences" (1933) 33 Col Law Rev 55 at 75–78; Howard, *Strict Liability*, Chapter 9.

12. (1933) 24 Cr App Rep 74; **SHC 125**; above, p. 46.

13. (1983) Times, 28 March, above, p. 46. Cf. *O'Sullivan v Fisher* [1954] SASR 33, discussed by Howard, op. cit. at 193; *Achterdam* 1911 EDL 336 (Burchell & Hunt, 114).

14. *Crime and the Criminal Law* (2nd ed.), 44. See also p. 63, criticised by Hogan, "Criminal Liability without Fault" (Leeds Univ Press, 1967); Hart, *The Morality of the Criminal Law*, 13 et seq.

15. Ibid., at p. 51.

That it was so unfit is undiscoverable by any precaution which a butcher can be expected to take. Ought the butcher to have acted as he did? Unless we want butchers to stop selling meat, or to take precautions so extreme as to be unreasonable (like employing an analyst)[16] it would seem that the answer should be in the affirmative; we want butchers, who have taken all reasonable precautions, to sell meat – the act of this butcher was not one which the law should seek to prevent. Some of the judges who upheld the conviction of *Prince* did so on the ground that men should be deterred from taking girls out of the possession of their parents, whatever the girl's age. This reasoning can hardly be applied to many modern offences of strict liability. We do not wish to deter people from driving cars, being concerned in the management of premises, financing hire purchase transactions or canning peas.[17] These acts, if done with all proper care, are not such acts as the law should seek to prevent. The fallacy in the argument lies in looking at the harm done in isolation from the circumstances in which it was brought about. Many acts, which have in fact caused harm, *ought* to have been done. The surgeon performing a justified operation with all proper skill may cause death.

Another argument that is frequently advanced in favour of strict liability is that, without it, many guilty people would escape – "that there is neither time nor personnel available to litigate the culpability of each particular infraction."[18] This argument assumes that it is possible to deal with these cases without deciding whether D had *mens rea* or not, whether he was negligent or not. Certainly D may be convicted without deciding these questions, but how can he be sentenced? Clearly the court will deal differently with (i) the butcher who knew that the meat was tainted; (ii) the butcher who did not know, but ought to have known; and (iii) the butcher who did not know and had no means of finding out. Sentence can hardly be imposed without deciding into which category the convicted person falls. Treating the offence as one of strict liability, in the case of jury trial, merely removes the decision of these vital questions of fact from the jury and puts them in the hands of the judge; in the case of summary trial, it removes the questions from the sphere of strict proof according to law and leaves them to be decided in the much more informal way in which questions of fact relating purely to sentence are decided. *Gosney*[19] illustrates this vividly. On the assumption (held, on appeal, to be wrong) that dangerous driving was an offence of strict liability, the judge, no doubt rightly, excluded evidence alleged to show that D was blameless. If the rules relating to proof at the trial have any value at all, it is extraordinary that they should not be applied

---

16. See Kennedy LJ cited above, p. 101 and see below, p. 115.
17. See *Smedleys Ltd v Breed*, below, p. 118. "Obviously any consequence is avoidable by the simple expedient of not engaging in the process at all. But that clearly is not what is meant unless the process itself is open to serious criticism as unnecessary or inefficient:" per Lord Hailsham [1974] 2 All ER 21 at 28.
18. Wechsler, "The Model Penal Code", in *Modern Advances in Criminology* (ed., J. Ll. J. Edwards) (1965), 73. The argument was met by the authors of the Code by "the creation of a grade of offense which may be prosecuted in a criminal court but which is not denominated criminal and which entails upon conviction no severer sentence than a fine or civil penalty or forfeiture".
19. [1971] 2 QB 674, [1971] 3 All ER 220.

to the most important facts in the case. That the sentence should be imposed by the judge on a basis of fact different from that on which the jury convicted is deplorable; but it is always possible in the case of strict liability unless the judge questions the jury as to the grounds of their decision – and there are difficulties about this.[20]

The argument which is probably most frequently advanced by the courts for imposing strict liability is that it is necessary to do so in the interests of the public. Now it may be conceded that in many of the instances where strict liability has been imposed, the public does need protection against negligence and, assuming that the threat of punishment can make the potential harmdoer more careful, there may be a valid ground for imposing liability for negligence as well as where there is *mens rea*. This is a plausible argument in favour of strict liability if there were no middle way between *mens rea* and strict liability – that is liability for negligence – and the judges have generally proceeded on the basis that there is no such middle way. Liability for negligence has rarely been spelled out of a statute except where, as in driving without due care, it is explicitly required. Lord Devlin has explained this:[1]

"It is not easy to find a way of construing a statute apparently expressed in terms of absolute liability so as to produce the requirement of negligence. Take, for example, an offence like driving a car while it has defective brakes. It is easy enough to read into a statute a word like 'wilfully' but you cannot just read in 'carelessly'. You cannot show that no one should carelessly drive a car with defective brakes; you are not trying to get at careless driving. What you want to say is that no one may drive a car without taking care to see that the brakes are not defective. That is not so easy to frame as a matter of construction and it has never been done."

The case against strict liability, then, is, first, that it is unnecessary. It results in the conviction of persons who have behaved impeccably and who should not be required to alter their conduct in any way. Secondly, that it is unjust. Even if an absolute discharge can be given (as in *Ball*)[2] D may feel rightly aggrieved at having been formally convicted of an offence for which he bore no responsibility. It is significant that Ball thought it worthwhile to appeal. Moreover, a conviction may have far-reaching consequences outside the courts,[3] so that it is no answer to say that only a nominal penalty is imposed.[4]

The imposition of liability for negligence would in fact meet the arguments of most of those who favour strict liability. Thus Roscoe Pound, in a passage which has been frequently and uncritically accepted as a justification for such offences, wrote:[5]

---

20. Cf. comment on *Lockyer v Gibb* [1966] Crim LR 504 and on *Sheppard* [1981] Crim LR 171 at 172, *Dalas* (1966) Times, 28th September; *Warner* [1967] 3 All ER 93, [1967] Crim LR 528; *Lester* [1976] Crim LR 389; *Foo* [1976] Crim LR 456 and commentaries on these cases.
1. *Samples of Lawmaking*, 76.
2. (1966) 50 Cr App Rep 266.
3. As in the case of *Sweet v Parsley* [1970] AC 132, [1969] 1 All ER 347.
4. This was accepted by the Privy Council in *Lim Chin Aik* [1963] AC 160 at 175 and by Lord Reid in *Warner* [1968] 2 All ER 356 at 366.
5. *The Spirit of the Common Law*, 52.

"The good sense of the courts has introduced a doctrine of acting at one's peril with respect to statutory crimes which expresses the needs of society. Such statutes are not meant to punish the vicious will but to put pressure upon the thoughtless and inefficient to do their whole duty in the interest of public health or safety or morals."

The "thoughtless and inefficient" are, of course, the negligent. The objection to offences of strict liability is not that these persons are penalised, but that others who are completely innocent are also liable to conviction. Though Lord Devlin was sceptical about the possibility of introducing the criterion of negligence in the lecture from which the above quotation is taken, in *Reynolds v Austin*[6] he stated from the bench the principle that strict liability should only apply when there is something that the defendant can do to promote the observance of the law – which comes close to requiring negligence.

If there were something which D could do to prevent the commission of the crime and which he had failed to do, he might generally be said to have failed to comply with a duty – perhaps a high duty – of care; and so have been negligent. One would have thought that what D ought to do would necessarily be limited by what was reasonable. A law requiring one to act unreasonably would seem odd indeed; but Lord Salmon was prepared to take this step in *Alphacell*. The section, he thought,[7]

"encourages riparian factory owners not only to take reasonable steps to prevent pollution but to do everything possible to ensure that they do not cause it."

This suggests that, however vast the expenditure involved, and however unreasonable it may be in relation to the risk, D is under a duty to take all *possible* steps. The factory owner might prefer to take the chance of paying the maximum fine of £200; but a "repetition or continuation of an earlier offence" may lead to liability to imprisonment for six months.[8] By now, the offence might be thought to have lost its character of being "not criminal in any real sense" but it could not cease to be an offence of strict liability; and it would still be no defence that reasonable steps (or, indeed, all possible steps) had been taken. Clearly Lord Salmon was right in saying that there was a great deal more in the case than the fine and costs of the trial, amounting to £44. Yet it may be doubted whether factory owners will in fact do more than is reasonable; and it is questionable whether they ought to be required to do so, at the risk – even though it be unlikely – of imprisonment. The contrary argument is that –

"... the existence of strict liability does induce organisations to aim at higher and higher standards."[9]

Possible developments: a "halfway house?" There are several possible compromises between *mens rea* and strict liability in regulatory offences.

1. D might be convicted without proof of any *mens rea* by the Crown; but acquitted if *he* proved, on a balance of probabilities, that he lacked *mens rea*;

6. [1951] 2 KB 135 at 150, [1951] 1 All ER 606 at 612; above, p. 105.
7. [1972] 2 All ER at 491. Cf. *Smedleys Ltd v Breed*, below, p. 118.
8. Criminal Law Act 1967, s. 2 (7).
9. Smith & Pearson, "The Value of Strict Liability" [1969] Crim LR 5 at 16.

i.e., that he had an honest belief in a state of facts which, had it existed, would have made his act innocent.

2. D might be convicted without proof of any *mens rea* by the Crown; but acquitted if he proved on a balance of probabilities that he lacked *mens rea* *and* was not negligent; i.e., that he had an honest *and reasonable* belief in a state of facts which, had it existed, would have made his act innocent.

3. D might be convicted without proof of any *mens rea* by the Crown, unless he tendered credible evidence of an honest and reasonable belief in a state of facts which, had it existed, would have made his act innocent; in which case, the onus would lie with the Crown to prove beyond reasonable doubt that he had no such honest belief or that his belief was not reasonable.

The first view finds support in numerous *dicta* to the effect that, where a section uses the word "knowingly", the onus of proving knowledge is on the Crown, but that where it does not do so, D may clear himself by proving that he had no *mens rea*.[10] This view has, however, been disapproved[11] on a number of occasions, particularly in recent times by the Privy Council[12] and by Lord Pearce.[13] Lord Reid, however, looked favourably upon it in *Sweet v Parsley*.

A "halfway house" has developed in Australia. There are two opinions as to the effect of the Australian cases, corresponding to views (2) and (3) above. The view which has been most strongly pressed[14] is (2) – that the onus of proving reasonable mistake is on D. According to view (3),[15] D bears only an evidential burden and, when he has introduced some evidence of mistake, the onus of proof is with the Crown.

In *Sweet v Parsley*, Lord Reid[16] seems to have contemplated all three approaches as possible improvements on unmitigated strict liability, but to have thought that *Woolmington*[17] would be an obstacle to the implementation of (1) or (2). Lords Pearce[18] and Diplock[19] looked with approval on the Australian doctrine; but Lord Diplock, relying on the remarks of Dixon J in the leading case of *Proudman v Dayman*[20] (in fact equivocal on this point), thought that it represented view (3). Lord Diplock's opinion involves none of the difficulties with *Woolmington* which Lord Pearce naturally encountered and is preferable in principle. It has been followed by the Court of Appeal in New Zealand.[1] View (3), it is submitted, has

---

10. *Banks* (1794) 1 Esp 144 (Lord Kenyon); *Prince* (1875) LR 2 CCR 154 at 161–2 (Brett J); *Sherras v De Rutzen* [1895] 1 QB 918 at 921 (Day J); *Harding v Price* [1948] 1 KB 695 at 700, [1948] 1 All ER 283 at 284 (Goddard LCJ); *Reynolds v G. H. Austin & Sons Ltd* [1951] 2 KB 135 at 145, [1951] 1 All ER 606 at 609 (Goddard LCJ).
11. *Roper v Taylor's Central Garages* [1951] 2 TLR 284 (Devlin J).
12. *Lim Chin Aik v R* [1963] AC 160 at 173.
13. *Warner* [1969] 2 AC 256 at 303, [1968] 2 All ER 356 at 386.
14. By Howard, "Strict Responsibility in the High Court of Australia" (1960) 76 LQR 547. Campbell, *NZ Essays* 1, at 16; Orchard in *Criminal Law Essays*, 114.
15. Which is Sir F. Adams' opinion of the Australian doctrine: *NZ Essays* 67, at p. 80 and is supported by *Kidd v Reeves* [1972] VR 563; *Mayer v Marchant* (1973) 5 SASR 567.
16. [1970] AC at 150.
17. Above, p. 31.
18. At p. 158.
19. At p. 164.
20. (1941) 67 CLR 536 at 541.
1. *Strawbridge* [1970] NZLR 909 at 916.

much to commend it; but it was studiously ignored in *Alphacell*[2] and we are still a long way from any replacement by judicial decision of strict liability in English law.

5 Statutory Defences

It is becoming common for the drastic effect of a statute imposing strict liability to be mitigated by the provision of a statutory defence. Under the Food Act 1984, s. 100:

"1) A person against whom proceedings are brought under this Act shall –
a) upon information duly laid by him, and
b) on giving to the prosecution not less than three clear days' notice of his intention,

be entitled to have any person to whose act or default he alleges that the contravention of the provisions in question was due brought before the court in the proceedings; and –

i) if, after the contravention has been proved, the original defendant proves that the contravention was due to the act or default of that other person, that other person may be convicted of the offence; and
ii) if the original defendant further proves that he has used all due diligence to secure that the provisions in question were complied with, he shall be acquitted of the offence."

In order to escape liability under this provision the defendant must prove two things: (a), probably beyond reasonable doubt, that the contravention was due to the act or default of the third party and, (b), on the balance of probabilities that he himself used all due diligence to comply with the requirements of the Act. If he can establish only (a) and not (b) then both the original defendant and the third party are liable to conviction. If the court is left in doubt as to who caused the contravention then the original defendant must be convicted and the third party acquitted.[3] The third party might be, for example, a servant of the original defendant or a supplier of the goods in question. If he is a supplier, he, in his turn, might join the person from whom he received the goods, and so on, until the manufacturer is joined – and he might join his servant. There is also a provision[4] for short-circuiting this complicated procedure, and acting directly against the person ultimately responsible without joining the intermediate parties.

It is not necessary to prove any *mens rea* or negligence on the part of the third party. So if a shopkeeper is charged with selling a toffee with a nail in it,[5] he can escape liability by showing that there was no negligence on his own part and that the nail was in the toffee when he received it from the manufacturer. It is not necessary to show that the manufacturer knew, or ought to have known, that the nail was in the toffee when supplied. Indeed

2. Above, p. 110.
3. *Moore v Ray* [1951] 1 KB 98, [1950] 2 All ER 561.
4. Section 100 (3).
5. *Lindley v G. W. Horner & Co Ltd* [1950] 1 All ER 234.

it is no defence for the manufacturer to satisfy the court that he has used every reasonable precaution to prevent any such occurrence. In other words, though a number of defendants may escape liability under this provision by showing that they got the offending article from someone else and were not themselves negligent, there must always be someone at the end of the line who will be subject to unmitigated strict liability.

Another limitation on the effectiveness of this particular defence is that it would seem that it will be of no avail if the third party who is in default is not identifiable so that no information can be laid (though, if he is identifiable and an information is laid it is immaterial that he cannot be brought before the court, because, for example, his whereabouts are not known).[6]

In *Parker v Alder*,[7] D, a milk salesman, in pursuance of a contract of sale delivered some milk in a pure unadulterated condition to a railway station for carriage to London. Under this contract, the property in the milk passed when it was delivered to London. When the milk was delivered it was found to be adulterated by 9 per cent of added water. The luckless D, without any fault on his part, had sold adulterated milk and the Divisional Court held that he was guilty of an offence under s. 6 of the Sale of Food and Drugs Act 1875. The statutory defence we have been considering was not then in force; but it would seem that, in spite of it, D would be in no better position today.

In addition to the general defence, s. 3 of the Act provides a defence to a charge under s. 2 of supplying food which is not of the substance demanded by the purchaser because it contains extraneous matter. It is a defence for the defendant to prove that "The presence of the matter was an unavoidable consequence of the process of collection or preparation." "Unavoidable" is interpreted literally and it is not a defence that D took all reasonable precautions. In *Smedleys Ltd v Breed*[8] a caterpillar was found in a tin of peas. D Ltd was held liable although –

"It was not suggested that there were any other practicable steps that the appellants should or could have taken to secure the exclusion of the caterpillar. Their process was not criticised. Its presence must have been due to human failure in the course of the visual inspection. The chances of it happening again were, if this were the only caterpillar found in a tin, 3,499,999 to 1 or, if all four complaints[9] related to caterpillars in tins, 874,999 to 1."[10]

As a defence, s. 3 is not extravagantly generous. The result is a law with which no one expects the defendants to comply, because compliance is impossible. Even the individual scrutiny of every pea would not necessarily avoid all extraneous matter.

Statutory defences do not always take this complicated form. More commonly they simply impose on the accused the burden of proving that he had no *mens rea* and was not negligent. Thus one who sells feeding stuffs

---

6. *Malcolm v Cheek* [1948] 1 KB 400, [1947] 2 All ER 881.
7. [1899] 1 QB 20.
8. [1974] AC 839 at 855, [1974] 2 All ER 21, HL, per Viscount Dilhorne.
9. Four complaints had been received in respect of three and a half million tins.
10. Per Viscount Dilhorne at p. 32.

containing deleterious ingredients is liable unless he proves "that he did not know and could not with reasonable care have known that the article contained" such an ingredient.[11] The effect of such a provision is that the prosecution need do no more than prove that the accused did the prohibited act and it is then for him to establish, if he can, that he did it innocently. Such provisions are a distinct advance; but they are still a deviation from the fundamental principle that the prosecution must prove the whole of their case; and an extensive use of offences of strict liability, even when so qualified, is to be deplored.

6 Proposals for Reform

The Law Commission proposed[12] a Criminal Liability (Mental Element) Bill, now incorporated in the draft Criminal Code,[13] which would provide a definition of intention, knowledge and recklessness[14] and establish a presumption for offences created after the passing of the Bill that intention, knowledge or recklessness should be required as to all the elements of the offence.[15] The onus would then be on Parliament, if it wished to create an offence requiring a lesser degree of *mens rea* or an offence of negligence or strict liability, to make this clear in the enactment. It is Parliament's responsibility to decide the nature of criminal liability. It is better that Parliament should have an actual intention in the matter, rather than a purely mythical one, attributed to it, perhaps many years later, in the haphazard manner inevitably associated with the accidents of litigation.

11. Fertilisers and Feeding Stuffs Act 1926, s. 7 (1). See too, Weights and Measures Act 1963, ss. 26 and 27; Trade Descriptions Act 1968, s. 24; Post Office Act 1953, s. 63 (1). The provision of a statutory defence may be an indication to the court that an offence of strict liability is intended. Cf. Sexual Offences Act 1956, s. 6, below, p. 441, and Obscene Publications Act 1959, s. 2 (5), below, p. 726.
12. Law Com. No. 89 (1978).
13. Cl. 24, "General requirements of fault", Law Com. No. 143. See pp. 71–72.
14. Above, pp. 55 and 62.
15. Law Com. No. 89 (1978). See also Law Com. Working Paper No 31.

7 The Effect of Particular Words[1]

Certain words, which have a bearing on whether *mens rea* need be proved, tend to be commonly used in criminal statutes and their interpretation in many cases has given them a more or less well-settled meaning which requires examination.

In *Brutus v Cozens*[2] the House of Lords held that the meaning of an ordinary word of the English language in a statute is not a question of law but of fact. This, however, is not universally true. The words considered in this chapter are ordinary words, but the question whether they import *mens rea* has always been treated as a question of law. In *Vickers*[3] the question was whether the word "assists" in s. 20 of the Misuse of Drugs Act 1971[4] imports *mens rea*. Scarman LJ referred to *Brutus v Cozens* and declared: "In ordinary English one who assists knows what he is doing and the purpose with which it is done." This appears to establish this aspect of the meaning of the word as a matter of law – it is not to be left to a jury to say whether "assist" imports knowledge or not. This, it is submitted, is right – though not easily reconcilable with *Brutus v Cozens*.

1 Knowingly

Thus, the word, "knowingly", as has already appeared repeatedly, is apt to introduce a requirement of *mens rea*[5] as to all the elements of the offence though it has not invariably been held to do so.[6] This seems to be the clearest word which can be used and it is probably safe to assume that the word will in future import a requirement of *mens rea* except, possibly, as to an exception clause in the definition of the crime.[7] It is usually necessary and sufficient to prove knowledge of all the elements of the *actus reus*. A handler of stolen goods must know or believe the goods to be stolen but it is

1. Edwards, *Mens Rea*; Williams, CLGP, Ch. 5; Howard, *Strict Responsibility*, Ch. 6.
2. [1973] AC 854, [1972] 2 All ER 1297. Cf. the remarkable difficulties experienced by the courts in giving a legal meaning to the word, "supply": *Maginnis*. [1987] AC 303, [1987] 1 All ER 907, HL, [1987] Crim LR 564.
3. [1975] 2 All ER 945 at 950–951, CA.
4. "A person commits an offence if in the United Kingdom he assists in or induces the commission in any place outside the United Kingdom of an offence punishable under the provisions of a corresponding law in force in that place."
5. See *Gaumont British Distributors Ltd v Henry* [1939] 2 KB 711, [1939] 2 All ER 808, *A-G v Cozens* (1934) 50 TLR 320 and *Taaffe* [1984] AC 539, [1984] 1 All ER 747, HL, above.
6. *Brooks v Mason* [1902] 2 KB 743; *Dacey* [1939] 2 All ER 641, overruled by *Hallam* [1957] 1 QB 569, [1957] 1 All ER 665. And see Sexual Offences Act 1956, ss. 25 and 26, below, p. 444.
7. See *Brooks v Mason*. And see *Wings Ltd v Ellis*, above, p. 53.

immaterial that he is ignorant or mistaken as to the nature of the goods.[8] A visitor may be guilty of knowingly remaining in the United Kingdom beyond the time limited by his leave even though, because of a mistake of law, he supposes the leave has not expired.[9] A mistake of fact would negative knowledge.

D is "knowingly" concerned in the fraudulent importation of goods if he imports whisky believing it to be brandy. His mistake is immaterial because he knows he is committing the *actus reus* of the crime charged. In principle, the answer should be different if D believes the whisky to be cannabis because the importation of cannabis carries a higher penalty and, therefore, under the *Courtie*[10] principle is a different offence. However, the legislative history of this particular section has led the courts to conclude that the *mens rea* required is knowledge that the thing is a prohibited thing, whatever the nature of it and whatever the penalty applicable.[11] It is, in effect, one of those cases where the *mens rea* for crime A will suffice for crimes B and C, and vice versa.

It is sufficient to prove what is sometimes called "wilful blindness": "it is always open to the tribunal of fact, when knowledge on the part of a defendant is required to be proved, to base a finding of knowledge on evidence that the defendant had deliberately shut his eyes to the obvious or refrained from inquiry because he suspected the truth but did not want to have his suspicion confirmed."[12] "Connivance", as this attitude of mind is sometimes called, is closely akin to recklessness.[13] It should be noted, however, that in one particularly important offence, handling goods knowing or believing them to be stolen,[14] the courts have taken a stricter view.

"Knowingly" requires knowledge at the time of committing the offence. A person who has once known of a fact but has forgotten it at the time of the act does not "know".[15]

If, as Devlin J says, "knowingly" only says expressly what is normally implied,[16] it is generally superfluous and its use in some but not all sections of a statute, puzzling. Three explanations have been offered: (1) that the sections where the word is not used create offences of strict liability – a view inconsistent with Devlin J's *dictum* and rejected in *Sherras v De Rutzen*[17] in favour of (2) that the absence of the word shifts the onus of proof on to the defence;[18] (3) Williams argues that the requirements of *mens rea* are

---

8. *McCullum* (1973) 57 Cr App Rep 645, below, p. 635.
9. *Grant v Borg* [1982] 2 All ER 257, [1982] 1 WLR 638, HL.
10. Above, p. 35.
11. *Shivpuri* [1987] AC1, [1986] 2 All ER 334, HL, confirming *Hussain* [1969] 2 QB 567, [1969] 2 All ER 1117, CA; *Ellis, Street and Smith* (1986) 84 Cr App Rep 235, [1987] Crim LR 44, CA and commentary. Cf. *Taaffe* [1984] AC 539 [1984] 1 All ER 747.
12. *Westminster City Council v Croyalgrange Ltd* [1986] 2 All ER 353 at 359. HL. See also *Evans v Dell* [1987] 1 All ER 349 at 353, per Hewart CJ and *Roper v Taylor's Central Garages Ltd* [1951] 2 TLR 284 at 288, *per* Devlin J.
13. See Edwards, *Mens Rea*, 202–205; Williams, CLGP, 159.
14. Below, p. 632.
15. *Russell (Raymond)* (1985) 81 Cr App Rep 315, [1985] Crim LR 231, CA and commentary. It is submitted that the criticism of *Russell* in *Martindale* [1986] 3 All ER 25, [1986] 1 WLR 1042, CA, is misconceived. Cf. [1986] Crim LR 736–737.
16. See *Roper*, above, pp. 103 and 116.
17. Above, p. 103.
18. See above, p. 116, footnote 10.

satisfied by "simple ignorance"[19] where "knowingly" is not used, but not where it is. For example, D makes a reproduction of a musical or dramatic performance without obtaining the consent of the performer. D does not know that this is an offence and consequently does not even consider whether the performers have consented or not. He is not guilty of "knowingly" committing the offence:[20] but, according to this view, he would be guilty (simple ignorance being equated with recklessness) if the statute had omitted the word "knowingly". In *Sherras v De Rutzen*,[1] the publican had a positive belief that the constable was off duty. According to this view, he would have been guilty if (being ignorant that it was against the law to serve constables on duty) he had not directed his mind to the question whether the constable was on or off duty. This third solution involves giving an extended meaning to recklessness in statutory offences; but it may well be the most satisfactory explanation of Parliament's action. If so, of course, "knowingly" does say something more than is normally implied.

2 Maliciously

Another adverb commonly found in statutes is "maliciously". Some offences containing this word are examined below.[2] At one time this adverb was taken, in its natural and popular meaning, to require a generally wicked intention and improper motive. Later,[3] however, the word came simply to denote a requirement of recklessness or intention with respect to the *actus reus* of the crime in question: that is, to import a requirement of *mens rea*. In some contexts it may denote the absence of a claim of right[4] or other lawful excuses.[5] It is therefore no longer sufficient for the judge to tell the jury that D was malicious if he did the act "wickedly".[6] The question is whether he knew of the circumstances and foresaw the consequences which constitute the *actus reus* of the offence charged; or, in some cases, which constitute harm of the same kind, though not necessarily of the same degree as that specified in the definition of the *actus reus*.[7]

3 Wilfully

The term "wilfully" has been less consistently interpreted. Sometimes it is held to import a requirement of *mens rea*.[8] Thus in *Eaton v Cobb*,[9] D, a motorist, was found not guilty of wilfully obstructing the free passage of the highway when, after looking in his mirror and seeing the road

---

19. CGLP §§ 54 and 59; above, p. 73.
20. *Gaumont British Distributors v Henry* [1939] 2 KB 711, [1939] 2 All ER 808.
  1. Above, p. 103.
  2. See pp. 400–403.
  3. *Fordham* (1839) 4 JP 397; *Prestney* (1849) 3 Cox CC 505; *Matthews and Twigg* (1876) 14 Cox CC 5.
  4. Edwards, *Mens Rea*, 21–27.
  5. *Solanke* [1969] 3 All ER 1383, [1970] 1 WLR 1; below, p. 336; discussed in *Arrowsmith* [1975] 1 All ER 463 at 471–472, CA.
  6. *Cunningham* [1957] 2 QB 396, [1957] 2 All ER 412; **SHC 63**; below, p. 404, footnote 3.
  7. *Mowatt* [1968] 1 QB 421, [1967] 3 All ER 47; **SHC 64**; below, p. 400.
  8. *Roper v Knott* [1898] 1 QB 868; *Morris v Edmonds* (1897) 77 LT 56; *Younghusband v Luftig* [1949] 2 KB 354, [1949] 2 All ER 72; *Wilson v Inyang* [1951] 2 KB 799, [1951] 2 All ER 237; *Bullock v Turnbull* [1952] 2 Lloyd's Rep 303; *Rice v Connolly* [1966] 2 QB 414, [1966] 2 All ER 649, below, p. 394.
  9. [1950] 1 All ER 1016. Cf. *Iannella v French*, above, p. 84, *Lowe* below, p. 350.

apparently clear, he opened his car door in the path of a cyclist. He wilfully opened the car door, but did not "wilfully obstruct". In other cases it has been held to do no more than impose a requirement that D's conduct be voluntary and not to extend to his knowledge of circumstances or foresight of consequences. D was held to have wilfully destroyed an oak tree in contravention of a tree preservation order although he was unaware of the order and believed that permission had been given for the tree to be felled.[10]

In *Hudson v MacRae*[11] it was held that D was guilty of unlawful and wilful fishing in water where another person had a private right of fishing, under s. 24 of the Larceny Act 1861,[12] though he believed the public had a right to fish there. And in *Cotterill v Penn*[13] it was held that D was guilty of "unlawfully and wilfully" killing a house pigeon under s. 23 of the Larceny Act 1861 (repealed) where he shot a bird honestly thinking it was a wild pigeon. It was enough that he shot the bird he aimed at, though it would have been different, according to Lord Blackburn in the former case and Lord Hewart in the latter, if the section had used the word "maliciously". In the earlier case of *Horton v Gwynne*[14] Darling J suggested that it would be different if D shot at a crow, missed and killed a pigeon. "Wilful", according to this view, required an intention to kill the bird that was killed, but not an intention to kill a *house pigeon*.

In the most recent and important authority, *Sheppard*,[15] Lord Diplock thought that in s. 1 of the Children and Young Persons Act 1933, "wilfully" might be capable of meaning only the intention to do one of the positive physical acts described in the section (assault, ill-treat, etc.) and not relate to the consequences ("in a manner likely to cause him unnecessary suffering or injury to health") but that it was not the natural meaning; and he observed that, if the word were given the narrow meaning, it would be otiose because, even in offences of strict liability, the law requires a voluntary act in the absence of any such word as "wilfully". This surely means that there must be some very strong reason for not applying the natural meaning.[16] Their Lordships held that "wilfully" in "wilfully neglects" was satisfied by (in effect) *Caldwell* recklessness[17] – D was wilful if he refrained from getting medical aid although he knew there was a risk that the child's health might suffer or where he was unaware of the risk because he did not care whether the child might be in need of medical treatment or not.[18]

It is submitted that the better view is that "wilful" should be held to apply to all the elements in the offence. So, on a charge of wilfully

---

10. *Maidstone Borough Council v Mortimer* [1980] 3 All ER 552, DC. It is otherwise if the order has not been deposited for inspection as required by the Act, for then it is invalid: *Vale of Glamorgan v Palmer and Bowles* (1983) 81 LGR 678, DC.
11. (1863) 4 B & S 585; *Wells v Hardy* [1964] 2 QB 447, [1964] 1 All ER 953.
12. See now Theft Act 1968, Sch. 2, para. 2.
13. [1936] 1 KB 53. Cf. Stallybrass in MACL at 460 et seq.
14. [1921] 2 KB 661.
15. [1981] AC 394, [1980] 3 All ER 899.
16. But cf. *Maidstone v Mortimer*, above.
17. Above, p. 100. The case was decided before *Caldwell* and may be regarded as a forerunner of that decision.
18. Lord Diplock at 87 and 90, Lord Edmund-Davies at 93–94 and Lord Keith concurring at 100 with Lord Diplock's answer to the certified question. Lords Fraser and Scarman dissented.

obstructing the police it was held that it was not sufficient that D did a deliberate act which in fact obstructed the officer; an intention to obstruct the police must be proved.[19] It seems an abuse of language to say that one who shoots a bird he believes to be a wild pigeon, wilfully *shoots a house pigeon*. If he was reckless, and shot at the bird, not knowing whether it was wild or tame, that is another matter.[20]

4 "Permitting", "Suffering", or "Allowing"

The meaning of these three words appears to be the same. The most commonly used is "permitting" and this has often been held to import a requirement of *mens rea*.[1] There must be either knowledge of the offending state of affairs or wilful blindness. It is not enough that there are reasonable grounds for suspicion that the state of affairs exists. The question is whether D in fact suspected.[2] This construction applies to permitting premises to be used for smoking cannabis,[3] permitting an employee to drive for a number of hours exceeding that permitted[4] and permitting the use of a vehicle with defective brakes[5] or an insecure load[6]. The courts have not always been consistent in their interpretation of "permits".

It had been held that D was guilty of permitting the use of an uninsured vehicle even though he believed on reasonable grounds that there was a policy of insurance in force.[7] This interpretation, with some exceptions,[8] has been followed in recent years.[9] Where the defendant permits the use of the vehicle, his belief that the use was insured is no defence. Where he does not permit the use of the vehicle – where, for example, it is taken without his authority – he is plainly not guilty. In *Newbury v Davies*[10] where D lent his car to E on the express condition that E should insure the car and E used it without doing so it was held that conditional permission was no permission at all when the condition was unfulfilled.[11] D was not liable. But in *Baugh v Crago*[12] where D merely believed that E was insured but did not

---

19. *Willmott v Atack* [1977] QB 498, [1976] 3 All ER 794, DC.
20. Cf. *Holroyd* (1841) 2 Mood & R 339 (wilful obstruction satisfied by recklessness).
   1. See cases referred to in comment on *Tapsell v Maslen* [1967] Crim LR 53.
   2. *Souter* [1971] 2 All ER 1151, [1971] 1 WLR 1187.
   3. *Souter* (above). The point is now made doubly sure by the Misuse of Drugs Act 1971, s. 8, which uses the expression "knowingly permits"; but the word "knowingly" adds nothing: *Thomas* (1976) 63 Cr App Rep 65, [1976] Crim LR 517, CA.
   4. *Grays Haulage Co v Arnold* [1966] 1 All ER 896, [1966] 1 WLR 534; *Knowles Transport Ltd v Russell* [1975] RTR 87, DC.
   5. *Fransman v Sexton* [1965] Crim LR 556; *Hill & Sons (Botley and Denmead) Ltd v Hampshire Chief Constable* [1972] RTR 29.
   6. *P. Lowery & Sons v Wark* [1975] RTR 45, DC.
   7. *Lyons v May* [1947] 2 All ER 1062. The supervising driver does not "permit" a provisional licence-holder to drive where the latter is the owner of the vehicle: *Thompson v Lodwick* [1982] Crim LR 690, DC.
   8. *Sheldon Deliveries Ltd v Willis* [1972] RTR 217.
   9. *Boss v Kingston* [1963] 1 All ER 177, [1963] 1 WLR 99; *Roberts v Warne* [1973] RTR 217; *Baugh v Crago*, below.
   10. [1974] RTR 367.
   11. *Sheldon Deliveries*, supra, was justified, *ex post facto*, on this ground. D, deliverers of cars, permitted an employee to take a car bearing trade plates to his home on Saturday so that he could begin his journey early on Monday. On Sunday he drove the car for his own purposes without the trade plates.
   12. [1975] RTR 453, [1976] Crim LR 73, DC, and commentary thereon. (Followed in *Ferrymasters Ltd v Adams* [1980] RTR 139, DC (permitting unlicensed driving).)

make that a condition, he was guilty. Thus D must be proved to have intended to permit the use of the vehicle; he need not be proved to have intended to permit the uninsured use.

"Permits" is held to require *mens rea* even when it is used in proximity to other words which are taken to impose strict liability. In *James & Son Ltd v Smee*[13] the court had to consider the Motor Vehicles (Construction and Use) Regulations 1951 under which it was an offence "If any person uses or causes or permits to be used" a vehicle in contravention of the regulations. "Using", "causing" and "permitting" are three separate offences; and the court held that *using* a vehicle in contravention of a regulation (in that it had a defective braking system) was an offence of strict liability;[14] but D was charged with *permitting* the use, "which, in our opinion, at once imports a state of mind". Knowledge of the defect, or wilful blindness, had to be proved. Similarly, selling liquor to a drunken person is an offence of strict liability,[15] but *permitting* drunkenness requires *mens rea*.[16] It will probably continue to be an offence of strict liability to *use* a vehicle not covered by a third party policy of insurance,[17] whatever the position regarding permitting such use.

Though attempts have been made[18] to distinguish between them, it is probable that "permitting" and "suffering" mean precisely the same thing.[19] In principle, the same *mens rea* should be required. It has been held in a number of cases that a licensee "suffers" gaming to be carried on in the licensed premises, only if he knows of, or connives at, the gaming.[20] Out of line with these authorities is the judgment of Manisty J in *Bond v Evans*[1] in which he held that *suffering* gaming is an offence of strict liability, pointing out (i) that in other sections the statute used the phrases "*knowingly* suffers" and "*knowingly* permits", and (ii) that the earlier statute had used "knowingly" in relation to suffering gaming but the present statute did not. These are no light arguments, but nevertheless they have not, as *Sherras v De Rutzen*[2] and *Harding v Price*[3] show, always been found conclusive. Stephen J concurred but his judgment, though not absolutely clear, is evidently based on the fact that the gaming was suffered by D's servant who has *mens rea* and for whose acts D was in the circumstances vicariously liable.[4] The case is distinguishable from earlier authorities on this ground.

If the consistent trend of modern authorities is followed, the use of the adverbs "knowingly" or "wilfully" to qualify "permitting" or "suffering"

---

13. [1955] 1 QB 78, [1954] 3 All ER 273.
14. *Green v Burnett*, decided at the same time as *James v Smee*.
15. *Cundy v Le Cocq*, above, p. 101.
16. *Somerset v Wade* [1894] 1 QB 574.
17. *Boss v Kingston* [1963] 1 All ER 177, [1963] 1 WLR 99.
18. E.g. by Darling J in *Rochford Rural District Council v Port of London Authority* [1914] 2 KB 916 at 924.
19. *Bond v Evans* (1888) 21 QBD 249 at 257, per Stephen J; *Somerset v Wade* [1894] 1 QB 574 at 576, per Matthew J.
20. *Bosley v Davies* (1875) 1 QBD 84, followed in *Redgate v Haynes* (1876) 1 QBD 89 and *Somerset v Hart* (1884) 12 QBD 360.
1. (1888) 21 QBD 249.
2. Above, p. 103.
3. [1948] 1 KB 695, [1948] 1 All ER 283.
4. See below, p. 162.

is superfluous, yet the very fact that they are used sometimes can give force to the argument that, where they are not used, strict liability is intended. The three possible solutions to the occasional use of the word "knowingly", which have already been considered, are however again applicable.[5]

5 Causing

Where D is alleged to have caused the doing of the prohibited act by another, E, it must be proved that the act was done on D's actual authority, express or implied, or in consequence of his exerting his capacity to control or influence E's acts. It is not sufficient that D was acting as the agent of C, on whose behalf E was also acting, and that D's acts were a link in the chain of causation of the prohibited act.[6]

"Causes" requires proof of a positive act[7] whereas other epithets such as "permits" do not; but the cases do not establish any general rule that it imports *mens rea*. On the one hand, D did not *cause* to be presented a play containing words disapproved by the Lord Chamberlain, so as to incur liability under the Theatres Act 1843, s. 15, if he did not know that the offending words were being included.[8] The owner of a steam engine did not cause it to be erected within twenty-five yards of the highway, contrary to the Highway Act 1835, if he had no knowledge that the machine was being so placed.[9] Nor, under the same Act, did a surveyor cause to be laid on the highway a heap of stone, if he did not know that the carter to whom he had given general directions as to the repairing of the road, was going to and did so lay the stones.[10] The manager of a colliery was not liable for causing horses belonging to the colliery to be ill-treated, when he had no knowledge of the cruelty.[11]

Each of these cases involved the intervention of a third party between D and the result alleged to be caused by him. This perhaps distinguishes *Alphacell*[12] where, as Lord Pearson pointed out –

"There was no intervening act of a trespasser and no act of God. There was not even any unusual weather or freak of nature."

But that distinction cannot apply to *Sopp v Long*[13] where a licensee was held to have caused a short measure of whisky to be delivered to a customer

---

5. *Lomas v Peek* [1947] 2 All ER 574, suggests that the words, when they qualify "permitting", are generally superfluous. They were omitted from an information charging an offence under the Licensing (Consolidation) Act 1910 which uses the words. It was held that the omission of these "technical words" was irrelevant. "If a man permits a thing to be done, it means that he gives permission for it to be done, and if a man gives permission for a thing to be done, he knows what is to be done or what is being done, and, if he knows that, it follows that it is wilful" – per Lord Goddard CJ. See also Viscount Dilhorne in *Alphacell Ltd v Woodward* [1972] 2 All ER 475 at 483–4, above, p. 110.
6. *A-G of Hong Kong v Tse Hung-Lit* [1986] AC 876, [1986] 3 All ER 173, PC.
7. *Price v Cromack* [1975] 2 All ER 113, [1975] 1 WLR 988.
8. *Lovelace v Director of Public Prosecutions* [1954] 3 All ER 481, [1954] 1 WLR 1468; see now Theatres Act 1968, s. 2, below, p. 736.
9. *Harrison v Leaper* (1862) 5 LT 640.
10. *Hardcastle v Bielby* [1892] 1 QB 709.
11. *Small v Warr* (1882) 47 JP 20.
12. [1972] 2 All ER 475 at 488; above p. 110.
13. [1970] 1 QB 518, [1969] 1 All ER 855, DC.

where he had delegated his authority through A and B to C who sold the short measure. He had given strict instructions to ensure compliance with the law. Since only the licensee can sell intoxicating liquor, the court thought that by every sale he "caused" to be delivered that which was sold. In *Lovelace*[14] it was accepted that D undoubtedly caused the presentation of the play as authorized but it was held that it would be unreal to say that he caused the presentation of the part which was unauthorised. Was it any more realistic in *Sopp v Long* to say that, because the defendant caused the delivery of the liquor sold, he caused delivery of the short measure? The court was influenced by the provision of a statutory defence (which was not relied on); but that was sufficiently explicable by the presence of other offences – such as *delivering* short measure – where there was no word apt to import *mens rea*. In *Ross Hillman Ltd v Bond*[15] the court opined that *Lovelace* and *Sopp v Long* are irreconcilable, unless the latter turns on the special position of the licensee; and that *Lovelace* is to be preferred. It was held that causing the unlawful use of a vehicle requires proof of prior knowledge of the facts amounting to the unlawful user – in that case, use with an excessive load. But *Alphacell* was not cited; and it continues to be impossible to state any universal rule of the construction of this word.

Edwards[16] argues that

"Whereas . . . 'permits', 'suffers' and 'allows' all denote passive acquiescence in the commission of the prohibited act, 'causes' is a far more positive epithet and indicates an express authorisation of the forbidden event."

It is, moreover, a stronger term than some of the verbs used to denote the conduct of an abetter or counsellor where *mens rea* is required.[17] Yet, clearly, there is no general rule that it imports *mens rea*.

6 Fraudulently

It would seem that nothing could be more apt to introduce a requirement of *mens rea* than the word "fraudulently" or the term "with intent to defraud"; and generally it is clear that this is their effect. A decision under the now repealed Merchandise Marks Act 1887, s. 2, that strict liability applied notwithstanding that it was a defence for D to prove that he "acted without intent to defraud"[18] can probably now be ignored. The word "fraudulently" and the phrase "with intent to defraud" both imply dishonesty[19] and the test is the same in commercial dealings as in other matters. It seems then that D has an intent to defraud if (i) he intends to do acts which, in the circumstances known to him, would, if carried out, defraud P and (ii) he knows that ordinary people would regard what he

---

14. See above, fn. 8.
15. [1974] QB 435, [1974] 2 All ER 287, DC.
16. *Mens Rea*, 254.
17. Below, p. 142.
18. *Kat v Diment* [1951] 1 KB 34, [1950] 2 All ER 657.
19. *Cox and Hodges* (1982) 75 Cr App Rep 291, CA.

proposes to do as dishonest.[20] A person is defrauded if he is deprived of "something which is his or to which he is or would be or might be entitled" or some proprietary right of his is injured,[1] or he is induced to act contrary to his public duty.[2]

7 Corruptly[3]

"Corruptly" means deliberately doing an act which the law forbids as tending to corrupt. So a promise to a voter that he would be paid his expenses of travelling to the poll on condition that he voted for the promisor was held to be made corruptly under s. 2 of the Corrupt Practices Prevention Act 1854.[4] No dishonest intention need be proved. It is difficult to see what, if anything, the word adds to the definition of the relevant offences. It is no answer to a charge of offering a bribe to a public servant under the Public Bodies Corrupt Practices Act 1889 to say that it was done only with the intention of exposing the public servant.[5] D acted corruptly because he deliberately did an act which the law forbids as tending to corrupt others. A gift for a past favour is received corruptly even though there was no prior agreement or understanding that payment would be made and D has exercised his judgment in the matter honestly. The offence lies not in showing favour but in accepting a reward for doing so.[6]

8 Possession

It is generally accepted one cannot "possess" without a mental element. In all of the many crimes where this word is used, some mental element is therefore imported into the offence. The problem has arisen most frequently in recent times in relation to the possession of drugs and these cases have been examined above.[7] To establish possession it must at least appear that D knew he had the thing, even though he did not know what it was. Yet he will not cease to have possession because he believes the thing to have been destroyed or forgets that he has the thing in his wallet[8] or in anything else of which he is in possession.[9] If the thing was in a container, D's possession of the container is prima facie evidence of possession of the contents, rebuttable by evidence of a mistake in the sense described by the majority in *Warner*.[10]

It should be noted that for some purposes, even knowledge of the existence of the thing is unnecessary to found possession. Thus an

---

20. *Ghosh* [1982] QB 1053, [1982] 2 All ER 689.

  1. *Scott v Metropolitan Police Commissioner* [1975] AC 819, [1974] 3 All ER 1032.

  2. The broad definition of "intent to defraud" expounded by Lord Radcliffe in *Welham v Director of Public Prosecutions* [1961] AC 103 [1960] 1 All ER 805, HL is not confined to the use of that phrase in the Forgery Act 1913 (repealed) but is of general application: *Terry* [1984] AC 374, [1984] 1 All ER 65, HL; *Grantham* [1984] QB 675 [1984] 3 All ER 166, CA.

  3. See. D. J. Lanham, "Bribery and Corruption", in *Criminal Law Essays*, 92, 104; Shyllon, "The Corruption of 'Corruptly'" [1969] Crm LR 250.

  4. *Cooper v Slade* (1858) 6 HL Cas 746 at 773, per Willes J. *Smith* [1960] 2 QB 423, [1960] 1 All ER 256; *Wellburn* (1979) 69 Cr App Rep 254; *Parker* (1985) 83 Cr App Rep 69.

  5. *Smith*, above, fn. 4.

  6. *Parker*, above, fn. 4.

  7. P. 107.

  8. *Martindale* [1986] 3 All ER 25, [1986] 1 WLR 1042, [1986] Crim LR 736. It may be different if D is alleged to be "knowingly" in possession; above, p. 121, fn. 15.

  9. *Buswell* [1972] 1 All ER 75, [1972] 1 WLR 64.

10. Above, p. 107.

intention to exclude others from one's property is enough, for some purposes, to found possession of things in or on the property.[11] Though the drug may have been planted in D's basket or his car without his knowledge, it would seem that he could sue for trepass if it were wrongfully removed by another; his general intention to exclude others being enough. When we are concerned with criminal offences of possession, however, it would seem likely that the more elaborate mental element specified in *Warner* will be required. It is obvious that this may prove a source of considerable difficulty to juries and those who have to direct them.

Concentration on the mental element must not be allowed to obscure the fact that possession has a physical element as well, consisting in a measure of control over the thing. A seaman is not in possession of drugs simply because he allows others to conceal them behind a bulkhead panel in his cabin.[12] A licensee, the employee of a company, is not in possession of a false measuring instrument used by a fellow employee in the sale of intoxicating liquor simply on the ground that he is the only person entitled to use the instrument to sell liquor. Some degree of control by him must be proved.[13]

---

11. *Elwes v Brigg Gas Co* (1886) 33 Ch D 562; *South Staffs Water Co v Sharman* [1896] 2 QB 44; *Hibbert v McKiernan* [1948] 2 KB 142, [1948] 1 All ER 860; *Woodman* [1974] QB 754, [1974] 2 All ER 955, CA; **SHC 478**; below, p. 511. Cf. *Parker v British Airways Board* [1982] QB 1004, [1982] 1 All ER 834, CA.
12. *Hussain* [1969] 2 QB 567, [1969] 2 All ER 1117. Cf. *Searle* [1971] Crim LR 592 and *Brown* [1970] 1 QB 105, [1969] 3 All ER 198, below, p. 583.
13. *Bellerby v Carle* [1983] 2 AC 101, [1983] 1 All ER 1031, HL, distinguishing *Sopp v Long*, above, p. 126.

8 Modes of Participation in Crime

1 Accomplices

The person who directly and immediately causes the *actus reus* of a crime is not necessarily the only one who is criminally liable for it. By the Accessories and Abettors Act 1861, s. 8 as amended by the Criminal Law Act 1977:

"Whosoever shall aid, abet, counsel or procure the commission of any indictable offence whether the same be an offence at common law or by virtue of any act passed or to be passed, shall be liable to be tried, indicted and punished as a principal offender."[1]

The effect of s. 1 of the Criminal Law Act 1967[2] is that this provision is now applicable to all offences whether they were formerly felonies or misdemeanours. Those who aid, abet, counsel or procure the commission of an offence are conveniently designated "secondary parties." The common law of felonies designated the actual perpetrator "the principal in the first degree" and distinguished secondary parties into principals in the second degree – those who participated at the time when the felony was actually perpetrated – and accessories before the fact – those who participated at an earlier time.[3] The abolition of felonies has made no change of substance. No one became liable to conviction, as a result of this reform, who was not liable before it; and no one is exempt from liability who was not exempt before. The modes of participation in crime which the law recognises are unchanged.

Notwithstanding the abolition of felonies it continues to be necessary for certain purposes to distinguish the "principal in the first degree" (hereafter, "principal") from secondary participants:

    a) in the case of all offences of strict liability for, even in these cases, secondary parties must be proved to have *mens rea*;[4]

---

1. Similar provisions relating to summary trial are to be found in the Magistrates' Courts Act 1980, s. 44.

2. Above p. 25. For proposals for further reform of the law, see Law Commission Working Paper No. 43.

3. It was traditional to state that the distinction was that the principal in the second degree was *present* at the commission of the offence; but in fact he might be a considerable distance away – in an American case (*State v Hamilton and Lawrie* 13 Nev 386 (1878) – signals from mountain top), 30–40 miles, so long as he was assisting or available to assist, at the time. Hawkins 2 PC c. 29, ss. 7 and 8; Foster 350.

4. Below, p. 142. In road traffic offences, where disqualification of the principal is obligatory, disqualification of secondary parties is discretionary: Road Traffic Act 1972, s. 93 (6).

b) in all cases where the offence is so defined that it can be committed as a principal in the first degree only by a member of a specified class (e.g. the holder of a justices' licence);[5]

c) where vicarious liability is in issue. In some offences vicarious liability may be imposed for the act of another who is a principal or does the act of a principal; but there is no vicarious liability for the act of a secondary party.[6]

The old cases on participation in felonies remain valid authorities on the limits of criminal liability. To be liable, a person who is not the principal must be proved to have aided, abetted, counselled or procured, though it is quite sufficient to show that he did one of these things. All four expressions imply the commission of the offence. "Counselling" must not be taken literally. Mere incitement to commit an offence, not followed by its actual commission, is not "counselling".[7] Secondary parties are liable when and where the offence aided, abetted, counselled or procured is committed. So an employer who sends a lorry, which he knows to be in a dangerous condition, from Scotland to England may be held liable in England for a death caused here because of the lorry's condition.[8]

The law of secondary parties is applicable to all offences, unless expressly or impliedly excluded. It is possible that it is impliedly excluded where statute creates offences of "using or causing or permitting to be used."[9] Occasionally, aiding, etc., is made the principal offence.[10]

1 The Principal

Where there are several participants in a crime the principal is the one whose act is the most immediate cause of the *actus reus*. In murder, for example, he is the man who, with *mens rea*, fires the gun or administers the poison which causes death; in theft, the man, who, with *mens rea*, appropriates the thing which is stolen; in bigamy, the person who, knowing himself to be already married, goes through a second ceremony of marriage; and so on. The *actus reus* may be directly brought about by the act of someone who is not a participant in the crime at all (that is, who has no *mens rea*, or who has some defence, such as infancy or insanity). Such a person is usually described as an "innocent agent" and, in such a case, the principal is the participant in the crime whose act is the most immediate cause of the innocent agent's act. If D sends through the post a letter-bomb to P who is injured by the explosion, the postman who delivers the letter is an innocent agent. So if D, intending to kill P, gives to P's daughter a poison which, he says, will cure P's cold, and she innocently administers the poison, causing P's death, then D is guilty as the principal offender.[11] If the daughter had

---

5. Below, p. 155.
6. Below, p. 169.
7. *Assistant Recorder of Kingston-upon-Hull, ex parte Morgan* [1969] 2 QB 58, [1969] 1 All ER 416.
8. *Robert Millar (Contractors) Ltd* [1970] 2 QB 54, [1970] 1 All ER 577, below, p. 148.
9. *Carmichael & Sons (Worcester) Ltd v Cottle* [1971] RTR 11. Cf. *Farr* [1982] Crim LR 745, CA, and commentary.
10. See Suicide Act 1961, below, p. 359.
11. (1634), Kelyng 53; *Michael* (1840) 9 C & P 356; below, p. 325.

had *mens rea* then she would, of course, have been the principal. Where D, a collector of money, makes a false statement to his employer's book-keeper, knowing that the statement will be entered in the books, and it is so entered by the innocent book-keeper, D is guilty, as a principal, of falsifying his employer's accounts.[12] Where D induces a child, aged eleven, to take money from a till and give it to D, D is a principal only if the child is exempt from criminal liability which, in the case of a child of that age, depends on whether he knows the act is wrong.[13] If the child does know his act is wrong, then he is the principal and D is a secondary party.[14]

There are some crimes to which the doctrine of innocent agency is inapplicable because it is impossible to say that D has personally commit-ted the *actus reus*.[15] Bigamy – except in the case of a marriage by proxy – is the clearest example. Compare it with murder. If D causes an innocent person, E, to kill P, it is right for the law to take the view that *D has killed P* – the *actus reus* of murder; but if D induces E, an innocent person, to go through a marriage with F, which D knows to be bigamous, it is impossible to say that *D has married during the lifetime of his wife* – the *actus reus* of bigamy. He has not done so. In the same category, it is submitted, are rape and other crimes involving sexual intercourse and the *dicta* in *Cogan and Leak*[16] that rape may be committed through an innocent agent are contrary to principle.

It is, of course, perfectly possible to have two or more principals in the first degree in the same crime. If D1 and D2 make an attack on P intending to murder him and the combined effect of their blows is to kill him, plainly both are guilty of murder[17] as joint principals.

What is the position when the principal himself is not present at the moment of the completion of the crime? If two or more persons conspire to employ an innocent agent both are liable as principals for the agent's acts and it is immaterial that the agent was instructed by the one in the absence of the other. The innocent agent's acts are considered the acts of both conspirators.[18] Where there is no innocent agent, the same considerations cannot apply. D1, in pursuance of an agreement with D2, leaves poison to be taken by P, or sets a trap into which P falls. It is thought that D2 will be liable as a secondary party.

The distinction between a joint principal and an abettor will sometimes be difficult to make. Generally it is immaterial in which capacity D2 is alleged to have participated in the crime. When it is necessary to dis-tinguish, the test would seem to be: did D2 by his own act (as distinct from anything done by D1 with D2's advice or assistance) contribute to the

---

12. *Butt* (1884) 15 Cox CC 564.
13. See below, p. 179. And see *Tyler* (1838) 8 C & P 616 (liability for act of lunatic).
14. *Manley* (1844) 1 Cox CC 104. The child was actually nine. A child under ten is now incapable of crime, so D would be the principal whether the nine-year-old knew the act was wrong or not. See also *Mazeau* (1840) 9 C & P 676.
15. Cf. *Woby v B and O* [1986] Crim LR 183, DC (boys under 18 not guilty of *buying intoxicating liquor in licensed premises* when they sent in an adult to buy it).
16. [1976] QB 217, [1975] 2 All ER 1059, [1975] Crim LR 584 and commentary thereon; below, p. 156. Cf. burglary, below, p. 597.
17. *Macklin and Murphy's* case (1838) 2 Lew CC 225; *Bingley* (1821) Russ & Ry 446 (A and B each forged part of a banknote).
18. *Bull and Schmidt* (1845) 1 Cox CC 281.

causation of the *actus reus*? Where the *actus* is a "state of affairs",[19] the test is: ignoring D1, does the statutory description of the state of affairs fit D2?

2 Secondary Participation

In *Attorney General's Reference (No. 1 of 1975)* Lord Widgery CJ said:

"We approach s. 8 of the 1861 Act on the basis that the words should be given their ordinary meaning, if possible. We approach the section on the basis also that if four words are employed here 'aid, abet, counsel or procure', the probability is that there is a difference between each of those four words and the other three, because, if there were no such difference, then Parliament would be wasting time in using four words where two or three would do."[20]

The four words had previously been regarded as technical terms and it is clear that they cannot be given their ordinary meaning in all respects. It has sometimes been said[1] that "aid and abet" is a single concept, "aid" denoting the *actus reus* and "abet" the *mens rea*. The natural meaning of s. 8 is however that stated in *A-G's Reference*. Moreover the words do connote a different kind of activity. The natural meaning of "to aid" is to "give help, support or assistance to"; and of "to abet", "to incite, instigate or encourage".[2] It is entirely clear that either type of activity is sufficient to found liability as a secondary party. "Abet", so defined, seems indistinguishable from "counsel". Perhaps there is no difference except that at common law "abet" connoted incitement at the time of the offence and "counsel" incitement at an earlier time. Participation in a conspiracy to commit an offence amounts to counselling if the offence is actually committed.[3]

All four words may be used together to charge a person who is alleged to have participated in an offence otherwise than as a principal in the first degree.[4] So long as the evidence establishes that D's conduct satisfied one of the words, that is enough.

It has also been said that "aiding and abetting" described the activity of the principal in the second degree and "counselling and procuring" that of the accessory.[5] Where it is necessary to distinguish between them, "abet" and "counsel" will be used henceforth to describe the two types of secondary participation. "Aid and abet" has however sometimes been used in relation to acts committed before the actual perpetration of the crime. If we are to have regard to the natural meaning of the words instead of regarding them as technical terms, this is desirable because some such acts

---

19. Above, p. 46.
20. [1975] 2 All ER 684 at 686.
   1. *Lynch v Director of Public Prosecutions for Northern Ireland* [1975] 1 All ER 913 at 941, per Lord Simon quoting the third edition of this work and Devlin J in *National Coal Board v Gamble* [1959] 1 QB 11 at 20; **SHC 156.**
   2. Oxford English Dictionary.
   3. Stephen, *Digest of the Criminal Law* (9th ed.), Article 28; Williams, CLGP, 363; *Pinkerton v US* (1946) 328 US 640. See, however, Lanham, "Complicity, Concert and Conspiracy" [1980] 4 Crim LJ 276. Secondary participation in a conspiracy (if there is such a thing – see *Crime, Proof and Punishment* at 28–29) might not lead to liability for the ulterior offence.
   4. *Re Smith* (1858) 3 H & N 227; *Ferguson v Weaving* [1951] 1 KB 814, [1951] 1 All ER 412.
   5. *Ferguson v Weaving*, above, at 818–819; **SHC 154,** Stephen, *Digest* (4th ed.), Articles 37–39. *Bowker v Premier Drug Co Ltd* [1928] 1 KB 217 ("aid and abet" implies presence).

are not very happily described either as counselling or as procuring though they merit criminal liability.

3 Secondary Parties: Causation and Consensus

"To procure means to produce by endeavour."[6] "You cannot procure an offence unless there is a causal link between what you do and the commission of the offence."[7] In *A-G's Reference* D2 who had added alcohol to D1's drink without D1's knowledge or consent was held to have procured D1's offence of driving with a blood/alcohol concentration above the prescribed limit[8] if it was proved that D2 knew that D1 was going to drive and that the ordinary and natural result of the added alcohol would be to bring D1's blood/alcohol concentration above the prescribed limit. D2 had caused the commission of the offence. This is in accordance with the natural meaning of "procure".[9] The natural meaning of "abet" and "counsel" on the other hand does not imply any causal element because, unlike "procure", these words do not even imply that the offence has been committed. Instigation, incitement, encouragement, counselling, may all be unsuccessful and they have occurred no less because the offence is not committed. Of course, the law is that the offence must have been committed before anyone can be convicted as an abettor or counsellor of it; but, when the offence has been committed, it is certainly still true to say that D2 "counselled" it, in the ordinary meaning of the word, even if his counsel was ignored by D1; and the same seems to be true of abetting. There is nevertheless the high authority of Stephen for the view that one who counsels or commands (as well as procures) is liable and, by implication liable only, for an offence "which is committed *in consequence* of such counselling, procuring, or commandment".[10] It is clearly the law that an attempt to counsel does not amount to counselling. Proffered advice or encouragement which has no effect on the mind of the principal offender is not counselling.[11] This is not to say that the counselling must be a cause of the commission of the offence. So to require would be to insist that, but for the counselling, the offence would not have been committed.[12] This would confine counselling (and abetting) much too narrowly. If it were incumbent on the prosecution to prove that the offence would not have been committed but for D2's advice or encouragement it seems safe to say that the point would figure much more prominently in the law reports. On the contrary, the facts of many cases where D2 has been held liable suggest that the offence would have been committed whether he had participated or not and no one seems to have suggested that this should be a defence. There must, however, be some connection between the counselling and the commission of the offence. It is probably not necessary to prove that D1 was influenced

6. *A-G's Reference (No. 1 of 1975)* [1975] 2 All ER 684 at 686; **SHC 145**; *Reed* [1982] Crim LR 819. See K.J.M. Smith, "Complicity and Causation" [1986] Crim LR 663; Beynon, "Causation, Omissions and Complicity", [1987] Crim LR 539.
7. Ibid., at 687.
8. Road Traffic Act 1972, s. 6(1), now substituted by Transport Act 1981, Sch. 8.
9. Cf. Glazebrook "Attempting to Procure" [1959] Crim LR 774.
10. Stephen, *Digest* (4th ed.) Art. 39.
11. *Clarkson* [1971] 3 All ER 344, [1971] 1 WLR 1402 (C–MAC); **SHC 163**.
12. ". . . it does not make any difference that the person [*sc.*, the person counselled] would have tried to commit suicide anyway": *A-G v Able* [1984] 1 All ER 277 at 288, per Woolf J.

in any way by D2 but he must at least be aware that he has the authority, or the encouragement, or the approval, of D2 to do the relevant acts.

"For example, if the principal offender happened to be involved in a football riot in the course of which he laid about him with a weapon of some sort and killed someone who, unknown to him, was the person whom he had been counselled to kill, he would not, in our view, have been acting within the scope of his authority; he would have been acting outside it, albeit what he had done was what he had been counselled to do."[13]

What has been said of counselling applies to abetting.[14] Aiding, likewise, does not imply any causal connection. D2 may come to the assistance of D1 and enable him to commit the offence more easily, earlier, or with greater safety and, if so, he is surely guilty even if the same offence would have been committed if he had not intervened.[15]

In *A-G's Reference (No. 1 of 1975)* D2's act of procuring was done without the knowledge or consent, and perhaps against the will, of D1. The case decides that this is immaterial where "procuring" is relied on. It was suggested that it might be different in the case of aiding, abetting and counselling – that these concepts might require a meeting of minds of secondary party and principal. If counselling and abetting must be operative, as suggested above, this is clearly right. The same does not seem necessarily to follow in the case of aiding, however. If D2 sees D1 committing a crime and comes to his assistance by, for example, restraining the policeman who would have prevented D1 from committing the crime, D2 is surely guilty even though his assistance is unforeseen and unwanted by D1 and unknown to him. The same might apply to aid given beforehand. D2, knowing that D1 is going to meet a blackmailer, P, slips a gun into D1's pocket in the hope that he will kill P – which he does.

To sum up – the law probably is that:
  i) "procuring" implies causation but not consensus;
 ii) "abetting" and "counselling" imply consensus but not causation;
iii) "aiding" requires actual assistance but neither consensus nor causation.

4 The Time Factor

Assistance given before the offence is committed will ground liability so it is only as regards the conclusion of the offence that time becomes important. Assistance given when the principal is no longer in the course of the commission of the offence – to enable him to escape or to reap the benefits of the commission of the offence – does not amount to abetting. Where D1 broke into a warehouse, stole butter and deposited it in the street thirty yards from the warehouse door, D2 who came to assist in carrying it off was held not guilty of abetting in larceny.[16] Assistance given to a murderer, after his victim is dead, to a rapist after the act of intercourse has

---

13. *Calhaem* [1985] QB 808, [1985] 2 All ER 266, CA, per Parker LJ.
14. See e.g. *Wilcox v Jeffery*; **SHC 163**; below, p. 137; *Du Cros v Lambourne*, below, p. 137.
15. See Le Fave and Scott, *Criminal Law*, 504.
16. *King* (1817) Russ & Ry 332; see also *Kelly* (1820) Russ & Ry 421.

concluded,[17] or to a bigamist after the second ceremony of marriage, cannot ground liability for the crime in question. One who, without any pre-arranged plan, joins in an attack on P after P has received a fatal injury, is not guilty of homicide (though he may be guilty of an attempt) if his action in no way contributes to P's subsequent death.[18]

5 Presence at the Crime

A person is not guilty merely because he is present at the scene of a crime and does nothing to prevent it.[19] To continue to sit beside the driver of a car until the end of a journey after learning that he is uninsured does not amount to abetting his uninsured driving.[20] If prohibited drugs, found in a van belonging to a party of tourists, are the property of and under the exclusive control of one of them, the others are not guilty of abetting simply because they are present and know of the existence of the drugs.[1] The abettor must either (a) be present in pursuance of an agreement that the crime be committed or (b) give assistance or encouragement in its commission. Both assistance or encouragement in fact and an intention to assist or encourage must be proved.[2] When this is proved, it is immaterial that D joined in the offence without any prior agreement.[3] In *Allan*[4] it was held that one who remains present at an affray, nursing a secret intention to help if the need arises but doing nothing to evince that intention, does not thereby become an abettor. Thus in the leading case of *Coney*[5] it was held that proof of mere voluntary presence at a prize-fight, without more, is, at the most, only prima facie and not conclusive evidence of abetting the battery of which the contestants are guilty. Presence at such an event is certainly capable of amounting to an actual encouragement. If there were no spectators there would be no fight and, therefore, each spectator, by his presence, contributes to the incentive to the contestants. As Matthew J (dissenting) said:[6]

"The chief incentive to the wretched combatants to fight on until (as happens too often) dreadful injuries have been inflicted and life endangered or sacrificed, is the presence of spectators watching with keen interest every incident of the fight."

Voluntary presence at such an event, then, is some evidence on which a jury might find that the accused was there with the intention of encouraging the fight. Coney's conviction was quashed because the majority of the court thought that the chairman's direction was capable of being understood to

17. The act does not conclude at the instant of penetration but continues at least as long as the penetration: *Mayberry* [1973] Qd R 211 at 229, (Skerman J, dissenting, p. 286, on this issue); *Kaitamaki* [1985] AC 147, [1984] 2 All ER 435.
18. *S v Thomo* 1969 (1) SA 385 (AD); Burchell & Hunt, 352.
19. *Atkinson* (1869) 11 Cox CC 330; but it is an offence to refuse to assist a constable to suppress a breach of the peace when called upon to do so: *Brown* (1841) Car & M 314.
20. *Smith v Baker* [1971] RTR 350.
1. *Searle* [1971] Crim LR 592 and commentary thereon.
2. *Clarkson* [1971] 3 All ER 344, [1971] 1 WLR 1402; **SHC 163**; *Jones and Mirrless* (1977) 65 Cr App Rep 250, CA.
3. *Rannath Mohan v R* [1967] 2 AC 187, [1967] 2 All ER 58.
4. [1965] 1 QB 130, [1963] 2 All ER 897; **SHC 162**; see also *Tansley v Painter* (1968) 112 Sol Jo 1005.
5. (1882) 8 QBD 534.
6. Ibid., at p. 544.

mean that voluntary presence was *conclusive* evidence of an intention to encourage. If the direction had made it clear that presence was prima facie evidence only, no doubt the conviction would have been sustained. So in *Wilcox v Jeffrey*[7] it was held that D's presence at a public performance by H, a celebrated alien performer on the saxophone, who had been given permission to land only on condition that he would take no employment, was a sufficient aiding and abetting of H in his contravention of the Aliens Order 1920. D's behaviour before and after the performance supplied further evidence of his intention to encourage; for he had met H at the airport and he afterwards reported the performance in laudatory terms in the periodical of which he was the proprietor.

It would seem that where the evidence establishes mere presence without any positive act, a prior agreement that the crime be committed must be proved. But if some positive act of assistance is voluntarily done, with knowledge of the circumstances constituting the offence, that is enough to sustain a conviction; and it is irrelevant, in the latter case, that the aid is not given with the motive or purpose of encouraging the crime.[8] So if D2 handed a gun to D1 knowing that D1 intended to shoot P, it would not avail D2 to say that he hoped that D1 would not use the gun.[9]

6 Participation by Inactivity

Where D has a right to control the actions of another and he deliberately refrains from exercising it, his inactivity may be a positive encouragement to the other to perform an illegal act, and, therefore, an aiding and abetting. A husband who stands by and watches his wife drown their children is guilty of abetting the homicide. His deliberate abstention from action gives encouragement and authority to his wife's act.[10] If a licensee of a public house stands by and watches his customers drinking after hours, he is guilty of aiding and abetting them in doing so.[11] Again in *Du Cros v Lambourne*,[12] it was proved that D's car had been driven at a dangerous speed but it was not proved whether D or E was driving. It was held that, nevertheless, D could be convicted. If E was driving she was doing so in D's presence, with his consent and approval; for he was in control and could and ought to have prevented her from driving in a dangerous manner. D was equally liable whether he was a principal or an abettor.[13] The result would presumably have been different if it had been E's own car, for D would then have had no right of control, and could only have been convicted if active instigation to drive at such speed had been proved. In such cases it must be proved that D2 knew of those features of D1's

---

7. [1951] 1 All ER 464; **SHC 163**.

8. *National Coal Board v Gamble* [1959] 1 QB 11, [1958] 3 All ER 203; **SHC 156**; below, p. 140.

9. Cf., however, *Fretwell* (1864) Le & Ca 443; below, p. 140.

10. *Russell* [1933] VLR 59.

11. *Tuck v Robson* [1970] 1 All ER 1171, [1970] 1 WLR 741, DC.

12. [1907] 1 KB 40; cf. also *Rubie v Faulkner* [1940] 1 KB 571, [1940] 1 All ER 285; *Harris* [1964] Crim LR 54.

13. Cf. *Swindall and Osborne* (1846) 2 Car & Kir 230: *Salmon* (1880) 6 QBD 79; *Iremonger v Wynne* [1957] Crim LR 624; Williams, CLGP 137, n. 23. There is, however, a difference regarding disqualification; above, p. 130, footnote 4. *Smith v Mellors* [1987] Crim LR 421.

driving which rendered it dangerous and failed to take action within a reasonable time.[14] In *Baldessare*, [15] D1 and D2 unlawfully took X's car and D1 drove it recklessly and caused P's death. It was held that D2 was guilty of manslaughter as an abettor. In this case (as prosecuting counsel put it)

"The common purpose to drive recklessly was . . . shown by the fact that both men were driving in a car which did not belong to them and the jury were entitled to infer that the driver was the agent of the passenger. It matters not whose hand was actually controlling the car at the time."

If, however, all that can be proved is that the offence was committed either by D1 or by D2, both must be acquitted.[16] Only if it can be proved that the one who did not commit the crime must have aided and abetted it can both be convicted.[17] This is as true where parents are charged with injury to their child as it is in the case of any other defendants. The only difference is that one parent may have a duty to intervene to prevent the ill-treatment of their child by the other when a stranger would have no such duty. It is for the prosecution to prove that the parent who did not inflict the injuries must have aided and abetted the infliction by failure to fulfil that duty or otherwise.

One whose participation in the relevant events does not involve advice or encouragement to commit the crime, and who does not assist the commission in any way, is not liable. Accepting a lift on a motor-cycle known to have been taken without consent does not amount to aiding and abetting the use of the vehicle without insurance.[18] It would have been different if the taking had been a joint enterprise.[19]

This rule received what has been regarded as a generous interpretation in *Taylor*.[20] A and B quarrelled and agreed to fight. They each agreed to put down £1 so that the £2 might be paid to the winner. D agreed to hold the stakes. A and B fought, A received injuries of which he died and B was convicted of manslaughter. D was not present at the fight. He paid over the £2 to B, not knowing at that time that A's life was in danger. It was held that D was not liable as an accessory. There was no evidence that he encouraged the two men to fight, and, as Bramwell B said, "Nothing that the accused did assisted or enabled the fight to take place."[1] The stake was, after all, a collateral transaction, and the fight could well have taken place without it.

7 Mens rea

i) *Intention to aid, etc.* It must be proved that D intended to do the acts which he knew to be capable of assisting or encouraging the commission of

---

14. *Dennis v Pight* (1968) 11 FLR 458 at 463.
15. (1930) 22 Cr App Rep 70.
16. *Richardson* (1785) 1 Leach 387.
17. *Russell and Russell* [1987] Crim LR 494, CA: *Lane and Lane* (1986) 82 Cr App Rep 5. *Gibson and Gibson* (1985) 80 Cr App Rep 24 is misleading and should be used with care. See commentary, [1984] Crim LR 615.
18. *D (an infant) v Parsons* [1960] 2 All ER 493, [1960] 1 WLR 797. Cf. *Bland* [1988] Crim LR 41, CA.
19. *Ross v Rivenall* [1959] 2 All ER 376, [1959] 1 WLR 713. Cf. s. 12(1) of the Theft Act 1968 and *Boldizsar v Knight* [1980] Crim LR 653, below, p. 587.
20. (1875) LR 2 CCR 147, criticised in Williams, CLGP, 365; Kenny, *Outlines*, 110.
1. (1875) LR 2 CCR 147 at 149.

the crime. That is not the same thing as an intention that the crime be committed. As Devlin J said:[2]

"If one man deliberately sells to another a gun to be used for murdering a third, he may be indifferent whether the third man lives or dies and interested only in the cash profit to be made out of the sale, but he can still be an aider and abettor."

So it is the intention to do the acts of assistance or encouragement which must be proved. If D has that intention it is no defence that his motives were unimpeachable.[3] In *Lynch v Director of Public Prosecutions for Northern Ireland*, where D2 drove D1 to the place where he knew that D1 intended to murder a policeman, D2's intentional driving of the car was aiding and abetting, "even though he regretted the plan or indeed was horrified by it".[4]

There is some difficulty in reconciling the implications of the decision in *Gillick's case*[5] (a civil action for a declaration) with this principle. The House of Lords held that, in certain circumstances, a doctor may lawfully give contraceptive advice or treatment to a girl under the age of sixteen without her parents' consent. The conditions of lawful treatment could include cases where the doctor knew that the provision of the advice or treatment would encourage or facilitate sexual intercourse by the girl with a man. The man, but not the girl, would commit an offence.[6] The doctor's motives would no doubt be unimpeachable, but that is generally no answer. Why is not the doctor (and the parents if they concurred in the advice, for they have no more right than the doctor to aid and abet crime) guilty of aiding and abetting the man's offence? His act may well be facilitated (through the girl's being more ready to have intercourse) and (if he knows of the contraception) encouraged by the doctor's acts.[7] The decision that the doctor's advice is lawful clearly implies that he does not aid and abet a crime but the reason is nowhere clearly stated. It seems most likely that Woolf J and the majority of the House thought he lacked the necessary intention. As noted above,[8] this seems to put an undue strain on the concept of intention. If a mother, knowing that her son is about to embark on an armed robbery and cannot be dissuaded, gives him a bullet-proof vest, with the sole and admirable motive of saving him from death or serious injury, is not her intention to enable him to perpetrate the robbery more safely an intention to aid and abet it? *Gillick's case* is better regarded as being based impliedly, if not expressly,[9] on necessity.

Mere recklessness, still less negligence, whether assistance be given, is probably not enough. D's realisation that he may have left his gun-

---

2. [1959] 1 QB 11 at 23, [1958] 3 All ER 203.

3. Woolf J in *Gillick v West Norfolk and Wisbech Area Health Authority* [1984] QB 581 at 589, [1984] 1 All ER 365 at 373. Woolf J's discussion of the criminal aspects of this case was adopted by Lords Scarman and Bridge in the House of Lords, [1986] AC 112.

4. [1975] AC 653 at 678, [1975] 1 All ER 913, per Lord Morris, approving the judgment of Lowry LCJ on this point. See **SHC 160**. *Fretwell* (1862) Le & Ca 161, below, p. 140, appears to be a merciful decision and unsound in principle.

5. Above, footnote 3.

6. Sexual Offences Act 1956, s. 6, below, p. 441.

7. For a full discussion of this question, see [1986] Crim LR 114.

8. P. 58.

9. See J. R. Spencer in *Criminal Law Essays* 148, 164.

cupboard unlocked and that his son has a disposition to commit armed robbery, is probably not sufficient to fix D with liability for the armed robbery and homicide which the son commits using one of D's guns. There was no intention to do any act of advice or assistance.

In *National Coal Board v Gamble*,[10] E, a lorry driver, had his employer's lorry filled with coal at a colliery belonging to the defendant Board. When the lorry was driven on to the weighbridge operated by the defendants' servant, F, it appeared, and F so informed E, that its load exceeded by nearly four tons that permitted by the Motor Vehicles (Construction and Use) Regulations. E said he would take the risk, F gave him a weighbridge ticket and E committed the offence by driving the overloaded lorry on the highway. The property in the coal did not pass until the ticket was handed over and, therefore, E could not properly have left the colliery without it. It was held that the Board, through F,[11] was guilty of the misdemeanour. The decision was based on the assumption that F knew he had the right to prevent the lorry leaving the colliery with the coal. Had he not known this, he should have been acquitted. Presumably F was indifferent whether E drove his overloaded lorry on the road or not – he probably thought that it was none of his business – but F's motive was irrelevant and it was enough that a positive act of assistance had been voluntarily done with knowledge of the circumstances constituting the offence.

This result is in accord with two previous decisions. In *Cook v Stockwell*,[12] D, a brewer, supplied large quantities of beer to some cottages, knowing very well that they were re-selling it, without being licensed to do so, to soldiers quartered near by. In *Cafferata v Wilson*,[13] D, a wholesaler, sold a firearm to E, who kept a general shop, but was not registered as a firearms dealer. Presumably D knew that E was going to re-sell the firearm, which he in fact did. In both cases D was held liable as an accessory to the illegal sale.

In these cases the suppliers were indifferent whether the crime was committed or not. In *Fretwell*[14] D reluctantly supplied an abortifacient to a woman when she threatened to kill herself if he did not do so. He hoped she would not use it but she did so and died. This was self-murder at common law but D was held not liable as an accessory because he was "unwilling that the woman should take the poison". A distinction between indifference and unwillingness of this nature is, however, too uncertain to form the basis of a legal rule.

Fretwell is perhaps best regarded as a case in which the court strained the principles governing the liability of accessories in order to mitigate the severity of the rule which treated suicide as murder.[15] Woolf J regards it "as confined to its own facts".[16]

10. [1959] 1 QB 11, [1958] 3 All ER 203; **SHC 156**, DC, Slade J dissenting.
11. See, however, below, p. 172, footnote 2.
12. (1915) 84 LJKB 2187.
13. [1936] 3 All ER 149.
14. Above, p. 139, footnote 4. Cf. Williams, CLGP, §124.
15. As to which, see below, p. 358.
16. *A-G v Able* [1984] 1 All ER 277 at 287, citing the 4th edition of the work (1978) pp. 120–121. But cf. *Gillick*, above, p. 139 and *Salford Health Authority*, above, p. 58.

National Coal Board v Gamble suggests a distinction between the cases (i) where the seller is aware of the illegal purpose of the buyer before ownership has passed to the buyer; and (ii) where the seller learns of that purpose for the first time after ownership has passed but before delivery. In (i) delivery amounts to abetting; in (ii) it does not. The seller is merely complying with his legal duty to give the buyer his own property.

"In a sense a man who gives up to a criminal a weapon which the latter has a right to demand from him aids in the commission of the crime as much as if he sold or lent the article, but this has never been held to be aiding in law."[17]

This seems a scarcely satisfactory distinction. If D delivers weedkiller to E, knowing that E intends to use it to murder his wife, it would be remarkable if D's guilt turned on whether the ownership passed before or after D learned of E's intention. The important thing is that he knows of it when he makes delivery. It should not be an answer that E has a right to possession of the thing in the civil law because the civil law should not afford a right in such a case.[18] In *Garrett v Arthur Churchill (Glass) Ltd*[19] D, who had bought a goblet as agent of E, was held guilty of being knowingly concerned in the exportation of goods without a licence, when, on E's instructions, he delivered E's own goblet to E's agent who was to take it to America.

"... albeit there was a legal duty in ordinary circumstances to hand over the goblet to the owners once the agency was determined, I do not think that an action would lie for breach of that duty if the handing over would constitute the offence of being knowingly concerned in its exportation."[20]

Probably then the seller is liable whether or not the ownership has passed before delivery. Williams's view, however, is that the seller ought to be liable in neither case. He argues:[1]

"The seller of an ordinary marketable commodity is not his buyer's keeper in criminal law unless he is specifically made so by statute. Any other rule would be too wide an extension of criminal responsibility."

Williams would now accept that:

"... the seller of a motor car would become a party to crime if he knew that the buyer proposed to drive the car himself and was subject to epileptic fits – because danger to life is involved; it is very like selling a revolver to a would-be murderer."[2]

An example given to demonstrate the extravagance of a general rule of liability of sellers is:

"... the vendor of a hotel would become a party to crime if he knew at the time of sale that the purchaser intended to carry on illegal after-hour trading."

---

17. [1959] 1 QB 11 at 20, per Devlin J.
18. See Williams, CLGP, s. 124 and Smith, [1972]B CLJ 197 at p. 208.
19. [1970] 1 QB 92, [1969] 2 All ER 1141. How far does this go? If X lends a picture to a museum, does the museum really commit an offence if, on demand, it returns the picture to X, knowing that he intends to export it without a licence?
20. [1969] 2 All ER at 1145, per Parker LCJ.
1. CLGP, §124 at p. 373. Cf. TBCL, 293–294.
2. 9 JSPTL (NS) at p. 171.

A rule based on the nature of the thing as "an ordinary marketable commodity" is not workable. Motor cars and weedkiller are ordinary marketable commodities. A more feasible distinction is one based on the seriousness of the offence contemplated. The example of the sale of the hotel would be less startling if the seller knew that it was to be used as a headquarters for espionage or as a brothel. This is the American approach:

> "The gravity of the social harm resulting from the unlawful conduct is used to determine whether mere knowledge of the intended use will be sufficient to carry the taint of illegality."[3]

The disadvantage of this rule is its uncertainty and no such distinction has been taken in English law. The cases suggest a general rule of liability of sellers. This is a fortiori the case with lenders or letters of articles or premises intended for unlawful purposes for here the owner has a continuing interest in and right to control the property.[4]

ii) *Knowledge of circumstances.* The secondary party must always have full *mens rea* in the sense of knowledge of, or wilful blindness towards, the circumstances which must be proved in order to constitute the offence:

> "Before a person can be convicted of aiding and abetting the commission of an offence he must at least know the essential matters which constitute that offence. He need not actually know that an offence has been committed, because he may not know that the facts constitute an offence and ignorance of the law is not a defence."[5]

"The essential matters which constitute the offence" are the circumstances existing at the time when the act of secondary participation is done. The *actus reus* may also include certain consequences, but these cannot be "known". To what extent the consequences must be foreseen is considered below.[6] The circumstances of the *actus reus* must be known, but there is some authority for the view that the *mens rea* of the principal offender need not.[7] The word "knows", which is generally used in this context, includes "wilful blindness". In one case at least the court went further and held that it was sufficient that D2 was merely reckless as to the material fact – that the learner-driver whom D2 was supervising had an excessive blood-alcohol concentration.[8] This is the sort of fact which it is very difficult actually to know.

This principle applies even in the case of an offence of strict liability: in such a crime the principal offender may, but a secondary party may not, be

---

3. Perkins and Boyce (3rd ed.) 746.
4. For example, the hotelier who lets a room to a man accompanied by a fourteen-year-old girl, knowing that he intends to seduce her. But cf. Gordon, 142–143.
5. *Johnson v Youden* [1950] 1 KB 544 at 546, [1950] 1 All ER 300 at 302, **SHC 153**; per Lord Goddard CJ; see above, p. 80. See also *Ackroyds Air Travel Ltd v Director of Public Prosecutions* [1950] 1 All ER 933 at 936; *Thomas v Lindop* [1950] 1 All ER 966 at 968; *Ferguson v Weaving* [1951] 1 KB 814, [1951] 1 All ER 412; **SHC 154**; *Bateman v Evans* (1964) 108 Sol Jo 522; *Smith v Jenner* [1968] Crim LR 99; *Dial Contracts Ltd v Vickers* [1971] RTR 386; *D. Stanton & Sons Ltd v Webber* (1972) 116 Sol Jo 667, [1972] Crim LR 544 and commentary thereon.
6. See p. 148.
7. Below, p. 155.
8. *Carter v Richardson* [1974] RTR 314, discussed by Williams [1975] CLJ 182 and *TBCL*, 309. But in *Giorgianni* (1984) 156 CLR 473 the High Court of Australia held that recklessness is not sufficient on a charge of aiding and abetting.

convicted without *mens rea*. The reason is that secondary participation is a common law notion. It was never necessary for a statute creating an offence to specify that it should also be an offence to aid, etc., its commission. The common law, now codified in the Accessories and Abettors Act 1861,[9] was that so to act created liability to conviction of the offence aided. It is natural that the normal principles of liability at common law should apply. The result, however, is to emphasise the anomalous nature of offences of strict liability, for the alleged aider who has no *mens rea* must be acquitted even if he was negligent[10] whereas the principal who has caused the *actus reus* must be convicted even if he took all proper care.

In *Callow v Tillstone*,[11] D, a veterinary surgeon, was charged with abetting the exposure for sale of unsound meat. At the request of a butcher, G, he examined the carcase of a heifer which had eaten yew leaves and been killed by the farmer just before it would have died of yew poisoning. He gave G a certificate that the meat was sound. The examination had been negligently conducted and the meat was tainted. G, relying on the certificate, exposed the meat for sale and was convicted. The justices, holding that D's negligence had caused the exposure, convicted him of abetting. It was held that his conviction must be quashed.[12] Thus, if Prince[13] had been assisted by a friend, D, who had driven him away with the girl in a hansom cab, it would have been a defence for D (even though it was not for Prince) to show that he believed the girl to be over sixteen or even (at least if he was unaware of the relevance of the age of sixteen) that he did not know what age she was. The same principle must apply, a fortiori, to offences where negligence as to circumstances will found liability. If D2 encourages D1 to marry, both believing honestly but mistakenly and on unreasonable grounds that D1's husband is dead, D1 may be convicted of bigamy but D2 cannot be convicted of abetting. This principle applies only to circumstances. Whether a secondary party may be liable for unforeseen consequences is considered below.[14]

iii) *Knowledge of type of crime.* Three principles are involved here.
  a) If A aids, abets, counsels or procures B to commit a crime of a certain type, neither party specifying any particular victim, time or place, A may be convicted as a secondary party to any crime of that type which B commits.
  b) If A aids, abets, counsels or procures B to commit a crime against a particular person, or in respect of a particular thing, A is not liable if B intentionally commits an offence of the same type against some other person, or in respect of some other thing.
  c) A is, however, equally liable with B for any acts done by B in the course of endeavouring to carry out the common purpose. If the

9. Above, p. 130. Cf. *McCarthy* [1964] Crim LR 225.
10. *Carter v Mace* [1949] 2 All ER 714 DC, is to the contrary, but in *Davies, Turner & Co Ltd v Brodie* [1954] 3 All ER 283, [1954] 1 WLR 1364, DC, that case was said to lay down no principle of law and to be decided on its own particular facts. See J. Montgomerie in (1950) 66 LQR 222.
11. (1900) 83 LT 411, DC; **SHC 128.**
12. See also *Bowker v Premier Drug Co Ltd* [1928] 1 KB 217 at 227.
13. Above, p. 41.
14. Below, p. 148.

common purpose is to cause grievous bodily harm to C, and B, endeavouring to do so, kills C, both A and B are guilty of murder. If the common purpose is to assault C, and B, endeavouring to do so, kills him, both A and B are guilty of manslaughter. If the common purpose is to wound C (so the case is within principle (ii) above) and B, endeavouring to wound C, wounds D, B is liable under the doctrine of transferred malice;[15] and so, therefore, is A.

The application of these principles is not free from difficulty and principles (a) and (b) require more detailed consideration.

Principle (a). A leading case is *Bainbridge*.[16] D purchased some oxygen-cutting equipment which was used six weeks later for breaking into a bank at Stoke Newington. D's story was that he had bought the equipment for one Shakeshaft, that he suspected Shakeshaft wanted it for something illegal – perhaps breaking up stolen goods – but that he did not know that it was going to be used for any such purpose as it was in fact used. It was held that it was essential to prove that D knew the type of crime that was going to be committed: it was not enough that he knew that some kind of illegality was contemplated; but that, if he knew breaking and entering and stealing was intended, it was not necessary to prove that he knew that the Midland Bank, Stoke Newington, was going to be broken into. It is the same where information on how to commit a crime of a particular type is given, though neither adviser nor advised has any particular crime in view when the advice is given.[17] Where D opened a bank account for E, giving E a false name, D was convicted of aiding and abetting E in the fraudulent use of the particular forged cheque which E subsequently drew upon the account. D had evinced an intention that the account be used as a vehicle for presenting forged cheques like the one in fact presented.[18] The House of Lords carried the principle to its logical conclusion in *Director of Public Prosecutions for Northern Ireland v Maxwell*.[19] If D gives assistance to E, knowing that E intends to commit a crime, but being uncertain whether E has crime X, or crime Y, or crime Z, in mind, D will be liable as a secondary party to whichever of those crimes E in fact commits. D drove E to an inn, realising that E intended either to plant a bomb or to shoot persons at the inn. In fact, E intended to plant, and did plant a bomb. D was liable for that offence. He would have been liable for murder if E had shot and killed. It would be otherwise if E had committed another type of crime which was not in D's contemplation when he did the relevant act. Nor is a "general criminal intention" enough. So an intention to abet another in the possession of a bag, whatever its contents may be, is insufficient to found an

---

15. Above, p. 73.
16. [1960] 1 QB 129, [1959] 3 All ER 200, CCA; **SHC 147**.
17. *Baker* (1909) 28 NZLR 536. Williams thinks the case is wrongly decided: CLGP §125. But is it distinguishable in principle from *Bainbridge?* Cf. *McLeod and Georgia Straight Publishing Co Ltd* (1970) 75 WWR 161 (newspaper liable for incitement through article on how to cultivate marijuana). In Scotland, merely giving the name of an abortionist does not amount to participation in the subsequent illegal abortion: *HM Advocate v Johnstone* 1926 JC 89.
18. *Thambiah v R* [1966] AC 37, [1965] 3 All ER 661, PC.
19. [1978] 3 All ER 1140, [1978] 1 WLR 1350, HL; **SHC 150**.

indictment for abetting the possession of cannabis.[20] If D had guessed that the bag contained either cannabis or some other article, proscribed or not, that should have been enough.

Where D has supplied E with the means of committing or information on how to commit a crime of a particular type, is he to be held liable for all the crimes of that type which E may thereafter commit? What if the Midland at Stoke Newington was the second, third or fourth bank which E had feloniously broken and entered with Bainbridge's apparatus? Williams questions whether D should be subject to such unforeseeable and perhaps far-reaching liability.[1] Yet, once it is conceded that D need not know the details of any specific crime, it is difficult to see why he should be liable for any one crime of the type contemplated and not for others.[2]

Bainbridge and *Maxwell* leave some unsolved problems. Whether a crime is of the same type as another may not always be easy to discover. If D lends a jemmy to E, contemplating that E intends to enter a house in order to steal, is D guilty of any offence if E enters a house intending to rape?[3] Clearly, D cannot be convicted of rape, because that is an offence of a different type; but he is probably guilty of burglary, because burglary was the crime he had in view – though this particular variety of burglary may be abhorrent to him. If D contemplates theft and E commits robbery, D is not guilty of robbery but might be convicted of the theft which is included in it.[4] Is theft an offence of the same type as removing an article from a place open to the public[5] or taking a motor vehicle without authority?[6] Is robbery an offence of the same type as blackmail?

Principle (b). This principle is most clearly expressed by Hawkins:[7]

"But if a man command another to commit a felony on a particular person or thing and he do it on another; as to kill A and he kill B or to burn the house of A and he burn the house of B or to steal an ox and he steal an horse; or to steal such an horse and he steal another; or to commit a felony of one kind and he commit another of a quite different nature; as to rob J S of his plate as he is going to market, and he break open his house in the night and there steal the plate; it is said that the commander is not an accessary because the act done varies in substance from that which was commanded."

The principle applies where there is a substantial variation from the proposed course of conduct. Hawkins also stated:[8]

"if the felony committed be the same in substance with that which was intended, and variant only in some circumstance, as in respect of the time or place, at which, or the mean whereby it was effected, the abettor of the intent is altogether as much an accessory as if there had been no variance

---

20. *Patel* [1970] Crim LR 274 and commentary thereon. Cf. *Fernandez* [1970] Crim LR 277.
1. CLGP, §124.
2. On the question of the withdrawal of an accessory before the fact, see below, p. 156.
3. See below, p. 595.
4. Below, p. 540.
5. Theft Act 1968, s. 11. Below, p. 578.
6. Theft Act 1968, s. 12. Below, p. 581.
7. 2 PC c 29, s. 21. See also Foster 369. Stephen, Digest (4th ed.) Art 43.
8. Ibid., s. 20.

at all between it and the execution of it; as where a man advises another to kill such a one in the night, and he kills him in the day, or to kill him in the fields, and he kills him in the town, or to poison him, and he stabs or shoots him."

The distinction depends on whether the variation is one "of substance" and any such distinction must produce difficult borderline cases. In *Dunning and Graham*, an unreported case at Preston Crown Court,[9] D had a grievance against P. E offered to set fire to P's house. D accepted the offer and gave E P's address. E went to P's house, changed his mind, and set fire to P's Mercedes instead. D did not know that P owned such a car. Nevertheless, Macpherson J held that it was open to the jury to convict D on the ground that she must have authorised or envisaged the possibility of property such as a car in the driveway being damaged by fire. If the car had been so damaged as a consequence of E's setting fire to the house, D would have been liable for arson of the car under principle (c), below. The actual case, however, seems to involve a deliberate variation from the plan. The result might be justified on the basis that D had authorised E to take revenge on P by damaging his property and that it did not really matter to her what the property was. Whether the variation is, or is not, one of substance, depends on the purpose of D as expressed to E.

The South African case of *Robinson*[10] provides a further controversial illustration of the difficulties of applying these principles. D1, D2 and E agreed with P that E should kill P to procure the money for which P's life was insured and to avoid P's prosecution for fraud. At the last moment, P withdrew his consent to die but E nevertheless killed him. It was not proved that D1 and D2 foresaw the possibility that E might kill P even if he withdrew his consent or that they had been reckless whether he did so kill him. It was held that the common purpose was murder with the consent of the victim and that E had acted outside that common purpose. D1 and D2, accordingly, were not guilty of murder – though they were guilty of attempted murder, since E had reached the stage of an attempt before P withdrew his consent. Holmes JA, dissenting, thought ". . . looking squarely at the whole train of events, the conspiracy was fulfilled in death, and there is no room for exquisite niceties of logic about the exact limits of the mandate in the conspiratorial common purpose." It is submitted that the better view is that of the majority. If E knows that a condition precedent of the agreement has not been performed, he is no longer engaged on the joint enterprise. If D agrees with E that E shall murder P if he finds out that P is committing adultery with D's wife and E, having discovered that P is not committing adultery, nevertheless kills him, D should not be liable for murder, though, if this conditional intention is enough, he may be liable for conspiracy to murder.

Principle (c). The doctrine of transferred malice applies to secondary parties as it does to principals.[11] Where E, intending to follow D's advice to

---

9. December, 1985.
10. 1968 (1) SA 666; **SHC 151**.
11. Hawkins, PC, Ch. 29, s. 22; Foster, *Crown Law*, 370; Stephen, *Digest*, Art. 41, illustration (1).

kill X, mistakes Y for X and kills Y, D as well as E is guilty of murder. If D advises E to burn X's house and E does so but the flames spread and burn Y's house, D as well as E is guilty of arson of Y's house. The difference between these cases and those falling under principle (b) is that here E has not deliberately departed from the course that D advised or assisted him to follow; E was attempting to put the agreed plan into execution and D is as responsible for the unintended results of the acts he has authorised or encouraged as E.

The old and famous case of *Saunders and Archer*,[12] in its result at least, is reconcilable with this principle. D1, intending to murder his wife, on the advice of D2, gave her a poisoned apple to eat. She ate a little of it and gave the rest to their child. D1 loved the child, yet he stood by and watched it eat the poison, of which it soon died. It was held that D1 was guilty of murder, but the judges agreed that D2, who, of course, was not present when the child ate the apple, was not an accessory to this murder.

If D1 had been absent when the child ate the apple it is thought that this would have been a case of transferred malice and D2 would have been liable; but D1's presence and failure to act made the killing of the child, in effect, a deliberate, and not an accidental, departure from the agreed plan. It was – as it is well put in Kenny,[13]

"as if Saunders had changed his mind and on a later occasion had used such poison as Archer had named in order to murder some quite different person of whom Archer had never heard."

Foster, however, stated the rule rather more widely than this:[14]

"So whenever the principal goeth beyond the terms of the solicitation, *if in the event the felony committed was a probable consequence of what was ordered or advised*, the person giving such orders or advice will be an accessory to that felony."

This would make a counsellor liable for negligence in failing to foresee what he ought, as a reasonable man, to have foreseen, which, it is submitted, would be going too far. It is true that he may be held liable for negligently unforeseen consequences where the principal in the first degree may likewise be held liable[15] but, where the crime is one requiring *mens rea*, it is submitted that actual foresight of the consequences in question must be proved equally for the counsellor as for the abettor. Take the following case: D advises E to steal money from P's house by breaking the gas-meter from the wall. E does so, with the result that the gas escapes and P is injured. It is established that E is guilty of maliciously administering a noxious thing[16] only if he actually foresaw that injury of the particular kind might be caused.[17]

Foster's rule would fix D with liability simply because the result was a probable consequence of his action. It is submitted that the true rule is that

12. (1576) 2 Plowd 473.
13. *Outlines*, 112.
14. *Crown Law*, 370. See, to the same effect, Stephen, *Digest*, Art 20.
15. *Baldessare* (1930) 22 Cr App Rep 70.
16. Offences against the Person Act 1861, s. 23; below, p. 403.
17. *Cunningham* [1957] 2 QB 396, [1957] 2 All ER 412; **SHC 63**; below, p. 404, footnote 3.

the counsellor must have such foresight of the consequence of his action as is necessary for the conviction of the principal in the first degree. In this example, D may be convicted only if he foresaw the likelihood that the coal gas would be administered to someone.

iv) *Liability of secondary party for unforeseen consequences.* Where two persons embark on a joint unlawful enterprise each is equally liable for the consequences of such acts of the other as are done in pursuance of the agreement. The abettor is, then, liable for unforeseen consequences to the same extent as the principal. So in *Baldessare*,[18] the driver was held liable for the unintended and unforeseen death which he caused and his passenger was equally liable. D was guilty of counselling death by dangerous driving when he instructed his employee to drive a vehicle knowing that it had a dangerously defective tyre and, in consequence, there was an accident and a person was killed.[19] If, in a crime requiring *mens rea*, one of the parties goes beyond what was agreed upon, then the other is not liable for the unforeseen consequences of that unauthorised act. In an old case three soldiers went to rob an orchard. Two climbed a pear tree while the third stood at the gate with a drawn sword. When the owner's son intervened, the sentinel stabbed and killed him. Holt CJ held that he was guilty of murder, but that the other two were innocent. It would have been otherwise if they had all set out with a common intention to oppose interference with deadly force.[20]

In a modern case,[1] two gangs of boys engaged in a fight on Clapham Common. One of them, E, carried a knife with which he inflicted a fatal stab wound. There being no evidence that D, another member of the same gang, knew that E carried a knife, it was held that D, though guilty of a common assault, was not an accomplice in the murder.[2] If E had killed with a blow of his fist, D would have been guilty of manslaughter, because the blow was delivered in pursuance of the agreement. But, because the use of a knife was not within his contemplation at all, he was not responsible for the death which resulted from it.[3]

If both parties have a common design to kill or cause grievous bodily harm, should it be necessary to do so in order to carry out their enterprise, and one of them kills in pursuance of that design, both are guilty of murder.[4] Difficulty arises where there is no common design but D was, or may have been, aware that E might act with intent to kill or cause grievous bodily harm. According to *Jubb and Rigby*[5] D is liable for a murder

18. Above, p. 138.
19. *Robert Millar (Contractors) Ltd* [1970] 2 QB 54, [1970] 1 All ER 577. It would seem that, while the driver might have been convicted even if he had not known of the dangerous state of the tyre if he *ought* to have known of it, the counsellor could only be guilty if he actually knew. The state of the tyre was a *circumstance* which made the driving dangerous and knowledge of the essential circumstances of the offence, as distinct from the consequences, must be proved against secondary parties. See above, p. 142.
20. (1697) Foster, 353.
  1. *Davies v Director of Public Prosecutions* [1954] AC 378, [1954] 1 All ER 507, HL.
  2. Cf. *Murtagh and Kennedy* [1955] Crim LR 315.
  3. Cf. *Caton* (1874) 12 Cox CC 624.
  4. *Betts and Ridley* (1930) 22 Cr App Rep 148, CCA.
  5. [1984] Crim LR 616.

committed by E only if he foresaw that it was "probable" that E would act with such intent. In *Chan Wing-siu*[6] the Privy Council took a less generous view. They held that it is not necessary that D should have thought this event more probable than not. This is surely right. If D knows that he and E have got away with 50 robberies in the past without E (who carries the gun) firing a shot, he should surely be liable for murder on the 51st occasion when E shoots to kill. The prosecution must prove that D knew there was "a substantial risk, a real risk, a risk that something might well happen". It must be something more than a risk which "may have been dismissed by him as altogether negligible".

If D does not contemplate any "real risk" that E will act with intent to cause grievous bodily harm but is aware that E may threaten harm or act with intent to cause some less degree of harm, then D is liable for the consequences of those contemplated acts; so that, if such an act results in death, D as well as E will be guilty of manslaughter. Where D knows that E carries a knife but does not contemplate any "real risk" that E will use it with intent to cause grievous bodily harm, what is the position if E does use it with such an intent and causes death? According to *Betty*,[7] D is liable for manslaughter (for which he had the *mens rea*) because the use of a knife is "within the scope of the concerted action". The court thought it would be different if E had used a revolver which D did not know he had. That would have been outside the scope of the concerted action.[8] Another view is that the act done by E with intent to cause grievous bodily harm is an act for which D is not liable at all because it was not contemplated by him as "a real risk". In *Anderson and Morris*[9] the judge had directed that, if there was a common design to attack P, D was guilty of manslaughter if, unknown to D, E had a knife and used it with intent to kill or cause grievous bodily harm, and did kill P. D's conviction of manslaughter was quashed. It was, no doubt, sufficient to exempt D from liability for homicide that the use of the knife was an act outside the scope of the common design; but there is a suggestion that the formation by E of the intention to kill or cause grievous bodily harm was also sufficient to do so.

This was followed and formed the ratio decidendi of *Lovesey and Peterson*.[10] The convictions of murder of both appellants were quashed because one of them had gone beyond the proved common design to rob by acting with intent to inflict grievous bodily harm and it was impossible to prove which. The court held that it could not substitute verdicts of manslaughter because, "if a common design to inflict grievous bodily harm is excluded, the jury may well have concluded that the killing was the unauthorised act of one individual for which the co-adventurers were not

6. *Chan Wing-siu v R* [1985] AC 168, [1984] 3 All ER 877, approved in *Ward* (1986) 85 Cr App Rep 71, [1987] Crim LR 338, CA.
7. (1963) 48 Cr App Rep 6, CCA; *Reid* (1976) 62 Cr App Rep 109, CA, is to the same effect. Cf. *Smith* [1963] 3 All ER 597, [1963] 1 WLR 1200, CCA.
8. 48 Cr App Rep 6 at 10. *Sed quaere?* See *Williams and Blackwood* (1973) WIR 329 (CA Jamaica) (D liable for stabbing where he incited beating up) and above, p. 145.
9. [1966] 2 QB 110 at 120, [1966] 2 All ER 644 at 648, CA.
10. [1970] 1 QB 352, [1969] 2 All ER 1077, CA.

responsible at all". The earlier cases[11] were not cited and are not easily reconcilable.

The fact that D *ought* to have been aware of a risk is not sufficient to convict him of being a secondary party to a crime, even a crime that may be committed by negligence. Though manslaughter is (or certainly was then[12]) a crime which might be committed by gross negligence, it was held in *Reid*[13] that the fact that D's conduct, in going to P's house with E who was armed with a revolver, was "grossly and utterly negligent" was not sufficient to render him liable for manslaughter when E murdered P with the revolver. D's conviction was upheld on the ground that he was in joint possession of the offensive weapon and must have intended at least to frighten by using it.

8 Secondary Participation and Inchoate Offences

It is an offence to incite, or to conspire, or to attempt, to commit an offence.[14] It is not an offence to attempt[15] or, it is submitted, to incite or to conspire[16] to do an act which would involve no more than secondary liability for the offence if it were committed. Knowing that D1 intends to drive his car, D3 urges D2 to "lace" D1's drink with so much alcohol that D1 will inevitably commit an offence under s. 6 (1) of the Road Traffic Act 1972[17] if he drives after consuming the drink. D2 agrees to do so and attempts to, or does, lace the drink. If D1 consumes the drink, drives his car and thus commits the offence under s. 6 (1), D2 and D3 will be guilty as secondary parties;[18] but if D1 declines the drink, or does not drive the car, D3 is guilty neither of incitement nor of conspiracy and D2 is guilty neither of conspiracy nor of attempt to commit the offence. The act incited, agreed upon, attempted and indeed done, is not the offence.[19]

In this example, D1 is guilty as the principal offender, notwithstanding his lack of *mens rea*, on the ground that the offence is assumed to be one of strict liability. Where the offence is one requiring *mens rea*, which the actual perpetrator of the *actus reus* lacks, then those who procured him to act will be liable because they, or one of them, will be the principals in the first degree. D3 urges D2 to stage his death and disappear so that D2's wife, D1, may claim the insurance money on D2's life. If D1 was not a party to the fraud and was intended to obtain the money innocently, D3 would be guilty of inciting D2 to obtain for another by deception as the principal offender;

---

11. Above, footnote 7.
12. See below, p. 352.
13. (1975) 62 Cr App Rep 109 at 112, CA.
14. Chapter 10, below.
15. Criminal Attempts Act 1981, s. 1(4) (b), below, p. 297; *Dunnington*, [1984] QB 472, [1984] 1 All ER 676, [1984] Crim LR 98, CA. Cf. *Chief Constable of Hampshire v Mace* (1986) 84 Cr App Rep 40, [1986] Crim LR 752.
16. *Hollinshead* [1985] 1 All ER 850 at 857–858, CA. The House of Lords left the question open: [1985] AC 975; [1985] 2 All ER 769. See Smith, "Secondary Participation and Inchoate Offences" in *Crime, Proof and Punishment*. 21. *Po Koon Tai*, Criminal Appeal No. 836 of 1979, Supreme Court of Hong Kong, is to the contrary so far as conspiracy is concerned.
17. As substituted by Transport Act 1981, Sch. 8.
18. *Attorney-General's Reference (No. 1 of 1975)*, above, p. 133.
19. The adulteration of the drink might possibly amount to the administration of a noxious thing, contrary to the Offences against the Person Act 1861, s. 24, below, p. 403.

D3 and D2 would be guilty of conspiring to commit the offence; and D2 would be guilty of an attempt to do so at the latest when the news of his death reached the insurers.[20] If D1 were a party, D2's acts would not be an offence[1] but the three would be guilty of conspiracy to defraud. Where D1 is guilty of incitement to commit a crime, D2 may be liable for abetting or counselling the incitement. Where D1 is guilty of an attempt to commit a crime, D2 may be liable for abetting or counselling the attempt.[2] In the case of conspiracy, however, one who abets or counsels appears to be a principal in the first degree in the conspiracy.

9 Conviction of Secondary Party and Acquittal of Principal Offender

Even if the alleged principal has been acquitted, a conviction of another as a secondary party may be logical. This is so even if it is assumed[3] that a secondary party may be convicted only when the principal himself is guilty. The acquittal of the alleged principal, so far from being conclusive that no crime was committed, would not even be admitted as evidence at a subsequent trial of the secondary parties.[4] A second jury may be satisfied beyond reasonable doubt that the crime was committed upon evidence which the first jury found unconvincing; evidence may be admissible against the secondary party which was not admissible against the principal, or fresh evidence may have come to light or the principal may have been acquitted because the prosecution offered no evidence against him. The position would seem to be the same where the secondary party is tried first and convicted and the principal is subsequently acquitted[5] and when the parties are jointly indicted. In *Hughes*,[6] after the prosecution had offered no evidence against E, he was acquitted and called as a witness for the Crown, with the result that D was convicted by the same jury as an accessory before the fact to E's alleged crime. Where principal and secondary party are tried separately, this result is supported by the analogous rule laid down in *Director of Public Prosecutions v Shannon*[7] that the acquittal of one party to a conspiracy does not invalidate the conviction of the only other party on an earlier or later occasion. *Shannon* left open the question whether the one party may be convicted of conspiracy when the other is acquitted at the same trial;[8] and in *Anthony*[9] it was said, *obiter*, that a jury cannot acquit E

20. *Director of Public Prosecutions v Stonehouse*, [1978] AC 55, [1977] 2 All ER 909, HL, below, p. 299.
  1. This assumes that *Robinson* [1915] 2 KB 342, CCA, is rightly decided and that these would be preparatory acts and not an attempt to obtain. Below, p. 295.
  2. *Hapgood and Wyatt* (1870) LR 1 CCR 221, CCR; *S v Robinson* 1968 (1) SA 666. Cf. Sexual Offences (Amendment) Act 1976, s 7 (2) (aiding, etc. attempted rape).
  3. Contrary to the view expressed below, p. 155.
  4. Under the Police and Criminal Evidence Act 1984, s. 74, convictions may now be admissible as evidence of the commission of an offence, but acquittals remain inadmissible.
  5. In *Rowley* [1948] 1 All ER 570, D's conviction was quashed when, after he had pleaded guilty as an accessory after the fact, the alleged principals were acquitted by the jury. But the decision is criticised in *Shannon* [1974] 2 All ER 1009 at 1020 and 1049; below p. 284.
  6. (1860) Bell CC 242.
  7. [1975] AC 717, [1974] 2 All ER 1009, HL; below, p. 284.
  8. The point is now settled by the Criminal Law Act 1977, and *Longman and Cribben* (1980) 72 Cr App Rep 121, below, p. 284; but *Shannon* is relevant to the common law governing secondary participation.
  9. [1965] 2 QB 189, [1965] 1 All ER 440. Cf. *Surujpaul v R* [1958] 3 All ER 300 at 302–303.

and at the same time find D guilty of counselling him to commit the crime. If E and D are tried together and the evidence tending to show that E committed the crime is the same against both, then it would be inconsistent to acquit E and convict D.[10] Where, however, there is evidence admissible against D but not against E that E committed the crime (as, for example, a confession by D that he counselled E to commit the crime and saw him commit it) it would be perfectly logical to acquit E and convict D of counselling him (and of conspiring with him). In *Humphreys and Turner*,[11] which was just such a case, Chapman J held that D might be convicted as a secondary party, distinguishing the dicta in *Anthony* as applicable only to felonies. It is submitted that, since the Criminal Law Act 1967 came into force, the rule stated in *Humphreys and Turner* is applicable to all offences.

10 Conviction of Secondary Party where there is no Principal

It is one thing for a court which is trying D2 alone to reject or ignore the holding of another court that D1 was not a principal in the first degree and to hold that he was; and that, therefore, D2 might be convicted as a secondary party to D1's crime. It is quite another thing for a court to hold at one and the same time, (i) that D1 was, in law, not guilty[12] and (ii) that D2 was guilty, as a secondary party, of D1's crime. These propositions seem to be inconsistent and irreconcilable with a passage in Russell[13] which has received judicial approval:[14]

"... when the law relating to principals and accessories as such is under consideration there is only one crime, although there may be more than one person criminally liable in respect of it; ... There is one crime, and that it has been committed must be established before there can be any question of criminal guilt of participation in it."

This seems, indeed, to be an obvious enough principle: a man cannot be guilty of having abetted a crime, or counselled it, unless the crime has actually been committed by the principal offender. But it cannot be accepted without qualification. The question arises where there are two crimes with the same *actus reus* but different *mens rea*, as with murder and manslaughter and offences under ss. 18 and 20 of the Offences against the Person Act 1861. There are two situations.

i) Where D, the alleged accessory, has the *mens rea* of the lesser offence but E acts with the *mens rea* of the greater. As noted above,[15] according to *Betty*,[16] and *Reid*[17] D may be convicted of manslaughter though E is guilty of murder. To the same effect is the ruling of Glyn-Jones J in *Murtagh and*

---

10. *Surujpaul v R* [1958] 3 All ER 300, [1958] 1 WLR 1050.
11. [1965] 3 All ER 689 (Liverpool Crown Court). Following in *Sweetman v Industries and Commerce Department*, [1970] NZLR 139. Cf. *Davis* [1977] Crim LR 542, CA and commentary.
12. Not merely that there was not enough evidence to convict him, but that there was evidence which established his innocence.
13. 12th ed. by J. W. C. Turner, 128.
14. *Surujpaul v R* [1958] 3 All ER 300 at 301, PC but cf. *Director of Public Prosecutions v Merriman* [1972] 3 All ER 42 at 59, per Lord Diplock.
15. P. 149.
16. (1963) 48 Cr App Rep 6, CCA.
17. (1976) 62 Cr App Rep 109, CA, above, p. 150.

Kennedy,[18] where a car mounted a pavement and ran down P, that if E, the driver, intended to kill, he was guilty of murder, and, if D, the passenger, intended only to frighten, he was guilty of manslaughter. As also noted above, there is some difficulty in reconciling these decisions with other Court of Appeal rulings, particularly *Lovesey and Peterson*.[19]

ii) Where D, the alleged accessory, has the *mens rea* of the greater offence, but E acts with the *mens rea* of the less. In *Howe* Lord Mackay (with whom Lords Bridge, Brandon and Griffiths agreed) stated:

"where a person has been killed and that result is the result intended by another participant, the mere fact that the actual killer may be convicted of the reduced charge of manslaughter for some reason special to himself does not, in my opinion, in any way result in a compulsory reduction for the other participant."[20]

Lord Mackay was agreeing with the Court of Appeal, who found the following example convincing:

"[D] hands a gun to [E] informing him that it is loaded with blank ammunition only and telling him to go and scare [P] by discharging it. The ammunition is in fact live (as [D] knows) and [P] is killed. [E] is convicted only of manslaughter. ... It would seem absurd that [D] should thereby escape conviction for murder."[1]

It would indeed be absurd. D has procured the very result he intended to produce and the law would be gravely defective if he were not liable for it. It may be confidently asserted that such a person will not in future escape liability. The contrary result was however thought to follow from *Richards*[2] which the Court of Appeal and Lord Mackay considered to be wrongly decided. D, a woman, hired E and F to beat up her husband "bad enough to put him in hospital for a month". She signalled to E and F when P left the house. They inflicted a wound upon P, not amounting to a serious injury. D was convicted of wounding with intent to cause grievous bodily harm but E and F were acquitted of that offence and convicted of the lesser offence of unlawful wounding. Following the opinion of Hawkins that "the offence of the accessory can never rise higher than that of the principal"[3] D's conviction was quashed and a conviction for unlawful wounding substituted. It was assumed that, under the old law of felonies, D would have been an accessory and not a principal in the second degree.[4] The result might have been different if D had been present, which seems an absurd distinction. *Richards* was heavily criticised and, in view of the disapproval expressed in *Howe*, though only obiter, may not be followed in future. *Richards* found a belated defender in Professor Kadish who argues (a) that D did not cause the actions of E and F because they were not her unwitting instruments but chose to act freely as they did and (b) she could not be held

18. [1955] Crim LR 315.
19. [1970] 1 QB 352, [1969] 2 All ER 1077, above, p. 149.
20. [1987] 1 All ER 771 at 799. Cf. s. 2 (4) of the Homicide Act 1957 – D's liability for murder not affected by E's diminished responsibility.
1. [1986] QB 626 at 641–642, [1986] 1 All ER 833 at 839–840. See the similar examples in the 5th edition of this work, 140.
2. [1974] QB 776, [1973] 3 All ER 1088, CA.
3. 2 PC, c. 29, s. 15.
4. Above, p. 130.

liable "for an aggravated assault [i.e., an assault with intent to cause grievous bodily harm] that did not take place".[5] However, D did, in a very real sense, cause the actions of E and F – they were acting in pursuance of her instructions, though not going as far as she wished; and the *actus reus* (wounding) which took place was (or so the decision seems to assume) the *actus reus* she intended. The only difference from the loaded gun case discussed above is that there E intended to carry out his instructions to the letter whereas in *Richards* E decided to carry them out only partially. It is submitted that that should make no difference.

(iii) Where D and E both have the *mens rea* for the greater offence but E's liability is reduced for some reason to that of a lesser offence. If E causes the *actus reus* in carrying out the agreed plan but his liability is reduced "for some reason special to himself",[6] such as provocation or diminished responsibility,[7] it seems clearly right that D should not be able to shelter behind E's personal exemption from liability for the greater offence. In the case considered in *Howe*, however, the reduction in E's liability did not depend on a personal consideration of this kind. E's defence was that he had agreed to shoot P out of fear of D, but that, when it came to the event, the gun went off accidentally. The killing was therefore unintentional and amounted to no more than manslaughter. The judge, following *Richards*, directed that, if the jury found E guilty only of manslaughter, then D could at most be guilty of manslaughter. The implication of the decision of the House is that this was wrong. It is submitted that it is right; that the true position is that if E has gone beyond a merely preparatory act and is attempting to commit the crime when he "accidentally" kills, both D and E are guilty of murder; but, if E is doing only a preparatory act when he happens to kill – he is driving to P's house with intent to blow it up when the bomb in his car goes off and kills P who has unexpectedly gone out for a walk – E is liable only for manslaughter and so is D. The killing which occurs is not the killing he intended, though the victim happens to be the same.[8]

If there is no *actus reus*, no one can be convicted. In *Morris v Tolman*,[9] D was charged with abetting the owner of a vehicle in using that vehicle for a purpose for which the vehicle had not been licensed. The statute (the Roads Act 1920) was so phrased that the offence could be committed only by the licence-holder. It was held that, there being no evidence that the licence-holder had used the vehicle for a purpose other than that for which it was licensed, D must be acquitted. Though he, in fact, had used the vehicle, that was not an *actus reus*. Again, in *Thornton v Mitchell*,[10] D, a bus conductor, negligently signalled to the driver of his bus to reverse, so that two pedestrians, whom it was not possible for the driver to see, were

---

5. "Complicity and Causation", (1985) 73 Cal. Law Rev. 323 at 329.
6. The phrase used by Lord Mackay in *Howe*, above, p. 153.
7. This case is covered by s. 2(4) of the Homicide Act 1957.
8. See commentary, [1987] Crim LR 481 at 484.
9. [1923] 1 KB 166.
10. [1940] 1 All ER 339. See R. D. Taylor, "Complicity and Excuses", [1983] Crim LR 656, for another way of looking at the problems raised by this case.

knocked down and one of them killed. The driver having been acquitted of careless driving, it was held that the conductor must be acquitted of abetting. Again, there was no *actus reus*. The driver's acquittal shows that he committed no *actus reus*, for careless driving is a crime which requires no *mens rea* beyond an intention to drive and D could not be said to have driven the bus. There would have been no such obstacle in the way of convicting D for manslaughter. That would simply have raised the question whether D's negligence was sufficiently great.[11]

An alternative way of looking at these cases would be to say that in each of them D was not liable because he was incapable of being a principal offender, not being a licence-holder or a driver, respectively.[12] This rule, however, would produce unsatisfactory results in a number of situations. It is well settled that a person can be convicted as a secondary party to a crime which he is personally incapable of committing as a principal offender. Thus a woman[13] or a boy under fourteen[14] could be convicted of abetting a rape; a bachelor could be convicted of abetting a bigamous marriage. Should the boy, or the woman or the bachelor be acquitted because the person committing the rape, or the person going through the ceremony of marriage was insane, or lacked *mens rea*, or was exempt from criminal liability for some other reason? D's conduct would certainly be none the less heinous, and though incapable of committing an *actus reus* personally, D would have caused one to occur and have done so with *mens rea*. It does not seem feasible to extend the doctrine of the innocent agent to this situation. If D, through an innocent agent, has killed P, it is not unreasonable for the indictment to state, "D . . . murdered P." If D, a bachelor, procures E to go through a ceremony of marriage, it would be quite plainly untrue for the indictment to state, "D . . . married . . ., during the life of his wife . . ." for he did not marry anyone, nor did he have a wife. Is there any reason why the indictment should not state, "E . . . married F, during the life of his wife . . . D . . . was present, aiding, abetting and assisting the said E to commit the said crime"? There are two cases where the result at least supports this view. In *Bourne*,[15] D, by duress, compelled his wife to have connection with a dog. He was charged with abetting her to commit buggery. It was argued that, as the wife could not be convicted, since she acted under the coercion of her husband,[16] he must be acquitted. This argument was rejected. The Court of Criminal Appeal assumed that the wife was entitled to be acquitted, but held that, nevertheless, D's conviction as an abettor could stand. In *Bourne*, according to one view, the wife, though excused by duress, committed the *actus reus* with *mens rea* for she knew exactly what she was doing.[17] Another view, however, is that

11. See above, p. 94, and below, p. 352.
12. See Williams, CLGP, §§120, 129 (4).
13. *Ram and Ram* (1893) 17 Cox CC 609.
14. *Eldershaw* (1828) 3 C & P 396, per Vaughan B. See below, p. 438.
15. (1952) 36 Cr App Rep 125, CCA; **SHC 138**, cf. *Kemp and Else*, below, p. 718, and *Matusevich and Thompson* [1976] VR 470.
16. See below, p. 238.
17. Cross (1953) 69 LQR 354. Lord Edmund-Davies in *Lynch v Director of Public Prosecutions for Northern Ireland* [1975] 1 All ER 913 at 952; below, p. 232. See also, Edwards (1953) 69 LQR 226.

intentionally to do an act, knowing of circumstances which prevent the act from being a crime, is not *mens rea*.[18] In the second case, *Cogan and Leak*,[19] there is no doubt that the person committing the *actus reus* lacked *mens rea*. D terrorised his wife, P, into submitting to sexual intercourse with E. The jury were directed, in accordance with the decision of the Court of Appeal in *Morgan*,[20] that E's alleged belief that P was consenting was no defence if it was not based on reasonable grounds. The decision of the House of Lords in *Morgan*[1] was given before E's appeal and, consequently, his conviction had to be quashed; but D's conviction for aiding and abetting was upheld. He had procured E to commit the offence.

"In the language of the law the act of sexual intercourse without the wife's consent was the *actus reus*; it had been procured by (D) who had the appropriate *mens rea*, namely his intention that (E) should have sexual intercourse with her without her consent."

The court preferred to regard D as the principal offender, acting through an innocent agent. There are objections to that,[2] apart from the technical rule that a man cannot rape his own wife.[3] It is simply untrue to say, as an indictment for rape as the principal offender must allege, that "D had sexual intercourse with P without her consent."

Whatever the reasoning and its merits, the result in both *Bourne* and *Cogan and Leak* is that the abetting or counselling of a mere *actus reus* is indictable. The result produced is just and logical. The most formidable objection is that the closely related crime of incitement requires proof that the inciter knew or believed the person incited to have *mens rea*.[4] But the difference is that the inciter is immediately liable for the act of incitement. The secondary party does not become liable as such until the *actus reus* is committed. Aiding, abetting, etc. and incitement are different concepts.

11 Withdrawal by a Secondary Party[5]

Where D has counselled E to commit a crime, or is present, aiding E in the commission of it, it may yet be possible for him to escape liability by withdrawal before E goes on to commit the crime. An effective withdrawal will not, however, affect any liability he may have already incurred for incitement, or conspiracy, or, if the withdrawal took place after E had done more than a merely preparatory act,[6] attempt, to commit the crime.[7]

---

18. Above, p. 35.
19. [1976] 2 QB 217, [1975] 2 All ER 1059, [1975] Crim LR 584 and commentary;; **SHC 139**. See Buxton "Vicarious Rape" (1975) 125 NLJ 1133, Williams [1975] CLJ 182.
20. [1976] AC 182, [1975] 1 All ER 8; **SHC 45**.
  1. Above, p. 86, below, pp. 207, 429.
  2. Above, p. 155.
  3. Below, p. 430.
  4. Below, p. 255.
  5. See Lanham, "Accomplices and Withdrawal", (1981) 97 LQR 575 Williams, TBCL, 310–311.
  6. Below, p. 287.
  7. Withdrawal does not affect liability for an attempt; below, p. 299.

Mere repentance, without any action, clearly leaves D liable.[8] His "innocent" state of mind at the time of the commission of the crime is no answer. He had *mens rea* when he did the act of counselling or aiding. What is an effective withdrawal may depend on the mode of D's participation in the contemplated offence. If it consisted only in advising or encouraging E to commit the crime, it is enough for him to tell E to desist.[9] If E then commits the crime he does so against E's advice and without his encouragement. It may be that E would never have committed the crime if D had not put it into his head in the first place; but then D may be properly and adequately dealt with by conviction of incitement. If D has counselled more than one person, then it seems that he must communicate his countermand to all of those who perpetrate the offence, for otherwise his counselling remains operative.[10]

To be effective, the communication must be such as "will serve unequivocal notice upon the other party to the common unlawful cause that if he proceeds upon it he does so without the further aid and assistance of those who withdraw."[11] The position might be different where D has supplied E with the means of committing the crime. Arguably, D must neutralise, or at least take all reasonable steps to neutralise, the aid he has given. If E ignores D's countermand and uses the thing or information with which D has supplied him to commit the crime, he has in fact been aided by D in doing so. Aid may be less easily neutralised than advice. Where D2 handed D1 a knife so that he could use it on anyone interfering in a burglary, D2 did not make a sufficient communication of withdrawal when, on the appearance of P, he said "Come on, let's go," and got out through a window. Something "vastly different and vastly more effective" was required and, possibly, nothing less than physical intervention to stop D1 committing the crime would be required.[12]

In that case, the "withdrawal" occurred at a very late stage and it does not follow that it is never possible effectively to withdraw by countermand where aid given by D continues to be effective. In *Grundy*[13] D had supplied E, a burglar, with information which was presumably valuable to E in committing the crime; but, for two weeks before E did so, D had been trying to stop him breaking in. It was held that there was evidence of an effective withdrawal which should have been left to the jury. In *Whitefield*[14] there was evidence that D had served unequivocal notice on E that, if he proceeded with the burglary they had planned together, he would do so without D's aid or assistance. The jury should have been told that, if they accepted the evidence, that was a defence. It may be that an effective withdrawal can be made more easily at the preparatory stage than where the

8. Hale, 1 PC 618; Stephen, *Digest* (4th ed.), Art. 42 Williams, CLGP, §§ 127; *Croft* [1944] 1 KB 295, [1944] 2 All ER 483; *Becerra*, below, footnote 11.
9. *Saunders and Archer* (1573) 2 Plowd 473.
10. *State v Kinchen* (1910) 52 So 185, quoted by Lanham, op. cit. at 591.
11. *Whitehouse* [1941] 1 WWR 112, per Sloan JA (Court of Appeal of British Columbia) approved in *Becerra* (1976) 62 Cr App Rep 212, CA. Cf. *Fletcher* [1962] Crim LR 551; *Grundy* [1977] Crim LR 543, CA.
12. *Becerra*, above, footnote 11.
13. [1977] Crim LR 543, CA.
14. (1984) 79 Cr App Rep 36.

crime is in the course of commission, as in *Becerra*. When the knife is about to descend, the only effective withdrawal may be physical intervention to prevent it reaching its target.

If a rejected countermand may be an effective withdrawal, as in *Grundy*, it is arguable that an attempt to countermand should be the same. D has done all in his power to communicate his countermand to E but failed. In all these cases, the countermand has, *ex hypothesi*, failed; and, if the question is whether D has done his best to prevent the commission of the crime, the answer does not depend on the reasons for the failure.[15] It may be argued that, where D has failed to communicate, he can escape only by going to the police; but this was not insisted on in *Grundy* when persuasion failed.

Where D does give timely warning to the police, the effect ought in most cases to be that the crime will be prevented; but this may not always be so and, even where it is, there remains D's potential liability for abetting E's attempt, if E has gone beyond mere preparation. Surely, however, efforts to prevent the commission of the crime by informing the police ought to be an effective withdrawal, whether D has or has not attempted to persuade E to desist. Apart from being the best evidence of repentance, it is conduct which the law should and does encourage.[16]

Withdrawal, it is submitted, must be voluntary. If D is arrested, he can hardly be said to have "withdrawn". His arrest does not undo any aid, advice or encouragement he may have already given and therefore does not absolve him from any potential liability he has already incurred.[17] Of course, it usually precludes any future secondary participation by him;[18] but in this section we are concerned with absolution from the potential liability arising from D's past acts.

It is sometimes suggested that withdrawal is effective only if there is a genuine "repentance". English courts are generally reluctant to go into questions of motive. D may have seen the light, or he may be acting out of malice against his accomplices or because of fear of detection or because he has decided that the risks outweigh the possible rewards. It is submitted that it should make no difference.

12 Victims as Parties to Crime[19]

It has been noted[20] that when a statute creates a crime it does not generally provide that it shall be an offence to aid, abet, counsel or procure it. Such a provision is unnecessary, for it follows by implication of law. There is, however, one exception to this rule. Where the statute is designed for the protection of a certain class of persons it may be construed as excluding by implication the liability of any member of that class who is the victim of the offence, even though that member does in fact aid, abet, counsel or procure

15. Contra, Lanham 590.
16. Cf. the large "discounts" on sentence which may be earned for information given after D has become liable for and been convicted of the offence. Above, p. 11.
17. *Johnson and Jones* (1841) Car & M 218. *Jackson* (1673) 1 Hale PC 464 at 465 appears contra but is an obscure and unsatisfactory case. See Lanham, op. cit. 577.
18. For a case where it did not, see *Craig and Bentley* (1952) Times, 10–13th December.
19. Hogan [1962] Crim LR 683; Criminal Law Revision Committee, Fifteenth Report (Cmnd. 9213), Appendix B.
20. Above, pp. 130 and 143.

the offence. The principle has been applied, so far, only in respect of certain sexual offences.

In *Tyrrell*[1] D, a girl between the ages of thirteen and sixteen, abetted E to have unlawful sexual intercourse with her. This was an offence by E under the Criminal Law Amendment Act 1885, s. 5.[2] It was held, however, that D could not be convicted of abetting because the Act

"was passed for the purpose of protecting women and girls against themselves."[3]

The decisions on sodomy with boys under the age of fourteen seem to be explicable only on the assumption that the courts have applied a similar principle.[4] On the other hand, it has been held that a woman who is not pregnant can be convicted of abetting the use upon herself by another of an instrument with intent to procure her miscarriage, although the clear implication of the statute[5] is that such a woman cannot be convicted of *using* an instrument on herself with that intent.[6] However, a pregnant woman can be convicted under the same section of using an instrument on herself so it cannot be argued that this section was passed for the protection of *women* and it would be curious that Parliament should have intended to protect non-pregnant women from themselves, but not pregnant women.

How far the rule in *Tyrrell* extends has not been settled. The court referred to "women" as well as girls and it may well be that it extends to the offences of procuration of women to be prostitutes and of brothel keeping which were in the 1885 Act and are now in the Sexual Offences Act 1956.[7] It will obviously extend to intercourse with girls under thirteen and defectives;[8] to permitting premises to be used for intercourse with young girls and defectives;[9] and to at least some offences of abduction.[10] It is not settled whether it applies to the prostitute who abets a man who is living off her earnings but it is thought that the better view is that she cannot be convicted.[11]

In all these cases, it seems clear that the protection of the law extends only to a person of the class who is a *victim*. Thus, it is thought, a girl under sixteen could be convicted of abetting E in having intercourse with another girl under sixteen; a boy under fourteen could be convicted of abetting E in sodomy with another boy under fourteen; a prostitute could abet E in keeping a brothel in which she was not a participant, or of living off the earnings of another prostitute.

1. [1894] 1 QB 710.
2. See now Sexual Offences Act 1956, s. 6; below, p. 441. The rule applies to incest with a girl under 16; below, p. 445.
3. Per Lord Coleridge CJ at 712. Both the Chief Justice and Mathew J pointed out that there was nothing in the Act to say that the girl should be guilty of aiding and abetting; but, it is submitted, no importance could be attached to that, for statutes hardly ever do.
4. Below, p. 47.
5. Offences against the Person Act 1861, s. 58; below, p. 366.
6. *Sockett* (1908) 72 JP 428; below, p. 283.
7. Below, p. 45.
8. Below, pp. 441 and 443.
9. Below, p. 444.
10. Below, p. 452. The rule was not applied in a Tasmanian case of abduction of a girl under eighteen: *Preston* [1962] Tas SR 141; but this turned on the construction of the Tasmanian Criminal Code.
11. Hogan [1962] Crim LR at pp. 692–693.

There are many instances outside sexual offences where laws are passed for the protection of a particular class of persons. For example, there is much legislation protecting tenants from rapacious landlords. In the civil law a tenant who has paid a premium illegally demanded by her landlord is not so tainted with his criminality as to be disabled from asserting her rights under the tenancy;[12] and it is possible that a principle similar to that in *Tyrrell* might be applied if a tenant were charged with abetting the landlord's offence.

13 Instigation for the Purpose of Entrapment[13]

Police or other law enforcement officers or their agents sometimes do acts for the purpose of entrapping, or getting evidence against offenders, which would certainly amount to counselling or abetting an offence if they were not done for that purpose. The difficult question is how far an officer may go without himself incurring liability for the offence. Law enforcement officers have no general licence to aid and abet crime. In *Sang*[14] Lord Diplock said:

"I would now refer to what is, I believe and hope, the unusual case, in which a dishonest policeman, anxious to improve his detection record, tries very hard with the help of an agent provocateur to induce a young man with no criminal record to commit a serious crime; and ultimately the young man reluctantly succumbs to the inducement ... The policeman and the informer who had acted together in inciting him to commit the crime should ... both be prosecuted and suitably punished."

It is not clear that the word "dishonest" adds anything to the postulated facts and it should make no difference that the policeman's motive is hatred of crime. It can hardly be necessary that the man induced to act should be "young"; and it might be even more serious to induce a man with a bad record who was "going straight", for the consequences for him would be worse. The essence of the dictum seems to be that a person who would not otherwise have committed a crime is induced to do so.[15] It may, however, be lawful to participate in an offence which has already been "laid on" and is going to be committed in any event, in order to trap the offenders.[16] In such a case it makes no difference that the police intervention may have affected the time or other circumstances of the commission of the offence.[17]

By these standards, judges in the past may have shown undue tolerance to incitement of offences by the police. In *Mullins*[18] when D, apparently acting with the authority of the police, attended a treasonable conspiracy, endeavoured to persuade strangers to join in and advocated the use of

---

12. *Grace Rymer Investments Ltd v Waite* [1958] Ch 831, [1958] 2 All ER 777.
13. Williams, CLGP, § 256; McClean, "Informers and Agents Provocateurs", [1969] Crim LR 527; Heydon, "The Problems of Entrapment" [1973] CLJ 268; Law Commission Working Paper No. 55 and *Report on Defences of General Application* (Law Com No. 83, 1977) where it is recommended that there should be no defence of entrapment but that consideration should be given to the creation of a new *offence* of entrapment. See Ashworth, "Entrapment" [1978] Crim LR 137.
14. (1979) 69 Cr App Rep 282 at 296.
15. Cf. *Birtles* [1969] 2 All ER 1131n, [1969] 1 WLR 1047.
16. *McCann* (1971) 56 Cr App Rep 359.
17. *McEvilly* (1973) 60 Cr App Rep 150.
18. (1848) 3 Cox CC 526.

violence, Maule J rejected an argument that D's evidence required corroboration as that of an accomplice. He said that a person employed by the government as a spy does not deserve to be blamed "if he instigates offences no further than by pretending to concur with the perpetrators". That dictum is of course acceptable; but D's conduct seems to have gone well beyond this, particularly in trying to persuade strangers to join in. In *Bickley*,[19] A, a woman acting on behalf of the police, asked P to give her something to procure an abortion and was held not to be an accomplice. It is of course certain that that particular offence would not have been committed if A had not asked for an abortifacient; but it may be that this sort of action can be justified where a person is reasonably suspected of carrying on a system or practice of committing offences of a particular type. In a case of this kind, the High Court of Justiciary thought that, without evidence obtained in this way, there would be wholesale flouting of the law.[20] Though Lord Goddard was unwilling to condone it,[1] it is probable that this practice is lawful.

It would be wise, however, for police authorities to bear in mind the recommendation of the Royal Commission on Police Powers:[2]

"As a general rule, the police should observe only, without participating in an offence, except in cases where an offence is habitually committed in circumstances in which observation by a third party is *ex hypothesi* impossible. Where participation is essential it should only be resorted to on the express and written authority of the Chief Constable."

Moreover, it cannot be the law that the police may properly participate in a crime to the point at which irreparable damage is done. A policeman who assists E to commit murder in order to entrap him must be guilty of murder. It is submitted that the same must be true of any injury to the person, unless it is trivial and P consents to it; and probably to any damage to property, unless the owner consents.

It is now established by *Sang*[3] that a person who has been induced by the police, whether lawfully or not, to commit a crime, has no defence of entrapment and the judge has no discretion to exclude the evidence which he has provided in consequence of the trap, on the ground that it was unfairly obtained. It is, however, a matter which may be taken into account in fixing the sentence so, where there was a possibility that a theft might not have been committed but for a police trap, D was sentenced as if he had been convicted of a conspiracy to steal rather than the actual theft.[4] Where the police have facilitated the commission of a crime, this fact must be revealed to the trial court.[5] With these cases of police intervention may be compared that of *Smith*[6] where a private citizen took it upon himself to instigate crime with the object of procuring a conviction and was himself convicted. But even in the case of a private citizen it is a defence that he was

19. (1909) 2 Cr App Rep 53, CCA.
20. *Marsh v Johnston* [1959] Crim LR 444, 1959, SLT 28.
 1. *Brannan v Peek* [1948] 1 KB 68 at 72 (cf. [1947] 2 All ER 572 at 573, 574).
 2. Cmd. 3297 (1928), 116.
 3. Above. On the question of discretion, see PACE 1984, s. 78.
 4. *McCann*, above, p. 160.
 5. *Macro* [1969] Crim LR 205.
 6. [1960] 2 QB 423, [1960] 1 All ER 256; above p. 128.

acting honestly and solely in order to betray his associates and ensure the recovery of any proceeds of the crime[7] – as where a taxi-driver drives burglars to the scene of the crime, with the intention of fetching police when he has left them there.

2 Vicarious Liability[8]

In the law of tort, a master is held liable for all acts of his servant performed in the course of the servant's employment. In the criminal law, a master is generally not so liable. In the leading civil case of *Lloyd v Grace, Smith & Co*,[9] a solicitor's managing clerk, without the knowledge of his employer, induced a widow to give him instructions to sell certain property, to hand over the title deeds and to sign two documents which were neither read over nor explained to her, but which she believed were necessary for the sale. The documents were, in fact, a conveyance to the clerk of the property, of which he dishonestly disposed for his own benefit. It was held that, since the clerk was acting within the scope of his authority, his employer was liable. Now it is very likely that the clerk was guilty of certain criminal offences – perhaps larceny of the title deeds and fraudulent conversion of the money; but it is perfectly clear that his employer could never have been made criminally liable for those acts for which he bore civil liability. An employer is similarly liable in tort where the fraud involves a forgery,[10] and for acts which amount to obtaining by deception, assault and battery, manslaughter and so on; but in none of these cases would he be criminally liable simply on the ground that his servant was acting in the course of his employment. The doctrine of vicarious liability in tort developed in the early part of the eighteenth century, but it was made clear by the leading case of *Huggins*[11] that there was to be no parallel development in the criminal law. Huggins, the warden of the Fleet, was charged with the murder of a prisoner whose death had been caused by the servant of Huggins's deputy. It was held that, though the servant was guilty, Huggins was not, since the acts were done without his knowledge. Raymond CJ said:[12]

> "It is a point not to be disputed, but that in criminal cases the principal is not answerable for the act of the deputy as he is in civil cases: they must each answer for their own acts, and stand or fall by their own behaviour. All the authors that treat of criminal proceedings proceed on the foundation of this distinction; that to affect the superior by the act of his

---

7. See *Clarke* (1984) 80 Cr App Rep 344, [1985] Crim LR 209, CA. *Mullins*, above, p. 160.
8. Williams, CLGP, Ch. 7, and "*Mens Rea* and Vicarious Responsibility" (1956) 9 CLP 57; Glazebrook, "Situational Liability" in *Reshaping the Criminal Law* 108; Pace, "Delegation – a Doctrine in Search of a Definition" [1982] Crim LR 627; L. H. Leigh, *Strict and Vicarious Liability*; F. B. Sayer "Criminal Responsibility for the Acts of Another" (1930) 43 Harv LR 689; Baty, *Vicarious Liability* (1916), especially Ch. X. For proposals for the reform of the law, see Law Commission Working Paper No. 43.
9. [1912] AC 716, HL.
10. *Uxbridge Permanent Building Society v Pickard* [1939] 2 KB 248, [1939] 2 All ER 344.
11. (1730) 2 Stra 883.
12. Ibid., at 885.

deputy, there must be the command of the superior which is not found in this case."

A master can be held liable for his servants' crimes, as a general rule, only where he is a participant in them within the rules stated in the preceding section. Two exceptions to this have already been noted:[13] in public nuisance and criminal libel a master has been held liable for his servants' acts although he is, personally, perfectly innocent. These were the only exceptions at common law; but now, by statute, there are many such offences.

1 Strict Liability and Vicarious Liability Distinguished

Vicarious liability is by no means the same thing as strict liability. The point requires emphasis for there is an unhappy judicial tendency to confuse the two concepts. A statute may require *mens rea* and yet impose vicarious responsibility. It has already been noted that supplying liquor to a constable on duty is an offence requiring *mens rea*,[14] yet a licensee may be vicariously liable for his servants' act in so doing[15] and the same considerations apply to the offence of suffering gaming to be carried on in licensed premises.[16] Conversely, it is clearly possible for a statute to create strict liability without imposing vicarious responsibility. Once a statute has been held to impose a duty, with strict liability, on a particular person, it is likely to be held that that person is liable for the acts of anyone through whom he performs that duty.[17] Where, however, the duty is not imposed on particular persons but on the public generally, vicarious liability is inappropriate. For example, the former offence of causing death by dangerous driving was, at one time, held to be an offence of strict liability, but it is surely inconceivable that vicarious liability would have been imposed.

As in the case of strict liability, so with vicarious liability it may well be argued that the development is the work of the courts rather than of Parliament. A statute rarely says in terms that one person is to be liable for another's crimes.[18] It is not uncommon, however, for the courts to detect such an intention in statutes which create summary offences. The reason most commonly advanced by the judges for holding a master liable is that the statute would be "rendered nugatory"[19] – and the will of Parliament thereby defeated – if he were not. Two quite distinct principles, differing somewhat in their effect, underlie the various decisions. In the first place, a person may be held liable for the acts of another where he has delegated to

13. Above, p. 99 and see "Contempt of Court", below, p. 767.
14. *Sherras v De Rutzen*, above p. 103.
15. *Mullins v Collins* (1874) LR 9 QB 292.
16. *Bosley v Davies* (1875) 1 QBD 84 (*mens rea* required); *Bond v Evans* (1888) 21 QBD 249 (licensee liable for servants' acts); Licensing Act 1872, s. 16.
17. *Dicta* to the effect that an offence of strict liability necessarily imposes vicarious responsibility are not difficult to find: see, e.g., *Barker v Levinson* [1951] 1 KB 342 at 345; [1950] 2 All ER 825 at 827; *James & Son Ltd v Smee* [1955] 1 QB 78 at 95, [1954] 3 All ER 273 at 280, per Slade J. *Bradshaw v Ewart-James* [1983] 1 All ER 12 at 14.
18. A striking example is the Transport Act 1982, s. 31, which provides that the owner of a vehicle (even if a corporation) shall be conclusively presumed to have been the driver at the time of the commission of certain offences and, "accordingly, that acts or omissions of the driver of the vehicle at the time were his acts or omissions."
19. *Mullins v Collins* (1874) LR 9 QB 292 at 295, per Blackburn and Quain JJ; *Coppen v Moore (No. 2)* [1898] 2 QB 306 at 314, per Lord Russell CJ; *Allen v Whitehead* infra.

that other the performance of certain duties cast on him by Act of Parliament. In the second place, a master may be held liable because acts which are done physically by the servant may, in law, be the master's acts. These two types of case require separate consideration.

2 The Delegation Principle[20]

A good illustration of the application of this principle may be found in the case of *Allen v Whitehead*.[1] Under the Metropolitan Police Act 1839, s. 44, it is an offence to

> "knowingly permit or suffer prostitutes or persons of notoriously bad character to meet together and remain in a place where refreshments are sold and consumed".

D, the occupier of a café, while receiving the profits of the business, did not himself manage it, but employed a manager. Having had a warning from the police, D instructed his manager that no prostitutes were to be allowed to congregate on the premises and had a notice to that effect displayed on the walls. He visited the premises once or twice a week and there was no evidence that any misconduct took place in his presence. Then, on eight consecutive days, a number of women, known to the manager to be prostitutes, met together and remained there between the hours of 8 p.m. and 4 a.m. It was held by the Divisional Court, reversing the Metropolitan Magistrate, that D's ignorance of the facts was no defence. The acts of the servant and his *mens rea* were both to be imputed to his master, not simply because he was a servant, but because the management of the house had been delegated to him.

So in *Linnet v Metropolitan Police Commissioner*[2] it was held, following *Allen v Whitehead*,[3] that one of two co-licensees was liable for the acts of the other in knowingly permitting disorderly conduct in the licensed premises, contrary to s. 44 of the same Act, although the other was neither his servant nor his partner,[4] but simply his delegate in "keeping" the premises.

The argument that vicarious responsibility is necessary to make the statute operative applies with especial force to cases of this type. Where the statute is so phrased that the offence can be committed only by the delegator, there would indeed be a real difficulty in making the statute effective without vicarious liability. Under the Metropolitan Police Act 1839, s. 44, the offence may be committed only by a person "who shall *have or keep* any house . . .". Presumably the manager in *Allen v Whitehead* was not such a person and if, therefore, the absentee "keeper" were not liable for his manager's acts, the statute could be ignored with impunity. The position is the same in many of the offences under the Licensing Acts; only the licensee can commit the offences. The difficulty has been well put by Lord Russell CJ:[5]

20. See Pace, "Delegation – A Doctrine in Search of a Definition" [1982] Crim LR 627.
   1. [1930] 1 KB 211.
   2. [1946] KB 290, [1946] 1 All ER 380.
   3. Above, footnote 1.
   4. Both were, in fact, the employees of a limited company. The company was not charged, no doubt for the good reason that it was not the licensee.
   5. In *Police Commissioners v Cartman* [1896] 1 QB 655 at 658. Yet when Parliament adds "or his servant" the court holds that the delegation principle still applies to the licensee: *Howker v Robinson*, below, p. 165.

"We may take as an illustration the case of a sporting publican who attends race-meetings all over the country, and leaves a manager in charge of his public-house; is it to be said that there is no remedy under this section[6] if drink is sold by the manager in charge to any number of drunken persons? It is clear that there is no machinery by which the person actually selling can be convicted; a penalty can only be inflicted on the licensee."

If the licensee's delegate sub-delegates his responsibilities, the licensee is liable for the sub-delegate's acts,[7] but he is not liable for the acts of an inferior servant to whom control of the premises has not been delegated.[8]

There is some doubt as to the degree of delegation which is necessary to bring the principle into operation. In a leading case, *Vane v Yiannopoulos*,[9] Parker LCJ said that:

"It must be shown that the licensee is not managing the business himself but has delegated the management to someone else ..."[10]

Lord Evershed[11] agreed with that and Lord Hodson said that the principle:

"... has never so far been extended so as to cover the case where the whole of the authority of the licensee has not been transferred to another."[12]

Lord Reid appears to have confined the principle to cases where the licensee is absent from the premises leaving another in charge.[13] It was held that the principle was inapplicable in that case where the licensee was on the premises at the time of the offence, but not on the floor where a waitress, whom he had instructed as to her rights to sell intoxicating liquor, made an illegal sale. But in *Howker v Robinson*[14] a licensee who was serving in the public bar was held liable for an illegal sale made by his barman in the lounge. This does not seem to be a case where the whole authority of the licensee had been transferred or where he was not managing the business himself. The court regarded the question whether there had been delegation as one of fact, which had been properly decided by the magistrates. *Winson*,[15] which the court followed, was entirely different, for there the licensee visited the premises only occasionally and had a manager who was in control.

In *Howker v Robinson* the degree of delegation was no greater than is essential in any public house with more than one bar and it is submitted that not only does it go too far but it leaves the law in an uncertain state; for it is apparently open to the magistrates to find as "a fact" that there has or has not been delegation where the licensee is on the premises. The

6. Licensing Act 1872, s. 13. Cf. *Cundy v Le Cocq*, above, p. 101, which establishes that the offence is also one of strict liability.
7. *Crabtree v Hole* (1879) 43 JP 799; *Sopp v Long* [1970] 1 QB 518, [1969] 1 All ER 855, above, p. 126.
8. *Allchorn v Hopkins* (1905) 69 JP 355.
9. [1965] AC 486, [1964] 3 All ER 820, HL; **SHC 191.**
10. [1964] 2 QB 739 at 745, [1964] 2 All ER 820 at 823.
11. [1965] AC at 505.
12. At p. 510.
13. At p. 497. Cf. Pace, loc. cit., 629, 636.
14. [1973] QB 178, [1972] 2 All ER 786, DC.
15. [1969] 1 QB 371, [1968] 1 All ER 197.

principle ought to be confined to the case where the licensee is not doing his job, but has handed it over to another.

According to Lord Parker, the delegation principle comes into play *only* in the case of offences requiring *mens rea*.[16] Where liability is strict, "the person on whom liability is thrown is responsible whether he has delegated or whether he has acted through a servant." According to this view, if D, the licensee, not having delegated his duties, is serving in the bar and E, the barmaid, without his knowledge, sells liquor (a) to a constable on duty and (b) to a drunken person, D is liable for the latter but not the former offence, since (a) requires *mens rea* but (b) does not. If this is right, it is the principle next to be discussed which applies in the case of offences of strict liability. The licensee is the "seller" for this purpose even though he is not the owner of property sold,[17] because, under the Licensing Acts, he is the only person who can lawfully "sell" intoxicating liquor on the premises.[18]

Some doubt was cast on the validity of the delegation principle by the House of Lords in *Vane v Yiannopoullos*.[19] Since there was no delegation in that case their lordships' remarks were *obiter*. Lords Morris and Donovan could find no statutory authority for the doctrine and, though they did not find it necessary to pronounce on its validity, Lord Donovan thought that "If a decision that 'knowingly' means 'knowingly' will make the provision difficult to enforce, the remedy lies with the legislature." Lord Reid found the delegation principle hard to justify; but while it may have been unwarranted in the first instance, it was now too late to upset such a long standing practice. Lord Evershed thought that a licensee may "fairly and sensibly" be held liable where he has delegated his powers and Lord Hodson expressed no opinion. Subsequent cases[20] show that the doctrine continues unimpaired. Such a long standing principle is perhaps unlikely now to be overruled by the House of Lords. It should not, however, be extended.[1] In *Bradshaw v Ewart-James*[2] the court declined to apply it to the case where the master of a ship delegated the performance of his statutory duty to his chief officer. That, however, was not a case of the full delegation which the doctrine seems to require, for the master remained on board and in command. As the master cannot personally direct the ship for 24 hours a day, some delegation is inevitable.

---

16. *Winson* [1969] 1 QB 371 at 382, [1968] 1 All ER 197; **SHC 173**.
17. He is not the seller for the purposes of the Sale of Goods Act 1979, s. 1. Pace (loc. cit.) points out that, as Parker J, his lordship, had stated the doctrine applied to the strict liability offence of using an unclean milk bottle: *Quality Dairies (York) Ltd v Pedley* [1952] 1 KB 275, [1952] 1 All ER 380, DC, but the ratio decidendi of that case clearly was that D had "used" the bottle through his agent and so was liable under the second principle, below, p. 167.
18. *Goodfellow v Johnson* [1966] 1 QB 83, [1965] 1 All ER 941, [1965] Crim LR 304 and commentary thereon. (D, a licensee, liable for sale of watered gin, contrary to the Food and Drugs Act 1955, by barmaid, a servant not of D but of his employer, a brewery.)
19. See footnote 9 on p. 165.
20. *Ross v Moss* [1965] 2 QB 396, [1965] 3 All ER 145; *Winson* [1969] 1 QB 371, [1968] 1 All ER 197.
   1. Cf. *Howker v Robinson* above, p. 165. Yet Bristow J, while considering himself bound by the authorities to apply the delegation principle, hoped that it might be overturned by the House of Lords: [1972] 2 All ER at p. 791.
   2. [1983] QB 671, [1983] 1 All ER 12, DC.

3 Where the Servant's Act is his Master's Act in Law

The most obvious application of the second principle occurs in the many cases where "selling" is the central feature of the *actus reus*, under statutes like the Trade Descriptions Act, the Food and Drugs Acts and the Fertilisers and Feeding Stuffs Act. Now a "sale" consists in the transfer of property in goods from A to B[3] and the seller, in law, is necessarily the person in whom the property is vested at the commencement of the transaction. It is not a great step, therefore, for the court to say that the employer has committed the *actus reus* of "selling" even though he was nowhere near when the incident took place. In *Coppen v Moore (No. 2)*,[4] D owned six shops, in which he sold American hams. He gave strict instructions that these hams were to be described as "breakfast hams" and were not to be sold under any specific name of place of origin. In the absence of D, and without the knowledge of the manager of the branch, one of the assistants sold a ham as a "Scotch ham". D was convicted, under the Merchandise Marks Act 1887, s. 2(2), of selling goods "to which any . . . false trade description is applied". Lord Russell CJ said:[5]

"It cannot be doubted that the appellant sold the ham in question, although the transaction was carried out by his servants. In other words he was the seller, although not the actual salesman. It is clear also, as already stated, that the ham was sold with a 'false trade description' which was material. If so, there is evidence establishing a prima facie case of an offence against the Act having been *committed by the appellant*".

The court was clearly influenced by the fact that D (like many other employers) carried on his business in a number of branches and could not possibly be in direct control of each one so that, if actual knowledge of the particular transaction had to be proved, he could hardly ever be made liable. The court did not, however, apply the principle of delegation which is to be found in the licensing cases. By construing the Act in accordance with the principles of the civil law and so holding that D had himself committed an *actus reus*, the court introduced a more far-reaching principle.[6] Comparison with *Allchorn v Hopkins*[7] will show that, under the delegation principle, D would not have been liable for the act of the assistant to whom control of the premises had not been delegated.[8]

There are many cases not involving a sale where a similar principle has been invoked. Just as it is the master who, in law, "sells" goods with which

---

3. This is so in the criminal as well as the civil law: *Watson v Coupland* [1945] 1 All ER 217.
4. [1898] 2 QB 306. One partner may similarly be liable for the acts of another: *Davies v Harvey* (1874) LR 9QB 433. Cf. *Parsons v Barnes* [1973] Crim LR 537.
5. Ibid., at 313.
6. If the same reasoning as that followed in *Coppen v Moore* had been used in the licence cases, where the offence involved "selling", a licensee who owned his stock might have been convicted, notwithstanding the absence of delegation. But this reasoning has not been followed: *McKenna v Harding* (1905) 69 JP 354; *Vane v Yiannopoullos* [1965] AC 486, [1964] 3 All ER 820. But see *Goodfellow v Johnson* [1966] 1 QB 83, [1965] 1 All ER 941, [1965] Crim LR 304 and commentary thereon.
7. Above, p. 165 footnote 8.
8. It was within the scope of the servant's authority in *Coppen v Moore*, above, to sell hams. A master is not liable where a servant boy, who has no authority to sell anything, supplies his master's whisky to a customer out of hours: *Adams v Camfoni* [1929] 1 KB 95. In this case there was no sale by the master.

his servant is actually dealing, so too is he "in possession" of goods which are actually in his servant's hands[9] and so can be made liable for offences of "being in possession" (of which there are many[10]) through his servants. A producer of plays "presents" a play even though he may be miles away when it is performed and was liable, under s. 15 of the Theatres Act 1843 (now repealed[11]), if words were introduced, even without his knowledge, which had not been allowed by the Lord Chamberlain.[12]

The owners of a van, supplied to the bailiff of their farm, "keep" a van which is not "used solely for the conveyance of goods or burden in the course of trade" without a licence[13] if the bailiff uses it, without their knowledge or authority, to take his wife for a day out at Clacton.[14] A master "uses" his vehicle in contravention of the Motor Vehicles (Construction and Use) Regulations if his servant so uses it.[15] It is quite understandable that a court should hold that an employer "presents" a play or "keeps" a vehicle, for these verbs are apt to describe his function and inapt to describe that of his servants. It is less clear that this is so in the case of "uses". This could very well refer to the servant's use.

4 Mode of Participation of Master and Servant

In those cases where it is only the licensee, keeper of the refreshment house, or other designated person in whom it is an offence to do the act in question, it is apparent that the licensee, etc., who is held vicariously liable is a principal for he alone possesses the personal characteristic which is an essential part of the *actus reus* and no one else is qualified to fill that role. The servant who actually performs the act is plainly incapable of being a principal, but it seems that he may be convicted as an abettor,[16] – strange though this appears when he is the only participant in the crime who is present.

Where the *actus reus* does not include a personal characteristic of the master and the servant is capable of being a principal, then it seems that he may be held to be a joint principal with his master. In crimes of "selling" and being "in possession" the court allows the prosecution the best of both worlds by having regard to the legal act when dealing with the master and the physical act when dealing with the servant. So it is held that the servant, as well as the master, "sells"[17] or is "in possession";[18] and the servant

9. Infra.
10. For examples, see above, p. 128.
11. See Theatres Act 1968; below, p. 736.
12. *Grade v Director of Public Prosecutions* [1942] 2 All ER 118. The defendant had in fact been called up for service in the R.A.F. The result would have been different if D had been charged with "causing" the play to be presented: *Lovelace v Director of Public Prosecutions* [1954] 3 All ER 481, [1954] 1 WLR 1468, above, p. 126, footnote 8.
13. Contrary to s. 27 of the Revenue Act 1869.
14. *Strutt v Clift* [1911] 1 KB 1.
15. *Green v Burnett* [1955] 1 QB 78, [1954] 3 All ER 273; but not where a partner, or person authorised ad hoc, uses the vehicle, if there is also an offence of permitting: *Crawford v Haughton* [1972] 1 All ER 535, [1972] 1 WLR 572, DC; *Garrett v Hooper* [1973] Crim LR 61; *Cobb v Williams* [1973] Crim LR 243.
16. *Griffiths v Studebakers Ltd* [1924] 1 KB 102; *Ross v Moss* [1965] 2 QB 396, [1965] 3 All ER 145.
17. *Hotchin v Hindmarsh* [1891] 2 QB 181. Cf. *Goodfellow v Johnson* [1966] 1 QB 83, [1965] 1 All ER 941.
18. *Melias Ltd v Preston* [1957] 2 QB 380, [1957] 2 All ER 449.

whose "use" of a vehicle was held to be use by his master was convicted in *Green v Burnett* (above) as a principal. It is submitted that when the servant is capable of being a principal it is logical to hold him liable as such (for he is the real offender) and not as an abettor.

The precise nature of the delegate's liability is of more than academic interest for two reasons. First, if the crime is one of strict liability, *mens rea* must nevertheless be proved if he is to be convicted as an abettor but not if he is a principal.[19] Secondly, where there is a statutory defence enabling one held vicariously liable to escape if he can bring the "actual offender" before the court, it is difficult to suppose that the production of an abettor (even though he is the real offender) will suffice, but a joint principal certainly will.[20]

5 No Vicarious Liability for Abetting, or Attempting Crimes

Abetting is a common law notion and therefore, as we have seen,[1] requires *mens rea* even where the offence abetted is one of strict liability. For the same reasons there can be no vicarious responsibility for abetting an offence, even though the offence itself may be one imposing vicarious liability. In *Ferguson v Weaving*[2] D, a licensee, was charged with abetting several of her customers in consuming liquor on the licensed premises outside the permitted hours, contrary to the Licensing Act 1921, s. 4. It appeared that she had taken all proper means to ensure that drinking ceased when "Time" was called. But the waiters in the concert room, contrary to their instructions, made no attempt to collect the customers' drinks and, while D was visiting the several other rooms in the premises, the offence was committed. It was assumed that control of the concert room had been delegated. While accepting that the waiters might have been guilty of abetting, the court was emphatic that D could not be. Lord Goddard CJ said:[3]

"She can aid and abet the customers if she knows that the customers are committing an offence, but we are not prepared to hold that their knowledge can be imputed to her so as to make her, not a principal offender, but an aider and abettor. So to hold would be to establish a new principle in criminal law and one for which there is no authority."

Had there been a substantive offence of *permitting* drinking on licensed premises after hours, it is fairly clear that the court could have held D guilty; for in that case the acts, and the *mens rea*, of the servant would have been attributed to her.

An attempt is likewise a common law notion, and it has been said that there can be no vicarious liability for attempting to commit a crime, even though the crime attempted imposes vicarious liability.[4]

---

19. Above, p. 142.
20. *Melias Ltd v Preston* above.
   1. Above, p. 142.
   2. [1951] 1 KB 814, [1951] 1 All ER 412; **SHC 154**. See also *Thomas v Lindop* [1950] 1 All ER 966; *John Henshall (Quarries) Ltd v Harvey* [1965] 2 QB 233, [1965] 1 All ER 725. *Provincial Motor Cab Co Ltd v Dunning* [1909] 2 KB 599 overlooks this principle and is a doubtful decision.
   3. [1951] 1 KB 814 at 821, [1951] 1 All ER 412 at 415.
   4. *Gardner v Akeroyd* [1952] 2 QB 743, [1952] 2 All ER 306.

6 The Special Position of Corporations[5]

A corporation is a legal person but it has no physical existence and cannot, therefore, either act or form an intention of any kind except through its directors or servants. As each director and servant is also a legal person quite distinct from the corporation, it follows that a corporation's legal liabilities are all, in a sense, vicarious. If a corporation's criminal liability for the acts of its servants and agents were co-extensive with that of a natural person, it could be made liable only for those crimes which fall within the narrow limits which govern the vicarious liability of natural persons. A corporation's liability is in fact much wider than that, and therefore requires separate consideration.

It was formerly thought that a corporation could not be indicted for a crime at all.[6] Personal appearance was necessary at assizes and quarter-sessions and the corporation, having no physical person, could not appear. In the Court of King's Bench, however, appearance by attorney was allowed and a way out of this difficulty was found by removing the indictment into that court by writ of certiorari;[7] but now this is unnecessary and, by statute,[8] a corporation may appear and plead through a representative. A second difficulty which has gone was that at one time all felonies were punished by death and, as the corporation was incapable of suffering the prescribed punishment, there was no point in trying it. Further objections which have been raised are that, since a corporation is a creature of the law, it can only do such acts as it is legally empowered to do, so that any crime is necessarily ultra vires; and that the corporation, having neither body nor mind, cannot perform the acts or form the intents which are a prerequisite of criminal liability. The ultra vires doctrine, however, seems to have been ignored in both the law of tort and crime and to apply only in the law of contract and property,[9] while the minds and bodies of the officers and servants of the corporation have been taken to supply its lack of mental and physical faculties. This has been done in two distinct ways:

a) By holding that a corporation is vicariously liable for the acts of its servants and agents where a natural person would similarly be liable; for example, in public nuisance at common law,[10] or when a statute imposes vicarious responsibility.[11]

b) By holding that (i) in every corporation there are certain persons (designated "controlling officers" in the draft Criminal Code)[12] who control and direct its activities, and (ii) those persons, when acting in the company's business, are considered to be the "embodiment of the

---

5. See Williams, CLGP, Ch. 22: R. S. Welch, "The Criminal Liability of Corporations" (1946) 62 LQR 345; L. H. Leigh (1977) 9 Ottawa LR 247. For proposals for reform, see Law Commission Published Working Paper No. 44.
6. *Anon* (1701) 12 Mod Rep 560, per Holt CJ.
7. *Birmingham and Gloucester Rly Co* (1842) 3 QB 223.
8. Criminal Justice Act 1925, s. 33.
9. Cf. Winfield, *Text Book of the Law of Tort* (4th ed.), 128.
10. *Great North of England Rly Co* (1846) 9 QB 315.
11. *Griffiths v Studebakers Ltd* [1924] 1 KB 102; *Mousell Bros Ltd v London and North Western Rly Co* [1917] 2 KB 836.
12. Law Com. No. 143, para. 11–6, and cl. 34.

company"[13] for this purpose. Their acts and states of mind are the company's acts and states of mind and it is held liable, not for the acts of its servants, but for what are deemed to be its own acts.

The type of case where it is most obviously proper that a corporation should be held liable arises where a statute imposes a duty upon a corporation to act and no action is taken. It was in such cases that the earliest developments took place. In 1842, in *Birmingham and Gloucester Rly Co*,[14] a corporation was convicted for failing to fulfil a statutory duty. Four years later, in *Great North of England Rly Co*,[15] counsel sought to confine the effect of that decision to cases of non-feasance where there was no agent who could be indicted, arguing that, in the case of misfeasance, only the agents who had done the wrongful acts were liable. The court held that the distinction was unfounded. Even if it were discoverable, it was incongruous that the corporation should be liable for the one type of wrong and not the other. From holding that a corporation could be liable for breach of a statutory duty it was not a great step forward to impose liability in those cases where a natural person would similarly be liable for his servants' acts – for example in public nuisance at common law, or where statute imposes vicarious responsibility.[16]

Non-vicarious liability of corporations. There was a further important development in 1944. In that year it was held in three cases that a corporation may be held liable for acts of its employees which would certainly *not* render liable a natural person in the same situation. The principle has been well stated by Denning LJ:[17]

"A company may in many ways be likened to a human body. It has a brain and a nerve centre which controls what it does. It also has hands which hold the tools and act in accordance with directions from the centre. Some of the people in the company are mere servants and agents who are nothing more than hands to do the work and cannot be said to represent the mind or will. Others are directors and managers who represent the directing mind and will of the company and control what it does. The state of mind of these managers is the state of mind of the company and is treated by the law as such."[18]

A person is not a "controlling officer" simply because his work is brain work and he exercises some managerial discretion, since not all such persons "represent the directing mind and will of the company and control what it does."[19] The manager of a supermarket belonging to a company owning hundreds of supermarkets is not the company's "brains" and does

13. *Essendon Engineering Co Ltd v Maile* [1982] RTR 260, [1982] Crim LR 510.
14. (1842) 3 QB 223.
15. (1846) 9 QB 315.
16. *Mousell Brothers v London and North Western Rly Co* [1917] 2 KB 836; *Griffiths v Studebakers Ltd* [1924] 1 KB 102.
17. *H. L. Bolton (Engineering) Co Ltd v T. J. Graham & Sons Ltd* [1957] 1 QB 159 at 172.
18. Thus, it is thought that a company could be guilty of abetting an offence through its managing director – though there is no *vicarious* liability in abetting (above, p. 169). See *Robert Millar (Contractors) Ltd* [1970] 2 QB 54, above p. 131.
19. *Tesco Supermarkets Ltd v Nattrass* [1972] AC 153 at 171, HL, per Lord Reid, 187 per Lord Dilhorne, 200 per Lord Diplock; **SHC 181**.

not act as the company.[20] Companies have been held to be not criminally liable for the acts of a depot engineer[1] or a weighbridge operator.[2] In the leading case of *Tesco Supermarkets Ltd v Nattrass*[3] it was said that the company may be criminally liable for the acts only of:

". . . the board of directors, the managing director and perhaps other superior officers of a company [who] carry out the functions of management and speak and act as the company,"

per Lord Reid,[4] or of a person:

". . . who is in actual control of the operations of a company or of part of them and who is not responsible to another person in the company for the manner in which he discharges his duties in the sense of being under his orders,"

per Viscount Dilhorne.[5]

Lord Diplock[6] thought that the question is to be answered by

". . . identifying those natural persons who by the memorandum and articles of association or as result of action taken by the directors or by the company in general meeting pursuant to the articles are entrusted with the exercise of the powers of the company."

Lord Pearson too thought that the constitution of the company concerned must be taken into account; and Lords Dilhorne, Pearson and Diplock thought that the reference in the "common form" provision, discussed below,[7] to "any director, manager, secretary or other similar officer of the body corporate" affords a useful indication. If those persons who are responsible for the general management of the company delegate their duties to another, then the acts of that other will be the acts of the company.[8]

Once the facts have been ascertained, it is a question of law whether a person in doing particular things is to be regarded as the company or merely as the company's servant or agent.[9] Accordingly the judge should direct the jury that if they find certain facts proved, then they must find that the act and intention of the agent is the act and intention of the company. It is not sufficient to direct that the company is liable for its 'responsible agents" or "high executives", for such persons are not necessarily the company.[10] The test is the same whether the offence be serious or trivial.

In the *Tesco* case, the company, being charged with an offence under the Trade Descriptions Act 1968, relied on the statutory defence that they had taken all reasonable precautions and exercised all due diligence and that the commission of the offence was due to the act or default of "another person", namely the branch manager, who had failed to supervise the

20. Ibid.
1. *Magna Plant Ltd v Mitchell* [1966] Crim LR 394.
2. *John Henshall (Quarries) Ltd v Harvey* [1965] 2 QB 233, [1965] 1 All ER 725.
3. Above, footnote 19.
4. At p. 171.
5. At p. 187.
6. At p. 200.
7. See p. 175.
8. [1972] AC 153 at 193.
9. [1972] AC 153 at 170, 173, per Lord Reid.
10. *Sporle* [1971] Crim LR 706.

assistant who actually committed the offence. Since the manager was the "hands" and not the "brains" of the company, it was held that the defence was available. It would have been otherwise if it had been not the manager but a director who had failed in his duty.

In *Director of Public Prosecutions v Kent and Sussex Contractors Ltd:*[11] D Ltd was charged with offences under a Defence of the Realm regulation which required an intent to deceive. The justices found that the transport manager of the company had the requisite intention but dismissed the information on the ground that an act of will or state of mind could not be imputed to the company. The Divisional Court held that there was ample evidence that the *company* had done the act in question, with intent to deceive.

That decision was approved by the Court of Criminal Appeal in *ICR Haulage Ltd*,[12] where the convictions of a company, its managing director and nine other persons of a common law conspiracy to defraud were upheld. Stable J said[13]

"... the acts of the managing director were the acts of the company and the fraud of that person was the fraud of the company."

Now a natural person could never be held vicariously liable for a common law conspiracy, and the case is therefore an excellent illustration of the wider liability of corporations.

In *Moore v I. Bresler Ltd*[14] the company was convicted of making certain returns in respect of purchase tax, which were false in material particulars, with intent to deceive, contrary to the Finance (No. 2) Act 1940, s. 35. The returns were actually made by the secretary of the company, and the sales manager of the branch concerned, and were made with the object of concealing the fraudulent sale which these two had made of the company's property. Welch criticises the case[15] on the ground (inter alia) that, in identifying these two agents with the company, the court went too far down the scale, but it may perhaps be justified in this respect on the ground that the company secretary was involved. *Kent and Sussex Contractors* seems more doubtful in that only the transport manager appears to have acted.

A corporation's state of mind. Where the offence is one of strict liability, the corporation may be held liable for the acts of any of its servants or agents where those acts are, in law, the company's acts, under the principle discussed above;[16] but where the offence requires *mens rea*, it must be proved that a controlling officer had the *mens rea*.[17] Similarly, where a defence requires evidence of a belief or other state of mind, this must usually be the belief or state of mind of a controlling officer;[18] but the belief

11. [1944] KB 146, [1944] 1 All ER 119.
12. [1944] KB 551, [1944] 1 All ER 691. Cf. *McDonnell* [1966] 1 QB 233, [1966] 1 All ER 193, below, p. 281.
13. [1944] KB at 559, [1944] 1 All ER at 695.
14. [1944] 2 All ER 515.
15. (1946) 62 LQR at 358.
16. "Where an agent's act is the defendant's act in law," p. 167.
17. *Tesco Supermarkets Ltd v Nattrass* [1972] AC 153 [1971] 2 All ER 127. Draft criminal code, cl. 34, (2).
18. *GJ Coles & Co Ltd v Goldsworthy* [1958] WAR 183. See Orchard in *Criminal Law Essays*, 114, 117, 118–119.

of one will not suffice if another, especially if he is superior to the first, knows that that belief is ill founded.[19] Probably, as the draft code states, all controlling officers who are concerned in the offence must have the required state of mind. If, however, no controlling officer is involved and all the employees or agents who are involved do have the required state of mind, the defence ought clearly to be available. If a branch manager, not being a controlling officer, finds a controlled drug in supplies delivered to his branch and takes control of it, intending to hand it to the police, the company may surely rely on this intention to establish the defence provided by s. 5(4) of the Misuse of Drugs Act 1971, if it is charged with unlawful possession of the drug.[20]

Limitations on corporate liability. There are certain existing limitations on the liability of a corporation. (1) It can only be convicted of offences which are punishable with a fine. These include most offences;[1] but exclude murder. (2) There are other offences which it is quite inconceivable that an official of a corporation should commit within the scope of his employment; for example, bigamy, rape, incest and, possibly, perjury.[2]

In *Cory Bros & Co*,[3] it was held that a corporation could not be indicted for any felony or for a misdemeanour involving personal violence, but in *ICR Haulage Ltd* Stable J pointed out that this was a branch of law which had developed and, if the matter came before the court today, the result might well be different.[4] A corporation has subsequently been tried for manslaughter but acquitted on the merits.[5] *Dicta* to the effect that a corporation cannot be convicted of fraudulent conversion[6] (now a variety of theft) are almost certainly out of date, and it is probable that the only limitations on the criminal liability of corporations are those stated above.

The social purpose underlying corporate criminal liability does not appear to have been considered by the English courts. The fine imposed is ultimately borne by the sharcholders who, in most cases, are not responsible, in any sense, for the offence. If they really had control over the directors and so over the management of the company, this might afford some justification; but it is generally recognised that they have no such control over large, public companies.[7] Moreover fines may be inflicted on

---

19. *Brambles Holdings Ltd v Carey* (1976) 15 SASR 270 at 280.
20. See Draft Criminal Code, Sch. 1, illustration 34(vi).
   1. See Magistrates' Courts Act 1980, s. 32 and Powers of Criminal Courts Act 1973, s. 30.
   2. Even in some of these cases it is not inconceivable that a corporation might be held liable as a secondary party. E.g., the managing director of an incorporated Marriage Advisory Bureau negotiates a marriage which he knows to be bigamous.
   3. [1927] 1 KB 810.
   4. [1944] KB 551 at 566, [1944] 1 All ER 691 at 694. Cf. the rejected argument of Artemus Jones KC in *Cory Bros Ltd*: "The old difficulties as to procedure and punishment having disappeared, it follows that the *dicta* of the judges to the effect that a corporation cannot be indictable for a felony have ceased to have any application on the principle *cessante ratione legis cessat ipsa lex.*"
   5. *Northern Star Mining Construction Co Ltd, Glamorgan Assizes*, February 1, 1965, unreported. *In Spooner, ex p* (1987) Times, 10 October, CA, the court expressed the opinion, obiter, that a corporation may be convicted of manslaughter. Cf. *Robert Millar (Contractors) Ltd*, above, p. 131.
   6. *Grubb* [1915] 2 KB 683.
   7. Pennington, (3rd ed.) *Company Law*, pp. 500 et seq.

the Boards of nationalised industries, where there are no shareholders and the consumers of the product, who ultimately pay the fine, have no rights whatever to appoint or dismiss the officials concerned.[8]

Since the persons actually responsible for the offence may, in the great majority of cases, be convicted, is there any need to impose this additional penalty? Arguments in favour of corporate liability are that there may be difficulty in fixing individuals with liability where someone among the "brains" of the corporation has undoubtedly authorised the offence. Corporate liability ensures that the offence will not go unpunished and that a fine proportionate to the gravity of the offence may be imposed, when it might be out of proportion to the means of the individuals concerned. The imposition of liability on the organisation gives all of those directing it an interest in the prevention of illegalities – and they are in a position to prevent them, though the shareholders are not. Since, moreover, the names of the officers will mean nothing to the public, only the conviction of the corporation itself will serve to warn the public of the wrongful acts – operating buses with faulty brakes, or selling mouldy pies – which are committed in its name. None of these reasons seems to be very compelling and the necessity for corporate criminal liability awaits demonstration.

Statutory liability of officers. It is now common form to include the following provision in statutes creating offences likely to be committed by corporations:

"Where an offence . . . committed by a body corporate is proved to have been committed with the consent or connivance of, or to be attributable to any neglect on the part of, any director, manager, secretary or other similar officer of the body corporate or any person who was purporting to act in any such capacity, he as well as the body corporate shall be guilty of that offence and shall be liable to be proceeded against and punished accordingly."

Whether a director or other officer is under a duty is a question which can be answered only by looking at the facts of each case; and the onus of proving that there was a duty which has been neglected is on the prosecution.[9]

So far as "consent" and "connivance" are concerned the provision probably effects only a slight extension of the law; for the officer who expressly consents or connives at the commission of the offence will be liable as a secondary party under the principles considered above. There may be a consent which does not amount to counselling or abetting, however; and the words "attributable to any neglect on the part of"[10] clearly impose a wider liability in making the officer liable for his negligence in failing to prevent the offence.

---

8. In 1951 the Yorkshire Electricity Board was fined £20,000 for contravening a Defence Regulation. It has been suggested that the object of such a prosecution was to demonstrate that nationalised industries are not above the law.

9. *Huckerby v Elliott* [1970] 1 All ER 189. "Manager" means someone managing the affairs of the company and not, e.g. the manager of a store: *Tesco Supermarkets Ltd v Nattrass* [1972] AC 153 at 178.

10. These words are omitted from s. 18 of the Theft Act 1968, below, p. 638.

Unincorporated bodies. An unincorporated association is not a legal person at common law and therefore could not incur criminal liability though its members could. In *A-G v Able*[11] Woolf J, dealing with an alleged offence under the Suicide Act 1961, said, "It must be remembered that the [Voluntary Euthanasia Society] is an unincorporated body and there can be no question of the society committing an offence." Sometimes, however, statute expressly imposed criminal liability on unincorporated bodies as when the Trade Union and Labour Relations Act 1974 provided that trades unions and employers' associations are guilty of an offence under s. 12 if they refuse or wilfully neglect to perform certain duties imposed by the Act. However, by the Interpretation Act 1978, Sch 1, the word "person" in any Act includes, unless the contrary intention appears, "a body of persons corporate or incorporate"; and, by Sch 2, "Application of Act to Existing Enactments": "The definition of 'person', so far as it includes bodies corporate, applies to any provision of an Act whenever passed relating to an offence punishable on indictment or on summary conviction." The effect appears to be that in Acts passed after the commencement of the Interpretation Act 1978 (1 January 1979) unincorporated associations are "persons" and are liable to be convicted of any offence where the definition uses the word "person" – as is usual. So when the Banking Act 1987, s. 98 (1) assumes rather than provides that offences under the Act may be committed by unincorporated associations, it does so rightly.

When an unincorporated association is prosecuted, presumably the court must proceed by analogy to the law relating to corporations. Such associations have officials corresponding to the controlling officers of corporations and it is inconceivable that the association is liable for the act of any one of its members who has no part in the general management of its affairs.

11. [1984] QB 795, [1984] 1 All ER 277, 286, above, p. 140.

9 General Defences

Where D has caused an *actus reus* with the appropriate *mens rea*, he will generally be held liable. But this is not invariably so for there are certain defences which may still be available even in this situation. As well as special defences which apply in the case of particular crimes, there are certain defences which apply in the case of crimes generally and it is these with which we are concerned in this chapter.

The common law distinguished between justification and excuse. Some homicides, like that done by the public hangman in carrying out the sentence of the court, were justifiable. Others, like killing by misadventure and without culpable negligence, were merely excusable. In both cases the accused who successfully raised the defence was acquitted of felony but, if the homicide was merely excusable, his goods were forfeited. In 1828 forfeiture was abolished and, ever since, there has been no difference, so far as the defendant is concerned, between the various general defences. If successfully raised, they result in a verdict of not guilty.

Recently, however, there has been a revival of interest in a distinction between justification and excuse.[1] No one suggests that there is any difference so far as the acquittal of the person relying on the defence is concerned but it is said that the distinction affects third parties in that (i) it is lawful to resist an aggressor whose agression is merely excused but not one whose aggression is justified; and (ii) there may be a conviction for aiding and abetting one who is merely excused[2] but not one who is justified. As Fletcher (whose work inspired the current interest) acknowledges,[3] Anglo-American criminal law has never recognised these (as he thinks) fundamental distinctions. The proposed distinctions bear little resemblance to the justifiable and excusable homicides of the common law and there is disagreement between the protagonists as to which defence should fall into which category.

Applying the theory as expounded by Fletcher, a person arresting "anyone who is in the act of committing an arrestable offence" would be justified but a person arresting "anyone whom he has reasonable grounds for suspecting to be [but who is not in fact] committing such an offence" is merely excused. But both acts are equally "justified" by the law – the Police

---

1. Fletcher, *Rethinking Criminal Law*, Ch. 10; Williams, "The Theory of Excuses" [1982] Crim LR 732; Alldridge (1986) 50 J Cr L 274; Robinson (1982) 82 Col Law Rev 199.
2. As in *Bourne* (1952) 36 Cr App Rep 125 and *Cogan and Leak* [1976] QB 217, [1975] 2 All ER 1059, above, p. 155.
3. Op. cit., footnote 1, above.

and Criminal Evidence Act 1984, s. 24(4) (a) and (b), declares that both are acts that a person *may* do. In doing so, he incurs no civil or criminal liability. It is true, however, that the first "arrestee" would not be entitled to use force in self-defence (if the arrestor was using only reasonable force) whereas the second might be.[4]

The law does recognise that a person's act may be excused in the criminal law, while incurring civil liability. A person who makes an unreasonable mistake of fact which, if it were true, would amount to reasonable grounds for suspecting another to be in act of committing an arrestable offence, has a defence to a criminal prosecution for false imprisonment or assault (because he lacks *mens rea*) but remains liable for the corresponding torts: it is not the act which the 1984 Act says he *may* do. Here the terminology of justification and excuse seems appropriate. The act is "unlawful", but the actor is excused from criminal liability.

Any attempt to categorise defences as justifications or excuses would, in the present state of the law, be premature and it is not made in the following pages.

1 Infancy

Infants are persons under eighteen years of age. As such, they are (with some exceptions) incapable of making contracts or wills but the law imposes no such limitations on their ability to commit crimes, for, as Kenny put it,

> "a child knows right from wrong long before he knows how to make a prudent speculation or a wise will".[5]

For the purpose of the criminal law, infants are divided into three categories.

1 Children under Ten Years

The first category is those who are entirely exempt from criminal responsibility in all circumstances. At common law a child was so exempt until the day before his seventh birthday.[6] Now responsibility begins on the tenth birthday.[7] The rule is commonly stated as a conclusive presumption that the child is *doli incapax*. Even though there may be the clearest evidence that the child caused an *actus reus* with *mens rea*, he cannot be convicted once it appears that he had not, at the time he did the act, attained the age of ten. Nor is this a mere procedural bar; no crime at all is committed by the infant with the result that one who instigated him to do the act is a principal

---

4. Below, p. 245.
5. *Outlines*, 80.
6. A person now attains a particular age at the commencement of the relevant anniversary of the date of his birth: Family Law Reform Act 1969, s. 9(1).
7. Children and Young Persons Act 1933, s. 50, as amended by the Children and Young Persons Act 1963, s. 16, which raised the age from eight. The Ingleby Committee had recommended that the age be raised to twelve. Cmnd. 1911 (1960).

and not a secondary party.[8] And where a husband and wife were charged with receiving from their son (aged seven years) a child's tricycle, knowing it to have been stolen, it was held that they must be acquitted on the ground that, since the child could not steal, the tricycle was not stolen.[9] The only remedy in the case of a child under ten who has done an act which would be a crime if done by an older person is to bring "care proceedings"[10] in a juvenile court. This is not a criminal proceeding, so there is no lower age limit nor is there a finding of guilt; yet the result may be that the child is sent to a community home, which might be regarded as a punishment. Ten is a comparatively low age for the beginning of criminal responsibility; but, as the Ingleby Committee pointed out:[11]

"In many countries the 'age of criminal responsibility' is used to signify the age at which a person becomes liable to the 'ordinary' or 'full' penalties of the law. In this sense, the age of criminal responsibility in England is difficult to state: it is certainly much higher than eight."[12]

2 Children over Nine and under Fourteen Years

A child aged not less than ten but under fourteen years is exempt from criminal responsibility unless the prosecution prove, not only that he caused an *actus reus* with *mens rea*, but also that he did so with what is traditionally called "a mischievous discretion".[13] Hale wrote that this involved proof that the child could "discern between good and evil at the time of the offence committed".[14] The modern test is stated in *Gorrie*.[15] A thirteen-year-old boy was charged with the manslaughter of a schoolmate, who died from an infection resulting from a slight wound with a penknife. Salter J told the jury that they must be satisfied:

"that when the boy did this he knew what he was doing was wrong – not merely what was wrong, but what was gravely wrong, seriously wrong."

This passage was adopted in *J M (a minor) v Runeckles*[16] where the court held that it is not necessary to prove that the child knew that the act was morally wrong; he must know that it is "seriously" wrong in the sense that it is not merely naughty or mischievous. The fact that the offence committed is of such a nature that any normal child of the defendant's age would know it is seriously wrong is not apparently sufficient to rebut the presumption unless the prosecution proves that he was of normal mental capacity.[17] But it is not necessary in all cases to call evidence to prove that the defendant is a normal child of his age. His behaviour before and after the offence may be sufficient to show that he knew he was doing something

8. Above, p. 131.
9. *Walters v Lunt* [1951] 2 All ER 645; and cf. *Marsh v Loader* (1863) 14 CBNS 535.
10. See Children and Young Persons Act 1969, s. 1.
11. Cmnd. 1191, p. 30. For the special rules governing the treatment of children and young persons, see Children and Young Persons Acts 1933, 1963 and 1969; Cross, *The English Sentencing System* (3rd ed.), 75.
12. As the age then was. Above, p. 178, footnote 6.
13. Hale, 1 PC 630.
14. 1 PC 26.
15. (1919) 83 JP 136.
16. (1984) 79 Cr App Rep 255, DC.
17. *JBH and JH (Minors) v O'Connell* [1981] Crim LR 632, DC; *IPH v Chief Constable of South Wales* [1987] Crim LR 42, DC.

seriously wrong. In 1748 a boy of ten was convicted of murder on evidence which showed that, after killing a five-year-old girl, he had concealed the body and told lies about what happened.[18]

In *J M v Runeckles* the court held that there was ample evidence in the nature of the act (a blow with a milk bottle and a stab with a broken part of it), the fact that D ran away from the police and hid, and the content and handwriting of her statement, these being commensurate with the ability of an average thirteen-year-old. But the younger a child, the stronger is the evidence required to establish mischievous discretion.[19]

Since it is now the duty of every court, in dealing with a child or young person, to "have regard to the welfare of the child or young person",[20] and merely retributive punishment is ruled out, it has been argued[1] that this test is now out of date:

"It saves the child not from prison, transportation or the gallows, but from the probation officer, the foster parent, or the approved school. The paradoxical result is that, the more warped the child's moral standards, the safer he is from the correctional treatment of the criminal law."

The Ingleby Committee were impressed by similar arguments and by evidence that, because courts find difficulty in applying the presumption and differ in the degree of proof they require, there is inconsistency in the administration of the law. They recommended that the *doli incapax* presumption be abolished. This recommendation has not been implemented but an alternative to criminal proceedings has been provided in the case of "children" (persons under fourteen) and "young persons" (persons under seventeen) by the Children and Young Persons Act 1969[2], s. 1, in the form of "care proceedings". These may be instituted in a juvenile court by any local authority, constable or person authorised by the Home Secretary. The court must be satisfied that the child or young person is in need of care and control which he is unlikely to receive unless the court makes an order and also that one of a number of conditions is satisfied. Condition (f) is:

"he is guilty of an offence excluding homicide."

In the case of homicide, only criminal proceedings may be instituted; but in the case of any other offence care proceedings are an alternative *if* the infant is in need of care and control which he is unlikely otherwise to receive. When reliance is placed on condition (f), known as "the offence condition", the usual conditions of criminal liability apply. The mischievous discretion must be proved. The onus and standard of proof and rules of evidence are those of criminal proceedings. The limitation period for summary offences applies, as do the rules relating to previous acquittal or conviction; and the infant may appeal against a finding that he has committed an offence. Only when the court has found that the offence condition is satisfied does it go on to consider (according to the rules of civil cases) whether the infant is in need of care and control.

---

18. *York* (1748), see Fost 70.
19. *X v X* [1958] Crim LR 805.
20. Children and Young Persons Act 1933, s. 44(1).
  1. By Williams [1954] Crim LR 493 at 495.
  2. As amended by the Criminal Justice Act 1982. See articles on the Act in [1972] Crim LR 670–701.

It was intended that criminal proceedings should be brought only as a last resort and, in the case of infants under fourteen, eliminated altogether. Section 4 provides –

"A person shall not be charged with an offence, except homicide, by reason of anything done or omitted while he was a child" –

but it has not been brought into force. It was intended to raise the minimum age by stages, but it appears that it is unlikely to be raised in the foreseeable future. If section 4 should ever be fully implemented, children between ten and fourteen will continue to be capable of committing crime but not be liable to prosecution, except for homicide. Care proceedings are civil proceedings and a finding that the offence condition is satisfied is not a conviction.

There is another special rule of exemption for a boy under fourteen in that he cannot be convicted of rape,[3] offences involving sexual intercourse,[4] buggery[5] or, possibly, assault with intent to commit buggery.[6] The rule is theoretically based on a presumption of incapacity but,[7] as no evidence is admissible in rebuttal, it is in effect a rule of law. When a boy has done acts which, but for his age, would amount to one of these offences he may be convicted of an indecent assault. He may also be convicted of abetting another to commit those offences of which he is himself incapable.[8]

3 Persons over Fourteen Years

Above the age of fourteen an infant is presumed to be "responsible for his actions entirely as if he were forty".[9] In the case of these infants the prosecution need prove only the usual *mens rea* required in the case of a person of full age to obtain a conviction. There are however very important differences in the treatment of young persons convicted of crime in the modern law.[10] It has already been seen that care proceedings are an alternative, except in the case of homicide, to the prosecution of infants under seventeen; and the Children and Young Persons Act 1969, section 5, provides for restrictions on the prosecution of young persons. This provision has not been brought into force and there is no intention of bringing it into force at the present time. It would restrict the right to prosecute young persons to "qualified informants" specified in the Act, who might institute proceedings only subject to regulations made by the Home Secretary and where the informant was of the opinion that the case could not otherwise be adequately dealt with.

---

3. *Groombridge* (1836) 7 C & P 582.
4. *Waite* [1892] 2 QB 600. Whether a conviction for attempted rape or an offence involving sexual intercourse is possible is considered below, p. 438.
5. *Tatam* (1921) 15 Cr App Rep 132, holding that a boy under fourteen cannot be an accomplice to sodomy. But see below, p. 473.
6. *Philips* (1839) 8 C & P 736 (assault with intent to rape – no longer an offence), below, pp. 438, 474.
7. But see below, p. 438.
8. Above, p. 155.
9. *Smith* (1845) 1 Cox CC 260, per Erle J.
10. Jackson, *Enforcing the Law* (Revised ed.), Chapter 8; Cross *The English Sentencing System* (3rd ed.), 75. Criminal Justice Act 1982, Part I.

2 Insanity[11]

1 Insanity before the Trial

An accused person's sanity may become relevant at two stages before the trial. It is inaccurate to speak of "a defence" in these preliminary proceedings, for the effect of a finding of insanity of the appropriate kind is to prevent the accused being tried at all. It is thought convenient to deal briefly with these matters here, however, because of their very close relationship with the defence of insanity at the trial.

Where D has been committed in custody for trial, and the Home Secretary is satisfied by reports from at least two medical practitioners that he is suffering from mental illness, or severe mental impairment,[12] he may order that D be detained in a hospital, if he is of opinion having regard to the public interest that it is expedient to do so.[13] The Home Secretary exercises this power only

"where the prisoner's condition is such that immediate removal to a mental hospital is necessary, that it would not be practicable to bring him before a court, or that the trial is likely to have an injurious effect on his mental state."[14]

The prisoner is normally brought to trial when he is well enough.[15] The basis for this practice is –

"that the issue of insanity should be determined by the jury whenever possible and the power should be exercised only when there is likely to be a scandal if the prisoner is brought up for trial . . ."[16]

The second stage is when the accused is brought up for trial. He may then be found unfit to plead on arraignment under s. 4 of the Criminal Procedure (Insanity) Act 1964.[17] The question at this stage is whether he is able to understand the charge and the difference between pleas of guilty and not guilty, to challenge jurors, to instruct counsel and to follow the evidence. If he is able to do these things, he has a right to be tried if he so wishes, even though he is not capable of acting in his best interests.[18] The same principle must, theoretically, be applicable where the prosecution contend that D is fit to plead and he denies it; but it might be more leniently applied in such a case.

It was held in *Podola*[19] that a man is fit to plead where an hysterical amnesia prevents him from remembering events during the whole of the

---

11. Walker, *Crime and Insanity in England*; Williams, CLGP, Chapter 10. Proposals for the reform of the law are made in the Report of the Committee on Mentally Abnormal Offenders (The Butler Report – hereinafter Butler) Cmnd. 6244, 1975. Emmins, [1986] Crim LR 605.
12. See below, p. 199, footnote 20.
13. Mental Health Act 1983, ss. 47, 48.
14. RCCP, Cmd. 8932, p. 76 referring to the corresponding power under the Criminal Lunatics Act 1884. See Butler, para. 3.38.
15. Butler, para. 3.38.
16. RCCP, Cmd. 8932, loc. cit.
17. Replacing s. 2 of the Criminal Lunatics Act 1800.
18. *Robertson* [1968] 3 All ER 557, [1968] 1 WLR 1767, CA.
19. [1960] 1 QB 325, [1959] 3 All ER 418; **SHC 186**. The jury had found that Podola was not suffering from hysterical amnesia and the question before the Court of Criminal Appeal concerned the onus of proof of that issue; but the Court held that this question could only arise if the alleged amnesia could in law bring Podola within the scope of s. 2 of the Criminal Lunatics Act 1800. The Court's decision on this point thus appears to be part of the *ratio decidendi* of the case.

period material to the question whether he committed the crime alleged, but whose mind is otherwise completely normal. The court was prepared to concede that a deaf mute is "insane" – the word used in the Criminal Lunatics Act 1800 – but declined

"to extend the meaning of the word to include persons who are mentally normal at the time of the hearing of the proceedings against them and are perfectly capable of instructing their solicitors as to what submission their counsel is to put forward with regard to the commission of the crime."[20]

But is a person suffering from hysterical amnesia so capable? If the actual facts justify a defence of accident or alibi but D is unable to remember them, the defence, in the absence of volunteer witnesses, cannot be raised. On the other hand it would be unsatisfactory if, for example, there could be no trial of a motorist who had suffered concussion in an accident, alleged to have been caused by his reckless driving, and who could not remember what he did. It would be still less satisfactory in the case of one whose failure to recall the relevant events arose from drunkenness.[1]

The issue may be raised by the judge on his own initiative or at the request of the prosecution or the defence. Where neither party raises the issue, the judge should do so if he has doubts about the accused's fitness.[2] He may resolve his doubts by reading the medical reports, but it is undesirable for him to hear medical evidence.

If the question is raised by either party, or if the judge has doubts, the issue must be tried by a jury specially empanelled for the purpose.[3] If the accused is found unfit to plead, the court makes an order that he be admitted to the hospital specified by the Home Secretary,[4] where he may be detained without limitation of time, the power to discharge him being exercisable only with the Home Secretary's consent.[5]

The general view expressed by witnesses before the Royal Commission on Capital Punishment was that:

"someone who is certifiably insane may often nevertheless be fit to plead to the indictment and follow the proceedings at the trial and that, if he is, he should ordinarily be allowed to do so, because it is in principle desirable that a person charged with a criminal offence should, whenever possible, be tried, so that the question whether he committed the crime may be determined by a jury. Moreover, we were told that, as is not unnatural, persons who have been found insane on arraignment and ordered to be detained during H.M. pleasure sometimes exhibit a strong sense of grievance on the ground that they have not been proved to have

20. [1960] 1 QB at 356, [1959] 3 All ER at 433. The word "insane" is not used in s. 4 of the 1964 Act; but the law is unchanged. Cf. Cmd. 2149, p. 7.

1. *Broadhurst v R* [1964] AC 441 at 451, [1964] 1 All ER 111 at 116, PC. Butler (by majority) recommends the retention of the *Podola* rule.

2. *MacCarthy* [1967] 1 QB 68, [1966] 1 All ER 447, discussed by A. R. Poole, "Standing Mute and Fitness to Plead" [1966] Crim LR 6.

3. Criminal Procedure (Insanity) Act 1964, s. 4(4). Butler recommends that the issue should be decided by the judge unless (i) the medical evidence is not unanimous, and (ii) the defence want a jury; paras. 10.20–10.23.

4. Criminal Procedure (Insanity) Act 1964, s. 5(1) (c) and Sch. 1.

5. Mental Health Act 1983, ss. 23 and 41 (as amended by the Mental Health (Amendment) Act 1982).

committed any crime and ought not therefore to be detained in an institution for 'criminal lunatics'."[6]

Podola's case also decides, overruling earlier authorities, that, where D raises the issue of fitness to plead, the onus of proving that he is unfit is on him. By analogy to the rule prevailing when a defence of insanity is raised at the trial,[7] D is required to prove his case, not beyond reasonable doubt, but on a balance of probabilities. If the issue is raised by the prosecution and disputed by the defence then the burden is on the prosecution and the matter must be proved beyond reasonable doubt.[8] If the issue is raised by the judge and disputed by D, presumably the onus is again on the prosecution.[9]

The effect of *Podola*'s case is that a man may be convicted although a jury was not satisfied that he was capable of making out a proper defence at his trial. Moreover the reasoning of the court has been criticised[10] on the ground, *inter alia*, that the prosecution, in bringing the charge at all, is implicitly alleging that D is fit to stand his trial; and that he, in denying that he is so fit, is merely denying that the prosecution have established all the elements in their case.

Time of trial of fitness to plead. A difficult problem may arise where there is evidence both of a substantive defence to the charge and of unfitness to plead. Until recently the predominant view[11] appeared to be that, where the court was aware of the issue as to unfitness, it was its duty to see that that issue was tried, even though no application was made by either prosecution or defence, before allowing the trial of the general issue to proceed. If it should then be found that D was unfit he was deprived of his right to raise the substantive defence. He might then be ordered to be detained indefinitely although there was a defence witness in court who could prove that D was ten miles away at the time of the alleged crime.[12] There were however two cases in which Devlin[13] and Finnemore[14] JJ respectively held that the general issue should be tried first, and the question whether D was fit to plead should be tried and determined by the jury only if the general issue was determined against him.[15]

The conflict is now resolved by s. 4 of the Criminal Procedure (Insanity) Act 1964. The general rule remains that the question of fitness to plead is to

6. Report, Cmd. 8932, p. 78. The terms, "Her Majesty's Pleasure" and "criminal lunatic" are no longer used. In fact only about half the prisoners found unfit to plead are detained in Broadmoor or other special hospitals, the remainder being detained in local hospitals: Cmd. 2149, para. 21(4). Butler recommends that the judge should have a discretion as to the disposal of the person under disability; paras. 10.27–10.29.

7. See below, p. 185.

8. Per Edmund Davies J at first instance, [1960] 1 QB 325 at 329, [1959] 3 All ER 418 at 442; *Robertson* [1968] 3 All ER 557, [1968] 1 WLR 1767, CA.

9. According to Podola's counsel, Mr Lawton, it had been the normal practice in recent years for the prosecution to call the evidence.

10. By Dean [1960] Crim LR 79 at 82.

11. *Beynon* [1957] 2 QB 111, [1957] 2 All ER 513 (Byrne J); *Podola* [1960] 1 QB 325 at 349–350, [1959] 3 All ER 418 at 429, CCA; **SHC 186**.

12. Per Devlin J in *Roberts* [1954] 2 QB 329 at 335–336, [1953] 2 All ER 340 at 344.

13. *Roberts* [1954] 2 QB 329, [1953] 2 All ER 340.

14. *Pickstone* [1954] Crim LR 565.

15. In both cases the jury returned a verdict of not guilty, so it was unnecessary to determine whether he was fit to plead.

be determined as soon as it arises[16] but the judge is now given a discretion to postpone it until any time up to the opening of the case for the defence, where, having regard to the nature of D's supposed disability, he considers it is expedient and in D's interests to do so.[17] The discretion to postpone must, as a rule, be exercised where there is a reasonable chance that the prosecution case will be successfully challenged.[18] This is so even where the disability is such that, whatever the outcome, D is bound to be detained.[19] But if the prosecution case is very strong and D very disabled then postponement may be inexpedient. If the trial of the issue is postponed and at the end of the case for the prosecution there is insufficient evidence to justify a conviction, then the jury should be directed to acquit. If, on the other hand, there is a substantial case against the accused, the issue of fitness to plead will be determined there and then by another jury specially empanelled for the purpose or by the trial jury as the judge shall direct. Where the defence on the substantive issue depends on some positive evidence (for example, of alibi) rather than on the weakness of the prosecution's case, it would be possible to request the judge to call the witness before the end of the prosecution's case.[20]

2 Insanity at the Trial[1]

If the accused is found fit to plead or, if that issue is not raised, he may raise the defence of insanity at his trial. It is important to notice that, whereas at the two preliminary stages we were concerned with the accused's sanity *at the time of the inquiry*, at the trial the question concerns the accused's sanity *at the time when he did the act*. The fact that he was insane in the medical sense is not in itself sufficient to afford a defence. There is a legal criterion of responsibility defined by the common law and set out in authoritative form in the "M'Naghten Rules", formulated by the judges in 1843. Daniel M'Naghten, intending to murder Sir Robert Peel, killed the statesman's secretary by mistake. His acquittal of murder[2] on the ground of insanity provoked controversy and was debated in the House of Lords, which sought the advice of the judges and submitted to them a number of questions. The answers to those questions became the famous Rules.[3] Answers to hypothetical questions, even by all the judges, are not, strictly speaking, a source of law; but in *Sullivan*[4] it was accepted by the House of Lords that the Rules have provided a comprehensive definition since 1843. In a sense, the Rules are now obsolete since they are invoked by way of defence on only one or two occasions each year. The Rules are, however, still of great importance both because they remain the legal test of

16. Criminal Procedure (Insanity) Act 1964, s. 4(3).
17. Ibid., s. 4(2). The court has power to remand for treatment: Mental Health Act 1983, s. 36.
18. *Webb* [1969] 2 QB 278, [1969] 2 All ER 626.
19. *Burles* [1970] 2 QB 191, [1970] 1 All ER 642.
20. See Cmd. 2149, para. 24. Butler proposes that the issue should be tried at the outset, that there should be a power to postpone trial where disability is found and that there should be a "trial of the facts" where there is no prospect of recovery: para. 10.19.
   1. See generally, Williams, CLGP, Chapter 9; Ellenbogen, "The Principles of Criminal Law relating to Insanity", 1 *Journal of Criminal Science*, 178.
   2. 4 St Tr NS 847.
   3. 10 Cl & F 200; **SHC 188**.
   4. [1984] AC 156, [1983] 2 All ER 673.

responsibility of the mentally abnormal and because they set a limit to the defences of automatism and, in theory, of diminished responsibility. The basic propositions of the law are to be found in the answers to Questions 2 and 3:[5]

"... the jurors ought to be told in all cases that every man is presumed to be sane, and to possess a sufficient degree of reason to be responsible for his crimes, until the contrary be proved to their satisfaction; and that to establish a defence on the ground of insanity, it must be clearly proved that, at the time of the committing of the act, the party accused was labouring under such a defect of reason, from disease of the mind, as not to know the nature and quality of the act he was doing, or, if he did know it, that he did not know he was doing what was wrong."

It will be seen that there are two lines of defence open to an accused person: (i) he must be acquitted if, because of a disease of the mind, he did not know the nature and quality of his act; (ii) even if he did know the nature and quality of his act, he must be acquitted if, because of a disease of the mind, he did not know it was "wrong". The two limbs of the rule require separate consideration but the first question, under either limb, is whether D was suffering from "a defect of reason from disease of the mind". If D was unaware of the nature and quality of his act for some other reason, he will usually be entitled to a simple acquittal on the ground that he lacked the necessary *mens rea*. Moreover the onus of proof will remain on the Crown, whereas it will shift to D once he tenders evidence of a defect of reason arising from disease of the mind. If D was unaware that his act was "wrong" for some other reason, this will generally not amount to a defence at all for neither ignorance of the law nor good motive normally affords a defence.

When a defendant puts his state of mind in issue, the question whether he has raised the defence of insanity is one of law for the judge. Whether D, or indeed his medical witnesses, would call the condition on which he relies "insanity", is immaterial. The expert witnesses may testify as to the factual nature of the condition but it is for the judge to say whether that is evidence of "a defect of reason, from disease of the mind", because, as will appear, these are legal, not medical, concepts.

In the leading case of *Sullivan*,[6] the defence to a charge of assault occasioning actual bodily harm was that D attacked P while recovering from a minor epileptic seizure and did not know what he was doing. The House of Lords held that the judge had rightly ruled that this raised the defence of insanity. D had then pleaded guilty to the charge, of which he was manifestly innocent, and his conviction was upheld.

i) *Disease of the mind.* Whether a particular condition amounts to a disease of the mind within the Rules is not a medical but a legal question to be decided in accordance with the ordinary rules of interpretation.[7] It seems that any disease which produces a malfunctioning of the mind is a disease of

5. 10 Cl & F at 210.
6. [1984] AC 156, [1983] 2 All ER 673, HL; **SHC 199**.
7. *Kemp* [1957] 1 QB 399 at 406, [1956] 3 All ER 249 at 254, per Devlin J, approved by Lord Denning in *Bratty*, below, p. 189.

the mind. It need not be a disease of the brain. Arteriosclerosis, a tumour on the brain, epilepsy, diabetes, all physical diseases, may amount in law to a disease of the mind if they produce the relevant malfunction. A malfunctioning of the mind is not a disease of the mind when it is caused by some external factor – a blow on the head causing concussion, the consumption of alcohol or drugs, or the administration of an anaesthetic. Contrary to the dictum of Devlin J in *Kemp*,[8] it is clear that the law considers not only the state of mind in which D was, but how it came about. Devlin J thought that the object of the inclusion of the words "disease of the mind" was to exclude "defects of reason caused simply by brutish stupidity without rational power"; but it seems the words exclude more than that. In *Quick*[9] D who had inflicted actual bodily harm called medical evidence to show that he was a diabetic and that he was suffering from hypoglycaemia and was unaware of what he was doing. Bridge J ruled that he had raised a defence of insanity, whereupon D pleaded guilty. On appeal it was held that the alleged mental condition was caused not by D's diabetes but by his use of insulin prescribed by the doctor. This was an external factor and the defence of automatism should have been left to the jury. If the condition had been caused by the diabetes then it would seem that the defence would have been insanity.

In *Kemp* D made an entirely motiveless and irrational attack on his wife with a hammer. He was charged with causing grievous bodily harm to her with intent to murder her. It appeared that he suffered from arteriosclerosis which caused a congestion of blood in his brain. As a result he suffered a temporary lapse of consciousness during which he made the attack. It was conceded that D did not know the nature and quality of his act and that he suffered from a defect of reason but it was argued on his behalf that this arose, not from any mental disease, but from a purely physical one. It was argued that, if a physical disease caused the brain cells to degenerate (as in time, it might), then it would be a disease of the mind; but until it did so, it was said, this temporary interference with the working of the brain was like a concussion or something of that sort and not a disease of the mind. Devlin J rejected this argument and held that D was suffering from a disease of the mind. He said:[10]

"The law is not concerned with the brain but with the mind, in the sense that 'mind' is ordinarily used, the mental faculties of reason, memory and understanding. If one reads for 'disease of the mind' 'disease of the brain,' it would follow that in many cases pleas of insanity would not be established because it could not be proved that the brain had been affected in any way, either by degeneration of the cells or in any other way. In my judgment the condition of the brain is irrelevant and so is the question of whether the condition of the mind is curable or incurable, transitory or permanent."

8. [1957] 1 QB 399 at 407, **SHC 191**.
9. [1973] QB 910, [1973] 3 All ER 347, [1973] Crim LR 434 and commentary; **SHC 175**.
10. [1957] 1 QB at 407, [1956] 3 All ER at 253.

In the earlier case of *Charlson*[11] where the evidence was that D was "acting as an automaton without any real knowledge of what he was doing" as a result of a cerebral tumour, Barry J directed the jury to acquit if the defence might reasonably be true. Devlin J distinguished *Charlson* on the ground that there the doctors were agreed that D was not suffering from a mental disease. As this is a question of law the distinction seems unsound[12] and in *Bratty*[13] Lord Denning approved *Kemp* and disagreed with *Charlson*. Lord Denning put forward his own view of a disease of the mind:

"it seems to me that any mental disorder which has manifested itself in violence and is prone to recur is a disease of the mind. At any rate it is the sort of disease for which a person should be detained in hospital rather than be given an unqualified acquittal."

Quick casts some doubt on this dictum. The definition might fit a diabetic, but "no mental hospital would admit a diabetic merely because he had a low blood sugar reaction", and it might be felt to be "an affront to common sense" to regard such a person as insane; yet the Court saw the weakness of the argument, agreeing with Devlin J that the disease might be "curable or incurable ... transitory or permanent"; and the fact that the Home Secretary might have a difficult problem of disposal did not affect the matter. Lord Denning's dictum has also been criticised on the ground that it is tautologous and that a disease of the mind may manifest itself in wrongful acts other than violence, such as theft.[14]

Cases in other jurisdictions have raised the question whether a "dissociative state" resulting from a "psychological blow" amounts to insane or non-insane automatism. In *Rabey*[15] D, a student who had become infatuated by a girl, P, discovered that P did not regard him particularly highly and reacted by hitting her on the head with a rock that he had taken from a geology laboratory. He was acquitted of causing bodily harm with intent on the ground of automatism. The trial judge accepted that D was in a dissociative state consequent upon the psychological blow of his rejection, which, he held, was an external factor, analogous to a blow to the skull, where the skull is thin, causing concussion. The Ontario Court of Appeal allowed the prosecution's appeal and ordered a new trial. A further appeal to the Supreme Court of Canada was dismissed. That court approved the judgment of Martin J, who took the view that "the ordinary stresses and disappointments of life which are the common lot of mankind do not constitute an external cause ...".[16] The exceptional effect which this ordinary event had on D "must be considered as having its source primarily in the [D's] psychological or emotional make-up". Notwithstanding the powerful dissent by Dickson J, it is submitted that this is right and

11. [1955] 1 All ER 859, [1955] 1 WLR 317.
12. A similar argument was rejected in *Sullivan* [1983] 2 All ER 673 at 677. The nomenclature adopted by the medical profession may change but the meaning of "disease of the mind" in the Rules remains unchanged.
13. *Bratty v A-G for Northern Ireland* [1963] AC 386 at 410–412, [1961] 3 All ER 523 at 533–534, HL; **SHC 180**.
14. Walker, *Crime and Insanity in England*, 117.
15. (1977) 37 CCC (2d) 461, affirming [1980] SCR 513, 54 CCC (2d) 1. See also *Parnerkar* [1974] SCR 449, (1973) 10 CCC (2d) 253 and cases discussed by Mackay in [1980] Crim LR 350.
16. (1980) 54 CCC (2d) at p. 7.

that in such a case, if the evidence as to the dissociative state is accepted at all,[17] it should be treated as evidence of insanity. Once the judge has so categorised the defence, the onus of proving on a balance of probabilities that he was in a dissociative state is on D. If he and his medical witnesses are to be believed, he was not guilty, but he is a highly dangerous person. Who is to say that the next ordinary stress of life will not lead him unconsciously to wield a deadly weapon?[18] Martin J left open the question of the effect of an extraordinary event of such severity that it might reasonably be expected to cause a dissociative state in the average person. This, it is submitted, is a case of non-insane automatism because D has done nothing to show that he is any more dangerous to others than anyone else; and he should be simply acquitted.

"External" and "internal" factors. The distinction between external causes, which may give rise to a defence of non-insane automatism, and internal factors which can only give rise to a defence of insanity has been subjected to criticism.[19] There is however some reason in it, in that the internal factor will usually be a continuing condition which may cause a recurrence of the prohibited conduct whereas the external factor – the blow on the head, the injection, the inhalation of toxic fumes,[20] etc. will usually have a transitory effect. Of course, the blow on the head may inflict permanent damage, in which case that damage will be an internal factor, giving rise to a defence of insanity. Difficult to reconcile with the theory, however, is the opinion[1] that sleep-walking is non-insane automatism. This appears clearly to arise from an internal factor and, prima facie, presents a danger of recurrence.

The reach of the M'Naghten rules in extending to epileptics and diabetics is wide, but all the cases involve apparently purposive conduct and it may be that the Rules should be limited to cases of that type. A convulsive movement of a person in an epileptic fit may result in injury to person or property but it would seem absurd either to convict the epileptic or hold him to be insane. In *Bratty v A-G for Northern Ireland,*[2] D took off a girl's stocking and strangled her with it. There was medical evidence that he was suffering from psychomotor epilepsy which might have prevented him from knowing the nature and quality of his act. It was held to be evidence of insanity. This is very far removed from a convulsive movement of the body. It is a complex operation which has every appearance of being controlled by the brain. Whether or not D could have prevented himself from acting in this way, he appears to be a very dangerous person and, in the absence of some other form of protection for the public, a simple

---

17. Cf. the scepticism of Williams about the acceptance of the evidence of "overenthusiastic psychiatrists" in relation to the similar case of *Parnerkar* [1974] SCR 449, 10 CCC (2d) 253; TBCL (1st ed.) 612–613.
18. In fact, D's expert witness said D had no predisposition to dissociate; but the court, while bound to take account of medical evidence, may also take account of the facts of the case and apply its common sense to all the evidence.
19. See the dissent by Dickson J in *Rabey* (1981) 114 DLR (3d) 193; Mackay, "Non-Organic Automatism", [1980] Crim LR 350; Williams, TBCL, 671.
20. *Oakley* (1986) 24 CCC (3d) 351 at 362, per Martin JA.
1. *Bratty v A-G for Northern Ireland* [1963] AC 386, [1961] 3 All ER 523 at 535, per Lord Denning.
2. [1963] AC 386, [1961] 3 All ER 523.

verdict of acquittal seems inappropriate. Sullivan's conduct, like that of Kemp, Charlson, Quick and Rabey also seems to have been apparently purposive and, though he was less obviously a danger to the public than Bratty, his case may be indistinguishable in principle.

ii) *Disease of the mind in combination with other factors.* There are three types of factors which may prevent D from knowing the nature of his act.

    a) Those tending to an absolute acquittal, such as concussion, the taking of a *medically prescribed* drug or anaesthetic, and other "external" factors, including, in the case of crimes of "specific intent" only, intoxication arising from the voluntary taking of drink or drugs.

    b) Those tending to an acquittal on the ground of insanity – diseases of the mind.

    c) Those not amounting to a defence at all – in the case of crimes not requiring specific intent, intoxication arising from the voluntary taking of drink or drugs.

The various factors may operate consecutively or concurrently. There is little authority on the complex questions which may arise and such as there is does not seem well thought out. It is sufficient to demonstrate, however, that this is a practical and not merely an academic problem. The following answers are necessarily somewhat speculative.

Consecutive operation. (i) Intoxication causes automatism. D, because he is drunk, sustains concussion and does the allegedly criminal act in a state of automatism resulting from the concussion. In *Stripp*[3] the Court of Appeal thought, *obiter*, that D should be acquitted on the ground of automatism. That seems right – the intoxication is too remote from the act. (ii) Automatism causes intoxication. D having sustained concussion, drinks a bottle of vodka under the impression that it is water and does the allegedly criminal act, not knowing what he is doing because he is intoxicated. Since the intoxication is involuntary, both causes lead to an acquittal and D must be acquitted. (iii) Intoxication causes insanity. This is dealt with in *Beard*[4] which settles that insanity caused by drink operates in the same manner as insanity arising from any other cause. (iv) Insanity causes intoxication or automatism. "Insanity" in the *M'Naghten* sense can strictly have no application here because it applies only in relation to a particular criminal act, whereas getting drunk or causing oneself concussion is probably not a criminal act at all and certainly not the criminal act we are concerned with. However, D may not know the nature and quality of the act which causes the condition. The intoxication is involuntary, so D should be acquitted. In so far as the automatism is caused by the insanity, it is the result of an internal cause which looks as if the net result should be, not guilty on the ground of insanity; but it would seem odd that, if D's insanity leads him to drink excessively, he should be acquitted absolutely whereas if it takes the form of banging his head against a wall until he does not know what he is

---

3. (1979) 69 Cr App Rep 318, 323, CA. No foundation for automatism was laid.
4. Below, p. 210.

doing he should be subject to restraint. Policy may be best served by a verdict of not guilty on the ground of insanity in both cases. (v) Automatism causes insanity. It is difficult to envisage a convincing case but, if it should arise, probably the answer should be as in the case where automatism and insanity are concurrent causes and for the same reason.[5]

Concurrent operation. (i) Intoxication and automatism. Intoxication is no defence to a charge of a crime not requiring specific intent because this is thought necessary for the protection of the public. If the public needs protection against one whose condition is wholly brought about by intoxication, it also needs protection against one whose similar condition is partially so brought about. D should be found guilty of the offence. (ii) Intoxication and insanity. D does not know what he is doing, partly because of a disease of the mind and partly because he is drunk. The choice is (or should be) between a verdict of not guilty on the ground of insanity and, in a crime not requiring specific intent, one of guilty. This seems to have been the situation in *Burns*.[6] D was charged with indecent assault, a crime not requiring specific intent. He may not have been aware of what he was doing, partly because of brain damage and partly because of drink and drugs taken, otherwise than on prescription. The court accepted that, if D did not know what he was doing, he was entitled to an absolute acquittal. It is difficult to see how this can be right, since neither of the concurrent causes entitled D to be absolutely acquitted.[7] Analogy with *Beard* might suggest that the right verdict is not guilty on the ground of insanity but the House of Lords in *A-G for Northern Ireland v Gallagher*[8] thought otherwise, unless the alcohol caused some quite different type of disease, such as delirium tremens.[9] (iii) Automatism and insanity. The choice is between a verdict of acquittal and one of not guilty on the ground of insanity. Since D has been put in jeopardy only because his mental state has been affected by an external factor (not being merely one of the ordinary stresses and disappointments of life[10]), a misfortune, the verdict of acquittal seems more appropriate.[11]

iii) *Defect of reason.* The disease of the mind must have given rise to a defect of reason. It seems that the powers of reasoning must be impaired and that a mere failure to use powers of reasoning which one has is not within the Rules. When D claimed that she had taken articles from a supermarket without paying for them because of absentmindedness resulting from depression, it was held that, even if she was suffering from a

---

5. Below.
6. (1973) 58 Cr App Rep 364, [1975] Crim LR 155 and commentary, below, p. 213.
7. The court took account of the possibility that D might not have appreciated the effect which the drink and drunks might have; but it seems unlikely that such unawareness will displace the general rule excluding a defence of intoxication in crimes not requiring specific intent.
8. [1963] AC 349, [1961] 3 All ER 299, below, p. 219. (Effect of drink on a psychopath.)
9. Combination of mental abnormality and drink resulting in a substantial impairment of mental responsibility does not amount to a defence of diminished responsibility: *Fenton*, below, p. 205.
10. *Rabey*, above, p. 188.
11. Above, p. 189.

disease of the mind, she had not raised the defence of insanity but was simply denying that she had *mens rea*.[12]

iv) *The nature and quality of his act*. The phrase "nature and quality of his act" refers to the physical nature and quality of the act and not to its moral or legal quality.[13] Illustrations given by leading writers are:

"A kills B under an insane delusion that he is breaking a jar"[14]

and

"the madman who cut a woman's throat under the idea that he was cutting a loaf of bread."[15]

Of course, a man who was under such a delusion as these, apart altogether from insanity, could never be convicted of murder,[16] simply because he had no *mens rea*. The important practical difference, however, is that, if the delusion arose from a disease of the mind, he will be liable to be indefinitely detained in a special hospital whereas, if it arose from some other cause, he will go entirely free. A person whose acts are involuntary because he is unconscious does not "know the nature and quality of his act".[17]

v) *Knowledge that the act is wrong*. The question is not whether the accused is able to distinguish between right and wrong in general, but whether he was able to appreciate the wrongness of the particular act he was doing at the particular time. It has always been clear that if D knew his act was contrary to law, he knew it was "wrong" for this purpose. Thus in their first answer the judges in *M'Naghten's* case said:[18]

". . . notwithstanding the party accused did the act complained of with a view, under the influence of insane delusion, of redressing or revenging some supposed grievance or injury, or of producing some public benefit, he is nevertheless punishable, according to the nature of the crime committed, if he knew at the time of committing such crime that he was acting contrary to law; by which expression we understand your lordships to mean the law of the land."

Even if D did not know his act was contrary to law, he was still liable if he knew that it was wrong "according to the ordinary standard adopted by reasonable men".[19] The fact that the accused thought his act was right was irrelevant if he knew that people generally considered it wrong. This again seems to be supported by the Rules:[20]

"If the question were to be put as to the knowledge of the accused solely and exclusively with reference to the law of the land, it might tend to confound the jury, by inducing them to believe that an actual knowledge of the law of the land was essential to lead to a conviction: whereas the law is administered upon the principle that everyone must be taken

12. *Clarke* [1972] 1 All ER 219; **SHC 190**.
13. *Codère* (1916) 12 Cr App Rep 21.
14. Stephen, *Digest* (8th ed.), 6.
15. Kenny, *Outlines*, 76.
16. Manslaughter, however, might be another matter.
17. *Sullivan* [1983] 2 All ER 673 at 678, HL.
18. 10 Cl & F at 209.
19. *Codère* (1916) 12 Cr App Rep 21 at 27.
20. 10 Cl & F at 210.

conclusively to know it, without proof that he does know it. If the accused was conscious that the act was one which he ought not to do, and if that act was at the same time contrary to the law of the land, he is punishable."

A modern case, however suggests that the courts are concerned only with the accused's knowledge of legal wrongness.

In *Windle*,[1] D, unhappily married to a woman, P, who was always speaking of committing suicide and who, according to medical evidence at the trial, was certifiably insane, killed P by the administration of 100 aspirins. He then gave himself up to the police, saying, "I suppose they will hang me for this." A medical witness for the defence said that D was suffering from a form of communicated insanity known as *folie à deux*. Rebutting medical evidence was called, but the doctors on both sides agreed that he knew he was doing an act which the law forbade. Devlin J thereupon withdrew the issue from the jury. So far the decision accords perfectly with the law as stated above but, in the Court of Criminal Appeal, Lord Goddard CJ, in upholding the conviction, said:[2]

"Courts of law can only distinguish between that which is in accordance with the law and that which is contrary to law. ... The law cannot embark on the question and it would be an unfortunate thing if it were left to juries to consider whether some particular act was morally right or wrong. The test must be whether it is contrary to law. ...

In the opinion of the court there is no doubt that in the M'Naghten Rules 'wrong' means contrary to law and not 'wrong' according to the opinion of one man or of a number of people on the question whether a particular act might or might not be justified."

It is thought that *Windle*[3] is in accordance with authority in rejecting the arguments of the defence that D should be acquitted if, knowing his act to be against the law, he also believed it to be morally right. But the effect of the *obiter dictum* – it was no more than that – that "wrong" means simply "legally wrong", would seem to be to widen the defence by making it available to a man who knows that his act is morally wrong but, owing to disease of the mind, fails to appreciate that it is also legally wrong. Such a case was not before the court and seems unlikely to arise.

The High Court of Australia has refused to follow *Windle*. In *Stapleton v R*[4] they made a detailed examination of the English law, before and after *M'Naghten* and came to the conclusion that *Windle* was wrongly decided. Their view was that if D believed his act to be right according to the ordinary standard of reasonable men he was entitled to be acquitted even if he knew it to be legally wrong. This would extend the scope of the defence, not only beyond what was laid down in *Windle*, but beyond what the law was believed to be before that case. While such an extension of the law may

1. [1952] 2 QB 826, [1952] 2 All ER 1; **SHC 190**.
2. [1952] 2 QB 826 at 833, 834, [1952] 2 All ER 1 at 1, 2.
3. Above, footnote 1.
4. (1952) 86 CLR 358; see also *Weise* [1969] VR 953, especially at 960 et seq., per Barry J.

be desirable, it is difficult to reconcile with the M'Naghten Rules and to justify on the authorities.[5] It is unlikely to be followed by the courts in England.

vi) *Insane delusions.* The judges were asked in *M'Naghten's* case:

"If a person under an insane delusion as to existing facts commits an offence in consequence thereof, is he thereby excused?"

They replied:[6]

"... the answer must, of course, depend on the nature of the delusion: but making the same assumption as we did before, namely, that he labours under such partial delusion only, and is not in other respects insane, we think he must be considered in the same situation as to responsibility as if the facts with respect to which the delusion exists were real. For example, if under the influence of his delusion he supposes another man to be in the act of attempting to take away his life, and he kills that man, as he supposes, in self-defence, he would be exempt from punishment. If his delusion was that the deceased had inflicted a serious injury to his character and fortune, and he killed him in revenge for such supposed injury, he would be liable to punishment."

This seems to add nothing to the earlier answers. The insane delusions that the judges had in mind seem to have been factual errors of the kind which prevent a man from knowing the nature and quality of his act or knowing it is wrong. The example given seems to fall within those rules.

The proposition that the insane person "must be considered in the same situation as to responsibility as if the facts with respect to which the delusion exists were real" must be treated with caution. It must always be remembered that there must be an actual *actus reus*, accompanied by the appropriate *mens rea*, for a conviction. Suppose that D strangles his wife's poodle under the insane delusion that it is her illegitimate child. If the supposed facts were real he would be guilty of murder – but that is plainly impossible as there is no *actus reus*.[7] Nor is there any crime in respect of the dog, for there is no *mens rea*. The rule seems merely to emphasise that delusions which do not prevent D from having *mens rea* will afford no defence. As Lord Hewart CJ rather crudely put it, "the mere fact that a man thinks he is John the Baptist does not entitle him to shoot his mother".[8] A case often discussed is that of a man who is under the insane delusion that he is obeying a divine command. Some American courts have held that such a belief affords a defence. Yet if the accused knows that his act is forbidden by law, it seems clear he is liable. Stephen certainly thought that this was so:[9]

---

5. *Stapleton v R* is discussed in a note by N. Morris (1953) 16 MLR 435, which is criticised by Montrose (1954) 17 MLR 383.

6. 10 Cl & F at 211; **SHC 188**.

7. Nor, notwithstanding *Shivpuri*, below, p. 304, should an insane delusion entail liability for an attempt.

8. Hewart, *Essays*, 224.

9. 2 HCL 160, n. 1.

"My own opinion is that if a special divine order were given to a man to commit murder, I should certainly hang him for it, unless I got a special divine order not to hang him."

vii) *Irresistible impulse.* It is recognised by psychiatrists that a man may know the nature and quality of an act, may even know that it is wrong, and yet perform it under an impulse that is almost or quite uncontrollable. Such a man has no defence under the Rules. The matter was considered in *Kopsch*:[10] D, according to his own admission, killed his uncle's wife. He said that he strangled her with his necktie at her own request. (If this was an insane declusion, it would not, of course, afford a defence under the rules stated above.) There was evidence that he had acted under the direction of his subconscious mind. Counsel argued that the judge should have directed the jury that a person under an impulse which he cannot control is not criminally responsible. This was described by Lord Hewart CJ as a

"fantastic theory . . . which if it were to become part of our criminal law, would be merely subversive."[11]

The judges have steadily opposed the admissibility of such a defence on the ground of the difficulty – or impossibility – of distinguishing between an impulse which proves irresistible because of insanity and one which is irresistible because of ordinary motives of greed, jealousy or revenge. The view has also been expressed that the harder an impulse is to resist, the greater is the need for a deterrent.[12]

The law does not recognise irresistible impulse even as a symptom from which a jury might deduce insanity within the meaning of the Rules.[13] If, however, medical evidence were tendered in a particular case that the uncontrollable impulse, to which the accused in that case had allegedly been subject, was a symptom that he did not know his act was wrong, it would be open to the jury to act on that evidence.[14] But it is not permissible for a judge to make use in one case of medical knowledge which he may have acquired from the evidence in another, in his direction to the jury.[15]

Although the M'Naghten Rules remain unaltered a partial defence of irresistible impulse has, as will appear below,[16] now been admitted into the law through the new defence of diminished responsibility.

viii) *Burden of proof.* The M'Naghten Rules laid down that

"every man is presumed to be sane, and to possess a sufficient degree of reason to be responsible for his crimes, until the contrary be proved to [the jury's] satisfaction; and that to establish a defence on the ground of insanity, it must be clearly proved, etc."[17]

10. (1925) 19 Cr App Rep 50, CCA. See also *True* (1922) 16 Cr App Rep 164; *Sodeman* [1936] 2 All ER 1138, PC.
11. (1925) 19 Cr App Rep 50 at 51.
12. As a Canadian judge, Riddell J, put it: "If you cannot resist an impulse in any other way, we will hang a rope in front of your eyes, and perhaps that will help": *Creighton* (1909) 14 CCC 349.
13. *A-G for State of South Australia v Brown* [1960] AC 432, [1960] 1 All ER 734, PC.
14. Ibid. See also *Sodeman* (1936) 55 CLR 192 at 203.
15. [1960] AC 432 at 449.
16. See p. 204.
17. 10 Cl & F at 210.

It seems from these words that the judges were intending to put the burden of proof squarely on the accused, and so it has always been subsequently assumed.[18] Insanity is stated to be the one exception at common law to the rule that it is the duty of the prosecution to prove the prisoner's guilt in all particulars.[19] He does not have to satisfy that heavy onus of proof beyond reasonable doubt which rests on the prosecution but is entitled to a verdict in his favour if he proves his case on a balance of probabilities, the standard which rests on the plaintiff in a civil action. If the jury think it is more likely than not that he is insane within the meaning of the Rules, then he is entitled to their verdict.

When, however, consideration is given to what has to be proved to establish insanity under the first limb of the Rules, there is an apparent conflict with the general rule requiring the prosecution to prove *mens rea*. This requires proof that the accused was either intentional or reckless with respect to all those consequences and circumstances of his act which constitute the *actus reus* of the crime with which he is charged. But this, in effect, is to prove that the accused *did* know the nature and quality of his act. The general rule, therefore, says that the prosecution must prove these facts; the special rule relating to insanity says that the defence must disprove them. Williams argues[20] that the only burden on the accused is the "evidential" one of introducing sufficient evidence to raise a reasonable doubt in the jury's minds; and that the burden of *proof* is on the prosecution. This solution appears to be the only way of resolving the inconsistency; but, as yet, not even the difficulty, let alone the suggested solution, has been judicially recognised in England.[1]

This problem does not arise when the accused's defence takes the form that he did not know that his act was wrong. Here he is setting up the existence of facts which are quite outside the prosecution's case and there is no inconsistency in putting the onus on the accused. It is very strange that the onus of proof should be on the Crown if the defence is based on the first limb of the Rules and on the accused if it should be on the second. Yet the authorities[2] seem clearly to establish that the onus in the case of the second limb is on the accused. It is not possible to argue that the courts really meant the evidential burden, for they have said very clearly that the burden is one of proof "on balance of probabilities", the same standard that the plaintiff in a civil action must satisfy. Whatever may be the position regarding the first limb of the defence then, it seems clear that, under the second, the onus is on the accused.

The anomaly is emphasised by the decision of the House of Lords in *Bratty v A-G for Northern Ireland*[3] that, where the defence is automatism arising otherwise than through a disease of the mind, the burden of proof is on the prosecution. It is difficult to see why a man whose alleged disability

18. *Stokes* (1848) 3 Car & Kir 185; *Layton* (1849) 4 Cox CC 149; *Smith* (1910) 6 Cr App Rep 19; *Coelho* (1914) 30 TLR 535; *Bratty v A-G for Northern Ireland* [1963] AC 386, [1961] 3 All ER 523.
19. *Woolmington v Director of Public Prosecutions* [1935] AC 462; **SHC 39**.
20. CLGP, p. 165.
1. Cf., however, *Cottle* [1958] NZLR 999 at 1019 per North J.
2. *Sodeman v R* [1936] 2 All ER 1138: *Carr-Briant* [1943] KB 607, [1943] 2 All ER 156.
3. [1963] AC 386, [1961] 3 All ER 523; **SHC 180**.

arises from a disease of the mind should be convicted whereas one whose alleged disability arises from some other cause, would, in exactly the same circumstances, be acquitted.[4]

ix) *The special verdict of insanity and the right of appeal.* Where a defence under the M'Naghten Rules was established, the correct verdict until 1964 was

"guilty of the act or omission charged but insane, so as not to be responsible, according to law, for his actions at the time when the act was done or the omission made."

Despite the form of the verdict it was well settled that it was one of acquittal and no appeal lay from the finding either of guilty of doing the act charged, or of insanity.[5]

The anomalous form of the "guilty but insane" verdict had been repeatedly criticised and, by s. 1 of the Criminal Procedure (Insanity) Act 1964, it is provided that it shall be replaced by a special verdict that "the accused is not guilty by reason of insanity". Although it may seem, at first sight, highly illogical to give the accused a right of appeal from an acquittal, this too was a highly desirable reform which was effected by the 1964 Act. If it were the case that a special verdict of insanity could be found only where D himself had so pleaded, it would be reasonable that there should be no appeal; but this was not the case. Thus it will be recalled that in *Kemp*[6] D's contention was that he should be entirely acquitted, but it was held that the medical evidence established insanity within the M'Naghten Rules. The issue was decided against D, yet he had no right of appeal. A similar position arose where, after the Homicide Act, 1957, D raised the defence of diminished responsibility and the prosecution were thereupon allowed to introduce evidence of insanity within the M'Naghten Rules.[7] For these reasons, a right of appeal to the Court of Appeal and the House of Lords is provided by s. 12 of the Criminal Appeal Act 1968, subject to the same conditions as apply in criminal appeals generally. The right of appeal is not limited to the case where the issue is decided against D's contention in the court below. It is now possible for D to appeal against the finding (no longer express but now implicit in the verdict) that he did the act or against the finding that he was insane when he did so.

x) *Function of the jury.* It has been laid down for defences of both insanity and diminished responsibility that:[8]

".... it is for the jury and not for medical men of whatever eminence to determine the issue. Unless and until Parliament ordains that this

---

4. The Butler proposals on onus of proof appear below, p. 200.
5. *Felstead v R* [1914] AC 534; *Duke* [1963] 1 QB 120, [1961] 3 All ER 737.
6. Above, p. 187.
7. Below, p. 201.
8. *Rivett* (1950) 34 Cr App Rep 87 at 94; *Latham* [1965] Crim LR 434; *Walton v R* [1978] 1 All ER 542, [1977] 3 WLR 902; [1977] Crim LR 747, PC.

question is to be determined by a panel of medical men, it is to a jury, after a proper direction by a judge, that by the law of this country the decision is to be entrusted."

The jury must, however, act on the evidence; so that, if the medical evidence is all one way (and in favour of the accused) and there is nothing in the facts or surrounding circumstances which could lead to a contrary conclusion, then a verdict against the medical evidence will be upset.[9] If there are facts which, in the opinion of the court, justify the jury in coming to a different conclusion from the experts then their verdict will be upheld. The jury hardly seems an appropriate body to decide betweeen conflicting experts, still less to reject their united opinion on a matter of this sort.

Probably a jury may not find a defendant to be insane in the absence of some medical evidence to that effect.[10]

xi) *Proposals for reform.* Almost from the moment of their formulation the Rules have been subjected to vigorous criticism, primarily by doctors, but also by lawyers. The Rules, being based on outdated psychological views, are too narrow, it is said, and exclude many persons who ought not to be held responsible. They are concerned only with defects of reason and take no account of emotional or volitional factors whereas modern medical science is unwilling to divide the mind into separate compartments and to consider the intellect apart from the emotions and the will. There is clearly something gravely wrong when, as in *Quick, Clarke* and *Sullivan,*[11] a person who, on the evidence, is not guilty of an offence will plead guilty to it rather than submit to a verdict of not guilty on the ground of insanity. The propriety of accepting such a plea seems doubtful but it was not questioned by the Court of Appeal in *Sullivan* and the House of Lords left the matter open[12] while affirming the appellant's conviction of a crime of which he was not guilty. The problem would be alleviated by abandoning the term "insanity", and giving the courts broad powers of disposal on a verdict of not guilty on grounds of mental disorder, removing the liability to indefinite detention and much of the stigma. In 1923 a committee under the chairmanship of Lord Atkin recommended that a prisoner should not be held responsible.

"when the act is committed under an impulse which the prisoner was by mental disease in substance deprived of any power to resist."[13]

The recommendation was not implemented. In 1953 the Royal Commission on Capital Punishment[14] made much more far-reaching proposals. They thought that the question of responsibility is not primarily a matter of law or of medicine, but of morals and, therefore, most appropriately

9. *Matheson* (1958) 42 Cr App Rep 145; *Bailey* [1961] Crim LR 828.
10. Cf. *Dix*, below, p. 202.
11. Above, pp. 187, 192 and 186, respectively.
12. [1983] 2 All ER 673 at 676.
13. Cmd. 2005.
14. Cmd. 8932.

decided by a jury of ordinary men and women. They thought that the best course would be to abrogate the rules altogether and –

> "leave the jury to determine whether at the time of the act the accused was suffering from disease of the mind (or mental deficiency) to such a degree that he ought not be held responsible."[15]

This meant abandoning the assumption that it is necessary to have a rule of law defining the relation of insanity to criminal responsibility; but the Commission thought this assumption had broken down in practice anyway.[16] As an alternative, which they thought less satisfactory but better than leaving the Rules unchanged, the Commission recommended that a third limb be added to the Rules: that the accused "was incapable of preventing himself from committing it . . ."[17]

The Butler Committee adopts a new approach.[18] The defence proposed would have two limbs. A special verdict of "not guilty on evidence of mental disorder" would be given where:

i) evidence is given of mental disorder for the purpose of negativing *mens rea* and the jury find that D did the act but did not have *mens rea*. Any form of mental disorder would suffice; but transient states, not related to other forms of mental disorder and arising from the administration, maladministration or non-administration[19] of alcohol or drugs or from physical injury, would be expressly excluded; and

ii) at the time of the act or omission charged D was suffering from severe mental illness or severe subnormality. Severe subnormality was then[20] defined in s. 4(2) of the Mental Health Act 1959 as ". . . a state of arrested or incomplete development of mind which includes subnormality of intelligence and is of such a nature or degree that the patient is incapable of living an independent life or of guarding himself against serious exploitation, or will be so incapable when of an age to do so." There is at present no statutory definition of severe mental illness and the Committee proposes one:

> "A mental illness is severe when it has one or more of the following characteristics:
>
> a) Lasting impairment of intellectual functions shown by failure of memory, orientation, comprehension and learning capacity.

---

15. Ibid., para. 333. Cf. Walker's criticism, op. cit. at 110–111: "By what criterion could one tell whether this or that case 'ought' to have been included? Could the criterion be expressed in words, or was it ineffable?"

16. The Commission was impressed by Lord Cooper's view that "However much you charge a jury as to the M'Naghten Rules or any other test, the question they would put to themselves when they retire is – 'Is this man mad or is he not?'"; Report, para. 322.

17. Cmd. 2005.

18. Paras. 18.14–18.36. The Butler proposals are incorporated in the draft Criminal Code, cl. 38 (see Law Com. No. 143, Ch. 12, and Griew "Let's Implement Butler on Mental Disorder and Crime", (1984) 37 CLP 47).

19. Cf. *Quick*, above, p. 187.

20. The Mental Health Act 1983, s. 1(1) replaces the concepts of subnormality and severe subnormality with those of mental impairment and severe mental impairment. "Severe mental impairment" means "a state of arrested or incomplete development of mind which includes severe impairment of intelligence and social functioning and is associated with abnormally aggressive or seriously irresponsible conduct on the part of the person concerned." But the draft Code retains the 1959 Act definition for this purpose: Law Com No. 143, para. 12–8.

b) Lasting alteration of mood of such degree as to give rise to delusional appraisal of the patient's situation, his past or his future, or that of others, or to lack of any appraisal.

c) Delusional beliefs, persecutory, jealous or grandiose.

d) Abnormal perception associated with delusional misinterpretation of events.

e) Thinking so disordered as to prevent reasonable appraisal of the patient's situation or reasonable communication with others."

The second limb of the proposals involves a major change of principle in that no causal connection between the abnormality and the commission of the criminal act need be proved. The committee think that the mental conditions described are of such severity that causal connection can safely be presumed. Under the proposal, D's belief that he was John the Baptist,[1] presumably a grandiose delusional belief, *would* be a defence to a charge of murdering his mother. It is perhaps not obvious that D should have a defence to a charge of robbing a bank or reckless driving because he had a jealous delusional belief that his wife was committing adultery. Of course, the belief must spring from mental illness and not a mere mistake. Might the question, what is a mental illness? be as difficult as the question, what is a disease of the mind?

The committee proposes, in relation to the first limb of the proposed rule, that the onus of proving *mens rea* should always be on the Crown. If the Crown fails to prove this, D must be acquitted; but there remains the choice between an absolute acquittal or a special verdict. D should be entitled to an absolute acquittal unless the jury are satisfied on a balance of probabilities that he was mentally disordered. The second limb requires the jury to choose between conviction and a special verdict and, in order to avoid confusing the jury, it is suggested that the same rule should apply – the jury (who, *ex hypothesi*, are now satisfied beyond reasonable doubt that D had *mens rea*) should be directed to convict unless satisfied on a balance of probabilities that D was suffering from severe mental illness or severe subnormality.[2]

The M'Naghten Rules still have their defenders and the case for them has been most cogently put by Lord Devlin:

"As it is a matter of theory, I think there is something logical – it may be astringently logical, but it is logical – in selecting as the test of responsibility to the law, reason and reason alone. It is reason which makes a man responsible to the law. It is reason which gives him sovereignty over animate and inanimate things. It is what distinguishes him from the animals, which emotional disorder does not; it is what makes him man; it is what makes him subject to the law. So it is fitting that nothing other than a defect of reason should give complete absolution."[3]

1. Above, p. 194.
2. Para. 18.39.
3. "Mental Abnormality and the Criminal Law" in *Changing Legal Objectives* (Ed. R. St J. MacDonald, Toronto, 1963) 71 at 85. Cf. A. F. Goldstein, *The Insanity Defence* (1967).

3 Diminished Responsibility[4]

The Homicide Act 1957, s. 2, introduced into law a new defence to murder, known as "diminished responsibility", which entitles the accused not to be acquitted altogether, but to be found guilty only of manslaughter.[5] By s. 2 (2) the Act expressly puts the burden of proof on the defendant and it has been held that, as in the case of insanity, the standard of proof required is not beyond reasonable doubt but on a balance of probabilities.[6] Consideration of this defence is, strictly speaking, out of place here, for it is not a general defence, but applies only to murder. In practice, however, the scope of the new defence is almost the same as insanity, for the Rules themselves are rarely relied on outside murder cases. Except in murder, the prospect of indefinite and possibly life-long confinement in hospital is far worse than the ordinary punishment for the crime. Similarly it is reasonable to suppose that defendants generally will prefer a conviction for manslaughter to an "acquittal" on the ground of insanity. Since the new defence includes all cases which also fall within the M'Naghten Rules (as well as other cases where there was formerly no defence) it is clear that the importance of the Rules in practice is much diminished.

Where D, being charged with murder, raises the defence of diminished responsibility and the Crown have evidence that he is insane within the Rules, they may adduce or elicit evidence tending to show that this is so. This is now settled by the 1964 Act, s. 6, resolving a conflict in the cases. In *Bastian*[7] Donovan J had held that it was the *duty* of the prosecution to set up insanity in these circumstances. This was remarkable in that the Crown was now contending for what was, technically, a verdict of acquittal, while D was asserting that he should be convicted of manslaughter! It was, nevertheless realistic. Obviously, a verdict of guilty of manslaughter will often be preferable from D's point of view to a verdict of not guilty on the ground of insanity; but the latter verdict may well be in the public interest and it seems right that the Crown should be allowed to seek to achieve it. The other view was put by Lawton J in *Price*:[8]

"Prosecutors prosecute. They do not ask juries to return a verdict of acquittal."

But Lawton J's more formidable objection to the *Bastian* procedure was that it deprived D of his right of appeal if the jury accepted the Crown's and rejected his submissions. That objection being removed by the 1964 Act there was no other obstacle of substance to the ratification by that Act of the

---

4. Williams (1960), 1 Med Sci & L., 41; Wootton (1960) 76 LQR 224; Sparks (1964) 27 MLR 9; Walker, *Crime and Insanity in England*, 138–164; Dell, "Diminished Responsibility Reconsidered", [1982] Crim LR 809. Griew, "The Future of Diminished Responsibility" [1988] Crim LR 75.
5. The defence is borrowed from the law of Scotland, where it was a judicial creation, originating in the decision of Lord Deas in *HM Advocate v Dingwall* (1867) 5 Irv 466. See T. B. Smith, [1957] Crim LR 354 and Lord Keith [1959] Jur Rev 109.
6. *Dunbar* [1958] 1 QB 1, [1957] 2 All ER 737. Where the medical evidence of diminished responsibility is based on certain facts, it is for the defence to prove those facts by admissible evidence: *Ahmed Din* (1962) 46 Cr App Rep 239; *Bradshaw* (1985) 82 Cr App Rep 79, [1985] Crim LR 733 and commentary.
7. [1958] 1 All ER 568 n, [1958] 1 WLR 413.
8. [1963] 2 QB 1 at 7.

Bastian rule.[9] The Act also provides for the converse situation. Where D sets up insanity, the prosecution may contend that he was suffering only from diminished responsibility.[10] Where D relies on some other defence, such as provocation, and evidence of diminished responsibility emerges, it seems that the most the judge should do is to draw the attention of D's counsel to it.[11] Diminished responsibility is an "optional defence".

Thus, strangely, the roles of the prosecution and defence may be reversed, according to which of them is contending that the prisoner is insane. It seems clear in principle that the Crown must establish whichever contention it puts forward beyond reasonable doubt.[12] It must follow that D rebuts the Crown's case if he can raise a doubt.

The Act does not deal with the situation where D's abnormality of mind is put in issue otherwise than by pleading insanity or diminished responsibility – for example, by raising the defence of automatism. However, the Criminal Law Revision Committee[13] did not think that the limited provision in the Act should throw any doubt on the right of the prosecution to call evidence in cases such as *Kemp*.[14] The prosecution may not, however, lead evidence of D's insanity where the defence have not put the abnormality of D's mind in issue,[15] even though this course is desired by the defence. The position would seem to be that, where the defence rely on the abnormality of mind of any kind, it is open to the prosecution to allege, and to call evidence to prove, that the abnormality amounts to insanity or diminished responsibility. The prosecution should supply the defence with a copy of any statement or report which a prison medical officer may have made on that crime and should make him available as a defence witness.[16]

As with insanity,[17] the decision is to be made by the jury, not the medical experts. They may reject unanimous medical evidence that D is suffering from diminished responsibility if there is anything in the circumstances of the case to justify them in doing so. They may not, however, find that the defendant is suffering from diminished responsibility unless there is medical evidence of an abnormality arising from one of the causes specified in the parentheses in s. 2(1) of the Act.[18] An abnormality arising from some other cause will not suffice. So the word "disease" is important. Alcoholism is enough if it injures the brain, causing gross impairment of judgment and emotional responses, or causes the drinking to be involuntary.[19] Medical evidence is "a practical necessity if the defence is to begin to run at all".[20] Where no medical evidence is called, there will always be the suspicion that medical opinion has been sought and found unfavourable.

9. The Act does not, however, say that it is the *duty* of the Crown to seek to establish insanity.
10. It had been so held at common law by Elwes J in *Nott* (1958) 43 Cr App Rep 8.
11. *Campbell* (1987) 84 Cr App Rep 255 at 259–260; *Kooken* (1982) 74 Cr App Rep 30.
12. *Grant* [1960] Crim LR 424, per Paull J.
13. Cmnd. 2149, para. 41.
14. Above, p. 187.
15. *Dixon* [1961] 3 All ER 460 n, [1961] 1 WLR 337, per Jones J.
16. *Casey* (1947) 32 Cr App Rep 91, CCA. See Samuels, "Can the Prosecution allege that the Accused is Insane?" [1960] Crim LR 453, [1961] Crim LR 308.
17. Above, p. 197.
18. Below, p. 202. Cf. *Byrne* [1960] 2 QB 396 at 402; *Dix* (1981) 74 Cr App Rep 306 at 311; *Purdy* [1982] 2 NSWLR 964, Roden J diss.
19. *Tandy* (1987) Times, 23 December.
20. *Dix*, above at 311.

1 The Nature of the Defence

The Homicide Act 1957, s. 2, enacts:

"(1) Where a person kills or is a party to the killing of another, he shall
not be convicted of murder if he was suffering from such abnormality of mind (whether arising from a condition of arrested or
retarded development of mind or any inherent causes or induced by
disease or injury) as substantially impaired his mental responsibility for his acts and omissions in doing or being a party to the
killing.

(2) . . .

(3) A person who but for this section would be liable, whether as
principal or as accessory, to be convicted of murder shall be liable
instead to be convicted of manslaughter."

In early cases where the defence was raised, it was held that it was the
duty of the judge, in summing up, simply to read the section to the jury and
invite them to apply the tests stated therein without further explanation; it
was not for the judge to re-define the definition which had been laid down
by Parliament. In *Spriggs*[21] prosecuting counsel argued that D had a high
intelligence quotient and could not, therefore, be suffering from abnormality of mind. There was evidence that D lacked ability to control his
emotions and his counsel submitted that such a condition came within the
ambit of s. 2. In summing up the judge gave no ruling as to these
conflicting submissions but simply left it to the jury to say whether they
were satisfied that the accused came within the statutory definition. It was
held by the Court of Criminal Appeal that this was a proper course. Yet it is
a well established rule that the interpretation of statutes is exclusively a
matter for the court, and this course left the jury free to choose between the
alternative interpretations of the section. It now seems clear, however, that
the decision in *Spriggs* is wrong and the true rule is that it was the duty of
the judge to direct the jury as to the meaning to be attached to s. 2.

In *Byrne*[1] the trial judge directed the jury as to the meaning of s. 2 and
did so in substantially the same terms as those urged by counsel for the
prosecution in *Spriggs*; that is, that difficulty or even inability of an accused
person to exercise will-power to control his physical acts could not amount
to such abnormality of mind as substantially impaired his mental responsibilities. The Court of Criminal Appeal held that this was a wrong direction
and that Byrne's conviction of murder must be quashed. Obviously the
jury in *Spriggs* may have elected to follow just such a view of the law and it
seems to follow that Spriggs's conviction of murder should have been
quashed. Subsequently in *Terry*[2] the court expressly stated that

". . . in the light of [the interpretation that this court put on the section in
Byrne] it seems to this court that it would no longer be proper merely to
put the section before the jury but that a proper explanation of the terms
of the section as interpreted in *Byrne* ought to be put before the jury."[3]

21. [1958] 1 QB 270, [1958] 1 All ER 300. Cf. *Rolph* [1962] Qd R 262.
1. [1960] 2 QB 396, [1960] 3 All ER 1.
2. [1961] 2 QB 314, [1961] 2 All ER 569.
3. [1961] 2 All ER at 574.

The facts of *Byrne*[4] were that D strangled a young woman in a Y.W.C.A. hostel and, after her death, committed horrifying mutilations on her body. Evidence was tendered to the effect that D, from an early age, had been subject to perverted violent desires; that the impulse or urge of those desires was stronger than the normal impulse or urge of sex, so that D found it very difficult or, perhaps, impossible in some cases to resist putting the desire into practice and that the act of killing the girl was done under such an impulse or urge. The court held that it was wrong to say that these facts did not constitute evidence which would bring a case within the section. Lord Parker CJ said:[5]

"'Abnormality of mind', which has to be contrasted with the time-honoured expression in the M'Naghten Rules, 'defect of reason', means a state of mind so different from that of ordinary human beings that the reasonable man would term it abnormal. It appears to us to be wide enough to cover the mind's activities in all its aspects, not only the perception of physical acts and matters and the ability to form a rational judgment whether an act is right or wrong, but also the ability to exercise will-power to control physical acts in accordance with that rational judgment."

Thus, the defence of irresistible impulse is at last admitted into the law (but only of murder) by way of diminished responsibility. The difficulties of proof, which deterred the judges from allowing the defence under the M'Naghten Rules, remain:

"... the step between 'he did not resist his impulse' and 'he could not resist his impulse' is, as the evidence in this case shows, one which is incapable of scientific proof. A fortiori, there is no scientific measurement of the degree of difficulty which an abnormal person finds in controlling his impulses."

The only way to deal with the problem is for the jury to approach it "in a broad common-sense way".[6] They are entitled to take into account not only the medical evidence but also the acts or statements of the accused and his demeanour and other relevant material. Even when they are satisfied that D was suffering from abnormality of mind there remains the question whether the abnormality was such as substantially to impair his mental responsibility – a question of degree and essentially one for the jury.

It is not necessary that the impulse on which D acted should be found by the jury to be *irresistible*; it is sufficient that the difficulty which D experienced in controlling it (or, rather, *failing* to control it) was *substantially* greater than would be experienced in like circumstances by an ordinary man, not suffering from mental abnormality.[7] The impairment need not be total, but it must be more than trivial or minimal.[8] Where a doctor testified that an epileptic defendant could be "vulnerable to an impulsive tendency and therefore occasional impulsive acts", it was held

4. [1960] 2 QB 396, [1960] 3 All ER 1; **SHC 316**.
5. [1960] 2 QB 396 at 403, [1960] 3 All ER 1 at 4.
6. [1960] 2 QB at 404, [1960] 2 All ER 1 at 5, per Lord Parker CJ; *Walton v R* [1978] 1 All ER 542, [1977] 3 WLR 902, PC.
7. *Byrne*, above, p. 204; *Simcox* [1964] Crim LR 402; *Lloyd* [1967] 1 QB 175, [1966] 1 All ER 107n. But cf. Sparks, op. cit., at 16–19.
8. *Lloyd* [1967] 1 QB 175, [1966] 1 All ER 107n.

that there was no evidence of diminished responsibility because (inter alia) the witness had not said that the impulse would *substantially* impair responsibility.[9] The test appears to be one of moral responsibility. A man whose impulse is irresistible bears *no* moral responsibility for his act, for he has no choice; a man whose impulse is much more difficult to resist than that of an ordinary man bears a diminished degree of moral responsibility for his act.

The court has from time to time approved directions following those given in Scottish cases and which, in effect, tell the jury what must be proved is a mental state "bordering on, though not amounting to insanity"[10] or "not quite mad but a border-line case".[11] Care must be taken in giving such a direction to avoid any suggestion that "insanity" in this context bears the very narrow meaning of that form of insanity which is a defence under the M'Naghten Rules. If the word is used at all it must be used in "its broad popular sense".[12] A depressive illness may found diminished responsibility, although it is by no means on the borderline of insanity. To tell the jury in such a case that D must be on that borderline is a material misdirection.[13] In such a case, reference to insanity is best avoided altogether.

It is thought, moreover, that this direction is generally unsatisfactory. It follows Scottish directions but the Scottish law of irresponsibility on the ground of insanity appears to be wider than the M'Naghten Rules[14] and diminished responsibility is now interpreted more favourably to the accused in England than in Scotland.[15] Under English law, persons who are actually insane in the "broad popular sense" may well be outside the scope of the M'Naghten Rules and have to rely on diminished responsibility.

Where the evidence is that D was suffering from an abnormality of mind of which one of the causes is an excess of alcohol, the jury must perform the difficult task of ignoring the effect of the alcohol and determine whether the other factors were sufficient to amount to a substantial impairment. They must be asked: "Has D satisfied you on the balance of probabilities that, if he had not taken drink, (i) he would have killed as he in fact did? and (ii) he would have been under diminished responsibility when he did so?"[16] If it was the drink which caused him to kill, he cannot rely on diminished responsibility. But, if an alcoholic's craving for drink is proved to be irresistible, the resulting abnormality at the time of the killing may be a defence.[17]

2 The Effect of the Introduction of Diminished Responsibility
Diminished responsibility has been pleaded with success in cases where one would have thought there was no chance of a defence of insanity

9. *Campbell* (1987) 84 Cr App Rep 255 at 259.
10. *HM Advocate v Braithwaite* 1945 JC 55, per Lord Cooper.
11. *Spriggs* [1958] 1 QB 270 at 276, [1958] 1 All ER 300 at 304, per Lord Goddard CJ.
12. *Rose v R* [1961] AC 496, [1961] 1 All ER 859.
13. *Seers* (1984) 79 Cr App Rep 261, CA, following the remarks of the Privy Council in *Rose v R* [1961] AC 496, [1961] 1 All ER 859.
14. Cf. T. B. Smith, *The United Kingdom; The Development of Its Laws and Constitution*, 719.
15. Walker, op. cit., 155–156.
16. *Atkinson* [1985] Crim LR 314, approving the commentary on *Gittens* [1984] QB 698, [1984] 3 All ER 252, in [1984] Crim LR 553 at 554.
17. *Tandy* (1987) Times, 23 December.

succeeding – mercy killers, deserted spouses or disappointed lovers who killed while in a state of depression, persons with chronic anxiety states, and so on.[18] It is surprising that there has been no spectacular increase in the number of persons escaping conviction for murder on the ground of their mental abnormality. In fact, the proportion of persons committed for trial for murder who escape conviction on the ground of their mental abnormality has remained much the same since the Homicide Act as it was before. The proportion found insane on arraignment and the proportion acquitted on the ground of insanity have sharply declined. This suggests that persons who were formerly found insane on arraignment or acquitted on the ground of insanity now plead diminished responsibility instead; and that only a very few persons escape conviction who would not have done so before 1957.[19] The difference is that instead of being compelled to send the mentally abnormal person to a mental hospital, the court may sentence him to imprisonment, put him on probation or make a hospital order as it thinks appropriate in its discretion. In view of the wide range of types of person who shelter under the umbrella of diminished responsibility, it seems desirable that there should be this flexibility in the means of dealing with them.[20]

3 Hospital Orders

It remains to notice that, of much wider practical importance than either insanity or diminished responsibility, is the courts' power to make hospital orders. Under s. 37 of the Mental Health Act 1983, a person who is proved to have committed an offence may be committed to a mental hospital or to the guardianship of a local social services authority. The offence must be one punishable with imprisonment and offences where the sentence is fixed by law (in effect, murder) are excluded. The order can be made only on the evidence of two medical practitioners (one approved by the Secretary of State as having special experience in the diagnosis or treatment of mental disorder) who agree that detention for treatment or reception into guardianship is warranted.

The Crown Court may, if it thinks it necessary for the protection of the public, make a "restriction order" for an indefinite or a specified period.[21] The offender then may not be discharged, given leave of absence or transferred to another hospital without the consent of the Home Secretary.

The relative importance of hospital orders in practice is seen by the fact that in 1986[1] no person charged with murder was found unfit to plead, only one was acquitted on the ground of insanity, 55 charges of murder were reduced to manslaughter on the ground of diminished responsibility, but hundreds of hospital and guardianship orders are made every year.

---

18. Wootton, *Crime and the Criminal Law*, 86.
19. Walker, op. cit. 158–160; Butler, Appendix 9.
20. For proposals for reform, see CLRC, Fourteenth Report (Cmnd. 7844), 38–44.
21. Mental Health Act 1983, s. 41.
 1. Criminal Statistics, England and Wales, 1986.
 2. Keedy, "Ignorance and Mistake in the Criminal Law" (1908), 22 Harv LR 75; Williams, CLGP, Ch. 5; Hall, *General Principles*, Ch. XI; Williams, "Homicide and the Supernatural" (1949), 65 LQR 491; Howard, "The Reasonableness of Mistake in the Criminal Law" (1961), 4 Univ QLJ 45.

4 Mistake[2]

It is settled by the "landmark decision"[3] in *Director of Public Prosecutions v Morgan*[4] that mistake is a defence where it prevents D from having the *mens rea* which the law requires for the crime with which he is charged. Where the law requires intention or recklessness with respect to some element in the *actus reus*, a mistake, whether reasonable or not, which precludes both states of mind will excuse.[5] Where the law requires only negligence, then only a *reasonable* mistake can afford a defence; for an unreasonable mistake, by definition, is one which a reasonable man would not make and is, therefore, negligent.[6] Where strict liability is imposed, then even a reasonable mistake will not excuse.[7]

A mistake which does not preclude *mens rea* (or negligence where that is in issue) is irrelevant and no defence. Suppose D believes he is smuggling a crate of Irish whiskey. In fact the crate contains Scotch whisky. Duty is, of course, chargeable on both. D believes he is importing a dutiable item and he is importing a dutiable item. The *actus reus* is the same whether the crate contains Irish or Scotch. He *knows*, because his belief and the facts coincide in this respect, that he is evading the duty chargeable on the goods in the crate. If D had believed the crate to contain only some non-dutiable item, e.g., foreign currency (even if he had mistakenly believed it was dutiable) he would have lacked the *mens rea* for the offence.[8] Mistake of law is generally no defence,[9] for usually knowledge that the act is forbidden by law is no part of *mens rea*; but where the *mens rea* involves some legal concept,[10] or the absence of a claim of right,[11] then it may do so.

The rules are simply an application of the general principle that the prosecution must prove its case, including the *mens rea* or negligence which the definition of the crime requires. The so-called "defence" is simply a denial that the prosection has proved its case. Where the natural inference from D's conduct in the particular circumstances is that he intended or foresaw a particular result, the jury are very likely to convict him if he introduces no testimony that he did not in fact foresee; but the onus of proof remains throughout on the Crown and, technically, D does not bear even an evidential burden,[12] as he does when he raises a defence of automatism.

3. *Beckford v R* [1987] 3 All ER 425, PC.
4. [1976] AC 182, [1975] 2 All ER 347; **SHC 45**, above, p. 98.
5. See above, p. 74. This remains true after *Caldwell* [1981] 1 All ER 961, above, p. 62. For example, D has sexual intercourse with P, having formed the mistaken belief that P is consenting. Recklessness is negatived and he is not guilty of rape.
6. Above, p. 91. Where *gross* negligence is required, an unreasonable but not grossly unreasonable mistake is a defence.
7. Above, p. 98.
8. See commentary on *Taaffe* [1983] Crim LR 536 at 537, CA, affirmed, [1984] AC 539.
9. Above, p. 80.
10. Above, p. 83.
11. Above, p. 84.
12. Williams, "The Evidential Burden" (1977) 127 NLJ 156 at 158. But there is an evidential burden on D to get a particular mistake before the jury. "Mistake is a defence . . . in the sense that it is raised as an issue by the accused. The Crown is rarely possessed of knowledge of the subjective factors which may have caused an accused to entertain a belief in a fallacious set of facts": *Pappajohn v R* (1980) 52 CCC (2d) 481 at 494, per Dickson J. The judge does not have to direct the jury in every case of murder: "You must be satisfied that D did not believe P was a turkey"; but he must give such a direction if D has testified that, when he fired, he thought P was a turkey.

Mistake has traditionally been treated as a special defence because, before *Morgan*,[13] these principles were rarely recognised. There were many *dicta* that *only* reasonable mistakes would excuse. Lord Lane CJ[14] and the House of Lords[15] have recently, in the light of *Morgan*, doubted the propriety of the requirement of reasonableness in earlier pronouncements by distinguished authorities. Statements that unreasonable mistakes can never excuse may be regarded as discredited but it does not follow that the cases in which they were uttered and applied are wrongly decided. Where the court held that a mistake was not a defence because it was unreasonable, there are two possibilities. The case may be wrongly decided, just as *Morgan* was wrongly decided at first instance and in the Court of Appeal.[16] Alternatively, the case may be taken to have decided that the crime in question was one which did not require *mens rea* as to the element in question. If the court rightly held that only a reasonable mistake would excuse, it held in effect that the law requires only negligence with respect to that element. Thus, in *Morgan*, the House showed no inclination to interfere with the bigamy cases[17] which assert that D's mistaken belief in the death of his first spouse, or the dissolution or nullity of the first marriage, is a defence only if it is reasonable. These cases may then be taken to fall into the second category and establish that neither intention nor recklessness but only negligence with respect to the existence of the first marriage need be proved. Thus Lord Fraser said, "bigamy does not involve any intention except the intention to go through a marriage ceremony." Lord Cross said; ". . . if the definition of the offence is on the face of it 'absolute' and the defendant is seeking to escape his prima facie liability by a defence of mistaken belief, I can see no hardship to him in requiring the mistake – if it is to afford him a defence – to be based on reasonable grounds." This view of bigamy is that the statute, on its true interpretation, required proof of nothing more than negligence.

In the leading case of *Tolson*[18] D believed on reasonable grounds that her husband had been drowned at sea and, more than five years later, married again reasonably believing herself to be a widow. By a majority of nine to five the court held that she was not guilty, but only because her belief was reasonable. The minority of five, it will be noted, held that the offence was one of strict liability, subject only to the statutory defence of seven years absence.[19] The case can fairly be regarded as one of statutory construction, laying down no general principle. The *dicta* – much cited in subsequent cases – that the common law allowed a defence only if it was honest and reasonable[20] must, since *Morgan*, be regarded as unsound.

One unfortunate aspect of the discussion of the bigamy cases in *Morgan* is that it suggests a very strict approach to the problem of the implication of

13. [1976] AC 182 at 192, [1975] 2 All ER 347; **SHC 45**; above, p. 86.
14. *Taaffe* [1983] 2 All ER 625 at 628.
15. *Westminster City Council v Croyalgrange Ltd* [1986] 2 All ER 353 at 399.
16. [1976] AC 182, [1975] 1 All ER 8; **SHC 45**.
17. See below, p. 714. The House also accepted the requirement of reasonable grounds for believing the use of force to be necessary in self-defence, but see *Williams*, above, p. 88.
18. (1889) 23 QBD 168, CCR; **SHC 105**.
19. See below, p. 711.
20. See, e.g., per Cave J at 181.

mens rea into statutory offences. The House was concerned with the common law offence of rape; but Lord Cross said that if the Sexual Offences Act had enacted in terms that a man who has sexual intercourse with a woman without her consent (the *actus reus* of rape) is guilty of an offence, he might well have held that only a reasonable mistake would be a defence. Presumably the only intention which Lord Cross would have required in this hypothetical case would have been an intention to have intercourse with a woman. These *dicta* therefore suggest that, where a statute uses no words expressly importing *mens rea*, the mental element which the court will require the prosecution to prove will be minimal – to go through a ceremony of marriage, to have sexual intercourse, etc., and that it will then be for the accused to introduce evidence sufficient to raise a doubt whether he did not, on reasonable grounds, have a belief inconsistent with some material element in the *actus reus*. This approach may be admirable where we are concerned with "quasi-criminal", "regulatory" or "welfare" offences; but it is submitted it should have no place in serious crimes.

A better approach, it is submitted, is that of the Court of Appeal in *Smith*.[1] Rejecting an argument that the only mental element required by the Criminal Damage Act 1971 was an intention to damage or destroy property, the Court held: "Applying the ordinary principles of *mens rea*, the intention and recklessness and the absence of lawful excuse required to constitute the offence have reference to property belonging to another." Similarly, in *Westminster City Council v Croyalgrange Ltd*[2] Robert Goff LJ referred to "the ordinary principle that, where it is required that an offence should have been knowingly committed, the requisite knowledge must embrace all the elements of the offence". It is submitted that the ordinary principles of *mens rea* require intention of recklessness as to all the elements of the *actus reus* unless that is excluded expressly or by implication; and the more serious the crime, the more reluctant should the court be to find an implied exclusion.

5 Intoxication

The law in this area has developed principally in cases where D was intoxicated by alcohol. In *Lipman*[3] it was held that the same principles apply to intoxication by other drugs but two recent cases, *Bailey*[4] and *Hardie*,[5] suggest that drugs must be divided into two categories. Where it is common knowledge that a drug is liable to cause the taker to become aggressive or do dangerous or unpredictable things, that drug is to be classed with alcohol. Where there is no such common knowledge, as in the case of a merely soporific or sedative drug, different rules apply. There are

---

1. [1974] QB 354, [1974] 1 All ER 632; **SHC 634**; below, p. 684.
2. [1985] 1 All ER 740 at 744, DC, affirmed [1986] 2 All ER 353, HL.
3. [1970] 1 QB 152, [1969] 3 All ER 410, **SHC 95**, below, p. 348.
4. [1983] 2 All ER 503, [1983] 1 WLR 760.
5. [1984] 3 All ER 848, [1985] 1 WLR 64, **SHC 98**.

obvious difficulties about classifying drugs in this way and, if the distinction survives at all, it would not be surprising if it leads to further case-law.

1 Intoxication by Alcohol and "Dangerous" Drugs

Intoxication is not, and never has been, a defence as such. It is no defence for D to say, however convincingly, that, but for the drink, he would not have behaved as he did. One of the effects of alcohol is to weaken the restraints and inhibitions which normally govern our conduct so a man may do things when drunk that he would never dream of doing while sober. But, if he had the *mens rea* required for the crime, he is guilty even though drink impaired or negatived his ability to judge between right and wrong[6] or to resist provocation, and even though, in his drunken state, he found the impulse to act as he did irresistible.

Intoxication also impairs a person's perception and judgment so he may fail to be aware of facts, or to foresee results of his conduct, of which he would certainly have been aware, or have foreseen, if he had been sober. So, intoxication may be the reason why the defendant lacked the *mens rea* of the crime charged. When D relies on evidence of intoxication he does so for the purpose of showing he lacked *mens rea*. This is its only relevance so far as liability to conviction is concerned.

In many of the cases where drunkenness is relevant, the defence, in substance, is one of mistake and the evidence of drunkenness is circumstantial evidence that the mistake was made. Two examples quoted by Lord Denning[7] are: (i) where a nurse got so drunk at a christening that she put the baby on the fire in mistake for a log of wood;[8] and (ii) where a drunken man thought his friend, lying in bed, was a theatrical dummy and stabbed him to death.[9] Lord Denning said there would be a defence to murder in each of these cases. These mistakes were highly unreasonable and, in the case of a sober man, it would be extremely difficult to persuade a jury that they were made. The relevance of the evidence of drunkenness is simply that it makes these mistakes much more credible. Similarly where D denies that he foresaw some obvious consequence of his action. A denial which would be quite incredible in the case of a sober man may be readily accepted when there is evidence that D was drunk.

In the leading case of *Beard* it was said that intoxication was a defence only if it rendered D incapable of forming the *mens rea*.[10] Proof of incapacity is of course conclusive that *mens rea* was not present; but it is now established that it is not necessary to go so far. It is a defence to a sober man that, though he was perfectly capable of forming the intent required, he did not do so on the occasion in question. Equally, a drunken man may be capable, notwithstanding his drunkenness, of forming the intent to kill and yet not do so. The nurse at the christening was capable of forming the intent to tend the fire, so she was probably capable of forming an intent to

6. *Director of Public Prosecutions v Beard* [1920] AC 479 at 502–504.
7. In *A-G for Northern Ireland v Gallagher* [1963] AC 349 at 381, [1961] 3 All ER 299 at 313; **SHC 93**.
8. (1978) 18 *Gentleman's Magazine*, 570; quoted in Kenny, *Outlines*, 29.
9. (1951) Times, 13 January.
10. [1920] AC 479 at 501–502, HL.

kill. The important thing is that she did not do so – and the drunkenness was highly relevant to rebut the inference which might otherwise have arisen from her conduct. The question is, taking D's intoxicated state into account, did he in fact form the necessary intent?[11] The onus of proof – again contrary to certain *dicta* in *Beard*[12] – is clearly on the Crown to establish that, notwithstanding the alleged intoxication, D formed the intent.[13]

1) *Intoxication and "Specific Intention"*

The principles stated above are applicable:

i) to crimes requiring a "specific intent"[14] whether the drink or drug was taken voluntarily or involuntarily;

ii) to all crimes where the drink or drug was taken involuntarily. So if D's lemonade is laced with vodka and he is unaware that he has consumed any alcohol, he can rely on evidence of his drunken condition.[15] Similarly, perhaps, where he has taken drink under duress; and

iii) to all crimes where the drink or drug is taken voluntarily but in *bona fide* pursuance of medical treatment or prescription. So in *Quick*[16] D could rely on evidence that he had taken insulin, though voluntarily, and it was recognised that an anaesthetic would have a similar effect. This is likely to be rarely applicable to drink but it might apply where, for example, brandy is administered to D after an accident.

The principles do not apply where D is charged with a crime not requiring a specific intent and the drink or drug was taken voluntarily. In *Director of Public Prosecutions v Majewski*[17] the House of Lords has confirmed the rule, obscurely stated in *Beard*,[18] that evidence of self-induced intoxication negativing *mens rea* is a defence to a charge of a crime requiring a specific intent but not to a charge of any other crime. In the case of a crime not requiring "specific intent" D may be convicted if he was voluntarily intoxicated at the time of committing the offence, though he did not have the *mens rea* required in all other circumstances for that offence and even though he was in a state of automatism at the time of doing the act. It is a rule of substantive law that, where D relies on voluntary intoxication as a defence to a charge of a crime not requiring "specific intent", the prosecution need not prove any intention or foresight, whatever the definition of the crime may say, nor indeed any voluntary act.[19] It follows

---

11. *Pordage* [1975] Crim LR 575, CA, following *dicta* in *Sheehan* [1975] 2 All ER 960, [1975] Crim LR 339 and commentary, CA. To the same effect are *Menniss* [1973] 2 NSWLR 113 and *Kamipeli* [1975] 1 NZLR 610.

12. [1920] AC 479 at 502.

13. *Sheehan*, above.

14. Below, p. 212.

15. But what of the much more common case where D has voluntarily taken some drink and his companions surreptitiously add more?

16. Above, p. 187. In *Majewski*, below, the Lord Chancellor pointed out that the drugs taken were not medically prescribed.

17. [1977] AC 142, [1976] 2 All ER 142, [1976] Crim LR 374 and commentary. Williams, 126 NLJ 658; A. D. Gold, "An Untrimmed Beard" (1976) 19 Crim LQ 34; Dashwood, "Logic and the Lords in *Majewski*" [1977] Crim LR 532 and 591.

18. [1920] AC 479.

19. The House approved *Lipman*, below, p. 348.

that s. 8 of the Criminal Justice Act 1967[20] has no application. There is, it appears, an implied qualification to every statute creating an offence and specifying a *mens rea* other than a specific intent. The *mens rea* must be proved – except, we must infer, where the accused was intoxicated through the voluntary taking of drink or drugs.

It seems that this rule applies whatever the degree of intoxication, provided that it prevented D from foreseeing or knowing what he would have foreseen or known had he been sober. It is true that Lord Elwyn-Jones at one point[1] posed the question before the House much more narrowly – as that of a man who "consciously and deliberately takes alcohol and drugs not on medical prescription, but in order to escape from reality, to go 'on a trip', to become hallucinated ...". Such a person is readily distinguishable from the ordinary "social drinker" who becomes intoxicated in the course of a convivial evening. The former, intending to reduce himself to a state in which he will have no control over his actions, might well be said to be in some sense reckless as to what he will do while in that state. The same cannot be said of the latter. But the general tenor of the speeches, as well as earlier and subsequent cases, is against any such distinction.[2]

The nature of "specific intent" is thus a matter of great importance but a careful scrutiny of the authorities, particularly *Majewski* itself, fails to reveal any consistent principle. In *Majewski*, "specific" was contrasted with "basic intent";[3] but some crimes requiring no ulterior intent – conspicuously murder – are also treated as crimes of "specific intent". Lord Simon suggested that the distinguishing factor is that "the *mens rea* in a crime of specific intent requires proof of a purposive element:" yet there need be no purposive element in the *mens rea* of murder; and rape, which is said not to be a crime of specific intent, obviously requires a purposive element. Lord Elwyn-Jones LC suggested that the test is that crimes not requiring specific intent are crimes that may be committed recklessly. Lord Edmund-Davies, a party to *Majewski*, was dismayed to think that, as a result of *Caldwell*, this opinion has prevailed[4] and it certainly now seems likely that any offence which may be committed either by *Cunningham* or *Caldwell* recklessness will be held an offence of "basic" and not "specific" intent.

The only safe conclusion seems to be that "crime requiring specific intent" means a crime where evidence of voluntary intoxication negativing *mens rea* is a defence; and the designation of crimes as requiring, or not requiring, specific intent is based on no principle but on policy. In order to know how a crime should be classified for this purpose we can look only to the decisions of the courts. These tell us that the following are crimes requiring specific intent.

20. Above, p. 85.
  1. [1977] AC 443 at 471.
  2. A. C. E. Lynch, "The Scope of Intoxication" [1982] Crim LR 139 (see also p. 392) makes a quite different distinction between "complete intoxication" (to which *Majewski* would apply) and "partial intoxication" (to which it would not); but there are many degrees of intoxication and the suggested distinction seems unworkable.
  3. Above, p. 70.
  4. Above, p. 62; [1982] AC 341 at 361, [1981] 1 All ER 961 at 972.

Murder,[5] wounding or causing grievous bodily harm with intent,[6] theft,[7] robbery,[8] burglary with intent to steal,[9] handling stolen goods,[10] endeavouring to obtain money on a forged cheque,[11] causing criminal damage contrary to s. 1(1) or (2) of the Criminal Damage Act 1971 where only intention to cause damage or, in the case of s. 1(2), only intention to endanger life, is alleged,[12] an attempt to commit any offence, and possibly the aiding and abetting of any offence.[13]

The following are crimes not requiring a specific intent: manslaughter (apparently in all its forms);[14] rape;[15] maliciously wounding or inflicting grievous bodily harm;[16] assault occasioning actual bodily harm;[17] assault on a constable in the execution of his duty;[18] indecent assault;[19] common assault;[20] taking a conveyance without the consent of the owner[1] and criminal damage where intention or recklessness, or only recklessness, is alleged.[2]

Contrary (at first sight) to the view stated above, there is some authority[3] that a jury must be directed to decide whether D was reckless, disregarding the evidence that he was intoxicated. In *Woods*[4] D, charged with rape, claimed that he was so drunk that he did not realise P was not consenting. He relied on s. 1(2) of the Sexual Offences (Amendment) Act 1976[5] which requires the jury to have regard to the presence or absence of reasonable grounds for a belief that the woman was consenting, "in conjunction with any other relevant matters". He said his intoxication was a relevant matter.

---

5. *Beard*, above; *Gallagher* [1963] AC 349, [1961] 3 All ER 299; *Sheehan* [1975] 2 All ER 960, [1975] 1 WLR 739, CA.
6. *Bratty v AG for Northern Ireland* [1963] AC 386, [1961] 3 All ER 523, per Lord Denning; *Pordage* [1975] Crim LR 575.
7. *Ruse v Read* [1949] 1 KB 377, [1949] 1 All ER 398 and *Majewski* per Lord Simon at 152.
8. As a corollary of theft.
9. *Durante* [1972] 3 All ER 962, [1972] 1 WLR 1612.
10. *Durante*, above.
11. *Majewski*, per Lord Salmon at 158.
12. *Caldwell* [1981] 1 All ER 961 at 964.
13. *Clarkson* [1971] 3 All ER 344 at 347. But in *Lynch v Director of Public Prosecutions* [1975] 1 All ER 912 at 942, Lord Simon said, approving the decision of the Northern Irish Court of Criminal Appeal, that they held that the *mens rea* of aiding and abetting did not involve a "specific intent". But (i) he may have used the term in a different sense; and (ii) there may be a difference depending on the nature of the alleged secondary liability – an intent to procure is different from an intent to aid; above, p. 133.
14. *Beard*, *Gallagher* and *Bratty v A-G for Northern Ireland* [1961] 3 All ER at 533, per Lord Denning; *Lipman* [1970] 1 QB 152, [1969] 3 All ER 410.
15. *Majewski*, above, per Lords Simon and Russell and *Leary v R* (1977) 74 DLR (3d) 103, SCC, discussed, 55 Can Bar Rev 691. But if this is right, *Cogan and Leak* above, p. 156 is wrongly decided; and *Morgan* above, pp. 86, 207 might have been decided shortly on this ground.
16. *Bratty* at 533, per Lord Denning; *Majewski*, above, per Lords Simon and Salmon.
17. *Bolton v Crawley* [1972] Crim LR 222; *Majewski*, above.
18. *Majewski*, above.
19. *Burns* (1973) 58 Cr App Rep 364.
20. A fortiori.
1. *MacPherson* [1973] RTR 157. *Diggin* (1980) 72 Cr App Rep 204 is not, as at first appeared: [1980] Crim LR 656, an authority on intoxicated taking: [1981] Crim LR 563; but see White, "Taking the Joy out of Joyriding" [1980] Crim LR 609.
2. Below, p. 581.
3. See Williams, TBCL, 427–428.
4. (1982) 74 Cr App Rep 312, CA.
5. Below, p. 429.

The court said that self-induced intoxication is not "a legally relevant matter" but "the subsection directs the jury to look carefully at all the other relevant evidence before making up their minds on this issue." The evidence of intoxication is undoubtedly logically relevant and may be the most cogent evidence. To ignore it, in coming to a conclusion, is to answer a hypothetical question. It is no longer, "did he believe she was consenting?" and must become, "would he have known she was consenting if he had not been drunk?" This is most obviously so in the case where D's intoxication has rendered him unconscious. Take *Lipman*.[6] How can a judge seriously tell a jury to decide whether D *did* intend to do an unlawful and dangerous act to P – ignoring the undisputed evidence that he was unconscious at the time? Without this "legally irrelevant" evidence, the *only* question the jury can sensibly answer is, "would he have known that such an act was dangerous if he had not been intoxicated?" On facts like those in *Lipman*, there is only one possible answer. It is most regrettable that juries should be faced with questions which are, with all respect, nonsensical, even if their common sense will lead them to consider the only matter really in issue.

It is now fatal for a person charged with a crime not requiring specific intent who claims that he did not have *mens rea* to support his defence with evidence that he had taken drink and drugs. By so doing he dispenses the Crown from the duty, which until that moment lay upon them, of proving beyond reasonable doubt that he had *mens rea*. *Mens rea* ceases to be relevant. Can the Crown escape from this duty by leading evidence, or extracting an admission in cross-examination, that D had taken drink so as to diminish his capacity to foresee the consequences of his acts? According to Lord Salmon[7] in *Majewski* the question the House was deciding was whether the accused could rely *by way of defence* on the fact that he had voluntarily taken drink. But there are other dicta which suggest that D is held liable without the usual *mens rea* because he has taken drink – the taking of the drink is the foundation of his liability[8] – a variety of *mens rea* – though not in the sense in which that term is used in this book. If that be right, there is no reason why the Crown should not set out to prove it instead of seeking to prove *mens rea* in the sense of intention or recklessness.

Where the offence is one of *Caldwell* recklessness, the impact of *Majewski* is reduced. Where, because he was intoxicated, D gave no thought to the existence of the risk, he was reckless and is liable to conviction without the invocation of the rule in *Majewski*. This was the position in *Caldwell* itself. But *Majewski* may still have a significant sphere

---

6. Below, p. 348.
7. P. 156.
8. "His course of conduct in reducing himself by drugs and drink to that condition in my view supplies the evidence of *mens rea*, of guilty mind, certainly sufficient for crimes of basic intent:" per Lord Elwyn-Jones LC at 150. "There is no juristic reason why mental incapacity (short of M'Naghten insanity) brought about by self-induced intoxication to realise what one is doing or its probable consequences should not be such a state of mind stigmatised as wrongful by the criminal law; and there is every practical reason why it should be": per Lord Simon at 153.

of operation.[9] D might say that he did consider whether there was a risk and decided there was none. He was then not *Caldwell*-reckless. But, if he would have appreciated the existence of the risk had he been sober, he will still be liable because of *Majewski*. D, about to have intercourse with P, asks himself, "Is she consenting?" and answers the question in the affirmative because, being drunk, he fails to observe what he would have observed when sober. He is not *Caldwell*-reckless but, if rape is a crime not requiring specific intent, he is guilty.

ii) *Majewski and Defences*

The *Majewski* rule has been held inapplicable where statute expressly provides that a particular belief shall be a defence to the charge. If D held that belief, he is not guilty, even though it arose from a drunken mistake that he would not have made when sober. In *Jaggard v Dickinson*[10] D had a friend, H, who had invited her to treat his house as if it were her own. When drunk, D went to a house which she thought was H's but which in fact belonged to R, who barred her way. D gained entry by breaking windows and damaging the curtains. Charged with criminal damage, contrary to s. 1(1) of the Criminal Damage Act 1971, she relied on s. 5(2) of that Act[11] which provides that a person has a lawful excuse if he believed that the person entitled to consent to the damage would have done so had he known of the circumstances. D said that she believed that H would, in the circumstances, have consented to her damaging his property. Since s. 1(1) creates an offence not requiring specific intent, D could not have relied on her drunkenness to negative her recklessness whether she damaged the property of another, but, it was held, she could rely on it to explain what would otherwise have been inexplicable and give colour to her evidence about the state of her belief. The court thought this was not the same thing as using drunkenness to rebut an inference of intention or recklessness. It seems, however, to be exactly the same thing.[12] Moreover, thought the court, s. 5(2) provides that it is immaterial whether a belief is justified or not if it is honestly held, and it was not open to the court to add the words "and the honesty of the belief is not attributable only to self-induced intoxication". Yet the courts have not hesitated to add similar words to qualify Parliament's express requirement of recklessness. The result is anomalous. Where the defendant did not intend any damage to property he may be held liable because he was drunk; but where he did intend damage to property but thought the owner would consent he is not liable, however drunk he may have been. Suppose that D, because he is drunk, believes that certain property belonging to P is his own and damages it. His belief is not a matter of defence under s. 5(2)[13] but negatives recklessness whether property *belonging to another* be damaged.[14] Even though D gave his drunken mind to the matter, and so was not *Caldwell*-

---

9. This is overlooked by Lord Diplock at [1981] 1 All ER 968a.
10. [1981] QB 527, [1980] 3 All ER 716.
11. Below, p. 688.
12. See above, pp. 210–211.
13. *Smith* (DR) [1974] QB 354, [1974] 1 All ER 632.
14. Ibid.

reckless, he is liable. If D, being drunk, destroys X's property believing that it is the property of Y who would consent to his doing so, this is a defence; but if he destroys X's property believing that it is his own, it is not.

In relation to common law defences, the law has gone quite the other way. Although it is now settled that when D sets up self-defence, he is to be judged on the facts as he believed them to be, whether reasonably or not,[15] a mistake arising from voluntary intoxication cannot be relied on, according to *O'Grady*,[16] even on charge of murder or other crime requiring specific intent. This was an obiter dictum because the appellant had been acquitted of murder and was appealing only against his conviction for manslaughter. The dictum seems, moreover, to have proceeded on the assumption that, on a charge of homicide, self-defence must be either a complete defence or no defence at all, which is not the case;[17] and the court's attention does not appear to have been drawn to the recommendations of the Criminal Law Revision Committee, complementing those which the court followed in *Gladstone Williams*.[15] The better view, it is submitted, is that a mistake arising from voluntary intoxication by alcohol or dangerous drugs may found a defence to crime requiring specific intent but not to one of basic intent.

2 Intoxication otherwise than by Alcohol or Dangerous Drugs

In *Bailey*[18] a diabetic failed to take sufficient food after insulin. He caused grievous bodily harm and his defence to charges under ss. 18 and 20 of the Offences against the Person Act was that, because of this failure, he was in a state of automatism. The recorder's direction to the jury that this was no defence was obviously wrong so far as s. 18 was concerned for that is an offence of specific intent. The Court of Appeal held[19] that it was also wrong for s. 20 because "self-induced automatism, other than that due to intoxication from alcohol or drugs, may provide a defence to crimes of basic intent". The court went on:

"The question in each case will be whether the prosecution has proved the necessary element of recklessness. In cases of assault, if the accused knows that his actions or inaction are likely to make him aggressive, unpredictable or uncontrolled with the result that he may cause some injury to others and he persists in the action or takes no remedial action when he knows it is required, it will be open to the jury to find that he was reckless."

The automatism seems to have been treated as arising from the failure to take food, rather than from the taking of the insulin, but the court hinted at a distinction between two types of drug:

"It is common knowledge that those who take alcohol to excess or certain sorts of drugs may become aggressive or do dangerous or unpredictable things. . . . But the same cannot be said, without more, of a man who fails to take food after an insulin injection."

15. *Gladstone Williams* [1987] 3 All ER 411, (1983) 78 Cr App Rep 276, above, p. 88.
16. [1987] 3 All ER 420, [1987] 3 WLR 321.
17. Below, p. 241.
18. [1983] 2 All ER 503, [1983] 1 WLR 760, CA.
19. P. 507.

In *Hardie*[20] D's defence to a charge of damaging property with intent to endanger the life of another or being reckless whether another's life be endangered, was that he had taken valium, a sedative drug, to calm his nerves and that this had resulted in intoxication precluding the *mens rea* for the offence. The judge, following *Majewski* and *Caldwell*, directed that this could be no defence. The Court of Appeal quashed the conviction. *Majewski* was not applicable because valium

"is wholly different in kind from drugs which are liable to cause unpredictability or aggressiveness. . . . if the effect of a drug is merely soporific or sedative the taking of it, even in some excessive quantity, cannot in the ordinary way raise a conclusive presumption against the admission of proof of intoxication for the purpose of disproving mens rea in ordinary crimes, such as would be the case with alcoholic intoxication or incapacity or automatism resulting from the self-administration of dangerous drugs."[1]

These cases then appear to apply where intoxication is self-induced otherwise than by alcohol or dangerous drugs. In these cases the test of liability is stated to be one of recklessness: "If he does appreciate the risk that [failure to take food] may lead to aggressive, unpredictable and uncontrollable conduct and he nevertheless deliberately runs the risk or otherwise disregards it, this will amount to recklessness."[2]

It is clear that the recklessness which must be proved is:

i) subjective, an actual awareness of the risk of becoming aggressive, etc., not recklessness of the *Caldwell* type; but

ii) "general" – not requiring foresight of the *actus reus* of any particular crime, such as is required in the case of a sober person charged with an offence of *Cunningham* recklessness. D will be liable for any crime of recklessness the *actus reus* of which he happens to commit under the influence of the self-induced intoxication. And –

iii) being aware that one may lose consciousness may be sufficient where a failure to exercise control may result in the *actus reus* of a crime, as in the case of careless or reckless driving.

3 Intoxication causing Insanity or Abnormality of Mind

If excessive drinking causes actual insanity, such as delirium tremens, then the M'Naghten Rules will be applied in exactly the same way as where insanity arises from any other causes:

". . . drunkenness is one thing and the diseases to which drunkenness leads are different things; and if a man by drunkenness brings on a state of disease which causes such a degree of madness, even for a time, which would have relieved him from responsibility if it had been caused in any other way, then he would not be criminally responsible."[3]

---

20. [1984] 3 All ER 848, [1985] 1 WLR 64.

1. P. 853. This overlooks the fact that the *Majewski* principle is stated to be a rule of substantive law and that the Criminal Justice Act 1967, s. 8, precludes conclusive presumptions of intention or foresight. Above, p. 85.

2. *Bailey* [1983] 2 All ER 503 at 507.

3. *Davis* (1881) 14 Cox CC 563 at 564, per Stephen J approved by the House of Lords in *Director of Public Prosecutions v Beard* [1920] AC 479 at 501.

It has already been seen[4] that there are serious difficulties in defining a "disease of the mind" and the distinction between temporary insanity induced by drink and simple drunkenness is far from clear-cut. The distinction becomes important in the case of a man who does not know that his act is wrong because of excessive drinking. If he is suffering from temporary insanity he is entitled to a verdict of not guilty on the ground of insanity; but if he is merely drunk he should be convicted.[5]

Self-induced intoxication must be ignored in deciding whether D was suffering from such an abnormality of mind as to amount to diminished responsibility unless it is proved that the craving for drink or drugs is in itself an abnormality of mind.[6] It has been argued[7] that drink can produce a toxic effect on the brain which would be an "injury" within s. 2 of the Homicide Act 1957;[8] but the court thought it very doubtful whether the *transient* effect of drink could amount to an injury. Presumably a permanent injury to the brain produced by drink would be held to be an injury within the section. Difficult questions may arise where a substantial impairment arises as a result of a combination of inherent abnormality and drink.[9]

4 Involuntary Intoxication

Involuntary intoxication includes both the case where a person's drink is "laced" with alcohol without his knowledge and that where he becomes intoxicated through taking drugs in accordance with a medical prescription.[10] There is little authority on the subject but it is clear that the rule in *Majewski* does not apply and it follows that involuntary intoxication negativing the *mens rea* of the offence charged, whether specific intent or basic intent, is a defence. Where it does not negative *mens rea*, it will not be a defence even though it may well be that D would not have committed the offence had he not been intoxicated; but it will then, of course, be a substantial mitigating factor.[11]

As intoxication is nearly always voluntary, it is probably for D to raise the issue if he wishes to contend that it is involuntary. The onus of proof will then generally be on the Crown:[12] but the Public Order Act 1986, s. 6(5), for the purposes of offences under that Act, requires D to "show" that his intoxication was not self-induced or caused by medical treatment. This was presumably intended to put the onus of proof on D; but "show", in contrast with "prove" which is used in other sections of the Act, might be taken to impose no more than an evidential burden.

---

4. Above, pp. 186–190.
5. In a case of simple drunkenness the judge should not introduce the question whether the prisoner knew he was doing wrong – for "it is a dangerous and confusing question" – per Lord Birkenhead in *Director of Public Prosecutions v Beard* [1920] AC 479 at 506.
6. *Fenton* [1975] Crim LR 712, above, p. 205, *Carraher v HM Advocate* 1946 JC 108; *HM Advocate v MacLeod* 1956 JC 20.
7. In *Di Duca* (1959) 43 Cr App Rep 167. See also *Dowdall* (1960) The Times, 22nd January.
8. Above, p. 203.
9. See p. 190, above and *Clarke and King* [1962] Crim LR 836.
10. Cf. *Quick* [1973] QB 910 and commentary, [1973] Crim LR 436–437.
11. Cf. *Davies* [1983] Crim LR 741 (Swansea Crown Court).
12. *Stripp* (1978) 69 Cr App Rep 318 at 323; *Bailey* [1983] 2 All ER 503 at 507.

5 Intoxication induced with the Intention of Committing Crime

Has D a defence if, intending to commit a crime, he takes drink or drugs in order to give himself Dutch courage and then commits the crime, having, at the time of the act, induced insanity within the M'Naghten Rules or such a state of drunkenness as to negative a "specific intent"? The problem was raised by *A-G for Northern Ireland v Gallagher*.[13] D, having decided to kill his wife, bought a knife and a bottle of whisky. He drank much of the whisky and then killed his wife with the knife. The defence was that he was either insane or so drunk as to be incapable of forming the necessary intent at the time he did the act. The Court of Criminal Appeal in Northern Ireland reversed his conviction for murder on the ground that the judge had misdirected the jury in telling them to apply the M'Naghten Rules to D's state of mind at the time before he took the alcohol and not at the time of committing the act. The majority of the House of Lords apparently did not dissent from the view of the Court of Criminal Appeal that such a direction would be

"at variance with the specific terms of the M'Naghten Rules which definitely fix the crucial time as the time of committing the act."[14]

They differed, however, in their interpretation of the summing up and held that it did direct the jury's attention to the time of committing the act. In that case, of course, it was not necessary to decide the problem because the jury, by their verdict, had found that D had *mens rea* and was not insane.

Lord Denning, however, seems to have taken the view that the Court of Criminal Appeal's interpretation of the summing up was correct and that the direction, so interpreted, was right in law. He said:[15]

"My Lords, I think the law on this point should take a clear stand. If a man, whilst sane and sober, forms an intention to kill and makes preparation for it knowing it is a wrong thing to do, and then gets himself drunk so as to give himself Dutch courage to do the killing, and whilst drunk carries out his intention, he cannot rely on this self-induced drunkenness as a defence to a charge of murder, nor even as reducing it to manslaughter. He cannot say he got himself into such a stupid state that he was incapable of an intent to kill. So also, when he is a psychopath, he cannot by drinking rely on his self-induced defect of reason as a defence of insanity. The wickedness of his mind before he got drunk is enough to condemn him, coupled with the act which he intended to do and did do."

The difficulty about this is that an intention to do an act some time in the future is not *mens rea*.[16] The *mens rea* must generally coincide with the conduct which causes the *actus reus*. If D, having resolved to murder his wife at midnight, drops off to sleep and, while still asleep, strangles her at midnight, it is thought that he is not guilty of murder (though he may be liable for manslaughter on the ground of his negligence). The case of deliberately induced drunkenness, however, is probably different. The true analogy, it is thought, is the case where a man uses an innocent agent as an

---

13. [1963] AC 349, [1961] 3 All ER 299, **SHC 93**.
14. See [1963] AC 349 at 376, [1961] 3 All ER 299 at 310.
15. [1963] AC 349 at 382, [1961] 3 All ER 299 at 314.
16. Above, p. 76.

instrument with which to commit crime. It has been seen[17] that if D induces an irresponsible person to kill, D is guilty of murder. Is not the position substantially the same where D induces in himself a state of irresponsibility with the intention that he shall kill while in that state? Should not the responsible D be liable for the foreseen and intended acts of the irresponsible D? So regarded, a conviction would not be incompatible with the wording of the M'Naghten Rules. The result, certainly, seems to be one required by policy and it is thought the courts will achieve it if the problem should be squarely raised before them.

6 Alternatives to *Majewski*

Majewski had been followed by the Supreme Court of Canada in *Leary*[18] but only by a majority of four to three, a powerful minority holding that D could rely on evidence of intoxication in any case and that there was no distinction between the so-called specific intents and other mental elements prescribed in the definition of crime. In the High Court of Australia in *O'Connor*[19] a majority of four to three agreed with the Canadian minority. So did the South African Appellate Division in *S v Chretien*.[20] The Australian majority were confident that they were not opening the flood-gates to hordes of drunken offenders ravaging the public with impunity; juries would not be taken in by spurious defences that D was drunk. The decision only confirmed the law laid down in the state of Victoria as long ago as 1964 and nothing disastrous had happened there. It is fair to say that Australia is probably alone in common law jurisdictions in departing from *Majewski*, but it is strongly supported by the unanimous decision in *Chretien*.

An alternative course is proposed by the Butler Committee.[1] This would require the creation of a new offence to be called dangerous intoxication. It would never be charged in the first instance but would come into operation only when D was acquitted of a "dangerous" offence – dangerous to the person. It is implicit in the proposal that *Majewski* would be repealed so far as these offences are concerned. Where D relied on evidence of intoxication to show that he did not have *mens rea*, the jury should be directed that, if they were not satisfied he had *mens rea*, but were satisfied that he did the act, they should convict him of this new offence.

This solution was considered by the CLRC in their examination of the law of offences against the person.[2] They found it unsatisfactory in that a conviction would merely record that the defendant had committed a dangerous act while intoxicated. It would be the same crime, whether he killed, or committed an act of rape, or a minor assault. Moreover, the problem of the intoxicated offender is not confined to offences against the person and a reform which is sound in principle should be capable of extension to other offences, such as taking away motor vehicles. But,

17. Above, p. 131.
18. [1978] 1 SCR 29, (1977) 33 CCC (2d) 473.
19. (1980) 54 ALJR 349; see also (1980) 54 ALJR 569.
20. 1981 (1) SA 1097 (A), discussed by J. M. Burchell, (1981) 98 SALJ 177.
   1. Cmnd. 6244, paras 18.51–18.59.
   2. CLRC/OAP/R, pp. 111–118.

whatever kind of harm was done, the conviction recorded and the maximum sentence would be the same (one year for a first and three years for a subsequent offence). One view is that this is right because D's fault lies in getting drunk and that is what is recorded against him. What he did afterwards was done by an accident or a mistake, albeit a drunken one, and so without fault in the criminal sense. The law has, however, always attached and will continue to attach importance to the harm done as well as to the harm intended or foreseen.

The majority of the CLRC thought that the best that could be done was to clarify the rule in *Majewski*, to allow evidence of intoxication to negative the *mens rea* of murder and the *intention* required for any offence, leaving D liable for an offence of recklessness where he had not appreciated a risk which he would have appreciated when sober. To the extent that this would clarify the present obscure distinction between offences of specific and basic intent, it would be an improvement. As under the present law, however, the verdict of a jury would not distinguish between an offender who was reckless and one who was intoxicated but not reckless. This is a material difference, because the two cases may call for different sentences. Moreover, where D is convicted of an offence of recklessness when he was not in fact reckless the verdict does not represent the truth. A minority of the CLRC therefore preferred a modification of the Butler proposal, under which the jury would find a special verdict that the defendant did the act alleged in a state of intoxication. The court would have the same sentencing powers as are available on conviction of the offence charged,[3] in order to ensure that the public could be adequately protected from a dangerous offender.

Dr Ashworth tentatively proposes[4] a radical solution. Given the widely held view that intoxication is the source of much violence and damage, "should the law not go further than the summary offences of public drunkenness and make intoxication itself a serious crime, as a kind of inchoate offence?" Since the fault consists in getting drunk and not (where *mens rea* is negatived) in doing the harm, the suggestion is attractive. But there are difficulties. Since the "criminal" act would be no part of the offence and be admissible in evidence, if at all, only for the purpose of establishing that D was intoxicated, it would follow that there would be a theoretical liability where he did nothing but lie in bed and sleep it off. In practice, it would be unlikely that any prosecution would be brought unless some damage was done and, if evidence of that were admitted, inevitably the court would regard it as a most material factor in fixing sentence. There would also be a difficult question of the degree of intoxication which it is necessary to prove. A quite small amount of alcohol affects judgment and so may in fact have prevented D from foreseeing consequences. Everyone is a little more dangerous when he has had only a small amount to drink but it is impossible to prohibit all taking of alcohol or drugs. Experience with road traffic offences revealed the impossibility of drawing a satisfactory distinction between different degrees of intoxication, even in relation to the special

3. A better proposal might be one which provided for a reduced maximum to mark the general difference in culpability between the reckless and the merely intoxicated offender.
4. [1980] Crim LR 556.

activity of driving. That has been solved by fixing a precise blood/alcohol level for drivers;[5] but it is impossible to suppose that this could be extended to a general law against having a certain percentage of alcohol in the blood. Furthermore we are concerned with all drugs, not merely alcohol.

There is no obviously right solution; but the minority proposal of the CLRC has the great virtue that it requires the jury to declare the facts as they find them, so giving the judge the best opportunity to impose the right sentence; which, after all, is the object of the whole exercise.

6 Necessity[6]

We are not concerned here with cases where a man is compelled by physical force to go through the motions of an *actus reus* without any choice on his part. In such cases he will almost[7] invariably have a defence on the more fundamental ground that he did no act.

> "If there be an actual forcing of a man, as if A by force takes the arm of B and the weapon in his hand and therewith stabs C whereof he dies, this is murder in A but B is not guilty."[8]

The problem now to be discussed is the more difficult one that arises where D is able to choose between two courses, one of which involves breaking the criminal law and the other some evil to himself or others of such magnitude that it may be thought to justify the infraction of the criminal law. In an American case the master of a ship was held not guilty of violating an embargo act by illegal entry into a port when, as the result of storms, this course was "necessary" for the preservation of the vessel and the cargo and lives of those on board.[9] This was not a case where the ship was driven, willy-nilly, by the storm, but one where the captain made a deliberate choice to break the law in order to avert a greater evil; and was held justified in doing so.

To what extent a defence of necessity prevails in English law has not been settled with any degree of certainty. Stephen thought it –

> "a subject on which the law of England is so vague that, if cases raising the question should ever occur the judges would practically be able to lay down any rule which they considered expedient."[10]

His own opinion on the matter was that

> "it is just possible to imagine cases in which the expediency of breaking the law is so overwhelmingly great that people may be justified in breaking it, but these cases cannot be defined beforehand, and must be adjudicated upon by a jury afterwards, the jury not being under the pressure of the motives which influenced the alleged offenders."[11]

---

5. Road Traffic Act 1972, s. 6, as substituted by Transport Act 1981, Sch. 8.
6. See Hall, *General Principles*, Ch. XII; Williams, CLGP, Ch. 17, and (1953), 6 CLP, 216; Stephen, *Digest*, Art. 11 and 2 HCL 108–110; Fuller "The Speluncean Explorers" (1949), 62 Harv. LR 616; Wechsler and Michael (1937) 37 Col LR 701 at 737–739.
7. Cf. *Larsonneur* (above, p. 46).
8. Hale, 1 PC 434.
9. *The William Gray* 29 Fed Cas 1300, No. 17, 694.
10. 2 HCL 108.
11. Ibid., 109.

In spite of these doubts, Williams has submitted "with some assurance" that the defence of necessity is recognised by English law[12] and, particularly, by the criminal law,[13] arguing that the

"peculiarity of necessity as a doctrine of law is the difficulty or impossibility of formulating it with any approach to precision."

Certainly the earlier writers generally quoted maxims supporting necessity as a defence[14] and, in 1550, Serjeant Pollard, in an argument which apparently found favour with the judges of the Exchequer Chamber, said:[15]

". . . in every law there are some things which when they happen a man may break the words of the law, and yet not break the law itself; and such things are exempted out of the penalty of the law, and the law privileges them although they are done against the letter of it, for breaking the words of the law is not breaking the law, so as the intent of the law is not broken. And therefore the words of the law of nature, of the law of this realm, and of other realms and of the law of God will also yield and give way to some acts and things done against the words of the same laws, and that is, where the words of them are broken to avoid greater inconveniences, or through necessity, or by compulsion . . ."

Moreover, it always seems to have been recognised that it was justifiable (in the conditions of those days) to pull down a house to prevent a fire from spreading,[16] for a prisoner to leave a burning gaol contrary to the express words of a statute and for the crew of a ship or a passenger[17] to jettison the cargo in order to save the ship. The judges have accepted *obiter* that it would be a defence to the common law misdemeanour of exposing an infected person in the streets to show that the defendant was taking her infected child to obtain medical advice.[18] It has long been recognised that it is lawful to kill one who makes an illegal attack if that is necessary in self-defence.[19] It has been held that prison officials may – indeed, must – forcibly feed prisoners if that is necessary to preserve their health and, a fortiori, their lives.[20] It was a defence to the statutory felony of procuring an abortion to show that the act was done in good faith for the purpose only of preserving the life of the mother,[1] although at that time there was no provision for such a defence in any statute.[2] A constable may direct other persons to disobey traffic regulations if that is reasonably necessary for the protection of life and property.[3] Lord Goff has said, "That there exists a defence of necessity at common law, which may in some circumstances be

---

12. 6 CLP, 216.
13. CLGP, 724, et seq.
14. See 6 CLP, at 218.
15. *Reniger v Fogossa* (1552) 1 Plowd 1 at 18.
16. See now the Criminal Damage Act 1971, below, p. 677.
17. *Mouse's Case* (1608) 12 Co Rep 63.
18. *Vantandillo* (1815) 4 M & S 73; below, p. 794.
19. Below, p. 240.
20. *Leigh v Gladstone* (1909) 26 TLR 139 (Alverstone LCJ). The decision is heavily criticised; see Zellick, [1976] *Public Law* at 159.
   1. *Bourne* [1939] 1 KB 687, [1938] 3 All ER 615; below, p. 365. Cf. *Morgentaler* (1975) 20 CCC (2d) 449 (SCC), discussed by Leigh, [1978] Crim LR 151.
   2. See now Abortion Act 1967, below, p. 369, and *T v T* [1988] 2 WLR 189, Fam. Div.
   3. *Johnson v Phillips* [1975] 3 All ER 682, [1976] 1 WLR 65, DC. Cf. *Wood v Richards* [1977] RTR 201, [1977] Crim LR 295, DC.

invoked to justify what would otherwise be a trespass to land, is not in doubt. But the scope of the defence is by no means clear." He found it unnecessary to decide the important question raised in that case, whether the defence could justify forcible entry (which would otherwise be a crime) into the private premises of another in the bona fide, but mistaken, belief that there exists an emergency on the premises by reason of the presence there of a person who has suffered injury and who may require urgent attention.[4] But, on the other hand, writers from Hale onwards have denied that necessity can be a defence to the larceny of food and clothing.[5] He put this on the ground that no such necessity could arise in England because the law provided for the relief of poverty. But Lord Denning justified the rule on the ground that –

"... if hunger were once allowed to be an excuse for stealing, it would open a door through which all kinds of lawlessness and disorder would pass."[6]

In that civil case it was held that homelessness did not justify an orderly entry into empty houses owned by the local authority.

"If homelessness were once admitted as a defence to trespass, no one's house could be safe. Necessity would open a door which no man could shut."[7]

Duress of circumstances. As will appear below,[8] if D commits what would otherwise be a crime (other than murder or some forms of treason) because E has threatened him with death or serious bodily harm if he does not, he may rely on the defence of duress. Suppose D does the same acts to avoid death or serious bodily harm but the threat comes not from a person, but from circumstances, or, if it comes from a person, it does not take the form, "Do this, or else ..." The compulsion on D to do the act is exactly the same. His moral culpability, or lack of it, is exactly the same. It would, it has been well said, be "the apotheosis of absurdity" to allow a defence of duress of threats while disallowing it for duress of circumstances.[9] There is now some authority for a defence of "duress of circumstances". In *Willer*[10] D was charged with reckless driving after he had driven very slowly on a pavement in order to escape from a gang of youths who were obviously intent on doing violence to him and his passengers. The trial judge declined to leave the defence of necessity to the jury. The Court of Appeal quashed D's conviction. It ought to have been left to the jury to say whether D drove "under that form of compulsion, i.e. under duress". But the compulsion was not the duress *per minas* which constitutes the defence of

4. *Richards and Leeming* (on appeal from 81 Cr App Rep 125), unreported, 10-7-86, HL. The House agreed with Lord Goff's speech. (We are indebted to Mr Anthony Hooper for drawing our attention to this case.) By s. 17(5) of the Police and Criminal Evidence Act "all the rules of common law under which a constable has power to enter premises without a warrant are hereby abolished". But does this abolish a justification which (if it exists at all) is available, not only to constables, but to persons generally?
5. See 1 PC 54 Blackstone, *Commentaries* iv. 31.
6. *Southwark London Borough v Williams* [1971] 2 All ER 175 at 179, CA.
7. Ibid.
8. P. 229.
9. Cross, 28 University of Toronto Law Journal 377.
10. (1986) 83 Cr App Rep 225, CA.

duress. The youths were not saying, "Drive on the pavement – or else . . ."
A better analogy is with private defence.[11] But it is best regarded simply as a
variety of necessity for it should make no difference whether D drove on the
pavement to escape from the youths, or a herd of charging bulls, a runaway
lorry, or a flood, if he did so in order to escape death or serious bodily harm.

The admission of such a defence of "duress of circumstances" seems to
be a logical consequence of the defence of duress which is inescapable
without absurdity.[12] Since it would be confined to cases where D feared
death or serious bodily harm, it would provide only a limited defence of
necessity but the limits would be consistent with those imposed on the
defence of duress.

In other parts of the common law world a general defence of necessity is
now recognised. Many American states have adopted the provision in the
American Model Penal Code.[13] The courts of Victoria have recognised the
existence of a general, if limited, defence in *Loughnan*[14] where D's defence
to a charge of escaping from prison was that he feared he would otherwise
be killed by other prisoners – but the defence was not made out on the facts.
In *Perka*[15] the Supreme Court of Canada held that necessity may be an
"excuse" but not a "justification" (there seems to be no practical difference
except that it perhaps made the court feel better) where D's acts are
"morally involuntary", the "involuntariness" being "measured on the
basis of society's expectation of appropriate and normal resistance to
pressure". In England it has been argued that there is a principle of
statutory interpretation –

". . . that it requires clear and unambiguous language before the courts
will hold that a statutory provision was intended to apply in which more
harm will, in all probability, be caused by complying with it than by
contravening it."[16]

This principle, if it exists, seems to be little noticed in modern times. In
Buckoke v Greater London Council[17] Lord Denning MR said, *obiter*:

"A driver of a fire engine with ladders approaches the traffic lights. He
sees 200 yards down the road a blazing house with a man at an upstairs
window in extreme peril. The road is clear in all directions. At that
moment the lights turn red. Is the driver to wait for 60 seconds or more,
for the lights to turn green? If the driver waits for that time, the man's
life will be lost."

Lord Denning accepted the view of both counsel that the driver would
commit an offence if he crossed the red light, adding –

". . . nevertheless such a man should not be prosecuted. He should be
congratulated."

Similarly, a medical emergency, though possibly a "special reason" for
not disqualifying, seems to be no defence to a charge of driving with

11. Below, p. 246.
12. See the draft Criminal Code (Law Com. No. 143), cl. 45.
13. Below, p. 229.
14. [1981] VR 443.
15. (1984) 13 DLR (4th) 1, **SHC 226**.
16. Ibid., at 93, citing *Reniger v Fogossa*, above, *Burns v Nowell* (1880) 5 QBD 444.
17. [1971] 1 Ch 655, [1971] 2 All ER 254 at 258; **SHC 223**. But see now S.I. 1975, No. 1536,
reg. 34(1) (b).

excessive blood alcohol, even though the driver is not impaired.[18] A person sleeping in a car which had been driven by another, who wakes up to find it running down a hill and steers it to safety, has no defence to a charge of driving while impaired by drink.[19] It can be argued[20] that Parliament could hardly have intended that the driver of the fire engine should stand at the red lights and watch a man burn to death or that the "driver" of the runaway car should let it take its course. It is odd to see the Master of the Rolls finding a breach of the criminal law a case for congratulation. A better answer might be to create an exception.

> "... it seems foolish to make rules (or to fail to make exceptions to rules) that discourage people from behaving as we would like them to behave. To the extent that the threat of punishment has deterrent efficacy, rules such as these would condition people confronted with dilemmas to make the wrong choice, either through action or inaction. And the actual imposition of punishment would serve no useful purpose since we assume these people are not in need of either restraint or reform."[1]

The case which has been most discussed in this connection is *Dudley and Stephens*.[2] Three men and a boy of the crew of a yacht were shipwrecked. After eighteen days in an open boat, having been without food and water for several days, the two accused suggested to the third man that they should kill and eat the boy. He declined but, two days later, Dudley killed the boy who was now very weak. The three men then fed on the boy's body and, four days later, they were rescued. The accused were indicted for murder. The jury, by a special verdict, found that the men would probably have died within the four days had they not fed on the boy's body, that the boy would probably have died before them and that, at the time of the killing, there was no appreciable chance of saving life, except by killing one for the others to eat.

The accused were convicted of murder, but the sentence was commuted to six months' imprisonment. The *ratio decidendi* is not obvious. Stephen said that he could discover no principle in the judgment[3] but Lord Simon thinks the *ratio decidendi* was the rejection of any defence of necessity.[4]

Lord Coleridge CJ, however, began by casting doubt on whether necessity really existed:

> "The verdict finds in terms that 'if the men had not fed upon the body of the boy they would *probably* have not survived,' and that 'The boy being in a much weaker condition was *likely* to have died before them.' They might possibly have been picked up next day by a passing ship; they might possibly not have been picked up at all; and in either case it is

---

18. Cf. *Brown v Dyerson* [1969] 1 QB 45, [1968] 3 All ER 39.
19. *Kitson* (1955) 39 Cr App Rep 66.
20. Glazebrook, op. cit., at 96.
   1. Packer, *The Limits of the Criminal Sanction*, 114.
   2. (1884) 14 QBD 273 **SHC 219**. On the instructions of Huddleston B the jury found the facts in a special verdict and the judge then adjourned the assizes to the Royal Courts of Justice where the case was argued before a court of five judges (Lord Coleridge CJ, Grove and Denman JJ, Pollock and Huddleston BB).
   3. *Digest* (8th ed.), 10, n. 2.
   4. *Lynch v Director of Public Prosecutions for Northern Ireland* [1975] 1 All ER 913 at 936 **SHC 211** below, p. 232.

obvious that the killing of this boy would have been an unnecessary and profitless act."[5]

It is arguable that the case decided nothing about necessity, in that it was based on the premise that no necessity existed. But there is no certainty in human affairs; in any emergency, however hopeless the situation may seem, there is always the possibility of some unforeseen intervention. And there was no *appreciable* chance of saving life, except by killing. It is, therefore, difficult to avoid the conclusion that *Dudley and Stephens* decided that it was no defence that the killing of one was necessary to preserve the lives of three. This view of the case is confirmed by the decision of the House of Lords in *Howe*[6] that duress can never be a defence to a charge of murder. Lord Hailsham,[7] like Lord Simon and Lord Kilbrandon in *Lynch*[8] thought that the two cases stood or fell together, so that to allow the defence of duress to murder would be to overrule *Dudley and Stephens*.[9]

Lord Coleridge CJ examined the pronouncements of writers of authority and found nothing in them to justify the extension of a defence to such a case as this. Killing by the use of force necessary to preserve one's own life in self-defence was a well-recognised, but entirely different, case from the killing of an innocent person. Moreover,

"If ... Lord Hale is clear – as he is – that extreme necessity of hunger does not justify larceny, what would he have said to the doctrine that it justified murder?"[10]

Apart from authority, the court clearly thought that the law ought not to afford a defence in such a case. They thought, first, that it would be too great a departure from morality; and, secondly, that the principle would be dangerous because of the difficulty of measuring necessity and of selecting the victim. The second reason is more convincing:

"Who is to be the judge of this sort of necessity? By what measure is the comparative value of lives to be measured? Is it to be strength or intellect, or what? It is plain that the principle leaves to him who is to profit by it to determine the necessity which will justify him in delibe- rately taking another's life to save his own."[11]

Williams finds as the "one satisfying reason" in the judgment that it was no more necessary to kill the boy than one of the grown men and adds: "To hinge guilt on this would indicate that lots should have been cast ...".[12] If the boy had agreed to be bound by the casting of lots, he would have been consenting to die; and consent in such a situation may be a defence. Captain Oates took his life when he left Scott and his companions; yet he was regarded, not as a felon, but as a hero. If the boy had not consented, the drawing of lots would be hardly more rational than trial by ordeal – yet more civilised than a free-for-all. In fact, the court disapproved, *obiter*, of a

5. 14 QBD at 279. Cf. Cardozo J: "Who shall know when masts and sails of rescue may emerge out of the fog?" *Selected Writings*, 390.
6. [1987] AC 417, [1987] 1 All ER 771, below, p. 232.
7. See p. 777.
8. [1965] AC 653 at 692 and 701–702.
9. On the case generally, see A. W. B. Simpson, *Cannibalism and the Common Law*.
10. 14 QBD at 283.
11. 14 QBD at 287.
12. CLGP, 744.

ruling in an American case, *US v Holmes*,[13] that the drawing of lots in similar circumstances would legalise a killing. Holmes, a member of the crew of a wrecked ship, was cast adrift in an overcrowded boat. In order to prevent the boat sinking, the mate gave orders to throw the male passengers overboard and Holmes assisted in throwing over sixteen men. No doubt, if his act was criminal at all, it was murder; but a grand jury refused to indict him for murder and so he was charged with manslaughter. The judge directed that the law was that passengers must be preferred to seamen; only enough seamen to navigate the boat ought to have been saved; and the passengers whom necessity requires to be cast over must be chosen by lot. As this had not been done (none of the officers or crew went down with the ship) the jury found him guilty.

Stephen thought the method of selection "over refined"[14] and Lord Coleridge thought this

"somewhat strange ground . . . can hardly . . . be an authority satisfactory to a court in this country."[15]

The English judges offered no alternative solution and, presumably, their view was that, in the absence of a self-sacrificing volunteer, it was the duty of all to die. This was also the view of the distinguished American judge, Cardozo J:

"Where two or more are overtaken by a common disaster, there is no right on the part of one to save the lives of some, by the killing of another. There is no rule of human jettison."[16]

Nor does it appear to make any difference that A's object was to save a number of persons; Dudley killed to save himself and two others. Yet there are difficulties about a logical application of this rule to all cases: would it not be lawful to open a dike with the effect of drowning the half-dozen inhabitants of a farm, if this was the only way of saving a dam from bursting and inundating a whole town?[17]

Perhaps the difference here is that the choice is clear; it is *either* the half-dozen *or* the hundreds who must perish; but in *Dudley* there was no clear choice between the boy on the one hand and the men on the other. It must be conceded that it was not "more necessary to kill him than one of the grown men."[18] It is arguable that it is "more necessary to save the hundred than the half-dozen." But this case is not absolutely clear. Suppose that the farmer, knowing all the facts, has a rifle with which he can kill the man opening the dam. Does the law deny him the right to shoot to kill in order to preserve his own life and the lives of his family? Is he not essentially in the same position as the first man on the plank? He is the one at present in

---

13. 26 Fed Cas 360 (1842).
14. 2 HCL 108.
15. 14 QBD at 285.
16. *Selected Writings*, 390.
17. American Model Penal Code, Tentative Draft No. 8, S3.02 Comments, p. 9: ". . . he can rightly point out that the object of the law of homicide is to save life, and that by his conduct he has effected a net saving of innocent lives . . . the numerical preponderance in the lives saved surely establishes an ethical and legal justification for the act."
18. (1884) 14 QBD at 287–288.

possession of safety. If it is lawful to drown him in order to preserve the hundred lives, then it must follow either that he is deprived of his right of self-defence and is under a duty to die a heroic and unresisting death[19] or that it is not unlawful for either man to kill the other.[20]

The American Model Penal Code propounds a general defence of necessity:

"Conduct which the actor believes to be necessary to avoid a harm or evil to himself or to another is justifiable, provided that:

a) the harm of evil sought to be avoided by such conduct is greater than that sought to be prevented by the law defining the offence charged . . ."[1]

No such general principle exists or is likely to be developed by English courts. Edmund Davies LJ has clearly formulated the judicial attitude:

". . . the law regards with the deepest suspicion any remedies of self-help, and permits these remedies to be resorted to only in very special circumstances. The reason for such circumspection is clear – necessity can very easily become simply a mask for anarchy."[2]

Except in cases where necessity has already been recognised as a defence, the courts are likely to be satisfied by their power to grant an absolute discharge in hard cases.[3]

The Law Commission, departing from the views of its Working Party, has recommended that there should be no general defence of necessity; and that, for the avoidance of doubt, it should be enacted that any such defence as does exist is abolished.[4] Provision should be made by statute for a defence to particular offences where appropriate.[5]

These recommendations have been subjected to very cogent criticism and the Law Commission's codification team found themselves unable to act on them. The draft Criminal Code provides for a limited defence of necessity – in effect that which is a logical consequence of the existence of the defence of duress – i.e., "duress of circumstances".[6]

7 Duress (or Compulsion) and Coercion[7]

The defences here to be considered are closely related to that of necessity. Once again, D is faced with a choice of evils: shall he break the criminal law or submit to the infliction of some evil on himself or on another? These might be regarded as special cases of necessity, the only peculiarity being

---

19. The law rarely, if ever, imposes such high standards; but cf. Hall, *General Principles*, 435.
20. See Huxley, "Proposals on the Defence of Necessity" [1978] Crim LR 141 at 146; and cf. below, p. 233.
1. Art. 3. Section 3.02. It is subject to qualifications not necessary to be noted here.
2. *Southwark London Borough v Williams* [1971] Ch 734, [1971] 2 All ER 175 at 181 **SHC 211**.
3. Glazebrook, op. cit., 118–119.
4. Report on Defences of General Application (Law Com. No. 83, 1977); criticised by Williams [1978] Crim LR 128; Huxley [1978] Crim LR 141.
5. See for example, Midwives Act 1951, s. 9.
6. Above, p. 224. See Law Com. No. 143, cl. 46.
7. Edwards (1951) 14 MLR 297; Williams, CLGP, Ch 18; Hall, *General Principles*, 436 et seq.; Ashworth (1975) 91 LQR 102; Wasik, [1977] Crim LR 453.

that need arises out of the wrongful threats of another to inflict some harm on D if he does not commit the criminal act.[8] The terms "duress", "compulsion" and "coercion" are often used as if they were synonymous; but some writers reserve "coercion" for a special defence available to wives under pressure from their husbands, and this convenient practice will be followed here.

1 Duress

Duress is a general defence but it does not apply to some forms of treason, murder (whether as a principal or as a secondary party) and possibly not to attempted murder.

Duress and Voluntariness

It has often been said that the duress must be such that D's act is not "voluntary", but it is clear that we are not here concerned with the kind of involuntariness which arises from automatism. As the courts recognise, duress does not negative intention.[9] D intends to do the act which, but for the duress, would be a crime. When D pleads duress he admits that he had a choice and chose to do the act with which he is charged, but denies that it is a crime.[10] He may say, "I had no choice", but that is not strictly true. The choice was not a very good one but he could have chosen to defy the threat – indeed, where he is required to commit murder, the courts insist that he must defy it – or face the prospect of conviction for murder and a sentence of imprisonment for life.

It is said that D's will must have been "overborne" by the threat. Presumably this means only that he would not have committed the offence but for the threat and that the threat was one which might cause a person of reasonable fortitude to do as he did. But the threat need not be the only motive for D's actions. In *Valderrama-Vega*[11] D was under financial pressure and had been threatened with disclosure of his homosexual inclinations – neither matter being capable of amounting to duress – but it was wrong to direct the jury that the threats of death or serious injury also alleged to have been made must have been the sole reason for his committing the offence. If he would not have committed the offence but for the latter threats, the defence was available even if he acted because of the cumulative effect of all the pressure on him. It is probably going too far to say that it is enough that the threats of death were "the last straw" because the law will look for something more substantial than "a straw" for an excuse; but threats of death or serious bodily harm can never be trivial, so it is probably sufficient to tell the jury that D has the defence if he would not have acted but for the threats. A direction that the defence was available only if D acted *solely* because of the relevant threats was upheld where it

---

8. Threats not directed to causing D to commit the particular crime do not amount to duress: *Dawson* [1978] VR 536 (not a defence to a charge of escape from prison that D feared for his life).

9. *Howe* [1987] 1 All ER 771 at 777, HL, per Lord Hailsham, LC, citing Lords Kilbrandon and Edmund-Davies in *Director of Public Prosecutions for Northern Ireland v Lynch* [1975] AC 653 at 703 and 709–710.

10. Cf. the discussion of *Steane* [1947] KB 997, [1947] 1 All ER 813, above, p. 57.

11. [1985] Crim LR 220 and commentary.

was suggested that he might also have been influenced by greed but the court thought it inadvisable to use that word in a summing up.[12]

Duress is a defence because—

". . . threats of immediate death or serious personal violence so great as to overbear the ordinary powers of human resistance should be accepted as a justification for acts which would otherwise be criminal."[13]

Duress has been accepted as a defence to manslaughter,[14] criminal damage,[15] arson,[16] theft,[17] handling,[18] perjury and contempt of court[19] and drug offences;[20] and courts have assumed that it would apply to buggery[1] and conspiracy[2] to defraud. It now seems safe to say that duress may be a defence to any crime, except some forms of treason, murder and, possibly, attempted murder.

Duress and treason. Although it is not uncommon for treason to be mentioned as a crime where duress is not a defence, it is quite clear that it may be a defence to at least some forms of treason.[3]

As long ago as 1419 in *Oldcastle*'s case[4] the accused who were charged with treason in supplying victuals to Sir John Oldcastle and his fellow rebels were acquitted on the ground that they acted *pro timore mortis, et quod recesserunt quam cito potuerunt.* The existence of the defence was admitted, *obiter*, by Lee CJ in *M'Growther*,[5] a trial for treason committed in the 1745 rebellion and by Lord Mansfield in *Stratton*:[6]

". . . if a man is forced to commit acts of high treason, if it appears really force, and such as human nature could not be expected to resist and the jury are of that opinion, the man is not guilty of high treason."

Much more recently, in *Purdy*[7] Oliver J directed a jury that fear of death would be a defence to a British prisoner of war who was charged with treason in having assisted with German propaganda in the second world war. Against this, Lord Goddard CJ said in *Steane*[8] that the defence did not apply to treason, but this remark appears to have been made *per incuriam*.

Hale[9] would allow the defence only in time of war or public insurrection and not in time of peace. In peacetime men may resort to the law for protection but this is not possible for one who falls into enemy or rebel

12. *Ortiz* (1986) 83 Cr App Rep 173.
13. *A-G v Whelan* [1934] IR 518, per Murnaghan J (Irish CCA); Elliott and Wood (2nd ed.) at 46.
14. *Evans and Gardiner* [1976] VR 517 and (No. 2) 523.
15. *Crutchley* (1831) 5 C & P 133.
16. *Shiartos* (Lawton J, Sept. 19, 1961, unreported but referred to in *Gill*, below).
17. *Gill* [1963] 2 All ER 688, [1963] 1 WLR 841, CCA.
18. *A-G v Whelan* [1934] IR 518.
19. *K* (1983) 78 Cr App Rep 82, CA.
20. *Valderrama-Vega* [1985] Crim LR 220, *Ortiz* (1986) 83 Cr App Rep 173.
1. *Bourne* (1952) 36 Cr App Rep 125.
2. *Verrier* [1965] Crim LR 732.
3. [1975] 1 All ER at 920, per Lord Morris; 940, per Lord Simon; 944, per Lord Kilbrandon.
4. (1419) 1 Hale PC 50; East 1 PC 70.
5. Fost (1746) 13; 18 State Tr 391.
6. (1779) 1 Doug KB 239.
7. (1946) 10 JCL 182.
8. [1947] KB 997 at 1005, [1947] 1 All ER 813 at 817.
9. 1 PC 49–51.

hands. The reasoning is unsatisfactory,[10] for legal remedies may not be available in peacetime to one who is in the hands of criminals; and it is clear that in wartime a man who commits treasonable acts when he could put himself under the protection of lawful authority has no defence. The distinction between peace and war is unsound. The true distinction is between one who can reasonably be expected to escape from the duress and one who cannot.

Treason is an offence which may take many forms varying widely in seriousness and it would be wrong to suppose that threats, even of death, will necessarily be a defence to every act of treason. In *Oldcastle*'s case[11] Hale emphasises that the accuseds' act was *only* furnishing of victuals and he appears to question whether, if they had taken a more active part in the rebellion, they would have been excused. Stephen thought the defence only applied where the offender took a subordinate part.

Duress and murder. It was stated in the books from Hale onwards that duress could not be a defence to a charge of murder. As Blackstone put it, a man under duress "ought rather to die himself than escape by the murder of an innocent".[12] There was, however, no clear judicial authority in point and in 1969 in *Kray*[13] an inroad was made into the supposed rule when Widgery LJ said that a person charged as an accessory before the fact to murder might rely on duress. In 1975, in *Lynch v Director of Public Prosecution for Northern Ireland*[14] the House of Lords, by a majority of three to two, held that a person charged with aiding and abetting murder – one who would have been a principal in the second degree under the law of felonies – could have a defence of duress. The position of the actual killer was left open and in *Abbott*[15] in 1976, again by three to two, the Privy Council distinguished *Lynch* and held that the defence was not available to the principal offender, the actual killer. This was an illogical and unsatisfactory position because it is by no means always the case that the actual killer is the most dominant or culpable member of a number of accomplices, but he alone was now excluded from the defence. The distinctions involved were technical and absurd.[16] Accordingly, when the matter came before the House in *Howe*[17] there was a strong case for either going forward and allowing the defence to all alleged parties to murder, or backward, and allowing it to none. The House chose the latter course, overruling its own decision in *Lynch*. The speeches emphasise different aspects, but the following reasons for the decision appear among them.

    i) The ordinary man of reasonable fortitude, if asked to take an innocent life, might be expected to sacrifice his own.[18] Lord Hailsham would not –

10. See the criticism by Stephen, 2 HCL 106–107.
11. (1419), Hale 1 PC 50.
12. Commentaries, iv, 30.
13. [1970] 1 QB 125, [1969] 3 All ER 941.
14. [1975] AC 653.
15. [1977] AC 755, [1976] 3 All ER 140.
16. *Graham* [1982] 1 All ER 801 at 804, per Lane LCJ.
17. [1987] 1 All ER 771, [1987] 2 WLR 568, [1987] Crim LR 480 (sub nom *Burke*) and commentary.
18. Pp. 779–780.

"regard a law as either 'just' or 'humane' which withdraws the protection of the criminal law from the innocent victim and casts the cloak of its protection on the coward and the poltroon in the name[19] of a 'concession to human frailty'."

ii) One who takes the life of an innocent person cannot claim that he is choosing the lesser of two evils.[20]

iii) The Law Commission had recommended[1] ten years previously that duress should be a defence to the alleged principal offender, but Parliament had not acted on that recommendation.[2]

iv) Hard cases could be dealt with by not prosecuting – in some cases the person under duress might be expected to be the principal witness for the prosecution[3] – or by the action of the Parole Board in ordering the early release of a person who would have had a defence if duress had been an available defence.[4]

It is submitted that none of these reasons is convincing.

i) If the defence were available, it would apply only when a jury thought a person of reasonable fortitude *would* have yielded to the threat. The criminal law should not require heroism. Moreover, there are circumstances in which the good citizen of reasonable fortitude not only would, but probably should, yield to the threat because –

ii) to do so might clearly be to choose the lesser of two evils, as where the threat is to kill D and all his family if he does not do, or assist in, an act which he knows will cause grievous harm but not death (though, ex hypothesi, it has resulted in death and so constitutes murder).

iii) Parliament's failure to act on the Law Commission recommendation proves nothing. The government has not given Parliament the opportunity to consider the matter. By parity of reason, Parliament might be taken to have approved of *Lynch*'s case, because there has been no move to overrule it.

iv) Even if he were not prosecuted, the "duressee" would be, in law, a murderer and, if he were called as a prosecution witness, the judge would be required to tell the jury that he was an accomplice in murder, on whose evidence it would be dangerous to act in the absence of corroboration. A morally innocent person should not be left at the mercy of administrative discretion on a murder charge.

The effect on other offences. The decision in *Howe* applies only to the law of murder. Lord Hailsham said that, in the case of a charge of attempted murder, the availability of the defence would require re-consideration while Lord Griffiths would declare (though plainly obiter) that duress is not available on such a charge.[5] If it were available, the law would involve the absurdity that an act, excusable when done, would become inexcusable

19. Referring to the fifth edition of this work at p. 215.
20. Lord Hailsham at 780.
 1. Report on Defences of General Application (Law Com No. 83).
 2. Lord Bridge at 784 and Lord Griffiths at 788.
 3. Lord Griffiths at 790.
 4. Lord Griffiths at 791, Lord Hailsham at 780–781.
 5. At pp. 780 and 790.

if death occurred within a year and a day of its having been done. The same anomaly applies to one who, under duress, causes grievous bodily harm with intent to do so. If death results within a year and a day, he becomes guilty of murder. The only way to prevent the excusable subsequently becoming inexcusable is to exclude the defence from s. 18 of the Offences against the Person Act as well.

The threat. What is a sufficiently serious threat to amount to duress? Hale speaks of threats of death and so do the judges in *M'Growther*[6] and *Purdy*;[7] Blackstone refers to "death or other bodily harm", Stephen to death or grievous bodily harm, Lord Goddard CJ in *Steane*[8] to violence or imprisonment, and Widgery LJ in *Hudson*[9] to death or serious personal injury. It seems that threats to kill or injure a third person may be sufficient. In *Hurley and Murray*[10] the Supreme Court of Victoria held threats to kill or seriously injure D's *de facto* wife amounted to duress. That principle would clearly extend to D's family and others to whom he owed a duty and, possibly, even to a complete stranger – for example one held as a hostage to be killed if D did not participate in the crime. Probably the gravity of the threat required varies with the enormity of the crime. The dictum of Lords Wilberforce and Edmund-Davies no longer applies to killing but is good for other acts:

"... the realistic view is that, the more dreadful the circumstances of the killing, the heavier the evidential burden of an accused advancing such a plea, and the stronger and more irresistible the duress needed before it could be regarded as affording any defence."[11]

There is no modern[12] case in which a threat of injury to property, as distinct from the person, has been admitted.[13] In *M'Growther*[14] D, who was a tenant of the Duke of Perth, called witnesses who proved that the Duke had threatened to burn the houses and drive off the cattle of any of his tenants who refused to follow him. Lee CJ directed that this could be no defence. But that was a case of treason and it does not necessarily follow that such a threat would not be enough on some lesser charge. If the evil D caused by submitting to the threat was clearly less than that which would have been inflicted had he defied it, there are cogent reasons for allowing a defence; even if the threat was not of death or even grievous bodily harm. Williams has argued strongly in favour of such a principle, which is, of course,

6. Supra.
7. Supra.
8. [1947] KB 997 at 1005, [1947] 1 All ER 813 at 816.
9. [1971] 2 QB 202, [1971] 2 All ER 244.
10. [1967] VR 526.
11. *Abbott v R* [1976] 3 All ER at 152.
12. Cf. *Crutchley* (1831) 5 C & P 133.
13. "... the threat may be to burn down [D's] house unless the householder merely keeps watch against interruption while a crime is committed. Or a fugitive from justice may say, 'I have it in my power to make your son bankrupt. You can avoid that merely by driving me to the airport.' Would not many ordinary people yield to such threats, and act contrary to their wish not to perform an action prohibited by law? Faced with such anomaly, is not the only answer, 'Well, the law must draw a line somewhere; and, as a result of experience and human valuation, the law draws it between threats to property and threats to the person," per Lord Simon [1975] 1 All ER at 932.
14. Above, p. 231.

closely analogous to that adopted in the American Model Penal Code in relation to necessity.[15] But this would deny a defence to D even though the injury threatened was one which he could not be expected to endure; and there would be grave difficulty in balancing the two evils against one another when they are of a completely different character.[16]

It is generally stated that the threat must be "immediate" or "imminent" and that, if the person under the compulsion is able to resort to the protection of the law, he must do so.

"The only force that doth excuse, is a force upon *the person*, and present fear of death; and his force and fear must continue all the time the party remains with the rebels. It is incumbent on every man, who makes force his defence to show an actual force, and that he quitted the service as soon as he could."[17]

In *Hurley*, however, D had ample opportunity to place himself under the protection of the police but the court held that the defence of duress might still be available because his *de facto* wife was held as a hostage by his oppressors. Though he himself was physically out of range, the threats against her were presently operative on his mind. *Hudson* goes further. Two young women, called as witnesses for the prosecution, gave false evidence because they had been threatened by a gang with serious physical injury if they told the truth, and they saw one of the gang in the gallery of the court. Duress was accepted as a defence to a charge of perjury. D could have put herself under the protection of the law by informing the court; and there were no threats to third parties. The court thought it immaterial that the threatened injury could not follow at once since (in its opinion) there was no opportunity for delaying tactics and she had to make up her mind whether to commit the offence while the threat was operating. The threat was no less compelling because it could not be carried out there if it could be effected in the streets of Salford the same night. The case thus turns on the point that police protection could not be effective. It extends the possible ambit of the defence widely for there must be few cases where the police can offer effective and permanent protection against such threats.[18]

The Facts and the Standard – Objective or Subjective

In *Howe* the House of Lords answered in the affirmative the question –

"Does the defence of duress fail if the prosecution prove that a person of reasonable firmness sharing the characteristics of the defendant would not have given way to the threats as did the defendant?"

The House held that the correct direction was that stated by Lane LCJ in *Graham*:[19]

---

15. Above, p. 229.
16. Law Commission Working Paper No. 55, paras. 14–17.
17. *M'Growther*, Fost (1746) 13 at 14, per Lee CJ.
18. See comment in [1971] Crim LR 359 and (by Goodhart) in 87 LQR 299 and 121 NLJ 909 and (by Zellick) in 121 NLJ 845. In *K* (1983) 78 Cr App Rep 82, CA, it was held that duress might be available as a defence to contempt of court committed in the witness box by a prisoner who had been threatened with reprisals against himself and his family, by the accused, a fellow prisoner.
19. [1982] 1 All ER 801 at 806, 74 Cr App Rep 235 at 241. Cf. *Lawrence* [1980] 1 NSWLR 122.

"Was [D], or may he have been, impelled to act as he did because, as a result of what he reasonably believed [E] had said or done, he had good cause to fear that if he did not so act [E] would kill him or . . . cause him serious physical injury? (2) If so, have the prosecution made the jury sure that a sober person of reasonable firmness, sharing the characteristics of [D], would not have responded to whatever he reasonably believed [E] said or did by taking part in the killing?"

The direction contains three objective elements. D must have *reasonably* believed; his belief must have amounted to *good cause* for his fear and his response must be one which might have been expected of a *sober person of reasonable firmness*. It is respectfully submitted that, in the first two respects, this lays down too strict a rule. D should surely be judged on the basis of what he actually believed and what he actually feared. If his actual fear was such that no person of reasonable firmness could have been expected to resist it, he should be excused. He may have been unduly credulous or stupid, but he is no more blameworthy than a person whose fear is based on reasonable grounds. In *Gladstone Williams*[20] the courts have now recognised that, for purposes of private defence, D should be judged on the facts as he believed them to be, whether reasonably or not, and it seems inconsistent in principle to apply a different test for duress. Lack of faith in the jury to detect the "bogus defence" probably lies at the root of the objective requirements. It is much the same as with mistake generally. The more tenuous the grounds for fear, the less likely is D to be believed.[1]

Since duress is (*pace* Lord Hailsham) a concession to human frailty[2] and some are more frail than others, it is arguable that the standard of fortitude required should also vary.[3] *Graham* is however consistent with the general approach of the law in deciding that this is fixed. It is for the law to lay down standards of conduct. When attacked, D may use only a reasonable degree of force in self-defence. In blackmail P is expected to display a measure of fortitude and not to be affected by trivial threats. Under provocation, D must display a reasonable degree of self-restraint. Similarly, *Graham* decides, a person under duress is required to display "the steadfastness reasonably to be expected of the ordinary citizen in his situation".[4] The court relied particularly on the analogy with the law of provocation as laid down in *Camplin*.[5] This suggests that the threat must be one which would overcome the will of a person having the ability to resist threats reasonably to be expected of an ordinary person of the sex and age of the defendant and in other respects sharing such of the defendant's characteristics as the jury think would affect the gravity of the threat to him.

---

20. [1987] 3 All ER 441, (1984) 78 Cr App Rep 276, above, p. 88, below, p. 241.
 1. Cf. Sexual Offences (Amendment) Act 1976, s. 1(2), below, p. 429.
 2. *Pace* Lord Hailsham in *Howe* [1987] 1 All ER 771 at 779–780.
 3. "It is arguable that the standard should be purely subjective and that it is contrary to principle to require the fear to be a reasonable one": per Lord Simon, [1975] 1 All ER at 931. Cf. Law Commission Working Paper No. 55, paras, 11–13 and Report (Law Com. No. 83) at 2.27–2.28. Cf. *Hudson* [1965] 1 All ER 721 at 724; **SHC 206**; above, p. 96.
 4. 74 Cr App Rep at 241.
 5. [1978] AC 705, [1978] 2 All ER 168, below, p. 337.

Similar principles probably apply to the doctrine requiring D to escape from duress if possible. His defence will fail if an ordinary person of his sex, age and other relevant characteristics, would have taken an opportunity to escape. Obviously, physical disabilities, for example that he was lame, would be taken into account.[6] Following *Graham*, however, he must presumably be taken to have been aware of opportunities of which he ought reasonably to have been aware. A better view, it is submitted, is that if he was not in fact aware of the opportunity to escape, he should not be penalised for his stupidity or slow-wittedness.

Duress by an association voluntarily joined.

"where a person has voluntarily, and with knowledge of its nature, joined a criminal organisation or gang which he knew might bring pressure on him to commit an offence and was an active member when he was put under such pressure, he cannot avail himself of the defence of duress."[7]

In *Sharp* D was a party to a conspiracy to commit robberies who said that he wanted to pull out when he saw his confederates equipped with guns, whereupon E threatened to blow his head off if he did not carry on with the plan. In the course of the robbery, E killed P. D's conviction for manslaughter was upheld after a jury, directed substantially as above, had rejected his defence of duress.

If D joins a group of people whom he knows to be dedicated to violence as a political end, or one which is overtly ready to use violence for other criminal ends, then he will inevitably forfeit any possible defence of duress. The defence is not inevitably barred because the duress comes from a criminal organisation which D has joined. It depends on the nature of the organisation and D's knowledge of it. If he was unaware of any propensity to violence, the defence will not be denied. The court so held in *Shepherd*[8] where D had voluntarily joined a gang of burglars. The question should have been left to the jury to decide whether he could be said to have taken the risk of violence from a member of the gang, simply by joining its activities.

Until these recent decisions there was no English authority on the point, but there was a wealth of persuasive authority in the criminal codes of many common law jurisdictions, the decision of the Court of Criminal Appeal in Northern Ireland in *Fitzpatrick* (duress no defence to a charge of robbery committed as a result of threats by the I.R.A. because D had voluntarily joined that organisation)[9] and the dicta of Lords Morris, Wilberforce and Simon in *Lynch*.[10] If D was compelled to join the violent organisation by threats of death or serious bodily harm then, in principle, he should not be deprived of the defence. Whether any lesser threat should suffice at this stage has not been decided. D's attempt to withdraw from the organisation, when the particular enterprise which resulted in the charge is in contemplation, is too late. But a man who joined the I.R.A. in his youth can hardly

---

6. But the fact that he was voluntarily drunk or drugged might be considered irrelevant.
7. *Sharp* [1987] QB 853, [1987] 3 All ER 103, per Lane LCJ.
8. (1987) 86 Cr App Rep 47, CA.
9. [1977] NILR 20.
10. [1975] AC 653.

be held to have forfeited his right to plead duress by that organisation for life. If he has done all he can to sever his connection with it before the particular incident was in contemplation, should he not be able to rely on the defence?

The onus of proof. The onus of disproving duress is on the Crown.[11] If no facts from which duress might reasonably be inferred appear in the prosecution's case, then D has the "evidential burden" of laying a foundation for the defence by introducing evidence of such facts.

Reform. The Law Commission favours the retention of the defence and its extension to all offences, including murder as a principal in the first degree; but excluding anyone who, voluntarily and without reasonable cause, is in a situation in which he knows he will, or may be, subjected to duress.[12]

2 Coercion

Though the terminology used by judges and writers is by no means uniform, the term "coercion" is generally reserved for a special defence that was available at common law only to a wife who committed certain crimes in the presence of her husband. It was then presumed that she acted under such coercion as to entitle her to be excused, unless the prosecution were able to prove that she took the initiative in committing the offence. The exact extent of the defence is uncertain. It did not apply to treason or murder; Hale[13] excluded manslaughter as well and Hawkins ruled out robbery.[14]

Earlier authorities allowed the defence only in the case of felonies but later it seems to have been extended to misdemeanours – but excluding brothel-keeping;

"for this is an offence touching the domestic economy or government of the home in which the wife has a principal share."[15]

Various theoretical justifications were advanced for the rule – the identity of husband and wife, the wife's subjection to her husband and her duty to obey him – but the practical reason for its application to felonies was that it saved a woman from the death penalty when her husband was able, but she was not, to plead benefit of clergy.[16] This reason disappeared in 1692 when benefit of clergy was extended to women, yet the rule continued and its scope increased.

In 1925, however, the presumption was abolished by the Criminal Justice Act 1925, s. 47:

"Any presumption of law that an offence committed by a wife in the presence of her husband is committed under the coercion of the husband is hereby abolished, but on a charge against a wife for any offence other than treason or murder, it shall be a good defence to prove that the

---

11. *Gill* [1963] 2 All ER 688, [1963] 1 WLR 841, CCA.
12. Report on Defences of General Application (Law Com. No. 83 1977). See A. T. H. Smith, [1978] Crim LR 122. Cf. above, p. 233.
13. 1 PC 45.
14. 1 PC 4; but the editor of the 8th ed. (J. Curwood) doubted this.
15. Blackstone, *Commentaries*, iv. 29.
16. Hale, 1 PC 45; 2 Lew CC 232n.

offence was committed in the presence of, and under the coercion of, the husband.''

At first sight, it would seem that all Parliament has done is to shift the burden of proof. But there are difficulties about this, for the question at once arises, proof of what? and it is not very easy to answer. "Coercion" at common law was really a fiction applied when the wife committed a crime in the presence of the husband and there was no evidence of initiative by the wife. The common law gives little guidance as to what is required now coercion is a matter of affirmative proof. One solution is to hold that it simply means the same as duress and puts the wife in the same situation as anyone else. The difficulty about that is that it would appear to put the wife in a *worse* position; for (i) the onus of disproving duress is on the Crown[17] and (ii) duress probably applies to some forms of treason.[18] The first difficulty might be got over by holding that the statute puts on the wife only the evidential burden (which defendants relying on duress have, but wives relying on coercion at common law did not) of introducing so much evidence as might raise a reasonable doubt whether she was under duress. The second difficulty is less easy to get over. Of course, it may be that, owing to the uncertainties of this branch of the criminal law, Parliament thought that duress did not apply to treason or murder and that wives have been put in a worse position by accident.

The better view is that coercion is a wider defence than duress and is available to wives in addition to the general defence.[19] "The Act can be regarded as merely an incomplete statement of the common law, and the common law still exists to supplement its deficiency."[20] This would seem to have been the real intention and the better view. In the debate on the Bill the Solicitor-General told the House that the section gives the married woman

"a rather wider and more extended line of defence than pure compulsion, because coercion imports coercion in the moral, possibly even in the spiritual realm, whereas compulsion imports something only in the physical realm."[1]

The recommendation of the Avory Committee[2] that wives should be put in the same position as persons generally was not adopted. Far from there being the "endless litigation" which one member feared, there are only three reported cases[3] in which the defence has been relied on.[4] It is by no means clear what a wife has to prove to succeed – moral and spiritual, as

---

17. Above, p. 238.
18. Above, p. 231.
19. Williams, CLGP, 765. See *Richman* [1982] Crim LR 507 (Bristol Crown Court).
20. Williams CLGP 765, approved by Lord Edmund-Davies [1975] 1 All ER 954. See also Lord Wilberforce at 930.
1. Parl Deb, H of C (1925), 188, col. 875.
2. Cmd. 1677.
3. *Pierce* (1941) 5 JCL 124 and *Richman*, above, footnote 12. Cf. *Bourne* (above, p. 155) where duress rather than coercion seems to have been relied on.
4. Perhaps the view of Mr Greaves-Lord, M.P., has proved correct: "... how many women are there who have been coerced like that, who dare go into the witness box in order to convict the very persons under whose coercion the woman had committed the crime?" Parl Deb, H of C, 188, col. 870.

distinct from physical, coercion are somewhat intangible. Edwards suggests – as possibilities – the wife who has been

"tamed into believing that failure to obey her husband's every command would inevitably result in her being doomed to suffer the fires of hell;"

or who has

"been inculcated with her husband's teaching that to steal from the rich to help the poor was right and just;"

and,

"what about threats not to provide any money to purchase food for the wife and children, or to desert the wife or to bring a concubine home to live under the same roof?"[5]

Williams suggests that

"perhaps it is enough to show that the wife is meek and tractable, under the domination of her husband, and unable to influence him."[6]

The answer to these questions must await the decisions of the court when such cases arise.

The defence will no doubt be confined, as it was at common law, strictly to the case of husband and wife and will not be extended to an unmarried couple living as man and wife.[7] Yet a woman in such a situation may be as much under coercion as any married woman; while children, to whom no such defence is available, may be even more under the influence of their parents. It does not extend to a wife by a polygamous marriage nor to a woman who wrongly believes she is married to her oppressor.[8]

It is thought that the very absence of cases in which it has been relied on goes a long way towards showing that it is an unnecessary anomaly at the present day. The Law Commission has recommended its abolition.[9]

8 Public and Private Defence

Force causing personal injury, damage to property, or even death may be justified or excused because the force was reasonably used in the defence of certain public or private interests. Public and private defence is therefore a general defence and appropriately considered at this point. The law is to be found in a variety of sources. Defence of the person, whether one's own or that of another, is still regulated by the common law, defence of property by the Criminal Damage Act 1971 and arrest and the prevention of crime by s. 3 of the Criminal Law Act 1967. Because of its haphazard growth, the law contains some inconsistencies and anomalies. The general principle, however, is that the law allows such force to be used as is reasonable in the circumstances of the particular case: and, for the purposes of offences requiring *mens rea*, what is reasonable is to be judged in the light of the

5. (1951) 14 MLR at 311.
6. CLGP, 766.
7. *Court* (1912) 7 Cr App Rep 127.
8. *Kara* [1988] Crim LR 42, CA.
9. Law Com. No. 83 (1977), 3.1–3.9.

circumstances as the accused believed them to be, whether reasonably or not. For example, if D believed that he was being attacked with a deadly weapon and he used only such force as was reasonable to repel such an attack, he has a defence to any charge of an offence requiring *mens rea* arising out of the use of that force. It is immaterial, so far as D's liability for an offence involving *mens rea* is concerned, that he was mistaken and unreasonably mistaken. But if the offence – e.g., manslaughter[10] – is one which may be committed by gross negligence or recklessness, then it would seem that a grossly negligent or reckless mistake would not excuse.

The question, "Was the force used reasonable in the circumstances as D supposed them to be?" is, with one exception,[11] a question, to be answered by the jury or magistrates. D's opinion that it was reasonable is not conclusive but the test of reasonableness, it has been held,[12] is not "purely objective". The force will commonly be used in a moment of crisis. In the case of self-defence the jury should be reminded they must not disregard the state of mind of the defendant altogether.[13] Lord Morris has said:[14]

"If there has been attack so that defence is reasonably necessary it will be recognised that a person defending himself cannot weigh to a nicety the exact measure of his necessary defensive action. If a jury thought that in a moment of unexpected anguish a person attacked had only done what he honestly and instinctively thought was necessary that would be most potent evidence that only reasonable defensive action had been taken. A jury will be told that the defence of self-defence, where the evidence makes its raising possible, will only fail if the prosecution show beyond doubt that what the accused did was not by way of self-defence."

These cases relate to self-defence but similar considerations may apply, depending on the circumstances, to force used to prevent crime or to effect an arrest, etc.

The authority for the proposition that D is to be judged on the facts as he believed them to be is *Gladstone Williams*,[15] now approved by the Privy Council in *Beckford v R*.[16] D was charged with an assault occasioning actual bodily harm to P. D's defence was that he was preventing P from committing an assault on Q. But P may have been lawfully arresting Q. The jury was directed that, if P was acting lawfully, D had a defence only if he believed *on reasonable grounds* that P was acting unlawfully. It was held that this was a misdirection. D had a defence if he honestly held that belief, reasonably or not. The court referred to the recommendation of the Criminal Law Revision Committee: "The common law of self-defence should be replaced by a statutory defence providing that a person may use such force as is reasonable in the circumstances as he believes them to be in

---

10. Whether manslaughter may be committed by gross negligence is discussed below, p. 352.
11. See s. 5 of the Criminal Damage Act 1971, below, p. 688.
12. *Whyte*, [1987] 3 All ER 416, CA.
13. Ibid.
14. *Palmer v R* [1971] 1 All ER 1077 at 1078, PC, applied in *Shannon* (1980) 71 Cr App Rep 192, [1980] Crim LR 438 and *Whyte*, supra.
15. (1984) 78 Cr App Rep 276, CA. But, where D is drunk, see *O'Grady*, above, p. 216.
16. [1987] 3 All ER 425, [1987] 3 WLR 611.

the defence of himself or any other person."[17] The court declared that this proposition represented the common law, as stated in *Morgan*[18] and *Kimber*.[19]

It is arguable that this ruling was obiter but, if so, the law has been settled beyond doubt by the decisions which have followed it.[20]

Force used in the Course of Preventing Crime or Arresting Offenders

The common law on this subject was both complex and uncertain;[1] but now, by the Criminal Law Act 1967, s. 3:

"(1) A person may use such force as is reasonable in the circumstances in the prevention of crime, or in effecting or assisting in the lawful arrest of offenders or suspected offenders or of persons unlawfully at large.

(2) Subsection (1) above shall replace the rules of the common law on the question when force used for a purpose mentioned in the subsection is justified by that purpose."

Section 3 states a rule both of civil and criminal law. When the force is "reasonable in the circumstances" it is justified in every sense. No civil action or criminal proceeding will lie against the person using it. The section says nothing specifically about any criminal liability of the user of the force. When that is in issue the ordinary principles of *mens rea* should apply. The use of force may be unjustified in the civil law because it is not in fact "reasonable in the circumstances"; but D may nevertheless be excused from liability for an offence requiring *mens rea* if it was "reasonable in the circumstances *as he believed them to be*". The Criminal Law Revision Committee,[2] the authors of the section, wrote:

"No doubt if a question arose on clause [now 'section'] 3, the court, in considering what was reasonable force, would take into account all the circumstances, including in particular the nature and degree of force used, the seriousness of the evil to be prevented and the possibility of preventing it by other means; but there is no need to specify in the clause the criteria for deciding the question. Since the clause is framed in general terms, it is not limited to arrestable or any other class of offences, though in the case of very trivial offences it would very likely be held that it would not be reasonable to use even the slightest force to prevent them."

It cannot be reasonable to cause harm unless (*a*) it was *necessary* to do so in order to prevent the crime or effect the arrest and (*b*) the evil which would follow from failure to prevent the crime or effect the arrest is so great that a reasonable man might think himself justified in causing that harm to avert that evil. It is likely, therefore, that even killing will be justifiable to prevent unlawful killing or grievous bodily harm, or to arrest a man who is

17. Fourteenth Report (Cmnd. 7844), para. 72(a).
18. Above, p. 86.
19. Above, p. 66.
20. *Jackson* [1985] RTR 257, CA; *Asbury* [1986] Crim LR 258, CA; *Fisher* [1987] Crim LR 334, CA; *Beckford v R* [1987] 3 All ER 425, [1987] 3 WLR 611, PC.
  1. See the first edition of this book at pp. 230–238.
  2. Cmnd. 2659, para. 23.

likely to cause death or grievous bodily harm if left at liberty. The whole question is somewhat speculative. Is it reasonable to kill or cause serious bodily harm in order to prevent rape? Or robbery, when the property involved is very valuable, and when it is of small value?[3] How much force may be used to prevent the destruction of a great work of art? It seems that the question, what amount of force is reasonable in the circumstances? is always for the jury and never a point of law for the judge.[4] If the prosecution case does not provide material to raise the issue, there is an evidential burden on the accused. If that burden is satisfied, the question for the jury is:

". . . Are we satisfied that no reasonable man (a) with knowledge of such facts as were known to the accused or [reasonably][5] believed by him to exist (b) in the circumstances and time available to him for reflection (c) could be of the opinion that the prevention of the risk of harm to which others might be exposed if the suspect were allowed to escape, justified exposing the suspect to the risk of harm to him that might result from the kind of force that the accused contemplated using."[6]

The standard of reasonableness should, as noted above, take account of the nature of the crisis in which the necessity to use force arises for, in circumstances of great stress, even the reasonable man cannot be expected to judge the minimum degree of force required to a nicety. In holding quite considerable force to be justified to prevent an obstruction of the highway by a violent and abusive driver, Geoffrey Lane J said:

"In the circumstances one did not use jewellers' scales to measure reasonable force . . ."[7]

The Criminal Law Act 1967 made no reference to the right of private defence – the right to use force in defence of oneself or another against an unjustifiable attack. The right of private defence still exists at common law; but if, and in so far as, it differed in effect from s. 3 of the 1967 Act, it has probably been modified by that section. Private defence and the prevention of crime are sometimes indistinguishable. If D goes to the defence of E whom P is trying to murder, he is exercising the right of private defence but he is also seeking to prevent the commission of a crime. It would be absurd to ask D whether he was acting in defence of E or to prevent murder being committed and preposterous that the law should differ according to his answer. He was doing both. The law cannot have two sets of criteria governing the same situation and it is submitted that s. 3 of the Criminal Law Act is applicable. The Act may be taken to have clarified the common law. Before the Criminal Law Act, the Court of Criminal Appeal equated

---

3. Where a butcher used a butcher's knife to frustrate the robber of his takings, his action met with the approval of the coroner, though the robber died; (1967), *The Times*, 16th September.
4. *Reference under s. 48A of the Criminal Appeal (Northern Ireland) Act 1968 (No. 1 of 1975)* [1976] 2 All ER 937 at 947, HL, per Lord Diplock.
5. Lord Diplock used the word "reasonably" and, in the light of his often stated opinion, it is likely that he would wish to continue to use it, were he still alive; but his remarks, in the light of *Gladstone Williams* and the cases following it, should be read as if "reasonably" were omitted.
6. Ibid.
7. *Reed v Wastie* [1972] Crim LR 221.

the defence of others with the prevention of crime. In *Duffy*[8] it was held that a woman would be justified in using reasonable force when it was necessary to do so in defence of her sister, not because they were sisters, but because "there is a general liberty as between strangers to prevent a felony". That general liberty now extends to all offences. The principles applicable are the same whether the defence be put on grounds of self-defence or on grounds of prevention of crime. The degree of force permissible should not differ, for example, in the case of an employer defending his employee from the case of a brother defending his sister – or, indeed, that of a complete stranger coming to the defence of another under unlawful attack. The position is the same where D acts in defence of property, whether his own or that of another, which P seeks to steal, destroy or damage.

Where D is acting in defence of his own person it may be less obvious that he is also acting in the prevention of crime but this will usually be in fact the case. D's purpose is not the enforcement of the law but his own self-preservation; yet the degree of force which is permissible is the same.[9] An inquiry into D's motives is not practicable.[10]

There were formerly technical rules about the duty to retreat before using force, or at least fatal force. This is now simply a factor to be taken into account in deciding whether it was necessary to use force, and whether the force was reasonable.[11] If the only reasonable course is to retreat, then it would appear that to stand and fight must be to use unreasonable force. There is, however, no rule of law that a person attacked is bound to run away if he can.

A demonstration by D at the time that he did not want to fight is, no doubt, the best evidence that he was acting reasonably and in good faith in self-defence; but it is no more than that. A person may in some circumstances so act without temporising, disengaging or withdrawing; and he should have a good defence.[12]

In *Browne*[13] Lowry LCJ said, with regard to self-defence:

"The need to act must not have been created by conduct of the accused in the immediate context of the incident which was likely or intended to give rise to that need."

Self-defence is clearly not available where D deliberately provoked the attack with the intention of killing, purportedly in self-defence.[14] Where D's act was merely "likely" to give rise to the need, the proposition, with respect, is more questionable. If D did not foresee that his actions would lead to an attack on him, it is submitted that he should not be deprived of his usual right of self-defence. Even if he did foresee the attack, he may still be entitled to act in self-defence if he did not intend it. D intervenes to stop P from ill-treating P's wife. He knows that P may react violently. P makes a deadly attack on D. Surely D's right of self-defence is unimpaired.

---

8. [1967] 1 QB 63, [1966] 1 All ER 62, CCA.
9. *Devlin v Armstrong* [1971] NI 13 at 33, CA; **SHC 380**; *McInnes* [1971] 3 All ER 295 at 302.
10. Above, p. 78.
11. *McInnes* supra. But cf. *Whyte* [1987] 3 All ER 416 at 419, CA.
12. This passage was approved by the Court of Appeal in *Bird* [1985] 2 All ER 513 at 516.
13. [1973] NI 96 at 107, CCA, discussed 24 NILQ 527.
14. Cf. *Mason* (1756) Fost 132; and the corresponding problem in provocation, below, p. 344.

Lowry LCJ also stated in *Browne*:[15]

"Where a police officer is acting lawfully and using only such force as is reasonable in the circumstances in the prevention of crime or in effecting the lawful arrest of offenders or suspected offenders, self-defence against him is not an available defence."

Again it may respectfully be questioned whether this proposition is not too wide. If D, an innocent person, is mistaken, even reasonably, by the police for a notorious gunman and they so attack him that he can preserve his life only by killing or wounding – an attack which would be reasonable if he were the gunman – does the law really deny him the right to resist?[16] Again, if D reasonably supposes that the police are terrorists, he surely commits no crime by resisting, even if the police are in fact acting lawfully and reasonably.

A person is not to be deprived of his right of self-defence because he has gone to a place where he might lawfully go, but where he knew he was likely to be attacked. There is no question of any duty to retreat at least until the parties are in sight of one another and the threat is imminent.[17]

In a very few cases the attacker may not be committing a crime because, for example, he is a child under ten, insane, in a state of automatism or under a material mistake of fact. If D is unaware of the circumstances which exempt the attacker, then s. 3 of the Criminal Law Act will still, indirectly, afford him a defence to any criminal charge which may be brought, provided he is acting reasonably in the light of the circumstances as they appear, reasonably or not, to him; for he intends to use force in the prevention of crime, as that section allows, and therefore has no *mens rea*. Where D does know of the circumstances in question, then s. 3 is entirely inapplicable, but it is submitted that the question should be decided on similar principles. A person should be allowed to use reasonable force in defending himself or another against an unjustifiable attack, even if the attacker is not criminally responsible.

Unknown circumstances of justification. The test proposed in the Criminal Law Revision Committee's 14th Report and adopted as the law in *Gladstone Williams* is stated exclusively in terms of the defendant's belief. Its terms do not apply where D is unaware of circumstances which, if he knew of them, would justify his use of force. This accords with *Dadson*.[18] This is no accident. The Committee gave careful consideration to the matter and concluded that the *Dadson* principle was correct.[19] However, s. 2 of the Criminal Law Act 1967 (which was itself a product of an earlier

15. [1973] NI 96 at 107.
16. The judgment of Winn LJ in *Kenlin v Gardner* [1967] 2 QB 510 [1966] 3 All ER 931 is ambivalent. *Albert v Lavin* [1981] 1 All ER 628, [1981] 2 WLR 1070, DC (reversed by the House of Lords on another point) supports the view in the text. And see the draft Criminal Code. cl. 47(3)(b) and (6) (Law Com 143) and *Ansell v Swift* [1987] Crim LR 194 (Lewes Crown Court). The question is elaborately discussed in *Lawson and Forsythe* [1986] VR 515. Young CJ thought it may be reasonable to assume that, in some circumstances, D may defend himself against a lawful attack; McGarvie J said that he may do so, approving the 5th edition of this work, 327–328, but Ormiston J thought self-defence was only lawful against an unlawful attack. Cf. *Fennell* [1970] 1 QB 428, [1970] 3 All ER 215, [1971] Crim LR 581 and commentary; **SHC 383**; below, p. 391.
17. *Field* [1972] Crim LR 435; cf. *Beatty v Gillbanks* (1882) 9 QBD 308.
18. Above, p. 37.
19. The discussion is not included in the Report, Cmnd. 7844, paras 281–287.

report of the CLRC, when that Committee was differently constituted) provides alternative justifications for arrest, (a) where the circumstances of justification exist, and (b) where the arrester reasonably suspects they exist; and the dual nature of the justification for arrest is emphasised by the form of the Police and Criminal Evidence Act 1984, s. 24, which has replaced s. 2 of the 1967 Act.[20] If the arrest is lawful, then reasonable force to effect it is also lawful under s. 3 of the 1967 Act. It does not follow that the same principles apply to self-defence. While the law relating to self-defence cannot sensibly be distinguished from that relating to the prevention of crime (where the aggressor is, or appears to be, committing a crime) self-defence and arrest will usually have separate spheres of operation. In *Thain*[1] it was held that the "unknown necessity" justification could not apply, even if circumstances justifying force to effect an arrest existed, if D was not acting in order to effect an arrest.

Defence of property.[2] Where D is charged with criminal damage and his defence is that he was acting in defence of his own property – as where he kills P's dog which, he claims, was attacking his sheep, the matter is regulated by the Criminal Damage Act 1971, which is considered below, p. 689. Where D is charged with an offence against the person, or any other offence, and his defence is that he was defending his property, he will generally be acting in the prevention of crime and, as in defence of the person, s. 3 is likely to be held to provide the criterion. It can rarely, if ever, be reasonable to use deadly force merely for the protection of property. Would it have been reasonable to kill even one of the Great Train Robbers to prevent them from getting away with their millions of pounds of loot, or to kill a man about to destroy a priceless old master? – even assuming that no means short of killing could prevent the commission of the crime.

In the modern case of *Hussey*[3] it was stated that it would be lawful for a man to kill one who would unlawfully dispossess him of his home. Even if this were the law at the time, it would seem difficult now to contend that such conduct would be reasonable; for legal redress would be available if the householder were wrongly evicted. It is thought that, in any event, the rule in *Hussey* would not extend to a trespasser who did not intend to dispossess the householder, even if the trespasser were guilty of an offence under Part II of the Criminal Law Act 1977.[4]

To what Offences is Public or Private Defence an Answer?
These defences are most naturally relied on as answers to charges of homicide, assault, false imprisonment and other offences against the person. It is not clear to what extent they may be invoked as defences to other crimes. Sometimes they may operate indirectly as by negativing recklessness.[5] *Willer*,[6] though regarded by the court as a case of duress,

---

20. Below, p. 861.
1. [1985] NILR Bulletin No 11, 31, CA (N. Ireland).
2. See Lanham, [1966] Crim LR 426.
3. (1924) 18 Cr App Rep 160, CCA **SHC 242**.
4. Below, p. 802. Cf. *Taylor v Mucklow* [1973] Crim LR 750 and commentary.
5. See *Renouf* [1986] 2 All ER 449, [1986] 1 WLR 522, 82 Cr App Rep 344, and *Sears v Broome* [1986] Crim LR 461, above, p. 61.
6. (1986) 83 Cr App Rep 225, CA, above, p. 224.

seems to be more appropriately classed as one where self-defence was an answer to a charge of reckless driving. But would D have had a defence if he had driven through a red light,[7] driven while disqualified or with an excess of alcohol in his blood? – assuming in each case that it was necessary to do these acts in order to escape death or serious bodily harm. If the law excuses killing in such circumstances, it is difficult to see why it should not excuse these much lesser crimes. If D becomes caught up in a shoot-out between police and dangerous criminals, picks up a revolver which has been dropped by a wounded policeman and fires it in order to defend his own life and that of the police, it would seem strange that he should have a defence to a charge of homicide but not to a charge of possessing a firearm without a licence. In *A-G's Reference (No 2 of 1983)*[8] D made and retained in his shop petrol bombs at a time when extensive rioting was taking place in the area. He was acquitted of an offence under s. 4(1) of the Explosive Substances Act 1883 of possessing an explosive substance in such circumstances as to give rise to a reasonable suspicion that he did not have it for a lawful object. It was a defence under the terms of the section for D to prove that he had it for a lawful object. The Court of Appeal held that there was evidence on which a jury might have decided that the use of the petrol bombs would have been reasonable force in self-defence against an apprehended attack. If so, D had the bombs for "a lawful object" and was not guilty of the offence charged. Yet it was assumed[9] that he was committing offences of manufacturing and storing explosives contrary to the Explosives Act 1875. The court agreed with the Court of Appeal in Northern Ireland in *Fegan*[10] that possession of a firearm for the purpose of protecting the possessor may be possession for a lawful object, even though the possession was unlawful, being without a licence. The common law of private defence will not be a defence to other offences apparently, though the court did say –

"In our judgment a defendant is not left in the paradoxical position of being able to justify acts carried out in self-defence but not acts immediately preparatory to it."[11]

The fears of the courts regarding a general defence of necessity[12] probably militate against a recognition that public and private defence may constitute a defence to crime generally; but, where contravention of *any* law is (i) necessary to enable the right of public or private defence to be exercised, and (ii) reasonable in the circumstances, it ought to be excused. It is open the courts to move in this direction.

Use of Force, Excessive in the Known Circumstances

Where D, being under no mistake of fact, uses force in public or private defence, he either has a complete defence or if he uses excessive force, no defence. If the charge is murder, he is guilty of murder or not guilty of

---

7. Cf. *Buckoke's case*, above, p. 225.
8. [1984] QB 456, [1984] 1 All ER 988, [1984] Crim LR 289 and commentary, CA.
9. At pp. 992–993.
10. [1972] NI 80.
11. P. 993.
12. Above, p. 229.

anything. There being no grossly negligent, or *Caldwell*-reckless, mistake of fact, there is no ground for convicting D of manslaughter. He may have believed the force was reasonable but if, even by the relaxed standard applied in this context,[13] it was not, he was making a mistake of law, which is not a defence, and he is guilty of murder. That is the law of England but for thirty years a line of cases in Australia held that killing by excessive force, even where there is no mistake of fact, should be manslaughter and not murder, if some force was justified.

"... if the occasion warrants action in self defence or for the prevention of felony or the apprehension of the felon but the person taking action acts beyond the necessity of the occasion and kills the offender the crime is manslaughter – not murder."[14]

The defence, as stated by the High Court in *Howe*[15] in relation to self-defence, applied where (1) D honestly and reasonably thought he was defending himself; and (2) homicide would have been justified if excessive force had not been used; but (3) D used more force than was reasonably necessary. This principle was mainly applied in self-defence cases,[15] but it originated in *McKay*,[16] which concerned the use of excessive force in the arrest of a felon and the defence of property and it is logical that, if it applies at all, it should apply to any of the defences now being considered.[17]

This doctrine was followed in some Canadian cases[18] but has been rejected by the Supreme Court. The English courts appear to have flirted with it but it has been regarded sceptically by members of the House of Lords[19] and firmly rejected both by the Privy Council[20] and the Court of Appeal.[1] Their Lordships were unconvinced by the Australian cases and saw no need for this refinement of the law.

"If there has been attack so that defence is reasonably necessary it will be recognised that a person defending himself cannot weigh to a nicety the exact measure of his necessary defensive action. If a jury thought that in a moment of unexpected anguish a person attacked had only done what he honestly and instinctively thought was necessary that would be most potent evidence that only reasonable defensive action had been taken. A jury will be told that the defence of self-defence, where the evidence makes its raising possible, will only fail if the prosecution show beyond doubt that what the accused did was not by way of self-defence."[2]

13. Above, p. 243.
14. *McKay* (1957) ALR 648 at 649, per Lowe J.
15. (1958) 100 CLR 448; *Bufalo* [1958] VR 363; *Haley* (1959) 76 WN NSW 550; *Tikos (No. 1)* [1963] VR 285 *Tikos (No. 2)* [1963] VR 306.
16. [1957] VR 560.
17. It has been argued the principle is of general application and should govern duress, coercion and necessity. Thus, even if duress, coercion and necessity do not afford a complete defence to murder, they might reduce the offence to manslaughter: Morris and Howard, op. cit., 142. The idea is undeniably attractive but it is as yet unsupported by authority.
18. *Gee* (1983) 139 DLR 587; *Brisson* (1983) 139 DLR 685.
19. *Reference under s. 48A of the Criminal Appeal (Northern Ireland) Act 1968 (No. 1 of 1975)* [1976] 2 All ER 937 at 956 and 959.
20. *Palmer v R* [1971] AC 814, [1971] 1 All ER 1077, [1971] 1 WLR 1600; **SHC 238**.
  1. *McInnes* [1971] 3 All ER 295; **SHC 240**.
  2. *Palmer v R* [1971] 1 All ER 1077 at 1088.

In *Zekevic*[3] the Australian High Court has now overruled its previous decisions on excessive self-defence and followed *Palmer*, bringing Australian law into line with that of England. It did so, not because it thought the principle applied in those cases was a bad one, but because of the complexity which had arisen from the Court's attempt to state the law in a form which took account of the onus of proof. The law was to be changed because it was too difficult for juries to understand and apply. In the meantime, the CLRC was persuaded that *Howe* was right in principle and recommended its adoption in relation to private defence of person and property and the prevention of crime[4]. It is submitted that the soundness of this recommendation is not impaired by *Zekevic*. The principle of *Gladstone Williams*[5] – which has not yet been followed in Australia – removes some of the complexity from the law and it ought to be capable of being stated in a form readily comprehensible by juries. The CLRC propose that murder be retained as a separate offence to cater for the most heinous homicides and a man who believes, however foolishly, that his act is justified in law, hardly falls into that category.

9 Superior Orders

Though there is little authority on this question, it is safe to assert that it is not a defence for D merely to show that the act was done by him in obedience to the orders of a superior, whether military or civil. Where a security officer caused an obstruction of the highway by checking all the vehicles entering his employer's premises, it was no defence that he was obeying his employer's instructions.[6] The Australian High Court has held that there is no place for a general defence of superior orders or of the Crown or executive fiat in Australian criminal law.[7] The fact that D was acting under orders may, nevertheless, be very relevant. It may negative *mens rea* by, for example, showing that D was acting under a mistake of fact or that he had a claim of right[8] to do as he did, where that is a defence; or, where the charge is one of negligence,[9] it may show that he was acting reasonably.

The only question (which has been discussed mainly in connection with military orders) is whether orders are a defence where they do not negative *mens rea* or negligence, but give rise to a reasonable mistake of law. *The Manual of Military Law*[10] now asserts as "the better view" that they do not. Dicta in some of the cases suggest that they might. In a South African case[11] which has been much cited, Solomon J said:

"I think it is a safe rule to lay down that if a soldier honestly believes he is

---

3. *Zecevic v DPP (Vic)* (1987) 61 ALJ 375. See Editorial, [1988] Crim LR 1.
4. CLRC/OAP/R, para. 228. Cf. P. F. Smith [1972] Crim LR 524.
5. Above, p. 241.
6. *Lewis v Dickson* [1976] RTR 431, DC.
7. *A v Hayden* (1984) 156 CLR 532.
8. *James* (1837) 8 C & P 131.
9. *Trainer* (1864) 4 F & F 105.
10. (1956) Part I, 117. Nichols "Untying the Soldier by Re-Furbishing the Common Law" [1976] Crim LR 181.
11. *Smith* (1900) 17 SCR 561; 17 CGH 561. But the case has not always been followed in South Africa. See Burchell and Hunt, 298–9.

doing his duty in obeying the commands of his superior, and if the orders are not so manifestly illegal that he must or ought to have known they are unlawful, the private soldier would be protected by the orders of his superior officer . . ."

The only English authority[12] directly on the point holds that it is not a defence to a charge of murder for D to show that he fired under the mistaken impression that it was his duty to do so. D was, no doubt, making a mistake of law, but there is no finding as to its reasonableness. If mistake of law does not afford a defence where it is reasonable on other grounds, it should not, in principle, afford a defence because it is reasonable as arising from the orders of a superior. If the result is harsh, it is because the rule (if it be the rule[13]) that reasonable mistake of law is not a defence is a harsh general rule.[14]

10 Impossibility[15]

Where the law imposes a duty to act, it has sometimes been held that it is a defence that, through no fault of his own, it was impossible for D to do so. A driver is not liable for failure to report an accident if he does not know the accident has happened.[16] The secretary of a limited company is not liable for failure to annex to an annual return, as required by the Companies Act 1985, a copy of a balance sheet laid before the company in general meeting where there is no such balance sheet in existence: "nobody ought to be prosecuted for that which it is impossible to do."[17] A person is not liable for failure to leave a particular place if he is unaware of the order requiring him to do so.[18] In New Zealand it has been held that a failure to leave the country after the revocation of a permit was not an offence if no airline would carry D because of the advanced state of her pregnancy.[19] Impossibility is a defence to a charge of failure to assist a constable to preserve the peace when called upon to do so.[20]

On the other hand, the failure of a driver to produce a test certificate is not excused by the fact that it is impossible for him to do so, the owner of the vehicle being unable or unwilling to produce it.[1] Failure by the owner of a vehicle to display the excise licence is not excused by the fact that, without any negligence or default on his part, it has become detached in his absence.[2]

We find here the inconsistency which is so common in relation to strict liability. It cannot be asserted, therefore, that any general defence of

---

12. *Thomas* (1816) Ms. of Bailey J, Turner and Armitage, *Cases on Criminal Law*, 67.
13. See above, p. 80.
14. For further discussion, see Stephen, 1 HCL, 204–206; Dicey, *Law of the Constitution* (10th ed.), 302–306; Williams, CLGP, 105.
15. Williams CLGP, 746–748.
16. *Harding v Price* [1948] 1 KB 695, [1948] 1 All ER 283, DC.
17. *Stockdale v Coulson* [1974] 3 All ER 154 at 157, DC, per Melford Stevenson J.
18. *Lim Chin Aik v R* [1963] AC 160, [1963] 1 All ER 223, PC.
19. *Finau v Dept of Labour* [1984] 2 NZLR 396.
20. *Brown* (1841) Car & M 314, per Alderson B; below, p. 767.
 1. *Davey v Towle* [1973] RTR 328, DC.
 2. *Strowger v John* [1974] RTR 124, DC; cf. *Pilgram v Dean* [1974] 2 All ER 751, DC.

impossibility is recognised at the present time. It has to be regarded as a question of the interpretation of the particular provision, with all the uncertainty that this entails.

When impossibility might be available as a defence, it will presumably fail if the impossibility has been brought about by D's own default.[3] The defence would also seem to be confined to cases where the law imposes a duty to act and not to cases of commission where the corresponding defence, if any, is necessity.[4]

11 Non-Compliance with Community Law

A defence of which more may be heard in the future is that the provision under which the defendant is charged is invalid because it conflicts with the law of the European Community.[5] In *Dearlove*[6] P charged a substantially higher price for goods which the buyer intended to sell on the home market than for goods intended for export. It was accepted that this policy contravened Article 85 (1) of the EEC Treaty. D conspired to obtain goods from P at the lower price by dishonestly representing that he intended to export them to Bulgaria. His conviction was upheld because the Theft Act 1968 could not be regarded as a statutory support of the offending pricing policy and the prosecution was brought by the Crown to protect the public. The result would have been the same if P had brought a private prosecution – the nature of the criminal proceedings would have been the same. But the Court accepted that, if the prosecution had undermined the effectiveness of Article 85 (1) or favoured or reinforced the contravention, the appeal would have been allowed. And it might also have been different if the prosecution had been brought under a regulation made to enforce the offending policy.

3. But cf. *Stockdale v Coulson*, supra, and comment at [1974] Crim LR 375.
4. See *Canestra* 1951 (2) SA 317 (AD) and Burchell and Hunt, 293–296.
5. See T. C. Hartley, "The Impact of European Community Law on the Criminal Process", [1981] Crim LR 75.
6. *Dearlove, Druker* (1988) Times, 28 January.

10 Incitement, Conspiracy and Attempt

1 Incitement

An inciter, it has been said –

"... is one who reaches and seeks to influence the mind of another to the commission of a crime. The machinations of criminal ingenuity being legion, the approach to the other's mind may take various forms, such as suggestion, proposal, request, exhortation, gesture, argument, persuasion, inducement, goading or the arousal of cupidity."[1]

A person may incite another by threats or pressure as well as by persuasion.[2] Incitement may be implied as well as express. To advertise an article for sale, representing its virtue to be that it may be used to do an act which is an offence, is an incitement to commit that offence[3] – even when accompanied by a warning that the act is an offence. But the mere intention to manufacture and sell wholesale a device which has no function other than one involving the commission of an offence is not an intention to incite the commission of that offence.[4]

The mere incitement of another to commit an indictable offence is a common law misdemeanour, whether the incitement is successful in persuading the other to commit, or to attempt to commit the offence or not. It was so held in the leading case of *Higgins*[5] where Lord Kenyon said:[6]

"But it is argued, that a mere intent to commit evil is not indictable, without an act done; but is there not an act done, when it is charged that the defendant solicited another to commit a felony? The solicitation is an act: and the answer given at the Bar is decisive, that it would be sufficient to constitute an overt act of high treason."

The act incited must be one which, when done, would be a crime by the person incited. So in *Whitehouse* it was not an offence at common law for a man to incite a girl of fifteen to permit him to have incestuous sexual intercourse.[7] Though the man commits incest by having intercourse with

---

1. Holmes, JA in *Nkosiyana*, 1966 (4) SA 655 at 658, AD.
2. *Race Relations Board v Applin* [1973] QB 815 at 827, CA, Civil Div., per Lord Denning MR, followed in *Invicta Plastics Ltd v Clare* [1976] RTR 251, [1976] Crim LR 131, DC.
3. *Invicta Plastics*, above. (Indication that "Radatec" may be used to detect police radar traps is an incitement to an offence under s. 1 (1) of the Wireless Telegraphy Act 1949.)
4. *James and Ashford* (1985) 82 Cr App Rep 226 at 232, distinguishing *Invicta Plastics*, above.
5. (1801) 2 East 5.
6. Ibid., at 170.
7. (1977) 65 Cr App Rep 33, CA, below, p. 445.

her, the girl commits no offence by permitting it. The Criminal Law Act 1977, s. 54, makes it an offence for a man to incite a girl under sixteen to have sexual intercourse with him but the general principle is unaffected. It is not the offence of incitement for anyone to urge a fifteen-year-old girl to have incestuous intercourse with a third party or for a man to urge an unrelated girl of fifteen,[8] or a defective woman,[9] to have intercourse with himself. Arguably, however, the latter cases are attempts by him to commit the offence.[10]

By analogy to *Bourne*[11] and *Cogan and Leak*,[12] it is arguable that incitement to commit the *actus reus* should be an offence.[13] D threatens E with grievous harm if she does not commit the act of buggery with a dog or encourages F to have sexual intercourse with D's wife, telling him, falsely, that she consents to his doing so. The argument that these acts should be aiding and abetting, if the act is committed, may be thought equally cogent that it should be incitement, if it is not. But the present law is that D must know or believe that the person incited has the *mens rea* of the offence;[14] and an extension of the law which is justifiable when the *actus reus* has occurred may be thought unjustifiable when it is merely in prospect. If such a principle were accepted, it would not affect cases like *Whitehouse* because there is no *actus reus* on the part of the person incited.

In principle, it would seem necessary that the incitement should have been communicated,[15] but the matter is of small practical importance[16] since, in the case of a failure of communication,[17] there would at least be an attempt to incite.[18]

Where under the rule in *Tyrrell*[19] a victim is incapable of being an abettor, he is equally incapable of incitement; but the procedural requirements of the ulterior offence – such as the consent of the Director of Public Prosecutions[20] – do not necessarily apply to a charge of incitement.

If the offence incited is actually committed, then, as seen above, D becomes a participant in the offence and may be dealt with accordingly.

---

8. Below, p. 441.
9. Below, p. 442.
10. Incitement of a person to commit an offence is not the offence of attempting to commit that offence; but the incitement of an innocent agent might be. See *Cromack* [1978] Crim LR 217 and commentary, and Smith in *Crime, Proof and Punishment*, 21. The cases posed in the text are different, being, arguably, attempts by D to do the act himself.
11. (1952) 36 Cr App Rep 125, above, p. 155.
12. [1976] QB 217, [1975] 2 All ER 1059, above, p. 156.
13. See R. Leng (1978) 41 MLR 725.
14. *Curr* [1968] 2 QB 944, [1967] 1 All ER 478, CA, below, p. 255.
15. *Banks* (1873) 12 Cox CC 393 (letter, suggesting the murder of a child not yet born, intercepted. Held an attempt to incite under Offences against the Person Act 1861, s. 4; (repealed)). Statutory offences of "soliciting" may be different; cf. *Horton v Mead* [1913] 1 KB 154; below, p. 466.
16. *Ransford* (1874) 13 Cox CC 9. Section 19 of the Misuse of Drugs Act 1971 expressly makes it an offence to attempt to incite another to commit an offence under that Act.
17. It is of *some* importance, because a magistrates' court has no power to convict of an attempt on a charge of the full offence.
18. An offence at common law: *Chelmsford JJ, ex parte Amos* [1973] Crim LR 437, DC.
19. Above, p. 159. Tyrrell was acquitted of incitement as well as abetting.
20. *Assistant Recorder of Kingston-upon-Hull, ex parte Morgan* [1969] 2 QB 58, [1969] 1 All ER 416.

1 The Crime Incited

i) *Offences generally*. Incitement to commit any criminal offence, even an offence triable only summarily, amounted to a misdemeanour at common law. It followed that the incitement was triable on indictment and punishable with fine and imprisonment at the discretion of the court.[1] It was highly anomalous that the mere incitement should be regarded as more serious than the actual commission of the offence, even though the use of the greater powers of sentencing might be defensible where the incitement was to commit a large number of summary offences.[2] Now, by the Magistrates' Courts Act 1980, s. 45, any offence consisting in the incitement to commit a summary offence is triable *only* summarily. Incitement to commit an offence triable either way is itself triable either way.[3] Incitement to commit an offence triable only on indictment continues to be triable only on indictment. Where incitement is tried summarily the offender is not liable to any greater penalty than he would be liable to on summary conviction of the completed offence, whether it is a summary offence[4] or an offence triable either way.[5] Where incitement is tried on indictment, it continues to be punishable with fine and imprisonment at the discretion of the court, whatever the penalty for the crime incited.

ii) *Other inchoate offences*. An indictment would lie at common law for inciting to conspire but the offences of incitement and attempt to conspire were abolished by s. 5 (7) of the Criminal Law Act 1977. A charge of incitement to attempt to commit an offence would generally be inept because to incite to attempt is to incite to commit. Where, however, in the circumstances known to the inciter, but not to the person incited, the completed act will amount only to an attempt, the contrary is arguable. For example, D gives E a substance which he knows to be harmless, telling E that it is poison and urging him to administer it to P. If E does as requested he will be guilty of an attempt to murder.[6] D could scarcely be said to have incited murder but it is arguable that he should be liable for inciting an attempt to murder. However, the Magistrates' Courts Act 1980, Schedule 1, paras. 34 and 35 appear to be drafted on the assumption that there is no such offence as an incitement to attempt;[7] and it may well be that this is the law. An incitement to incite is an offence except, possibly, when it amounts to an incitement to conspire. To allow an indictment for incitement to incite in the latter case would, it has been said, amount to an illegitimate evasion of s. 5 (7) of the Criminal Law Act 1977.[8] But the distinction is absurd and a better view would be that incitement to incite is untouched by the 1977 Act.

1. By the Magistrates' Courts Act 1952, s. 19 (8) and Schedule 1, para. 20, incitement to commit a summary offence could be dealt with summarily with the consent of the accused.
2. As in *Curr* [1968] 2 QB 944, [1967] 1 All ER 478, CA; **SHC 246.**
3. Magistrates' Courts Act 1980, s. 17 and Schedule 1, para. 35.
4. Criminal Law Act 1977, s. 30 (4).
5. Ibid., s. 28 (1).
6. Below, p. 303.
7. If there is such an offence, its exclusion from the schedules means that it is triable only on indictment even though the offence incited is triable either way or only summarily.
8. *Evans* [1986] Crim LR 470, CA; *Sirat* (1986) 83 Cr App Rep 41, [1986] Crim LR 245, CA.

iii) *Counselling and abetting*. There is probably no offence of incitement to counsel or abet an offence.[9] It is true that, in *Whitehouse*, the court did not quash the conviction on that short ground as they might have done; but the Criminal Law Act 1977, s. 30 (4), seems to be drafted on the assumption that there is no such offence and there is one decision to that effect by a circuit judge.[10] D paid E £50 to find someone to assault P. It was held that there was no case to answer on an indictment alleging that D incited E to assault P and that is not an offence to incite another to become "an accessory before the fact".

There may, however, be an incitement to incite, so D could have been charged with that unless (possibly) E was incited to conspire with X, a person yet unknown; and there may be a conspiracy to incite,[11] an offence of which both D and E would seem to be guilty – so such a situation is far from being without remedy.

2 Mens Rea

As in the case of counselling and abetting, it must be proved that D knew of (or deliberately closed his eyes to) all the circumstances of the act incited which constitute the crime in question. As with attempts, he must intend the consequences in the *actus reus*. If D incites E to inflict grievous bodily harm upon P, D is not guilty of incitement to murder, though both D and E will be guilty of murder if death should result from the infliction of the intended harm.[12] An intention to bring about the criminal result is of the essence of incitement. There must probably be, in addition, an element of persuasion or pressure,[13] which is not necessary in the case of counselling or abetting. If D sells a gun to E, knowing that E intends to murder P, it is probable that D is guilty of murder if E does kill P;[14] but, if E does not kill P, it would seem impossible, on those facts alone, to convict D of incitement.[15]

Among the circumstances is the *mens rea* of the person incited. If D believes that the person does not have *mens rea* for the crime in question, then he intends to commit that crime through an innocent agent, if it is capable of being so committed, and may become guilty as the principal or an abettor if the *actus reus* is completed,[16] but he is not guilty of incitement. In *Curr*[17] D was acquitted of inciting women to commit offences under the Family Allowances Act 1945 because it was not proved that the women had the guilty knowledge necessary to constitute that offence. The real question, it is submitted, should have been, not whether the women actually had

9. See Smith, *Crime, Proof and Punishment*, 21 at 29.
10. *Bochin and Bodin* [1979] Crim LR 176 and commentary (Judge Geoffrey Jones).
11. Incitement to conspire was abolished on the recommendation of the Law Commission by s. 5 (7) of the Criminal Law Act 1977; but the Commission saw no reason why conspiracy to incite should not continue in the law (Law Com. No. 76, para. 1.44) and it is unaffected by the 1977 Act.
12. Cf. *Whybrow* (1951) 35 Cr App Rep 141.
13. Above, p. 252; *Hendrickson and Tichner* [1977] Crim LR 356; *Christian*, below, p. 439. Cf. Buxton (1969) 85 LQR 252 at 256.
14. Above, p. 139.
15. Cf. *James and Ashford* (1985) 82 Cr App Rep 226 at 232, above p. 252.
16. Above, p. 131.
17. [1968] 2 QB 944, [1967] 1 All ER 478, CA; **SHC 246.**

the knowledge, but whether D believed they had. In that event he should have been guilty. But if he believed that they did not have the guilty knowledge, he was not guilty of incitement, whether they had it or not.[18] If D urges E to accept the gift of a necklace, which is in fact stolen, he is not guilty of inciting E to handle stolen goods if he believes E to be unaware that the necklace is stolen; even though in fact she is so aware.

2 Conspiracy

Conspiracy was a misdemeanour at common law. It was classically, if loosely, defined[19] as an agreement to do an unlawful act or a lawful act by unlawful means. The word "unlawful" was used in a broad sense. It included not only all crimes triable in England, even crimes triable only summarily, but also at least some torts, fraud, the corruption of public morals and the outraging of public decency. In this respect it went far beyond the other inchoate offences of incitement and attempt, where the result incited or attempted must be a crime. For many years the crime of conspiracy was believed to be even more extensive and to include any agreement to effect a public mischief; but in 1974 in *Director of Public Prosecutions v Withers*[20] the House of Lords held that an agreement which did not come within one of the heads referred to above was not indictable as a public mischief.

It is the ultimate aim of the Law Commission that conspiracy shall be confined to agreements to commit crimes.

"The crime of conspiracy should be limited to agreements to commit criminal offences: an agreement should not be criminal where that which it was agreed to be done would not amount to a criminal offence if committed by one person."[1]

This aim has received general approval. Its immediate implementation, however, was not thought to be appropriate because the abolition of conspiracy to defraud would leave an unacceptably wide gap in the law. It was therefore recommended that conspiracy to defraud should be preserved until the Law Commission could make recommendations for more comprehensive offences of fraud and these could be implemented. It was further decided that, pending the outcome of a review of the law relating to obscenity and indecency, it was undesirable to interfere with the law of conspiracy to corrupt public morals or to outrage public decency and that these too should for the present be preserved. The reform effected by the Criminal Law Act 1977 is therefore a limited and provisional reform. Notwithstanding some amendment by the Criminal Attempts Act 1981 and

---

18. Cf. *Bourne* (1952) 36 Cr App Rep 125; **SHC 138**; above p. 155.
19. By Lord Denman in *Jones* (1832) 4 B & Ad 345 at 349. But a few years later in *Peck* (1839) 9 Ad & El 686 at 690 he declared, "I do not think the antithesis very correct."
20. [1975] AC 842, [1974] 3 All ER 984. Conspiracy to commit the common law offence of public nuisance continues to be a potential source of expansion of the criminal law. See commentary on *Soul* (1980) 70 Cr App Rep 295, [1980] Crim LR 233, CA.
1. Law Com. No. 76, para. 1. 113; see also Law Commission Working Paper No. 50.

the Criminal Justice Act 1987, it remains an ill-drafted piece of legislation presenting numerous problems of interpretation and it is to be hoped that a more thoroughgoing and effective reform will not be long delayed. In the meantime, it is an offence of conspiracy triable only on indictment to agree –

   i) to commit any criminal offence triable within the jurisdiction, even an offence triable only summarily;

   ii) to defraud, whether or not the fraud amounts to a crime;

   iii) to do an act which tends to corrupt public morals or outrage public decency, whether or not the act amounts to a crime.

Whether a particular agreement is a conspiracy at common law or a statutory conspiracy under the Criminal Law Act, or both, is considered below. In all cases, however, the *actus reus* is the agreement which, of course, is not a mere mental operation, but must involve spoken or written words or other overt acts. If D repents and withdraws immediately after the agreement has been concluded, he is guilty[2] and his repentance is a matter of mitigation only.

1) *Common Law and Statutory Conspiracies*

Section 1 (1) of the Act creates the offence of statutory conspiracy. It provides in effect that it is a conspiracy to agree to commit *any* offence; but s. 1 (1) is subject to the following provisions of Part I of the Act. These include s. 5 (1) and (2) which (as amended by the Criminal Justice Act 1987) provide:

   "(1) Subject to the following provisions of this section, the offence of conspiracy at common law is hereby abolished.

   (2) Subsection (1) above shall not affect the offence of conspiracy at common law so far as relates to conspiracy to defraud."

The Act, as originally enacted, caused great difficulty and controversy over the relationship between statutory conspiracy and conspiracy to defraud at common law. Eventually the House of Lords decided in *Ayres*[3] that any agreement the performance of which would involve the commission of an offence must be indicted as a statutory conspiracy to commit that offence and not as a conspiracy to defraud. Statutory conspiracy and conspiracy to defraud were mutually exclusive. This led to great difficulties for prosecutors. Indictments and convictions for conspiracy to defraud had to be quashed because it was discovered that the carrying out of the agreement necessarily involved the commission of some offence, however trivial. The House substantially modified the effect of *Ayres*, as generally understood, in *Cooke*.[4] That decision brought new difficulties,[5] but, happily, these need not be pursued here because the Criminal Justice Act 1987, s. 12, restores the full scope of conspiracy to defraud at common law:

2. As in the *Bridgewater Case*, unreported, referred to by Lord Coleridge CJ in the *Mogul SS Case* (1888) 21 QBD 544 at 549.

3. [1984] AC 447, [1984] 1 All ER 619.

4. [1986] AC 909, [1986] 2 All ER 985.

5. See [1987] Crim LR 114.

"(1) If –

    a) a person agrees with any other person or persons that a course of conduct shall be pursued; and

    b) that course of conduct will necessarily amount to or involve the commission of any offence or offences by one or more of the parties to the agreement if the agreement is carried out in accordance with their intentions,

the fact that it will do so shall not preclude a charge of conspiracy to defraud being brought against any of them in respect of the agreement."

Statutory conspiracy and conspiracy to defraud are no longer mutually exclusive. An agreement to commit a crime involving fraud is both a statutory conspiracy and a conspiracy to defraud. The prosecutor will frequently have a choice which should be exercised in accordance with the guidance in the Code for Crown Prosecutors issued by the Director of Public Prosecutions under s. 10 (1) of the Prosecution of Offences Act 1985.

Statutory conspiracies and common law conspiracies to corrupt public morals or to outrage public decency remain mutually exclusive, as the Act makes plain. Where the conduct in which the parties have agreed to engage would amount to the commission of an offence if carried out by a single person, the agreement is a statutory conspiracy. Where it would not amount to an offence if carried out by a single person, it is conspiracy at common law. This too is full of potential difficulties because no one can say for certain whether an act by a single person tending to corrupt public morals or to outrage public decency is an offence at common law. Fortunately, it appears that such prosecutions are rarely brought so the difficulties have not yet arisen in practice.

2) *The Mens Rea of Conspiracy*

Conspiracy is a crime where it is more than usually difficult to distinguish between *actus reus* and *mens rea*. The *actus reus* may be said to be an agreement: but agreement is essentially a mental operation, though it must be manifested by acts of some kind. Because the mental element looms so large it is convenient to deal with it first.

1 Statutory Conspiracies[6]

The offence of statutory conspiracy is defined by s. 1 (1) and s. 1 (2) of the Act. Section 1 (1) (as amended by s. 5 of the Criminal Attempts Act 1981) provides:

---

6. For the background to Part I of the Criminal Law Act, see Law Commission Working Papers Nos. 50 (*Inchoate Offences*, 1973), 56 (*Conspiracy to Defraud*, 1974), 57 (*Conspiracies Relating to Morals and Decency*, 1974) and 63 (*Conspiracies to Effect a Public Mischief and to Commit a Civil Wrong*, 1975); and Report, *Conspiracy and Criminal Law Reform* (Law Com. No. 76, 1976). For the interpretation of the Act, see Griew, Annotations to the Act in *Current Law Statutes*; Smith [1977] Crim LR 598 and 638; Elliott [1978] Crim LR 202; and Williams (1977) 127 NLJ 1164 and 1188.

"Subject to the following provisions of this part of the Act, if a person agrees with any other person or persons that a course of conduct shall be pursued which, if the agreement is carried out in accordance with their intentions, either –

a) will necessarily amount to or involve the commission of any offence or offences by one or more of the parties to the agreement, or

b) would do so but for the existence of facts which render the commission of the offence or any of the offences impossible, he is guilty of conspiracy to commit the offence or offences in question."

i) *Intention to carry out the agreement*. The section assumes the existence of an intention of the parties to carry out the agreement. This is not surprising because the essence of conspiracy, like incitement and attempt, is the intent to cause the forbidden result. The Law Commission understood this well enough and their report[7] was quite unequivocal. The Draft Bill, and the Bill which was introduced into Parliament, provided that, where a person was charged with conspiracy to commit an offence, "both he and the other person or persons with whom he agrees must intend to bring about any consequence which is an element of that offence, even where the offence in question may be committed without that consequence actually being intended by the person committing it". Unwisely, this provision was deleted from the Bill because it was thought too complex; but, in agreeing to the amendment, the Lord Chancellor stated: "What has been sought to be done, and what I think has been conceded in the speeches made today, is that the law should require full intention and knowledge before conspiracy can be established."[8]

However, in *Anderson*,[9] Lord Bridge, in a speech with which all of the House agreed, had no hesitation in deciding that a person who has agreed that a course of conduct be pursued which, if pursued, will necessarily result in a crime, is guilty of statutory conspiracy, "irrespective of his intention". In that case, D was convicted of conspiring with a number of other persons to effect the escape of one of them from gaol. D had agreed to supply diamond wire to cut bars but said that he never intended the plan to be put into effect and believed that it could not possibly succeed. It was held that this was no defence. It was clear in that case that two or more of the alleged conspirators did intend to carry out the agreement, so D's conviction could have been upheld on the ground that he aided and abetted that conspiracy – which he undoubtedly did, encouraging the making or continuance of it by his offer of help.[10] But, if no intention need be proved on the part of one alleged principal offender in conspiracy, it need not be proved on the part of another. A conspiracy which no one intends to carry out is an absurdity, if not an impossibility. Moreover, s. 1 (2)[11] requires

---

7. Report on Conspiracy and Criminal Law Reform (Law Com. No. 76), paras 1. 25–1. 41. For the common law, see *Mulcahy* (1868) LR 3 HL 306 at 317, per Willes J.

8. HL Deb. vol 379, col. 55.

9. [1986] AC 27, [1985] 2 All ER 961, [1985] Crim LR 651 and commentary.

10. See commentary on the decision of the Court of Appeal, [1984] Crim LR 551, and, on conspiracy to aid and abet, below, p. 265.

11. Below, p. 265.

intention or knowledge as to facts or circumstances constituting an offence, and it would be very remarkable indeed if intention or knowledge were required for circumstances and not for consequences. It is submitted that *Anderson* should not be followed in this respect.

ii) *Intention to play some part in carrying out the agreement.* According to Lord Bridge in *Anderson*[12] the *mens rea* of conspiracy is established –

". . . if, and only if, it is shown that the accused, when he entered into the agreement, intended to play some part in the agreed course of conduct in furtherance of the criminal purpose which the agreed course of conduct was intended to achieve."

This *obiter dictum* appears to be a novel proposition. No authority was cited.[13] If it is right, there is no conspiracy where A incites B to murder C and B agrees to do so, A intending to play no further part in carrying out the agreement. A, of course, may be convicted of incitement but, if B is not guilty of conspiracy, he is not guilty of anything. It is submitted that the better view is that A and B are guilty of conspiracy to murder. There is nothing in the section, nor in the common law, to require participation in the carrying out of the agreement by each conspirator. All that need be contemplated is the commission of the offence "by one or more of the parties to the agreement".

iii) *The Meaning of "course of conduct".* The words, "the agreement", mean the agreement that a "course of conduct" shall be pursued. We thus have to envisage the contemplated course of conduct as having been pursued and to ask, would it, when completed, necessarily amount to or involve the commission of any offence?[14] But the phrase, "course of conduct", is ambiguous. It might mean only the actual physical acts which the parties propose shall be done; or it might include the consequences which they intend to follow from their conduct and the relevant circumstances which they know, or believe, or intend to exist. In *Director of Public Prosecutions v Nock*,[15] a case of common law conspiracy committed before, but decided after, the Act came into force, the House of Lords used the same phrase, "course of conduct", and gave it the former meaning. The defendants resolved to extract cocaine from a particular substance in their possession by subjecting it to a certain process. The substance contained no cocaine. They were held not guilty of conspiracy to produce a controlled drug. The "course of conduct" was the application of that process to that substance; and this would necessarily *not* amount to or involve the commission of the offence of producing a controlled drug.

Section 1 (1) (b), which was added by the Criminal Attempts Act 1981, is designed to ensure that this result does not follow in a case of statutory conspiracy. *Nock* is a case where the "existence of facts" – i.e., that there was no cocaine in the substance – rendered the commission of the offence of

---

12. [1985] 2 All ER 961 at 965.
13. *El Ghazal* [1986] Crim LR 52, CA, is to the contrary but was decided before *Anderson* was reported.
14. Cf. *Barnard* (1980) 70 Cr App Rep 28, [1980] Crim LR 235, CA and commentary.
15. [1978] AC 979, [1978] 2 All ER 654, [1978] Crim LR 483 and commentary.

producing a controlled drug impossible; and, but for that fact, the course of conduct would necessarily have resulted in the production of a controlled drug. The agreement in *Nock* would therefore now amount to a statutory conspiracy to produce a controlled drug. The phraseology is unhappy – the *absence* of cocaine must be regarded as the existence of a fact – but the effect seems to be that we look at the facts at the time of the agreement as the defendants believed them to be.

Section 1 (1) (b) removes any problem concerning the existence of facts at the time of the agreement and, as a corollary, consequences which depend on the existence of those facts – for example, the production of cocaine. The subsection has nothing to say, however, about (i) other consequences, not dependent on the existence of facts believed by the defendants to exist or (ii) the existence of facts precluding the commission of the crime at the time it is to be carried out. First, consequences. Suppose the defendants agree to kill P by putting poison in his tea. This, surely, must be conspiracy to murder; but the act of putting poison in the tea will not necessarily result in murder. P may decide not to drink it. So, if the course of conduct is putting poison in the tea, it is not conspiracy to murder – which is absurd.[16] Subsection (1) (b) has nothing to say in the matter because there is no question of impossibility. To avoid the absurdity, "course of conduct" must be read to include the intended consequences – in this case, the death of P.[17]

Next, circumstances. In determining whether conspiracy is committed, we have to look forward from the time of the agreement – will the pursuance of the agreed course of conduct necessarily amount to or involve the commission of an offence? Circumstances change. The commission of the offence may be perfectly possible at the time of the agreement and become impossible by the time it is to be performed. Where this may happen, how can we say that the pursuance of the course of conduct will *necessarily* amount to or involve the commission of an offence? Defendants agree to receive certain goods, which they know to be stolen, next Monday; but, before next Monday, the goods may cease to be stolen goods by being restored to lawful custody. D1 and D2 may agree to marry next Tuesday, knowing that D1's wife is alive; but, before next Tuesday, she may die. These events may be unlikely, but they are possible, and therefore it cannot be said that the receipt of the goods or the going through the marriage ceremony will necessarily amount to or involve the offences of handling stolen goods and bigamy respectively. If the contemplated receipt, or ceremony, is the "course of conduct", the agreements do not amount to conspiracy to handle or commit bigamy.[18] Clearly they ought to.

The obvious way out of this difficulty is to construe "course of conduct" to include material circumstances which the parties believe will exist, and that is a perfectly reasonable construction.

16. It would be conspiracy to attempt to commit murder, since putting poison in the tea necessarily amounts to an attempt. The Criminal Attempts Act 1981 does not rule out the possibility of such an offence, but it is an absurd concept. An agreement to attempt to do something is an agreement to do it.
17. This argument is more fully developed in [1977] Crim LR at 601–602. See also Williams (1977) 127 NLJ 1164 at 1165.
18. They might be conspiracies to attempt. See footnote 16, above.

There are two difficulties about this approach. One is s. 1 (2) of the Act.[19] This provides that a person is not guilty of conspiracy to commit an offence unless he "intends or knows" that circumstances necessary for the commission of the offence shall or will exist at the time when the conduct constituting the offence is to take place. In the examples just given, D cannot "know" that the circumstances will exist because, as we have seen, they may not do so; and it seems strange to say that he "intends" that they shall exist when he has, and knows he has, no control over their existence.[20] He "believes" they will exist; but s. 1 (2) does not use that word. Nevertheless, the result is so obviously the right one that it is almost certain that "intend or know" will be held to include "believe". The circumstance may be held to be intended because it is part of an intended result; or "know" may be construed broadly.

The second difficulty, which applies to both consequences and circumstances, is a new one, arising from the amendment made by the Criminal Attempts Act 1981, which added s. 1 (1) (b). If "course of conduct" includes the circumstances believed by the parties to exist, this provision was entirely unnecessary. It is necessary only if the *Nock*[1] interpretation of "course of conduct" is right. Parliament thus appears to have accepted that interpretation and to have taken the sting out of it, so far as impossibility at the time of the agreement is concerned. The trouble with this approach is that it leaves other stings elsewhere. However, the argument that course of conduct must include intended consequences and foreseen circumstances is so compelling that s. 1 (1) (b) should be regarded as an "avoidance of doubt" provision, strictly unnecessary, but there for the guidance of the unwary. *Nock* is a discredited, though not overruled,[2] decision on the common law and should not be applied to the interpretation of the Act.

iv) *Conspiracy to commit strict liability offences.* Section 1 (2) of the Act provides:

"Where liability for any offence may be incurred without knowledge on the part of the person committing it of any particular fact or circumstance necessary for the commission of the offence, a person shall nevertheless not be guilty of conspiracy to commit that offence by virtue of subsection (1) above unless he and at least one other party to the agreement intend or know that the fact or circumstance shall or will exist at the time when the conduct constituting the offence is to take place."

This provision is intended to ensure that strict liability and recklessness as to circumstances have no place in conspiracy. Intention or knowledge as to all the circumstances of the *actus reus* are to be required *even* where the agreement is to commit a crime which may be committed recklessly or a crime of strict liability. It is expressed to apply *only* to such conspiracies. A strict interpretation could thus lead to the conclusion that the intention or knowledge required by the subsection is *not* required where the offence in

---

19. Below.
20. For a further discussion of "intend or know", see 4th ed. of this book, 220–222 and [1977] Crim LR 602–605.
1. Above, p. 260.
2. See below, p. 301.

view *does* require knowledge. There is no express provision in s. 1 (1) requiring intention or knowledge as to circumstances. If D1 and D2 agree to take P out of the possession of her parents without their consent and D1 knows that she is only 15, there is no conspiracy if D2 believes she is 16 (or has no idea what age she is). Liability for this offence may be incurred without knowledge on the part of the person committing it of the fact of the girl's age; so s. 1 (2) is applicable. The following case has been put.

"But suppose in the same situation, D2's belief is that the girl is not in the possession of a parent or guardian (although D1 is under no misapprehension). It seems that D2 is guilty of conspiracy to commit the offence in section 20, Sexual Offences Act 1956, although if they did take the girl, D2 would not be guilty of that offence. Indeed it is precisely because he would not be so guilty, that he is guilty of conspiracy to commit the offence in section 20. Section 1 (2) fails to protect him because it only applies where liability for any offence may be incurred without knowledge ... of any fact or circumstance, and *Hibbert*[3] holds that there is no liability for the offence in section 20 without knowledge of the existence of a parent or guardian.[4]

It is difficult to suppose, however, that Parliament intended that the requirement of *mens rea* should be greater on a charge of conspiring to commit an offence of strict liability or recklessness than on a charge of conspiring to commit an offence requiring knowledge.[5] To avoid the "scandalous paradox"[6] revealed by the above example, reliance should be placed on the word "nevertheless" in s. 1 (2). Parliament might be taken to be saying "*Even* where liability for any offence may be incurred without knowledge, knowledge or intent is required on a charge of conspiracy"; and thus implying that, a fortiori, such knowledge or intent is required on a charge of conspiracy to commit an offence requiring knowledge.

v) *Existence of circumstance not known, intended or believed in.* It follows that the parties are not liable for conspiracy to commit any crime the *actus reus* of which includes a circumstance the existence of which they do not intend, or know of, or believe in. Suppose that D1 and D2 have been invited by E to have intercourse with E's wife, P. D1 and D2 confer together and are uncertain whether P is truly consenting or is merely submitting through fear of E. They agree, nevertheless, to have intercourse with her. P in fact is not consenting so, if they carry out the agreement, they they will commit rape. Their recklessness whether she consents or not is a sufficient *mens rea* for rape.[7] In the *actual* circumstances, the carrying out of the agreement "will necessarily amount" to rape; but it is not a conspiracy to rape because it would not be rape in the circumstances which the parties intend, or know, or believe, shall or will exist. Recklessness as to circumstances of the *actus reus* is not a sufficient *mens rea* on a charge of conspiracy to commit a crime even where it is a sufficient *mens rea* for the crime itself.

3. (1869) LR 1 CCR 184, above, p. 72.
4. Elliott [1978] Crim LR 204.
5. Smith [1977] Crim LR 606; Williams 127 NLJ 1166.
6. Elliott, loc. cit.
7. Sexual Offences Amendment Act 1976, below, p. 429.

vi) *Unforeseen but inevitable consequences*. As noticed above,[8] Parliament deleted the provision in the Bill requiring an intention to cause any consequence which is an ingredient in the crime the parties are alleged to have conspired to commit. It is, however, submitted above that, notwithstanding *Anderson*, the parties must intend to pursue the course of conduct agreed upon. If so, they must be proved to have intended the foreseen consequences. Exceptionally, the agreed course of conduct may be such that it will necessarily cause a consequence not foreseen by the parties. For example, they agree to inflict a particular type of bodily harm, not appreciating that it will necessarily cause death. On a literal interpretation of the Act they are guilty of conspiracy to murder. In principle, that would be a wrong result, because killing is not intended and possibly not even foreseen as a possibility. It is thought that, here too, the answer lies in the construction of "course of conduct".[9] This should be read not only to include the consequences which are intended by the parties, but also to be limited to such consequences, whether they will in fact necessarily result or not. This is justifiable because it is the *agreed* course of conduct that we are concerned with; and the agreement does not include causing death.

If D1 and D2 agree to cause grievous bodily harm to P they are guilty of conspiring to commit an offence under s. 18 of the Offences against the Person Act 1861 but they are not guilty of conspiracy to murder although, if they carry out their intention and consequently P dies, they will be guilty of murder.[10] Similarly, an agreement to behave with gross negligence towards P is not a conspiracy to commit manslaughter, even though the parties will be guilty of manslaughter if they carry out the agreement and kill P.[11]

vii) *Where only one party has mens rea*. Section 1 (2) makes it clear that, so far as the relevant circumstances are concerned, both parties to the agreement (or, where there are more than two parties, at least two of them) must have *mens rea*. If D1 and D2 agree to take P out of the possession of her parents without their consent and D1 knows that she is only 15, there is no conspiracy if D2 believes that she is 16.

The Law Commission's rejected subsection would have made similar provision for foresight of consequences, but there is no such provision in the Act. If, however, "course of conduct" is construed, as suggested above, to include intended consequences, and only intended consequences, the result is the same. There is no conspiracy to commit a particular crime unless at least two parties to the agreement intend that the consequences which are ingredients of that crime shall be caused. If D1 intends death and D2 intends grievous bodily harm, this is a conspiracy to cause grievous bodily harm but not a conspiracy to murder.

8. Above, p. 259.
9. Above, p. 260.
10. For an argument to the contrary, see 4th ed. of this work, 222–223 and [1977] Crim LR 638–639. Cf. Williams, 127 NLJ at 1169 and TBCL, 357–359.
11. A conspiracy to commit manslaughter seems a theoretical possibility in the case of a suicide pact or where the party to do the killing is suffering from diminished responsibility. Below, p. 298.

viii) *Agreement to do acts of secondary participation.* Persons may agree to
do an act which would render them liable to conviction as secondary parties
if that offence were committed. Is an agreement to aid and abet an offence a
conspiracy? The Criminal Attempts Act 1981[12] makes it clear that there can
be no attempt to aid and abet an offence but it leaves open the question
whether there can be a conspiracy to do so.[13]

D1 and D2, knowing that E intends to commit a burglary, agree to leave
a ladder in a place where it will assist him to do so. E is not a party to that
agreement. If E uses the ladder and commits burglary, D1 and D2 will be
guilty of aiding and abetting him to do so. Are they guilty of conspiracy to
commit burglary? If the course of conduct is placing the ladder, it seems
clear that they are not. Placing the ladder is not an offence, not even an
attempt to aid and abet burglary, since the Criminal Attempts Act 1981[14]
makes it clear that this is not an offence known to the law. It has been
argued above[15] that "course of conduct" should be interpreted to include
the consequences intended to follow from the conduct agreed upon,
including the action of a third party to the agreement – in that example, P,
who takes up the poisoned tea and drinks it. So it might be argued,
consistently with that, the course of conduct ought to include E's use of the
ladder in committing burglary. If that should be accepted, the next
question would be whether the burglary is "the commission of any offence
by one or more of the parties to the agreement". E is not a party to the
agreement, so the question becomes, do the words "commission of any
offence" include participation in the offence as a secondary party? Since all
the parties to a conspiracy to commit an offence will be guilty of that
offence if it is committed, but s. 1 (1) contemplates that it may be *committed*
by only one of them, it is clear that "commission" means commission by a
principal in the first degree. It is submitted therefore that an agreement to
aid and abet an offence is not a conspiracy under the Act.

The above paragraphs were approved by the Court of Appeal in
Hollinshead.[16] DD agreed to sell to X "black boxes", devices for altering
electricity meters to show that less electricity had been used than was the
fact. They expected X to re-sell the devices to consumers of electricity for
use in defrauding electricity boards. The House of Lords[17] did not find it
necessary to decide the matter and Lord Roskill said that it should be
treated as open for consideration *de novo* if the question arises again. But
there was clearly an agreement to aid and abet the consumers to commit
offences under the Theft Act 1978, s. 2, against the electricity boards and, if
that agreement were a statutory conspiracy, it could not under the
prevailing (though now repealed) rule in *Ayres*,[18] be a conspiracy to
defraud. By upholding the conviction for conspiracy to defraud, the House
implicitly decided that there was no statutory conspiracy and therefore that

12. Section 1 (4) (b).
13. The question is discussed by Smith in *Crime, Proof and Punishment*, 21, 35–36 and 40–41.
14. Below, p. 297.
15. P. 260.
16. [1985] 1 All ER 850 at 858.
17. [1985] AC 975.
18. Above, p. 257.

an agreement to aid and abet the consumers to commit an offence against the boards was not a statutory conspiracy.[19]

This, it is submitted, is the position under the Act. What of the common law? The Supreme Court of Hong Kong has held that there may be a common law conspiracy to aid and abet an offence. In *Po Koon-tai*,[20] the defendants, the owners of a ship in Hong Kong and the captain and crew on the high seas, agreed to land in Hong Kong certain refugees whom they had picked up at sea in desperate circumstances. The refugees were not alleged to be parties to the conspiracy but they committed the principal offence by landing in Hong Kong without permission. It was held that landing the refugees was "an unlawful act". The concept of the unlawful act in common law conspiracy was one of notorious elasticity but an English court might be reluctant to extend it to acts of aiding and abetting if the Criminal Law Act has been correctly interpreted above. The question arises only in the fields of fraud, corruption of morals and outraging public decency.

2 Conditional intention

i) *Statutory conspiracies*. The question of conditional intention requires separate consideration, particularly in the light of section 1 (1) of the Act. The parties may agree on alternative courses of action depending on the existence of some fact to be ascertained or some event which may or may not happen. If one of these courses of action involves the commission of a crime and the other does not, is this a conspiracy to commit the crime? Can it be said that, if the agreement is carried out in accordance with their intentions, the course of conduct pursued will *necessarily* amount to or involve the commission of an offence? Is not the agreement carried out in accordance with their intentions if, in the event, they take the non-criminal course? There are two decisions on the point. In *Reed*[1] A and B were held guilty of conspiring to aid and abet suicide[2] where they agreed that A would visit individuals contemplating suicide and either discourage them or actively help them, depending on his assessment of the appropriate course of action. In *Jackson*[3] A and B agreed with C that C should be shot in the leg so that, if he was convicted of the burglary for which he was being tried, the court would deal with him more leniently. They were guilty of conspiring to pervert the course of justice.

In each case, the court held that the following hypothetical case is distinguishable: A and B agree to drive from London to Edinburgh in a time which can be achieved without exceeding the speed limits, but only if the traffic which they encounter is exceptionally light. In this example, as in the two decisions, the parties have apparently agreed that, in a certain event, they will commit a crime. The difference appears to be that

---

19. See commentary on *Hollinshead* [1985] Crim LR 653 at 656.
20. [1980] HKLR 492.
  1. [1982] Crim LR 819, CA.
  2. Aiding and abetting suicide is a substantive offence, so the rule that there is no offence of conspiracy to aid and abet an offence does not apply. Above, p. 265, below, p. 359.
  3. [1985] Crim LR 442, CA.

exceeding the speed limit is only incidental to the main object of the agreement – getting from London to Edinburgh in a certain time. In the decided cases, procuring the suicide or perverting justice is, in a certain event, to be "the object of the exercise". Are burglars guilty of conspiracy to murder if they set out to commit burglary, having agreed that, if it is necessary to do so in order to complete the burglary or to escape, they will shoot to kill? Presumably not – shooting to kill would be incidental to the achievement of an objective which might be achieved without it. On the other hand, there is clearly a conspiracy where the parties' objective is to commit a crime – but not if it proves too difficult or too dangerous – as where A and B agree that they will abandon their intention to commit burglary in No. 10 King Street if they find the house surrounded by police.

ii) *Common law conspiracies.* There is little authority at common law on the adequacy of conditional intention. The fact that an agreement is subject to express or implied reservations does not necessarily preclude conspiracy.[4] It is open to the courts to hold that any conditional intention is enough. If the parties contemplate that, in a certain event, they will intentionally commit the unlawful act, they have a conditional intention. They agree to ask P to give them some money and, if he refuses, to make a statement they know to be false in order to persuade him. This would be a conspiracy to defraud. Possibly "conditional recklessness" would also be enough – in the last example, they agree that they will make the statement, realising that they do not know whether it is true or false.

3 The Object of the Conspiracy

a) *Statutory conspiracies.* An agreement to commit any offence, even an offence triable only summarily, is a conspiracy contrary to section 1 of the Act, triable on indictment.[5] Proceedings for conspiracy to commit any summary offence or offences may not be instituted except by or with the consent of the Director of Public Prosecutions[6] or, where prosecution for the summary offence itself so requires, by or with the consent of the Attorney-General.[7] Probably discretion will be exercised in the light of the reasons given by the Law Commission[8] for retaining the apparently anomalous rule that an agreement to commit a summary offence should be indictable. "We think that the only justification for prosecuting as conspiracy an agreement to commit summary offences is the social danger involved in the deliberate planning of offences on a widespread scale."

4. *Mills* (1963) 47 Cr App Rep 49, [1963] Crim LR 181, CCA, and commentary. Cf. *Hussein* [1978] Crim LR 219, CA, and commentary, below, p. 536.
5. There is one exception. An agreement to commit a summary offence, not punishable with imprisonment, is not a conspiracy if the offence is to be committed in contemplation or furtherance of a trade dispute: s. 1 (3). Section 3 of the Conspiracy and Protection of Property Act 1875 is repealed: s. 5 (11). See [1977] Crim LR at 650.
6. Section 4 (1).
7. Section 4 (2).
8. Law Com. No. 76, para. 1. 85. The Commission refer to *Blamires Transport Services Ltd* [1964] 1 QB 278, [1963] 3 All ER 170 as a typical example of the sort of case they had in mind. The conspiracy to contravene certain provisions of the Road Traffic Acts extended over two years and included a large number of offences, all triable only summarily.

Such indictments at common law were particularly objectionable because they enabled the conspiracy to be punished so much more heavily than the actual commission of the summary offence and because they enabled the indictment to be brought after the time limit for the institution of summary proceedings had expired. As appears below, the Act goes some way towards meeting these objections.[9]

There was an exception at common law where the offence punishable summarily was defined so as to consist in an agreement and that agreement would not be a conspiracy at common law or to commit an offence under some other statute. In such a case a conspiracy charge alleges "the very offence which is created by the Act ... and which the Act makes triable only as a summary offence"; and, therefore, no indictment would lie.[10] Such an agreement appears not to be a conspiracy under section 1 (1)[11] of the Act because it is the agreement itself, and not any course of conduct to be pursued, which amounts to the commission of an offence.[12]

An agreement to break a law which might be made in the future was not indictable at common law.[13] Suppose, however, that the parties agree to pursue a course of conduct which will offend against a statute passed but not in force at the time of the agreement. If, at the time of the agreement, a date has been fixed on which the statute will come into force and, if that date is before the agreed date of the course of conduct, it appears that there is a conspiracy. If the commencement date is fixed after the agreement and is before the agreed date of performance, the continuing agreement will become a conspiracy as soon as the date of commencement is fixed.

i) *Agreement in England to commit an offence abroad.* Section 1 (4) of the Act provides:

"In this Part of this Act 'offence' means an offence triable in England and Wales, except that it includes murder notwithstanding that the murder in question would not be so triable if committed in accordance with the intentions of the parties to the agreement."

This subsection (apart from the exception) codifies the law stated by the House of Lords in *Board of Trade v Owen*, where Lord Tucker justified the rule as follows:[14]

"The gist of the offence being the agreement, whether or not the object is attained, it may be asked why it should not be indictable if the object is

9. In *Blamires* the prosecution was brought several years after the offences had been committed. That would not be possible under the Act; but if the proceedings were instituted within the six-month limitation period, the fine of £1,000 would still be possible. It may be that the agreement, or part of it, amounted to a conspiracy to defraud (it was an agreement to make false records, presumably to deceive inspectors, cause them to act contrary to their duty and thereby, according to *Welham v Director of Public Prosecutions* [1961] AC 103, [1960] 1 All ER 805, to defraud them) in which case it must be indicted as such, and the limitation period is inapplicable.

10. *Barnett* [1951] 2 KB 425, [1951] 1 All ER 917, CCA, holding that there could be no indictment for a conspiracy amounting to a bidding agreement under the Auctions (Bidding Agreements) Act 1927. The agreement was not unlawful apart from the Act. (Offences under the Act are now triable on indictment: Auctions (Bidding Agreements) Act 1969 s. 1 (1)).

11. It would, in any case, probably be a conspiracy to defraud, if it were a conspiracy at all.

12. Cf. s. 5 (6) which declares that *conspiracies* under the enactments shall be governed by the rules laid down by ss. 1 and 2 but shall not also be offences under s. 1.

13. *West* [1948] 1 KB 709, [1948] 1 All ER 718.

14. [1957] AC 602 at 625, [1957] 1 All ER 411 at 415.

situate abroad. I think the answer to this is that it is necessary to recognize the offence to aid in the preservation of the Queen's Peace and the maintenance of law and order within the realm with which, generally speaking, the criminal law is alone concerned."

Thus an agreement in Dover to commit an assault in Calais is not indictable here for the assault would not be triable here. An agreement in Dover there to procure a girl under the age of twenty-one to have unlawful sexual intercourse in Calais with a third person is indictable in England for the procuration, if it occurred, would be triable here.[15] An agreement in England by a British citizen to commit murder abroad is indictable in England apart from the exception in section 1 (4) for murder by a British citizen is indictable in England wherever it is committed.[16] The exception goes further. An agreement in England by aliens to commit murder abroad is indictable here, though the murder, if committed abroad, would *not* be triable here. An agreement in England to obtain property by deception abroad is not indictable as a conspiracy to defraud merely because it will cause loss to a person in England.[17]

ii) *Agreement abroad to commit an offence in England.* The Act makes no express provision for this case. At common law, an agreement abroad to commit a crime in England is indictable if the parties act in England in concert and in pursuance of the agreement.[18] Whether such a conspiracy is indictable if the parties take no steps in England to implement it has not been decided. It is submitted that the better view is that any of the parties entering the jurisdiction during the continuance of the agreement should be indictable at common law.

iii) *Agreement abroad to commit an offence abroad.* D1 and D2, British citizens in France, agree to kill P in France or to go through a ceremony of marriage there, both knowing that D1 is married. The offences contemplated are triable in England so, literally, these are indictable conspiracies under the Act. It may be, however, that the presumption against the extra-territorial application of the criminal law will exclude agreements not made within the jurisdiction and not intended to have any effect therein.[19]

b) *Common Law Conspiracies*

i) *Conspiracy to defraud.* It was stated by the House of Lords in *Scott v Metropolitan Police Commissioner*[20] that:

"... it is clearly the law that an agreement by two or more by dishonesty to deprive a person of something which is his or to which he is or would

---

15. Sexual Offences Act 1956, s. 23 (1), below, p. 442.
16. Below, p. 309. Cf. bigamy, below, p. 706.
17. *A–G's Reference No. 1 of 1982* [1983] QB 751, [1983] 2 All ER 721. But see below, p. 275.
18. *Director of Public Prosecutions v Doot* [1973] AC 807, [1973] 1 All ER 940, revsg. *Doot* [1973] QB 73, [1972] 2 All ER 1046, 57 Cr App Rep 13. Acts done by innocent agents should be enough: *A–G (Hong Kong) v Yeung Sun-shun* [1987] HKLR 987.
19. Cf. the corresponding problem in attempts, below, p. 299.
20. [1975] AC 819, [1974] 3 All ER 1032.

be or might be entitled[1] and an agreement by two or more by dishonesty to injure some proprietary right of his, suffices to constitute the offence of conspiracy to defraud."[2]

In *Scott* D agreed with the employees of cinema owners that, in return for payment, they would abstract films without the consent of their employers, or of the owners of the copyright, in order that D might make copies infringing the copyright, and distribute them for profit. It was held that D was guilty of a conspiracy to defraud. It was immaterial that no one was deceived; the well-known definition of "defraud" by Buckley J in *Re London and Globe Finance Corporation Ltd.*[3], "to defraud is by deceit to induce a course of action", is not exhaustive. Larceny was an offence which had to be committed "fraudulently", but deceit has never been a necessary ingredient of theft. The majority of the authorities relied on were in fact conspiracies to steal or to do acts which included theft, though the defrauding was not necessarily confined to theft. In *Button*[4] DD were convicted of conspiracy to use their employer's vats and dyes to dye articles which they were not permitted to dye in order to make profits for themselves and so to defraud their employer of the profit. The dyes were no doubt stolen; but the employer did not have a proprietary interest in the profit so that the appropriation of it did not constitute a substantive offence.[5] The great majority of agreements to defraud will be agreements to commit offences under the Theft Acts but clearly there are cases amounting to fraud within the definition in *Scott* which are not substantive offences. An example is the appropriation of the profit in *Button*. The Criminal Law Revision Committee considered whether such conduct should be brought within the definition of theft and concluded:

"... although the conduct, when it occurs, is reprehensible enough to deserve punishment, it does not seem to us that it occurs often enough to involve a substantial problem or to require the creation of a new criminal offence."[6]

Parliament presumably accepted this view, as it certainly accepted, after full debate, that temporarily to deprive another of his property should not be theft; yet an agreement so to do is clearly capable of amounting to conspiracy under the decision in *Scott*. Likewise with the case where D1 and D2 agree to shift D1's boundary fence so as to appropriate P's land – an act which is not, by recent decision of Parliament, theft, but evidently a conspiracy to defraud.

It is clear that P is defrauded if he is induced to take an economic risk which he would not have taken but for a deception.[7] It is no answer that D

---

1. In *Tarling v Government of the Republic of Singapore* (1978) 70 Cr App Rep 77, [1978] Crim LR 490 the House of Lords by a majority held that the intention of company directors to make and retain a secret profit for which they would have been accountable to the shareholders was not evidence of an intention to defraud. See, however, Smith [1979] Crim LR 220 at 225–226.
2. Per Viscount Dilhorne at 1039.
3. [1903] 1 Ch 728 at 732, 733.
4. (1848) 11 QB 929.
5. (1956) 19 MLR 39.
6. Cmnd. 2977, p. 29.
7. *Allsop* (1976) 64 Cr App Rep 29, [1976] Crim LR 738, CA and commentary; cf. *Hamilton* (1845) 1 Cox CC 244, *Carpenter* (1911) 22 Cox CC 618.

believed that the speculation was a good one and that P had a good chance of making a profit. If P is induced to part with something of economic value, he is probably defrauded even if he does receive the promised return.[8]

The proposition in *Scott* is not an exclusive definition of conspiracy to defraud. It is confined to economic prejudice; but a person is also defrauded if he is deceived into acting contrary to his public duty.[9] So it would be a conspiracy to defraud to agree by deception to induce a public official to grant an export licence,[10] or to supply information[11] or to induce a professional body to accept an unqualified person as a member,[12] assuming, in each case, that it was the duty of the person so deceived not to do as asked in the actual circumstances of the case. If the public official is persuaded by means other than deception – for example, bribes or threats – to act contrary to his duty, he is obviously not defrauded and the agreement is not a conspiracy unless it can be said that those affected by the breach of duty have been defrauded – e.g. those persons about whom the confidential information is disclosed or, more likely, perhaps, the official's superiors whose duty to keep the information secret has been vicariously violated. Most conspiracies to pervert the course of justice consist in agreements to deceive a public official so that he acts contrary to his duty and are conspiracies to defraud.

Some of their lordships in *Withers*[13] thought that this principle is strictly confined to public officials, and does not extend to the case of a bank manager deceived into breaking his contractual duty. It may be different where the private person is induced to break his public duty as in *Newland*[14] where the manufacturer was induced to break the statute.

The concept of fraud favoured by the House in *Welham*[15] was a broad one and it may well be that fraud for the purposes of conspiracy extends beyond the instances here discussed.

Mens rea of conspiracy to defraud. In *Scott* Lord Diplock said "Where the intended victim of a 'conspiracy to defraud' is a private individual, the purpose of the conspirators must be to cause the victim economic loss by depriving him of some property or right corporeal or incorporeal, to which he is or would or might become entitled."[16] The word, "purpose", though commonly used in this context, seems wrong. In *A–G's Reference (No. 1 of 1982)*[17] (the "whisky label-case") the defendants were charged with

---

8. *Potger* (1970) 55 Cr App Rep 42; Smith, *Law of Theft* para. [184].
9. *Welham v Director of Public Prosecutions* [1961] AC 103, [1960] 1 All ER 805; below, p. 276. *Welham* was followed in *Terry* [1984] AC 374, [1984] 1 All ER 65, HL. (D, who uses an excise licence belonging to another vehicle intending to cause police officers to act on the assumption that it belongs to his vehicle, has an intention to defraud, even though he intends to pay the licence fee.)
10. *Board of Trade v Owen* [1957] AC 602, [1957] 1 All ER 411.
11. *Director of Public Prosecutions v Withers* [1975] AC 842, [1974] 2 All ER 984.
12. *Bassey* (1931) 22 Cr App Rep 160, CCA.
13. [1975] AC 842, [1974] 3 All ER 984.
14. [1954] 1 QB 158, [1953] 2 All ER 1067, CCA.
15. Above, footnote, 9.
16. [1975] AC 819 at 814.
17. [1983] QB 751, [1983] 2 All ER 721, [1983] Crim LR 534 and commentary.

conspiracy to defraud X Co by causing loss by unlawful labelling, sale and supply of whisky, falsely purporting to be "X label" products. The agreement was made in England but the whisky was to be sold in Lebanon. The ratio decidendi was that the trial judge had rightly held that he had no jurisdiction to try the indictment because the contemplated crime in Lebanon (obtaining by deception from the purchasers of the whisky) would not have been indictable in England. One reason for holding that there was no conspiracy to defraud X Co was that this was not the "true object" of the agreement. Damage to X Co would have been "a side effect or incidental consequence of the conspiracy and not its object".[18] This must now be considered in the light of the decision of the House of Lords in *Cooke*.[19] British Rail stewards boarded a train, equipped with their own food which they dishonestly sold to passengers, instead of that provided by their employers, intending to keep the proceeds of sale for themselves. They were probably guilty in law of going equipped to cheat the passengers and, when they sold food to them, of obtaining the price by deception.[20] Whether this was so or not, the House had no difficulty in holding that they were guilty of conspiracy to defraud British Rail. It is true that the House was preoccupied with the problem of distinguishing *Ayres*, the "whisky-label case" was not cited and it does not appear that it was argued that the loss to British Rail was "a side effect or incidental consequence". Nevertheless, it is clear that this was a case where the object of the conspirators was to make a profit out of the customers, not to defraud British Rail. Of course, one must agree with Lord Lane CJ in the "whisky-label case"[21] that, "It would be contrary to principle, as well as being impracticable for the courts, to attribute to defendants constructive intentions to defraud third parties based on what the defendants should have foreseen as probable or possible consequences." Constructive intentions are to be abhorred; but presumably the House in *Cooke* thought that a jury could properly find that the defendants must have known that their conduct would, inevitably, cause loss to British Rail. If so, it was right to hold that they *intended*[1] to defraud BR and it should be immaterial that this was not their purpose. The true purpose of conspirators is almost always to make a gain for themselves, not to cause loss to another. Conspirators act out of greed, not spite. Since they know they can make a gain only by causing a loss, they intend to cause that loss. Of course, the intention must be proved. Thus, the use abroad of a stolen cheque book and cheque card is capable of being fraud on a bank in England because the effect is to cause the bank in England to meet its legal or commercial obligation to honour the cheque; but, if D is charged with conspiracy to defraud the bank, the jury must be directed that he appreciated that his conduct would have this effect.[2] Subject to the jurisdictional problem, considered below, it is submitted that, on a proper direction, the whisky-label conspirators might properly

18. [1983] 2 All ER 724.
19. [1986] AC 909, [1986] 2 All ER 985, [1987] Crim LR 114.
20. Below, p. 557.
21. [1983] 2 All ER at 724.
 1. Above, p. 57.
 2. *McPherson and Watts* [1985] Crim LR 508, CA.

have been convicted of conspiracy to defraud the X Co. They were probably much more sophisticated than the BR stewards in *Cooke* and better able to appreciate the effect of their actions on third parties. This applies equally to the facts of the "Chanel case",[3] where the facts were similar.

Purpose, it is submitted, is not required. Intention is enough. Recklessness is probably not enough. The matter was considered in *Allsop*.[4]

D was a "sub-broker" for a hire-purchase finance company, P. His function was to introduce prospective hire-purchasers who wished to acquire cars. In collusion with others, he filled in application forms with false statements about the value of the cars and the payment of deposits so as to cause P to accept applications for hire-purchase finance which, otherwise, they might have rejected. He expected and believed that the transactions he introduced would be duly completed, so that P would achieve their contemplated profit to the advantage of all concerned, including D who got his commission. His defence was that he did not intend P to suffer any pecuniary loss or be prejudiced in any way. The judge directed the jury that they must be satisfied that D realised that his conduct was *likely to lead* to the detriment or prejudice of P. It was unsuccessfully argued that this was a misdirection, relying on the statement of Lord Diplock in *Scott v Metropolitan Police Commissioner*[5] that "the purpose of the conspirators must be to cause the victim economic loss . . .".

The judgment of the Court of Appeal is extremely confusing because the court said that they were taking the same view as that expressed by Lord Diplock in *Scott* and also that they were adopting and applying the view (now discredited[6]) expressed by Lord Diplock in *Hyam*,[7] that a consequence that is foreseen as likely is intended. Now it may then have been reasonable to argue that one who foresees a consequence as likely intends it; but it surely could not be said[8] that, because he foresees that it is likely, it is his purpose. Both of Lord Diplock's dicta could not be applied to conspiracy to defraud. The ratio decidendi of the case must be determined by looking at the facts and the decision. The court found that P was defrauded when he was induced to do the very acts which D intended him to do. P paid an excessive price for cars and advanced money to persons who were not as creditworthy as they were alleged to be. This not merely put him at risk of being defrauded, but actually defrauded him: "Interests which are imperilled are less valuable in terms of money than those same interests when they are secure and protected".[9] The result intended by D was, in law, the defrauding of P; and P was in law defrauded. It is wholly immaterial whether D would have regarded that result as "fraud". If he did not, he was making a mistake of law. So regarded, the case is not about recklessness at all and does not decide that anything less than intention in the strict sense will suffice for conspiracy to defraud.

3. *Pain, Jory and Hawkins* (1985) 82 Cr App Rep 141.
4. (1976) 64 Cr App Rep 29.
5. [1975] AC 819, [1974] 3 All ER 1032.
6. See above, p. 56.
7. [1975] AC 55 at 86.
8. With the greatest respect to Lord Devlin in *Chandler v Director of Public Prosecutions* [1964] AC 763 at 804–805.
9. (1976) 64 Cr App Rep at 32.

The intention to defraud is readily discernible in *Allsop* where there could be no question of P believing he had any right to do what he did. More difficult is the case where company directors take a risk with the company's property, perhaps hoping to make a large profit and so benefit the shareholders. If the risk taken was such that "no director could have honestly believed ... it was in the interest of that company that the risk should be taken",[10] then the company is defrauded. Whether a risk is unjustifiable is a question of judgment and a matter of degree. There is no clear dividing line between right and wrong, such as was crossed in *Allsop* when false statements were made. Whether the risk is so grave that no director could believe it justified is equally a matter of judgment and degree. Conspiracy to defraud thus lacks the precision that we should normally look for in an offence. In *Landy*[11] the Court of Appeal proposed a model of how an indictment should be drawn for the facts of that case. The words italicised by the authors illustrate these points.

> "Causing and permitting the Bank to make *excessive* advances to *insub-stantial* and *speculative* trading companies incorporated in Liechtenstein and Switzerland, such advances being *inadequately* guaranteed and without *proper* provision for payment of interest."[12]

Dishonesty is an essential constituent of the *mens rea* but there has been controversy about what "dishonesty" means in this context. In *Landy*[13] the court appeared to think that the ultimate test was whether the *defendant* thought his conduct dishonest. In *McIvor*[14] the court reiterated this view, holding that the test in theft is different; but, shortly afterwards in *Ghosh*[15] it was held that the same test should be applied in conspiracy to defraud as in theft. The standard of honesty is that of ordinary decent people and D is dishonest if he realises he is acting contrary to that standard. In theft, D is not dishonest if he believes he has a right to do the act in question and this must also apply in conspiracy. If, however, he knows that no "ordinary decent company director" would take the risk in question, then he knows that the risk is an unjustifiable one and it is dishonest for him to take it.[16] The test proposed in *Sinclair*[17] accords with this. If *no* director could have believed the risk was justified, it follows that the defendant did not; but it would seem right that the jury should be directed that they must find this is so.

Fraud – by whom? In statutory conspiracy it is expressly provided that the contemplated offence is to be committed "by one or more of the parties to the agreement".[18] In *Hollinshead*[19] the Court of Appeal held that this was a

10. *Sinclair* [1968] 3 All ER 241, 52 Cr App Rep 618.
11. [1981] 1 All ER 1172, 72 Cr App Rep 237.
12. [1981] 1 All ER at 1179.
13. [1981] 1 All ER 1172 at 1181.
14. [1982] 1 All ER 491, [1982] 1 WLR 409.
15. [1982] QB 1053, [1982] 2 All ER 689. See *Cox and Hodges* [1983] Crim LR 167 and commentary (fraudulent trading).
16. For a remarkable difference of opinion in the House of Lords as to whether there was evidence of dishonesty, see *Tarling v Government of the Republic of Singapore* (1978) 70 Cr App Rep 77. See, on this case, Smith, [1979] Crim LR 220.
17. Above, footnote 10.
18. Criminal Law Act 1977, s. 1(1)(a), above, p. 259.
19. [1985] 1 All ER 850 at 857, above, p. 265.

restatement of the common law, so the same principle applied to conspiracy to defraud: the contemplated fraud must be one which is to be perpetrated by one of the parties to the agreement in the course of carrying it out. But complete execution of the agreement to sell the black boxes would not defraud anyone. The parties contemplated that the fraud would be carried out by other persons, not yet ascertained, who would buy the boxes and use them to defraud the electricity boards. The court therefore quashed the convictions for conspiracy to defraud – but they were restored by the House of Lords. The House held that the "purpose" of the defendants was to cause economic loss to the electricity boards. This is difficult to understand. Their purpose was to make a profit by selling the devices to the (as they thought) middleman. Presumably they did not care what happened to the boxes after that. If they had been accidentally destroyed in a fire, they would not consider that their enterprise had failed. On the contrary they might have been pleased at the prospect of selling some more. The House seems to have been much influenced by the fact that the boxes were "dishonest devices" with only one "purpose", which was to cause loss. But "purpose" is here used in the sense of "function". An inanimate thing cannot have a "purpose" (any more than it can be "dishonest") in the sense in which that word is used in the law of conspiracy. However that may be, *Hollinshead* seems to broaden the law of conspiracy to defraud to include the case where the defendants contemplate that the execution of their agreement will enable some third party to perpetrate a fraud.

Jurisdiction over conspiracy to defraud. An agreement in England to carry out a fraud abroad is not indictable as a conspiracy to defraud in England. But the question remains, where is the fraud committed? Where DD, by acts done abroad, cause P in England to incur obligations to do acts in England, it seems that P is defrauded in England and there is an indictable conspiracy to defraud.[20] But what if the fraud committed abroad merely causes an economic loss to P in England? In the *"whisky-label* case" it seems to be assumed that this is not an indictable conspiracy to defraud. Yet is not P equally defrauded whether the act is done at home or abroad? When, in the near future, British Rail can go through the Channel tunnel will they be any less defrauded by sales made by the dishonest stewards after the train has passed the middle of the Channel?

In cases like *Scott*,[1] the *whisky-label case* and *Cooke* P is caused a loss in two ways. Take *Scott*: (i) Because of the circulation of the pirated copies, P will sell fewer legitimate copies; and (ii) DD intended to keep the profits from the sale of the pirated copies for which, in law, they were bound to account to P.[2] The same applies to the sale of the bogus whisky and food in the other two cases. In the case of the BR stewards, it might be argued that they were continuing to defraud in the second respect in England, because they would fail to account on their return. But that is an evasion of the

20. *McPherson and Watts* [1985] Crim LR 508, above, p. 272. Cf. *Beck* [1985] 1 All ER 571, [1985] 1 WLR 22.
1. Above, p. 270.
2. *Reading v A-G* [1951] AC 507, [1951] 1 All ER 617.

substance of the matter. The truth is that P is equally defrauded in these cases wherever P does the acts in question. Lord Radcliffe has said:[3]

"Now I think that there are one or two things that can be said with confidence about the meaning of this word 'defraud'. It requires a person as its object; that is, defrauding involves doing something to someone. Although in the nature of things it is almost invariably associated with the obtaining of an advantage for the person who commits the fraud, it is the effect on the person who is the object of the fraud that ultimately determines its meaning."

Just as a person can be killed or wounded only in the place where he is, so, arguably, he can be defrauded only in the place where he is. It may be that this would extend the limits of jurisdiction beyond the traditional understanding of their boundaries; but fraud is now much more international than ever before and, in the absence of clear authority to the contrary, the way may be open for the courts to take this step.[4]

ii) *Conspiracy to corrupt public morals.* In *Shaw v Director of Public Prosecutions* the House of Lords (Lord Reid dissenting) held that a conspiracy to corrupt public morals is an offence. D published the Ladies' Directory which advertised the names and addresses of prostitutes with, in some cases, photographs and, in others, particulars of sexual perversions which they were willing to practise. He was convicted of (1) conspiring to corrupt public morals; (2) living on the earnings of prostitution[5] and (3) publishing an obscene article, contrary to the Obscene Publications Act 1959, s. 2 (1).[6] His conviction on all counts was upheld by the Court of Criminal Appeal and the House dismissed his further appeal in respect of counts (1) and (2). Lord Tucker, with whose speech the majority agreed, was of the opinion that there was an offence of conspiring to commit a public mischief and that the corruption of public morals was a public mischief; but he did not reject the view of the Court of Criminal Appeal that to corrupt public morals is a substantive offence. Lord Simon in *Director of Public Prosecutions v Withers*[7] concluded that there were three possible *rationes decidendi*.

    i) There is a substantive offence of corrupting public morals, so an agreement to do so is a conspiracy.

    ii) The corruption of public morals is a separate head of conspiracy.

    iii) There is an offence of conspiracy to effect a public mischief and the corruption of public morals is a public mischief.

Lord Simon held that it was open to the House to reject *ratio* (iii) and, indeed, the decision does so. Since Lord Tucker did not decide that there is a substantive offence of corrupting public morals, it seems clear that the

---

3. *Welham v Director of Public Prosecutions* [1961] AC 103 at 123, [1960] 1 All ER 805 at 808, HL.

4. See also *Tomsett* [1985] Crim LR 369, CA, and commentary and the discussion of *Tarling's case* (1979) 70 Cr App Rep 77 in [1979] Crim LR 221.

5. Below, p. 460.

6. Considered below, p. 719. Leave to appeal on that count was refused by the Court of Criminal Appeal. See the puzzling remarks by Lord Reid [1962] AC 220 at 280, [1961] 2 All ER 446 at 460 ; and see [1961] Crim LR 473, n. 2a.

7. [1974] 3 All ER 984 at 1003. Above, p. 256.

ratio must be taken to be (ii). It is therefore uncertain whether an agreement to corrupt public morals is a statutory conspiracy; but judges of first instance may consider themselves bound by the decision of the Court of Criminal Appeal to hold that it is. *Shaw* was followed in *Knuller*[8] where, Lord Diplock dissenting, the House held that an agreement to publish advertisements to facilitate the commission of homosexual acts between adult males in private was a conspiracy to corrupt public morals, although such conduct is no longer a crime.[9] Lord Reid maintained his view that *Shaw* was wrongly decided but held that it should nevertheless be followed in the interests of certainty in the law. Given the existence of the offence, he thought there was sufficient evidence of its commission here:

"... there is a material difference between merely exempting certain conduct from criminal penalties and making it lawful in the full sense ... I read [the Sexual Offences Act 1967[10]] as saying that, even though it may be corrupting, if people choose to corrupt themselves in this way that is their affair and the law will not interfere. But no licence is given to others to encourage the practice."[11]

In *Shaw*, Lord Simonds used language which suggested that the House was asserting the right to expand the scope of the criminal law:[12]

"In the sphere of criminal law I entertain no doubt that there remains in the courts of law a residual power to enforce the supreme and fundamental purpose of the law, to conserve not only the safety and order but also the moral welfare of the State, and that it is their duty to guard it against attacks which may be the more insidious because they are novel and unprepared for."

In *Knuller*, however, the House was emphatic that there is no residual power to create new offences. That is a task for Parliament.

"What the courts can and should do (as was truly laid down in *Shaw*'s case) is to recognise the applicability of established offences to new circumstances to which they are relevant."[13]

Moreover, a finding that conduct is liable to corrupt public morals is one not lightly to be reached. It is not enough that it is liable to "lead morally astray." Lord Simon of Glaisdale went so far as to say that –

"The words 'corrupt public morals' suggest conduct which a jury might find to be destructive of the very fabric of society."[14]

iii) *Conspiracy to outrage public decency.* A majority of the House in *Knuller* (Lords Reid and Diplock dissenting) held that there is a common law offence of outraging public decency[15] and, consequently, it is an offence to

---

8. [1973] AC 435, [1972] 2 All ER 898.
9. Below, p. 471.
10. Below, p. 471.
11. [1972] 2 All ER at 904.
12. [1962] AC 220 at 267, [1961] 2 All ER 446 at 452. For a judicial view to the contrary, see Stephen, 3 HCL 359. See Seaborne Davies, *Annual Survey of English Law* (1932), 276–277. For criticism of *Shaw*, see Seaborne Davies (1962), 6 JSPTL (NS) 104; Goodhart (1961) 77 LQR 560; Hall Williams (1961) 24 MLR 626; and [1961] Crim LR 470.
13. [1972] 2 All ER at 932, per Lord Simon of Glaisdale.
14. Cf. Lord Devlin's views, above, p. 19.
15. See below pp. 468–470; following *Mayling* [1963] 2 QB 717, [1963] 1 All ER 687, CCA.

conspire to outrage public decency. The particular offences previously recognised – keeping a disorderly house, mounting an indecent exhibition and indecent exposure – were particular applications of a general rule. It is not an answer to show that outrageously indecent matter is only on the inside pages of a book or magazine which is sold in public. But –

"... 'outrage', like 'corrupt' is a very strong word. 'Outraging public decency' goes considerably beyond offending the susceptibilities of, or even shocking, reasonable people ... [T]he offence is concerned with recognised minimum standards of decency, which are likely to vary from time to time ... [N]otwithstanding that 'public' in the offence is used in a locative sense, public decency must be viewed as a whole; and ... the jury should be invited, where appropriate, to remember that they live in a plural society, with a tradition of tolerance towards minorities, and that this atmosphere of tolerance is itself part of public decency."[16]

Lords Simon and Kilbrandon (Lord Morris dissenting) thought that the jury had not been adequately directed in accordance with these principles and, accordingly, that the conviction must be quashed.

3) *The Actus Reus of Conspiracy*

1 The Agreement

It may be that an agreement in the strict sense required by the law of contract is not necessary[17] but the parties must at least have reached a decision[18] to perpetrate the unlawful object. In *Walker*[19] a conviction was quashed although it was "perfectly clear" that D had discussed with others the proposition of stealing a payroll, because it was not proved that they had got beyond the stage of negotiation when D withdrew.

If A agrees to sell B certain goods, known to both to be stolen, at "a price to be agreed between us", they have not (apart from the question of illegality) reached the stage of a concluded contract.[20] Is there an indictable conspiracy? It is thought that there probably is; though it is arguable that the situation is no different from that where the parties are bargaining as to the price of stolen goods and are clearly, therefore, still at the stage of negotiation.

It is probably not essential that the agreement should have been made prior to the concerted action. If, when D1 is taking steps towards the commission of a crime D2 comes to his assistance and the two work in concert, they might thereby be held to have conspired;[1] but if D1 is unaware of, or rejects D2's assistance, there is no conspiracy,[2] though D2 might be held to be an abettor of any offence or attempt consummated by D1.[3] The same principles probably apply to statutory conspiracy.

16. [1972] 2 All ER at 936, per Lord Simon.
17. See Orchard, "Agreement in Criminal Conspiracy" [1974] Crim LR 297 and 335.
18. Cf. Williams, CLGP, 212.
19. [1962] Crim LR 458. *Mulcahy v R* (1868) LR 3 HL 306 at 317.
20. *May and Butcher Ltd v R* [1934] 2 KB 17n, HL.
   1. *Leigh* (1775) 1 Car & Kir 28n. *Tibbits and Windusk* [1902] 1 KB 77, CCR.
   2. *State v Tally* (1894) 102 Ala 25; Michael & Wechsler's Cases 699; *Hawkesley* [1959] Crim LR 211 (QS).
   3. *Rannath Mohan v R* [1967] 2 AC 187, [1967] 2 All ER 58, PC.

2 Proof of the Agreement

The question of what is a sufficient agreement to found a charge of conspiracy is one of several questions in the criminal law which are aggravated by a confusion between the substantive law and the law of evidence. The actual agreement in most cases will probably take place in private and direct evidence of it will rarely be available. A very frequent way of proving it is by showing that the parties concerted in the pursuit of a common object in such a manner as to show that their actions must have been co-ordinated by arrangement beforehand.[4] The danger is that the importance attached to the acts done may obscure the facts that these acts do not in themselves constitute a conspiracy, but are only evidence of it. If the jury are left in reasonable doubt, when all the evidence is in, whether the two accused persons were acting in pursuance of an agreement, they should acquit, even though the evidence shows that they were simultaneously pursuing the same object.[5]

It may not be necessary to show that the persons accused of conspiring together were in direct communication with one another. Thus, it may be that the conspiracy revolves around some third party, X, who is in touch with each of D1, D2, D3, though they are not in touch with one another (a "wheel conspiracy"); or D1 may communicate with X, X with D2, D2 with Y, Y with D3 (a "chain conspiracy"). Provided that the result is that they have a common design – for example, to rob a particular bank – D1, D2 and D3 may properly be indicted for conspiring together though they have never been in touch with one another until they meet in the dock. It must be proved, of course, that each accused has agreed with another guilty person in relation to that single conspiracy.[6]

"What has to be ascertained is always the same matter: is it true to say . . . that the acts of the accused were done in pursuance of a criminal purpose held in common between them?"[7]

These propositions, for which there is ample authority,[8] are stated in the case of *Meyrick*,[7] though that case itself seems a questionable application of them. D1 and D2, night-club proprietors, each offered bribes to a police sergeant, E, to induce him to connive at breaches of the licensing laws. They were convicted of conspiring to, inter alia, contravene the licensing laws.

4. *Cooper and Compton* [1947] 2 All ER 701; *Hammersley* (1958) 42 Cr App Rep 207. Lord Diplock thinks that it is "a legal fiction" (*Director of Public Prosecutions v Bhagwan* [1970] 3 All ER 97 at 104) and "the height of sophistry" (*Knuller (Publishing, Printing and Promotions) Ltd v Director of Public Prosecutions* [1972] 2 All ER 898 at 921) that the offence lies not in the concerted action but in the inferred anterior agreement; but the law is clear that it is the agreement that is the offence. The concerted action is evidence of the crime, but not the crime itself.

5. Where there are counts for both conspiracy and the ulterior crime and the only evidence of conspiracy is the collaboration of the parties in the completion of the ulterior crime, the only logical verdicts are guilty of both conspiracy and the ulterior crime or not guilty of both. Thus in *Cooper and Compton* [1947] 2 All ER 701, the court quashed a verdict of guilty of conspiracy as inconsistent with a verdict of not guilty of larceny. Conversely, in *Beach and Owens* [1957] Crim LR 687, a verdict of guilty of attempt to pervert the course of justice was quashed as inconsistent with a failure to agree on a conspiracy count.

6. *Ardalan* [1972] 2 All ER 257 at 261.

7. *Meyrick* (1929) 21 Cr App Rep 94 at 102. Cf. *Griffiths* [1966] 1 QB 589, [1965] 2 All ER 448.

8. See e.g. *Cooper and Compton*, above; *Sweetland* (1957) 42 Cr App Rep 62.

The jury were directed that there must be a "common design" and, by their verdict of guilty, they so found but it is difficult to see how the evidence justified this finding. The design of each night club proprietor was simply to evade the licensing laws in respect of his own premises.

Meyrick was distinguished in *Griffiths*[9] on the rather unconvincing ground that

"... the conspiracy alleged [in *Meyrick*] was ... in relation to a comparatively small geographical area, namely Soho. In view of the size and nature of the locality, there were clearly facts upon which a jury could come to the conclusion that the night club proprietors in that district well knew what was happening generally in relation to the police."[10]

Even if D1 and D2 each knew that the other had made a similar agreement with E, it would seem that there were two conspiracies not one. Paull J has put the following example:

"I employ an accountant to make out my tax return. He and his clerk are both present when I am about to sign the return. I notice an item in my expenses of £100 and say: 'I don't remember incurring this expense.' The clerk says: 'Well, actually I put it in. You didn't incur it, but I didn't think you would object to a few pounds being saved.' The accountant indicates his agreement to this attitude. After some hesitation I agree to let it stand. On those bare facts I cannot be charged with fifty others in a conspiracy to defraud the Exchequer of £100,000 on the basis that this accountant and his clerk have persuaded 500 other clients to make false returns, some being false in one way, some in another, or even all in the same way. I have not knowingly attached myself to a general agreement to defraud."[11]

It is submitted that the position would be no different if the accountant had said: "We do this for all our clients"; there would still have been a series of conspiracies, not one general conspiracy. The convictions in *Griffiths* were indeed quashed on the ground that the evidence, while perhaps sufficient to establish a series of separate conspiracies, did not establish the single "wheel conspiracy" alleged. A count charging a general conspiracy is not bad because the evidence offered to prove it includes subsequent subsidiary conspiracies.[12] If A and B set up an organisation to plant bombs, that is a conspiracy and indictable as such, though the overt acts offered to prove it consist in further agreements to plant particular bombs. Those further agreements are indictable as separate conspiracies, notwithstanding the existence of the general conspiracy;[13] and acquittal or conviction of one such alleged conspiracy is no bar to trial for another.

3 Conspiracy where the Contemplated Offence is Committed

The courts discourage the charging of conspiracy where there is evidence of the complete crime:

"... when the proof intended to be submitted to a jury is proof of the actual commission of crime, it is not the proper course to charge the

9. (1965) 49 Cr App Rep 279.
10. Ibid., at 291.
11. Ibid. Cf. the argument of Maddocks in *Meyrick* (1929) 45 TLR 421 at 422.
12. *Greenfield* [1973] 3 All ER 1050, [1973] 1 WLR 1151.
13. *Coughlan (Martin)* (1976) 63 Cr App Rep 33, [1976] Crim LR 631, CA.

parties with conspiracy to commit it, for the course operates, it is manifest, unfairly and unjustly against the parties accused; the prosecutors are thus enabled to combine in one indictment a variety of offences, which, if treated individually, as they ought to be, would exclude the possibility of giving evidence against one defendant to the prejudice of others, and which deprive defendants of the advantage of calling their co-defendants as witnesses."[14]

Though these sentiments have been approved by the Court of Criminal Appeal,[15] it is not at all clear that evidence is admissible on a conspiracy charge which would not be admissible on a joint trial for the complete crime. In both cases D1 may be prejudiced by evidence admissible only against D2. The real objection to conspiracy, as it has been commonly used in recent years, has been pointed out by Williams.[16] It is –

"... to the use of a conspiracy count to give a semblance of unity to a prosecution which, by combining a number of charges and several defendants, results in a complicated and protracted trial. The jury system is unworkable unless the prosecution is confined to a relatively simple issue which can be disposed of in a relatively short time."

No better illustration could be imagined than *Griffiths*[17] where a supplier of lime, his accountant and seven farmers were charged with conspiracy to defraud the government of the subsidy payable to farmers for spreading lime on their land. In addition to the conspiracy count, there were 24 other counts alleging substantive offences of false pretences. There were 60 prosecution and 35 defence witnesses and 263 exhibits including accounts and schedules. The jury had to return no less than 78 verdicts and the trial lasted 10 weeks – at the end of which, not surprisingly, all the convictions had to be quashed.

4 Two or More Parties

It must be proved that D conspired with another but the other need not be identified.[18] If the managing director of a company resolves to perpetrate an illegality in the company's name, but communicates this to no one, there is no conspiracy between him and the company. To allow an indictment would be to

"offend against the basic concept of a conspiracy, namely an agreement of two or more to do an unlawful act . . . it would be artificial to take the view that the company, although it is clearly a separate legal entity can be regarded here as a separate entity or a separate mind . . ."[19]

In statutory conspiracies there are three cases in which the requirement of two parties is not satisfied. By section 2 (2) of the Act, a person is not guilty of a statutory conspiracy –

14. Cockburn CJ, in *Boulton* (1871) 12 Cox CC 87 at 93.
15. *West* [1948] 1 KB 709 at 720, [1948] 1 All ER 718 at 723.
16. CLGP, 684; and see *The Proof of Guilt* (3rd ed), Ch. 9 and "The Added Conspiracy Count" (1978) 128 NLJ 24.
17. Above, p. 280. The headnote is wrong in stating that a "wheel conspiracy" is not known to the law: *Ardalan* [1972] 2 All ER 257 at 262.
18. *Phillips* (1987) 86 Cr App Rep 18, CA.
19. *McDonnell* [1966] 1 QB 233, [1966] 1 All ER 193 (Nield J). Cf. *ICR Haulage Co.*, above, p. 173.

"... if the only other person or persons with whom he agrees are (both initially and at all times during the currency of the agreement) persons of any one or more of the following descriptions, that is to say –
a) his spouse;
b) a person under the age of criminal responsibility; and
c) an intended victim of that offence or of each of those offences."

Paragraph (a) almost certainly states the rule of the common law, although no English case has ever so decided.[20] The common law rule was based upon the fiction that husband and wife were one person with one will. The application of the rule to statutory conspiracies is based upon a social policy of preserving the stability of marriage.[21]

The common law rule applies only where the parties are married at the time of the agreement. Marriage after the conspiracy or during its continuance is no defence.[1] Clearly the same rule applies under the Act.

For the purposes of paragraph (b) a person is under the age of criminal responsibility "so long as it is conclusively presumed by section 50 of the Children and Young Persons Act 1933,[2] that he cannot be guilty of any offence"[3] – that is, he is under the age of ten. The Act makes no provision for the case of a child between ten and fourteen.[4] If such a child has a "mischievous discretion" there is clearly a conspiracy. If such a discretion is not proved the child is not guilty but, if there is an agreement in fact, the adult party probably is. There appears to be no common law authority on agreements with children but principle suggests that the rule should be the same as for statutory conspiracies.

The Act does not define "victim". It is suggested that a person is a victim of an offence when the offence is held to exist for his protection with the effect that he is not a party to that offence when it is committed by another with his full knowledge and co-operation.[5] Thus there would be no conspiracy where D agreed with a girl under sixteen to take her out of the possession of her parents without their consent, or to have sexual intercourse with her, or to have intercourse with a defective. On the other hand, an agreement by an adult to commit buggery with a fourteen year old boy, or to commit an act of gross indecency with a ten year old boy who has a "mischievous discretion" is a conspiracy. In these cases the boy as well as the man will be guilty of the offence if the act takes place so he cannot be regarded as a "victim". Again there seems to be no common law authority in point and the question seems unlikely to arise on a charge of conspiracy at common law since an agreement to defraud with the victim of the fraud is difficult to imagine.

Where one of two parties to an agreement would be immune from prosecution for the ulterior offence for some reason other than the three

---

20. See, e.g., Hawkins 1 PC, c. 27, s. 8 and *Mawji v R* [1957] AC 126, [1957] 1 All ER 385, PC. There may be a conspiracy between husband and wife in the civil law: *Midland Bank Trust Co Ltd v Green* (No. 3) [1979] Ch 496, [1979] 2 All ER 193 (Oliver J).
21. Law Com. No. 76, paras, 1.46–1.49.
  1. *Robinson's Case* (1746) 1 Leach 37.
  2. Above, p. 178.
  3. Section 2 (3) of the Act.
  4. Above, p. 179.
  5. Above, p. 158.

stated in the section, it seems that both may be convicted of either a common law or a statutory conspiracy as is appropriate. By s. 1 (1) it is sufficient if *one* of the parties will necessarily be guilty of the offence if the agreement is carried out. This is also so at common law. In *Duguid*,[6] D agreed with E to remove a child of whom E was the mother, from the possession of her lawful guardian. This would have been a crime by D under the Offences Against the Person Act 1861, section 56; but that section provided that no person who was inter alios the mother of the child should be liable to be prosecuted for the offence. The Court upheld D's conviction of conspiracy, declining to decide whether E could have been convicted of either the conspiracy or the ulterior offence. Section 56 has been repealed by the Child Abduction Act 1984[7] but the principle of *Duguid* appears to be unaffected by the 1977 Act. A similar question would arise if a parent (E) were charged with conspiring to commit an offence under s. 2 of the 1984 Act. Though E cannot commit the offence D may conspire with him to do so; and it may be that E is also guilty of conspiracy.[8] Similarly, a woman continues (theoretically, for in practice prosecutions are not brought) to be liable for conspiring to procure an abortion on herself although she could commit no ulterior offence as she is not in fact pregnant.[9] The result may be technically justified on the ground that D would have been guilty as an aider and abettor if the offence had been completed;[10] but it has been criticised as "gravely wrong for it sets at naught the limitation upon responsibility imposed by Parliament."[11]

It would be otherwise if *both* parties were immune from prosecution for the ulterior offence. If the mother and a man believing himself on reasonable grounds to be the father of an illegitimate child agree to remove the child from lawful custody, there is no conspiracy to commit an offence under s. 4 of the 1984 Act because neither party can commit that offence.

The Act does not deal with an agreement with a mentally disordered person so the common law, whatever it may be, applies to all conspiracies. The Law Commission thought express provision unnecessary because "a purported agreement with a person who is so mentally disordered as to be incapable of forming the intent necessary for the substantive offence will not be an agreement within clause 1 (1) of the draft Bill [now, in substance, section 1 (1) of the Act]."[12] This seems to be right in the case of a mentally disordered person who does not know the nature and quality of the proposed act; but a person who, through mental disorder, does not know the proposed act is "wrong" may be perfectly capable of forming the intent to commit it with full knowledge of the facts and circumstances.[13] In such a case it is arguable that a mentally normal party to the agreement is guilty of a statutory conspiracy though the mentally abnormal person is not because

---

6. (1906) 21 Cox CC 200.
7. Below, p. 415.
8. The course of conduct will necessarily amount to the commission of the offence by *one* of the parties: s. 1 (1), above, p. 129.
9. *Whitchurch* (1890) 24 QBD 420.
10. *Sockett* (1908) 72 JP 428.
11. Williams, CLGP, 673, criticised by Hogan in "Victims as Parties to Crime", [1962] Crim LR 683; and see below, p. 367.
12. Law Com. No. 76, p. 22, note 67.
13. Cf. *Matusevitch v R* (1977) 51 ALJR 657 at 670, per Aickin J.

it is sufficient that the carrying out of the agreement will amount to an offence by *one of the parties*.[14] What is the position where there is an agreement by D1 and D2 to kill where D2 would have a defence of diminished responsibility on a charge of murder? If the killing is to be done by D1 it will be murder and so the agreement is a conspiracy to murder. If it is to be done by D2, D1 will still be guilty of murder by virtue of s. 2 (4) of the Homicide Act 1957.[15] However if, as submitted above,[16] "commission of any offence" means commission as principal in the first degree, this appears to be a conspiracy to commit manslaughter.

Another case with which the Act does not deal specifically is that where E purports to conspire with D but has no intention of going through with the plan. The question was formerly of no practical importance because D could be convicted of an attempt to conspire, but the Act rules that out. The point has not arisen in England but in some jurisdictions it has been decided that there is no conspiracy.[17] It might be argued that, looking at the facts objectively, there is such an agreement as (apart from the illegality) would be enforceable in the law of contract and that therefore there is an *actus reus*. D, who, with *mens rea*, has caused the *actus reus* should be guilty. An answer to this argument is that there is no *actus reus* unless E agrees in fact, i.e. that an actual subjective agreement is required. If *Anderson*[18] is followed and E held to be guilty of conspiracy notwithstanding his lack of intention, the problem disappears.

5 Acquittal of the other Alleged Conspirators

Where D is alleged to have conspired with one other person, E, the acquittal of E, either before or after the trial of D, was no bar to, or ground for quashing, as the case may be, the conviction of D.[19] This was where the parties were tried separately. Where they were tried together there was some doubt whether it was ever right to convict D and acquit E – or vice versa.[1] These doubts are resolved by s. 5 (8) and (9) of the Act which governs both common law and statutory conspiracies.

"5 (8) The fact that the person or persons who, so far as appears from the indictment on which any person has been convicted of conspiracy, were the only other parties to the agreement on which his conviction was based have been acquitted of conspiracy by reference to that agreement (whether after being tried with the person convicted or separately) shall not be a ground for quashing his conviction unless under all the circumstances of the case his conviction is inconsistent with the acquittal of the other person or persons in question.

(9) Any rule of law or practice inconsistent with the provisions of subsection (8) above is hereby abolished."

14. Section 1 (1), above, p. 259.
15. Above, p. 153, footnote 20.
16. Above, p. 265.
17. *Harris* [1927] NPD 347 (South Africa); *O'Brien* [1954] SCR 666 (Canada); *Delaney v State* (1932) 164 Tenn 432 (Tennessee); *State v Otu* [1964] NNLR 113 (Nigeria). Cf. *Thomson* (1965) 50 Cr App Rep 1. See Fridman in (1956) 19 MLR 276.
18. Above, p. 259.
19. *Director of Public Prosecutions v Shannon* [1975] AC 717, [1974] 2 All ER 1009, HL.
1. Ibid.

There may be evidence – usually a confession – which is admissible against D but not against E, which shows that D conspired with E. In these circumstances it is perfectly logical for the jury to be satisfied, as against D, that he conspired with E, but not satisfied, as against E, that he conspired with D. It is only when the evidence against D and E is of equal weight, or nearly so, that the judge should direct the jury that they must either acquit both or convict both – being careful to add that, if they are unsure about the guilt of one, both must be acquitted.[2]

4) *Sentence*

A person convicted of a common law conspiracy was liable to imprisonment and a fine at the discretion of the court; but under the Criminal Justice Act 1987, s. 12, conspiracy to defraud is now punishable with a maximum of ten years' imprisonment. A person convicted of a statutory conspiracy is liable to a sentence of imprisonment for a term not exceeding the maximum provided for the offence which he has conspired to commit.[3] Where the conspiracy is to commit more than one offence, the maximum is the longer or longest of the sentences provided for. Where the offence is triable either way the maximum for conspiracy is the maximum provided for conviction on indictment. Power to impose life imprisonment is provided in the case of conspiracy to commit (i) murder or any other offence the sentence for which is fixed by law; (ii) any offence for which a sentence of imprisonment for life is provided and (iii) an indictable offence punishable with imprisonment for which no maximum term is provided.[4]

The power to impose a fine without limit is unaffected by the Act. S. 3 (1) preserves the general power of the Crown Court under the Powers of Criminal Courts Act 1973, s. 30 (1), to impose a fine in lieu of or in addition to dealing with the offender in any other way. A conspiracy to commit an offence punishable with a maximum fine of £10 is thus punishable with a fine without limit except, of course, that it must not be unreasonable in all the circumstances.

5) *Powers of Arrest*

Since the Police and Criminal Evidence Act 1984, s. 24 (1), came into force all offences carrying a maximum of five years' imprisonment or more are arrestable offences,[5] whether the maximum derives from an enactment or

---

2. *Longman and Cribben* (1980) 72 Cr App Rep 121, [1981] Crim LR 38 and commentary. Cf. the similar problem which arises with secondary parties, above, p. 151. *Roberts* (1983) 78 Cr App Rep 41, [1985] Crim LR 218.
3. Section 3 (3).
4. Section 3(2).
5. See above, p. 25.

from the common law. As conspiracy to defraud is now punishable with a maximum of ten years' imprisonment under the Criminal Justice Act 1987, s. 12 (3), it is an arrestable offence. So are common law conspiracies to corrupt public morals or outrage public decency because they are punishable at common law with imprisonment at the discretion of the court.

Statutory conspiracies are arrestable offences if the offence, or one of the offences, which the parties have conspired to commit, is punishable with a maximum of five years or more.

6) *Periods of Limitation*

Section 4 (4) of the Act provides that where –
   "a) an offence has been committed in pursuance of any agreement; and
   b) proceedings may not be instituted for that offence because any time limit applicable to the institution of such proceedings has expired, proceedings under section I above for conspiracy to commit that offence shall not be instituted against any person on the basis of that agreement."

One of the objections to conspiracy charges at common law, especially charges of conspiracy to commit a summary offence, is that they enable a limitation period to be evaded. This provision meets that criticism, at least to some extent. S. 4 (4) only applies where the offence has been committed. Thus an agreement to commit an offence which is subject to a period of limitation remains indictable indefinitely if the offence is never committed and never will be committed because the parties have abandoned the plan. There is no point from which the period of limitation can begin to run.

7) *Rationale of Conspiracy*

Why should the mere agreement to commit an offence be a crime?[6] A commonly accepted reason is that it enables the criminal law to intervene at an early stage to prevent the harm involved in the commission of the ulterior offence.[7] This argument is not completely convincing, however, for it does not explain why agreements differ from other acts manifesting an intention to commit a crime, which are not offences unless sufficiently proximate to amount to attempts. A declaration by one person of his unshakeable resolution to commit a crime and the taking of preparatory steps (not in themselves offences) do not amount to a crime. The law thus attaches importance to the act of agreement, "over and above its value as an indicator of criminal intent."[8] It is a step towards the commission of a crime to which the law has long attached a peculiar significance. The

6. See Ian H. Dennis, "The Rationale of Criminal Conspiracy", (1977) 93 LQR 39; Williams, CLGP, para. 226; Sayre (1922) Harv LR 393.
7. Law Commission Working Paper, para. 12: "the most important rationale". The Law Commission agreed: Law Com. No. 76, 1.5.
8. Dennis, op. cit., footnote 6, above.

combination of minds, bent on the commission of the unlawful act, is taken to dispense with the need for proximity where only one person is involved.

It is argued that the effect of the combination is to increase the risk that the crime will be committed and the danger to the proposed victim, or to the public. Yet the risk and the danger are not necessarily greater than those arising from the resolve and the preparatory acts of a determined individual. Perhaps the basis, never clearly articulated by our courts, is that there is something inherently wicked in a "plot" to commit crime.[9]

None of this explains why an agreement to do an act, which is not a crime, may be a conspiracy. The traditional explanation is as follows.

"The general principle on which the crime of conspiracy is founded is this, that the confederacy of several persons to effect any injurious object creates such a new and additional power to cause injury as requires criminal restraint; although none would be necessary were the same thing proposed, or even attempted to be done, by any person singly."[10]

This, however, does not explain why the confederacy, however powerful, should be criminal when even the actual achievement of the same injurious object by an individual – or, indeed, by the confederates – is not in itself an offence. The rationale of this aspect of conspiracy is now generally rejected and we are moving to a stage where it will be of historical interest only. ". . . the offence of conspiracy to do an unlawful, though not criminal, act ought to have no place in a modern system of law."[11] The only significant exception to this principle is now the law of conspiracy to defraud; and it is intended that that will go when the law relating to fraud has been amended.

3 Attempt

An attempt to commit any indictable offence was a misdemeanour at common law. The common law[12] was repealed by the Criminal Attempts Act 1981 (in this section of the book referred to as "the Act") which came into force on 27th August 1981. Section 1 (1) of the Act creates a new statutory offence.

"If, with intent to commit an offence to which this section applies, a person does an act which is more than merely preparatory to the commission of the offence, he is guilty of attempting to commit the offence."

1 Mens Rea in Attempts

Exceptionally, *mens rea* is here discussed before *actus reus* because, as has often been remarked,[13] the mental element assumes paramount importance in attempts. The *actus reus* may be a perfectly innocent and harmless act as

9. See Dennis, op. cit. pp. 51–52.
10. Criminal Law Commission, 7th Report (1843), p. 90.
11. Law Com. No. 76, 1.9.
12. See the fourth edition of this book at pp. 246–264.
13. See, e.g., *Whybrow* (1951) 35 Cr App Rep 141; **SHC 270.**

where D, intending to murder P, puts sugar in his tea, believing that it is not sugar but a deadly poison. The *actus reus* may be *any* act, provided it is done with intent to commit the offence and goes beyond mere preparation.

Where, as is commonly the case, the complete offence may be committed with a *mens rea* falling short of an intention to commit the offence, the requirements of the law on a charge of attempt are stricter. An intention to cause grievous bodily harm is a sufficient *mens rea* for murder, but that is plainly not an intent to commit murder and so is insufficient on a charge of attempted murder. Nothing less than an intention to kill will do.[14] Recklessness is a sufficient *mens rea* for most non-fatal offences against the person and for criminal damage and many other offences but it is not a sufficient *mens rea* on a charge of attempting to commit any of them.[15]

As has been seen,[16] however, intention has a variable meaning in the criminal law so the question arises, what does "intent to commit an offence" mean in s. 1 (1) of the Act? It was held in *Pearman*[17] that the word "intent" in section 1 has the same meaning as in the common law of attempts. They applied *Mohan*[18] where the Court of Appeal held that there must be proved –

"... a decision to bring about, in so far as it lies within the accused's power, the commission of the offence which it is alleged the accused attempted to commit, no matter whether the accused desired that consequence of his act or not."

The concluding words are difficult to reconcile with the main proposition which certainly seems to embody the notion of trying to cause, or striving for, a result.

In *Pearman* the court thought that these words –

"are probably designed to deal with a case where the accused has, as a primary purpose, some other object, for example, a man who plants a bomb in an aeroplane, which he knows is going to take off, it being his primary intention that he should claim the insurance on the aeroplane when the freight goes down into the sea. The jury would not be put off from saying that he intended to murder the crew simply by saying that he did not want or desire to kill the crew, but that was something that he inevitably intended to do. Similarly, for example, a man who is cornered by the police when he is in a car may have the primary purpose of simply escaping from that situation. If he drives straight at the police officers at high speed, a jury is likely to conclude that he intended to injure a police officer and maybe cause him serious grievous bodily harm."[19]

This seems to be substantially the same as the meaning given to intention in the criminal law generally, after the recent cases, culminating in *Nedrick*.[20]

This, however does not solve all the problems. The notion of attempt requires an intended result. It does not necessarily require intention with

14. Cf. *Whybrow* (1951) 35 Cr App Rep 141; **SHC 270**; *O'Toole* [1987] Crim LR 759, CA.
15. *Millard and Vernon* [1987] Crim LR 393.
16. Above, p. 55.
17. (1984) 80 Cr App Rep 259, CA.
18. [1976] QB 1, [1975] 2 All ER 193; **SHC 271**.
19. (1984) 80 Cr App Rep 259 at 263.
20. Above, p. 55.

respect to material circumstances. So in *Pigg*,[1] before the Act, it was assumed without argument that a man might be guilty of attempted rape if he tried to have sexual intercourse with a woman, being reckless whether or not she consented to his doing so. Though the point was not spelt out in any case, it is submitted that this was right in principle, at least until *Caldwell* recklessness supplanted *Cunningham* recklessness[2] in the case of some crimes. The *mens rea* of the complete crime should be modified only in so far as it is necessary in order to accommodate the concept of attempt. If recklessness as to circumstances is a sufficient *mens rea* for the complete crime, it should be so for an attempt. Griew, however, argues[3] that under the Act intention must apply to "the whole situation necessary to constitute the offence"; and that therefore a man attempting to have sexual intercourse with a woman who does not in fact consent will not be guilty of attempted rape if he is merely reckless whether she is consenting or not. His aim must be not merely sexual intercourse, but non-consensual sexual intercourse, or he must at least have known that non-consensual sexual intercourse was the certain outcome of the achievement of his objective. Thus, it would not be enough that he knew that it was highly probable that the woman was not consenting (even if foresight of high probability were regarded generally as "intention"), still less that he knew that this was merely probable, or possible or that, if he had stopped to think, he would have known it. It is thought doubtful whether the courts will go as far as this.[4] In *Morgan*, Lord Hailsham said:[5]

"... if the intention of the accused is to have intercourse *nolens volens*, that is recklessly and not caring whether the victim be a consenting party or not, that is equivalent on ordinary principles to an intent to do the prohibited act without the consent of the victim."

If the courts take that view of intent, then *Cunningham* recklessness[6] as to circumstances is enough. As a matter of policy, it is submitted that the result would be right.[7] The difficulty is to reconcile it with the Act. One way of doing so is to treat this state of mind as a conditional or qualified intent: "If she is not consenting, then I intend to have intercourse with her without her consent." To apply *Caldwell* recklessness would, however, be going altogether too far, even on the assumption that *Caldwell* recklessness is sufficient for the complete crime. A man who never contemplated non-consensual sexual intercourse as a possibility could be held to have intended such intercourse only by a fiction of a kind which should have no place in the criminal law.

Conditional intent. Great practical difficulty and much academic debate was caused by the decision of the Court of Appeal in *Husseyn*.[8] The defendants

---

1. [1982] 2 All ER 591, 74 Cr App Rep 352, [1982] Crim LR 446 and commentary.
2. Above, p. 62.
3. See Notes on the Act in *Current Law Statutes* and, to the same effect, Buxton, [1984] Crim LR 25; Glanville Williams takes the opposite view, [1983] Crim LR 365.
4. The question was raised in *Millard* but left open. Cf. *Mousir* [1987] Crim LR 561, CA.
5. (1975) 61 Cr App Rep 136 at 164–167.
6. Above, p. 62.
7. An analogous problem arises where recklessness is required as to a result not being part of the *actus reus*: *O'Toole* [1987] Crim LR 759, CA and commentary.
8. (1977) 67 Cr App Rep 131n, [1978] Crim LR 219 and commentary.

opened the door of a van in which there was a holdall containing valuable sub-aqua equipment. They were charged with attempted theft of that equipment. The judge directed the jury that they could convict if the defendants were about to look into the holdall and, if its contents were valuable, to steal them. The Court of Appeal[9] held that this was a misdirection: "it cannot be said that one who has it in mind to steal only if what he finds is worth stealing has a present intention to steal". This caused particular difficulties in the law of burglary because most persons charged with that crime intend to steal, not some specific thing, but anything they find which they think is worth stealing. The Court of Appeal got over this difficulty by holding that *Husseyn* applied only where, as in that case, the indictment named the specific thing which the defendant was alleged to have attempted to steal. It would have been different, apparently, if the indictment had charged an attempt to steal "some or all of the contents" of the holdall – or car, handbag or house, as the case may be. This purely procedural device was rightly criticised. In *Husseyn*, for example, the only thing in the holdall was the sub-aqua equipment. If the defendant was guilty of attempting to steal "some or all of the contents" he was obviously guilty of attempting to steal the sub-aqua equipment – there were no other contents; but if the indictment charged him with that he had to be acquitted! The Act does not expressly do anything about this absurd and unworthy distinction which remains part of the law.[10] The Act does, however, remove the major obstacle to a rational solution to the problem, namely the decision in *Haughton v Smith*.[11] So long as this case remained law, the defendant could only be convicted of attempting to steal something that was in the holdall, car, room or other place, because there could be no attempt to steal something that was not there.[12] In *Husseyn* the jury must have found that D intended to steal anything in the holdall that he found to be of value. If he would have taken the sub-aqua equipment had he found it, he had certainly done an act which was more than merely preparatory to stealing it and he ought to be found guilty of attempting to do so. It might not, however, be possible for the jury to be satisfied that he would have taken that item. If he would not have taken it, it follows that he was looking for other things – we know not what and perhaps he did not know either – which were not there. He was attempting to steal all right, but his attempt was doomed to failure. This no longer matters since the Act reversed *Haughton v Smith*. He was no different in this respect from the man who attempts to steal from an empty pocket. The only difficulty is about the form of the indictment. The formula approved by the Court of Appeal, "some or all of the contents", is unsatisfactory because the jury may not be satisfied that he intended to steal *any* of the contents and may indeed be satisfied that he did not intend to steal any of them. The indictment would

---

9. *A–G's References* (Nos. 1 and 2 of 1979) [1980] QB 180, [1979] 3 All ER 143, [1979] Crim LR 585; **SHC 511**; see also *Walkington* [1979] 2 All ER 716, [1979] Crim LR 526 and commentary.
10. *Smith and Smith* [1986] Crim LR 166, CA.
11. [1975] AC 476, [1973] 3 All ER 1109, below, p. 305.
12. Though there was an understandable inclination on the part of the Court of Appeal to carry on as if that case did not exist. See *Bayley v Easterbrook* [1980] Crim LR 503 and commentary.

be accurate, however, if it simply stated, "attempted to steal from a holdall". This represents the truth, whether there is anything there that he would have stolen or not. The failure to specify any subject-matter is not an objection because there is in fact no subject-matter to be specified. The defendant must be dealt with on the basis that he intended to take anything he thought worth taking, whatever it might be. The problem is exactly the same in the empty pocket case.

In *Husseyn*, the Court followed *Easom*,[13] where D picked up a woman's handbag in a theatre, rummaged through the contents and put it back having taken nothing. The handbag was attached by a thread to a policewoman's wrist. D's conviction for stealing the handbag and the specified contents – tissues, cosmetics, etc., was quashed because there was no intention permanently to deprive the owner of these. Consequently, the court held, he was not guilty of attempting to steal the handbag or contents. Whether he was rightly acquitted of theft is debated[14] but, assuming he was, he was also innocent of attempting to steal the specific contents, but he was clearly guilty of an attempt to steal what was not there. Plainly, he was looking for money and therefore the handbag was, in effect, empty. *Easom*, too, seems a suitable case for a charge of attempting to steal from a handbag. The court posed a much-discussed example. "If a dishonest postal sorter picks up a pile of letters intending to steal any which are registered, but, on finding that none of them are, replaces them, he has stolen nothing." This is true; but he was then (before *Haughton v Smith*) and is now, guilty of attempting to steal registered letters.

2 Actus Reus in Attempt

Before the Act there was an *actus reus* if the defendant had taken such steps towards the commission of the offence as were properly described as "an attempt" to commit it, in the ordinary meaning of that term. Many steps may be taken towards the commission of a crime which could not properly be so described. D, intending to commit murder, buys a gun and ammunition, does target practice, studies the habits of his intended victim, reconnoitres a suitable place to lie in ambush, puts on a disguise and sets out to take up his position. These are all acts of preparation but could scarcely be described as attempted murder. D takes up his position, loads the gun, sees his victim approaching, raises the gun, takes aim, puts his finger on the trigger and squeezes it. He has now certainly committed attempted murder; but he might have desisted or been interrupted at any one of the stages described. At what point had he gone far enough to be guilty of an attempt? The answer given by the common law was that it was a matter of fact: was the act sufficiently proximate to murder to be properly described as an attempt to commit it? More detailed formulations of the principle proved unsuccessful, being capricious in their operation or

---

13. [1971] 2 QB 315, [1971] 2 All ER 945.
14. See Williams, TBCL, 651–653 and [1979] Crim LR 530, footnote 3; below, p. 496.

simply unhelpful.[15] This is not surprising when it is recalled that the principle has to apply to all crimes and that crimes are very diverse in their nature. The only well-settled rule was that if D had done the last act which, as he knew, was necessary to achieve the consequence alleged to be attempted, he was guilty.[16] The converse, however, did not apply. An act might be sufficiently proximate although it was not necessarily the last act to be done. In *White*[17] D was held guilty of attempted murder by the attempted administration of a dose of poison though he may well have contemplated further doses, and further doses may have been necessary, to kill.

The test stated in s. 1 (1) of the Act is in substance that proposed by the Law Commission.[18] The Commissioners found that there is no "magic formula" to define precisely what constitutes an attempt and that there is bound to be some degree of uncertainty in the law. The proximity test was the only one broadly acceptable. Even its imprecision was not without advantages: "its flexibility does enable difficult cases to be reconsidered and their authority questioned"; and "where cases are so dependent on what are sometimes fine differences of degree, we think it is eminently appropriate for the question whether the conduct in a particular case amounts to an attempt to be left to the jury". The purpose of the proximity test was to prevent too great an extension of criminal liability, by excluding mere acts of preparation. The Commission thought it "undesirable to recommend anything more complex than a rationalisation of the present law". They rejected a definition in terms of proximity because of the danger of a formula which suggested that only the last act could be an attempt. They therefore decided that the formula should direct attention, not to when the commission of the offence begins, but to when mere preparation ends. The preparatory act test is more apt in one respect. "Proximity" suggested that the attempter had to come "pretty near"[19] to success; yet, where the attempt is to do the impossible, success is an infinity away. There is no such conceptual difficulty about preparatory acts to do the impossible – by one who does not know it is impossible, of course! It seems that no substantial change in the law was intended. If any change has been made, it is to extend the scope of attempts because, if there is any "middle ground" between mere preparation and a proximate act, an act in the middle ground now constitutes an attempt whereas formerly it did not do so. However, it seems more likely that preparation and commission overlap than that there is any gap between them.

Every step towards the commission of an offence, except the last one, could properly be described as "preparatory" to the commission of the

---

15. The most interesting effort was called the "equivocality theory". This is discussed in the fourth edition of this book at 253–255, but it is probably now of only historical interest, so far as English law is concerned.
16. Even this, not very ambitious, rule was doubted by Lord Edmund-Davies in *Stonehouse* [1978] AC 55 at 86, [1977] 2 All ER 909 at 933, but his Lordship's doubts seem to relate to the last act of a secondary party which, admittedly, does not necessarily constitute an attempt. See [1977] Crim LR 547–549.
17. [1910] 2 KB 124; **SHC 278**. See also *Linneker* [1906] 2 KB 99.
18. See Law Com. No. 102, 2.45–2.52.
19. O. W. Holmes J, *Commonwealth v Kennedy* (1897) 170 Mass. 18.

offence. The assassin crooks his finger around the trigger preparatory to pulling it. If the section were so interpreted, only the last act would amount to an attempt – a result which the Law Commission's formula was intended to avoid. The key word is "merely".[20] Not all preparatory acts are excluded. When does an act cease to be *merely* preparatory? The answer, it seems, must be when the actor is engaged in the commission of the offence which he is attempting – as Rowlatt J put it many years ago, when he is "on the job".[1] Whether he is seems to be still, as it was before the Act, the ultimate question.

Whether an act is "more than merely preparatory to the commission of the offence" is a question of fact. In a jury trial, it is of course for the judge to decide whether there is evidence sufficient in law to support such a finding and it is then for the jury to decide (i) what acts the defendant did and (ii) whether they were more than merely preparatory.[2] If the judge decides there is not sufficient evidence, he directs a verdict of not guilty. Where he decides there is sufficient evidence, he must leave both questions of fact to the jury, even where the only possible answer in law is that the defendant is guilty. Where, for example, the evidence is that the defendant has done the "last act", he may not tell the jury that, if they find that D did that act, that *is* an attempt even though, in law, this is so. The judge may express a strong opinion, but he must not appear to take the question of fact out of the hands of the jury.[3]

It has been argued[4] that the judge and jury, in performing their respective functions, are not entitled to have regard to the word "attempt". The question to be determined is, in the words of s. 4 (3), simply whether the defendant "did an act falling within subsection (1) of [section 1]"; and that subsection does not use the word "attempt". While there is great force in this argument, it is submitted that it should not prevail. As observed above, all acts but the last are preparatory. How then are we to determine whether an act is more than *merely* preparatory? To be more than merely preparatory, it must also be something else. What? Some other concept not mentioned in the section must be invoked to give it a sensible meaning. The answer seems to be that the act must be part of the commission of the intended offence, an act that is done by a defendant "on the job", that it is, in a word, an "attempt".

Since the Act provides for the first time a statutory definition of attempt, the cases on attempt at common law are no longer binding. They may,

---

20. Griew, *Current Law Statutes*, says that "If 'merely' adds anything at all, it is only emphasis"; but elsewhere in his note he recognises that all acts but the last are in one sense preparatory and that the phrase, "merely preparatory", indicates that "there may, in any criminal transaction, be a point before which it is appropriate to describe the actor as not yet engaged in the commission of the offence but as *only* preparing to commit it". (Our italics.) "Only" equals "merely". Thus, Griew seems to agree that not all preparatory acts are excluded, but only those that are "only" or "merely" preparatory.

  1. *Osborn* (1919) 84 JP 63.

  2. See s. 4 (3) of the Act, which, in substance, codifies the common law as to the functions of judge and jury: *Stonehouse* [1978] AC 55, [1977] 2 All ER 909.

  3. If he does and the jury convict, the conviction is likely to be upheld under the proviso to s. 2 of the Criminal Appeal Act 1968.

  4. Griew, *Current Law Statutes*; see above, p. 289.

however, be regarded as persuasive because the Act is (in this respect) intended to be no more than a rationalisation of the common law.

The test of proximity at common law was expressed in various ways. One way, which gave attempts very narrow scope, was that of Lord Diplock in *Stonehouse* where, having cited the opinion in *Eagleton*[5] that only acts "immediately connected" with the offence can be attempts, he continued:[6] "In other words the offender must have crossed the Rubicon and burnt his boats."

Both before and after the Act, this passage seems to have been popular with defending counsel – not unnaturally, because it gives the narrowest possible scope to the law of attempts. It is accepted as the law in *Widdowson*.[7] This graphic test is most misleading. The point about crossing the Rubicon is that there is no going back, no possibility of an effective change of mind. The intending arsonist who struck the match beside the haystack with the intent of setting fire to it would not be guilty, nor would the intending assassin who put his finger round the trigger, preparatory to pulling it. The "Rubicon test" is inconsistent with such cases as *White*[8] where D was held guilty of attempted murder by the administration of poison even though he contemplated, as was the fact, that further doses were necessary in order to kill. The assassin who has pressed the trigger has "burnt his boats" and so too may have Stonehouse[9] but many persons have been convicted of attempts although there was the possibility of repentance. In *Boyle and Boyle*,[10] where the defendants damaged a door of a house with a view to entering and stealing and were convicted of attempted burglary, the court said that the conviction could be upheld whether the Rubicon test or that stated by Stephen (*infra*) were applied; but is that so? Having damaged the door, the defendants could have desisted and departed – but they were surely rightly convicted – they were "on the job." Happily the Court of Appeal has now repudiated the Rubicon test: in *Gullefer*[11] it was held that it need not be proved that the defendant has reached a point from which it is impossible for him to retreat. The rival test formulated by Stephen[12] is –

"'An attempt to commit a crime is an act done with intent to commit that crime and forming part of a series of acts which would constitute its actual commission, if it were not interrupted."

This, though constantly cited, is unhelpful. Merely preparatory acts may form "part of a series of acts which would constitute the actual commission of the crime if not interrupted", but they do not amount to an attempt. In *Gullefer* Lane LCJ said that the words of the Act give as clear a guidance as possible and it is submitted that that is correct.

Some decisions at common law which were thought by judicial and academic critics to take too restrictive a view of attempts may now be

5. (1855) Dears CC 376, 515.
6. [1978] AC 55 at 68.
7. (1985) 82 Cr App Rep 314 at 318–319, CA, [1986] Crim LR 233 and commentary.
8. [1910] 2 KB 124, CCA.
9. Below, p. 299.
10. (1987) 84 Cr App Rep 270.
11. [1987] Crim LR 195, CA.
12. *Digest of the Criminal Law* (9th ed.).

reconsidered. Notable among these is *Robinson*.[13] D, a jeweller, having insured his stock against theft, concealed some of it on his premises, tied himself up with string and called for help. He told a policeman who broke in that he had been knocked down and his safe robbed. The jewellery was insured for £1,200. The policeman was not satisfied with the story and discovered the property concealed on the premises. D confessed that he had hoped to get money from the insurers. His conviction for attempting to obtain by false pretences was quashed. If this case still represents the law, a judge, on these facts, should direct a jury to acquit of the attempt. Notwithstanding the criticisms, it is by no means clear that this conduct ought to be regarded as more than merely preparatory. The stage had been set; but the business of obtaining money from the insurance company was yet to begin. D was undoubtedly preparing to commit a crime but it is not obvious that he had yet begun to commit it. Even if *Robinson* has been overruled by the Act, it is not possible to say that what he did amounts to an attempt but only that there is evidence on which a reasonable jury might so find. The indications are that *Robinson* is still good law. *Ilyas*[14] and *Widdowson* were rather similar cases where convictions for attempt were quashed. In *Ilyas* the charge was of attempt at common law but the case was decided after the Act came into force and the court used terminology similar to that of the Act. But both *Ilyas* and *Widdowson* were influenced by the misleading Rubicon test. Nevertheless, it is thought that *Robinson* should still be decided in the same way. His acts were merely preparatory.

In *Comer v Bloomfield*[15] the defendant went a step further than Robinson. Having crashed his van, he pushed it into a nearby wood, reported to the police that it had been stolen and wrote to his insurers stating that the van had been stolen and inquiring whether he could claim for it. He was acquitted by magistrates of attempting to obtain money by deception and the Divisional Court held that the magistrates were entitled to conclude that the making of a preliminary inquiry was insufficiently proximate to the actual obtaining. If the magistrates had convicted the defendant, it may be that the conviction would have been upheld on the ground that there was evidence on which they might find that the act was sufficiently proximate. Some such inconsistency in result must be anticipated when the question is treated as one of fact. Even if *Robinson* does represent the law, Bloomfield's inquiry might well be held to be evidence of a more than merely preparatory act; D had set about the business of getting money from the insurers.

Perhaps the most striking case of all is *Komaroni and Rogerson*[16] where the defendants followed a lorry for 130 miles, waiting in vain for the driver to leave it unattended so that they could steal it. Streatfield J held that this was mere preparation. It seems likely that this might be held to be evidence of an attempt under the Act.

13. [1915] 2 KB 342, 11 Cr App Rep 124, CCA. Cf. *Button* [1900] 2 QB 597, CCR.
14. (1983) 78 Cr App Rep 17.
15. (1970) 55 Cr App Rep 305.
16. (1953) 103 L Jo 97.

3 Attempt by Omission

A crime of omission where the *actus reus* does not include any consequence of the omission is by its nature incapable of being attempted.[17] This is not true of an offence including a consequence which may be committed by one having a duty to act. If the parents of a child deliberately withhold food from the child with the intent to kill it, they have set out to commit murder.[18] In fact, they are attempting to commit murder but, in the rare case where it cannot be proved that they did any act contributing to the death, it seems probable that, under the Act, they are no longer guilty of that offence.[19] They have done no act, as required by s. 1 (1). Though the government seems to have supposed that an attempt could be charged in such a case,[20] it would require bold judicial interpretation to read "act" to include "omission". Cases will be rare where an intent to commit an offence by omission can be proved. Where it can be so proved, there seems to be an unfortunate gap in the law.

4 Successful Attempts

It has sometimes been argued that failure is essential to the very nature of an attempt so that success precludes a conviction for attempting to commit a crime.[1] For a rather technical reason, this was true of attempts to commit felonies at common law. There was a rule that a misdemeanour committed in the course of committing a felony "merged" in the felony. Since an attempt to commit a felony was a misdemeanour, it ceased to exist when the felony was committed. This doctrine was almost certainly abolished, so far as trial on indictment is concerned, as long ago as 1851,[2] though the matter was disputed. With the abolition of felonies by the Criminal Law Act 1967 this doctrine of merger disappeared and s. 6 (4) of the Act provided:

"... where a person is charged on indictment with attempting to commit an offence or with an assault or other act preliminary to an offence, but not with the completed offence, then (subject to the discretion of the court to discharge the jury with a view to the preferment of an indictment for the completed offence) he may be convicted of the offence charged notwithstanding that he is shown to be guilty of the completed offence."

This provision does not extend to summary trial and there was some doubt about the position in magistrates' courts until the Divisional Court held in *Webley v Buxton*[3] that an attempt to commit a misdemeanour does not merge in the completed offence at common law. D, sitting astride a

---

17. Below, p. 298.
18. *Gibbins and Proctor* (1918) 13 Cr App Rep 134, above, p. 49. Cf. Gunn and Smith [1985] Crim LR 705 at 706, footnote 9.
19. They are of course guilty of the offence of wilful neglect of a young person under the Children and Young Persons Act 1933.
20. See *Dennis* [1982] Crim LR 7.
  1. Hall, GPCL, 577: "... attempt implies failure ...". Fletcher *Rethinking*, 131. In *Commonwealth v Crow* (1931) 303 Pa 91 at 98, the court said "A failure to consummate a crime is as much an essential element of an attempt as the intent and performance of an overt act towards its commission."
  2. By the Criminal Procedure Act 1851, s. 12, now repealed by the Criminal Law Act 1977.
  3. [1977] QB 481, [1977] 2 All ER 595, [1977] Crim LR 160.

motor-cycle, used his feet to push it eight feet across a pavement. He was charged with attempting to take a conveyance for his own use without the consent of the owner. The slightest movement of the conveyance is enough to constitute the full offence.[4] It was held that, though the justices were satisfied that he was guilty of the full offence, they had properly convicted him of the attempt. The Act makes no provision in the matter, following the recommendation of the Law Commission,[5] so the matter is governed by the common law as stated in *Webley v Buxton*.

As a matter of principle, this seems right. At a certain point in the transaction, D is guilty of an attempt. The attempt may fail for many reasons, or it may succeed. There is no reason why, if it succeeds, it should cease to be the offence of attempt which, until that moment, it was. The greater includes the less. If D is convicted of attempted murder while his victim, P, is still alive and P then dies of injuries inflicted by D, D is now liable to be convicted of murder; but the conviction for attempt is not invalidated. It would, of course, be improper to convict D of both the attempt and the full offence at the same time. To that extent, the attempt merges in the completed offence.

5 Offences which may be Attempted

By s. 1 (4), the section applies to any offence triable in England and Wales as an indictable offence – i.e., any offence triable only on indictment, or triable either way,[6] – except conspiracy, whether common law or statutory,[7] and offences of assisting an arrestable offender or compounding an arrestable offence contrary to ss. 4 (1) and 5 (1) respectively of the Criminal Law Act 1967.[8] It is an offence under the Act, as it was at common law, to attempt to commit the common law offence of incitement.[9] This is to deal with the case where a communication, which would be an incitement if it arrived, is intercepted. The Act makes clear that it is not an offence to attempt to aid, abet, counsel, procure or suborn the commission of an offence:[10] s. 1 (4) (b). Where, however, aiding, etc., is the principal offence as in s. 2 (1) of the Suicide Act 1961[11] or s. 4 of the Sexual Offences Act 1967,[12] an attempt to aid, etc. is an offence. Section 1 (4) (b) does not apply because these are not instances of aiding, etc., *an offence*.

Apart from the statutory exceptions there may be other crimes where an attempt is impossible. Stephen thought there was a large number of such offences[13] but his examples are not wholly convincing. There are five types

---

4. Below, p. 582.
5. Law Com. No. 102, 2.113.
6. Above, p. 28.
7. Above, p. 254.
8. Below, pp. 758–766. Reasons for excluding the offences under the Criminal Law Act 1967 are given in Law Com. No. 102 at 2.124–2.126.
9. Above, p. 253.
10. *Dunnington* [1984] QB 472, [1984] 1 All ER 676, 78 Cr App Rep 171. For the common law, see Smith, "Secondary Participation and Inchoate Offences", in *Crime, Proof and Punishment*, 21.
11. Below, p. 359. *McShane* (1977) 66 Cr App Rep 97, [1977] Crim LR 737. Smith in *Crime, Proof and Punishment* at 32.
12. Below, p. 473.
13. 2 HCL 227.

of offence where no attempt is possible. (1) Where any act done with the appropriate intent amounts to the complete crime.[14] Such crimes are rare but one may be the form of treason known as compassing the Queen's death.[15] The offence requires proof of an overt act but it seems that any act done with intent to kill the Queen would be enough. (2) A crime defined as an omission[16] where the *actus reus* does not include any consequence of the omission, as in the case of misprision of treason or some statutory offences of omission. (3) An offence which may be committed recklessly or negligently but not intentionally. The only example which comes readily to mind is involuntary manslaughter. The essence of this crime is that the killing is unintentional. An intentional killing (in the absence of diminished responsibility, the conditions for infanticide, provocation[17] or a suicide pact) is necessarily murder. Section 1 (1) of the Act requires an intent to commit the offence which D is charged with attempting but an intent to commit involuntary manslaughter is not a concept known to the law. (4) It is difficult to conceive of an attempt where the *actus reus* is a state of affairs, such as "being found" in particular circumstances.[18] (5) At common law it was doubtful whether an attempt to commit an offence triable only summarily was a crime. Under the Act, it is clear that it is not, unless the provision creating the offence expressly provides that it shall be. Such "an attempt under a special statutory provision" (s. 3 (1) of the Act) is now governed by the same principles as attempts under the Act.

a) *Attempt in England to commit an offence abroad.* Where the offence, if it were completed, would be triable on indictment in England, the attempt is likewise indictable. If D, a British citizen, in England posts a letter bomb to P in France, intending to kill P, he is liable to conviction for attempted murder as soon as the letter is posted;[19] but, if he intends only to injure P, he is not guilty of an attempt to cause him grievous or actual bodily harm. Murder abroad by a British citizen is triable in England but lesser offences against the person are not. If D were an alien, then he could not be tried in England for attempted murder. This seems anomalous, particularly since two aliens acting in concert could since 1977 be convicted of conspiracy in England to commit murder abroad.[20] If D posts a letter in England, attempting to obtain property by deception from P in France, he appears to be guilty of an attempt if he intends that the ownership or possession of the property shall be transferred to him in England;[1] but if both are to be transferred in France (e.g. to D's agent there) it is possible that the

---

14. In *Rogers v Arnott* [1960] 2 QB 244, [1960] 2 All ER 417 it was said that, for this reason, there could be no attempt to commit fraudulent conversion under s. 20 of the Larceny Act 1916; but it seems clear that there may be an attempt to appropriate property belonging to another, i.e., to steal, contrary to s. 1 of the Theft Act 1968, which has replaced fraudulent conversion.
15. Below, p. 827.
16. Attempt by omission generally is considered, p. 296.
17. For attempted infanticide, see *K A Smith* [1983] Crim LR 739, below, p. 363; and for attempt under provocation, *Bruzas* [1972] Crim LR 367, below, p. 33.
18. Above, p. 46.
19. Above, p. 292; below, p. 310.
20. Above, p. 269.
1. Smith, *Theft*, para. 191.

completed offence would not be triable in England, in which case there is no indictable attempt.

b)*Attempt abroad to commit an offence in England*. This is less clear than the previous case because English courts do not usually take jurisdiction over acts committed abroad; but it seems almost certain that the Act does not change the position previously established, namely that an attempt to procure the commission of a crime within the jurisdiction is indictable here, though all D's acts are done abroad, at least if they are intended to, and do, have an effect in England. The House of Lords so held in *Director of Public Prosecutions v Stonehouse*.[2] D, in Miami, falsely staged his death by drowning with the intention that his innocent wife in England should claim life assurance monies. He was guilty of attempting to enable his wife to obtain by deception. The "effect" was the communication through the media to her and the insurance companies of the false statement that he had died. It is submitted that, where D has gone beyond mere preparation, the better view is that it is immaterial that no effect occurs in England.[3] Why should the result have been different if D had been "rescued" from the sea and confessed before any report of his death appeared in England?

c) *Attempt abroad to commit an offence abroad*. D, a British citizen, being in France, attempts to kill P in France or, knowing himself to be married, attempts to go through a ceremony of marriage there. If he succeeds he will be liable to conviction in England of murder and bigamy. Exceptionally, English law assumes jurisdiction over these crimes when committed abroad by a British citizen. Literally, then, the attempt is an offence under the Act but it may be that the presumption against the extra-territorial operation of the criminal law[4] requires the words "does an act" to be construed as applicable only to acts done within the jurisdiction, or having, or being intended to have, some effect therein.

6 Withdrawal

It is logical that, once the steps taken towards the commission of an offence are sufficiently far advanced to amount to an attempt, it can make no difference whether the failure to complete the crime is due to a voluntary withdrawal by the prisoner, the intervention of the police, or any other reason. In *Taylor*[5] it was held that an attempt was committed where D approached a stack of corn with the intention of setting fire to it and lighted a match for that purpose but abandoned his plan on finding that he was being watched. In some jurisdictions, logic has given way to policy and a defence of free and voluntary desistance is allowed.[6] Following the recommendation of the Law Commission,[7] the Act makes no change in this

---

2. [1978] AC 55, [1977] 2 All ER 909, [1977] Crim LR 544 and commentary. Cf. *Baxter* [1972] 1 QB 1, [1971] 2 All ER 359.
3. This was, in effect, the opinion of Lord Diplock. Lord Keith of Kinkel thought the contrary. The other judges expressed no opinion. Cf. Law Commission Working Paper No. 29 (1970).
4. See Griew, *Current Law Statutes*, General Note.
5. (1859) 1 F & F 511; See also *Lankford* [1959] Crim LR 209.
6. See Stuart, [1970] Crim LR at 519–521.
7. Law Com. No. 102, 2.131–2.133.

respect. The principal argument in favour of a withdrawal defence is that it might induce the attempter to desist – but this seems unlikely. The existence of the defence would add to the problems of law enforcement authorities.

4 Impossibility

The problem to be discussed is peculiar to the "inchoate" offences which are the subject of this chapter. If it is impossible to commit a crime, obviously no one can be convicted of committing it. It does not follow that no one can be convicted of inciting another, or conspiring or attempting to commit it. It is a fact that people sometimes do incite, conspire and attempt to do what is impossible. This happens only when the defendant does not realise that what he has in view is impossible, i.e., he is making a mistake of some kind.

The law has long recognised that, in some circumstances, a conviction for incitement, conspiracy or attempt to commit an offence might be proper, although the commission of that offence was impossible. There has been great controversy about the circumstances in which impossibility will afford a defence and those in which it will not.

One category of case can be shortly disposed of. That is where the crime is "impossible" in the sense that the intended result is not a crime at all but D, because of his ignorance or mistake of criminal law, believes that it is. Here, the law is the same for all three inchoate offences and it is clear that none of them is committed. Suppose that D comes from a land where adultery is a crime and he thinks that it is a crime in England. He may incite the commission of adultery, agree to commit adultery and attempt to commit adultery. The "offence" he has in mind is non-existent, its "commission" is impossible and he has committed no inchoate offence. In *Taaffe*[8] D imported into the United Kingdom certain packages which he believed to contain foreign currency. He thought it was a crime to import foreign currency. It was not. He could not, on those facts, be committed of any offence or of an attempt to commit any offence. The intention to import foreign currency, believing it to be a crime, though morally reprehensible, was not the *mens rea* of any crime – any more than an intention to commit adultery in England is a *mens rea*. The conduct he had in mind was not the *actus reus* of any offence. In fact, Taaffe had committed the *actus reus* of a crime because the contents of the package were cannabis and it is an offence to import cannabis; but there was no *mens rea* to complement that *actus reus*.

In all the other cases to be considered D has the *mens rea* of the ulterior offence – he intends that it shall be committed; but because of some *fact* as to which he is ignorant or mistaken, either –

a) the result he intends cannot be achieved or

---

8. [1984] AC 539 [1984] 1 All ER 747, HL, [1983] 2 All ER 625, CA. See commentary on the decision of the Court of Appeal, [1983] Crim LR 536.

b) the result he intends, if achieved, will not be the crime that he believed would be committed.

Into category a) fall cases where the means used are inadequate to achieve the intended result and where the subject matter or victim of the intended offence does not exist. Category b) comprises cases where some circumstance, which is an element of the intended crime, does not exist. D believes that he is committing a crime, because he is making a mistake, not of criminal law, but of fact. For example, he intends that he (or the person incited or with whom he conspires) shall have sexual intercourse with P, whom he believes to be fifteen. P is sixteen and consequently the "result" (intercourse with P) will not be the crime that D intended. At one time,[9] it was thought that the distinction between categories a) and b) was material but, as the law now stands, it has no part to play.

It might be expected that the same general principles of the common law would apply to all cases of of incitement, conspiracy and attempt and this probably was the case.[10] The law now, however, is that

i) incitement and common law conspiracy are governed by the common law;

ii) statutory conspiracy and attempt are governed by the Criminal Law Act 1977, s. 1 (1), as amended,[11] and the Criminal Attempts Act 1981, s. 1 (2) and (3), respectively.

The common law. The common law was laid down, for attempts, in *Haughton v Smith*,[12] and for conspiracy, in *Director of Public Prosecutions v Nock*.[13] The result of these decisions is that impossibility is a general defence at common law. It seems that the only exception is that D may be convicted where the impossibility results from the inadequacy of the means used, or to be used, to commit the offence. So, for example, D will not be guilty of incitement where –

a) The subject matter of the offence does not exist. D incites E to steal from P's safe. P's safe is empty.

b) The victim of the offence does not exist. D incites E to murder P. P is already dead.[14]

c) The subject-matter of the offence lacks some quality which is an element of the offence. D and E believe a certain diamond to have been stolen. D incites E to receive it. It has not been stolen.[15]

d) The victim of the offence lacks some quality which is an element of the offence. D and E believe P to be aged fifteen. In fact she is sixteen. D incites E to have sexual intercourse with her.

On the other hand, D may be guilty of incitement where –

---

9. See the first three editions of this work.
10. In *Fitzmaurice* [1983] QB 1083, [1983] 1All ER 189. CA, followed in *Sirat* (1986) 83 Cr App Rep 41, [1986] Crim LR 245, it was held that the principles stated in *Haughton v Smith* and *Nock* apply to incitement.
11. Above, p. 259.
12. [1975] AC 476, [1973] 2 All ER 896.
13. [1978] AC 979, [1978] 2 All ER 654, above, p. 260.
14. *Sirat* (1986) 83 Cr App Rep 41 at 43.
15. *Haughton v Smith*, supra.

a) He gives E a jemmy and urges him to use it to break into P's safe and steal a diamond. The diamond is in the safe, but it is impossible to break in with the jemmy.

b) He gives E some poison and tells him to administer it to P so as to kill him. The dose is inadequate to kill anyone.

The statutory law. For statutory conspiracies the law is to be found in the Criminal Law Act 1977, s. 1 (1)[16] as amended by the Criminal Attempts Act 1981 and, for attempts, it is in the Criminal Attempts Act 1981, s. 1 (2) and (3) which provides:

"(2) A person may be guilty of attempting to commit an offence to which this section applies even though the facts are such that the commission of the offence is impossible.

(3) In any case where –

a) apart from this subsection a person's intention would not be regarded as having amounted to an intent to commit an offence; but

b) if the facts of the case had been as he believed them to be, his intention would be so regarded, then for the purposes of subsection (1) above he shall be regarded as having an intent to commit that offence."

Subsection (3) is strictly unnecessary but it was wise to include it as a matter of caution. It is unnecessary because under it no one will "be regarded as having an intent to commit that offence" who does not in fact have that intent. It would be wholly wrong to impute a non-existent intent to a defendant and the Act does not do so. In other words the subsection does nothing – except forestall the following fallacious argument.

i) D (believing them to be stolen) intends to handle certain goods.

ii) Those goods are not stolen.

iii) Therefore D does not intend to handle stolen goods.

Subsection (3) says he shall be regarded as having an intent to handle stolen goods. Of course, he has such an intent anyway. The fact that the goods are not stolen, being unknown to him, is wholly irrelevant in determining his intention.

The gist of the two provisions is that for both conspiracy and attempt there must be an intention to commit the offence[17] contemplated, whereupon it is immaterial that it is *in fact* impossible to commit that offence if, in the case of conspiracy, there has been an agreement to commit it and in the case of an attempt, a more than merely preparatory step towards its commission. The provisions have no application to the cases considered above[18] where it is, *in law*, impossible to commit "the offence" D intended to commit.

The proper construction of the Criminal Attempts Act has been a matter of acute controversy but it is now settled by the decision of the House of Lords in *Shivpuri*.[19]

16. Above, p. 259.
17. For conspiracy, pace Lord Bridge in *Anderson*, above, p. 259.
18. P. 300.
19. [1987] AC 1, [1986] 2 All ER 334, [1986] Crim LR 536.

It seems reasonable to assume that the same interpretation will be put on the amended s. 1 (1) of the Criminal Law Act 1977 (statutory conspiracy) for that section was amended by the Criminal Attempts Act 1981, s. 5, to keep the law of attempt and conspiracy in line in this respect.

In the case of attempts, it must be proved that D had an intention to commit the crime in question. Once that is established, the only question is whether, with that intent, he has done an act which is "more than merely preparatory" to the commission of the offence. Since, ex hypothesi, the offence is impossible, it is the offence envisaged by D to which the act in question must be more than merely preparatory. The effect is that the court must ask, "would the act have been more than merely preparatory to the commission of the offence if the facts had been as D believed them to be?"

In the case of conspiracy, it must be proved that D agreed with another or others that a course of conduct be pursued which, in the circumstances believed by the parties to exist, will, in the event of their intention being achieved, amount to or involve the commission of the offence. It has been argued above[20] that this is the only sensible interpretation of the phrase, "course of conduct", and that the amendment by the 1981 Act was strictly unnecessary. The 1981 amendment may, however, be taken to reinforce this opinion. It is then immaterial that the circumstances are in fact such that the offence is impossible, or that the results can never be achieved.

In the following examples, D will be guilty both of conspiracy and attempt.

i) D and E agree that they will use D's jemmy to break into P's safe and steal a diamond. D tries to do so. It is quite impossible to break into the safe with that jemmy. D and E are guilty of conspiracy and D of an attempt to steal the diamond. (It is immaterial whether the diamond is in the safe or not.)

ii) D and E agree that they will administer a poison, which D has acquired, to P in order to kill him. D administers the poison. The poison would not kill anyone. D and E are guilty of conspiracy, and D of an attempt, to murder P.

iii) D and E agree that they will steal from P's safe. D attempts to break open the safe. It is empty. D and E are guilty of conspiracy, and D of attempt, to steal from the safe.

iv) D and E agree that they will murder P. D shoots at P's heart but P is already dead. D and E are guilty of conspiracy to murder and D of attempted murder.

v) D and E agree that they will receive from F certain goods which they believe to be stolen goods. D takes possession of the goods. The goods are not stolen goods. D and E are guilty of conspiracy, and D of an attempt, to handle stolen goods.

vi) D and E agree that D will have sexual intercourse with P, a girl whom they believe to be aged fifteen. D has sexual intercourse with her. In fact she is sixteen. D and E are guilty of conspiracy, and D of an attempt, to have sexual intercourse with a girl under the age of sixteen.

20. P. 260.

Examples iii) and iv) would not have been offences at common law under the principles established in *Haughton* v *Smith* and *Nock* but those decisions are now generally recognised to have been unduly restrictive. It is the cases exemplified by illustrations (v) and (vi) which have been the subject of much controversy.[1] The reason is that, in these cases, if D succeeds in doing the precise thing that he set out to do, he will not commit a crime. D takes possession of the very goods he intended to take possession of – no other – and that is no offence, for the goods are not stolen goods. D has sexual intercourse with the girl he intends to have intercourse with. She is sixteen and consents so there is nothing unlawful. How then can his taking steps towards the accomplishment of something which is no crime be a conspiracy or an attempt to commit it? Bramwell B ridiculed the idea in *Collins*[2] in 1864. He put the case of D who takes an umbrella from his club, intending to steal it. It turns out to be his own umbrella. Bramwell B thought it absurd that D should be convicted of attempting to steal it. Arguments of this kind prevailed in the House of Lords in *Anderton v Ryan*[3] (1985) but were then rejected in *Shivpuri*[4] (1986) barely a year later.

In *Anderton v Ryan* D bought a video recorder for £110. Later she said to police, "I may as well be honest, it was a stolen one I bought . . .". She was charged with handling and attempted handling. The prosecution, presumably believing that they were unable to prove that the recorder had in fact been stolen, offered no evidence on the first charge. The magistrates were not satisfied that the recorder had been stolen, though D believed it had. They dismissed the charge. The Divisional Court allowed the prosecution's appeal[5] but the House of Lords, Lord Edmund-Davies dissenting, restored the decision of the magistrates. The Criminal Attempts Act 1981, s. 1 (3), said Lord Roskill, "does not compel the conclusion that an erroneous belief in the existence of facts which, if true, would have made his completed act a crime makes him guilty of an attempt to commit that crime". Because the House thought the conclusion absurd, they were not going to reach it unless compelled to. In *Shivpuri* D was arrested by customs officials while in possession of a suitcase. He admitted that he knew it contained prohibited drugs. Analysis showed that the material in the suitcase was not a prohibited drug but a vegetable material akin to snuff. He was convicted of attempting to be knowingly concerned in dealing with a prohibited drug, contrary to s. 1 (1) of the Criminal Attempts Act 1981 and s. 170 (1) (b) of the Customs and Excise Management Act 1979. His appeal was dismissed by the Court of Appeal[6] and, overruling *Anderton v Ryan*, by the House of Lords. No distinction is to be drawn between "objectively innocent" acts (taking one's own umbrella, receiving non-stolen goods, handling snuff) and "guilty" acts, for the

---

1. The decisive article which influenced the decision in *Shivpuri* is Glanville Williams, "The Lords and Impossible Attempts", [1986] CLJ 33. For earlier writing, see Hogan [1984] Crim LR 584 and 135 NLJ 454, Williams 135 NLJ 337 and commentaries at [1985] Crim LR 44, 504, [1986] Crim LR 51.
2. 9 Cox CC 497 at 498.
3. [1985] AC 560, [1985] 2 All ER 355.
4. [1987] AC 1, [1986] 2 All ER 334.
5. [1985] 1 All ER 138, [1984] Crim LR 483.
6. [1985] QB 1029, [1985] 1 All ER 143.

purposes of the law of attempts. The law is as stated above.[7] Since it must be proved that D intended to commit the crime in question, he is morally at least as bad as the person who actually commits the offence and, where the offence may be committed with some lesser degree of *mens rea*, perhaps worse; and he is as dangerous to whatever interest the particular law is designed to protect as the person who actually commits the offence. It is sometimes objected that he is punished solely for his thoughts but this is not true because it must be proved (in the case of an attempt) that he has taken such steps to put his intention into execution as would (if the facts were as he believed) be more than merely preparatory to the commission of the offence. In the case of conspiracy (not expressly considered in *Shivpuri* but presumably governed by the same principles) he must have agreed with another that the offence be committed – the usual *actus reus* of conspiracy. It is also argued that the conclusion offends against the principle of legality (no one shall be convicted of doing something which has not been declared by the law to be an offence). But the issue in these cases was the proper construction of the statute. If Parliament has said (and the House ultimately decided that it has) that it is to be an offence (attempt) to do any more than a merely preparatory act with intent to commit an offence, the law may be criticised for being too wide-ranging; but the conviction of one who does any such act with that intent can no longer be criticised for breaching the principle of legality.

The breadth of the law is such that there may be cases where prosecution would be ill-advised. Bramwell B's man who took his own umbrella would no doubt be surprised to find himself charged with attempting to steal his own umbrella. D who has *succeeded* in having sexual intercourse with P, a sixteen-year-old girl, might be astonished to find himself charged in consequence with *attempting* to have sexual intercourse with a girl under sixteen. As such acts are objectively innocent, the offence is unlikely to come to light unless D advertises the fact that he acted with *mens rea*. There will be other cases, however, where a prosecution is in the public interest. The would-be drug smuggler, exemplified by *Shivpuri*, is an example. It may well be that their Lordships' change of mind was not uninfluenced by the fact that *Anderton v Ryan* would have required them to turn such dangerous persons loose on the public. Perhaps the most important case in practice is that of the person who receives goods wrongly believing them to be stolen. Mrs Ryan's was an unusual and trivial case. Typical of the case where a prosecution is likely to be brought is *Haughton v Smith* itself. A van, heavily laden with stolen corned beef, was intercepted by the police. Having discovered that the intended recipient was D, the police allowed it to proceed on its way, but under the control of disguised policemen. D received the goods, believing them to be stolen. But the beef ceased to be stolen goods when the police took control of it.[8] The House held that he was not guilty of attempted handling but now he could plainly be convicted. The public interest called for his conviction no less than if the police had never intercepted the goods.

7. P. 303.
8. Below, p. 617.

Impossibility in future. It would be rash to predict that *Shivpuri* solves all the problems relating to impossibility. The fact that Lord Hailsham, with whom Lord Elwyn-Jones and Lord Mackay concurred, offered reasons why *Anderton v Ryan* was distinguishable (even though they concurred in overruling it) may encourage subsequent attempts to distinguish *Shivpuri* on similar lines. To do so would, however, be to resurrect in a slightly different form arguments which were in substance rejected in *Shivpuri*.[9] It is, of course, anomalous that, for incitement, impossibility should continue to be governed by the common law, particularly as that was left in such an unsatisfactory state by *Haughton v Smith* and *Nock*. It is submitted that the matter would be put on a sound basis by the enactment of the proposal of the draft Criminal Code, cl. 54 (1).[10]

"A person may be guilty of incitement, conspiracy or attempt to commit an offence although the commission of the offence is impossible, if it would be possible in the circumstances which he believes or hopes exist or will exist at the relevant time."

9. See the analysis of Lord Hailsham's speech at [1986] Crim LR 539–541.
10. See Law Com. No. 143, 14.40–14.41.

Part II

Particular Crimes

11 Homicide

1 Murder

The classic definition of murder is that of Coke:

> "Murder is when a man of sound memory, and of the age of discretion, unlawfully killeth within any county of the realm any reasonable creature *in rerum natura* under the king's peace, with malice aforethought, either expressed by the party or implied by law, so as the party wounded, or hurt, etc. die of the wound or hurt, etc. within a year and a day after the same."[1]

1) *Who Can Commit Murder*

"A man of sound memory, and of the age of discretion" means simply a man who is responsible according to the general principles which have been discussed above. Such a man is not insane within the M'Naghten Rules; he is over nine and, if under fourteen, he has a "mischievous discretion"; and, since 1957,[2] he does not suffer from diminished responsibility.

2) *Where Murder Can Be Committed*

If the killing is by a British citizen, it need no longer take place within "any county of the realm". Murder and manslaughter are among the exceptional cases where the English courts have jurisdiction over offences committed abroad. By s. 9 of the Offences against the Person Act 1861 and s. 3 of the British Nationality Act 1948 a murder or manslaughter committed by a British citizen on land anywhere out of the United Kingdom may be tried in any county or place in England as if it had been committed there.[3] Homicides on a British ship[4] or aircraft[5] are also triable here, whether committed by a British subject or not; but not those on a foreign ship, outside territorial waters.[6]

1. 3 Inst 47.
2. See s. 2 of the Homicide Act 1957, above, p. 201.
3. See CLRC, OAP/WP, p. 67, OAP/R 125.
4. Not only when sailing on the high seas, but also when in the rivers of a foreign territory at a place below bridges, where the tide ebbs and flows and where great ships go: *Anderson* (1868) LR 1 CCR 161.
5. Civil Aviation Act 1949, s. 62.
6. Jurisdiction over offences within territorial waters is given by the Territorial Waters Jurisdiction Act 1878, s. 2. And see Continental Shelf Act 1964, s. 3.

3) *Who Can Be The Victim*[7]

"A reasonable creature *in rerum natura*" includes any human being. The only problems are at what stage in the process of birth a foetus becomes a person; and at what stage in the process of death a person becomes a corpse. It is not murder to kill a child in the womb or in the process of leaving the womb. At common law it was a "great misprision" (misdemeanour)[8] and it is now an offence under s. 58 of the Offences against the Person Act 1861,[9] or, where the child is capable of being born alive, under the Infant Life (Preservation) Act 1929.[10] To be the victim of a murder the child must be wholly expelled from the mother's body and it must be alive.[11] The cord and the after-birth need not have been expelled from the mother nor severed from the child.[12] The child, it is commonly said, must have an existence "independent of the mother".[13] The tests of independent existence which the courts have accepted are that the child should have an independent circulation, and that it should have breathed after birth. But there are difficulties about both these tests.

In *Brain* Park J said:[14]

"... it is not essential that it should have breathed at the time it was killed; as many children are born alive and yet do not breathe for some time after their birth."

And, according to Atkinson, there is no known means of determining at what instant the foetal and parental circulations are so dissociated as to allow the child to live without the help of the parental circulation; and this dissociation may precede birth.[15] There is thus some uncertainty about the precise moment at which the child comes under the protection of the law of murder, though the question does not seem to have troubled the courts in recent years. The last reported case the CLRC could trace was in 1874.[16] The committee recommends that the test should be that the victim should have been born and have an existence independent of its mother.

If the child is poisoned or injured in the womb, is born alive and then dies of the poison or injury, this may be murder or manslaughter.[17] In *West*[18] Maule J directed the jury:

"... if a person intending to procure abortion does an act which causes a child to be born so much earlier than the natural time that it is born in a

7. Seaborne Davies, "Child-killing in English Law", MACL 301; Williams, *Sanctity of Life and the Criminal Law*, 19–23; S. B. Atkinson, "Life, Birth and Live Birth" (1904) 20 LQR 134.

8. 3 Co Inst 50. According to Hale, 1 PC 433, "a great crime". Willes J said in 1866 (BPP 21, p. 274) that the crime was obsolete. (See MACL at 310.)

9. Below, pp. 366.

10. Below, p. 364.

11. *Poulton* (1832) 5 C & P 329, per Littledale J; *Brain* (1834) 6 C & P 349 (Park J); *Sellis* (1837) 7 C & P 850 (Coltman J).

12. *Reeves* (1839) 9 C & P 25 (Vaughan J); *Trilloe* (1842) 2 Mood CC 260 (Erskine J and CCR).

13. See the cases cited by Atkinson, 20 LQR at 143.

14. (1834) 6 C & P 349 at 350.

15. 20 LQR at 145.

16. *Handley* (1874) 13 Cox CC 79. Cmnd. 7844, para. 35.

17. 3 Co Inst 50; Hawkins, 1 PC, c. 31, §16; East, 1 PC 228; contra Hale, 1 PC 433.

18. (1848) 2 Cox CC 500. See also *Kwok Chak Ming* (Hong Kong, 1963) discussed in [1963] Crim LR 748 and Temkin, "Pre-natal Injury, Homicide and the Draft Criminal Code", [1986] CLJ 414.

state much less capable of living and afterwards dies as a consequence of its exposure to the external world, the person who by her misconduct so brings a child into the world and puts it merely into a situation in which it cannot live is guilty of murder."

In such a case, D would have the *mens rea* sufficient, at that time, for murder, since she intended to commit a felony.[19] It was held in *Senior*[20] that where the pre-natal injury was caused by gross negligence or with a *mens rea* sufficient only for manslaughter, and death after birth resulted from it, then, similarly, a conviction for manslaughter was appropriate. It would be logical to go on to hold that gross pre-natal neglect of the child by the mother, resulting in death after birth, should also be manslaughter; but this step has not been taken, and the rule appears to apply only to acts and not omissions.[1] Similar problems could arise as to the moment at which life ends, though these do not seem, in practice, to have troubled the courts. Is P dead, and therefore incapable of being murdered, if his heart has stopped beating but a surgeon confidently expects to start it again, by an injection or mechanical means?[2] Is P dead if he is in a "hopeless" condition and "kept alive" only by an apparatus of some kind?[3] There is, at present, no certain answer to these questions which are being raised in an acute form by heart transplant operations. The current medical view is that the test is one of brain death and that this can be diagnosed with certainty.[4] The law has not yet evolved a definition of its own and the CLRC declined to propose one[5] both because of the fluid state of medical science and the repercussions that such a definition might have on other branches of the law.

All persons appear to be "under the Queen's peace" for this purpose, even an alien enemy, "unless it be in the heat of war, and in the actual exercise thereof."[6] So also it is murder at common law if a man condemned to death be executed by someone other than the officer lawfully appointed, or if the officer lawfully appointed carries out the execution by an unauthorised method, as where he beheads a man condemned to be hanged.[7] In *Page*[8] an argument that an Egyptian national who had been murdered in an Egyptian village by a British soldier was not within the Queen's peace, was rejected.[9]

19. Under 9 Geo. IV, c. 31, s. 13.
20. (1832) 1 Mood CC 346.
   1. *Knights* (1860) 2 F & F 46; *Izod* (1904) 20 Cox CC 690; and see the discussion by Davies, MACL at 308–309.
   2. Williams, *Sanctity of Life and the Criminal Law*, 18.
   3. Elliott (1964) 4 Med Sci & L 77; and see ibid., at 550; I. M. Kennedy, "Alive or Dead?" (1969) 22 CLP 102; "Switching Off Life Support Machines", [1977] Crim LR 443; Hogan "A Note on Death" [1972] Crim LR 80; Skegg, "Irreversibly Comatose Individuals: Alive or Dead?" [1964] CLJ 130; and Report of the Broderick Committee (1969) Cmnd. 4810, paras. 808–812.
   4. *British Medical Journal and The Lancet*, 31 February, 1979. Cf. *Malcherek* [1981] 2 All ER 422, [1981] 1 WLR 690, below, p. 317.
   5. CLRC/OAP/R, para. 37.
   6. Hale, 1 PC 433.
   7. Ibid.
   8. [1954] 1 QB 170, [1953] 2 All ER 1355 (C–MAC).
   9. The real issue in that case was whether the court-martial assembled in the Canal Zone had jurisdiction to try the case. It was admitted that, if D had been brought to this country and tried here, no question could have arisen as to the nationality of the victim. The court-martial was held to have jurisdiction under the Army Act.

4) *Death Within a Year and a Day*

The reason for this arbitrary rule lies in the difficulty of tracing the causation when there is a long interval between the infliction of the injury and the death:

"... for if he die after that time, it cannot be discerned, as the law presumes, whether he died of the stroke or poison, etc. or a natural death."[10]

This may have been a sound basis for the rule in Coke's time, but the retention of the rule in the present state of medical science can be justified only on the ground that one who has injured another should not remain indefinitely at risk of prosecution for murder.[11] But the rule undoubtedly remains valid both for murder and manslaughter.[12] Thus in *Dyson*[13] D, who had inflicted injuries on a child in November, 1906, and again in December, 1907, was indicted for the manslaughter of the child which died on March 5, 1908. The judge directed the jury that they could find D guilty if they considered death to have been caused by the injuries inflicted in November, 1906. The Court of Criminal Appeal set aside the conviction:

"It is still undoubtedly the law of the land that no person can be convicted of manslaughter where the death does not occur within a year and a day after the injury was inflicted, for in that event it must be attributed to some other cause."[14]

The law takes no note of a part of a day. If the blow is struck at any time on January 1, 1973, death must occur before midnight on January 1, 1974, to be within the rule. Time runs, it is submitted, not from the date of D's act but from that of the infliction of the injury, where these are different. This is in accordance both with the original rationale of the rule and considerations of policy. For example, D plants a bomb on January 1, 1981. It goes off on January 2, 1982, and gravely injures P. D is guilty of homicide if P dies before January 3, 1983. If the relevant date were that of D's act, he could not be made liable at all.[15]

5) *The Problem of Causation*[16]

The year and a day rule is a convenient starting point for the whole question of causation. What must be caused is some acceleration of death. Since everyone must die sooner or later, it follows that every killing is merely an acceleration of death; and it makes no difference for this purpose that the victim is already suffering from a fatal disease or injury or is under

10. 3 Co Inst 52.
11. CLRC, OAP/WP, para. 44, OAP/R, para. 39.
12. *Quaere*, for other statutory forms of homicide, for example, causing death by reckless driving.
13. [1908] 2 KB 454.
14. Ibid., at 456.
15. See CLRC/OAP/R, para. 40. The CLRC recommends that, in the case of pre-natal injury, time should run from the date of birth.
16. Hart and Honoré, *Causation in the Law* (2nd ed.), especially Chs. XII–XIV; Williams, "Causation in Homicide", [1957] Crim LR 429 and 510; Camps and Harvard, "Causation in Homicide – A Medical View", [1957] Crim LR at 576.

sentence of death. Thus, in *Dyson*, the facts of which are given above, Lord Alverstone CJ said:[17]

"The proper question to have been submitted to the jury was whether the prisoner accelerated the child's death by the injuries which he inflicted in December, 1907. For if he did the fact that the child was already suffering from meningitis from which it would in any event have died before long, would afford no answer to the charge of causing its death."

The administration of pain-saving drugs presents difficult problems. In the case of *Adams*[18] Devlin J directed the jury that there is no special defence justifying a doctor in giving drugs which would shorten life in the case of severe pain: "If life were cut short by weeks or months it was just as much murder as if it were cut short by years." He went on:

"But that does not mean that a doctor aiding the sick or dying has to calculate in minutes or hours, or perhaps in days or weeks, the effect on a patient's life of the medicines which he administers. If the first purpose of medicine – the restoration of health – can no longer be achieved, there is still much for the doctor to do, and he is entitled to do all that is proper and necessary to relieve pain and suffering even if measures he takes may incidentally shorten life."

These passages are not easy to reconcile. If the doctor gives drugs with the object of relieving the pain and suffering of a dying man knowing that the drugs will certainly shorten his life, then he intends to shorten life. If, as Devlin J held, and as must surely be the case, the doctor has a defence, it cannot be because his act has not caused death nor because he did not intend so to do. Perhaps this is a case in which motive affords an excuse.[19] Would not a legatee, who administered the same drugs with the object of hastening his inheritance, be guilty of murder if his action accelerated the death to any appreciable extent?[20]

Alternatively, it may be that there is a defence in these cases only where the drugs are not a "substantial" cause of death; for, if the doctor is entitled to shorten life at all to save pain, presumably he may do this only where death is inevitable within a short time; hence the contrast made by the learned judge between "weeks or months" and "minutes or hours".[1]

1 A Question of Fact and Law

Causation is generally a question of fact for the jury but, in answering the question, they must apply the legal principles which it is the judge's duty to

---

17. [1908] 2 KB at 457. And see Hale, 1 PC 428; *Fletcher* (1841) Russell 417; *Martin* (1832) 5 C & P 128 at 130.
18. [1957] Crim LR 365; (1957) *The Times, 9th April;* Sybille Bedford, *The Best We Can Do*, at 192, Devlin, *Easing the Passing* (1985); Hart and Honoré, op. cit., at 344.
19. See, for an alternative explanation, Beynon, "Doctors as Murderers", [1982] Crim LR 17.
20. But the doctor who, following accepted medical practice, administered drugs which shortened life, would not be guilty because he knew that P had left him a legacy and was pleased at the prospect of receiving it sooner. See above, p. 78.
1. See, for an alternative explanation, Helen Beynon, [1982] Crim LR 17–19.

explain to them.[2] According to *Blaue*,[3] where "there is no conflict of evidence and all the jury has to do is to apply the law to the admitted facts, the judge is entitled to tell the jury what the result of that application will be": but that may require reconsideration in the light of *Stonehouse*.[4] The judge may certainly direct the jury that they must acquit where there is no evidence that D caused death, but it is not so clear that he may tell them that they must find that D did cause death (or any other result) even where that is the only reasonable conclusion. If it is not for the judge to decide the issue, still less is it for medical experts. Their function is to inform the court as to the medical facts. It is then for the jury to find the facts and apply the legal principles under the direction of the judge.

2 The "But For" Principle

The first principle is that D's act cannot be the cause of an event if the event would have occurred in precisely the same way had that act never been done. It must be proved that, *but for*, D's act, the event would not have occurred.[5] In the traditional terminology, the act must be a *sine qua non* of the event. But this is only a starting point. There are many acts which are *sine qua non* of an event but are not, either in law or common sense, the cause of it. If D invites P to dinner and P is run over and killed on the way, P would not have died but for the invitation; but no one would say "D killed P", and D has not caused his death in law. In *Jordan*,[6] the wound was certainly a *sine qua non* of the death for it led directly to the medical treatment, but it did not necessarily follow that it was, in law, a cause of the death. That depended on the application of the further principles considered below. Thus, the case of *Jordan* has been criticised[7] because medical experts were permitted to say that certain medical treatment, and not a wound inflicted by D, was the cause of P's death.[8] Whether the wound was "a cause", for the purpose of the decision, was a question of law, not of medicine. Certainly it was relevant and proper for the court to know if the medical treatment was effective to cause death, either in conjunction with, or independently of, the wound; and perhaps all that the witnesses intended to say was that the treatment alone was the medical cause of death.

3 Contributory Causes

It is clear that the act of the accused need not be the sole or the main cause of death. It is wrong to direct a jury that D is not liable if he is less than one-fifth to blame.[9] In *Dyson* it would have been immaterial that the blows

2. *Pagett* (1983) 76 Cr App Rep 279, CA.
3. [1975] 3 All ER 446 at 450, CA, below, p. 319 .
4. [1978] AC 55, [1977] 2 All ER 909 above, p. 293. The principle is a general one, not confined to the question whether an act constitutes an attempt. Cf. *Pagett* (1983) 76 Cr App Rep 279 at 291.
5. Even this basic rule may have exceptions, but only in very unlikely circumstances, e.g., D and E, independently and simultaneously, shoot at P. D's bullet goes through P's heart and E's bullet blows his brains out. It seems safe to assume that both will be held to have caused P's death. Cf. Hall, *General Principles* 267.
6. Discussed in detail, below, p. 322.
7. By Williams at [1957] Crim LR 431 and by Camps and Havard at [1957] Crim LR 582.
8. Cf. *Cato*. [1976] 1 All ER 260 at 264, below, p. 348 where the medical experts said it was not for them to state the cause of death; they spoke to facts, and deductions therefrom were for the jury.
9. *Hennigan* [1971] 3 All ER 133.

would not have caused death but for the meningitis; it was enough that the death would not have been caused by the meningitis at the time when it occurred but for the blows.[10] Contributory causes may be the acts of others including the acts of the deceased himself. The contributory negligence of the plaintiff in civil actions of negligence was an absolute defence at common law, but no such principle applied in the criminal law. In *Swindall and Osborn*[11] where one or other of the two accused ran over and killed an old man, Pollock CB directed the jury:

"The prisoners are charged with contributing to the death of the deceased, by their negligence and improper conduct, and, if they did so, it matters not whether he was deaf or drunk or negligent, or in part contributed to his own death; for in this consists a great distinction between civil and criminal proceedings . . . each party is responsible for any blame that may ensue, however large the share may be. . . . Generally, it may be laid down, that, where one by his negligence, has contributed to the death of another, he is responsible. . . ."

A case in which the negligence of third parties contributed to P's death is *Benge*.[12] D, a foreman platelayer, employed to take up a certain section of railway line, misread the time-table so that the line was up at a time when a train arrived. He placed a flagman at a distance of only 540 yards, instead of 1,000 yards as required by the company's regulations and entirely omitted to place fog signals, although the regulations specified that these should be put at 250-yard intervals for a distance of 1,000 yards. At D's trial for manslaughter it was urged that, in spite of his mistakes, the accident could not have happened if the other servants of the company had done their duty – if the flagman had gone the proper distance or if the engine driver had been keeping a proper look-out, which he was not. Pigott B ruled that this was no defence; if D's negligence mainly or substantially caused the accident, it was irrelevant that it might have been avoided if other persons had not been negligent.

Evidence of P's negligence may, however, be relevant in showing that D was not negligent at all or that his negligence was not gross.

The death is not attributable to the accused if the culpability of his act in no way contributed to it. In *Dolloway*[13] D was driving a cart on a highway with reins not in his hands but loose on the horse's back. A three-year-old child ran into the road a few yards in front of the horse and was struck by one of the wheels and killed. Erle J directed the jury that, if the prisoner had reins and by using the reins could have saved the child, he was guilty of manslaughter; but that, if they thought he could not have saved the child by the use of the reins, then they should acquit him. If D had not been driving the cart at all the incident could not have occurred; and in that sense, he "caused" it; but it was necessary to go further and show that the death was

---

10. *Johnson* (1827) 1 Lew CC 164, is difficult to reconcile with this principle. D struck P who died. The evidence was that P would not have died if he had been sober. Hullock B directed an acquittal. The case is inconsistent with *Murton* (1862) 3 F & F 492, and other cases and its correctness has frequently been questioned. See Roscoe, *Criminal Evidence* (16th ed.), 769 and Russell, 416, n 79.
11. (1846) 2 Car & Kir 230 above, p. 137. See also *Walker* (1824) 1 C & P 320 (Garrow B).
12. (1865) 4 F & F 504. Cf. *Ledger* (1862) 2 F & F 857.
13. (1847) 2 Cox CC 273.

due to the culpable element in his act – the negligence in not using the reins.

4 A Substantial Cause

It is sometimes said[14] that the act must be a "substantial" cause but this seems to mean only that D's contribution must not be so minute that it will be ignored under the "de minimis" principle.[15] It may therefore be misleading to direct a jury that D is not liable unless his conduct was a "substantial" cause.[16] Killing is merely an acceleration of death and factors which produce a very trivial acceleration will be ignored. For example:

D and P are roped mountaineers. P has fallen over a thousand-foot precipice and is dragging D slowly after him. D cuts the rope and P falls to his death five seconds before both P and D would have fallen. Or where two persons independently inflict wounds on P:

". . . suppose one wound severed the jugular vein whereas the other barely broke the skin of the hand, and as the life blood gushed from the victim's neck, one drop oozed from the bruise on his finger . . . metaphysicians will conclude that the extra drop of lost blood hastened the end by the infinitesimal fraction of a second. But the law will apply the *substantial factor* test and for juridical purposes the death will be imputed only to the severe injury in such an extreme case as this."[17]

These are, perhaps, rather unlikely examples but the principle would apply, for example, to the person visiting the dying man and contributing to his exhaustion by talking with him; and probably to the administration of pain-killing drugs which accelerate death.[18]

The problem of an intervening cause, which is discussed below[19] is sometimes put on the basis of substantial cause. Thus Hall writes:

"For example, a slight wound may have necessitated going to a doctor or drugstore, and *en route* the slightly injured person was struck by an automobile or shot by his mortal enemy. The slight wound, though a necessary condition of the death, did not contribute substantially to it."[20]

5 Intervening Acts or Events

Difficult problems may arise where, after D has inflicted an injury on P, some other act or event intervenes before death.

D is not responsible for the death where P dies as the result of some subsequent act or event which would have caused death in just the same way even if D had not inflicted the injury on P: for example, D administers poison to P but, before it takes any effect on P's body, P dies of a heart attack[1] or is shot dead by E. Here it is clear D is not guilty of homicide, even

---

14. See for example, *Benge*, above, *Smith* [1959] 2 QB 35 at 42–43, [1959] 2 All ER 193 at 198 (below, p. 322); Hall, *General Principles*, 283; Perkins (1946) 36 J Cr L & Cr at 393, and *Criminal Law*, 606–607.
15. *Cato* [1976] 1 All ER 260 at 265–266; ". . . it need hardly be added that [that cause] need not be substantial to render the accused guilty": *Malcherek* [1981] 2 All ER 422 at 428.
16. *Hennigan*, above, p. 314.
17. Perkins and Boyce, *Criminal Law*, (3rd ed.) 779. But cf. *Garforth* [1954] Crim LR 936.
18. Above, p. 313.
19. Infra.
20. Hall, *General Principles*, at 283, 393.
1. Cf. *White*, above p. 45; *Pankotai* [1961] Crim LR 546.

though the dose of poison was a fatal one. He must be judged by what actually happened, not by what would have happened but for subsequent events.

It is not, however, every intervening act or omission of a causal nature which will relieve D from liability for the subsequent death. There are three different grounds on which he might still be held to have caused the death.

1. The injury inflicted by D may still be "an operating cause and a substantial cause"[2] of P's death. The intervening act may be a further injury inflicted by E, not in itself mortal, but causing death when combined with the injury inflicted by D. D and E are both guilty of homicide. If P's wound is treated negligently by E, or by P himself, and P dies of the ill-treated or non-treated wound, D is liable. In *People v Lewis*[3] P, having received a mortal gunshot wound from which he would have died within the hour, cut his throat and died within five minutes. D was held liable for manslaughter on the ground that the original wound was an operating cause. "Here, when the throat was cut, [P] was not merely languishing from a mortal wound; he was actually dying; and after the throat was cut he continued to languish from both wounds. Drop by drop the life current went out from both wounds, and at the very instant of death the gunshot wound was contributing to the event."[4] The answer would presumably have been different if P had blown his brains out, and died instantly, for then the bleeding from the gunshot wound would not have contributed.

In *Malcherek*[5] D inflicted upon P injuries which resulted in brain damage. She was put on a life support machine. Some days later, after carrying out five of the six tests[6] for brain death prescribed by the Royal Colleges, doctors disconnected the machine and half an hour later she was pronounced dead. The judge withdrew the question of causation from the jury, ruling that there was no evidence on which they could decide that D did not cause P's death. On appeal, it was argued that there was evidence on which the jury could have found that the doctors caused death by switching off the machine. The appeal was dismissed. There was no doubt that the injury inflicted by D was an operating and substantial cause of death. Whether or not the doctors were also a cause of death was immaterial. They were not on trial;[7] D was. It was enough that one cause of P's death was the injury inflicted by D.

2. P may die as the result of some act or event which would not have occurred but for the act done by D and which is a natural consequence of D's act – that is, it was foreseeable as likely to occur in the normal course of

---

2. *Smith* [1959] 2 QB at 42–43, per Parker LCJ; **SHC 33**; below, p. 322. On "substantial" see above, p. 316.

3. 124 Cal 551 (1899) Sup Ct of California.

4. But was the contribution of the gunshot wound substantial or de minimis? Cf. the example given by Perkins, above, p. 316 and Hart and Honoré, 243.

5. [1981] 2 All ER 422, [1981] 1 WLR 690. The appeal of *Steel*, heard at the same time was materially the same.

6. There were reasons for not applying the sixth test.

7. The court remarked, obiter, that they thought the suggestion that the doctors had caused the death "bizarre" – they had done their skilful best to save life, but failed and so discontinued treatment.

events. Though any injury which D may have inflicted is not an "operating cause" in the sense discussed in the previous paragraph, D is still held to have caused the death. If, however, the act or event was not the natural consequence of D's act, then D is not liable. The propositions are illustrated by the examples given by Perkins:[8]

". . . if one man knocks down another and goes away leaving his victim not seriously hurt[9] but unconscious, on the floor of a building in which the assault occurred, and before the victim recovers consciousness he is killed in the fall of the building which is shaken down by a sudden earthquake, this is not homicide. The law attributes such a death to the 'Act of God' and not to the assault, even if it may be certain that the deceased would not have been in the building at the time of the earthquake, had he not been rendered unconscious. The blow was the occasion of the man's being there, but the blow was not the cause of the earthquake, nor was the deceased left in a position of obvious danger. On the other hand if the blow had been struck on the seashore, and the assailant had left his victim in imminent peril of an incoming tide which drowned him before consciousness returned, it would be homicide."[10]

P's being drowned in the latter example was a "natural" consequence of D's action – that is, a consequence which might be expected to occur in the normal course of events. P's being killed by the falling building in the former was an abnormal and unforeseeable consequence.

Human intervention, where it consists in a foreseeable act instinctively done for the purposes of self-preservation, or in the execution of a legal duty, does not break the chain of causation. In *Pagett*,[11] D, to resist lawful arrest, held a girl in front of him as a shield and shot at armed policemen. The police instinctively fired back and killed the girl. D was held to have caused her death and to be guilty of manslaughter.[12] Though the court regarded the officers' instinctive act as "involuntary", they also held that neither a reasonable act of self-defence nor an act done in the execution of a duty to prevent crime or arrest an offender, using such force as is reasonable in the circumstances, will break the chain of causation. A truly involuntary act clearly does not break the chain – D so startles E that E involuntarily drops a weight he is carrying which causes damage. There is no true intervening "act" and D has caused the damage. But acts of self-defence or in the prevention of crime are by no means necessarily in this class. It would seem that it cannot be "reasonable" for anyone intentionally to kill P, an innocent person, in order to save his own life[13] or to arrest X; and whether it is reasonable for him to take a risk of killing P must be doubtful. *Pagett* does not deal with the case where the officer's intervening

8. (1946) 36 J Cr L & Cr at 393.
9. The result would appear to be the same if he were seriously hurt.
10. Cf. *Hallett* [1969] SASR 141 where the court followed this passage in relation to similar facts.
11. (1983) 76 Cr App Rep 279.
12. Since the jury acquitted of murder, it must be taken that they were not satisfied D had the necessary *mens rea* as then defined in *Hyam* [1975] AC 55 – that he knew it was probable that the girl would suffer death or grievous bodily harm.
13. *Dudley and Stephens* (1884) 14 QBD 273, above, p. 226; *Howe* [1987] AC 417, [1987] 1 All ER 771, HL. Cf. commentary on *Pagett* [1983] Crim LR 394.

act is unlawful, but it does not necessarily follow that D's act does not continue to be a cause of death. There may be two unlawful causes.

The same principles should apply in determining whether the killing of an innocent bystander, or another policeman, by police bullets should be taken to be caused by D. It is obvious that the police marksman also causes death.[14] His liability was not the issue in *Pagett*; but, if the shooting was a reasonable act of self-defence, the result, so far as he was concerned, was accidental death.[15]

Where an intervening act causing death is not foreseeable,[16] it breaks the chain of causation whether it is intentional, negligent or merely accidental. The surgeon to whom the injured P is taken for an operation deliberately kills him; or the ambulance driver, taking P to the hospital, negligently drives into a canal and drowns him; or a careless nurse gives him a deadly poison in mistake for a sleeping pill; or, as in a Kentucky case, *Bush v Commonwealth*,[17] the medical officer attending P inadvertently infects him with scarlet fever and he dies of that. None of these is an act which might be expected to occur in the ordinary course of events and they free D from liability. But if the injured P is receiving proper and skilful medical attention and he dies from the anaesthetic or the operation D will be liable. The receipt of such medical attention may be regarded as the natural consequence of the infliction of the wound. At one time the cases concerning medical treatment seemed to lay down a stricter rule, and this is considered in more detail below.

3. This third case is in the nature of an exception to the second. In the criminal law, as in the civil, the defendant must "take his victim as he finds him," and this applies to the victim's mind as well as his body. If then, D's act causes P to do an act, or make an omission, which causes P's death, D may be held liable although P's intervening conduct was not the natural consequence of D's act – it was not foreseeable that P was likely so to behave. In *Blaue*[18] D stabbed P, a young girl, and pierced her lung. She was told that she would die if she did not have a blood transfusion. Being a Jehovah's Witness, she refused on religious grounds. She died from the bleeding caused by the wound. D was convicted of manslaughter and argued that P's refusal to have a blood transfusion, being unreasonable, had broken the chain of causation. It was held that the judge had rightly instructed the jury that the wound was a cause of death. Lawton LJ said:[19]

---

14. *Cf. Malcherek*, above, p. 317.
15. The court said that its comments were confined to homicide: but the same principles must surely apply to a case of wounding.
16. *Dalby* [1982] 1 All ER 916, [1982] 1 WLR 425, below, p. 351 (supply of controlled drug to addict who was likely to take it and suffer harm and who did so and died) seems (*pace Goodfellow* (1986) 83 Cr App Rep 23) to turn on the law of constructive manslaughter (which requires an act causing *direct* harm) rather than any general principle of causation. The case did not decide that D might not have been convicted of manslaughter on the ground of gross negligence.
17. (1880) 78 Ky 268 (Kentucky Court of Appeals).
18. [1975] 3 All ER 446, [1976] Crim LR 648 and commentary. *Smithers* (1976) 34 CCC (2d) 427 (Sup. Ct. of Canada) is to the same effect. Immaterial that death was caused in part by malfunctioning epiglottis, where kick was contributing cause, outside the *de minimis* range.
19. At 450.

"It has long been the policy of the law that those who use violence on other people must take their victims as they find them. This in our judgment means the whole man, not just the physical man. It does not lie in the mouth of the assailant to say that his victim's religious beliefs which inhibited him from accepting certain kinds of treatment were unreasonable. The question for decision is what caused the death. The answer is the stab wound."

In this case, the wound was "an operating cause and a substantial cause;" but the principle stated may be capable of wider application. If the victim of a rape were to be so outraged as to commit suicide by shooting herself it might be argued that it was the bullet which caused the death and not the rape. Certainly the rape is not "an operating and substantial cause" in the same sense as the wound in *Blaue*; but the rapist must take his victim as he finds her. His act caused the act which caused her death. This has been thought[20] to be a better ground for the decision in *People v Lewis* and the court would have so decided the case if they had been satisfied that the first act was the cause of the second. They thought, however, that P's suicide might have been from remorse or a desire to shield D. If P had committed suicide because of the pain of the wound, then D could have been held liable even if the gunshot wound were not "an operating and substantial cause" in the sense discussed above – if, for example, P had killed himself instantly by shooting.[1]

This principle, which would impose liability upon D for unforeseeable intervening acts causing death, is probably confined to acts or omissions by the victim. If the parents of the victim of the supposed rape were to kill her on the ground that their religion required them to liquidate a defiled daughter, it is thought that D would not be liable for the death. If, however, in *Blaue*, P had been too young to make a decision about a blood transfusion and her parents had succeeded on religious grounds in preventing a transfusion being given, it is thought that the wound would have remained an operating and substantial cause, so D would still have been liable.

An intervening act by the original actor will not break the chain of causation so as to excuse him, where the intervening act is part of the same transaction;[2] but it is otherwise if the act which causes the *actus reus* is part of a completely different transaction. For example, D, having wounded P, visits him in hospital and accidentally infects him with smallpox of which he dies.

---

20. Hart and Honoré, 223.

   1. Similar reasoning has been applied in a civil action, *Pigney v Pointers Transport Services Ltd* [1957] 2 All ER 807, [1957] 1 WLR 1121, where Pilcher J held that a suicide eighteen months after an accident was caused by the accident; the injury caused a state of acute anxiety neurosis which caused the victim to take his own life. It was no answer that the man's own disposition contributed to the anxiety neurosis – the defendant must take his victim as he found him. Cf. the cases where P loses his life accidentally in trying to escape from D; below, p. 326.

   2. See above, p. 76; Russell, 53–60, where the cases are set out; Williams, CLGP, 65; Hart and Honoré, *Causation in the Law*, 333.

6 Death caused by Medical Treatment of an Injury

The nineteenth century cases seem to lay it down that, where the immediate cause of death is the medical treatment received by P consequent upon his injury by D, D is guilty of homicide, whether the treatment was proper or improper, negligent or not. If the treatment was given bona fide by competent medical officers, evidence was not admissible to show that it was improper or unskilful. In the earlier cases, this rule was applied only where the wound was dangerous to life. Later, and logically, it was extended to less serious injuries.

In *Pym*[3] Erle J refused to admit evidence that it was the operation and not the wound which caused the death, and that the operation was unnecessary. In *McIntyre*[4] Coleridge J directed that it was murder if D, intending to kill, inflicted mortal injuries upon P, even though the immediate cause of P's death was the entry into her lungs of brandy given by a surgeon to restore her; if, however, the injury was not a mortal one, then D was guilty of an assault.[5] In *Clark and Bagg*[6] where the injuries were not of a dangerous character, Wightman J directed the jury that, if they found that death occurred from bad medical treatment, they should find a verdict of assault. But in *Davis and Wagstaffe*,[7] Mathew J after consultation with Field J, went further. The injury which D inflicted upon P in that case was admittedly not mortal, and P died as the result of the administration of chloroform in the course of an operation to mend a broken jaw. Mathew J directed the jury that:

". . . if although there might be no intent to do more than assault, still an injury was inflicted by one man on another which compelled the injured man to take medical advice, and death ensued from an operation advised by the medical man, for that death the assailant was in the eye of the law responsible."

This was logical. If D inflicts upon P an injury which renders advisable an operation, and P is killed by the anaesthetic, it is difficult to see why D has "caused" death any more where the injury is grievous than where it is slight. D's contribution to P's death consists, in both cases, in putting him in the situation in which an anaesthetic must be administered. If he intended the grievous or the slight injury, he had the *mens rea*, in the one case of murder, in the other of manslaughter; and he should be guilty of homicide in both cases or neither. Mathew J's ruling would not allow the question to be gone into at all in either case:

"For it would never do to have a serious injury by one man on another, and have the issue raised that death was due to want of skill on the part of the medical men."

These cases must now be regarded in the light of the decisions of the Court of Criminal Appeal in *Jordan*[8] and *Smith*[9].

---

3. (1846) 1 Cox CC 339 at 341; he said that Rolfe B was of the same opinion.
4. (1847) 2 Cox CC 379.
5. The jury in fact convicted of manslaughter.
6. (1842) 6 JP 508.
7. (1883) 15 Cox CC 174.
8. (1956) 40 Cr App Rep 152; **SHC 31.**
9. [1959] 2 QB 35, [1959] 2 All ER 193; **SHC 33.**

In *Jordan* D stabbed P who was admitted to hospital and died eight days later. At the trial,

> "it did not occur to the prosecution, the defence, the judge or the jury that there could be any doubt but that the stab caused death."[10]

In the Court of Criminal Appeal, the fresh evidence of two doctors was allowed to the effect that in their opinion death had not been caused by the stab wound, which was mainly healed at the time of the death, but by the introduction (with a view to preventing infection) of terramycin after the deceased man had shown he was intolerant to it and by the intravenous introduction of large quantities of liquid. This treatment, according to the evidence, was "palpably wrong." The court held that if the jury had heard this evidence they would have felt precluded from saying that they were satisfied that the death was caused by the stab wound and they quashed the conviction. The case has been interpreted by Williams[11] as one where the medical treatment was grossly negligent, but he argues[12] that any degree of negligence which would be recognised by the civil courts should be enough. The court did not say in express terms that there was evidence of negligence, gross or otherwise, though it may reasonably be inferred that "palpably wrong" treatment is negligent.

While anxiously disclaiming any intention of setting a precedent[13] they stated the basis of their decision in even broader terms. They were "disposed to accept it as law that death resulting from any normal treatment employed to deal with a felonious injury may be regarded as caused by the felonious injury;" but it was "sufficient to point out here that this was not normal treatment." Surely treatment which is "not normal" is not necessarily negligent, even in the civil law.

The case gave rise to some concern in the medical profession and it was predicted[14] that the result of it would be that if, in future, the victim of a homicidal assault died as a result of the medical treatment instituted to save his life, it would not be considered homicide by the assailant if the treatment could be shown to be "not normal".

How far it is safe to rely on *Jordan* is doubtful, in view of the fact that it was distinguished by the Court of Criminal Appeal in *Smith*[15] and by the Court of Appeal in *Blaue*[16] as "a very particular case depending upon its exact facts." In *Malcherek* the court thought that if a choice had to be made between *Jordan* and *Smith*, *Smith* was to be preferred; but they did not believe it was necessary to choose. In *Blaue*, *Jordan* was thought to be "probably rightly decided on its facts". It is submitted that this is so and that it should be followed where the facts are indistinguishable in principle. *Smith* is distinguishable. In the course of a fight between soldiers of different regiments, D stabbed P twice with a bayonet. One of P's

---

10. See (1956) 40 Cr App Rep 152 at 155.
11. [1957] Crim LR at 430.
12. Ibid., at 513.
13. But no court has the right to preclude future courts from considering the effects of its decisions.
14. By Camps and Havard, "Causation in Homicide – A Medical View" [1957] Crim LR 576 at 582–583.
15. [1959] 2 QB 35 at 43, [1959] 2 All ER 193 at 198.
16. [1975] 3 All ER 446. Likewise in *Evans and Gardiner (No. 2)* [1976] VR 523 at 531.

comrades, trying to carry P to the medical reception station, twice tripped and dropped him. At the reception station the medical officer, who was trying to cope with a number of other cases, did not realise that one of the wounds had pierced a lung and caused haemorrhage. He gave P treatment which, in the light of the information regarding P's condition available at the time of the trial, was "thoroughly bad and might well have affected his chances of recovery." D's conviction of murder was upheld and counsel's argument, that the court must be satisfied that the treatment was normal, and that this was abnormal was brushed aside.

". . . if at the time of death the original wound is still an operating cause and a substantial cause, then the death can properly be said to be the result of the wound, albeit that some other cause of death is also operating. Only if it can be said that the original wounding is merely the setting in which another cause operates can it be said that the death does not result from the wound. Putting it in another way, only if the second cause is so overwhelming as to make the original wound merely part of the history can it be said that death does not flow from the wound."[17]

Jordan's case was evidently one in which the wound was merely the setting in which (according to the new evidence) the medical treatment operated to cause death.

It is submitted that the following propositions at present represent the law:

1) Medical evidence is admissible to show that the medical treatment of a wound was the cause of death and that the wound itself was not.[18] This is so whether or not the wound is mortal.

2) If the medical treatment killed P, quite independently of the wound, and was grossly negligent, the wound is merely the setting for and not the cause of death.[19] *Jordan* must be equated with the case where a nurse inadvertently administers a deadly poison to the patient.

3) If the medical treatment killed P quite independently of the wound, but was not grossly negligent,[20] it is submitted that D remains guilty of homicide – murder, if he had malice aforethought, manslaughter if he had not,[1] ". . . the fact that the victim has died, despite or *because of* medical treatment for the initial injury given by *careful and skilled* medical practitioners, will not exonerate the original assailant from the responsibility for the death."[2]

---

17. Per Lord Parker CJ [1959] 2 QB 35 at 42–43, [1959] 2 All ER 193 at 198.
18. *Jordan* must be authority for this at least. Moreover at the trial in *Smith* Dr. Camps gave evidence, that, with proper treatment, P's chances of recovery were as high as 75 per cent.
19. But in *Evans and Gardiner* (above, footnote 16) it was held that death was caused by stabbing when, 11 months later, P died because of a growth of tissue consequential on an operation necessitated by the stabbing, "however inept or unskilful the medical treatment".
20. Or, if *Jordan* be given the wider interpretation, not negligent.
   1. The proposition from *Smith* quoted above, is capable of a wider construction, exempting D *whenever* the treatment is the immediate cause of death, the original wound in such a case becoming merely part of the history. It is thought that such a radical departure from the authorities can hardly have been intended.
   2. *Malcherek* [1981] 2 All ER 422 at 428. (Authors' italics.)

7 The Effect of Neglect by the Injured Person

The common law rule is that neglect or maltreatment by the injured person of himself does not exempt D from liability for his ultimate death. In *Wall's* case,[3] where the former governor of Goree was convicted[4] of the murder of a man by the illegal infliction on him of a flogging of 800 lashes, there was evidence that P had aggravated his condition by drinking spirits. MacDonald LCB, told[5] the jury:

". . . there is no apology for a man if he puts another in so dangerous and hazardous a situation by his treatment of him, that some degree of unskilfulness and mistaken treatment of himself may possibly accelerate the fatal catastrophe. One man is not at liberty to put another into such perilous circumstances as these, and to make it depend upon his own prudence, knowledge, skill or experience what may hurry on or complete that catastrophe, or on the other hand may render him service."

In *Holland*[6] D waylaid and assaulted P, cutting him severely across one of his fingers with an iron instrument. P refused to follow the surgeon's advice to have the finger amputated, although he was told that if he did not his life would be in great danger. The wound caused lockjaw, the finger was then amputated, but it was too late and P died of lockjaw. The surgeon's evidence was that if the finger had been amputated at first, P's life could probably have been saved. Maule J told the jury that it made no difference whether the wound was in its own nature instantly mortal, or whether it became the cause of death by reason of the deceased not having adopted the best mode of treatment. The question was whether, in the end, the wound inflicted by the prisoner was the real cause of death. *Holland* was followed in *Blaue*.[7] The argument[8] that medical science has advanced greatly since 1841 and that a refusal to undergo medical treatment, reasonable then, would be unreasonable now, did not impress the court. Whether P's conduct was reasonable or not was irrelevant.

8 Intended Consequences

It is sometimes said that intended consequences cannot be too remote. This, however, is not always true, for the *sine qua non* rule remains applicable. Thus, in *White*[9] the consequence intended by D – the death of his mother – occurred; but its occurrence had nothing to do with D's act in administering the poison and would have happened just the same if D had done nothing. Even where the *sine qua non* rule is satisfied, the consequence, though intended, may be too remote where it occurs as a result of the intervention of some new cause. So in the cases of *Bush*[10] and *Jordan*[11] it may be that D intended P's death, and P's death occurred; moreover, in neither case would death have occurred without D's act; but in the one case it was caused by scarlet fever and not by D's bullet; and in the other it was

3. (1802) 28 State Tr 51.
4. Twenty years after the event.
5. Ibid., at p. 145.
6. (1841) 2 Mood & R 351.
7. Above, p. 320. Cf. *Mubila* 1956 (1) S A 31.
8. By Hart and Honoré, *Causation in the Law*, at 360.
9. Above, p. 45; **SHC 278.**
10. (1880) 78 Ky 268; above, p. 319.
11. (1956) 40 Cr App Rep 152; **SHC 31.**

caused by medical treatment and not by D's knife. Where the death occurs in the manner intended by D he will be guilty even if the course of events was not what he expected, for example, he shoots at P's head, but the bullet misses, ricochets and kills P by striking him in the back. The case of *Michael*[12] is perhaps a rather extreme example of this:

D's child, P, was in the care of a nurse, X. D, intending to murder the child, delivered to X a large quantity of laudanum, telling her it was a medicine to be administered to P. X did not think the child needed any medicine and left it untouched on the mantelpiece of her room. In X's absence, one of her children, Y, aged five, took the laudanum and administered a large dose to P who died. All the judges held that the jury were rightly directed that this administration by "an unconscious agent" was murder.

Hart and Honoré[13] criticise the case on the ground that the child was
"not in any sense an agent, conscious or unconscious, of the mother, who intended [X] alone to give the poison to the child; but the decision may be justified on the ground that, in our terminology, the act of the child of five did not negative causal connexion between the prisoner's act and the death."

According to this view, the result would have been different if Y had been, not five, but fifteen.

It does not appear that Y knew, from the labelling of the bottle or otherwise, that this was "medicine" for P. If she did know this, and acted on that knowledge, then there seems no difficulty in imputing the death to D, whatever Y's age. No such fact being reported, however, the case must be treated as one where Y's intervention was in no way prompted by D's instructions. Thus, if Y had taken the poison herself, her death would have been just as much caused by D's act as was P's in the actual case; but it would require an extension of the decision to hold D guilty in such a case, for Y's death was not an intended consequence.[14] If such an extension be not made, the result is quite arbitrary, for it was pure chance whether Y administered the poison to P, or to herself or another child.

9 Special Instances of Causation

There are a few instances of causation which require special mention, by reason of the state of the authorities.

i) *Killing by mental suffering or shock.* The view of earlier writers was that the law could take no cognisance of a killing caused merely by mental suffering or shock, because "no external act of violence was offered, whereof the common law can take notice and secret things belong to God."[15] Stephen thought[16] that the fear of encouraging prosecutions for witchcraft was the reason for the rule and that it was "a bad rule founded on ignorance now dispelled."

12. (1840) 9 C & P 356.
13. Op. cit., at 301.
14. But the doctrine of transferred malice (above p. 73) would support such an extension.
15. Hale, 1 PC 429; and see East, 1 PC 225.
16. *Digest*, 217, n 9.

"Suppose a man were intentionally killed by being kept awake till the nervous irritation of sleeplessness killed him, might not this be murder? Suppose a man kills a sick person intentionally by making a loud noise when sleep gives him a chance of life; or suppose knowing that a man has aneurism of the heart, his heir rushes into his room and roars in his ear, 'Your wife is dead!' intending to kill and killing him, why are not these acts murder? They are no more 'secret things belonging to God' than the operation of arsenic."

This view now represents the law. Hale's proposition was first modified in *Towers*[17] where D violently assaulted a young girl who was holding a four-and-a-half-months'-old child in her arms. The girl screamed loudly, so frightening the baby that it cried till it was black in the face. From that day it had convulsions and died a month later. Denman J held that there was evidence to go to the jury of manslaughter. In the case of an adult person, he said that murder could not be committed by using language so strong or violent as to cause that person to die:

"mere intimidation, causing a person to die from fright by working upon his fancy, was not murder";

but that rule did not apply to a child of such tender years as this;

". . . if the man's act brought on the convulsions or brought them to a more dangerous extent, so that death would not have resulted otherwise, then it would be manslaughter."[18]

This was extended to the case of an adult person by Ridley J in *Hayward*.[19] D, who was in a condition of violent excitement and had expressed his determination to "give his wife something", chased her from the house into the road using violent threats against her. She fell dead. She was suffering from an abnormal heart condition, such that any combination of physical exertion and fright or strong emotion might cause death. Ridley J directed the jury that no proof of actual physical violence was necessary, but that death from fright alone, caused by an illegal act, such as a threat of violence, was enough.

ii) *Killing by frightening P into taking his own life*. This was recognised to be homicide at an earlier stage than the previous category. In *Pitts*[20] Erskine J held that D was guilty of murder if P had thrown himself into a river and been drowned from the apprehension of immediate violence by D. A similar principle was applied where P accidentally fell from a window in an attempt to escape immediate violence.[1] In these cases it was said that the apprehension of immediate violence must be "well-grounded." This qualification was not made in *Halliday*[2] where D was convicted of wilfully and maliciously inflicting grievous bodily harm[3] on his wife who had jumped from a window and broken a leg in escaping from him. If P is

---

17. (1874) 12 Cox CC 530.
18. Ibid., at 533.
19. (1908) 21 Cox CC 692.
20. (1842) Car & M 284.
  1. *Curley* (1909) 2 Cr App Rep 96 at 109, CCA.
  2. (1889) 61 LT 701, CCR, followed in *Lewis* [1970] Crim LR 647. See below, p. 399.
  3. Clearly manslaughter if she had died: *Mackie* [1973] Crim LR 54 (Cusack J) and *Boswell* [1973] Crim LR 307 (Judge Gower).

unusually timorous and jumps when a person of average firmness and common sense would not do so, should not D (so far as causation is concerned) take his victim as he finds him?[4]

iii) *Killing by perjury.* It is sometimes said[5] that it is not homicide if D, by giving false evidence, procures the conviction and execution of P. There is no conclusive authority on the point. In *McDaniel*[6] D and others were in fact convicted of the murder of P by falsely swearing to his guilt of robbery (in order to obtain the reward) for which P was hanged; but judgment was respited "upon a doubt whether an indictment for murder would lie in this case:" and the Attorney-General declined to argue that it would, so the prisoners were discharged. Blackstone wrote[7] that he had

"grounds to believe it was not from any apprehension that the point was not maintainable, but from other prudential reasons."

The "prudential reasons" appear to be

"to avoid the danger of deterring witnesses from giving evidence upon capital prosecutions, if it must be at the peril of their own lives."

East[8] says that Lord Mansfield CJ took the same view of the law and that he and the other judges supported the indictment.

The balance of authority is then, perhaps, against the rule; but if it exists, it is thought that it has nothing to do with causation[9] but it is a rule of policy, closely analogous to that which protects a witness from an action for defamation[10] or for damages for the injury suffered by conviction upon perjured evidence.[11]

6) *The Mens Rea of Murder*

The *mens rea* of murder is traditionally called "malice aforethought". This is a technical term and it has a technical meaning quite different from the ordinary popular meaning of the two words. The phrase, it has been truly said,

"is a mere arbitrary symbol ..., for the 'malice' may have in it nothing really malicious; and need never be really 'aforethought'."[12]

Thus a parent who kills a suffering child out of motives of compassion is "malicious" for this purpose; and there is sufficient aforethought if an intention to kill is formed only a second before the fatal blow is struck. Neither ill-will nor premeditation is necessary.

---

4. *Blaue*, above, p. 319.
5. The earlier authorities said that it was murder; but Coke (3 Inst 48) said that it was "not holden for murder at this day." Foster, *Crown Law* at 131, supported this, citing the case of *Titus Oates* (1685) 10 State Tr 1227, who, he thinks, would certainly have been charged with murder by perjury if that had been a crime. East, 1 PC 333, is non-committal. Hawkins accepted the older view: 1 PC, c. 13, §5, 7.
6. (1756) 1 Leach 44.
7. *Commentaries*, iv, 196.
8. 1 PC 333, n (a).
9. Cf. Hart and Honoré, *Causation in the Law*, at 405.
10. *Watson v M'Ewen*, [1905] AC 480.
11. *Hargreaves v Bretherton* [1959] 1 QB 45, [1958] 3 All ER 122; *Marrinan v Vibart* [1963] 1 QB 528, [1962] 3 All ER 380.
12. Kenny, *Outlines* (15th ed) 153.

The meaning of the term is of the utmost importance, for it is the presence or absence of malice aforethought which determines whether an unlawful killing is murder or manslaughter.

"Murder is unlawful homicide with malice aforethought. Manslaughter is an unlawful homicide without malice aforethought."[13]

Malice aforethought is a concept of the common law. It has a long history but, since *Moloney*,[14] it is no longer necessary to explore this in order to expound the modern law. We can now state that it consists in –

　1) an intention to kill any person or,

　2) an intention to cause grievous bodily harm to any person.

"Intention" has the meaning attributed to it in *Hancock*[15] and *Nedrick*[16] examined above.

"Grievous bodily harm", at one time broadly interpreted to mean any harm sufficiently serious to interfere with health and comfort, must now be applied in its ordinary natural meaning. "Grievous" means "really serious"[17] and the word "really" probably adds nothing but emphasis to the fact that the harm intended must be (actually or really) serious.[18]

In 1960 in the notorious case of *Director of Public Prosecutions v Smith* the House of Lords laid down a largely objective test of liability in murder – the test was "not what the defendant contemplated, but what the ordinary reasonable man or woman would in all the circumstances of the case have contemplated as the natural and probable result". In *Hyam*[19] the House declined to overrule *Smith*, holding that its effect had been modified by s. 8 of the Criminal Justice Act 1967; but in *Frankland and Moore v R*[20] the Privy Council (comprising five judicial members of the House of Lords), acting on the dicta of Lord Diplock in *Hyam*,[1] Lord Bridge in *Moloney*[2] and Lord Scarman in *Hancock*,[3] held that in so far as it laid down an objective test, *Smith* did not represent the common law of England. Though the Privy Council cannot formally overrule a decision of the House of Lords, it can probably be taken, for all practical purposes, that *Smith* is overruled. Section 8 did not, after all, modify the law of murder; and the function of that section in relation to murder, as to all other crimes, is not to define what *mens rea* must be proved, but only *how* the *mens rea* required by the common law or other statutes, is to be proved.

Although the common law of malice aforethought is now fully stated in the rule requiring an intention to cause death or grievous bodily harm, it is

---

13. Per Stephen J in *Doherty* (1887) 16 Cox CC 306 at 307.
14. [1985] AC 905, [1985] 1 All ER 1025, above, p. 56.
15. [1986] AC 455, [1986] 1 All ER 641, HL.
16. [1986] 3 All ER 1, [1986] 1 WLR 1025, CA, above, p. 56.
17. *Director of Public Prosecutions v Smith* [1961] AC 290 at 334, [1960] 3 All ER 161 at 171.
18. *Saunders* [1985] Crim LR 230.
19. [1975] AC 55 at 70–71.
20. [1987] AC 576 [1987] 2 WLR 1251 on appeal from the Isle of Man, where at the time of the homicides, the English common law, unamended by the equivalent of s. 8 of the Criminal Justice Act 1967, prevailed.
　1. [1975] AC 55 at 94.
　2. [1985] AC 905 at 921 and 928.
　3. [1986] AC 455 at 473.

necessary to refer to s. 1 of the Homicide Act 1957 which modified the common law.

"1) Where a person kills in the course or furtherance of some other offence, the killing shall not amount to murder unless done with the same malice aforethought (express or implied) as is required for a killing to amount to murder when not done in the course or furtherance of another offence.

2) For the purposes of the foregoing subsection, a killing done in the course or for the purpose of resisting an officer of justice, or of resisting or avoiding or preventing a lawful arrest, or of effecting or assisting an escape or rescue from legal custody, shall be treated as a killing in the course or furtherance of another offence."

The purpose of this section was, as the shoulder-note indicates, to limit malice aforethought by the "Abolition of 'constructive malice'". This took two forms. (i) It was murder to kill in the course or furtherance of a violent felony (or possibly any felony) so that an intention to commit the felony (e.g., rape or robbery) was a sufficient *mens rea* where death resulted. (ii) It was murder to kill while attempting to prevent lawful arrest or bring about escape from lawful arrest or custody, so that an intention to do these things was also malice aforethought where the act caused death. Subsection (1) abolishes the first, and subsection (2) the second, form of constructive malice. While eliminating constructive malice, the section leaves in existence "express" and "implied" malice. Although these terms have been used for centuries, their meaning is obscure and is certainly not any ordinary natural meaning that they might bear.[4] In the light of the common law, as we know it to be, "express malice" must be taken to mean the intention to kill and "implied malice" the intention to cause grievous bodily harm. Though the terms remain on the statute book, there is in practice no need to use them and the sooner they are buried the better.

It was at one time argued that s. 1 also abolished intention to cause grievous bodily harm as a head of malice aforethought – an argument which required some other meaning to be given to "implied malice" since that is expressly preserved. The argument was that the only reason why intention to cause grievous bodily harm was malice aforethought before 1957 was that in 1803 Lord Ellenborough's Act created a felony of causing grievous bodily harm with intent to do so. If death resulted, that was murder because, and only because, the killing was in the course or furtherance of that felony. The argument was rejected in *Vickers*[5] but accepted by Lords Diplock and Kilbrandon in *Hyam* where the matter was left open because Lord Cross was not prepared to decide between the conflicting views. In *Cunningham*[6] the House confirmed that intention to cause grievous bodily harm survived the Homicide Act as a head of *mens rea*, having ante-dated Lord Ellenborough's Act as a form of malice aforethought, distinct from constructive malice.

---

4. See Lord Hailsham in *Cunningham* [1981] 2 All ER 863 at 867.
5. [1957] 2 QB 664, [1957] 2 All ER 741, CCA (a court of five judges).
6. [1982] AC 566, [1981] 2 All ER 863, HL.

7) *The Sentence for Murder*

Until the Homicide Act 1957 all persons convicted of murder were automatically sentenced to death. By s. 5 of that Act certain types of murder were singled out and designated "capital murder". These continued to be punishable by death, while the remaining types of murder were punishable by imprisonment for life. In effect we had two degrees of murder.

The distinction between the two degrees of murder proved to be most unsatisfactory, and the death penalty for murder was suspended by the Murder (Abolition of Death Penalty) Act 1965, which is to continue permanently in force.[7] The distinction between capital and non-capital murder has thus disappeared, and all persons convicted of murder must now be sentenced to imprisonment for life. The mandatory sentence for murder is unique in English law and the Criminal Law Revision Committee (CLRC) has given long and anxious consideration to the question whether the judge should not have a discretion as in all other crimes. In the event, the Committee was deeply and almost evenly divided on the issue. Their Report[8] sets out the arguments on both sides in some detail but makes no recommendation. In *Cunningham*[9] Lord Hailsham stated his reservations about giving the judges the same discretion they have in other offences, but this was on the assumption that murder and manslaughter might be amalgamated into a single offence. If, as the CLCR intend, both murder and manslaughter continue in the law, the difficulties are no greater than in any other case where the maximum discretionary sentence is life imprisonment.

On sentencing a murderer, the judge may recommend to the Home Secretary the minimum period which should elapse before the prisoner is released on licence. The CLRC has recommended that the judge, when minded to make a minimum recommendation, should invite the defence to make representations and should state publicly the factors on which he bases his recommendation, if he makes one; and that there should be a right of appeal against a recommendation.[10]

8) *Proposals for Reform*

The Law Commission's proposals for a statutory definition of murder[11] were never implemented and the latest proposal for the reform of the law of murder comes from the Criminal Law Revision Committee. They recommend that it should be murder:

  a) if a person, with intent to kill, causes death and
  b) if a person causes death by an unlawful act intended to cause serious injury and known to him to involve a risk of causing death.[12]

7. By virtue of affirmative resolutions of both Houses of Parliament on 16th and 18th December 1969.
8. Fourteenth Report CLRC/OAP/R, pp. 19–27.
9. [1981] 2 All ER at 870.
10. CLRC/OAP/R, 28–31.
11. *Imputed Criminal Intent: Director of Public Prosecutions v Smith.*
12. CLRC/OAP/R, 14.

"Intent" is here used to mean the state of mind of a person "(i) who wants the particular result to follow from his act or (ii) who though he may not want the result to follow, knows that in the ordinary course of things it will do so."[13]

2 Manslaughter

1) *Voluntary and Involuntary*

Manslaughter is a diverse crime, covering all unlawful homicides which are not murder. A wide variety of types of homicide fall within this category, but it is customary and useful to divide manslaughter into two main groups which are designated "voluntary" and "involuntary" manslaughter, respectively. The distinction is that in voluntary manslaughter D may have the malice aforethought of murder, but the presence of some defined mitigating circumstance reduces his crime to the less serious grade of criminal homicide. Where these circumstances are present, then, D may actually intend to kill and do so in pursuance of that intention and yet not be guilty of murder.[14] At common law, voluntary manslaughter occurred in one case only, where the killing was done under provocation. But now, by statute, two further categories must be added. Under the Homicide Act 1957, killing is now manslaughter and not murder, notwithstanding the presence of malice aforethought, where (i) D is suffering from diminished responsibility;[15] and (ii) where D kills in pursuance of a suicide pact.[16] Diminished responsibility has already been considered, and the problem of the suicide pact is looked at in connection with the new statutory crime of abetting suicide.[17] This section, then, will be devoted to killing under provocation.

2) *Provocation*[18]

In deciding whether D intended death or grievous bodily harm, the jury must consider evidence of provocation with all other relevant evidence.[19] If they are not satisfied that he had the necessary *mens rea*, they must acquit. But even if they decide he did have *mens rea*, provocation may still be a defence to a charge of murder[20] at common law, entitling D to be convicted

---

13. Ibid., para. 10.
14. *A-G of Ceylon v Perera* [1953] AC 200, PC; *Lee Chun Chuen v R* [1963] AC 220, [1963] 1 All ER 73; *Parker v R* [1964] AC 1369, [1964] 2 All ER 641; contra, per Lord Simon in *Holmes v Director of Public Prosecutions* [1946] AC 588 at 598 HL.
15. Section 2.
16. Section 4.
17. Below, p. 359.
18. Ashworth, "The Doctrine of Provocation", [1976] CLJ 292.
19. Section 8 of the Criminal Justice Act 1967, above, p. 85; *Williams* [1968] Crim LR 678; *Ives* [1970] 1 QB 208, [1969] 3 All ER 470.
20. Provocation is not a defence to a charge of wounding or any charge other than murder according to *Cunningham* [1959] 1 QB 288, [1958] 3 All ER 711. In *Bruzas* [1972] Crim LR 367 Eveleigh J held that it is not a defence to a charge of attempted murder; but see commentary and CLRC/OAP/R, para. 98.

of manslaughter. The common law rule was stated by Devlin J in what the Court of Criminal Appeal described as a "classic direction", as follows:

> "Provocation is some act, or series of acts, done by the dead man to the accused, which would cause in any reasonable person, and actually causes in the accused, a sudden and temporary loss of self-control, rendering the accused so subject to passion as to make him or her for the moment not master of his mind."[1]

The common law rule has been modified by the Homicide Act 1957, s. 3, which provides:

> "Where on a charge of murder there is evidence on which the jury can find that the person charged was provoked (whether by things done or by things said or by both together) to lose his self-control, the question whether the provocation was enough to make a reasonable man do as he did shall be left to be determined by the jury; and in determining that question the jury shall take into account everything both done and said according to the effect which, in their opinion, it would have on a reasonable man."

This section does not replace the whole of the previous law of provocation – it does not, for example, state what the effect of a successful plea of provocation is. The section assumes the existence of the dual test of the common law: (i) was the defendant provoked to lose his self-control?, a subjective question, and (ii) was the provocation enough to make a reasonable man do as he did?, an objective question.

Whether the defendant was provoked to lose his self-control is a question of fact. In accordance with the general rule, it is for the judge to say whether there is any evidence of that fact. Sufficient evidence may appear in the case presented by the Crown. If not, there is an evidential burden on the defendant. If no evidence that the defendant was provoked to lose his self-control is adduced by the Crown or the defendant, then the judge will withdraw the defence from the jury. Since the burden of proof is on the Crown, evidence which might leave a reasonable jury in reasonable doubt whether or not the defendant was provoked is sufficient. Once the judge has decided there is sufficient evidence that the defendant was provoked, whether or not the defence has been raised expressly by D or his counsel,[2] he must leave it to the jury to answer the questions, (i) *was* the defendant provoked to lose his self-control? and (ii) was the provocation enough to make a reasonable man do as he did? Since the Act, the judge may not withdraw the defence from the jury on the ground that in his opinion there is no evidence on which they could answer the second question in the affirmative.[3]

I Provocation by things done or said

Since provocation continues to be a defence at common law it might have been held that the words "provoked" and "provocation" in the section bear the limited meaning they had at common law, subject only to the

---

1. *Duffy* [1949] 1 All ER at 932n.
2. *Mancini v Director of Public Prosecutions* [1942] AC 1, [1941] 3 All ER 272.
3. This seems to be a unique exception to the rule that the judge must not allow a matter of fact (or opinion) to be decided when there is no evidence of it. The CLRC recommends repeal of this rule: CLRC/OAP/R, para. 88.

limited changes expressly made by the section. This has not been the approach of the courts.[4] These words have been given their ordinary natural meaning, free of the technical limitations of the common law. In *Doughty*[5] it was held that the judge was bound by the plain words of the section to leave provocation to the jury where there was evidence that the persistent crying of his baby had caused D to lose his self-control and kill it. Whatever the position may have been at common law, the provocation does not have to be an illegal or wrongful act. There must be "things done or things said" and the crying of the baby was presumably regarded as a "thing done". Mere circumstances, however provocative, do not constitute a defence to murder. Loss of control by a farmer on finding his crops destroyed by a flood, a financier ruined by a crash on the stock market or an author on his manuscript being destroyed by lightning, could not, it seems, excuse a resulting killing. "Act of God" could hardly be regarded as "something done" within s. 3. Since, where there is a provocative act, it no longer need be done by the victim, this distinction begins to look a little thin. If D may rely on the defence where the crops or the manuscript were destroyed by an unknown arsonist or the stock exchange crash was engineered by other anonymous financiers, why should it be different where no human agency was involved? The "provocation" is no more and no less.

2 Provocation and Third Parties[6]

i) *By whom the provocation may be given.* Section 3 removes certain limitations on the defence as formulated in *Duffy*. That formulation limited the nature of operative provocation to acts done (i) by the dead man (ii) to the accused. Evidence would thus not be admissible of acts done (i) by third parties or (ii) to third parties. Under s. 3, however, there is no such limitation and the only question seems to be whether the evidence is relevant to the issue – namely whether D was provoked to lose his self-control. The test of relevance should be – would a reasonable man regard the act in question as having a provocative effect on the person charged? So it was held in *Davies* where D killed his wife, P, following upon her adultery with Q, that the judge was wrong to direct that P's conduct and, by implication, not Q's, was to be taken into account.[7]

The defence was available, even at common law, if the blow was *aimed* at the provoker. If, by accident, it missed him and killed an innocent person, P, then the doctrine of transferred malice[8] operated and D was guilty of manslaughter only. In *Gross*[9] D, provoked by blows from her husband, fired at him, intending to kill him but missed and killed P. It was held that

4. *Edwards v R* [1973] AC 648l, [1973] 1 All ER 152, PC, below, p. 343 may be an exception.
5. (1986) 83 Cr App Rep 319.
6. See O'Regan, "Indirect Provocation and Misdirected Retaliation", [1968] Crim LR 319.
7. [1975] QB 691, [1975] 1 All ER 890. Cf. the earlier decision to the same effect by Lawton J in *Twine* [1967] Crim LR 710, where D's girl friend's conduct caused D to lose his self-control and strike and kill the man she was with.
8. Above, p. 73.
9. (1913) 23 Cox CC 455 (Darling J); and see *Porritt* [1961] 3 All ER 463, [1961] 1 WLR 1372.

". . . if the firing at the person intended to be hit would be manslaughter, then, if the bullet strikes a third person not intended to be hit, the killing of that person equally would be manslaughter and not murder."[10]

If D knew it was virtually certain that he would hit P, he would have an independent *mens rea* with respect to P, probably sufficient to fix him with liability for murder[11] at common law; but now the provocation given by the third party would be a defence.

ii) *Acts directed against third parties.* It is said that at common law provocation must consist in something done to D. Most commonly, provocation has consisted in some kind of physical attack on D. The case of the adulterous spouse might also be considered as one where something is "done to" D by the guilty pair. At least they are committing a matrimonial offence against him. Suppose, however, that D came upon P committing rape on his wife and instantly killed him. It is conceived that this would have been sufficient provocation at common law; it could hardly have been less provoking because the wife was not consenting. In *Fisher*,[12] Park J said obiter,[13] that if a father came upon a man in the act of committing an unnatural act with his young son and instantly killed him, this, by analogy to the adultery rule, would probably have been a sufficient provocation. In *Harrington*[14] Cockburn CJ contemplated the possibility that a violent assault upon his daughter by her husband might be sufficient to reduce D's killing of the husband to manslaughter, but did not decide the point. Whatever the position at common law, however, it is now clear that if there is evidence that D was in fact provoked to lose his self-control, the defence must be left to the jury even though the provocative act was directed against another.

3 The Subjective Condition

The jury should be directed to consider the subjective condition first.[15] In deciding this question of fact they are, naturally, entitled to take into account all the relevant circumstances; the nature of the provocative act and all the relevant conditions in which it took place, the sensitivity or otherwise of D and the time, if any, which elapsed between the provocation and the act which caused death. D's failure to testify to his loss of self-control is not necessarily fatal to his case. Provocation is commonly set up as an alternative to the complete defence of self-defence. The admission of loss of self-control would weaken or destroy the alternative defence; and the courts recognise that D has a tactical reason for not expressly asserting what may be the truth.[16]

If D is of an unusually phlegmatic temperament and it appears that he did not lose his self-control, the fact that a reasonable man in like

10. 23 Cox CC at 456.
11. Above, p. 75.
12. (1837) 8 C & P 182.
13. The judge ruled as a matter of law that there had been a sufficient cooling time.
14. (1886) 10 Cox CC 370. And see *Terry* [1964] VR 248.
15. *Brown* [1972] 2 All ER 1328 at 1333.
16. *Bullard v R* [1957] AC 635, [1961] 3 All ER 470 n; *Rolle v R* [1965] 3 All ER 582; *Lee Chun Chuen v R* [1963] AC 220, [1963] 1 All ER 73.

circumstances would have done so will not avail D in the least. A traditional example of extreme provocation is the finding of a spouse in the act of adultery;[17] but if D, on so finding his wife, were to read her a lecture on the enormity of her sin and then methodically to load a gun and shoot her, it is probable (for it remains a question of fact) either that the judge would rule that there was no evidence that D lost his self-control or that the jury would find that he did not. In that case, D would be guilty of murder and it would be irrelevant that the jury may think that a reasonable man in like circumstances would lose his self-control.

Although the House of Lords has stated that the Act "abolishes all previous rules as to what can or cannot amount to provocation"[18] it appears that the subjective condition is unchanged. In *Ibrams*[19] the Court of Appeal has, after *Camplin*,[20] reaffirmed that there must be a "sudden and temporary loss of self-control", as Devlin J put it in *Duffy*,[1] and approved that judge's further words:

"Indeed, circumstances which induce a desire for revenge are inconsistent with provocation, since the conscious formulation of a desire for revenge means that a person has had time to think, to reflect, and that would negative a sudden temporary loss of self-control, which is of the essence of provocation."

In *Ibrams*, D had received gross provocation but the last act occurred on October 7. The attack was carefully planned on October 10 and carried out on October 12. It was held that the judge was right to rule that there was no evidence of loss of self-control. Provocation may extend over a long period of time provided it culminates in a sudden explosion, sparked off by some relatively trivial incident.[2]

Great importance is attached in many of the cases to the presence of "cooling time" between the act of provocation and the killing. In *Hayward*[3] Tindal CJ told the jury that the question for their consideration was –

"... whether the mortal wound was given by the prisoner while smarting under a provocation so recent and so strong that the prisoner might not be considered at the moment the master of his own understanding; in which case, the law, in compassion to human infirmity, would hold the offence to amount to manslaughter only: or whether there had been time for the blood to cool, and for reason to resume its seat, before the mortal wound was given, in which case the crime would amount to wilful murder."[4]

17. Killing, in such a case "is of the lowest degree of [manslaughter]; and therefore ... the court directed the burning in the hand to be gently inflicted, because there could not be a greater provocation": Blackstone, *Commentaries*, iv, 192. And see the leading case of *Manning* (1671) T Raym 212.
18. *Camplin* [1978] AC 705 (1978) 67 Cr App Rep 14 at 19, **SHC 321**.
19. (1982) 74 Cr App Rep 154, **SHC 327**.
20. Below, p. 337.
  1. [1949] 1 All ER 932n.
  2. See a valuable article, "Cumulative Provocation and Domestic Killing" by Martin Wasik, [1982] Crim LR 29, discussing, *inter alia*, some cases and practices which are difficult to reconcile with *Duffy* and *Ibrams*.
  3. (1833) 6 C & P 157.
  4. Ibid., at 159. This direction was approved by the Court of Criminal Appeal in *Hall* (1928) 21 Cr App Rep 48. See also *Lynch* (1832) 5 C & P 324; *Eagle* (1862) 2 F & F 827; and cf. *Fisher*, above, p. 334.

Shortness of time in that case was in D's favour, but against him was the fact that he fetched the weapon from two or three hundred yards away. If this showed "contrivance and design", that was inconsistent with the "violent and ungovernable passion" which was necessary for the defence to succeed.

Cooling time is obviously a fact of very great importance in deciding this particular question; but it should always be remembered that it is not a matter of law, but one item of evidence in answering the question: was D deprived of his self-control when he did the fatal act?

The CLRC (OAP/R, para. 84) proposed no change in what they took to be the present law:

"... the defence applies only where the defendant's act is caused by the provocation and is committed suddenly upon the provoking event, not to cases where the defendant's violent reaction has been delayed; but the jury should continue to take into consideration previous provocations before the one which produced the fatal reaction."

4 The Objective Condition[5]

In the older cases, the courts laid down as a matter of law what was, and what was not, capable of amounting to provocation.[6] It usually consisted of a violent act against the defendant, though two other instances were well recognised, that where a husband discovered his wife in the act of adultery and killed either or both of the guilty pair and that where a father found and promptly killed a man committing sodomy with his son.[7] In *Holmes v Director of Public Prosecutions*[8] the House of Lords held that, as a matter of law, a confession of adultery was insufficient provocation where a husband killed his wife; and added that "in no case could words alone, save in circumstances of a most extreme and exceptional character", reduce the crime to manslaughter. The reasonable man did not make his appearance until *Welsh*[9] in 1869. Thereafter even when the act was recognised as capable of amounting to provocation, it probably had to pass the reasonable man test.

This test was applied by the Court of Criminal Appeal in the important case of *Lesbini*.[10] The girl in charge of a firing range in an amusement arcade made some impertinent personal remarks about D. He asked for a revolver, ostensibly to shoot at the range, and shot her dead. At his trial for murder, his defences of accident and insanity were rejected by the jury. On appeal, it was argued that the jury should have been directed on provocation and *Welsh* did not apply where, as in the present case, D suffered from defective control and want of mental balance. Avory J interjected that it would seem to follow from this that a bad-tempered man would be entitled to a verdict of manslaughter where a good-tempered one would be liable to be

---

5. See Williams, "Provocation and the Reasonable Man", [1954] Crim LR 740; Edwards "Another View", [1954] Crim LR 898.
6. See, e.g., Hawkins 1 PC c. 13, s. 36; East, 1 PC 233.
7. *Fisher* (1837) 8 C & P 182.
8. [1946] AC 588, [1946] 2 All ER 124.
9. (1869) 11 Cox CC 336.
10. [1914] 3 KB 1116.

convicted of murder[11] and the court held that, to afford a defence, the provocation must be such as would affect the mind of a reasonable man, which was manifestly not so in the present case.

Before the Homicide Act the judges took it upon themselves to instruct the jury as to the characteristics of the reasonable man. The defendant might be mentally deficient[12] but the jury still had to consider the effects of the provocation on a normal person. Moreover, he (or she) was normal in body as well as mind. The fact the defendant was seven months pregnant was irrelevant to the application of the objective test.[13] In *Bedder v Director of Public Prosecutions*,[14] D, a youth of eighteen who was sexually impotent, attempted in vain to have sexual intercourse with P, a prostitute. She jeered at him and attempted to get away. He tried to hold her and she slapped him in the face, punched him in the stomach and kicked him in the genitals. D knew of his impotence and had allowed it to prey on his mind. The House of Lords held that the jury had been correctly directed to consider what effect P's acts would have had on an ordinary person, not a man who is sexually impotent. Mental and physical characteristics were, in the view of the House of Lords, inseparable.

The Homicide Act, s. 3 made three changes in the law. (i) It made it clear that "things said" alone may be sufficient provocation, if the jury should be of the opinion that they would have provoked a reasonable man, thus reversing *Director of Public Prosecutions v Holmes*.[15] (ii) It took away the power of the judge to withdraw the defence from the jury on the ground that there was no evidence on which the jury could find that a reasonable man would have been provoked to do as D did, reversing *Mancini*.[16] (iii) It took away the power of the judge to dictate to the jury what were the characteristics of the reasonable man, reversing *Bedder*.

It was not until the decision of the House of Lords in *Camplin*,[17] more than 20 years after the Act, that the second and third effects were fully recognised. The Court of Appeal in that case were of the opinion that *Bedder* was binding on them. The House of Lords decided that the effect of s. 3 is to overrule that case and all others which defined any characteristic of the reasonable man except his powers of self-control and the fact that he is sober.

In *Camplin* D, a fifteen-year-old boy, killed P, with a kitchen utensil known as a chapati pan. D's story was that P had buggered him against his will and then laughed at him when he was overcome by shame, whereupon he lost his self-control and made the fatal attack. The trial judge declined the invitation of D's counsel to instruct the jury to consider the effect of the provocation on a boy of fifteen. He directed that the test was the effect of the provocation, not on a reasonable boy, but on a reasonable man. The Court of Appeal held that this was a misdirection and distinguished *Bedder*

---

11. For a discussion of this argument, see the 4th edition of this work, 304–306.
12. *Alexander* (1913) 9 Cr App Rep 139.
13. *Smith* (1915) 11 Cr App Rep 81.
14. [1954] 2 All ER 801, [1954] 1 WLR 1119.
15. [1946] AC 588, [1946] 2 All ER 124.
16. [1942] AC 1, [1941] 3 All ER 272.
17. [1978] AC 705, [1978] 2 All ER 168, **SHC 321**.

on the ground that youth, and the immaturity which naturally accompanies youth, are not deviations from the norm, but norms through which everyone must pass. Youth is not a personal idiosyncrasy and certainly not a physical infirmity or disability like Bedder's impotence.[18] The House of Lords dismissed the Director's appeal on the broader ground that *Bedder* is, in effect, overruled by s. 3 of the 1957 Act. Their lordships were much influenced by the fact that, under the Act, words alone may be a sufficient provocation. This accentuates the anomalies, inconveniences and injustices which would flow from a continued application of the *Bedder* principle, for the gravity of verbal provocation will frequently depend on the particular characteristics or circumstances of the person to whom a taunt or insult is addressed. In a case of provocation by words, personal characteristics could not be ignored without absurdity. To allow such characteristics to be taken into account where the provocation was verbal so undermined the *Bedder* principle that it should no longer be followed, whatever the nature of the provocation.

This conclusion, it is submitted, is well justified by the words of the Act. S. 3 is to be given its natural meaning[19] and tells us that the question for the jury is "whether the provocation was enough to make a reasonable man do as [D] did." What is "the provocation"? It seems obviously to be the things done or things said – which may or may not have been a sufficient provocation at common law – which the jury have found to have provoked the accused. The section goes on to direct that the jury –

"shall take into account *everything* both done and said according to the effect which, *in their opinion*, it would have on a reasonable man."

The words we have italicised are inconsistent with the continuance of *Bedder* as a rule of law. "Everything" includes a taunt of impotence where that in fact provoked the accused and the effect of it on a reasonable man is a question for the opinion of the jury.

The result of *Camplin*, as Lord Simon pointed out, is to bring the common law, as modified by the Homicide Act, into line with the New Zealand Crimes Act 1961.[20] This provides by s. 169 (2):

"Anything done or said may be provocation if –

(a) In the circumstances of the case it was sufficient to deprive a person having the power of self-control of an ordinary person, but otherwise having the characteristics of the offender, of the power of self-control; and

(b) It did in fact deprive the offender of the power of self-control and thereby induced him to commit the act of homicide."

The reasonable man must now be endowed by the jury with the age, sex and other personal characteristics of the accused, whether normal or abnormal. The characteristics may be taken into account by the jury – it is a matter for their opinion – both in assessing the gravity of the provocation addressed to the accused and in determining what degree of self-control is to be expected of him. The jury should be directed as follows:[1]

18. [1978] 1 All ER at 1241.
19. *Davies* [1975] QB 691, [1975] 1 All ER 890.
20. As explained in *McGregor* [1962] NZLR 1069.
 1. Per Lord Diplock at p. 175.

"The judge should state what the question is using the very terms of the section. He should then explain to them that the reasonable man referred to in the question is a person having the power of self-control to be expected of an ordinary person of the sex and age of the accused, but in other respects sharing such of the accused's characteristics as they think would affect the gravity of the provocation to him; and that the question is not merely whether such a person would in like circumstances be provoked to lose his self-control but also would react to the provocation as the accused did."

The judge may tell the jury that a man is not entitled to rely on "his exceptional excitability (whether idiosyncratic or by cultural environment or ethnic origin) or pugnacity or ill-temper or on his drunkenness."[2] The judge should remind the jury of any material characteristics of the defendant[3] and may suggest considerations which may influence the jury in forming their opinion but he must make it clear that it is for them and no one else to decide what weight, if any, ought to be given to them. The evidence of witnesses as to how they think a reasonable man with the characteristics of the accused would react to the provocation is not admissible.

The question of what is meant by "characteristics" was further elucidated by the Court of Appeal in *Newell*,[4] following the judgment delivered by North J in the New Zealand case of *McGregor*:

"The characteristic must be something definite and of sufficient significance to make the offender a different person from the ordinary run of mankind, and have also a sufficient degree of permanence to warrant its being regarded as something constituting part of the individual's character and personality."

By the terms of the decision in *Camplin* and of the New Zealand Crimes Act, the jury are obviously not entitled to give weight to such permanent characteristics as unusual excitability or pugnacity of the defendant or his disposition to lose his temper readily; and transitory states of mind, such as a mood of depression, excitability or irascibility are equally excluded.

North J went on:

"Moreover, it is to be equally emphasised that there must be some real connection between the nature of the provocation and the particular characteristic of the offender by which it is sought to modify the ordinary man test. The words or conduct must have been exclusively or particularly provocative to the individual because, and only because, of the characteristic of the offender by which it is sought to modify the ordinary man test ... In short there must be some direct connection between the provocative words or conduct and the characteristic sought to be invoked as warranting some departure from the ordinary man test."

The jury is now entitled and bound to take into account two classes of fact: (i) the events which have happened and which might have a tendency to cause a reasonable man with the relevant characteristics of the defendant

2. Per Lord Simon, who did not think this list necessarily exhaustive. *McCarthy* [1954] 2 QB 105, [1954] 2 All ER 262 remains good law.
3. *Burke* [1987] Crim LR 336, CA.
4. (1980) 71 Cr App Rep 331, [1980] Crim LR 576, CA, **SHC 325**.

to lose his self-control; and (ii) those relevant characteristics. The two matters are inter-related. The fact that a man is impotent is a relevant characteristic if the alleged provocation consists in taunts of impotence but it would be irrelevant if the provocation were taunts about the defendant's race, religion, stupidity or dishonesty.

In *Newell*, D was a chronic alcoholic who was very depressed by the defection of the young woman with whom he had been living for some time and to whom he was strongly attached. When D and his friend, P, were both very drunk, P made derogatory remarks about the woman which caused D immediately to lose his self-control and make a violent attack on P, killing him. The judge asked the jury: "Would a sober man, in relation to that drunken observation, batter his friend over the head with a nearly two poundweight ashtray?" That was held to be a proper direction. The only matter which could possibly be described as a characteristic was D's chronic alcoholism but, without deciding that it was, the court held that it had nothing to do with the words by which D was said to be provoked.

The application of these principles may make considerable demands on a jury. In *Raven*,[5] D aged 22, had a mental age of approximately nine years, regrettably, no doubt, a permanent characteristic, and had lived in "squats" for two to three years of his life. The jury were directed to consider the reasonable man as having lived the same type of life as D for 22 years, but with his retarded development and mental age.

5 The Relationship between the Provocation and the Mode of Resentment

In *Mancini v Director of Public Prosecutions*[6] D was charged with the murder of P who had been stabbed to death by an instrument with a two-edged blade, a sharp point and sharp sides, at least five inches long. D's story was that P was attacking him with an open pen-knife and MacNaghten J told the jury that, if they believed this story, they should return a verdict of not guilty (on the ground of self-defence.) He did not direct them that, if they rejected the defence of self-defence, they still might find D guilty of manslaughter on the ground of provocation; and D appealed on the ground that he ought to have done so. His conviction was affirmed. By their verdict, the jury had rejected his story of the attack with the pen-knife; and the case had, therefore, to be treated as one in which, at the most, P made an unarmed attack on D. If there had been evidence of provocation, it would have been the judge's duty to direct the jury on it, even though the defence had not been set up;[7] but here there was no evidence. An attack by hand or fist

"would not constitute provocation of a kind which could extenuate the sudden introduction and use of a lethal weapon like this dagger, and there was, therefore, ... no adequate material to raise the issue of provocation."[8]

5. [1982] Crim LR 51 and commentary.
6. [1942] AC 1, [1941] 3 All ER 272, HL.
7. Above, p. 332.
8. [1942] AC at 10, [1941] 3 All ER at 278.

The House stated the law in general terms as follows:[9]

". . . it is of particular importance . . . to take into account the instrument with which the homicide was effected, for to retort, in the heat of passion induced by provocation, by a simple blow, is a very different thing from making use of a deadly instrument like a concealed dagger. In short, the mode of resentment must bear a reasonable relationship to the provocation if the offence is to be reduced to manslaughter."

Clearly such a case could not be decided in this way today. If there was evidence that D was provoked to lose his self-control, the judge could not decline to leave the defence to the jury because the resentment did not bear a reasonable relationship to the provocation. It was in this respect, no doubt, that Lord Diplock in *Camplin* said that *Mancini* is no longer to be treated as an authority on the law of provocation.[10] It would now be wrong to tell the jury, "fists might be answered with fists but not with a deadly weapon",[11] because if fists were answered with a deadly weapon, this would be to take out of the jury's hands a question which is exclusively for them and on which their opinion is decisive. So it has been said that the "reasonable relationship rule" is not a rule of law and that it is wrong for the judge, who has directed them on the subjective and objective conditions, to go on to tell them that there is a third condition, viz that the retaliation must be proportionate to the provocation.[12] Yet in a sense, the reasonable relationship rule still is a rule of law because the defence is made out only if the provocation was enough to make the reasonable man "do as he did". Thus, it would be right for the judge to direct the jury: "If you are satisfied that a reasonable man, though he might have answered with fists, would not have answered with the deadly weapon used by D, then you *must* reject the defence of provocation." This is no more than the application of the words of the section to the facts. The difference, since the Act, is that it is for the jury, not the judge, to decide whether the answer with a deadly weapon was the act of a reasonable man.

Since 1978, the decision in *Camplin* has removed much of the "inequity" said to arise from the test. The main argument, in favour of the test, that the bad-tempered man should be treated in the same way as the good-tempered man, has been subjected to cogent criticism.[13] If the good-tempered man kills when he has not lost his self-control, he deserves to be convicted of murder and no injustice is done to him if the man who has lost his self-control is convicted only of manslaughter. On the other hand, it is the business of the law to lay down standards of conduct and this is a standard of self-restraint, similar to the standards of fortitude and resolution which are required by the law in the defence of duress and blackmail. One difference, however, is that here we are not concerned with criminal liability or no criminal liability, but only with a matter of mitigation – in practice, with untying the judge's hands to enable him to impose an appropriate sentence instead of requiring him to impose the sentence of

9. [1942] AC at 9, [1941] 3 All ER at 277, per Lord Simon.
10. 67 Cr App Rep at 21. See commentary on *Brown* [1972] Crim LR 506.
11. Per Devlin J in *Duffy* [1949] 1 All ER 932n.
12. *Brown* [1972] 2 QB 229, [1972] 2 All ER 1328.
13. Williams, [1954] Crim LR 751; Kenny, *Outlines*, 178.

imprisonment for life. The CLRC has recommended that the question for the jury should be whether, on the facts as they appeared to the defendant, the provocation can reasonably be regarded as a sufficient ground for the loss of self-control leading the defendant to react against the victim with murderous intent,[14] and that, in answering this question, the defendant should be judged with due regard to all the circumstances, including any disability, physical or mental, from which he suffered.[15] This proposal would remove the objective test and, with it, much unnecessary technicality from the law.

It will be noted that, under section 3 of the Homicide Act, the subjective and objective tests differ. The questions are: (i) did D *lose his self control?* and (ii) was the provocation enough to make the reasonable man *do as D did?* It can hardly have been intended, however, that the jury should consider whether a reasonable man in full control of himself would have done what D did for the logical effect of that would be to eliminate the defence from the law. The objective test must be construed as it was in *Phillips v R:*[16]

"... the question ... is not merely whether in their opinion the provocation would have made a reasonable man lose his self-control but also whether, having lost his self-control, he would have retaliated in the same way as the person charged in fact did."

This assumes that a person who has lost his self-control acts with more or less ferocity according to the degree of provocation which caused the loss of self-control. The Privy Council has rejected the argument –

"... that loss of self-control is not a matter of degree but is absolute; there is no intermediate stage between icy detachment and going berserk. This premise, unless the argument is purely semantic, must be based upon human experience and is, in their Lordships' view, false. The average man reacts to provocation according to its degree with angry words, with a blow of the hand, possibly, if the provocation is gross and there is a dangerous weapon to hand, with that weapon."[17]

Whatever scientific opinion may be,[18] this certainly seems to be the view of human conduct on which the section is based; and the objective condition requires affirmative answers to two questions: (i) would the reasonable man have lost his self-control? and (ii) would he then have retaliated as D did?

6 Provocation arising from a Mistake of Fact
The authorities suggest that, where D is provoked partly as the result of a mistake of fact he is entitled to be treated as if the facts were as he mistakenly supposed them to be. Thus in *Brown*[19] D, a soldier, wrongly, but apparently reasonably, supposed that P was a member of a gang who were attacking him and his comrade. He struck P with a sword and killed

14. CLRC/OAP/R, para. 81.
15. Ibid., para. 83.
16. [1969] 2 AC 130 at 137, PC; **SHC 328**.
17. Ibid., 137. See White, "A Note on Provocation" [1970] Crim LR 446.
18. Brett, "The Physiology of Provocation" [1970] Crim LR 634.
19. (1776) Leach 148.

him. The judges were clearly of the opinion that this was only man-slaughter. In the other cases the mistake arose from drunkenness. In *Letenock*[20] the Court of Criminal Appeal substituted a verdict of man-slaughter in the case of a soldier who had stabbed a corporal, where

"The only element of doubt in the case is whether or not there was anything which might have caused the applicant, *in his drunken condition*, to believe that he was going to be struck."[1]

This decision is unaffected by *McCarthy*[2] which was not concerned with a mistake of fact but with the effect of the alcohol on D's self-restraint. So in *Wardrope*,[3] Edmund Davies J told the jury both that the provocation "must be such as to deprive a reasonable man, not a drunken man . . . of self-control" and that

"A person whose mind was so impaired by drink as to imagine himself attacked was entitled[4] to take such steps in defending himself as were necessary to meet the imagined attack as if it were real or not exaggerated. . . ."

It is recognised that a drunken mistake may negative the *mens rea* of murder[5] and it is consistent that such a mistake should be relevant in determining whether the killing should be reduced to manslaughter on the ground of provocation. A drunken mistake is almost inevitably an unrea-sonable one; and it seems clear that it is immaterial whether the mistake is reasonable or not for this purpose. The jury must look at the reactions of the reasonable man in the circumstances which D supposed to exist.

7 Self-Induced Provocation

In *Edwards v R*[6] D visited P with intent to blackmail him. P responded by attacking D with a knife. D wrested the knife from P and killed him. At D's trial for murder in Hong Kong, the judge declined to leave the defence of provocation to the jury. In the Privy Council, Lord Pearson said:

"On principle it seems reasonable to say that (1) a blackmailer cannot rely on the predictable results of his own blackmailing conduct as constituting provocation sufficient to reduce his killing of the victim from murder to manslaughter, and the predictable results may include a considerable degree of hostile reaction by the person sought to be blackmailed, for instance vituperative words and even some hostile action such as blows with a fist; (2) but if the hostile reaction by the person sought to be blackmailed goes to extreme lengths it might constitute a sufficient provocation even for the blackmailer; (3) there would in many cases be a question of degree to be decided by the jury."

20. (1917) 12 Cr App Rep 221, CCA.
 1. Ibid., at 224.
 2. [1954] 2 QB 105, [1954] 2 All ER 262.
 3. [1960] Crim LR 770.
 4. Wardrope also raised the defence of self-defence and the use of the word "entitled" (cf. *Southgate* [1963] 2 All ER 833) suggests that it was to this defence that the judge was here referring; but he could hardly have intended the jury to consider D's mistake of fact for the purpose of the one defence and not for the other. Such a mistake, properly taken into account for purposes of self-defence, may not lead to a complete acquittal since it is said that drunken mistakes can at best reduce murder to manslaughter.
 5. Above, pp. 210–215.
 6. [1973] AC 648, [1973] 1 All ER 152, PC; **SHC 329**.

Since P did go to extreme lengths, the defence ought to have been left to
the jury. Though the Privy Council did not refer to it, a provision in
precisely the same words as s. 3 of the Homicide Act was in force in Hong
Kong. It is difficult to reconcile the section with the above principles. As a
fact, D might have been provoked to lose his self-control by an attack
predictably caused by his own blackmailing. How can the judge in such a
case withdraw the defence from the jury, consistently with the section?[7] It
would seem that the most he could do would be to advise the jury as to how
they should decide the objective question.

It has been questioned[8] whether this view would not open a defence for
one who *deliberately* induces provocation – D provokes P to do a provocative act so that D may kill him and rely on the defence of provocation. Such
a situation seems far-fetched. If it did occur, it should, it is submitted, be
decided on the same lines as *A-G for Northern Ireland v Gallagher*[9] – D
should be held liable for the acts which, when unprovoked, he intended to
do under provocation. The judge should find there is no evidence that D
was provoked.

8 Provocation by a Lawful Act

It has been argued that "The law would be self-contradictory if a lawful act
could amount to provocation,"[10] but it is submitted that this proposition
will not bear examination.[11] To taunt a man with his impotence or his wife's
adultery may be cruel and immoral, but it is not unlawful and it may,
surely, amount to provocation. So, we now know, may the crying of a
baby.[12] Where P's act is one which he is not merely at liberty to do but
which is positively praiseworthy, it is scarcely conceivable that a jury would
find that it would provoke a reasonable man to lose his self-control; but
under the terms of s. 3 it must be a question for the jury in each case. It is
impossible, as a matter of law, to divide acts which P is at liberty to do into
classes of "good" and "bad".

3) *Involuntary Manslaughter*

This category includes all varieties of unlawful homicide which are
committed without malice aforethought. It is not surprising, therefore, that
the fault required takes more than one form. And, as the limits of malice
aforethought are uncertain, it follows inevitably that there is a corresponding uncertainty as to the boundary of manslaughter. The difficulties
do not end there, for there is another vague borderline between manslaughter and accidental death. Indeed, Lord Atkin said[13] that

7. Such a course was held to be justified in *Leung Ping-Fat* [1973] HKLJ 342; **SHC 330**. *Sed quaere?*
8. By Ashworth [1973] Crim LR 483.
9. Above, p. 219.
10. Howard, *Australian Criminal Law* (2nd ed.) 93.
11. See *Browne* [1973] NI 96 at 108, per Lowry LCJ: "I should prefer to say that provocation is something *unwarranted* which is likely to make a reasonable person angry or indignant."
12. *Doughty* (1986) 83 Cr App Rep 319, above, p. 333.
13. In *Andrews v Director of Public Prosecutions* [1937] AC 576 at 581, [1937] 2 All ER 552 at 554–555.

"... of all crimes manslaughter appears to afford most difficulties of definition, for it concerns homicide in so many and so varying conditions ... the law ... recognises murder on the one hand based mainly, though not exclusively,[14] on an intention to kill, and manslaughter on the other hand, based mainly, though not exclusively,[15] on the absence of intent to kill, but with the presence of an element of 'unlawfulness' which is the elusive factor."

This "elusive factor" is obviously difficult to define; but it would seem to comprise at least two, and perhaps three, varieties of fault.

1) An intention to do an act[16] which, whether D knows it or not, is unlawful and dangerous in the sense that it is likely to cause direct[17] personal injury, though not necessarily serious injury.

2) Where D does an act which creates an obvious and serious risk of causing personal injury to another –
   (a) not giving thought to the possibility of there being any such risk; or
   (b) having recognised that there was some risk involved, going on to take it.
   It is not certain whether there continues to exist a third head of liability;

3) An intention to do an act, or to omit to act where there is a duty to do so,[18] being grossly negligent whether death or serious personal injury be caused.

1 Intention to do an Unlawful and Dangerous Act

Constructive Manslaughter

Coke laid it down that an intention to commit any unlawful act was a sufficient *mens rea* for murder[19] so that if D shot at P's hen with intent to kill it and accidentally killed P, this was murder, "for the act was unlawful". This savage doctrine was criticised by Holt CJ[20] and by the time Foster wrote his *Crown Law*,[1] it appears to have been modified by the proviso that the unlawful act must be a felony. Thus, if D shot at the hen intending to steal it, the killing of P was murder. This was the doctrine of constructive murder which survived until the Homicide Act 1957. From Foster's time there existed a twin doctrine of constructive manslaughter; that any death caused while in the course of committing an unlawful act, other than a felony, was manslaughter. An act was unlawful for this purpose even if it was only a tort, so that the only *mens rea* which needed to be proved was an intention to commit the tort.

---

14. See above, p. 327.
15. See above, p. 331.
16. In *Lowe*, below, p. 350 it was held, distinguishing unlawful acts, that an unlawful omission causing death was not manslaughter. *Sed quaere?*
17. *Dalby* [1982] 1 All ER 916, 74 Cr App Rep 348.
18. In *Stone and Dobinson* [1977] QB 354, [1977] 2 All ER 341, CA below, p. 352, an omission to care for P, to whom a duty was owed, was the foundation of liability.
19. 3 Inst. 56. See Turner, MACL 195 at 212 et seq. for a discussion of the historical development.
20. *Keat* (1697) Comb 406 at 409.
1. (1762) – see p. 258.

Thus, in *Fenton*[2] D threw stones down a mine and broke some scaffolding with the result that a corf being lowered into the mine overturned and P was killed. Tindal CJ told the jury that D's act was a trespass and the only question was whether it caused P's death.

Even in the nineteenth century, this doctrine was not accepted without reservation by the judges. A notable refusal to follow it is the direction of Field J in *Franklin*.[3] D, while walking on Brighton pier

"took up a good sized box from the refreshment stall on the pier and threw it into the sea."

The box struck P and killed him. The prosecution urged that, quite apart from the question of negligence, it was sufficient to show that the death was caused by an unlawful act – the tort against the refreshment stallkeeper; and relied on *Fenton*. Field J (with whom Mathew J agreed) held that the case must go to the jury "on the broad ground of negligence". Expressing his abhorrence of constructive crime, the judge asserted that

"the mere fact of a civil wrong committed by one person against another ought not to be used as an incident which is a necessary step in a criminal case."[4]

One *nisi prius* ruling, however, could not undermine so well-established a doctrine and it has continued to the present day, though in a modified form. In *Church*[5] the Court of Criminal Appeal held that it is wrong to direct a jury that to cause death by an unlawful act in relation to a human being is necessarily manslaughter.

"For such a verdict inexorably to follow, the unlawful act must be such as all sober and reasonable people would inevitably recognise must subject the other person to, at least, the risk of some harm resulting therefrom, albeit not serious harm."[6]

The importance of *Church* lies in the fact that it restricted the category of unlawful acts to acts "dangerous" in the sense described. Before *Church*, there was no doubt that death caused by such an act was manslaughter.[7] It was less clear that an unlawful act which was not obviously dangerous to human beings would not be sufficient if, by chance, it caused the death of a human being. In *Director of Public Prosecutions v Newbury*[8] where the House of Lords applied *Church*, Lord Salmon said that some crimes:

"need only what is called a basic intention,[9] which is an intention to do the acts which constitute the crime. Manslaughter is such a crime . . ."

2. (1830) 1 Lew CC 179.
3. (1883) 15 Cox CC 163.
4. Ibid., at 165.
5. [1966] 1 QB 59, [1965] 1 All ER 72; **SHC 332**. See also *Creamer* [1966] 1 QB 72 at 82, [1965] 3 All ER 257 at 262: "A man is guilty of involuntary manslaughter when he intends an unlawful act and one likely to do harm to the person and death results which was neither foreseen nor intended."
6. [1966] 1 QB 59 at 70.
7. *Larkin* [1943] 1 All ER 217 at 219; **SHC 335**.
8. [1977] AC 500, [1976] 2 All ER 365, HL. The House, approving the law as stated in *Larkin* and *Church*, disapproved dicta of Lord Denning MR in *Gray v Barr* [1971] 2 QB 554, [1971] 2 All ER 949, CA, which suggested that it must be proved that D *realised* that his act was likely to cause harm.
9. Lord Salmon is using "basic intent" in a sense quite different from that used above, p. 70. An intention to cause the *actus reus* of manslaughter is of course an intention to murder.

There must then be an intention to do an act which is in fact unlawful and dangerous. If D knows all the relevant facts, it is irrelevant that he does not realise that the act is unlawful or that it is dangerous. Lord Salmon said:

"In judging whether the act was dangerous, the test is not did the accused recognise that it was dangerous but would all sober and reasonable people recognise its danger."

The test of dangerousness is objective. The proposition of Edmund-Davies J in *Church* described the type of act from which a charge of manslaughter may result, not the intention (real or assumed) of the accused.[10] Hence s. 8 of the Criminal Justice Act 1967[11] had no effect on the law as stated in that case. D's ignorance that the act is unlawful cannot excuse him, if it is ignorance of the criminal law.[12] A material mistake of fact or civil law certainly, if reasonable, might, in principle, excuse. For this type of manslaughter the following conditions must be satisfied:

i) There must be an unlawful act.

ii) The act must be unlawful for some reason other than the negligent manner of its performance.

It is possible that there is a third condition – that the act must be one which causes "direct" harm. Each of these matters requires further discussion.

i) *The unlawful act.* It must be proved that the act was unlawful for frequently it is lawful for one person to inflict some slight degree of bodily harm on another. If the infliction of such slight harm should cause death, this will be accidental death and not a crime. A shoulder charge in the course of a game of football is a lawful act[13] and, if it chance to cause death, this will not be unlawful. It would be otherwise if precisely the same charge were inflicted on a person who had not consented to receive such treatment and who was not participating in the game. And, if excessive violence were used, even in the course of a lawful game, a resultant death would be manslaughter.[14] Similarly, a woman's consent to sexual intercourse is no defence if excessive force is used and death results.[15]

It is lawful in some circumstances for one person to inflict a degree of physical chastisement on another. A father may so chastise his children and may delegate this power to a schoolteacher.[16] If this should cause death, it will not be criminal, provided that D neither knew nor, as a reasonable

10. [1976] 2 All ER 370, per Lord Edmund-Davies.
11. Above, p. 85.
12. Above, p. 80.
13. Below, p. 383.
14. *Moore* (1898) 14 TLR 229. What is excessive force is a difficult question. One answer would be: force greater than that to which P consented; and he consented to such force as the rules of the game allow. But in *Moore*, Hawkins J refused to allow the rules to be put in evidence by the Crown "for it is not criminal and not necessarily either dangerous or malicious to break them." On the other hand, in *Bradshaw* (1878) 14 Cox CC 83, Bramwell LJ admitted evidence of the rules of the game for the defence as tending to show that D was not actuated by any malicious motive or intention and was not acting in a manner which he knew to be likely to be productive of death or injury. See below, p. 383. Cf. *A. W. Killingback's Application*, [1976] CLY 426 (Crim Inj Comp Bd).
15. *Sharmpal Singh* [1962] AC 188, PC.
16. *Cleary v Booth* [1893] 1 QB 465; but see below, p. 386.

man, ought to have known that death or grievous bodily harm was likely to result. If the chastisement is unlawful and it causes death, this is man-slaughter.[17]

In Lamb[18] D pointed a loaded gun at his friend, P, in jest. He did not intend to alarm P and P was not alarmed. Because they did not understand the way in which a revolver works, both thought that there was no danger; but, when D pulled the trigger, he shot and killed his friend. The pointing of the gun was not an assault because P did not apprehend any injury and because D did not intend him to do so; nor was it an attempt to assault. It was therefore a misdirection to tell the jury that this was an unlawful and dangerous act. It was not "unlawful in the criminal sense of that word" and it was not in point that D may have been civilly liable.

In Newbury the unlawful act consisted in throwing a piece of paving stone from the parapet of a bridge as a train approached. The question for the House of Lords was whether D could properly be convicted if he did not foresee that his act might cause harm to another. It was not, and, the House thought, could not be argued that the act was lawful. On the hypothesis that no injury to the person was foreseen the unlawfulness may have consisted in (i) the tort of trespass[19] or (ii) the offence of criminal damage or (iii) an offence of endangering passengers contrary to s. 34 of the Offences against the Person Act 1861.

Another decision which is unsatisfactory in this respect is Cato[20] where D caused P's death by injecting him with heroin with his consent. The court, accepting that the administration was not an offence under the Misuse of Drugs Act and assuming for this purpose that it was not an offence under s. 23 of the Offences against the Person Act 1861,[1] said "the unlawful act would be described as injecting the deceased [P] with a mixture of heroin and water which at the time of the injection and for the purposes of the injection Cato had unlawfully taken into his possession." The act was thus closely associated with other acts which are offences but it is submitted that neither this nor the fact that the act excites strong moral condemnation should be enough.

Where the prosecution rely on an unlawful act which does not require a specific intent and D was intoxicated at the time, it is immaterial that he lacked the mens rea of the crime in question and even that he was unconscious: Lipman[2] where D killed P by cramming a sheet into her mouth and striking her while he was on an L.S.D. "trip" and believed he was in the centre of the earth being attacked by snakes. Though the jury convicted on the grounds that D was reckless or grossly negligent when,

17. Hopley (1860) 2 F & F 202; Pennington [1958] Crim LR 690.
18. [1967] 2 QB 981, [1967] 2 All ER 1282, CA; SHC 334.
19. A tort should not be regarded as a sufficient unlawful act. Cf. Franklin, above, p. 346 and Lamb, supra.
20. [1976] 1 All ER 260.
    1. Below, p. 403. In fact, Cato was convicted of the offence under s. 23 so the remarks discussed in the text may be regarded as obiter.
    2. [1970] 1 QB 152, [1969] 3 All ER 410; SHC 95. The case was heavily criticised. See Hooker [1969] Crim LR 547; Orchard [1970] Crim LR 132; Glazebrook [1970] CLJ 21; Buxton [1970] Annual Survey of Commonwealth Law, 128 and 134. It was not followed in Australia: Haywood [1971] VR 755 (Crockett J) but has now been affirmed by the House of Lords in Majewski (above, p. 211).

quite consciously, he took the drugs, the Court of Appeal upheld the conviction by applying the *Church* doctrine. The unlawful act was the battery committed on P while D was unconscious.

ii) *Unlawfulness arising otherwise than through negligence.* This requirement is implicit in the formulation of the rule. An act which all sober and reasonable people would realise entailed the risk (*sc.*, an unjustifiable risk) of harm to others almost certainly becomes the tort of negligence when harm results and therefore the reference to "an unlawful act" would be otiose if it did not mean unlawful in some other respect. This is in accordance with the well-established rule[3] that negligence sufficient to found civil liability is not necessarily enough for criminal guilt, that death caused in the course of committing the tort of negligence is not necessarily manslaughter. But the limitation goes further than this: there are degrees of negligence which are *criminally* punishable which are yet not sufficient to found a charge of manslaughter. If, then, the unlawfulness, whether civil or criminal, of the act arises solely from the negligent manner in which it is performed, death caused by the act will not necessarily be manslaughter. This follows from the decision of the House of Lords in *Andrews v Director of Public Prosecutions.*[4]

In that case Du Parcq J told the jury that if D killed P in the course of dangerous driving contrary to s. 11 of the Road Traffic Act 1930 he was guilty of manslaughter. Lord Atkin (who clearly regarded dangerous driving as a crime of negligence)[5] said that, if the summing up had rested there, there would have been misdirection:

"There can be no doubt that this section covers driving with such a high degree of negligence as that, if death were caused, the offender would have committed manslaughter. But the converse is not true, and it is perfectly possible that a man may drive at a speed or in a manner dangerous to the public, and cause death, and yet not be guilty of manslaughter."[6]

Lord Atkin expressly distinguished[7] between acts which are unlawful because of the negligent manner in which they are performed and acts which are unlawful for some other reason:

"There is an obvious difference in the law of manslaughter between doing an unlawful act and doing a lawful act with a degree of carelessness which the legislature makes criminal."

His Lordship's next sentence implies that killing in the course of unlawful acts generally *was* manslaughter:

"If it were otherwise a man who killed another while driving without due care and attention would *ex necessitate* commit manslaughter."

This passage has been severely criticised[8] and it is certainly unhappily phrased. "... doing a lawful act with a degree of carelessness which the

---

3. Below, p. 353.
4. [1937] AC 576, [1937] 2 All ER 552; **SHC 341.**
5. See above, p. 91. The offence of dangerous driving is now abolished. Below, p. 482.
6. [1937] AC at 584, [1937] 2 All ER at 556, 557.
7. [1937] AC at 585, [1937] 2 All ER at 557.
8. Turner, MACL at 238.

legislature makes criminal" is a contradiction in terms, for the act so done is plainly not a lawful act. But the distinction evidently intended, viz., between acts which are unlawful because of negligent performance and acts which are unlawful for some other reason, is at least intelligible and, in view of the established distinction between civil and criminal negligence, a necessary limitation.

In *Lowe*,[9] the Court of Appeal held that D is not guilty of manslaughter simply on the ground that he has committed the offence under s. 1(1) of the Children and Young Persons Act 1933 of neglecting his child so as to cause unnecessary suffering or injury to its health, and that neglect has caused death. The Court disapproved *Senior*[10] which, on similar facts, held that this was manslaughter. *Lowe* has now been overruled on its interpretation of the 1933 Act and *Senior* to some extent rehabilitated by *Sheppard*[11] – but not on this point, on which, it is thought, *Lowe* and not *Senior* represents the law. Death had certainly been caused by unlawful and dangerous conduct, but the Court distinguished between omission and commission.

". . . if I strike a child in a manner likely to cause harm it is right that if the child dies I may be charged with manslaughter. If, however, I omit to do something with the result that it suffers injury to its health which results in its death, we think that a charge of manslaughter should not be an inevitable consequence even if the omission is deliberate."

If the omission is no more than an act of negligence then it is right that the doctrine of the unlawful and dangerous act does not apply and D is not guilty in the absence of gross negligence; but if the omission is truly *wilful* – a deliberate omission to summon medical aid, knowing it to be necessary, there seems to be no valid ground for the distinction.[12]

iii) *Likely to cause harm.* The act must be one which any sober and reasonable man would realise was likely to cause "harm". The harm need not be serious but to be "harm" it must presumably involve some degree of pain or injury. A mere touching is presumably not harm.

A battery which kills is necessarily manslaughter if it is intended (as most batteries are) to cause any degree of physical harm.[13] If the battery is not intended to cause harm – as in the case of a mere touching without consent – the question is whether any reasonable man would necessarily have foreseen the risk of some harm resulting – a question which in most such cases must surely be answered in the negative. It is clear that an assault, as distinct from a battery, is sufficient if it is committed in such circumstances that the reasonable man would realise that it is likely to cause bodily injury. In *Conner*[14] D was guilty of manslaughter where she threw a piece of iron at her child intending to frighten it and accidentally killed another of her own children as it came in through the door. In *Larkin*,[15] O had been

9. [1973] QB 702, [1973] 1 All ER 805.
10. [1899] 1 QB 283.
11. [1981] AC 394, [1980] 3 All ER 899, 72 Cr App Rep 82, HL.
12. See editorial comment in [1976] Crim LR 529.
13. *Alabaster* (1912) 47 LJN 397; *Woods* (1921) 85 JP 272; *Garforth* [1954] Crim LR 936, CCA.
14. (1835) 7 C & P 438.
15. [1943] 1 All ER 217; **SHC 335**. The case is reported only on another point in [1943] 1 KB 174.

committing "adultery" with D's mistress, P. D took a razor and, according to his story, pulled it out of his pocket with the intention only of terrifying O by the show of the razor. P, being groggy with drink, swayed against him and her throat was cut by the razor as he held it out for the purpose of frightening O. Oliver J told the jury that if this story were true, D was guilty of manslaughter and the Court of Criminal Appeal held that this was a correct direction. The distinction was again between acts which are unlawful only because negligently performed and acts which are otherwise unlawful:

"If a person is engaged in doing a lawful act, and in the course of doing that lawful act behaves so negligently as to cause the death of some other person, then it is for the jury to say, upon a consideration of the whole of the facts of the case, whether the negligence proved against the accused person amounts to manslaughter, and it is the duty of the presiding judge to tell them that it will not amount to manslaughter unless the negligence is of a very high degree; the expression most commonly used is unless it shows the accused to have been reckless as to the consequences of the act. That is where the act is lawful. Where the act which a person is engaged in performing is unlawful, then, if at the same time it is a dangerous act, that is an act which is likely to injure another person, and quite inadvertently he causes the death of that other person by that act, then he is guilty of manslaughter."[16]

Whether frightening is itself "harm", so that an act which is likely only to frighten amounts to manslaughter if it in fact kills, is less clear. In *Reid*,[17] causing fright by threats to use firearms was regarded as harm. P was in fact shot dead and whether the court would have taken the same view if the guns had not been loaded and P had died of fright is open to question.

iv) *Causing harm "directly"*. In *Dalby*[18] the court said that, in this type of manslaughter, D's act must be "directed at" P and likely, in itself, to cause some injury; but in *Goodfellow*[19] it was held that there is no requirement that the act be directed at P, saying that the court in *Dalby* meant no more than that "there must be no fresh intervening cause between the act and death". In fact, the decision in *Dalby* was certainly not based on the ground that D did not cause P's death – the point of law certified for the House of Lords postulated an "act [not directed at P] which is the substantial cause of the death" and the court left open the question whether D was guilty of manslaughter by gross negligence, which it could scarcely have done if it had decided that D did not cause P's death. This implies that there is a requirement of directness in addition to the ordinary requirement of the absence of any *novus actus interveniens*[20] sufficient to break the chain of causation.

16. Ibid., at 219, per Humphreys J.
17. (1976) 62 Cr App Rep 109. Cf. *Edmonds* [1963] 2 QB 142, [1963] 1 All ER 828, CCA, below, p. 424 (fright an "injury to the person" only if capable of producing injury through the operation of shock).
18. [1982] 1 All ER 916, [1982] 1 WLR 425, CA.
19. (1986) 83 Cr App Rep 23.
20. Above, p. 316.

In *Goodfellow*[1] D, because he wished to be re-housed, set fire to his council house, causing the deaths of his wife, friend and child. He was convicted of manslaughter. It was held to be immaterial that his act was not "directed at" the deceased; but the fire was, of course, a direct cause of their deaths. The conviction was upheld on the grounds both of unlawful act, and of reckless manslaughter. Reference was made to *Mitchell*[2] and *Pagett*.[3] *Mitchell* presents no difficulty in this regard. It was a case of transferred malice where an act done directly to O caused the death of P. *Pagett* is more problematical. It was not D's act of firing at the police which directly caused P's death, but the return fire by the officers.

In *Dalby* no reference was made to *Cato*[4] where D caused the death of P by injecting him with heroin with P's consent. An act done with P's consent would not be appropriately described as "directed at" him but it was certainly done directly to him, unlike the mere supply of the drug in *Dalby*. There must, however, remain some doubt whether there is any requirement that an unlawful act causing death should have been done directly by D to P.

2 Reckless Manslaughter

For many years the courts have used the terms "recklessness" and "gross negligence" to describe the fault required for involuntary manslaughter, other than constructive manslaughter, without any clear definition of either term. It was not clear whether these terms were merely two ways of describing the same thing, or whether they represented two distinct conditions of fault. The fifth edition of this work adopted the latter view, distinguishing between gross negligence manslaughter, where the gross negligence must be whether death or serious injury be caused, and reckless manslaughter where the recklessness might be as to death, personal injury, whether serious or slight, and[5] possibly any injury to "health or welfare". The matter must now be re-considered in the light of the decisions in *Lawrence* and *Caldwell*[6] and their application to manslaughter by the House of Lords in *Seymour*[7] and by the Privy Council in *Kong Cheuk Kwan v R*.[8] In *Seymour* it was held that the law was the same for manslaughter as for the statutory offence of causing death by reckless driving[9] and therefore that the *Lawrence* test was applicable, subject in a manslaughter case to the omission of reference to a risk of substantial damage to property. In *Kong Cheuk Kwan* the Privy Council expressly approved[10] of a comment made by Watkins LJ in delivering the judgment of the Court of Appeal in *Seymour*:[11]

---

1. (1986) 83 Cr App Rep 23, CA.
2. [1983] QB 741, [1983] 2 All ER 427, 76 Cr App Rep 293 CA, above, p. 73.
3. (1983) 76 Cr App Rep 279, CA, above, p. 318.
4. [1976] 1 All ER 260, above p. 348.
5. Following *Stone and Dobinson* [1977] QB 354, [1977] 2 All ER 341.
6. [1982] AC 341 and 510 respectively, above, p. 62.
7. [1983] 2 AC 493, [1983] 2 All ER 1058.
8. (1985) 82 Cr App Rep 18, [1985] Crim LR 787.
9. Below, p. 485.
10. At p. 26.
11. (1983) 76 Cr App Rep 211 at 216.

". . . we are of the view that it is no longer necessary or helpful to make reference to compensation and negligence. The *Lawrence* direction on recklessness is comprehensive and of general application to all offences, including manslaughter involving the driving of motor vehicles recklessly and should be given to juries without in any way being diluted. Whether a driver at the material time was conscious of the risk he was running or gave no thought to its existence, is a matter which affects punishment for which purposes the judge will have to decide, if he can, giving the benefit of doubt to the convicted person, in which state of mind that person had driven at the material time."

The reference to "compensation and negligence" clearly relates to the classic statement of the gross negligence doctrine by Hewart LCJ in *Bateman*.[12]

"In explaining to juries the test which they should apply to determine whether the negligence, in the particular case, amounted or did not amount to a crime, judges have used many epithets such as 'culpable', 'criminal', 'gross', 'wicked', 'clear', 'complete'. But whatever epithet be used and whether an epithet be used or not, in order to establish criminal liability the facts must be such that, in the opinion of the jury, the negligence of the accused went beyond a mere matter of compensation between subjects and showed such disregard for the life and safety of others, as to amount to a crime against the State and conduct deserving of punishment."

This passage has been criticised[13] on the grounds that (i) it is circular in that it tells the jury to convict if they think that D is guilty of a crime and (ii) it leaves a question of law to the jury. These criticisms are well founded; yet, if we are to have a crime based on a certain degree of negligence, no other test is possible – the jury must say whether the negligence is bad enough to attract criminal liability. The "*Bateman* test" has the virtue that it draws attention to the fact that there exists civil liability for less degrees of negligence and that criminal liability should be reserved for gross aberrations.

Bateman received general approval from Lord Atkin in *Andrews*, though he noted its circular nature[14] and it seems to have been accepted as an authoritative statement until *Seymour*.

If there still exists a gross negligence test, separate from that of *Lawrence* recklessness, *Kong Cheuk Kwan* was surely a case in which the jury ought to have been directed on it. It arose out of a collision in clear sunny weather between two hydrofoils carrying passengers from Hong Kong to Macau and the appellant was in command, and at the helm, of one of them. The clear implication is that there is no such separate test. If so, the law of involuntary manslaughter has been significantly simplified.[15] This conclusion may, however, be premature, for the courts may not have realised the

12. (1925) 19 Cr App Rep 8 at 11. (Negligent medical treatment by a doctor causing death.)
13. By Turner, MACL 211 Russell, 592–594.
14. [1937] AC at 583, [1937] 2 All ER at 556 and see the Court of Criminal Appeal [1937] WN 69.
15. Writers trying to elucidate the law have, however, experienced great difficulty in doing so. See articles at [1983] Crim LR 764 and 776 and [1984] Crim LR 467, 476 and 479.

full significance of that step. If the *Lawrence* direction is "comprehensive and of general application" to manslaughter, then so is the "lacuna".[16] Lamb[17] who, at the time, the Court of Appeal confidently thought might have been convicted of manslaughter on the ground of "criminal negligence", could no longer be so convicted. While the elimination of gross negligence as sufficient fault for manslaughter has been recommended by the Criminal Law Revision Committee[18] and may be no bad thing, it would be a significant change in the law as it was understood to be before *Lawrence* and one to which many judges would certainly be unsympathetic. Moreover, in *Andrews*, Lord Atkin[19] seems to have foreseen the lacuna (or something very like it) and thought it no answer to the charge. In *Goodfellow*, Lane LCJ said that the question in *Kong Cheuk Kwan* was whether the defendant was "guilty of recklessness (or gross negligence)". In fact, the Privy Council said nothing about gross negligence; but the use of the words in parentheses suggests that the Lord Chief Justice is aware of the problem and will not necessarily regard *Lawrence* recklessness as the exclusive test when the time comes to decide the matter. A dual test is justifiable only if there is some difference in the results which have to be proved to have been foreseen or foreseeable. For *Lawrence*, it is "physical injury to some other person" – nothing, be it noted, about injury to "health or welfare". If gross negligence is a separate criterion, then it would seem reasonable, as suggested in earlier editions of this work, that it be negligence as to death or serious injury. If gross negligence as to any injury will suffice, that, as noted earlier, makes nonsense of the *Lawrence* test of recklessness and results in a simple (and savage) test of gross negligence liability for a very serious offence.

In *Jennings v United States Government*[20] the House of Lords rejected the argument that "motor manslaughter" had been abolished by the creation in 1956 of the offences of causing death by dangerous and by reckless driving and the repeal in 1977 of the former offence. "Motor manslaughter" is not a separate legal category. It is just involuntary manslaughter where the implement causing death happens to be a motor vehicle. The law is no different where the death is caused by a gun, a hydrofoil, or a train. Causing death by reckless driving and manslaughter clearly overlap but are not exactly co-incident for it appears that, if D takes an obvious and serious risk of causing substantial damage to property and happens to cause death, he will be guilty of the statutory offence, but not of manslaughter. A statement in *Seymour*[1] that "in order to constitute the offence of manslaughter the risk of death being caused by the manner of the defendant's driving must be very high" has been charitably explained in *Kong Cheuk Kwan* as being advice to prosecutors as to the cases in which it might still be appropriate to charge the common law rather than the statutory offence. That is not what it said but is how it should, and no doubt will, be treated.

16. Above, p. 65.
17. Above, pp. 65 and 348.
18. Fourteenth Report, Cmnd. 7844, para. 121.
19. [1937] AC 576 at 581, [1937] 2 All ER 552 at 555.
20. [1982] 3 All ER 104.
 1. (1985) 82 Cr App Rep 18 at 25.

Reform. The Criminal Law Revision Committee has recommended that involuntary manslaughter be abolished and replaced by a new offence of causing death recklessly, punishable with a maximum of 14 years imprisonment.[2] "Recklessly" is used in the sense proposed by the Law Commission.[3]

3 Offences Ancillary to Murder

Parliament was not content to leave to the common law the punishment of acts preliminary to murder. The Offences against the Person Act 1861 created offences of conspiracy, solicitation, attempt and threats to murder. The offences of attempt were particularly complicated[4] and were repealed by the Criminal Law Act 1967. Attempts to commit murder are now governed by the Criminal Attempts Act 1981.[5] The conspiracy provision was repealed by the Criminal Law Act 1977 and conspiracy to murder is governed by that Act.

1) *Solicitation*

By s. 4 of the Offences against the Person Act 1861 (as amended by the Criminal Law Act 1977) it is an offence punishable with life imprisonment to

"solicit, encourage, persuade or endeavour to persuade or . . . propose to any person, to murder any other person."

This provision adds nothing to the common law of incitement except perhaps on a jurisdictional point. It is expressly provided that the person to be murdered need not be a British subject or within the jurisdiction; but this would generally not be necessary at common law either, since murder by a British citizen is indictable here though committed abroad.[6] The section, however, would catch an alien who, within the jurisdiction, incited the commission of murder abroad and who might otherwise be immune under the rule in *Board of Trade v Owen*.[7]

The offence may be committed by the publication of an article in a newspaper and it is immaterial that the readers of the newspapers are not identified.[8] It seems, however, that the offence is not committed unless the mind of the person solicited, etc., is reached. Lord Alverstone CJ so held in *Krause*,[9] applying this limitation even to "endeavour to persuade" which might be thought to cover an unsuccessful attempt to communicate. He held, however, that there was a common law attempt to commit the

2. CLRC, OAP/R, paras. 88–94.
3. Law Com. No. 89.
4. See the first edition of this book, pp. 250–253.
5. Above, p. 287.
6. Above, p. 309. Cf. Greaves's note on the subject in Russell, 612, n. 2.
7. [1957] AC 602, [1957] 1 All ER 411; above, p. 268.
8. *Most* (1881) 7 QBD 244.
9. (1902) 66 JP 121. Contrast *Horton v Mead*, below, p. 466.

statutory offence where it was not proved that the offending letters, though sent, had ever reached the addressee.[10] If it is proved that the letter or other publication did reach the addressee, it is not necessary to prove that his mind was in any way affected by it.[11]

In deciding whether the words amount to a solicitation, etc., the jury will take account of (a) the language used; (b) the occasion on which it was used; (c) the persons to whom the words were used, and (d) the circumstances surrounding their use. In *Diamond*,[11] where Coleridge J so directed in leaving to the jury an article extolling the virtues of the assassins of tyrants, the occasion was just after an attempt on the life of the Viceroy of India, and the persons addressed were not "a debating society of philosophers or divines" but "anybody whom the paper would reach in this country or in Ireland."

The proposed victims need not be named, provided that they are a sufficiently well-defined class. Where the indictment used the words "sovereigns and rulers of Europe" Phillimore J thought "rulers" a somewhat vague word, but there were some eighteen or twenty sovereigns in Europe and that was a sufficiently well-defined class.[12]

2) *Threats to Kill*

Section 16 of the Offences against the Person Act 1861 created an offence of making written threats to murder.[13] The Criminal Law Act 1977, Schedule 12, replaces that provision with a new and broader section 16.

"A person who without lawful excuse makes to another a threat, intending that that other would fear that it would be carried out, to kill that other or a third person shall be guilty of an offence and liable on conviction on indictment to imprisonment for a term not exceeding ten years."

The offence is triable either way.[14] It follows closely the pattern of section 2 of the Criminal Damage Act 1971[15] which relates to threats to destroy or damage property. The threat may take any form[16] and presumably may be implied as well as express.[17] In principle, it is thought that a threat should be "made to another" only when communicated; but, since it has been held that a "demand" is "made" within section 21(1) of the Theft Act when and where a letter containing it is posted,[18] it is at least possible that the same might be decided in the case of a threat. The words "to another" make no difference, since the demand under section 21 must impliedly be made to another.

10. See also *Banks* (1873) 12 Cox CC 393 at 399, per Quain J.
11. (1920) 84 JP 211; *Most*, supra; *Krause*, supra.
12. *Antonelli and Barberi* (1905) 70 JP 4.
13. See the third edition of this book, p. 266.
14. Criminal Law Act 1977, Schedule 2.
15. Below, p. 700.
16. Below, p. 701.
17. Cf. *Solanke* [1969] 3 All ER 1383, [1970] 1 WLR 1.
18. *Treacy v Director of Public Prosecutions* [1971] AC 537, HL; below, p. 589.

There would be a lawful excuse for making the threat if, in the circumstances known to D, the killing would be excusable if the threat were carried out, as where D makes the threat in self-defence.[19] A threat to kill may, however, be excusable where actual killing would not. To cause fear of death might be reasonable to prevent crime or arrest an offender whereas actually to kill would be quite unreasonable.[20] In many cases it will be desirable to tell the jury this.[1] Where there is some evidence of a lawful excuse, the onus is on the Crown to prove its absence and the question is always one for the jury.[2]

3) Concealment of Birth

This offence when first created by statute in 1623[3] was limited to (i) an illegitimate child who (ii) was born alive and whose body was disposed of so as to conceal its death (iii) by its mother. The current statute, the Offences against the Person Act 1861, s. 60, is subject to none of these limitations; it applies to any child, legitimate or not and whether born alive or not, whose body is disposed of so as to conceal its birth, by anyone. The section provides:

"If any woman shall be delivered of a child, every person who shall, by any secret disposition of the dead body of the said child, whether such child died before, at, or after its birth, endeavour to conceal the birth thereof, shall be guilty of [an offence triable either way] and being convicted thereof shall be liable, at the discretion of the court, to be imprisoned for any term not exceeding two years. . . ."

The expressed object of the original statute was to catch those women who would otherwise escape on a murder charge through the difficulty of proving live-birth and it was provided, indeed, that the woman should suffer death as in the case of murder. Under a later Act,[4] which repealed the 1623 provision, conviction of the new offence thereby created was possible only after an acquittal on an indictment for murder; but the current offence is an independent substantive crime for which an indictment will lie in the first instance. It was formerly the law that a person acquitted of murder, infanticide or child destruction might be convicted, on the same indictment, of concealment of birth; but this rule was abolished by the Criminal Law Act 1967, Sch. 2.

The test of a "secret disposition" seems to be whether there was a likelihood that the body would be found. So, said Bovill CJ, it would be a secret disposition

"if the body were placed in the middle of a moor in the winter, or on the top of a mountain, or in any other secluded place, where the body would not be likely to be found."[5]

19. See above, p. 240.
20. The two preceding sentences were approved by the Court of Appeal in *Cousins* [1982] 2 All ER 115 at 117.
  1. *Cousins*, supra.
  2. *Cousins*, supra.
  3. 21 Jac. 1. c. 27.
  4. 43 Geo. 3 c. 58.
  5. *Brown* (1870) LR 1 CCR 244.

If a body were thrown from a cliff top to the sea-shore, it might be a secret disposition if the place were secluded, not if it were much frequented.[6] So where the body was left in a closed but unlocked box in D's bedroom in such a way as to attract the attention of those who daily entered the room, it was held that there was no secret disposition.[7]

The accused must be proved to have done some act of disposition after the child has died. If the living body of the child is concealed and thereafter dies in the place of concealment, this offence is not committed,[8] though it is probable that murder or manslaughter is.

According to Erle J in *Berriman*[9] the child must have

"arrived at that stage of maturity at the time of birth that it might have been a living child";

so that the concealment of a foetus but a few months old would be no offence.[10]

4) *Other Offences*

It is a common law misdemeanour to dispose of or destroy a dead body with intent to prevent an inquest from being held.[11] It is an offence under the Perjury Act 1911 wilfully to make a false statement relating to births or deaths, or the live birth of a child.[12] And it is a summary offence under the Births and Deaths Registration Act 1953, s. 36, to fail to give information concerning births and deaths when under a duty, as defined in the Act, to do so.

4 Complicity in Suicide and Suicide Pacts[13]

It was felony at common law for a sane person of the age of responsibility to kill himself either intentionally or in the course of trying to kill another.[14] Such a suicide was regarded as self-murder. Though the offender was, in the nature of things, personally beyond the reach of the law, his guilt was not without important consequences at common law, since it resulted in the forfeiture of his property. The results were more important, however, where the attempt failed, for then:

6. Ibid.

7. *George* (1868) 11 Cox CC 41. Cf. *Sleep* (1864) 9 Cox CC 559; *Rosenburg* (1906) 70 JP 264.

8. *Coxhead* (1845) 1 Car & Kir 623 (decided under 9 Geo. 4, c. 31, but the principle is the same); *May* (1867) 10 Cox CC 448.

9. (1854) 6 Cox CC 388 at 390.

10. *Colmer* (1864) 9 Cox CC 506 is to the contrary but is doubted by Russell, 611, n. 69 and Archbold, 20–94.

11. Below, p. 756. Cf. *Hunter* [1972] Crim LR 369.

12. Below, p. 749.

13. For general discussions, see Williams, *The Sanctity of Life*, Ch. 7; St. John Stevas, *Life, Death and the Law*, Ch. 6; Second Report of the Criminal Law Revision Committee, Cmnd. 1187 (1960).

14. Hawkins, 1 PC 77.

i) Since D had attempted to commit a felony he was guilty, under ordinary common law principles, of the misdemeanour of attempted suicide.[15]

ii) If D, in the course of trying to kill himself, killed another, he was guilty of murder under the doctrine of transferred malice.[16]

Though suicide was regarded as "not a very serious crime",[17] an intention to commit it was thus the *mens rea* of murder. Moreover, one who was an accessory or principal in the second degree to the suicide of another was likewise guilty of murder as a secondary party. It followed that the survivor of a suicide pact was also guilty of murder, for, even if he did not actually kill, he was an aider and abettor, or at least an accessory before the fact to the other party's self-murder.

Suicide has now ceased to be a crime by virtue of the Suicide Act 1961 which simply provides that

"The rule of law whereby it is a crime for a person to commit suicide is hereby abrogated."

It inevitably follows that (i) attempted suicide has also now ceased to be criminal; and (ii) that there is no room for the doctrine of transferred malice where D kills P in the course of trying to kill himself, for there is no malice to transfer.

In the latter case, D's liability will now depend on the general principles of murder and manslaughter. Thus, if the death of P were utterly unforeseeable, it would be accidental death; if a reasonable man would certainly have foreseen the likelihood of killing (or, perhaps, seriously injuring) another, it will probably be manslaughter; and, if D himself foresaw this as virtually certain it may be murder.[18]

1) *Complicity in Another's Suicide*

Section 2 of the Suicide Act creates a new offence:

"A person who aids, abets, counsels or procures the suicide of another or an attempt by another to commit suicide, shall be liable on conviction on indictment to imprisonment for a term not exceeding fourteen years."

The words "aids, abets, counsels or procures", are those used to define secondary participation in crime[19] but here they are used to define the principal offence. The interpretation of the words should be the same.[20] As in the law of secondary participation the words imply that the crime has been committed or attempted.[1] Advising another to commit suicide does not amount to abetting or counselling unless and until that other does

---

15. Not the felony of attempted murder under Offences against the Person Act 1861, s. 15: *Burgess* (1862) 9 Cox CC 247; *Mann* [1914] 2 KB 107. Section 15 has been repealed by the Criminal Law Act 1967.

16. *Hopwood* (1913) 8 Cr App Rep 143; *Spence* (1957) 41 Cr App Rep 80. Above, p. 73.

17. *French* (1955) 39 Cr App Rep 192, per Lord Goddard CJ.

18. See above, p. 327.

19. Cf. the Accessories and Abettors Act 1861, ss. 2, 8 and the Magistrates' Courts Act 1980, s. 44; above, p. 130.

20. See *Reed* [1982] Crim LR 819, CA; *A-G v Able*, infra.

1. Above, p. 131.

commit suicide. Since the aiding, etc., is the principal offence, an indictment will lie for an attempt to aid, etc. so that unsuccessful advice or
encouragement is punishable as an attempt.[2] The distribution of a booklet
giving advice to any person who wishes to commit suicide on how to do so
efficiently and painlessly is not necessarily an offence under the section. In
A-G v Able,[3] Woolf J refused to grant a declaration that the distribution
was unlawful, holding that an offence would be committed only if the
distributor intended that the booklet would be used by someone contemplating suicide and that he would be (and in fact was) assisted or
encouraged to do so. This is in accordance with the ordinary law of
secondary participation.[4]

There were very sound reasons for the abolition of the felony of suicide.
The felon was beyond the reach of punishment; the legal sanction was not
an effective deterrent – there were some 5,000 suicides a year; and the effect
was merely to add to the distress and pain of the bereaved relatives. The
most important practical effect of the Act, however, was its repeal by
implication of the crime of attempted suicide. This also recognised the
realities of the situation for it had been the practice for many years to
institute proceedings only where it was necessary for the accused's protection, for example, because no relatives and friends were willing to give help.
Thus, in 1959, of a total of 4,980 suicide attempts known to the police (and
an estimated total of 25,000 actual concealed from the police) only 518
prosecutions were brought. The protection of the attempter may now be
secured under Part II of the Mental Health Act 1983.

The new crime of complicity in suicide is one which covers a variety of
situations varying almost infinitely in moral culpability; from D who
encourages P to commit suicide for the purpose of inheriting his property,
to that of D who merely supplies a deadly drug to a suffering and dying P
who is anxious to accelerate the end. In order to achieve consistency in the
bringing of prosecutions, this is made one of those crimes in which the
consent of the Director of Public Prosecutions is required.[5]

2) *Suicide Pacts*

A party to a suicide pact who aids, abets, counsels or procures the other
party to commit suicide is of course guilty of the offence under s. 2 of the
Suicide Act.[6]

The survivor of such a pact may, however, have either himself killed the
deceased or have procured a third party to do it. Such cases do not fall
within the Suicide Act, but within the Homicide Act 1957, s. 4(1), which,
as amended by the Suicide Act provides:

2. *McShane* [1977] Crim LR 737, CA, discussed by Smith in *Crime, Proof and Punishment*, 21
at 32–33.
3. [1984] QB 795, [1984] 1 All ER 277, QBD.
4. Above, pp. 133–148. See K. J. M. Smith, [1983] Crim LR 579.
5. Williams argues in favour of the legalisation of the abetting of a suicide for unselfish
reasons: *The Sanctity of Life*, 271–276.
6. Until the enactment of the Suicide Act, this was manslaughter under the Homicide Act
1957, s. 4.

"It shall be manslaughter and shall not be murder for a person acting in pursuance of a suicide pact between him and another to kill the other[7] or be party to the other being killed by a third person."

"Suicide pact" is defined by s. 4(3) of the Homicide Act as

"a common agreement between two or more persons having for its object the death of all of them, whether or not each is to take his own life, but nothing done by a person who enters into a suicide pact shall be treated as done by him in pursuance of the pact unless it is done while he has the settled intention of dying in pursuance of the pact."

The onus on a charge of murder of establishing the defence of suicide pact is put by s. 4(2) on the accused and the standard of proof required is, no doubt, a balance of probabilities.

The distinction between complicity in suicide and manslaughter by suicide pact is not entirely satisfactory. The latter, being punishable with life imprisonment, is evidently the more serious crime; yet, since the person guilty of it always intends to die himself, it is difficult to see how it can compare in moral heinousness with the case of D who incites P to die in order that he may live and enjoy P's property.

The distinction between the two crimes will frequently be very fine. If D and P agree to gas themselves and D alone survives, it appears that he will be liable under the Homicide Act if he turned on the tap[8] and under the Suicide Act if P did. It may frequently be difficult to establish who did such an act and this is recognised by the provision in s. 2(2) of the Suicide Act that, on the trial of an indictment for murder or manslaughter, the jury may find the accused guilty of complicity in suicide if that is proved. If D is charged with murder and he establishes on a balance of probabilities that P committed suicide in pursuance of a suicide pact he is entitled to be acquitted of murder and may presumably be convicted of complicity in suicide since he has, in effect, admitted his guilt. If, however, D were charged with complicity and it appeared that he had killed P, he would have to be acquitted.

5 Infanticide[9]

The Infanticide Act 1938, s. 1(1), provides:

"Where a woman by any wilful act or omission causes the death of her child being a child under the age of twelve months, but at the time of the act or omission the balance of her mind was disturbed by reason of her not having fully recovered from the effect of giving birth to the child or by reason of the effect of lactation consequent upon the birth of the child, then, notwithstanding that the circumstances were such that but for this

---

7. If, otherwise than in pursuance of a suicide pact, D kills P at P's request, D is of course guilty of murder. Cf. *Robinson*, above, p. 146.
8. But if D pours out a glass of poison and P takes it, he will be liable under the Suicide Act.
9. Seaborne Davies, "Child-Killing in English Law" (1937) 1 MLR 203; MACL 301; Williams, *The Sanctity of Life*, 25–45.

Act the offence would have amounted to murder, she shall be guilty of [an offence], to wit of infanticide, and may for such offence be dealt with and punished as if she had been guilty of the offence of manslaughter of the child."

This enactment replaces a statute of 1922 which confined the defence to a "newly-born" child, a term which the Court of Criminal Appeal had held to be inapplicable to a child of thirty-five days, so that the mother was convicted of murder.[10] The 1922 Act was itself the result of an agitation over very many years during which it was practically impossible to get convictions of murder by mothers of their young children because of the disapproval by public and professional opinion of a law which regarded such killings as ordinary murders. Where a conviction was obtained, the judge had to pronounce a sentence of death which everyone, except perhaps the prisoner, knew would not be carried out. A number of reasons were advanced why infanticide should be considered less reprehensible than other killings: (i) The injury done to the child was less, for it was incapable of the kind of suffering which might be undergone by the adult victim of a murder; (ii) the loss of its family was less great; (iii) the crime did not create the sense of insecurity in society which other murders caused; (iv) generally, the heinousness of the crime was less, the motive very frequently being the concealment of the shame of the birth of an illegitimate child; and (v) where the killing is done by the mother, her responsibility may be reduced by the disturbance of her mind caused by the stress of the birth. It is, of course, the last of these considerations which is the governing one in the present legislation. The killing of an infant by persons other than the mother, or by the mother if the balance of her mind is not disturbed, remains murder.

The Act provides by s. 1(2) that a woman indicted for the murder of her child under the age of twelve months may be acquitted of murder and convicted of infanticide if the conditions of s. 1(1) are satisfied.

Where the charge is murder, an evidential burden on the issue of disturbance will fall on D; but the onus of *proof* remains with the Crown. Where the charge is infanticide, the onus of proving disturbance appears to be on the Crown; but this, of course, is unlikely to be contested.

It appears that the principles on which the Act was based may be no longer accepted and that mental illness is not now considered to be a significant cause of infanticide. In most cases the relationship of incomplete recovery from the effects of childbirth or lactation to the child-killing is remote.[11] When the Infanticide Act was passed, there was no defence of diminished responsibility to murder. The Butler Committee thought that that defence would now probably cover all cases and recommended the abolition of the separate offence of infanticide.[12] The CLRC disagreed, at first on the ground that, so long as the prosecution are unable to charge

10. *O'Donoghue* (1927) 20 Cr App Rep 132.
11. Butler Report, Cmnd. 6244 at paras. 19.23–19.24.
12. Ibid.

manslaughter by reason of diminished responsibility, infanticide has the advantage that it avoids the necessity of charging the mother with murder;[13] and later on the ground that diminished responsibility might not cover all the circumstances which in practice may be held to justify an infanticide verdict. According to the Royal College of Psychiatrists, these include "(1) overwhelming stress from the social environment being highlighted by the birth of a baby, with the emphasis on the unsuitability of the accommodation etc; (2) overwhelming stress from an additional member to a household struggling with poverty; (3) psychological injury, and pressures and stress from a husband or other member of a family from the mother's incapacity to arrange the demands of the extra member of the family; (4) failure of bonding between mother and child through illness or disability which impairs the development of the mother's capacity to care for the infant." In order to bring the law into line with its practical operation, and because of the difficulty of establishing a direct connection between giving birth and the imbalance of the woman's mind, the CLRC recommend that the test should be whether the balance of her mind was disturbed by reason of the effect of giving birth to the child *or circumstances consequent upon that birth*.[14] A dissentient view was that the effect would be to make adverse social conditions a defence to child killing.[15] Because of the decision to recommend the broadening of the offence (in law, if not in practice) the Committee abandoned its earlier tentative recommendation that the killing of older children of the family should be infanticide and not murder;[16] and that the maximum penalty should be five years imprisonment and not two, as they had previously been disposed to think.[17]

The Criminal Law Revision Committee thought that, because of the way in which the offence is drafted, it is not possible to charge a person with attempting to commit infanticide[18] but McCowan J has held that such an indictment will lie.[19]

6 Child Destruction and Abortion[20]

1 *Child Destruction*

It has already been observed that it is not murder to kill a child in the womb or while in the process of being born.[1] Though the killing of the child in the

---

13. CLRC/OAP/WP 26. The committee tentatively suggested that a person apparently suffering from diminished responsibility should be indictable for manslaughter but later withdrew this proposal: CLRC/OAP/R, para. 95.
14. CLRC/OAP/R, paras. 103–106.
15. See Annexes 7 and 8 to the Report.
16. Para. 106.
17. Para. 108.
18. CLRC/OAP/R, para. 113.
19. *K. A. Smith* [1983] Crim LR 739 and commentary.
20. See Williams, *The Sanctity of Life and the Criminal Law*, 139–223 (1958), and "The Legalization of Medical Abortion" *The Eugenics Review*, April, 1964; B. M. Dickens, *Abortion and the Law* (1966).
1. See above, p. 310.

womb after quickening was a misdemeanour at common law, the present law on the subject is statutory. Section 58 of the Offences against the Person Act 1861 (subject to the Abortion Act 1967[2]) prohibits attempts to procure miscarriage from any time after the conception of the child until its birth; and s. 1 of the Infant Life (Preservation) Act 1929 prohibits the killing of any child which is capable of being born alive. The two offences thus overlap. Procuring a miscarriage so as to kill a child capable of being born alive may amount to both offences. Killing a child in the process of being born is not procuring a miscarriage and can amount only to child destruction. Section 1 of the Infant Life (Preservation) Act provides:

"(1) Subject as hereinafter in this subsection provided, any person who, with intent to destroy the life of a child capable of being born alive, by any wilful act causes a child to die before it has an existence independent of its mother, shall be guilty of an offence, to wit, of child destruction, and shall be liable on conviction thereof on indictment to imprisonment for life: Provided that no person shall be found guilty of an offence under this section unless it is proved that the act which caused the death of the child was not done in good faith for the purpose only of preserving the life of the mother.

(2) For the purposes of this Act, evidence that a woman had at any material time been pregnant for a period of twenty-eight weeks or more shall be prima facie proof that she was at that time pregnant of a child capable of being born alive."

While the actual physical condition in which a foetus would be after birth is a matter for expert medical evidence, whether a foetus at that stage of development can properly be described as "a child capable of being born alive" is a question of law for the court. In *C v S*[3] the medical experts disagreed as to whether a foetus at the stage it will normally have reached by the 18th to the 21st week could be so described. The court held, in the light of the evidence that it would never be capable of breathing, that it could not.[4] Although the Abortion Act 1967, s. 5(1), uses the phrase, "protecting the life of the viable foetus", in respect of the provisions of the 1929 Act, it is not certain that "viable" means the same as "capable of being born alive". "Viable" may be taken to mean not only being born alive but surviving, in which case the phrase in the 1967 Act is more restrictive.

The jury may convict of this offence on an indictment for murder, manslaughter, infanticide or an offence under s. 58 of the Offences against the Person Act 1861; and on an indictment for child destruction, they may convict of an offence under s. 58 of the Offences against the Person Act 1861.

The Abortion Act 1967 now legalises abortion in certain circumstances and subject to certain formalities, but it is provided that this shall not affect the offence of child destruction. Where a foetus capable of being born alive is destroyed, it is no defence to show that the conditions prescribed in the 1967 Act were satisfied. Conversely, if the formalities prescribed by the

---

2. See below, p. 369.
3. [1987] 1 All ER 1230, [1987] 2 WLR 1108, CA (Civ. Div.).
4. Ibid., at 1238–1239 (Heilbron J). Cf. Wright, [1984] Crim LR 347; Tunkel and Wright, [1985] Crim LR 133.

1967 Act are not complied with, it may be no defence to a charge under s. 58 of the Offences against the Person Act to show that the act was done in good faith for the purpose only of preserving the life of the mother. Where the foetus is capable of being born alive, it is safe to procure an abortion only if both (a) the conditions of the 1967 Act are satisfied and (b) it is done in good faith for the purpose only of preserving the life of the mother. It has been recommended that subsection (2) should be repealed and the Abortion Act 1967 amended to authorise abortions up to the twenty-fourth week of pregnancy but not thereafter.[5]

A wider meaning was given to the words "for the purpose only of preserving the life of the mother" by Macnaghten J in *Bourne*.[6] This was *obiter*, so far as the Infant Life Preservation Act was concerned, since the charge was brought under the Offences against the Person Act 1861; but Macnaghten J took the view that those words represented the common law and were implicit in the 1861 Act by virtue of the word "unlawfully". He said:

"As I have said, I think those words ['for the purpose of preserving the life of the mother'] ought to be construed in a reasonable sense, and if the doctor is of opinion, on reasonable grounds and with adequate knowledge, that the probable consequence of the continuance of the pregnancy will be to make the woman a physical or mental wreck, the jury are quite entitled to take the view that the doctor who under these circumstances and in the honest belief, operates, is operating for the purpose of preserving the life of the mother."[7]

Both before and after this, however, the judge stressed that the test was whether the operation was performed in good faith for the purpose of preserving the *life* of the girl and the passage may be intended to refer only to such inquiries to health as will shorten life for the judge had said:[8]

". . . life depends upon health and health may be so gravely impaired that death results."

Informed medical opinion construed the judgment in the wider sense[9] and this appears to have been vindicated. In *Bergmann and Ferguson*[10] Morris J is reported to have said that the court will not look too narrowly into the question of danger to life where danger to health is anticipated. Then in *Newton and Stungo*[11] Ashworth J stated in his direction to the jury:

"Such use of an instrument is unlawful unless the use is made in good
faith for the purposes of preserving the life *or health* of the woman",

adding that this included mental as well as physical health. Newton was acquitted of manslaughter by criminal negligence, but convicted of manslaughter by unlawfully using an instrument[12] and of the offence under s. 58. He did not appeal (obviously the direction was favourable to him) and

5. See below, p. 370.
6. [1939] 1 KB 687, [1938] 3 All ER 615.
7. [1939] 1 KB at 693, 694, [1938] 3 All ER at 619.
8. [1939] 1 KB at 692, [1938] 3 All ER at 617.
9. Havard [1958] Crim LR at 605.
10. (1948) unreported; *The Sanctity of Life*, 154; 1 BMJ 1008.
11. [1958] Crim LR 469, fully considered by Havard in "Therapeutic Abortion", [1958] Crim LR 600.
12. That is, constructive manslaughter; see above, p. 345.

we thus have no appellate ruling on the question; but it is thought likely that Ashworth J's view would be accepted by the appellate courts.

The criterion of the defence as it has been applied by the courts is a subjective one; that is, the question is not whether the operation is in fact necessary to preserve the life of the mother but whether D believes it to be necessary.[13] In answering this question the court will take account of the size of the fee, a large fee being evidence of bad faith;[14] and whether D followed accepted medical practice.[15] What is the position if the operation was in fact necessary, but was performed by D in bad faith, to oblige, as he thought, the mere convenience of the woman and for a high fee? One view might be that there is no *actus reus* here,[16] but it is thought more likely that the defence will be limited to the case of a bona fide belief.[17] Thus, in *Newton*, it does not seem to have been decided that an operation was unnecessary; only that Newton did not bona fide believe it to be necessary.[18]

These cases all relate to s. 58 of the 1861 Act, where they are probably no longer in point.[19] Since they purport to be an interpretation of the proviso in the 1929 Act, however, they cannot be ignored in considering child destruction. On the other hand it is quite possible that the court, when actually confronted with the interpretation of the proviso, might take a stricter and narrower view of what constitutes the preservation of the life of the mother.

2) *Attempting to Procure Miscarriage*

The common law misdemeanour of abortion applied only after the child had quickened in the womb. To procure an abortion before this occurred was no crime. A statute of 1803[20] enacted that it should be a felony punishable by death to administer a poison with intent to procure the miscarriage of a woman quick with child and a felony punishable with imprisonment or transportation for fourteen years to administer poison with a like intent to a woman who was not proved to be quick with child. The distinction between quick and non-quick women gave rise to complications and it disappeared in the re-enactment of the law by the Offences against the Person Act 1837[1] which established the law substantially in its modern form. The current statute is the Offences against the Person Act 1861, which provides by s. 58:

13. *Bergmann and Ferguson* cited in *The Sanctity of Life*, 165.
14. A significant difference between the case of Newton and that of Stungo (who was acquitted) seems to have been that Stungo took a very small fee, Newton a high one.
15. See Havard [1958] Crim LR at 607, 608.
16. Cf. The discussion of *Dadson*, above, p. 37.
17. Cf. Williams, *The Sanctity of Life*, 166, who would agree with this conclusion on the ground that the crime is in the nature of an attempt. But it is just as much a substantive crime as burglary.
18. But even if it was necessary to carry out the operation, it was probably not necessary to carry it out in the way it was done – in a consulting room, the patient being sent back to a hotel in a taxi afterwards.
19. Infra.
20. 43 Geo. III. c. 58.
 1. 7 Will & 1 Vic. c. 85.

"Every woman being with child who, with intent to procure her own miscarriage, shall unlawfully administer to herself any poison or other noxious thing, or shall unlawfully use any instrument or other means whatsoever with the like intent, and whosoever, with intent to procure the miscarriage of any woman, whether she be or be not with child, shall unlawfully administer to her or cause to be taken by her any poison or other noxious thing, or shall unlawfully use any instrument or other means whatsoever with the like intent, shall be guilty of an offence, and being convicted thereof shall be liable . . . to imprisonment for life. . . ."

The extension of the law was of great practical importance, since most self-induced abortions occur before quickening. Certain modern anti-pregnancy techniques appear to offend against the law because they function after fertilisation of the ovum.[2]

The statute makes it clear beyond all doubt that the offence may be committed by the woman herself as well as by others, the only distinction being that if the woman herself is charged, it must be proved that she is in fact pregnant, whereas this is not necessary if the accused is someone other than the mother herself.

The Act is not confined to the use of a "poison or other noxious thing" or "any instrument"; the "other means" include manual interference, even though no instrument is employed and the medical evidence is that the act could not, in the circumstances, cause a miscarriage.[3] The *actus reus* consists simply in the *administration* of the poison or other noxious thing or the *use* of the instrument or other means.

The Act distinguishes between "poison" and "noxious thing" and it has been held that in the case of something other than a "recognised poison" the thing must be administered in such quantity as to be in fact harmful though not necessarily abortifacient.[4] A sleeping pill has been held not to be noxious;[5] and the administration in harmless quantities of oil of juniper was no *actus reus*;[6] but Denman J said that it would be otherwise if a thing, innocuous when administered in small quantities, were to be administered in such quantities as to be noxious. Field and Stephen JJ thought that if the thing were a "recognised poison" the offence might be committed even though the quantity given was so small as to be incapable of doing harm. The distinction is hardly a logical one for "recognised poisons" may be beneficial when taken in small quantities and in such a case the thing taken is no more poisonous than the oil of juniper was noxious.

It has been observed that the section makes a distinction between the case where the woman administers, etc., the thing to herself and that where it is administered to her by another. In the former case the woman must be proved to be with child, in the latter case, she need not. The importance of this distinction has been diminished by the decision in *Whitchurch*[7] that a

---

2. See Tunkel [1974] Crim LR 461.
3. *Spicer* [1955] Crim LR 772.
4. *Marlow* (1964) 49 Cr App Rep 49 (Brabin J); *Douglas* [1966] NZLR 45. Cf. *Marcus* [1981] 2 All ER 833, below, p. 403.
5. *Weatherall* [1968] Crim LR 115 (Judge Brodrick) below, p. 405.
6. *Cramp* (1880) 5 QBD 307.
7. (1890) 24 QBD 420; above, p. 283.

woman who is not pregnant may be convicted of conspiring with another to procure her own abortion and by the decision in *Sockett* that such a woman[8] may be convicted of aiding and abetting in the offence of the other, if it is complete. Thus, in effect, the woman will be excused on the ground that she is not with child only in cases where she is not acting in concert with another. While one view is that this interpretation has "set at naught" the intention of Parliament,[9] it has been argued elsewhere[10] that it would have been perfectly reasonable for Parliament to discriminate between the non-pregnant woman who calls in the back-street or professional abortionist and the non-pregnant woman who administers to herself an abortifacient in the solitude of her own bedroom. The point is perhaps not of great practical importance as it appears that it is not the practice to prosecute the mother today.[11]

3) *Knowingly Supplying or Procuring Poison, etc.*

Section 59 of the Offences against the Person Act makes a substantive crime of certain preparatory acts, some of which might amount to counselling or abetting the offence under s. 58. It provides:

"Whosoever shall unlawfully supply or procure any poison or other noxious thing, or any instrument or thing whatsoever, knowing that the same is intended to be unlawfully used or employed with intent to procure the miscarriage of any woman, whether she be or be not with child, shall be guilty of a misdemeanour, and being convicted thereof shall be liable ... to imprisonment ... for any term not exceeding five years ..."

It has recently been held[12] that the word "procure", on the first occasion on which it is used in the section, means "get possession of something of which you have not got possession already"; so D's conviction was quashed when there was no evidence as to how or when he had come into the possession of the instruments and the judge had directed the jury that the word was

"wide enough to include getting instruments or getting them together or preparing them for use".[13]

This leaves a gap in the legislation. As Crown counsel said:[14]

"... if a defendant went to a chemist and bought an instrument to abort A, he would have committed an offence, but if he then put the instrument away in a cupboard and later, for the purpose of aborting B went to the cupboard and took the instrument he would not have committed an offence."

The words, "knowing that the same is intended to be unlawfully used" have been construed in an extraordinarily wide sense and one highly

8. (1908) 72 JP 428; above, p. 159.
9. Williams, CLGP, 673.
10. Hogan, [1962] Crim LR at 690.
11. Cf. *The Sanctity of Life* at 146; *Peake* (1932) 97 JPN 353.
12. *Mills* [1963] 1 QB 522, [1963] 1 All ER 202, following *Scully* (1903) 23 NZLR 380.
13. [1963] 1 QB at 524.
14. Ibid. at 526.

unfavourable to the accused. Their natural meaning is surely that some person other than the accused must intend the unlawful user and that the accused must know of that intention. But it has been held that it is enough if the accused *believes* that the poison, e.c., is to be so used, so that it is no defence for him to show that the person supplied did not intend to use it[15] or that the person supplied was a policeman who had obtained the thing by false representations about a purely fictitious woman.[16] This construction was defended by Erle CJ, the rest of the Court concurring, on the extraordinary ground that

> "The defendant knew what his own intention was, and that was that the substance procured by him should be employed with intent to procure miscarriage."[17]

This attitude contrasts strikingly with the strict construction of the word "procure"; and these two cases, which have been dissented from in Victoria,[18] though followed elsewhere in the Commonwealth,[19] deserve reconsideration.

4) *The Abortion Act 1967*[20]

The law relating to abortion is modified in important respects by the Abortion Act 1967. In the Act:

> "'the law relating to abortion' means ss. 58 and 59 of the Offences against the Person Act 1861, and any rule of law relating to the procurement of abortion."

Section 1 of the Act provides:

> "**1 Medical termination of pregnancy**. – (1) Subject to the provisions of this section, a person shall not be guilty of an offence under the law relating to abortion when a pregnancy is terminated by a registered medical practitioner if two registered medical practitioners are of the opinion, formed in good faith –
>
> (a) that the continuance of the pregnancy would involve risk to the life of the pregnant woman, or of injury to the physical or mental health of the pregnant woman or any existing children of her family, greater than if the pregnancy were terminated; or
>
> (b) that there is a substantial risk that if the child were born it would suffer from such physical or mental abnormalities as to be seriously handicapped.
>
> (2) In determining whether the continuance of a pregnancy would involve such risk of injury to health as is mentioned in paragraph

---

15. *Hillman* (1863) 9 Cox CC 386, CCR.
16. *Titley* (1880) 14 Cox CC 502 (Stephen J).
17. (1863) 9 Cox CC at 387.
18. *Hyland* (1898) 24 VLR 101.
19. *Scully* (1903) 23 NZLR 380; *Nosworthy* (1907) 26 NZLR 536; *Neil* [1909] St R Qd 225; *Freestone* [1913] TPD 758; *Irwin v R* (1968) 68 DLR (2d) 485.
20. See Hoggett, "The Abortion Act 1967", [1968] Crim LR 247: *A Guide to the Abortion Act 1967* (Abortion Law Reform Association). On the working of the Act, see H. L. A. Hart, "Abortion Law Reform: The English Experience" (1972), 8 MULR 389; M. Simms [1970] Crim LR 567, 573 and [1971] Crim LR 86; J. M. Finnis, [1971] Crim LR 3.

(a) of subsection (1) of this section, account may be taken of the pregnant woman's actual or reasonably foreseeable environment.

(3) Except as provided by subsection (4) of this section, any treatment for the termination of pregnancy must be carried out in a hospital vested in the Minister of Health or the Secretary of State under the National Health Service Acts, or in a place for the time being approved for the purposes of this section by the said Minister or the Secretary of State.

(4) Subsection (3) of this section, and so much of subsection (1) as relates to the opinion of two registered medical practitioners, shall not apply to the termination of a pregnancy by a registered medical practitioner in a case where he is of the opinion, formed in good faith, that the termination is immediately necessary to save the life or to prevent grave permanent injury to the physical or mental health of the pregnant woman."

As noted above, the Act affords no defence to the killing of a viable child and twenty-eight weeks or more of pregnancy is prima facie proof of viability. It has been argued that the period of twenty-eight weeks is too long, having regard to modern methods of sustaining prematurely born infants.[1] The Lane Committee has recommended the law should be amended to provide a definite upper time limit of twenty-four weeks – abortions up to that time (the other conditions of the Act being satisfied) should be lawful, abortions thereafter unlawful.[2]

The Secretary of State for the Social Services has exercised the powers given to him by s. 2 to require the opinion of medical practitioners to be certified in a particular form and notice of the termination of pregnancy and other information to be given. The question of the good faith of the doctors is essentially one for the jury. A verdict of bad faith where there is no evidence as to professional practice and medical probabilities is often likely to be regarded by the Court of Appeal as unsafe; but this depends on the nature of the other evidence.

"An opinion may be absurd professionally and yet formed in good faith; conversely an opinion may be one which a doctor could have entertained and yet in the particular circumstances of a case may be found either to have been formed in bad faith or not to have been formed at all."[3]

If one or both of the doctors has expressed an opinion in bad faith but the operation is performed by a third, D, who is unaware of the bad faith, the conditions of the Act are not satisfied but it is submitted that D has a defence. He lacks *mens rea* for, on the facts as he believes them to be, his act is a lawful one. The doctor in bad faith might, however, be convicted under the doctrine of *Cogan and Leak*.[4]

The defences provided by the Act are available "when a pregnancy is terminated by a registered medical practitioner". When the conditions in the Act are satisfied and the pregnancy is terminated by the doctor, there is no *actus reus*. Those who assist him are therefore guilty of no offence. The

1. By the Peel Committee, HMSO, 1972.
2. Cmnd. 5579 (1974), para. 283.
3. *Smith* [1974] 1 All ER 376 at 381.
4. [1976] QB 217, [1975] 2 All ER 1059, above, p. 156.

Act obviously did not contemplate that every action in the steps leading to an abortion would be done personally by the doctor. If, however, the doctor were to delegate more and more of the process to others, there would come a point when it could no longer be said that the pregnancy had been terminated "by a registered medical practitioner" – and at that point it would become unlawful. In *Royal College of Nursing of the United Kingdom v Department of Health and Social Security*,[5] the House of Lords by a majority of three or two, reversing a unanimous Court of Appeal and restoring the judgment of Woolf J, held that a particular process for the extra-amniotic method of termination of pregnancies was lawful, notwithstanding the substantial part played by nurses in that process. According to Lord Diplock, what the Act requires is that –

"... a registered medical practitioner ... should accept responsibility for all stages of the treatment for the termination of the pregnancy. The particular method to be used should be decided by the doctor in charge of the treatment for the termination of the pregnancy; he should carry out any physical acts, forming part of the treatment, that in accordance with accepted medical practice are done only by qualified medical practitioners, and should give specific instructions as to the carrying out of such parts of the treatment as in accordance with accepted medical practice are carried out by nurses or other members of the hospital staff without medical qualifications. To each of them, the doctor, or his substitute, should be available to be consulted or called on for assistance from beginning to end of the treatment."

Thus if the doctor were to direct the whole procedure by correspondence or over the telephone, the operation would presumably be unlawful.

Treatment to terminate a pregnancy, which, if the treatment were successful, would be lawfully terminated, is lawful treatment,[6] notwithstanding (as apparently happens in 1 to 2 per cent of cases) an ultimate failure to terminate the pregnancy. If the conditions of the Act are otherwise fulfilled and known to be fulfilled, the steps taken to procure abortion are taken without *mens rea* – there is no intent *unlawfully* to administer anything or *unlawfully* to use any instrument. There is moreover no *actus reus* for the legalisation of an abortion must include the steps which are taken towards it.

Section 1(1) (a) clearly affords a greater protection than did *Bourne*. Indeed, on a literal reading, it could justify the termination of most pregnancies in their early stages, since some risk is necessarily involved in child-bearing whereas the risks involved in an abortion operation at this stage are very slight.[7] The Act also allows the interests of the children of the woman's family to be taken into account for the first time. These expressions are not defined in the Act, but it has been argued[8] that "family"

5. [1981] AC 800, [1981] 1 All ER 545.
6. Per Lord Edmund-Davies, citing the 4th edition of this book at 346, [1981] 1 All ER at 573.
7. "... it follows that a pregnancy may lawfully be terminated in order to secure a relatively small improvement in the woman's medical condition": *A Guide to the Abortion Act* 1967, p. II. The Act is not, however, interpreted in this way by the medical profession and administrators: Hart (1972) 8 MULR at 393–394.
8. Hoggett, op. cit. at 249; *A Guide to the Abortion Act 1967*, p. 6.

means the sociological and not the legal unit, so as to include illegitimate children and perhaps children who have been accepted as members of the family. The view has been expressed[9] that a person over twenty-one could be a child of the family for this purpose if, for example, he were severely subnormal. The eugenic justification for abortion provided by s. 1(1) (b) is also an innovation in the law. It presents difficulties of interpretation as to what is a "substantial risk" and when physical and mental abnormalities amount to serious handicaps. While these questions must be of great concern to the medical profession, it is perhaps unlikely that they will require consideration by the courts.

By s. 5(2) of the Abortion Act:

"For the purposes of the law relating to abortion, anything done with intent to procure the miscarriage of a woman is unlawfully done unless authorised by section 1 of this Act."

It seems clear that this is intended entirely to supersede the law as laid down in *Bourne*.[10] Abortions, and the steps to procure them which are proscribed, are unlawful unless they can be justified by the 1967 Act. It is submitted, however, that this provision cannot have been intended entirely to eliminate the operation of general defences to crime. To take extreme examples, a child under the age of ten or a person within the M'Naghten rules could surely not be convicted of committing or (slightly more likely) abetting an abortion. If this is conceded, then duress ought equally to operate as a defence; and if duress, why not necessity? And so we are back to admitting *Bourne's* case into the law. A possible interpretation of the Act would be to allow general defences, other than necessity. Construing s. 5(2) in the light of the previous law, a court might conclude that its obvious purpose was to overrule *Bourne*; and that it would be unreasonable to extend its operation beyond that.

A limited defence of necessity would seem desirable in principle. The defence would necessarily be limited in scope by the fact that, in the great majority of cases where it is necessary to procure an abortion, this is lawful by statute so that there is no room for the operation of any broader defence. But suppose that a qualified doctor who is not a registered medical practitioner and so does not come within the terms of s. 1(4) above, forms the opinion in good faith that immediate termination of a pregnancy is necessary in order to save the life of the mother who is in a remote place and beyond the help of any registered medical practitioner. Is it the law that he must let the woman die when he could save her by terminating the pregnancy?

In *Bourne* Macnaghten J took the view that there was not only a right but a duty to perform the operation where a woman's life could be saved only by the doctor procuring an abortion:

---

9. Ibid.
10. Above, p. 365. Cf. the Canadian case of *Morgentaler* [1976] 1 SCR 616, (1975) 20 CCC (2d) 449 discussed by L. H. Leigh in [1978] Crim LR 151 and *Davidson* [1969] VR 667 (Menhennit J).

"... if a case arose where the life of a woman could be saved by performing the operation and the doctor refused to perform it because of his religious opinions and the woman died, he would be in grave peril of being brought before this court on a charge of manslaughter by negligence. He would have no better defence than a person who, again from some religious reason, refused to call in a doctor to attend his sick child, where a doctor could have been called in and the life of the child could have been saved."[11]

Section 4 of the Abortion Act now provides:

"(1) Subject to subsection (2) of this section, no person shall be under any duty, whether by contract or by any statutory or other legal requirement, to participate in any treatment authorised by this Act to which he has a conscientious objection:

Provided that in any legal proceedings the burden of proof of conscientious objection shall rest on the person claiming to rely on it.

(2) Nothing in subsection (1) of this section shall affect any duty to participate in treatment which is necessary to save the life or to prevent grave permanent injury to the physical or mental health of a pregnant woman."

The same people whose acts are rendered lawful by s. 1 are given by s. 4 the right in conscience to object to performing those same acts. A person cannot claim that right in respect of an act which would not have amounted to an offence before the Abortion Act came into force. So a secretary was not entitled, by s. 4, to refuse to type a letter arranging an abortion rendered lawful by s. 1. It was held that she would not, under the old law, have been guilty of the abortion as a secondary party; her intention would have been merely to carry out her contract of employment, not to counsel or procure.[12]

Section 4(2) does not create any duty, but it does appear to recognise at least the possibility of a duty at common law. The only authority for this appears to be *Bourne*. It will be noted that Macnaghten J dealt only with the case where the woman died, whereas the Act refers to grave permanent injury to physical or mental health. Macnaghten J appeared to regard the doctor's liability as one arising from gross negligence; and this is indeed confined to cases where death is caused.[13] There is no general criminal liability for causing grievous bodily harm by gross negligence as distinct from recklessness. If, however, the doctor is under a duty to act, and he knows all the circumstances giving rise to that duty and foresees the consequences of not fulfilling it, it would seem that he has the *mens rea* necessary to found a conviction for causing grievous bodily harm contrary to s. 18 of the Offences against the Person Act 1861.[14] The only doubtful link in this argument appears to be the existence of the duty; but the Act strengthens the case for its existence. Clearly, a doctor with conscientious

11. [1939] 1 KB at 693, [1938] 3 All ER at 618; **SHC 224**.
12. *Salford Health Authority, ex p Janaway* (1988) Times, 5 January CA (Civ. Div.), above, pp. 58, 139–140.
13. Above, p. 353.
14. Below, p. 397.

objections could fulfil his duty by referring the patient to another doctor who does not have such objections; and it is submitted that the doctor has a duty to do this where an abortion is necessary to save the woman from death or grave permanent injury. The question of a duty to participate in the operation can arise only where there is no effective substitute for the doctor concerned. Where the patient has conscientious objections there can be no duty to perform the operation since, clearly, it can only be lawfully performed with consent.

7 Genocide

The Genocide Act 1969 gives effect to the Genocide Convention, Article II. It is an offence under the Act to commit any of the acts falling within the definition of genocide in Article II. This provides:

"In the present Convention, genocide means any of the following acts committed with intent to destroy, in whole or in part, a national, ethnical, racial or religious group, as such:

(a) Killing members of the group;

(b) Causing serious bodily or mental harm to members of the group;

(c) Deliberately inflicting on the group conditions of life calculated to bring about its physical destruction in whole or in part;

(d) Imposing measures intended to prevent births within the group;

(e) Forcibly transferring children of the group to another group."

The offence is punishable with fourteen years imprisonment unless it consists of the killing of any person, in which case it is punishable with life imprisonment.

12 Non-Fatal Offences against the Person

1 Assault and Battery[1]

Assault and battery are two distinct crimes at common law;[2] but it is common in ordinary usage, and even in statutes, to use the term "assault" to cover both. By s. 47 of the Offences against the Person Act 1861 a "common assault", which includes battery, is an offence triable either way and punishable on indictment with one year's imprisonment; and by s. 42, it is punishable on summary conviction with two months' imprisonment or a fine not exceeding level 3 on the standard scale.[3]

By s. 42, where the matter comes before the court "upon complaint by or on behalf of the party aggrieved", a common assault is triable only summarily and is punishable with two months' imprisonment or a fine not exceeding level 3 on the standard scale. This section was probably "intended to be reserved for cases of minor assault of the kind which commonly arise from disputes between neighbours, where the charge is brought by or on behalf of the complainant himself, the police seeing no need to intervene".[4]

By s. 43 it is a separate offence of aggravated assault,[5] triable only summarily and punishable with six months' imprisonment or a fine not exceeding level 4 on the standard scale, where the victim is a male child under fourteen or any female and the justices are of the opinion that the offence is of so aggravated a nature that it cannot be sufficiently punished under s. 42. It is immaterial whether the matter comes before the court upon complaint of the party aggrieved or otherwise.[6] "Aggravated" here means aggravated in some way which does not amount to a distinct offence recognised by the law, and does not include rape, attempted rape or an indecent assault.[7]

---

1. Turner, "Assault at Common Law", MACL 344; Williams "Assault and Words", [1957] Crim LR 219.
2. So a conviction for "assault or battery" must be quashed: *Jones v Sherwood* [1942] 1 KB 127. And see *Mansfield JJ ex parte Sharkey* [1985] 1 All ER 193 at 203, per Lane LCJ.
3. This paragraph was approved by the Court of Appeal in *Beasley* (1981) 73 Cr App Rep 44 at 47.
4. *Harrow JJ ex parte Osaseri* [1986] QB 589 at 663, [1985] 3 All ER 185 at 192, per Nolan J, DC.
5. *Harrow JJ*, supra, applying *Courtie* [1984] AC 463, [1984] 1 All ER 740, above, p. 35.
6. These curious provisions are criticised by Griew, "Common Assault and the Statute Book", [1983] Crim LR 710.
7. *Re Thompson* (1860) 6 H & N 193 (rape); *Baker* (1883) 47 JP 666 (indecent assault).

An assault is any act by which D, intentionally or recklessly,[8] causes P to apprehend immediate and unlawful personal violence.[9] A battery is any act by which D, intentionally or recklessly, inflicts unlawful personal violence upon P.[10] But "violence" here includes any unlawful touching of another, however slight, for, as Blackstone wrote:[11]

> "the law cannot draw the line between different degrees of violence, and therefore prohibits the first and lowest stage of it; every man's person being sacred, and no other having a right to meddle with it, in any the slightest manner."

As Lane LCJ put it:

> "An assault (sc. meaning "battery") is any intentional touching of another person without the consent of that person and without lawful excuse. It need not necessarily be hostile, or rude, or aggressive, as some of the cases seem to indicate."[12]

Presumably the same applies to assault in the strict sense – it is enough that P apprehends some unwanted touching. It is however neither an assault nor a battery for D to pull himself free from P who is detaining him, even though D uses force.[13]

It should be noted that assault and battery are also torts; and many, though not all, of the principles appear to be equally applicable in both branches of the law. Consequently, some of the cases cited below are civil actions.

1) *Elements of Assault*

1 Actus Reus

The typical case of an assault as distinct from a battery is that where D, by some physical movement, causes P to apprehend that he is about to be struck. D rides or drives at P, or acts so as to appear to P to be on the point of striking, stabbing or shooting him. Assault was once regarded as attempted battery. D had embarked on an act which, if not suspended or evaded, would immediately result in an impact of some kind on P. Many attempted batteries are assaults, but this is not necessarily so. D's acts may be unobserved by P, as where D approaches P from behind, or P is asleep, or insensible, or too young to appreciate what D appears likely to do. And there may be an assault where D has no intention to commit a battery but only to cause P to apprehend one.[14]

There is a tendency to enlarge the concept of assault by taking a generous view of "immediacy" and including threats where the impending impact is more remote than in the typical assaults instanced above. In *Lewis*[15] D was

---

8. *Venna* [1976] QB 421, [1975] 3 All ER 788, CA (a case of battery but the same principle surely applies to assault); *Logdon v Director of Public Prosecutions* [1976] Crim LR 121, DC.
9. A definition in almost identical terms was approved in *Fagan v Metropolitan Police Commissioner* [1969] 1 QB 439, [1968] 3 All ER 442 at 445; **SHC 25**; below, p. 380.
10. *Rolfe* (1952) 36 Cr App Rep 4.
11. *Commentaries*, 3, 120, cited by Goff LJ in *Collins v Wilcock* [1984] 3 All ER 374 at 378.
12. *Faulkner v Talbot* [1981] 3 All ER 468 at 471, applied in *Thomas* (1985) 81 Cr App Rep 331 at 334; and see *Collins v Wilcock* [1984] 3 All ER 374 at 379, DC; *Wilson v Pringle* [1987] QB [1986] 2 All ER 440, CA (Civ. Div.), criticised by Wood J. in *T v T* [1988] 2 WLR 189 at 200, 203, Fam Div.
13. *Sheriff* [1969] Crim LR 260.
14. *Logdon v Director of Public Prosecutions* [1976] Crim LR 121.
15. [1970] Crim LR 647, CA.

held guilty of maliciously inflicting grievous bodily harm and therefore impliedly of an assault,[16] although D was uttering threats from another room. In *Logdon v Director of Public Prosecutions*[17] it was held that D committed an assault by showing P a pistol in a drawer and declaring that he would hold her hostage. In *Smith v Superintendent of Woking Police Station*[18] D committed an assault by looking through the window of a bed-sitting room at P in her night-clothes, intending to frighten her and doing so. The court distinguished the example given in the 4th edition of this book – "There can be no assault if it is obvious to P that D is unable to carry out his threat, as where D shakes his fist at P who is safely locked inside his car." Kerr LJ said, "That may be so, but those are not the facts of the present case."

There may be an assault although D has no means of carrying out the threat.[19] The question is whether he intends to cause P to believe that he can and will carry it out and whether P does so believe. The question arises where D points an unloaded or imitation gun at P.

If P knows the gun is unloaded or an imitation, there is no assault, for then he could not be put in fear.[20] If P believes it is, or may be a real, loaded gun, there is an *actus reus*, for now he suffers the apprehension which is an essential element of the crime.[1]

It has been generally accepted that mere words cannot constitute an assault. It has been held in Canada[2] that there was no assault where a man with a jacket over his arm went up to the box-office of a theatre and said to the cashier, "I've got a gun, give me all your money or I'll shoot." It would probably have been different if it had been proved that D simulated the pointing of a gun. In England, there seems to be no more authority for the proposition than a dictum of Holroyd J in *Meade and Belt*[3] that "no words or singing are equivalent to an assault". The proposition has been rightly questioned by modern writers.

"If the plaintiff turns a corner to be confronted by a motionless robber who, with gun in hand, commands 'Hands up', why should not this be an assault?"[4]

Moreover,

"The opinion would deny the possibility of an assault (as opposed to a battery) in pitch darkness, when a gesture cannot be seen but menacing words can be heard."[5]

In *Wilson*[6] Lord Goddard said of the accused:

"He called out 'Get out the knives', *which itself would be an assault*, in addition to kicking the gamekeeper."

16. But see now *Wilson* [1984] AC 242, [1983] 3 All ER 448 below, p. 399.
17. Supra.
18. (1983) 76 Cr App Rep 234.
19. *Pace* Tindal CJ in *Stephens v Myers* (1830) 4 C & P 349.
20. *Lamb*, above, p. 65.
  1. *Logdon v Director of Public Prosecutions*, supra.
  2. *Byrne* [1968] 3 CCC 179 (Br Col C of A). Cf. *Logdon v Director of Public Prosecutions*, supra, where D showed P the gun.
  3. (1823) 1 Lew CC 184.
  4. Street, *Torts*, 26.
  5. Williams [1957] Crim LR at 224.
  6. [1955] 1 All ER 744 at 745.

This was a mere dictum – but it surely counterbalances that in *Meade*? In a civil case, the Court of Appeal held that a threat forcibly to eject P was an assault.[7]

It is clear that a threat to inflict harm at some time in the future cannot amount to an assault[8] – an apprehension of immediate personal violence is essential. As already noted, an oral threat even to murder P, and even if made in his presence, was not an offence until 1977 unless it amounted to an assault.

Whether or not words may amount to an assault, it is clear that they may negative one. In the famous case of *Tuberville v Savage*[9] D laid his hand upon his sword, saying, "If it were not assize time I would not take such language." If D had said nothing, it is clear that the court would have held this to be evidence of an assault; but

"the declaration of [D][10] was, that he would not assault him, the judges being in town."[11]

If the words had not accompanied the act, but followed it, again there would presumably have been an assault, for the words could not undo a crime already constituted by the apprehension aroused in P.

In *Blake v Barnard*,[12] Lord Abinger applied the same principle to the situation where D presented a pistol at P's head and said that if P was not quiet he would blow his brains out. This differs from *Tuberville v Savage* in that D's declared intention not to shoot was conditional on P's doing as he was told. It has been forcefully argued[13] that this is a vital distinction and that D should not have been acquitted of an assault on that ground –

"Otherwise, indeed, the highwayman who says 'Your money or your life,' at the same time presenting a weapon, would not be guilty of assault at common law – a proposition which it is impossible to believe."

Thus in *Read v Coker*,[14] where D and his servants had surrounded P, tucking up their sleeves and aprons, and had threatened to break his neck *if he did not leave the premises*, the Court of Common Pleas had no doubt that this was an assault. Yet P was already a trespasser in that case, having been told to go. The threat amounted to an assault presumably only because it was of excessive force.[15] If P threatens to punch D and D produces a knife, saying that, if P does so, he will "cut him to bits," D is guilty of an assault if the violence he has threatened goes beyond what was reasonably necessary as a means of self-defence.[16]

---

7. *Ansell v Thomas* [1974] Crim LR 31.
8. *Stephens v Myers*, above, p. 377; and see *Police v Greaves* [1964] NZLR 295; *Fagan v Metropolitan Police Commissioner* [1969] 1 QB 439, [1968] 3 All ER 442; **SHC 25** below p. 380, footnote 5.
9. (1669) 1 Mod Rep 3. But cf. *Light* (1857) Dears & B 332.
10. D was in fact the plaintiff in an action for assault arising out of a fight which followed the incident described.
11. Ibid.
12. (1840) 9 C & P 626.
13. By Williams [1957] Crim LR at 220.
14. (1853) 13 CB 850.
15. Cf. *Osborn v Veitch* (1858) 1 F & F 317 (Pointing a gun at half-cock ("cocking it is an instantaneous act") to resist an unlawful arrest held an assault, because "To shoot a man is not a lawful way of repelling an unlawful assault": per Willes J).
16. *Rozsa v Samuels* [1969] SASR 205. But cf. *Cousins*, above, p. 357.

It has generally been assumed that an act of some kind is an essential ingredient of assault; but a modern case[17] suggests the possibility of an assault by omission. Where D inadvertently causes P to apprehend immediate violence and subsequently wilfully declines to withdraw the threat, his omission might constitute an assault.

2 Mens Rea

It is now clear that the *mens rea* of assault is an intention to cause P to apprehend immediate and unlawful violence, or recklessness whether such apprehension be caused.[18] The question now is whether this means *Cunningham* or *Caldwell* recklessness.[19] *Venna*, the leading case, was decided before *Caldwell* and therefore held that it was the former.[20] It is submitted that this was, and is still, right. We are concerned not with the use of the word "reckless" in a statute but with the common law. Assault is akin to those offences against the person which are statutorily defined in the 1861 Act and which, because the word "maliciously" is used, require *Cunningham* recklessness. Negligently to cause such apprehension may amount to a tort but is not a criminal offence. The *mens rea* of battery would also presumably be enough on a charge of assault. D strikes at P from behind, intending to injure him without attracting his attention, but P turns round and, seeing the blow coming, avoids it. D is guilty of assault as well as attempted battery.

It is often said that D must have had a *hostile* intention in assault and battery.[1] So far as assault is concerned, this adds nothing to intentionally or recklessly causing apprehension. It would be no defence that D was friendly with P and did it for a joke – unless P's consent could be implied.

3 Attempt to Assault

It has been questioned whether there can be an attempt to assault, since assault itself was regarded as an attempt to commit a battery. It is submitted that, since assault itself is now wider than attempted battery, there is no reason why there should not be attempt to commit it; as where D points an unloaded gun at P, intending to frighten him, but P, knowing the gun is unloaded, is unperturbed.[2]

2) *Battery*

1 Actus Reus

This consists in the infliction of unlawful personal violence by D upon P. It

17. *Fagan v Metropolitan Police Commissioner* [1969] 1 QB 439, [1968] 3 All ER 442, below, p. 380.
18. *Venna* [1976] QB 421, [1975] 3 All ER 788, CA; *Logdon v Director of Public Prosecutions* [1976] Crim LR 121, DC.
19. Above, p. 62.
20. The judge, in the direction to the jury which was approved by the Court of Appeal, said: "If he lashes out with his feet *knowing* that there are officers about him and *knowing* that by lashing out he will probably or is likely to kick somebody ... then he is equally [sc., as if he intended to kick another] guilty of the offence." (Authors' italics.)
   1. *Coward v Baddeley* (1859) 28 LJ Ex 260; *Fairclough v Whipp* [1951] 2 All ER 834; *Director of Public Prosecutions v Rogers* [1953] 2 All ER 644, [1953] 1 WLR 1017. Cf. below, p. 448; *Wilson v Pringle* [1986] 2 All ER 440.
   2. "Is Criminal Assault a Separate Substantive Crime or is it an Attempted Battery?" (1945) 33 Ky LJ 189; *State v Wilson* (1955) 218 Ore 575; 346 P (2d) 115. See also [1980] Crim LR 780.

used to be said that every battery involves an assault; but this is plainly not so, for in battery there need be no apprehension of the impending violence. A blow from behind is not any less a battery because P was unaware that it was coming. It is generally said that D must have done some act and that it is not enough that he stood still and obstructed P's passage[3] like an inanimate object. But suppose D is sitting at the corner of a corridor with his legs stretched across it. He hears P running down the corridor and deliberately remains still with the intention that P, on turning the corner, shall fall over his legs. Why should not this be a battery? It would be if D had put out his legs with the intention of tripping up P. There is certainly no battery where D has no control over the incident, as where his horse unexpectedly runs away with him;[4] but this might be put on the ground of lack of *mens rea*. It might be otherwise if D foresaw, when he mounted, that there was an unacceptable risk that this might happen. There may be a battery where D inadvertently applies force to P and then wrongfully refuses to withdraw it. In *Fagan*,[5] where D accidentally drove his mini-car on to a constable's foot and then intentionally left it there, the court held that there was a continuing act, not a mere omission.

Since the merest touching without consent is a criminal offence, the exigencies of everyday life demand that there be an implied consent to that degree of contact which is necessary or customary in the ordinary course.

"Generally speaking, consent is a defence to battery; and most of the physical contacts of ordinary life are not actionable because they are impliedly consented to by all who move in society and so expose themselves to the risk of bodily contact. So nobody can complain of the jostling which is inevitable from his presence in, for example, a super-market, an underground station or a busy street; nor can a person who attends a party complain if his hand is seized in friendship, or even if his back is (within reason) slapped. Although such cases are regarded as examples of implied consent, it is more common nowadays to treat them as falling within a general exception embracing all physical contact which is generally acceptable in the ordinary conduct of daily life."[6]

Touching a person for the purpose of engaging his attention has been held to be acceptable[7] but physical restraint is not. A police officer who catches hold of a boy, not for the purpose of arresting him but in order to detain him for questioning, is acting unlawfully.[8] So is a constable who takes hold of the arm of a woman found soliciting in order to caution her. The fact that the practice of cautioning prostitutes is recognised by statute does not imply any power to stop and detain.[9] But to "detain" without any

---

3. *Innes v Wylie* (1844) 1 Car & Kir 257.
4. *Gibbon v Pepper* (1695) 2 Salk 637.
5. [1969] 1 QB 439, [1968] 3 All ER 442 above, pp. 49, 378 and 379.
6. *Collins v Wilcock* [1984] 3 All ER 374 at 378, per Robert Goff LJ.
7. *Wiffin v Kincard* (1807) 2 Bos & PNR 471; *Coward v Baddeley* (1859) 4 H & N 478. *Donnelly v Jackman* [1970] 1 All ER 987, [1970] 1 WLR 562, where a police officer was held to be acting in the execution of his duty although he persisted in tapping P on the shoulder when P had made it clear that he had no intention of stopping to speak, is "an extreme case": [1984] 3 All ER 374 at 379.
8. *Kenlin v Gardiner* [1967] 2 QB 510, [1966] 3 All ER 931.
9. *Collins v Wilcock*, supra, footnote 6.

actual touching cannot be a battery. If the detention is effected by the threat of force, then it may be false imprisonment.

For this purpose the person of the victim includes the clothes he is wearing; Parke B ruled that there was a common assault where D slashed P's clothes with a knife:

"surely it is an assault on a man's person to inflict injury to the clothes on his back. In the ordinary case of a blow on the back, there is clearly an assault, though the blow is received by the coat on the person."[10]

It is apparently not necessary that P should be able to feel the impact through the clothes. In *Thomas*[11] where D touched the bottom of P's skirt and rubbed it, the court said, obiter, "There could be no dispute that if you touch a person's clothes while he is wearing them that is equivalent to touching him."

Most batteries are directly inflicted, as by D's striking P with his fist or an instrument, or by a missile thrown by him, or by spitting upon P. But it is not essential that the violence should have been so directly inflicted. Thus Stephen and Wills JJ thought there would be a battery where D digs a pit for P to fall into, or, as in *Martin*,[12] he causes P to rush into an obstruction. It is submitted that it would undoubtedly be a battery to set a dog on another.[13] If D beat O's horse causing it to run down P, this would be battery by D.[14] No doubt the famous civil case of *Scott v Shepherd*[15] is equally good for the criminal law. D throws a squib into a market house. First E and then F flings the squib away in order to save himself from injury. It expodes and injures P. This is a battery by D. If there is no violence at all, there is no battery; as where D puts harmful matter into a drink which is consumed by P.[16]

2 Mens Rea

The Court of Appeal has held:

"... the element of *mens rea* in the offence of battery is satisfied by proof that the defendant either intentionally or recklessly applied force to the person of another."[17]

For the reasons given above,[18] it is submitted that this means *Cunningham*, not *Caldwell* recklessness.[19]

Since the *mens rea* of assault is not classed as a "specific intent", it is not a defence that D had no *mens rea* because of the effect of drink or drugs.[20]

---

10. *Day* (1845) 1 Cox CC 207.
11. (1985) 81 Cr App Rep 331 at 334, CA.
12. Below, p. 399.
13. But note the caution of the court in *Dume* (1986) Times, 16 October, CA.
14. *Gibbon v Pepper* (1695) 2 Salk 637 (obiter).
15. (1773) 2 Wm Bl 892.
16. *Hanson* (1849) 2 Car & Kir 912; but see below, p. 403.
17. *Venna* [1975] 3 All ER 788 at 793; **SHC 355**.
18. P. 379.
19. Above, p. 63.
20. *Majewski* [1977] AC 443, [1976] 2 All ER 142, HL, above, p. 211.

3) *Defences to Assault and Battery*

1 Consent

i) *Effect of consent*. It is of the essence of both offences that they are done against the will of the victim.[1] Consent therefore negatives either crime and the onus of proving the absence of consent is on the Crown.[2] Fraud does not necessarily negative consent. It does so only if it deceives P as to the identity of the person or the nature of the act.[3] In *Clarence*[4] P consented to intercourse with D and, although she would not have consented had she been aware of the disease which D knew he was suffering, this was no assault. If D told P that he was going to inject him with a vaccine and then injected a poison instead, it is thought that this would be a battery, but if he injected the vaccine with a dirty needle, there would, as in *Clarence*, be no battery even though D knew that P would not have consented to injection with a dirty needle. Where D1, a doctor, by falsely pretending that D2 was a medical student, obtained P's consent to D2's presence at a vaginal examination of P, it was held that there was no assault because the fraud was not as to the nature and quality of what was to be done.[5] In *Burrell v Harmer*[6] consent was held to be no defence to a charge of assault occasioning actual bodily harm, where D tattooed boys aged 12 and 13, causing their arms to become inflamed and painful. The court took the view that the boys were unable to understand the nature of the act. But in what sense did they not understand it? Consent may also be negatived by duress. A threat to imprison P unless he submitted to a beating would probably invalidate P's consent. Possibly a threat to dismiss from employment[7] or to bring a prosecution[8] would have a similar effect. If the test is whether the threat would be sufficient to overcome the will of a reasonably firm person, the outcome must depend to some extent on the relationship between the gravity of the threat and the act to which P is asked to submit. Duress may be implied from the relationship between the parties – for example where D is acting as a schoolmaster, and P is a thirteen year-old pupil.[9] As in rape and indecent assault,[10] submission is not consent. But an unfounded belief in P's consent is a defence, whether the belief is based on reasonable

---

1. *Christopherson v Bare* (1848) 11 QB 473. *A-G's Reference (No. 6 of 1980)* [1981] 2 All ER 1057 at 1058.

2. *Donovan* [1934] 2 KB 498, following *May*, [1912] 3 KB 572.

3. But cf. the rule in trespass to land and, therefore, in burglary, below, p. 597.

4. (1888) 22 QBD 23; below, p. 000.

5. *Bolduc and Bird* (1967) 63 DLR (2d) 82 (Supreme Ct. of Canada, Spence J diss), reversing British Columbia CA 61 DLR (2d) 494. Cf. *Rosinski* (1824) 1 Mood CC 19.

6. [1967] Crim LR 169 and commentary thereon. It is now an offence to tattoo a person under the age of 18, except tattooing by a doctor for medical reasons: Tattooing of Minors Act 1969.

7. *McCoy* 1953 (2) SA 4 (AD) (threat to ground air hostess negativing consent on assault charge).

8. *State v Volschenk* 1968 (2) PH H283 (threat to prosecute held *not* to negative consent on rape charge).

9. *Nichol* (1807) Russ & Ry 130.

10. Below, pp. 433 and 446.

grounds or not, provided only that it is honestly held. *"Cunningham* recklessness"* whether P consents is a sufficient *mens rea*.[11]

ii) *Limitations on consent*.[12] There are limits to the right of any person to consent to the infliction of physical harm on himself. Consent to being killed is ineffective. It is no defence to a charge of murder for D to say that P asked to be killed. On the other hand, P's consent to D's taking a high degree of risk of killing him is effective where it is justified by the purpose of the act, as it may be in the case of a surgical operation. Where the act has some social purpose, recognised by the law as valid, it is a question of balancing the degree of harm which will or may be caused against the value of that purpose. "Prize fights", though not unlawful as such,[13] have regularly been held to amount to batteries. Any entertainment value they may have is thought by the courts to be outweighed by risks of grave physical injury to the contestants. No prosecutions have been brought in respect of contests conducted with the greatest publicity in accordance with the Queensberry rules and, notwithstanding the clear risk of injury and occasionally death which is involved, it must be assumed that these are lawful. Fights without gloves, or in other circumstances which aggravate the risk of serious injury, are unlawful. In *Coney*[14] Cave J said:

"The true view is, I think, that a blow struck in anger, or which is likely or is intended to do corporal hurt, is an assault, but that a blow struck in sport, and not likely, nor intended to cause bodily harm, is not an assault, and that, an assault being a breach of the peace and unlawful, the consent of the person struck is immaterial. If this view is correct a blow struck in a prize-fight is clearly an assault; but playing with single-sticks or wrestling do not involve an assault; nor does boxing with gloves in the ordinary way, and not with the ferocity and severe punishment to the boxers deposed to in *R v Orton*."[15]

The condition that the blow must be "not intended to cause bodily harm", seems hardly consistent with the rest of the passage. A right hook delivered by Muhammed Ali with the avowed intention of knocking his opponent unconscious could not be said to be not intended to cause bodily harm; yet it appears to be lawful. The assumed value of the sport is taken to justify P's consenting to D's trying to knock him out. Where, however, two youths of 18 and 17 decided to settle an argument by a fight with fists (presumably bare) and the one sustained a bleeding nose and bruises to his face it was held that the other was guilty of assault occasioning actual bodily harm.

"... it is not in the public interest that people should try to cause or should cause each other actual bodily harm for no good reason. Minor

11. *Morgan* [1976] AC 182, [1975] 2 All ER 347, HL; **SHC 45**; above, pp. 86, 207, and below, p. 429; *Albert v Lavin* [1981] 1 All ER 628, DC. Absence of consent is "a definitional element" of assault. Above, p. 88.
12. Williams, "Consent and Public Policy" [1962] Crim LR 74 and 154.
13. *Pallante v Stadium Pty Ltd (No. 1)* [1976] VR 331.
14. (1882) 8 QBD 534 at 539; above, p. 136.
15. (1878) 39 LT 293. The contestants wore gloves but it was held that the jury were rightly directed that it was a prize-fight if they intended to fight on until one gave in from exhaustion or injury.

struggles are another matter. So, in our judgment, it is immaterial whether the act occurs in private or in public; it is an assault if actual bodily harm is intended and/or caused. This means that most fights will be unlawful regardless of consent."[16]

The court went on to say:

"Nothing which we have said is intended to cast doubt on the accepted legality of properly conducted games and sports, lawful chastisement or correction, reasonable surgical interference, dangerous exhibitions etc. These apparent exceptions can be justified as involving the exercise of a legal right, in the case of chastisement or correction, or as needed in the public interest, in the other cases."

So the shoulder charge, delivered in the course of a game of soccer, which would clearly be unlawful if it were inflicted on an unwilling passer-by, is lawful because P has consented to D's doing what the rules of the game reasonably permit. Prima facie, P has consented to that and nothing more; and therefore *Moore*[17] holding the rules inadmissible in evidence seems a dubious decision. Some players however think they consent to certain acts in breach of the rules which they know are very likely to occur in the ordinary course of play. Proof of breach of the rules ought to establish at least a prima facie case.[18] Consent by boys to rough and undisciplined play may be a defence to a charge of inflicting grievous bodily harm if there is no intention to cause injury. Consent, or a genuine belief in consent, even an unreasonable belief, apparently negatives recklessness: *Jones*[19] where boys were injured by being tossed in the air by schoolmates. The decision recognises that boys have always indulged in rough and undisciplined play among themselves and probably always will; but the non-consenting child is rightly protected by the criminal law.

Consent to a surgical operation for a purpose recognised as valid by the law is effective[20] and this includes a sex-change operation[1] and, presumably, cosmetic surgery and organ transplants. It is otherwise where the purpose is one which the law condemns.

So Coke tells us that in 1604,

"a young strong and lustie rogue, to make himself impotent, thereby to have the more colour to begge or to be relieved without putting himself to any labour, caused his companion to strike off his left hand":

---

16. *A-G's Reference (No. 6 of 1980)* [1981] 2 All ER 1057 at 1059; **SHC 359**. The implication of this passage that causing bodily harm is unlawful though no bodily harm is intended is puzzling. Actual bodily harm may occasionally be caused by an assault not intended to cause harm, as where D's unwanted pat on the head cracks P's eggshell skull; but no question of consent seems to arise in such a case. Perhaps the reference is to reckless assaults. P's consent to take the risk is not an answer unless there is some justification, other than mere consent. Consent to the administration of a noxious thing likely to endanger life is not a defence: *Cato* [1976] 1 All ER 260, [1976] 1 WLR 110. Cf. *McLeod* (1915) 34 NZLR, 430. See commentary at [1981] Crim LR 554.
17. (1898) 14 TLR 229. Cf. *Billinghurst* [1978] Crim LR 553 (Judge Rutter).
18. The rules are admissible in favour of the defence, as tending to negative "malice"; *Bradshaw* (1878) 14 Cox CC 83.
19. [1987] Crim LR 123, CA.
20. Stephen, *Digest*, Art. 310. See Skegg, [1974] Crim LR 693 and (1973) 36 MLR 370.
 1. *Corbett v Corbett* [1971] P 83 at 99.

and that both of them were convicted of mayhem.[2] Maiming, even with consent, was unlawful because it deprived the king of a fighting man. In early Victorian times when soldiers, as part of their drill, had to bite cartridges, a soldier got a dentist to pull out his front teeth to avoid the drill. Stephen J thought that both were guilty of a crime.[3] Denning LJ followed these instances in discussing, obiter, the legality of a sterilisation operation:

"When it is done with the man's consent for a just cause, it is quite lawful, as, for instance, when it is done to prevent the transmission of an hereditary disease; but when it is done without just cause or excuse, it is unlawful, even though the man consents to it. Take a case where a sterilisation operation is done so as to enable a man to have the pleasure of sexual intercourse without shouldering the responsibilities attaching to it. The operation is then plainly injurious to the public interest."[4]

This was unnecessary to the decision, the other judges were careful to express no opinion and Lord Denning's opinion is no longer tenable on the particular point,[5] but it illustrates the continuing influence of public policy. In *Cowburn*,[6] a man with uncontrollable sexual impulses was willing to undergo a castration operation but the Court of Criminal Appeal declined to give its blessing to the operation as the issue was not before it. The legality of such operations has not been settled by any judicial decision; but it now seems highly improbable that they would be held to be unlawful. Public policy might well be served[7] rather than offended by an operation such as that proposed in *Cowburn*: but "public policy" is a notoriously elusive and slippery doctrine. It was invoked to justify conviction for a relatively slight degree of harm in *Donovan*.[8] D, for his sexual gratification, beat a seventeen-year-old girl with a cane in circumstances of indecency. He was convicted of both indecent assault and common assault. The judge failed to direct the jury that the onus of negativing consent was on the Crown, but the Court of Criminal Appeal held that, if the blows were likely or intended to cause bodily harm, this omission was immaterial because D was guilty whether P consented or not. The conviction was quashed because the question whether the blows were likely or intended to cause bodily harm was not put to the jury, and

"There are many gradations between a slight tap and a severe blow . . .".[9] Thus, P's consent to "a slight tap" would have been operative notwithstanding D's evil motives. But it was clearly these motives which rendered unlawful a degree of force which, in other circumstances, might have been

---

2. 1 Co Inst 127a and b.
3. *Digest* (3rd ed.) 142.
4. *Bravery v Bravery* [1954] 3 All ER 59 at 67, 68.
5. The National Health Service (Family Planning) Amendment Act 1972 authorises the provision of voluntary vasectomy services.
6. [1959] Crim LR 590. Cf. *T v T* [1988] 2 WLR 189, Fam. Div.
7. See Havard [1959] Crim LR 554 at 555: "The Scandinavian experience has shown that voluntary castration is particularly efficacious in these cases and may permit an early rehabilitation in the community."
8. [1934] 2 KB 498.
9. Ibid., at 510. See Leigh, "Sado-Masochism, Consent and the Reform of the Criminal Law," (1976) 39 MLR 130.

permissible. In *A-G's Reference (No. 6 of 1980)*[10] the Court of Appeal, while rejecting the tautologous reasoning of *Donovan*,[11] confirmed its effect, namely that the intentional infliction of any degree of bodily harm, however slight,[12] is a battery unless P consents *and* the action can be positively justified by some public interest, such as that which validates "manly sports". This gives the criminal law the widest possible range,[13] or potential range, and leaves much to the opinion of the judges as to what is, and what is not, in the public interest.

2 Lawful Correction

Parents are entitled to inflict moderate and reasonable physical chastisement on their children; but –

> "If it be administered for the gratification of passion or rage or if it be immoderate or excessive in its nature or degree, or if it be protracted beyond the child's powers of endurance or with an instrument unfitted for the purpose and calculated to produce danger to life and limb . . . ."[14]

– then it is unlawful. If the chastisement is moderate, it would be impracticable for the courts to inquire very closely into the validity of the parent's motives. Where the force is immoderate, his motives are irrelevant. Immigrant parents must conform to English standards.[15] At common law, school teachers are in the same position as parents with regard to the conduct of the child at, or on its way to or from school.[16] A "member of staff" of a school, as defined in s. 47 (10) of the Education (No. 2) Act 1986 now has no right, by virtue of his position as such, to administer corporal punishment to a "pupil" as defined in s. 47 (5) of that Act. Presumably corporal punishment would still be lawful if administered by a teacher on the authority of a parent. In a school to which the definitions in the 1986 Act do not apply, the common law position continues. Section 1 of the Children and Young Persons Act 1933, which makes it an offence, inter alia, wilfully to assault a person under sixteen, provides that nothing in the section "shall be construed as affecting the right of any parent, teacher, or other person having the lawful control or charge of a child or young person to administer punishment to him."

The ancient right to chastise a servant, an apprentice or (if such a right ever existed), a wife,[17] is now obsolete.

---

10. Above, p. 384.
11. "If an act is unlawful in the sense of being in itself a criminal act, it is plain that it cannot be rendered lawful because the person to whose detriment it is done consents to it. No person can license another to commit a crime."
12. In *Donovan* there were seven or eight red marks on P's body. This was sufficient evidence of bodily harm to go to the jury.
13. Stephen thought "everyone has a right to consent to the infliction upon himself of bodily harm not amounting to a maim": *Digest of Criminal Law* (4th ed.) 148–149. The influential American Model Penal Code allows consent as a defence where the harm is "not serious".
14. *Hopley* (1860) 2 F & F 202 at 206, per Cockburn CJ. Cf. *Smith* [1985] Crim LR 42, CA.
15. *Derriviere* (1969) 53 Cr App Rep 637, CA.
16. *Cleary v Booth* [1893] 1 QB 465; *Newport (Salop) JJ* [1929] 2 KB 416; *Mansell v Griffin* [1908] 1 KB 160.
17. *Jackson* [1891] 1 QB 671.

2 Aggravated Assaults

The Offences against the Person Act 1861 singles out certain varieties of assault as being especially heinous and provides a more severe punishment for them. Some of these were, no doubt, intended to deal with matters causing public concern at the time, and appear rather curious today.

Thus, obstructing or assaulting a clergyman in the discharge of his duties in a place of worship or burial place, or who is on his way to or from such duties is an offence triable either way, punishable on indictment with two years' imprisonment under s. 36. Assaulting a magistrate or other person in the exercise of his duty concerning the preservation of a vessel in distress or a wreck is an offence punishable on indictment with seven years' imprisonment under s. 37.

Such provisions are rarely invoked at the present day and need not be considered further. But s. 38, now in part replaced by s. 51 of the Police Act 1964, is still important. Under s. 38 it is an offence triable either way and punishable on indictment with two years' imprisonment to assault any person with intent to resist or prevent the lawful apprehension or detainer of one's self or of any other person for any offence.

1) *Assault on, Resistance to, or Obstruction of Constables*

By s. 51 of the Police Act 1964:

"(1) Any person who assaults a constable in the execution of his duty, or a person assisting a constable in the execution of his duty, shall be guilty of an offence and liable on summary conviction to a fine not exceeding level 5 on the standard scale or to imprisonment for a term not exceeding six months or to both.

(2) Subsection (2) of section 17 of the Firearms Act 1968, shall apply to offences under subsection (1) of this section.

(3) Any person who resists or wilfully obstructs a constable in the execution of his duty, or a person assisting a constable in the execution of his duty, shall be guilty of an offence and liable on summary conviction to imprisonment for a term not exceeding one month or to a fine not exceeding level 3 on the standard scale, or to both."

Though the section is headed "Assaults on Constables", there are three crimes here, only one of which necessarily amounts to an assault. Resistance to a constable may occur without an assault, as where D has been arrested by P and tears himself from P's grasp and escapes.[18] Obstruction, as appears below, embraces many situations which do not amount to an assault. On the other hand, both resistance and obstruction clearly may include assaults. The nature of assault and resistance require no further consideration but obstruction presents problems and is examined in some detail below. The first question – when is a constable[19] acting in the course

---

18. *Sheriff* [1969] Crim LR 260.
19. I.e. a person holding the *office*, not the rank of constable. A prison officer acting as such is a constable for this purpose: Prison Act 1952,. s. 8.

of his duty? – is common to all three crimes. But the *mens rea* of assault and resistance, on the one hand, and obstruction on the other require separate consideration.

1 A Constable Acting in the Execution of his Duty[20]

When a policeman is acting in the course of his duty is a question which can give rise to difficult problems. A constable directing a motorist to leave the road to take part in a traffic census, before there was a statutory power to do so,[1] was not acting in the execution of his duty since his right at common law to regulate traffic derives only from his duty to protect life and property.[2] There are many things which a constable on duty may do which he is probably not under any "duty" in the strict sense to do; that is, he would commit no crime or tort or even breach of police regulations by not doing it. It might be rescuing a stranded cat or helping to deliver a baby. Older cases[3] suggested that a constable was not in the execution of his duty for the purposes of this section unless he was doing something that he was obliged to do, but in *Coffin v Smith*[4] the divisional court rejected an argument on these lines and doubted those authorities. Officers, who had been summoned to a boys' club to ensure that certain people left, were assaulted. It was held that they were there in fulfilment of their duty to keep the peace and were plainly acting in the execution of their duty. In one of the doubted cases, *Prebble*,[5] where a constable at the request of a landlord, turned some persons out of a public house and was held not to be acting in the execution of his duty, the court found there was no nuisance or danger of breach of the peace, and it may possibly be distinguishable as a case where the officer was doing no more than assist a citizen in the enforcement of private rights. A constable may be acting in the execution of his duty by being present, and by intervening when a breach of the peace occurs or is imminent, but acting outside his duty if he takes it upon himself to expel a trespasser.[6] In a leading case, *Waterfield*,[7] the Court of Criminal Appeal said:

---

20. On the duties of the police, see *Metropolitan Police Commissioner, ex parte Blackburn* [1968] 2 QB 118, [1968] 1 All ER 763, CA, and *(No. 3)* [1973] 2 QB 241, [1973] 1 All ER 324, CA; Lidstone, "A Policeman's Duty not to Take Liberties" [1976] Crim LR 617; U. Ross, "Two Cases on Obstructing a Constable" [1977] Crim LR 187.

   1. See now the Road Traffic Act 1974, s. 6.

   2. *Hoffman v Thomas* [1974] 2 All ER 233, DC. In the pursuance of that duty, a constable may require a motorist to disobey a traffic regulation: *Johnson v Phillips* [1975] 3 All ER 682, DC; and remove a vehicle to the police station when the driver is arrested: *Liepéns v Spearman* [1985] Crim LR 229. Cf. *Saunders* [1978] Crim LR 98 (Judge Heald) and commentary.

   3. *Prebble* (1858) 1 F & F 325 and *Roxburgh* (1871) 12 Cox CC 8. See also *Betts v Stevens* [1910] 1 KB 1 and 4th ed. of this book at 361–372.

   4. (1980) 71 Cr App Rep 221.

   5. Above, footnote 3.

   6. In *Chief Constable of Devon and Cornwall, ex parte Central Electricity Generating Board* [1982] QB 458, [1981] 3 All ER 826, 835 the Chief Constable appeared to take the view that he had no right to intervene to expel trespassers, even where they were committing a criminal obstruction, unless a breach of the peace was imminent. Lawton LJ said the CEGB had no right to call on the police to supply "muscle-power" to remove the obstructors; and if the obstructors allowed themselves to be removed without struggling or causing uproar, "the police will have no reason for taking action, *nor should they*": pp. 836–837. (Authors' italics.)

   7. [1964] 1 QB 164 at 170, [1963] 3 All ER 659 at 661.

"In the judgment of this court it would be difficult, and in the present case it is unnecessary, to reduce within specific limits the general terms in which the duties of police constables have been expressed. In most cases it is probably more convenient to consider what the police constable was actually doing and in particular whether such conduct was prima facie an unlawful interference with a person's liberty or property. If so, it is then relevant to consider whether (a) such conduct falls within the general scope of any duty imposed by statute or recognised at common law and (b) whether such conduct, albeit within the general scope of such a duty, involved an unjustifiable use of powers associated with the duty."

If the police officer's conduct falls within the scope of the general "duty" to prevent crime and to bring offenders to justice, then it would seem to be within the protection of the statute, if it was lawful. If, in the course of carrying out his duty to prevent crime and to bring offenders to justice, the officer exceeds his powers, then he is no longer acting in the execution of his duty for this purpose.[8] In *McArdle v Wallace*,[9] P was held to be acting in the execution of his duty as a constable when he entered a café to make inquiries regarding some property which he thought might have been stolen. He was told to leave but did not do so and was then assaulted. At the time of the assault he was no longer acting in the execution of his duty since he became a trespasser when he refused to leave: for a constable can hardly have a duty to break the law. A police officer investigating crime is entitled to speak to any person from whom he thinks useful information can be obtained, even though that person declares that he is unwilling to reply;[10] but the officer has no power to detain for questioning so the use of reasonable force to escape from such detention is not an assault;[11] and the use of excessive force, while a common assault (or wounding, etc.) would not be an offence under s. 51. Where, however, P tapped D on the shoulder, not intending to detain him but in order to speak to him, it was held that P was acting in the course of his duties, though it seems clear that D did not consent to this contact. The court thought that –

"... it is not every trivial interference with a citizen's liberty that amounts to a course of conduct sufficient to take the officer out of the course of his duties."[12]

8. *Ludlow v Burgess* [1971] Crim LR 238, CA; *Pedro v Diss* [1981] 2 All ER 59, 72 Cr App Rep 193. Where D is arrested or detained by an officer unlawfully, for example, where the officer has not used words of arrest or told D the grounds therefor; the officer is not acting in the execution of his duty. Likewise where he searches P without giving reasons: *McBean v Parker* [1983] Crim LR 399; *Brazil v Chief Constable of Surrey* (1983) 77 Cr App Rep 237, DC. Similarly where an officer enters a dwelling house, otherwise than in hot pursuit, without a warrant, to search for evidence of crime: *McLorie v Oxford* [1982] 3 All ER 480, [1982] Crim LR 603.
9. [1964] Crim LR 467; cf. *Davis v Lisle* [1936] 2 KB 434, [1936] 2 All ER 213 *Robson v Hallett* [1967] 2 All ER 407; *McGowan v Chief Constable of Kingston-upon-Hull* [1968] Crim LR 34; *Kay v Hibbert* [1977] Crim LR 226, DC. *Jones and Jones v Lloyd* [1981] Crim LR 340, DC.
10. Code of Practice C. 38 (issued under the Police and Criminal Evidence Act 1984); *Weight v Long* [1986] Crim LR 746.
11. *Kenlin v Gardner* [1967] 2 QB 510, [1966] 3 All ER 931 *Ludlow v Burgess* [1971] Crim LR 238. Cf. *Daniel v Morrison* (1980) 70 Cr App Rep 142, DC.
12. *Donnelly v Jackman* [1970] 1 All ER 987; **SHC 375**, criticised in [1970] Crim LR at 220 and 33 MLR 438; and followed in *Pounder v Police* [1971] NZLR 1808 (constable committing "a trivial trespass"). Cf. *Squires v Botwright* [1972] RTR 462, DC; *Inwood* [1973] 2 All ER 645, CA. See Lanham, "Arrest, Detention and Compulsion" [1974] Crim LR 288.

That the commission of a crime or tort can ever be part of the duty of a constable is an unacceptable proposition; and the case is an "extreme" one,[13] explicable only on the ground that the trespass committed by the constable was a momentary and trivial incident in an otherwise lawful course of conduct. In *Bentley v Brudzinski*,[14] on very similar facts, a different result was reached. Where the question is whether something is trivial or *de minimis*, it is perhaps to be expected that assessments will differ. *Waterfield*[15] is a more difficult case. P, a constable, had been informed that a car had been involved in a serious offence. Evidently acting on the instructions of a superior officer, he attempted to prevent D, the owner of the car, from removing it from the place on the road where it was parked. D drove the car at P, thus assaulting him, in order to remove it. The court held that P was not "entitled" to prevent removal of the car[16] and therefore was not acting in the execution of his duty. The difficulty is that the judgment nowhere specifies in what respect P's act was unlawful. He simply stood in front of the car. It has been pertinently asked, why, if it was not an unlawful act, was it not one that P might properly do in fulfilment of the general duty to bring offenders to justice?[17] It may be, however, that the answer is that P was guilty of obstructing the highway under the Highways Act 1959;[18] but there was no finding that the road was a highway.

Probably the most important application of the provision is in the context of the constable's duty to prevent breaches of the peace which he reasonably apprehends.[19] If it appears (i) that facts existed from which a constable could reasonably have anticipated a breach, as a real and not merely as a remote possibility; and (ii) that he did so anticipate, then he is under a duty to take such steps, whether by arrest or otherwise,[20] as he reasonably thinks are necessary.[1] In *Piddington v Bates*, it was held that P was acting in the course of his duty in forbidding D to join two persons picketing the entrance to certain premises. Notwithstanding the provisions of the Trade Disputes Act 1906, and now the Trade Union and Labour Relations Act 1974,[2] authorising "one or more" persons to picket, the police have a duty to limit the number of pickets if it is necessary to maintain the peace.

Even where no breach of the peace is anticipated, a constable may be under a duty to give instructions to members of the public – for example, to remove an obstruction from the highway – and a deliberate refusal to obey

13. *Collins v Wilcock* [1984] 3 All ER 374 at 378, above, p. 380.
14. [1982] Crim LR 825, DC and commentary.
15. [1964] 1 QB 164, [1963] 3 All ER 659.
16. The case has since been doubted on this point: *Ghani v Jones* [1970] 1 QB 693 at 707, CA. Where a constable in uniform requires a vehicle to stop under s. 159 of the Road Traffic Act 1972, the driver commits an offence if he fails to do so. He has a duty to remain at rest for a reasonable period; but it seems that the constable has no right under the section physically to stop or to detain the driver or vehicle: *Lodwick v Sanders* [1985] 1 All ER 577 at 582–584 [1985] Crim LR 210, per Webster J. But if the constable reasonably suspects the vehicle to be stolen by the driver he is entitled to seize and detain it and arrest the driver: ibid.
17. See "The Arrest of a Motor-Car", by P. J. Fitzgerald, [1965] Crim LR 23.
18. Now s. 137 of the Highways Act 1980. Below, p. 799.
19. *Duncan v Jones* [1936] KB 218. See below, p. 411.
20. *King v Hodges* [1974] Crim LR 424.
1. *Piddington v Bates* [1960] 3 All ER 660.
2. Section 15.

such an instruction may amount to an obstruction of the police. It is in the course of a constable's duty to require pickets to move where they would otherwise obstruct lawful passage on the highway by others.[3]

2 Mens Rea in Cases of Assault and Resistance

The only *mens rea* required is an intention to assault (or, presumably, to resist) and it is no defence that D was reasonably unaware that P was a constable, still less that he was on duty. It was so held by a recorder in a direction to a jury in *Forbes*[4] *and Webb* which six judges in *Prince*[5] accepted as correct; and in *Maxwell*[6] *and Clanchy* the Court of Criminal Appeal, holding that there was evidence to support a jury's finding that D knew P was a policeman, said, obiter, that they wished to cast no doubt on *Forbes*; it was followed in *Mark*;[7] and in *Reynhoudt*[8] a majority of the High Court of Australia (Taylor, Menzies and Owen JJ, Dixon CJ and Kitto J dissenting) arrived at a similar result on the construction of the equivalent provision in Victorian legislation. It is submitted that the better view is that of the dissenting judges in *Reynhoudt* – that at least the chance of P's being a peace officer in the execution of his duty must be foreseen by D when he makes the assault.[9] Such a view avoids any difficulty arising from the fact that s. 36[10] of the 1861 Act uses the words "to the knowledge of the offender", whereas no such words were used in s. 38 or its successor.

Nevertheless, the present English law is that laid down in *Forbes*. This is implicit in *McBride v Turnock*,[11] where D struck at O, who was not a constable, and hit P, who was. Although he had no intention of assaulting P, the Divisional Court held he was guilty of assaulting a constable in the execution of his duty. The *mens rea* for this crime being only that of a common assault, D's "malice" was transferable.[12] No better illustration could be given of the unsatisfactory nature of the rule in *Forbes*.

If D, whether reasonably or not, is unaware that P is a constable and believes in the existence of circumstances of justification or excuse, he should now have a defence.[13] If, however, D knows that P is a constable, it seems that even an honest and reasonable belief that the constable is acting outside the course of his duty will not always be a defence, if the belief is mistaken. In *Fennell*[14] the court assumed that a father might lawfully use

3. *Kavanagh v Hiscock* [1974] QB 600, [1974] 2 All ER 177, CA, applying *Broome v Director of Public Prosecutions* [1974] AC 587, [1974] 1 All ER 314, HL.
4. (1865) 10 Cox CC 362.
5. (1875) LR 2 CCR 154.
6. (1909) 73 JP 176, 2 Cr App Rep 26.
7. [1961] Crim LR 173 (Judge Maxwell Turner).
8. (1962) 36 ALJR 26; **SHC 381**.
9. This was the view of the majority of the court in *Galvin (No. 2)* [1961] VR 740, overruling *Galvin (No. 1)* [1961] VR 733. Barry J thought actual knowledge necessary. Sholl J adhered to his view in *Galvin (No. 1)* that the offence was one of strict liability. See also *McLeod* (1955) 111 CCC 106.
10. Above, p. 387.
11. [1964] Crim LR 456.
12. Above, p. 73.
13. *Gladstone Williams* [1987] 3 All ER 411, (1984) 78 Cr App Rep 276, above, p. 88. *Mark*, supra, requiring reasonable grounds for the belief, can no longer be regarded as good law.
14. [1971] 1 QB 428, [1970] 3 All ER 215, [1970] Crim LR 581 and commentary, CA; **SHC 383**.

reasonable force to free his son from unlawful arrest by the police; but he acted at his peril and, if the arrest proved to be lawful, he was guilty. The court thought it would be otherwise if D mistakenly believed that a relative or friend was in imminent danger of injury and used reasonable force to prevent that.

3 Wilful Obstruction[15]

i) *The meaning of obstruction.* There must be obstruction in fact. An act done with intent to obstruct but which fails to do so is not the offence – but it may be an attempt.[16] A wide interpretation of "obstruction" has been accepted in England. It is not necessary that there should be any interference with the officer himself by physical force or threats. To give a warning to a person who has committed a crime so as to enable him to escape detection by police is enough. Thus in *Betts v Stevens*,[17] D committed the offence by warning drivers who were exceeding the speed limit that there was a police trap ahead. In the earlier case of *Bastable v Little*[18] it had been held that D was not guilty of the offence when he warned a driver, who was not proved to be committing an offence, of the speed trap. This distinction did not appeal to the divisional court in *Green v Moore*[19] which thought *Bastable v Little* "a very curious decision based on a highly eccentric view of the facts" and one which "should be strictly confined to the facts as the court found them". The court conceded that, if the warning was addressed to motorists who had not exceeded the speed limit and was intended to discourage them from *ever* doing so, the decision was right. But they thought that a more realistic view of the facts was that D intended to warn the drivers to slow down until they had passed through the speed trap, after which they might race away with impunity. So the distinction is between advising a person to *suspend* his criminal activity, so that he will not be found out by the police, which is an offence; and advising him to give it up altogether – in which case he will not be found out by the police – which is not an offence. In *Green v Moore*, D was a probationer constable who "tipped off" the landlord of his local pub that a police "support group" were waiting to catch him in the dastardly act of selling liquor out of hours. Thereafter, naturally, the landlord kept strictly within the letter of the law. D was aware that "the landlord did not give a high priority to the strict observance of licensing hours", and the court construed his warning as one that the sale of liquor out of hours had better be *suspended* until the support group moved on to deal with some other nefarious activity. If he had said, "Fred, the sale of liquor out of hours simply isn't on – give it up, once and for all" – the efforts of the support group would have been equally frustrated, but that would have been no offence. The "suspension theory" can only operate where the person "tipped off" is known or believed to be engaged in a continuing criminal activity or system. If he is dissuaded from

15. See Coutts (1956) 19 MLR 411.
16. *Bennett v Bale* [1986] Crim LR 404, DC and commentary.
17. [1910] 1 KB 1.
18. [1907] 1 KB 59.
19. [1982] QB 1044, [1982] 1 All ER 428; **SHC** 377. Cf. *Moore v Green* [1983] 1 All ER 663, DC.

persisting in what is or appears to be a "one-off" offence, which he is about to commit, there is no room for the suspension theory. In *Green v Moore*, D knew of the landlord's illegal practice.

Where the police tell an offender to desist from an offence his deliberate refusal may amount to an obstruction, as where D is obstructing the highway and refuses to obey the instructions of a constable to move.[20] It is not necessary that the constable should anticipate a breach of the peace. A constable has no power to arrest D for obstructing him, unless the obstruction was such that it actually caused, or was likely to cause, a breach of the peace.[1]

Presumably it must be proved that some named officer was obstructed;[2] it would hardly be enough that D warned E in general terms that if he did not stop committing an offence he would be found out; or if he advised E to get a television licence because the detector van was visiting his street next week – apart from the fact that the operators of the van would not be constables.

Hinchliffe v Sheldon[3] might be thought to go further than *Betts v Stevens*[4] in that it was only suspected, and not proved, that an offence was being committed; but there the warning was tantamount to a physical obstruction.[5] D, a publican's son, shouted a warning to his parents that the police were outside the public house. It was 11.17 p.m. and the lights were on in the bar, so presumably the police suspected that liquor was being consumed after hours. There was a delay of eight minutes before the police were admitted and no offence was detected. *Bastable v Little*[6] was distinguished on the ground that the police had a right to enter the licensed premises under the Licensing Act 1953.[7] Whether an offence was being committed or not, an entry under this statutory right was in execution of their duty; and their *entry* was obstructed.

Lord Goddard CJ defined "obstructing" as

"Making it more difficult for the police to carry out their duties."[8]

This is far wider than was necessary for the decision. But the dictum has been applied in New Zealand in a case where D, a bystander, merely advised E not to answer any questions put to him by P, a police officer, investigating a suspected offence.[9] E was perfectly entitled to remain silent but his doing so undoubtedly made it more difficult for P to carry out his

20. *Tynan v Balmer* [1967] 1 QB 91, [1966] 2 All ER 133; *Donaldson v Police* [1968] NZLR 32.
  1. *Wershof v Metropolitan Police Comr* [1978] 3 All ER 540 (May J); *Gelberg v Miller* [1961] 1 All ER 291, [1961] 1 WLR 153.
  2. *Syce v Harrison* [1981] Crim LR 110.
  3. [1955] 3 All ER 406, [1955] 1 WLR 1207.
  4. Above, p. 392.
  5. See Coutts, op. cit.
  6. Above, p. 392.
  7. See now Licensing Act 1964, s. 186 (1). The police must have reasonable grounds for suspecting that an offence is being or is about to be committed: *Valentine v Jackson* [1972] 1 All ER 90, [1972] 1 WLR 528.
  8. [1955] 3 All ER at 408.
  9. *Steele v Kingsbeer* [1957] NZLR 552; distinguished in *Dash v Police* [1970] NZLR 273 (solicited advice, disinterestedly given, to a motorist not to take a breath test, which he was not bound to take; held, not "wilful" obstruction).

duty of investigating crime. An earlier decision[10] in the Supreme Court of Victoria is to the contrary and is to be preferred. Surely a solicitor who advises his client to say nothing cannot be guilty of an offence, though he undoubtedly makes things more difficult for the police; and why should a solicitor be in a different situation from anyone else?

In England, it has been held that refusal to answer a constable's question, though it undoubtedly makes it more difficult for the police to carry out their duties, does not amount to wilful obstruction: *Rice v Connolly*.[11] The fact that the refusal is expressed in abusive and obscene terms should in principle make no difference.[12] If D's language amounts to some other offence, such as that under the Public Order Act 1986, s. 4,[13] he should be charged with that. *Ricketts v Cox*[14] seems a doubtful decision. The court accepted the finding of the justices that the "totality of [the defendants'] behaviour and attitude at this stage amounted to an obstruction . . .", but all that could be added to the total was the abusive, obscene and hostile attitude of the defendants, reprehensible, no doubt, and galling to the officers but still the assertion of an actual right.[15] While the report does refer to some unspecified threat by D, the court attaches no particular significance to it and the decision seems to be based on the generally "obstructive" nature of D's behaviour.

Telling the police a false story is quite different from merely remaining silent and clearly an obstruction.[16] Refusing to reveal the whereabouts of a prohibited drug is not an obstruction; but burying it to hide it from an officer searching for it might be, when the officer's task is made more difficult.[17] These difficulties would not arise if the Act had been held to be limited to physical interference; and it has been held[18] to be so limited in Scotland where "obstruct" has been construed *ejusdem generis* with "assault" and "resist".[19] D was held not guilty when he told lies to the police to conceal an offence of which he was guilty. There is much to be said in favour of the Scottish view.[20]

One who is guilty of obstruction is, ex hypothesi, in breach of a legal duty; but it is not necessary that the act relied on as an obstruction should be unlawful independently of its operation as an obstruction of the police.[1] It appears that the conferment of powers and imposition of duties on the police, may, impliedly, impose duties on others not to impede the exercise by the police of these powers and duties. The right of a constable to enter

10. *Hogben v Chandler* [1940] VLR 285.
11. [1966] 2 QB 414, [1966] 2 All ER 649, DC.
12. See Marshall J in *Rice v Connolly* at 420.
13. Below, p. 790.
14. (1981) 74 Cr App Rep 298, DC.
15. See commentary at [1982] Crim LR 184. The partial retraction by the commentator at [1982] Crim LR 484 seems unnecessary.
16. *Rice v Connolly* (supra); *Mathews v Dwan* [1949] NZLR 1037.
17. See note on *Syce v Harrison* [1981] Crim LR 110n.
18. *Curlett v M'Kechnie* 1938 SCJ 176.
19. The re-arrangement of these offences by the Police Act precludes the application of the *ejusdem generis* rule; but it could have been applied when they were contained in the Offences against the Person Act 1861.
20. See Coutts, op. cit.
1. *Dibble v Ingleton* [1972] 1 QB 480, [1972] 1 All ER 275. See [1972] CLJ 193.

licensed premises when he reasonably suspects an offence is being committed implies a duty under the Police Act on the licensee and others to let him in.[2] The right of a constable to require a driver in certain circumstances to provide a specimen of breath[3] implies a duty on the motorist (though he has not been arrested) to remain "there or nearby" until 20 minutes have elapsed since he had his last drink and the constable has had a reasonable opportunity to carry out the test.[4] Since the consumption of further alcohol will render impossible a valid breath test, which it is the constable's right to take, the driver is also under an implied duty not to drink alcohol. So it will amount to obstruction if, knowing that a breath test may be required, the driver runs away or consumes alcohol[5] whether or not the police have arrived on the scene.[6] If, when D is found to have consumed an excess of alcohol, it is the duty of a constable to remove D's car from the highway, there is an implied duty on D to hand over the keys of the car.[7]

Whether a duty thus to co-operate with the police is to be implied depends on whether this is a compelling inference from the nature of the police duty or right. To some extent it is a question of policy – witness the ruling that there is no duty to answer police questions but there is a duty not to give misleading answers.[8] In *Dibble v Ingleton*[9] the court distinguished between "positive acts" which will amount to obstruction and omissions which will not. Of course, here as elsewhere,[10] the law penalises acts more readily than omissions but this is only one factor and omissions may amount to obstruction even when the omission is not an offence independently of s. 51.[11]

ii) *Mens rea.* Unlike "assault" and "resist", obstruction must be "wilful". D must intend to behave in such a way as to make it more difficult for the police to carry out their duties. His conduct need be neither hostile to, nor aimed at, the police, as some cases[12] have suggested: *Lewis v Cox*[13] where D persisted in opening the door of a van in which Q, who had been arrested, was about to be driven away. D's purpose was not to obstruct the police but to find out where Q was being taken, but, since he must have known that he was preventing the police officer from driving off, the justices were bound to find that he intended to make it more difficult for them to carry out their duty.[14] Similarly in *Hills v Ellis*[15] where D laid his hand on a constable's

2. *Hinchliffe v Sheldon*, above, p. 393.
3. Road Traffic Act 1972, s. 8, as substituted by Transport Act 1981, Sch. 8.
4. *Director of Public Prosecutions v Carey* [1970] AC 1072 at 1097, [1969] 3 All ER 1662 at p. 1680.
5. *Dibble v Ingleton* above. *Cunliffe v Bleasdale* [1972] Crim LR 567, per Melford Stevenson J. Cf. *Britton* [1973] RTR 502, CA.
6. *Neal v Evans* [1976] RTR 333, [1976] Crim LR 384.
7. *Stunt v Bolton* [1972] RTR 435, [1972] Crim LR 561.
8. *Rice v Connolly*, above.
9. Supra.
10. Above, p. 48.
11. For example, *Stunt v Bolton*, supra.
12. *Willmott v Atack* [1977] QB 498, [1976] 3 All ER 794; *Hills v Ellis* [1983] QB 680. [1983] 1 All ER 667; **SHC 383**.
13. [1984] 3 All ER 672, [1985] QB 509.
14. Cf. the discussion of intention, above, p. 55.
15. Footnote 12, above.

arm to draw his attention to the fact that, as D believed, he was arresting the wrong man. *Forbes* is inapplicable to a charge of obstruction. In *Ostler v Elliott*[16] it was held that D's reasonable belief that the police officers were robbers was a defence to wilful obstruction. Since *Gladstone Williams*[17] the only question would be whether the belief was truly held, reasonably or not.

In *Rice v Connolly*[18] it was said that "wilfully" means not only "intentionally" but also "without lawful excuse." This is difficult to follow. "Wilfully" must surely refer to the state of mind of the defendant. But whether he has a lawful excuse for what he does generally depends on D's conduct and the circumstances in which he acts.[19] In that case, D would have been no more "wilful" if he had told a false story. The difference seems to lie in the conduct which the court considers to be permissible. "Wilfully" may of course import the absence of any *belief* on D's part of circumstances of lawful excuse.[20] If the story told by D were in fact false, but D believed it to be true, the constable might be obstructed, but he would not be "wilfully" obstructed.

2) *Assault Occasioning Actual Bodily Harm*

By s. 47 of the Offences against the Person Act 1861, an assault occasioning actual bodily harm is an offence triable either way and punishable on indictment with five years' imprisonment. "Bodily harm", according to the House of Lords in *Director of Public Prosecutions v Smith*[1]

"needs no explanation. 'Grievous' means no more and no less than 'really serious'."

It seems to follow that, under s. 47, the harm need not be really serious.

In *Miller*,[2] Lynskey J quoted the statement formerly contained in Archbold:[3]

"Actual bodily harm includes any hurt or injury calculated to interfere with the health or comfort of the prosecutor . . ."

Lynskey J held that this included a hysterical and nervous condition resulting from an assault, taking the view that an injury to the state of a man's mind is actual bodily harm.

Since – absurdly – the maximum punishment for this offence is the same as that for maliciously inflicting grievous bodily harm contrary to s. 20 of the same Act – which until recently was also held to require proof of an assault[4] – it would seem that the prosecutor could, with advantage, almost

---

16. [1980] Crim LR 584. Note that, if he had assaulted the officers, his reasonable belief that they were not officers would not, in itself, have been a defence to a charge of assaulting them in the execution of their duty. See commentary at [1980] Crim LR 585.
17. [1987] 3 All ER 411, (1983) 78 Cr App Rep 276, CA, above, p. 88.
18. Above, p. 394.
19. See comment at [1966] Crim LR 390.
20. Cf. above, pp. 35, 122.
   1. [1961] AC 290 at 334, [1960] 3 All ER 161 at 171; Above, p. 328.
   2. [1954] 2 QB 282 at 292, [1954] 2 All ER 529 at 534; below, p. 431; **SHC 362**. Cf. *Burrell v Harmer* [1967] Crim LR 169 and commentary thereon; above, p. 382.
   3. 32nd ed., 959.
   4. Below, p. 399.

always indict for an offence under s. 47, whatever the degree of harm caused, thus incurring the burden of proving a less degree of harm.

The *mens rea* would appear to be merely that of an assault.[5] Once assault is proved, the only remaining question is one of causation – did the assault cause the actual bodily harm? This is an objective matter.[6] So, where D assaulted P by trying to take off her coat and she jumped out of a moving car and sustained injury, the only question was whether P's action was the natural consequence of the assault.[7] Only if her act was something that no reasonable man could be expected to foresee would the chain of causation be broken.

3 Wounding and Grievous Bodily Harm

Sections 18 and 20 of the Offences against the Person Act 1861 create offences of wounding and causing or inflicting grievous bodily harm. By s. 18, as amended by the Criminal Law Act 1967:

"Whosoever shall unlawfully and maliciously by any means whatsoever wound or cause any grievous bodily harm to any person with intent to do some grievous bodily harm to any person or with intent to resist or prevent the lawful apprehension or detainer of any person, shall be guilty of an offence, and being convicted thereof shall be liable to imprisonment for life."

By s. 20:

"Whosoever shall unlawfully and maliciously wound or inflict any grievous bodily harm upon any other person, either with or without any weapon or instrument shall be guilty of [an offence triable either way] and being convicted thereof shall be liable to imprisonment for five years."

The two sections are closely associated with one another and it is convenient to consider them together. Each creates two offences, one of wounding and the other of causing (s. 18) or inflicting (s. 20) grievous bodily harm.

1) *The Actus Reus*

1 To Wound

In order to constitute a wound, the continuity of the whole skin must be broken.[8] Where a pellet fired by an air pistol hit P in the eye but caused only an internal rupturing of blood vessels and not a break in the skin, there was

---

5. Above, p. 379.
6. Above, p. 45.
7. *Roberts* (1971) 56 Cr App Rep 95, [1972] Crim LR 27; **SHC 363**.
8. *Moriarty v Brookes* (1834) 6 C & P 684.

no wound.[9] It is not enough that the cuticle or outer skin be broken if the inner skin remains intact.[10] Where P was treated with such violence that his collarbone was broken, it was held that there was no wound if his skin was intact.[11] It was held to be a wound, however, where the lining membrane of the urethra was ruptured and bled, evidence being given that the membrane is precisely the same in character as that which lines the cheek and the external and internal skin of the lip.[12]

It was held that there was no wounding under the 1837 Act[13] where P, in warding off D's attempt to cut his throat, struck his hands against a knife held by D and cut them;[14] and where P was knocked down by D and wounded by falling on iron trams.[15] That Act did not contain the words "by any means whatsoever", and it is probable that these cases would now be decided differently. Even under the earlier law, D was guilty where he struck P on the hat with a gun and the hard rim of the hat caused a wound.[16]

It was formerly held that wounding must be the result of a battery but it is probably now sufficient that the wound be directly inflicted whether by a battery or not.[17]

2 To Cause or Inflict Grievous Bodily Harm

"Grievous bodily harm" was formerly interpreted to include any harm which seriously interferes with health or comfort;[18] but in *Smith*[19] the House of Lords said that there was no warrant for giving the words a meaning other than that which they convey in their ordinary and natural meaning. Grievous bodily harm may cover cases where there is no wounding as, for instance, the broken collarbone in *Wood*.[20] Conversely, there might be a technical "wounding" which could not be said to amount to grievous bodily harm.

Where s. 18 uses the word "cause", s. 20 uses "inflict". The effect is that s. 18 may be wider than s. 20. In a series of cases[21] from 1861 until 1983 it was held or assumed that the words "inflict" and "wound" both imply an "assault". D could be convicted of an offence under s. 20 only if it was proved that he wounded or caused grievous bodily harm by committing an assault. It followed that, when D was charged with an offence under s. 20, he could be convicted on that indictment of common assault, because that

9. *C (a minor) v Eisenhower* [1984] QB 331, (1983) 78 Cr App Rep 48, DC.
10. *M'Loughlin* (1838) 8 C & P 635.
11. *Wood* (1830) 1 Mood CC 278.
12. *Waltham* (1849) 3 Cox CC 442. Contrast *Jones* (1849) 3 Cox CC 441.
13. 7 Will. 4 & 1 Vic. c. 85, s. 4.
14. *Beckett* (1836) 1 Mood & R 526 (Parke B); *Day* (1845) 1 Cox CC 207; above, p. 381. Cf. *Coleman* (1920) 84 JP 112.
15. *Spooner* (1853) 6 Cox CC 392.
16. *Sheard* (1837) 2 Mood CC 13.
17. *Wilson*, below, p. 399. Cf. *Taylor* (1869) LR 1 CCR 194; *Austin* (1973) 58 Cr App Rep 163, CA.
18. *Ashman* (1858) 1 F & F 88.
19. [1961] AC 290, [1960] 3 All ER 161; above, p. 328; followed in *Metharam* [1961] 3 All ER 200.
20. Above, footnote 11.
21. *Yeadon and Birch* (1861) 9 Cox CC 91; *Taylor* (1869) LR 1 CCR 194; *Clarence* (1888) 22 QBD 23; *Snewing* [1972] Crim LR 267; *Carpenter* (30th July, 1979, unreported, cited [1983] 1 All ER 1004).

was an "included offence". But there was a second line of cases[1] where the alleged requirement of an assault was simply ignored and convictions were upheld although it was very difficult, if not impossible, to discern an assault on the facts.

In 1983, in *Wilson*,[2] the House of Lords resolved the matter by deciding that "inflict" does not, after all, imply assault.[3] The House followed the Australian case of *Salisbury*[4] where it was said that, though "inflict" does not imply assault, it does have a narrower meaning than "cause". Unlike "cause", "inflict" implies the direct application of force. This, however, is almost a distinction without a difference for the direct application of force usually is an assault – or, strictly, a battery, which is probably what "assault" meant in this context. *Wilson* dispenses us from the need to look for an assault in this second line of cases, but the requirement of directness presents equal difficulties. In those cases D was held guilty under s. 20 where, for example, he so frightened P that he jumped through a window[5] or accidentally injured himself by putting his hand through a glass door under[6] "a well-grounded apprehension of violence". Similarly in *Martin*[7] where, shortly before the end of a performance in a theatre. D put out the lights and placed an iron bar across the doorway. He was convicted of inflicting grievous bodily harm on those injured in the panic. We need no longer search for the invisible assault in these cases, but it is almost equally difficult to discern any *direct* application of force. Certainly force was applied in each case in the sense that there was an impact, causing injury to P. The presence of force in this sense is sufficient to distinguish *Clarence*,[8] the leading authority for the overruled proposition that inflict implies assault. D, knowing that he was suffering from gonorrhea, had intercourse with his wife and infected her. No doubt he had caused her grievous bodily harm but the court held that he had not "inflicted" it because he had not committed an assault. Today, he might be acquitted on the different ground that, because P consented (though in ignorance of his condition), there was no application of force. The actual decision in *Clarence* has not been overruled. In that case, the harm was surely caused "directly" so the distinguishing feature appears to be simply "force". The position appears to be that if force is applied, directly or indirectly by D, harm is "inflicted". If harm is caused without the use of force, it is not inflicted, but, if grievous, and intentionally caused, it may be the subject of an indictment under s. 18.

1. *Halliday* (1869) 61 LT 701; **SHC 419**; *Lewis* [1970] Crim LR 647, CA; *Mackie* [1973] Crim LR 54; *Boswell*]1973] Crim LR 307 and *Cartledge v Allen* [1973] Crim LR 530, DC.
2. [1984] AC 242 at 260, [1983] 3 All ER 448 at 455.
3. The House nevertheless contrived to hold that a person charged under s. 20 could be convicted on that indictment of a common assault by virtue of s. 6(3) of the Criminal Law Act 1967 – a much criticised decision. See Glanville Williams, [1984] CLJ 290 and commentary at [1984] Crim LR 37.
4. [1976] VR 452 at 461.
5. *Halliday* (1869) 61 LT 701.
6. *Cartledge v Allen* [1973] Crim LR 530.
7. (1881) 8 QBD 54 CCR.
8. (1888) 22 QBD 23.

2) *The Mens Rea*

1 Malice

Both sections contain the word "maliciously". It is settled that this word means "intentionally or recklessly" and "reckless" is used in the *Cunningham*, not the *Caldwell*, sense.[9] The next question is, what is the harm that must be intended or risked? The answer might be expected to be, wounding or grievous bodily harm;[10] but the law has developed differently. It is enough that D foresaw that some physical harm, not necessarily amounting to grievous bodily harm or wounding, might occur.[11] It is not enough, however, that D intended to frighten, whether the charge is one of wounding[12] or inflicting grievous bodily harm.[13]

Where, under s. 18, the charge is of causing grievous bodily harm with intent to do grievous bodily harm, the word "maliciously" obviously has no part to play. Any *mens rea* which it might import is comprehended within the ulterior intent. Where the charge is wounding with intent to do grievous bodily harm, the word can be given meaning, though the occasion to invoke it is unlikely to arise. It is possible for D to intend to do grievous bodily harm, without intending to wound. If he in fact wounds and is charged accordingly, then it is arguable that it must be proved, not only that he intended to cause grievous bodily harm, but also that he foresaw that he might wound, otherwise the wounding is not malicious.

Where the charge is of wounding or causing grievous bodily harm with intent to resist lawful apprehension, then there is no difficulty in giving meaning to "maliciously" and it is submitted that meaning should be given to that word. A mere intent to resist lawful apprehension should not found liability for a charge of wounding or causing grievous bodily harm. It is submitted that the Court of Appeal went too far in *Mowatt*[14] in saying that "In section 18 the word 'maliciously' adds nothing."

The observation was obiter, the court in that case being concerned with an appeal from conviction under s. 20. The court held that, under this section, –

"... the word 'maliciously' does import upon the part of the person who unlawfully inflicts the wound or other grievous bodily harm an awareness that his act may have the consequence of causing some physical harm to some other person. That is what is meant by 'the particular kind of harm' in the citation from Professor Kenny.[15] It is quite unnecessary that the accused should have foreseen that his unlawful act might cause

---

9. Above, p. 62. *Cunningham* [1957] 2 QB 396, [1957] 2 All ER 412, CCA; *Mowatt* [1968] 1 QB 421, [1967] 3 All ER 47; *W (a minor) v Dolbey* [1983] Crim LR 681, DC; *Grimshaw* [1984] Crim LR 108, CA. The court in *Dume* (1986) Times, 16 October, seems to have been unduly hesitant.
10. Cf. above, p. 70.
11. *Mowatt*, supra and below, p. 401; *Sullivan* [1981] Crim LR 46.
12. *Flack v Hunt* (1979) 70 Cr App Rep 51.
13. *Sullivan* [1981] Crim LR 46, CA.
14. [1968] 1 QB 421, [1967] 3 All ER 47; **SHC 64**. See Buxton, "Negligence and Constructive Crime" [1969] Crim LR 112. See also *Ward* (1872) LR 1 CCR 356.
15. *Outlines of Criminal Law* (19th ed) 211. The citation is the passage approved by the Court of Criminal Appeal in *Cunningham* [1957] 2 QB 396, [1957] 2 All ER 412; **SHC 63**; above, p. 62; below, p. 404.

physical harm of the gravity described in the section, *i.e.*, a wound or serious physical injury. It is enough that he should have foreseen that some physical harm to some person, albeit of a minor character, might result."

If this be correct for s. 20, then it is submitted that it is also correct for s. 18, where the ulterior intent alleged is an intent to resist lawful apprehension. It is submitted, however, that the statement in *Mowatt* is unsound in principle.[16] A person who intends some injury less than wounding or grievous bodily harm intends to commit another offence under the Offences against the Person Act, that of assault occasioning actual bodily harm contrary to s. 47.[17] This appears to be a less serious offence than that under s. 20 and it is wrong that the *mens rea* of the less offence should suffice for liability for the greater. In fact, offences under both s. 20 and s. 47 are punishable with five years' imprisonment.[18] This is quite irrational, and no doubt happens because the Act, like most of the 1861 legislation, is a rag-bag of offences brought together from a variety of statutes with little or no attempt to introduce uniformity or consistency. Thus the accused who intends harm of a minor character and is convicted of an offence under s. 20 cannot be more severely punished than for the offence which he intended; but this should not be allowed to obscure the violation of principle involved. A rational system, if it distinguished at all between causing actual and causing grievous bodily harm, would provide for different penalties and the *mens rea* of the less should not be sufficient to found liability for the greater offence.

Whatever consequence it is that must be foreseen, it is clear that there must be proof that the accused person actually foresaw that consequence. Any doubt there may have been about this has been dispelled by the Criminal Justice Act 1967, s. 8.[19] *Mowatt* was decided before the Act came into force, and certain observations in the case are therefore suspect. It was said[20] that where the act:

"... was a direct assault which any ordinary person would be bound to realise was likely to cause some physical harm to the other person ... and the defence put forward on behalf of the accused is not that the assault was accidental or that he did not realise that it might cause some physical harm to the victim, but is some other defence such as that he did not do the alleged act or that he did it in self-defence, it is unnecessary to deal specifically in the summing up with what is meant by the word 'maliciously' in the section."

This suggests that the jury need not be directed on the issue because they are bound to infer that D foresaw the result by reason of its being a natural

---

16. But *Mowatt* was followed in *Sullivan* [1981] Crim LR 46, CA, and, in *Jones* [1987] Crim LR 123, the court indicated only that counsel would have great difficulty in persuading them that *Mowatt* was, in this respect, wrong.

17. Above, p. 396.

18. Thus the prosecution might always use s. 47 where the onus on the Crown is much less, so that s. 20 would become redundant except where the jury acquit on a charge under s. 18 and convict instead of an offence under s. 20, which they may do though that offence be not expressly charged: Criminal Law Act 1967, s. 6 (3).

19. Above, p. 85.

20. [1968] 1 QB 421 at 426–427, [1967] 3 All ER 47 at 50.

and probable consequence of his actions. This is directly contrary to the words of s. 8. Under s. 10 of the Criminal Justice Act 1967, formal admissions may be made; but, if D has not admitted his malice, then it is submitted that it must be proved like every other element in the crime. The fact that the evidence appears to the judge to be overwhelming is not a good reason for not leaving it to the jury.

2 The Ulterior Intent

Section 18 alone requires an ulterior intent which may be either an intent to do grievous bodily harm or an intent to resist or prevent the lawful apprehension or detainer of any person. Recklessness is not enough.[1] A count is not bad for duplicity because it specifies the ulterior intent in the alternative; the intents specified "are variations of method rather than creations of separate offences in themselves", according to *Naismith*[2] – though it is difficult to see how an ulterior intent can be equated with a "method".

The intent specified in the indictment must be proved. It is not enough to prove another variety of intent described in the section. So D had to be acquitted where the various counts of the indictment charged intent to murder, to disable, or to do some grievous bodily harm and the jury found that the acts were done to resist and prevent D's apprehension *and for no other purpose*.[3] But if D intends to prevent his apprehension and, in order to do so, intends to cause grievous bodily harm, he may be convicted under an indictment charging only the latter intent. It is immaterial which is the principal and which the subordinate intent.[4]

Intention has the same meaning as in the law of murder[5] so the prosecution must prove either (i) that it was D's purpose to cause grievous bodily harm or, if it was not his purpose, (ii) that he knew that grievous bodily harm was a virtually certain consequence of his act. In case (ii), that is evidence from which the jury may infer that he had the requisite intent.[6]

If D intends to cause grievous bodily harm to O and, striking at O, he by accident wounds another person P, he may be indicted for wounding P with intent to cause grievous bodily harm to O.[7] If D intends to cause grievous bodily harm to O, and strikes the person he aims at who is in fact P, he may be convicted of wounding P with intent to cause grievous bodily harm to P.[8]

1. *Re Knight's Appeal* (1968) 12 FLR 81.
2. [1961] 2 All ER 735, [1961] 1 WLR 952. (C-MAC).
3. *Duffin and Marshall* (1818) Russ & Ry 365; cf. *Boyce* (1824) 1 Mood CC 29.
4. *Gillow* (1825) 1 Mood CC 85. Cf. *Cox* (1818) Russ & Ry 362. In *Woodburne and Coke* (1722) 16 State Tr 53, the defence to an indictment charging intent to maim and disfigure was that D intended to kill. Lord King CJ directed (at p. 81) that the latter intent did not exclude the former. Willes J and Eyre B expressed some dissatisfaction with this case: East, 1 PC 400; and cf. *Sullivan* (1841) Car & M 209.
5. *Bryson* [1985] Crim LR 669; cf. *Belfon* [1976] 3 All ER 46, CA.
6. Above, p. 56.
7. *Monger* [1973] Crim LR 301, per Mocatta J holding that D could not be convicted where the indictment alleged intent to harm P. This is in accord with *Ryan* (1839) 2 Mood & R 213 and *Hewlett* (1858) 1 F & F 91 but contrary to *Hunt* (1825) 1 Mood CC 93 and *Jarvis, Langdon and Stear* (1837) 2 Mood & R 40. Cf. the doctrine of transferred malice, above, p. 73 and comment on *Monger* in [1973] Crim LR 302.
8. *Smith* (1855) Dears CC 559 at 560; *Stopford* (1870) 11 Cox CC 643.

The intent to cause grievous bodily harm requires no further consideration. The intent to resist lawful apprehension is obviously negatived if the attempted apprehension is believed to be, and is, unlawful.[9] But if the apprehension is lawful, it has been held that[10] it is no defence that D believed it unlawful. This was put on the ground that ignorance of the law was not a defence. It does not follow that D should be convicted if he wrongly believed in a state of *facts* such that, if it had existed, the arrest would have been unlawful. In such a case he should be acquitted.[11] It is, moreover, arguable that even a mistake of law should afford a defence, being a mistake of civil law which negatives *mens rea*.[12]

4 Administering Poison

1 *The Actus Reus*

Sections 23 and 24 of the Offences against the Person Act 1861 create offences, punishable with ten and five years' imprisonment respectively, with a similar *actus reus*. In each case, the definition includes the words –

"... unlawfully ... administer to or cause to be administered to or taken by any other person any poison or other destructive or noxious thing. ..."[13]

But under s. 23, the *actus reus* includes a further element –

"... so as thereby to endanger the life of such person, or so as thereby to inflict upon such person any grievous bodily harm ...".

A poison is "administered" by D if it is left by him for P who takes it up and consumes it;[14] but it seems that it is not administered until it is taken into the stomach.[15] To leave the poison, intending it to be taken, would be an attempt. To squirt fluid at another is not to "administer" it.[16]

In *Marcus*,[17] a case under s. 24, "noxious" was broadly interpreted. A substance which may be harmless if taken in small quantities is noxious if administered in sufficient quantity to injure, aggrieve or annoy.[18] The meaning is taken to be coloured by the purpose which D may have in view. It is not necessary that the substance should be injurious to bodily health: "by 'noxious' is meant something different in quality from and of less importance than poison or other destructive things." The court quoted the

---

9. *Walker* (1854) Dears CC 358; *Sanders* (1867) LR 1 CCR 75.
10. *Bentley* (1850) 4 Cox CC 406.
11. *Gladstone Williams* [1987] 3 All ER 411, (1983) 78 Cr App Rep 276, CA, above, p. 88.
12. Above, p. 83.
13. The meaning of poison, etc., is considered above, p. 367.
14. *Harley* (1830) 4 C & P 369; *Dale* (1852) 6 Cox CC 14. D would more appropriately be charged with "causing ... to be taken".
15. *Cadman* (1825) *Carrington's Supplement*, 237. The report to the contrary in Ryan and Moody 114 is said to be inaccurate: *Harley* (above) per Parke J: and 6 Cox CC 16 n (c). But see *Walford* (1899) 34 L Jo 116, per Wills J.
16. *Dones* [1987] Crim LR 682 (CCC) and commentary.
17. [1981] 2 All ER 833, [1981] 1 WLR 774, CA.
18. Following *Hennah* (1877) 13 Cox CC 547 and *Cramp* (1880) 5 QBD 307. Cf. *Marlow* (1964) 49 Cr App Rep 49 (Brabin J).

Shorter Oxford Dictionary meaning, "injurious, hurtful, harmful, un-wholesome", and opined that the insertion of the celebrated snail in the ginger beer bottle in *Donoghue v Stevenson*[19] with intent to annoy would have amounted to the offence. It was held that the insertion of sedative and sleeping tablets into a bottle of milk was an attempt to commit an offence under s. 24. While the tablets would cause no more than sedation or possibly sleep, they might be a danger to a person doing such normal but potentially hazardous acts as driving or crossing the street.

The court "explained" *Cato*,[20] a case under s. 23, where it was said that a thing could not be noxious merely because it was harmful if taken in large quantities. That observation was not "explicable" but wrong. The actual decision, however, that heroin is a noxious thing even where it is adminis-tered to a person with a high tolerance to whom it is unlikely to do any particular harm, is presumably right. Heroin is noxious because "it is liable to cause injury in common use".[1] It was no answer that P was experienced in taking heroin and had a high tolerance; nor was P's consent a defence.[2]

Because the interpretation of "noxious" in s. 24 was coloured by the words, "injure, aggrieve or annoy", it is arguable that in s. 23 the word must be read in the light of the fact that the substance must endanger life or inflict grievous bodily harm, and it is indeed difficult to see how a substance with a potential only to aggrieve or annoy could result in the *actus reus*.

2) *The Mens Rea*

Under s. 23 the only *mens rea* required is intention or recklessness as to the administration of a noxious thing. This, at least, is plainly required by the use in the section of the word "maliciously"; and, of course, it has been so held in the leading case of *Cunningham*.[3] It may be, however, on present authority, that the requirement of malice does not extend to the second part of the *actus* – so as to endanger life or inflict grievous bodily harm.

Section 24 requires an ulterior intent:

"with intent to injure aggrieve or annoy such person".

When a drug is given to P with intent to keep him awake, it seems that whether this amounts to an intention to injure depends on whether D has a malevolent or a benevolent purpose. If D, a homosexual man, gives the drug to P, a small boy, with the motive of ingratiating himself with P or rendering him susceptible to sexual offences, he has an intent to injure:

---

19. [1932] AC 562.
20. [1976] 1 All ER 260, [1976] 1 WLR 110; **SHC 368**; cf. *Dalby* [1982] 1 All ER 916, [1982] 1 WLR 425, CA.
  1. [1976] 1 All ER at 268.
  2. See also *McShane* [1977] Crim LR 737, CA.
  3. [1957] 2 QB 396, [1957] 2 All ER 412; **SHC 63**; D tore the gas meter from the wall of an unoccupied house to steal money from it. The gas seeped into the neighbouring houses and was taken by P, whose life was endangered. D's conviction under s. 23 was quashed because the judge directed the jury only that "malicious" meant "wicked". See now Criminal Damage Act 1971, s. 1 (2), below, p. 677.

Hill.[4] It would probably be otherwise if D's intention was to enable P to stay awake to enjoy the fireworks or greet his father on return from work. The administration of a drug to the pilot of an aircraft to keep him awake is probably not an offence. The administration of the same drug for the purpose of carrying out a prolonged interrogation may be.[5] This casts doubt on *Weatherall*.[6] D put a sleeping tablet in P's tea to enable him to search her handbag for letters proving that she was committing adultery. It was held that there was insufficient evidence of intent to injure, aggrieve or annoy: but there was surely evidence of a "malevolent" purpose, as there would be if D gave P a sleeping tablet with intent to rape her. The test of malevolence is presumably objective. The paedophile's belief that the drugged child will enjoy and profit from the sexual experience is unlikely to be regarded as capable of being a "benevolent" purpose.

The contrast between "so as thereby to" in s. 23 and "with intent to" in s. 24; suggests that no *mens rea* is required as to the second part of the *actus* in s. 23; and it was so held in *Cato*. The requirement of "malice" was satisfied by the deliberate injection of heroin into P's body. No foresight of danger to life or the infliction of grievous bodily harm was required.

In *Cunningham*, the court thought the jury should have been told that D must have foreseen that the coal gas might cause injury to someone. They did not say he must have foreseen that life would be endangered. This is an extraordinary result, in that a less culpable state of mind is required for the more serious offence than the less.

By s. 25, a person charged under s. 23 may be convicted of an offence under s. 24. But a person charged under s. 24 may not be convicted of an offence under s. 23.[7]

5 False Imprisonment

False imprisonment, like assault and battery, is both a misdemeanour at common law and a tort. The civil remedy is much more commonly invoked and most of the cases on this subject are civil actions. But, as will appear, it is probable that there are some important distinctions between the crime and the tort.

False imprisonment is committed where D unlawfully and intentionally or recklessly restrains P's freedom of movement from a particular place. "Imprisonment" is probably a wider term than, and includes, "arrest".[8]

4. (1986) 83 Cr App Rep 386; **SHC 369.**
5. Examples taken from *Hill* supra.
6. [1968] Crim LR 115 (Judge Broderick).
7. Cf. *Stokes* (1925) 19 Cr App Rep 71.
8. *Rahman* (1985) 81 Cr App Rep 349 at 353, CA. *Brown* [1977] Crim LR 291, CA, and commentary thereon and articles by Telling [1978] Crim LR 320 and Lidstone [1978] Crim LR 332.

1) *The Actus Reus*

1 Imprisonment

The "imprisonment" may consist in confining P in a prison,[9] a house,[10] even P's own house,[11] a mine[12] or a vehicle;[13] or simply in detaining P in a public street[14] or any other place. It is not necessary that he be physically detained. There may be an arrest by words alone, but only if P submits. If P is not physically detained and does not realise he is under constraint he is not imprisoned.[15] If P agrees to go to a police station voluntarily, he has not been arrested though the constable would have arrested him if he had refused to go.[16] If it is then brought home to P that he will not be allowed to leave until he provides a laboratory specimen, it has been suggested that, though he has never been "arrested", he is "under arrest".[17] If the distinction is valid it would seem to be enough for false imprisonment that P is "under arrest". It is enough that D orders P to accompany him to another place and P goes because he feels constrained to do so. P is not imprisoned if, on hearing D use words of arrest, he runs away or makes his escape by a trick.[18] An invitation by D to P to accompany him cannot be an imprisonment if it is made clear to P that he is entitled to refuse to go. Thus Lord Lyndhurst CB thought there was no imprisonment where D asked a policeman to take P into custody, and the policeman objected, but said that if D and P "would be so good as to go with him", he would take the advice of his superior.[19] The distinction between a command, amounting to an imprisonment, and a request not doing so, is a difficult one.[20] Probably Alderson B went too far in *Peters v Stanway*[1] in holding that P was imprisoned if she went to the police station with a constable voluntarily but nevertheless in consequence of a charge against her.

Though some of the older authorities[2] speak of false imprisonment as a species of assault it is quite clear that no assault need be proved.[3] In *Linsberg*,[4] the Common Sergeant held that P, a doctor, was falsely imprisoned where D locked the door to prevent him leaving a confinement. The restraint need be only momentary, so that the offence would be complete if

---

9. *Cobbett v Grey* (1850) 4 Exch 729.
10. *Warner v Riddiford* (1858) 4 CB-NS 180.
11. *Termes de la Ley*, approved by Warrington and Atkin LJJ (1920) 122 LT at 51 and 53.
12. *Herd v Weardale Steel, Coal and Coke Co Ltd* [1915] AC 67.
13. By driving at such a speed that P dare not alight: *McDaniel v State* (1942) 15 Tex Crim R 115; *Burton v Davies* [1953] QSR 26.
14. Blackstone, *Commentaries*, iii, 127; *Ludlow v Burgess* [1971] Crim LR 238.
15. *Alderson v Booth* [1969] 2 QB 216, [1969] 2 All ER 271.
16. *Campbell v Tormey* [1969] 1 All ER 961, [1969] 1 WLR 189.
17. Ibid., per Ashworth J.
18. *Russen v Lucas* (1824) 1 C & P 153.
19. *Cant v Parsons* (1834) 6 C & P 504.
20. Williams in *Police Power and Individual Freedom* at p. 43.
1. (1835) 6 C & P 737, followed in *Conn v David Spencer Ltd* [1930] 1 DLR 805.
2. For example, Hawkins, 1 PC, c. 60, §7; *Pocock v Moore* (1825) Ry & M 321.
3. *Grainger v Hill* (1838) 4 Bing NC 212; *Warner v Riddiford* (1858) 4 CB-NS 180.
4. (1905) 69 JP 107.

D tapped P on the shoulder and said, "You are my prisoner."[5] But a battery is not necessarily an imprisonment. In *Bird v Jones*[6] P was involved in

"a struggle during which no momentary detention of his person took place."

It is not an imprisonment wrongfully to prevent P from going in a particular direction, if he is free to go in other directions. This was decided in *Bird v Jones*,[7] where Coleridge J said:

"A prison may have its boundary large or narrow, visible and tangible, or, though real, still in the conception only;[8] it may itself be moveable or fixed: but a boundary it must have. . . ."

It would be otherwise if P could move off in other directions only by taking an unreasonable risk;[9] it could hardly be said that a man locked in a second-floor room was not imprisoned because he could have climbed down the drainpipe.

There is little authority on the question how large the area of confinement may be. It has been suggested that it would be tortious to confine P to a large country estate or the Isle of Man;[10] but it could hardly be false imprisonment to prevent P from leaving Great Britain, still less to prevent him from entering. But a person who has actually landed and is not allowed to leave an airport building is imprisoned.[11] Is P also imprisoned, then, if he is not allowed to leave the ship which has docked in a British port?

It has been held by the Court of Appeal, Duke LJ, dissenting, in *Meering v Graham-White Aviation Co Ltd*[12] that it is irrelevant that P does not know he is imprisoned. Atkin LJ said:

"It appears to me that a person could be imprisoned without his knowing it. I think a person can be imprisoned while he is asleep, while he is in a state of drunkenness, while he is unconscious, and while he is a lunatic ... though the imprisonment began and ceased while he was in that state."

A contrary decision of the Court of Exchequer[13] was not cited and the case has been heavily criticised;[14] but the arguments advanced against awarding damages in this situation are not applicable to the crime. D's conduct may not be damaging to P if P knows nothing about it, but it is not necessarily any less blameworthy for, in most cases, the fact that P remains in ignorance must be a matter of mere chance.

---

5. *Simpson v Hill* (1795) 1 Esp 431, per Eyre CJ; *Sandon v Jervis* (1859) EB & E 942, ". . . a mere touch constitutes an arrest, though the party be not actually taken;" per Crowder J.
6. Infra.
7. (1845) 7 QB 742 (Denman CJ dissenting).
8. For example, P is forbidden to move more than ten yards from the village pump.
9. Street, *Torts*, 29.
10. Street, *Torts*, 28. In *Re Mwenya* [1960] 1 QB 241, [1959] 3 All ER 525, a writ of *habeas corpus* was sought for P who was confined to an area of some 1,500 square miles but he was released before it became necessary to decide whether he was imprisoned for the purpose of *habeas corpus*.
11. *Kuchenmeister v Home Office* [1958] 1 QB 496, [1958] 1 All ER 485.
12. (1919) 122 LT 44. Two policemen were stationed outside the door of a room to prevent P leaving. He was effectively imprisoned as if the door had been locked. Cf. *Alderson v Booth*, above, p. 406.
13. *Herring v Boyle* (1834) 1 Cr M & R 377.
14. Williams in *Police Power and Individual Freedom* at 45–46; Street, *Torts*, 31.

Like other crimes, false imprisonment can be committed through an innocent agent. So D is responsible for the *actus reus* if, at his direction or request, a policeman takes P into custody,[15] or he signs the charge-sheet when the police have said they will not take the responsibility of detaining P unless he does;[16] but merely to give information to a constable, in consequence of which he decides to make an arrest has been held not to be actionable, at all events if D is bona fide.[17] A fortiori, it should not be *criminal*, for lack of *mens rea*; but why should D not be guilty if he deliberately supplies false information to a constable who, acting on his own authority but relying exclusively on D's information, arrests P? D has surely caused the *actus reus* with *mens rea* and may be liable for the ministerial act of the constable as distinct from the judicial act of the magistrate.[18] Where D is initially liable for false imprisonment his liability ceases on the intervention of some judicial act[19] authorising the detention or on any other event, breaking the chain of causation.[20]

Whatever may be the position in the law of tort,[1] it is thought that it would be immaterial in the criminal law that the imprisonment was not "directly" caused by D; and that it would be sufficient that he caused it with *mens rea* – as by digging a pit into which P falls and is trapped.[2]

Another question in the law of tort is whether it is possible falsely to imprison by mere omission in view of the requirement of a trespass. In *Herd v Weardale Steel Coal and Coke Co Ltd*[3] P voluntarily descended into D's mine and, in breach of contract, stopped work and asked to be brought to the surface before the end of the shift. D's refusal to accede to this request was not a false imprisonment: he was under no duty to provide facilities for P to leave in breach of contract. Clearly, the result would be different if D were to take positive steps to prevent P from leaving in breach of contract,[4] as by locking him in a factory. Buckley and Hamilton LJJ[5] thought that mere omission could not have been false imprisonment, even if it occurred when the shift was over. P's only civil remedy would have been in contract; but the House of Lords expressed no opinion on this point.

---

15. *Gosden v Elphick and Bennett* (1849) 4 Exch 445.

16. *Austin v Dowling* (1870) LR 5 CP 534. It is otherwise if D signs the charge sheet as a matter of form, when the police are detaining P on their own responsibility: *Grinham v Willey* (1859) 4 H & N 496.

17. *Gosden v Elphick and Bennett*, supra; *Grinham v Willey*, supra; "We ought to take care that people are not put in peril for making complaint when a crime has been committed," per Pollock CB.

18. See *Austin v Dowling* (1870) LR 5 C & P 534 at 540.

19. *Lock v Ashton* (1848) 12 QB 871. Cf. *Marrinan v Vibart* [1963] 1 QB 528, [1962] 3 All ER 380.

20. *Harnett v Bond* [1925] AC 669. D's report caused P to be taken to an asylum; D was not liable for the imprisonment after the doctor at the asylum had examined P and decided to detain him. Cf. *Pike v Waldrum* [1952] 1 Lloyds Rep 431.

1. Street, *Torts*, 30.

2. Cf. *Clarence* (1888) 22 QBD 23 at 36, per Wills J.

3. [1915] AC 67, HL.

4. Unless, perhaps, the contract was that P should be entitled to leave only on the fulfilment of some reasonable condition: *Robinson v Balmain New Ferry Co Ltd* [1910] AC 295, PC. *Sed quaere* whether one is entitled to restrain another from leaving even if it is a breach of contract for him to do so? The contract can hardly be specifically enforceable.

5. [1913] 3 KB at 787 and 793.

In *Mee v Cruikshank*,[6] Wills J held that a prison governor was under a duty to take steps to ensure that his officers did not detain a prisoner who had been acquitted. In that case there were acts of imprisonment by the prison officers but they were not the servants of D, the governor, and it seems to have been D's omission which rendered him liable in tort. Surely it ought to be false imprisonment if D, a gaoler, is under a duty to release P at midnight and deliberately omits to unlock his cell until noon the following day?[7] And it ought to make no difference that D's duty to release P arises out of a contract:

"If a man gets into an express train and the doors are locked pending its arrival at its destination, he is not entitled, merely because the train has been stopped by signal, to call for the doors to be opened to let him out."[8]

But if he is kept locked in for a day at his destination this surely ought to be false imprisonment. And if the technicalities of the forms of action preclude a remedy in tort this is no reason why the omission should not be held to be criminal.

2 Unlawful Restraint

The imprisonment must be "false", that is unlawful. A parent may lawfully exercise restraint over a child, so long as he remains within the bounds of reasonable parental discipline and does not act in contravention of a court order.[9] Where a girl of 14 or 15 was fostered out by her father with the consent and assistance of the local authority and he abducted her against her will and with intent to take her to her country of origin, it was for the jury to say whether they were satisfied that this was outside the bounds of legitimate parental discipline and correction.[10]

The question most commonly arises in connection with the exercise of powers of arrest. If such powers are exceeded, there is a false imprisonment. The principal powers are as follows.

i) *Arrest by a constable under a valid warrant.* Where the justice lacks jurisdiction to issue the warrant, the constable is statutorily protected[11] from any action if he acts in obedience to it. As the term "action" is inappropriate to a criminal proceeding, a constable could not rely on the Act as a defence to criminal prosecution; but he would probably have a good defence on the ground of lack of *mens rea*.[12] An arrest under warrant for a civil matter is unlawful if the arresting officer does not have the warrant in his possession.[13]

---

6. (1902) 20 Cox CC 210.
7. See *Moone v Rose* (1869) LR 4 QB 486; *Lesley* (1860) Bell CC 220; and cf. *Peacock and Hoskyn v Musgrave and Porter* [1956] Crim LR 414 (where damages were awarded for detention by the police, originally justified, but unreasonably prolonged) and *Lambert v Hodgson* (1823) 1 Bing 317.
8. *Herd v Weardale Steel Coal and Coke Co Ltd* [1915] AC 67 at 71, per Lord Haldane.
9. *Rahman* (1985) 81 Cr App Rep 349, CA. Cf. *D* [1984] AC 778, [1984] 1 All ER 574, below, p. 412.
10. *Rahman*, supra, at 354. In fact, D pleaded guilty, and his appeal was dismissed.
11. The Constables Protection Act 1750.
12. Below, p. 412.
13. *De Costa Small v Kirkpatrick* (1979) 68 Cr App Rep 186, [1979] Crim LR 41.

ii) *Arrest by a constable or other person for an arrestable offence.* The Police and Criminal Evidence Act 1984, s. 24 provides:

"(4) Any person may arrest without a warrant –
   (a) anyone who is in the act of committing an arrestable offence;
   (b) anyone whom he has reasonable grounds for suspecting to be committing such an offence.
(5) Where an arrestable offence has been committed, any person may arrest without a warrant –
   (a) anyone who is guilty of the offence;
   (b) anyone whom he has reasonable grounds for suspecting to be guilty of it.
(6) Where a constable has reasonable grounds for suspecting that an arrestable offence has been committed, he may arrest without a warrant anyone whom he has reasonable grounds for suspecting to be guilty of the offence.
(7) A constable may arrest without a warrant –
   (a) anyone who is about to commit an arrestable offence;
   (b) anyone whom he has reasonable grounds for suspecting to be about to commit an arrestable offence."

Section 24 (3) provides that the above subsections apply to conspiring, attempting, inciting, aiding, abetting, counselling or procuring an arrestable offence and that these acts are also arrestable offences.

It will be noted that arrest is always lawful where D reasonably suspects P to be in the act of committing the arrestable offence, even though in fact P is not doing so: but that where D reasonably suspects that P *has committed* an arrestable offence, the arrest is unlawful if that offence has not been committed by anyone, unless D happens to be a constable. This, in effect, re-enacts the rule laid down for arrest for felony in *Walters v W. H. Smith & Sons Ltd.*[14] D suspected on reasonable grounds that P had stolen a number of books from his book stall. He arrested him on a charge of stealing a particular book. Though other books had certainly been stolen, this one had not been stolen by P or anyone else. Because the offence for which the arrest was made had not been committed, D was held liable in damages. The Criminal Law Revision Committee thought it right to preserve the rule, although they pointed out that it may be

"a trap to a private person who is careful instead of precipitate about deciding whether to arrest a person. If, for example, a store detective saw a person apparently shoplifting, he could arrest him under clause 2 (2) [now s. 24 (4)(b) of PACE] on the ground that he had reasonable cause to suspect him of being in the act of committing an arrestable offence, and he would not be liable for unlawful arrest even if it turned out that he was wrong; but if he preferred out of caution to invite the other to the office to give him an opportunity of clearing himself, and then arrested him on being satisfied that he was guilty, the detective would be liable if this turned out to be wrong."[15]

14. [1914] 1 KB 595.
15. Cmnd 2659, para. 14.

The justification for the rule is that an increase in the powers of arrest of private persons would not be acceptable to public opinion and that it is desirable, where it is at all doubtful whether an offence has been committed, for a private person to put the matter in the hands of the police.[16] This hardly allows, however, for the case where the citizen has no opportunity to inform the police and must either let the suspected person escape or make an arrest himself.

The powers of arrest of a constable are wider under s. 24 than those of other persons in three respects. An arrest by a constable of a person reasonably suspected of having committed an arrestable offence is not unlawful even though the offence in question has never been committed. Secondly, a constable may arrest a person reasonably suspected to be *about to commit* an arrestable offence, whereas other persons must wait until he is *in the act* of committing the offence. Thirdly, a constable who has made an arrest may do what is reasonable to investigate the matter and discover whether his reasonable suspicions are well founded; but a private person must hand the arrested person over to a constable or magistrate as soon as possible.[17]

iii) *Where a constable or other person arrests for breach of the peace committed in his presence, or where he reasonably believes that such a breach will be committed in the immediate future by a person unless he is arrested, or where a breach has been committed and he reasonably believes that a renewal of it is threatened.*[18] There is a breach of the peace whenever harm is actually done or is likely to be done to a person, or in his presence to his property, or a person is in fear of being so harmed through an assault, an affray, a riot, or other disturbance.[19] Public alarm, excitement or disturbance is not of itself a breach of the peace, unless it arises from actual or threatened violence.

iv) *Arrest by a constable under the "general arrest conditions".* By s. 25 (1) of the Police and Criminal Evidence Act, a constable who has reasonable grounds for suspecting that any offence which is not an arrestable offence has been committed or attempted, or is being committed or attempted, by X, may arrest X if it appears to him that the service of a summons is impracticable or inappropriate because of the "general arrest conditions" specified in the section. The conditions are, broadly, (i) the constable is unable to ascertain X's true name and address or a satisfactory address for service of a summons; or (ii) the constable has reasonable grounds for believing that the arrest is necessary to prevent X from causing or sustaining physical injury to himself, causing physical injury to others,

---

16. Ibid., para. 15.
17. *Dallison v Caffrey* [1965] 1 QB 348, [1964] 2 All ER 610 at 616–617, CA, per Lord Denning. It is lawful for a private detective to take a suspected shoplifter to his employer for a decision whether to prosecute; *John Lewis & Co Ltd v Tims* [1952] AC 676, [1952] 1 All ER 1203, HL, but it is not, apparently, lawful for the private arrester of a child to take the child to his father to deal with; *Brewin* [1976] Crim LR 742 (Recorder Jowitt) and commentary.
18. *Howell* (1981) 73 Cr App Rep 31 at 36.
19. Ibid at 37. Lord Denning has said that even the lawful use of force is a breach of the peace: *Chief Constable of Devon* [1981] 3 All ER 826 at 832; but this can hardly subject the person using such force to arrest.

causing loss of or damage to property, committing an offence against public decency, causing an unlawful obstruction of the highway; or to protect a child or other vulnerable person from X.[20]

v) *Arrest under the powers preserved by Schedule 2 of the Police and Criminal Evidence Act 1984.* Numerous statutory powers of arrest without warrant were abolished by s. 26 of the 1984 Act which, however, preserved the powers specified in Schedule 2.

Arrest unlawful, unless information given. Where a person is arrested, otherwise than by being informed he is under arrest, he must be so informed as soon as practicable afterwards. No arrest is lawful unless the person arrested is informed of the ground of the arrest at the time or as soon as is practicable thereafter; and this is so even where the ground for the arrest is obvious. If the arrested person escapes before it is reasonably practicable for him to be informed that he is under arrest, or the ground for the arrest, the arrest is not rendered unlawful.[1]

2) *Mens Rea*

Since the great majority of the cases are civil actions, there is little authority on the nature of the *mens rea* required for false imprisonment but in *Rahman*[2] the court stated that "False imprisonment consists in the unlawful and intentional or reckless restraint of a victim's freedom of movement from a particular place." Though the court did not specify what kind of recklessness it had in mind, it is submitted that it must be *Cunningham* recklessness.[3] It would be very difficult to reconcile a requirement of mere *Caldwell* recklessness with the decision in *Gladstone Williams*[4] that even an unreasonable mistake will negative the *mens rea* of assault committed in the course of making an arrest. Assault and false imprisonment are both common law offences and are so closely related that it is inconceivable that a different principle of *mens rea* should apply to the one than the other. As suggested above, D would not have been criminally liable in *Walters v W H Smith & Son Ltd* because he believed on reasonable grounds that the felony for which he arrested P had been committed; and, today, it should make no difference that there were no reasonable grounds for his belief, so long as it was honestly held. This makes no difference, of course, to the position in the civil law and D remains liable to pay damages to P in the circumstances of that case.

---

20. Does this provision imply that any person other than a constable, acting on the same necessity, does so unlawfully? Above, p. 222.

   1. These rules, in s. 28 of the 1984 Act, replace the common law as stated in *Christie v Leachinsky* [1947] AC 573, [1947] 1 All ER 567.

   2. (1985) 81 Cr App Rep 349 at 353, CA, above, p. 409.

   3. Above, p. 62.

   4. [1987] 3 All ER 411, 78 Cr App Rep 276.

3) *Kidnapping*

In *R v D*[5] the House of Lords gave an authoritative account of the law of kidnapping.

"First, the nature of the offence is an attack on, and infringement of, the personal liberty of an individual. Second, the offence contains four ingredients as follows: (1) the taking or carrying away of one person by another, (2) by force or by fraud, (3) without the consent of the person so taken or carried away and (4) without lawful excuse. Third, until the comparatively recent abolition by statute of the division of criminal offences into the two categories of felonies and misdemeanours (see s. 1 of the Criminal Law Act 1967), the offence of kidnapping was categorised by the common law as a misdemeanour only. Fourth, despite that, kidnapping was always regarded, by reason of its nature, as a grave and (to use the language of an earlier age) heinous offence. Fifth, in earlier days the offence contained a further ingredient, namely that the taking or carrying away should be from a place within the jurisdiction to another place outside it; this further ingredient has, however, long been obsolete and forms no necessary part of the offence today. Sixth, the offence was in former days described not merely as taking or carrying away a person but further or alternatively as secreting him; this element of secretion has, however, also become obsolete, so that, although it may be present in a particular case, it adds nothing to the basic ingredient of taking or carrying away."

It is the absence of consent of the person taken which is relevant, even where that person is a child. In the case of a young child, lacking the understanding or intelligence to give consent, the absence of consent is a necessary inference. In the case of an older child, it is a question of fact for the jury whether (i) the child has sufficient understanding and, if so, (ii) it in fact consented. Lord Brandon thought that a jury would usually find that a child under 14 lacked sufficient understanding to give consent; but this may underestimate the capacity of the modern child.

It was held in *Reid*[6] that a husband may be convicted of kidnapping his wife and in *D* that a father may be guilty of kidnapping his child. It was recognised that, until modern times, it may be that an indictment of a father for kidnapping his child would have failed because of the paramountcy of his position in the family; but common law principles adapt and develop in the light of radically changed social conventions and conditions. Lord Bridge held that parental kidnapping includes the case (as in *D*) where the parent acts in contravention of the order of a competent court, leaving open the question whether a parent might be convicted in any other circumstances; but the majority preferred to hold simply that the parent is guilty where he acts "without lawful excuse". What is a lawful excuse is left completely at large; and whether a taking by a parent in other circumstances amounts to kidnapping is likely to be resolved in the same way

---

5. [1984] AC 778, [1984] 2 All ER 449, [1984] Crim LR, 558.
6. [1973] QB 299, [1972] 2 All Er 1350.

whether the court proceeds by the route of deciding (as the majority would) whether there is a lawful excuse or by deciding (as Lord Bridge would) whether the offence extends to those further circumstances. If a 12-year-old child refuses to return home from a visit to his grandmother's and his father forcibly carries him off, he surely commits no offence. The majority would say, presumably, because the father has a lawful excuse and Lord Bridge, because kidnapping does not extend to those circumstances. The result is the same. The question must be whether the parent has gone beyond what is reasonable in the exercise of parental authority.

Where P is not D's child and D is not acting in pursuance of any statutory authority or power of arrest, "lawful excuse" is likely to be narrowly confined. In *Henman*[7] D was guilty of attempted kidnapping when he tried to take by force an acquaintance whom he believed to be in moral and spiritual danger from a religious sect to which she belonged. There was no lawful excuse because there was no "necessity recognised by the law as such" for D's conduct.

The crime is complete when P is deprived of his liberty and carried away from the place where he wished to be.[8] The requirements of carrying away and the use of force or fraud seem to be the only factors distinguishing kidnapping from false imprisonment. It seems that every kidnapping is also a false imprisonment but a detention without any taking away or force or fraud (D merely turns the key locking P in the room) is only the latter offence. Where D has carried P away by force or fraud, he may be convicted of both offences.[9] Kidnapping is an aggravated form of false imprisonment[10] so the rules of lawful excuse are, no doubt, the same. Since both offences are common law misdemeanours, punishable with imprisonment or fine at the discretion of the court, the significance of the element of aggravation is that it enables the kidnapper to be labelled as such and given an appropriate penalty.

4) *Taking of Hostages*

The Taking of Hostages Act 1982 creates an offence of exceptional breadth in that it extends to a person of any nationality acting anywhere in the world, or indeed, in outer space. It is committed by anyone who detains another and, in order to compel a State, international governmental organisation or person to do or abstain from doing any act, threatens to kill, injure or continue to detain the hostage. It is punishable with imprisonment for life. Proceedings may not be instituted except by or with the consent of the Attorney-General.

---

7. [1987] Crim LR 333, CA.
8. *Wellard* [1978] 3 All ER 161, [1978] 1 WLR 921.
9. *Brown* [1985] Crim LR 398, CA (5 years' imprisonment concurrent on both counts upheld).
10. East, 1 PC, 429.

5) *Abduction of Children*

The Child Abduction Act 1984 creates two offences of abduction of a child under the age of sixteen.

The first offence may be committed only by a person "connected with" the child who takes or sends the child out of the United Kingdom "without the appropriate consent".

A person "connected with" a child is the child's parent or guardian, a person to whom custody has been awarded by a court, whether solely or jointly, or, in the case of an illegitimate child, a man in respect of whom there are reasonable grounds for believing him to be the father. The "appropriate consent" is the consent of each person who is the child's parent or guardian or to whom custody has been awarded; or, if the child is the subject of a custody order, the leave of the court; or the leave of the court granted under s. 7 of the Guardianship of Minors Act 1971 or s. 1 (3) of the Guardianship Act 1973.

The Act provides defences of which D bears an evidential burden and the prosecution the burden of proof where:

a) D believes that he has the appropriate consent or that he would have it if the person or persons whose consent is required were aware of all the relevant circumstances; or

b) he has taken all reasonable steps to communicate with those persons but has been unsuccessful; or

c) – except where the child is the subject of a custody order or where D acts in breach of a direction under s. 7 of the Guardianship of Minors Act 1971 or s. 1 (3) of the Guardianship Act 1973 – the consent has been unreasonably refused.

The second offence is committed by a person other than the parent or guardian or a person having custody under a court order who, without lawful authority or reasonable excuse, takes or detains the child –

a) so as to remove him from the lawful control[11] of any person having lawful control of him; or

b) so as to keep him out of the lawful control of any person entitled to lawful control of him.

It is provided that it is a defence for D to "show" – which, in the context, must mean "prove" –

a) that he believed the child had attained sixteen; and

b) in the case of an illegitimate child, he had reasonable grounds for believing himself to be the father.

The offences under the Act are different in principle from the common law offences of false imprisonment and kidnapping. The essence of the common law offences is that they are acts done without the consent of the person imprisoned or kidnapped whereas the essence of the statutory offences is that they are done without the consent of the person entitled to give the appropriate consent or having lawful control. Though the definition of the second offence does not use the word "consent", it seems clear that a child is not "removed from" or "kept out of" lawful control if the

11. See *Mousir* [1987] Crim LR 561, CA.

person in control consents to what is done. It is provided that "taking" includes D's inducing the child to accompany him or another and "detaining" includes inducing the child to remain with D or another, and there is no requirement of force or fraud. The child may be ready and willing, but the offence will still be committed.

Notwithstanding this distinction between the offences, it is provided that no prosecution shall be instituted for an offence of kidnapping if it was committed (a) against a child under the age of sixteen and (b) by a person "connected with the child", except by or with the consent of the Director of Public Prosecutions.

Both offences are punishable, on summary conviction, by six months' imprisonment or a fine not exceeding the statutory maximum, or both and, on indictment, by imprisonment for seven years.

6 Firearms and Offensive Weapons

One way of discouraging serious offences against the person is by regulating the use of firearms and offensive weapons and there is a good deal of criminal legislation on this subject.

1) *The Firearms Act 1968*

The Firearms Act 1968 contains detailed regulations about firearms.[12] It is an offence under s. 1 to purchase, acquire or possess any firearm or ammunition without a firearm certificate.[13] Shot guns, defined as smooth bore, with a barrel not less than 24 inches in length, are excepted from s. 1 but governed by similar provisions in s. 2. A rifle, converted to smooth bore, is a shot gun even though it is still capable of firing bullets and incapable of firing shot gun cartridges.[14]

In *Hussain*[15] it was stated that possession of a firearm without a certificate was an absolute offence; but D must of course have that degree of knowledge which is necessary to constitute possession.[16] Moreover, it appears that D knew the precise nature of the instrument in his possession and his ignorance, if any, was that it was a firearm within the meaning of the Act, which is a mistake of law. "Possession" has been widely construed, so that where D1 left a shotgun in D2's house while they went on holiday, to be cleaned by D2 on his return, both were in possession, D1 having "proprietary possession" and D2 "custodial possession."[17]

---

12. The Firearms Act 1982 extends the provisions of the 1968 Act, with certain exceptions, to any imitation firearm which is so constructed or adapted as to be readily convertible into a firearm to which s. 1 of the 1968 Act applies.
13. Firearms Act 1968, s. 1.
14. *Hucklebridge* [1980] 3 All ER 273, [1980] 1 WLR 1284, CA.
15. [1981] 2 All ER 287, 42 Cr App Rep 143, CA.
16. *Warner v Metropolitan Police Comr*, above, p. 107.
17. *Hall v Cotton* [1987] QB 504, [1986] 3 All ER 332.

The Act provides for the grant, renewal, variation, revocation and production of certificates[18] and exempts various classes of persons from the necessity of holding a certificate.[19] It is a summary offence to manufacture, sell, transfer, repair, test or prove any firearm, or have it in one's possession for any of these purposes, or to expose it for sale or transfer, unless registered as a firearms dealer[20] and the Act makes detailed provision for registration.[21] It imposes restrictions on the purchase or possession of firearms and air weapons by young persons[1] and prohibits the sale of them to drunk or insane persons.[2] A person who has been sentenced to preventive detention or corrective training or imprisonment for three years or more is prohibited from possessing a firearm or ammunition at any time. A person who has been sentenced for less than three years but not less than three months is prohibited from possessing a firearm or ammunition for five years from the date of his release. It is an offence to sell, etc., a firearm or ammunition to a person so prohibited.[3]

The Act creates a number of more serious offences which deserve more detailed consideration.

1 Prohibited Weapons

The Act distinguishes a separate category of prohibited weapons. These are weapons considered suitable for use only by the armed services and which have no proper function in civilian life.

A "prohibited weapon" is defined as one which is –

a) "... so designed or adapted that, if pressure is applied to the trigger, missiles continue to be discharged until pressure is removed ..." (an automatic weapon) or

b) "... designed or adapted for the discharge of any noxious liquid, gas or other thing"

and

c) "... any ammunition containing or designed or adapted to contain, any such noxious thing."[4]

An automatic continues to be a prohibited weapon though it will not at present fire because of some temporary fault[5] or because it is completely dismantled.[6] And it is immaterial that the trigger pressure is difficult to sustain.

It is an offence, punishable with two years' imprisonment, to manufacture, sell, transfer, purchase, acquire or have in one's possession any prohibited weapon without the consent of the Defence Council.

---

18. Firearms Act 1968, ss. 26–32.
19. Ibid., ss. 7–12; *Woodage v Moss* [1974] I All ER 584, DC.
20. Firearms Act 1968, s. 3.
21. Ibid., ss. 33–39. *Ackers v Taylor* [1974] I All ER 771, DC.
  1. Firearms Act 1968, ss. 22–24.
  2. Ibid., s. 25.
  3. Ibid., s. 21.
  4. Firearms Act 1968, s. 5(1).
  5. Ibid. Cf. *Pannell* (1982) 76 Cr App Rep 53, CA.
  6. *Pannell* (1982) 76 Cr App Rep 53.

2 Use of Firearms or Imitation Firearms to Resist Arrest; and Possession of them, in relation to Certain Offences

By s. 17 (1) of the Act it is an offence, punishable with life imprisonment,

"To make or attempt to make any use whatsoever of a firearm or imitation firearm with intent to resist or prevent the lawful arrest or detention of himself or any other person."

By s. 17 (2), it is an offence punishable with fourteen years' imprisonment,

"If a person, at the time of his committing, or being arrested for an offence specified in Schedule 1 to this Act, has in his possession a firearm or imitation firearm ... unless he shows that he had it in his possession for a lawful object."

The schedule specifies a wide range of offences under the Criminal Damage Act 1971, the Offences against the Person Act 1861, the Vagrancy Act 1824, the Prevention of Crimes Act 1871, the Theft Act 1968, the Police Act 1964, and the Sexual Offences Act 1956.

The sentence under s. 17 (1) may be in addition to any imposed for any offence for which he is lawfully arrested or detained and that under s. 17 (2) may be in addition to any imposed for an offence in the Schedule.

"Firearm" is particularly defined by s. 57 (1) for the purposes of this section as

"a lethal barrelled weapon of any description from which any shot, bullet or other missile can be discharged, and includes

(a) any prohibited weapon, whether it is such a lethal weapon as aforesaid or not".

This definition has been widely interpreted. In *Read v Donovan*[7] Lord Goddard went so far as to say that "lethal weapon" means "a weapon capable of causing injury ..." This dictum was wider than was necessary for the decision, for there was evidence that the weapon was capable of killing at up to twenty feet. Lord Parker later said in *Moore v Gooderham*,[8] that he did not feel that "too much attention" can be attached to that definition. In that case the court accepted, surely rightly, that the injury must be of a kind which may cause death. The court nevertheless held that an airgun was a lethal weapon because it might cause death if fired point-blank at some particularly vulnerable part. The question is not whether the weapon was designed or intended to cause death but whether it might do so if misused.

"Imitation firearm" means

"any thing which has the appearance of being a firearm"[9] at whatever is the relevant time for the particular offence[10] – except a weapon which has the appearance of a weapon 'designed or adapted for the discharge of any noxious liquid, gas or other thing'[11] – "whether or not it is capable of discharging any shot, bullet or other missile."

7. [1947] KB 326 at 327, [1947] 1 All ER 37.
8. [1960] 3 All ER 575 at 577.
9. In Canada it has been held that a pointed finger cannot be an imitation firearm. There must be an instrument of some kind: *Sloan* (1974) 19 CCC 190.
10. *Morris and King* (1984) 79 Cr App Rep 104.
11. It is not obvious why an imitation gas pistol, for example, should be excluded from the Act.

A real weapon which is incapable of firing is an imitation firearm within the definition. This was held in *Debreli*,[12] where D was in possession of an automatic pistol with the firing pin removed. Having regard to the mischief aimed at by the Act, the court held that it was sufficient that the weapon looked like a firearm and it was immaterial that it was not fabricated as an imitation. The court thus avoided the absurdity that a rubber model of an automatic pistol would have been within the Act but not the real pistol used in that case.

Rather remarkably, in view of the seriousness of the offence involved, it has been held that s. 17 (1) imposes strict liability in one respect. In *Pierre*,[13] the court held that it was unnecessary that D should know that the thing used is a firearm as defined in the section. No doubt it is necessary to prove that D intended to use the thing which he did use[14] and which is a firearm within the meaning of the section; but if D supposes it is something other than a firearm he will have no defence. Presumably the same construction must be applicable to s. 17 (2): it must be proved that D knows he has the thing,[15] but he need not know its nature. However, here it would be open to D to establish, on a balance of probabilities, that he had the thing for a lawful object. Thus, if D has in his possession, for purposes of amateur dramatics, an object which he believes to be an imitation gas-pistol but which in fact is a real one and he happens to commit an offence within Schedule 1, he may be able to establish a defence; but if he encounters and strikes[16] with the pistol a police officer who is attempting to arrest him he will have no defence. Yet if the thing had been an imitation his offence would only have been the summary offence under s. 51 of the Police Act 1964,[17] punishable with six months' imprisonment.

In another respect, however, a benevolent construction has been put on s. 17 (2). On a literal reading of the sub-section the offence is committed when D is lawfully arrested for one of the specified offences, whether he has actually committed it or not. But in *Baker*[18] the court held that it must be proved not only that D was lawfully arrested for such an offence but also that he actually committed it.

"The other construction results in the absurdity that a man who has committed no offence at all of the nature specified in Sched. 3 [now Sched. 1] might be liable to seven years' [now fourteen years'] imprisonment as opposed to two years merely because a policeman had reasonable grounds for suspecting that he had committed one of those offences."[19]

Section 17(2) is nevertheless a wide-ranging provision. D would appear to be liable under it even if at the time of his arrest many years had elapsed

12. [1964] Crim LR 53.
13. [1963] Crim LR 513, CA; followed in *Howells* [1977] QB 614, [1977] 3 All ER 417, CA, (honest and reasonable belief that firearm an antique no defence to charge under s. 58 (2)).
14. Cf. *Cugullere* [1961] 2 All ER 343; below, p. 427.
15. *McGuire and Page* [1963] Crim LR 572, where D1 is in possession, D2 must be shown to have knowledge and joint control.
16. It is evidently not necessary that use should be made of the firearm as such – the Act says "any use whatsoever".
17. Above, p. 387.
18. [1961] 2 QB 530, [1961] 3 All ER 703.
19. [1962] 2 QB at 532, 533 [1961] 3 All ER at 704.

since he committed the specified offence and his possession of the firearm was in no way connected with it.

3 Possessing Firearms with Intent

By s. 16 of the Firearms Act 1968 it is an offence punishable with life imprisonment,

> ". . . for a person to have in his possession any firearm or ammunition with intent by means thereof to endanger life or cause serious injury to property, or to enable another person by means thereof to endanger life or cause serious injury to property, whether any injury to person or property has been caused or not."

The definition of "firearm" for the purpose of this section includes, as well as those things which are firearms for the purposes of s. 17,[20]

> "(b) any component part of such a lethal or prohibited weapon; and
>
> (c) any accessory to any such weapon designed or adapted to diminish the noise or flash caused by firing the weapon."[1]

On the other hand, imitation firearms are not within the section since one would hardly possess these with the necessary intent.

It is not necessary that the weapon should be presently capable of causing any injury whatsoever. A dummy revolver with the barrel and cartridge chambers only partially bored[2] and a revolver with holes pierced in the sides of the barrel so as to make it ineffective for the purpose of firing live ammunition[3] have both been held to be within the Act either because the whole thing, or the whole thing less the defective parts, was a "component part" of a lethal weapon.

It is likely that *Pierre*[4] would again be applicable but this is perhaps less serious as, even though D is unaware that the thing is a firearm as defined in the Act, he must be proved to believe that it is capable of endangering life or causing serious injury to property. A mistaken belief that the thing was an imitation might thus afford a defence, by negativing the intent. The intention need not be immediate and may be conditional – to use the firearm if occasion arises.[5] The contemplated danger to life need not be within the United Kingdom.[6] The offence continues so long as possession and intention co-exist.

There must be an intention to endanger the life of another; it is not sufficient that D intends to commit suicide.[7]

The offence is clearly useful in penalising preparations for murder, etc., which would not amount to attempts – though there is obviously difficulty in establishing intent where no action has been taken.

---

20. Above, p. 418.
  1. Firearms Act 1968, s. 57 (1). This is the general definition of "firearm" in the Act except where otherwise expressly provided.
  2. *Cafferata v Wilson* [1936] 3 All ER 149; *Freeman* [1970] 2 All ER 413.
  3. *Muir v Cassidy* 1953 SLT (Sh Ct) 4.
  4. Above, p. 419.
  5. *Bentham* [1973] 1 QB 357, [1972] 3 All ER 271, CA. Cf. *Buckingham* (1976) 63 Cr App Rep 159.
  6. *El-Hakkaoui* [1975] 2 All ER 146, CA.
  7. *Norton* [1977] Crim LR 478.

4 Carrying and Trespassing with Firearms

By s. 20 of the Firearms Act 1968:

"(1) A person commits an offence if, while he has a firearm with him, he enters or is in any building or part of a building as a trespasser and without reasonable excuse (the proof whereof lies on him).

(2) A person commits an offence if, while he has a firearm with him, he enters or is on any land as a trespasser and without reasonable excuse (the proof whereof lies on him)."

An offence under s. 20 (1) is punishable on indictment with five years' imprisonment and an offence under s. 20 (2) is punishable on summary conviction with three months. The constituents of the offence under s. 20 (1) bear an obvious kinship with the definition of burglary, to which reference may be made.[8]

By s. 18:

"(1) It is an offence for a person to have with him a firearm or imitation firearm with intent to commit an indictable offence, or to resist arrest or prevent the arrest of another, in either case while he has the firearm or imitation firearm with him."

This offence, which is punishable with fourteen years' imprisonment, differs from that under s. 16 in that the range of the ulterior intent is much wider and the *actus reus* is narrower[9] in that to "have with" one is less extensive than merely to have in one's possession. The phrase denotes a more personal form of possession[10] – "there must be a very close physical link and a degree of immediate control over the weapon by the man alleged to have the firearm with him."[11] If D has gone out, leaving the firearm at home, he may be guilty of an offence under s. 16, but not under s. 18. As the side-note indicates, s. 18 is concerned with "carrying" but a man not carrying a weapon may have it with him if it is immediately available to him.[12] If D is carrying a weapon for an innocent purpose and, on impulse, uses it to commit an indictable offence he is held to have had it with him with intent, contrary to s. 18.[13] The principle of *Jura*[14] under the Prevention of Crime Act 1953, does not apply to this section.

By s. 19:

"A person commits an offence if, without lawful authority or reasonable excuse (the proof whereof lies on him) he has with him in a public place[15] a loaded shot gun or loaded air weapon, or any other firearm (whether loaded or not) together with ammunition suitable for use in that firearm."

This offence, which is punishable with five years' imprisonment, is closely related to that in the Prevention of Crime Act 1953 and the

---

8. Below, p. 595. Smith, *Law of Theft*, paras. 331 et seq.
9. But s. 18 extends to imitation firearms and not to ammunition, while s. 16 extends to ammunition but not to imitation firearms.
10. *Murphy* [1971] NI 193, CCA.
11. *Kelt* (1977) 65 Cr App Rep 74 at 78, CA.
12. Ibid.
13. *Houghton* [1982] Crim LR 112, CA.
14. [1954] 1 QB 503, [1954] 1 All ER 696, CA, below, p. 424.
15. A firearm kept behind the counter in a shop is in a "public place"; *Anderson v Miller* [1976] Crim LR 743, DC.

discussion of the constituents of the offence under that statute[16] is probably applicable to s. 19 in so far as the same expressions are used. To carry a loaded shot gun or air weapon is not an offence under the Prevention of Crime Act unless it is intended for causing injury to the person. No such intent need be proved under s. 19. The defence of "reasonable excuse" seems to vest a wide discretion in the court.[17] The definition of "public place"[18] is wider for the purposes of s. 19 than for the purposes of the Prevention of Crime Act, in that it apparently includes a place to which the public have access, whether they are permitted to or not.

2) *The Prevention of Crime Act 1953*[19]

The Prevention of Crime Act 1953 is, according to its long title:
"An Act to prohibit the carrying of offensive weapons in public places, without lawful authority or reasonable excuse."
It goes much further than the Firearms Act 1968 in that, (i) in general, the mere carrying of the offensive weapon in a public place is an offence without proof of any ulterior intent or the commission of any other offence and (if it is a firearm) without proof that it was loaded or that ammunition was carried; and (ii) it extends to a much wider range of weapons. The Act provides:
"1.—(1) Any person who without lawful authority or reasonable excuse, the proof whereof shall lie on him, has with him in any public place any offensive weapon shall be guilty of an offence, and shall be liable –
(a) on summary conviction, to imprisonment for a term not exceeding three months or a fine not exceeding £1,000, or both;
(b) on conviction on indictment, to imprisonment for a term not exceeding two years or a fine, or both.
(2) Where any person is convicted of an offence under subsection (1) of this section the court may make an order for the forfeiture or disposal of any weapon in respect of which the offence was committed."

1 Offensive Weapons

"Offensive weapon" is defined by s. 1 (4), as amended by the Public Order Act 1986, to mean
"any article made or adapted for use for causing injury to the person, or intended by the person having it with him for such use by him or by some other person."
It will be noted that this definition is narrower than that of "weapon of offence" in s. 10 (1) (b) of the Theft Act 1968. It does not include, as the

16. Infra.
17. See *Taylor v Mucklow* [1973] Crim LR 750 and below, p. 425.
18. Section 57 (1).
19. *Brownlie* [1961] Crim LR 19.

Theft Act does, articles made, adapted or intended for *incapacitating* a person.[20]

There are three categories of offensive weapon: (i) Articles *made for causing injury* would include a service rifle or bayonet, a revolver, a cosh, knuckle-duster,[1] dagger or flick knife.[2] (ii) Articles *adapted for causing injury* would include razor blades inserted in a potato or cap-peak, a bottle broken for the purpose, a chair-leg studded with nails and so on. "Adapted" probably means altered so as to become suitable.[3] It is not certain whether the intention of the adaptor is relevant.[4] Is an *accidentally* broken milk bottle "adapted for use for causing injury to the person"? It is submitted that it is not and that if the article was not adapted with intent, it can only be an offensive weapon in category (iii) below. It has been held that a bottle broken for the purpose of committing suicide is adapted for causing injury to the person;[5] but since the question is whether it is an offensive weapon and "offensive" implies an attack on another, the "injury" which (it is submitted) the adaptor must contemplate, must be injury to another. (iii) It is very important to distinguish the third category of articles which are neither made nor adapted for causing injury, but are carried for that purpose. Whether D carried the article with the necessary purpose is essentially a question of fact.[6] Articles which have been held to be carried with such intent include a sheath-knife,[7] a shot-gun,[8] a razor,[9] a sandbag,[10] a pick-axe handle,[11] a stone,[12] and a drum of pepper.[13] *Any* article is capable of being an offensive weapon; but if it is of such a nature that it is unlikely to cause injury when brought into contact with the person, then the onus of proving the necessary intent will be very heavy.

The importance of the distinction is that, in the case of articles "made or adapted", the prosecution have to prove no more than possession in a public place.[14] D will then be convicted unless he can prove, on a balance of probability, that he had lawful authority or reasonable excuse. But if the article falls into the third category the onus is on the prosecution to show

20. Below, p. 609; Smith, *Law of Theft*, paras. [365]–[370].
   1. ". . . bludgeons, properly so-called, clubs and anything that is not in common use for any other purpose but a weapon are clearly offensive weapons within the meaning of the legislature" (the Smuggling Acts): (1784) 1 Leach 342 n (a).
   2. An offensive weapon *per se* because judicially noticed as such *Simpson* [1983] 3 All ER 789, [1983] 1 WLR 1494, CA; cf. *Gibson v Wales* [1983] 1 All ER 869, DC, [1983] Crim LR 113 and commentary.
   3. Cf. *Davison v Birmingham Industrial Co-operative Society* (1920) 90 LJKB 206; *Flower Freight Co Ltd v Hammond* [1963] 1 QB 275, [1962] 3 All ER 950; and *Herrmann v Metropolitan Leather Co Ltd* [1942] Ch 248, [1942] 1 All ER 294; *Maddox v Storer* [1963] 1 QB 451, [1962] 1 All ER 831.
   4. *Maddox v Storer* [1963] 1 QB 451, [1962] 1 All ER 831.
   5. By the Crown Court in *Bryan v Mott* (1975) 62 Cr App Rep 71. The point was not decided by the Divisional Court.
   6. *Williamson* (1978) 67 Cr App Rep 35, [1978] Crim LR 229, CA.
   7. *Woodward v Koessler* [1958] 3 All ER 557.
   8. *Gipson* [1963] Crim LR 281; *Hodgson* [1954] Crim LR 379.
   9. *Petrie* [1961] 1 All ER 466; *Gibson v Wales* [1983] 1 All ER 869.
   10. Ibid.
   11. *Cugullere* [1961] 2 All ER 343.
   12. *Harrison v Thornton* (1966) 110 Sol Jo 444, [1966] Crim LR 388, DC.
   13. 120 JP 250. Also, no doubt, a stiletto heel which can be a very dangerous weapon: (1964) The Times, 25th September.
   14. *Davis v Alexander* (1970) 54 Cr App Rep 398.

that it was carried with intent to injure.[15] The prosecution must satisfy the jury that the article is either offensive *per se* (made or adapted) or, if it is not, that D had it with him with intent. If some of the jury think it is the one, and some of the other, the case, it is submitted, is not made out.[16] The question in *Woodward v Koessler*[17] was whether D intended to "cause injury to the person" if he intended merely to frighten or intimidate by displaying a knife. It is now established that this is too wide. An intention to frighten or to intimidate is not enough. If there is no intention to cause physical injury, there must be an intention to cause injury by shock – and only in very exceptional circumstances could evidence of such an intention be found.[18]

A conditional intention to use the article is sufficient but it must be an intention to use the article in the future. If D sets out from Berkshire intending, if the occasion arises, to use a domestic knife for causing injury in Cornwall, the knife is an offensive weapon so long as it is carried in a public place and the intention continues. Once D believes that there is no possibility of the knife being used for causing injury – because, for example, his purpose has been accomplished – it ceases to be an offensive weapon.[19] It may, therefore, be no offence to carry the knife – whether or not it had been used – from Cornwall back to Berkshire.

After some hesitation, the courts have construed the Act in the light of its long title. It is aimed at the *carrying* of offensive weapons *in public places*. It is not aimed at the actual *use* of the weapon, which can invariably be adequately dealt with under some other offence. In *Jura*[20] D was holding an air rifle at a shooting gallery when, on a sudden provocation, he shot and wounded a woman. It was held that he had a reasonable excuse for *carrying* the rifle though not, of course, for using it in that way. But he had committed one offence, not two. It was as if a gamekeeper at a shooting party were suddenly to lose his temper and shoot at someone. If, then, D is lawfully in possession of the article, whether it be an offensive weapon per se or not, his decision unlawfully to use and immediate use of it does not amount to an offence under the Act. In *Dayle*[1] D took a car jack from the boot of his car and threw it at P in the course of a fight. In *Ohlson v Hylton*[2] D, a carpenter, took a hammer from his tool bag in the course of a fight and struck P. In neither case was D guilty of an offence under the Act.

It seems that if D is not in possession of the article until an occasion for its use arises and he then takes it up for immediate use, he commits no offence under the Act. The law was so stated in *Ohlson v Hylton*:[3]

15. *Petrie* [1961] 1 All ER 466; *Leer* [1982] Crim LR 310, CA.
16. *Flynn* (1985) 82 Cr App Rep 319, [1986] Crim LR 239 and commentary.
17. [1958] 3 All ER 557.
18. *Edmonds* [1963] 2 QB 142, [1963] 1 All ER 828, CA; *Rapier* (1979) 70 Cr App Rep 17, CA.
19. *Allamby* [1974] 3 All ER 126, CA. Cf. *Ellames* [1974] 3 All ER 130.
20. [1954] 1 QB 503, [1954] 1 All ER 696, CA.
1. [1973] 3 All ER 1151, CA.
2. [1975] 2 All ER 490, DC. See also *Police v Smith* [1974] 2 NZLR 32 (guest in restaurant using table knife offensively); *Humphreys* [1977] Crim LR 225, CA (penknife).
3. [1975] 2 All ER 490 at 496.

"To support a conviction under the Act the prosecution must show that the defendant was carrying or otherwise equipped with the weapon, and had the intent to use it offensively before any occasion for its actual use had arisen."[4]

This interpretation avoids the formidable difficulty which would otherwise arise where D picks up an article in the course of a fight, allegedly for self-defence. The onus of proving that this was an unreasonable step for the purposes of self-defence is on the Crown but, if it was capable of being an offence under the Act, it would be for D to prove he had a reasonable excuse.

An "occasion" has a beginning and it must also have an end.[5] If D picks up a glass to defend himself in the course of a pub brawl he does not commit an offence under the Act; but suppose, when the fight is over, he declines to put the glass down and insists on carrying it home through two miles of streets? Probably the "occasion" has come to an end, and the question is whether D has a reasonable excuse.

2 Lawful Authority or Reasonable Excuse

It may be that the existence of lawful authority is a pure question of law, whereas whether there is a reasonable excuse is a question of fact, subject to the usual judicial control.[6] "Lawful authority" presents difficulties. Before the Act, it was presumably generally lawful to be in possession of an offensive weapon in a public place – otherwise there would have been no necessity for the Act. Now it is generally unlawful. "Lawful authority" postulates some legal exception to the general rule of the Act; yet none is provided for and the words themselves are certainly not self-explanatory. In *Bryan v Mott* Lord Widgery CJ said[7] that "lawful authority" refers to those "people who from time to time carry an offensive weapon as a matter of duty – the soldier with his rifle and the police officer with his truncheon." It seems that the "duty" must be a public one – an employer cannot authorise his employees to carry offensive weapons simply by getting them to contract to do so.

Whether there is a reasonable excuse is said to depend on whether a reasonable man would think it excusable to carry the weapon[8] but the courts have construed the provision strictly and exercised close control over magistrates and juries. It is not enough that D's intentions were entirely lawful.[9] It is not necessarily a reasonable excuse that the weapon is carried only for self-defence. To have a defence D must show that there was "an imminent particular threat affecting the particular circumstances in which the weapon was carried."[10] One who is under constant threat, it is said, must resort to the police. He commits an offence if he regularly goes

---

4. *Powell* [1963] Crim LR 511, CCA, and *Harrison v Thornton* [1966] Crim LR 388, DC, appear to be wrongly decided in the light of this principle.
5. Cf. *Giles* [1976] Crim LR 253 (Judge Jones).
6. *Peacock* [1973] Crim LR 639; *Leer* [1982] Crim LR 310, CA.
7. (1976) 62 Cr App Rep 71 at 73, DC.
8. *Bryan v Mott*, above, p. 423, footnote 5.
9. *Bryan v Mott*, above. Cf. s. 17 (2) of the Firearms Act 1968, above, p. 423, where possession "for a lawful object" is a defence.
10. *Evans v Hughes* [1972] 3 All ER 412 at 415, DC; *Evans v Wright* [1964] Crim LR 466.

out armed for self-defence. So there was held to be no excuse for carrying an iron bar though D had reasonable cause to fear and did fear that he would be violently attacked and intended to use the bar for defence only.[11] It is not reasonable for an Edinburgh taxi-driver to carry two feet of rubber hose with a piece of metal inserted at one end, though he does so for defence against violent passengers whom taxi-drivers sometimes encounter at night.[12] It has been held that possession of a broken milk-bottle (an article adapted for causing injury) is not excused by the fact that D intended to use it to commit suicide.[13] It is an offence for security guards at dance halls to carry a truncheon "as a deterrent" and as "part of the uniform."[14] If, as the court said, "weapons must not be carried as a matter of routine or as part of a uniform," where stand the thousands of men said to be employed by private security forces and to be armed with batons?[15]

3 A Public Place

Section 1 (4) of the Prevention of Crime Act 1953 provides:

"'public place' includes any highway and any other premises or place to which at the material time the public have or are permitted to have access whether on payment or otherwise."

This is very similar to the interpretation which has been placed upon s. 196 of the Road Traffic Act 1972 and to the definition of public place, etc., in other Acts.[16] It should always be borne in mind that the same term may bear different meanings according to the context in which it is found and that whether a place is public is a question of fact.[17] A householder impliedly invites persons having legitimate business to walk up his garden path to the door, but this does not render the garden a "public place". The class of persons invited to enter is too restricted to constitute them "the public".[18] On the other hand, the landing of a block of flats has been held to be a public place on the ground that the public had access in fact, whether or not they were permitted to have it.[19] In the absence of a notice restricting entry, there was evidence on which justices could find that the unrestricted access of the public to a council estate extended to the stairways and landings of the flats. The jury are, of course, entitled to draw reasonable inferences; so that where D produced an air pistol in a private dwelling-house which he was visiting, it was open to them to infer that he brought it to or took it away from the house through the public street.[20]

---

11. Ibid. See also *Bradley v Moss* [1974] Crim LR 430, DC; *Pittard v Mahoney* [1977] Crim LR 169, DC.
12. *Grieve v Macleod* 1967 SLT 70.
13. *Bryan v Mott*, above.
14. *Spanner* [1973] Crim LR 704, CA.
15. 69 Law Soc Gaz 673.
16. And see the discussion of the meaning of public place for other purposes at pp. 466–467.
17. *Theodolou* [1963] Crim LR 573.
18. *Edwards and Roberts* (1978) 67 Cr App Rep 228, [1978] Crim LR 564 (a case under s. 5 of the Public Order Act 1936).
19. *Knox v Anderton* (1983) 76 Cr App Rep 156 [1983] Crim LR 114, DC and commentary. Cf. *Heffey* [1981] Crim LR 111 (Judge Nance).
20. *Mehmed* [1963] Crim LR 780.

4 Mens Rea

The Court of Criminal Appeal has held that the words "has with him in any public place" mean "*knowingly* has with him in any public place."[1]

> "If some innocent person has a cosh slipped into his pocket by an escaping rogue, he would not be guilty of having it with him within the meaning of the section, because he would be quite innocent of any knowledge that it had been put into his pocket."[2]

So D is not guilty, though he has put an offensive weapon in his car if, at the time of the alleged offence, his forgetfulness of its existence or presence in the car is so complete as to amount to ignorance that it is there at all.[3] Whether D must know of the facts which make the thing an offensive weapon within the Act has not been decided. Is D guilty if he has with him in a public place a revolver which he believes to be an imitation but which is real? Analogy with the Firearms Act 1968[3] would suggest that he is, but principle, it is submitted, requires acquittal.

3) *The Customs and Excise Management Act 1979*

By s. 86 of the Customs and Excise Management Act 1979 any person who is "armed with any offensive weapon or disguised in any way" when committing "smuggling" offences against the Act is liable on conviction on indictment to three years' imprisonment.

4) *The Night Poaching Act 1828*

Where three or more persons "unlawfully enter or be in" any land by night, for the purpose of taking or destroying game, and any of them is
> "armed with any gun, crossbow, fire arms, bludgeon, or any other offensive weapon",

all are guilty of an offence punishable on summary conviction by six months' imprisonment or a fine not exceeding level 3 on the standard scale or both[4] under s. 9 of the Night Poaching Act 1828.

5) *Bomb Hoaxes: Criminal Law Act 1977*

The bomb hoax, always irritating and sometimes frightening, was dealt with in a variety of ways before 1977. If a demand were made by the

---

1. *Cugullere* [1961] 2 All ER 343 at 344. Cf. *Warner v Metropolitan Police Commissioner* [1968] 2 All ER 356; **SHC** 110; above, p. 107.

2. Ibid. Cf. *Roper v Taylor's Garages Ltd* [1951] 2 TLR 284 at 288, per Devlin J; above, p. 103; and contrast the cautious approach of the court to a similar problem arising under the Dangerous Drugs Regulations 1953 where the question whether possession must be accompanied by *mens rea* was left open: *Carpenter* [1960] Crim LR 633.

3. *Russell* (1984) 81 Cr App Rep 315, [1985] Crim LR 231, CA. Cf. *Martindale* [1986] 3 All ER 25, [1986] 1 WLR 1042.

4. *Pierre*, above, p. 419.

hoaxer, it might be treated as blackmail.[5] If, as is usually the case, it involved a threat to damage property, s. 2 of the Criminal Damage Act 1971[6] might be invoked. In other cases, the hoax amounted to the offence of wasting the time of the police.[7] On one occasion at least, the clumsy weapon of public nuisance was used.[8] The Criminal Law Act 1977, s. 51 now provides a special offence.

"51.—(1) A person who –

(a) places any article in any place whatever; or

(b) dispatches any article by post, rail or any other means whatever of sending things from one place to another, with the intention (in either case) of inducing in some other person a belief that it is likely to explode or ignite and thereby cause personal injury or damage to property is guilty of an offence.

In this subsection "article" includes substance.

(2) A person who communicates any information which he knows or believes to be false to another person with the intention of inducing in him or any other person a false belief that a bomb or other thing liable to explode or ignite is present in any place or location whatever is guilty of an offence.

(3) For a person to be guilty of an offence under subsection (1) or (2) above it is not necessary for him to have any particular person in mind as the person in whom he intends to induce the belief mentioned in that subsection.

(4) A person guilty of an offence under this section shall be liable –

(a) on summary conviction, to imprisonment for a term not exceeding three months or to a fine not exceeding £1,000, or both;

(b) on conviction on indictment, to imprisonment for a term not exceeding five years."

The gist of the offences is the *mens rea*. The *actus reus* of section 51 (1) (a) is an act which everyone does every day. Under section 51(2) the information communicated may in fact be true; it is sufficient that D believes it to be false. If he believes that the information is, or may possibly be, true, then it obviously cannot be an offence to pass it on.

5. Below, p. 588. *King* [1976] Crim LR 200.
6. Below, p. 700. *Farrell* [1976] Crim LR 318.
7. Below, p. 758. *Bikram* [1974] Crim LR 55.
8. *Madden* [1975] 3 All ER 155. CA; below, p. 795.

13 Sexual Offences[1]

1 Rape

Section 1 (1) of the Sexual Offences Act 1956 provides:
"It is an offence for a man to rape a woman."
By s. 37 Schedule 2 the maximum punishment is life imprisonment.

That Act told us nothing more about the crime and so its definition was a matter of common law until the law was declared by the Sexual Offences (Amendment) Act 1976.

"1. (1) For the purposes of section 1 of the Sexual Offences Act 1956 (which relates to rape) a man commits rape if
(a) he has unlawful sexual intercourse with a woman who at the time of the intercourse does not consent to it; and
(b) at the time he knows that she does not consent to the intercourse or he is reckless as to whether she consents to it;
and references to rape in other enactments (including the following provisions of this Act) shall be construed accordingly."

The subsection codifies the law as laid down by the House of Lords in *Director of Public Prosecutions v Morgan*[2] where the argument that an unreasonable belief in consent could not be a defence was rejected. That decision caused widespread but largely unfounded concern which led to the appointment of an advisory group under Heilbron J to consider whether early changes in the law of rape were necessary. The Group made recommendations[3] for important reforms in the law of evidence and procedure on prosecutions for rape; but they concluded that *Morgan* was right in principle and recommended its codification. Much of the criticism of the decision appeared to assume that it meant that D had to do no more than assert that he believed P consented to ensure his acquittal; and, accordingly the Heilbron Group recommended the declaratory provision now to be found in s. 1 (2) of the Act:

"(2) It is hereby declared that if at a trial for a rape offence the jury has to consider whether a man believed that a woman was consenting to sexual intercourse, the presence or absence of reasonable grounds for such a belief is a matter to which the jury is to have regard, in

---

1. CLRC, Fifteenth Report, Sexual Offences, Cmnd. 9213 (1984); Hogan "On Modernising the Law of Sexual Offences" in *Reshaping the Criminal Law* 174. Hughes, "Consent in Sexual Offences" (1962) 25 MLR 319; Koh, "Consent in Sexual Offences", [1968] Crim LR 81.
2. [1975] 2 All ER 347; **SHC 45**; above, p. 86.
3. Cmnd. 6352 (1975). See [1976] Crim LR 97.

conjunction with any other relevant matters, in considering
whether he so believed."

This, of course, is a matter of common sense, in no way peculiar to rape. Whenever a jury has to decide whether a person knew a fact or foresaw a consequence, the fact that a reasonable man would have known the fact or foreseen the consequence is evidence tending to show that the accused knew or foresaw; but the decision must be made in the light of the whole of the evidence, including the accused's own testimony, if he gives it, that he did not know or foresee as the case may be. It is unfortunate that a matter of common sense should be enacted at all, particularly that it should be enacted in relation to one offence. So long, however, as it is understood that subsection (2) is a public relations provision and does not enact a rule peculiar to rape, it is harmless.

1 The Actus Reus

i) *Unlawful sexual intercourse.* The phrase, "unlawful sexual intercourse", has been held, for the purposes of some sections of the Sexual Offences Act 1956, to mean "illicit" intercourse, that is, intercourse outside the bonds of marriage.[4] The common law rule almost certainly was that a husband could not be convicted of raping his wife as a principal in the first degree.[5] Parliament considered an amendment to the Sexual Offences Amendment Bill which would have made it possible for a husband to be convicted of raping his wife but in the end decided to refer the question to the Criminal Law Revision Committee.[6] The Act thus tends to confirm the generally accepted view of the common law.

It was stated by Hale[7] that

"the husband cannot be guilty of a rape committed by himself upon his lawful wife, for by their mutual matrimonial consent and contract the wife hath given up herself in this kind unto her husband which she cannot retract."

This view of the law seems to have been so generally accepted that there was no recorded prosecution of a husband for himself committing rape upon his wife until 1949[8] when Byrne J in *Clarke*[9] accepted Hale's statement of the law as generally correct but held that an indictment would lie in that case, because the justices had made an order providing that the wife should no longer be bound to co-habit with the accused.[10]

"The position, therefore, was that the wife, by process of law, namely, by marriage, had given consent to the husband to exercise the marital right during such time as the ordinary relations created by the marriage

---

4. *Chapman* [1959] 1 QB 100, [1958] 3 All ER 143, CCA, (s. 19 (1)); *Jones* [1973] Crim LR 710, CA (s. 17 (1)).
5. Cf., however, *Cogan and Leak* [1976] QB 217, [1975] 2 All ER 1059, CA, above p. 156.
6. 911 H. of C. Official Report (5th Series) 1976, cols. 1957–1958.
7. 1 PC 629.
8. Morris and Turner, (1952–55) 2 Univ QLJ at 256.
9. [1949] 2 All ER 448.
10. Similarly in *O'Brien* [1974] 3 All ER 663, Park J held that a decree nisi of divorce effectively terminated a marriage and it was possible thereafter for the husband to rape the wife. Similarly where an injunction has been granted to restrain a husband from molesting his wife or where he has given an undertaking to the court not to do so: *Steele* (1977) 65 Cr App Rep 22, [1977] Crim LR 290.

contract subsisted between them, but by a further process of law, namely the justices' order, her consent to marital intercourse was revoked."[11]

In *Miller*,[12] the only direct authority, Lynskey J, after a careful examination of the authorities, concluded that Hale's proposition was correct and that the husband, who was charged with rape, had no case to answer. In that case, the wife had presented a petition for divorce before the act of intercourse but Lynskey J held, distinguishing *Clarke*, that this was immaterial. He said, obiter, that if there had been an agreement to separate, particularly if it had contained a non-molestation clause, the wife's consent would have been revoked.

Though doubts were expressed by some of the judges in *Clarence*,[13] the rule as stated by Hale has been generally accepted for so long, not only in England, but in other common law jurisdictions that, for practical purposes, it must be taken to be the common law.[14]

The question now is as to the meaning of "unlawful" in section 1 of the Act. If this were interpreted strictly to mean "outside matrimony and not otherwise," the effect would be to reverse *Clarke*.[15] That was certainly not Parliament's intention and the section should not be so interpreted. Thus, intercourse by a husband with a wife may be "unlawful" where there has been a judicial separation or decree nisi of divorce or nullity, an injunction against molestation, an undertaking to the court not to molest or a formal deed of separation, even though it does not contain a non-cohabitation clause or a non-molestation clause.[16] There may be other cases. In *Clarence* Stephen J thought the husband's act was unlawful because it constituted cruelty and, as such, a cause for judicial separation; but the disappearance of the "matrimonial offence" from family law weakens the case for arguing that such intercourse is "unlawful" and capable of being rape if the other conditions are satisfied.

A husband may be convicted as a secondary party to a rape[17] committed by another on his wife; for, as Hale puts it,[18]

"tho in marriage she hath given up her body to her husband, she is not to be by him prostituted to another."[19]

The basis for the general rule as stated by Hale is plainly fictitious – the wife may in fact have withdrawn her consent and the civil law recognises that she may properly do so in certain circumstances. She is not bound to submit to inordinate or unreasonable demands by her husband[20] and may refuse intercourse because her husband has been guilty of a matrimonial offence, which she does not wish to condone, or because he is suffering from a venereal disease.[1] The criminal law should not be based upon

11. [1949] 2 All ER at 449.
12. [1954] 2 QB 282, [1954] All ER 529; **SHC 362**.
13. (1888) 22 QBD 23; above, p. 382.
14. Cf. CLRC/SO/WP, at para. 28: "For the purposes of this Working Paper we adopt the generally accepted opinion . . .".
15. Above and *O'Brien*, above footnote 10.
16. *Roberts* [1986] Crim LR 188, CA.
17. *Cogan and Leak* [1976] QB 217, [1975] 2 All ER 1059, CA, above, p. 156.
18. Loc. cit.
19. See *Lord Castlehaven*'s case (1631) 3 State Tr 401.
20. Bromley, *Family Law* (7th ed.) 109.
 1. *Foster v Foster* [1921] P 438.

fictions. It may be, however, that the continuance of the rule can be justified on grounds of policy:

"If the wife is adamant in her refusal the husband must choose between letting his wife's will prevail, thus wrecking the marriage, and acting without her consent. It would be intolerable if he were to be conditioned in his course of action by the threat of criminal proceedings."[2]

The law does not, however, leave the wife defenceless against violence by her husband. In *Miller*,[3] Lynskey J held that though the husband had a right to sexual intercourse, he was not entitled to use force or violence in order to exercise that right:

"If he does so, he may make himself liable to the criminal law, not for the offence of rape, but for whatever other offence the facts of the particular case warrant. If he should wound her, he might be charged with wounding or causing bodily harm, or he may be liable to be convicted of common assault."[4]

The CLRC has unanimously recommended that rape should be extended to all cases where husband and wife are not co-habiting but recognises the difficulty of producing a satisfactory definition. A narrow majority of members were opposed to the complete abolition of the rule that a husband cannot rape his wife. In their opinion, the criminal law should interfere as little as possible in family relationships. An accusation of a husband by his wife of rape would in many cases preclude the reconciliation which would otherwise follow in a few days. The police would be bound to investigate the accusation, asking intimate questions which would be greatly resented by husbands and children. Proof of rape, always difficult, would be especially so in the case of a co-habiting husband and wife. The minority point to the fact that large numbers of men and women today cohabit without marrying and that the law of rape applies there without, so far as appears, any adverse consequences. But should the wife be denied a protection which is extended to the co-habiting woman?[5]

ii) *Sexual intercourse.* The phrase "carnal knowledge", formerly favoured in statutes, was replaced in the consolidation by the Sexual Offences Act by "sexual intercourse". Section 44 provides some guidance as to the meaning of that term:

"Where on the trial of any offence under this Act, it is necessary to prove sexual intercourse (whether natural or unnatural), it shall not be necessary to prove the completion of the intercourse by the emission of seed, but the intercourse shall be deemed complete upon proof of penetration only."

By section 7 (2) of the Sexual Offences (Amendment) Act 1976, s. 44, so far as it relates to natural intercourse,[6] applies for purposes of rape. The slightest penetration will suffice and it is not necessary to prove that the

2. Morris and Turner, op. cit., at 259, quoting Lord Dunedin in *G v G* [1924] AC 349 at 357: "It is indeed permissible to wish that some gentle violence had been employed. . . ."

3. [1954] 2 QB 282, [1954] 2 All ER 529; **SHC 413**. Cf. *Sharmpal Singh* [1962] AC 188.

4. Ibid. at 292 and 534. But the husband's immunity may extend to charges of indecent assault committed in the course of sexual intercourse: *Caswell* [1984] Crim LR 111; *Kowalski* [1988] Crim LR 124.

5. Fifteenth Report, Sexual Offences, Cmnd. 9213, paras. 2.55–2.85.

6. *O'Sullivan* [1981] Crim LR 406. There is no such offence as rape *per anum*.

hymen was ruptured.[7] The purpose of s. 44 is to remove doubts as to the minimum conduct needed to constitute sexual intercourse. "Complete" is used in the sense of having come into existence, not in the sense of being at an end.[8] Intercourse continues until the man withdraws. In *Kaitamaki*, it was held that it follows that D commits rape if, having penetrated with consent, or believing he has consent, he declines to withdraw on consent being revoked or on realising that P does not consent. So rape may be committed by omission. It is debatable whether this is right. Is not penetration without consent an essential part of the *actus reus* which must be accompanied by *mens rea*?[9]

iii) *The absence of consent.* The absence of P's consent is an essential part of the *actus reus* and must be proved by the prosecution. Earlier authorities emphasised the use of force; but it is now clear that lack of consent is the crux of the matter and this may exist though no force is used. A subtle change of emphasis occurred in the middle of the nineteenth century in the cases of *Camplin*[10] and *Fletcher*.[11] The test is not "was the act against her will?" but "was it without her consent?" This may seem, as it has to at least one judge,[12] a distinction without a difference; but it emphasises that it is not necessary for the Crown to prove a positive dissent by the woman; it is enough that she did not assent. So convictions were upheld where D had intercourse with a woman whom he had rendered insensible by giving her liquor in order to excite her;[13] and again where D had intercourse with a woman who was asleep.[14]

Inconsistently with this development, courts and writers continued up to 1976 to cite the traditional seventeenth century definition of rape as having intercourse without consent "by force, fear or fraud". The Heilbron Committee,[15] however, adopted the statement of the law in this book and in *Olugboja*[16] the Court of Appeal, while not persuaded that this was wrong, held that, whatever the law may have been before the 1976 Act, Parliament had adopted and incorporated in the Act the statement in the Heilbron report, so that –

"... the question now is simply: 'At the time of sexual intercourse did the woman consent to it?' It is not necessary for the prosecution to prove that what might otherwise appear to have been consent was in reality merely submission induced by force, fear or fraud, although one or more of these factors will no doubt be present in the majority of cases of rape."[17]

7. *Russen* (1777) 1 East PC 438; *Hughes* (1841) 9 C & P 752; *Lines* (1844) 1 Car & Kir 393.
8. *Kaitamaki* [1985] AC 147, [1984] 2 All ER 435, PC, construing the corresponding provision in the New Zealand Crimes Act 1961, s. 127; *Mayberry* [1973] Qd R 229, above, p. 17.
9. See the dissent by Woodhouse J in the New Zealand Court of Appeal, [1980] 1 NZLR 59; **SHC 20**.
10. (1845) 1 Den 89.
11. (1859) Bell CC 63.
12. Lawson J in *Dee* (1884) 15 Cox CC 579 at 595 (Irish CCR).
13. *Camplin* (1845) 1 Den 89.
14. *Mayers* (1872) 12 Cox CC 311; *Young* (1878) 14 Cox CC 114.
15. Cmnd. 6352 (1975), p. 3, citing the 3rd ed., p. 326.
16. (1981) 73 Cr App Rep 344.
17. 73 Cr App Rep at 350.

There are similar problems with fraud. At present the only fraud recognised as vitiating consent is the impersonation of a husband or deception as to the nature of the act.

Olugboja said that the jury should be directed that consent is to be given its ordinary meaning and, if need be, that there is a difference between consent and submission. This conceals a great difficulty – namely what is the difference between consent and submission? A person submits when he or she yields, or gives in, to pressure of some kind. A woman may reluctantly submit to sexual intercourse only because her fiancé threatens that he will break off their engagement if she does not. Such a case is very far removed from rape but it seems to be be one of submission. At the other extreme, a woman may submit because the man is holding a knife at her throat. This is plainly rape. The distinction cannot, however, be justified by a distinction between consent and submission. In both cases the woman yields because a threat is made. Submission may indeed be induced by a promise. The woman gives in only because the man promises that he will marry her if she does so. No one would say that is rape if the man intends to keep the promise (and it is clearly not rape in law if he does not) but is it not a case of submission? The dictum of Coleridge J in *Day*:[18] "every consent involves a submission; but it by no means follows that a mere submission involves consent", seems, on reflection, to be the wrong way round. A woman who joyously embraces her reluctant lover undoubtedly consents to the intercourse which follows but it would seem inappropriate, to put it mildly, to say that she "submits" to that which she ardently desires and provokes. On the other hand, a woman who gives in to threats does in fact consent, however reluctantly. In *Olugboja*[19] reference is made to an unreported case in which Winn J held that a constable had no case to answer where he induced P to consent to sexual intercourse by threatening to report her for an offence; whereas in *Wellard*[20] D was said to have a previous conviction for rape (for which he was sentenced to six years' imprisonment) by masquerading as a security officer and inducing a girl to consent by threatening to report to her parents and the police that she had been seen having intercourse in a public place.

It is doubtful if the bounds of the crime of rape can be satisfactorily drawn by a distinction between consent and submission. It is so vague that, as the above cases suggest, both judges and juries may have quite different ideas as to its application. The CLRC's recommendation[1] is that sexual intercourse obtained by threats of immediate force against the woman or any other person "should continue to be rape" but that intercourse obtained by other threats, including threats of force which can be carried out only at some time in the future, should not be rape but should be punishable under s. 2 of the Sexual Offences Act 1956[2] with an increased penalty.

18. (1841) 9 C & P 722 at 724.
19. At 347–348.
20. Above, p. 414, (1978) 67 Cr App Rep 364 at 368. The court made no comment on the propriety or otherwise of the conviction.
  1. Fifteenth Report, 2.29.
  2. Below, p. 439.

Where D had intercourse with a girl of thirteen years of weak intellect, it was held that the jury were rightly told that he was guilty if they were satisfied that the girl was incapable of giving consent or exercising any judgment on the matter.[3] Willes J said[4] that a consent produced by mere animal instinct would be sufficient to prevent the act from constituting a rape and this was followed by Keating J[5] and approved by Kelly CB.[6] Palles CB, however, described this as a doctrine

"abhorrent to our best feelings, and ... discreditable to any jurisprudence in which it may succeed in obtaining a place."[7]

It is submitted that his view that consent must be an intelligent act is the better view.

No doubt it is also rape to have intercourse with a child too young to understand the nature of the act; but there is no fixed age limit below which consent is impossible as a matter of law.[8] It is a question of fact in each case and therefore it is a misdirection to tell a jury that, as a matter of law, a child of six cannot consent. Yet, since

"... it would be idle for anyone to suggest that a girl of that age had sufficient understanding and knowledge to decide whether to consent or resist"

a conviction may be upheld, notwithstanding such a misdirection.[9] The effect seems to be much the same as if it were a rule of law.

The 1956 Act provides, by s. 1 (2), that

"a man who induces a woman to have sexual intercourse with him by impersonating her husband commits rape."

This provision, re-enacting the Criminal Law Amendment Act 1885, s. 4, reverses a line of decisions[10] culminating in *Barrow*[11] where the Court for Crown Cases Reserved held that the woman's consent to sexual intercourse was a defence even though she was deceived into thinking that D was her husband. However, in *Flattery*[12] four of the five judges in the Court for Crown Cases Reserved thought that *Barrow* ought to be reconsidered; and in *Dee*[13] the Irish Court for Crown Cases Reserved dissented from it and upheld the impersonator's conviction. The *Barrow* line of cases might still be of importance where D obtains intercourse by impersonating some person other than a husband. It is submitted that this should be rape. It is true that, where the husband is impersonated, there is also an error as to the nature of the transaction – it is not marital intercourse

---

3. *Fletcher* (1859) Bell CC 63.
4. Ibid.
5. In *Fletcher* (1866) LR 1 CCR 39.
6. In *Barratt* (1873) LR 2 CCR 81.
7. In *Dee* (1884) 15 Cox CC 579 at 594.
8. *Harling* [1938] 1 All ER 307 at 308. "It may well be that in many cases the prosecution would not want much evidence beyond the age of the girl to prove non-consent, but in every charge of rape the fact of non-consent must be proved to the satisfaction of the jury": per Humphreys J. By s. 46 of the Sexual Offences Act 1956 "woman" in that Act includes "girl".
9. *Howard* [1965] 3 All ER 684, CCA.
10. *Jackson* (1822) Russ & Ry 487, CCR; *Saunders* (1838) 8 C & P 265; *Williams* (1838) 8 C & P 286; *Clarke* (1854) Dears CC 397.
11. (1868) 11 Cox CC 191.
12. (1877) 2 QBD 410.
13. (1884) 15 Cox CC 579.

but adultery – whereas if D impersonates another, the transaction is both understood to be and is adultery or fornication – but such an error has never been held sufficiently fundamental to found an indictment for rape. Sexual intercourse is, however, a relationship in which personality is supremely important and consent to have intercourse with A is not consent to have intercourse with B. The *Barrow* line of cases is presumably authority against this view but it contained a fundamental inconsistency in that it held that D was guilty of an assault; yet consent should have been equally a defence there as in rape and the cases might be treated, as they were in *Dee*, as depending on the narrow view of rape which was rejected in *Fletcher*.[14]

If D had intercourse with P by impersonating, for example, P's fiancé, it is submitted that *Barrow* should be overruled and D convicted of rape.[15]

Where D, by fraud, deceives the woman as to the nature of the transaction, it is well established that this is rape. So in *Flattery*[16] D was convicted where P submitted to intercourse with him under the impression that he was performing a surgical operation. It is an offence under the Sexual Offences Act 1956, s. 3

"for a person to procure a woman, by false pretences or representations, to have sexual intercourse in any part of the world."

It seems probable that this section covers conduct such as that of Flattery but that it also extends to a much wider range of frauds of a much less fundamental character; and it has been held by the Court of Criminal Appeal in *Williams*,[17] a case with substantially the same facts as *Flattery*, that such conduct is still indictable as rape.

Probably any fraud which does not go to the nature of the act or the identity of the man is not sufficient to destroy consent. So misrepresentations by a man as to his wealth, social position or freedom to marry would not render intercourse thereby obtained rape.[18] Even where the woman is induced by fraud to suppose that she is already married to D, her consent to intercourse affords a defence.[19]

The CLRC's recommendation[20] is that it should continue to be rape to obtain sexual intercourse by fraud as to the nature of the act or by impersonation of P's husband and that it should also be rape to obtain intercourse by impersonation of another man. Other cases of obtaining intercourse by fraud should be dealt with under s. 3 of the Sexual Offences Act 1956.[1]

iv) *Fundamental mistake not arising from fraud.* Though stress in the cases has been laid on the element of fraud it is thought that this is not the crucial

---

14. (1859) Bell CC 63; above, p. 435.
15. But cf. *Collins* [1973] QB 100, [1972] 2 All ER 1105, below, p. 596.
16. (1877) 2 QBD 410.
17. [1923] 1 KB 340.
18. See Stephen J in *Clarence* (1888) 22 QBD 23 at 44. Cf. Canadian Criminal Code, s. 298.
19. *Papadimitropoulos v R* (1958) 98 CLR 249, [1958] ALR 21; **SHC 450**; where it is pointed out that there is no reported instance of an indictment for rape based on the fraudulent character of the ceremony.
20. Fifteenth Report, 2.24–2.25.
 1. Below, p. 439.

matter; and that if D had intercourse with P, knowing that she was under a mistake, not induced by him, either as to his identity or as to the nature of the act, that would be rape.[2]

If the man obtains the woman's consent without the use of force, threats or fraud he is not guilty of rape or any offence, though he may have resorted to various other devices – soft lights, sweet music, flattery – and drink. It is a misdirection to tell a jury that D is guilty of rape if he encouraged P to drink in the hope that her resistance would collapse.[3]

2 The Mens Rea

Although the Act does not spell this out, it seems clear there must be an intention to have sexual intercourse with a woman who is not D's wife.[4] Additionally, D must know that P does not consent or be reckless whether she consents. There is no doubt that the Heilbron Group had in mind *Cunningham* recklessness.[5] It appeared for a time as if *Caldwell*[6] had defeated that intention. In *Pigg*[7], applying *Caldwell*, it was held that "A man is reckless if he was indifferent and gave no thought to the possibility that [P] might not be consenting in circumstances where, if any thought had been given to the matter, it would have been obvious that there was a risk that she was not consenting . . .". It is difficult to understand how a man can be indifferent to something the possibility of which he has not envisaged. In *Satnam S*[8] the court recognised this and other difficulties, pointing out that *Caldwell* was concerned with recklessness as to the consequences of D's act whereas in rape we are concerned with recklessness as to P's state of mind. It was held that the definition of rape should be based on s. 1 of the 1976 Act and *Morgan* without regard to *Caldwell* and *Lawrence*. Though the *mens rea* is formulated in various ways, it seems that there is, in substance, a return to *Cunningham* recklessness. If D is aware that there is any possibility that P is not consenting and proceeds to have intercourse, he does so recklessly. Lord Hailsham in *Morgan* required an "intention of having intercourse, willy-nilly, not caring whether the victim consents or not".[9] Another way of putting it is to ask, "Was D's attitude one of 'I could not care less whether she is consenting or not, I am going to have intercourse with her regardless.'"[10]

It is submitted therefore that the *mens rea* is an intention to have sexual intercourse with P, (i) knowing that P does not consent, or (ii) being aware that there is a possibility that she does not consent.

2. See *Papadimitropoulos v R* (1958) 98 CLR 249 at 260.
3. *Lang* (1975) 62 Cr App Rep 50, CA. Cf. s. 4 (1) of the Sexual Offences Act 1956, below, p. 440.
4. D would not be guilty of rape on the ground that his marriage to P was void because P was already married to another, if the fact was unknown to D; or where P, having successfully impersonated D's wife, unsuccessfully resisted his attempts to have sexual intercourse.
5. Above, p. 62.
6. Above, p. 62. Contrast the attention paid to the intentions of the Heilbron Group in *Olugboja*, above, p. 433.
7. [1982] 2 All ER 591, [1982] Crim LR 446 CA, and commentary.
8. (1983) 78 Cr App Rep 149, [1985] Crim LR 236.
9. [1976] AC 182 at 215.
10. *Taylor* (1984) 80 Cr App Rep 327; *Haughian* (1985) 80 Cr App Rep 334.

In *Bashir*[11] it was said that the trial judge had acted "very wisely" in amending the indictment in respect of a single act of alleged rape so that it charged D with knowing that P did not consent in one count and being reckless in a second count. The verdict then assists the judge in the imposition of sentence.

3 Boys under Fourteen; and Women

As noted above,[12] there is an irrebuttable presumption in criminal law[13] that a boy under the age of fourteen is incapable of committing rape, any other crime of which sexual intercourse is an ingredient, or sodomy.[14] This is an absurd rule, capable of producing injustice. If two boys, aged 16 and 13 respectively, were charged with rape of a girl and it was proved that one boy had intercourse with the girl while the other abetted, but it could not be proved which of the boys did the act, both would have to be acquitted because, if it was in fact the 13-year old, the law says it did not happen at all. The CLRC has recommended the abolition of the irrebuttable presumption.[15] There are conflicting *dicta* whether he may be convicted of an attempt. It is submitted that he should be liable to conviction. The law does not say that the completed act is no offence, it says that the completed act can never happen. It does not say that the boy may not try to make it happen. Plainly he may, and, at least since the Criminal Attempts Act 1981, the presumed impossibility should be no answer.[16] This would mitigate the difficulty pointed out above – both boys could be convicted of the attempt. A difficulty in the way of this opinion may be the cases which decided that a boy under 14 could not be convicted of assault with intent to commit rape.[17]

It is clear, however, that a boy under fourteen may be convicted of counselling or abetting a rape,[18] as may a woman.[19]

2 Other Offences Involving Sexual Intercourse

The meaning given to "consent" in rape left a number of cases where consent was in some way imperfect, but which were not crimes at common law. The law has therefore been supplemented by several statutory crimes involving sexual intercourse where consent has been improperly obtained by threats, false pretences or the administration of drugs; or where the woman, though consenting in fact, is deemed by the law to be incompetent to consent on account of age or mental handicap. Except where otherwise stated the offences are punishable with two years' imprisonment.

11. (1982) 77 Cr App Rep 59.
12. See p. 181.
13. There is no such presumption in civil cases: *L v K* [1985] Fam 144, [1985] 1 All ER 961. (Ewbank J).
14. *Groombridge* (1836) 7 C & P 582; *Waite* [1892] 2 QB 600, CCR; *Cratchley* (1913) 9 Cr App Rep 232; *Tatam* (1921) 15 Cr App Rep 132.
15. Fifteenth Report, 2.48.
16. Above, p. 300.
17. *Eldershaw* (1828) 3 C & P 396; *Philips* (1839) 8 C & P 736. Cf. Williams, CLGP 634.
18. *Eldershaw*, supra.
19. *Ram and Ram* (1893) 17 Cox CC 609; above p. 155.

1 Procurement of Woman by Threats or by False Pretences

By s. 2 (1) of the Sexual Offences Act 1956:

"It is an offence for a person to procure a woman, by threats or intimidation, to have unlawful sexual intercourse in any part of the world."

By s. 3 (1) of the Sexual Offences Act 1956:

"It is an offence for a person to procure a woman, by false pretences or false representations, to have unlawful sexual intercourse in any part of the world."

These offences, which were originally enacted by the Criminal Law Amendment Act 1885, were probably intended to deal with the person who procures the woman to have intercourse with a third party but have been held to apply also to the man who causes the woman to have intercourse with himself.[20] Whereas rape is indictable only if the sexual intercourse takes place within the jurisdiction, here it may take place in any part of the world, but the act of procuring must of course be done[1] within the jurisdiction. The creation of these offences in no way limited the common law of rape[2] nor does their existence limit the statutory offence which has replaced it.

Both offences are punishable by two years' imprisonment. These offences are not committed unless sexual intercourse actually takes place. Persuading a girl to agree to have intercourse and to accompany a man for that purpose is not "procuring" if the intercourse does not take place; but it is an attempt to procure.[3] "To procure" means to produce by endeavour.[4] Proof that the threats or false pretences induced P to submit to sexual intercourse will inevitably establish this.

These offences can be committed by any person, whether male or female, but a boy under fourteen cannot be convicted of procuring intercourse with himself because of the irrebuttable presumption that he is incapable.[5] It is possible, however, that he might be convicted of an attempt to procure.[6]

Threats. As has been seen, there is some uncertainty as to what threats are sufficiently grave to negative consent for the purpose of rape. Whatever the limits in rape, it is possible that less grave threats will suffice for this much less serious offence. Threats to injure a third party may be enough.[7] Suppose that, for example, D threatens that, if P does not consent, he will (a) tell the police of a theft she has committed; (b) tell her father of her previous immorality; (c) dismiss her from her present employment; (d) not

20. *Williams* (1898) 62 JP 310 by the Recorder who declined to state a case (s. 3 (1)). Cf. *Cook* [1954] 1 All ER 60, below, p. 443.
1. Or, strictly, "begun", because the procuring is complete only when the intercourse takes place.
2. *Williams* [1923] 1 KB 340, CCA (s. 3 (1)).
3. *Johnson* [1964] 2 QB 404, [1963] 3 All ER 577, [1963] Crim LR 860, and commentary thereon. See also Glazebrook, [1959] Crim LR 774.
4. *Christian* (1913) 78 JP 112; below, p. 456; *Attorney General's Reference (No. 1 of 1975)* above, p. 133.
5. On the question of an attempt to have intercourse by a boy under fourteen see above, p. 438.
6. See above, p. 438.
7. Cf. *Wilson* (1973) 58 Cr App Rep 304 at 307, CA.

give her a rise in salary; (e) never take her to the pictures again. Clearly, a line must be drawn somewhere before we reach the last case. Once we go beyond the threats of violence, it is not obvious on what principle the line should be drawn. Perhaps it must be a threat which a person of the age and with the other characteristics of the woman could not reasonably be expected, in the circumstances, to resist.[8]

False pretences. There is a similar uncertainty about the meaning of false pretences. In *Williams,*[9] Hewart CJ said that "it is obvious" that the words of the section go "far beyond the case of rape". It seems likely that it extends to cases where there is no mistake as to the nature of the act. Certainly cases of impersonation, if they are not rape, will be offences under s. 3. It may be that any false pretence which in fact induces P to give a consent which she would not otherwise have given is enough. But it is just arguable (the property offences involving deception do not support the argument) that the pretence must be one which would influence a reasonable woman. Suppose, for example, that D tells P that intercourse improves the voice, or is a certain cure for rheumatism? Whether the restricted meaning given to "false pretences" under the Larceny Act 1916 applies to s. 3 does not seem to have been decided. If it does, "false pretences" is confined to misrepresentation of present fact and, for example, it would be no offence for D to procure intercourse with P by misrepresenting that it was his intention to marry her.[10] But the words "or false representations" suggest that the wider meaning should be adopted.

The CLRC has recommended that these offences should continue in their present wide terms.[11] Although rarely used, they are useful to deal with the occasional case which does not amount to rape but should not be allowed to fall outside the criminal law. The penalty for the s. 2 offence should be increased to five years and the reference to "false pretences or false representations" should be replaced by "deception".[12]

2 Administering Drugs to Obtain or Facilitate Intercourse
By s. 4 (1) of the Sexual Offences Act 1956:
"It is an offence for a person to apply or administer to, or cause to be taken by, a woman any drug, matter or thing with intent to stupefy or overpower her so as thereby to enable any man to have unlawful sexual intercourse with her."

It will be noted that this offence is complete when the drugs, etc., have been applied, administered, etc., with the ulterior intent;[13] and it is not necessary that intercourse should have taken place or been attempted. No doubt this section also applies to the man who seeks to have intercourse himself, and, clearly, the offence can be committed by any person male or female.

---

8. Cf. Blackmail, below, p. 588; duress, above, p. 235.
9. [1923] 1 KB 340, above, p. 436.
10. Cf. *Dent*, below, p. 549, footnote 9.
11. Fifteenth Report, 2.107–2.112.
12. Below, p. 544.
13. Cf. *Shillingford* [1968] Crim LR 282.

3 Intercourse with a Girl under Thirteen

By s. 5 of the Sexual Offences Act 1956:[14]

"It is an offence for a man to have unlawful sexual intercourse with a girl under the age of thirteen."

4 Intercourse with a Girl under Sixteen

By s. 6 of the Sexual Offences Act 1956:

"(1) It is an offence [triable either way], subject to the exceptions mentioned in this section, for a man to have unlawful sexual intercourse with a girl under the age of sixteen.

(2) Where a marriage is invalid under section two of the Marriage Act 1949 or section one of the Age of Marriage Act 1929 (the wife being a girl under the age of sixteen), the invalidity does not make the husband guilty of an offence under this section because he has sexual intercourse with her, if he believes her to be his wife and has reasonable cause for the belief.

(3) A man is not guilty of an offence under this section because he has unlawful sexual intercourse with a girl under the age of sixteen, if he is under the age of twenty-four and has not previously been charged with a like offence, and he believes her to be of the age of sixteen or over and has reasonable cause for the belief.

In this subsection, 'a like offence' means an offence under this section or an attempt to commit one, or an offence under paragraph (1) of section five of the Criminal Law Amendment Act 1885 (the provision replaced for England and Wales by this section)."

The offence under s. 5 is punishable with life imprisonment. Since they were amended by the Criminal Law Act 1967, the offences under ss. 5 and 6, which were formerly mutually exclusive, overlap, so that a man who has intercourse with a girl under thirteen commits both offences. It is clear that these sections must be read in the light of *Prince*.[15] It follows that a belief that the girl is over thirteen, no matter how reasonable it may be, will not afford a defence to a charge under s. 5 and that a belief that the girl is over sixteen is a defence to a charge under s. 6 only if it is reasonable and held by a man under twenty-four who has not previously been charged with a like offence. The defence is available only to one who has an actual belief that the girl was over sixteen; reasonable cause for such a belief does not afford a defence to one who never directed his mind to the question of the girl's age.[16] A man is "charged" for the purposes of this section when he first appears before a court having jurisdiction to determine the matter.[17] Thus, if the other conditions of the defence are satisfied, D will not be guilty of an offence under the section if he has unlawful sexual intercourse with a girl under sixteen after being committed for trial for a like offence, even though he be convicted of the first offence before the second one comes before the

---

14. This replaces the Criminal Law Amendment Act 1885, s. 4.
15. (1875) LR 2 CCR 154; **SHC 102**; above, p. 41; see especially per Blackburn J at 171.
16. *Banks* [1916] 2 KB 621; *Harrison* [1938] 3 All ER 134. Yet the Criminal Law Amendment Act in terms required only "reasonable cause to believe" and made no mention of actual belief. A fortiori, then, this interpretation must apply to the present statute.
17. *Rider* [1954] 1 All ER 5, per Streatfeild J.

court of trial; otherwise if he appears before the court of trial for the first offence before he commits the second. Presumably the rationale of the sub-section is that the defence should be available to a young man who has not had brought to his attention in a formal way the serious consequences of a mistake as to the girl's age. If so, does not the restrictive interpretation of "charge" extend the defence too far? When D has been committed for trial he is well aware of the risks involved in his conduct.

When the present offence was originally enacted in 1885 the age of marriage for a girl was fixed by the common law at twelve and it so remained until the Age of Marriage Act 1929 which raised it to sixteen.[18] Intercourse with a girl under sixteen is now necessarily unlawful, except in the case of a marriage valid under a foreign law. In the latter case there is no *actus reus* under s. 5 or s. 6.[19]

The onus of proving (on a balance of probabilities) all the elements of a defence under sub-ss. (2) or (3) of s. 6 is on the accused.[20] Thus a jury ought to convict a man if they thought that there was an even chance that he believed on reasonable grounds that the girl was his wife or that the conditions of sub-s. (3) were fulfilled.[1]

5 Procuration[2] of Girl under Twenty-One

It is no crime to have unlawful sexual intercourse with a girl over the age of sixteen. But, by s. 23 (1) of the Sexual Offences Act 1956:

"It is an offence for a person to procure a girl under the age of twenty-one to have unlawful sexual intercourse in any part of the world with a third person."

As already noted in connection with other sections, procuration implies causation by the endeavours of the accused and the offence is not complete until intercourse takes place.[3] It is likely that the principle of *Prince*[4] is again applicable, so that a reasonable belief that the girl is over twenty-one will afford no defence.

A man who procures a girl under twenty-one to have intercourse with himself commits no offence; but if he agrees with a third person that the third person shall procure the girl for him, then he may be convicted under this section as an abettor and also of conspiracy to commit an offence under this section.[5]

6 Intercourse with a Defective

Section 7 of the Sexual Offences Act 1956, as amended by the Mental Health Act 1959, provides:

18. See now the Marriage Act 1949, s. 2.
19. *Alhaji Mohamed v Knott* [1969] 1 QB 1, [1968] 2 All ER 563, [1968] Crim LR 341 and commentary thereon.
20. Section 47 of the Act provides: 'Where in any of the foregoing sections the description of an offence is expressed to be subject to exceptions mentioned in the section, proof of the exception is to lie on the person relying on it."
   1. For proposals for reform of the law, see CLRC/SO/WP, 24–28.
   2. The Act uses "procurement" in ss. 2, 3 and 9 and "procuration" in ss. 22 and 23 but it does not appear that there is any difference in the meaning of these terms. Cf. *Broadfoot* [1976] 3 All ER 753, CA, below, p. 456.
   3. *Johnson* [1964] 2 QB 404, [1963] 3 All ER 577; *Mackenzie and Higginson* (1910) 6 Cr App Rep 64.
   4. (1875) LR 2 CCR 154; above p. 41.
   5. *Mackenzie*, above, following *Whitchurch*, above, p. 283.

"(1) It is an offence, subject to the exception mentioned in this section, for a man to have unlawful sexual intercourse with a woman who is a defective.

(2) A man is not guilty of an offence under this section because he has unlawful sexual intercourse with a woman if he does not know and has no reason to suspect her to be defective."

By s. 45, as amended, "'defective' means a person suffering from a state of arrested or incomplete development of mind which includes *severe impairment of intelligence and social functioning*."[6] The italicised words do not give examples of deficiency but specify two conditions which must be present in every case for a person to be "defective". They are not terms of art. Severe impairment is to be measured against the standard of normal persons.[7]

7 Procurement of a Defective

By s. 9 of the Sexual Offences Act 1956:

"(1) It is an offence, subject to the exception mentioned in this section, for a person to procure a woman who is a defective to have unlawful sexual intercourse in any part of the world.

(2) A person is not guilty of an offence under this section because he procures a defective to have unlawful sexual intercourse, if he does not know and has no reason to suspect her to be a defective."

Procurement (or "procuration")[8] implies causation by the endeavours of the accused so that it would seem that a girl is not procured to have intercourse if the initiative comes from her.[9] The problem can hardly arise under s. 2 or s. 3 when false pretences or duress have been proved. But it may arise under s. 9.

It is not clear that this section applies, as do ss. 2, 3 and 23, to the case of a man who procures a defective to have intercourse with himself. In *Cook*[10] Stable J held that D had no case to answer although one morning he asked P to go back to bed and then went and had intercourse with her. The judge pointed out that while the Mental Deficiency Act 1913 made it an offence to have intercourse with a mental defective in an institution or out on licence, there was in that Act no such provision for mental defectives generally. Stable J did not, however, clearly rule that it was no offence for D to procure P to have sexual intercourse with D, but seems rather to have held that the element of persuasion involved in procuration was lacking.[11] Any gap in the law revealed by this case is now closed by s. 7[12] and any procuration by D of P to have sexual intercourse with himself is an offence under that section. Only in one situation is the question whether s. 9 applies to this case now of importance; some attempts to procure may not amount to attempts to have intercourse.[13]

6. Cf. the definition of "severe mental impairment", above p. 199, footnote 20.
7. *Hall* [1987] Crim LR 831. For onus of proof, see above, p. 442, footnote 20.
8. See above, p. 420, footnote 20.
9. See above, p. 439, footnote 4.
10. [1954] 1 All ER 60.
11. "He did not get the girl to come into his house. He did not get her away from her mother." But surely there was evidence that D procured P *to have intercourse*?
12. See above, p. 442.
13. See [1963] Crim LR at 861.

It is clear that, under ss. 7 and 9, it would be a defence for D to establish that he reasonably[14] did not advert to the question whether P was a defective or not. It would not be necessary for him to prove that he considered the question and decided she was not.[15]

8 Sexual Intercourse with Mentally Disordered Patients

Without prejudice to s. 7 of the Sexual Offences Act 1956 and subject to a similar exception, it is an offence under s. 128 of the Mental Health Act 1959, punishable with two years' imprisonment, for an officer, employee or manager of a hospital or mental nursing home to have sexual intercourse with a woman receiving treatment in the hospital or home or, if the intercourse is on the premises, who is receiving treatment there as an out-patient. Similarly in the case of a man having intercourse with a woman who is a mentally disordered patient subject to his guardianship or in his custody or care.

9 Permitting Use of Premises for Intercourse

Sections 25, 26 and 27 of the Sexual Offences Act 1956 create offences ancillary to those in ss. 5, 6 and 7 respectively. Where the owner or occupier of premises, or any person who has or acts or assists in the management or control of any premises, induces or knowingly suffers to resort to or be on those premises, for the purpose of having unlawful sexual intercourse with men or with a particular man–

 i) a girl under thirteen, he is, by s. 25, guilty of an offence punishable with life imprisonment;

 ii) a girl under sixteen or

 iii) a woman who is defective, he is, by ss. 26 and 27 respectively, guilty of an offence punishable with two years' imprisonment. The offence under s. 26 is triable either way.

Although each of these sections uses the expression "induce or knowingly suffer", it is not clear that *mens rea* is required for s. 27 alone provides for an exception:

"A person is not guilty of an offence under this section because he induces or knowingly suffers a defective to resort to or be on any premises for the purpose mentioned, if he does not know and has no reason to suspect her to be a defective."

It is implicit in this that D may "knowingly suffer" a defective to be on the premises, although he does not know she is a defective, if he has reason[16] so to suspect. If, as might reasonably be expected, "knowingly suffer" bears the same meaning in each of these closely related provisions, it would follow that D might likewise "knowingly suffer" girls under thirteen and sixteen respectively to be on the premises for the purpose of intercourse, although he believes them to be over those ages; and in the absence of the exception which applies to s. 27, it may be immaterial that that belief is a perfectly reasonable one – that is, *Prince*[17] is applicable and a

14. But see *Hudson* [1965] 1 All ER 721; and comment at [1965] Crim LR 172.
15. Contrast the position under s. 6 and *Harrison*, above, p. 441.
16. Cf. above, pp. 124–126.
17. Above, p. 41.

person who knowingly suffers *girls* (of whatever age) to be on his premises for this purpose does so at his peril.[18] In *McPherson*[19] it was held that in such circumstances, D may be guilty of *inducing*, if not knowingly suffering, the girls to be there.

10 Incest

There remains one offence involving sexual intercourse which does not depend in any way upon a deficiency in the consent of the woman. This is incest, which consists in sexual intercourse between persons within a specified degree of consanguinity. Incest was not a crime at common law or at all until 1908, but was dealt with by the ecclesiastical courts. The Marriage Act 1949, Schedule I, sets out the degrees of relationship within which marriage is prohibited and, if celebrated, void, but it is only in the case of a much narrower range of relationships that sexual intercourse is a criminal offence. The law is now to be found in ss. 10 and 11 of the Sexual Offences Act 1956:

"10.–(1) It is an offence for a man to have sexual intercourse with a woman whom he knows to be his grand-daughter, daughter, sister or mother.

(2) In the foregoing subsection 'sister' includes half-sister, and for the purposes of that subsection any expression importing a relationship between two people shall be taken to apply notwithstanding that the relationship is not traced through lawful wedlock.

11.–(1) It is an offence for a woman of the age of sixteen or over to permit a man whom she knows to be her grandfather, father, brother or son to have sexual intercourse with her by her consent.

(2) In the foregoing subsection 'brother' includes half-brother, and for the purposes of that subsection any expression importing a relationship between two people shall be taken to apply notwithstanding that the relationship is not traced through lawful wedlock."

Where the female is, and is alleged by the indictment to be, a girl under thirteen, the offence is punishable with life imprisonment and an attempt to commit it with seven years. In other cases, the maximum is seven years for the full offence and two years for an attempt. A prosecution for incest or attempted incest may not be commenced except by or with the consent of the Director of Public Prosecutions.

The statute makes it clear[20] that the prohibition applies equally to illegitimate as to legitimate blood relationships, so that D may be convicted of incest with his illegitimate grand-daughter, etc. Presumably the basis of the law is eugenic.

It would seem that a consent by a woman sufficient to negative a charge of rape will not necessarily amount to a permission to the man for the

---

18. This construction is supported by the legislative history of the section. See [1980] Crim LR 655–656. But for another view, see Williams, [1981] Crim LR 796.
19. [1980] Crim LR 654.
20. Cf. *Winch* [1974] Crim LR 487.

purpose of this offence. In *Dimes*[1] it was held that D's acquittal of rape on the ground of P's consent did not necessarily mean that P was an accomplice in incest:

"There is a distinction between submission and permission."[2]

Mens rea must be proved; so D has a defence if he believes that his wife's daughter, P, is the child of an adulterer.[3]

Probably a significant reason for the existence of this offence is the horror and disgust that the idea of it arouses. That, according to the principles of the Wolfenden report,[4] which have gained wide acceptance, is not a good reason for its retention in the law. Another practical reason may be that the genetic risks of incest appear to be very high. The law does not, however, prohibit sexual intercourse by a person with a serious hereditary disease where the genetic risks may be even higher. That is not a conclusive argument, because the offence of incest imposes a relatively slight restriction on liberty – it excludes the right to have intercourse, not altogether, but only with close relatives; and it applies to everyone. If the offence of incest in its present form were to be abolished, it would probably be thought necessary to provide protection for persons under 21 from the lustful attentions of other members of the family.[5]

It is an offence under section 54 of the Criminal Law Act 1977, punishable summarily with six months' and on indictment with two years' imprisonment, for a man or boy to incite to have sexual intercourse with him a girl under the age of sixteen whom he knows to be his granddaughter, daughter, sister or half-sister. Again, it is immaterial that the relationship is illegitimate. A girl under sixteen who permits incestuous intercourse commits no offence and, consequently, the incitement was not an offence at common law.[6] It is still no offence to incite a girl under sixteen to have incestuous sexual intercourse with a third party.

3 Indecent Assault and Indecency with Children[7]

Under the Sexual Offences Act 1956, as amended by the Sexual Offences Act 1985, it is an offence punishable with ten years' imprisonment to commit an indecent assault on a man or a woman.[8] Both offences are triable either way. Generally, consent is a defence but, in both cases, it is provided

---

1. (1911) 7 Cr App Rep 43.
2. But cf. above, p. 434.
3. *Carmichael* [1940] 1 KB 630, [1940] 2 All ER 165. Cf. *Baillie-Smith* (1977) 64 Cr App Rep 76, CA.
4. See above, p. 19.
5. CLRC, Fifteenth Report, 63–73.
6. *Whitehouse* (1977) 65 Cr App Rep 33; above, p. 253.
7. See generally A. N. Macksey, "The Criminal Law and the Woman Seducer", [1956] Crim LR at 446 and 529.
8. Section 15.

that a person under sixteen or who is a defective cannot give any consent which would prevent an act being an assault for the purposes of these sections. If D does not know and has no reason to suspect that P is a defective, P's consent is a defence, although P is in fact a defective.[9] There is no similar provision with respect to persons under sixteen so once again it is clear that *Prince*[10] is applicable and that a reasonable belief that P is over that age is not a defence if he or she is in fact under it. As in rape, a consent exacted by force, or by fraud as to the nature of the transaction[11] is not a defence. Nor, according to *Donovan*,[12] is consent a defence if the probable consequence of the assault is the infliction of bodily harm; and that decision seems to have received confirmation of its result if not of its reasoning.[13]

Where D has gone through a form of marriage with a girl under sixteen and the marriage is invalid, his "wife's" consent to indecent acts is a defence, although she is under sixteen, if D believes on reasonable grounds that she is his wife.[14] There is no similar provision in s. 15 with respect to a woman who has gone through a form of marriage with a boy under sixteen and the implication would seem to be that she would have no defence. Perhaps such a case is unlikely to arise, but it is possible, and the omission of the defence from s. 15 seems to be an oversight.

Where a man under the age of twenty-four is charged under s. 6 with intercourse with a girl under sixteen and establishes a defence on the ground that he reasonably believed her to be over sixteen, he may be convicted on a second count for an indecent assault under s. 14.[15] In *Laws*[16] the Court of Criminal Appeal rightly said that

"it is indeed a grotesque state of affairs that the law offers a defence upon the major charge but excludes that defence if the minor charge is preferred."

Yet the anomaly was re-enacted, after these observations, in the consolidation of the law in 1956.

A not dissimilar curiosity is that boys under fourteen, who must be acquitted of any charge involving sexual intercourse because of their presumed incapacity, may be convicted of indecent assault on evidence that they did in fact have intercourse.[17] This discrepancy seems less objectionable, however, since the acquittal on the major charge is on a "technicality", whereas an acquittal under s. 6 (3) is based on the absence of *mens rea* or even negligence.

9. Sections 14 (4) and 15 (4); and see *Hudson*, above p. 96, footnote 13.
10. (1875) LR 2 CCR 154; **SHC 31**; above, p. 41.
11. *Case* (1850) 1 Den 580.
12. [1934] 2 KB 498; **SHC 407.**
13. *A–G's Reference (No. 6 of 1980)*, above, pp. 383 et seq.
14. Section 14 (3) which is in similar terms to s. 6 (2), above, p. 441.
15. *Forde* [1923] 2 KB 400; *Keech* (1929) 21 Cr App Rep 125; *Maughan* (1934) 24 Cr App Rep 130.
16. (1928) 21 Cr App Rep 45 at 46.
17. *Waite* [1892] 2 QB 600; *Williams* [1893] 1 QB 320.

1 The Requirement of an Assault

The term "assault" is here used both in its strict sense and to include a battery.[18] So in *Rolfe*[19] D was convicted where he moved towards a woman with his person exposed, inviting her to have connection with him, even though he did not touch her. More frequently there is actual physical contact in cases of indecent assault.

There can be no assault unless D does something to P or acts so as to cause P to apprehend that D is going to do something to him. So in *Fairclough v Whipp*[20] D was acquitted where he invited a girl aged nine to touch his exposed person. The ratio decidendi of this case appears to be that an invitation to somebody to touch the invitor cannot amount to an assault. In *Burrows*,[1] where the facts were similar except that the child was a boy, the court followed its earlier decision but added that the invitation could not be an assault

"because there was no hostile act towards the child, and, unless there is a hostile act, there can be no assault."[2]

This causes difficulty. In indecent assaults D's attitude to P will frequently not be "hostile" in the ordinary sense, but unduly affectionate![3] "Hostile", it is submitted, cannot mean more than against the will of P. But, if this is so, how can hostility be an essential element in an offence against a child under sixteen, where consent is irrelevant? Yet in *Director of Public Prosecutions v Rogers*[4] D was acquitted expressly on the ground of the absence of any *hostile* act though he did put his arm around his eleven-year-old daughter and led her upstairs in order that she should masturbate him. Lack of hostility was presumably also the ground of the acquittal in *Williams v Gibbs*,[5] where D took some little girls paddling and, in drying them, was guilty of conduct for which "every right minded person would feel disgust." These cases go well beyond *Fairclough v Whipp*,[6] for something was done by D to P. In holding that the action must be hostile, the court seems to have ignored the statutory rule that the child's consent is irrelevant. The Court of Appeal has now held in *M'Cormack*[7] that an indecent act done to a girl of fifteen, with her consent and without hostility, is an indecent assault and in *Faulkner v Talbot*[8] Lane LCJ said that an

18. Above, p. 375.
19. (1952) 36 Cr App Rep 4.
20. [1951] 2 All ER 834. It has been argued that this was wrong because "A battery may be committed if the impact is occasioned by the movement of the victim himself against some stationary matter, provided that the accused has intentionally caused that impact . . ."; A. N. Macksey, "The Criminal Law and the Woman Seducer", [1956] Crim LR at pp. 453 and 542. Cf. the argument by D. W. Elliott in relation to s. 20 of the Offences against the Person Act 1861, [1974] Crim LR 15. Earlier cases supported this view: *Police v Marchant* (1938) 2 J C L 324; *Boxer* (1944) discussed at 8 J C L 168–170.
   1. [1952] 1 All ER 58n, 35 Cr App Rep 180.
   2. 35 Cr App Rep at 182. Cf. *Willmot v Atack*, above, p. 395.
   3. "Offenders frequently approach their victims with gentleness and there is no doubt, too, that in many cases the child is a willing party to, and in some cases even the instigator of, the act which takes place": Cmnd. 247 at p. 36.
   4. (1953) 37 Cr App Rep 137.
   5. [1958] Crim LR 127.
   6. Supra.
   7. [1969] 2 QB 442, [1969] 3 All ER 371. Similarly in the case of a boy under sixteen: *Kallides* (CA unreported, referred to in [1977] 3 All ER at 479).
   8. [1981] 3 All ER 468, [1981] 1 WLR 1528, 74 Cr App Rep 1, DC; **SHC 404**.

assault "need not be hostile or rude or aggressive, as some of the cases seem to indicate". It seems that the line of cases following *Fairclough v Whipp* can be justified, if at all, only on the ground that the courts thought that nothing indecent was done by D to P. This was the approach of the Court in *Sutton*[9] where it was held that the touching of naked boys under sixteen by D, who was taking pornographic photographs, was not indecent since the touching was merely to indicate a pose.

Where, as in *Burrows*,[10] both the persons concerned are male, a charge of gross indecency under s. 13[11] will lie; but where one of the parties is a female and D does nothing to P there is no possible charge under the Sexual Offences Act.[12] The Divisional Court pointed out the necessity for an amendment of the law on several occasions and now, by the Indecency with Children Act 1960—

"Any person who commits an act of gross indecency with or towards a child under the age of fourteen, or who incites a child under that age to such an act with him or another, shall be liable on conviction on indictment to imprisonment for a term not exceeding two years or on summary conviction to imprisonment for a term not exceeding six months, to a fine not exceeding [£2,000] or both."

Since this makes mere incitement the offence, it is immaterial that the child does not act on the invitation to touch the accused. Inactivity on D's part is enough if, in the opinion of the jury, it amounts to an invitation to the child to start, or to continue, conduct amounting to gross indecency.[13] The offence would also be committed if D suggested to two children, at least one of whom was under fourteen, that they should commit a gross indecency together.

So far as persons over fourteen are concerned, the law is unchanged and an assault as defined in *Fairclough v Whipp* and its successors must be proved. The problem of the "hostile act" may still arise in relation to children between fourteen and sixteen.

2 Circumstances of Indecency

The assault must be "accompanied with circumstances of indecency on the part of" the prisoner.[14] In *Beal v Kelley*[15] where this definition was approved, D exposed his person to a boy of fourteen and asked him to handle it. The boy refused whereupon D got hold of the boy's arm and pulled him towards himself. D argued that it was not enough to prove an assault with an indecent motive and that it must be established that the assault itself was of an indecent nature. The act of pulling another towards oneself is not, without more, indecent; but no act can be divorced from the

9. [1977] 3 All ER 476, CA, [1977] Crim LR 569 and commentary thereon. See the Protection of Children Act 1978 which creates offences of taking, permitting to be taken, possessing or publishing, indecent photographs of persons under 16 and *Owen* [1988] 1 WLR 134, [1988] Crim LR 120, CA.
10. Above, p. 448.
11. Below, p. 474.
12. It might be indecent exposure at common law or under the Vagrancy Act 1824, below, pp. 470.
13. *Speck* [1977] 2 All ER 859, CA.
14. Archbold (32nd ed.), §2981.
15. [1951] 2 All ER 763.

circumstances in which it takes place and it was surely right to hold that the circumstances in this case rendered the assault indecent. In *Leeson*[16] it was held that to kiss a young girl about the face and neck against her will and with suggestions of sexual intercourse was an indecent assault. No doubt the spoken words were "a circumstance of indecency".

If there are no circumstances of indecency, D's secret indecent intention cannot turn an assault by him into an indecent one.[17] In *George*,[18] D attempted to remove a girl's shoe from her foot because it gave him sexual gratification. Streatfeild J, rejecting an argument that D's indecent motive made this an indecent assault, held that there were no circumstances of indecency; and in *Thomas*[19] it was held that touching the bottom of a girl's skirt was not indecent although D may have had an indecent intent. It might have been different if he had touched the girl's limbs through the skirt or if there had been a request by D for a kiss. Even where D behaved indecently while assaulting a boy he was held not guilty of an indecent assault because he did not handle the boy indecently and the indecent behaviour was unseen by, and unknown to, the boy.[20]

Though the general term, "indecent assault", covers both, there is a difference between indecent assault and indecent battery. In *Court*[1] it was said: "If there was touching [therefore battery], it was not necessary to prove that the victim was aware of the assault or of the circumstances of indecency. If there was no touching [therefore not battery] then to constitute an indecent assault the victim must be shown to have been aware of the assault and of the circumstances of indecency." The *actus reus* of assault, as distinct from battery, is the apprehension caused in the mind of the victim and, if the assault is to be an indecent assault, that apprehension must include the circumstances of indecency. In the case of an indecent battery P need not be aware of the circumstances of indecency – the indecent touching of a sleeping or unconscious person is an indecent battery.

In *Court*, it was held[2] that, while D must know of, or be reckless as to the existence of, the circumstances of indecency, it need not be proved that his purpose or motive was indecent. Whether the circumstances known to D are "circumstances of indecency" is, it seems, an objective question. If the event would appear indecent to the reasonable observer, it is immaterial that there is no indecency in the mind of D, or, it seems, P. The jury were entitled to find that D's spanking a 12-year-old on her buttocks outside her shorts constituted an assault in circumstances of indecency and evidence of his motive – "buttock fetishism" – though not essential, was relevant as evidence of the nature of the act.

If indecent purpose is no part of the offence a decent purpose must, in some circumstances, constitute a defence. Touching of the body is not

16. (1968) 52 Cr App Rep 185.
17. *Kilbourne* [1972] 3 All ER 545 at 551, CA.
18. [1956] Crim LR 52.
19. (1985) 81 Cr App Rep 331, CA.
20. *Johnson* [1968] SASR 132 (Bray J).
  1. [1987] 1 All ER 120 at 122, CA.
  2. Holding that *Pratt* [1984] Crim LR 41 (Crown Court) was wrongly decided. See commentary at [1987] Crim LR 136.

indecent if done in the course of a proper medical examination, though it may be an indecent assault if it was done with an indecent purpose.[3] It is not simply a question of consent. Whether an intimate handling by a doctor of an unconscious person, or a person under sixteen, is an indecent assault must depend on whether he has a genuine medical purpose. If he does, his act is lawful, even though he derives some secret sexual gratification from his work. But if he carries out the same intimate examination when he knows that there are no medical grounds for doing so, he commits an indecent assault. A disciplinary purpose may also be relevant. If the child's parent had administered exactly the same beating as that in *Court* because the child had misbehaved, would that have been an indecent assault? Would such an assault by a shopkeeper be indecent if he believed the child had been shoplifting and administered the beating solely out of anger?

3 Assaults by Women

Under ss. 14 and 15 of the Sexual Offences Act 1956 it is an offence for "a person" to commit an indecent assault and it is clear that this includes a woman as well as a man. It was held in *Hare*[4] that a woman who instigated a twelve-year-old boy to have intercourse with her and infected him with venereal disease was guilty of an offence under s. 62 of the Offences against the Person Act 1861, the predecessor of the present s. 15. This was in spite of the fact that ss. 61–63 of the 1861 Act were headed "Unnatural Offences". The court held that the words of the heading could not control the plain meaning of the statute.[5] In the present Act, ss. 14 and 15 fall under the heading "Assaults" and not under "Unnatural Offences".

It is not an offence for a woman to induce or permit a boy under the age of sixteen to have sexual intercourse with her. If she does so and there is no evidence that she did anything more than lie passively, no offence is committed. If, however, before, during or after the sexual intercourse, she does to the boy any act which would be an indecent assault if it were done without his consent – such as touching his penis – then she is guilty of an indecent assault although he does consent to or encourage the act in question. It is strange that an act which is merely a prelude or a postlude to sexual intercourse should be an offence when the sexual intercourse is not but, given that s. 15 applies to an act by a woman, the conclusion is inevitable. The section, as interpreted, states in effect that a woman commits an indecent assault if she indecently handles a boy under sixteen with his consent and it is impossible to say that what was an assault when it was done ceases to be an assault when the episode culminates in sexual intercourse.[6]

In *Hare* the court said obiter that a woman might be guilty of an indecent assault on another woman. This seems to have been held by Lopes J in

---

3. *Armstrong* (1885) 49 JP 745. Cf. *Bolduc and Bird*, above, p. 382.
4. [1934] 1 KB 354.
5. That headings and sidenotes are not part of the Act and cannot be used as an aid to construction has now been held by the House of Lords in *Chandler v Director of Public Prosecutions* [1964] AC 763, [1962] 3 All ER 142. C. K. Allen criticises the principle of interpretation applied in *Hare* as "the extreme of literalism": *Law in the Making* (7th ed.) 524.
6. *Faulkner v Talbot* (1981) 74 Cr App Rep 1, DC.

Armstrong[7]; and, indeed, there is no reason for interpreting "person" more narrowly in s. 14 than in s. 15.[8]

It has been suggested that

"*Hare* is an authority for the proposition that an indecent assault may be committed passively."[9]

It is submitted, however, that this is not so, for a woman's part in voluntary sexual intercourse, particularly where she is the instigating party, may reasonably be presumed to involve the doing by her of acts, which, if done without consent, would be battery.

4 Abduction of Women[10]

1 Classification of Abduction Offences

The Sexual Offences Act 1956 re-enacts four offences of abducting women and girls. There are three offences where the abduction consists in *taking the girl from the possession of her parent or guardian.*[11] Only in the first of these, under s. 20, does the Act provide that the taking must be "without lawful authority or excuse." These words did not appear in s. 55 of the Offences against the Person Act 1861 which s. 20 of the 1956 Act replaced. That section merely used the word, "unlawfully". It was argued in *Tegerdine*[12] that the effect was that good motives, based on reasonable belief, could be an excuse; so that the putative father who took a child out of the possession of the mother, because he reasonably believed it was not being well cared-for, should have a defence. The court held otherwise. The change in wording did not alter the law, the 1956 Act being a consolidation Act. The word "lawful" in the section governs "excuse" as well as "authority". The meaning of "lawful excuse" as distinct from "authority" is obscure. It may be that it would cover such cases as where D takes the girl because it is necessary to do so in order to save her from unlawful violence or injury.

In each of the other offences the section requires proof of an unlawful intention of some kind and it would probably not be a defence that the defendant would otherwise have had lawful authority simply to take the girl. His right to do so would be vitiated by his unlawful intention.[13]

i) *Girls under sixteen* (s. 20). The girl must be (a) unmarried and (b) taken against the will of the parent or guardian. There need be no sexual motive.

---

7. (1885) 49 JP 745.

8. The Wolfenden Committee found no instance of an assault by one female on another "which exhibits the libidinous features that characterise sexual acts between males". In most cases where a woman is convicted under s. 14 it is as aider and abettor of a man in an assault upon another woman: Cmnd. 247, p. 38.

9. Macksey [1956] Crim LR at 355. In *Mason* Veale J held that *Hare* was not authority for this proposition, the court being solely concerned with the question whether a woman can commit an indecent assault.

10. Cf. the offences of false imprisonment, kidnapping and child abduction, above, pp. 415.

11. In each case, "guardian" means "any person having the lawful care or charge of the girl".

12. (1982) 75 Cr App Rep 298, [1983] Crim LR 163, CA and commentary.

13. Cf. *Dadson*, above, p. 37.

ii) *Girls under eighteen* (s. 19). In addition to conditions (a) and (b), it must be proved (c) that the girl was taken with intent that she should have unlawful sexual intercourse with men or with a particular man.

iii) *Defective women of any age* (s. 21). The woman may or may not be married but must be taken (a) against the will of the parent or guardian; and (b), as in (ii), with the intention that she shall have unlawful sexual intercourse with men or with a particular man.

iv) *Abduction of woman by force or for the sake of her property.* Under the fourth offence of abduction[14] the woman who is taken away or detained need not have been in anyone's possession. It is an offence to take away or detain a woman of any age (a) against *her* will (b) with the intention that she shall marry or have unlawful sexual intercourse with the taker or any other person, and (c) either by force or for the sake of her property or expectations of property.

Offences (i), (ii) and (iii) are punishable with two years' imprisonment. Offence (iv) is punishable with fourteen years' imprisonment.

2 The "Taking"

In offences (i), (ii) and (iii) a *taking* must be proved; in offence (iv) a *taking*[15] or *detaining*. So in *Alexander*,[16] D's conviction of offence (i) was quashed where the recorder said that the offence consisted in keeping the girl secretly and preventing her parents knowing her whereabouts. While this might have been detaining, it was certainly not taking.

The word "takes" does not imply the use of any force, actual or constructive, and it is irrelevant that the girl freely consents to go.[17] Even if the girl takes the initiative, D is still guilty if he assists her to leave with him; as where D, at the girl's suggestion, brought a ladder to her window so that she might elope with him.[18] If any kind of persuasion is exercised by D, a fortiori he is guilty. If, however, –

"she was determined to leave her home, and showed the prisoner that that was her determination, and insisted on leaving with him – or even if she was so forward as to write and suggest to the prisoner that he should go away with her, and he yielded to her suggestion, taking no active part in the matter . . ."[19]

he would not be guilty.

D need not be present when the girl leaves, if she does so as the result of his persuasion.[20] If she leaves her father's possession without persuasion or assistance from D, then he cannot be guilty of taking, though he may be of detaining. A girl does not, however, leave her father's possession merely

14. Sexual Offences Act 1956, s. 17.
15. Though the cases interpreting this word are mainly on s. 20 (and its predecessors) it is reasonable to assume that they apply to all the offences.
16. (1912) 107 LT 240; *Olifier* (1866) 10 Cox CC 402.
17. *Mankletow* (1853) Dears CC 159. "Suppose you take a person to the Playhouse, does it follow that it is against the will of the person taken?" per Alderson B.
18. *Robins* (1844) 1 Car & Kir 456; cf. *Biswell* (1847) 9 LTOS 394.
19. *Jarvis* (1903) 20 Cox CC 249 at 251, per Jelf J. Cf. *Handley* (1859) 1 F & F 648.
20. *Olifier* (1866) 10 Cox CC 402; *Frazer* (1861) 8 Cox CC 446.

because she is out of the house for a particular purpose,[1] unless it is her intention not to return home.[2]

"Taking" does not require a permanent deprivation and so in *Timmins*[3] D was guilty where he took a girl away for three days and slept with her at night. The court's view was that this deprived the father of possession of the girl because it

"placed her in a situation quite inconsistent with the existence of the relation of father and daughter."[4]

In *Baillie*[5] the girl was absent from her father's house only for a matter of hours but the court seems to have regarded this as a permanent deprivation since in that time D married her so that the father

"never could have the custody of her in the same sense as before her marriage."[6]

The offence can hardly be committed by a boy who takes his girl-friend for a walk against her father's will. Some more radical infringement of the parents' right to control their daughter, as by keeping her away overnight, must surely be proved. In *Jones*[7] Swanwick J ruled that there must be a substantial interference with the possessory relationship of parent and child and that an attempt to take a ten year old girl for a walk with the intention of indecently assaulting her was not an attempt to breach such a relationship.

The taking must be assumed to be against the will of the parent if it appears that, had he been asked, he would have refused his consent.[8] Where, however, the parent permits the daughter to follow a lax course of life[9] or does not take reasonable care of her,[10] this may be evidence of consent to the taking.

3 The Mens Rea

The celebrated case of *Prince*[11] was, of course, decided on the forerunner of s. 20 and the principle of that case applies to all these offences, except where it is expressly modified. In offence (i) (s. 20) a belief even on reasonable grounds that the girl is above the specified age is no defence; but in offence (ii) (s. 19) it is a defence for D to prove, on a balance of probabilities,[12] that he believed on reasonable grounds that the girl was over eighteen. Similarly, in offence (iii) (s. 21) it is a defence for D to show that he did not know and had no reason[13] to suspect the woman to be a defective.

In all the offences except (i) (s. 20), the ulterior intent described in the section must, of course, be proved by the prosecution.

---

1. *Mankletow* (1853) Dears CC 159 at 165.
2. *Mycock* (1871) 12 Cox CC 28.
3. (1860) 8 Cox CC 401.
4. Ibid., at 404.
5. (1859) 8 Cox CC 238.
6. Ibid., at 239.
7. [1973] Crim LR 621. Cf. *Mears* [1975] Crim LR 155 (Judge Watkin Powell).
8. *Handley* (1859) 1 F & F 648, per Wightman J.
9. *Primelt* (1858) 1 F & F 50.
10. *Frazer* (1861) 8 Cox CC 446.
11. (1875) LR 2 CCR 154; **SHC 102**; above, p. 41.
12. Sexual Offence Act 1956, s. 47.
13. See *Hudson* [1966] 1 QB 448, [1965] 1 All ER 721; above, p. 96, footnote 13.

In offences (i) to (iii) it must be shown that D knew that the girl was in the possession of a parent or guardian.[14] In principle, it should be enough that D is reckless whether the girl is in such a possession, and it would seem that in both *Hibbert* and *Green*[14] D ought to have been convicted on that ground.

5 Offences Relating to Prostitution[15]

"... prostitution is proved if it be shown that a woman offers her body for purposes amounting to common lewdness for payment in return."[16] In so defining prostitution in *Webb*[17] Lord Parker CJ rejected an argument that prostitution is limited to cases in which the woman offers herself for ordinary sexual connection and approved the decision in *de Munck*[18] where a conviction for procuring a girl to become a common prostitute was upheld although it was proved that the girl was virgo intacta. It was enough that the girl had exposed herself to men in order to gratify their passions and that the accused had procured her so to do. *Webb* went rather farther. Though the nature of the lewdness was not proved in *de Munck*, it may perhaps be assumed that the men did something to the girl. In *Webb* the girl was employed as a masseuse and was expected, as part of her employment, to masturbate clients who so desired. The court rejected an argument that the role of the prostitute must be passive and that active indecency of this nature could not be prostitution.

"Indeed, it can be said with some force that some activity on her part is of the very essence of prostitution. It cannot matter whether she whips the man or the man whips her; it cannot matter whether he masturbates himself on her or she masturbates him."[19]

Some provisions in the sexual offences legislation apply only to "common" prostitutes. In *Morris-Lowe*[20] it was held that the word "common" is not mere surplusage. It denotes a woman who offers herself commonly for lewdness. The performance of a single act of lewdness with a man on one occasion for reward does not make a woman a common prostitute. The court did not decide that it makes her a prostitute, though that seems to be the surprising implication of the decision that "common" adds something. adds something.

Prostitution, as such, is not criminal. It is, however, in the opinion of the Wolfenden Committee,[1]

"a social fact deplorable in the eyes of moralists, sociologists and ... the great majority of ordinary people."

14. *Hibbert* (1869) LR 1 CCR 184; *Green* (1862) 3 F & F 274.
15. R. Jerrard, "Prostitution and the Law", (1979) 143 JP 531, 545, 560, 692.
16. Per Darling J in *de Munck* [1918] 1 KB 635 at 637; cited with approval in *Webb* [1964] 1 QB 357 at 366; [1963] 3 All ER 177 at 179, CCA.
17. Last note. See also *Kelly v Purvis*, below, p. 458.
18. [1918] 1 KB 635.
19. [1963] 3 All ER at 179.
20. [1985] 1 All ER 400, [1985] Crim LR 50 and commentary, CA.
  1. Report, Cmnd. 247, p. 79. See CLRC Working Paper on Offences relating to Prostitution (1982), 1–8.

Thus the law actively discourages prostitution in a number of ways. It is criminal to cause or encourage others to become common prostitutes; in some circumstances to allow premises to be used for prostitution; to live on the earnings of prostitution; and to loiter or solicit for purposes of prostitution. These crimes require further examination.

1 Causing or Encouraging Women to become Common Prostitutes

By s. 22 (1) of the Sexual Offences Act 1956:

"It is an offence for a person—

(a) to procure a woman to become, in any part of the world, a common prostitute; or

(b) to procure a woman to leave the United Kingdom, intending her to become an inmate of or frequent a brothel elsewhere; or

(c) to procure a woman to leave her usual place of abode in the United Kingdom, intending her to become an inmate of or frequent a brothel in any part of the world for the purposes of prostitution."

As with the other cases of procuring,[2] the offence is not complete till the woman becomes a common prostitute, or leaves the United Kingdom, or leaves her usual place of abode, as the case may be: and, though it has been said[3] that the word "procure" is not a term of art, it seems that the element of persuasion or invitation must be present. There must be a causal connection so that, if the woman would have embarked on the conduct in question of her own volition without D's act, there is probably no procurement.[4] If a woman is already a common prostitute it is impossible to procure her to become one; and, if D believes her to be a common prostitute, he cannot be guilty of the offence, or of an attempt to commit it.

Procuration of a girl under twenty-one,[5] though not an offence directly involving prostitution, is also highly relevant. By s. 24, it is an offence to detain a woman against her will in a brothel or in any premises with intent that she shall have unlawful sexual intercourse. And by s. 28:

"(1) It is an offence for a person to cause or encourage the prostitution of, or the commission of unlawful sexual intercourse with, or of an indecent assault on, a girl under the age of sixteen for whom he is responsible.

(2) Where a girl has become a prostitute, or has had unlawful sexual intercourse, or has been indecently assaulted, a person shall be deemed for the purposes of this section to have caused or encouraged it, if he knowingly allowed her to consort with, or to enter or continue in the employment of, any prostitute or person of known immoral character."[6]

---

2. Above, p. 131.

3. *Broadfoot* [1976] 3 All ER 753, CA.

4. *Broadfoot*, supra, referring to *A–G's Reference (No. 1 of 1975)*, above, p. 133 and *Christian* (1913) 23 Cox CC 541, above, p. 439. Cf. *Beck* [1985] 1 All ER 571, [1985] 1 WLR 22, CA, below, p. 577.

5. Sexual Offences Act 1956, s. 23; above, p. 442.

6. Subsections (3) and (4) of this section define the persons who are "responsible" for a girl for the purposes of the section – broadly, a parent or legal guardian or any person having possession or control or custody of her. Sub.-s. (5) provides that a girl who appears to the court to be under sixteen may be presumed to be so, unless the contrary is proved.

This offence seems to overlap to a large extent with ss. 21, 6 and 14. If there is a difference, only prostitution, not "common" prostitution, is required. One who caused the prostitution of, or sexual intercourse with, or an indecent assault on, a girl under sixteen would usually be guilty as a counsellor or abettor under s. 21 and s. 6 (or s. 5 if the girl was under thirteen) and s. 14 respectively. One who "encouraged"[7] these offences would be guilty of incitement to commit them. Causing or encouraging prostitution will also, in the great majority of cases, necessarily involve counselling or abetting or inciting sexual intercourse or indecent assault on the girl, though, owing to the wide definition of prostitution, the section may occasionally cover cases outside these limits.[8] Perhaps the real value of the section lies in the wide meaning given to "cause or encourage" by sub-s. (2). The conduct there described might be insufficient to support a charge of aiding or abetting or incitement.

The section may be wider in one other respect. It may well be that *Prince*[9] governs the section yet again and, if so, a belief even on reasonable grounds that the girl was over sixteen would be no defence. Such a belief would afford a defence to a charge of counselling or abetting or incitement;[10] it would, in any event, be difficult to establish in the case of a person responsible for a girl actually under sixteen.

By s. 29 (1) of the Sexual Offences Act 1956:

"It is an offence, subject to the exception mentioned in this section, for a person to cause or encourage the prostitution in any part of the world of a woman who is a defective."

Reasonable ignorance that the woman is a defective is a defence under the section.[11] If there is a difference, only prostitution, not "common" prostitution, is required.

It seems that very few cases of procuration come to the notice of the police, probably because most women who become prostitutes do so because they want to and the element of persuasion implicit in procuring is lacking.[12]

2 The Use of Premises for Prostitution

i) *Brothel keeping.* By s. 33 of the Sexual Offences Act 1956:

"It is an offence for a person to keep a brothel, or to manage,[13] or act or assist in the management of, a brothel."

By s. 34:

"It is an offence for the lessor or landlord of any premises or his agent to let the whole or part of the premises with the knowledge that it is to be used, in whole or in part, as a brothel, or, where the whole or part of the

---

7. Cf. *Drury* (1974) 60 Cr App Rep 195.
8. Cf. *Webb*, above, p. 455.
9. (1875) LR 2 CCR 154; **SHC 102**; above, p. 41.
10. Above, pp. 138 and 255.
11. Sexual Offences Act 1956, s. 29 (2). And cf. *Hudson* [1965] 1 All ER 721; above, p. 96, footnote 13.
12. Cmnd. 247 at p. 112.
13. Keeping or managing a brothel is a continuing offence which may extend over a long period of time: *Anderton v Cooper* (1980) 72 Cr App Rep 232, DC.

premises is used as a brothel, to be wilfully a party to that use continuing."

And by s. 35 (1):

"It is an offence for the tenant or occupier, or person in charge, of any premises knowingly to permit the whole or part of the premises to be used as a brothel."

The Act does not define "brothel" but this term has a definite meaning at common law. It is a common law misdemeanour to keep a disorderly house and a brothel or bawdy house is one variety of disorderly house. For the purposes of ss. 33, 34 and 35 of the Sexual Offences Act 1956, it is now provided by the Sexual Offences Act 1967, s. 6, that premises shall be treated as a brothel

". . . if people resort to it for the purpose of lewd homosexual practices in circumstances in which resort thereto for lewd heterosexual practices would have led to its being treated as a brothel for the purposes of those sections."

Lewd sexual practices are not confined to sexual intercourse. It is sufficient that more than one woman offers herself as a participant in physical acts of indecency for the sexual gratification of men, whether for payment or not.[14]

At common law a brothel is

"a place resorted to by persons of both sexes for the purpose of prostitution;"[15]

and there must be at least two women plying their trade as prostitutes in that place. Now it would seem that a place may be a brothel though persons of only one sex resort to it. It is presumably necessary that two women, or two men, or a man and a woman ply their trade there. If two persons are using the premises for prostitution, the place is a brothel and it is immaterial that one of them is the occupier.[16] But in *Singleton v Ellison*[17] a woman occupied premises at which she alone received a number of men for the purposes of prostitution. It was held that she was rightly acquitted of keeping a brothel. In *Caldwell v Leech*[18] the occupier was acquitted where he permitted a single woman to use the premises for prostitution. Where a building comprised three floors and D let the first and second floors to one woman and the third floor to another, knowing both to be prostitutes, he was acquitted of letting the premises with knowledge that they were to be used as a brothel[19] when it appeared that the two flats were separate premises, each being occupied by one prostitute only.[20] But in *Donovan v Gavin*[1] it was held that a brothel may be constituted by rooms independently let for separate occupation, "if they are sufficiently close to each

---

14. *Kelly v Purvis* [1983] 1 All ER 525; *Winter v Woolfe* [1931] 1 KB 549, 95 JP 20.
15. *Singleton v Ellison* [1985] 1 QB 607 at 608, per Wills J.
16. *Gorman v Standen* [1964] 1 QB 294, [1963] 3 All ER 627.
17. Above, footnote 15.
18. (1913) 109 LT 188, Ridley J dissenting and Pickford J concurring with regret. Ridley J would have confined *Singleton v Ellison*, above, to the case where the sole prostitute was also the occupier. Pickford J regretted that he did not think that case could be so confined.
19. See s. 34 of the Sexual Offences Act 1956.
20. *Strath v Foxon* [1956] 1 QB 67, [1955] 3 All ER 398.
 1. [1965] 2 QB 648, [1965] 2 All ER 611, DC. Cf. *Durose v Wilson* (1907) 96 LT 645; *Abbott v Smith* [1965] 2 QB 662, n9 [1964] 3 All ER 762.

other to constitute in effect what might be called a nest of prostitutes", at least if there is some common management of the business of prostitution or if (as in this case) at least two of the prostitutes are collaborating in their business.

A single prostitute may, however, be convicted of the common law offence of keeping a disorderly house if he or she provides services which are available to the public so as to outrage public decency or to injure the public interest "to such an extent as to call for condemnation and punishment". It is immaterial that the services are provided to only one client at a time.[2] The Disorderly Houses Act 1751 refers to "any bawdy-house or other disorderly house", recognising that a brothel is only one type of disorderly house. The offence has been held to cover the keeping of premises where card games are played for very high stakes and the showing of indecent films, as well as where various sexual services are provided. The Metropolitan Police claim to prosecute only when there are complaints from the public and the offence may be invoked where services of a sado-masochistic nature are offered, usually by one woman, in order to avoid prosecution for brothel keeping,[3]

ii) *Tenant permitting premises to be used for prostitution.* By s. 36 of the Sexual Offences Act 1956:

"It is an offence for the tenant or occupier of any premises knowingly to permit the whole or part of the premises to be used for the purposes of habitual prostitution."

A tenant who sub-lets part of the premises to a woman whom he knows to be a prostitute is not guilty of an offence under the section; "tenant" in the section means tenant in occupation.[4] A fortiori, it would be no offence if the whole of the premises were sub-let. But if a tenant allowed a mere licensee to use the premises for prostitution, he would no doubt be guilty although he was not actually living on the premises himself.

The effect of ss. 33–36, then, is that it is an offence for a landlord to let premises, knowing that they are to be used as a brothel, or to be wilfully a party to their being so used; for anyone to keep a brothel, or to act or assist in the management of one; or for the tenant or occupier knowingly to permit even one woman to use any part of those premises for habitual prostitution. But it is not an offence for a landlord to let premises knowing that they are to be used for prostitution by one woman, or to be party to the use of the premises by a single prostitute; nor is it an offence for the tenant herself to practise prostitution on the premises.

If D lets a flat to T whom he knows to be a prostitute, and T carries on the business of prostitution in the flat, no offence is committed.[5] If D has let flats to a number of other prostitutes, even within a single building, and

---

2. *Tan* [1983] QB 1053, [1983] 2 All ER 12.
3. CLRC 17th Report, 3.8.
4. *Siviour v Napolitano* [1931] 1 KB 636, decided under the Criminal Law Amendment Act 1885, s. 13, which used the words "tenant, lessee or occupier. . .". The decision would apply, a fortiori, to the present section.
5. T cannot be said to "permit" the flat to be used for prostitution for "permitting" means letting someone else do something: *Mattison v Johnson* (1916) 85 LJKB 741. Cf. *James & Son v Smee*, above, p. 125.

each carries on her business independently of the others, no offence is committed by anybody, provided that it is clear that each woman has exclusive possession of her flat so as to constitute it separate premises for legal purposes.[6] But even the landlord of prostitutes who is careful so to arrange his affairs as to fall outside the provisions so far examined may yet fall foul of the rule next to be considered.

3 A Man Living on the Earnings of Prostitution

By s. 30 of the Sexual Offences Act 1956:

"(1) It is an offence for a man knowingly to live wholly or in part on the earnings of prostitution.

(2) For the purposes of this section a man who lives with or is habitually in the company of a prostitute, or who exercises control, direction or influence over a prostitute's movements in a way which shows he is aiding, abetting or compelling her prostitution with others, shall be presumed to be knowingly living on the earnings of prostitution, unless he proves the contrary."[7]

By s. 4 of the Street Offences Act 1959 the maximum penalty for this offence was increased from two to seven years. This provision replaces that in the Vagrancy Act 1898, as amended by s. 7 of the Criminal Law Amendment Act 1912, which in turn replaced a provision in the Vagrancy Act 1824. It has been said by Lord Simonds, however, that no assistance in its interpretation is to be derived from its ancestry.[8]

According to the Wolfenden Committee,[9]

"In its simplest and most usual form, 'living on the earnings of prostitution' consists of an arrangement by which a man lives with a prostitute and is wholly or mainly kept by her. Such a man is commonly known as a 'ponce' or souteneur."

There may be difficulties in proving the existence of such a relationship, but, once established, there is no doubt that the offence is proved. It is now clear, however, that the meaning of the section extends beyond this, and difficult questions have arisen as to its limits. In deciding these questions,

"the second subsection is probative and explanatory of the first but not an exhaustive definition of it."[10]

One view of the words of s. 30 (1) would be that anyone who received money from a prostitute, knowing that she had earned it by practising her

---

6. The neighbours of such premises may have a remedy in the civil courts. In *Thompson-Schwab v Costaki* [1956] 1 All ER 652, the Court of Appeal held that the user of premises for prostitution and the perambulations of the prostitutes and their customers may amount to such an interference with the comfortable and convenient enjoyment of nearby houses as to be an actionable nuisance. An interlocutory injunction was granted.

7. The presumption imposes a burden of proof on the balance of probabilities on D; but he may satisfy the burden by cross-examination of the prosecution witnesses: *Grant* [1985] Crim LR 387, CA. See *Clarke* [1976] 2 All ER 696, [1977] Crim LR 110, CA; *Bell* [1978] Crim LR 233, CA.

8. *Shaw v Director of Public Prosecutions* [1962] AC 220 at 263, [1961] 2 All ER 446 at 449: "The Act of 1824 may be regarded as a convenient peg on which to hang divers offences to which the words 'vagabondage and roguery' would not be entirely appropriate."

9. Report, Cmnd. 247, p. 99. For proposals for reform of the law, see CLRC, Seventeenth Report, Cmnd. 9688.

10. Per Lord Simonds [1962] AC 220 at 263, [1961] 2 All ER 446 at 449.

profession, is guilty of an offence. It is agreed on all hands that such an interpretation would be far too wide. Its effect would be that no one could receive payment for the supply of food, clothing, lodging or other necessaries to the prostitute.

The opposite view would be that anyone who gives value, whether goods or services to the prostitute and is paid by her, is living on his own earnings, not on hers, and is not guilty. This view, too, is generally rejected.

"To give effect to it would be to exclude from the operation of the Act the very persons, the tout, the bully or protector, whom it was designed to catch. For they would surely claim that they served the prostitute, however despicable their service might seem to others."[11]

Somewhere between these two views a line must be drawn and, in a series of cases since 1954, the courts have attempted to draw it. Two situations must be considered

1. It is clear that the offence is committed where D, for reward and with the intention of furthering prostitution, supplies goods or services or premises which in their nature are referable to the prostitution and nothing else.[12] In the leading case of *Shaw v Director of Public Prosecutions*[13] the whole object of the *Ladies' Directory* was to facilitate the business of the advertisers and it was agreed by all the judges in that case that D, in receiving payment from the prostitutes for the advertisements, was living on their earnings within the meaning of the section. The majority so held for the reason given above. Lord Reid alone thought that the seller of goods, etc., exclusively for prostitution is not necessarily guilty. In his view, it must also appear that D's occupation is "parasitic" – and Shaw's ("He was really no more than a tout . . .") was.[14] However, this is not a necessary element of the offence, at least where the presumption in s. 30 (2) applies. It is then irrelevant to consider the quality of the "living on".[15]

The same principle governs in *Calvert v Mayes*,[16] where D allowed his parked car to be used for prostitution or drove prostitutes and their clients to secluded places in the countryside where they might have intercourse. Slightly more difficult are the further instances alleged in *Mayes* where the intercourse took place in the back of the car while servicemen were being driven to their base; but the fact that free transport was provided satisfied the court that the *sole reason* for hiring the car was the facilitation of prostitution. In such cases it is immaterial that the charge made is reasonable – in *Mayes* the court accepted that D would have been paid the same sum of money if the journey had been a legitimate one and in *Shaw* it

---

11. Lord Simonds [1962] AC at 263, 264, [1961] 2 All ER at 450.
12. Cf. the test suggested by Bramwell B for civil cases where a prostitute is sued for goods supplied: to afford a defence it must appear that ". . . the thing supplied must be not merely such as would be necessary or useful for ordinary purposes, and might also be applied to an immoral one; but that they must be such as would under the circumstances not be required, except with that view": *Pearce v Brooks* (1866) LR 1 Exch 213 at 215. Would not the supplier of the ornamental brougham in that case and the laundress of the clients' nightcaps in *Lloyd v Johnson* (1798) 1 Bos & P 340 (who recovered the price!), now be guilty of living on the earnings of prostitution?
13. [1962] AC 220, [1961] 2 All ER 446. The facts are set out above, p. 276.
14. Ibid at 270 and at 453, 454.
15. *Wilson* (1983) 78 Cr App Rep 247, CA.
16. [1954] 1 QB 342, [1954] 1 All ER 41.

was held to be irrelevant that the charges for the advertisements in the *Ladies' Directory* were reasonable.[17]

In *Thomas*,[18] D let a prostitute have the use of a room for prostitution between 9 p.m. and 2 a.m. each night. Pilcher J, who was upheld by the Court of Criminal Appeal, directed that this amounted to the offence if the rent was grossly inflated. But, as Lord Simonds has pointed out,[19] there was strong evidence there that the accommodation was provided for prostitution and nothing else, in which case it should have been irrelevant whether the rent was inflated or not.

2. It seems that the offence is also committed where D receives the price of the supply of goods or services or premises which, though not exclusively referable to prostitution, will be used to further it in some way but only where D makes an exorbitant charge because the woman is a prostitute. In *Silver*[20] Judge Maude directed an acquittal of a landlord who let premises to a woman and charged her an exorbitant rent ("a prostitute rent") because he knew that she intended to practise prostitution there. In *Thomas*, the Court of Criminal Appeal upheld a ruling by Pilcher J that, in such circumstances,[21] there was a case to leave a jury and in *Shaw* the majority were disposed to favour this view. In the latter case Lord Simonds (with whom Lords Tucker, Morris and Hodson concurred on this point) distinguished the case where the flat is let only for prostitution, as in *Thomas*, and went on:[1]

"But, if the flat is let for occupation, I am not prepared to say that the landlord commits an offence merely because he knows that his tenant is a prostitute and must be assumed to know that she will there ply her trade. The prostitute must live somewhere just as she must eat and drink to live. It is, I think, too fine a distinction to say that a grocer supplying her with groceries does not, but a landlord letting her a flat does, commit an offence. It is true that the flat is the scene of her prostitution, but if she did not eat and drink she would not have a body to prostitute. Therefore, in such a case as *Silver* (where the flats appear to have been let for occupation) the landlord can only be convicted of an offence upon the ground that the rent is exorbitant. This may be a tenable view upon the footing that, to the extent to which the rent is in excess of normal, he extorts it from the prostitute upon no other ground than that she is a prostitute."

Lord Reid agreed[2] with the majority on this point:

"In reality he is not then merely acting as landlord; he is making her engage in a joint adventure with him which will bring to him a part of her immoral earnings over and above the rent."

Would it not then follow that a grocer overcharging a prostitute because she was a prostitute would be guilty of the offence? The problem is unlikely

17. [1962] AC 220 at 229, [1961] 1 All ER 330 at 335, CCA.
18. [1957] 2 All ER 181.
19. [1962] AC 220 at 265, [1961] 2 All ER 446 at 451.
20. [1956] 1 All ER 716.
21. Pilcher J attached no importance to the fact, noted above, that the premises were apparently let for prostitution and nothing else.
  1. [1962] AC 220 at 265, 266. [1961] 2 All ER 446 at 451.
  2. [1962] AC at 271, [1961] 2 All ER at 454.

to arise. Prostitutes are vulnerable to overcharging for premises, because it is difficult for them to find accommodation; but they can get groceries – and most other goods and services – as easily as anyone else.

Thus, though the matter is not free from doubt,[3] it seems likely that the landlord who lets premises for prostitution commits no offence provided that the rent is the reasonable or normal rent for those premises. The Wolfenden Committee rejected proposals that this loophole in the law should be closed:[4]

"As long as society tolerates the prostitute, it must permit her to carry on her business somewhere. That she ought not to be allowed to carry it on in public will be apparent . . .; and the law, for a variety of reasons, rightly frowns on the brothel. The only remaining possibility is individual premises. We have therefore reached the conclusion that it would not be right to amend the law in such a way as to make guilty of a criminal offence a person who lets premises to a prostitute who uses them, even to his knowledge, for the purpose of her own habitual prostitution."

This accords with the general attitude of the law towards prostitution. Life is not to be made impossible for the prostitute. She must have food, clothing, clean linen and the other necessities (or, indeed, luxuries) of life, not exclusively referable to prostitution. The civil courts do not discourage tradesmen from supplying these by refusing to allow them to recover the price and the criminal courts will not construe the statute so widely as to make the supply a criminal offence. As regards premises, the civil law goes farther than the criminal for it is clear that the landlord who lets premises for prostitution[5] cannot recover the rent,[6] however reasonable it might be. But, while it would be intolerable for the civil law to allow recovery of money which, when recovered, would be regarded as the earnings of prostitution for the purposes of the section, it is not unreasonable to use the milder sanction of the civil law to discourage landlords while withholding the bigger guns of the criminal law.

The money paid must be "the earnings of prostitution." So D does not commit the offence where, without the knowledge of prostitutes, he supplies their addresses and telephone numbers to men for payment.[7] The money paid has not been earned by prostitution. It was different where D was "letting the room and letting the services of the woman" and received the price from the men. Here the money was earned by the woman.[8] In *Farrugia*[9] a cab driver engaged by an escort agency to drive prostitutes to their customers was held guilty although the fare was paid by the customers; the prostitutes provided opportunities of earning money. In the

---

3. Professor Goodhart argues that the landlord is guilty even if the rent is reasonable: ". . . rent, however exorbitant, is still rent. Thus if the normal rent of a hotel room is doubled at the time of a coronation, the whole of the payment remains rent. The nature of the services cannot be affected by the amount that is charged for them . . .": 77 LQR at 563.
4. Cmnd. 247 at p. 104.
5. Or even for use by a mistress: *Upfill v Wright*, [1911] 1 KB 506.
6. Nor can he recover possession of the premises until the lease is terminated: *Alexander v Rayson* [1936] 1 KB 169 at 186.
7. *Ansell* [1975] QB 215, [1974] 3 All ER 568, CA.
8. *Calvert v Mayes*, above.
9. (1979) 69 Cr App Rep 108, CA.

opinion of the court, the money "came from the intended prostitution". Here the money was not earned by the prostitute. If, however, she had paid the fare, the case would have been clear and, arguably, it should make no difference that the money was paid by the customer on her behalf.

It will have been noted that the offence under s. 30 of the Sexual Offences Act 1956 can be committed only by a man.[10] This continues to be so, as far as female prostitution is concerned; but, by s. 5 of the Sexual Offences Act 1967, it is an offence punishable with seven years' imprisonment for a man or woman knowingly to live wholly or in part on the earnings of prostitution of another man.

4 A Woman Exercising Control over a Prostitute

A closely related offence under s. 31 of the Sexual Offences Act 1956 may be committed only by women:

"It is an offence for a woman for purposes of gain to exercise control, direction or influence over a prostitute's movements in a way which shows she is aiding, abetting or compelling her prostitution."

As in the case of complicity in suicide,[11] statute here makes it an offence to aid and abet an act which, in itself, is no crime.

5 Loitering or Soliciting in Public Places[12]

In all the offences so far considered, the crime is committed not only by the prostitute but by another. The legislation now to be considered is aimed at the prostitute herself. Its object is not the suppression or discouragement of prostitution, but the elimination of an offence against public order and decency arising from the activities of prostitutes in public places. The present law is to be found in the Street Offences Act 1959 which provides in s. 1:

"(1) It shall be an offence for a common prostitute to loiter or solicit in a street or public place for the purpose of prostitution.

(2) A person guilty of an offence under this section shall be liable, on summary conviction, to a fine not exceeding level 2 on the standard scale or, for an offence committed after a previous conviction, to a fine not exceeding level 3 on the standard scale.

(3) A constable may arrest without warrant anyone he finds in a street or public place and suspects, with reasonable cause, to be committing an offence under this section."

This provision was enacted as a result of the report of the Wolfenden Committee[13] and it repeals and replaces a number of earlier enactments. The law is strengthened in a number of respects: (1) It is no longer necessary to establish "annoyance" on the part of any member of the public. This was difficult to prove because men solicited by prostitutes were almost invariably unwilling to give evidence and the standard of proof

---

10. May a woman counsel or abet? p. 438, footnotes 18 and 19, above.
11. Above, p. 359.
12. See Report of the Home Office Working Party on Vagrancy and Street Offences (1974).
13. Cmnd. 247 (1957).

accepted by the courts was far from uniform. (2) The Act is not limited to urban areas as was the previous legislation. And (3) the penalties have been greatly increased. A "cautioning system" is in operation under which a woman is not arrested until she has been cautioned on two occasions and is seen loitering or soliciting on a third occasion.[14]

The terms "common prostitute", "loiter", "solicit" and "in a street or public place" require further examination.

i) *Common prostitute*. The Wolfenden Committee, rejecting criticisms of this term, observed[15] that it is

"a description of a trade or calling that is not itself unlawful, and that there are parallels for prohibiting to members of one trade or calling actions which for other persons are not offences;"

and they found no evidence that injustice results from its use in legislation. Its value is said to be that it protects from arrest a respectable woman who, through ignorance or indiscretion, loiters, quite innocently but so as to give rise to reasonable suspicion in the mind of a policeman that she is doing so for the purposes of prostitution. But if a policeman reasonably suspects that D is loitering for the purposes of prostitution, does he not thereby necessarily also suspect that she is a common prostitute? Before the decision in *Morris-Lowe*[16] the CLRC concluded that the word "common" no longer serves any useful purpose and, being regarded by some as unduly pejorative, should be dropped.[17] If the word really does add anything (which is doubted) the implementation of this recommendation would broaden the scope of the offence in theory but probably have no practical effect.

ii) *Loiter*. This word "loiter" has been used in other Acts of Parliament and it is probable that the meaning attributed to it in those Acts dealing with a similar mischief is applicable. Under the Street Betting Act 1906 it was an offence to loiter in a street for the purpose of betting. In *Williamson v Wright*[18] the Court of Session held there was no evidence of loitering when a car slowed down on a single occasion to pick up betting slips. Lord Anderson said that loitering

"is just travelling indolently and with frequent pauses" and "involves an idea of a certain persistence or repetition."

Lord Alness thought that loitering "connotes the idea of lingering" – which was absent in that case. Lord Hunter was inclined to think the word appropriate only to a pedestrian but Lord Anderson was quite clear that a person may loiter in a car; and this was accepted by a Divisional Court in *Bridge v Campbell*[19] where it was held that D was loitering for the purpose of the Vagrancy Act 1824 when he followed a vehicle in his van and repeatedly stopped when that vehicle stopped.

---

14. Home Office Circular 108/1959 and CLRC Working Paper on Prostitution, 3.15 to 3.21.
15. Cmnd. 247 at p. 88.
16. [1985] 1 All ER 400, [1985] 1 WLR 29, CA, above, p. 455.
17. CLRC, Sixteenth Report, Cmnd. 9329.
18. 1924 JC 57.
19. [1947] WN 223.

iii) *Solicit.* Soliciting is conduct amounting to an importuning of prospective customers. The prostitute must be physically present, so that the offence is not committed where she displays a card on a notice board in a street, inviting men to visit her for the purpose of prostitution.[20] If one has regard to the mischief at which the Act is aimed, this limitation upon its effect is clearly right.[1] It is probably not necessary that the prostitute's invitation should ever be received. It is enough that it is made and it is irrelevant that the prospective clients are deaf, blind, or merely daydreaming and unaware that they are being solicited.[2] There is undoubtedly an attempt to solicit in such cases and this is no less severely punishable, but the point is not academic as magistrates' courts have no power to convict of an attempt on a charge of committing the full offence.[3] Solicitation may be by acts done and it is unnecessary to prove that D used any words. It was enough in *Horton v Mead* that he

"smiled in the faces of gentleman, pursed his lips, and wriggled his body."[4]

iv) *In a street or public place.* By s. 1 (4) of the Street Offences Act 1959:

"For the purposes of this section 'street' includes any bridge, road, lane, footway, subway, square, court, alley or passage, whether a thoroughfare or not, which is for the time being open to the public; and the doorways and entrances of premises abutting on a street (as hereinbefore defined), and any ground adjoining and open to a street, shall be treated as forming part of the street."

The meaning of "street" is thus a wide one yet it will be noted that the sub-section does not provide an exclusive definition. The term "public place" is not defined at all and is more likely to occasion difficulty. That term is to be found in many statutes and formerly had a meaning at common law as part of the definition of affray.[5] Clearly its meaning may vary according to the context. Generally, however, it is construed to mean a place to which the public has access in fact, whether as of right or not and whether only on payment or not. Such a construction is supported in the present case by the use of the phrase "for the time being open to the public" in connection with "street"; for "public place" probably must be construed ejusdem generis with "street".[6] If so, the term might include privately-owned fields to which the public have access for the purpose of viewing point-to-point racing,[7] a car-park belonging to a dance-hall[8] or

---

20. *Weisz v Monahan* [1962] 1 All ER 664. Cf. *Burge v Director of Public Prosecutions*, below, p. 476.

1. It might be noted that a shopkeeper publishing such notices for reward might possibly be convicted of (i) conspiracy to corrupt public morals: *Shaw v Director of Public Prosecutions* (above, p. 276); (ii) publishing an obscene article (cf. the *Ladies Directory*, below, p. 730), and (if a man) (iii) living on the earnings of prostitution.

2. *Horton v Mead* [1913] 1 KB 154, a case under s. 1 (1) of the Vagrancy Act 1898 (see now, Sexual Offences Act 1956, s. 32); below, p. 476.

3. Criminal Law Act 1967, s. 6 (4) applies only to trial on indictment.

4. [1913] 1 KB 154 at 157.

5. See 5th ed. of this work, p. 738.

6. As "public place" is construed *ejusdem generis* with "road" in the Road Traffic Acts: *Elkins v Cartlidge* [1947] 1 All ER 829.

7. *Collinson* (1931) 23 Cr App Rep 49.

8. *Williams v Boyle* [1963] Crim LR 204.

public house,[9] the grounds of a hospital to which visitors and their friends are admitted,[10] an omnibus[11] or train, a village hall at which there is a dance open to members of the public,[12] and a public house[13] during licensing hours.

It has been emphasised in recent cases, however, that whether a place is public is a question of degree and fact.

"If only a restricted class of person is permitted or invited to have access, the case would fall on the side of the place being private. If only a restricted class is excluded the place would be public."[14]

Soliciting takes place *in* a street or public place where the solicitation takes effect there, even though D may be outside the street or public place. In *Smith v Hughes*[15] D attracted the attention of men in the street by tapping on the window pane, and by gestures invited them in and indicated the price of her services. Applying the "mischief rule" of construction, the Divisional Court dismissed her appeal:[16]

"Everybody knows that this was an Act intended to clean up the streets, to enable people to walk along the streets without being molested or solicited by common prostitutes. Viewed in that way, it can matter little whether the prostitute is soliciting while in the street or is standing in a doorway or on a balcony, or at a window, or whether the window is shut or open or half-open; in each case her solicitation is projected to and addressed to somebody walking in the street."

A similar result was reached where the prostitute was motionless but dressed in an alluring fashion and illuminated by a red light.[17] The test appears to be whether D's conduct in fact has a tendency to induce persons in the street to approach her for purposes of prostitution and whether she intends it to have such an effect. It does not follow that the result would be the same if the prostitute failed to attract anyone's attention,[18] for in *Smith v Hughes* Hilbery J thought that solicitation was not complete until the signals reached the men.[19]

6 Soliciting of Women by Men

The decision in *Crook v Edmondson*[20] that a man did not commit an offence under s. 32 of the Sexual Offences Act 1956 by soliciting a woman in a public place to have intercourse with him, left an unfortunate gap in the law. Solicitation of women by men, especially by "kerb-crawling", caused

9. *Elkins v Cartlidge*, supra; *Waters* [1963] Crim LR 437.
10. *Powell* [1963] Crim LR 511, above, p. 425.
11. *Holmes* (1853) Dears CC 207.
12. *Morris* (1963) 47 Cr App Rep 202.
13. *Mapstone* [1963] 3 All ER 930.
14. *Waters* [1963] Crim LR 437 at 438.
15. [1960] 2 All ER 859. What of the opposite case where D, in the street, attracts the attention of men in private premises?
16. [1960] 2 All ER 859 at 861. The decision is criticised by Williams in *Crime, Proof and Punishment*, 71.
17. *Behrendt v Berridge* [1976] 3 All ER 285, DC.
18. This is probably immaterial if the prostitute is in the street: *Horton v Mead*, above, p. 466.
19. Cf. the problem arising under the Public Order Act 1936; *Wilson v Skeock* (1949) 113 JP 294; *Ward v Holman* [1964] Crim LR 541.
20. [1966] 2 QB 81, [1966] 1 All ER, 833, below, p. 477.

great annoyance, not only to women solicited, but also to the residents of neighbourhoods where the practice was prevalent. Following the recommendations of the CLRC,[1] the Sexual Offences Act 1985 creates two new offences. Both are punishable on summary conviction with a fine, not exceeding level 3 of the standard scale. The first offence is kerb-crawling:

"1.–(1) A man commits an offence if he solicits a woman (or different women) for the purpose of prostitution –

(a) from a motor vehicle while it is in a street or public place; or

(b) in a street or public place while in the immediate vicinity of a motor vehicle that he has just got out of or off,

persistently or, subject to section 5 (6) below, in such manner or in such circumstances as to be likely to cause annoyance to the woman (or any of the women) solicited, or nuisance to other persons in the neighbourhood."

Section 5 (6) excludes the operation of the words after "persistently" in s. 1 (1) in any area where the Prosecution of Offences Act 1985 is not in force. In such an area the offence is committed only where the soliciting is persistent, not where it is not persistent but is likely to cause annoyance. This qualification was intended to preclude over-zealous police application of the new Act.

The second offence is persistent soliciting:

"2.–(1) A man commits an offence if in a street or public place he persistently solicits a woman (or different women) for the purpose of prostitution."

"Street" is defined for the purposes of the Act by s. 4 (4) in precisely the same terms as s. 1 (4) of the Street Offences Act 1959.[2] And "man" includes boy, and "woman", girl.

6 Indecent Exposure[3]

1 Indecent Exposure at Common Law

i) *The actus reus.* It is a common law misdemeanour[4] to commit an act outraging public decency in public and in such a way that more than one person sees, or is at least able to see, the act. The most common way of committing this offence is by indecently exposing the body.

A wide view is taken of "in public". In *Wellard*[5] Grove J said that a public place is one where the public go, no matter whether they have a right to or not. But earlier cases seem to go farther than this. D may himself be on

---

1. Sixteenth Report, Cmnd. 9329.
2. Above, p. 466.
3. See report of Home Office Working Party on Vagrancy and Street Offences; Leigh, [1975] Crim LR 413.
4. *Sidney* (1663) 1 Sid 168; *Knuller*, above, p. 277.
5. (1884) 14 QBD 63.

private premises, to which the general public do not have access, and so may those who see him. In *Bunyan and Morgan*,[6] D was in the parlour of a public house and was witnessed through the window of another room of the house; and in *Thallman*[7] D was on the roof of a private house and could be seen only from the windows of other houses. These could hardly be described as places "where the public go" yet both were convicted. It is doubtful if "in public" adds anything to the requirement that two or more persons must have been able to see the act.[8]

It has been held to be no offence where only one person was able to see that act;[9] but it has never been held that two persons must have actually seen it. In *Elliot*[10] it was submitted that it was enough that D exposed himself in a place where he might have been seen, although *no one* saw him. The court was evidently divided, three to two (but which way does not appear) and asked for the case to be re-argued. They later changed their minds and no judgment was delivered. In the modern case of *Mayling*[11] the Court of Criminal Appeal did not go farther than to say that it is clear that more than one person must *at least have been able* to see the act; but two persons actually saw it in that case. The point is therefore not settled. It seems artificial to insist on two persons having seen the act; but, if this is not required, what is the test? Must two persons have been present? Or is it enough that D exposed himself in a street or at a window where two or more persons might have been expected to pass by and see him though no one did? As a practical matter, of course, there will almost invariably be one witness of the act, for otherwise it would not be provable except by confession.

It is not necessary to prove that anyone was actually disgusted or annoyed. This was decided in *Mayling*,[12] where the court pointed out that a requirement of actual disgust would be incompatible with a rule that the offence could be established by proof that persons could have seen, but did not see, the act. Probably the exposure must grossly transgress generally accepted bounds of decency and tend gravely to offend the average person.[13] Whether it does so will depend on time, place and circumstance.

ii) *The mens rea.* It is unnecessary to prove any sexual motive or any intention to insult or annoy. Lady Godiva would have been guilty, notwithstanding her admirable motives, at least if there had been two

---

6. (1844) 1 Cox CC 74.
7. (1863) 9 Cox CC 388.
8. Cf. Lord Denham CJ in *Watson* (1847) 2 Cox CC 376 at 377: "... a nuisance must be public; *that is*, to the injury or offence of several," and Willes J in *Harris and Cocks* (1871) 11 Cox CC 659 at 661. See also Lord Coleridge CJ and Huddleston B in *Wellard* as reported in 15 Cox CC 559 at 562, 563.
9. *Reubegard* (1830) cited in 1 Den 344; *Webb* (1848) 1 Den 338; *Watson*, supra; *Farrell* (1862) 9 Cox CC 446.
10. (1861) Le & Ca 103.
11. [1963] 2 QB 717, [1963] 1 All ER 687.
12. Ibid.
13. *Moloney v Mercer* [1971] 2 NSWLR 207 (Taylor J) and *Knuller*, above, p. 277.

peeping Toms. In *Crunden*[14] D was convicted when he undressed and swam (presumably naked) opposite the East Cliff at Brighton in view of a row of houses. It was held irrelevant that his object was to procure health and enjoy a favourite recreation, not to outrage decency or corrupt the public morals.

It is submitted that it must at least be proved that D intended that, or was reckless whether, the exposure might be seen by two or more persons who do not consent to see it. In *Bunyan and Morgan*[15] the recorder seems to have held that negligence would suffice and that, although D had been seeking privacy, it was enough that there was a reasonable probability of his being discovered. This seems to be contrary to principle.

The offence may be committed by a female as well as a male person,[16] and the exposure need not necessarily be to persons of the opposite sex. If, however, three men were to bathe together naked, in a place in which they would reasonably expect not to be observed by anyone else, it is thought that no offence would be committed because this could not be said to outrage public decency. But it is quite otherwise if a man masturbates himself in the view of other men.[17] Is the offence committed if a mixed party of men and women bathe naked together? It is thought not (unless they are liable to be observed by others) because their consent negatives the outraging of decency. If it were not so, nudist camps would be illegal.

2 Indecent Exposure under the Vagrancy Act 1824

By s. 4 of the Vagrancy Act 1824:

"... every person wilfully, openly, lewdly and obscenely exposing his person with intent to insult any female ... shall be deemed a rogue and vagabond. ...."

The offence is punishable summarily by three months' imprisonment or a fine not exceeding level three on the standard scale; or, on a second conviction and committal to the Crown Court for sentence, by one year's imprisonment.

Unlike the common law offence this crime is limited to exposure by a male to female and requires an ulterior intent to insult. The word "person" means "penis"[18] so that –

"however deliberate be the intent to insult the female, and however great the insult she feels, the exposure of the backside is not within the section."[19]

The section was formerly limited to public places, but this limitation was removed by the Criminal Justice Act 1925 s. 42. The exposure is committed "openly" even though it occurs in D's own bedroom.[20] The vast majority of charges of indecent exposure are brought under this Act.[1]

14. (1809) 2 Camp 89; *Reed* (1871) 12 Cox CC 1.
15. (1844) 1 Cox CC 74.
16. *Elliot* (1861) Le & Ca 103.
17. For example, *Mayling*, supra.
18. *Evans v Ewels* [1972] 2 All ER 22, DC; contra, *Norton v Rowlands* [1971] CLY 2384 (QS).
19. *Sexual Offences* (ed. Radzinowicz), 427.
20. *Ford v Falcone* [1971] 2 All ER 1138.
 1. *Sexual Offences* 427.

7 Unnatural Offences

1 Buggery

Buggery at common law consists in intercourse per anum[2] by a man with a man or woman;[3] or intercourse per anum or per vaginam[4] by a man or a woman[5] with an animal. It can be committed by a husband with his wife.[6] As in rape, penetration must be proved, but emission need not.[7]

Consent is no defence. Indeed, the consenting party is also guilty of the offence, not merely as an abettor but as a principal offender.[8] The person effecting the intercourse is known as the "agent" and the other party as the "patient".

Buggery has never been defined by statute and its elements are still governed by the common law. At common law it was a single offence, whatever the age or sex of the parties, whether or not they both consented and whether or not an animal was involved. This was unaffected by the Sexual Offences Act 1956 s. 12 (1) which provided:

"It is an offence for a person to commit buggery with another person or with an animal."

That subsection, incorporating the common law of buggery, is still the basis of the law, but it is now qualified by the Sexual Offences Act 1967, which provides that it is not an offence for consenting men, who have attained the age of twenty-one, to commit buggery in private. The Act introduced a new scale of penalties[9] according to the circumstances of the particular buggery. The effect of *Courtie*[10] is that, since 1967 (though no one seems to have realised this until 1984) there are four distinct offences of buggery, punishable with life, ten years, five years and two years respectively.

Section 1 of the Sexual Offences Act 1967 provides[11] that it shall not be an offence for a man to commit buggery or gross indecency with another man provided that:

i) the act is done in private,
ii) the parties consent and
iii) the parties have attained the age of twenty-one.

An act is not done in private for this purpose if (i) more than two persons take part or are present; or (ii) the act is done in a lavatory to which the public have or are permitted to have access, whether on payment or otherwise. Where these conditions are not satisfied, whether a place is private seems to be a question of fact and the jury must take into account all

2. Other unnatural forms of intercourse are not within the meaning of the term: *Jacobs* (1817) Russ & Ry 331; but may amount to indecent assault or an act of gross indecency; see below, p. 475.
3. *Wiseman* (1718) Fortes Rep 91.
4. East says "in any manner": 1 PC 480.
5. *Bourne* (1952) 36 Cr App Rep 125; **SHC 138**; above, p. 155. Cf. Coke, 3 Inst 59 "... a great lady had committed buggery with a baboon and conceived by it ..."!
6. *Jellyman* (1838) 8 C & P 604.
7. *Reekspear* (1832) 1 Mood CC 342; *Cozins* (1834) 6 C & P 351. Where penetration is impossible, D may be convicted of an attempt. See *Brown* (1889) 24 QBD 357 and p. 300, above.
8. Stephen, *Digest*, Art. 221.
9. Below, p. 475.
10. [1984] AC 463, [1984] 1 All ER 740, above, p. 35.
11. Section 1.

the circumstances – the nature of the place, the time, the lighting, the likelihood of a third person coming on the scene and so on.[12]

A person suffering from severe mental handicap[13] cannot consent for the purposes of the Act. It is a defence for D to prove "that he did not know and had no reason to suspect" P to be suffering from severe mental handicap. It seems probable that it would be no defence to show that D1 believed D2 to be over twenty-one if he was in fact under that age.[14]

The Act expressly puts on the Crown the onus of proving that the act was

i) not done in private, or

ii) without consent or

iii) that any party was under twenty one.

There is, however, an evidential burden on D to raise these issues.[15]

An act of buggery or gross indecency continues to be an offence where it is done on a United Kingdom merchant ship by a member of the crew of that ship with another man who is a member of the crew of that or any other United Kingdom merchant ship.[16] The Act does not affect the provisions of the Army Act 1955, or the Air Force Act 1955, under which disgraceful conduct of an unnatural kind is punishable with two years' imprisonment,[17] or the Naval Discipline Act 1957[18] under which disgraceful conduct of an indecent kind is similarly punishable.

A consenting party under twenty-one continues to be guilty of an offence but proceedings against him for participating in any buggery or gross indecency may not be instituted except with the consent of the Director of Public Prosecutions.[19]

It continues to be an offence under s. 12 (1) of the 1956 Act for a man to commit buggery with a woman,[20] though both parties consent, or for a man or a woman to commit buggery with an animal, whether in private or not. And although a homosexual act between adult males in private is no longer an offence, there may be a conspiracy to corrupt public morals by publicly encouraging such acts.[1]

It seems to be the law that a person under fourteen, whether male or female, cannot be convicted as a principal offender either as agent or as patient.[2] Clearly, as regards the female and the male patient this does not depend upon any presumption of sexual incapacity. Coke,[3] Hale[4] and East[5]

12. *Reakes* [1974] Crim LR 615. (The commentary should refer to proof beyond reasonable doubt, *not* proof on a balance of probabilities).
13. This means the same as "defective" in Sexual Offences Act 1956, s. 45. Above, p. 443, footnote 7.
14. Cf. *Prince* (1875) LR 2 CCR 154; **SHC 102**; above, p. 41.
15. *Spight* [1986] Crim LR 817, CA and commentary.
16. Section 2.
17. Section 66 of both Acts.
18. Section 37.
19. If consent is not obtained, any proceeding is a nullity: *Angel* [1968] 2 All ER 607n, [1968] Crim LR 342; but consent is not required on a charge of incitement to commit the offence: *Assistant Recorder of Kingston-upon-Hull, ex parte Morgan* [1969] 1 All ER 416.
20. *Harris* (1971) 55 Cr App Rep 290, CA.
1. *Knuller v Director of Public Prosecutions* [1973] AC 435, [1972] All ER 898; **SHC 261**; above, p. 277.
2. Cf. Hogan, [1962] Crim LR 683; Williams, [1964] Crim LR 686.
3. 3 Inst. 59.
4. 1 PC 670.
5. 1 PC 480.

put this rule upon the child's want of discretion; but, if this is so, then the child over ten ought to be liable to conviction on proof of mischievous discretion. However, in *Tatam*[6] the Court of Criminal Appeal ruled that three boys under fourteen with whom D had committed buggery were not accomplices, "being unable at law to commit that offence." This presumably means that they could be convicted neither as principals nor as abettors. Yet, somewhat remarkably, it seems that a child under fourteen could be convicted of abetting D to commit buggery upon P. This was held in *Cratchley*,[7] where a boy of under ten, who kept watch, was held not to be an accomplice in the buggery of P by D but only on the ground of lack of evidence of guilty knowledge.[8] If the child's immunity really depends on presumed lack of discretion, the presumption ought equally to be rebuttable, or irrebuttable, whether D is the patient or the abettor of a buggery upon another. The only basis on which the present rule can be justified is that the law is designed to protect the patient[9] – which seems to be contrary to fact. It may well be that the present rule is due to a misunderstanding by the courts and subsequent writers of Hale, Coke and East who probably meant no more than that a person under fourteen is not liable unless a mischievous discretion is proved.

Where the agent is a boy under fourteen, the patient, if over fourteen, may nevertheless be convicted,[10] a result difficult to reconcile with the conclusive presumption of incapacity.

2 Procuring Others to Commit Lawful Homosexual Acts
Section 4 of the Sexual Offences Act 1967 creates a new offence, triable either way and punishable on indictment with two years' imprisonment, of procuring another man to commit with a third man an act of buggery which, by reason of s. 1 of the Act, is not an offence.

3 Assault with Intent to Commit Buggery: and Attempts
By s. 16 (1) of the Sexual Offences Act 1956:
> "It is an offence for a person to assault another person with intent to commit buggery."

The offence is punishable with ten years' imprisonment. An attempt to commit buggery is likewise punishable, though it is no longer[11] a statutory offence. Most cases under s. 16 (1) will also amount to an attempt but there may be occasional instances where the statutory provision is useful, as where D assaults P, intending to carry him off and commit buggery some hours later.[12] Here the act would probably not be sufficiently proximate to

---

6. (1921) 15 Cr App Rep 132.
7. (1913) 9 Cr App Rep 232.
8. The case is distinguishable from *Tatam*, above, only on the assumption that, in the latter case, none of the boys aided and abetted the buggery of another.
9. Cf. *Tyrrell*, above, p. 159.
10. *Allen* (1849) 1 Den 364. It is perhaps not surprising that the court was anxious to uphold the conviction in that case: D induced a boy of twelve to bugger him.
11. It was formerly included in s. 62 of the Offences against the Person Act 1861. Now the only statutory reference to attempt is in the Second Schedule to the 1956 Act, providing for the punishment.
12. And cf. *Lankford* [1959] Crim LR 209.

be an attempt but would amount to the statutory offence. On the other hand an attempt covers cases obviously not within the statute, as where D attempts buggery with an animal or, perhaps, approaches a sleeping P and does a sufficiently proximate act which does not amount to an assault or battery.

The necessity for an assault also means that consent must be a defence to a charge under the section, and this even though the other party be under sixteen (for there is here no statutory provision to the contrary) but old enough to understand the nature of the act;[13] but where a charge under s 16 (1) would fail only because of consent, the act is almost certainly an indecent assault under s. 15 by the one party where the other is under sixteen. And, whatever the age of the parties, it may amount to a gross indecency under s. 13[14]. Consent would be no defence, however, to a charge of attempt to commit buggery and here both parties might be convicted if their acts were sufficiently proximate.

Whether a boy under fourteen may be convicted of attempted buggery depends on the same arguments as are considered above[15] in relation to attempted rape.

4 Indecency between Men

By s. 13 of the Sexual Offences Act 1956:

"It is an offence [triable either way] for a man[16] to commit an act of gross indecency with another man, whether in public or private, or to be a party to the commission by a man of an act of gross indecency with another man, or to procure the commission by a man of an act of gross indecency with another man."

As noted above,[17] this is now qualified by the Sexual Offences Act 1967, s. 1. This Act also provides, by s. 4 (3), that it shall not be an offence under s. 13 of the 1956 Act for a man to procure the commission *with himself* of an act of gross indecency by another man where that act, by reason of s. 1 of the 1967 Act, is not an offence. It continues to be an offence under s. 13 for a man to procure another man to commit with a third man an act of gross indecency, though the act, by reason of s. 1 of the 1967 Act, is not an offence. The effect of *Courtie*[18] is that there are two offences of gross indecency – (i) by a man of or over twenty-one with a man under that age (five years) and (ii) other offences (two years).

It is an offence under the Criminal Attempts Act 1981 to attempt to procure the commission of an act of gross indecency by one man with another;[19] or to incite another to procure such an act,[20] at least if it is not an incitement to conspire[1] and, possibly, even if it is.

---

13. *Wollaston* (1872) 12 Cox CC 180: consent negatives an assault. The point seems to have been overlooked in *Cratchley*.
14. Infra.
15. Above, p. 438.
16. "Man" includes "boy": s. 46.
17. See p. 471.
18. [1984] AC 463, [1984] 1 All ER 740, above, p. 35.
19. *Hampshire v Mace* [1986] Crim LR 752, CA.
20. *Bentley* [1923] 1 KB 403.
 1. *Sirat* (1985) 83 Cr App Rep 41, [1986] Crim LR 245, above, p. 254.

The nature of "gross indecency" does not seem to have been further defined by the courts, save that it has been held that[2] there is no need for actual physical contact, if two men concert to behave in an indecent manner. It is enough that

"two men put themselves in such a position that it can be said that a grossly indecent exhibition is going on."

According to the evidence before the Wolfenden Committee:[3]

". . . the offence usually takes one of three forms; either there is mutual masturbation; or there is some form of intercrural contact; or oral-genital contact (with or without emission) takes place. Occasionally the offence may take a more recondite form; techniques in heterosexual relations vary considerably, and the same is true of homosexual relations."

The distinction between "indecency" and "gross indecency" is not clear. It has been suggested, as an example, that if

"two male persons kissed each other under circumstances which showed that the act was immoral and unnatural",

this would be indecent but not grossly indecent.[4]

The offence requires the co-operation of two men acting in concert.[5] If D's indecent act is directed against another person who does not consent, the act cannot amount to an offence under the section.[6] If D's act is directed towards procuring the co-operation of the other in the act of indecency, then it may amount to an attempt to commit an offence under the section, if the other is unwilling to collaborate. The act may also of course be an indecent assault.[7]

Where the charge is one of *procuring*, the same considerations apply as where that term is used elsewhere in the Act.[8]

5 Penalties for Buggery and Gross Indecency

The Sexual Offences Act 1967, s. 3, provides a new scale of penalties for, and, following *Courtie*, series of offences of, buggery and gross indecency as follows: –

Buggery

    i) If with a boy under the age of sixteen or with a woman or an animal – life.

    ii) If with a man who is sixteen or over who did not consent – ten years.

    iii) If with a man between sixteen and twenty-one who consented where D is twenty-one or over – five years.

    iv) a) If with a man of twenty-one or over who consented (whatever D's age) – two years.

        b) If with a man of sixteen or over who consented and D is under twenty-one – two years.

---

2. *Hunt* [1950] 2 All ER 291.
3. Cmnd. 247, p. 38. See also *Sexual Offences* (ed. Radzinowicz), 349.
4. *The Criminal Law Amendment Act* (4th ed.) (1963), by Mead and Bodkin, cited in *Sexual Offences*, p. 349.
5. *Hornby and Peaple* [1946] 2 All ER 487.
6. *Preece and Howells* [1976] Crim LR 392, CA.
7. *Pearce* (1952) 35 Cr App Rep 17, CA.
8. Above, p. 439. See also *Jones* [1896] 1 QB 4; *Bentley* [1923] 1 KB 403.

Attempted buggery

    i) If with a boy under the age of sixteen or with a woman or an animal – ten years.[9]

    (ii) If with a man of sixteen or over – the maximum for the completed offence (above).[10]

Committing or procuring gross indecency

    i) If by a man of or over twenty-one with a man under that age – five years.

    ii) In other cases two years.

The draughtsman of the 1967 Act was probably unaware that he was creating a series of offences and might have drafted them differently had he been able to foresee *Courtie*. The effect is that the offences are mutually exclusive – a man buggering a fifteen-year-old boy believing him to be sixteen (and vice versa) intends to commit one offence and commits another – raising the 'kind of problems faced by the court in *Prince*[11] and suggesting that the offences are likely to be construed to impose strict liability with respect to age and, perhaps, to sex – but not, it is to be hoped, consent.

6 Solicitation by Men[12]

By s. 32 of the Sexual Offences Act 1956:

"It is an offence for a man persistently to solicit or importune in a public place for immoral purposes."

There is no distinction between importuning and soliciting.[13] The meaning of "solicit" and "public place" would seem to be the same here as in the Street Offences Act 1959 and has already been sufficiently considered in that connection.[14]

This offence differs from that under the Street Offences Act in that the soliciting must be "persistent". In *Dale v Smith*[15] it was said that the word implies "a degree of repetition, of either more than one invitation to one person or a series of invitations to different people". It was held that it was enough that there were two invitations. It may be that a single act of "continuing solicitation" would be enough. In *Burge*[16] the alleged solici-tation consisted in the display of a card. As it was held on appeal[17] that this could not be soliciting since D was not physically present, the point did not, in the end, require decision, but the Chairman of Quarter Sessions thought that a display, even for half an hour, would be persistent.

Although this section is being discussed under "Unnatural Offences", it seems that its original object was to penalise soliciting by men on behalf of female prostitutes.[18] "Immoral purposes" however is not defined, and is

9. Sexual Offences Act 1967, s. 3 (1) and Powers of Criminal Courts Act 1973, s. 18 (2).
10. Ibid.
11. Above, p. 41.
12. See Cohen, "Soliciting by Men" [1982] Crim LR 349.
13. *Field v Chapman* [1953] CLY 787.
14. Above, p. 464.
15. [1967] 2 All ER 1133 at 1136. Cf. *Barker v Barker* [1949] P 219 at 221; [1949] 1 All ER 247 at 248; *Broad v Broad* (1898) 78 LT 687.
16. [1961] Crim LR 412.
17. *Burge v Director of Public Prosecutions* [1962] 1 All ER 666 n. Cf. *Weisz v Monahan*, above, p. 466.
18. Cmnd. 247 at p. 42.

clearly wide enough to cover both homosexual and heterosexual behaviour. In *Crook v Edmondson*[19] it was held that a man does not solicit for immoral purposes within s. 32 by soliciting a woman to have intercourse with himself. The court did not define "immoral purposes" but said that a possible view is "such immoral purposes as are referred to in this part of the Act". It is surprising that "unlawful sexual intercourse" should not be regarded as an immoral purpose. That case was, however, distinguished in *Dodd*[20] where kerb-crawlers solicited fourteen-year old girls who were in the street for innocent purposes. The defendants' purpose was not merely immoral but illegal. It is not, however, necessary that the purpose should be illegal. In *Ford*[1] it was held to be no answer to a charge of soliciting another man that both parties were over 21 and that homosexual activity between them in private would not be an offence. There was a case to go to the jury and it was a question of fact whether the conduct contemplated was or was not immoral. So in *Grey*[2] where the judge directed that homosexual activity was, as a matter of law, "immoral" the Court of Appeal held that there had been a misdirection and a material irregularity. They nevertheless upheld the conviction under the proviso to s. 2 (1) of the Criminal Appeal Act 1968, holding that the legislative history showed that Parliament had no intention of excluding importuning by males for the purposes of engaging in homosexual activity. This leaves the law in a most unsatisfactory state. Juries and magistrates may have different views on the immorality or otherwise of homosexual activity so the application of the law may be uneven and unjust. If a judge misdirects a jury that homosexual activity is immoral, the conviction may well be upheld under the proviso; and if magistrates decide that it is not, they may be held to have decided against the weight of the evidence and be directed to convict. Clearly the matter ought to be resolved as a matter of law, one way or the other.

---

19. [1966] 2 QB 81, [1966] 1 All ER 833, DC, Sachs J dissenting. But D may be bound over to be of good behaviour on the ground that such conduct is *contra bonos mores* – "contrary to a good way of life": *Hughes v Holley* (1986) 86 Cr App Rep 130, DC.
20. (1977) 66 Cr App Rep 87, CA.
1. [1978] 1 All ER 1129, [1977] Crim LR 688 and commentary, CA.
2. [1982] Crim LR 176, CA.

14 Road Traffic Offences[1]

The advent of the motor vehicle created problems with which the existing law was ill-equipped to deal. The threat of proceedings for manslaughter might deter the motorist from driving with wilful disregard for human life, but where some harm less than death was caused other offences against the person were hardly pertinent at all. These offences, in the main, require that the harm should be caused intentionally or recklessly. It is rare for a motorist to intend harm though perhaps not so rare for him to be reckless as to whether or not he causes harm, particularly if recklessness does not require the driver to be aware of the obvious risk which he is taking.[2] Though the motorist who causes harm may often be at fault, the harm he causes is ordinarily both undesired and unforeseen by him. But it must not be thought that there is little or no room for offences of intention and recklessness in road traffic. There are many offences (such as speeding, driving whilst unlicensed, driving whilst uninsured) where the offence is ordinarily committed intentionally or recklessly though it does not follow that such offences will require proof of intention or recklessness. Generally it is only in relation to the causing of harm to the person or property that the motorist is neither intentional nor reckless.

There were some provisions of statutes which applied to motorists, but only, as it were, by chance. Under the Highway Act 1835, s. 72, for example, it was an offence to drive any carriage on the pavement and this could be applied to the motor carriage, and under the Town Police Clauses Act 1847, s. 28, the furious driving of any horse or carriage was an offence and this was applied to motorists. And it is still an offence under s. 35 of the Offences against the Person Act 1861 for a person, having charge of a carriage or vehicle, to cause bodily harm by wanton or furious driving.[3] But for the main part the law barely concerned the motorist at all. There were no tests of driving proficiency, no registration requirements, no compulsory insurance, and virtually no driving offences. The common law could not fill gaps like these and the result is that for practical purposes the regulation of road traffic is almost entirely statutory. And the bulk of the legislation is considerable. The principal Act, the Road Traffic Act 1972, runs to two hundred and nine sections and ten schedules, and that is a large body of law.[4]

1. Elliott & Street, *Road Accidents* (1968).
2. As to which see below, p. 483.
3. This provision is not a dead letter; see *Cooke* [1971] Crim LR 44, QS where D could not be charged under the Road Traffic legislation because the offence was not committed on a road, and *Mohan* [1976] QB 1, [1975] 2 All ER 193, CA; SHC 271; above, p. 288.
4. Note that the 1972 Act is a consolidating measure which, with only minor amendments, re-enacts the former law. Consequently the cases decided under earlier legislation remain authoritative.

It is not possible in a work of this kind to treat the plethora of road traffic offences in a comprehensive way and attention is concentrated on careless driving, reckless driving and causing death by reckless driving since a discussion of these contributes to an understanding of the general principles of the criminal law.

1 Careless Driving

The Road Traffic Act 1972, s. 3, provides –

"If a person drives a motor vehicle on a road without due care and attention, or without reasonable consideration for other persons using the road, he shall be guilty of an offence."[5]

The offence, which is summary only, is punishable by a fine at level 4 on the standard scale, or, in the case of a second or subsequent conviction, by imprisonment for three months or a fine at level 4 or both.[6]

In order to determine whether the offence of careless driving is committed, the test, as Lord Goddard CJ said in *Simpson v Peat*[7] is: was D exercising that degree of care and attention that a reasonable and prudent driver would exercise in the circumstances? The relevant standard, according to Lord Hewart CJ,

"is an objective standard, impersonal and universal, fixed in relation to the safety of other users of the highway. It is in no way related to the degree of proficiency or degree of experience attained by the individual driver."[8]

It is accordingly no defence that a learner driver is doing his best if the care exercised falls short of that to be expected from the reasonably competent driver;[9] nor is any special standard applicable to experienced drivers, such as police drivers who may be trained to meet exacting standards of proficiency,[10] and even though they may have to cope with emergencies which are not the lot of ordinary drivers.[11] Faced by an emergency the issue

---

5. Section 18 creates similar offences in respect of cycling.

6. Road Traffic Act 1972, Sch. 4, Road Traffic Act 1974, Sch. 5, and Criminal Law Act 1977, Sch. 6.

7. [1952] 2 QB 24, [1952] 1 All ER 447 at 449, DC.

8. *McCrone v Riding* [1938] 1 All ER 157 at 158, DC. The standard is the same as that applied in a civil action for negligence. Hence the Court's view in *Hume v Ingleby* [1975] Crim LR 396, that while D "might have no answer to a civil claim he was not guilty of an offence [of careless driving]" can only be explained in relation to different standards of proof. References in a criminal case to rules of civil law affecting the onus of proof (such as res ipsa loquitur) are probably best avoided though it is open to justices to infer negligence from facts affording no other reasonable explanation.

9. *McCrone v Riding* [1938] 1 All ER 157; *Preston JJ, ex p Lyons* [1982] RTR 173, [1982] Crim LR 451, DC. See Wasik [1982] Crim LR 411. Inexperience may be relevant to sentence: *Mabley* [1965] Crim LR 377.

10. *Woods v Richards* (1977) 65 Cr App Rep 300, DC.

11. In coping with such emergencies the police driver owes the ordinary duty of care to other persons lawfully (*Gaynor v Allen* [1959] 2 QB 403, [1959] 2 All ER 644) or unlawfully (*Marshall v Osmond* [1983] QB 1034, [1983] 2 All ER 225, DC) on the highway. The test is whether D is driving with due care *in all the circumstances*, including the emergency with which he is faced (*Woods v Richards* (1977) 65 Cr App Rep 300, DC) and the nature of the unlawful conduct with which he has to deal (*Marshall v Osmond*).

is not whether by taking some other course of action harm may have been avoided but whether D's reaction to the emergency was a reasonable one.[12]

Another view of the nature of liability for careless driving was given by Lord Diplock in *Lawrence*.[13] "Section 3", he said,

"creates an absolute offence in the sense in which that term is commonly used to denote an offence for which the only mens rea needed is simply that the prohibited physical act (actus reus) done by the accused was directed by a mind that was conscious of what his body was doing, it being unnecessary to show that his mind was also conscious of the possible consequences of his doing it. So s. 3 takes care of this kind of inattention or misjudgment to which the ordinarily careful motorist is occasionally subject without its necessarily involving any moral turpitude, although it causes inconvenience and annoyance to other users of the road."

This is a puzzling passage. Offences of "absolute", perhaps more properly called "strict", liability are ordinarily contrasted with offences requiring a fault element, including offences which require proof of negligence.[14] In the case of an absolute offence it can be no defence to show that all reasonable care was taken but where an offence, such as careless driving, requires proof of negligence the prosecution must necessarily fail unless a want of due care is established.

There is a sense in which liability for careless driving might be said to be absolute. If D's driving falls short of the standard expected from the reasonably prudent driver, not only is it no defence for D to show that he was doing his level best but also it is no defence for him to show that it was in fact impossible for him to do any better. Drivers, being human, will inevitably make some errors of judgment in their driving lives but the assumption is, and for practical reasons must be, that the reasonably prudent driver makes none. In truth, the "reasonably prudent driver" is not the average driver but a mean standard. In this limited sense careless driving might be said to be an absolute offence but it is not clear that it is in any sense helpful to so classify it. The general basis on which persons are punished for offences of negligence is that they could have done better,[15] whereas people may be punished for offences of absolute liability even though they have taken all reasonable care.

Lord Diplock does, however, recognise that no liability can be incurred unless what was done by D was directed by a mind conscious of what he was doing. This is merely a particular instance of a general principle governing criminal liability. If D is unforeseeably afflicted by an epileptic seizure when driving he cannot be convicted of careless driving. D may thereby create considerable dangers for other road users, which perhaps explains why some cases seem to show a marked lack of sympathy to drivers

---

12. *R v Bristol Crown Court, ex p. Jones* (1986) 83 Cr App Rep 109, DC.
13. [1981] 1 All ER 974 at 981, HL.
14. Cf. his Lordship's view as expressed in *Tesco Supermarkets Ltd v Nattrass* [1971] 2 All ER 127 at 155, HL: "negligence connotes a reprehensible state of mind – a lack of care for the consequences of his physical acts on the part of the person doing them."
15. Above, p. 91.

raising automatism,[16] but without a real ability to control his actions D cannot be convicted of careless driving.

Nor must it be thought that, as Lord Diplock's dictum might be taken to imply, the offence of careless driving requires proof of inconvenience or annoyance to other road users. Careless driving is a conduct crime and not a result crime;[17] consequently it may be committed though no one is affected by the careless driving in question.

All the circumstances (which cannot be exhaustively stated but include such factors as the state of the road, the volume of traffic, weather conditions and so on) need to be considered by the justices in determining whether D's driving falls short of the relevant standard and the question is essentially one of fact for them. Only where the justices reach a decision which no reasonable bench could reach on those facts will the High Court interfere.[18] Consequently the High Court may uphold a decision to convict (or acquit) if it is one which may reasonably be reached on the facts and even though, had the decision been to acquit (or convict), that decision would equally have been upheld.[19] In criminal cases, as in civil actions for negligence, the courts resist any attempt to elevate "to the status of propositions of law what really are particular applications to special facts of propositions of ordinary good sense".[20]

The point may be illustrated by reference to cases involving the Highway Code. While the Code contains many precepts of good driving, and while the Act itself provides[1] that a failure to observe its provisions may be relied on in both criminal and civil proceedings as tending to establish or negative liability, it does not lay down for drivers a regime of inflexible imperatives. Since each case turns on its own particular facts it does not *always* (though it may usually) follow that a driver is necessarily careless in driving at such a speed that he cannot stop in the distance he sees to be clear,[2] nor in leaving insufficient braking distance between his vehicle and another's,[3] nor in failing to look behind before reversing,[4] though these are all precepts of driving practice set out in the Code.

Nor is D's driving necessarily careless merely because it constitutes some other driving offence. While the speed at which a vehicle is driven is often a relevant factor, it does not necessarily follow that D is guilty of careless driving merely because he is exceeding a speed limit.[5] Nor does it follow that a driver who is guilty of the offence of failing to accord precedence to a pedestrian on a crossing is guilty of careless driving.[6]

---

16. *Watmore v Jenkins* [1962] 2 QB 572, [1962] 2 All ER 868, DC; *Broome v Perkins* [1987] Crim LR 271, DC.
17. Above, p. 33.
18. *Bracegirdle v Oxley* [1947] KB 349, [1947] 1 All ER 126, DC.
19. *Jarvis v Fuller* [1974] RTR 160, DC. The same principles apply to a charge of inconsiderate driving: *Dilks v Bowman-Shaw* [1981] RTR 4.
20. *Easson v London and North Eastern Rly Co* [1944] 2 All ER 425 at 426, CA, per du Parcq LJ.
1. S. 37 (5).
2. *Jarvis v Fuller* [1974] RTR 160.
3. *Scott v Warren* [1974] RTR 104, DC. Cf. *Preston JJ ex p Lyons* [1982] RTR 173, DC.
4. *Hume v Ingleby* [1975] RTR 502, DC.
5. *Quinn v Scott* [1965] 2 All ER 588, [1965] 1 WLR 1004.
6. *Gibbons v Kahl* [1956] 1 QB 59, [1955] 3 All ER 345, DC.

Since the test is objective, and what is relevant is the driver's conduct, it cannot matter that the failure to exercise due care arose from a deliberate act of bad driving on D's part.[7] This is not to say that subjective factors must always be ruled out of account. Though no account is to be taken of such subjective factors as experience and skill,[8] knowledge of circumstances may be a relevant factor. It is clear, for example, that D could be convicted of careless driving where, because of his familiarity with the vehicle, he realises that it has a tendency to pull to the right when the brakes are applied at high speed,[9] while someone who was unfamiliar with the vehicle, and who was reasonably unaware of this tendency, could not.

Section 3 creates two distinct offences, careless driving and inconsiderate driving. In many cases the facts would constitute either offence but they are not identical since the latter, unlike the former, may be committed only where other persons are using the road. Inconsiderate driving is the more appropriate offence where, for instance, D drives his car through a puddle which he might have avoided and drenches pedestrians. It must be the driving which is inconsiderate; other inconsiderate conduct, such as kicking a cyclist,[10] will not do.

For the purposes of s. 3 "other persons using the road" includes the passengers in a vehicle driven by D.[11]

2 Reckless Driving

The Road Traffic Act 1972, s. 2,[12] provides:

"A person who drives a motor vehicle on a road recklessly shall be guilty of an offence."[13]

The offence is punishable on summary conviction by six months' imprisonment and/or a fine of the prescribed sum;[14] and on indictment by imprisonment for two years and/or a fine.[15]

Under the former law, as well as an offence of reckless driving there were offences of driving in a dangerous manner or at a dangerous speed. Dangerous driving was interpreted in such a way by the courts[16] that it

---

7. *Taylor v Rogers* (1960) 124 JP 217, [1960] Crim LR 271, DC.
8. Presumably no account is to be taken of age although D may lawfully drive a motor car at seventeen years and a motor cycle at sixteen. No doubt the same "impersonal and universal" standard would be applied. But what of careless cycling under s. 18 where D may be only ten years? In civil cases generally a child must exercise the care to be expected of a child of his age but where a child is engaged in an activity such as cycling on a road there is much to be said for holding him to the standard of the reasonably experienced cyclist. Cf. Fleming, *Torts* (4th ed.) at p. 112. But a child of ten to fourteen years is criminally liable only if he knows his act to be wrong: above, p. 178. How is this doctrine to be applied in the case of negligent crimes?
9. *Haynes v Swain* [1975] RTR 40, [1974] Crim LR 483, DC.
10. *Downes v Fell* [1969] Crim LR 376, DC.
11. *Pawley v Wharldall* [1966] 1 QB 373, [1965] 2 All ER 757.
12. This is a substituted section by virtue of s. 50 (1) of the Criminal Law Act 1977.
13. There is a similar offence in respect of cyclists, s. 50 (2) of the Criminal Law Act 1977 substituting a new section for s. 17 of the Road Traffic Act.
14. Magistrates' Courts Act 1980, s. 32.
15. Road Traffic Act 1972, Sch. 4.
16. See the 3rd Edn of this work at p. 371.

covered a broad range of conduct and, at one end of the spectrum, it was virtually indistinguishable from careless driving. The James Committee[17] thought it would suffice to retain only the offence of reckless driving and Parliament accepted its recommendation to abolish the offence of dangerous driving.

Obviously the James Committee envisaged a clear distinction between reckless and careless driving which the former offence of dangerous driving had blurred. This was confirmed in *Lawrence*[18] where the House of Lords stated that there was no need to give to reckless driving an ambit so wide as to recreate the previous overlap with careless driving. Careless driving deals with driving that creates a risk of inconvenience or annoyance to others while reckless driving is concerned with driving which creates a real risk of causing injury to the person or substantial damage to property.

The House then considered the *mens rea* of reckless driving. As explained by Lord Diplock (with whom all their lordships agreed) "recklessly", as descriptive of physical acts such as driving a vehicle, refers not only to the driver's state of mind but also qualifies the manner of the driving. Following the tenor of *Caldwell*[19] Lord Diplock said that on a charge of reckless driving the jury should be satisfied of two things –

"[F]irst, that the defendant was in fact driving the vehicle in such a manner as to create an obvious and serious risk of causing physical injury to some other person who might happen to be using the road or of doing substantial damage to property; and, second, that in driving in that manner the defendant did so without having given any thought to the possibility of there being any such risk or, having recognised that there was some risk involved, had none the less gone on to take it."[20]

Given the creation of the obvious and serious risk, Lord Diplock thought that one of the two states of mind could normally be inferred but "regard must be given to any explanation [D] gives as to his state of mind which may displace the inference".

It is not clear what Lord Diplock had in mind in adding this delphic postscript to the main statement. Possibly his Lordship was thinking of the cases where D addresses his mind to the risk but decides that he can cope with it; that, for him, no risk is involved. Thus D may appreciate that oncoming traffic creates a risk when he is about to overtake but decides that he has the time and distance in which to overtake safely, that is, he decides that for him there is no risk. Such a case does not fall within either of the two states of mind specified because it is neither a case where D gives no thought to the risk, nor is it a case where, having given thought to it, he decides to run the risk.[1] If *Cunningham* recklessness[2] were applicable to such a case D, in this illustration, could be held reckless if (i) he realised the risk and (ii) the risk was one which it was unreasonable for him to take in

---

17. *The Distribution of Criminal Business between the Crown Court and Magistrates Courts,* 1975, Cmnd. 6323, paras. 123, 124 and Appendix K.
18. [1982] AC 510, [1981] 1 All ER 974, HL.
19. [1981] 1 All ER 961, HL, above, p. 62.
20. [1981] 1 All ER at 982.
 1. See Griew, "Reckless Damage and Reckless Driving" [1981] Crim LR 743.
 2. See above, p. 62.

the circumstances. Since *Cunningham* recklessness is apparently not applicable to reckless driving, it is not at all clear how a jury is to be directed in such a case. Griew,[3] in attempting to seek an explanation, suggests that if D addresses his mind to the risk and decides that he is competent to deal with it, he should not be guilty of reckless driving (though he will be guilty of careless driving) even though a serious and obvious risk of harm to person or property is in fact created. Such a case, adds Griew, would lack the "moral turpitude" which appears to be required for reckless, though not for careless, driving.[4] But it is difficult to see any meaningful distinction between one who realises the risk and incompetently decides he can cope with it, and one who, owing to incompetence, does not appreciate that there is any risk.

Arguably the definition of recklessness which the House of Lords has applied to reckless driving is not open to the same theoretical and practical objections that can be applied to the definition in criminal damage (*Caldwell* recklessness). Reckless driving differs from criminal damage in being a conduct crime and not a result crime;[5] driving may be properly regarded as reckless if it carries with it the risk of harm to person or property even though no such harm is foreseen or in fact materialises. There is of course a contrary argument. Reckless driving is a serious offence carrying a maximum of two years' imprisonment on conviction on indictment and, if it is to involve moral turpitude, this should be visited only on the driver who knowingly takes serious risks. Moreover the James Committee appeared to think that the test in relation to risk taking was intended to be subjective –

"[I]t (sc. reckless driving) is marked off from other offences by *the element of deliberate disregard* for the safety of others. As such, it is always a serious offence, clearly distinguishable from the minor driving offences and from a driver's failure to reach the standard of care and competence demanded of him in the interests of the public."[6]

But given the decision in *Lawrence* it would be idle to pretend that reckless driving is confined to deliberate, conscious, risk taking. It includes this of course, but also extends to the driver who gives no thought to the risk, if that risk would have been obvious to the ordinary prudent driver. The Court of Appeal has subsequently advised[7] that it would be prudent for trial judges not to seek to paraphrase the direction laid down in *Lawrence* but to follow it to the letter.[8]

As with careless driving, reckless driving has regard not merely to the handling of the controls of the vehicle but also to other factors which render the driving of the vehicle a danger to others. To drive at speed a

---

3. Op. cit. at pp. 750, 751.
4. Griew admits, op. cit. at p. 751, that his argument "may be too much dictated by a desire to limit the effect of the decision in *Lawrence*".
5. See above, p. 33. Lord Diplock noted this: [1981] 1 All ER at 981.
6. Cmnd. 6323, Appendix K. Italics supplied.
7. *Madigan* (1982) 75 Cr App Rep 145, CA, confirming that the standard is that to be expected of the ordinary prudent driver, not the defendant. Above, p. 479.
8. Griew, op. cit. at p. 745 points out that the direction may need to be modified where the alleged recklessness relates not to the *manner* of the driving but to driving a vehicle known to be mechanically defective or where a driver is subject to a sudden loss of consciousness. Cf. *Haynes v Swain* [1975] RTR 40, above, p. 482.

vehicle which D knows, or ought to know, has defective brakes would be to drive carelessly and, if an obvious and serious risk of harm to person or substantial damage to property was created, would be to drive recklessly. Similarly, to drive a vehicle with an insecure load may constitute careless or reckless[9] driving. Knowledge which D has, or ought to have, of his own deficiencies may also be relevant in determining whether he has driven carelessly or recklessly. If D chooses to drive a vehicle with his legs encased in plaster where he knows, or ought to know, that his ability to drive is impaired, he may be convicted of careless or reckless driving. It follows that if D knows, or ought to know, that his ability to drive is impaired by drink or drugs he would be guilty of careless driving and, if he creates an obvious and serious risk of harm to the person or of substantial damage to property, of driving recklessly.[10]

3 Causing Death by Reckless Driving

Under the former law it was an offence to cause death by reckless or dangerous driving but in line with the recommendation of the James Committee to restrict the driving offence to reckless driving, the offence of causing death has been restricted to death caused by reckless driving. The James Committee was prepared to go further and favoured the abolition of the offence altogether.[11] The Criminal Law Revision Committee has made the same recommendation[12] but the government shows no sign yet of acting on it. Section 1 of the Road Traffic Act 1972[13] provides –

"A person who causes the death of another person by driving a motor vehicle on a road recklessly shall be guilty of an offence."

The offence is triable only on indictment and is punishable by imprisonment for five years and/or a fine.[14]

At common law, and it is still the law, a motorist who causes death by his driving may be convicted of manslaughter.[15] In practice juries have been traditionally reluctant to convict motorists of manslaughter which was why the statutory offence was introduced.[16]

The offence requires proof, at the very least, of reckless driving by D, that is, reckless driving as defined by *Lawrence*[17] and discussed in the last section. The speeches in that case were exclusively concerned with the offence of reckless driving;[18] the House was not asked to consider, nor did

9. *Crossman* [1987] RTR 49, CA.
10. *Griffiths (Rupert)* [1984] Crim LR 628, CA.
11. Cmnd. 6323, Appendix K.
12. CLRC/OAP/WP, para. 99; CLRC/OAP/R, paras. 140–143.
13. As substituted by s. 50 (1) of the Criminal Law Act 1977 which was brought into force on 1st December 1977.
14. Road Traffic Act 1972, Sch. 4.
15. *Jennings v United States Government* [1983] 1 AC 624 [1982] 3 All ER 104, HL.
16. Originally in the Road Traffic Act 1956, s. 8. In *Andrews v Director of Public Prosecutions* [1937] AC 576, [1937] 2 All ER 552; **SHC 341**, the House of Lords declined to extend the doctrine of constructive manslaughter to the negligent motorist, see above, p. 349.
17. [1982] AC 510, [1981] 1 All ER 974, HL.
18. Lawrence was initially charged with, and convicted of, causing death by reckless driving but his conviction was quashed by the Court of Appeal owing to misdirections by the trial judge.

it, whether the offence of causing death by reckless driving differed in any respects from reckless driving.

There is an obvious difference which relates to the *actus reus*. Causing death by reckless driving requires that someone be killed by the driving whereas reckless driving requires no harmful result in fact. The former is thus a result crime while the latter is a conduct crime. Had the House been so asked, it seems clear enough that, having authoritatively defined recklessness for the purpose of reckless driving, it would not have sanctioned some other definition for the purposes of causing death by reckless driving. So if death is in fact caused by the driving, all that needs to be proved is that D has the *mens rea* for reckless driving as defined by *Lawrence*. This view has been endorsed by the Court of Appeal in *Seymour*.[19]

This means that D would commit the offence, if death in·fact ensued, where the driving created a serious risk of substantial damage *only to property* if he either gave no thought to that risk, or, having considered that risk, decided to take it.

This would appear to be a very harsh result. In effect gross negligence as to the risk of substantial harm to property would suffice as the *mens rea* of a serious offence against the person. Moreover it would hardly appear to be consistent with Lord Atkin's observation[20] that:

"It is difficult to visualise a case of death caused by 'reckless' driving, in the connotation of that term in ordinary speech, which would not justify a conviction for manslaughter."[1]

This dictum appears clearly to have been endorsed by the decision of the House of Lords in *Jennings v United States Government*.[2] A more acceptable formulation, therefore, would be to confine causing death by reckless driving to the case where the driving creates a serious risk of injury only to the person to which D gave no thought or which he decided to take. But this formulation is also difficult to reconcile with Lord Atkin's dictum. It envisages that D may be convicted of causing death by reckless driving where he is grossly negligent as to personal injury and it is very doubtful if this would suffice to support a conviction for manslaughter.[3]

A third formulation would require foresight of death or, at least, of personal injury. This would be consistent with Lord Atkin's view since there is some authority for the proposition that one who foresees personal injury to another and decides to take the risk of causing it is guilty of manslaughter if death ensues. To accept this third formulation would, however, involve recognising a materially different definition of recklessness in the context of causing death by dangerous driving from the

---

19. [1983] 2 AC 493, [1983] Crim LR 260, and commentary.
20. *Andrews v Director of Public Prosecutions* [1937] AC 576 at 583, [1937] 2 All ER 552 at 556, HL.
   1. Manslaughter for this purpose *excludes* constructive manslaughter since the House in *Andrews* specifically declined to extend this doctrine to the negligent motorist.
   2. [1982] 3 All ER 104, [1982] 3 WLR 450.
   3. Recklessness (i.e. *Cunningham* recklessness requiring actual foresight) as to any personal injury would suffice for manslaughter as would gross negligence as to death or (possibly) serious harm, see above, pp. 352–355. Gross negligence as to any personal injury does not appear to be a sufficient mens rea for manslaughter.

definition accorded by *Lawrence* to recklessness in the context of reckless driving simpliciter.

In order to prove the offence of causing death by reckless driving the prosecution must prove that the reckless driving caused death. In *Hennigan*,[4] it was held that it is not necessary to show that the reckless driving was the sole cause or even a substantial cause; it is enough that it is "a cause" and is something more than de minimis. The principles appear to be the same as apply in relation to homicide generally which are discussed elsewhere.[5]

Where D is charged with causing death by reckless driving, the jury may return a verdict of reckless driving if they are not satisfied that D's driving was the cause of death.[6] Such a verdict might properly be returned in circumstances parallel to *Dallaway*,[7] but it is a verdict which juries sometimes return in the teeth of clear evidence that the driving was the cause of death.[8]

4. [1971] 3 All ER 133, CA.
5. Above, pp. 312–327.
6. Road Traffic Act 1960, s. 2 (2).
7. (1847) 3 Cox CC 273; above, p. 315.
8. *Curphey* [1957] Crim LR 191.

15 Theft and Related Offences

The law of theft was codified by the Theft Acts 1968 and 1978.[1] These Acts provide a code relating to virtually all offences against property involving fraud, with the notable exception of forgery. On two previous occasions, in the Larceny Acts of 1861 and 1916, the law relating to theft has been the subject of major legislation but the Theft Acts of 1968 and 1978 are quite unlike these earlier enactments. In general terms it may be said that the aim of the Acts of 1861 and 1916 was to consolidate the various statutory provisions and to state these in a convenient and accessible form. The Theft Acts of 1968 and 1978 proceed on another basis altogether. Although the Criminal Law Revision Committee, which was charged with the task of reforming the law,[2] saw that there were advantages in retaining the old system with some necessary amendment to repair its defects, they decided that the time had come

> "for a new law of theft and related offences, based on a fundamental reconsideration of the principles underlying this branch of the law and embodied in a modern statute."[3]

The Theft Acts of 1968 and 1978 constitute that modern legislation and are new law in a way in which the Larceny Acts of 1861 and 1916 were not new law. This has consequences of fundamental importance so far as the interpretation of the Theft Acts is concerned.[4] Even in the case of a statute which purports to codify the common law:

> "The proper course is, in the first instance, to examine the language of the statute and to ask what is its natural meaning uninfluenced by any considerations derived from the previous state of the law, and not to start with inquiring how the law previously stood, and then, assuming that it was probably intended to leave it unaltered, to see if the words of the enactment will bear an interpretation in conformity with this view."[5]

In practice the Larceny Act 1916 was often construed on the tacit assumption that there was no intention to alter the previous law and the

1. See Smith, *The Law of Theft*, 5th ed. (hereinafter Smith, *Theft*); Griew, *The Theft Acts 1968 and 1978* 5th ed. (hereinafter Griew, *Theft*).
2. See Eighth Report, *Theft and Related Offences* Cmnd. 2977, HMSO; hereinafter referred to as Cmnd. 2977, and Thirteenth Report (1977), Cmnd. 6733; hereinafter referred to as Cmnd. 6733.
3. Cmnd. 2977, para. 7.
4. See Brazier, "The Theft Act: Three Principles of Interpretation" [1974] Crim LR 701.
5. *Bank of England v Vagliano Bros* [1891] AC 107 at 144 per Lord Herschell. The court was considering the Bills of Exchange Act 1882, but the observation applies to codifying statutes generally. And see the observations of Edmund Davies LJ in *Bonner* [1970] 2 All ER 97n, CA.

earlier case law lost little or no authority. Such an approach to the Theft Acts would be wholly wrong, and any assumption that there was no intention to alter the previous law would be completely misconceived.

Nevertheless reference to earlier cases would be permissible in certain restricted circumstances. A clear instance would be where the Theft Act refers to concepts of the civil law, such as "trust", "equitable interest", or "proprietary right or interest". Obviously civil cases, whether decided before or after the Act, would be authoritative to explain these concepts. But in cases under the Act the courts have on occasion displayed some impatience with arguments based on "the finer distinctions in civil law."[6] This attitude, though laudable in its aim to achieve simplicity, is difficult to defend.[7] All offences relating to the appropriation of property can be defined intelligibly only in relation to a law of property. That law is the civil law and sometimes the question of mine and thine (and this is a fundamental question in this context) must involve nice questions of civil law.[8]

But while a reference to civil cases to explain civil concepts is generally permissible, reference to prior criminal cases will be rarely permissible. One case where such reference may be made is where the Theft Acts use expressions taken from earlier legislation which have acquired a settled meaning. For example, it would be permissible to refer to earlier decisions to elucidate the meaning of "menaces" in connection with the offence of blackmail under s. 21 of the 1968 Act. Strictly the earlier cases on the meaning of "menaces" are no longer authoritative but reference to them is legitimate and it is most likely they would be followed.[9] The word "menaces" had acquired a special meaning which was rather wider than that which it has in ordinary parlance and accordingly it may be assumed, since the draftsmen could have chosen another word such as "threats", that by retaining "menaces" the intention was to retain its earlier meaning. But this process cannot be carried too far and certainly affords no pretext for any wholesale reference to the earlier law. Before any reference can be made it must be clear from the context in which the expression is used in the Theft Act that it is being used in its special sense. For example, it would not be relevant to consider earlier authorities on the meaning of "robbery" since s. 8 itself defines robbery exhaustively and that definition may or may not accord with the former position.

Beyond this limited point it would not be relevant to refer to previous decisions.[10] If codification of the kind exemplified by the Theft Acts is to operate effectively it must be "within its field the authoritative, comprehensive and exclusive source of that law".[11] If a code is not so regarded it is in danger of failing to develop or reform the law.[12] But earlier cases often provide convenient fact situations in which to consider the effect of the

---

6. *Baxter* [1971] 2 All ER 359 at 363, CA; *Morris* [1983] 3 All ER 288 at 294, HL. But cf. *Walker* [1984] Crim LR 112, CA. Cf. Brazier, op. cit, at p. 706.

7. But Brazier thinks otherwise, op. cit. at p. 708.

8. See Smith, "Civil Law Concepts in the Criminal Law" [1972B] CLJ 197; Williams, "Theft, Consent and Illegality" [1977] Crim LR 127 and 205.

9. See further below, p. 589.

10. As to the Reports of the CLRC, see above, p. 63.

11. Scarman, *Codification and Judge-Made Law* (1966) at p. 7.

12. Ibid., p. 8.

provisions of the Theft Acts and for that purpose some reference is made to them in the ensuing pages. In the interpretation of the Acts the courts have aimed to give words and expressions their ordinary meaning so as to avoid undue technicality and subtlety. This is a sensible approach clearly enough but it has led, and not only in the context of the Theft Act,[13] to the practice of leaving the interpretation, at least of "ordinary" words and expressions, to be decided by the jury.[14] This may be a less desirable development. The interpretation even of ordinary words would seem to be pre-eminently a matter for the court if consistency of interpretation is to be achieved. To leave interpretation in the hands of the jury is to risk juries taking different views on comparable facts. Even such ordinary words in the Theft Act as "dishonesty", "force", "building" etc. may involve definitional problems on which a jury requires guidance if like is to be treated as like. But there is House of Lords authority[15] for this innovation in the interpretation of statutes and it looks as though we shall have to live with it for some time yet.

A last point by way of introduction. The Theft Act 1968 has not proved quite the success that was hoped for.[16] One offence proved so troublesome that it had to be replaced in the 1978 Act,[17] and in some other respects cracks are beginning to show through. The legislation, and the administration of criminal justice accordingly, would benefit from a review.

1 Theft

By s. 1 (1) of the Theft Act 1968:
> "A person is guilty of theft if he dishonestly appropriates property belonging to another with the intention of permanently depriving the other of it; and 'thief' and 'steal' shall be construed accordingly."

And by s. 7 a person guilty of theft is liable to ten years' imprisonment.

There is much about this definition which is self-explanatory and the vast majority of instances which actually occur will be covered with further elaboration. It is worth noting that before turning to the elaboration.

---

13. See Glanville Williams, "Law and Fact" [1976] Crim LR 472; Elliott, "Law and Fact in Theft Act Cases" [1976] Crim LR 707.
14. See the discussion of dishonesty, below, p. 525.
15. *Brutus v Cozens* [1973] AC 854, [1972] 2 All ER 1297. But in *Chandler v Director of Public Prosecutions* [1964] AC 763, [1962] 3 All ER 142, HL; **SHC 51**, Lord Radcliffe said, at 149, "The Act of Parliament [the Official Secrets Act 1911] in this case has introduced the idea of purpose as a determining element in the identification of the offence charged *and lawyers therefore, whose function it is to attribute meaning to words and to observe relevant distinctions between different words, cannot escape from this duty* merely by saying that 'purpose' is a word which has no sharply defined context. They must do the best they can to find what its content is in the context of this Act." – italics supplied.
16. While the statistic is a crude one and may to some extent be explained by other factors, a LEXIS search shows that reported appeals more than doubled in the first ten years of the operation of the Theft Act 1968 as against the last ten years of the Larceny Act 1916. A comparable search relating to the Malicious Damage Act 1861 and the Criminal Damage Act 1971, however, shows a six-fold increase in reported appeals.
17. See below, p. 544.

1) *The Actus Reus*

The *actus reus* of theft consists in the appropriation of property belonging to another.

1 Appropriation[18]

By s. 3 (1) of the Theft Act 1968:

"Any assumption by a person of the rights of an owner amounts to an appropriation, and this includes, where he has come by the property (innocently or not) without stealing it, any later assumption of a right to it by keeping or dealing with it as owner."

Broadly, appropriation, in the context of the Theft Act, conveys the idea of annexing something or treating something as one's own. But while this notion is conveyed by appropriation it is important to keep in mind that s. 3 (1) itself provides the only relevant definition and according to this subsection "*any* assumption by a person *of the rights* of an owner" amounts to an appropriation.

Throughout the discussion of appropriation which follows it may be important to bear in mind that what is being discussed is what constitutes an appropriation and not what constitutes theft. Theft requires an appropriation but it does not follow that an appropriation necessarily constitutes theft since there are other elements that need to be present before theft is constituted.

a) *Appropriation as an unauthorised act.* The meaning of appropriation was considered by the House of Lords in *Morris*[19] and, even if it is not the last word on the matter, it provides a convenient starting point. The case concerned the appeals of D and E against their convictions of theft. Both had perpetrated what is now the common fraud of label-switching in a self-service store, substituting a lower price label for a higher price label on goods which they were about to purchase, the only difference being that D was arrested after he had paid the lower price at the check-out while E was arrested before he had passed through the check-out. D could therefore have been convicted of obtaining the goods by deception contrary to s. 15 of the Act and his counsel argued that it was "somewhat anomalous" that he was liable to be convicted of obtaining by deception goods which he had already stolen. E might have been convicted of attempting to obtain by deception if his conduct was sufficiently proximate but his counsel denied that it was and further submitted that E had not appropriated the goods merely by switching the price labels.

Both the Court of Appeal[20] and the House of Lords dismissed their appeals but the House of Lords did so on a view of appropriation significantly narrower than that of the Court of Appeal and a comparison may be helpful. The Court of Appeal considered that the appropriation took place when D and E removed the articles from the shelves with intent

---

18. See Koffman, "The Nature of Appropriation" [1982] Crim LR 331; Stuart, "Reform of the Law of Theft" (1967) 30 MLR 609.
19. [1984] AC 320, [1983] 3 All ER 288, **SHC 411**.
20. [1983] 2 All ER 448.

to take them through the check-out without paying for them. This was a usurpation of one of the owner's rights. Notwithstanding that the owner might consent to their removing the goods from the shelves it was nevertheless a taking for their own use and accordingly an appropriation. The goods had therefore been appropriated *before* the label-switching took place; the label-switching was treated as a second appropriation, as a "later assumption of a right . . . by keeping or dealing with it as owner".

This was to give the widest possible meaning to appropriation. It meant that any assumption of control with intent to treat the property as one's own would be an appropriation even though there was no overt conduct on D's part to which P would take exception, and that appropriation would be theft if done with the required intent. The House of Lords preferred a narrower view. Delivering a speech in which all their lordships concurred, Lord Roskill said:[1]

"In the context of s. 3 (1), the concept of appropriation involves not an act expressly or impliedly authorised by the owner but an act by way of adverse interference with or usurpation of those rights."

It seems clear that this was to define appropriation in narrower terms and that the appropriation took place when D and E switched the labels[2] and not when D and E removed them from the shelves with intent to switch the labels. Hence, and considering earlier shoplifting cases, the House approved *McPherson*[3] and *Eddy v Niman*.[4] In the former there was held to be an appropriation where D removed goods from the shelves and placed them not in the wire basket as the owner would have approved but in her own shopping bag, an action clearly not authorised by the owner and adverse to the owner's right. In the latter D, bent on stealing goods, placed them in the basket provided but then lost his nerve and abandoned the basket in the shop. It was held that there was no appropriation because nothing was done that was inconsistent with the owner's rights. However Lord Roskill thought[5] that in *Eddy v Niman* Webster J went too far in saying[6] that there must be "some overt act . . . inconsistent with the true owner's rights" since Lord Roskill thought that the act need not necessarily be overt. This is a puzzling observation[7] and it puzzled the Court of Appeal in *Fritschy*.[8] P, who had authorised D to remove Krugerrands from London to Switzerland, became suspicious when he heard no more from D so he called in the police. D was charged with stealing the Krugerrands in England and the judge directed the jury that they might convict if satisfied that when D collected them in London he intended to dispose of them regardless of P's rights. The Court of Appeal quashed D's conviction and

---

1. [1983] 3 All ER 288 at 293.
2. *Anderton v Wish* (1980) 72 Cr App Rep 23, [1980] Crim LR 319, DC, which is to this effect, was approved.
3. [1973] Crim LR 191, CA.
4. (1981) 73 Cr App Rep 237, [1981] Crim LR 502, DC. See ATH Smith, "Shoplifting and the Theft Acts" [1981] Crim LR 586.
5. [1983] 3 All ER 228 at 294.
6. (1981) 73 Cr App Rep 237 at 241.
7. But consider appropriation by keeping or dealing as owner, below, p. 494. And cf. *A-G's Reference (No. 1 of 1983)* [1985] QB 182, [1984] 3 All ER 369, CA, below, p. 519.
8. [1985] Crim LR 745.

referring to Lord Roskill's view that the act need not necessarily be overt said:

"We have found this comment difficult to understand and we were tempted to say that some subsequent act on the part of an accused person, for example in the present instance disposing of the goods in Switzerland, could be evidence to justify a finding of an earlier appropriation: in this instance at the time when [D] received the Krugerrands [in London]. But having regard to Lord Roskill's earlier requirement of an act by way of adverse interference with or usurpation of an owner's rights, we found this conclusion impossible. There was here no evidence of any act by [D] within the jurisdiction that was not authorised by [P]. That, in the light of . . . *Morris* is fatal to the charge of theft."

The essence of appropriation would therefore seem to lie in conduct of D's which is observable as conduct that is inconsistent with or is a usurpation of the owner's rights; a simple way of looking at it might be to ask: was what D did something that he was not authorised by the owner to do?[9]

It may of course be argued that while a shopkeeper authorises an honest customer to take goods from shelves and place them in the receptacle provided, he does not authorise dishonest customers to do so. Commonly shoplifters place goods in the receptacle merely so that they can move them to a less well observed part of the store to effect a transfer of goods to their own persons. The answer would seem to be that the *conduct* of the shoplifter *is* authorised so long as it falls within the conduct permitted of shoppers. It is not merely that as a practical matter it will be difficult or impossible to prove an intent to steal until D acts in an unauthorised fashion for in some cases such proof will not be difficult to come by. In *Skipp*[10] D, posing as a genuine haulage contractor, collected loads from three separate places and then made off with them. On these facts a jury would inevitably have concluded that he intended to steal each of the loads as he collected it. Paradoxically D's counsel contended for this conclusion since D had been convicted on a single count for stealing all three loads and it was argued that the count was bad for duplicity. It was held there was only one appropriation which took place after the collection of the three loads at the point where D diverted them from their true destination. Until then D had done nothing which was inconsistent with the rights of the various owners since he was doing only what he was authorised to do.

To the same effect is *Meech*[11] though factually more complex. D was asked by P to bank and cash a cheque but because the cheque was for £1,450 the bank asked D to wait until it was cleared. Before clearance D discovered that P had dishonestly acquired the cheque so he resolved to cheat P by staging a fake robbery, to be effected by his confederates E and

---

9. "The question is – and is only – whether the defendant acted in relation to the [property] in a manner which the owner would have the right to act": *Stein v Henshall* [1976] VR 612 at 615.
10. [1975] Crim LR 114, CA.
11. [1974] QB 549, [1973] 3 All ER 939, CA. Cf. *Peter Jackson Pty Ltd v Consolidated Insurance of Australia Ltd* [1975] VR 480 where it was held that a servant authorised to take money to a bank did not steal it until he departed from the authorised route to the bank though he intended to steal from the outset.

F, while D was taking the proceeds to P. This was done but the fraud was discovered and D, E and F were convicted of theft. On appeal E and F argued that D had stolen the money when he withdrew it from the bank with dishonest intent and that while they might have been liable as handlers they were not liable as thieves. It was held, however, that the appropriation took place at the time of the staged robbery for it was then that "the performance of the obligation [by D to P] finally became impossible".[12] *Skipp* and *Meech* were approved in *Morris*.[13]

On the other hand Lord Roskill in *Morris*[14] doubted the "difficult case" of *Dip Kaur v Chief Constable of Hampshire*.[15] There D was looking at shoes, some pairs priced £6.99 and some pairs priced £4.99, when she noticed that a £6.99 pair carried a £6.99 price-tag on one shoe and a £4.99 tag on the other. Making no attempt to conceal the price-tags she presented the shoes hoping the cashier would see only the £4.99 tag and charge that price. The cashier did but D's conviction for theft was quashed on the grounds that the contract of sale was merely voidable and not void. The reason which Lord Roskill gave for his disapproval of the case, that it is "on any view wrong" to introduce the niceties of the civil law into this branch of the criminal law, cannot, with respect, be accepted and it is difficult to see how the decision in *Dip Kaur* is inconsistent with the view of appropriation advanced in *Morris*. D had done nothing with the shoes, either in presenting them to the cashier or in accepting delivery of them, that she was not authorised to do. D had of course tricked the cashier into delivering them but so did D in *Skipp* trick the deliverers into handing over goods by posing as a genuine haulage contractor.

Probably inconsistent with *Morris* is *Monaghan*[16] where D's conviction for theft was upheld when she took away money from a customer and placed it in her employer's till without ringing it up, intending to remove the money later in the day. It is difficult to see that she *did* anything she was not authorised to do unless it can be said that she was authorised to put money in the till only after ringing up the purchase. On the other hand a shop assistant is clearly not authorised to sell goods other than at the price she knows that her employer requires for them and if she marks the goods at less than their true value[17] or charges the customer less than their true value[18] she appropriates the goods.

b) *Appropriation by keeping and dealing.* To assume the rights of another would seem clearly to require conduct on D's part demonstrating such an assumption and so would a dealing. It is difficult to conceive of an

---

12. It would also seem that *Hircock* (1978) 67 Cr App Rep 278, CA, holding that a hire-purchaser was guilty of stealing a car only when he departed from the terms of the agreement, is inferentially approved by *Morris*.
13. [1984] AC 3ao, [1983] 3 All ER 288.
14. [1983] 3 All ER 288 at 294.
15. [1981] 2 All ER 430, [1981] 1 WLR 578, DC.
16. [1979] Crim LR 673, CA.
17. *Pilgram v Rice-Smith* [1977] 2 All ER 658, [1977] 1 WLR 671, DC.
18. In *Bhachu* (1976) 65 Cr App Rep 261, CA, the court thought the appropriation took place when the customer removed the goods but, following *Morris*, it would seem that the appropriation took place when the assistant rang up the lower price. Cf. *A-G for Hong Kong v Nai-Keung* [1988] Crim LR 125, PC.

assumption or dealing where D has done nothing at all in relation to the goods and even though he has made up his mind to steal the goods.[19] Does "keeping", however, go somewhat further?

Suppose that D, having borrowed P's cycle for a period, resolves on the expiry of the period to keep it. It would clearly be an appropriation to refuse to return it on demand,[20] or to deny P access to it, or for D claim it as his own. Such conduct shows that he is keeping it as owner. It would also constitute appropriation if D were to use the cycle after the expiry of the loan because this is an assumption of one of the owner's rights.[1] But what if D on the expiry of the loan merely leaves the cycle where it is in his garage hoping that P will forget about it and intending to keep it. At first sight it would seem inconsistent with *Morris* to say that D has appropriated the cycle since there is no conduct in relation to the cycle, and a mere mental resolution to steal cannot be an appropriation. But once the period of loan has elapsed D's possession is no longer authorised; his possession is now adverse to the owner's rights. Literally the case falls within the section since D is "keeping ... it as owner" and there would appear to be no warrant for giving the words other than their plain meaning. Of course proof of D's intention may be hard to come by but, assuming an admission by him, he satisfies the requirement of keeping as owner. It may be that in *Morris* Lord Roskill had appropriation by keeping as owner in mind when he said that the act of appropriation need not necessarily be overt.[2]

c) *Appropriation and the rights of an owner.* Section 3 (1) provides that "Any assumption of the rights of an owner" amounts to an appropriation. The Act does not provide, nor does English law otherwise provide, any definitive statement as to what are the rights of an owner[3] but, leaving that aside for now,[4] the phrase is, perhaps, capable of two interpretations. It might mean any assumption of *all* the rights of an owner, or it might mean an assumption of *any* of the rights of an owner. Clearly the latter view would give a more expansive view of appropriation than the former.

Counsel for D in *Morris* argued for the former interpretation. Certainly it looks odd to say that D has stolen an article when he subsequently acknowledges P's ownership of the article by offering to buy it from P, albeit at a price which, as D knows, P did not put it on offer. Lord Roskill dealt shortly with the point:[5]

"[I]f one reads the words 'the rights' at the opening of s. 3 (1) literally and in isolation from the rest of the section, the submission of counsel for [D] undoubtedly has force. But the later words 'any assumption of a right' in

---

19. But see *A-G's Reference (No. 1 of 1983)* [1985] QB 182, [1984] 3 All ER 369, CA, below, p. 519.
20. Cf. *Wakeman* (1912) 8 Cr App Rep 18.
  1. On which see infra. Very little may be required to show that D has assumed the owner's rights. Cf. *Walters v Lunt* [1951] 2 All ER 645; DC; *Poynton* (1862) 9 Cox CC 249.
  2. See above, p. 492.
  3. For a general discussion of an owner's rights see Honoré, *Oxford Essays in Jurisprudence*, 112–120.
  4. See appropriation as conversion, below, p. 496.
  5. [1983] 3 All ER 288 at 293. In this matter the House followed the Court of Appeal which had set aside the doubts it expressed in *Oxford v Peers* (1980) 72 Cr App Rep 19. *Morris* was followed in *Chan Man-sin v A-G of Hong Kong* [1988] 1 All ER 1, PC.

sub-s. (1) and the words in sub-s. (2) 'no later assumption by him of rights' seem to me to militate strongly against the correctness of the submission. Moreover the provisions of s. 2 (1) (a)[6] also seem to point in the same direction. It follows therefore that it is enough for the prosecution if they have proved in these cases the assumption by the defendants of *any* of the rights of the owner of the goods in question . . ."
This view has been criticised[7] but, as appears from *Morris*, it represents the current thinking of both the House of Lords and the Court of Appeal. Merely to damage goods (to scratch the paintwork of a car for example) would be an appropriation (an assumption of a right of the owner) though it would not, standing alone, amount to theft for other reasons. Oddly enough Lord Roskill in *Morris*[8] thought that a mischief-maker who swapped labels in a store merely to cause confusion would not, without more, be appropriating the goods. Clearly the mischief-maker would not be guilty of theft but the act, which is one which only the owner may lawfully do or authorise, seems clearly to amount to an appropriation within the general definition advanced in *Morris*. So, too, there would seem to have been an appropriation in *Easom*[9] where D sifted through the contents of P's handbag (tissues, cosmetics etc.) and, finding nothing worth his while to take, returned it to its former place. D's conviction for stealing the handbag and its contents was inevitably quashed since he did not intend to steal these.[10] But it would seem clear that what he did amounted to an appropriation of the handbag and its contents because what he did was not authorised by the owner.

d) *Appropriation and conversion.* The Criminal Law Revision Committee took the view that "appropriates" meant the same as "converts" in the former offences of fraudulent conversion under s. 20 (1) (iv) of the Larceny Act 1916.[11] Consequently it might be permissible in this context to have regard to decisions on the meaning of conversion in the former law of larceny though, as it turns out, there are few helpful decisions in point. Some help might be gleaned from decisions on what constitutes conversion for the purposes of the law of tort but the analogy, if it is to be pursued at all, must be pursued with some caution. "Appropriates" has a statutory definition in s. 3 (1) and while this may not be an exhaustive definition[12] the interpretation given to it which extends it to any assumption of any of the owner's rights would seem to give to appropriation an ambit significantly wider in the criminal law than conversion bears in the law of tort. Moreover the policies of the criminal law and the civil law differ in that the criminal

---

6. Below, p. 526.
7. Smith, *Theft*, para. 34.
8. [1983] 3 All ER 288 at 293.
9. [1971] 2 QB 315, [1971] 2 All ER 945, CA.
10. No doubt D intended to steal money, should he have found any, and he could have been convicted of attempting to steal money. See above, p. 289.
11. Cmnd. 2977, para. 35. The Committee apparently preferred "appropriates" only on the ground that "converts" was a lawyer's word which was not as meaningful to the layman as "appropriates".
12. The CLRC regarded it (Cmnd. 2977, para. 34) as a partial definition as did Lord Roskill in *Morris* [1983] 3 All ER 288 at 292.

law emphasises the conduct and intentions of D whereas the civil law places the emphasis on some serious interference in fact with the property and this may lead to conduct being treated as an appropriation which would not amount to conversion in the civil law.[13]

e) *Appropriation and possession.* The most common form of appropriation, and by far, is by an unauthorised taking by one who is not in possession from the owner who is in possession. Originally larceny was confined to such takings, an unfortunate straightjacket on the offence loosened only gradually by judicial ingenuity and legislative intervention. All that is behind us and appropriation is in no way geared to possession. A person in or out of possession can appropriate property and the test of appropriation is the same for both cases: has D assumed any of the rights of the owner?

A person lawfully in possession of another's property may accordingly appropriate that property by doing with it something he is not authorised to do. Where P deposits jewels with D for safe custody it would be an appropriation for D to wear the jewellery. A fortiori it would be an appropriation for D to pledge or sell the jewellery. Where P hires a car to D for a period, D appropriates the car if he uses it after the period has expired.[14]

Moreover it would seem that D may appropriate property where he is not in possession of it and does not seek to take possession of it. For D to destroy goods in situ would amount to an appropriation[15] since this is obviously an assumption of the owner's rights even though D never had nor acquires possession of the property. Suppose, then, that D sells the crown jewels, securely guarded in the Tower of London, to a gullible tourist. A clear case of deception but has D appropriated the crown jewels? The issue, in less extravagant but nevertheless engaging circumstances, arose in *Pitham and Hehl.*[16] E, knowing that his friend P was in prison and in no position to interfere, took D1 and D2 to P's house where he purported to sell P's furniture to them. The issue was whether D1 and D2 were properly convicted as handlers[17] and this required of course that there was *stolen* furniture for them to handle which in turn required an appropriation of the furniture. Lawton LJ, on behalf of the court, dealt with the matter quite shortly:[18]

---

13. In *Jackson* (1864) 9 Cox CC 505, Martin B thought that many acts (none were specified) might amount to the tort of conversion but not the crime. In *Bonner* [1970] 2 All ER 97n at 98, it appears that Edmund Davies LJ did *not* accept a submission that there must be a conversion for the purposes of the civil law before there could be an appropriation. In *Rogers v Arnott* [1960] 2 All ER 417 at 419, Donovan J thought the analogy between civil and criminal conversion was "misleading" because the tort is not actionable without special damage. But cf. Street, *Torts*, at p. 31, n. 13.

14. In *Jackson* (1864) 9 Cox CC 505 where D, who had been lent P's coat for a day, was found some days later wearing the coat on a ship bound for Australia. Martin B held that there was no evidence of a conversion of the coat. This decision *may* be consistent with the civil cases on conversion for there is apparently no case holding that a mere excess of permitted use constitutes a conversion (Street, *Torts*, at p. 39, n. 3) but it would seem clear that D has now appropriated the coat by assuming the right to use it when he is not authorised to do so.

15. Were D charged with theft it might be difficult to prove that he was acting dishonestly and he would be more appropriately charged under the Criminal Damage Act 1971.

16. (1977) 65 Cr App Rep 45, [1977] Crim LR 285, CA.

17. See below, p. 627.

18. (1977) 65 Cr App Rep 45 at 49.

"What was the appropriation in this case? . . . What had [E] done? He had
assumed the rights of the owner. He had done that when he took [D1 and
D2 to P's house] showed them the property and invited them to buy what
they wanted. He was then acting as the owner. He was then, in the words
of the statute, 'assuming the rights of the owner'. The moment he did
that he appropriated [P's] goods to himself. The appropriation was
complete."

Assuming that E in *Pitham* purported to be the owner, or to have the
owner's authority, and was at least at the outset so treated by D1 and D2,[19]
the decision, that there was an *appropriation*,[20] may be defended.[21] Had E
taken a tenancy of P's house during P's sojourn in prison a purported sale
of the furniture, of which he is now in possession, would constitute an
appropriation. It can hardly be less an appropriation because E merely
appears to be in possession of the furniture. P is at risk of losing his
furniture if D1 and D2 remove the property or of having a claim brought
against him if they do not remove it before P's return. In neither case are
P's rights usurped in the sense that P's title to the furniture is lost but his
rights are clearly interfered with and that interference arises because E has
purported to assume P's rights as owner.

In *Pitham*, it is assumed, E was in apparent possession of the furniture
and was in a position to deliver the furniture to D1 and D2. In the example
given above D is not in apparent possession of the crown jewels and is in no
position to deliver them to the gullible tourist. Because the illustration is a
preposterous one (and D is anyway guilty of obtaining by deception) it is
tempting to say that the conclusion that D has appropriated the crown
jewels is equally preposterous. But the definition of appropriation in s. 3 (1)
makes no reference to possession; any assumption of any right of an owner
suffices and, with or without possession, a purported sale by D of P's
property seems to be an assumption of P's rights as owner.

Williams, however, regards it as "jurisprudentially preposterous"[1] to say
that where D is not in possession of property he can steal[2] that property
when he is in no position to transfer ownership or make delivery of the
property[3] because the purported sale is a wholly nugatory effort to usurp
one of the powers of the owner.[4] The argument is not without force but
s. 3 (1) says that any assumption of the rights of an owner (and to purport to
sell another's property would appear to be such an assumption) "amounts-

19. Perhaps an unlikely conclusion in view of the fact that E, D1 and D2 gained entry to the
house by breaking a window and the preferable interpretation of the facts is that D1 and D2,
abetted by E who was paid for his help, went to the house to steal the furniture. See Williams,
TBCL, at p. 763; Smith, *Theft*, para. 27.
20. But whether there was a *theft* additionally involves a consideration of the intent
permanently to deprive which is considered below, p. 535.
21. For the purposes of the civil law of conversion a mere sale which does not involve a transfer
of ownership or a delivery of possession is not a conversion: *Lancashire Wagon Co v Fitzhugh*
(1861) 6 H & N 502; *Consolidated Co v Curtis & Son* [1892] 1 QB 495 at 498, per Collins J.
But, as pointed out above, p. 496, appropriation bears a significantly wider meaning than
conversion.
1. TBCL at p. 765.
2. But, see supra, n. 20, the issue here is only whether D *appropriates* the property.
3. If as a result of the "sale" the buyer takes the property away, D would be guilty of theft
through an innocent agent.
4. But in *Chan Man-sin v A-G of Hong Kong* [1988] 1 All ER 1, PC, it was held that there
could be an appropriation though in law the owner did not lose his property.

to" an appropriation. "Amounts to" here seems to mean "is". There would seem to be no warrant for qualifying the wording by some such requirement that the assumption must in fact threaten P's title to, or enjoyment of, the property.

If it is the case, as it is argued here that it is, that D may appropriate property without ever having or acquiring possession then some strange results ensue. D intends to hijack a lorry containing video-recorders if he can find a buyer for the goods. E agrees to buy them. D has now appropriated the goods though the lorry is in Nottingham and he is in Leeds and much needs to be done before he can get his hands on the goods.

f) *Appropriation and consent.* An act is not authorised by P merely because it is something which P expects, or even hopes, that D will do. Where P has reason to suspect that his property is being stolen, he may lay a trap (as by placing marked property in an accessible place) in order to catch D on whom the suspicion has fallen. D appropriates the marked property as soon as he takes possession of it; P has fully anticipated that D will take the property but D's appropriation is not authorised. But suppose that P goes further than this. Suppose that D suggests to E that E should take P's property and hand it to D at an arranged place. E tells P of the plan and P, with a view to catching D red-handed, authorises E to deliver the property as arranged.[5] Here P has consented to D having possession but he has not authorised the appropriation and D becomes a thief when he takes delivery of the goods from E.

It would be quite different if P authorised the appropriation. If P, learning of the plan from E, whimsically decided to make D a gift of the property that D was minded to steal and instructed E to deliver it, D would not be guilty of theft[6] since D cannot appropriate property in which he now has the entire proprietary interest. In this illustration P knows all the facts and has decided to make D the owner of the property; nothing thereafter done by D can amount to an appropriation of it. Similarly, if property is delivered under a contract of sale, D is not a thief if he then decides to make off with the goods without paying for them.[7]

Sometimes, of course, P is tricked into parting with the property. P gives money to D because D falsely tells him that he is collecting for charity, or P delivers goods to D in return for a cheque D knows to be worthless. Whenever a deception is used to obtain property the wisest course is to resort to s. 15 of the 1968 Act which is specifically designed to meet the case but it is nevertheless necessary to consider whether D is a thief.

Consider the difficult case of *Lawrence.*[8] On arrival in London P, an Italian student who spoke little English, showed a piece of paper to D, a taxi-driver, on which was written an address. The address was not far away and the normal fare would have been about 10/-, but D said it was a long way off and would be expensive. When P tendered a £1 note D said this

5. These are essentially the facts of *Turvey* [1946] 2 All ER 60, CCA, where D's conviction for larceny under the former law was quashed.
6. Though he may be convicted of attempting to steal.
7. D may be guilty of making off without payment, below, p. 569.
8. [1971] 1 QB 373, [1970] 3 All ER 933, CA; affirmed sub nom. *Lawrence v Metropolitan Police Comr.* [1972] AC 626, [1971] 2 All ER 1253, HL; **SHC 434**.

would not be enough and from P's wallet, which P was holding open, he took a further £1 note and a £5 note. On appeal against D's conviction for theft it was argued that D had not stolen the money because P had consented to its being taken by D. This argument was based on a requirement in the former law of larceny that a taking must be without the consent of the owner, and it seemed to get the case off on the wrong footing. P's consent to the *taking* as such would no more be a bar to a conviction of theft than the consent of the employer who set the trap so that D could be caught red-handed. The Court of Appeal held that P's consent was, as such, no defence, and when the House of Lords was asked whether s. 1 (1) of the Theft Act was to be construed as though it contained the words "without the consent of the owner" it answered with an emphatic No, and expressed surprise that the question should have been asked at all.

But this does not end the matter. There are two further problems to consider.

The first is whether P has consented, not merely to the *taking* of his property, but to parting with his entire interest in it. If P consents to transfer his entire proprietary interest then D cannot be convicted of theft;[9] this is so even though D is acting dishonestly. The point is illustrated by *Edwards v Ddin*[10] where D, who had just had three gallons of petrol put in his tank by an attendant at a garage, drove off without paying. It was held that D could not be convicted of theft. The ownership of the petrol passed when it was poured into D's tank so that when D drove off the petrol was entirely his; there was no property belonging to another of which he could divest P.[11]

It is not clear whether D in *Edwards v Ddin* intended from the outset to cheat P or whether he made up his mind to do so only after the petrol had been placed in his tank but, so far as the offence of theft is concerned, it could, on the view of the law submitted here, make no difference.[12] On the former hypothesis D has tricked P into delivering the petrol and no doubt P never would have consented to make D the owner of the petrol had he known that D was not going to pay for it. P was cheated into transferring ownership but he nevertheless intended to transfer it. This may be a simple case but anyone familiar with the civil cases on fraud and mistake will know that it is not always easy to determine whether the fraud does or does not have the effect of preventing the transfer of ownership from P to D. This may become a crucial question *if D is charged with theft*. In practice the difficulty can be circumvented if D has made a deception and thereby induced P to transfer the property to him.[13] If in *Edwards v Ddin* it could

9. Unless the case is caught by s. 5(4) which is considered below, p. 518.
10. [1976] 3 All ER 705, 63 Cr App Rep 218, DC; *Greenberg* [1972] Crim LR 331, QS; and *Corcoran v Whent* [1977] Crim LR 52, DC, are to the same effect. See further below, p. 520.
11. The position is the same at a self-service filling station. If D, intending not to pay, fills his tank with petrol and makes off, the property in the petrol passes and he may not be convicted of theft; see above p. 491.
12. But on the view of the law taken by the Court of Appeal in *Lawrence* [1971] 1 QB 373 at 375, [1970] 3 All ER 933, below, p. 521 – that facts which would establish a charge of deception may also support a charge of theft – it would make a difference and D could be convicted of theft. See further below, p. 521.
13. And whether or not there is a deception D may in such cases commit the offence of making off without payment contrary to s. 3 of the 1978 Act.

have been shown that all along D did not intend to pay that would have been a deception as to his intention to pay and by that deception he obtained the petrol. Similarly, it is submitted, *Lawrence*[14] would have presented no problems had D been charged with deception. By his conduct he represented that £1 would not suffice for the fare and by that deception he obtained the money. It is then quite unnecessary to determine whether D obtained ownership of the money because the offence under s. 15 may be committed whether D obtains ownership *or* possession *or* control.

The moral is plain. If D has by fraud caused P to part with his property the simple and sensible course is usually to charge him with deception contrary to s. 15. But this course was not adopted in *Lawrence* and it was therefore necessary to determine whether ownership of the money passed from P to D. If it did then it could not be shown that D appropriated property belonging to another, and whether it did depended on P's intention. Clearly the ownership of the first £1 (D was not charged with stealing this) passed to D by delivery. The ownership of the £6 would have equally passed by delivery by the same token. As it happened, however, P did not deliver the money; it was taken from P's wallet by D and when he took the money it was at that very moment still the property of P. It is only necessary that the property should belong to another at the instant of appropriation and, as Viscount Dilhorne put it, "[T]he money in the wallet which [D] appropriated belonged to [P]."[15]

The second problem is whether P's consent to what is done by D prevents D's conduct from amounting to an appropriation. In *Lawrence* Viscount Dilhorne, while accepting that D's belief in P's consent is relevant on the issue of dishonesty, apparently denied that consent could ever be relevant to the issue of appropriation:

"Belief or the absence of belief that the owner had ... consented to the appropriation is relevant to the issue of dishonesty, not to the question whether or not there has been an appropriation."[16]

But a consideration of what P has consented to is surely relevant in considering whether D has done something in relation to the property that he is not authorised to do for until D has done something he is not authorised to do there can be no appropriation: *Morris*.[17] In what respect was D in *Lawrence* dealing with the money in an unauthorised way? In *Morris* Lord Roskill said, "That there was in [*Lawrence*] an appropriation was beyond question."[18] But perhaps it is not quite beyond question. Suppose that in *Lawrence* D had somehow conveyed to P that the correct fare was £5 and P had handed over £5. P has been defrauded of course but nothing done thereafter by D with the money can amount to an appropriation since it becomes D's money. However, it is to be noted that in *Lawrence* Viscount Dilhorne did not think that P had consented: "In my opinion, the facts of this case to which I have referred fall far short of

14. [1972] 1 QB 373, [1971] 2 All ER 1253, HL; **SHC 434**.
15. [1971] 2 All ER 1253 at 1255.
16. [1971] 2 All ER 1253 at 1255.
17. [1984] AC 320, [1983] 3 All ER 288, above, p. 491.
18. [1983] 3 All ER 288 at 292.

establishing that [P] consented."[19] If it was the case, then, that P had really
no idea of what D was taking from his wallet or was too bewildered or timid
to protest the taking,[20] then the way is open to holding that there was an
appropriation and on that ground[1] the decision may be defended.

g) *Appropriation, consent and intimidation.* Where P is obliged to hand
over property because he has been intimidated by D into so doing, P might
be said to assent to the handing over but he is unlikely in any real sense to
assent to the appropriation of his property by D, and accordingly D may be
convicted of theft. Difficulty arises where D demands that P transfer
ownership to him, as by forcing P to make a gift or sale of the property. It
might be thought on principle that P does not in fact transfer ownership.
There is no real intention on P's part to do so; the property still belongs to
him and D may be convicted of stealing it.

It is thought that this is the position of law. Though there are cases
supporting the view that duress renders a contract voidable rather than
void,[2] it has been cogently argued[3] that duress ought to render a contract
void. Textbook writers who formerly favoured the voidable theory now
express themselves more cautiously.[4] If duress renders a contract voidable
only, then D would not commit theft because ownership would be
transferred notwithstanding the intimidation, and the property would
belong to D, not to P.

Again the problem may be obviated: this time by charging D with
blackmail contrary to s. 21 of the Act.[5] In this sort of situation D is making
an unwarranted demand with menaces and, so far as blackmail is concerned, it does not matter whether D obtains ownership or not. The
problem would not be obviated, however, by charging D with robbery
under s. 8 since robbery is merely an aggravated form of stealing. Suppose
that D wishes to purchase a particular painting from P but P is unwilling to
sell. D thereupon threatens P with violence unless he does sell so P hands
over the painting and receives payment. D might now be convicted of
blackmail, but can he be convicted of theft or robbery? It is submitted that
he can. The civil cases, such as they are, are hardly decisive since the result
in them would have been the same whether the contract was considered
void or voidable. It is difficult to resist the conclusion that:

---

19. [1971] 2 All ER 1253 at 1254.
20. "It may well be that when [in cross-examination through an interpreter] P used the word
'permitted', he meant no more than that he had allowed the money to be taken. It certainly was
not established at the trial that he had agreed to pay a sum far in excess of the legal fare for the
journey and so had consented to the acquisition by [D] of the £6": [1971] 2 All ER 1253 at
1254.
  1. Alternatively it may be said that when P proffered the wallet he authorised D only to take
the correct fare and in taking more than that D was doing what he was not authorised to do.
Contra, Williams [1977] Crim LR 208n.
  2. *Whelpdale's Case* (1604) 5 Co Rep 119a; *Barton v Armstrong* [1976] AC 104, [1975] 2 All
ER 465, PC.
  3. By Lanham, "Duress and Void Contracts" (1966) 29 Mod LR 615. And see Hooper,
"Larceny by Intimidation" [1965] Crim LR 532 and 592.
  4. See, e.g., Cheshire, Fifoot and Furmston's, *The Law of Contract* (11th ed.), 296; Treitel,
The Law of Contract (7th ed.), 312.
  5. Below, p. 588.

". . . in all contracts it is essential that there should be consent. Not even the officious by-stander would care to testify that a person with a gun to his head appeared to consent to the transaction in hand, whatever kind of contract was involved."[6]

So far it has been assumed that the duress takes the form of physical harm to P, actual or threatened. But what if the threat is not one to use physical violence? Suppose, for example, that D, a newspaper proprietor, tells P that unless P pays him money he will attack the creditworthiness of P's business in his newspaper, and P pays the money demanded.[7] This is best treated as a case of blackmail, but could D also be convicted of stealing the money? Does D become the owner of the money or does the money still belong to P? Again an earlier case implies that ownership does not pass to D in this situation, but the particular point was not argued.[8] Much might depend on the nature of the threat;[9] not every threat will necessarily nullify P's assent to the appropriation. The common sense approach would be

". . . to pose the question 'was there consent' or perhaps 'would the officious by-stander say that [P] consented to the transaction?' This would be a question of fact in each case, though the nature of the threat would always be a very important factor."[10]

In cases of doubt, however, it would be better, if the facts will support it, to charge blackmail or deception.

h) *The exception in favour of bona fide purchasers.* Notwithstanding that there is no general limitation on liability for theft in favour of persons acquiring property innocently in the first place, s. 3 (2) of the Act imposes a particular limitation in favour of bona fide purchasers. Section 3 (2) provides:

"Where property or a right or interest in property is or purports to be transferred for value to a person acting in good faith, no later assumption by him of rights which he believed himself to be acquiring shall, by reason of any defect in the transferor's title, amount to theft."

The Criminal Law Revision Committee explained this exception as follows:[11]

"A person may buy something in good faith, but may find out afterwards that the seller had no title to it, perhaps because the seller or somebody else stole it. If the buyer nevertheless keeps the thing or otherwise deals with it as owner, he could . . . be guilty of theft. It is arguable that this would be right; but on the whole it seems to us that, whatever view is

---

6. Lanham, "Duress and Void Contracts" (1966) 29 MLR 615, 619. Cf. *McGrath* (1869) LR 1 CCR 205; *Lovell* (1881) 8 QBD 185; and see further Smith, *Theft*, paras. 43–44.

7. Cf. *Boyle and Merchant* [1914] 3 KB 339.

8. *Boyle and Merchant*, see last footnote.

9. Cf. *Chapman* [1974] Crim LR 488, CA. D was convicted of theft when by his "overbearing conduct" he caused P, an elderly man, to sell property to him.

10. Lanham, op. cit., 621. And see above, p. 382. Cf. *Clear* [1968] 1 QB 670, [1968] 1 All ER 74, CA – "[T]here is no intent to steal unless there is an intent to take without the true consent of the [owner] . . . But there can be such an intent without that person being deprived of "that element of free, voluntary action which alone constitutes consent" in the words used by Wilde B".

11. Cmnd. 2977, para. 37.

taken of the buyer's moral duty, the law would be too strict if it made him guilty of theft."

The exception is in favour only of a person acquiring his interest in good faith and for value. It would extend to a pledgee or a person acquiring a lien as well as a buyer of property; but if a pledgee, having discovered the pledgor's lack of title, were to, say, destroy the property he might be guilty of theft because he is assuming rights greater than those which he believed he had acquired.

i) *Appropriation as a continuing act.* For certain purposes it may be important to determine whether appropriation is an instantaneous act, or whether it is a continuing one and, if so, for how long it continues.

At one extreme it might be suggested that the appropriation continues so long as the stolen property continues to be in D's possession. This would create obvious difficulties with the offence of handling. Handling is a more serious offence than theft and is constituted by receiving (and other dealings in) stolen goods "otherwise than in the course of the stealing".[12] If the appropriation continued while the thief had possession there would be little or no scope for handling so the notion that appropriation continues so long as the thief has possession must be rejected.

At the other extreme it may be suggested that appropriation is an instantaneous act. This view was apparently taken in *Pitham and Hehl*[13] where D invited E and F to make offers for P's furniture. It was held that by offering P's furniture for sale[14] D stole it; the property instantly became stolen property and it was held that E and F could be convicted of handling because their receiving was not in the course of the stealing.

The third possibility is that appropriation continues for so long as the thief can sensibly be regarded as in the act of stealing. This was the view taken in *Hale*[15] where the court rejected an argument that D and E were not guilty of robbery in using force against P seconds after property had been seized ... The appropriation was of course complete when the property was seized but it could fairly be regarded as continuing during the time taken to remove it from the house. This view, with respect, is sensible and ought to be the one which is preferred.

2 Property

The property which may be stolen is defined in s. 4 of the Theft Act 1968, and the broad effect of this section is that all property may be stolen subject to certain exceptions in relation to land, wild growth and wild creatures. Section 4 (1) provides the general definition:

"'Property' includes money and all other property, real or personal, including things in action and other intangible property."

The one limitation on the generality of this definition, apart from the specified exceptions, is that the property must be capable of appropriation.

---

12. Below, p. 626.
13. (1976) 65 Cr App Rep 45, CA, above p. 627.
14. See above, p. 497.
15. (1978) 68 Cr App Rep 415, [1979] Crim LR 596, CA, below, p. 542. Cf. *Gregory* (1982) 74 Cr App Rep 154, CA.

It is easy enough to visualise how tangible property, such as land or goods, may be appropriated, but the definition also extends to intangible property and it may be as well to illustrate how intangible property may be appropriated. The short answer, of course, is that intangible property may be appropriated by any assumption of the rights of an owner in respect of it.[16] Thus a debt might be appropriated by D where he causes the bank[17] to debit P's account and to credit his own.[18] D may not yet have withdrawn from his account the money so credited, but he has already appropriated the debt which the bank owes to P. So if D causes the Q company to transfer P's shares into D's name in the company's books, D has appropriated the shares.[19] In *Kohn*[20] D, an accountant, given cheques by his employers to meet their liabilities, drew cheques on their accounts for his own purposes. His conviction for theft was upheld; the employers' bank accounts were choses in action (i.e. each employer was owed the money that stood to his credit) and to cause the accounts to be diminished[1] was an appropriation of the chose belonging to the employers. On the other hand where D, knowing that his own account is overdrawn, uses his banker's card so that the bank is obliged to meet cheques drawn by him, D does not steal from the bank.[2] The bank is obliged to meet the cheque and its funds are thereby diminished but no chose has been appropriated; nothing which the bank owes to X has been transferred to Y.

On the face of it all property is capable of appropriation but there was formerly doubt whether electricity was capable of appropriation since the dishonest use, wasting or diverting of electricity is a separate offence under s. 13 of the Theft Act, and the Criminal Law Revision Committee observed that:

"This has to be a separate offence because owing to its nature electricity is excluded from the definition of stealing in . . . [s.] 1 (1) of the [Act]."[3]

The Committee's view was endorsed in *Low v Blease*[4] where it was held that, electricity not being property capable of appropriation, D could not be convicted of burglary in entering premises and making a telephone call from them. It has also been held[5] that confidential information, though it has a value and can be sold, is not property within s. 4 (1); accordingly an undergraduate was not guilty of theft where he unlawfully acquired an examination paper and returned it after he had read its contents.[6] While it

---

16. See *Storrow and Poole* [1983] Crim LR 332.

17. It is not enough that D himself by making false entries in the bank's books or by interfering with the bank's computerized accounts causes other accounts to be diminished and his own account to be enhanced for this does not involve an application by D of the choses in action belonging to the other customers: *Thompson* [1984] 3 All ER 565, [1984] 1 WLR 962, CA.

18. Cf. *Davenport* [1954] 1 All ER 602. See now *Chan Man-sin v A-G for Hong Kong* [1988] 1 All ER 1, PC.

19. See Smith, *Theft*, para. 100 for further discussion.

20. (1979) 69 Cr App Rep 395, CA. See further Griew, "Stealing and Obtaining Bank Credits" [1986] Crim LR 356.

1. The appropriation may have been complete when D drew up the cheques in an unauthorised way, see Smith, *Theft*, para. 106.

2. *Navvabi* [1986] 3 All ER 102, [1986] 1 WLR 1311, CA.

3. Cmnd. 2977, para. 85, below, p. 539.

4. [1975] Crim LR 513, DC.

5. *Oxford v Moss* (1978) 68 Cr App Rep 183, [1979] Crim LR 119.

6. But see commentary at [1979] Crim LR 119.

does seem to be the case that the "theft" of information is a serious problem for which the civil law may not provide adequate remedies, it would also seem, as Griew observes,[7] that the Theft Act is not the appropriate instrument to deal with this specialised kind of mischief.

a) *Limitations on the theft of land.* It should be appreciated at the outset that it would have been technically possible to make land stealable in general, since land is just as capable of appropriation as goods; such limitations as there are arise from policy considerations. Take, for example, the case (which has apparently occurred from time to time) where D moves the boundary fence between his and P's property and thus annexes some of P's land. Supposing this is done dishonestly there are no obstacles in the way of treating this as theft. D has appropriated land belonging to P with intent to deprive him permanently of it. But the Criminal Law Revision Committee, for a number of reasons[8] (such as that appropriating land by encroachment was not so widespread or socially evil that civil remedies were insufficient,[9] the civil law might give D a good title by occupation for twelve years and it would be odd if he remained even theoretically guilty of theft for ever afterwards), felt that such a case ought not to be treated as theft and s. 4 (2) gives effect to this view. Section 4 (2) of the Theft Act 1968 provides:

"A person cannot steal land, or things forming part of land and severed from it by him or by his directions, except in the following cases, that is to say –

(a) when he is a trustee or personal representative, or is authorised by power of attorney, or as liquidator of a company, or otherwise, to sell or dispose of land belonging to another, and he appropriates the land or anything forming part of it by dealing with it in breach of the confidence reposed in him; or

(b) when he is not in possession of the land and appropriates anything forming part of the land by severing it or causing it to be severed, or after it has been severed; or

(c) when, being in possession of the land under a tenancy, he appropriates the whole or part of any fixture or structure let to be used with the land.

For purposes of this subsection 'land' does not include incorporeal hereditaments; 'tenancy' means a tenancy for years or any less period and includes an agreement for such a tenancy, but a person who after the end of a tenancy remains in possession as statutory tenant or otherwise is to be treated as having possession under the tenancy, and 'let' shall be construed accordingly."

i) *Appropriation by trustees etc.*[10] The rule here is that land, or things forming part of the land, are capable of being stolen. Thus a trustee may appropriate land held in trust by an unauthorised disposition. Of

---

7. *Theft*, pp. 16–17. See further Hammond, "Theft of Information" (1984) 100 LQR 252.
8. Cmnd. 2977, paras. 40–44.
9. But the Committee observed (ibid., para. 42) that moving boundaries was a "real problem, especially in crowded housing estates." Cf. the offence under s. 11 (below p. 578) which seems to owe its origin to *three* known instances of its occurrence.
10. See Brazier, "Criminal Trustees?" (1975) 39 Conv (NS) 29.

course an unauthorised dealing is not of itself theft since the other requirements of the offence must be present. If, for example, a trustee is authorised to sell the land only to A and he sells it to B because B is offering a much better price, the unauthorised sale by the trustee may not be dishonest.

ii) *Appropriation by persons not in possession.* Here, as has been shown, the rule is that land as such cannot be stolen by a person not in possession. However a person not in possession can steal anything forming part of the land by severing it or by appropriating it after it has been severed. Thus it may be theft where D helps himself to the topsoil in P's garden, or to a gate, or to rose bushes, or even to growing grass.[11] In each case the appropriation is complete upon severance,[12] but where the thing is already severed, as where the gate is lying in P's yard for repair, the appropriation would be complete, at the latest, when D takes control of it.

iii) *Appropriation by tenants of fixtures.* A tenant cannot steal the land of which he stands possessed nor things forming part of the land. If D, a tenant, removes topsoil from the demised premises to sell to a neighbour he is appropriating property of another (the landlord) but he is not guilty of theft. But if D's son, who is living with D, removes the topsoil for the same purpose the son would be guilty of theft because he is not "in possession" of the land although he happens to live there.

A tenant may be guilty of theft, however, where he appropriates (and here severance is not required) any fixture or structure let to be used with the land. A fixture here means something annexed to land for use or ornament, such as a washbasin, cupboards or fireplace, and a structure seems to mean some structure of a moveable or temporary character, such as a garden shed or a greenhouse. A house would not be a structure in this sense.

b) *Limitations on the theft of things growing wild.* Section 4 (3) of the Act provides:

"A person who picks mushrooms growing wild on any land, or who picks flowers, fruit or foliage from a plant growing wild on any land, does not (although not in possession of the land) steal what he picks, unless he does it for reward or for sale or other commercial purpose.

For purposes of this subsection 'mushroom' includes any fungus, and 'plant' includes any shrub or tree."

In some ways it might be thought that s. 4 (3) is rather an unnecessary provision. It exempts from liability for theft one who picks wild mushrooms, or one who picks flowers, fruit or foliage "*from* a plant" (thus a

---

11. In 1972 a man was prosecuted at Leeds Crown Court for stealing Cleckheaton railway station by dismantling and removing it. He was acquitted on the merits, the jury accepting that on this bold enterprise he was acting under a claim of right. But railway stations are stealable by severance.

12. Note that if D is caught in the act of severing he is guilty only of an attempt. By attempting to sever D is of course assuming the rights of an owner and in other circumstances, (above, p. 495), this alone constitutes a complete appropriation. But in this case the effect of the subsection is to insist upon severance to complete the theft.

person who takes the whole plant may be convicted of theft) growing wild
on land unless done for sale or other commercial purpose. Picking holly
branches round about Christmas time for the purpose of sale may amount
to theft as may picking elderberries for making wine if the purpose is to sell
the wine. The whole matter might have been left to the common sense of
the prosecutor who would hardly institute proceedings where the appropriation was trivial. Of course this would leave the aggrieved landowner
free to take proceedings in such trivial cases, but generally under the
criminal law the person aggrieved is free to take proceedings in the most
trivial case and this does not apparently lead to any serious abuse.
However, the Criminal Law Revision Committee thought that

> "a provision could reasonably be criticized which made it even techni-
> cally theft in all cases to pick wild flowers against the will of the
> landowner."[13]

c) *Limitations on the theft of wild creatures.* Section 4 (4) of the Act
provides:

> "Wild creatures, tamed or untamed, shall be regarded as property; but a
> person cannot steal a wild creature not tamed nor ordinarily kept in
> captivity, or the carcase of any such creature, unless either it has been
> reduced into possession by or on behalf of another person and possession
> of it has not since been lost or abandoned, or another person is in course
> of reducing it into possession."

Wild animals while at large are not owned by anyone, nor does a
landowner have a proprietary interest in such animals even where they
constitute game. The landowner has the right to take wild animals and once
a wild animal is caught or killed it immediately becomes the property of the
landowner where this takes place, but he has no proprietary interest in such
animals while at large. Technically the person catching or killing the animal
would not, at that precise moment, be guilty of theft since he is not then
appropriating the property of another. But since, as has been shown,[14] a
person may commit theft, even where he has come by the property
innocently, by any subsequent assumption of ownership, there would be no
difficulty in finding such an assumption at a later stage. Indeed, unless the
catcher immediately releases it, or the killer does nothing about appropriating the carcase, each would be guilty of theft.

Though this would be the position under the general law of theft, s. 4 (4)
creates an exception which is, substantially, in favour of poaching. Thus if
D takes rabbits running wild on P's land he is not guilty of theft, though he
may commit an offence in relation to poaching,[15] and in this case it does not
become theft though the poacher takes the rabbit for purposes of sale.

---

13. Cmnd. 2977, para. 47. The Conservation of Wild Creatures and Wild Plants Act 1975
makes it an offence to kill, possess or sell certain creatures; and to pick, uproot or destroy
certain wild plants.
14. Above, p. 497.
15. For poaching offences see Stone's *Justices' Manual*, 4–4251 et seq.

It is, however, possible to steal wild creatures where these have been tamed or are ordinarily kept in captivity. A tiger may be stolen from a zoo, and if it has escaped it may be stolen while at large because it is "ordinarily" kept in captivity. Wild animals may also be stolen when they are in process of being reduced into possession by or on behalf of another. A lazy poacher who picks up the pheasants shot from the skies by P is a thief, as is a gamekeeper who keeps for himself a pheasant which he shot for his employer. And if P, having shot a pheasant, cannot find it in the brush and gives up the search, a subsequent appropriation by D makes him a thief from the landowner.[16]

3 Belonging to Another

At first sight it is a perfectly obvious proposition that a man may steal only the property of another. But appearances can be deceptive. In the vast majority of cases there is of course no difficulty. D snatches P's handbag; the handbag is owned and possessed by P and clearly D has appropriated property belonging to P. In some cases, however, it may not be quite so clear to whom the handbag belongs or whether it belongs to anyone at all.

Moreover property in a given case may belong to both D and P; they may, for example, be joint owners of the property. Obviously there is no reason in principle why D should not be treated as a thief if he dishonestly appropriates P's share. This was the view taken by the Court of Appeal in *Bonner*[17] where it was held that a partner can steal partnership property.

It is easy enough to accept the good sense of the idea that D may steal property belonging to himself if it also belongs to another, but there are also situations in which, though the property in law belongs only to D, it is desirable that his dishonest appropriation of it should be treated as theft. Take a simple illustration suggested by the facts of *Hassall*.[18] There members of a club paid sums of money each week to D, the treasurer, on the understanding that the following Christmas D would return to each member the total sum paid in; but in fact D misappropriated the money. In this situation D becomes the owner of the money (it was never expected that D should return to each member the identical coins given him) and the relationship between D and the members is essentially that of trustee and beneficiaries. Here is a situation where the property in law belongs to D,[19] but it is a case in which D ought to be treated as a thief and ought not to be allowed to shelter behind his legal ownership. Accordingly, s. 5 provides that in some cases, notwithstanding that D is the owner of the property, the property shall be treated as belonging to another so long as that other has some proprietary right or interest in the property. Once more the basic idea is simple enough to grasp but it can lead to difficulties in application.

This, in broad outline, explains the purport of s. 5. The section may now be looked at in more detail.

16. As to abandoment, see below, p. 524.
17. [1970] 2 All ER 97, [1970] 1 WLR 838.
18. (1861) Le & Ca 56.
19. See further below, p. 513.

a) *Property belonging to another: the general rule.* Section 5 (1) of the Theft Act 1968 provides:

> "Property shall be regarded as belonging to any person[20] having possession or control of it, or having in it any proprietary right or interest (not being an equitable interest arising only from an agreement to transfer or grant an interest)."

In the ordinary case property is stolen from one who both owns and possesses it by one who has no interest in the property whatever. Section 5 (1) covers this case of course but it goes much further. Suppose that P lends a book to Q and that Q is showing the book to R when D snatches the book from R's hands and makes off with it. Here D has stolen the book (who has control of it), and Q (who has possession of it), and P (who also has a proprietary interest – ownership – in it).

As we have just seen it does not matter that the property happens to belong to D in one of these senses if at the same time it also belongs to P and it is D's intention dishonestly to deprive P permanently of his interest. Thus in the above illustration if R were dishonestly to appropriate the book he would steal it from both P and Q,[1] and if Q were to dishonestly appropriate the book he would steal it from P.

Conversely D, an owner, may steal the book from P, his bailee. While the book is in P's possession it belongs to P for the purposes of s. 5 (1) which does not place any limitations on the class of persons who may steal from him. Of course the circumstances in which D's appropriation of his own property will amount to theft will not be of common occurrence since D may easily be able to show a claim of right.[2] But consider *Turner (No. 2)*.[3] D had left his car with P for repair, promising to pay for the repairs when he returned to collect the car the following day. D, however, returned a few hours later and surreptitiously took back his car. Although D claimed that he was entitled to do as he did, it was clear from the circumstances that he was acting dishonestly, and his conviction for stealing the car from P was affirmed.

At first sight this seems obviously right because D was out to cheat P of his repairer's lien; even as against the owner D the car could be properly regarded as belonging to P so long as he had his lien. Unfortunately the trial judge told the jury to disregard the question of the lien and the case is accordingly authority for saying that D may steal from his own bailee at will, that is although D is entitled to determine the bailment *at any time*. Such a bailee so long as he remains in possession undoubtedly has a

---

20. The person to whom the property belongs will usually be known and identified in the indictment, but if the owner is unknown D may be charged with stealing the property of a person unknown provided that this does not result in D being unable to ascertain the nature of the case he has to meet. Cf. *Gregory* [1972] 2 All ER 861 at 866, CA (handling property of person unknown); and see *Anglim and Cooke v Thomas* [1974] VR 363 at 374 (SC of Victoria).

1. Cf. *Thompson* (1862) Le & Ca 225. D made off with a sovereign which P handed him to buy a ticket for her because she was unable to make her way through the crowd before a ticket office. This would be theft by D. Cf. *Rose v Matt* [1951] 1 KB 810, [1951] 1 All ER 361, DC.

2. Below, p. 526.

3. [1971] 2 All ER 441, CA; **SHC 423** Cf. *Meredith* [1973] Crim LR 253; **SHC 424**.

proprietary right or interest against third parties, but it seems odd to regard him as having such an interest against the bailor when the latter has decided, whether by notice or otherwise, to determine the bailment. That P has lawful possession of the property is not in itself enough. So in *Meredith*,[4] where D surreptitiously removed his car from a police pound where it had been lawfully placed by the police for causing an obstruction, it was held that D could not be convicted of stealing the car. The police were lawfully in possession of it so that a third party could have stolen it from them but as against D they had no right to retain it though they did have a right to enforce the statutory charge for its removal. The police, unlike the repairer in *Turner (No. 2)*,[5] were not bailees of the car but (disregarding the repairer's lien) the repairer in *Turner (No. 2)* seems to have been in a position analogous to that of the police in *Meredith*.

   i) *Possession or control*. To a degree possession and control may overlap, and it is not important to pursue any possible distinction between them because property is treated as belonging to P if he has either possession or control. It is the limits of these concepts which are important, not the difference between them.

   Possession requires both an intention to possess and some degree of dominion in fact. If P and D both see a wallet on the pavement, both may have the same intent to possess it, but until one of them seizes it neither has possession. Once P seizes it he has both possession and control. If he hands it to D just to show D what he has got, it would normally be said that P retains possession while D has control.

   Possession and control are not, however, always as clear cut as in this illustration. There P's intent existed in respect of a specific article and he reduced it into his actual control – he had it in his hands. But it is not necessary to have, or ever to have had, control of a thing in this sense in order to have possession. An Electricity Board may have possession of the coins inserted in a domestic meter although the Board does not know at any given moment how many coins, if any, are in the meter.[6] Similarly, a householder normally has possession of the whole contents of his house even though he cannot itemise his goods. He may consign unwanted articles to his attic or cellar and forget about them, but he still retains possession. It is not, then, essential that P's intent should exist in respect of a specific thing: it may be enough for P's intent to exist in respect of all the goods situate about his premises. In *Woodman*[7] P sold all the scrap metal on certain disused business premises to Q; Q removed most of it but left some as being too inaccessible to be worth the expense of removal. D then entered the premises to take some of this scrap and was held to have been rightly convicted of its theft. P continued to control the site and

---

4. [1973] Crim LR 253 CC; **SHC 424.**
5. [1971] 2 All ER 441, supra.
6. Cf. *Martin v Marsh* [1955] Crim LR 781. But see [1956] Crim LR 74.
7. [1974] QB 754, [1974] 2 All ER 955, CA; **SHC 421** See also *Hibbert v McKiernan* [1948] 2 KB 142, [1948] 1 All ER 860, DC (theft of golf balls lost on club premises); *Williams v Phillips* (1957) 41 Cr App Rep 5, DC (theft of refuse from dustbins).

his conduct in erecting fences and posting notices showed that he intended to exclude others from it; that was enough to give him control of the scrap which Q did not wish to remove.[8]

ii) *Any proprietary right or interest.* Property is also to be regarded as belonging to any person having in it "any proprietary right or interest". Obviously, then, property may be stolen from the owner although at the time of the appropriation the owner is not in possession or control; and even though the owner may never have been in possession or control. If D sells goods to P (ownership passing to P) and D remains in possession, a dishonest appropriation by E will be theft from both D and P. Moreover if D dishonestly appropriates the goods he steals them from P.[9] The section extends to "*any* proprietary right or interest", and whether a person has a proprietary right or interest is a question of civil law. A person who owns, possesses or controls property has a proprietary right or interest in the property, but in what other circumstances a proprietary right or interest may exist is somewhat speculative.[10] In an American case[11] P purchased flowers from D which he laid on the grave of a friend; D entered the cemetery that night and took back the flowers in order to sell them again. It was held that P retained a proprietary interest in the flowers so that D could steal them from P, and it was indicated that Q, the owner of the cemetery, would also have a proprietary interest so that the flowers could be stolen from Q as well. But in this case it could fairly be said that P retained possession of the flowers,[12] and that Q, at least if he looked after the cemetery lot, would have control of them. In *Rose v Matt*[13] Lord Goddard CJ spoke of a pledgee as having a "special property" in the pledge, but the special property is possession.

D may appropriate property which belongs to P in any of the senses described in s. 5 (1). It does not matter that P's interest is precarious or that it may be short-lived; wild birds reared by P may belong to P although they may "betake themselves to the woods and fields" as soon as they are old enough to fly.[14] It does not matter that someone

---

8. Cf. *Rowe* (1859) 8 Cox CC 139, where D, employed to clean out P's canal, was convicted of stealing in appropriating iron found by him on the bed of the canal. For a case holding that P became the owner of coins thrown into his fountain for luck, see (1964) Times, 8th August. But cf. *Bridges v Hawkesworth* (1851) 21 LJQB 75, which is authority for the proposition that a person finding property in the public part of a shop is entitled to the property as against the shopkeeper; consequently the property so found does not belong to the shopkeeper and cannot be stolen from him. Cf. *Parker v British Airways Board* [1982] 1 All ER 834, CA. Presumably the finder of goods on the highway is entitled to the goods as against the highway authority. For a general discussion of the finder's rights as against the landowner see Street, *Torts*, 34.

9. And of course (see above, p. 510) P may steal the goods from D by, say, surreptitiously removing them without payment.

10. Arguably anyone who can sue in trespass, detinue or conversion in respect of the property has a proprietary right or interest. Perhaps anyone who may trace the property at law or in equity has a proprietary right or interest.

11. *Bustler v State* (1944) 184 SE 2d 24 (SC of Tennessee).

12. Cf. *Edwards and Stacey* (1877) 13 Cox CC 384. As for abandonment, see below, p. 524.

13. [1951] 1 KB 810, [1951] 1 All ER 361 (pledgor of clock dishonestly re-took it from pledgee).

14. Cf. *Shickle* (1868) LR 1 CCR 158.

exists who has a better right to the property than P: a thief may steal from a thief.[15] Any power to exclude others, however small, will suffice.

iii) *Equitable interests*: "Any proprietary right or interest" extends to both legal and equitable proprietary interests. Where property is subject to a trust it belongs to both the trustee (legal interest) and beneficiary (equitable interest) and it may be stolen from either.[16] But in the case of equitable interests s. 5 (1) introduces a limitation, and property is not to be regarded as belonging to a person who has an equitable interest arising only from an agreement to transfer or grant an interest. The limitation is of no great practical importance. In some circumstances an agreement to sell may give the intending buyer an equitable interest in the property[17] and this provision makes it clear that the seller cannot commit theft by reselling the property to another.

b) *Trust property*.[18] Section 5 (2) of the Theft Act 1968 provides:

"Where property is subject to a trust, the persons to whom it belongs shall be regarded as including any person having a right to enforce the trust, and an intention to defeat the trust shall be regarded accordingly as an intention to deprive of the property any person having that right."

In the ordinary case appropriation of trust property by a trustee is covered not only by this subsection but also by s. 5 (1) because the beneficiary ordinarily has a proprietary interest and accordingly the trust property belongs to the beneficiary within s. 5 (1). But in some exceptional circumstances there may be no ascertained beneficiary. This occurs in the case of "purpose" trusts whether charitable[19] or private,[20] where the object is to effect some purpose rather than benefit ascertainable individuals. To meet such cases s. 5 (2) goes further than s. 5 (1) by providing that the property is to be treated as belonging to anyone who has a right to enforce the trust.[1]

c) *Property received for a particular purpose*. It has already been mentioned[2] that it is in some circumstances right that D should be convicted of theft notwithstanding that he is the legal owner of the property, and the case of *Hassall*[3] was given as an illustration of the kind of situation envisaged. In *Hassall*, though D became the legal owner of the money paid in, it would be clear, even to someone who knew no law, that D was not free to do what he liked with the money. He was under an obligation to deal with the money in

---

15. Cf. *Clarke*, referred to at [1956] Crim LR 369–70; *Meech* [1974] QB 549, [1973] 3 All ER 939, CA; above, p. 493.
16. See further s. 5 (2), infra.
17. See Smith, *Theft*, paras. 63–64.
18. Brazier, "Criminal Trustees?"(1975) 39 Conv (NS) 29.
19. E.g., where money is given to D in trust for the improvement of schools in a particular locality.
20. E.g., where money is given to D in trust for the maintenance of a tomb, or for the upkeep of animals.
1. In the foregoing examples this would be, respectively, the Attorney-General and the person entitled to the residue of the estate.
2. Above, p. 510.
3. (1861) Le & Ca 56; above, p. 509.

a particular way. He might have kept the money in a box or he might have kept it in an account at the bank, but, one way or another, he had to keep the fund in existence. Consequently D's dishonest appropriation of the fund would now amount to theft by virtue of s. 5 (3)[4] which provides:

"When a person receives property from or on account of another, and is under an obligation to the other to retain and deal with that property or its proceeds in a particular way, the property or proceeds shall be regarded (as against him) as belonging to the other."

It is easy enough to appreciate that in *Hassall* D was under an obligation to deal with the money deposited in a particular way but it is more difficult to say, in general terms, when a person "is under an obligation to the other to retain and deal with that property or its proceeds in a particular way." The obligation referred to is a *legal* obligation, a moral or social obligation will not do.[5] The essential notion is that D must be under a fiduciary obligation with regard to the property which he receives. The idea of fiduciary obligation conveys accurately the essential requirement: the property, though it may be owned only by D, must be earmarked in D's hands for certain purposes of P's.

Take a simple case of loan. P lends D £10 – and, having received the money, D dishonestly decides never to repay P and subsequently denies that P made the loan. D is not guilty of theft. Clearly D is acting dishonestly and the view might be taken that his case is indistinguishable from that of a Hassall who misappropriates £10 from his workmates' holiday fund; but he is not a thief under the Theft Act. He does not appropriate property belonging to another, and the property (the £10) cannot under the Act be regarded as belonging to another since he was under no obligation whatever to deal with it in a particular way. It was D's to deal with as he liked.[6]

But suppose that D had agreed to do certain work for P and that P made D an advance of £10 on the agreed price for the job. If D does not do the

---

4. It would seem to be the case that D's appropriation of the money would amount to theft even without s. 5 (3). The depositors surely retain a proprietary right or interest in the money deposited in such circumstances. Indeed in all cases falling within s. 5 (3) it seems clear that the person from, or on whose account, the property is received would have a proprietary right or interest and thus the case would be covered by s. 5 (1). However, s. 5 (3) does make the point explicitly clear.

5. *Gilks* [1972] 3 All ER 280, CA; *Mainwaring* (1981) 74 Cr App Rep 99. But in *Cullen* (1974) unreported (No. 968/C/74) D's conviction was upheld where, living with P as his wife, she appropriated money given her for housekeeping – notwithstanding *Balfour v Balfour* [1919] 2 KB 571, the court found a "plain" legal obligation. But where people, not members of a family, share premises and the outgoings, it becomes easy to infer that legal relationships are intended so that if one of their number, given money or cheques to meet the outgoings, appropriates the money or cheques the case falls within s. 5 (3): *Davidge v Bunnett* [1984] Crim LR 297, DC. In *Meech* [1974] QB 549, [1973] 3 All ER 939, CA, the facts of which are given above, p. 493, it was concluded that D was under a legal obligation to pay the proceeds of the cheque to P. No doubt D was properly convicted because P had a proprietary right or interest in the money but it is questionable whether D was under a legal obligation in respect of the proceeds of the cheque because P would have been unable to recover them in a civil action. See further Smith, *Theft*, paras. 72–74.

6. Cf. *Police v Leaming* [1975] 1 NZLR 471 – D not guilty of theft in obtaining an illicit commission in the course of his employment because no trust arises in the case of an illicit commission; the relationship between an employer and a servant who has obtained an illicit commission is that of creditor and debtor.

work, and never intended to do it, it may be that D can be convicted of obtaining the £10 by deception; but he cannot be convicted of stealing the £10. Again the money belongs only to him, and, although it was advanced to him in connection with a particular transaction, it was not received by him to deal with in a particular way. D may again spend the £10 as he likes. However it is just in this sort of situation that D, in order to ensure an advance payment, will tell P that he needs cash in advance in order to procure materials for the job. When this happens D will often be guilty of obtaining the money by deception, but he is also guilty of theft because he is now under an obligation to deal with the money in a particular way.

Consequently, whether property has been received under an obligation to deal with it in a particular way depends upon the particular circumstances of the case. If, for example, P were to pay a deposit to D, a trader, for goods to be supplied under a contract of sale, the normal inference from such a transaction would be that D is under no obligation to deal with the deposit in a particular way. D might well pay the deposit into his trading account but he could draw on that account as he wished and would not be obliged to keep in existence a fund representing P's deposit. If, on the other hand, P were to give D, his secretary, £100 with instructions to go to a travel agency and purchase a ticket for a flight, the normal inference would be that D is under an obligation to deal with the £100 in a particular way. In such a case it would normally be clearly envisaged by both parties that D will apply that particular £100 to the purchase of the ticket; but in the first illustration it would not normally be envisaged by the parties that the trader will apply the deposit to the particular purpose of purchasing the goods that P has ordered.

The difficulties are well illustrated by *Hall*.[7] D, a partner in a firm of travel agents, had received money from P and others as deposits for air trips to America. The flights never materialised and the deposits, which had been paid into the firm's general trading account, were never returned. The Court of Appeal had no difficulty in accepting the jury's verdict that D had acted dishonestly in spending this money, but quashed D's conviction for theft on the ground that D had not received the money under an obligation to deal with it in a particular way. The court reached this conclusion with obvious reluctance –

"Nevertheless, when a client goes to a firm carrying on the business of travel agents and pays them money, he expects that in return he will, in due course, receive the tickets and other documents necessary for him to accomplish the trip for which he is paying, and the firm are 'under an obligation' to perform their part to fulfil his expectation and are liable to pay him damages if they do not. But, in our judgment, what was not here established was that these clients expected them 'to retain and deal with that property or its proceeds in a particular way', and that an 'obligation' to do so was undertaken by [D]. We must make clear, however, that each

---

7. [1972] 2 All ER 1009, CA; **SHC 426**; and see *Hayes* (1976) 64 Cr App Rep 82.

case turns on its own facts. Cases could, we suppose, conceivably arise where by some special arrangement (preferably evidenced by documents), the client could impose on the travel agent an 'obligation' falling within s. 5 (3)."[8]

The case shows that it is not enough that a debtor dishonestly dissipates his assets so that when the time comes for payment he has no funds from which to meet his obligations, and it makes no difference that the debtor has dissipated *his* funds in order to defeat his creditors.

Consider another example. Where D, following a sponsored charity event, receives money from sponsors he is, it has been held,[9] and though he becomes the debtor of the charity for the amount involved, under no obligation to retain and deal with that money or its proceeds in a particular way and accordingly he does not steal that money by dishonestly using it for his own purposes. No doubt it is different where money is collected for a charity in a collecting box; here the normal inference must be that the collector is obliged to deal with the box and its contents in a particular way.[10] Account has to be taken of the terms, implied as well as express, of the arrangement between D and P. Where D, a broker, is engaged to collect premiums on behalf of P, D may steal the premiums if the agreement provides that they vest in P[11] but not if the agreement merely makes D P's debtor for the amount of the premiums paid.[12] In both cases the broker has been dishonest and in both the insurer is the loser but in the one case the broker is a thief and in the other he is not; a distinction which may be effected by a few strokes of the pen.

A liability to pay P is accordingly not enough unless D is obliged to keep a fund representing that property in existence. If an employee receives a bribe in contravention of his duty to his employer, the employer may recover the amount of the bribe in a civil action; but the employee cannot steal the bribe by keeping it for himself since the employer acquires no proprietary interest in the bribe or its proceeds.[13] Similarly, if an employee makes a secret profit by selling at his employer's shop goods of his own or of a third party, the employee does not steal the profit by keeping it to himself.[14] The employer may recover the profit by action but he does not acquire in it any proprietary interest in the monies received or their proceeds.

The contract of sale or return is worth noting in this connection. In the ordinary case of sale or return P delivers goods to D on the terms that D will return them within a certain time unless D decides to buy them. Should D sell the goods to a third party he makes himself, vis-à-vis P, the buyer of the goods and must pay the agreed purchase price to P. Suppose then that P delivers jewellery to D which D sells to Q and then absconds with the purchase price. D cannot be convicted of stealing the jewellery for

---

8. [1972] 2 All ER 1009 at 1011.
9. *Lewis v Lethbridge* [1987] Crim LR 59, DC.
10. S. 5 (3) may not be necessary to deal with the case since the collector is merely a bailee of the box and its contents.
11. *Brewster* (1979) 69 Cr App Rep 375, [1979] Crim LR 798, CA.
12. *Robertson* [1977] Crim LR 629 (Judge Rubin QC).
13. *Powell v MacRae* [1977] Crim LR 571, DC.
14. *A-G's Reference (No. 1 of 1985)* [1986] QB 491, [1986] 2 All ER 219, CA.

he has not appropriated it.[15] Does D steal the proceeds? It is submitted that he does not because his only obligation is to pay P the agreed purchase price;[16] he is not, when he receives the money from Q, under any obligation to deal with it in any particular way. In other words, the buyer under a sale or return transaction is in the same position as any other purchaser of goods who has not paid the price: he is no more than P's debtor for the price.

It might be thought that another reason why the buyer under a contract of sale or return is not under an obligation to deal with the proceeds in a particular way is that he receives the proceeds from Q and not from P. But this will not do. Section 5 (3) applies when D receives property "from or on account of another" and clearly D may receive property from Q on the account of P.[17]

Thus it is not necessary that the fiduciary duty should arise out of the transaction between D and the person delivering the property to him; it is enough that D's fiduciary duty arises out of a relationship with a person other than the deliveror. To go back to the sale or return illustration: D's immunity there was not based on the fact that he received the money from Q; it was based on the fact that he did not receive the money from Q on P's account. It would be another matter if D had been simply an agent for the sale of the jewellery. Then D would not become the buyer of the jewellery at all, and the money paid by Q would belong to P and not to D. In this situation D might in fact become the owner of the money (as where it is expected that D will account for the money but is not expected to hand over the very coins and notes which he receives); nonetheless D has a duty to keep the fund of money in existence and his appropriation of it may amount to theft.

From the foregoing discussion it may be seen that whether property has been entrusted for a particular purpose may involve complex questions of law and fact. On principle (a) where the transaction is wholly in writing it ought to be for the judge to rule as a matter of law whether there has been an entrusting for a particular purpose; and (b) where the transaction is oral, or partly oral and partly in writing, it ought to be for the judge to rule what may in law amount to an entrusting for a particular purpose and for the jury to determine whether the property was so entrusted in fact.[18] *Mainwaring*[19] contains an unequivocal statement to this effect –

"Whether or not an obligation arises is a matter of law, because an obligation must be a legal obligation. But a legal obligation arises only in certain circumstances, and in many cases the circumstances cannot be known until the facts are established. It is for the jury, not the judge, to establish the facts.

What, in our judgment, a judge ought to do is this: if the facts relied upon by the prosecution are in dispute he should direct the jury to make their findings on the facts, and then say to them: 'If you find the facts to

15. See above, p. 491.
16. Cf. Hughes, "Sale or Return, Agents and Larceny" [1963] Crim LR 312, 411.
17. Cf. *Grubb* [1915] 2 KB 683.
18. Cf. *Hall* [1972] 2 All ER 1009 at 1012, 1013.
19. (1981) 74 Cr App Rep 99 at 107, CA. Suggestions to the contrary appearing in *Hayes* (1977) 64 Cr App Rep 82, CA, may now be disregarded.

be such-and-such, then I direct you as a matter of law that a legal obligation arose to which s. 5 (3) applies.'"

It was accordingly held in *Mainwaring* that the trial judge was wrong to direct the jury that the defendants were as a matter of law under an obligation. His direction was based on the interpretation of certain receipts and had the issue been exclusively governed by the interpretation of these documents, it is submitted that he would have been right to rule on their effect. But in that case the issue turned on further factors, such as whether certain monies had or had not been paid; the resolution of these facts was the province of the jury and the judge should have instructed them on which findings they might find that the money had been received under an obligation to deal with it in a particular way. In determining whether there is a legal obligation the intentions of the parties must of course be considered, and it may also be relevant to consider such factors as the relationship between them, the nature of the property, previous similar dealings between them, and business practice in similar transactions.[20]

d) *Property got by mistake.* Section 5 (4) of the Theft Act provides:

"Where a person gets property by another's mistake, and is under an obligation to make restoration (in whole or in part) of the property or its proceeds or of the value thereof, then to the extent of that obligation the property or proceeds shall be regarded (as against him) as belonging to the person entitled to restoration, and an intention not to make restoration shall be regarded accordingly as an intention to deprive that person of the property or proceeds."

This provision may be explained by reference to the facts of *Moynes v Coopper*.[1] In this case D, a labourer employed by P, was given an advance of pay by the site agent amounting to £6 19s. 6½d. Unaware that this advance had been made, P's wages clerk paid D the full weekly wage of £7 3s. 4d. and D dishonestly kept all of the money.

The difficulty with this case is that in law the whole of the £7 3s. 4d. belongs to D. The wages clerk made a mistake of course, but his mistake was not such as would prevent ownership of all the money passing to D. Had the clerk known of the advance he would have paid D only 3s. 9½d; nevertheless the clerk did intend to pay the full amount, and he was authorised as P's wages clerk to pay wages. The case is now covered by s. 5 (4) and D steals the excess payment if he dishonestly appropriates it; although D becomes the owner of the money he is under a legal obligation, at the very least, to repay the value of the excess payment.

But why, it may be asked, is all this trouble taken to deal with this particular kind of debtor? In terms of moral turpitude only the finest shading separates a Moynes from the ordinary debtor who dishonestly decides not to repay his loan. Under the former law Moynes was in fact acquitted, but in view of the criticism which his acquittal attracted it was no doubt felt necessary to bring such conduct within the net of the criminal law.

---

20. *Wakeman v Farrar* [1974] Crim LR 136, DC.
  1. [1956] 1 QB 439, [1956] 1 All ER 450.

It may be helpful to consider a mistake of common occurrence in giving too much change. Suppose that a barman makes an error and gives to a customer more change than he is entitled to. The customer realises that a mistake has been made but nevertheless dishonestly[2] decides to keep the excess. Section 5 (4) makes the customer a thief if, but only if, the customer is under a legal obligation to make restoration (in whole or in part) of the money *or* its proceeds *or* the value thereof. The Theft Act provides no guidance on when the customer incurs such an obligation; that can only be determined by reference to the relevant civil law.

The barman may have made one of a variety of mistakes. He may (a) deliver the correct change but to the wrong person; or (b) having correctly calculated the change as 20p, hand the customer a £1 coin thinking it a 20p piece; or (c) incorrectly calculate the change due as £1 when it should have been 20p and pay £1 to the customer. Section 5 (4) covers all three cases but it is not strictly necessary to cover cases (a) and (b) because in these cases the barman's mistake is such that ownership does not pass. The barman retains a proprietary right in the money and s. 5 (1) provides for them.

Case (c) is different. The barman has made a mistake but he has not made a mistake as to whom he is paying the money, nor as to the amount paid. The customer becomes the owner of the money and unless some special provision is made for the case he cannot be convicted of theft. The case is not covered by s. 5 (3) because the customer is under no legal obligation to retain and deal with *that* money or *its* proceeds in a particular way. The customer is, however, obliged to make restoration (to the *value* of 80p in the illustration given) but the obligation does not extend to the coin delivered or its proceeds. Section 5 (4) does of course cover the situation where D is under an obligation to make restoration of the property or its proceeds (and thus there will be some overlap between s. 5 (4) and s. 5 (3)) but s. 5 (4) extends to the case where D's obligation is to restore an amount (the value) equivalent to the sum by which he has been mistakenly enriched.

Section 5 (4) was applied in *A-Gs Reference (No. 1 of 1983)*.[3] D's salary was paid into her bank account by direct debit and on one occasion her employers mistakenly overpaid her by £74.74. The question for the court was: assuming that she dishonestly decided not to restore that money, would she have been guilty of theft. In law she became the owner of the money and, as Lord Jane CJ pointed out, had no special provision been made for the case that would have been an end to the matter. But s. 5 (4) provided for the case. While she, as owner of the chose in action against the bank, was not under an obligation to restore the chose or its proceeds, she was under an obligation to restore the value thereof to her employers.

But it is important to consider why D was under an obligation to make restoration. It is settled law that if owing to a mistake of fact P believes that he is legally obliged to make a payment when he is not, he is entitled to recover the equivalent of the sum so paid.[4] The issue whether D was under

2. It is assumed here that such an appropriation is dishonest but it is a matter on which, perhaps, views may differ, see below, p. 525.

3. [1985] QB 182, [1984] 3 All ER 369, CA. Cf. *Hamid Shadrokh-Cigaei* (1988) Times, 23 February.

4. *Norwich Union Fire Insurance Society Ltd v William H Price Ltd* [1934] AC 455.

a legal obligation was resolved without difficulty in this case but it will be appreciated that it will not always be so straightforward. The law of unjust enrichment[5] is not free from considerable subtlety. This may mean that D's liability for theft may turn upon a consideration of fine points of civil law remote from the central question of D's dishonesty. But this is not the only context in which complex issues of civil law may have to be determined. But while theft must take account of the civil law of mine and thine, s. 5 (4) goes to the very limit in treating property which in law belongs to D as belonging to P provided P has a right of restitution of the value of that property.

There was no evidence in *A-Gs Reference* that D had spent the money that was overpaid or that she had done any act in relation to it. But to meet a possible argument that in doing nothing D cannot intend permanently to deprive the owner, s. 5 (4) further provides that an intention not to make restoration shall be regarded as an intention permanently to deprive.[6]

It will be evident from the foregoing discussion that "obligation" in s. 5 (4) can only refer to a legal obligation imposed by the civil law. This is confirmed by *Gilks*[7] though the case has its complications. P, a bookmaker, mistakenly believing that D had backed a winning horse, overpaid D on the bets he had placed and D, aware of the error, dishonestly decided not to return the overpayment. Since P had made no mistake either as to the amount or the recipient, ownership of the money passed to D. The court was clear that s. 5 (4) was inapplicable. This being a wagering transaction P had no right of restitution in respect of the overpayment so D could be under no legal obligation to make restoration. But the court went on, relying upon an antique and questionable authority under the law of larceny,[8] to uphold D's conviction on the grounds that since P would not have made the overpayment but for his mistake, ownership in the money did not pass to D. This is at odds with the civil law and the holding needs to be reconsidered.

Thus far it has been assumed that P's mistake is self-induced and not induced by any deception on D's part. There is clearly no warrant for drawing any such distinction under s. 5 (4): if property is got by mistake, however induced, D may be convicted of theft *provided* the other elements in the subsection are met. It follows that in some cases D may be convicted of either deception or theft. *Cundy v Lindsay*[9] provides a convenient example of such a case. There the rogue Blenkarn, having induced P to believe that he was dealing with the respected firm of Blenkiron & Co., dishonestly made off with goods consigned by P to Blenkiron & Co. The effect of Blenkarn's fraud was to induce a fundamental mistake; P never intended to deal with Blenkarn so ownership never passed to him. When Blenkarn got his hands on the goods they were still the property of P[10] and Blenkarn could be convicted of theft as well as deception.

5. See Goff & Jones, *The Law of Restitution* (3rd edn., 1986), Ch. 3.
6. But this does not cover a further point. Was there an appropriation? See above, p. 494.
7. [1972] 3 All ER 280, [1972] 1 WLR 1341, CA.
8. *Middleton* (1873) LR 2 CCR 38.
9. (1878) 3 App Cas 459, HL.
10. Blenkarn may be convicted of theft without resort to s. 5 (4); at the time of the appropriation of the property P is still their owner.

In *Cundy v Lindsay* the effect of the fraud was to render the contract void or, more properly stated, the fraud prevented a contract from being formed. More usually fraud renders a contract voidable, that is to say that there is a contract which may (notice *may* not *must*) be set aside by the defrauded party. A classic example is provided by *King's Norton Metal Co Ltd v Edridge,*[11] *Merrett & Co Ltd* where the rogue Wallis induced P to sell and consign goods on credit to him by pretending that he ran a prosperous business. A clear case of obtaining by deception but the question is whether it is also theft by virtue of s. 5 (4). No doubt if Blenkarn and Wallis were in a prison cell together they would be hard put to find any distinction between their frauds but students of the law of contract will know that there was an important difference so far as the civil law is concerned. It is submitted here that there is an equally important distinction so far as the criminal law is concerned. Wallis, unlike Blenkarn, becomes the owner of the goods; they are *his* goods until such time as P elects to set aside (and he may if he wishes choose to confirm it) the contract. But until such time as P sets aside the contract D is under no obligation to make restoration of the goods or their proceeds or the value thereof. He has an obligation to pay the price for the goods but that is a personal obligation he has to P; until such time as the contract is set aside the goods are his. Section 5 (4) requires that at the time of the appropriation D "is" under an obligation; it is not enough that he may become under an obligation. When the contract is set aside by P, D will become under an obligation to restore the goods to P for they are now P's goods and not D's and an appropriation after the contract has been set aside may amount to theft.[12]

The effect of s. 5 (4), it is submitted, is that while it may enable some cases of deception to be treated as theft, it falls way short of enabling all cases of deception to be treated as theft. Some cases of deception may also be treated as theft without resort to s. 5 (4). Whenever as a result of D's deception P is not deprived of his entire proprietary right or interest in the goods (as where D by deception obtains a loan of the goods intending to make off with them) D may be convicted of theft as well as deception. But whenever P is deprived of ownership then, and unless P has a right to restitution so that s. 5 (4) applies, it is thought that D cannot be convicted of theft.

Lawrence[13] might have provided definitive guidance on the relationship between theft and deception. In the Court of Appeal it was argued that D was guilty of obtaining by deception and that accordingly he could not be convicted of theft. This argument is wrong in principle because, as has been indicated above, at least some cases of deception may also constitute theft. It was, with respect, rightly rejected by the Court of Appeal but that court was prepared to go further and said that the fact that a charge could be brought under s. 15 in no way operated to prevent a charge being brought under s. 1, and concluded:

11. (1897) 14 TLR 98, CA.
12. Once again, though, there would be no need to rely on s. 5 (4); D is simply appropriating property belonging to another.
13. [1971] 1 QB 373, [1970] 3 All ER 933, CA; [1972] AC 626, [1971] 2 All ER 1253, HL, above, p. 499.

"It may be that the result of our decision is that in any case where the facts would establish a charge under s. 15 (1) they would also establish a charge under s. 1 (1)."[14]

This conclusion, incidentally, was reached without resort to s. 5 (4). The Court of Appeal then asked the House of Lords whether the two offences were mutually exclusive and that question, quite rightly, was answered in the negative. Viscount Dilhorne was content to say merely that some cases of deception might be charged as theft.[15] It is a pity that the Court of Appeal did not ask whether all cases of deception might be charged as theft. Viscount Dilhorne might have answered that question in the negative since he was of the opinion that there were some cases which fell only within s. 15 and some cases which fell only within s. 1. But there remains the view of the Court of Appeal that all cases of deception may be charged as theft.[16]

e) *Property of corporations.* Property may of course belong to a corporation just as much as to an individual, and may be stolen from a corporation.[17] Normally the legal personality of a corporation continues, notwithstanding changes in membership, until the corporation is dissolved, but in the case of a corporation sole (a bishop of the Established Church for example) a vacancy may occur owing to the death of the incumbent. Section 5 (5) accordingly provides:

"Property of a corporation sole shall be regarded as belonging to the corporation notwithstanding a vacancy in the corporation."

This subsection accordingly provides for a very special case but it may be convenient here to consider other problems which arise in connection with corporations and theft.

Theft is a crime which a corporation may commit provided the conditions for corporate criminal liability are met.[18] Thus if the directors of a company were dishonestly to appropriate property belonging to a rival firm to use in the company's business, the company as well as the directors may be convicted of theft. Nor is there any bar to convicting a director, even if he is the majority shareholder, of stealing from the company. A director is no more entitled to appropriate the company's typewriter than is his secretary. But what if D and E are the sole directors of and shareholders in the company – may D and E steal the typewriter if they take it for their own purposes? May D and E use the company's assets for any purpose of their own though they know that the company's creditors will be defeated thereby without danger of conviction for theft?[19]

---

14. [1970] 3 All ER 933 at 936.
15. [1971] 2 All ER 1253 at 1256.
16. See further, Griew, "Theft and Obtaining by Deception" [1979] Crim LR 292; Williams, "Theft and Voidable Title" [1981] Crim LR 666; Smith "Theft and Voidable Title: A Reply" [1981] Crim LR 677.
17. If D and E hold all the shares in a company they cannot, acting in concert, steal the company's assets for they own them: [1982] Crim LR 829. But either D or E, acting alone, may steal the assets which are jointly owned: *Bonner* [1970] 2 All ER 97n, [1970] 1 WLR 838, above, p. 509.
18. Above, p. 170.
19. Such conduct may amount to the offence of defrauding creditors contrary to the Insolvency Act 1986, s. 207 but this carries only two years' imprisonment which may be thought inadequate for some cases.

If X is in business on his own account he is free to dispose of the assets of the business (for they are his assets) as he wishes and no question of theft can arise even if he dissipates the assets to defeat creditors. If Y and Z form a partnership it is established that either may steal from the other by appropriating the other's share.[20] But it is clear that Y and Z together cannot steal the partnership property (for it is their property) and again even if done to defraud creditors.

Where a company is involved it is not so straightforward.[1] D and E may be the sole directors of and shareholders in DE Ltd but the assets of the company are not theirs; the company is a separate legal entity and is the owner of its own assets. On the face of it D and E may steal the assets of DE Ltd (may appropriate property of *another*) by using the assets for their own purposes. But if D and E do not own the assets of DE Ltd, they control its affairs; DE Ltd can only speak and act through D and E.

The problem was considered in *A-G's Reference (No. 2 of 1982)*.[2] D and E, directors of and sole shareholders in several companies, drew cheques on the accounts of the companies to pay their own creditors and to support their extravagant lifestyle. It was accepted by counsel for D and E that all the elements of theft were present (there was an appropriation of property belonging to another with intent permanently to deprive) except for dishonesty. He argued that by s. 2 (1) (b) of the Act[3] a person does not act dishonestly if he believes that he has "the other's consent" to the appropriation, and here the companies, through the persons who were in entire charge of their affairs, had given their consent to the appropriations. This was rejected on the grounds that none of the companies could be regarded as "the other" for the purposes of this provision. This was not to say that D and E might not have had a defence (they may have believed they had in law a right to deprive the companies of their assets) but the court thought that a jury might properly have concluded on these facts that D and E were acting dishonestly and convicted them of theft.

The argument in *A-G's Reference* thus centred on dishonesty and that there was an appropriation was conceded. In *Roffel*,[4] where the facts were substantially the same, this concession was not made and the High Court of Victoria held,[5] following *Morris*,[6] that there was no appropriation by D and E of the assets of the company. *Morris* required that for an appropriation there must be an unauthorised dealing in the property of another; here the dealings in the assets of the company had been authorised by the company. On this view D and E were not guilty of theft whether the transactions authorised by D and E in the company's behalf were *intra vires* or *ultra vires* the company; in *A-G's Reference* it had been conceded that the

---

20. *Bonner* [1970] 2 All ER 97n, [1970] 1 WLR 838 CA, above, p. 509.
  1. See Sullivan, "Company Controllers, Company Cheques and Theft" [1983] Crim LR 512; Nessen, "Company Controllers, Company Cheques and Theft – An Australian Perspective" [1986] Crim LR 154.
  2. [1984] QB 624, [1984] 2 All ER 216. The reference was from [1982] Crim LR 829. See Dine [1984] Crim LR 397; Sullivan [1984] Crim LR 405.
  3. Below, p. 527.
  4. [1985] VR 511; see comment by Smith (1985) 9 Crim LJ 320.
  5. Applying provisions *in pari materia* with those of the Theft Act 1968.
  6. [1984] AC 320, [1983] 3 All ER 288, HL, above, p. 491.

defendants would have been guilty of theft had the transactions been *ultra vires*.

It is submitted that the view taken in *Roffel* is to be preferred. D is not a thief where he spends his own money on himself even if it is done to defeat creditors. It can make no difference that D gives his money to E for E to spend on himself, whether E is aware of D's impending insolvency or not.[7] By parity of reasoning, if DE Ltd makes a gift of its assets to F, F cannot steal them.[8] In principle it can make no difference that DE Ltd makes the gift to D and E, the sole directors and shareholders.

f) *Ownerless property*. A person cannot steal property that is not owned by another at the time of the appropriation. If there is no person to whom the property belongs in any of the senses set out in s. 5, that property cannot be stolen.

Though "property" and "belonging to another" are widely defined in the Act it would still appear to be the law that a corpse cannot be stolen. In *Doodeward v Spence*,[9] a decision of the High Court of New South Wales where the English authorities are examined, it was held that, while there could be no right of property in a corpse buried in the ordinary way, a proprietary interest could be acquired by one who expended work and skill on the corpse with a view to its preservation on scientific or other grounds. Since the rule of common law is hardly one dictated by logic or by practical considerations (there is no reason why the executors should not at least have possession of the corpse[10]), the limitation suggested in *Doodeward v Spence* seems a sensible one. While it may not be a practical problem in this context, it would be surprising if tissue removed from a dead body for the purpose of a transplant was not at least in the lawful possession of the surgeon.[11]

Property that is capable of belonging to another may be ownerless because it has never been made the subject of ownership. D can commit no offence in taking a swarm of bees not previously owned by another. Conversely, property which has at one time been owned may become ownerless by abandonment. But abandonment is not something to be lightly inferred: property is abandoned only when the owner is indifferent

7. There are provisions in the Insolvency Act 1986 (ss. 339 and 341) under which the court may, on the application of the trustee in bankruptcy, make such order as it thinks fit for restoring the position to what it would have been if the debtor had not entered the transaction in question. But at no stage does the trustee have a proprietary right or interest in the assets given to E nor any right of restitution in respect of them.

8. The Insolvency Act contains provisions parallel to those in the last note applicable to companies.

9. (1908) 9 R (NSW) 107. See A. T. H., Smith, "Stealing the Body and its Parts" [1976] Crim LR 622.

10. Cf. the Human Tissue Act 1961 which, for the purposes of authorising the removal of tissue from a dead body, speaks of "the person lawfully in possession of his body after his death".

11. Cf. *Welsh* [1974] RTR 478, CA where a driver who had provided a specimen of urine for analysis and subsequently poured the specimen down the sink was convicted of stealing the urine. In *Rothery* [1976] RTR 550, CA where a driver provided a specimen of blood which he subsequently removed, his conviction for stealing the capsule and its container was affirmed; apparently he was not charged with stealing the contents (that is his own blood) but it would seem that he would have no answer to such a charge.

to any future appropriation of the property by others. It is not enough that P has no further use for the goods. A farmer who buries diseased animals has no further use for them but he would clearly intend that others should not make use of them and retains ownership of the carcases.[12] A house-holder who puts rubbish in his dustbin has no further use for the rubbish but he puts it there to be collected by the corporation and not as an invitation to all comers to help themselves.[13] Nor is property abandoned because the owner has lost it and has given up the search. A wife may have lost her wedding ring and long since given up the search but she will not have abandoned it.

2) *Mens Rea*

An appropriation of property belonging to another amounts to theft if it is done (1) dishonestly, and (2) with the intention of permanently depriving the other of it.

1 Dishonesty[14]

Everyone has some idea of what is honest and what is dishonest conduct. Perhaps no two people would have absolutely identical views, but most people would find that their views substantially coincide. And it may be safely guessed, the views of most other people would substantially coincide with those of the law. After all, the law seeks here only to represent the standards of right thinking members of society generally. Consequently the bulk of cases give rise to no problems whatever. But there is in some cases – as always – room for some difference of view, as where D appropriates money to which he believes himself morally entitled, or where he appropriates money which he intends to repay, or goods which he intends to replace.

"Dishonestly" in the Theft Act 1968 replaces the requirement in the former law that D should act "fraudulently and without a claim of right made in good faith". The Criminal Law Revision Committee felt that "dishonestly" was a better word than "fraudulently", being easier for the layman to understand.[15] In this instance some reference to the cases on fraudulent conduct is inevitable in order to elucidate what is dishonest conduct. Such cases are no longer authoritative of course,[16] but in so far as they are indicative of attitudes to the conduct in question it would be hard to gainsay their relevance. It is unlikely that attitudes will change very much on this issue whether the relevant adverb is "fraudulently" or "dishonestly".

---

12. Cf. *Edwards and Stacey* (1877) 36 LT 30.
13. Cf. *Williams v Phillips* (1957) 121 JP 163.
14. See Harvey, "What Does Dishonesty Mean" [1972] Crim LR 312; Elliott, "Dishonesty Under the Theft Act" [1972] Crim LR 625; Elliott "Dishonesty in Theft: A Dispensable Concept" [1982] Crim LR 395; Campbell, "The Test of Dishonesty in *Ghosh*" (1984) 43 LJ 349; Griew, "Dishonesty – the Objections to *Feely* and *Ghosh*" [1985] Crim LR 341.
15. Cmnd. 2977, para. 39.
16. See above, p. 489.

The Committee thought that "dishonestly" would probably stand without definition,[17] but decided on a partial definition. Section 2 accordingly provides:

"(1) A person's appropriation of property belonging to another is not to be regarded as dishonest –

(a) if he appropriates the property in the belief that he has in law the right to deprive the other of it, on behalf of himself or of a third person; or

(b) if he appropriates the property in the belief that he would have the other's consent if the other knew of the appropriation and the circumstances of it, or

(c) (except where the property came to him as trustee or personal representative) if he appropriates the property in the belief that the person to whom the property belongs cannot be discovered by taking reasonable steps.

(2) A person's appropriation of property belonging to another may be dishonest notwithstanding that he is willing to pay for the property."

a) *Belief in legal right.* D does not commit theft where he appropriates property in the belief that he is in law entitled to deprive P of the property. Thus if D mistakenly believes that he owns P's umbrella, his appropriation of it would not be dishonest whether his mistake, or ignorance, is of fact or law. Moreover, s. 2 (1) (a) makes it clear that D will not commit theft where he appropriates P's umbrella in the belief that it belongs to E on whose behalf D is acting.[18] It may be that E dishonestly told D that the umbrella was his; nevertheless if D acts in good faith he will not be guilty of theft though E will be.

Of course it is all very easy and all very reasonable to make mistakes about umbrellas. One umbrella often looks uncommonly like another. But what if D's mistake is unreasonable? D may make an unreasonable mistake of fact or law, or he may unreasonably believe that he has a legal right which the law does not recognise at all. Suppose, for example, that D, honestly believing that upon marriage a wife's property belongs in law to her husband, sells his wife's clothes. His belief is (probably) unreasonable and the law recognises no such claim. It seems clear, however, that he would not be guilty of theft. The Act says that D's appropriation is not to be regarded as dishonest "if he appropriates the property in the belief that *he* has in law the right to deprive the other of it". It would be difficult to read into this any objective requirement of reasonableness. Support for this view is afforded by *Small*[19] where it was held a misdirection to tell the jury that D would not be acting dishonestly if he reasonably believed the goods had been abandoned. Strictly a person who believes property to be abandoned cannot intend to appropriate the property *of another* and the issue of dishonesty does not arise, but the case contains a clear ruling that while the reasonableness of a belief is a factor to be considered in

17. Loc. cit.
18. Cf. *Knight and Roffey* (1781) 2 East PC 510.
19. [1987] Crim LR 778, CA, Cf. *Kell* [1985] Crim LR 239, CA.

determining whether it is honestly held, the issue is whether the belief was so held and not whether it is reasonable.

b) *Belief in the other's consent.* Obviously D is not acting dishonestly where, as he knows, P is willing that D should appropriate his property and deprive him permanently of it. It may happen, however, that P is not in fact given the opportunity to express assent or dissent, but D believes that he would have done so had he been asked. Section 2 (1) (b) makes it clear that D is not a thief if he believes that P would have assented. Again, the single criterion appears to be the honesty of D's belief and it does not matter that it is in the circumstances unreasonable.[20]

But D must believe not only that P would have consented to the appropriation but that P would have consented to the appropriation in the particular circumstances. D may believe that his next-door neighbour would consent to his appropriating a pint of milk from his doorstep when D himself had forgotten to leave an order for the milkman; but may believe that his neighbour would not consent to D's appropriating the milk in order to sell it at a profit to a thirsty hitch-hiker who is passing by.

c) *Belief that property has been lost.* Property which has been lost, as opposed to abandoned, continues to belong to the loser and accordingly anyone appropriating lost property would normally be appropriating property belonging to another. But where the owner of lost property cannot be found by taking reasonable steps no one regards the appropriation of that lost property as dishonest; better that D should have the use of it rather than it be put to no use at all. Section 2 (1) (c) provides accordingly.

Here again it seems clear enough that if D honestly believes that the person to whom the property belongs cannot be traced by taking reasonable steps, he is not a thief, although any reasonable person would have appreciated that the owner could be traced by taking the most simple measures.[1] D may be stupid in not appreciating that the owner of the wig he finds on the floor of the law court cannot be traced by taking reasonable steps, but stupidity is no substitute for dishonesty. What are reasonable steps would depend on the circumstances, including of course the value of the thing found and the place where it is found. It may be that when D finds, say, a number of banknotes he believes that the owner cannot be traced, but some days later learns of facts which lead him to believe that the owner can be traced. If D now appropriates the money he is acting dishonestly and may be convicted of theft. If, however, D is fortunate enough to have spent the money before he learns that the owner might be traced he cannot be convicted of theft. His appropriation when it took place was not dishonest and now, when he might have acted dishonestly, there is nothing left to appropriate.

d) *Other cases.* Section 2 (1) contains only a partial definition and conduct is not to be regarded as dishonest simply because it cannot be brought

20. *Small*, last note.
1. Ibid.

528 THETHE FT AND RELATED OFFENCES

within the subsection. Nor does it follow from this subsection that D's conduct is necessarily dishonest because D knows that he had no legal right to the property or that P does not consent or that the owner can be traced.

Two further subsections touch on the question of dishonesty. One is s. 1 (2) which provides:

"It is immaterial whether the appropriation is made with a view to gain or is made for the thief's own benefit."

Normally, of course, people steal to gain something for themselves,[2] but this subsection makes it clear that an appropriation may amount to theft although this motive is lacking.

"The subsection will prevent argument that it is not theft to take something which is useless to the taker or to take something with the intention of immediately destroying it."[3]

Thus it may be theft for D to destroy or hide away ledgers belonging to P because the ledgers provide evidence that D's friend has been misappropriating P's money.[4]

The other provision is s. 2 (2) which states:

"A person's appropriation of property belonging to another may be dishonest notwithstanding that he is willing to pay for the property."

This subsection meets a possible argument that an appropriation cannot amount to theft by virtue only of the fact that D is willing to pay for the property. Obviously all the circumstances must be considered along with D's willingness to pay. In an old case[5] a traveller met a fisherman and, upon the latter's refusal to sell him any fish, took some from him by force and threw down money much above its value. It was doubted whether the traveller was acting dishonestly but it is thought that in circumstances such as these the traveller could now be convicted of theft or of robbery. Certainly it would be an undesirable principle that D should be able to take what he wants from another without fear of any criminal sanction provided only that he is willing to pay. Nevertheless, as will appear, it is possible to imagine circumstances in which it is arguable that D's intention to pay, or to repay, shows that he is not acting dishonestly.

The Theft Act does not, then, provide an exhaustive definition of dishonesty.[6] As a practical matter the definition covers most situations of any common occurrence, but there are other situations where the question of dishonesty may be said to be at large. It is prudent to heed Hale's warning that in cases of stealing,

"the variety of circumstances is so great, and the complications thereof so mingled, that it is impossible to prescribe all the circumstances evidencing a felonious intent, but the same must be left to the due and attentive consideration of the judge and jury."[7]

---

2. As to gain see s. 34 (2) of the Act, below, p. 592. Note that where s. 4 (3) applies (above, p. 507) D commits theft only where, in effect, he has a view of gain.
3. Cmnd. 2977, Annex. 2.
4. Cf. *Cabbage* (1815) Russ & Ry 292.
5. *The Fisherman's Case* (1584) 2 East PC 661.
6. For an argument that "dishonestly" might have been exhaustively defined, see MacKenna, "The Undefined Adverb in Criminal Statutes" [1966] Crim LR 548, 553.
7. 1 PC 509.

Hale, however, offered no precise guidance on the respective functions of judge and jury, nor does the Theft Act offer any guidance on the matter. Essentially there would appear to be three possible approaches. The first would require the judge as a matter of law to define dishonesty. He must of course leave the determination of the facts to the jury but he would instruct the jury that if they find the facts to be this then D is dishonest but if they find the facts to be that then D is not dishonest. This would enable divisional courts, the Court of Appeal and even the House of Lords to state what is and what is not dishonest so that a single standard could be articulated.

A second approach is to put the matter entirely in the hands of the jury. In its extreme form this approach would simply ask the jury to consider whether D believed, and however outrageous his conduct appeared to the rest of us, he was acting dishonestly and accordingly D's views of what is honest or dishonest become paramount. The courts did toy for a while with this approach[8] but it has obvious dangers. Are we really to say, for example, that someone who genuinely believes that it is all right to rob the rich in order to feed the poor is not a thief? Are we to say that someone who knows that his standards are at odds with the rest of society cannot be convicted of theft because he believes that he is right and the rest of us are wrong?

The third approach, the via media, which Hale would have apparently approved, is to share the task between judge and jury. The judge lays down the guidelines, the jury applies them to the facts of the particular case. This is now the received wisdom endorsed by the Court of Appeal in *Ghosh*.[9] The court, accepting that the law was in "a complicated state", sought to put the law on a clear footing. It was held that the jury should be directed that D acts dishonestly if (i) his conduct would be regarded as dishonest by the ordinary standards of reasonable and honest people; and (ii) D realises that his conduct is so regarded. If (i) and (ii) are met, it matters not that (iii) D himself does not regard his conduct as dishonest.

To the extent that *Ghosh* is a rejection of the second approach[10] it is, perhaps, to be welcomed but it still leaves problems in its wake.

As to (i) the issue is pre-eminently one for the jury –

"Jurors, when deciding whether an appropriation was dishonest can be reasonably expected to, and should, apply the current standards of ordinary decent people. In their own lives they have to decide what is and what is not dishonest. We can see no reason why, when in a jury box, they should require the help of a judge to tell them what amounts to dishonesty ... It is clear in our judgment that the jury should have been

---

8. *Boggeln v Williams* [1978] 2 All ER 1061, [1978] 1 WLR 873, DC. See also *Feely* [1973] QB 530, [1973] 1 All ER 341, CA; *Landy* [1981] 1 All ER 1172, [1981] 1 WLR 355, CA; *McIvor* [1982] 1 All ER 491, [1982] 1 WLR 409, CA.
9. [1982] QB 1053, [1982] 2 All ER 689; **SHC 437**.
10. The second approach was taken by the New Zealand Court of Appeal in *Williams* [1985] 1 NZLR 294 where *Ghosh* was not followed. The court held that a jury should be directed that D does not act dishonestly, even where it is proved that he knows that he is acting contrary to his legal obligations, if it is reasonably possible that D was (subjectively) acting honestly, however mistakenly. But in *Salvo* [1980] VR 401 the Supreme Court of Victoria adopted the first approach. It was held that it is for the trial judge to tell the jury, having regard to the alleged facts, what are the constituents of dishonesty.

left to decide whether the defendant's alleged taking of money had been dishonest. They were not, with the result that a verdict of guilty was returned without having given thought to what was probably the most important issue in the case."[11]

No doubt any jury would take the view that it is dishonest to claim payment for work that has not been done,[12] or that it is dishonest to travel on buses intending to avoid payment. In *Ghosh* the court was of the view that a jury would equally have no difficulty in deciding that it is dishonest to rob the rich to feed the poor, or that it is dishonest for anti-vivisectionists to remove animals from laboratories.

But a jury can only surmise as to what conduct is regarded by ordinary people as dishonest. No evidence can be led on this issue so the jurors have only their own knowledge and experience to guide them. This is not to suggest that juries would be capricious but juries might legitimately differ on how they believe that ordinary people would regard the conduct in question.[13]

Consider the "borrowing" cases.[14] It sometimes happens that people take money from others without their consent but with a view to repaying it.[15] D may take some small change from the firm's petty cash to pay a taxi-driver who cannot change D's £10 note;[16] E may take a few pounds from the firm's till to lay a wager on a horse;[17] F may take several hundred pounds from the firm's safe to pay for a family holiday.[18] Whether these takings would be considered dishonest by ordinary people would no doubt involve a consideration of such factors as the amount involved, whether the firm had expressly prohibited "borrowing", whether the taking was open or clandestine and so on. On the propriety and honesty of such "borrowing" views may differ widely.[19] Consider the following case supposed by Lawton LJ delivering the judgment of the Court of Appeal in *Feely*:[20]

"It is possible to imagine a case of taking by an employee in breach of instructions to which no one would, or could reasonably, attach moral obloquy; for example that of a manager of a shop, who having been told that under no circumstances was he to take money from the till for his own purposes, took 40p from it, having no small change himself, to pay

11. *Feely* [1973] 1 All ER 341 at 345.
12. *Ghosh* [1982] QB 1053, [1982] 2 All ER 689.
13. Consistency of result could be achieved if (i) was regarded as a question of law for the judge, but, following the fashion set by the House of Lords in *Brutus v Cozens* [1973] AC 854, [1972] 2 All ER 1297, (see above, p. 490), the issue is treated as one of fact for the jury. See Griew, *Dishonesty and the Jury* (Leicester UP, 1974).
14. For a general discussion of the "borrowing" cases see Lowe, "The Fraudulent Intent in Larceny" [1956] Crim LR 78; Smith, "Fraudulent Intent in Larceny" [1956] Crim LR 238; Elliott, "Dishonesty Under the Theft Act" [1972] Crim LR 625.
15. In such cases D does not borrow the money; he deprives P permanently of the money he takes intending to repay an equivalent amount.
16. An example instanced in *Feely* [1973] QB 530, [1973] 1 All ER 341.
17. *Sinclair v Neighbour* [1967] 2 QB 279, [1966] 3 All ER 988, CA.
18. *McIvor* [1982] 1 All ER 491, [1982] 1 WLR 409, CA.
19. In *Sinclair v Neighbour* [1966] 2 QB 279, [1966] 3 All ER 988, where D took the money to lay a wager on a horse, the trial judge thought that the action was reprehensible but not dishonest. In the CA Sachs LJ was firmly of the view that D's conduct was dishonest but Sellers LJ thought that views might differ.
20. [1973] 1 All ER 341 at 346.

for a taxi hired by his wife who had arrived at the shop saying that she only had a £5 note which the cabby could not change. To hold that such a man was a thief and to say that his intention to put the money back in the till when he acquired some change was at the most a matter of mitigation would tend to bring the law into contempt. In our judgment a taking to which no moral obloquy can reasonably attach is not within the concept of stealing either at common law or under the Theft Act 1968.''
At first sight this seems to be an example of robust common sense. No one would regard this conduct by the employee, though apparently in breach of the employer's instruction to take not a penny from the till, as dishonest. But just suppose that the employer is present in the shop that day and, told by the employee that he is strapped for change to pay the taxi driver, he yet resolutely refuses to allow the employee to take the 40p. The employee thereupon knocks the employer senseless and takes the 40p. Are we to say, assuming the employee intends to repay the 40p, that the employer has not been robbed (i.e. that his 40p has not been stolen by force)? This would be an astonishing conclusion. Strapped for change to pay a taxi driver, is D entitled to forcibly deprive any passer-by he meets of the 40p he requires without fear of conviction for theft or robbery because he intends to repay? The answer must be a resounding No. This is not to say that Lawton LJ's employee is to be convicted of theft. However vehement an employer's instructions not to take money from the till, an employee may yet face circumstances where he can honestly say that if his employer had in mind the circumstances that have occurred (e.g. the temporary inability to find change for the taxi driver) the employer would have consented and the employee's salvation is thus provided by s. 2 (1) (b). If, however, the employee knows that the employer would under no circumstances what-ever allow an employee to use the employer's money for the employee's own convenience,[1] it is difficult to see how the appropriation can be other than dishonest.

On the *Ghosh* view, however, a jury may, using no more than its own intuition in the matter, take the view, or may not take the view, that such an appropriation is dishonest. It is by no means impossible that differently composed juries may take different views. Having regard to the serious consequences of a conviction for theft it cannot be right that on the same facts a jury in Leeds may acquit while a jury in Nottingham may convict.

As to (ii) the jury must be satisfied that D realises his conduct is so regarded. In *Ghosh*[2] the court supposed the case of a man who comes from a country where all public transport is free and he assumes it is the same here so he boards a bus with no intention of paying. He is not to be regarded as acting dishonestly because he is unaware of the circumstances which render this conduct dishonest and is therefore unaware that his conduct would be regarded as dishonest.

This is entirely understandable; no one would wish to condemn the unwitting foreigner's conduct as dishonest. But does this open the door to

---

1. Bank managers, as the simplest inquiry shows, view with horror the notion that employees of the bank may in *any* circumstances use the bank's money for their own purposes.
2. [1982] 2 All ER 689 at 696.

the modern Robin Hood who thinks that ordinary people do not consider robbing the rich to feed the poor to be dishonest; or the anti-vivisectionist who is convinced that ordinary people up and down the country do not regard freeing animals from laboratories to be dishonest? The answer must be that it does. Commenting on *Boggeln v Williams*,[3] where D had reconnected his electricity supply after the Electricity Board had disconnected it for failure to pay bills, the court in *Ghosh* said[4] that such a case –

> "will depend on the view taken by the jury whether the defendant may have believed what he was doing was in accordance with the ordinary man's idea of honesty. A jury might have come to the conclusion that the defendant in that case was disobedient or impudent, but not dishonest in what he did."

No doubt the circumstances in which D can claim to act honestly where his conduct is considered generally to be dishonest will be rare. But not, perhaps, unheard of. Not everyone has the sort of upbringing that acquaints him with community standards of what is honest and what is dishonest. Some may be totally unaware of what the community standards are and others may have the most outlandish ideas of what they are. *Ghosh* does not tell us how to deal with the former and assumes that we must accept the latter. No doubt jurymen try to take a commonsense view, but one man's common sense may not be the same as another's.

The correct approach, it is respectfully submitted, is the first approach. It is for the judges to define dishonesty against the background of the partial definition in s. 2. They may get it wrong but they are subject to correction by appellate courts. Arguably the appellate courts may get it wrong but they are subject to scrutiny and they can change their minds. At all events the meaning of dishonesty is then open for public scrutiny. Before *Brutus v Cozens*[5] no one would have doubted, and without in any way interfering with the jury's prerogative to find the facts, that it was the judge's function to explain the law including, most obviously it might be thought, the meaning of words in statutes. There is now a judicial movement to pass the buck to the jury where the word (and "dishonesty" is an archetypal word in this context) is an "ordinary" English word. It is this development which has confused the meaning of dishonesty and, it may be added, much else besides. The direction in *Ghosh* goes some of the way to recognising the problem but falls short of resolving it.

2 Intention Permanently to Deprive

Theft requires an intention permanently to deprive the other of his property, and while the Theft Act contains provisions making it an offence in certain cases to use the property of another,[6] it should be noted that even in these instances the offence created is not theft. Stealing at common law always required an intention permanently to deprive and that requirement is now expressed in the basic definition of theft in s. 1 (1) of the Act.[7]

3. [1978] 2 All ER 1061, [1978] 1 WLR 873.
4. [1982] 2 All ER 689 at 969.
5. [1973] AC 854, [1972] 2 All ER 1297, AC.
6. See below, p. 578.
7. For an argument that temporary deprivation should be theft see Williams, [1981] Crim LR 129.

There need not, of course, be any permanent deprivation in fact; D may be guilty of theft even though P is never in any danger of losing his property so long as D appropriates with the intent.[8] Conversely, the fact of permanent deprivation is insufficient if there was no intent. But it must be clear that the facts – the history of what D did with the goods – will often have an important bearing on the proof of D's intent. If, for instance, D was found respraying the car which he took from P without his permission, the jury is likely to favour the inference that D's intent was to deprive P permanently of it. If, on the other hand, D had taken P's lawn-mower without permission, and left it in full view of P's house after he had used it to mow his own lawn, the jury is likely to favour the inference that it was not D's intent to deprive P permanently of it. In every case it is for the jury to determine, on the evidence, whether D did so intend, so that where the evidence as to D's intent is circumstantial the judge will instruct the jury that they *may* infer the intent from evidence pointing to that conclusion, but it would be an error of law for the judge to direct that because the evidence points to that conclusion they *must* infer the intent, and the conviction may be quashed on appeal. The meaning of the intent to deprive permanently and its relation to the accompanying problem of proof may be illustrated by reference to the situation in which D takes P's goods and then abandons them. Suppose, for instance, that D takes P's car and subsequently abandons it. If D's intention was to use the car for some temporary purpose then he does not steal it. Nor need D take any steps to return the car, so it follows that as a matter of fact it is often difficult to make out a case of car stealing because it will be difficult for P to show (even if D has been apprehended in possession) that it was D's intent to steal the car rather than use it temporarily.[9] It is less difficult where what D has taken is P's umbrella. If D takes P's car in Nottingham and abandons it in London it would be virtually impossible to get a conviction of theft; if D does the same with P's umbrella a conviction of theft is a virtual certainty. It is not a case of treating cars and umbrellas differently for the jury will be asked to apply the same test to both. Everyone knows that if an umbrella is borrowed in Nottingham and abandoned in London it will be lost forever to its owner, and ordinarily D will know and intend this.

In the general run of cases there are no problems, other than evidential ones, in establishing that D intended permanent deprivation, that he intended to make the property his own. But substantial difficulties can arise. It is obvious, for example, that if D dishonestly appropriates a bottle of whisky which he drinks he has deprived P of it; less obvious, perhaps, where D takes a rail ticket which he intends to return to British Rail at the end of his journey, or where he pawns goods belonging to P intending to redeem and restore them to P at some future stage. It is to meet problems of this kind that s. 6 was introduced.[10] Section 6 does not contain an exhaustive definition of the intent permanently to deprive, it merely

---

8. Cf. *Egginton* (1801) 2 Leach 913.
9. Hence it was made a statutory offence merely to take P's car without P's consent.
10. See Spencer, "The Metamorphosis of Section 6 of the Theft Act" [1977] Crim LR 653.

clarifies its meaning in certain respects. In most cases it will be unnecessary to go beyond s. 1 (1) and unwise to do so.[11] Section 6 is there to deal with a number of difficult cases of uncommon occurrence. The section provides:

"(1) A person appropriating property belonging to another without meaning the other permanently to lose the thing itself is nevertheless to be regarded as having the intention of permanently depriving the other of it if his intention is to treat the thing as his own to dispose of regardless of the other's rights, and a borrowing or lending of it may amount to so treating it if, but only if, the borrowing or lending is for a period and in circumstances making it equivalent to an outright taking or disposal.

(2) Without prejudice to the generality of subsection (1) above, where a person, having possession or control (lawfully or not) of property belonging to another, parts with the property under a condition as to its return which he may not be able to perform, this (if done for purposes of his own and without the other's authority) amounts to treating the property as his own to dispose of regardless of the other's rights."

a) *Disposal regardless of the other's rights.* In the foregoing illustration concerning the umbrella it is assumed that D knows the umbrella will be lost forever to P and that he intends this. D thus means P permanently to lose the thing and there is no problem whatever concerning intent. But it might be that when D disposes of P's property he is merely indifferent as to whether it will be recovered by P; D might even hope that the property will somehow be restored to P, but realises that in the circumstances this is unlikely. Where D is thus indifferent it may be difficult to say that he is "meaning the other permanently to lose the thing itself". However s. 6 (1) provides that D is nevertheless to be regarded as having the intention of permanently depriving P of it if "his intention is to treat the thing as his own to dispose of regardless of the other's rights".

Note that it is not enough that D is treating the property as his own. In borrowing P's property without P's consent and using it there is an appropriation of the property and D is treating it as his own; but he does not steal the property unless he intends, in addition, to treat it as his own to dispose of regardless of P's rights. Any such disposal will suffice.

Suppose, for example, that D appropriates property belonging to P intending all along to sell it back to P.[12] He will certainly be guilty of obtaining by deception if he carries through his fraud, but it is necessary to decide whether he is a thief when he appropriates the property. It seems clear enough that he is, for he intends to treat the property as his own to dispose of regardless of P's rights. It can hardly be argued that he is not treating the property as his own to dispose of since D proposes to represent to the true owner himself that he is the owner or is authorised by the owner to sell. Nor can it be seriously argued that he is not acting regardless of the owner's rights. D is of course aware of the owner's rights and it is his very awareness which shows that he is acting regardless of them. In such a case this is a clear usurpation of dominion by D since he affects to be the owner.

Contrast *Holloway*.[13] D, who was employed by P to dress skins and was paid by the piece, took some already dressed skins from P's warehouse and then claimed payment for dressing them. Here D, though guilty of obtaining or attempting to obtain by deception, does not steal the skins. He does not mean P to be permanently deprived of them nor does he treat them *as his own* to dispose of regardless of P's rights; all along D acknowledges that the skins belong to P.[14] The fact that D obtains a payment from P for the restoration of his property (for example, the deposit paid in respect of empty bottles belonging to P) does not make D guilty of theft if the payment is one which P is in any event obliged to pay for the restoration of his property;[15] that D has come by the bottles dishonestly does not make him a thief from P.

Section 6 (1) states that a person treating property as his own to dispose of "*is* to be regarded" as having an intent permanently to deprive even though he does not in fact intend that the owner should be deprived in fact. The case instanced above where D appropriates P's property with a view to selling it back to him provides a convenient illustration. Here D "is to be regarded" as intending permanently to deprive though it is part of his fraud that P's property should be restored to him, albeit only after P has paid for it. In such a case, however, P is in at least some danger of being permanently deprived of his property for if, for whatever reason, he refuses to buy back his goods, it can hardly be supposed that D would thereupon make a present of them to P and he would no doubt seek to dispose of the property elsewhere. There is really no difficulty in saying that D intends permanent deprivation where he appropriates P's property with a view to its sale at a profit to D, and permanent deprivation is no less intended because D has P in mind as one of the possible buyers. Even before the Theft Act 1968 came into force it was held that in such a case D intended permanently to deprive.[16]

But what if P is at no risk of being deprived of his property? The example has been given above[17] of the rogue who sells the crown jewels to a gullible tourist. It was argued that the rogue appropriates the jewels because to purport to sell another's property (whether or not the seller is in possession) is an assumption of a right of an owner; the issue here is whether the rogue can be said to intend to deprive the owner permanently of the jewels. On a literal interpretation of s. 6 (1) the rogue may be said to be deemed to have such an intention because he "is" to be so regarded in disposing of them regardless of the owner's rights. But it may be that the courts would not go this far and not only because a solemn declaration that the crown

---

13. (1849) 1 Den 370.
14. It may be there is a more fundamental reason why Holloway would not now be guilty of stealing the skins; there may be no appropriation of the skins. Cf. Smith, *Theft*, paras. 5 and 128. But cf. *Morris* [1983] 3 All ER 288, above, p. 491.
15. *Johnstone, Comerford and Jalil* [1982] Crim LR 454 (Mr Recorder Chadwick). Cp. *Pick* [1982] Crim LR 238 (Judge Jolly).
16. *Hall* (1849) 1 Den 381. See further *Chan Man-sin v A-G for Hong Kong* [1988] 1 All ER 1, PC.
17. P. 498.

jewels, still secure in the Tower, had been stolen by a purported sale in Piccadilly Circus would cause some hilarity.

In such a case as this it would not have been held under the former law of larceny that the rogue had an intention permanently to deprive[18] and in *Lloyd* Lord Lane CJ said[19] that the court "would try to interpret s. 6 in such a way as to ensure that nothing is construed as an intention permanently to deprive which would not prior to the 1968 Act have been so construed". The difficulty is that when the relevant circumstances specified in s. 6 exist D "*is* to be regarded", not "*may* be regarded" as having that intent. It may be, however, that it is unrealistic to say that D has acted "regardless" of P's rights when what he has done poses no threat to P's rights.

It would be different if in pursuance of the sale of P's property D delivers possession of the property to the buyer or puts the buyer in a position where he can take possession of them[20] and here D steals the goods (appropriates with intent permanently to deprive) when the sale takes place.

b) *Conditional intention.* A problem which has much exercised the courts in recent years has been that of so-called conditional intent.[1] The problem concerned whether D could be convicted of theft, or of an attempt, where he had no specific property in mind but had resolved to steal if there was anything to be taken or if the property on examination proved to be worth his while to take. The problem was further complicated by the House of Lords decision in *Haughton v Smith*[2] which held that the crime of attempt could not be committed where the *actus reus* was, other than as to means, physically impossible to achieve.

The difficulty created by *Haughton v Smith* has been removed by the Criminal Attempts Act 1981 and physical impossibility is no longer a bar to a conviction for an attempt.[3] The other difficulty has been shown to be not one of substance. D must of course be proved to have an intention to steal but D may have such an intention though his implementation of it is subject to certain conditions (for example, that he is not being observed, or that the goods he seeks are in the place he thinks them to be). So if D looks through P's handbag intending to steal money, he no less intends to steal money though he has no means of knowing that there is any money there and, in the result, the handbag contains no money. If D opens P's car, or a box belonging to P, intending to steal anything that may prove of value, he may be convicted of attempting to steal property belonging to P though, in the result, he finds nothing in the car or box that he considers worth stealing.[4]

18. Cf. *Bloxham* (1943) 29 Cr App Rep 37, CCA. Nor was there an attempt where the seller took no steps to put the buyer in possession of the property.
19. [1985] 1 All ER 661 at 666.
20. Cf. *Pitham and Hehl* (1976) 65 Cr App Rep 45, [1977] Crim LR 285, CA, above, p. 497.
    1. See *Easom* [1971] 2 QB 315, [1971] 2 All ER 945, CA; *Husseyn* (1977) 67 Cr App Rep 131, CA; *Walkington* [1979] 2 All ER 716, [1979] 1 WLR 1169, CA; *A-G's References (Nos. 1 and 2 of 1979)* [1980] QB 180, [1979] 3 All ER 143, CA. See above, p. 289.
    2. [1875] AC 476; [1973] 3 All ER 1009.
    3. See above, p. 300.
    4. Above, p. 291. Cf. *Bayley and Easterbrook* [1980] Crim LR 503, CA.

D cannot of course be charged with attempting to steal, and still less of stealing, property which he is not minded to appropriate. If D's only interest in looking through P's handbag is money, he cannot be charged with attempting to steal the remaining contents of the handbag. Thus care may be required in drafting the charge in such cases but if D is bent upon stealing the fact that he has not yet found what he is looking for, or that it is not there, cannot mean that he lacks an intention to steal.

c) *Borrowing or lending*. Where D merely borrows P's umbrella and uses it without P's consent there is an appropriation, but if D intends to return the umbrella to P at some future date – definite or indefinite – he would not be "meaning" P permanently to lose it. Nor, by merely intending to use the umbrella indefinitely, does he intend to treat it as his own *to dispose of* regardless of P's rights. However s. 6 (1) provides that a borrowing or lending may amount to so treating it "if, but only if, the borrowing or lending is for a period and in circumstances making it equivalent to an outright taking or disposal".

Suppose, then, that D intends to return the property in a year's time, five years' time or fifty years' time. Would the borrowing in any or all of these cases amount to an outright taking? On the whole it would seem that this provision was not inserted to leave it to the court to determine how long a period of borrowing is equivalent to an outright taking. If D intends to return the property at some future stage then, without more, it is difficult to see how this could be equivalent to an outright taking – it necessarily falls short of an outright taking.[5] Moreover this sort of problem is not merely academic, it is almost fanciful. People do not ordinarily borrow property for one, five or fifty years as the case may be; property is either borrowed (i.e. D intends to return it) or it is appropriated permanently.

So it is reasonable to suppose that the draftsman had some other sort of case in mind. This is borne out by the fact that the borrowing or lending must be "for a period *and* in circumstances" making it equivalent to an outright taking or disposal. Something *more* than a borrowing is contemplated. "Borrowing," said Lord Lane CJ in *Lloyd*:[6]

"is *ex hypothesi* not something which is done with an intention permanently to deprive. [The second half of s. 6 (1)], we believe, is intended to make it clear that a mere borrowing is never enough to constitute the necessary guilty mind unless the intention is to return the 'thing' in such a changed state that it can truly be said that all its goodness or virtue is gone."

The provision, then, is aimed at the sort of case where D borrows P's theatre season ticket and uses it to gain admission to a series of performances. It would thus apply to the case where D takes a railway ticket in order to get a free ride; he intends that the ticket should be restored to P at the end of his journey, but the ticket is now worthless and his borrowing of it has been for a period and in circumstances making it equivalent to an

5. So in *Warner* [1971] Crim LR 114, CA, it was held that the trial judge was wrong in directing the jury that D could be convicted of theft if he intended to retain the property indefinitely.

6. [1985] 2 All ER 661 at 667, CA; **SHC 444**. Cf. *Coffey* [1987] Crim LR 498, CA.

outright taking. The same argument may be applied to a cheque which D obtains from P. In the ordinary course of events the cheque will be cashed and returned to the drawer, P, so there is no permanent deprivation of the cheque as a piece of paper. But, as *Duru*[7] makes clear, this ignores that the cheque has left P's hands as something of value and is returned to him as a mere scrap of paper. In such a case D has patently treated the cheque as his own to dispose of regardless of P's rights.

But there are difficulties. Suppose, for example, that D borrows a season ticket and uses it for nineteen out of the twenty performances[8] for which it is valid and then returns it to P for the last performance. Is this use by D equivalent to an outright taking? If it is so treated then the courts would again be faced with considerable difficulties in drawing the line. More important, if it is admitted that something short of an intention to use the ticket to view all twenty performances will suffice (say ten or fifteen) then dishonest use will in some circumstances amount to theft. A principle that was firmly kept out at the front door will have been allowed in at the back.

d) *The thing.* Rather curiously s. 6 (1) speaks of "the thing" where it might have been expected to use "the property". The explanation may be that the draftsman sought to make it clear that the kind of case provided for was one where P is to get the thing itself, in a literal sense, restored to him but it is D's intention that the thing shall be worthless in the real sense. The thing (the cancelled cheque, or used rail or season ticket) is restored to P but the article as property of value is not restored to him.

e) *Parting with property under a condition as to its return.* Section 6 (2) is meant to provide for the case where D (who will most often be a bailee of the property though the position is the same here even if D has taken the property in the first place without P's consent) pledges P's property without P's authority. If D intends to redeem the property and return it to P in due course he would not ordinarily be said to mean to deprive P permanently of the property. The difficulty with such cases arises because it may be uncertain whether D will be able to redeem the goods – the very fact that he has pawned them tends to show that he is lacking in funds. Accordingly s. 6 (2) provides that D is to be treated as having an intention permanently to deprive P if he parts with the property under a condition "which he *may* not be able to perform".

The subsection clearly implies that if D parts with the property, by pledging or otherwise, under a condition as to its return which he knows he can perform then D would not be guilty of theft. Yet in such a case D, by pledging P's property without authority, is treating the property as his own to dispose of regardless of P's rights within s. 6 (1) and s. 6 (2) is expressed

---

7. [1973] 3 All ER 715, CA; cf. *Downes* (1983) 77 Cr App Rep 260, CA. Cf. Smith, *Theft*, para. 134. *Duru* was a prosecution under s. 15 but the same principles are applicable.
8. The example given at HC Vol. 769, col. 472.

to be without prejudice to the generality of s. 6 (1). Presumably, though, s. 6 (1) is to be read subject to s. 6 (2) to this extent otherwise s. 6 (2) would be devoid of any worthwhile meaning.

f) *Deprivation of the owner's interest.* Normally a thief intends to deprive permanently in the fullest sense, that is, he intends to make the property his own. In such a case it does not matter that the person from whom the property is stolen is the owner or a person, such as a bailee, who has a limited interest. But it might happen that D, while not intending to deprive the owner permanently of the property, nevertheless intends to deprive, say, a bailee of his interest. For example, knowing that P has hired a car for the duration of his holiday D appropriates the car for the period of that holiday intending to return it to the owner. Since theft is the dishonest appropriation of property belonging to another with the intention of depriving that other permanently of it, and since the property belongs to the bailee, it seems that D will be guilty of theft if, knowing of P's limited interest as bailee, he dishonestly deprives him permanently of it.

2 Abstracting Electricity

It has been shown[9] why the Criminal Law Revision Committee thought it necessary to make special provision for electricity and the view that electricity is not property capable of being appropriated has been confirmed by the courts.[10] Section 13 accordingly provides:

"A person who dishonestly uses without due authority, or dishonestly causes to be wasted or diverted, any electricity shall on conviction on indictment be liable to imprisonment for a term not exceeding five years."

No doubt this provision will ordinarily be applied to the case where D dishonestly[11] uses some device to by-pass his electricity meter, but it is in fact capable of some curious applications.[12] Strictly there might be an offence under this section where D borrows an electrically driven, hand-operated, milk float, though there would be no theft of the float nor an offence of taking a conveyance under s. 12.[13] But proceedings under s. 13 in such a case are perhaps very unlikely; there might be some reluctance to prosecute when the substance of what D does is not criminal even though there is technically some incidental offence.[14] Moreover, in this sort of situation, it may be that D does not at all advert to the fact that he is causing the electricity to be used.

9. Above, p. 505.
10. *Low v Blease* [1975] Crim LR 513, DC.
11. See *Boggeln v Williams* [1978] Crim LR 242, 122 Sol Jo 94, DC, above, p. 529.
12. Cf. Smith, *Law of Theft*, paras. 294–298.
13. See below, p. 578.
14. Prosecutions have been brought for stealing the petrol consumed where D has borrowed a motor vehicle, but this was never regarded as satisfactory and the offence of taking motor vehicles was introduced. Cf. *Low v Blease*, above, p. 505, where it was apparently assumed that a dishonest user of a telephone may commit the offence under s. 13.

It was perhaps for these reasons that the Post Office Act 1953, s. 65, is amended by the Theft Act[15] to create a specific offence of dishonestly using a public telephone or telex system with intent to avoid payment.[16] This gets at the substance of the mischief and avoids any difficulty.

It is enough under s. 13 that D dishonestly causes electricity to be wasted or diverted; he need not be shown to have made any use of the electricity for himself. An employee who out of spite for his employer puts on all the lighting and heating appliances in the office would commit the offence.

3 Robbery[17]

By s. 8 of the Theft Act 1968:

"(1) A person is guilty of robbery if he steals, and immediately before or at the time of doing so, and in order to do so, he uses force on any person or puts or seeks to put any person in fear of being then and there subjected to force.

(2) A person guilty of robbery, or of an assault with intent to rob, shall on conviction on indictment be liable to imprisonment for life."

As defined robbery is essentially an aggravated form of theft; and if there is no theft, or attempted theft, there can be no robbery or attempted robbery. So it would not be robbery where D by force takes a car from P in the belief that he has the legal right to it;[18] or where D by force takes a car from P not intending to deprive P permanently of it. In the first case D may be guilty of an assault, and in the latter of both an assault and an offence under s. 12 of the Theft Act, but in neither case is he guilty of robbery.

The offence of robbery is complete when the theft is complete, that is when the appropriation is complete. So in *Corcoran v Anderton*[19] where D and E sought to take P's handbag by force, it was held that the theft was complete when D snatched the handbag from P's grasp though it then fell from D's hands and the defendants made off without it. It is arguable that the theft in such a case is complete when D struggles with P for possession of the handbag for by that conduct he is assuming the rights of an owner.[20] In the case of robbery the appropriation must normally be by taking[1] since it is difficult to imagine realistic situations in which robbery might be effected by other modes of appropriation.[2]

---

15. Sch. 2, para. 8 But this does not cover 999 calls since no payment is involved; see p. 758 below.
16. Punishable, on summary conviction, by three months' imprisonment and/or a fine of £100; and, on indictment, by two years' imprisonment. As to the intent, cf. *Corbyn v Saunders* [1978] Crim LR 169, DC.
17. See Andrews, "Robbery" [1966] Crim LR 524.
18. Cf. *Skivington* [1968] 1 QB 166, [1967] 1 All ER 483; *Robinson* [1977] Crim LR 173, CA.
19. (1980) 71 Cr App Rep 104, [1980] Crim LR 385.
20. See above, p. 491.
1. See above, p. 497.
2. See Andrews, op. cit., 527, for possible instances.

1 Use or Threat of Force in Order to Steal

Any use or threat of "force" against the person suffices. "Force" is undefined and in the prevailing climate of judicial opinion it can come as no surprise that it has been identified as an ordinary English word the meaning of which is to be determined by the jury.[3] But no jury could reasonably find that the slight physical contact which might be involved where D picks P's pocket would amount to a use of force. But very little may be required to turn a case of theft into one of robbery and to push or nudge the victim so as to cause him to lose his balance is capable of being a use of force.[4]

Under the former law robbery was thought of as stealing accomplished by force against the person, the force being used to overpower P's will to resist and not merely to seize the property.[5] The CLRC appeared to have the same distinction in mind for they said that they would "not regard mere snatching of property, such as a handbag, from an unresisting owner as using force for the purpose of the definition".[6] The distinction was meant to be conveyed by the words in s. 8, ". . . if he steals . . . and in order to do so, he uses force on any person or seeks to put any person of being then and there subjected to force". But in *Clouden*[7] the distinction was rejected and D's conviction for robbery was upheld where he wrenched a shopping basket from P's hand and ran off with it. In the view of the court the former distinction could not stand with the words of the section and it was open to a jury to find on these facts that force had been used on P with intent to steal. *A fortiori* it will be robbery where, for example, a struggle, even a fleeting one, takes place for possession of a handbag,[8] or where an earring is snatched tearing the lobe of the ear.[9]

A threat of force may be implied as well as express. So long as D intends P to understand, and P does so understand, that force will be used against him if he seeks to prevent the theft, the theft is accomplished by the threat of force. Where D threatens P with force unless P complies with D's demands and at a later stage takes property from an unprotesting P, D may be convicted of robbery if he intends, and P understands, the threat to continue, even though D's original threats were not made for the purpose of taking P's property.[10]

It is not necessary that the force used or threatened should amount to an assault. D may threaten a use of force and satisfy the requirements of the offence of robbery although P is not made to apprehend the immediate infliction of force on him which is necessary to constitute an assault.[11] Since "force" is an ordinary word it is for the jury to determine its meaning as a matter of fact.[12]

---

3. *Dawson and James* (1976) 64 Cr App Rep 170, CA.
4. *Dawson*, last note.
5. *Gnosil* (1824) 1 C & P 304; *Harman's Case* (1620) 2 Roll Rep 154.
6. Cmnd. 2977, para. 65.
7. [1987] Crim LR 56, CA.
8. *Corcoran v Anderton* (1980) 71 Cr App Rep 104, [1980] Crim LR 385, DC.
9. Cf. *Lapier* (1784) 1 Leach 320.
10. *Donaghy and Marshall* [1981] Crim LR 644 (Judge Chavasse).
11. *Tennant* [1976] Crim LR 133, CC.
12. *Dawson and James* (1976) 64 Cr App Rep 170, CA.

2 On Any Person

In most cases of robbery D will use or threaten force against the person to whom the property belongs.[13] But the offence is not so limited. Provided the force is used or threatened *in order* to steal it will be robbery.

"If, for example, the only force used at the time of the [Great Train Robbery] in 1963 had been on a signalman, this would under the [Act] have been sufficient."[14]

It does not matter that the person against whom the force is used or threatened has no interest whatever in the property; it would be robbery to overpower the same signalman because his signal-box overlooks a factory from which the thieves wish to steal and they fear that he will notice them and raise the alarm. It would seem to amount to robbery where D threatens to use force on Q in order to overcome P's reluctance to part with his money, as where D holds P's child over a river and threatens to throw her in unless P hands over his wallet.[15] Such a case is more naturally treated as one of blackmail under s. 21 of the Act, but it seems to fall literally within s. 8.[16]

3 Immediately Before or At the Time of Stealing

Strictly interpreted this expression might suggest that force used only a second after the theft is technically complete would not suffice for robbery, a view which may be said to receive further support from the requirement that the force be used "in order to steal". The argument was advanced in *Hale*.[17] D and E entered P's house and while D was upstairs stealing a jewellery box, E was downstairs tying up P. The Court of Appeal declined to quash their convictions for robbery though the appropriation of the jewellery box might have been completed before the force was used. The appropriation, said the court, should be regarded as a continuing act and it was open to the jury on these facts to conclude that it continued while P was tied up. The matter needs to be looked at in a common sense way; while the force must be used at the time of the theft and in order to steal, the theft needs to be looked at in its entirety.

But a line has to be drawn somewhere. If, having taken property from P without using or threatening force, D is stopped by a police officer in the street outside and knocks him down in order to avoid arrest, this would not amount to robbery. Force used to retain possession of property not obtained by force would not ordinarily be thought of as robbery.[18] Even on a broad view the use of force is neither at the time of, nor in order to commit, the theft.[19]

"Immediately before" must add something to "at the time of" the theft. Clearly if a gang overpower P, the nightwatchman, at the main gate of a factory, this would be a use of force immediately before the theft, although

---

13. Above, p. 509.
14. Cmnd. 2977, para. 65. Cf. *Smith v Desmond and Hall* [1965] AC 960, [1965] 1 All ER 976.
15. Cf. *Reane* (1794) 2 Leach 616.
16. Cf. Smith, *Theft*, paras. 150–152.
17. (1978) 68 Cr App Rep 415, [1979] Crim LR 596, CA. Cf. *Gregory* (1982) 74 Cr App Rep 154, [1982] Crim LR 229, CA.
18. *Harman's Case* (1620) 2 Roll Rep 154.
19. Cf. Cmnd. 2977, para. 65.

some minutes must elapse before the gang reaches the part of the factory where the safe is housed.[20] And it can make no difference that P is not present in the factory at all; it would be robbery where some members of the gang by force detain P at his home while their confederates open the safe in the factory.

It is not enough that D gets P to part with property by threatening to use force on another, and future, occasion. This may well amount to blackmail but the fact that P is intimidated or frightened is not in itself enough for robbery unless he is put in fear of being "then and there" subject to force. But suppose a gang by threats of force persuade P, the factory nightwatchman, to stay away from work the following evening, and on that evening they steal from the factory uninterrupted. At the time of the theft the threat of force still operates on P's mind; he stays at home because he is afraid of what will happen if he goes to work. But this does not seem to amount to robbery. At the time of the theft P is not put in fear of being "then and there" subjected to force.

It does not seem to be possible to put any particular temporal limit on "immediately". All the circumstances have to be considered including the time when, and the place where, the force was used or threatened in relation to the theft. Force converts theft into robbery only when its use or threat is in a real sense directly part of the theft, and is used in order to accomplish the theft.

4 Mens Rea

Obviously robbery requires at least an intent to steal. But it seems to require more than this. It could be argued that if D intends to steal it will be robbery if in fact there is some use of force, or if in fact he puts someone in fear, whether he intends to do so or not. But it seems clear that D must use or threaten force *in order* to steal, and a merely accidental use of force would not be done in order to steal.[1] It is enough that D seeks to put another in fear of being subjected to force. Fear here means to apprehend, and it would be no less a robbery because P was not afraid. Even if P does not apprehend that he will be subjected to force (because, perhaps, plainclothes policemen are present and D has walked into a trap), it will be robbery if D sought to make him fear. But it would not be enough that P is in fact put in fear unless D intended to put P in fear. A timorous witness to a smash and grab raid might well fear that the thieves will turn on him, but if the thieves do not intend to put him in fear of being there and then subjected to force the offence cannot amount to robbery.

4 Offences Involving Deception

At common law it was never an offence, as such, to obtain property by deception. In more robust – or less sophisticated – times, it was not

---

20. It would surely be open to the jury so to find. Cf. *Hale* (1978) 68 Cr App Rep 415, [1979] Crim LR 596, supra.
  1. Cf. *Edwards* (1843) 1 Cox CC 32.

apparently regarded as particularly grave to obtain property by swindling. In a case in 1704,[2] Holt CJ, holding that it was not stealing where D obtained £20 from P by pretending that he was authorised by Q to collect it, observed, "Shall we indict one man for making a fool of another?" But by 1757 a statutory offence of obtaining property by false pretences had been created. The offence is now defined in s. 15 (1) of the Theft Act:

"A person who by any deception dishonestly obtains property belonging to another, with the intention of permanently depriving the other of it, shall on conviction on indictment be liable to imprisonment for a term not exceeding ten years."

Although property is widely defined for the purposes of s. 15, and includes things in action, there are many common frauds where, though D does not obtain any specific property belonging to P, he nevertheless obtains something of value. D might, for example, obtain a night's lodgings at an hotel by deception or by deception persuade his creditor to defer the payment of a debt. Frauds of this kind were first made criminal by the Debtors Act 1869 which made it an offence to obtain credit by fraud. The Debtors Act was superseded by s. 16 of the Theft Act 1968 which created an offence of obtaining a pecuniary advantage by deception. This offence gave rise to many difficulties in its interpretation (being memorably described by Edmund Davies LJ[3] as "a judicial nightmare") and, following recommendations of the Criminal Law Revision Committee,[4] s. 16 (2) (a) was repealed and superseded by offences of obtaining services by deception and of evasion of liability by deception in ss. 1 and 2 of the Theft Act 1978. The offence of obtaining a pecuniary advantage by deception is, however, retained and may be committed in the ways specified in s. 16 (2) (b) and (c). These offences have common features relating to (i) the deception; (ii) the obtaining; and (iii) dishonesty. In this section these matters are taken first and are followed by a treatment of those matters, which relate in the main to the nature of what is obtained, where the offences diverge.

1) *The Deception*[5]

By s. 15 (4):

"For the purposes of this section 'deception' means any deception (whether deliberate or reckless) by words or conduct as to fact or as to law, including a deception as to the present intentions of the person using the deception or any other person."

Section 16 (3) expressly incorporates this definition for the purposes of the offence under s. 16 (1), and it is incorporated by s. 5 (1) of the Theft Act 1978 for offences under ss. 1 and 2 of that Act.

---

2. *Jones* (1704) 2 Ld Raym 1013.
3. In *Royle* (1971) 56 Cr App Rep 131 at 136.
4. 13th Report (1977) Cmnd. 6733 (hereinafter Cmnd. 6733). See also CLRC Working Paper, *Section 16 of the Theft Act 1968* (1974).
5. See A. T. H. Smith, "The Idea of Criminal Deception" [1982] Crim LR 721.

1 Deliberate or Reckless Deception

In line with general theory concerning criminal liability D may be convicted not only where he knows that what he represents as true is untrue[6] but also where he represents as true that which, as he is aware, may or may not be true. Of course D cannot be convicted of deception should what he represents to be true turn out to be true[7] because P would not have been deceived. Clearly there would be no offence where D represents as true that which he believes to be true but which, as he ought as a reasonable man to have known, is false. Recklessness ordinarily involves a subjective awareness which is absent from negligence.[8] Moreover the offence of deception requires dishonesty and negligence is no substitute for dishonesty.[9]

2 Words or Conduct

The deception may take the form of either words or conduct.[10] Usually the words or conduct will involve an express assertion of a fact which is untrue, but sometimes the words or conduct of D may be intended to imply certain facts though there is no express assertion of those facts. An obvious case is where D obtains goods or services by giving a cheque in payment. The giving of a cheque does not imply that D then has funds in the bank to meet it for he may have authority to overdraw his account; but he does represent as fact that the cheque is a valid order for the payment of its amount at the bank on which it is drawn.[11] D may therefore be convicted of an offence only if he knows that it will not be met or is reckless whether it is or not.

A case which is difficult to reconcile with these principles is *Greenstein*.[12] D and others applied to P for large numbers of shares and with each application they sent a cheque to cover the purchase price. They knew that they did not have funds in the bank to meet the cheque at the time of the application, but they also knew from experience that they would be allocated only a proportion of the shares applied for and that when the shares were allocated P would return a cheque for the difference between

---

6. Cf. The Rehabilitation of Offenders Act 1974. D would not be guilty of an offence in, for example, obtaining employment by concealing a "spent" conviction.

7. Cf. *Deller* (1952) 36 Cr App Rep 184, CCA; above, p. 36; but he may commit an attempt.

8. See above, p. 61. Given the requirement for dishonesty, it is thought that *Caldwell* recklessness cannot apply to deception offences. Contra Archbold, 18–102.

9. *Staines* [1975] Crim LR 651, CA. Cf. *Derry v Peek* (1889) 14 App Cas 337. And see below, p. 555. The Prevention of Fraud (Investments) Act 1958, s. 13, as amended by s. 21 (1) of the Protection of Depositors Act 1963, imposes criminal liability for "the reckless making (dishonestly or otherwise)" of statements in certain circumstances. But under s. 15 of the Theft Act dishonesty is of course required in all cases.

10. *Harris* (1975) 62 Cr App Rep 28, CA, booking in at hotel implies an intention to pay. Cf. *Barnard* (1837) 7 Car & P 784 – D, knowing it was the practice for Oxford shops to extend credit to students, obtained goods on credit by stating that he was a student. Bolland B said that even if nothing had passed in words the jury might find a pretence in the fact that D wore a cap and gown.

11. *Halstead v Patel* [1972] 2 All ER 147 at 151, DC. Cf. *Hazelton* (1874) LR 2 CCR 134. In *Charles* [1976] 3 All ER 112, HL, Lord Diplock, at p. 113, and Viscount Dilhorne, at p. 116, with whom Lords Salmon and Fraser of Tullybelton agreed, thought that there was in effect only one representation, that the cheque would be honoured on presentation. A postdated cheque similarly involves a representation that it will be honoured on the due date: *Gilmartin* [1983] QB 953, [1983] 1 All ER 829, CA.

12. [1976] 1 All ER 1, [1975] 1 WLR 1353, CA.

their cheque for the full purchase price and the actual purchase price. This return cheque they would immediately bank so that their own cheque, which was presented after the allocation of shares, would be met either on first or, at worst, second presentation. They had been told by their bankers that this practice was irregular and they knew that P would not have issued the shares had P realised that by their scheme they were getting for themselves a larger proportion of shares than bona fide applicants. Indeed to combat this practice which is known as "stagging" P had in some cases asked applicants to give an assurance that their cheques would be met on first presentation and the defendants had given this.

The defendants claimed that they did not dishonestly obtain the shares by deception because their experience in these stagging operations showed that the cheques would be met. But it was held that in so far as the defendants represented that each cheque was a valid order it was not, because, as they knew, they had no authority whatever to draw cheques for these large amounts – cheques which could only be met if the defendants succeeded in deceiving P into thinking that their applications were genuine. Yet a cheque does not cease to be a valid order[13] merely because D does not have the funds to meet it provided it is in his expectation (however arrived at) that there will be funds in the bank to meet it on presentation. But in those cases where the defendants had given an assurance that the cheque would be met on first presentation it might be thought that the road to conviction was plainer. After all they knew there was at least a risk that the cheques would not be met until second presentation and were accordingly reckless in giving that undertaking. This argument found favour with the court. But the definition of deception, though it includes statements of intention,[14] does so only where the statement is untrue as to the *present* intentions of D. How can a statement that a cheque will be met on first presentation some time hence amount to a statement of the present intentions of the defendants?[15]

At all events it may be seen that the giving of a cheque, without more, involves certain implicit representations of fact. These days it is common to use a cheque card when paying by cheque and the nature of the representation involved in using a cheque card was examined by the House of Lords in *Charles*.[16] Essentially cheque cards are issued by banks to overcome the reluctance of payees to accept cheques which they fear may be dishonoured on presentation. Provided certain simple conditions are fulfilled the bank guarantees that cheques up to a certain amount will be honoured. Consequently when a cheque card is used D cannot be guilty of deception in representing that the cheque will be met; even if D knows that there will be no funds to meet the cheque and that he has no authority to overdraw he also knows that the cheque will be honoured by his bank. But in *Charles* it was held that where D draws a cheque using a cheque card he represents to the payee that as between himself (D) and his bank he is authorised to use the card. If, therefore, D's authority to use the card has been withdrawn or

13. See Smith, *Theft*, para. 170.
14. See below, p. 544.
15. See Smith, *Theft*, para. 172.
16. [1977] AC 177, [1976] 3 All ER 112. See *Bevan* (1986) 84 Cr App Rep 143, CA, below p. 559, n. 6.

if D uses the card to cash cheques beyond the amount authorised by his bank, there is a deception.

It is not enough, however, to show that certain facts may be reasonably inferred from D's words or conduct. But given that D intends (or is reckless whether) his words and conduct should impliedly represent other facts to P, and they do so, there is no difficulty in finding that D has deceived P. Under a contract of sale the seller may charge whatever he can get for his goods and does not imply that his price is fair. But where parties are in a position of trust and, as D knows, P has left it to him to make a fair charge, D, in making an exorbitant charge, may commit the offence for he implicitly represents the exorbitant charge as a fair one; D's silence when making the exorbitant charge is as eloquent as if he said he was going to make only a modest profit.[17]

Where a statement of fact is properly inferred from D's words or conduct there is no difficulty in finding a deception. But what if D, realising that P has deceived himself, takes no steps to undeceive him? Suppose that D offers a boat for sale knowing that the hull is rotten. He is under no obligation to reveal defects in goods which he sells and he cannot be guilty of an offence though he knows that P buys the boat believing the hull to be sound.[18] But what if D had at some stage during the negotiations honestly represented the hull to be sound only to discover before the actual sale that it was rotten?[19] In such a case there seems no reason why D's representation should not be regarded as a continuing one so that if he goes through with the sale without correcting the error he obtains P's money on the basis of a representation which he now knows to be false. So in *Director of Public Prosecutions v Ray*[20] it was held that where a meal is ordered in a restaurant the customer represents that he will pay on presentation of the bill and that representation continues until the bill is paid. Hence if the customer changes his mind and decamps just before the presentation of the bill, it can be said that a representation, true when it was made, has become false and it may be relied upon as a deception if it deceives the waiter.[1] This may be an extreme instance of the application of the principle concerning continuing representations but the principle is sound in itself. Suppose, for example, that D is in receipt of social security benefits calculated on the basis that she is separated from her husband[2] and, notwithstanding that she has returned to her husband, she continues to draw benefit at the higher rate. It would be only common sense to regard her original representation that she was separated from her husband as a continuing one, and in continuing to draw benefit she is representing as true that which is now palpably false.

3 Fact or Law

The deception will nearly always be one of fact but s. 15 (4) makes it clear that a deception as to law suffices. So a lawyer might commit the offence

---

17. *Silverman* [1987] Crim LR 574.
18. It would be otherwise if D had moved the boat from the slipway into the water in order to conceal the rotten state of the hull, cf. *Schneider v Heath* (1813) 3 Camp 506.
19. Cf. *Incledon v Watson* (1862) 2 F & F 841.
20. [1974] AC 370, [1973] 3 All ER 131, HL.
  1. But see further below, p. 551.
  2. Cf. *Moore v Branton* [1974] Crim LR 439, DC.

where, dishonestly intending to prefer one beneficiary to another, he represents to the executors that "heirlooms" in the testator's will means all the personal chattels of the testator.

A statement of fact is not the same thing as a statement of opinion but as a practical matter it is often difficult to distinguish the two. Regard has to be had, so far as the offence of deception is concerned, to D's knowledge and intentions, and the effect produced in the mind of P. If D says in a testimonial concerning X that X is honest this would normally be taken as a statement of opinion, but it is a statement of fact to the extent that it will be taken to imply that D knows of no circumstances which show X to be dishonest. Thus if D knows that X is dishonest his statement is untrue in point of fact,[3] and it can make no difference that he expresses himself in the form, "It is my opinion that X is honest."

But in ordinary commerce people are given to making extravagant claims about the quality of property in order to induce its sale. It may often happen that D knows that (or does not care whether) his claim is untrue. Take, for example, the case of *Bryan* (1857),[4] where D obtained money from P by pledging with him certain spoons which D represented as being of the best quality, equal to Elkington's A (this being a high quality silver spoon manufactured by Elkington), and to have as much silver on them as Elkington's A. D's spoons were in fact of very inferior quality, and were not worth the sum advanced. D was convicted of obtaining by false pretences, the jury finding that he knew his representations to be untrue. It was held, quashing D's conviction, that dishonestly to exaggerate the quality of goods was not within the offence; in so far as there was a representation of fact – that the spoons pledged were silver spoons – this was true, even though they did not have the quality represented.

But there is much force in the dissenting judgment of Willes J in this case.[5] He regarded as crucial the fact that D's representation was dishonestly made with intent to defraud P, and to the extent that D claimed his spoons had on them as much silver as Elkington's A it could be demonstrated, as D well knew, that they had not. To the more general argument that to uphold D's conviction might interfere with the course of trade, Willes J replied that the court ought to prevent trade being carried out in this fashion.

It would seem to be quite open to a court to uphold a conviction for deception under s. 15 of the Theft Act on facts like these. D knew perfectly well, as the jury found, that his spoons were not as good as Elkington's A and to that extent there was an assertion of fact. Willes J might have been ahead of the commercial morality of his time but there is no reason to suppose that standards of fair dealing might have improved since then.[6]

This is not to say that any person who knowingly exaggerates the quality of his goods will commit the offence of deception. Regard must be had to the effect produced in the mind of P. There is a deal of give and take in

3. Cf. *Smith v Land and House Property Corpn* (1884) 28 Ch D 7.
4. Dears & B 265.
5. Ibid., at 280.
6. Cf. *Jeff and Bassett* (1966) 51 Cr App Rep 28. Note that the Trade Descriptions Act 1968 deals in a comprehensive way with false descriptions applied to goods and services "in the course of a trade or business".

commercial transactions and P is unlikely to be deceived by mere puffs. On the sale of a car it is thought that D would not be guilty of deception when he asserts that the car is "a good runner" for no one is really deceived by puffs of this kind.

4 Statements of Intention

In the tort of deceit it has long been the rule that a false statement of intention is actionable. In *Edgington v Fitzmaurice*,[7] where the directors of a company were held liable for falsely stating in a prospectus that the company was raising money to improve buildings when the real object was to use the money to discharge existing liabilities, Bowen LJ said:

"There must be a misstatement of an existing fact; but the state of a man's mind is as much a fact as the state of his digestion. It is true that it is very difficult to prove what the state of a man's mind at a particular time is, but if it can be ascertained it is as much a fact as anything else. A misrepresentation as to the state of a man's mind is therefore a misstatement of fact."[8]

In view of this it might be thought unnecessary to provide expressly in s. 15 that deception included "a deception as to the present intentions of the person using the deception or any other person", but it was probably necessary to do so because, under the former law it had been held[9] that a false statement of intention was not a false pretence. The directors in *Edgington v Fitzmaurice*[10] would thus now be liable under the criminal as well as the civil law; and, it might be noted, the case provides an example of a deception as to the intentions of another person, namely, the company.

It is accordingly enough that D merely orders goods on credit having no intention to pay. It is of course right that such a person should be convicted but care must be taken that these offences are not employed against the recalcitrant debtor. Mere failure to pay a debt is no proof of dishonest intent and the jury must be carefully directed on drawing the line between the dishonest customer and one who bites off more than he can chew.[11]

2) *The Obtaining*

To establish an offence under ss. 15 or 16 of the 1968 Act or ss. 1 and 2 of the 1978 Act it must be shown that the false representation deceived P and operated to enable D to obtain the property, the pecuniary advantage, the service or the evasion of liability.

The authorities clearly favour the view that offences of deception require some person to be deceived.[12] It is not possible to deceive a machine. If D

---

7. (1885) 29 Ch D 459, CA.
8. Ibid., at 483.
9. *Dent* [1955] 2 QB 590, [1955] 2 All ER 806, CCA.
10. (1885) 29 Ch D 459, CA.
11. Cf. *Ingram* [1956] 2 All ER 639 at 641, per Donovan J. In *Carpenter* (1911) 76 JP 158, the jury found D guilty of obtaining credit by fraud but added a recommendation to mercy on the grounds of his age and optimistic temperament.
12. "For a deception to take place there must be some person or persons who will have been deceived.": *Director of Public Prosecutions v Ray* [1973] 3 All ER 131 at 137, per Lord Morris. See also *Aston and Hadley* [1970] 3 All ER 1045 at 1048, per Megaw LJ; *Welham v Director of Public Prosecutions* [1960] 1 All ER 805 at 808, per Lord Radcliffe.

operates a cigarette machine with a washer he may be convicted of stealing the cigarettes[13] but is no more guilty of an offence under s. 15 than one who uses a screwdriver. So if D uses a false token on a parking meter in order to get free parking,[14] or on an automatic turnstile to get a free ride on a train,[15] he commits no offence under s. 2 of the 1978 Act. But if the machine is controlled or supervised by P and as a result of D's dishonest use of the machine P is caused to do or refrain from doing something then it can be said that D has obtained by his deception.

The deception must then operate on the mind of P and *cause* him to part with the property or confer the pecuniary advantage. The deception need not be addressed personally to P and it is enough that it is contained in a newspaper or prospectus and causes members of the public to act on it.

Obviously these offences cannot be committed, though there may be an attempt, where P is not taken in by the deception even though he does in fact part with the property or confer the advantage.[16] Even where P is deceived there can be no offence unless he is caused by it to do or refrain from doing something. In *Laverty*[17] a stolen car, the number plates of which had been changed by D, was sold to P and the deception alleged was that the car did not bear its original number plates. It was held that D's conviction could not stand on that deception. P bought the car because he thought that D was authorised to sell it, and provided he was so authorised, there was no evidence to show that P would have minded at all that the car did not bear its original plates.[18] But in *Sullivan*[19] D's conviction was upheld where he sold dartboards advertising himself as the "actual maker" of them. This was a lie because he was not the maker but it is difficult to see how this lie would have induced the purchasers to buy the dartboards and in *Laverty* the court said that it was "very anxious not to extend the principle in *Sullivan* more than is necessary."[20]

---

13. Cf. *Hands* (1887) 16 Cox CC 188.
14. Cf. *Davies v Flackett* (1972) 116 Sol Jo 526, DC; where D on leaving a car park which required paying 5p in a machine to raise the exit barrier, drove off without paying when he saw the barrier being held open by a stranger. The court left open whether an offence could be committed without a human mind, but it is thought that this would now provide the best ground for the decision. See Bystander, "Deceiving a Machine" (1972) 69 Law Soc Gaz 416; Smith, "Some Comments on Deceiving a Machine" (1972) 69 Law Soc Gaz 576.
15. Frauds of this kind may be covered by other legislation. The Road Traffic Regulation Act 1967, s. 42 (4), makes it a summary offence (£50 fine) to operate a parking meter other than by using the proper coin; the Regulation of Railways Act 1889, s. 5 (3), makes it a summary offence (£50 fine) to travel with intent to avoid payment of fare.
16. *Hensler* (1870) 11 Cox CC 570, above, p. 45. This is not to suggest that P must be totally convinced of the truth of D's representation. As Griew (*Theft*, 113) rightly points out, a person is deceived by a representation if, though he has certain doubts about its truth, he nevertheless accepts it and acts on it.
17. [1970] 3 All ER 432, CA.
18. It is otherwise where D alters the number plates (e.g. alters the last letter from H to M) and causes P to believe that the car is less old than it is.
19. (1945) 30 Cr App Rep 132, CCA.
20. [1970] 3 All ER 432 at 434. But cf. *Etim v Hatfield* [1975] Crim LR 234, DC, where *Sullivan* was followed and *Laverty* was distinguished. There was an obvious deception in *Etim v Hatfield* because D presented demands through the Post Office for social security benefits to which he was not entitled, and the difficulty in the case arose from the fact that no Post Office employee was called to give evidence. But whoever the clerk was he *must* have paid the money only because of the deception.

Another case where it is not at first sight easy to see the causal connection between the deception and the obtaining is *Director of Public Prosecutions v Ray*.[1] Here it was held that D, a customer in a restaurant, was rightly convicted of obtaining a pecuniary advantage by deception when, after a meal had been consumed but before the bill had been paid, he decamped from the premises while the waiter was out of the dining room. While it can be accepted that the waiter would not have left the room had he known that a customer had changed his mind about paying, it does not follow that he left the room because he assumed that D's original representation that he would pay remained unchanged. But a majority of the House of Lords held otherwise. The waiter was variously described as being put off his guard[2] or lulled into a false sense of security[3] so that there was evidence on which the justices could properly conclude that the deception induced the waiter to leave the room thereby enabling D to evade the debt.[4] In such cases as these it is of course proper to examine or cross-examine P with a view to proving or disproving that his mind was affected by the deception. *Director of Public Prosecutions v Ray* does not establish that the customer must necessarily obtain by deception in these circumstances, only that on the evidence before the justices it was proper to infer that this customer did.[5] To this extent the question whether the deception is an effective cause of the obtaining is a question of fact[6] though there is, as always, a preliminary question of law as to whether the facts are reasonably capable of supporting the inference drawn.

It would seem to follow that if P says he did not care whether D's representation was true or false the case against D must fail because his deception cannot be an effective cause of the obtaining. The issue arose for consideration in *Charles*.[7] D had purchased gambling chips at a casino by using his cheque card to cash cheques to a total value of £750 and it was argued that D's deception in falsely representing that he was authorised to use the card[8] was not an effective cause in inducing P, an employee of the casino, to accept the cheques. P admitted that he accepted cheques from customers only where a cheque card was produced because, as he put it, "It is the bank who takes the risk . . . we make no inquiries as to a customer's credit-worthiness or as to the state of his account with the bank." It would seem to follow therefore that D's deception did not cause P to accept the cheques. In view of this evidence it is surprising that the House of Lords considered that P accepted the cheques only because he was deceived by D into believing that D had authority to use the card. It is true that P admitted that he would not have cashed the cheques had he known that D

---

1. [1974] AC 370, [1973] 3 All ER 131, HL; **SHC 458**.
2. [1973] 3 All ER 131 at 136, per Lord MacDermott.
3. [1973] 3 All ER 131 at 142, per Lord Hodson.
4. See commentary at [1974] Crim LR 181 for a discussion of the law relating to the dishonest diner and Theft Act 1978, s. 3, below, p. 569.
5. D would not have committed this offence if he had decamped while the waiter was in the room. It is not enough that there is a deception *followed by* the obtaining unless the deception, by operating on P, is a *cause* of the obtaining. This point seems to have been overlooked in *McHugh* (1977) 64 Cr App Rep 92, CA.
6. Cf. *Hayat* [1976] Crim LR 508, CA.
7. [1977] AC 177, [1976] 3 All ER 112, HL.
8. As to which see above, p. 546.

was *not* authorised, but on his own admission P did not know this, *nor was there any evidence that he cared to find out about it*. On the facts *as interpreted by the House* the conviction could be upheld; *if* P had accepted the cheques because he was deceived into thinking that D had authority then the case could be regarded as one of obtaining by deception.

The courts returned to the problem in *Lambie*.[9] D was the holder of a credit card (Barclaycard) with a stipulated credit limit of £200. Knowing that she was over this limit, D tendered her card to P, a shop assistant employed by Q, to purchase goods to the value of £10.50. Having ascertained that D's name was not on the stop-list and made the other routine checks of the card and the voucher to ascertain that all was in order, P delivered the goods. In her evidence P said that when a credit card was produced she had no means of knowing what was the stipulated limit nor of knowing anything of the holder's dealings with the bank issuing the card. "I am only concerned," she said, "that my store gets paid," and she knew that if the transaction was carried out in the proper way then her store would be paid.

Quashing D's conviction for obtaining a pecuniary advantage by deception, the Court of Appeal sought to distinguish *Charles* on the grounds (i) that P did not in fact rely on the false representation (that D was authorised to use the card) made by D; and (ii) that a credit card differed from a cheque card in that the former, though not the latter, involved a prior contract between the bank issuing the credit card and the retailer.

These distinctions were rejected by the House of Lords which restored D's conviction. As to (ii) it was held, rightly with respect, that there was no relevant distinction for this purpose between a cheque card and a credit card; both amount to guarantees by the bank which can be enforced by someone accepting them according to their terms. As to (i) it was held (in the teeth of P's evidence) that the *only* inference to be drawn from P's evidence was that she was induced to part with the goods by D's implicit representation that D was authorised to use the card for had P known that D was not authorised to use the card then P would not have gone through with the transaction.

The decisions in *Charles* and *Lambie* have been subject to criticism.[10] Both cases ignore the fact that in neither was P induced to part with property on any assumption that D's use of the card was authorised. P's evidence in *Lambie* made clear (and P's evidence in *Charles* was hardly less clear) that she was concerned only that the shop was paid and she knew that if she followed certain procedures, which had nothing to do with D's creditworthiness other than making sure that D was not on the stop-list, the shop would be paid whatever D's position was vis-à-vis Barclaycard.

In neither *Charles* nor *Lambie* did the House of Lords question the requirement that the deception must cause the obtaining. The House was saying that the requirement is satisfied where, had P known the true facts, he would not have dealt with D. No doubt, in both *Charles* and *Lambie*, P would not have dealt with D had he known that D lacked authority but this

---

9. [1981] 1 All ER 332, [1981] 1 WLR 78; CA; [1982] AC 449, [1981] 2 All ER 776, HL.
10. See Smith, [1980] Crim LR 725, [1981] Crim LR 712; Williams, TBCL at p. 846.

is not the same thing as saying that P dealt with D because he believed that D had authority; P dealt with D in both cases *only* because he knew that if a certain procedure was followed he (or his employer) would be paid. That is the attraction of cheque cards and credit cards, and that is why the banks thought to invent them.

If, then, these cases throw no doubt on the requirement that the deception must be the cause of the obtaining, they must be regarded as special exceptions to the requirement. The decisions in *Charles* and *Lambie* were no doubt influenced by the opportunities for fraud which were perceived as following from the use of cheque cards and credit cards and, unless the requirement that the deception must cause the obtaining is to be brushed aside, must be confined to these situations.

Of course D may be deceived by an implied pretence just as much as an express one so long as he is induced to part with property or confer a pecuniary advantage. The question is whether the deception, whether express or implied, is an operative cause of the obtaining. The point seems to have been overlooked by the Court of Appeal in *Rashid*.[11] D, a British Rail steward, was found in possession of sliced loaves and a bag of tomatoes when about to board a train. On a charge of going equipped to cheat contrary to s. 25, the prosecution's case was that D intended to obtain money from passengers by passing off his own sandwiches as those of British Rail and pocket the proceeds. The conviction was quashed owing to various misdirections but the court was of the opinion that the offence could be proved only if an effective and operative deception was practised without which the passengers would not have purchased D's sandwiches. The court thought that on a proper direction no jury would have convicted because it would be a matter of "complete indifference" to the passengers what was the origin of the sandwiches so long as they were value for money.

Yet if the passengers had known that D was perpetrating a fraud on his employers, would they have purchased the sandwiches? No doubt the passenger may not consciously advert to the origin of the sandwiches, but the case is not on all fours with the cheque card case where P is moved to accept the cheque by the bank's guarantee of payment irrespective of D's authority. Had he thought about it, the passenger would have assumed that he was buying British Rail sandwiches and it is because of this implied representation that he is induced to buy. Not surprisingly in *Doukas*[12] the Court of Appeal, on facts essentially similar to *Rashid*, declined to follow the opinion expressed in that case. D, a waiter, was found in possession of bottles of wine which he planned to sell to his employer's customers for his own profit, and his conviction for going equipped to cheat was upheld. The jury was entitled to find that the hypothetical customer, who must be reasonably honest, would not lend his support to a swindle being conducted by D against his employers.[13]

It is possible to argue that a buyer who purchases goods without consciously adverting to their origin has not been deceived though he has

11. [1977] 2 All ER 237, 64 Cr App Rep 201.
12. [1978] 1 WLR 372, [1978] 1 All ER 1061, CA.
13. But cf. the observations of Lord Bridge in *Cooke* [1986] 2 All ER 985 at 990.

been defrauded. It may be said that to be deceived a man must be induced into an affirmative belief that something is true which is false. Against this it can be argued that people enter into many routine transactions on certain implicit assumptions whether they are consciously adverted to or not. One who buys goods assumes that the buyer is either the owner or is authorised to sell whether he consciously thinks about it or not. It must follow that if he deals with British Rail or with an hotelier he must assume that the goods emanate from British Rail or the hotelier. And it cannot be a matter of indifference to him whether the goods supplied belong to British Rail or the hotelier. Quite apart from the fact that he would not lend himself to a fraud in purchasing goods supplied by an employee, he would not willingly forgo his legal remedies against British Rail or the hotelier should the goods prove to be defective. So too a tenant or lodger will assume that a person letting premises is authorised to let since his own position is precarious if that person is a trespasser who is not authorised to let.[14]

It is a self-evident proposition from the foregoing discussion that the deception must precede the obtaining of the property or pecuniary advantage. Thus where D ordered petrol and, on then being asked by the attendant whether it was to be charged to D's firm, replied that it was and it was so charged, it was held that D could not be convicted on that representation[15] of obtaining the petrol by deception. D had already obtained ownership and possession[16] of the petrol before the representation was made.[17] On these facts D might have been convicted of evading a liability by deception because the debt was evaded by, and consequent upon, the deception.

In many cases D obtains property by making both true and false representations, and here D may be convicted of the offence if the representations which are false are an effective, though not necessarily the exclusive, cause of the obtaining. If, for example, D obtains money from P by representing, falsely, that he holds high military rank, and by representing, truly, that the money is required for investment in a company,[18] his deception may be held to be an effective cause of P's parting with his money since he parts with it on the basis that D is a man of standing. But it does not follow that the deception is an effective cause of the obtaining simply because P would not have parted with his property had he been aware that a representation made by D was false. In *Clucas*,[19] D and E falsely represented to P, a bookmaker, that they were acting as commission agents on behalf of several other persons and in that way P was induced to take from them a bet on credit; the horse backed won and P paid on the bet. It was held under the former law that D and E did not obtain the winnings by their false pretence and it seems that they would not now obtain the

---

14. *Edwards* [1978] Crim LR 49, CA, and commentary.
15. Had the prosecution been able to prove that from the outset D intended to avoid paying for the petrol D could have been convicted.
16. D might obtain ownership of property without deception and then get possession of that property from P by deception (cf. *Phillips v Brooks Ltd* [1919] 2 KB 243) and in such a case he may be convicted under s. 15.
17. *Collis-Smith* [1971] Crim LR 716, CA.
18. Cf. *Hamilton* (1845) 1 Cox CC 244.
19. [1949] 2 KB 226, [1949] 2 All ER 40, CCA.

winnings by deception.[20] It was quite clear in this case that P would not have accepted the bet had he known that D and E were not acting for others – indeed at one stage P suspected that all was not as it appeared and was unwilling to pay without further assurances – but the reason why he paid up was that they had backed a winning horse.

With the facts of *Clucas* it is instructive to contrast the facts of *Button*.[1] D had entered races, for which prizes were offered, in the name of E and gave particulars of former running performances which were true of E and which were only modest; on the basis of this D was given a favourable handicap and he romped home in both his races. So much so that suspicion was aroused and the upshot was that D did not stay to take the prize. It was held that D could be convicted under the former law of an attempt to obtain by false pretences, and it seems that he would now be convicted of an attempt to obtain by deception. Here the deception was the effective cause of D winning the race and thereby qualifying for the prize, whereas the deception in *Clucas* in no way improved D's chances of picking the winner. There is a ruling in *Lewis*[2] that where D gets employment by deception (in that case D falsely represented that she was a qualified teacher) he cannot be convicted of obtaining his salary by deception because he is paid in respect of the work done and not in respect of his appointment. *Lewis* was doubted in *King*.[3] The matter, said the court, fell to be determined as one of fact and that where D and E persuaded P to engage them to fell some trees by falsely claiming that they were from a firm of tree surgeons and that the felling was necessary to prevent damage, they were properly convicted of an attempt to obtain by deception. This seems entirely right since without the false representations they would not have been given the contract. On the other hand it cannot be supposed that where D gets employment by deception he continues down the years to obtain his salary by deception when his performance is found by his employer to be satisfactory. When the deception ceases to be an operative cause of obtaining the salary is presumably a matter of fact for the jury to determine.

The deception is no less the cause of the obtaining though it would not have deceived a reasonably prudent person so long as it in fact deceives P. D cannot escape the consequences of his dishonesty by showing his victim to have been unusually gullible.[4]

3) *Dishonesty*

The offences under both s. 15 and s. 16 require dishonesty. Although no definition of dishonesty is provided, nor is there any adaptation of the partial definition of dishonesty in s. 2, it would seem right that dishonesty

20. But they would commit an offence under s. 16 of the Act, below, p. 558.
   1. [1900] 2 QB 597.
   2. (1922) Somerset Assizes, Rowlatt J: Russell, at 1186n. The case is specifically provided for in s. 16, below, p. 560.
   3. [1987] QB 547, [1987] 1 All ER 547, CA.
   4. Cf. *Giles* (1865) Le & Ca 502.

should bear, so far as possible, the same meaning for offences of deception as it has for theft. Accordingly:

"Owing to the words 'dishonestly obtains' a person who uses deception in order to obtain property to which he believes himself entitled will not be guilty; for though the deception may be dishonest, the obtaining is not. In this respect ... the offence will be in line with theft, because a belief in a legal right to deprive an owner of property is for the purpose of theft inconsistent with dishonesty and is specifically made a defence by the partial definition of 'dishonestly' in [s.] 2 (1) (a). (The partial definition in [s.] 2 (1) is not repeated in [s. 15 (1)]. It would be only partly applicable to the offence of criminal deception, and it seems unnecessary and undesirable to complicate the [Act] by including a separate definition in [s.] 15.)"[5]

And no doubt the same general considerations apply to s. 16 and to ss. 1 and 2 of the 1978 Act. Consequently reference may be made to the discussion of dishonesty in connection with theft.[6] *Ghosh*[7] (where the charge was laid under s. 15) is of particular relevance and the considered restatement of the law in that case must apply throughout the Acts.

Obviously the partial definition of dishonesty in s. 2 (1), other than in s. 2 (1) (a), can have little application to obtaining offences but it would surely be permissible for the judge to tell the jury that D *may* act dishonestly for the purposes of deception offences though he does not obtain the property with a view to gain or for D's own benefit,[8] or notwithstanding that he intends to pay for the property.[9] The Criminal Law Revision Committee obviously thought the partial definition provided an analogy for deception cases because, in the passage cited above, the analogy is used to support their view that D would not be acting dishonestly in using a deception to obtain property to which he believes himself to be entitled.[10]

In other cases the *Ghosh* doctrine presumably governs. No doubt, as with theft, the jury will experience no difficulty in most cases in determining whether D's conduct is dishonest according to the standards of ordinary decent people, but there are bound to be some cases where the question of dishonesty does not admit of an obvious answer. If, for example, the directors in *Edgington v Fitzmaurice*[11] were to be charged with obtaining money by deception no jury could decide that it was other than dishonest for them to state that the money was required to expand the business of the firm when it was really required to pay off pressing creditors. But suppose the company was experiencing what the directors believed to be a short term cash-flow problem and in order to maintain public confidence and

---

5. Cmnd. 2977, para. 88. *Woolven* (1983) 77 Cr App Rep 231, CA, confirms the CLRC's thinking. Cf. *Williams* (1836) 7 C & P 354. See *Parker* (1910) 74 JP 208; below, p. 658.

6. Above, p. 525.

7. [1982] QB 1053, [1982] 2 All ER 689, CA, above, p. 529.

8. Cf. s. 1 (2).

9. Cf. s. 2 (2). See *Potger* (1970) 55 Cr App Rep 42, CA; where it was held that an intention to give full value did not necessarily negative dishonesty. Cf. *Balcombe v Desimoni* [1972] ALR 513.

10. So that D in *Parker* (1910) 74 JP 208, below, p. 658, would not be guilty of an offence under s. 15 in obtaining payment of a debt owed by P by sending P a letter purporting to come from P's superiors. Cf. *Williams* (1836) 7 C & P 354.

11. (1885) 29 Ch D 459, above, p. 549.

preserve the jobs of their employees they raised money by untruthfully stating that it was required for expansion. Is it at all fanciful to suggest that a jury in Birmingham might view that quite differently from one in London?

4) *Obtaining Property by Deception: Section 15*

1 Property belonging to another

The offence [under s. 15] may be committed in respect of any "property belonging to another". By s. 34 (1) of the Theft Act, s. 4 (1)[12] and s. 5 (1)[13] – which contain the primary definitions of "property" and "belonging to another" – are applied generally for the purposes of the Act.

Consequently "money and all other property, real or personal, including things in action and other intangible property" may be obtained by deception, and the limitations imposed by s. 4 on property which may be stolen do not apply to deception. So far as land is concerned the most obvious case is that of an imposter claiming trust property or a deceased person's estate,[14] but it would extend to any case where D by deception obtains the whole of another's interest in land. So far as things in action are concerned D might commit the offence where, for example, by deception he induces P to transfer or assign a debt, a copyright or patent, or other intangible property.

Since "property belonging to another" is to be given the same meaning it has for theft under s. 5 (1),[15] it follows that D may commit an offence under s. 15 where by deception he obtains property of which he is the owner. If, for example, in circumstances such as occurred in *Rose v Matt*,[16] D had by deception induced P to part with possession of the clock, he could be convicted of the offence under s. 15.

2 Ownership, possession or control

Section 15 (2) provides:

"For the purposes of this section a person is to be treated as obtaining property if he obtains ownership, possession or control of it, and 'obtain' includes obtaining for another or enabling another to obtain or retain."

Frequently D obtains ownership, possession and control of the property but the obtaining of any one of these suffices. If D by deception induces P to sell goods to him the offence is complete when ownership is transferred which may occur before the goods are delivered. If D by deception obtains a loan of the property the offence is complete, if all the other requirements are met, when D gets possession or control of them.

Most often D will obtain the goods for himself but the offence is also committed where D obtains for another or enables another to obtain or retain. Thus the offence might be committed where, for example, D by

12. Above, p. 504.
13. Above, p. 510.
14. Cmnd. 2977, para. 91.
15. Above, p. 510.
16. Above, p. 512.

deception induces P to transfer the ownership in property to E; or where by deception D induces P, who has lent goods to E, not to enforce his right to recover goods from E. In such cases E may be a confederate but D may commit the offence whether E is a confederate or not.

But D would commit no offence under s. 15 where, for example, owing P £10, he dishonestly tells P that he has paid him and that P must have forgotten about it. Here D does not obtain any property belonging to P.[17] Nor would D commit this offence where he enables himself to retain property belonging to P, as where he tells P that he has lost a book which P lent him.[18] He might commit deception by telling P that E has lost the book which P lent to E, for this might enable E to retain the book; but not by telling P that E has repaid a loan which P made to E because this does not enable E to retain property belonging to P.

3 Mens rea

Those elements of *mens rea* which are common to the offences under ss. 15 and 16, and ss. 1 and 2 of the 1978 Act, *viz.* the making of a deliberate or reckless deception and dishonesty, have been discussed elsewhere.[19] In addition the offence under s. 15 requires an intention permanently to deprive and an intention to obtain the property. As to the former s. 15 (3) provides that s. 6 applies with the necessary adaptation of the reference to appropriating and reference may be made to the discussion elsewhere.[20]

There must, lastly, be an intention to obtain the property for oneself or another by the deception. If, for example, during the course of negotiations for the purchase of goods on credit D tells P what he thinks to be an inconsequential lie (say that he was on active service during the war) he would not commit this offence though P is in fact induced to let him have the goods on credit because he is an ex-serviceman. D did not intend by the deception to obtain the goods. Nor would it be enough that D intends to cause loss to P unless he intends to obtain the property for himself or another.[1]

5 Obtaining a Pecuniary Advantage by Deception: Section 16

It was pointed out at the beginning of this section that the offence of obtaining a pecuniary advantage under s. 16 (2) (a) was found to create such formidable difficulties of interpretation that it has been repealed and replaced by new offences under ss. 1 and 2 of the 1978 Act. Otherwise the

---

17. But D commits an offence under s. 2 of the 1978 Act; below, p. 564.
18. But D would be guilty of stealing the book.
19. See above, pp. 545 and 555.
20. See above, p. 532.
 1. See Smith, *Theft*, paras. 208–209. Cf. *Balcombe v Desimoni* [1972] ALR 513.

offence of obtaining a pecuniary advantage is retained but it may be committed only in the ways specified in paragraphs (b) and (c).[2]

Section 16 provides:

"1) A person who by any deception dishonestly obtains for himself or another any pecuniary advantage shall on conviction on indictment be liable to imprisonment for a term not exceeding five years.

2) The cases in which a pecuniary advantage within the meaning of this section is to be regarded as obtained for a person are cases where –

b) he is allowed to borrow by way of overdraft, or to take out any policy of insurance or annuity contract, or obtains an improvement of the terms on which he is allowed to do so; or

c) he is given the opportunity to earn remuneration or greater remuneration in an office or employment, or to win money by betting.

3) For the purposes of this section 'deception' has the same meaning as in section 15 of this Act."

The definition of pecuniary advantage in s. 16 (2) is an exhaustive one. Proof that some pecuniary advantage was obtained by D will not suffice unless it falls within the definition; and if the case falls within the definition it is irrelevant that D in fact obtained no pecuniary advantage since the section states that D is *deemed* to have obtained the advantage if its terms are met.[3]

1 Overdrafts and Insurance Polices

D may commit an offence, by virtue of s. 16 (2) (b), where by deception he is allowed to borrow by way of overdraft; as where he tells his banker that he requires the credit to enable him to sell goods abroad when he intends to purchase a car. An overdraft is ordinarily regarded as a facility whereby a person may, if he so wishes, overdraw his account to a stated limit;[4] where a loan is arranged with a bank (say for the purchase of a car) this would not be regarded as an overdraft.[5] It has been held that D is "allowed" to borrow by way of overdraft where by use of the cheque guarantee card issued to him by the bank, the bank is bound to honour cheques issued by D to an amount in excess of that standing to D's credit.[6]

The paragraph also applies to insurance policies and annuity contracts obtained by deception,[7] as where D secures a policy, or a policy on better

---

2. But only one offence is created: *Bale v Rosier* [1977] 2 All ER 160, [1977] 1 WLR 263. The charge must specify the pecuniary advantage which D is alleged to have obtained: *Aston and Hadley* [1970] 3 All ER 1045, [1970] 1 WLR 1584, CA.

3. *Director of Public Prosecutions v Turner* [1973] 3 All ER 124 at 126, per Lord Reid.

4. So the offence is complete when D obtains the facility to overdraw; it is not necessary that D should have used the facility: *Watkins* [1976] 1 All ER 578 (Crown Court).

5. Griew, *Theft*, 164.

6. *Waites* [1982] Crim LR 369, CA. This seems a surprising decision as it would surely astonish bankers to learn that by issuing such cards they are *allowing* their customers to borrow by way of overdraft to an unspecified amount. But *Waites* was followed in *Bevan* (1986) 84 Cr App Rep 143, [1987] Crim LR 129, CA.

7. The offence may be committed although, as a result of the deception, D could not enforce the contract against P: *Alexander* [1981] Crim LR 183, CA.

terms, by falsely stating that he is a non-smoker where this is material to the issue of the policy or its terms.

2 Opportunity to Earn by Employment or Win by Betting

As has been shown[8] the offence of obtaining by deception contrary to s. 15 is not committed unless the deception is an effective cause of the obtaining of the property. Consequently that offence is not committed where D by deception induces a bookmaker to take bets on credit since it is the backing of the winning horse that is the effective cause of the obtaining.[9] The case is now expressly covered by s. 16 (2) (c) and the offence may be committed whether D is allowed to bet on credit or cash terms.

Section 16 (2) (c) may well have been introduced because of a ruling in *Lewis*[10] that D cannot be convicted of obtaining his salary by deception because his salary is paid in respect of work done and not in respect of the appointment. This ruling has been doubted[11] and it may well be that the case is covered by s. 15. Nevertheless, paragraph (c) continues to provide for the case where D obtains employment, or greater remuneration in that employment, by deception.

Paragraph (c) refers to "office or employment". An office can be held by one who is employed and if that office carries additional remuneration this offence may be committed if it is obtained by deception. But an office may exist without any contract of service, as where D is appointed chairman of a voluntary society and if that office is remunerated, as by an honorarium, it would be an offence to obtain the opportunity to earn that remuneration by deception. In *McNiff*[12] it was held that the tenancy of a public house was not an office. Nor had the tenant obtained the opportunity to earn remuneration in employment because the tenant earns the opportunity to earn money by his own efforts and is not remunerated by the brewery. Since an office may exist without a contract of service there would seem to be no reason for confining "employment" to cases where there is a contract of service. Giving "employment" its ordinary meaning it would seem to extend to contracts for services.

3 Mens rea

Those elements of *mens rea* which are common to the offences under both s. 15 and s. 16, viz. the making of a deliberate or reckless deception and dishonesty, have been discussed elsewhere.[13] In addition the offence under s. 16 requires an intention to obtain the pecuniary advantage for oneself or another. It is not enough that D obtains a pecuniary advantage unless his deception was made in order to gain it; nor is it enough that D's deception

---

8. Above, p. 549.
9. Cf. *Clucas* [1949] 2 KB 226, [1949] 2 All ER 40; above, p. 555.
10. Above, p. 555.
11. In *King* [1987] QB 547, [1987] 1 All ER 547, CA, above, p. 555.
12. [1986] Crim LR 57, CA.
13. See above, pp. 545 and 555.

inflicts some pecuniary loss on P unless it was made in order to obtain for D or another the pecuniary advantage.[14]

6 Obtaining Services by Deception

Section 1 of the Theft Act 1978 provides –

"1) A person who by any deception dishonestly obtains services from another shall be guilty of an offence.

2) It is an obtaining of services where the other is induced to confer a benefit by doing some act, or causing or permitting some act to be done, on the understanding that the benefit has been or will be paid for."

By s. 4 the offence is triable either way; on summary conviction it is punishable by imprisonment for a term not exceeding six months and/or a fine not exceeding the prescribed maximum (presently £1,000), and on indictment by imprisonment for a term not exceeding five years and/or a fine.

The notion behind this offence is that a person's labour is something of economic value. Labour is not property but a man may contract for value to provide it. It is therefore made an offence by deception to obtain the services of another.

1) *Deception*

Section 5 (1) provides that "deception" has the same meaning as in s. 15.[15] Two further points may be noted. One is that the deception must cause P to provide the services on the understanding that they will be paid for. It is not an offence for D by deception to cause P to provide services without charge. A reason for this might be that in such a case P has suffered no economic loss because no price has been put on his services but the offence may otherwise be committed notwithstanding that P suffers no economic loss. If D gets P to mow his lawn by pretending that he has sprained his ankle but at the same time offers P £10 for the job, the offence will be committed when D does the job if he is in part induced to do so because he believes the story of the sprained ankle. But as with the offence under s. 15 of the 1968 Act,[16] a person's conduct may be dishonest for the purposes of theft notwithstanding that he intends to pay for the service.[17] No doubt a jury would be reluctant to find D's conduct dishonest where no economic loss is in fact caused and the deception plays only a minor part in influencing P to act but a conviction in such circumstances can be supported.

14. See above, p. 558, and Smith, *Theft*, para. 218.
15. Above, p. 545.
16. See *Potger* (1970) 55 Cr App Rep 42, CA, above, p. 556
17. Above, p. 528.

The other point is that the service be obtained by deceiving P. It is not enough that the service is obtained by stealth and that a charge for the service is avoided. D does not commit this offence where he secretly enters a cinema or cricket ground or where he induces a taxi-driver to carry him by threats.

2) *Services*

"Services" is widely defined.[18] It is constituted by:

    a) any act done by P provided that (a) it confers a benefit on someone other than P, and (b) it is done on the understanding that it has been or will be paid for; or

    b) any act which P causes or permits to be done whether by D or another provided that (a) it amounts to a benefit or confers a benefit on someone other than P, and (b) it is caused or permitted on the understanding that it has been or will be paid for.

This is a wide definition. Typically it will extend to cases where D by deception induces P to provide him with board and lodging, or to provide an amenity such as the use of social or sporting facilities, or to provide goods on hire. In such cases as these P would be seen as providing what would ordinarily be thought of as a service but it is to be noted that s. 1 (2) provides the definition of service and it appears to go further than what is ordinarily understood as a service. *Any* act which meets the stated criteria *is* a service. While a sale of goods is not usually thought of as a provision of services, P does an act (delivers goods) which confers a benefit and, perhaps more naturally thought of as falling within s. 15 of the 1968 Act, it seems clearly to fall within this section. An obtaining of goods on hire-purchase terms is an obtaining of services,[19] and it cannot be a relevant difference that the purchase price is paid at once rather than in instalments.[20] Accordingly there would seem to be a considerable overlap between this offence and the offence under s. 15 of the 1968 Act, and the offence will also overlap with the offences under s. 16 of the 1968 Act.

P must, however, be induced to do some *act*; a mere omission will not suffice. But this limitation is not likely to be of any great practical significance since the offence extends to inducing P to cause or permit some act to be done. Permission may be given by passive acquiescence as where P allows D to park a car in P's lot or allows D to take a boat which is offered for hire.

Where D induces an act which confers a benefit the offence is complete when P does the act; where D induces P to permit an act it is arguable that

---

18. The CLRC initially had in mind a narrower offence involving deception as to the prospect of payment (see Working Paper, paras. 26–29 and 31–34) but this was rejected by Parliament and the Committee's redraft took account of Parliament's expressed preference for an offence of obtaining services, widely defined.

19. *Widdowson* (1986) 82 Cr App Rep 314, CA.

20. In *Halai* [1983] Crim LR 624, CA, it was held that a mortgage advance was not a service because it was a lending of money for property. *Halai* was distinguished in *Widdowson* but not convincingly (see comment at [1986] Crim LR 233); lending money is an act which confers a benefit on D and it is "paid for" in interest charges.

the offence is complete when the permission is given but it is submitted that a preferable view is that the offence is complete only when an act is done pursuant to that permission. The latter view seems more consistent with the wording of s. 1 (2): "causing or permitting some act to be done".

3) *The Benefit*

In typical cases proving that a benefit has been conferred will present no difficulty; the very fact that the act induced is on the understanding that it has been or will be paid for is pregnant evidence that it confers a benefit. People do not undertake to pay for lodgings, sporting facilities or the hire of chattels unless a benefit is conferred. That benefit need not be conferred on D; it is enough that P is induced to confer a benefit on another.

"Benefit" cannot mean something which turns out to be to D's profit or to be beneficial to him; it must refer to something which in law is regarded as a benefit. An apt test would seem to be whether the benefit would constitute consideration sufficient to support a contract. It would appear to follow from this that if the alleged benefit would constitute an illegal consideration for the purposes of the law of contract, it cannot be a benefit for the purposes of this offence.[1] This is not to suggest that an enforceable contract is required between P and D before an offence may be committed. The section does not suggest any such limitation. If, for example, a minor by deception induces P to provide non-necessary services P cannot enforce payment by D. There is, however, no reason why the services cannot constitute a benefit for clearly they do constitute a benefit; there is also an "understanding" that they will be paid for and accordingly there is no reason why D should not be convicted of the offence.

4) *The Understanding*

The offence, as has been pointed out, is not committed where by deception P is induced to provide services without charge for there is no understanding that such services will be paid for. Where there is an understanding that the services have been or will be paid for,[2] it will ordinarily be an understanding that D has paid or will pay for an act done by P. But the offence is not so limited and extends to the situations where the understanding is that E has paid or will pay for the service (as where D represents that his employer will pay his hotel bill) and where the understanding is that Q has been or will be paid (as where P, an employee, is induced to do an act on the understanding that Q, his employer, has been or will be paid for it).

---

1. See Smith, *Theft*, paras. 225–229.
2. No price needs to be fixed; it is enough that the parties understand that by ordinary commercial practice the service is to be paid for.

5) *Payment*

In the ordinary run of case the understanding will be that the services will be paid for in monetary form (cash, cheque or credit card). Suppose, however, that D by deception induces P to provide services in return for services or goods, for example, that if P digs D's garden then D will paint P's house or will provide P with a power drill. "Paid for" presumably has the same meaning as "payment" and it does not strain the ordinary meaning of the word to extend it to recompense in forms other than money. Payment may be said to describe any of the ways in which an obligation may be discharged.[3] On this view D in the examples given would commit the offence.

6) *Dishonesty*

The offence requires dishonesty and reference may be made to the discussion of this matter above.[4]

7 Evasion of Liability by Deception

Section 2 of the Theft Act 1978 provides –

"1) Subject to subsection (2) below, where a person by any deception –

    a) dishonestly secures the remission of the whole or part of any existing liability to make a payment, whether his own liability or another's; or

    b) with intent to make permanent default in whole or in part on any existing liability to make a payment, or with intent to let another do so, dishonestly induces the creditor or any person claiming payment on behalf of the creditor to wait for payment (whether or not the due date for payment is deferred) or to forgo payment; or

    c) dishonestly obtains any exemption from or abatement of liability to make a payment;

    he shall be guilty of an offence.

2) For purposes of this section 'liability' means legally enforceable liability; and subsection (1) shall not apply in relation to a liability that has not been accepted or established to pay compensation for a wrongful act or omission.

    3) For purposes of subsection (1) (b) a person induced to take in payment a cheque or other security for money by way of conditional satisfaction of a pre-existing liability is to be treated not as being paid but as being induced to wait for payment.

    4) For purposes of subsection (1) (c) 'obtains' includes obtaining for another or enabling another to obtain."

---

3. Cf. *White v Elmdene Estates Ltd* [1959] 2 All ER 605 at 610, per Lord Evershed MR.
4. At pp. 525 and 555.

The offence is triable and punishable in the same way as the offence under s. 1.[5]

The offence[6] under s. 2 was intended by the CLRC to penalise much of the conduct which was within s. 16 (2) (a) of the Theft Act 1968 which it replaces. In broad terms s. 2 deals with the dishonest debtor. It does not make it an offence dishonestly to resolve not to pay a debt, nor does it make it an offence to take measures (avoiding contact with the creditor, moving house, for example) though these measures are taken with a view to evading liability to meet the debt.[7] The section deals with the person who *by deception* dishonestly seeks to evade a liability to make payment, or to get the creditor to wait for or forgo payment, or to obtain an exemption from or abatement of a liability to make payment.

1) *Securing Remission of a Liability*

Section 2 (1) (a) envisages that there is an existing liability and that D by deception secures the remission of the whole or part of that liability. "An example", said the CLRC,[8]

"would be where a man borrows £100 from a neighbour and, when repayment is due, tells a false story of some family tragedy which makes it impossible for him to find the money; this deception persuades the neighbour to tell him that he need never repay the loan."

On the face of it this seems an obvious case falling within s. 2 (1) (a); P certainly intends to remit the debt and believes that he has done so. But in law the debt is not remitted for if D's fraud is discovered P may still claim his £100; moreover P's claim continues undiminished during the period when he remains deceived. So far as the debt of £100 is concerned no change has been brought about by D's fraud which in law causes the debt to be remitted. Only if the paragraph is read so as to be satisfied where P *believes* the debt to be remitted would this case fall within it and such an interpretation (though it would achieve the result intended by the CLRC) would be a bold one.

It was held in *Jackson*[9] that there was an offence under paragraph (a) where D obtained petrol from P by tendering a stolen credit card. That P would thereafter look to the authority issuing the card for payment meant, in the view of the court, that D had secured the remission of a liability. No doubt P would so look and no doubt most often the authority would pay. But the authority might refuse to pay because their conditions were not met

---

5. Above, p. 561.
6. It is not clear whether the section creates one offence or three. S. 16, which it replaces, was held to create one offence (*Bale v Rosier* [1977] 2 All ER 160, [1977] 1 WLR 263, DC). In *Holt* [1981] 2 All ER 854, [1981] 1 WLR 1000, CA, Lawson J was not sure whether the paragraphs simply described different ways of committing the same offence or whether there were conceptual differences. While the paragraphs overlap, it would seem they have different functions and it seems preferable to regard the section as creating three offences: see Smith, *Theft*, para. 232.
7. Such conduct may be an offence under s. 3, below, p. 569.
8. Cmnd. 6733, para. 13.
9. [1983] Crim LR 617, CA.

and in that event D would be liable to P. D's liability is not remitted simply because it is probable that someone else will meet it.

While this view of paragraph (a) robs it of much of its intended effect the fraudster can take little comfort from that since such cases fall within paragraph (b) in that P has been induced to forgo payment; "forgo" is entirely apt to describe what it is that P is induced to do in such a situation.[10] Of course paragraph (b) additionally requires an intent to make permanent default but proof of that would be easy to come by where D has persuaded P to remit the debt.

Paragraph (a) assumes an existing liability which P is persuaded to remit. It cannot therefore apply where D persuades P that there was no existing liability as, for example, where P, unsure to which of his friends he lent £10 at a party – in fact it was D – is persuaded by D that he must have lent the money to someone else. Such a case, however, falls within paragraph (b).

2) *Inducing Creditor to Wait for or Forgo Payment*

The operation of s. 2 (1) (b) may be illustrated by reference to the facts of *Director of Public Prosecutions v Turner*.[11] D, who owed P some £38 for work done and was being pressed for payment, told P that he had no ready cash and persuaded P to accept a cheque knowing that it would be dishonoured. Such conduct falls within s. 2 (1) (b) if, and only if, D intends to make permanent default on the debt. If, as seemed likely in *Turner* itself, D simply wanted to rid himself temporarily of the importunings of his creditor in order to give himself a breathing space, and was bent on settling the debt at a later stage, he would not commit an offence.

The effect of D's deception must be to make the creditor "wait for . . . or forgo" payment. "Forgo" appears to require that P in some way desists from looking for payment. It would be apt to cover the case where P, a waiter in a restaurant, is falsely told by D, a diner, that Q, another waiter, has taken payment for the meal.[12] "Wait" is more apt to cover the case whereby a strategem (for example sending his son to the door to say "Daddy's out", or returning bills marked "Not known at this address") D delays his creditor. The creditor in such cases does not forgo payment but is made to wait for it.

Section 2 (3) provides that where P is induced to accept a worthless cheque in payment, as happened in *Turner*, he is to be treated as not being paid and being induced to wait for payment. Strictly the acceptance of a cheque as payment suspends the creditor's remedies until the cheque is either honoured or dishonoured; this provision, however, provides that for the purpose of s. 2 (1) (b) the creditor is induced to wait for payment.

---

10. In *Holt* [1981] 2 All ER 854, [1981] 1 WLR 1000, counsel submitted that paragraph (a) required the legal consequence that the debt be extinguished while under paragraph (b) the forgoing of a liability did not require that the liability be extinguished. Lawson J found "great difficulty in introducing these concepts into the construction of the subsection".
11. [1974] AC 357, [1973] 3 All ER 124, HL.
12. *Holt* [1981] 2 All ER 854, [1981] 1 WLR 1000.

3) *Obtaining an Exemption from or an Abatement of Liability*

Section 2 (1) (c) differs from s. 2 (1) (a) and (b) in that the latter assume an existing liability and a subsequent deception, whereas (c) is concerned with a deception which induces P to confer an exemption from or abatement of a prospective liability. The provision was explained by the CLRC[13] –

"The ratepayer who makes a false statement in order to obtain a rebate to which he is not entitled is acting dishonestly and is practising a deception in order to obtain an abatement of his liability to pay rates and, accordingly, would be guilty of an offence under clause 2 (1) (c). The wording of this provision, 'where a person by any deception ... dishonestly obtains any exemption from or abatement of liability to make a payment' is intended to cover cases where the deception has induced the victim to believe that there is nothing due to him or that the amount due to him is less than would be the case if he knew the true facts. Another example of the application of this part of clause 2 is the case where a person by deception obtains services at a reduced rate (for example, air travel at a special rate for students when the traveller is not a student)."

There is, however, a difficulty with the operation of paragraph (c) of the same nature as that which, as it has been suggested,[14] applies to paragraph (a). Suppose D, a ratepayer, makes false statements in order to secure a reduction in his rates and the rating authority accordingly assess his rates at £200 rather than the proper rateable value which is £300. D does not thereby obtain an "abatement of liability" because his liability to pay £300 continues undiminished. Of course at some stage the rating authority will make a demand for £200 and at that stage they will, as a result of the continuing deception by D, be induced to forgo part of the existing liability to pay £300 and the case falls within paragraph (b). But strictly, and though this was not the result intended by the CLRC, the case does not fall within paragraph (c) which is, on this view, likely to be of only limited application. Again the gap is not a serious one because at a later stage D will normally commit an offence under paragraph (b) and, indeed, by submitting the false claim to the rating authority he would appear to be guilty of an attempt.

In *Sibartie*,[15] however, it was held that D was guilty of an attempt to commit the offence under paragraph (c) where, on passing a ticket inspector, he flashed (i.e. held it up so briefly that the inspector could not read it) an invalid season ticket. The court said the proper approach to paragraph (c) was to consider its "ordinary meaning" and ask whether D's conduct came within that. D could be taken as representing that he was the holder of a valid ticket, that he was not under a liability to pay, and was thus trying to obtain an exemption from his liability to pay the fare. So he was but, assuming he successfully deceives the inspector, he has not persuaded the inspector to remit the liability but rather to believe there is no liability. And whatever liability D has is not in law remitted. What D has done is to persuade the inspector to forgo a payment which is due and the case falls within paragraph (b).

13. Cmnd. 6733, para. 15.
14. See above, p. 565, and Smith, *Theft*, para. 239.
15. [1983] Crim LR 470, CA.

4) *Legally Enforceable Liability*

By s. 2 (2) an offence under s. 2 (1) may be committed only where the liability is legally enforceable. The section thus has no application to a "liability" which is unenforceable because it is illegal or against public policy or is for any other reason unenforceable; a minor cannot commit an offence under this section if the transaction to which it relates is one that is unenforceable against him.

Nor does s. 2 (1) apply in relation to a liability which has not been accepted or established to pay compensation for a wrongful act or omission. "Without this provision", said the CLRC,[16]

"there would be room for argument that subsection (1) (a) of the clause applies where, for example, a person lies about the circumstances of an accident in order to avoid the bringing of civil proceedings for negligence against him. We think that the dividing line is reached where liability is not disputed even though the amount of that liability is. On this basis it would be an offence under clause 2 (1) (a) for an antique dealer to lie about the age and value of jewellery sent to him for valuation which had been lost as a result of his admitted negligence, but not for him to lie about the circumstances of the loss in disputing an allegation of negligence. We see no justification for extending the criminal law to cases where the existence of any liability is disputed: the claimant can launch civil proceedings if he thinks he had been deceived when he absolved the other party from liability."

The "dividing line" is a fine one. The jeweller commits an offence under the section if by deception he induces P to settle on the basis that the jewellery is worth £100 when it is worth £500, but not if by deception he induces P to believe that he has not been negligent so that P drops his claim altogether.

8 Cheating

Cheating was a misdemeanour at common law and was developed most vigorously during the eighteenth century and it appears to require a large and liberal definition to encompass the authorities. Hawkins[17] defined cheating as

". . . deceitful practices, in defrauding or endeavouring to defraud another of his own right by means of some artful device, contrary to the plain rules of common honesty."

The common law offence of cheating still retains some importance because though s. 32 (1) of the Act abolishes cheating (along with common law offences against property) it does so only "except as regards offences relating to the public revenue". The punishment is imprisonment and/or a fine without limit.

---

16. Cmnd. 6733, para. 16.
17. 1 PC 318.

As a practical matter the offence of cheating has been used, on any scale at all, only in connection with frauds against the public revenue. In *Hudson*[18] the Court of Criminal Appeal upheld D's conviction on a charge of making false statements to the prejudice of the Crown and the public revenue with intent to defraud where it appeared that D had falsely stated to the Inland Revenue the profits of his business. It was argued that the indictment disclosed no offence known to the law, but the court, relying on dicta of Lord Mansfield CJ in *Bembridge*,[19] and statements by Hawkins[20] and East,[1] held that it was an offence for a private individual, as well as a public officer, to defraud the Crown and public.

The Criminal Law Revision Committee was minded to abolish the offence and its retention was the result of special pleading by the revenue authorities who wished to retain it for serious revenue frauds where penalties under other provisions were seen by them as inadequate. Perhaps, too, the revenue was attracted by the expansive terminology of Hawkins' definition. At all events the revenue's fondest hopes for cheating must have been realised by *Mavji*.[2] D had dishonestly evaded value added tax to the tune of over £1,000,000. Charged, as he might have been, under s. 38 (1) of the Finance Act 1972 with the fraudulent evasion of tax he would have been liable to a maximum of two years' imprisonment and/or a fine of £1,000 or three times the tax whichever was the greater. Convicted, as he was, of cheating he was sentenced to six years' imprisonment and made criminally bankrupt in the sum of £690,000. The Court of Appeal, affirming D's conviction and sentence, rejected counsel's submission that cheating required a positive act such as a deception and not merely an omission to make a VAT return. The court held that D was under a duty to make such a return and his failure to do so with intent to cheat the revenue of money to which it was entitled constituted the offence.

So to hold was, with respect, a novel extension of the offence. *Hudson*,[3] which was treated in *Mavji* as the leading case, appears to assume that cheating requires the use of a false representation or false device. Even the expansive language of Hawkins is conditioned by the requirement "by means of some artful device". What artful device was employed by D in *Mavji*?

9 Making off without Payment[4]

By s. 3 of the Theft Act 1978 –

"1) Subject to subsection (3) below, a person who, knowing that payment on the spot for any goods supplied or service done is required or

---

18. [1956] 2 QB 252, [1956] 1 All ER 814, discussed by "Watchful" [1956] BTR 119.
19. (1783) 22 State, Tr 1 at 156.
20. 1 PC 322.
    1. 2 PC 821.
    2. [1987] 2 All ER 758, [1987] 1 WLR 1388, CA.
    3. Supra.
    4. See Spencer, "The Theft Act 1978" [1979] Crim LR 24, 35; Syrota, "Annotations to Theft Act 1978" in Current Law Statutes.

expected from him, dishonestly makes off without having paid as required or expected and with intent to avoid payment of the amount due shall be guilty of an offence.

2) For purposes of this section 'payment on the spot' includes payment at the time of collecting goods on which work has been done or in respect of which service has been provided.

3) Subsection (1) above shall not apply where the supply of the goods or the doing of the service is contrary to law, or where the service done is such that payment is not legally enforceable.

4) Any person may arrest without warrant anyone who is, or whom he, with reasonable cause, suspects to be, committing or attempting to commit an offence under this section."

By s. 4 the offence, which is triable either way, is punishable on summary conviction by imprisonment and/or a fine not exceeding the prescribed maximum (presently £1,000), and on indictment by imprisonment for a term not exceeding two years and/or a fine.

This offence aims to deal in a simple and straightforward way with conduct commonly called "bilking". It deals with the man who, having consumed a meal in a restaurant, or filled the tank of his car with petrol, or having reached his destination in a taxi, decamps without paying. These cases, as we have seen,[5] for all their factual simplicity create considerable difficulties in relation to offences of theft and deception. There are no such difficulties under s. 3. There is no requirement whatever that D's conduct should otherwise amount to theft or deception or even that he has practised any deception.

It might be noted that the offence creates an exception to the general principle that it is not an offence dishonestly to avoid the payment of a debt. The exception is, however, limited and understandable. In the ordinary case a dishonest debtor can be coerced into payment without employment of criminal sanctions; where bilking is involved it is usually a matter of enforcement on the spot or never. Hence by s. 3 (4) a power of arrest is conferred for, without this, the enforcement of the law would be jeopardised.

1) *Makes off*

"Makes off" might be thought of as having a pejorative connotation implying some stealth in the person making off. Certainly it extends to such cases (the diner who waits till the manager leaves the room or decamps via the cloakroom) but it cannot be confined to such cases. A motorist who drives off after filling his tank with petrol is properly said to make off though it is done openly and without stealth; so too a heavyweight boxer whose departure cannot be prevented by a timorous P. "Makes off" appears to mean simply that D leaves one place (the place where the payment is required) for another place. Nor does the offence require that D

---

5. See, for example, *Director of Public Prosecutions v Ray* [1974] AC 370, [1973] 3 All ER 131, HL, above, p. 551; *Edwards v Ddin* [1976] 3 All ER 705, [1976] 1 WLR 942.

should have made off from P's premises such as an hotel or a restaurant; the spot from which D makes off is simply the place where payment is required and may be a newsvendor's stand or an ice-cream van on the highway. If D has not left the first place he has not made off but if he is in the process of leaving there may be an attempt.[6]

If D leaves with P's consent it may be more difficult to say that D has made off. Suppose that D, having determined never to pay, gives his correct name and address to P and is allowed to go. It would seem difficult to say that D had made off; D has left without paying but the offence requires something more than that. Suppose, though, that E, who also intends never to pay, gives a false name and address to P and is allowed to go. The cases differ in that D can be traced and coerced into payment while E cannot be traced at all. Spencer[7] argues that the difference is material. The mischief aimed at, he says, is the bilking customer who cannot be traced and he supports this by reference to the power of arrest afforded P; it would be highly undesirable if P could arrest a customer of whose identity he is aware, that power being required for the unidentifiable bilker.

Spencer's argument has force but is not easy to square with the language of s. 3. Assume that D is P's best customer of many years' standing. One day D determines not to pay and decamps from the premises via the lavatory window. All the elements of the offence appear to be present unless it is to be said that D did not make off. It may puzzle us all to wonder why D should have thought that he could get away with it but he seems clearly to have made off. A customer in a wheelchair would surely make off if he decamps without paying though he does not at all fancy his chances of outpacing the restaurateur.

Nor does s. 3 obviously give rise to the interpretation that D does not make off if he gives a correct identification but E does make off if he gives a false one. Suppose in the latter case that P orders a taxi for E and bids him a cheery farewell. Can it really be said that E has made off?[8]

If, however, P permits D to leave the spot where payment is required for a purely temporary purpose (for example to answer a telephone call or to collect his wallet from his overcoat which he has deposited in the cloak-room) expecting him to return to settle up, it is submitted that D commits the offence if he then decamps. In such cases P has not consented to D leaving without paying. So where P, a taxi driver, permits D to leave so that D, as he claims, may go into his house to get the fare it would appear that D, if he then decamps, has made off within the section.

2) *Goods Supplied or Service Done*

The offence requires that the goods be *supplied* or that a service be *done*. Most obviously goods are supplied where P delivers them to D but the

---

6. *Brooks and Brooks* (1983) 76 Cr App Rep 66, [1983] Crim LR 188, CA; making off, said the Court, "may be an exercise accompanied by the sound of trumpets or a silent stealing away after the folding of tents".
7. [1983] Crim LR 573.
8. Cf. *Hammond* [1982] Crim LR 611, below, p. 573.

offence cannot be limited to the case of delivery by P. Petrol is clearly supplied to D at a self-service filling station though D supplies himself and, by the same token, goods taken from the shelves in a self-service store are supplied.[9] Supplied in this context connotes goods proffered by P and accordingly taken by D. Hence it would not be an offence under this section (though it may be theft) for D to take goods in a shop which is not self-service; such goods are not proffered until tendered by P or his assistant. It is thought that goods may be supplied though D has a dishonest intent from the outset and accordingly steals the goods; it can hardly have been intended that theft and making off should be mutually exclusive since the effect would be mischievous.

Where service is concerned the service must be "done". Obvious examples of a service done is the provision of hotel accommodation or a meal in a restaurant but it will also apply to the collection of goods, such as clothes, shoes or cars, on which work has been done. A service may be done (as goods may be supplied) though nothing is done by P other than proffering the service of which D takes advantage, as where D is permitted to park his car on P's lot.

There is no definition of "service" in s. 3 as there is of "services" in s. 2 but it is not easy to see that any difference of significance was intended and reference may be made to the discussion above.[10]

3) *Unenforceable Debts*

The offence under s. 3, unlike the offence under s. 1, cannot be committed where the supply of the goods or the doing of the service is contrary to law; or where the service done is such that payment is not legally enforceable. The reason for the distinction is that while the aim of s. 1 is to punish fraud, the aim of s. 3, as seen by the CLRC,[11] is to protect legitimate business. Thus it is no offence for D to make off from a brothel, or from a betting shop without paying for services rendered.

Whether a supply of goods or services is contrary to law or whether payment for a service is not legally enforceable involves a consideration of the general law and cannot be detailed here. But the distinction which the section makes may be illustrated by reference to an impecunious minor. If a landlord supplies intoxicating liquor to a minor the transaction is contrary to law and the minor commits no offence in making off without payment. If the minor has a service provided which is not a "necessary" (say flying lessons) he commits no offence in making off since payment for the service is not legally enforceable. If the minor is supplied with non-necessary goods (say eleven fancy waistcoats) and makes off he commits the offence; while payment for the waistcoats is not legally enforceable, the supply of these *goods* is not contrary to law.

---

9. *Contra* Griew, *Theft*, 178, and A. T. H. Smith [1981] Crim LR 590.
10. At p. 562.
11. Cmnd. 6733, para. 19.

4) *Without Having Paid*

Normally this case presents no problems; D has either paid or he has not. But two points may be made. The first is where D pays by cheque supported by a cheque card or uses a credit card. It may be that as between D and his bank he is exceeding his authority but it is submitted that P is none the less paid. In the result it may be the bank that has to pay for the goods or service supplied by P to D but, so far as P is concerned, he is paid for he knows that, whatever the state of D's finances, he will get his money.

The second concerns payment by a worthless cheque, that is a cheque that D knows will not be met. In this case (unlike the first) P looks to D for payment and, believing that he has been paid, allows D to leave. It has been argued that a bad cheque is no more a payment than counterfeit money[12] but in *Hammond*[13] the trial judge thought there was a difference in that one who takes a cheque without a cheque card knows he is taking a risk. He further suggested that if P takes such a cheque and allows D to depart, it cannot be said that D makes off. It would follow that if P unwittingly accepts counterfeit money and allows D to depart, no more can D be said to make off.

The difficulty of the case, then, lies not so much in saying that D has left "without having paid", for a payment in counterfeit money or by a worthless cheque is not a payment, but in the effect which the apparent payment has on P. If as a result he agrees to D's departure it is difficult to say that D makes off.

5) *Mens Rea*

The offence requires that D should make off (i) dishonestly; (ii) knowing that payment on the spot is required or expected from him; and (iii) with intent to avoid payment.

1 Dishonestly

Reference may be made to the general discussion of dishonesty.[14] It does not matter at what stage D decides to act dishonestly so long as he is dishonest when he makes off. While dishonesty is a question for the jury D would not be dishonest in refusing to pay for goods or a service genuinely believed by him to be deficient.

2 Knowing that Payment on the Spot is Required or Expected of Him

The offence is concerned only with cases where payment on the spot is required. Such transactions are difficult to define in abstract terms but usually easy enough to identify.[15] They can be identified by regard to

---

12. Griew, *Theft*, 181.
13. [1982] Crim LR 611 (Judge Morrison).
14. Above, p. 555.
15. S. 3 (1) provides that it includes "payment at the time of collecting goods on which work has been done or in respect of which service has been provided". But this seems to have been added *ex abundanti cautela* and adds nothing. See Smith, *Theft*, para. 245.

normal trading practices though these may in particular instances be modified by the course of dealing between the parties.[16] If D honestly believes that the transaction is on credit terms, he cannot be convicted of this offence for he is not acting dishonestly and he does not *know* the transaction to be a spot transaction. And where D believes that payment is to be made by another (for example, where he believes that E will pay for the meal) he does not commit the offence because he neither acts dishonestly nor does he know that payment is to be required of him.[17]

3 Intention to Avoid Payment

Unlike s. 2 (1)(b) of the 1978 Act with which s. 3 invites comparison, the latter does not in terms require an intention to make permanent default and commentators tended to favour the view that, and always providing that D was acting dishonestly, an intention temporarily to avoid payment would suffice. *Allen*[18] holds, and rightly it is respectfully submitted, that the offence requires an intention to make permanent default. D had left an hotel without settling his bill and the trial judge directed the jury that all that was required was an intention to make default at the time payment was required. The Court of Appeal held, however, that an intention to make permanent default was required because s. 3 required both (i) a making off without paying on the spot; and (ii) an intent to avoid payment. In view of the requirement in (i), (ii) made sense only if permanent default was intended. The House of Lords endorsed this view and drew further support for it by reference to the fact that the Criminal Law Revision Committee had intended permanent default to be necessary.[19]

10 False Accounting and Other Frauds

1) *False Accounting*

By s. 17 of the Theft Act:

"1) Where a person dishonestly, with a view to gain for himself or another or with intent to cause loss to another, –

    a) destroys, defaces, conceals or falsifies any account or any record or document made or required for any accounting purpose; or

    b) in furnishing information for any purpose produces or makes use of any account, or any such record or document as aforesaid, which to his knowledge is or may be misleading, false or deceptive in a material particular;

he shall, on conviction on indictment, be liable to imprisonment for a term not exceeding seven years.

---

16. It cannot be enough that P requires a payment to be made on the spot, e.g. seeing D who owes him £10 lent a month ago, P demands payment on the spot. The reference is to those transactions where payment customarily follows immediately upon the provision of the goods or service.
17. *Brooks and Brooks* (1983) 76 Cr App Rep 66, [1983] Crim LR 188, CA.
18. [1985] AC 1059, [1985] 1 All ER 148, HL.
19. Cmnd. 6733, para. 18.

2) For purposes of this section a person who makes or concurs in making in an account or other document an entry which is or may be misleading, false or deceptive in a material particular, or who omits or concurs in omitting a material particular from an account or other document, is to be treated as falsifying the account or document."

Where D falsifies any document or record made for an accounting purpose he might often commit offences independently of this section. He might, for example, commit forgery or he might commit, or attempt to commit, an offence under s. 2 of the 1978 Act. But the offence under s. 17 is wider than forgery or evading liability in some respects.

1 Actus Reus

The offence may be committed by any person who falsifies etc. any document "made or required" for an accounting purpose. A document is "made" for an accounting purpose where that is the purpose of the document; but a document may be "required" for an accounting purpose though made for some other purpose so long as it is required, if only in part, for an accounting purpose.[20] The offence may be committed whether or not the person to whom the document is addressed accepts or acts on it.

"Any account or any record" is wide enough to include a mechanical accounting device such as a computer, a taximeter,[1] or a turnstile which records paying customers.[2] The admission of two persons through one movement of the turnstile amounts to falsification by the omission of a material particular. The section further extends to any document, so long as it is made or required for *any* accounting purpose, though the document itself is not in the nature of an account and though the falsification does not relate to figures. So if D enters in a hire-purchase proposal false particulars relating to a company director, the case would fall within the plain words of s. 17 (1)(a). If D, or E, were to use that document in furnishing information to P, the case would fall within s. 17 (1)(b) if the information was material. The information is so material if it is something that matters to P in making up his mind about action to be taken on the document.[3] D or E may commit the offence in furnishing information not only where they know of the falsification, but also where they know that the document *may* be false or misleading in a material particular; evidently wilful blindness suffices.

But some account of P's must be falsified by D or as a result of information provided by D. It is not enough that D is, as by selling his own property as P's, cheating P if that transaction is not recorded in any account of P's.[4]

2 Mens Rea

The *mens rea* of the offence requires that D (i) intentionally or recklessly falsifies etc. the document, or so uses a document knowing[5] it is false; and

---

20. *A–G's Reference (No. 1 of 1980)* [1981] 1 All ER 366, [1981] 1 WLR 34, CA.
1. Cf. *Solomons* [1909] 2 KB 980.
2. *Edwards v Toombs* [1983] Crim LR 43, DC.
3. *Mallett* [1978] 3 All ER 10, [1978] 1 WLR 820, CA.
4. *Cooke* [1986] AC 909, [1986] 2 All ER 985, HL.
5. Which may include wilful blindness as to falsity.

(ii) does so dishonestly and with a view to gain for himself or another, or with intent to cause loss to another.

So far as dishonesty is concerned reference may be made to the discussion elsewhere.[6] No doubt dishonesty should be interpreted here so as to accord with the meaning given it in other sections of the Act.

So far as view to gain and intent to cause loss are concerned "gain" and "loss" are defined in s. 34 (2) (a)[7] which is discussed elsewhere.[8] In this context it may be worth emphasising that there might be a view to gain or an intent to cause loss in falsifying the account although the gain or loss has already taken place. "Gain", for instance, includes a gain by keeping what one has, so it is clear that D would commit an offence under s. 17 where, having already appropriated property of P's, he destroys, defaces, conceals or falsifies an account so that he will not be found out, or to put off the evil day when he will be called to account.[9]

In this connection it is worth considering the facts of *Wines*,[10] where D falsified accounts to exaggerate the profit which the radio department, of which he was in charge, was making in order to induce his employer to continue his employment. In such a case there may be no appropriation, or intended appropriation, of any money or goods belonging to the employer, but clearly D is acting dishonestly, and it seems he has both a view to gain (he does this to keep his job and its salary) and an intent to cause loss (in so far as he realises that his employer would make greater profits with an efficient manager).

2) *False Statements by Company Directors*

Section 19 of the Act provides:

"1) Where an officer of a body corporate or unincorporated association (or person purporting to act as such), with intent to deceive members or creditors of the body corporate or association about its affairs, publishes or concurs in publishing a written statement or account which to his knowledge is or may be misleading, false or deceptive in a material particular, he shall on conviction on indictment be liable to imprisonment for a term not exceeding seven years.

2) For purposes of this section a person who has entered into a security for the benefit of a body corporate or association is to be treated as a creditor of it.

3) Where the affairs of a body corporate or association are managed by its members, this section shall apply to any statement which a member publishes or concurs in publishing in connection with his functions of management as if he were an officer of the body corporate or association."

---

6. See above, p. 525 and p. 555.
7. Set out below, p. 592.
8. See below, p. 593.
9. *Eden* [1971] Crim LR 416, CA.
10. [1953] 2 All ER 1497, CCA.

In two senses the offence created by this section is a narrow one. Firstly, it may be committed only by an officer[11] of a body corporate or unincorporated association. Secondly, it may be committed only where the intent is to deceive[12] members or creditors of the corporation or association about its affairs. But in another sense the offence is a wide one for it extends to the publication of any written statement or account which may be misleading in a material particular. It is not necessary to show that there is any view to gain or intent to cause loss in publishing the statement or account, though no doubt either or both will often be present. The offence might be committed where an officer, in order to inspire confidence in the company, falsely publishes that a well-known person has been appointed to the board. Possibly the offence might be committed where an officer publishes in the accounts a payment as having been made to the Conservative Party where it has in fact been paid to the Labour Party.

3) *Suppression of Documents*

By s. 20:
"1) A person who dishonestly, with a view to gain for himself or another or with intent to cause loss to another, destroys, defaces or conceals any valuable security, any will or other testamentary document or any original document of or belonging to, or filed or deposited in, any court of justice or any government department shall on conviction on indictment be liable to imprisonment for a term not exceeding seven years.

2) A person who dishonestly, with a view to gain for himself or another or with intent to cause loss to another, by any deception procures the execution of a valuable security[13] shall on conviction on indictment be liable to imprisonment for a term not exceeding seven years; and this subsection shall apply in relation to the making, acceptance, indorsement, alteration, cancellation or destruction in whole or in part of a valuable security, and in relation to the signing or sealing of any paper or other material in order that it may be made or converted into, or used or dealt with as, a valuable security, as if that were the execution of a valuable security.

3) For purposes of this section 'deception' has the same meaning as in section 15 of this Act, and 'valuable security'[14] means any document creating, transferring, surrendering or releasing any right to, in or over property, or authorising the payment of money or delivery of any property, or evidencing the creation, transfer, surrender or release of any such right, or the payment of money or delivery of any property, or the satisfaction of any obligation."

11. The officers of a body corporate are frequently defined in the articles or by-laws of a corporation.
12. As to intent to deceive, see *Welham v Director of Public Prosections* [1961] AC 103, [1960] 1 All ER 805, HL.
13. *Beck* [1985] 1 All ER 571 extends execution to action taken on the security; the decision is criticised by Griew, *Theft*, 175. Cf. *Bevan* (1986) 84 Cr App Rep 143, CA.
14. See *Benstead and Taylor* (1982) 75 Cr App Rep 276, [1982] Crim LR 456, CA.

Despite its length this provision is not likely to be of great practical importance.

"It seemed to us that it might provide the only way of dealing with a person who, for example, suppressed a public document as a first step towards committing a fraud but did not get so far as attempting to commit the fraud. In accordance with the scheme of the [Act] the offence is limited to something done dishonestly[15] and with a view to gain or with intent to cause loss[16] to another."[17]

11 Temporary Deprivation

In general, as has been seen,[18] it is not an offence dishonestly to use the property of another unless there is an intention to deprive the other permanently of the property. There is a case to be made out for creating a general offence (which need not necessarily be termed theft) of dishonest use, but the Criminal Law Revision Committee decided against any such course and their view, though subject to vigorous assault in Parliament, was accepted. The Committee were of the opinion – and, it is submitted, were quite rightly of the opinion – that such a considerable extension of the criminal law was not called for by any existing serious evil.[19] But there are particular cases in which temporary deprivation of property is a serious evil. The taking of motor vehicles (which was first made an offence by s. 28 of the Road Traffic Act 1930) is one obvious instance; and the taking of vessels (which was first made an offence by s. 1 of the Vessels Protection Act 1967) is another. These offences are now dealt with in s. 12 of the Theft Act which extends the prior law by making it an offence to take a much wider range of conveyances.

To the offence of taking conveyances the Theft Act adds a further and new offence of temporary deprivation; that of removing articles from places open to the public. Before the Act there had been a number of notorious "removals" such as the removal from the National Gallery of Goya's portrait of the Duke of Wellington, and the Committee thought the problem "serious enough to justify the creation of a special offence".[20]

1) *Removal of Articles from Places Open to the Public*

Section 11 of the Theft Act 1968 provides:
"1) Subject to subsections (2) and (3) below, where the public have access to a building in order to view the building or part of it, or a collection or part of a collection housed in it, any person who without lawful

15. See above, p. 525 and p. 555.
16. See below, p. 592.
17. Cmnd. 2977, para. 106.
18. Above, p. 532.
19. Cmnd. 2977, para. 56.
20. Ibid, para. 57 (ii).

authority removes from the building or its grounds the whole or part of any article displayed or kept for display to the public in the building or that part of it or in its grounds shall be guilty of an offence.

For this purpose 'collection' includes a collection got together for a temporary purpose, but references in this section to a collection do not apply to a collection made or exhibited for the purpose of effecting sales or other commercial dealings.

2) It is immaterial for purposes of subsection (1) above, that the public's access to a building is limited to a particular period or particular occasion; but where anything removed from a building or its grounds is there otherwise than as forming part of, or being on loan for exhibition with, a collection intended for permanent exhibition to the public, the person removing it does not thereby commit an offence under this section unless he removes it on a day when the public have access to the building as mentioned in subsection (1) above.

3) A person does not commit an offence under this section if he believes that he has lawful authority for the removal of the thing in question or that he would have it if the person entitled to give it knew of the removal and the circumstances of it.

4) A person guilty of an offence under this section shall, on conviction on indictment, be liable to imprisonment for a term not exceeding five years."

1 Actus Reus

On the face of it the offence under s. 11 is one of some complexity. As we have seen[1] the intention was to deal with a specific mischief and care has been taken to confine the operation of the section to that mischief. The following points arise for consideration.

a) *Public access to a building in order to view*. The public must have access to the building and the access must be *in order* to view the building (or part of the building) or a collection (or part of a collection) housed in it. The public might have access to a building (a shopping precinct or arcade for example) where collections are from time to time exhibited in the lanes connecting the shops; but here access exists in order to shop and it is only incidental to access that the public may view the collection. If, however, the collection is housed in a part of the precinct and access is given to that part so that a collection may be viewed, it would be within the section.

Access must be public access; access limited to a particular section of the public will not suffice.[2] It does not matter that the public are required to pay for the privilege of access, whether the purpose of imposing the charge is merely to cover expenses or to make a profit.[3] But the access must be to a building or part thereof. So if D removes a statuette displayed in the open in a municipal park this would not be within the section. If, however, the

---

1. Supra.
2. But the exclusion of a particular class, for example, the exclusion of children from an exhibition considered unsuitable for them, would not prevent access being public access.
3. But see below, p. 580.

park consists of a building and its grounds, and the public have access to the building in order to view, D's removal of the statuette would be within this section.

Normally, no doubt, D will have entered in consequence of the owner's invitation[4] to the public to view. But, so long as the public have access to view, D may commit the offence although he entered as a trespasser, or although he is the owner's guest and is temporarily residing in the building.

b) *Articles displayed or kept for display.* The offence proscribes the removal of any articles displayed or kept for display, and is not confined to works of art. The coronation stone in Westminster Abbey (something which the Committee expressly considered[5]) is clearly for this purpose an article displayed to the public though it is not a work of art. The criterion is only whether the article, which may be priceless in either sense of the term, is displayed or kept for display to the public.

"Display" here is presumably used in the sense of exhibit and not merely in the sense of able to be seen; the article must be displayed or exhibited *to the public.*[6] Consequently the removal of a fire extinguisher would not be within the section even though it can be seen by members of the public,[7] but it would be within the section if the fire extinguisher was exhibited as an example of an early type of extinguisher, or was in fact an up-to-date extinguisher which was exhibited as an example of good design.

It is enough that the article, though not displayed, is "kept" for display, as where a painting is kept in the gallery's store-room.[8]

c) *Removal.* To complete the offence the article must be removed from the building or from its grounds. But the removal, as s. 11 (2) makes clear, need not be during the times at which the public have access. If the collection is permanently[9] exhibited (which would be the case, for example, with municipal galleries and museums) removal at any time, even on a bank holiday when the building is closed to the public, may amount to an offence. But if the exhibition is temporary only, the removal must take place on a day when the public have access to the building in order to view.

d) *Commercial exhibitions.* As has been seen,[10] s. 11 applies notwithstanding that the owner charges the public for admission, and even though he admits the public only to make profit. But, whether the owner charges for admission or not, the section does not apply where the owner admits the public only to view a collection,[11] where the collection is "made or exhibited for the purpose of effecting sales or other commercial dealings".

4. *Barr* [1978] Crim LR 244 (Deputy Judge Lowry) and commentary.
5. Cmnd. 2977. Cp. *Barr* [1978] Crim LR 244, CA.
6. So linked in *Barr.*
7. Cf. Smith, *Theft*, 269.
8. Cf. *Durkin* [1973] QB 786, [1973] 2 All ER 872, CA.
9. In this context "permanently" means for an indefinite period: *Durkin* [1973] 1 QB 786, [1973] 2 All ER 872, CA.
10. Above, p. 579.
11. Note that if the owner admits the public to view the building as well as the collection D may commit the offence by removing anything displayed (including articles forming part of the collection) although the collection is exhibited for commercial purposes. Cf. Smith, *Theft*, para. 276.

It may seem odd that the law draws this distinction between exhibitions for commercial and non-commercial purposes. The reason given for it is that, but for this restriction upon the offence, the offence would be very wide indeed, and would have created a very substantial exception to the general principle that temporary deprivation should not be a criminal offence.[12] It would have meant, for example, that a removal from the premises of the ordinary commercial bookseller would have been an offence.

As it stands the limitation applies only where the collection is made or exhibited *for the purpose* of sale or other commercial dealings. If then a commercial bookseller, for the purpose of encouraging local art, arranges exhibitions in a room of his bookshop to which the public are admitted, the removal by D of the paintings, or of any other article displayed or kept for display in his premises, would fall within the section. Nor can it make any difference that the artists themselves hope that the exhibition of their work will lead to its sale.

2 Mens Rea

D must intend to remove the article from the building or its grounds. Dishonesty is not required but D would not be guilty of an offence if he removed an article in the belief (and clearly the test of D's belief is here subjective) that he had lawful authority or that the person entitled to give consent would have done so.[13] Strictly it would be an offence for D to remove a statuette from the house to the garden because he thinks the setting better, provided he believes the person entitled to give consent would not have done so.

2) *Taking Conveyances*[14]

Section 12 of the Theft Act 1968 provides:

"1) Subject to subsections (5) and (6) below, a person shall be guilty of an offence if, without having the consent of the owner or other lawful authority, he takes any conveyance for his own or another's use or, knowing that any conveyance has been taken without such authority, drives it or allows himself to be carried in or on it.

2) A person guilty of an offence under subsection (1) above shall on conviction on indictment be liable to imprisonment for a term not exceeding three years.

3) (Repealed.)[15]

4) If on the trial of an indictment for theft the jury are not satisfied that the accused committed theft, but it is proved that the accused committed an offence under subsection (1) above, the jury may find him guilty of the offence under subsection (1).

12. The clause as originally drafted would have excluded not only the case where the public was invited to view the contents for a commercial object, but also where the public was invited to view the building for a commercial object. The latter limitation was removed; cf. last footnote.
13. See further in connection with the offences under s. 12; below, p. 584.
14. See White, "Taking the Joy out of Joy-Riding" [1980] Crim LR 609.
15. The power of arrest formerly in this subsection is now in PACE, 1984, s. 24(2)(d).

5) Subsection (1) above shall not apply in relation to pedal cycles; but, subject to subsection (6) below, a person who, without having the consent of the owner or other lawful authority, takes a pedal cycle for his own or another's use, or rides a pedal cycle knowing it to have been taken without such authority, shall on summary conviction be liable to a fine [level 3 on the standard scale].

6) A person does not commit an offence under this section by anything done in the belief that he has lawful authority to do it or that he would have the owner's consent if the owner knew of his doing it and the circumstances of it.

7) For purposes of this section –

a) 'conveyance' means any conveyance constructed or adapted for the carriage of a person or persons whether by land, water or air, except that it does not include a conveyance constructed or adapted for use only under the control of a person not carried in or on it, and 'drive' shall be construed accordingly; and

b) 'owner', in relation to a conveyance which is the subject of a hiring agreement or hire-purchase agreement, means the person in possession of the conveyance under that agreement."

1 Taking for Own or Another's Use

The offence is committed where D "takes any conveyance for his own or another's use." This requires more than that D should use the conveyance for some purpose (say to sleep or shelter in it) since he must also take it. It has accordingly been held that the offence can be completed only by a taking, that is some movement, however slight, of the conveyance.[16] In the case of a motor vehicle the taking will be most frequently accomplished by driving but the taking may be accomplished in some other way, as by pushing or towing or even by removing the conveyance on a transporter. In *Pearce*[17] D's conviction was upheld when he took an inflatable dinghy and drove off with it on his trailer; the court rejecting an argument that the offence could be committed only where D took the conveyance by moving it in its own medium. The essence of the offence was thought by the Criminal Law Revision Committee to be stealing a ride.[18] Strictly, however, D may steal a ride without committing this offence. A hitch-hiker who jumps on to the back of a passing lorry literally steals a ride but does not commit the offence since in no sense has he *taken* the vehicle for his own or another's use. So too if D, without boarding the conveyance, releases the handbrake of a car so that it runs down an incline, or releases a boat from its moorings so that it is carried away by the tide, this would not fall within the section.[19] In neither case is the conveyance taken by D for his own or another's use.

---

16. *Bogacki* [1973] QB 832, [1973] 2 All ER 864, CA. Cf. *Miller* [1976] Crim LR 147, CA and *Diggin* (1980) 72 Cr App Rep 204, [1980] Crim LR 656, CA; below, p. 587. Without actual movement there may be an attempt to take.
17. [1973] Crim LR 321, CA.
18. Cmnd. 2977, para. 84.
19. Even though the owner temporarily loses the use of his car or boat and is as equally inconvenienced as by a taking. D may commit an offence of criminal damage if he intends that, or is reckless whether, the boat may be damaged.

Considering these last two examples the Court of Appeal in *Bow*[20] expressed the firm view that the reason why D was not guilty of an offence was that although the conveyance had been moved, it would not have been used as a conveyance. In other words "use" means, and means only, use as a conveyance. No doubt in the vast majority of cases D's purpose in taking the conveyance is to betake himself from one place to another but it is not entirely clear that the offence is, or ought to be, confined to such takings. In *Pearce* it does not clearly appear why D took the dinghy but in *Marchant and McCallister*[21] the Court of Appeal assumed that the conviction was based on D's intended use of the dinghy as a conveyance and confirmed that taking a conveyance with intent to use it on some future occasion as a conveyance sufficed.[1] *Bow* suggests, and *Marchant* appears clearly to confirm, that if D in *Pearce* had some use other than use as a conveyance in mind (e.g. to use it as a paddling pool for his children) he could not be convicted under s. 12. *Stokes*[2] is to the same effect. There it was held that D did not commit the offence where he pushed P's car around the corner to make P think it had been stolen.[3] The courts have interpreted s. 12 (1) as though the words "as a conveyance" had been inserted after "use". But on the face of it "use" is capable of extending to uses other than use as a conveyance.[4] The mischief aimed at is surely that the use of the conveyance is denied to P and it can be of no account to him to what use D puts it.

Even if use is restricted to use as a conveyance any such use suffices. It is enough that D releases a boat from its moorings so that he can be carried downstream in it.

So in *Bow*, where D released the handbrake of P's car and coasted some 200 yards down a narrow road in order to make egress for his own car, it was conceded that no distinction could be drawn between driving the motor and allowing it to coast. But it was argued that D had not used the car as a conveyance, merely to move it as an obstruction. The court accepted that to push an obstructing vehicle a yard or two to get it out of the way would not involve the use of the vehicle as a conveyance,[5] but where the vehicle was necessarily used as a conveyance, the taker cannot be heard to say that it was not for that use. Yet D did not use P's car in order to convey himself from one end of the lane to the other. It so happened that to remove it as an obstruction required its removal not for 2 yards but for 200. It is not easy to see why, if all D is doing is to remove a conveyance as an obstruction, the distance involved should make all that difference.[6]

Thus far it has been assumed that D is not in possession or control of the conveyance but it may happen that D already has lawful possession or

20. (1977) 64 Cr App Rep 54, [1977] Crim LR 176 and commentary; **SHC 475**.
21. (1985) 80 Cr App Rep 361.
  1. Equally a conditional intent (e.g. an intent to use should it prove suitable) will suffice.
  2. [1983] RTR 59, LA.
  3. The outcome of the case may have been different had D got into the car and steered it round the corner.
  4. See White, op. cit. at p. 611.
  5. In such circumstances D might in any case have lawful authority for the removal, see below, p. 584.
  6. In *Bow* D was probably engaged in a poaching expedition and P's car had been deliberately placed to block D's egress. But if D finds a vehicle blocking the highway he is presumably entitled to remove it whether he is on his way to or from a crime.

control and the question arises whether D can be said to "take" the conveyance by using it in an unauthorised way. Suppose, for example, that D, authorised to use P's van in the course of P's business, uses the van to take his family to the seaside. It seems clear that under this section he may commit the offence for he now "takes [the van] for his own ... use". D does not have the consent of P for the taking for his own use. This was the view taken by the Court of Appeal in *McGill*,[7] a case decided under s. 217 of the Road Traffic Act 1960. D, given permission to use P's car to drive E to the station and on condition that he returned it immediately, subsequently drove it elsewhere and did not return it for some days. D's conviction for taking the car without the consent of the owner, in relation to his use after the trip to the station, was upheld. The same result must follow under this provision of the Theft Act where there is no requirement for driving away and where the emphasis is squarely placed on taking "for his own or another's use". So in *McKnight v Davies*[8] the conviction of a lorry driver was upheld when instead of returning the lorry to the depot at the end of the working day he used it for his own purposes and did not return it till the early hours of the following morning.

McGill and *McKnight v Davies* were cases where the use by D was wholly at variance with the terms of the bailment or the terms of the employment so there was no difficulty in finding a taking for D's own use. It is thought, however, that not every deviation by a bailee from the terms of the bailment, or of an employee from the terms of his employment, would constitute a taking for his own use. There must be a use which is so at variance with the terms of the contract as to show that D has replaced use on behalf of another by use on his own behalf.[9] But there is an exception in the case of a hirer under a hire-purchase agreement. His unauthorised use cannot amount to an offence because by s. 12 (7) he is treated as owner for the purposes of the section.

2 Without Owner's Consent or Lawful Authority

The ordinary run of case where D takes P's vehicle without reference to P presents no problem. It follows from the discussion in the previous paragraph that where D has made reference to P, and has obtained P's permission to use the vehicle for a particular purpose and for a given time, D may be convicted of the offence if he uses it beyond that time for a different purpose: *McGill*.[10] There is no difficulty in such a case in saying that D has taken the vehicle for his own use, and that particular use is clearly one to which P has not consented.

McGill is a clear case. Suppose, however, that D had falsely represented that he was licensed to drive in order to borrow P's car for the trip to the

7. [1970] RTR 209, CA.
8. [1974] RTR 4, DC; **SHC 477**.
9. "Not every brief, unauthorised diversion from his proper route by an employee in the course of his working day will necessarily involve a 'taking' of the vehicle for his own use.": *McKnight v Davies* [1974] RTR 4 at 8, per Lord Widgery CJ. See also *Wibberley* [1966] 2 QB 214, [1965] 3 All ER 718, CCA; *Phipps* [1970] RTR 209. In determining whether an employee has taken his employers' vehicle it would seem proper to consider whether for civil purposes D is acting in the course of his employment.
10. [1970] RTR 209, CA; above, footnote 7.

station. There is perhaps no compelling reason why D should not be guilty of the offence since he knows perfectly well that P has "consented" only because he has been misled. But on a strict interpretation of the section all that is required is that P should have consented to D taking the car for the trip to the station (the taking for D's own use) and to this P may be said to have consented even though he would never have consented had he known that D was unlicensed. The point arose in *Whittaker v Campbell*.[11] D and E required a vehicle to transport goods but D was not licensed to drive and E had only a provisional licence. Somehow they came into possession of T's licence and D, representing himself as T, hired a vehicle from P. Their convictions for taking a vehicle without consent were quashed. The court thought that while there might be a taking without consent where the owner is by force compelled to part with possession, where he is induced to do so by fraud it could not be said "in commonsense terms" that he had not consented to the taking. The court then considered whether the offence would be committed where the fraud is such as to induce a fundamental mistake and thought that it would not make sense, having regard to the mischief at which the offence was aimed, to have D's liability turn upon whether the transaction was voidable for fraud or void for mistake. The distinction, as students of the law of contract will know, is a troublesome one and on the "commonsense" view there may be something to be said for not burdening students of the criminal law with it. But suppose that D personates P's brother on the telephone and induces P to agree the loan of his car to his brother and to leave the keys in an accessible spot while P is out of town. If D then avails himself of his trick to take possession of the car while P is away, it would be an astonishing conclusion to say that P had consented to D taking his car.

In *Whittaker v Campbell* there was no suggestion of any misrepresentation as to the use to which D and E proposed to put the vehicle and their actual use was within the terms of the hire. Suppose, however, that D obtains possession by specifying a use to which he knows P will consent while having in mind a use to which he knows P would not consent. D might, for example, secure P's consent to the use of his vehicle for the transportation of goods from Leeds to London knowing that P would not consent had he known that the goods were stolen. The case is essentially indistinguishable from *Whittaker v Campbell*. P has consented to the use of his vehicle for that journey though he would not have agreed to incur criminal liability as a handler of stolen goods. Suppose, though, that D's purpose is not to drive to London and back but to take the vehicle on a fortnight's holiday to the south of France. The point arose in *Peart*.[12] D persuaded P to lend him a van by pretending that he needed it for an urgent appointment in Alnwick and that he would return it by 7.30 p.m. In fact D wanted the van for a journey to Burnley where he was found with the van by the police at 9.00 p.m., and he knew all along that P would not have consented to this use. It was held, quashing D's conviction, that P's consent was not vitiated by the deception since P had merely been deceived

11. [1984] QB 318, [1983] 3 All ER 582, DC; **SHC 479**.
12. [1970] 2 QB 672, [1970] 2 All ER 823, CA.

as to the purpose for which the car was to be used and reliance was placed on this decision by the court in *Whittaker v Campbell*.

But there are difficulties with *Peart*. By reason of the direction given to the jury by the trial judge, the Court of Appeal had to consider the position at the time when the van was borrowed in the afternoon –

> "There was no issue left to [the jury] whether, in this particular case, there could have been a fresh taking ... at some time after it was originally taken away at 2.30 p.m. The consent which has to be considered is thus a consent at the time of taking possession of the van with licence to drive and use it."[13]

It seems then that even if he did not commit an offence at the time of the taking he would, like the defendants in *McGill* and *McKnight v Davies*,[14] have done so as soon as he departed from the Alnwick road and set course for Burnley. There is, however, a difference. In *McGill* and *McKnight v Davies* there was no evidence that the defendants had the unauthorised use in mind when they obtained possession but that proof was not lacking in *Peart* – D frankly admitted it – and it is submitted the case ought to be reconsidered. *Given* the use for a journey to which P had consented, D *took* it for a journey for which no consent was given. As a practical matter it will often be necessary to prove a departure from the stated use in order to prove that D intended to use the vehicle in other than the authorised way but this cannot affect the substantive law.

D commits no offence where he takes a vehicle, even without the consent of the owner, when acting under "other lawful authority". This is appropriate to cover cases where local authorities or the police are authorised under various statutory powers to remove vehicles, and where D is acting under some general ground of exculpation such as self-defence or duress. No doubt D would be acting lawfully in moving P's vehicle a few yards so that he can obtain access to the highway for his own vehicle, even though he may know that P does not consent to the removal.[15]

3 Conveyance

"Conveyance" as defined by s. 12 (7) (a) has been held to contemplate a mechanical contrivance of some kind. While it includes such conveyances as cars and motor-cycles, it does not include horses;[16] horses are clearly not constructed, though they may be suitable, for the carriage of persons, and the argument that they might be adapted by the use of halter and bridle was rejected.

Because the essence of the offence was thought to be stealing a ride,[17] conveyance is defined, in effect, to exclude conveyances which are not meant for riding.[18] Thus, though it would be an offence to take an aircraft, hovercraft or railway engine, it is not an offence within this section to take a

---

13. [1970] 2 All ER 823 at 824. It seems surprising that the proviso was not applied.
14. Above, p. 584.
15. But see *Bow* (1977) 64 Cr App Rep 54, CA, above p. 583.
16. *Neal v Gribble* (1978) 68 Cr App Rep 9, [1978] RTR 409.
17. Cf. Cmnd. 2977, para. 84. Earlier (para. 82) the Committee seemed to have viewed the mischief of the offence as the danger, loss and inconvenience which often result from it. See Hansard, H.L. Vol. 290, col. 141.
18. But on this see above, p. 582.

handcart or certain kinds of milk-float which, though power driven, are operated by a person who is not carried in or on it. A bath chair might fall within the definition but not a perambulator.

4 Driving or Being Carried

Where D takes a conveyance without consent or other lawful authority, it is an offence for E, knowing the conveyance has been so taken, to drive it or allow himself to be carried in or on it. A hitch-hiker would not be guilty of an offence where, unknown to him, the driver is using his employer's van, contrary to his instructions, to go to Blackpool for the day. If the driver tells the hitch-hiker that he is so using the van then the hitch-hiker will be liable if he allows himself to be carried further.[19] E's mere presence in the conveyance, knowing that it has been taken without consent or authority, does not suffice unless he allows himself to be "carried" in or on it and this requires some movement of the conveyance.[20]

It could happen that D believes he has authority to take the conveyance but E knows he has not. In such a case E would be guilty of an offence since he knows[1] it was taken without authority. And no doubt E knows the conveyance has been taken without authority, and may be convicted under this provision, though he knows that D has in fact stolen the conveyance.[2]

5 Pedal Cycles

Section 12 (5) creates an offence of taking pedal cycles which is broadly similar in its incidents to the offence under s. 12 (1). A small difference is that the offence under 12 (5) is not committed by one who allows himself to be carried on the cycle knowing that it has been taken without authority. And, of course, the offence is summary only.

6 Mens Rea

Section 12 (6) provides that a person does not commit an offence by anything done in the belief that he has lawful authority to do it or that the owner would have consented. The test of belief appears clearly to be subjective. If D honestly believes that P has consented to his use of P's car, it is not relevant to inquire whether P did in fact consent or whether P would have consented had he known that D was uninsured,[3] or even that D was unlicensed to drive. If D takes a vehicle "without having the consent of the owner" and does not believe that the owner would have consented had he known of the taking, he may be convicted though the owner subsequently says that he would have consented;[4] the offence is constituted not by taking a conveyance without the owner's consent, but in taking it without *having* the consent of the owner. If D takes a conveyance not caring whether the owner would or would not have consented, it would seem that he may be convicted for, in such a case, he does not *believe* that the owner

---

19. *Boldizsar v Knight* [1980] Crim LR 653, DC.
20. *Miller* [1976] Crim LR 147, CA; *Diggin* (1980) 72 Cr App Rep 204, [1981] RTR 83, CA.
 1. See above, p. 120 and infra.
 2. Cf. *Tolley v Giddings* [1964] 2 QB 354, [1964] 1 All ER 201.
 3. *Clotworthy* [1981] RTR 477, CA.
 4. *Ambler* [1979] RTR 217, CA.

would have consented. But where E is charged with driving or allowing himself to be carried in a conveyance taken by D, it must be shown that E *knew* that D had taken the conveyance without authority; presumably wilful blindness on E's part will suffice but it may be[5] that nothing short of actual knowledge will suffice. Hence E would be acquitted where he thinks it quite possible that D might have taken the vehicle without authority but makes no inquiries to ascertain whether this is so or not.

Taking a conveyance has been held to be a crime of basic intent so that evidence of intoxication is not relevant as tending to show that D lacked mens rea.[6]

12 Blackmail[7]

Originally the word blackmail was used to describe the tribute paid to Scottish chieftains by landowners in the border counties in order to secure immunity from raids on their lands. In the early stages of its development the crime of blackmail seems to have been pretty well coextensive with robbery and attempted robbery,[8] but over the years the definition has been extended to embrace more subtle methods of extortion. The law is now set out in s. 21 of the Theft Act:

"1) A person is guilty of blackmail if, with a view to gain for himself or another or with intent to cause loss to another, he makes any unwarranted demand with menaces; and for this purpose a demand with menaces is unwarranted unless the person making it does so in the belief—

    a) that he has reasonable grounds for making the demand; and

    b) that the use of the menaces is a proper means of reinforcing the demand.

2) The nature of the act or omission demanded is immaterial, and it is also immaterial whether the menaces do or do not relate to action to be taken by the person making the demand.

3) A person guilty of blackmail shall on conviction on indictment be liable to imprisonment for a term not exceeding fourteen years."

1 The Demand

A demand may take any form, and, no doubt, may be implicit as well as explicit. D may be guilty of blackmail where, for example, he apprehends P in the act of stealing and conveys to P, without any formal demand, that if P pays him money he will hear no more of the matter.[9] The humblest form of

---

5. Cf. *Tolley v Giddings* [1964] 2 QB 354, [1964] 1 All ER 201. Cf. the offence of handling; below, p. 639.

6. *MacPherson* [1973] RTR 157, CA, above, p. 209. For a contrary view see White, op. cit. at p. 618.

7. MacKenna, "Blackmail" [1966] Crim LR 467; Hogan "Blackmail" [1966] Crim LR 474; C. R. Williams "Demanding with Menaces: A Survey of the Australian Law of Blackmail" (1975), 10 Melb LR 118, especially at pp. 136–144.

8. Winder, "The Development of Blackmail" (1941) 5 MLR 21.

9. Cf. *Collister and Warhurst* (1955) 39 Cr App Rep 100.

request may be a demand if it contains a menace which is to materialise on failure to comply with the request.[10] But, whether express or implied, there must be a demand. If, having caught P in the act of stealing, D receives and accepts an offer to buy his silence, D might commit the offence of withholding for gain information relating to an arrestable offence[11] but he would not be guilty of blackmail.

Normally the demand will be for money or other property but s. 21 (2) provides that "the nature of the act or omission demanded is immaterial". This is not as far reaching as may appear at first sight because in any event the offence can be committed only if D has a view to gain or an intent to cause loss, and this refers to gain or loss in money or other property.[12] The provision seems to have been included[13] to forestall a possible argument that D's demand must be for some specific property. D might, for example, demand with menaces that he be given employment or demand that P append his signature to a valuable security provided by D;[14] in such cases he may be guilty of blackmail if he acts with a view to gain although he does not demand any property of P.

A demand may be complete though it has not been communicated to P because, say, P is deaf; and a demand by letter is made when it is posted.[15]

2   Menaces

The word "menace" is an ordinary English word which in many cases will convey its own meaning to a jury without need for elaboration.[16] On one view it might connote only threats of violence to persons or property, but under the former law relating to blackmail "menace" was given a much wider meaning. In this case it seems clear that it was intended to retain the former law; the Criminal Law Revision Committee was of course well aware of the meaning "menace" had acquired and deliberately chose to use this word when they might have chosen some other.[17]

In *Thorne v Motor Trade Association*,[18] Lord Wright said[19] that a menace was a threat of "any action detrimental to or unpleasant to the person addressed". This is of course to define menace very widely. The Committee chose menaces in preference to threats because, "notwithstanding the wide meaning given to "menaces" in *Thorne's Case* ... we regard that word as stronger than "threats", and the consequent slight restriction on the scope of the offence seems to us right". In view of Lord Wright's definition of menaces it might be thought that any distinction between menaces and

10. Cf. *Robinson* (1796), 2 East P.C. 1110, where the words "Remember, Sir, I am now only making an appeal to your benevolence" were held in the circumstances capable of importing a demand. Cf. *Harry* [1974] Crim LR 32; **SHC 483**; below, p. 590.
11. Below, p. 758.
12. Theft Act, s. 34; below, p. 592.
13. Cf. Cmnd. 2977, Annex 2.
14. Cf. *Phipoe* (1795) 2 Leach 673, where Mrs. Phipoe armed with a carving knife "in the French language threatened, amidst the most opprobious expressions, to take away [P's] life" unless he signed a promissory note on paper and with materials provided by her.
15. *Treacy v Director of Public Prosecutions* [1971] AC 537, [1971] 1 All ER 110, HL.
16. *Lawrence and Pomroy* (1971) 57 Cr App Rep 64, CA.
17. Cmnd. 2977, para. 123.
18. [1937] AC 797, [1937] 3 All ER 157.
19. [1937] AC at 817, [1937] 3 All ER at 167.

threats is wholly illusory, but it does perhaps serve to emphasise that the law will not treat as a menace words or conduct which would not intimidate or influence anyone to respond to the demand. So in *Harry*[20] where the organisers of a student Rag had written to shopkeepers offering them immunity from any "inconvenience" resulting from Rag activities, the trial judge ruled that there was not sufficient evidence of a menace. Some shopkeepers had complained of the veiled threat in the letter but this menace was not, to use the words of Sellers LJ in *Clear*,[1] "of such a nature and extent that the mind of an ordinary person of normal stability and courage might be influenced or made apprehensive so as to accede unwillingly to the demand." This is not to say that there can be no menace unless P is intimidated. D may be guilty of blackmail where he threatens to assault P unless P pays him money, though P is in no way frightened and squares up to D with the result that D runs away.[2] Here D intends to intimidate P when he makes the demand and it can make no difference that P is unmoved. D's intention seems to be the crucial factor here.[3] D may make what is literally a demand with menaces ("give me that book or I'll knock your block off"), but if he believes that in the circumstances his threat will not be taken seriously by P there is no intention to use the threat to reinforce the demand. It may be, of course, that P is an unusually timid soul and promptly parts with the book in the belief that D will assault him if he does not. There will still be no offence unless D knows of P's timidity and believes that in the circumstances P will part with the book because of the threat. D must intend that his threat should operate on the mind of P to cause P to comply with his demand, and this must involve a consideration of D's knowledge of all the circumstances[4] including his knowledge as to whether P is courageous or cowardly.[5]

3 Unwarranted Demand

Not every demand accompanied by a menace will amount to blackmail. It will be appreciated at once that it ought not to be blackmail to demand payment of a debt and to threaten civil proceedings in the event of failure to comply. There is a menace (a threat of action detrimental to or unpleasant to the person addressed) but it is in the circumstances a perfectly lawful demand accompanied by a justifiable threat. At the other extreme a demand by D for property to which he is not legally entitled accompanied by a threat to kill P would be thought of as an obvious instance of blackmail.

But between these two extremes less clear cut cases emerge. D may threaten to post P as a defaulter unless he pays a gaming debt;[6] D may threaten to publish memoirs which expose discreditable conduct of P's unless P buys them from her;[7] or D may threaten to expose P's immoral

---

20. [1974] Crim LR 32 (Judge Petre); **SHC 483**.
  1. [1968] 1 All ER 74 at 80, CA.
  2. Cf. *Moran* [1952] 1 All ER 803n, CCA.
  3. Cf. *Clear* [1968] 1 QB 670, [1968] 1 All ER 74, CA.
  4. Cf. *Clear* [1968] 1 All ER 74 at 80.
  5. *Garwood* [1987] Crim LR 476.
  6. Cf. *Norreys v Zeffert* [1939] 2 All ER 187.
  7. Cf. the case discussed in Lord Denning's *Report*, Cmnd. 2152, 31–36.

relationship with her unless P pays money which he had promised her.[8] Whether the conduct in any or all of these cases *ought* to be blackmail might give rise to a good deal of argument, but the solution provided in s. 21 (1) of the Theft Act is that D's demand will be unwarranted unless made in the belief (a) that there are reasonable grounds for making it, *and* (b) that the use of the menaces is a proper means of enforcing the demand.

The test is then essentially a subjective one. Suppose that D has had an immoral relationship with P and P promises that he will pay D £100 for the favours which he has received; P fails to keep his promise whereupon D threatens to expose the relationship to P's wife unless he pays.[9] D's liability would now turn upon whether she believed that she had reasonable grounds for demanding the £100, *and* believed that her threat to expose P's immorality was a proper way of enforcing the demand. All the circumstances have to be taken into account in so far as they are relevant as tending to show or negative that her belief was genuine. D might have believed (wrongly) that she was legally entitled to the £100 and that it was lawful for her to threaten to expose P to get it; if that were her belief she would surely believe the demand reasonable and the menace proper. She might have believed she was morally entitled to enforce payment in this way, and this would be enough provided she believed in fact that this was reasonable and proper. One person (a lawyer for example) might feel that he was morally entitled to something and yet recognise that his moral claim would not afford him reasonable grounds for making the demand. Another person might genuinely think that his moral right affords him reasonable grounds. In practice, it may be thought, D does not think precisely in terms of the legality or morality of his conduct, but more in terms whether it is, in a broad way, reasonable.

In *Harvey, Ulyett and Plummer*[10] D and his confederates paid P £20,000 for what P claimed was a consignment of cannabis but which turned out to be "a load of rubbish". Incensed by this swindle, the defendants kidnapped P's wife and child and made threats of serious bodily harm to them and to P unless the money was returned. No doubt a lawyer (or even a tolerably well informed layman) would have appreciated that in these circumstances the money was not recoverable since it was paid in pursuance of an illegal contract. Such a person might have difficulty in forming a belief that he has reasonable grounds for the demand. But in *Harvey* the particular defendants no doubt felt that they had been swindled ("ripped off to the tune of £20,000" as the trial judge put it) and it was for the jury to determine whether as a matter of fact they believed that their demand was reasonable.

It has been argued[11] that it is not right that D's own moral standards should determine the rightness or wrongness of his conduct; that the law should give "efficacy to the defendant's moral judgments whatever they may be".[12] The answer to this may be that as a practical matter most people

---

8. Cf. *Bernhard* [1938] 2 KB 264, [1938] 2 All ER 140.
9. Cf. *Bernhard* [1938] 2 KB 264.
10. (1981) 72 Cr App Rep 139, CA.
11. By MacKenna J "Blackmail" [1966] Crim LR 467, 469.
12. See *Lambert* [1972] Crim LR 422 (Newcastle Crown Court); **SHC 490**, where Judge John Arnold appears to have accepted that this is the effect of the section.

do act according to generally accepted legal and moral standards, and the cases must be rare where D can *genuinely* rely on his own moral standards where these are seriously at odds with accepted standards. If D knows that the threat he proposes is to commit a crime, he cannot accordingly maintain that he believes such a threat to be proper.[13] It is not enough that D feels that his conduct is justified or that it is in some way right for him; "proper" in this context involves a consideration of what D believes would be generally thought of as proper. It is not enough that D believes his conduct to be justified, that it is in some way right for him, if he does not also believe that his conduct would be generally regarded as proper. The test of D's belief is of course a subjective one but that belief refers to an external standard; D cannot, therefore, take refuge in his own standards when he knows that these are not thought proper by members of society generally.

Conversely, and because of the subjective nature of the test, D may be guilty of blackmail where he thinks he has no reasonable grounds for his demand or that the use of the menaces is improper, even though, viewed objectively, his demand is perfectly reasonable and his threat perfectly proper. Concentrating to this extent on D's state of mind as the criterion of criminality may be something of an innovation in English criminal law, but cases where the matter arises must inevitably be rare.

Section 21 (2) provides that it is immaterial whether the menaces relate to action to be taken by the person making the demand. Consequently if D makes a demand of P and threatens that E will assault P if he does not comply, this may amount to blackmail. Perhaps this was clear enough without express provision for it, but the provision was included to prevent any possible argument.[14]

4 View to Gain or Intent to Cause Loss

It has been noted above[15] that the requirement of a view to gain or intent to cause loss operates as a limiting factor on the offence of blackmail. Many might describe as blackmail a threat by D to prosecute P for theft unless she has sexual intercourse with him, but this, though it may constitute some other offence,[16] would not amount to blackmail under s. 21 (1) of the Act. The Theft Act is concerned with invasions of economic interests, and gain and loss are defined accordingly in s. 34 (2) (a):

"... 'gain' and 'loss' are to be construed as extending only to gain or loss in money or other property, but as extending to any such gain or loss whether temporary or permanent; and—

  i) 'gain' includes a gain by keeping what one has, as well as a gain by getting what one has not; and

  ii) 'loss' includes a loss by not getting what one might get, as well as a loss by parting with what one has."

In the ordinary case of blackmail D will have both a view to gain and an intent to cause loss; by demanding money from P by threats D will

---

13. *Harvey, Ulyett and Plummer* (1980) 72 Cr App Rep 139, CA.
14. Cmnd. 2977, Annex 2.
15. At p. 589.
16. See above, p. 439. There is a view to gain where D at gun point demands that a doctor gives him an injection of morphine (morphine is property) to relieve pain: *Evans (Ronald)* (1987) Times, 1 December.

ordinarily wish to gain the money for himself and cause the loss of it to P. But either suffices. D may commit the offence where he intends to cause loss to P without making a gain for himself; as where, by threats, he demands that Q destroy property belonging to P. And clearly in this case D intends to cause loss to "another" though the person threatened is not the person to whom the loss is caused.

Conversely there may be a view to gain although there is no intent to cause loss. D might demand that P appoint him a director in P's company; here D has a view to gain for himself but it may well be that, far from intending to cause P loss, he intends to bring him increased profits.

Most often D's view to gain will be transparently obvious since a blackmailer's prime objective is normally to get money or other property from P. And normally D will intend to deprive P permanently of the property. Section 34 (2) (a) makes it clear, however, that gain and loss extend to a temporary, as well as a permanent, gain or loss. D might be guilty of blackmail, for example, where by threats he demands that P make a loan of property. But will any view to gain – no matter how remote – suffice?[17] Clearly there may be a view to gain although the gain is not to materialise for a period of time, or even though the gain may never materialise.

D might by threats cause P to destroy Q's will on the assumption that this will be to D's financial advantage; it can make no difference that Q is on his death bed or is in the best of health, or that Q has made another will revoking the one destroyed. The essence of blackmail is the demand with menaces and the offence is then complete whether D succeeds thereafter in making a gain or not.[18] What seems to be important is that D should have the view of gain in his mind when he makes the demand; the fact that it has crossed his mind at some stage that there may be a gain involved might not be enough. One of his objectives in making the demand (though he may well have others) must be to make a gain for himself. Equally where it has to be shown that D *intended* to cause loss to another, it would not be enough that D foresaw some likelihood of loss unless he also intended to cause the loss.[19]

Sub-paragraphs (i) and (ii) of s. 34 (2) (a) were introduced to meet a possible argument that D would not be acting with a view to gain, or with intent to cause loss, where the gain or loss had already taken place. For example, D, who owes P £10, might by threats demand that P forgo his claim; it is now quite clear that D is acting with a view to gain.

A further problem is whether D can be said to have a view to gain or intent to cause loss where he acts under a legal claim of right to the property demanded. Suppose that D, who is in fact owed £10 by P, threatens to expose to P's employers the fact that P is a homosexual unless P pays the debt. Obviously D can satisfy the requirement that he believes he has reasonable grounds for making the demand, but it may be supposed (as must almost invariably be the case) that D does not believe that the use of the menace is a proper means of reinforcing the demand.

17. See Smith, *Theft*, para. 320.
18. Cf. *Moran* [1952] 1 All ER 803n.
19. See above, p. 560.

It was clearly intended by the Criminal Law Revision Committee that D might be guilty of blackmail if he failed to meet either of the criteria in paragraphs (a) and (b) of s. 21 (1), and irrespective of whether D acted under a legal claim of right to the property demanded:

"The essential feature of the offence will be that the accused demands something with menaces when he knows either that he has no right to make the demand or that the use of the menaces is improper. This, we believe, will limit the offence to what would ordinarily be thought should be included in blackmail. The true blackmailer will know that he has no reasonable grounds for demanding money as the price of keeping his victim's secret: *the person with a genuine claim will be guilty unless he believes that it is proper to use the menaces to enforce his claim.*"[20]

The offence of blackmail is, however, governed in all cases by the requirement of view to gain or intent to cause loss, and it can be argued[1] that where D demands property to which he is *legally* entitled, he has no view to make a gain for himself or to cause loss to another; D makes no gain in getting what he is legally entitled to, and P sustains no loss in paying his lawful debts. In other statutory contexts gain is sometimes treated as economic gain or profit, but it has also been said to mean acquisition and is not necessarily to be equated with profit.[2] To give it the latter meaning in the context of the Theft Act would certainly be consistent with the Committee's intentions,[3] and in *Lawrence and Pomroy*,[4] where D and E were convicted of blackmail in making threats to recover a debt, it appears to have been assumed by the Court of Appeal, though the point was not directly argued,[5] that D and E had a view to gain.

5 Unlawful Harassment of Debtors

Section 40 of the Administration of Justice Act 1970 creates an offence of unlawful harassment of debtors, which, because it may overlap blackmail, may be noted at this point. The offence, which is summary only and is punishable by fine,[6] is committed by one who, with the object of coercing another person to pay money claimed as a debt under a contract, (a) harasses the debtor by demands which by reason of their frequency or manner of making are calculated to subject the debtor or members of his household to alarm, distress or humiliation; or (b) falsely represents that criminal proceedings lie for non-payment; or (c) falsely represents that he is authorised in some official capacity to enforce payment; or (d) utters a document falsely represented to have an official character.

---

20. Cmnd. 2977, para. 121, italics supplied.
　1. Hogan, "Blackmail" [1966] Crim LR 474, 476. Cf. Smith *Theft*, paras 313–315, cf. Griew, *Theft*, 170.
　2. Cf. Smith, *Theft*, para. 315 and authorities there cited. Cf *Blazina* [1925] NZLR 407 on the meaning of "extort or gain" in the New Zealand Crimes Act 1908.
　3. As expressed in the passage cited at n. 5, above. But the Committee also characterised blackmail as an offence of dishonesty (cf. paras. 118 and 122) and one who demands that to which he believes he is legally entitled is not acting dishonestly: cf *Skivington* [1968] 1 QB 166, [1967] 1 All ER 483, CA, and *Robinson* [1977] Crim LR 173, above, p. 540.
　4. (1973) 57 Cr App Rep 64, CA.
　5. But the point was argued in *Parkes* [1973] Crim LR 358 (Judge Dean); **SHC 491**, where it was ruled that a person demanding money undoubtedly owed to him did have a view to gain.
　6. Level 5 on the standard scale.

Clearly, and whatever may be the position in relation to the offence of blackmail, it can be no defence to a charge under this provision that the debt was owed. The offence was created to curb the growing practice of enforcing the payment of debts in a fashion that is unreasonable, unfair or improper; such as where a creditor calls at the debtor's house to make a demand and is accompanied by a brace of large, fierce and hungry-looking alsatians.[7] The offence is wider than blackmail in that it may cover conduct that the creditor believes to be proper as a means of enforcing the debt. Under paragraph (a) it is enough that the demands are "calculated to" cause distress, and this will probably be interpreted to import an objective standard (calculated in the eyes of reasonable people) so that it will be no defence that D himself did not calculate to cause distress.

13 Burglary and Aggravated Burglary

1) *Burglary*

Section 9 of the Theft Act provides:

"1) A person is guilty of burglary if—
   a) he enters any building or part of a building as a trespasser and with intent to commit any such offence as is mentioned in subsection (2) below; or
   b) having entered any building or part of a building as a trespasser he steals or attempts to steal anything in the building or that part of it or inflicts or attempts to inflict on any person therein any grievous bodily harm.
2) The offences referred to in subsection (1) (a) above are offences of stealing anything in the building or part of a building in question, of inflicting on any person therein any grievous bodily harm or raping any woman therein, and of doing unlawful damage to the building or anything therein.
3) References in subsections (1) and (2) above to a building shall apply also to an inhabited vehicle or vessel, and shall apply to any such vehicle or vessel at times when the person having a habitation in it is not there as well as at times when he is.
4) A person guilty of burglary shall on conviction on indictment be liable to imprisonment for a term not exceeding fourteen years."

1 The Actus Reus

a) *Enters.* The common law rules relating to entry were developed with not a little ingenuity and a fondness for technicality. Broadly[8] an entry at common law was constituted by (i) the entry of any part of D's body within the building; or (ii) the insertion of an instrument for the purpose of abstracting property but not if inserted merely to further entry by D. It was

---

7. Which may constitute an affray, see below, p. 789.
8. For more detailed discussion see earlier editions of this work and Smith, *Theft*, paras. 333–335.

assumed in Parliament that the common law rules would continue to apply.[9] But it is questionable how far the incorporation of all the common law's technicality would be consistent with the ordinary interpretation of s. 9 that D is guilty of burglary only if "he enters any building" with intent to commit, or "having entered any building . . . he" commits, the specified offences.

Whether a person can properly be described as being outside a building, or in the process of entry, or as being inside the building, may be said to be determinable in a commonsense way. On a commonsense view a person standing outside a building with one hand inside the door frame would not be regarded as being in the building (though he may be regarded as in the process of entry and thus guilty of attempt) while a person standing inside a building with his hand outside the door frame would be regarded as being in the building.

This view gains some support from *Collins*.[10] Here it was crucial to know whether D had entered a building (in his case via a bedroom window) before or after an invitation to enter had been made. The Court of Appeal appeared to approach the problem in a commonsense way –

"Unless the jury were entirely satisfied that [D] made an *effective and substantial entry* into the bedroom without [P] doing or saying anything to cause him to believe she was consenting to his entering it, he ought not to be convicted of burglary."[11]

No reference was made to the common law rules of entry but there was at least an implicit rejection of the common law rule that entry by any part of D's body sufficed[12] since the entry must be "effective and substantial".

In *Brown*,[13] however, the Court of Appeal said that "substantial" was an unhelpful addition to "effective" and that the jury ought to be asked only to consider whether the entry was effective. It was held here that the jury was entitled to find that there had been an effective entry where D, though standing on the pavement outside a shop, had the top half of his body through a broken window and was rummaging among the goods inside. But effective for what purpose? The court cannot have meant effective for the purpose of committing the ulterior offence since, on this view, D would not have been guilty of burglary if the goods he sought to steal inside were beyond his reach. This cannot be right. Nor does it make any more sense to say that the entry must be effective for the purposes of constituting an entry since such a direction could only bemuse a jury. It makes more sense, however, to say that an entry must have been effected and leave it to the jury to decide in a commonsense way whether D is sensibly to be regarded as being outside the building, in the process of entry, or as having entered.[14]

---

9. 290 H.L. (5th Series) cols. 85–86.
10. [1973] QB 100, [1972] 2 All ER 1105, CA; **SHC 492**.
11. [1972] 2 All ER 1105 at 1111, per Edmund Davies LJ; italics supplied.
12. Otherwise, remarked Odgers in [1972A] 30 Camb LJ, "burglary may well . . . vary with the length of a part much more private than the prisoner's foot".
13. [1985] Crim LR 212, CA.
14. This could result in different juries taking different views on the same facts and a preferred view would be for the judge to direct the jury on which factual bases D would have or have not entered; the facts are for the jury, the law for the judge. But this view is out of favour with the judges.

The offence, it might be noted, is not to commit theft at a time when D is trespassing. In *Brown* D unquestionably trespassed and did so with intent to steal but the offence requires entry *by D* as a trespasser.

This leads on to a consideration whether, in conformity with s. 9, it can be said that D enters a building when he inserts within a building an implement for the purposes of forcing a lock or catch. If this is done by D as part of a plan to enter the building which is then interrupted, D is clearly guilty of attempt but even at common law this was not regarded as a complete entry. But may it be said (as it was at common law and might be said to be at least inferentially supported by *Brown*) that if the implement is inserted for the purpose of abstracting goods that this constitutes an entry by D? If the implement is regarded as an extension of D's arm, it makes little sense to say that it is not an entry if done to effect an entry but is an entry if done to abstract goods. There is not even the slightest hint of any such distinction in s. 9. It is accordingly submitted that either both should constitute entry by a trespasser or neither and it is thought that the courts will prefer the view that both should do so.

But what if D uses an innocent agent? It may be supposed that D employs a boy under the age of criminal responsibility to enter buildings and abstract property. The boy, of course, is guilty neither of burglary nor theft but it is clear law that D may perpetrate at least some crimes by using another as his tool or agent.[15] The answer in this context, it is submitted, turns upon the interpretation to be given to s. 9. This says that a person is guilty of burglary if "*he enters* any building as a trespasser ... or *having entered* as a trespasser he ...*" (italics supplied) and the question is whether these words are apt to extend to entry by another on his behalf. If they do, they must equally extend to the case where D trains a dog, or even a programmed robot, to enter premises to abstract goods. Essentially the boy under age, the dog and the robot are instruments and the arguments adduced in the preceding paragraph are applicable. All such cases must be regarded as constituting an entry by D or none so regarded, and again it is thought that the courts will favour the view that all such cases constitute an entry.

b) *As a trespasser*. Trespass is a legal concept and resort must be made to the law of tort in order to ascertain its meaning.[16] It would appear that as a matter of civil law any intentional, reckless or negligent entry into a building is a trespass if the building is in fact in the possession of another who does not consent to the entry. In all cases of burglary it must be shown that D entered the building as a trespasser in the civil law. If there is no civil trespass then there can be no burglary. If, for example, D is dragged by his drunken friends into P's house and D steals a vase there, D would be guilty of theft but not of burglary.

But while it is essential that D is a trespasser in the civil law, this alone is not enough. Liability in tort is strict to the extent that a mistake, even a

---

15. See above, p. 131.
16. Salmond on *Torts* (18th ed.) 36; Winfield on *Tort* (12th ed.), 335; Street, *Law of Torts* (7th ed.), 13, 63.

reasonable one, is no defence. D is no less a trespasser although he mistakenly believes that the house he enters is his own, or mistakenly believes that he has a right of entry. But to commit burglary *mens rea* is required and, in this particular, this requires that D know (or be reckless as to) the facts which constitute him a trespasser. In *Collins*[17] D, having discovered that P was lying asleep and naked on her bed, stripped off his clothes and climbed on to the window sill of the bedroom. At this moment P awoke and, mistakenly believing that the naked form at the window was her boyfriend, beckoned D in. D then got into P's bed and it was only after D had intercourse with her that P realised her error. D's conviction for burglary (entering as a trespasser with intent to commit rape) was quashed because the trial judge had, in terms, indicated to the jury that it would suffice if D's conduct amounted to a trespass in the civil law. "In the judgment of this court," said Edmund Davies LJ—

> "there cannot be a conviction for entering premises 'as a trespasser' within the meaning of s. 9 . . . unless the person entering does so knowing that he is a trespasser and nevertheless deliberately enters, or, at the very least, is reckless whether or not he is entering the premises of another without the other party's consent."[18]

In relation to the particular facts of this case the issue whether D was a trespasser or a lawful visitor would seem to involve a consideration of two matters: (i) D's belief as to P's (the girl's) authority to authorise his entry to the premises; and (ii) whether that authority was given before or after he had entered the premises.

The second matter is the easier to deal with and may be disposed of simply. It may be assumed that P had the necessary authority and further assumed that as D stood on the ladder outside the window he had determined to have intercourse with P by force. If he had reached P's bedside before any invitation had been extended to him he would already be guilty of burglary for he had already entered with intent to rape and P's subsequent consent could not alter that. But he would not be guilty of burglary had the invitation been extended while he still stood on the ladder.[19] One difficulty of the case, which has been discussed above, lay in determining whether he has entered before or after the invitation was made.

Once D had entered as a lawful visitor he cannot commit burglary though he thereafter commits any or all of the offences specified in s. 9. In the civil law there is a doctrine, trespass *ab initio*, by virtue of which one who enters premises under the authority of the law becomes a trespasser, and is deemed to have trespassed from the moment of entry, if he abuses his authority. *Collins*,[20] however, settled that whatever the status of this quaint doctrine in the civil law, it had no application to the offence of burglary.

---

17. [1973] QB 100, [1972] 2 All ER 1105, CA; **SHC 492.**
18. [1972] 2 All ER 1105 at 1110.
19. Provided he understood the invitation as one extended to him (i.e. he was unaware of P's mistake as to his identity) to have consensual intercourse causing him to abandon his intention to have intercourse by force. Supposing, for example, that D's purpose was to set fire to the house he would enter as a trespasser despite the invitation for the purposes of intercourse. See further below, p. 601.
20. [1972] 2 All ER 1105 at 1111.

Having lawfully entered premises D may become a trespasser if, required to leave by the occupier, he fails to leave within a reasonable time. Assuming that D does not do so and thereafter steals he would steal while trespassing but would not commit burglary unless he thereafter entered another part of the building and stole there. Burglary requires entry of a building or part as trespasser.

The first point is not so easily disposed of. An entry is not trespassory if the person entitled to consent to it gives his consent. Who is that person is determined by reference to the civil law. Trespass is an interference with possession. Burglary is therefore committed against the person in possession of the building, or part of the building, entered. Where the premises are let, the burglary is committed against the tenant and not against the landlord. Even if the tenant is only a tenant at will, he may maintain trespass. So may a deserted wife, even if she has no proprietary interest in the matrimonial home.[1] The guest at a hotel does not usually have possession of his room,[2] nor does a lodger.[3] Where D breaks into the hotel bedroom, or the lodger's room, he commits burglary against the hotelier or the landlord, not against the guest or lodger. If the hotelier enters the guest's room, or the landlord the lodger's with intent to steal, this is not burglary because there is no trespass. Depending on the terms of the contract, the position may be similar where an employee occupies premises belonging to his employer for the more convenient performance of his duties as servant.[4]

Obviously the person who is in lawful possession of the premises may give the relevant consent but that person, unless he is the sole occupant of the premises, will expressly or impliedly authorise others to permit entry to the premises. An occupier of a house may authorise his wife and children to invite others to the house and these others become lawful visitors even though the occupier is unaware of their entry. A company may authorise employees to permit others to enter the premises and may give to one employee a more extensive authority than another. Rarely will the occupier set out the authority of others in writing and the extent of their authority will have to be determined from the practice of the parties. If D is in fact authorised to enter he cannot enter as a trespasser though he believes he is not authorised. In such a case, D may be guilty of attempt.

Just as the occupier can confer authority, he may withhold or limit it. He may, for example, forbid his spouse ever to invite to the house his mother-in-law, or he may tell his daughter that her boyfriend is not to step over his threshold.

But what becomes of significance here is not merely whether the occupier has authorised entry by D, or authorised another to permit D's entry, but what D's perceptions are about the authorisation. Burglary requires *mens rea* which for this purpose requires that he knows (or at least be reckless as to) the facts which constitute him a trespasser. If D mistakenly believes that the occupier has consented to his entry, or mistakenly believes that the

---

1. *National Provincial Bank v Ainsworth* [1965] AC 1175, [1965] 2 All ER 472, but see now Matrimonial Homes Act 1967.
2. Street, *Torts* (7th ed.) 62.
3. It is necessary to look at the particular contract; it *may* give the lodger possession.
4. *Mayhew v Suttle* (1854) 4 E & B 347; *White v Bayley* (1861) 10 CBNS 227.

occupier has authorised another to consent to his entry, he lacks the necessary *mens rea* for entry as a trespasser and cannot be convicted of burglary, however unreasonable his belief.[5]

In *Collins* it was argued that P, the daughter, could not give an effective consent to D's entry since it was P's mother and not she who was the occupier and that D knew that (or was reckless whether) the mother would not have assented to his entry in the dead of night to have sexual intercourse with her daughter. The court said that whatever the position was in the law of tort, it was "unthinkable" to accept such a proposition in the criminal law. With respect, the court went astray here. No doubt had D in *Collins* called to deliver a newspaper in the afternoon and P had invited him in for a cup of tea he would have assumed that she was authorised to do so and he would not then enter as a trespasser even if, unknown to D, P's father had expressly forbidden her to invite any male into the house. But this was not quite what happened in *Collins*. If D had known that P was not the occupier he may properly be regarded as entering as a trespasser had he known (or was reckless whether) the occupier would not have consented to a naked stranger climbing through her bedroom window to have intercourse with his daughter in the dead of night. If D had believed that the occupier would have consented or had believed that the occupier had delegated to P the authority to consent to an entry in these circumstances then he would not enter as a trespasser for the purposes of the law of burglary. But if he did not believe (or was reckless whether) the occupier was consenting, or had authorised P to consent to, his entry there seems no difficulty in holding that he entered as a trespasser.

The courts returned to the problem in *Jones and Smith*.[6] D, P's son, was no longer living with P but he was a welcome visitor to P's house and, according to P, was free to enter at any time. One night D, together with his friend E, entered P's house and stole two television receivers. Although P loyally maintained at the trial that his son was always free to enter the family home, the Court of Appeal held that the jury was entitled to conclude that in entering his father's house with intent to steal D had knowingly exceeded the permission given to him and D's conviction for burglary was affirmed.

The problem in *Jones and Smith* was not on all fours with that in *Collins*. The equivalence really concerns the position of D in *Collins* and E in *Jones and Smith*. E in *Jones and Smith* could hardly have thought, any more than D in *Collins*, that the occupier would have consented to his entry to steal the television receiver. To show that he had not entered as a trespasser E would have had to have argued that he believed that the son, D, was authorised to permit friends to enter his father's house to steal television receivers. This would be a preposterous argument and was not advanced.[7]

---

5. It is assumed here that an honest belief in consent to entry suffices. An argument might be advanced, following the *Caldwell* doctrine, that D is reckless if there is a serious risk that the occupier has not authorised the entry and D gave no thought to such risk, but if D has considered the issue and formed the view that he is authorised this case falls outside *Caldwell*.

6. [1976] 3 All ER 54, [1976] 1 WLR 672, CA.

7. An argument which seems to have been advanced was that E entered the house at the invitation of D with no intention to steal. Had this been accepted E, if he had believed that D was authorised to permit E's entry, would not have entered as a trespasser.

The real issue in *Jones and Smith* on trespassory entry thus concerned D and the question was whether he believed that the "general" permission given by his father extended to an entry in the dead of night to steal property from his father's house. On the facts the jury were entitled to conclude, despite his father's assertions to the contrary, that the father would not have consented to this entry and that D was aware of that.[8]

The view taken of trespassory entry in *Jones and Smith* is certainly consistent with the civil cases which define trespass for the purposes of the law of tort.[9] If a person authorised to enter one part of the premises enters another, or authorised to enter for one purpose enters for another, he becomes a trespasser. So the High Court of Australia construing a similar provision in *Barker v R*[10] held that D entered P's house as a trespasser where, given permission to enter the house to keep an eye on things while P was away, he entered the house to steal P's property. There is of course the difference between the civil and criminal law in that for liability under the latter *mens rea* is required; it must be proved not only that D exceeded his authority but that he was aware (or was reckless whether) he had done so.

The view that, subject to the requirement for *mens rea*, the civil concept of trespass applies has its critics. Dissenting in *Barker v R*, Murphy J said[11] that it led to the conclusion that a guest invited to another's house for dinner would become a burglar if he had entered with intent to steal a teaspoon. It would mean, to take another example, that a shoplifter would be guilty of burglary so soon as he enters a shop since he enters for a purpose alien to the shopkeeper's invitation.

It does not do to dismiss such cases as fanciful on the grounds that proof that the guest or the shoplifter had formed the intent to steal on entry would be hard to come by; it might be much less than difficult if the shoplifter is wearing a specially adapted coat. Are such persons really to be treated as burglars? Williams argues[12] that they should not and if a person is authorised to enter premises his entry should not become trespassory for the purposes of burglary merely because D has determined to avail himself of the invitation to commit one of the specified crimes. Moreover, as Murphy J added, if the wide view is adopted determining the nature of the authorisation, and whether D's intent is alien to it, may raise issues more suitable for metaphysics than for a criminal trial.

It is submitted that the arguments, in concentrating on whether D had exceeded the terms of his authorisation, have perhaps neglected a consideration of what P's reaction would have been had he known of D's intentions. It does not follow that P would inevitably exclude D from his premises

---

8. Since E had entered as a trespasser and D was aware that he had so entered a simpler course would have been to find E guilty as principal and D as abettor thus short-circuiting the discussion whether D was a trespasser.

9. *Taylor v Jackson* (1898) 78 LT 555; *Hillen and Pettigrew v ICI (Alkali) Ltd* [1936] AC 65; *The Carlgarth* [1927] P. 93 at 110, per Scrutton LJ; *Gross v Wright* [1923] 2 DLR 171; *Farrington v Thompson and Bridgland* [1959] VR 286. Cf *Byrne v Kinematograph Reuters Society Ltd* [1958] 2 All ER 579, [1958] 1 WLR 762. Helpful surveys of the relevant authorities can be found in the judgments in *Barker v R* (1983) 57 ALJR 426.

10. (1983) 57 ALJR 426.

11. (1983) 57 ALJR 426 at 432.

12. TBCL 847.

though he knows of D's intent to steal. Restaurateurs would not necessarily turn away a customer even though they know that he is prone to stealing spoons. Shopkeepers do not necessarily refuse admission even to known shoplifters and commonly simply warn their staff that a known shoplifter is in the store in order that precautions may be taken. It is at least implicit in *Smith and Jones* that if the jury had believed the father's assertion that his son was free to enter the house even to steal the television receiver then the son's entry would not have been trespassory.

It is thought that it is not helpful in this context to distinguish between a general invitation to enter premises (where the entry is not to be regarded as trespassory though D has purposes in mind which he realises would lead to his exclusion had P known of them) and an invitation limited to a particular purpose or purposes (where the entry is to be regarded as trespassory if D enters for other than the stated purposes).[13] It is respect-fully submitted that the court in *Jones and Smith* was right to reject the submission that a person who enters premises under a general permission can never be a trespasser.[14] However general the terms in which an invitation is expressed (e.g. my house is open to you at any time for any purpose) it can hardly be sensibly supposed that this includes the occasion when you enter to do me serious bodily harm or to burn my house to the ground.

Similar considerations apply where D obtains entry by fraud. D may, for example, obtain entry by pretending that he is the person authorised to read the gas or electricity meter. Were D a genuine official of the gas or electricity board he would, under the principles discussed above, enter as a trespasser despite being given permission to enter if he does so with a secret intention to commit one of the specified offences. D can hardly be in any better a position if he is not a genuine official but gains entry by pretending that he is.

In *Collins* it was said:

"We hold that, *for the purposes of s. 9* of the Theft Act 1968, a person entering a building is not guilty of trespass if he enters it without knowledge that he is trespassing . . ."[15]

but it may be that there is a significant distinction between the offence under s. 9 (1) (a) and under s. 9 (1) (b). Suppose that D enters P's house mistakenly believing it to be his own. Realising his mistake D is about to leave when he sees P's umbrella, and, on impulse, he steals it. Clearly D is not a burglar by virtue of s. 9 (1) (a), but is the case covered by s. 9 (1) (b)? He did not enter the building with knowledge that he was a trespasser, but when he steals he then knows that he entered as a trespasser. At the time when the crime is committed, which under s. 9 (1) (b) is the time of the commission of the ulterior offence and not the time of entry, it would seem that he has *mens rea* in respect of all the constituents of the offence.

c) *Any building or part of a building.* The meaning of "building" in various statutes has frequently been considered by the courts.[16] Clearly the

13. Cf. Pace [1985] Crim LR 716 at 718.
14. [1976] 3 All ER 54 at 58.
15. [1972] 2 All ER 1105 at 1109. Italics supplied.
16. See *Manning and Rogers* (1871) LR 1 CCR 338.

meaning of the term varies according to the context and many things which have been held to be buildings for other purposes will not be buildings for the purpose of the Theft Act – for example, a garden wall, a railway embankment or a tunnel under the road. According to Lord Esher MR, its "ordinary and usual meaning is, a block of brick or stone work, covered in by a roof".[17] It seems clear, however, that it is not necessary that the structure be of brick or stone to be a building within this Act. Clearly all dwelling houses are intended to be protected and these may be built of wood; while "the inhabited vehicle or vessel" which is expressly included is likely to be built of steel or of wood.

To be a building, the structure must have some degree of permanence and it seems clear that it would not include a tent even though the tent was someone's home. The outbuildings of a house seem to be buildings for the purposes of the Act so that burglary may now be committed in a detached garage, a wooden toolshed or a greenhouse. Similarly, farm buildings such as a stable, cow-byre, pig sty, barn or silo and industrial buildings such as factories, warehouses and stores.[18] Other cases are more difficult. It is not uncommon for trespassers to enter unfinished buildings and do damage. If they enter with intent to cause damage are they now guilty of burglary? An unfinished building was a building within s. 6 of the Malicious Damage Act 1861. Why not for the purposes of burglary? Clearly there is a difficult question as to the point in its erection at which a structure becomes a building. In *Manning and Rodgers*,[19] Lush J said:

". . . it is sufficient that it should be a connected and entire structure. I do not think four walls erected a foot high would be a building."

In that case all the walls were built and finished and the roof was on. It may be that a roof will be thought necessary for a structure to be a building under the present Act, for it clearly is not intended to extend to a walled garden, yard or paddock. What if there is a roof but no walls, as in the case of a bandstand? There is no obvious answer to borderline cases such as this but they are likely to be rare.

i) *The extent of a "building"*. – Under the old law, the entry had to be into a particular dwelling house, office, shop, garage, etc. A single structure might contain many dwelling houses – for example a block of flats – many offices, shops or garages. If D got through the window of Flat 1 with intent to pass through it, go upstairs and steal in Flat 45, the breaking and entering of Flat 1 was neither burglary nor housebreaking for D did not intend to commit a felony therein.[20] It was probably not even an attempt, not being sufficiently proximate to

17. *Moir v Williams* [1892] 1 QB 264. Cf. Byles J in *Stevens v Gourley* (1859) 7 CBNS 99 at 112 – "a structure of considerable size and intended to be permanent or at least to endure for a considerable time"; **SHC 499**.
18. Contrast *B and S v Leathley* [1979] Crim LR 314 (Carlisle CC) and *Norfolk Constabulary v Seekings and Gould* [1986] Crim LR 167. (Norfolk CC.) In the former it was held that a freezer container detached from its chassis, resting on railway sleepers and used to store frozen food, was a building; while in the latter it was held that two similar containers still on their wheeled chassis remained vehicles though they were being used by a supermarket to provide temporary storage space.
19. (1871) LR 1 CCR 338.
20. Cf *Wrigley* [1957] Crim LR 57.

the intended crime. If D broke into a flat above a jeweller's shop with intent to break through the ceiling and steal in the shop, he could be convicted of burglary in the flat only if it could be said that he broke and entered the flat with intent to commit a felony therein, namely to break and enter the shop.[1] The difficulty about this argument is that while the breaking may reasonably be said to have occurred in the flat, the entering, strictly speaking, took place in the shop. On that view, there was no intent to commit a felony in the flat and it was not, therefore, burglary or house-breaking to break and enter it.

It is not entirely clear how this situation is affected by the Theft Act. It really depends on what is the extent of a "building".[2] In its ordinary natural meaning, this term could certainly include a block of flats. If that meaning be adopted, D's getting into the window of Flat 1 as a trespasser with intent to pass through it, go upstairs and steal in Flat 45 is an entry of a building as a trespasser with intent to steal therein – that is, it is burglary. Similarly the intending jewel thief would be guilty of burglary when he entered the flat above the jeweller's shop as a trespasser. The effect would be to make the full offence of what was previously, at the most, an attempt, and probably was only an act of preparation. There seems no good reason, however, why the law should not be extended in this way. On the contrary, there is everything to be said for enabling the police to intervene at the earliest possible moment to prevent such offences; and for forestalling defences such as "I had no intention to steal in the flat – I was only using it as a passage to another flat which I never reached". It is submitted therefore that the word "building" should be given its natural meaning.

ii) *Part of a building.* – It is sufficient if the trespass takes place in part of a building so that one lodger may commit burglary by entering the room of another lodger within the same house, or by entering the part of the house occupied by the landlord. A guest in a hotel may commit burglary by entering the room of another guest. A customer in a shop who goes behind the counter and takes money from the till during a short absence of the shopkeeper would be guilty of burglary even though he entered the shop with the shopkeeper's permission. The permission did not extend to his going behind the counter.[3]

What is "a part" of the building may be a difficult and important question. Take a case put by the Criminal Law Revision Committee.[4]

1. Cf. comment on *Wrigley*, last note, at [1957] Crim LR 58. An intention to break through the floor would not be sufficient ulterior intent if damage to the building was contemplated.
2. In *Hedley v Webb* [1901] 2 Ch 126, Cozens-Hardy J held that two semi-detached houses were a single building for the purpose of determining whether there was a sewer within the meaning of the Public Health Act 1875, s. 4. In *Birch v Wigan Corporation* [1953] 1 QB 136, [1952] 2 All ER 893, the Court of Appeal (Denning LJ dissenting) held that one house in a terrace of six was a "house" within the meaning of s. 11 (1) and (4) of the Housing Act 1936 and not "part of a building" within s. 12 of that Act. But, since the sections were mutually exclusive, the house could not be both a "house" and "part of a building" for the purpose of the Act. Otherwise, Denning LJ would have been disposed to say that the house was both and Romer LJ also thought that "for some purposes and in other contexts two 'houses' may constitute one building". Cf. Smith, *Theft*, paras. 348–351.
3. *Walkington* [1979] 2 All ER 716, [1979] 1 WLR 1169, infra.
4. Cmnd 2977, para. 75.

D enters a shop lawfully[5] but conceals himself on the premises until closing time and then emerges with intent to steal. When concealing himself he may or may not have entered a part of the building to which customers are not permitted to go; but even if he did commit a trespass at this stage, he may not have done so with intent to commit an offence in that part of the building into which he has trespassed. For example, he hides in the broom cupboard of a supermarket, intending to emerge and steal tins of food. Entering the broom cupboard, though a trespass committed with intent to steal, is not burglary, for he has no intent to steal in the part of the building which he has entered as a trespasser. When he emerges from the broom cupboard after the shop has closed, he is a trespasser and it is submitted that he has entered a part of the building with intent to steal. He is just as much a trespasser as if he had been told in express terms to go, for he knows perfectly well that his licence to remain on the premises terminated when the shop closed.[6] Suppose, however, having entered lawfully, he merely remained concealed behind a pile of tins of soup in the main hall of the supermarket. This was not a trespass because he had a right to be there. When he emerged and proceeded to steal, still in the main hall of the supermarket, was he entering another part of the building? It is submitted that every step he took was "as a trespasser", but it is difficult to see that he entered any part of the building as a trespasser; the whole transaction took place in a single part of the building which he had lawfully entered.

The word "part" has no precise meaning in relation to buildings. Its significance for the purpose of the section is that a man may lawfully enter one part of a building, yet be a trespasser if he sets foot upon another. This was the view taken in *Walkington*.[7] D, having entered a department store, entered an area bounded by a moveable three-sided counter where he opened a till. It was held that there was evidence on which the jury could find that the counter area was a part of the building from which the public were excluded and that if D knew that, he entered it as a trespasser. Buildings, it now seems clear, fall into two parts: those parts where D is entitled to be and those where he is not.

If D is lawfully in Flat 1 and, without leaving the building, he enters Flat 2 as a trespasser with intent to pass through it into Flat 3 and steal therein, his entry into Flat 2 does not constitute burglary if each flat is regarded as a separate part. He has not entered *Flat 2*, with intent to steal *therein*. Yet, as we have seen, if he had entered Flat 2 from outside the building as a trespasser, there would have been no problem; he would have entered the *building* as a trespasser with intent to steal *therein*. If the section will bear a construction which

---

5. I.e., without intent to steal; above, p. 601.
6. The Criminal Law Revision Committee thought "The case is not important, because the offender is likely to go into a part of the building where he has no right to be, and this will be a trespassory entry into that part". But he has no right to be in any part of the building after closing time and the only question, it is submitted, is whether he went into *another* part.
7. [1979] 2 All ER 716, [1979] 1 WLR 1169, CA.

will avoid this absurd result, it is submitted that that construction should be adopted.[8] If the view put forward in the previous paragraph be adopted, D has trespassed in the part of the building into which he is not allowed to go, with intent to steal in that part and he is guilty of burglary.

iii) *Inhabited vehicle or vessel.* – The obvious cases which are brought within the protection of burglary by this provision are a caravan or a houseboat which is someone's home. There seems to be no reason whatever why a home should lack the ordinary protection of the law because it is mobile and this extension is welcome. Its limits should be noted. "Inhabited" implies, not merely that there is someone inside the vehicle, but that someone is *living* there. My saloon car is not an inhabited vehicle because I happen to be sitting in it when D enters against my will. The caravan or houseboat which is a man's home is, however, expressly protected, whether or not he is there at the time of the burglary. He may, for example, be away on his holidays.

The provision is not free from difficulty. Many people now own "dormobiles" or motorised caravans which they use for the ordinary purposes of a motor car during most of the year but on occasions they live in them, generally while on holiday. While the vehicle is being lived in, it is undoubtedly an inhabited vehicle. When it is being used for the ordinary purposes of a motor car it is submitted that it is not an inhabited vehicle. The exact moment at which the dormobile becomes an inhabited vehicle may be difficult to ascertain.[9]

Very similar problems will arise in connection with boats with living accommodation. Ships where the passengers or crew sleep aboard are clearly covered. The person who trespasses into a passenger's cabin on the *Queen Elizabeth II* in order to steal is clearly guilty of burglary.[10]

According to ordinary principles, D should not be convicted unless he knew of the facts which make the thing entered "a building" in law, just as *Collins*[11] shows that D must know (or be reckless as to) the facts which constitute him a trespasser. Suppose D enters a dormobile parked by the side of the road. If he knew that P was living in the vehicle, there is no problem. But what if he did not know? It would now seem that he must be acquitted of burglary, unless it can be shown that he was at least reckless whether anyone was living there or not; and this involves showing that the possibility was present to his mind.

---

8. For further consideration of this problem see Smith, *Theft*, para. 350; Griew, *Theft* 76–78.
9. Cf. *Bundy* [1977] 2 All ER 382, [1977] 1 WLR 914, CA, below p. 613.
10. Presumably, in such a case, the trespass is committed against the owners since, under modern conditions, they, and not the master, are in possession of the ship: *The Jupiter (No. 3)* [1927] P 122 at 131; affd. [1927] P 250. The passengers would seem to be in the same situation as the guests in a hotel. See above, p. 599.
11. [1973] QB 100, [1972] 2 All ER 1105; **SHC 492**; above, p. 598.

2 Mens Rea

a) *Intention to enter as a trespasser. Collins*[12] shows that it must be proved on a charge of burglary that D knew (or was reckless as to) the facts which, in law, make his entry trespassory. It would follow that if D sets up an honest belief in a right to enter, it would be for the Crown to prove that the belief was not held.[13]

b) *The ulterior offence.* It must be proved that D, *either –*
- i) entered with intent to commit one of the following offences:
  - a) stealing,
  - b) inflicting grievous bodily harm,
  - c) rape,
  - d) unlawful damage to the building or anything therein;

  or
- ii) entered and committed or attempted to commit one of the following offences:
  - a) stealing,
  - b) inflicting grievous bodily harm.

For these purposes D has one of the relevant intents though his intent is conditional – that he will steal if there is anything worth stealing in the building, or that he will cause grievous bodily harm to P if P is there. That there is nothing in the building worth stealing or that P is out of town is no bar to D's conviction.[14]

- i) *Stealing. –* This clearly means theft, contrary to s. 1. So D is not guilty if he enters with intent to commit an offence contrary to s. 15 or s. 16 of the Act. Where the facts would support either a charge of deception under s. 15 or of theft under s. 1, D may be convicted of burglary if the other elements of the offence are present. Thus D gains admission to P's house or place of business by pretending to be E, the agent of a person well-known to P. This is an entry as a trespasser.[15] D then induces P to sell goods to E, and departs, taking the goods and leaving a forged cheque. There is, of course, no contract with E, the ownership in the goods remains in P, and D has dishonestly appropriated property belonging to another with the intention of permanently depriving the other of it. He is guilty of theft (as well, of course, as obtaining by deception) and, therefore, he is guilty of burglary.[16] But the position is different where the facts will support only a charge of deception. Suppose D gains admission to P's building by pretending that her (D's) husband is ill and then, by the same pretence, induces P to lend her £20 intending to deprive P

12. [1973] QB 100, [1972] 2 All ER 1105.
13. As to the reasonableness of the belief, see above, p. 598.
14. *A-G's References (Nos. 1 and 2 of 1979)* [1979] 3 All ER 143, CA. See the discussion above, p. 289.
15. Above, p. 602.
16. So if D enters a building as a trespasser intending there to purchase from E furnishings which, as D knows, belong to P who has not authorised E to sell, D is guilty of burglary; D may also be guilty of handling but he has entered a building as a trespasser with intent to appropriate P's goods and is accordingly guilty of burglary. Cf *Gregory* [1982] Crim LR 229, CA.

permanently of it. Here too D enters as a trespasser but the offence committed inside may be obtaining by deception and not theft (because the ownership of the money passes to D)[17] and therefore burglary is not committed. The difference lies in whether the property passes or not. If D goes into P's shop and induces P to let him have a television set on credit by giving a false address and false references, the nature of D's crime depends on the nature of the transaction in the civil law. If it is hire or hire-purchase, the ownership does not pass and D is guilty of theft as well as obtaining by deception; if it is a credit sale, the ownership passes and D is guilty only of obtaining by deception. Thus, it is burglary in the former case[18] but not in the latter.

ii) *Grievous bodily harm.* – Section 9 (1) (b), unlike s. 9 (1) (a), does not require the infliction of the grievous bodily harm to be an offence.[19] Such harm may be inflicted (for example, by accident or in self-defence) without its being an offence. It was argued in *Jenkins*[20] that an indictment alleging that D entered as a trespasser and "inflicted grievous bodily harm upon [P] therein" was bad, because no offence was alleged. This argument, rightly as the court thought, was abandoned but it is not clear why the court so thought. It may have been (i) because para. (b) does not require the infliction to be an offence; or (ii) that it does so require but it is sufficient to follow the words of the section without specifying the offence. The latter, it is submitted, is the only tenable construction for it would be a surprising view that made even a trespasser guilty of burglary by lawfully (or inadvertently) inflicting the harm.

If para. (b) requires the commission of an offence, it is necessary to determine to which offence it refers. It must extend to the offences under ss. 20 and 23 of the Offences against the Person Act since both use the expression "inflict any grievous bodily harm". But *Jenkins* decides that, however "inflicts" is to be interpreted in the context of s. 20,[1] it is not to be confined in this context to conduct involving an assault. It is accordingly suggested that the offence under s. 18 of the 1861 Act must also be included, as must murder since the greater must include the less. If D is charged under para. (a) proof that he entered with *intent* to commit one of these offences will be required; under para. (b) recklessness would suffice if recklessness suffices for the particular offence.

iii) *Rape.* – This offence has been sufficiently considered above. Entry with intent to rape is a species of burglary which might produce some

---

17. But on this cf. *Lawrence* and discussion thereon above, p. 521.

18. Assuming that entry with intent to commit a fraud of this nature is a trespass: see above, p. 602.

19. The bill as drafted by the Criminal Law Revision Committee, and as introduced into Parliament, did so expressly provide. That the Act does not, is an accidental result of an amendment.

20. [1983] 1 All ER 1000, CA. Cf. Smith, *Theft*, para. 359.

1. See *Wilson (Clarence)* [1983] 1 All ER 993, above, p. 399: *Jenkins* and *Wilson* were reversed by the House of Lords [1984] AC 242, [1983] 3 All ER 448 but on grounds which do not affect the discussion in the text.

rather odd-looking examples of that crime. For example, D drags P into a barn or persuades her to go into the barn with him, with intent to rape her. If D is trespassing in the barn, this is burglary.

iv) *Unlawful damage to the building or anything therein.* – Again the causing of the damage must amount to an offence. It might be any of the offences of causing damage created by the Criminal Damage Act 1971. In the case of every one of the offences which is likely to be invoked under this provision, the *actus reus* must be committed intentionally or recklessly.

Where the charge is one of entering with intent, it follows that an actual intent at the time of entry to cause the harm in question must be proved. In many such cases D's intent may be conditional at the time of entry, in the sense that he intends to steal if there is anything worth stealing, or intends to cause grievous bodily harm if P, his enemy, happens to be in the building. Such a conditional intent is now no bar to a conviction for burglary.[2]

2) *Aggravated Burglary*

By s. 10 of the Theft Act:

"1) A person is guilty of aggravated burglary if he commits any burglary and at the time has with him any firearm or imitation firearm, any weapon of offence, or any explosive; and for this purpose—

a) 'firearm' includes an airgun or air pistol and 'imitation firearm' means anything which has the appearance of being a firearm, whether capable of being discharged or not; and

b) 'weapon of offence' means any article made or adapted for use for causing injury to or incapacitating a person, or intended by the person having it with him for such use; and

c) 'explosive' means any article manufactured for the purpose of producing a practical effect by explosion, or intended by the person having it with him for that purpose.

2) A person guilty of aggravated burglary shall on conviction on indictment be liable to imprisonment for life."

The reason given by the Criminal Law Revision Committee for the creation of this offence is that "burglary when in possession of the articles mentioned . . . is so serious that it should in our opinion be punishable with imprisonment for life. The offence is comparable with robbery (which will be so punishable). It must be extremely frightening to those in the building, and it might well lead to loss of life."[3]

1 The Articles of Aggravation

"Firearm" is not defined in the Act, except to the extent that it includes an airgun or air pistol. The term is given a very wide meaning by the Firearms

---

2. See above, p. 289.
3. Cmnd. 2977, para. 80.

Act 1968,[4] but since that statutory definition has not been incorporated in the Theft Act it is submitted that the word should not be given a meaning any wider than that which it naturally bears; and that, therefore, the term "imitation firearm" be similarly limited.

The definition of "weapon of offence" is wider than that of "offensive weapon" in s. 1 (4) of the Prevention of Crime Act 1953,[5] in that it includes (as well as everything within the 1953 Act) any article made for *incapacitating* a person, any article adapted for *incapacitating* a person, and any article which D has with him for that purpose. Articles *made* for incapacitating a person might include a pair of socks made into a gag, and articles *intended* for incapacitating a person might include sleeping pills to put in the night-watchman's tea, a rope to tie him up, a sack to put over his head, pepper to throw in his face, and so on.

The definition of "explosive" closely follows that in s. 3 (1) of the Explosives Act 1875 which, after enumerating various explosives, adds:

"... and every other substance, whether similar to those above mentioned or not, used or manufactured with a view to produce a practical effect by explosion or by a pyrotechnic effect ..."

It will be observed that the definition in the Theft Act is narrower. The Explosive Substances Act, if read literally, is wide enough to include a box of matches – these produce a "pyrotechnic effect"; but it seems clear that a box of matches would not be an "explosive" under the Theft Act. The main difficulty about the definition – and this is unlikely to be important in practice – lies in determining the meaning of "practical effect". Perhaps it serves to exclude fireworks which, so it has been said in connection with another Act, are "things that are made for amusement".[6]

2 "At the Time" of Commission of Burglary

It must be proved that D had the article of aggravation with him *at the time* of committing the burglary. Where the charge is one of entry with intent this is clearly at the time of entry. Where the charge is one of committing a specified offence, having entered, it is at the time of commission of the specified offence. It is not enough to prove an armed entry by D as a trespasser unless that entry is accompanied by one of the specified intents. If, then, D, having no such intent at the time of entry, discards his weapon and thereafter commits one of the specified offences he is not guilty of aggravated burglary though he would be so guilty if he re-armed himself for this purpose.[7]

3 "Has with Him"

This again closely follows the wording of the Prevention of Crime Act 1953. As appears above, the words in that Act mean "*knowingly* has with

---

4. Above, p. 416.
5. Above, p. 422.
6. *Bliss v Lilley* (1862) 32 LJMC 3, per Cockburn CJ, and Blackburn J; but Wightman J thought that a fog-signal was a "firework". Cf *Bouch* [1982] 3 All ER 918, CA.
7. *Francis* [1982] Crim LR 363, CA.

him",[8] in the sense that D must be proved to have known that he had the thing which is an offensive weapon. It may be predicted with some confidence, therefore, that proof will be required that D knew that he had the article of aggravation with him at the appropriate time. It is submitted that, in principle, proof should also be necessary that he knew the thing had the characteristics of an article of aggravation.

The expression "has with him" has been the subject of a number of decisions in the context of the Prevention of Crime Act 1953. The contexts of the Prevention of Crime Act and the Theft Act are so similar at this point that it is safe to assume that cases under the one will govern the interpretation of the other. Recent decisions under the Prevention of Crime Act[9] have established that the law is directed against those who take weapons about with them for an offensive purpose. From them it appears that D would not commit an offence under s. 10 in using his jemmy to attack a householder if it was taken solely to effect entry and with no thought to use it as a weapon; and still less would D commit this offence in seizing something nearby, such as a candlestick, and using this to attack another who surprised him in the act of burglary. But if D arms himself and then proceeds to the commission of the offence, he may properly be said to have with him an article for use in the course of or in connection with the burglary though he has so armed himself only moments beforehand. In *O'Leary*[10] D, having entered P's house as a trespasser, took up a kitchen knife and proceeded upstairs where by use of the knife he forced P to hand over property. It was held that he was rightly convicted of aggravated burglary. Burglary is committed under s. 9 (1) (b) at the time when the ulterior offence is committed, and before its commission in this case D had armed himself for use in connection with it.

14 Possession of Articles for Housebreaking, etc.

By s. 25 (1) and (2) of the Theft Act:

"1) A person shall be guilty of an offence if, when not at his place of abode, he has with him any article for use in the course of or in connection with any burglary, theft or cheat.

2) A person guilty of an offence under this section shall on conviction on indictment be liable to imprisonment for a term not exceeding three years."

This provision is expressed to be directed against acts preparatory to:

i) burglary contrary to s. 9
ii) theft contrary to s. 1

8. *Cugullere* [1961] 2 All ER 343 at 344; above, p. 427.
9. *Dayle* [1973] 3 All ER 1151, CA; *Ohlson v Hylton* [1975] 2 All ER 490, DC. See above, p. 424.
10. (1986) 82 Cr App Rep 341, CA.

iii) criminal deception contrary to s. 15[11]

iv) taking and driving away a conveyance, contrary to s. 12[12]

1) *The Actus Reus*

The *actus reus* consists in the accused's having with him any article. Clearly the article need not be made or adapted for use in committing one of the specified offences. It is sufficient that the *mens rea* is proved in respect of the article, that is, that the accused intended to use it in the course of, or in connection with, one of the specified offences. The heading to the section is misleading in referring to "implements" of housebreaking. "Article", which is used in the section and is therefore the governing word, is much wider than implement. Thus the article may be a tin of treacle intended for use in removing a pane of glass, or a pair of gloves to be worn to avoid leaving fingerprints, and it is implicit in recent decisions that it may be a sliced loaf and a bag of tomatoes[13] or bottles of wine[14] which D intends to pass off as the property of his employer.

The offence is thus very wide in its scope. But there must be some limits. Thus D can hardly be committing an offence by wearing his shoes or any other item of everyday apparel. Yet it was argued above that gloves for the avoidance of fingerprints would entail liability.[15] This suggests that the article must be one which D would not be carrying with him but for the contemplated offence. If it is something which he would carry with him on a normal, innocent expedition, it should not fall within this section. So there might be a difference between a pair of rubber gloves and a pair of fur-lined gloves with D was wearing to keep his hands warm on a freezing night, even though he did intend to keep them on so as to avoid leaving fingerprints. The latter pair of gloves is hardly distinguishable, for this purpose, from D's overcoat which seems to fall into the same category as his shoes. If D is carrying a pair of plimsolls in his car to facilitate his cat-burgling, this seems a plain enough case; but what if he has simply selected his ordinary crepe-sole shoes for wear because they are less noisy than his hobnails?

The expression "has with him"[16] is the same as in s. 10 (1) (b) of the Act. Questions as to D's knowledge of the nature of the thing can hardly arise here, since it must be proved that he intended to use it in the course of or in connection with one of the specified offences. No doubt D has an article with him if it is in his immediate possession or control; so that he will be guilty if the article is only a short distance away and he can take it up as he needs it; as where a ladder has been left in a garden by an accomplice and D enters the garden intending to use the ladder to make an entry. If the article

---

11. By s. 25 (5), "cheat" means an offence under s. 15.
12. By s. 25 (5), "theft" in this section includes an offence under s. 12 (1).
13. *Rashid* [1977] 2 All ER 237, 64 Cr App Rep 201, CA.
14. *Doukas* [1978] 1 All ER 1061, [1978] 1 WLR 372, CA.
15. Cf *Ellames* [1974] 3 All ER 130, CA; **SHC 502**; below, p. 613, where gloves were included in the charge.
16. See above, p. 611.

is found in D's car some distance from the scene of the crime this will be evidence that D was in possession of the article when driving the car. The tenor of recent decisions on the interpretation of "has with him" indicates that mere momentary possession will not suffice,[17] as where D is apprehended on picking up a stone which he intends to use to break a window in order to commit burglary. But in *Minor*[18] it seems to have been decided that D may be convicted of going equipped (in this case to steal petrol from cars) though he did not take the equipment (petrol cans and a hose) with him and somehow came across it while he was removing the cap from the petrol tank of a car. It appears to have been regarded as enough that the theft "was to be posterior to the acquisition of the articles". On this view the burglar who picks up a nearby stone to break a window would commit the offence of going equipped but it is respectfully submitted that "has with him" requires more than that the acquisition of the article should precede the theft.

"Place of abode" connotes a place, that is a site, where D lives.[19] Clearly no offence is committed when D has articles for housebreaking etc. in his own home, but place of abode is apt to cover the whole of the premises where D lives so that D does not commit the offence by having the articles in his garage or even in his car while that is on his premises. Once D steps into the street with the articles or drives off with them in his car the offence may be committed. Though a car or a caravan may constitute a place of abode while stationary at some site, they can never constitute a *place* of abode while D is in transit and if he then has the articles with him he may commit the offence.[20]

2) *Mens Rea*

The *mens rea* for the offence would appear to consist in:
  i) knowledge that one possesses the article; and
  ii) an intention to use the article in the course of or in connection with any of the specified crimes.

It was held in *Ellames*[1] that the intent to use must necessarily relate to use in the future so that D was not guilty of this offence where the evidence showed only that he was in possession of certain articles (masks, guns, gloves, etc.) after a robbery and was trying to get rid of them. But given an intent to use the article in the future the expression "in the course of or in connection with" any burglary, theft or cheat is wide enough to cover not only articles intended for use in the perpetration of the crime but also articles intended for use before or after its commission. The string used by

17. Above, pp. 424 and 611.
18. [1987] 52 JP 30, DC.
19. *Bundy* [1977] 2 All ER 382, CA.
20. *Bundy* [1977] 2 All ER 382, CA.
  1. [1974] 3 All ER 130, CA; **SHC 502**.

614 CHAPTER 15. THEFT AND RELATED OFFENCES

D in *Robinson*[2] to tie himself up as part of his preparation to defraud the insurers could properly be said to be intended for use "in connection with" the commission of the crime of deception. Equally a car intended for use to make an escape after the commission of a robbery falls within the offence. But the article must be intended for some direct use in connection with the crime and it has been held that D's possession of a stolen driving licence so that he could obtain a job which would give him an opportunity to steal is not within the offence.[3]

In *Ellames*[4] the view was expressed that D could commit the offence where he possessed the articles for future use by another, so that D would have been guilty in that case had he been hiding away the guns etc. for their future use by others. And it was also the view of the court that it was not necessary to show that D intended the article to be used in connection with a particular theft or cheat; the section requires only intended use in connection with *any* burglary, theft or cheat. No doubt a conditional intent (for example, possessing a jemmy to use if necessary) suffices but D must have made up his mind, even if only contingently, to use the article. If D had not so determined he does not commit the offence.[5]

Section 25 (3) provides:

"Where a person is charged with an offence under this section, proof that he had with him any article made or adapted for use in committing a burglary, theft or cheat shall be evidence that he had it with him for such use."

This is probably no more than enactment of the general rules regarding proof of intent.[6] It puts upon D an evidential burden. If he offers no explanation then the jury may be told that there is evidence upon which they may find that he had the necessary intent; but it is submitted that they should be told so to find only if satisfied beyond reasonable doubt that he in fact had that intent.[7] If D does offer an explanation then the jury should be told to acquit if they think it may reasonably be true and to convict only if satisfied beyond reasonable doubt that the explanation is untrue.[8]

Where the article in question is not made or adapted for use in any specified offence, mere proof of possession without more will not amount to prima facie evidence – i.e., the case will have to be withdrawn from the jury. It is a question of law for the judge, at what point proof of other incriminating circumstances amounts to a case fit for submission to the jury.

---

2. [1915] 2 KB 342; above, p. 295.
3. *Mansfield* [1975] Crim LR 101, CA.
4. [1974] 3 All ER 130, [1974] 1 WLR 1391, CA.
5. So in *Hargreaves* [1985] Crim LR 243, CA, the jury were misdirected when told they could convict if satisfied that D might have used the article.
6. Cf. Criminal Justice Act 1967, s. 8; above, p. 85.
7. Cf. the case where the alleged receiver is proved to have been in possession of recently stolen property and offers no explanation: *Abramovitch* (1914) 11 Cr App Rep 45.
8. The decision in *Patterson* [1962] 2 QB 429 that the onus of proof under the Larceny Act 1916, s. 28 was on the accused, was based on the express wording of that section and is entirely inapplicable to the new provision.

15 Handling Stolen Goods

By s. 22 of the Theft Act:

"1) A person handles stolen goods if (otherwise than in the course of the stealing) knowing or believing them to be stolen goods he dishonestly receives the goods, or dishonestly undertakes or assists in their retention, removal, disposal or realisation by or for the benefit of another person, or if he arranges to do so.

2) A person guilty of handling stolen goods shall on conviction on indictment be liable to imprisonment for a term not exceeding fourteen years."

1) *The Actus Reus*

The questions which require consideration are: what are "goods"? when are they "stolen"? and what is "handling"?

1 Stolen Goods

By s. 34 (2) (b):

"... 'goods', except in so far as the context otherwise requires, includes money and every other description of property except land, and includes things severed from the land by stealing."

It will be noted that this definition differs from and is narrower than the definition of "property" for the purposes of theft in s. 1 (1).[9] Since, however, land generally is excluded from theft by s. 4 (1), the effect seems to be that, with small exceptions to be discussed below, the property which can be the subject of handling is co-extensive with that which can be the subject of theft.

a) *Things in action.* Things in action are expressly mentioned in s. 4 (1) and not in s. 34 (2) (b). They must however be included in the words "every other description of property except land". The remaining question is whether the context of s. 22 *requires* the exclusion of things in action. If s. 22 were confined, like the old law, to *receiving*, no doubt the context would so require. The context might be said to so require if a thing in action could not be handled in *all* the ways specified in s. 22 (1) since it may be assumed that it was intended that anything which could be handled under the sub-section could be handled in all the ways specified or in none. If "receiving" in s. 22 is given the same meaning as it bore under the former law (where it referred to taking control of a physical thing) it would not be apt to apply to things in action. Expressions such as "realisation" or "disposal" are, however, entirely apt to include dealings with things in action. But if "receiving" is given its ordinary meaning unfettered by connotations drawn from the earlier law (and there would seem to be no good reason for so fettering it) there is no reason why D cannot receive a thing in action. If D opens a bank account into which he pays stolen money

---

9. Above, p. 504.

and subsequently assigns the balance to E, it does not seem to be an abuse of language to say that E receives that balance.

The Court of Appeal appears to be prepared to take this view. In *A-G's Reference (No. 4 of 1979)*[10] it was said—

"[I]t is clear that a balance in a bank account, being a debt, is itself a thing in action which falls within the definition of goods and may therefore be goods which directly or indirectly represent stolen goods for the purposes of s. 24 (2) (a)."

It is submitted that this view is in accord with the interpretation of the Act and makes good sense.

b) *Land.* "Land" which is stolen contrary to s. 4 (2) (b)[11] can always be the subject of handling since the stealing necessarily involves severance of the thing in question. A fixture or structure which is stolen contrary to s. 4 (2) (c), on the other hand, may or may not be severed from the land. Only if it is severed can it be the subject of handling. If E, an outgoing tenant, dishonestly sells to D, the incoming tenant, a fixture belonging to P, D cannot be guilty of handling (whether or not his act is in the course of stealing) if the fixture is not severed; nor, of course, is F guilty of handling if he, knowing all the facts, takes over the premises, including the fixture, from D; yet he has knowingly taken possession of a stolen fixture.

Land which is stolen contrary to s. 4 (2) (a) will rarely be capable of being handled since the kind of conduct contemplated by s. 4 (2) (a) will not normally involve severance.

Land may be the subject of both obtaining by deception and blackmail, both of which are stealing for this purpose.[12] Again, severance may or may not take place and handling is possible only if it does so.

c) *Meaning of "stolen".* By s. 24 (4):

"For purposes of the provisions of this Act relating to goods which have been stolen (including subsections (1) to (3) above) goods obtained in England or Wales or elsewhere either by blackmail or in circumstances described in section 15 (1) of this Act shall be regarded as stolen; and 'steal', 'theft' and 'thief' shall be construed accordingly."

By s. 24 (1):

"The provisions of this Act relating to goods which have been stolen shall apply whether the stealing occurred in England or Wales or elsewhere, and whether it occurred before or after the commencement of this Act, provided that the stealing (if not an offence under this Act) amounted to an offence where and at the time when the goods were stolen; and references to stolen goods shall be construed accordingly."

Thus goods are "stolen" for the purposes of the Act if:

i) they have been stolen contrary to s. 1;

ii) they have been obtained by blackmail contrary to s. 21.

iii) they have been obtained by deception contrary to s. 15 (1);

---

10. [1981] 1 All ER 1193 at 1198, [1981] Crim LR 51 and commentary.
11. Above, p. 506.
12. Infra.

iv) they have been the subject of an act done in a foreign country which was (a) a crime by the law of that country and which (b), had it been done in England, would have been theft, blackmail or obtaining by deception contrary to s. 1 or s. 21 or s. 15 (1) respectively.

d) *The "thief" must be guilty.* If the alleged thief is not guilty, then the handler cannot be convicted for there are no *stolen* goods for him to handle.[13] So if the alleged thief turns out to have acted under a claim of right to the property, then the goods appropriated cannot be stolen goods and there can be no conviction for handling them,[14] even though D believed the goods had been stolen.[15] In such circumstances, however, the receiver is now guilty of attempting to handle stolen goods;[16] or of stealing the property.

If the appropriator of the goods is guilty of theft, it is submitted that the goods appropriated may be the subject of handling although the appropriator is immune from prosecution by reason, for example, of diplomatic immunity.[17] The thief could be prosecuted for the theft if diplomatic immunity were waived. The handler may be convicted whether that immunity is waived or not – unless, of course, he too is entitled to diplomatic immunity.

It is submitted that the question whether the thief was guilty must be decided on the evidence of that fact produced at the trial of the handler.[18] Thus the fact that the "thief" has been acquitted is no bar to the prosecution of an alleged handler of the goods which he has been acquitted of stealing and should not even be admitted as evidence that the goods were not stolen. On the other hand, the fact that the alleged thief has been convicted establishes that the goods are stolen unless D can prove otherwise on the balance of probabilities.[19] The fact that D believed the goods to be stolen cannot, in itself, constitute proof that the goods were stolen;[1] but admissions on matters of fact within D's knowledge (for example, that the goods were purchased at a gross undervalue, that identifying marks had been removed from articles) may be such as to entitle the jury to conclude that the goods were stolen.[2]

2 When Goods Cease to be Stolen
By s. 24 (3) of the Act:

"But no goods shall be regarded as having continued to be stolen goods after they have been restored to the person from whom they were stolen

---

13. But cf *Close* [1977] Crim LR 107, CA.
14. *Walters v Lunt* [1951] 2 All ER 645, thus remains good law.
15. *Haughton v Smith* [1975] AC 476, [1973] 3 All ER 1109, HL, remains good law on this point.
16. *Shivpuri* [1987] AC 1, [1986] 2 All ER 334, HL, overruling *Anderton v Ryan* [1985] AC 560, [1985] 2 All ER 355, HL.
17. Cf *Dickinson v Del Solar* [1930] 1 KB 376; *AB* [1941] 1 KB 454; *Madan* [1961] 2 QB 1.
18. Cf *Dabek* [1973] Crim LR 527, CA.
19. PACE, 1984, s. 74, reversing the rule in *Hollington v Hewthorn* [1943] KB 587, [1943] 2 All ER 35. The rule was abolished for civil proceedings by the Civil Evidence Act 1968.
1. *A-G's Reference (No. 4 of 1979)* [1981] 1 All ER 1193, [1981] 1 WLR 667.
2. *McDonald* (1980) 70 Cr App Rep 288, [1980] Crim LR 242, CA; *Hulbert* (1979) 69 Cr App Rep 243, CA; *Korniak* (1983) 76 Cr App Rep 145, [1983] Crim LR 109, CA.

or to other lawful possession or custody, or after that person and any other person claiming through him have otherwise ceased as regards those goods to have any right to restitution in respect of the theft."

It is obvious that goods which have once been stolen cannot continue to be regarded as "stolen" so long as they continue to exist thereafter. A line must be drawn somewhere; and the Act draws it in the same place as did the common law. So if the stolen goods are taken from the thief by the owner or someone acting on his behalf, or by the police,[3] and subsequently returned to the thief so that he may hand them over to a receiver, the receiver will not be guilty of handling because the goods are no longer stolen goods.[4]

Difficult questions may continue to arise whether goods have in fact been "restored to the person from whom they were stolen or to other lawful possession or custody". It cannot be enough that P (the owner or his agent) knows that D has stolen the goods and follows D to his destination so that the handler can be caught red-handed;[5] nor that in such circumstances P marks the goods after the theft for the purpose of their identification in the hands of the handler.[6] A more difficult case is *King*.[7] A parcel containing the stolen goods (a fur coat) was handed by E, the thief, to a policeman who was in the act of examining the contents when the telephone rang. The caller was D, the proposed receiver. The policeman discontinued his examination, D was told to come along as arranged, he did so and received the coat. It was held that D was guilty of receiving stolen goods on the ground that the coat had not been reduced into the possession of the police – though it was admitted that there was no doubt that, in a very few minutes, it would have been so reduced, if the telephone had not rung. The case has, however, been criticized. It is easy to see that if the police are examining a parcel to see whether it contains stolen goods they do not take possession of the contents until they decide that this is what they are looking for.[8] In *King*, however, E had admitted the theft of the coat and produced the parcel. One might have expected, therefore, that the policeman had in fact made up his mind to take charge of it before the telephone rang. The decision presumably proceeds on the assumption that he had not done so. On that assumption the decision would presumably be the same under the Theft Act[9] for it was held in *Re A-G's Reference (No. 1 of 1974)*[10] that whether the police officer has taken possession depends primarily on the intentions of the police officer. In that case a police officer, correctly suspecting that goods in the back of a car were stolen, immobilised the car by removing the rotor arm and kept watch until D returned to the car. He

---

3. *Re A-G's Reference (No. 1 of 1974)* [1974] QB 744, [1974] 2 All ER 899, CA; **SHC 504**.

4. Cf. *Dolan* (1855) Dears CC 436; *Schmidt* (1866) LR 1 CCR 15; *Villensky* [1892] 2 QB 597.

5. In *Haughton v Smith* [1975] AC 476, [1973] 3 All ER 1109, where the police accompanied the driver of a van containing stolen goods to its destination in order to trap the handler, Lords Hailsham and Dilhorne questioned whether the prosecution was right to concede that the goods had been restored to lawful custody.

6. *Greater London Metropolitan Police Comr v Streeter* (1980) 71 Cr App Rep 113.

7. [1938] 2 All ER 662, CCA.

8. Cf. *Warner v Metropolitan Police Comr* [1969] 2 AC 256, [1968] 2 All ER 356.

9. In *Re A-G's Reference (No. 1 of 1974)* [1974] 2 All ER 899 at 904, Lord Widgery CJ said that *King* "might be thought to be a rather bold decision".

10. [1974] QB 744, [1974] 2 All ER 899, CA; **SHC 504**.

questioned D and in view of the unsatisfactory nature of D's replies arrested him. It was held that the jury ought to have been asked to consider whether the officer had decided before D's appearance to take possession of the goods or whether he was of an entirely open mind, intending to decide when he had questioned D. Possession[11] requires both an intent to possess and some act of possession. To immobilise a car does not necessarily involve an intent to possess it or its contents but, along with other circumstances, it may afford evidence of such an intent.

It is now quite clear that the goods cease to be stolen in the case where the police are acting without the authority of the owner for they are clearly in "other lawful possession or custody of the goods".[12] Indeed, it would seem to be enough that the goods fall into the possession of any person who intends to restore them to the person from whom they were stolen. If, however, the thief makes a present of the goods to E who does not know that they are stolen, E's possession, though not unlawful in the criminal law, is not a sufficient "lawful possession or custody".

Section 24 (3) also provides that the goods lose their character of stolen goods if the person from whom they were stolen has ceased to have any *right to restitution* in respect of the theft. Whether a "right to restitution" exists is a question of civil law, and now turns on the provisions of the Torts (Interference with Goods) Act 1977. By s. 3 of this Act, in an action for wrongful interference with goods, courts are empowered, inter alia, to order delivery of the goods to the claimant. The remedy is discretionary (s. 3 (3) (b)) and it would appear that the claimant would be ordinarily confined to damages. Nevertheless it is thought that the phrase "right to restitution" in s. 24 (3) of the Theft Act extends to any case in which the claimant *may* obtain an order for the specific restitution of the goods. Thus goods continue to be stolen so long as the claimant is entitled to seek the return of his goods in an action for wrongful interference.[13]

The provision seems to have been intended to bear a still wider meaning. The Criminal Law Revision Committee explained it as follows:[14]

"This is because, if the person who owned the goods when they were stolen no longer has any title to them, there will be no reason why the goods should continue to have the taint of being stolen goods. For example, the offence of handling stolen goods will . . . apply also to goods obtained by criminal deception under [s. 15]. If the owner of the goods who has been deceived chooses on discovering the deception to ratify his disposal of the goods he will cease to have any title to them."

It is clear that "title" is here used in a broad sense to include a right to rescind. The Committee clearly has in mind a case where property passes

---

11. For the purposes of s. 24 (3) possession *or control* suffices. Arguably in both the above cases the police officer had at least control of the goods but control, like possession, must involve an intent to take charge.

12. Cf. the dictum of Cresswell J in *Dolan* (1855) Dears CC 436 that goods retained their stolen character in this situation. Presumably the police in *King* were acting with the owner's authority. The point is not discussed, but it would seem likely that the theft had been reported to the police by the owner.

13. *A-G's Reference (No. 4 of 1979)* [1981] Crim LR 51 and commentary.

14. Cmnd. 2977, para. 139.

from P to D at the moment when the goods are obtained by deception. In such a case, P, strictly, has no "title" and his right to recover the goods (or much more likely, their value) will only arise on his rescinding the contract.[15] Such a potential right it is submitted, is clearly a "right to restitution" within the Act.

3 Goods Representing those Originally Stolen may be Stolen Goods

By s. 24 (2) of the Act:

"For the purposes of those provisions references to stolen goods shall include, in addition to the goods originally stolen and parts of them (whether in their original state or not), –

a) any other goods which directly or indirectly represent or have at any time represented the stolen goods in the hands of the thief as being the proceeds of any disposal or realisation of the whole or part of the goods stolen or of goods so representing the stolen goods; and

b) any other goods which directly or indirectly represent or have at any time represented the stolen goods in the hands of a handler of the stolen goods or any part of them as being the proceeds of any disposal or realisation of the whole or part of the stolen goods handled by him or of goods so representing them."

The Criminal Law Revision Committee stated[16] of this provision:

"It may seem technical; but the effect will be that the goods which the accused is charged with handling must, at the time of the handling or at some previous time, (i) have been in the hands of the thief or of a handler, and (ii) have represented the original stolen goods in the sense of being the proceeds, direct or indirect, of a sale or other realisation of the original goods."

The effect is best explained by an example. If D steals an Austin car, exchanges it with B for a Bentley, exchanges the Bentley with C for a Citroën and sells the Citroën to E for £500; the Austin, Bentley, Citroën and £500 are now all stolen. Although only one car was actually stolen there are now in circulation three stolen cars and five hundred stolen pounds. The position would be exactly the same if D were not the thief but a receiver of the Austin. Clearly this provision can lead to indefinite multiplication of the stolen goods. Whenever any article which is actually stolen or notionally stolen under s. 24 (2) is exchanged for another, that other article is stolen *unless* the person to whom it is delivered is neither the thief nor a handler. So, if in the above example, B knew the Austin to be stolen, anything which he might receive for it would also be stolen; whereas, if C was an innocent receiver of the Bentley, anything which he received for it would lack the taint of stolen goods.

If in this illustration D hands to F the £500 then F, if he knows its provenance, is guilty of handling. Suppose, though, that D banks the £500 in his account where there is additional *lawfully* earned money, and that D

---

15. Cf. Smith, *Theft*, paras 83–86, where it is argued, in relation to s. 5 (4), that a person holding property under a voidable title is not "under an obligation to make restoration"; above, p. 521.

16. Cmnd. 2977 at p. 66.

subsequently draws a cheque on that account in favour of F, who again knows its provenance, for £500. In these circumstances F may be convicted of handling stolen goods if the prosecution can prove that the cheque for £500 represents, at least in part, the proceeds of the £500 which D received for the Citroën.[17] Such proof is obviously forthcoming where the account, but for the stolen £500, stands at less than £500 for in this case some part of D's cheque for £500 necessarily represents some of the proceeds of the stolen money. But if the balance of lawfully obtained money in the account stands at more than £500, can it be proved that D's cheque to F for £500 represents money other than that which was lawfully obtained? This point was left open in *A-G's Reference (No. 4 of 1979)*[18] but it is submitted that if F knows the provenance of the £500 paid to him, it would be difficult to maintain that the money in his hands *represented* money lawfully banked by D. If, as between D and F, it is intended to represent the proceeds of the stolen car, it must represent those proceeds. Proof of what D and F intended here might be hard to come by, but in the normal run of case it is surely open to the jury to infer that D's payment was intended to come from the tainted monies in the account.[19]

Goods which are notionally stolen, like goods which are actually stolen, continue to bear that taint until the conditions laid down in s. 24 (3) of the Act are satisfied in respect of the notionally stolen goods.[20]

4 Forms of Handling

The term "handling" has been adopted because "receiving" – the only way of committing the offence under s. 33 (1) of the Larceny Act 1916 – is now one of several ways in which the new offence can be committed. These are:

i) *Receiving* the goods.

ii) *Undertaking* the retention, removal, disposal or realisation of the goods by or for the benefit of another person.

iii) *Assisting* in the retention, removal, disposal or realisation of the goods by or for the benefit of another person.

iv) *Arranging* to do (i), (ii), (iii).

It has been decided that s. 22 creates only one offence.[1] Since that offence may be committed in four or six or even eighteen ways, a contrary decision would have had a disastrously complicating effect on the section, giving wide scope to possible objections on the ground of duplicity.

a) *Receiving*. All forms of handling other than receiving or arranging to receive are subject to the qualification that it must be proved that D was acting "for the benefit of another person". If there is no evidence of this – as will frequently be the case – then it must be proved that D *received* or

---

17. *A-G's Reference (No. 4 of 1979)* [1981] 1 All ER 1193, [1981] 1 WLR 667, CA.
18. Last note.
19. Ibid. at 1199.
20. Smith, *Theft*, paras 396–397.
   1. *Griffiths v Freeman* [1970] 1 All ER 1117, DC. But see also *Ikpong* [1972] Crim LR 432, CA and *Willis and Syme*, ibid., and *Deakin* [1972] 3 All ER 803, CA; **SHC 587**; *Nicklin* [1977] Crim LR 221, CA. But in *Bloxham* [1982] 1 All ER 582, at 584, Lord Bridge thought it "well settled" that this section creates two offences.

arranged to receive the goods and evidence of no other form of handling will suffice. The Act does not define receiving in any way and it must be assumed that all the old authorities remain valid.

To establish receiving, it must be proved, then, that D took possession or control of the stolen property or joined with others to share possession or control of it. "Receiving" the thief who has the goods in his possession does not necessarily amount to receiving the goods. If the thief retains exclusive control, there is no receiving.[2] There may, however, be a joint possession in thief and receiver, so it is unnecessary to prove that the thief ever parted with possession – it is sufficient that he shared it with the alleged receiver. In *Smith*[3] it was held that a recorder had correctly directed a jury when he told them that if they believed "that the watch was then in the custody of a person with the cognizance of the prisoner, that person being one over whom the prisoner had absolute control, so that the watch would be forthcoming if the prisoner ordered it, there was ample evidence to justify them in convicting . . ." Lord Campbell CJ said that if the thief had been employed by D to commit larceny, so that the watch was in D's control, D was guilty of receiving. In such a case D was an accessory before the fact to larceny and today he would be guilty of theft. If the facts were as put by Lord Campbell, when did D become a receiver? As soon as the theft was committed? If so, we have the extraordinary result that D became guilty of both theft and receiving at the same moment. But, if this moment is not selected, it is difficult to see what other is appropriate. This may, however, appear less anomalous under the new law than under the old. Virtually all handling is now theft, so it is the general rule that the two offences are committed simultaneously. In the ordinary case, however, the offence is handling because there has been a previous theft. The peculiarity of the present problem is that there has been no *previous* theft so it may be that D becomes a handler only by some act done *after* the theft.

As is clear from *Smith*, actual manual possession or control by D need not be proved. It is enough if the goods are received by his servant or agent with his authority.[4] The receipt may be for a merely temporary purpose such as concealment from the police.[5] It is unnecessary that the receiver should receive any profit or advantage from the possession of the goods. If D took possession of the goods from the thief without his consent, this was formerly only larceny (from the thief) and not receiving.[6] There seems to be no reason why it should not be both theft and handling under the Act, since it is clear that the two offences can be committed by one and the same act.

It continues to be essential for the judge to give a careful direction as to possession or control.[7] If the only evidence against D is that he ran away on being found by the police in a house where stolen property had been left, there would appear to be no case to leave to a jury. Likewise where the

2. *Wiley* (1850) 2 Den 37.
3. (1855) Dears CC 494.
4. *Miller* (1854) 6 Cox CC 353.
5. *Richardson* (1834) 6 C & P 335.
6. *Wade* (1844) 1 Car & Kir 739.
7. *Frost and Hale* (1964) 48 Cr App Rep 284.

evidence is consistent with the view that D went to premises where stolen goods were stored with the intention of assuming possession, but had not actually done so[8] or where the only evidence of receiving a stolen car is that D's finger-print was found on the driving mirror.[9] The mere fact that the stolen goods were found on D's premises is not sufficient evidence. It must be shown that the goods had come either by invitation or arrangement with him or that he had exercised some control over them.[10] D is not necessarily in possession of a stolen safe simply because he assists others in trying to open it.[11]

b) *Arranging to receive.* Where it is impossible to prove an actual receipt, the evidence may show that D has arranged to receive the goods. Where D has merely made preparations to receive and has not yet reached the stage of an attempt to do so, the preparations may constitute a sufficient arrangement. The difficulties in a case like *King*[12] will be overcome if it appears that the arrangement to receive was concluded before there was a possibility of the goods ceasing to be stolen. Presumably it is enough if the proposed receipt is by a servant or agent. It must be made after the theft, since D must know or believe the goods to be stolen when he makes the arrangement.[13]

Though there is no such express requirement, it is difficult to envisage an arrangement which does not involve an agreement with another. Such an agreement will almost always amount to a conspiracy to receive so the extension of the law effected by this provision is less far-reaching than might appear. Clearly, however, an arrangement made with an innocent person is enough, as is an arrangement which does not involve another party at all, if that can be envisaged.

The offence of handling is complete as soon as the proposed receipt is arranged. It is immaterial (except as to sentence) that D repents or does nothing in pursuance of the arrangement.

c) *Undertaking and assisting.* The provisions of the Act relating to handling by *undertaking* and *assisting* extend the law to cover cases which were formerly not criminal at all. They are far-reaching and overlapping. "Undertaking" presumably covers the case where D sets out to retain, etc., the stolen goods, on his own initiative and appears more apt to describe the activity of the seller of stolen goods rather than that of the buyer. "Assisting" seems more apt to cover the case where D joins the thief or another handler in doing so.[14]

How this provision extends the ambit of the former law may be illustrated by reference to former cases where the conduct in question did not amount to receiving as it was then defined. D negotiates the sale to F of

8. *Freedman* (1930) 22 Cr App Rep 133. But this might be sufficient evidence of an arrangement to receive.
9. *Court* (1960) 44 Cr App Rep 242.
10. *Cavendish* [1961] 2 All ER 856.
11. *Tomblin* [1964] Crim LR 780.
12. Above, p. 618. And similarly the difficulties of *Haughton v Smith* [1975] AC 476, [1973] 3 All ER 1109, HL, above p. 618.
13. *Park* (1987) Times, 14 December.
14. But cf *Deakin* [1972] 3 All ER 803, CA.

goods which he knows to have been stolen by E. D is never in possession or control of the goods.[15] He would appear to have undertaken or assisted in the disposal of stolen goods. D assists E to lift from a van a barrel of gin which he knows to have been stolen by E or another. Even if he never has possession or control[16] he has assisted or undertaken the removal of the stolen goods. D's fifteen-year-old son, E, brings home a bicycle which he has stolen. D assists in its retention if (i) he agrees that E may keep the bicycle in the house, or (ii) he tells the police there is no bicycle in the house, or (iii) he gives E a tin of paint so that he may disguise it.

D lights the way for E to carry stolen goods from a house to a barn, so that he may negotiate for the purchase of them.[17] D has assisted in the removal of the goods and would be no less liable to conviction (though his sentence might be lighter) if that was the full extent of his intended dealing with the goods.

The undertaking or assisting must under the Act relate to the retention etc. of the goods. Merely to use goods known to have been stolen does not suffice because use alone does not assist in their retention etc. So where D brings stolen equipment to his garage and E uses that equipment knowing it to have been stolen, E does not thereby assist D to retain the equipment.[18] But consider *Kanwar*.[19] D brought home some furnishings which E, his wife, knowing them to be stolen, used to furnish parts of their house. The police entered the house under a search warrant without any thought of arresting E; but when E lied to them about the provenance of the furnishings she was arrested, charged, and subsequently convicted of assisting D to retain the furnishings. On appeal it was recognised that proof of use was not proof of assisting, but E's conviction was upheld on the grounds that (i) assistance did not have to take the form of physical assistance and that merely verbal assistance would do; and (ii) telling lies to the police (even though the police were not taken in by them) amounted to such assistance when made for the purpose of protecting D. Point (i) must be right because D may be assisted to retain stolen goods by lies told by E which put the police off the scent. As to point (ii) the court said[20] –

"It would be absurd if a person dishonestly concealing stolen goods for the benefit of a receiver could establish a defence by showing that he was caught in the act. In the present case, if, while the police were in one part of the house, [E], in order to conceal the painting had put it under a mattress in the bedroom, it would not alter the nature of her conduct that the police subsequently looked under the mattress and found the picture because they expected to find it there or that they had caught her in the act of putting it there."

At first sight this is a common-sense view but it involves reading s. 22 (1) as though it read that something done *with intent to* assist etc. constitutes

---

15. Cf. *Watson* [1916] 2 KB 385.
16. *Gleed* (1916) 12 Cr App Rep 32; *Hobson v Impett* (1957) 41 Cr App Rep 138.
17. *Wiley* (1850) 2 Den 37.
18. *Sanders* (1982) 75 Cr App Rep 84, CA. The fact that E had used the equipment would be some evidence that he had *received* it.
19. [1982] 2 All ER 528, [1982] Crim LR 532, CA, and commentary.
20. [1982] 2 All ER at 529.

handling; literally interpreted, however, the subsection appears to require something that in fact assists etc.[21]

What becomes clear, then, is that E does not undertake or assist in the retention etc. by D simply because E is thereby advantaged. A wife does not assist in the *retention* of a TV receiver which she knows to be stolen by her husband *merely* because she watches programmes on it; nor does she assist in the *retention* of paintings which she knows to be stolen by him *merely* because she decides how they might be displayed to best effect. If the husband purchases Buckingham Palace with stolen money, his wife does not assist in retention or disposal of the stolen money though she can hardly wait to take up residence. Nor would the wife assist in the disposal of the stolen money merely because her husband insists that the palace be conveyed to them in their joint names. In *Coleman*,[1] though the premises purchased with the money were much less grandiose, it was held that a husband (in this case it was the wife who had stolen the money) could not be convicted of handling on proof only that a flat was purchased with the stolen money which was conveyed to both himself and his wife. It would have been different if the husband had given advice as to the disposal of the stolen money. It would have sufficed to convict him had he negotiated for the purchase of the flat, or if he had advised her to invest in real estate rather than leave the money on deposit at the bank, or even if he had encouraged her to buy the flat. But passive acquiescence by E in D's retention etc. of stolen property does not, as such,[2] render E a handler however much E may benefit from the enjoyment and use of the property.

d) *Arranging to undertake or assist*. The extension of the law to undertaking and assisting is far-reaching, but the Act goes still further. The mere arrangement to do any of the acts amounting to undertaking or assisting amounts to the complete offence of handling. So it would presumably be enough that D agreed to negotiate the sale of the stolen goods, to lift down the barrel of stolen gin or to do any act for the purpose of enabling E to retain, remove or dispose of the stolen goods. "Receiving", "undertaking" and "arranging" all suggest that some conduct is required though as little as a nod or a wink might suffice in particular circumstances. "Assisting", however, may be constituted by inactivity provided it is in circumstances where that inactivity does in fact provide assistance.[3]

Take a simple case. D, a wife, could hardly be constituted a handler because E, her husband, each dawn returns to *his* house with the fruits of the night's burglaries. As has been shown above, D would not become a handler even if she used the goods, provided such use did not involve assistance in their retention etc. Knowledge of the whereabouts of stolen goods cannot constitute D a handler; nor does D become a handler simply by refusing to answer police questions as to the whereabouts of the goods[4]

21. Since E would be in any case guilty of an attempt to assist etc., the point is not of practical importance.
1. [1986] Crim LR 56, CA.
2. But cf. handling by omission, infra.
3. See above, p. 137.
4. Though D may become a handler (assist in the retention of the goods) if lies are told to put the police off the scent: *Kanwar* [1982] 2 All ER 528, [1982] 1 WLR 845 above, p. 624.

since there is no obligation to help the police with their inquiries.[5] So in *Brown*,[6] where E secreted stolen goods in D's flat and told D he had done so, it was held a misdirection to tell the jury that assisting in the retention of the goods could be inferred from D's refusal to reveal the presence of the stolen goods when questioned by the police about them.

The conviction in *Brown* was, however, upheld by applying the proviso. D had tacitly, if not expressly, permitted E to hide the goods on his premises and had thereby assisted in their retention. This is not to say that knowledge of the presence of stolen goods on his premises constitutes the occupier a handler. Obviously D does not assist in the retention of stolen goods because he invites to his premises E who, to D's knowledge, is wearing a stolen overcoat even if D puts it in the cloakroom for the duration of E's stay. But if D's premises are used, as they were used in *Brown*, to house the goods and D allows them to remain there he can properly be said to be assisting in their retention just as plainly as if he had initially given permission. What is important here is that D has control of premises and has chosen to allow their use for the storage of stolen goods.

Pitchley[7] is to the same effect. E, D's son, gave D stolen money telling him that he had won it on the horses and D paid it into his bank account. Two days later D became aware that the money was stolen but he did nothing about it until questioned by the police four days later. D's conviction for handling by assisting in the retention of the stolen money[8] was upheld because he had continued to retain possession after he became aware that the money was stolen. D had assumed control of the money and had, with guilty knowledge, retained control for the benefit of E.[9]

5 Otherwise than in the Course of the Stealing

Whatever the form of handling alleged, it must be done "otherwise than in the course of the stealing". This provision was obviously necessary if a great many instances of perfectly ordinary theft were not automatically to become handling as well. Thus, without the provision, virtually every instance of theft by two or more persons would have been handling by one or other or, more likely, both of them, since they would inevitably render mutual assistance to one another in the removal of the goods. Given the decision to keep handling as a separate crime, the provision was, then, necessary – but it adds further unfortunate complications to an already complicated offence.

The position was in fact much the same under the old law of receiving because of the rule that a principal in the felony of larceny could not be guilty of receiving as a principal in the first degree.[10] If D received the goods in the course of the stealing, it followed that he was a principal in the larceny and this necessarily meant that he could not be convicted of receiving. If a servant stole money from his master's till and handed it to an

---

5. See above, p. 394.
6. [1970] 1QB 105, [1969] 3 All ER 198, CA.
7. (1973) 57 Cr App Rep 30, CA; **SHC 510**. Cf. *Tamm* [1973] Crim LR 115.
8. The decision overlooks the fact that when D acquired his knowledge there was no longer any "stolen" money to handle (see Smith, *Theft*, para. 407) but this does not affect the point at issue.
9. Cf. theft by "keeping [goods] as owner", above, p. 494.
10. See Smith, *Theft*, paras. 409–410.

accomplice in his master's shop, the accomplice was guilty of larceny and not guilty of receiving.[11] Similarly, if a man committed larceny in the room in which he lodged and threw a bundle of stolen goods to an accomplice in the street, the accomplice was guilty of larceny and not guilty of receiving.[12] "If one burglar stands outside a window", said Alderson B, "while another plunders the house and hands out the goods to him, he surely could not be indicted as a receiver".[13] It seems to follow that in cases such as these, the same result would be reached under the Theft Act – i.e., in each case D is guilty of theft and not guilty of handling. This result necessarily follows from the words, "otherwise than in the course of the stealing", whether or not the rule survives (under which the cases cited were decided) that a principal in larceny cannot be a principal in the first degree in receiving. These cases show that larceny was a continuing offence. As soon as the thief moved the thing a fraction of an inch the larceny was complete in the sense that, if he had been stopped at that moment, he could have been successfully indicted for the complete crime. The commission of the offence nevertheless continued at least until the point, in those cases, where the goods were put into the accomplice's hands.

It is arguable that theft is not a continuing offence in the way that larceny was.[14] If this argument were accepted, it might well follow that the receipt, on the facts of these cases, is not "in the course of the stealing". This argument receives support from *Pitham and Hehl*.[15] E, knowing that P was in prison and in no position to interfere, planned to steal furniture from P's house. He told D1 and D2 that he had furniture to sell, took them with him to P's house, and there sold them such furniture as they wished to buy at a considerable under-value. It was held by the Court of Appeal that E stole the furniture when he appropriated it by inviting D1 and D2 to buy it;[16] the way was thus open to upholding the conviction of D1 and D2 for handling because the handling took place *after* the appropriation was complete and was therefore not in the course of stealing. On the face of it this decision seems to render the words "in the course of the stealing" entirely nugatory. While stealing may be an instantaneous act, "in the course of the stealing" must mean something more. If in *Pitham and Hehl* D1 and D2 had known that E planned to steal the furniture and had gone to P's house to help him to steal it, it surely could not be realistically argued that their acts were not in the course of the stealing. As it happened there was no proof that they knew that E planned to steal – it was only when the furniture was offered to them at an under-value that they realised that E had stolen the furniture. This made their conduct look more like handling than stealing; nevertheless it is difficult to see how they could be said to have handled the furniture "otherwise than in the course of the stealing."[17]

---

11. *Coggins* (1873) 12 Cox CC 517.
12. *Perkins* (1852) 5 Cox CC 554.
13. Ibid. at 555.
14. Smith, *Theft*, para. 49, above, p. 135; cf *Figures* [1976] Crim LR 744.
15. (1977) 65 Cr App Rep 45, CA.
16. The offer to sell was an assumption of P's rights and therefore an appropriation, see above p. 497.
17. Cf. *Hale* (1978) 68 Cr App Rep 415, [1979] Crim LR 596 distinguished in *Gregory* (1982) 74 Cr App Rep 154, CA.

If E had stolen the furniture at some earlier stage so that the purchase and removal by D1 and D2 could be said to be a separate transaction it would have been proper to convict them of handling. Of course a line still has to be drawn somewhere and there are bound to be difficult borderline cases. Some guidance in drawing that line may be found in the authorities on the law of larceny.[18] So where E broke into a warehouse, stole butter and deposited it in the street some thirty yards from the warehouse door, D who then came to assist in carrying it off was not guilty of larceny as a principal offender.[19] Similarly where D waited half a mile from the scene of a proposed larceny and there received a horse stolen by E.[20] Doubtless, in these cases, D was guilty of receiving and would be so guilty on similar facts under the Theft Act.

These cases suggested that the theft continued at least while the thief was on the premises in which he perpetrated it and while "the job" was incomplete. But is E still in the course of theft as he walks down the garden path with the swag? as he drives home? and as he shows it to his wife in the kitchen? On the other hand, is the theft necessarily in the course of commission because the stolen property has not yet been removed from the premises on which it was stolen, if E had completed "the job" and all that remains is for others to take possession of the goods? It is thought that, in such a case, E is no longer in the course of stealing.[1] If so, some of the old cases on larceny are no longer in point. Thus in *Atwell and O'Donnell*[2] goods were left in the warehouse in which they had been stolen for *some time thereafter* and the court held that it was a continuing transaction as to those who joined in the plot *before the goods were finally carried away from the premises.* Presumably until this occurred, the asportation was incomplete. It seems clear that the course of stealing under the Theft Act does not continue so long. If E appropriates goods in his employer's warehouse and conceals them so that they may be taken by D who comes to the warehouse a week later, is it to be said that D's taking is in the course of stealing? Surely not. It is thought that E must still be "on the job" – vague though that phrase may be – if the receipt is to be "in the course of the stealing".

From the terms of s. 22 (1), at least at first sight, it would seem that to sustain a charge of handling the prosecution must prove that D handled the goods "otherwise than in the course of the stealing". This may create problems for the prosecutor since the circumstances may be such, as where D is found in possession of stolen goods some days after the theft, that while it is clear that D is either the thief or the handler it cannot be established beyond reasonable doubt whether he was the thief or the handler.

The problem was considered in *Cash*.[3] Found in possession of the proceeds of burglaries about a week after the burglaries had taken place, D

18. See also s. 5 (1) (a) of the Homicide Act 1957 and *Jones* [1959] 1 QB 291; *H. M. Advocate v Graham*, 1958 SLT 167.
19. *King* (1817) Russ & Ry 332; cf *Gruncell and Hopkinson* (1839) 9 C & P 365.
20. *Kelly* (1820) Russ & Ry 421.
1. A view reinforced by *Pitham and Hehl*, above, p. 627.
2. (1801) 2 East PC 768.
3. [1985] QB 801, [1985] 2 All ER 128, [1985] Crim LR 311, CA. But cf. *A-G of Hong Kong Yip Kai-foon* [1988] 1 All ER 153, PC.

gave no explanation for his possession and at his trial elected not to give evidence. Convicted on a single count of handling his counsel argued on appeal that the prosecution had to prove affirmatively that D had not stolen the goods, that is to prove beyond reasonable doubt that D came by the goods otherwise than in the course of the stealing. The Court of Appeal disagreed. Lord Lane CJ said that where there was no evidence whatsoever indicating that D was the thief, the jury was entitled to infer that he was a handler; in such a case the words "otherwise than in the course of the stealing" have little importance and the jury should not even be told about them. The decision may be said to afford a practical answer to what is a practical problem but it boldly ignores what seems to be a requirement of the offence of handling, namely, proof that the handling was not in the course of the theft. The better solution would surely be to add a count for theft whenever it is unclear whether D is thief or handler. Handling goods usually amounts to the theft of them as well so that a jury, not satisfied that D came by the goods otherwise than in the course of the stealing and thus cannot be convicted of handling, may still convict him of theft whether D appropriated the goods by taking them or receiving them as a handler.

6 For the Benefit of Another Person

Where a person steals goods it will ordinarily be with a view to some benefit to himself.[4] If D steals money he will spend it to his own benefit; if he steals goods he will use the goods to his own benefit or sell them and use the proceeds to his own benefit. When D disposes of stolen goods, a benefit usually accrues to another; the purchaser of the stolen car may be said to be benefitted by his use of the stolen car, the dealer who purchases the stolen TV receiver may make a profit on its resale, and so on. In such cases D has assisted in the disposal or realisation of the stolen goods and thus (irrespective of whether the purchaser or dealer is aware that the goods are stolen) would be guilty of handling unless some further qualification were introduced into the offence.

This qualification is provided, or was intended to be provided, by the requirement that the disposal etc. be "by or for the benefit of another person". In the illustration just given a benefit had accrued to the purchaser and the dealer but the disposal etc. is done by D for his own benefit and is not, or ought not to be considered, for their benefit simply because some profit may incidentally accrue to them.

The Criminal Law Revision Committee was concerned that the thief should not become a handler simply because he did one of the acts of disposing etc.; such an act makes the thief a handler only if it is "by or for the benefit of another" –

"[S]ince the offence will apply only to undertaking or assisting in the disposal or other dealing 'by or for the benefit of another person', *a thief will not be guilty of handling by keeping or disposing of the goods for his own benefit.*"[5]

---

4. This is not to suggest that theft requires any such view of benefit.
5. Cmnd. 2977, para. 131. Italics supplied.

Section 22 (1) is, however, somewhat unfortunately drafted.[6] It contemplates that handling (otherwise than by way of receiving) may be committed by undertaking or assisting in one of the specified acts (disposing, realising etc.) by *or* for the benefit of another.

Fortunately the House of Lords in *Bloxham*[7] has held that s. 22 (1) is to be interpreted in accordance with the intentions of the Criminal Law Revision Committee. It could not be said, therefore, that a disposal by D for his own benefit was for the benefit of another simply because some profit accrued to the other. Accordingly where D, an innocent purchaser of a stolen car, subsequently realised it was stolen and sold it to P, he did not sell the car "for the benefit of another". Nor, of course, would it make any difference that D had initially stolen the car rather than acquired it innocently. The 1968 Act strives to maintain a distinction between thieves and handlers and a thief is not to attract the heavier penalties accorded to the handler by disposing of stolen goods for his own benefit. This is not to say that a thief cannot in any circumstances handle the goods which he steals and the circumstances in which he may do so are examined in the following two sections.

7 Innocent Receipt and Subsequent Retention with Mens Rea

If D receives the stolen goods innocently, either, that is, believing them not to be stolen or knowing them to be stolen but intending to return them to the true owner, of course, he commits no offence.[8] Suppose he subsequently discovers the goods to be stolen or decides not to return them to the true owner or disposes of them. He has dishonestly undertaken the retention of or has disposed of stolen goods knowing them to be stolen. Whether he is guilty of an offence depends on a number of factors.

  1. Where D does not get ownership of the goods. (The normal situation where goods are stolen.)
  i) D gives value for the goods
    a) D retains or disposes of the goods for his own benefit. This is not theft because of s. 3 (2);[9] nor is it handling by undertaking, assisting or arranging since it is not for the benefit of another.[10] D might be guilty of handling by aiding and abetting the receiving by the person to whom he disposes of the goods, if that person has *mens rea*.
    b) D retains or disposes of the goods for the benefit of another. This is not theft (s. 3 (2)) but is handling.
  ii) D does not give value.
    a) D retains or disposes of the goods for his own benefit. This is theft but not handling unless it amounts to aiding and abetting receipt by another.
    b) D retains or disposes of the goods for the benefit of another. This is theft and handling.

6. See Blake, "The Innocent Purchaser and s. 22 of the Theft Act" [1972] Crim LR 494; Spencer, "The Mishandling of Handling" [1981] Crim LR 682; Smith, *Theft*, para 411.
7. [1983] AC 109, [1982] 1 All ER 582; HL **SHC 514**.
8. *Alt* [1972] Crim LR 552, CA.
9. Above, p. 503.
10. *Bloxham* [1983] AC 109, [1982] 1 All ER 582, HL.

2. Where D gets ownership of the goods. (Because the rogue obtained them by deception and acquired a voidable title or because of some exception of the nemo dat rule.)

a) D gives value for the goods.

Retention or disposal of the goods cannot be theft since P had no property in the goods, nor handling since P has lost his right to restitution,[11] his right to rescind being destroyed on the goods coming into the hands of D who was a bona fide purchaser for value.

b) D does not give value.

Again this cannot be theft, since P has no property in the goods, but it may be handling since P's right to rescind and secure restitution of his property is not extinguished by the goods coming into the hands of one who does not give value. It will be handling if this is so *and* D either aids and abets a guilty receipt by another or disposes of the goods for the benefit of another.

8 Handling by the Thief[12]

The common law rules regulating the liability of a thief to a charge of receiving goods feloniously stolen by him were complicated. The present position appears to be that any thief may be convicted of handling goods stolen by him by receiving them – if the evidence warrants this conclusion.[13] In the majority of cases the thief can only be guilty of handling by receiving where he is abetting the receipt by another because he is already in possession or control and therefore cannot receive as the principal offender. In some circumstances, however, a thief might be convicted of handling the stolen goods by receiving them as the principal offender. For example, D steals goods and, in the course of the theft, delivers them to E. Two days later E returns the goods to D.

9 Advertising for the Return of Stolen Goods

By s. 23 of the Theft Act 1968 it is an offence publicly to advertise for the return of stolen goods indicating that no questions will be asked about how the person returning the goods came by them. The antecedents of this offence go back to 1828 and it was retained, after some hesitation on the part of the CLRC, because it was thought that advertisements of this kind might encourage dishonesty.[14] Though such advertisements may encourage dishonesty in others, dishonesty is not required of the perpetrator. Indeed the offence has been held to be one of strict liability so that the advertising manager of a newspaper in which such an advertisement appeared committed the offence though he was unaware that it had appeared in the paper.[15]

---

11. Above, p. 619.
12. A. T. H. Smith, "Theft and/or Handling" [1977] Crim LR 517.
13. *Dolan* (1976) 62 Cr App Rep 36, CA; *Stapylton v O'Callaghan* [1973] 2 All ER 782, DC.
14. Cmnd. 2977, para. 144.
15. *Denham v Scott* (1983) 77 Cr App Rep 210, DC.

2) *The Mens Rea*

1 Knowledge or Belief[16]

It must be proved that the goods were stolen and that D handled them "knowing or believing them to be stolen goods." The Criminal Law Revision Committee thought that this provision would extend the law:

"It is a serious defect of the present law that actual knowledge that the property was stolen must be proved. Often the prosecution cannot prove this. In many cases indeed guilty knowledge does not exist, although the circumstances of the transaction are such that the receiver ought to be guilty of an offence. The man who buys goods at a ridiculously low price from an unknown seller whom he meets in a public house may not *know* that the goods were stolen, and he may take the precaution of asking no questions. Yet it may be clear on the evidence that he believes that the goods were stolen. In such cases the prosecution may fail (rightly, as the law now stands) for want of proof of guilty knowledge."[17]

It may be accepted that it would be a serious defect to confine D's liability to the case where he *knows* the goods are stolen. In one sense it may be questioned whether D can ever know that the goods are stolen. Even if D witnesses the "theft" he cannot know that the "thief" may not be acting under, say, a claim of right or under duress. But to give "knowing" such a restricted meaning in this context would be unrealistic. For practical purposes D may be said to know that goods are stolen when from the available facts he concludes they are stolen and either does not consider whether they may not be stolen, or, having considered the possibility, he discounts it. "Believing" was added to enlarge D's liability beyond the case where he knows the goods to be stolen. The question concerns the extent of that enlargement.

Take the Committee's example of the man who buys goods at a ridiculously low price from an unknown seller in a pub. At one extreme he may conclude that the goods are not stolen, in which case he incurs no liability; or at the other he may conclude that the goods are stolen with no ifs or buts, in which case he knows the goods are stolen. Between the two extremes he may consider that there is merely a risk that the goods are stolen, or he may conclude that while he does not know the goods are stolen (he may here refrain from asking questions to put the matter beyond doubt) he is as sure as may be that they are. In both cases D takes a risk that the goods are stolen; low in the first case, high in the second.

Looked at as a matter of principle, ought a person who acquires goods aware of a risk that they may be stolen to be considered a handler if the goods turn out to be stolen? Williams argues that such a rule would be an undue restraint on commerce. "People", he says,[18] "must be free to buy unless they positively know that the goods are stolen. The public interest in free trade is greater than the public interest in attempting to close every

---

16. See Griew, "Consistency, Communication and Codification – Reflections on Two Mens Rea Words" in *Reshaping the Criminal Law*, ed by Glazebrook, 1978, at p. 57.
17. Cmnd. 2977, 64. Cf *Woods* [1969] QB 447, [1968] 3 All ER 709, CA.
18. TBCL at p. 875. See further Williams, "Handling, Theft and the Purchaser who takes a Chance" [1985] Crim LR 432.

possibility of stolen goods being sold." Spencer, on the other hand and while he accepts that one who merely takes a risk that goods are stolen should not be a handler, argues[19] that D ought to be accounted a handler if he concludes that it is more probable than not that the goods are stolen and that "believing" should be so interpreted.

The courts have been sorely troubled by the interpretation of "knowing or believing". One way of tackling (or avoiding) the problem is to adopt the judicially popular stance of saying these are ordinary English words and their interpretation can be left to the jury without enlargement or explanation by the trial judge. This view has judicial support. In *Harris*[20] Lawton LJ said on behalf of the Court of Appeal:

"In our judgment the words 'knowledge or belief' are words of ordinary usage in English. In most cases, but not all, all that need be said to a jury is to ask them whether that which is alleged by the prosecution, namely receipt, knowing or believing that the goods were stolen, has been established."

But, and assuming the correctness of this approach, the court recognises that while it will do for most cases it will not do for all. *Harris* was a case where the jury were told that if the only inference to be drawn from the facts was that the goods were stolen they were entitled to infer that D knew or believed them to be so. This was regarded by the Court of Appeal as a straightforward case where the jury needed to be directed only in the words of the statute. In at least some cases, however, the issue may not be so straightforward. The inference that the goods were stolen may be less compelling or D may claim that he was less than sure that the goods were stolen and in such cases the meaning of "knowing or believing" needs to be explained to the jury.

The cases are clear that it is a misdirection to tell the jury that it is enough that D suspected that the goods were stolen;[1] mere recklessness as to the provenance of goods does not constitute knowledge or belief. It is also a misdirection to say that D knows or believes where D thinks it more probable than not that the goods are stolen.[2] And care must be taken in expressions along the lines of closing the mind to the obvious. While knowledge or belief *may* be inferred from the fact that D deliberately closed his eyes to the circumstances,[3] it is a misdirection to say that D knows or believes goods to be stolen if, suspecting that goods are stolen, he deliberately shuts his eyes to the consequences.[4] The vice of such a direction is that they may lead a jury to equate suspicion with knowledge or belief.

19. "Handling, Theft and the Mala Fide Purchaser" [1985] Crim LR 92 and 440.
20. (1987) 84 Cr App Rep 75 at 78. See also *Grainge* [1974] 1 All ER 928, [1974] 1 WLR 619, CA; *Smith* (1977) 64 Cr App Rep 217, CA; *Reader* (1978) 66 Cr App Rep 33, CA.
  1. *Grainge* [1974] 1 All ER 928, [1974] 1 WLR 619, CA; still less does it suffice to prove the circumstances were such that D ought to have realised the goods were stolen: *Atwal v Massey* [1971] 3 All ER 881.
  2. *Reader* (1978) 66 Cr App Rep 33. Cp. *Spencer* [1983] QB 771, [1985] 1 All ER 673, [1985] Crim LR 101 and 440.
  3. *Griffiths* (1974) 60 Cr App Rep 14 at 18, CA.
  4. *Griffiths* (1974) 60 Cr App Rep 14, CA; *Ismail* [1977] Crim LR 557, CA; *Smith* (1977) 64 Cr App Rep 217, CA; *Pethick* [1980] Crim LR 242, CA; *Bellenie* [1980] Crim LR 437, CA; *Moys* (1984) 79 Cr App Rep 72, CA.

These cases merely indicate what does not constitute knowledge or belief. In *Hall*[5] Boreham J, delivering the judgment of the Court of Appeal, concluded that the time had come to give guidelines on the appropriate directions to be given to the jury:

"We think that a jury should be directed along these lines. A man may be said to know that goods are stolen when he is told by someone with first hand knowledge (someone such as the thief or the burglar) that such is the case. Belief, of course, is something short of knowledge. It may be said to be the state of mind of a person who says to himself: 'I cannot say I know for certain that these goods are stolen, but there can be no other reasonable conclusion in the light of all the circumstances, in the light of all that I have heard and seen.' Either of those two states of mind is enough to satisfy the words of the statute. The second is enough (that is, belief) even if the defendant says to himself: 'Despite all that I have seen and all that I have heard, I refuse to believe what my brain tells me is obvious.' What is not enough, of course, is mere suspicion. 'I suspect that these goods may be stolen, but it may be on the other hand that they are not.' That state of mind, of course, does not fall within the words 'knowing or believing'."

While it may be accepted that D knows goods are stolen when so informed by one who has first hand knowledge (provided D believes him of course!) this is merely an example of a case where D has knowledge and it is not a definition of knowledge. It is submitted that D knows goods are stolen when he concludes that they are and either does not consider the possibility that they may not be or considers that possibility and dismisses it. Prima facie "believing" adds something to "knowing",[6] but, according to *Hall*, not very much. The first example given by Boreham J, that of the man who says he cannot be sure but there is no other reasonable conclusion, might be said to know the goods are stolen because he has considered the possibility they are not and discounted it. The second example of the man who refuses to believe what his brain tells him is obviously problematical. D might receive goods from his mother in circumstances which all point to their being stolen and yet refuses to believe that his mother could be a thief.[7] It was once thought to be obvious that the sun went round the earth but some people were not entirely convinced. People can, and do, believe in the preposterous. The essence of belief is conviction and doubts are not inconsistent with conviction. A person may believe, and be properly said to believe, that he knows the way from X to Y notwithstanding that just to be on the safe side he takes a road map with him. So D may believe goods to be stolen provided that that is his conviction and notwithstanding that he has not dismissed from his mind the possibility that they may not be stolen after all.

---

5. (1985) 81 Cr App Rep 260 at 264.

6. Williams, TBCL at p. 875, says that "believing" was an unnecessary and therefore misleading addition to the section. It might equally be said that "knowing" is surplusage in that it conveys nothing that would not be conveyed by "believing".

7. Conversely a man may believe goods to be stolen though all the available evidence points the other way and if the goods are in fact stolen he may be convicted of handling.

But if D knows or believes that the goods which he handles are stolen goods, it need not be proved that D realised the nature of those goods. If D handles a container knowing that it contains stolen goods he commits the offence though he is surprised to discover that the container has contents other than those he imagined;[8] and it would seem to make no difference, provided the goods are in fact stolen, that D is misled as to their nature.

2 Dishonesty

Dishonesty was an essential ingredient of the old crime of receiving though it was not expressed in the statute. The inclusion of the word "dishonestly"[9] thus makes no change in the law. D may receive goods knowing or believing them to be stolen and yet not be guilty if, for example, he intends to return them to the true owner or the police.[10] A claim of right will amount to a defence, but it will be difficult to establish such a claim where D knows or believes the goods to be stolen except in the case put above, where he intends to return the goods to the owner.

3 Proof of Mens Rea

The common law rules concerning proof of *mens rea* on a receiving charge hold good under the Act. Accordingly, where D is found in possession of recently stolen property the judge may direct the jury that they *may* infer guilty knowledge or belief if D offers no explanation of his possession or if they are satisfied beyond reasonable doubt that any explanation he has offered is untrue. The onus of proof remains on the Crown throughout, and, whether D offers an explanation or not, he should be convicted only if the jury are satisfied beyond reasonable doubt that he had the guilty knowledge or belief.[11]

Because of the difficulty of proving guilty knowledge, the Larceny Act provided for the admission of certain evidence on a receiving charge which would not be admissible in criminal cases generally. The Theft Act has corresponding provisions. By s. 27 (3):

"Where a person is being proceeded against for handling stolen goods (but not for any offence other than handling stolen goods),[12] then at any stage of the proceedings, if evidence has been given of his having or arranging to have in his possession the goods the subject of the charge, or of his undertaking or assisting in, or arranging to undertake or assist in, their retention, removal, disposal or realisation, the following evidence shall be admissible for the purpose of proving that he knew or believed the goods to be stolen goods:

a) evidence that he has had in his possession, or has undertaken or assisted in the retention, removal, disposal or realisation of, stolen goods from any theft taking place not more than twelve months before the offence charged;[13] and

8. *McCullum* [1973] Crim LR 582, CA.
9. Cf. *Ghosh* [1982] QB 1053, [1982] 2 All ER 689, CA; above, p. 529.
10. Cf. *Matthews* [1950] 1 All ER 137.
11. *Abramovitch* (1914) 11 Cr App Rep 45; *Aves* [1950] 2 All ER 330; *Hepworth*, [1955] 2 QB 600, [1955] 2 All ER 918.
12. Cf. *Anderson* [1978] Crim LR 223 (Judge Stroyan).
13. As to which see *Bradley* (1979) 70 Cr App Rep 200, [1980] Crim LR 173, and commentary.

b) (provided that seven days' notice in writing has been given to him of the intention to prove the conviction) evidence that he has within the five years preceding the date of the offence charged been convicted of theft or of handling stolen goods."[14]

16 Miscellaneous Matters

1) *Husband and Wife*

For many purposes husband and wife occupy a special position under the law and have special rules relating to themselves. This was so under the former law of larceny but now s. 30 of the Theft Act 1968 provides:

"1) This Act shall apply in relation to the parties to a marriage, and to property belonging to the wife or husband whether or not by reason of an interest derived from the marriage, as it would apply if they were not married and any such interest subsisted independently of the marriage.

2) Subject to subsection (4) below a person shall have the same right to bring proceedings against that person's wife or husband for any offence (whether under this Act or otherwise) as if they were not married, and a person bringing any such proceedings shall be competent to give evidence for the prosecution at every stage of the proceedings.

3) (Repealed.)

4) Proceedings shall not be instituted against a person for any offence of stealing or doing unlawful damage to property which at the time of the offence belongs to that person's wife or husband, or for any attempt, incitement or conspiracy to commit such an offence, unless the proceedings are instituted by or with the consent of the Director of Public Prosecutions:

Provided that –

a) this subsection shall not apply to proceedings against a person for an offence –

i) if that person is charged with committing the offence jointly with the wife or husband; or

ii) if by virtue of any judicial decree or order (wherever made) that person and the wife or husband are at the time of the offence under no obligation to cohabit; and

b) this subsection shall not prevent the arrest, or the issue of a warrant for the arrest, of a person for an offence, or the remand in custody or on bail of a person charged with an offence, where the arrest (if without a warrant) is made, or the warrant of arrest issues on an information laid, by a person other than the wife or husband."

---

14. These provisions have attracted both judicial and academic criticism: see *Fowler* [1987] Crim LR 769.

The substantial effect of s. 30 (1) is to make spouses liable in respect of offences against each other's property as though they were not married. Consequently either spouse may, for example, steal property belonging to the other. It may just be worth pointing out here that while it is clear that a spouse may steal property belonging exclusively to the other, it is equally clear that a spouse may steal property jointly owned with the other spouse since one co-owner may steal from another.[15]

By s. 30 (2) one spouse may prosecute the other, subject to s. 30 (4), for *any* criminal offence whether that offence is committed by a spouse on the person or property of the other, or whether by a spouse against a third party. A wife might, for example, prosecute her husband for stealing property belonging to a child of the marriage or for assaulting his mother-in-law.

While it is desirable that a spouse should have the general protection of the criminal law from depredations by the other, it will be appreciated that an over-readiness to institute proceedings by the one against the other, or by a third party against one spouse for an offence on the other spouse, can only be divisive, and hardly conducive to the continuation of a satisfactory domestic relationship. It is for this reason that s. 30 (4) provides that proceedings may not be instituted except by or with the consent of the Director of Public Prosecutions.[16] But note that the Director's consent need only be sought where the offence consists of "stealing or doing unlawful damage to property which at the time of the offence belongs to that person's wife or husband". Neither a wife nor a police officer, then, would need the Director's leave to institute proceedings for an assault on the wife by the husband, nor to prosecute the husband in respect of *any* offence committed by him on a third party.

Moreover, the Director's leave is not required in the two cases excepted by s. 30 (4) (a). The idea behind these exceptions is that in neither case does the risk of vexatious or divisive proceedings – which is the basis for the Director's control – exist. Thus a husband may, without the Director's leave, bring proceedings in respect of an appropriation of his property at a time when he was no longer bound to cohabit. And a third party may similarly bring proceedings where the spouses are jointly charged in respect of an offence relating to property belonging to one of them;[17] an example of this might be where H sets fire to his house in order to endanger the life of another[18] and W aids him in the enterprise.

2) *Corporations and Their Officers*

So far as offences under the Theft Act generally are concerned, the liability of corporations for them falls to be determined in accordance with the general principles applicable to the liability of corporations for crime.[19]

15. Above, p. 509.
16. *Withers* [1975] Crim LR 647.
17. Cf. Smith, *Theft*, paras. 450, *et seq.*
18. See below, p. 696.
19. See above, p. 170.

Where a corporation commits a crime it must be the case that the crime has been committed by a person, or persons, in control of the corporation's affairs.[20] Such persons are of course liable in accordance with the ordinary principles governing liability for crime. In this particular s. 18 contains a special provision relating to the offences of obtaining property by deception, obtaining a pecuniary advantage by deception, and false accounting. The section provides:

"1) Where an offence committed by a body corporate under section 15, 16 or 17 of this Act is proved to have been committed with the consent or connivance of any director, manager, secretary or other similar officer of the body corporate, or any person who was purporting to act in any such capacity, he as well as the body corporate shall be guilty of that offence, and shall be liable to be proceeded against and punished accordingly.

2) Where the affairs of a body corporate are managed by its members, this section shall apply in relation to the acts and defaults of a member in connection with his functions of management as if he were a director of the body corporate."

This provision was explained by the Criminal Law Revision Committee as follows:[1]

"The [section] follows a form of provision commonly included in statutes,[2] where an offence is of a kind to be committed by bodies corporate and where it is desired to put the management[3] under a positive obligation to prevent irregularities, if aware of them. Passive acquiescence does not, under the general law, make a person liable as a party to the offence, but there are clearly cases (of which we think this is one) where the director's responsibilities for his company require him to intervene to prevent fraud and where consent or connivance amount to guilt."

The inference from this seems to be that, but for some such provision, the director might not in some circumstances be liable under the general principles governing liability for crime. Suppose, for example, that D, a director, learns that E, a fellow director, proposes to raise an overdraft from a bank by stating that it is required to enable the company to purchase plant when it is required to pay off creditors, but that D does nothing about it and the overdraft is authorised by the bank. The effect of s. 18 appears to be that D incurs criminal liability in respect of the obtaining of the pecuniary advantage by deception because the offence has been committed with his consent. There would be no need to show that D communicated to E his approval of the deception. Possibly, however, D would be liable under general principles for he has a clear duty to control the actions of E in this

20. A corporation may of course be vicariously liable for crimes even though the crime is not committed by a person in control of its affairs: see above, p. 171. But vicarious liability would not apply in connection with offences under the Theft Act.
1. Cmnd. 2977, para. 104.
2. See further, above, p. 175.
3. Note that s. 18 imposes criminal liability only on the management; this may include (s. 18 (2)) any member who is in fact in control even though he may not formally hold a managerial post.

situation and his deliberate failure to perform his duty may make him an abettor.[4]

3) *Restitution*[5]

Section 28 of the Theft Act[6] provides:

"1) Where goods have been stolen, and either a person is convicted of any offence with reference to the theft[7] (whether or not the stealing is the gist of his offence) or a person is convicted of any other offence, but such an offence as aforesaid is taken into consideration in determining his sentence, the court by or before which the offender is convicted may on the conviction, whether or not the passing of sentence is in other respects deferred, exercise any of the following powers: –

  a) the court may order anyone having possession or control of the goods to restore them to any person entitled to recover them from him; or

  b) on the application[8] of a person entitled to recover from the person convicted any other goods directly or indirectly representing the first-mentioned goods (as being the proceeds of any disposal or realisation of the whole or part of them or of goods so representing them), the court may order those other goods to be delivered or transferred to the applicant; or

  c) the court may order that a sum not exceeding the value of the first mentioned goods shall be paid out of any money of the person convicted which was taken out of his possession on his apprehension to any person who, if those goods were in the possession of the person convicted, would be entitled to recover them from him.

2) Where under subsection (1) above the court has power on a person's conviction to make an order against him both under paragraph (b) and under paragraph (c) with reference to the stealing of the same goods, the court may make orders under both paragraphs provided that the person in whose favour the orders are made does not thereby recover more than the value of those goods.

3) Where under subsection (1) above the court on a person's conviction makes an order under paragraph (a) for the restoration of any goods, and it appears to the court that the person convicted has sold the goods to a person acting in good faith, or has borrowed money on the security of them from a person so acting, the court may order that there shall be paid to the purchaser or lender, out of any money of

---

4. See above, p. 137. *Tamm* [1973] Crim LR 115, CA.
5. Macleod, "Restitution under the Theft Act 1968" [1968] Crim LR 577.
6. As substituted by s. 64 (1) and Sch. 5 of the Criminal Justice Act 1972, and amended by s. 65 (4) and Sch. 12 of the Criminal Law Act 1977.
7. The Criminal Justice Act 1972, s. 6 (3), provides that the powers under s. 28 may be exercised where D is convicted of any other offence, but the court in determining sentence takes into consideration an offence specified by s. 28.
8. *Thibeault* (1983) 76 Cr App Rep 201, [1983] Crim LR 102, CA.

the person convicted which was taken out of his possession on his apprehension, a sum not exceeding the amount paid for the purchase by the purchaser or, as the case may be, the amount owed to the lender in respect of the loan.

4) The court shall not exercise the powers conferred by this section unless in the opinion of the court the relevant facts sufficiently appear from evidence given at the trial or the available documents, together with admissions made by or on behalf of any person in connection with any proposed exercise of the powers; and for this purpose 'the available documents' means any written statements or admissions which were made for use, and would have been admissible, as evidence at the trial, the depositions taken at any committal proceedings and any written statements or admissions used as evidence in those proceedings.

5) Any order under this section shall be treated as an order for the restitution of property within the meaning of sections 30 and 42 of the Criminal Appeal Act 1968 (which relate to the effect on such orders of appeals).

6) References in this section to stealing are to be construed in accordance with section 24 (1) and (4) of this Act."

On the face of it this is a formidable provision, but the idea behind it (and its anticipated operation) is simple enough. Suppose a straightforward case (and most of them are straightforward) where D has stolen P's watch. Here D is liable to be prosecuted in respect of the crime and proceeded against in respect of the tort. Obviously it would be convenient if the whole matter could be disposed of in one action, and s. 28 provides a procedure for doing this.[9] Equally obviously criminal courts (and especially magistrates' courts where most criminal cases are dealt with) are unsuitable for the trial of complex issues which may arise where goods have been dishonestly obtained and transferred to third parties. It is not intended that they should; and

"In practice the power will be exercisable only where there is no real dispute as to ownership. It would seriously hamper the work of the criminal courts if at the end of a trial they had to investigate disputed titles."[10]

Consequently s. 28 provides that the court *may* exercise the powers thereby conferred, and s. 28 (4) provides that the court *shall not* exercise any such power unless the relevant facts sufficiently appear. Accordingly it was held in *Ferguson*[11] that the trial judge was wrong in making a restitution order where an issue was raised whether the money found in D's possession was the proceeds of a robbery in which D had taken part or was money belonging to D's mistress. The court said it was only in "the plainest cases" that a criminal court would be justified in making a restitution order.

---

9. Cmnd. 2977, para. 164. Cf. *Church* (1970) 55 Cr App Rep 65, CA. A restitution order is to compensate P, not to punish D: *Pope* [1978] Crim LR 303.
10. Ibid.
11. [1970] 2 All ER 820, CA; cf. *Stamp v United Dominions Trust Ltd* [1967] 1 QB 418, [1967] 1 All ER 251.

Section 28 does not authorise the seizure of stolen goods or their proceeds from D. While the police otherwise have powers to retain property believed to be stolen property or its proceeds which is found in the possession of D,[12] there is no power to retain any such property simply because the police think it likely that, in the event of D's conviction, an order may be made against him for restitution or compensation.[13]

i) *Circumstances in which Order may be made.* The goods[14] must have been stolen at some stage, and goods obtained by blackmail or deception are stolen for this purpose.[15] The goods need not have been stolen by D, but D must be convicted of an offence with reference to the theft whether or not stealing is the gist of *his* offence. An order might be made, for example, where the gist of D's offence lies in giving assistance to E knowing that E has stolen the goods;[16] stealing is not the gist of D's offence here, but he has been convicted of an offence with reference to the theft.

ii) *Contents of an Order.* Upon D's conviction the court may order *any* person (the order might, for example, be made against a person who has in good faith purchased the goods from the thief, or against the police) having "possession or control" of the goods to restore them to any person entitled to recover them from him (para. (a)).[17]

The court may in addition, though this time only on the application of the person entitled to recover from the person convicted,[18] order any goods, which directly or indirectly represent the stolen goods, to be restored to the applicant. For example, D may have stolen P's gold watch which he exchanges for a necklace which he then sells to E, a handler; P may recover the necklace from E upon E's conviction for handling (para. (b)). Similarly upon P's application, and where for instance E has in turn sold the necklace, the court may order E to pay P the value of the watch out of any money taken from E upon his apprehension (para. (c)).

It might happen that when D is apprehended he has both the necklace and money in his possession but the necklace is worth less than the watch. In this sort of case the court is empowered to order D to give up the necklace to P along with money to make up the difference between the value of the necklace and the value of the watch: s. 28 (2).

Clearly a person may be in possession or control of the goods though the goods are not in his actual custody.[19] But where an order is made in respect of money under s. 28 (1) (c) this may only be done "out of any money of the person convicted which was taken out of his possession on his apprehension." On the face of it, and in view of the contrast with "possession or

12. *Chief Constable of Kent v V* [1983] QB 314, [1982] 3 All ER 36, CA.
13. Whether such order might be made under s. 28 or under s. 35 of the Powers of Criminal Courts Act 1973 (below, p. 644): *Malone v Metropolitan Police Comr* [1980] QB 49, [1979] 1 All ER 256, CA.
14. See s. 34 (2) (b); above, p. 615.
15. Section 28 (6): see s. 24 (4); above, p. 616.
16. See above, p. 623.
17. The person entitled to recover would be the person with the best right to possess: cf. Smith, *Theft*, para. 430.
18. *Thibeault* [1983] Crim LR 102.
19. See above, p. 622.

control" under s. 28 (1) (a), it might be thought that this referred to money taken[20] from the person of D at the time of his apprehension. In *Ferguson*,[1] however, it was held that money taken from D's deposit box nearly two weeks after his arrest was money taken "out of his possession on his apprehension". In *Parker*,[2] decided before *Ferguson*, the court had been unwilling to decide whether money in a wallet, apparently thrown away by D shortly before his arrest and found by the police the following day, was money taken out of D's possession on apprehension, but the case seems clearly to be covered by *Ferguson* where it was said that "on his apprehension" is to be given "a commonsense meaning". Thus money is taken "out of his possession on his apprehension" if it is taken from his possession or control at or about the time of his apprehension. This may well be a commonsense view, but it is questionable if it was the intended one.[3]

Where, as the result of an order under para. (a), a bona fide purchaser or pledgee from the person convicted (D) with respect to the theft is ordered to restore the goods to P, that person may in turn recover from D, out of money in D's possession on apprehension, the amount he paid D for, or lent D upon, the goods.

iii) *Effect of Order*. In practice the powers conferred by s. 28 will be exercised in only the clearest cases and ordinarily the goods will be restored to the person who is the owner of them. It might happen, however, that the court has, in pursuance of s. 28, restored the goods to P and later Q claims the goods from P. It seems clear that Q is free to do so and is in no way prejudiced by the order restoring the goods to P. Certainly the fact of a conviction for theft does not affect civil rights for by s. 31 (2)

"Notwithstanding any enactment to the contrary, where property has been stolen or obtained by fraud or other wrongful means, the title to that or any other property shall not be affected by reason only of the conviction of the offender."

iv) *Police (Property) Act 1897*. Quite apart from the new procedure for restitution introduced by s. 28 of the Theft Act there exists a similar procedure under the Police (Property) Act 1897. Section 1 (1) of that Act provides:

"When any property has come into the possession of the police in connection with their investigation of a suspected offence . . . a court of summary jurisdiction may, on application, either by an officer of police or by a claimant of the property, make an order for the delivery of the property to the person appearing to the magistrate or court to be the owner thereof, or, if the owner cannot be ascertained, may make such

---

20. "Taken" must mean "lawfully taken". The section cannot be interpreted to confer a general power to seize money found upon D at the time of his apprehension, and whether there is such a power depends upon common law or statutory powers to that effect.
1. [1970] 2 All ER 820, [1970] 1 WLR 1246, CA.
2. [1970] 2 All ER 458, [1970] 1 WLR 1003, CA.
3. Cf. Cmnd. 2977, para. 166, "The offender may well have neither the original goods nor any other goods which represent them . . . but an equivalent sum of money may be found *in his possession and taken from him on his apprehension*." Italics supplied.

order with respect to the property as to the magistrate or court may seem meet."

There are, however, a number of important differences between the two procedures. First, the Police (Property) Act applies to property which has come into police possession in connection with *any* crime. Secondly, an owner may get an order for the delivery of his property though the offender is never apprehended, much less convicted. A third difference results from s. 1 (2) of the Police (Property) Act:

"An order under the section shall not affect the right of any person to take within six months from the date of the order legal proceedings against any person in possession of the property delivered by virtue of the order for the recovery of the property, but on the expiration of those six months the right shall cease."

If, then, an order has been made under s. 1 (1) delivering the property to P, it appears that Q may not take legal proceedings against P after the expiration of six months even though Q has a better right than P and has been guilty of no lack of diligence in pursuing his claim to the property.[4] Had the order been made under the Theft Act Q's claim would not be so barred.[5] Fourthly, the powers conferred by s. 1 (1) may be exercised only by a court of summary jurisdiction but the court is empowered, if the owner cannot be ascertained, to make such order with respect to the property as may seem meet.[6]

Fifthly, under the Police (Property) Act an order for the delivery of the property may be made only to the person "appearing . . . to be the owner thereof" whereas an order under the Theft Act may be made in favour of "any person entitled to recover" the goods from the person convicted. In *Raymond Lyons & Co Ltd v Metropolitan Police Commissioner*[7] it was held that "owner" in the former Act was to be given its broad popular meaning, that is:

"a person who is entitled to the goods in question, a person whose goods they are, not simply the person who happens to have them in his hands at any given moment."[8]

Accordingly a jeweller who had received a ring in suspicious circumstances and handed it to the police for them to pursue inquiries, was not entitled to an order for the delivery of the ring since he was not the owner.[9] For the purposes of the Theft Act, on the other hand, a person may be entitled to recover the goods although he is not the owner and, provided the other conditions are satisfied, an order may be made in favour of the claimant with the best right to possession. Determining who is the owner or who is

---

4. But it may be that an order under s. 1 (1) only bars a claimant who might have asserted his right in the original proceedings: cf. Smith, *Theft*, para. 445.

5. See above, p. 642.

6. Section 2 of the Police (Property) Act empowers a Secretary of State to make regulations for the disposal of property where the owner has not been ascertained and no court order has been made.

7. [1975] QB 321, [1975] 1 All ER 335, DC.

8. [1975] 1 All ER 335, at 338.

9. But the court will not make an order for delivery to the owner where it appears that another has a better right to immediate possession than the owner: *Marsh v Police Comr* [1945] KB 43, [1944] 2 All ER 392, CA. In such a case it may be that the court cannot order delivery to either claimant, see Smith, *Theft*, para. 444.

the person entitled may involve difficult questions of law. In the *Raymond Lyons* case Lord Widgery CJ emphasised that the summary procedure under the Police (Property) Act should not be used in cases involving "tricky questions of title or large sums of money."[10] He added that the same caveat applied to compensation orders under the Criminal Justice Act 1972 (now the Powers of Criminal Courts Act 1973) which are next considered.

v) *Powers of Criminal Courts Act 1973, s. 35.* This section confers general powers upon courts to make compensation orders, though a magistrates' court may not award compensation exceeding £1,000.[11] Inter alia, an order may be made in respect of any offence of which D is convicted (including one which is taken into consideration upon conviction) which causes any loss of, or damage to, property;[12] and where (the offence being one under the Theft Act 1968) the property is recovered but has been damaged. In determining whether to make, and the amount of, a compensation order the court must have regard to D's means so far as they are known or appear to the court. Thus where an order for restitution cannot be made under the Theft Act or the Police (Property) Act, the court may award P compensation for his loss of the goods, and the order is enforceable as a judgment debt. As with orders for restitution under s. 28 of the Theft Act, orders for compensation under s. 35 should be made only where the legal position is quite clear.[13]

10. [1975] 1 All ER 335 at 338.
11. Criminal Law Act 1977, s. 60 (1).
12. Whether or not the victim would have a civil action: *Chappell* (1984) 80 Cr App Rep 31, CA.
13. *Vivian* [1979] 1 All ER 48, [1979] 1 WLR 291, CA.

16 Forgery and Counterfeiting

Forgery and counterfeiting are now regulated by the Forgery and Counterfeiting Act 1981. This Act is largely based upon the recommendations of the Law Commission,[1] and forms part of the programme for the codification of the criminal law. Earlier legislation, in particular the Forgery Act 1913 and the Coinage Offences Act 1936, is repealed and the offence of forgery at common law is abolished. It follows that decisions under the former law are no longer binding though they may retain some persuasive authority and, in this text, may be referred to as vehicles for discussion.

1 Forgery

The forging of documents in itself rarely brings any advantage to the forger. The forgery is usually done as a preparatory step to the commission of some other crime, most often a crime involving deception, which will result in some material advantage (most obviously money or other property) to the forger. Since preparatory acts, falling short of attempts, are not as such made criminal by the law, it has been cogently argued[2] that, with the exception of special cases such as banknotes and coins, there is no need for a separate offence of forgery. The Law Commission did not accept this view. In its view –

"There is a number of reasons for not accepting the soundness of this premise. In the many and varied activities of modern society it is necessary to rely to a large extent on the authenticity of documents as authority for the truth of the statements which they contain."[3]

While the Commission recognised that it was unnecessary to rely on forgery where property was obtained by the use of forged documents, the

---

1. Law Com. No. 55, *Report on Forgery and Counterfeit Currency* (1973). See also the Commission's Working Paper No. 26, *Forgery* (1970). As to Reports of the CLRC, see above, p. 63.

2. By Griew [1970] Crim LR 548 and Glazebrook [1970] Crim LR 554. Yet many statutes create offences of possessing even apparently innocuous articles with intent to commit crimes.

3. Law Com. No. 55, para. 14. When introducing the Bill to the House of Lords (HL, Vol. 416, col. 605) Viscount Colville declined to enter "the philosophical ... or jurisprudential discussions" about the need to have an offence of forgery. To him it was right that forgers "who, after all, are a special form of criminal that we tend to recognise as such" should have legislation directed against them. The circularity of this reasoning was apparently lost on their lordships. Lord Elwyn-Jones favoured the retention of forgery because it was a fact that "forgeries do run into thousands each year as crimes".

necessity for an offence of forgery was strikingly illustrated by the kind of person who has in his possession numbers of forged documents (such as passports, credit cards, railway season tickets, even Cup Final tickets) where it would not be possible to bring home a charge of attempting to commit any offence. Perhaps it might be added, as a reason for retaining forgery, that it has long been regarded as a serious offence; history is on the side of the Law Commission.

1) *The Subject Matter of Forgery*

A person is guilty of forgery if he makes a false instrument and for this purpose "instrument" is defined by s. 8 –

"1) Subject to subsection (2) below, in this Part of this Act 'instrument' means –

a) any document, whether of a formal or informal character;

b) any stamp issued or sold by the Post Office;

c) any Inland Revenue stamp; and

d) any disc, tape, sound track or other device on or in which information is recorded or stored by mechanical, electronic or other means.

2) A currency note within the meaning of Part II of this Act is not an instrument for the purposes of this Part of this Act.

3) A mark denoting payment of postage which the Post Office authorise to be used instead of an adhesive stamp is to be treated for the purposes of this Part of this Act as if it were a stamp issued by the Post Office.

4) In this Part of this Act 'Inland Revenue stamp' means a stamp as defined in section 27 of the Stamp Duties Management Act 1891."

The terms "writing", "document" and "instrument" have been traditionally used in the criminal law to denote the subject matter of forgery. At common law the preference was for "writing", under the Forgery Act 1913 it was for "document", under the new legislation "instrument" is given pride of place but this is immediately defined to include "any document, whether of a formal or informal character".

An instrument will normally be written on paper but may be written on any material and the writing may consist in letters, figures or any other symbols used for conveying information. "Instrument" might convey the notion that the document must be of a formal nature (wills, deeds etc.) but since s. 8 (1) (a) extends to documents of an "informal" character this notion would clearly be too restrictive. It has been held under earlier legislation that a forged letter purporting to come from an employee and requesting money from the employer,[4] a telegram which had been ante-dated in order to defraud a bookmaker,[5] a certificate of competency to drive,[6] and a football pools[7] coupon were all documents and there is no

---

4. *Cade* [1914] 2 KB 209.
5. *Riley* [1896] 1 QB 309, CCR.
6. *Potter* [1958] 2 All ER 51, [1958] 1 WLR 638 (Paull J).
7. *Butler* (1954) 38 Cr App Rep 57, CCA.

reason to suppose that they would not be considered instruments within s. 8 (1) (a). It may often be relevant to ask, though it is not suggested as an exclusive test, whether the document is of such a kind that the recipient is expected to act on it in some way.

However widely defined, "instrument" cannot extend to manufactured articles as such. In common parlance a replica of a Stradivarius may be said to be a forgery but a violin cannot be regarded as a document. Nor is a painting as such a document. On the other hand an authentication certificate, purporting to come from an acknowledged expert and which ascribes that painting to a particular artist, is a document which may be forged,[8] and it is no less a document because it is pasted to the back of, or even directly written on the back of, the canvas. What, then, if D produces a facsimile Constable or Turner and further signs the painting in the style of the artist? In *Close*[9] it was argued that the signature was, in effect, a certificate authenticating the work and as such it would constitute a forgery. The argument was rejected. Cockburn CJ asked –

"If you go beyond writing where are you to stop? Can sculpture be the subject of forgery?"[10]

The court went on to regard the signature as no more than a mark put upon the painting by the artist with a view to identifying it. *Close* was decided at common law and, on essentially similar facts, a ruling was given in *Douce*[11] that the signature constituted a document within the 1913 Act because it purported to convey information about the picture. The Law Commission proposed to settle this argument in favour of *Close* by defining "instrument" as "an instrument *in writing*"[12] but the Commission's wording has been modified in the Act.[13] If it were the practice of an artist to write on the back of his paintings the date and place of origin of his paintings and then add his signature, it would seem clear enough that this writing constitutes a document; if so there can only be the finest of lines between this and a signature on the face of the painting.

Perhaps an analogy is provided by the case where D alters the final letter on (i) the number plates, and (ii) the vehicle excise licence of his car.[14] This may be done to induce an intending purchaser to believe that the car is less old than in fact it is.[15] The number plates tell a lie but essentially this lie is as to the age of the car and it is thought that the number plates do not constitute a document for they are not intended to be acted on otherwise than as an identifying mark.[16] The vehicle excise licence is, however, a document; there is no difficulty in saying that it tells a lie about itself

8. *Pryse-Hughes* (1958) Times, 14th May.
9. (1857) Dears & B 460.
10. (1857) Dears & B 460 at 466.
11. [1972] Crim LR 105, QS.
12. Law Com. No. 55, para. 23, italics supplied.
13. Crystal-Kirk "Forgery Reforged" (1981) 49 MLR argues the painting in *Close* falls within the 1981 Act.
14. See *Clifford v Bloom* [1977] RTR 351; *Clayton* (1980) 72 Cr App Rep 135, [1981] Crim LR 186, CA.
15. The proffered explanation in *Clayton*, last note, was that D did not wish his friends to think he had come down in the world.
16. But it is an offence under the Road Vehicle (Registration and Licensing) Regulations 1971 fraudulently to alter number plates.

because it purports to have been issued in respect of a vehicle identified by a particular number when it was not so issued.

To be the subject of forgery the document, in the view of the Law Commission, must usually contain messages of two distinct kinds –

"The essence of forgery, in our view, is the making of a false document intending that it be used to induce a person to accept and act upon the message contained in it, as if it were contained in a genuine document. In the straightforward case a document usually contains messages of two distinct kinds – first a message about the document itself (such as the message that the document is a cheque or a will) and secondly a message to be found in the words of the document that is to be accepted and acted upon (such as the message that a banker is to pay a specified sum or that property is to be distributed in a particular way). In our view it is only documents which convey not only the first type of message but also the second type that need to be protected by the law of forgery."[17]

On this view it would not be forgery to make a false copy of a celebrity's autograph since the autograph conveys only one message (viz. about the genuineness of the signature) and there is no second message about the genuineness of the piece of paper on which the autograph is written. But where a cheque is forged by the insertion of a false signature two messages are conveyed; one that the signature is genuine and the other that the signature validates the order for the payment of money.

In this connection *Smith*[18] is worth comment. D had sold baking powder in wrappers substantially resembling the wrappers of one George Borwick, a well-known manufacturer of baking powder. It was held that the wrappers were not forgeries since they were not documents. The same result would appear to follow on the Law Commission view. The wrappers conveyed only one message, that they were George Borwick wrappers, and conveyed no further message concerning the genuineness of the document. They may have conveyed a second message about the lineage of the baking powder but there was no second message conveying the notion that the *wrapper* was to be accepted and acted upon.

The Law Commission was minded, and so provided in its Draft Bill, to exclude from the definition of "instrument" documents of historical interest only or as collector's items, but this does not form part of the Act. Suppose then that D makes a false copy of Shakespeare's will with a view to selling it as genuine. It is of course clear that if D makes a false copy of his father's will with a view to securing the inheritance for himself, this is a forgery. Both wills are made false with a view to dishonest gain but the Shakespeare will differs in one important respect. It is not produced with a view to affecting the devolution of Shakespeare's property and if P buys it he will do so not because the will, *qua* will, is going to affect his or anyone else's interests but merely for the intrinsic value of that piece of paper.

The essence of "instrument" or "document" is peculiarly difficult to define. To constitute an instrument for the purposes of forgery, the document must do more than merely convey information; it must be of

---

17. Law Com. No. 55, para. 22.
18. (1858) Dears & B 566.

such a nature that the information contained in it[19] as a document is intended to be acted on in some way, usually, though not necessarily exclusively, by purporting to affect the rights or interests of some person or persons.

By s. 8 (1) (d) the definition of "instrument" embraces "any disc, tape, sound track or other device on or in which information is recorded or stored[20] by mechanical, electronic or other means". This extension, if extension it be,[1] must be regarded as entirely right in an age when so much documentation is so processed. The extension will of course be in the same terms. If D produces a recording of what purports to be Mr Gladstone's voice, he is not guilty of forgery though he intends to defraud purchasers; the recording is no more a document for the purposes of the Act than the false Shakespeare will. Nor is D, a bank teller, guilty of forgery merely by causing false entries to be made in the bank's computer any more than he would be guilty of forgery in making false entries in the bank's ledgers.[2] Nor is E guilty of forgery if he obtains access to information stored in a computer by sending electronic signals which cause the computer to accept him as an authorised user.[3] If, however, D and E cause entries to be made which purport to be made or authorised by one who did not make them, they may be guilty of forgery.

2) *The Forgery*

By s. 9 of the Act –
  "1) An instrument is false for the purposes of this Part of this Act –
      a) if it purports to have been made in the form in which it is made by a person who did not in fact make it in that form; or
      b) if it purports to have been made in the form in which it is made on the authority of a person who did not in fact authorise its making in that form; or
      c) if it purports to have been made in the terms in which it is made by a person who did not in fact make it in those terms; or
      d) if it purports to have been made in the terms in which it is made on the authority of a person who did not in fact authorise its making in those terms; or
      e) if it purports to have been altered in any respect by a person who did not in fact alter it in that respect; or
      f) if it purports to have been altered in any respect on the authority of a person who did not in fact authorise the alteration in that respect; or

19. A document may be comprised of more than one part, e.g. a letter may be taken together with its envelope.
20. Cf. *Gold and Schifreen* [1987] 3 All ER 618, [1987] 3 WLR 803 below, p. 662.
  1. It has never been of any account in the law of forgery on what material, or in what symbols or code, the information is recorded.
  2. Cf. *Re Windsor* (1865) 6 B & S 522.
  3. *Gold and Schifreen* (1987) 3 All ER 618, [1987] 3 WLR 803. See below, p. 662.

     g) if it purports to have been made or altered on a date on which, or at a place at which, or otherwise in circumstances in which, it was not in fact made or altered; or

     h) if it purports to have been made or altered by an existing person but he did not in fact exist.

  2) A person is to be treated for the purposes of this Part of this Act as making a false instrument if he alters an instrument so as to make it false in any respect (whether or not it is false in some other respect apart from that alteration)."

1 Falsity in General

The definition given by s. 9 of "falsity" is exhaustive and the governing notion is that the document must not only tell a lie, it must also tell a lie about itself.[4] Telling a lie does not become a forgery because it is reduced to writing; it is the document which must be false and not merely the information in it.

In its ordinary application the distinction is easy enough to grasp. If an applicant for a job falsely states his qualifications in his letter of application, the letter is not a forgery; but if he writes a reference which purports to come from his employer, the reference is a forgery. The reference is false within s. 9 (1) (a) because it purports to have been made in the form in which it is made by a person (the employer) who did not make it in that form. A cheque is similarly false if D signs it in the name of P.

The application of s. 9 (1) (a) is straightforward and no serious difficulties are likely to be encountered in the application of the next three cases instanced in the sub-section. Paragraph (b) deals with the case where D makes a document which purports to be made on P's authority (even though it does not purport to be made by P himself) when P's authority has not been given. It can make no difference, incidentally, if D has the same name as P provided that D intends his signature, or his authorisation, to be taken for the signature or authorisation, of P.

Paragraphs (c) and (d) in effect parallel (a) and (b) in relation to cases where P has in fact made or authorised the instrument in certain terms but D alters those terms. Thus (c) extends to the case where P draws a cheque for £10 and D makes the amount appear as £100; while (d) deals with the case where P, having authorised D to make out the cheque for £10, D in fact enters, £100.

Paragraphs (e) and (f) contain further parallel provisions in relation to alterations. Usually the maker of an instrument is at liberty to alter it (he may, for instance, alter the name of the payee or the amount to be paid on a cheque); but where another alters it, the alteration purporting to be made or authorised by the maker, the other makes a false instrument. In this connection the facts of *Hopkins and Collins*[5] provide a convenient illustration. D and E, the secretary and treasurer of a football supporters' club, received monies raised by members and made disbursements on behalf of the club. Over a period of time they (i) entered in the books amounts less

---

4. The aphorism appears to have been coined by Kenny, *Outlines*, 375.
5. (1957) 41 Cr App Rep 231, CCA.

than were paid in; (ii) entered amounts in excess of what was paid out; and (iii) altered certain of the entries. It is clear that their accounts were inaccurate but to keep inaccurate accounts is not a forgery. The accounts tell a lie but to be false within s. 9 (1) (e) or (f) they must tell a lie about themselves. So far as (i) and (ii) are concerned the accounts merely told a lie; they purported to be the accurate accounts of D and E when they were the inaccurate acounts of D and E. But what of (iii), the alterations? Paragraphs (e) and (f) do not render a document false merely because it has been altered; the alteration is a forgery only if it purports to be made or authorised by one who did not make or authorise it. Thus so long as the alterations were made or authorised by D and E they were not forgeries.

Suppose, however, that only D, the secretary, had been acting dishonestly, and suppose further that only E, the treasurer, was authorised to keep the accounts. If D, without E's authority, altered entries so that the alterations appeared to have been made or authorised by E, the accounts would be forged. To constitute a forgery the hand of Jacob must purport to be the hand of Esau.

A document is accordingly not forged merely because it contains false information and has been prepared by D to perpetrate a fraud. If D, with a view to defrauding P, procures E to execute documents which are to be used to convince P that D is a man of substance or of good character, the documents, so long as they purport to be executed by E, are not forged even though the transactions or facts to which they purport to relate are a complete sham.[6]

But a case which appears to be at odds with the foregoing is *Donnelly*.[7] D, a jeweller, at E's behest, gave E a written valuation of certain items of jewellery, the valuation stating that D had examined the jewellery. In fact there was no jewellery to be valued: the valuation was a sham and part of a plan to defraud insurers. Upholding D's conviction for forgery the Court of Appeal said that it was only concerned to determine whether the valuation certificate was a false instrument by virtue of s. 9. The court held that it was because it fell foul of s. 9 (1) (g) in that it had been made "otherwise in circumstances" in which it was not in fact made. "In our judgment," said the court[8] –

"the words coming at the end of paragraph (g) 'otherwise in circumstances ...' expand its ambit beyond dates and places to *any* case in which an instrument purports to be made when it was not in fact made. This valuation purported to be made *after* [D] had examined the items of jewellery. ... He did not make it after examining these items because they did not exist. That which purported to be a valuation after examination of items was nothing of the kind: it was a worthless piece of paper."

Obviously the valuation certificate told a lie, but did it tell a lie about the *circumstances* in which it was made? If it did then a begging letter in which the beggar, or someone on his behalf, falsely states that he is bedridden or

6. Cf. *Dodge and Harris* [1972] 1 QB 416, [1971] 2 All ER 1523, CA.
7. (1984) 79 Cr App Rep 76; **SHC 520**.
8. At p. 78.

unemployed, is equally a forgery because the circumstances to which the writer alludes are untrue. This would be a remarkable extension of the law of forgery as previously understood but *if* this is the conclusion to which s. 9 (1) (g) inexorably leads then it would have to be accepted.[9]

This construction is, however, open to serious question, and, it is submitted, cannot stand with the decision of the House of Lords in *More*[10] where Lord Ackner, in a speech with which all their lordships agreed, firmly stated that s. 9 (1) requires the document to tell a lie about itself. "It is common ground," he said[11] –

> "that the consistent use of the word 'purports' in each of the paragraphs (a) to (h) inclusive of s. 9 (1) of the Act imports a requirement that for an instrument to be false it must tell a lie about itself, in the sense that it purports to be made by a person who did not make it (or altered by a person who did not alter it) or otherwise purports to be made or altered in circumstances in which it was not made or altered."

While *Donnelly* receives no mention in *More*, it must be clear that the former cannot stand with the latter; the valuation certificate in *Donnelly* told a lie but did not tell a lie about itself.

Paragraph (g) of s. 9 (1) deals with the case where the document purports to be made or altered on a date or at a place or otherwise in circumstances where it was not in fact made or altered. This would deal, for example, with the case where D alters the date on a will or deed to make it appear to antedate another will or deed.[12] Nor is the will or deed any less false because it is D's own will or deed; a will or deed which purports to be executed on the 1st of the month tells a lie about itself if it was in fact executed on the 10th and D, provided he acts with *mens rea*, is guilty of forgery.[13]

2 Falsity and Non-existing Persons

Much the most difficult provision in s. 9 (1) is paragraph (h). Most frequently false documents purport to be made or authorised by some existing person known to the person intended to be affected by the contents of the document. Sometimes, however, D may find it equally, or better, suits his purpose to invent the name of a person by whom the document purports to be made. Suppose, for instance, that D and E apply for a job and in order to bolster their prospects D falsely makes a reference purporting to come from Sir George X while E falsely makes a reference

---

9. Counsel for the Crown in *Donnelly* conceded that the valuation certificate would not have been a forgery either at common law or under the Forgery Act 1913 but argued that it was now a forgery by virtue of s. 9 (1) (g).
10. [1987] 3 All ER 825, [1987] 1 WLR 1578 discussed below, p. 654.
11. At p. 830.
12. Cf. *Wells* [1939] 2 All ER 169, 27 Cr App Rep 72, CCA; D was convicted of forgery where he altered the date on a settlement so as to ante-date the provisions of an Act of Parliament in order to avoid the payment of tax on the settlement.
13. Under the 1913 Act there was a requirement that a document must be forged in a *material* particular. Arguably on facts such as those in *Wells*, last note, D would not have been guilty of forgery in ante-dating the settlement if he had failed to ante-date it sufficiently to avoid the tax. There is now no requirement for materiality and D on facts such as *Wells* may be guilty of forgery even though the alteration does not achieve its intended effect. D may also be guilty of forgery if he alters it to make it false in any respect whether or not it is false in some other respect: s. 9 (2).

purporting to come from Sir Peter Y. In fact there is no Sir George X who is merely D's invention, but there is a Sir Peter Y who was formerly E's employer. E's reference is clearly a forgery and, on the face of it, there is no reason why D's case should be treated any differently; certainly D's case falls within s. 9 (1) (h).

But consider the facts of *Hassard and Devereux*.[14] D, a company bookkeeper made out cheques to a company creditor, B.S.A., and after the cheques had been signed by directors, he altered the cheques to B. S. Andrews and handed them to his confederate, E. Obviously these cheques were forgeries (s. 9 (1) (b)) and we are not concerned with them. D and E now needed to cash these cheques so they gave them to F who opened an account in the name of B. S. Andrews, F representing herself as Andrews and giving her correct address. F then drew a cheque on this account. While F's conviction for forgery under the 1913 Act was upheld and was a questionable decision under that Act, the question which now arises is whether this cheque is a forgery by virtue of s. 9 (1) (h). It might be said that the case falls literally within the paragraph; the cheque purports to be made by an existing person (B. S. Andrews) who did not in fact exist.

Yet any person may assume an alias. Authors frequently do. If, for example, an author called X chooses to write under the name of Y and has his royalties paid to Y in which style he opens a bank account, is he guilty of forgery if he draws cheques on that account in the name of Y? The answer must be an obvious No. Y is not someone who does not exist; he is someone who does exist, Y being a mere alias for X. Clearly if the bank knows that X and Y are one and the same person there can be no question of forgery. It can hardly become forgery because the bank is unaware of the true name of Y, knowing him only in the style of Y. Nor can the cheques be regarded as forgeries because X has opened a bank account in the name of Y to avoid paying tax on his royalties.

It is suggested, therefore, that the assumption of an alias by D, by which alias he is known to P, falls outside s. 9 (1) (h), and documents presented by D to P in the style of his alias are not documents which are made by a person who did not in fact exist.

A somewhat similar problem is presented by the facts of *Martin*.[15] D, whose name was Robert Martin and who was well known to P, purchased from P a pony and trap, giving in payment a cheque. The cheque was signed in P's presence but was, unnoticed by P at the time, signed in the style of William Martin and was drawn on a bank at which D had no account. Literally the case might be said to fall within s. 9 (1) (h) but viewed realistically P knew precisely who had made and signed the cheque; whatever signature appeared on the cheque P knew that the maker was D. The document in the circumstances did not tell a lie about itself and it is thought that it would not constitute a forgery.

To go back to *Hassard and Devereux*. No doubt the bank, had it been aware that B. S. Andrews was not F's real name, would not have honoured the cheque or, at least, would have required a convincing reason why it

14. [1970] 2 All ER 647, [1970] 1 WLR 1109, CA.
15. (1879) 6 QBD 34.

should. But the bank was not misled by anything which appeared on the face of the cheque into thinking that it was honouring a cheque other than the cheque of the person presenting it for payment whether that person chose to call herself F or B. S. Andrews. The cheque does not purport to be made by an existing person who does not exist; it purports to be made by an existing person who chooses to assume one name rather than another.

This seems clearly to follow from *More*.[16] D came by a cheque made out to M.R. Jessell with which he opened an account at a building society in the name of Mark Richard Jessell and later drew on that account by completing a withdrawal form in the name of Mark Richard Jessell. Affirming D's conviction for forgery, the Court of Appeal held that the withdrawal form came within s. 9 (1) (h) since it purported to have been made by an existing person who did not in fact exist. The House of Lords disagreed and quashed the conviction. As Lord Ackner pointed out[17] –

"[D] was a real person. . . . The withdrawal form clearly purported to be signed by the person who originally opened the account and in this respect it was wholly accurate. Thus, in my judgment, it cannot be validly contended that the document told a lie about itself. . . ."

This, with respect, is entirely right. It follows that while there is no mention in *More* of *Hassard and Devereux* (presumably because the latter is a decision under the repealed 1913 Act) if the facts of *Hassard* were to recur a conviction for forgery under the 1981 Act could not be sustained.

This does not mean that s. 9 (1) (h) is devoid of effect though the scope for its application is probably not extensive. It would apply where D makes a document purporting to emanate from E (E being purely a fiction in the sense that neither D nor any accomplice of D's is going to assume the alias of E and represent himself as such to P) the case must fall within s. 9 (1) (h) and D is guilty of forgery.[18] Thus the case instanced at the beginning of this section, where D presents to P a reference purporting to emanate from Sir George X, there being no Sir George X, would be one of forgery. Another case falling within the paragraph might be where D writes begging letters to P apparently emanating from distressed ex-servicemen called X, Y and Z, where X, Y and Z are merely figments of D's imagination.

All in all it would seem that paragraph (h) can apply only in restricted circumstances and it may be that Williams was right in suggesting[19] that we ought to be spared the complexity which arises from the application of the law of forgery to documents in the name of fictitious persons.

3 Falsity by Omission

At first sight it may seem odd to suggest that forgery may be committed by omission since if anything requires positive and painstaking effort it might be said that this is so of the craft[20] of the forger. But appearances can be

16. [1987] 3 All ER 825, [1987] 1 WLR 1578.
17. [1987] 3 All ER 830.
18. Cf. *Gambling* [1975] QB 207, [1974] 3 All ER 479, CA.
19. [1974] Crim LR 71 at 80.
20. Regrettably the photocopier and even kitchen cleansers (which can be used to remove signatures from credit and cheque cards) have brought forgery within the reach of the artisan as well as the artist.

deceptive. Though such cases may be of rare occurrence, it is possible to predicate cases of forgery by omission. If, for example, P, a blind man, dictates his will to D and D, with a view to gain for himself or another or with intent to cause loss to another, omits certain provisions, the will appears to be a forgery. The will purports to be made or authorised in the terms in which it is made by a person (P) who did not in fact make or authorise its making in those terms and thus falls within s. 9 (1) (c) or (d). In order for an omission to constitute forgery its effect must be to render the document false within s. 9 (1), that is, it must result in the document telling a lie about itself. If in *Hopkins and Collins*[1] D and E had simply failed to enter in the club's books monies which were paid in by members, the accounts would not be forged. Their accounts would be inaccurate but they would not be false within any of the definitions in s. 10 (1); they would remain what they purported to be: a statement of accounts prepared by D and E.

3) *Mens Rea: Intent to Prejudice*

Sections 1–5 of the Act create various offences involving forgery. For purposes of convenience the *mens rea* of the various offences may be regarded as having two aspects. There is first of all the mental element required in relation to the making, using or possession of the false instrument and this aspect is considered in relation to the specific offences in the next section. The second aspect, which governs the offences under ss. 1–4 and certain of the offences under s. 5, is the requirement that D should intend that P should be induced, by reason of accepting the false instrument as genuine, to do some act to his own or another's prejudice. It is this aspect which is discussed in this section. Before turning to this, however, it follows that as the *mens rea* of forgery has these two aspects, it is necessary that it be proved both that D intended to make etc. the false instrument and that he intended thereby to induce another to act to his prejudice. In *Tobierre*[2] it was accordingly held that D's conviction was to be quashed where the trial judge appeared to have directed the jury that it was enough that D intended a false instrument to be accepted as genuine and did not, or did not adequately, explain that it must be proved also that D intended another to thereby act to his prejudice.

By s. 10 of the Act which *exhaustively* defines "induce" and "prejudice" –

"1) Subject to subsections (2) and (4) below, for the purposes of this Part of this Act, an act or omission intended to be induced is to a person's prejudice if, and only if, it is one which, if it occurs –
   a) will result –
      i) in his temporary or permanent loss of property; or
      ii) in his being deprived of an opportunity to earn remuneration or greater remuneration; or

1. (1957) 41 Cr App Rep 231, above, p. 650.
2. [1986] 1 All ER 346, [1986] 1 WLR 125 CA; *Garciá* [1988] Crim LR 115, CA.

        iii) in his being deprived of an opportunity to gain a financial advantage otherwise than by way of remuneration; or

     b) will result in somebody being given an opportunity –

        i) to earn remuneration or greater remuneration from him; or

        ii) to gain a financial advantage from him otherwise than by way of remuneration; or

     c) will be the result of his having accepted a false instrument as genuine, or a copy of a false instrument as a copy of a genuine one, in connection with his performance of any duty.

2) An act which a person has an enforceable duty to do and an omission to do an act which a person is not entitled to do shall be disregarded for the purposes of this Part of this Act.

3) In this Part of this Act references to inducing somebody to accept a false instrument as genuine, or a copy of a false instrument as a copy of a genuine one, include references to inducing a machine to respond to the instrument or copy as if it were a genuine instrument or, as the case may be, a copy of a genuine one.

4) Where subsection (3) above applies, the act or omission intended to be induced by the machine responding to the instrument or copy shall be treated as an act or omission to a person's prejudice.

5) In this section 'loss' includes not getting what one might get as well as parting with what one has."

Essentially "prejudice" may be of two kinds, viz. the causing of economic loss or the causing of conduct in contravention of a duty.

1 Economic Loss

Usually an instrument is forged with a view to the economic benefit (in terms of money or other property) of the forger and consequential economic loss to the victim. Gain and loss are usually two sides of the same coin but the section treats separately of loss caused and advantage gained.

Most obviously D intends to induce P to act, or omit to act, to his prejudice if as a result P will be deprived, permanently or temporarily, of property (s. 10 (1) (a) (i)). This is most commonly the forger's intention and is typically instanced by the forgery of cheques, credit cards and other instruments in order to induce another to act to his prejudice. So if D falsifies a cheque guarantee card to induce P to part with money, or falsifies a credit card to induce Q to part with goods, he may be convicted of forgery. The fact that Q may, as is often the case with credit cards, claim reimbursement from R (a bank) cannot mean that Q has not been induced to act to his prejudice; Q has lost, and D intended to induce the loss of, the goods.

In practice most cases will be covered by s. 10 (1) (a) (i) but the section goes on to deal with other cases of much less frequent occurrence. Section 10 (1) (a) (ii) deals with the sort of case where P is seeking, say, employment or promotion in employment, and D writes a letter to the employer purporting to come from someone whose opinion is respected by the employer and which is intended to ensure that P does not get the post or the promotion. Such cases may be of limited occurrence but when they occur an instrument has been made false with a view to P's prejudice and there is no reason why they should not fall within the ambit of forgery.

Section 10 (1) (a) (iii) may have been included *ex abundanti cautela*. A case may be supposed where D and E are bidding for a contract to supply vehicle components to P. D might forge a letter purporting to come from someone who has done busines with E which asserts that E cannot be relied on to keep delivery dates. If E does not get the contract he has not been deprived of property within s. 10 (1) (a) (i). Nor might the case fall within s. 10 (1) (a) (ii) since "remuneration" ordinarily connotes a payment for services rendered and may not be apt to cover the case where someone loses his profit margins under a contract for the supply of goods. Accordingly sub-paragraph (iii) was included to make it clear that such a case falls within the Act.

. Section 10 (1) (b) is concerned with financial advantage and there is no need to prove loss to any particular victim. Usually that advantage will accrue to the forger or an accomplice but an offence may be committed though the beneficiary is unaware of the fraud. If D forges a testimonial with a view to securing the employment, or promotion, of someone in P's firm, it does not matter whether that someone is D himself, or someone who has procured the forged testimonial or someone who is wholly ignorant of D's action. The case falls within s. 10 (1) (b) (i) since "somebody" is given an opportunity to earn remuneration or greater remuneration. Nor does it matter that the someone who gets the job, or the promotion, fully justifies the remuneration, or greater remuneration, or, indeed, brings financial gain to P.

Section 10 (1) (b) (ii) deals with the case where a financial advantage, otherwise than by way of remuneration, is sought. So if in the bidding for a contract D forges a letter extolling the virtues of his own (or another bidder's) products an offence may be committed. Again, it cannot matter that D's (or the other's) products are in fact the best and the cheapest. The section makes it clear that an act or omission intended to be induced "is" to another's prejudice if the case falls within the section.

Normally D may falsify an instrument with a view to giving himself (or another) an advantage over other competitors, or seek to disadvantage another competitor, but a case may fall within s. 10 though D is the sole applicant for a job or a sole bidder for a contract.

2 Performance of Duty

Under the former law it was unclear how far the *mens rea* of forgery extended beyond an intent to cause economic loss. The argument is now, in a sense, settled by s. 10 (1) (c) – a victim is prejudiced if it is intended that he should accept a false instrument as genuine "in connection with his performance of any duty".

In formulating this provision the Law Commission sought,[3] on the one hand, to include such cases as forging a security pass to gain access to premises, forging a certificate of competency to drive, and forging documents in such circumstances as *Welham v Director of Public Prosecutions*[4]

3. Law Com. No. 55, paras. 28-37.
4. [1961] AC 103, [1960] 1 All ER 805, HL.

where documents were forged not with the intention of causing financial loss but with the intention of avoiding statutory restrictions on borrowing. On the other hand, the Commission wished to exclude cases where the prejudice was trivial or inconsequential, such as a forged invitation to a social function done with the intention of raising a laugh at the victim's expense.

The Act seeks to achieve this balance by the employment of the concept of "duty". "Duty" here must refer to a legal duty and cannot extend to what might be regarded as a social or moral duty. It will extend, however, to a duty arising under contract as well as a duty imposed by law independently of contract. Thus such cases as *Harris*[5] (where papers were forged to secure the release of a prisoner from jail); *Toshack*[6] (where a seaman forged a certificate of good conduct so that the Trinity House examiners would let him take an examination); *Moah*[7] (where a testimonial was forged to gain admission to the police force); and *Bassey*[8] (where a student forged papers to gain admission to the Inner Temple) would all fall within s. 10 (1) (c).

But where it is not intended to induce anyone to act in contravention of a duty no offence is committed under the Act. The Law Commission instances the case of the bogus invitation to a party with a view to raising a laugh. It is understandable that the heavy hammer of forgery should not be used on so small a nut,[9] even though real inconvenience may be caused.[10]

It is not enough that an instrument is falsified with a view to deceiving P unless there is an intention to induce an act or omission which constitutes "prejudice" as defined. It would not constitute forgery, for example, to falsify a birth certificate if D's *only* object is to convince people of his legitimacy, or to falsify a degree certificate if D's *only* object is to make his friends believe that he has had a university education. And to constitute forgery D must intend by the false document to prejudice the victim or some other party; it is not enough that acceptance of the false document will result in someone doing, or not doing, something to D's prejudice. Literally "a person's prejudice" in s. 10 might be read as including D himself but in *Utting*[11] the Court of Appeal rightly regarded such a submission as absurd.

3 Claim of Right

This issue may be conveniently introduced by reference to the facts of *Parker*,[12] a decision under the former law. D, who had made a loan of £3 to P and was unable to get payment from P, wrote P a letter, purporting to

---

5. (1833) 1 Mood CC 393.
6. (1849) 1 Den 492.
7. (1858) Dears & B 550.
8. (1931) 22 Cr App Rep 160.
9. Yet the heavy hammer would be applicable if the invitation was intended to induce a doorman or butler to admit the bearer to the party.
10. What if the bogus invitation was sent as a means of getting P out of the way while D burgles his premises? Has D, by reason of getting P to accept the invitation as genuine, induced an act which, if it occurs, will result in P's loss of property within s. 10 (1) (a) (i)?
11. [1987] Crim LR 636.
12. (1910) 74 JP 208.

come from the War Office, which asked P to give D's demand his best attention without delay. On these facts D has obviously made a false instrument within s. 9 but he is not guilty of forgery by reason of s. 10 (2) which provides that an act which a person has an enforceable duty to do (or an omission which he has an enforceable duty not to do) is to be disregarded for the purposes of the section. Arguably P suffers no "prejudice" within s. 10 (1) if he is merely made to pay that which he already owes[13] but s. 10 (2) puts the matter beyond doubt. The "enforceable duty" must of course be one which is imposed by law or arises under contract.

In *Parker* the debt was in fact owing but it is submitted that an honest belief[14] in entitlement suffices even if the belief is unreasonable. But it is not enough that D genuinely believes that his action is justified.[15] D may feel that he has been unfairly overlooked for promotion on previous occasions but if on the next occasion he falsifies a testimonial intending to induce P to promote him all the requirements of forgery are satisfied. The Law Commission said:

"If a person makes a false instrument intending that it be used as genuine to prejudice another by inducing him to act contrary to his duty it is irrelevant that that person may genuinely believe that he is entitled to what he is trying to obtain. However firmly he may believe, for example, that he is entitled to a driving licence, he intends another to act contrary to his duty if he intends to induce him to issue such a licence against a false certificate of competency to drive, as it is the issuing officer's duty to issue a licence only against the presentation of a valid certificate of competence."

Suppose, then, that D forges the acceptance to a bill of exchange in the name of E and claims that when he did so he intended all along to meet the bill and has in fact now paid the bankers who honoured the bill so that no actual loss has been sustained by anyone.[16] The case appears to fall within the Act. By the forged signature D has induced the bankers to honour the bill and by this D gains a financial advantage.[17] D cannot be relieved of liability by s. 10 (2) because it cannot be asserted that the bankers have any enforceable duty to honour a forged bill; had the bankers known that they were in the position of accepting a bill without the usual security of an acceptor they would have been in duty bound to reject it.

It follows that while a claim of legal right may negative an intent to cause another to act to his prejudice, it is not ordinarily relevant to consider whether D was acting dishonestly. Some might say that the forger of the acceptance to a bill who all along intends to meet the bill is not acting dishonestly, but this would not affect his liability for forgery since he has intentionally made a false instrument with intent thereby to induce another

13. Cf. the discussion in connection with blackmail, above, p. 594.
14. The Law Commission, Law Com. No. 55, para. 35 considered adding "dishonestly" to the mental element but did not think that it was "either necessary or helpful".
15. Cf. *Hagan* [1985] Crim LR 598, CA, holding it irrelevant that D may have made no personal gain from the property obtained and may have applied it to entirely worthy causes. The case was decided under the 1913 Act but the same result would follow under the 1981 Act.
16. These are the facts of *Geach* (1840) 9 C & P 499.
17. In effect D obtains credit or time to pay.

to do that which it is his duty not to do. This is confirmed by *Campbell*.[18] E, a plausible rogue, told D that having returned a car to a seller, the only way the seller could repay the purchase price was for him to make out a cheque in a fictitious name. D then obliged E by endorsing the cheque in the fictitious name to herself and paying it into her account, later drawing out the money which she paid to E. It was never doubted but that D had been duped and that she thought she was acting honestly in that no one would be the loser. Affirming her conviction for forgery the Court of Appeal said that the trial judge was right to rule that dishonesty was not a necessary element of forgery. Both elements of the *mens rea* were present here; she intended the bank to accept the false signature on the cheque as genuine and by reason thereof to cause the bank to do that which it was its duty not to do. It was thus irrelevant that she intended no permanent or temporary loss to the bank.

But suppose that in *Campbell* E's plausibility had been such that she convinced D that the drawer of the cheque had authorised D to endorse it in his name. Obviously if D signs an instrument "D on behalf of X" wrongly but honestly believing that he has X's authority to do so, the instrument is not a forgery; it has not been made false so as to appear genuine. At common law the same result obtained where D, wrongly but honestly believing that he had X's authority, simply signed the instrument in the name of X.[19] But by s. 9 (1) (a) such an instrument is literally false since it purports to be made in the form in which it is made by a person who did not make it in that form. Yet an instrument may be valid though not signed by the maker so long as it is signed on his authority. A will is valid notwithstanding that another signs it in the testator's name so long as it is signed by the direction and in the presence of the testator; and a bill of exchange is valid if the drawer's signature is written on it by another with the drawer's authority. If the instrument is valid because the signature is authorised, it would be absurd to say that it is a false instrument and such an instrument may properly be regarded as being *made* by the person, P, authorising the use of his signature. If, however, D does not have P's authority to sign, though D believes that he has, the instrument would be invalid. Nevertheless it is submitted that D would not be guilty of forgery either because D does not intend to make the instrument purport to be other than an instrument *made* by P, or because, believing the instrument to be valid, D cannot intend another to act on it to his prejudice. But if on these facts D honestly believed he was authorised by E to accept in E's name he would not intend the bankers to do anything to their own, or any other person's, prejudice.[20] Similarly D would not be guilty of forgery where he enters a larger amount in a bill or cheque where he is authorised to enter a smaller amount if he honestly believes he is authorised to enter the larger amount.[1]

---

18. (1985) 80 Cr App Rep 47, CA; **SHC 524**.
19. *Forbes* (1835) 7 C & P 224; *Clifford* (1845) 2 Car & Kir 202.
20. Cf. *Forbes* (1835) 7 C & P 224.
 1. Cf. *Clifford* (1845) 2 Car & Kir 202.

4 Forgery and Machines

Normally an instrument is forged with a view to causing loss to a person, or bringing a gain to a person, or causing a person to act in contravention of a duty. But nowadays D may use a forged instrument to cause a machine to operate to his advantage. Forgery postulates that "somebody" is induced to accept a false instrument as genuine and by reason of that to do or refrain from doing some act, and thus may not be apt to cover such cases. "The increasing use of more sophisticated machines", said the Law Commission,[2]

> "has led us to include within 'instruments' capable of being forged the discs, tapes and other devices mentioned in paragraph 25, which may cause machines into which they are fed to respond to the information or instructions upon them, and, of course, there are machines which are designed to respond to an instrument in writing. It is necessary, therefore, to make provision to cover in such cases the intention to cause a machine to respond to a false instrument as if it were a genuine instrument. There also has to be provision for treating the act or omission intended to flow from the machine responding to the instrument as an act or omission to a person's prejudice."

Sections 10 (3) and (4) implement the Commission's view. Take a simple illustration. If D uses a false instrument (say a cash card) to obtain cash from a machine (a bank's cash dispenser) he steals the money.[3] While this would seem to be enough to meet the case the position under the Act is that D is guilty of forgery if he made the instrument for this purpose, or of using a false instrument if he is not the maker. He is apparently so guilty though no *person* is ever induced to treat the false card as genuine;[4] the false card was made with a view to "inducing *the machine* to respond" to the false card as genuine (s. 10 (3)), and by s. 10 (4) the prejudice resulting "*shall* be treated" as an act to a person's prejudice.

In many cases where D, by the use of false instruments or otherwise, causes a machine to record information as made or authorised by one who did not make it, some person will be induced to act on it as genuine and the case is one of forgery in the ordinary way. However, with the increasing mechanisation of accounting, it may be the case, and may increasingly become the case, that D achieves his purpose in having his or another's account credited with monies though no *person* is ever deceived. D may still be convicted of a forgery offence because he has induced the machine to accept the false as genuine and the resulting prejudice is treated as being to a person.

These cases are ones where economic loss is caused. But prejudice is not confined to economic loss and extends to causing a person to act in

---

2. Law Com. No. 55, para. 36.
3. Cf. *Hands* (1887) 56 LT 370, above, p. 550.
4. In the Explanatory Notes to the Draft Bill (Law Com. No. 55) the Commission said of its provision (which is not reproduced in *identical* terms in the Act) that it "is required to deal with those cases where the false instrument, whether it be an instrument in writing or a disc, tape, sound track or other device, is made or used to cause a machine to respond to it as if it were a genuine instrument. The use of a false card to cause a bank's cash dispensing machine to pay out money would not be within [section] 3 standing alone as there would be no intention of inducing somebody to accept it as genuine and to act upon it."

contravention of a duty since "prejudice" referred to in s. 10 (4) is a reference to any of the forms of prejudice in s. 10 (1). If D causes the bank's computer to accept information which purports to be made or authorised by one who did not make or authorise it with a view to inducing P (an employee of the bank) to act in contravention of his duty this is forgery in the ordinary way. But we are also to contemplate, presumably, that the computer can be induced to act in contravention of its duty! If, then, D makes a false pass to gain access to premises (for example, to a car park or a building) via a machine which is programmed to respond to authorised passes, the case appears to fall literally within these provisions; the machine has accepted the false pass as genuine and its response is to be treated as a response to a person's prejudice.

The difficulties are illustrated by *Gold and Schifreen*.[5] Here D and E, two skilled 'hackers', obtained unauthorised access to P's computer on which information was stored by causing the computer to accept them as authorised users. The Court of Appeal quashed their convictions for forgery on two grounds. One was that the signals which caused the computer to treat them as authorised users were never 'recorded or stored' within the Act; they appeared only momentarily on a screen and were then immediately expunged. The other reason was that the extension of forgery to discs, tapes etc. did not alter the need for the requirement that for forgery the document must tell a lie about itself. Here, it seems, D and E simply caused the computer to accept *them* as authorised users. In effect they simply told a lie (viz, we are authorised users) and the case might be likened to D writing a password on a piece of paper which tricks the sentry into admitting him.

The court in *Gold* was evidently unhappy about what it regarded as a procrustean attempt to use the Act for situations for which it was not designed. There are certainly difficulties here and it may be that the effect of s. 10 (3) and (4) is not quite so far reaching. Take again the case where D uses a false cash card to get money from the dispenser. At some subsequent stage P, a bank employee, will react to the information stored in the dispenser and D intends P then to act to his own or another's prejudice. At this stage P cannot be induced so to act by accepting the false cash card as genuine for he cannot have seen it; that would normally require that D could not be convicted of a forgery offence but s. 10 (3) meets this difficulty by providing that references to a false instrument include a reference to inducing a machine to respond to a false instrument as genuine. The false information, in effect, becomes the false instrument which P is induced to accept as genuine. On this view the "act or omission intended to be induced" in s. 10 (4) is P's (a person's) act or omission following upon the machine responding to the false instrument.

5 Causation

Forgery extends not merely to the case where by reason of accepting the false instrument as genuine P is intended to be induced to act, or fail to act, to his prejudice but also to the case where P is intended to be caused so to

5. [1987] 3 All ER 618, [1987] 3 WLR 803.

act, or not to act, to the prejudice of any other person. As has been shown,[6] a false testimonial may be sent by D to P in order to induce P to appoint D, or to appoint E or not to appoint F, and all three situations fall within the ambit of forgery. But it is not enough that the false instrument results in prejudice to someone; the prejudice must result from a person (or persons) having accepted the false instrument as genuine and being induced thereby to do or refrain from doing something to his or another's prejudice. Prejudice clearly results to F if as a result of the false reference F is not considered for the job and is denied the opportunity to earn remuneration, but the offence lies, not in F being prejudiced, but in P being induced to act to F's prejudice.

Suppose that D wishes to acquire a vehicle from P, a dealer, and because D does not have the wherewithal he is referred by P to Q, a finance company, to arrange a hire-purchase of the vehicle. D signs the hire-purchase proposal in the name of R, R being a creditworthy individual which D is not. Having satisfied himself that R is creditworthy, Q confirms the proposal with P and P delivers the vehicle.[7] Supposing that P is prejudiced by delivering the vehicle to D,[8] it would not be apt to allege in an indictment that D has made a false instrument intending to induce P to act to his prejudice. The victim must be a person who, by reason of being induced to treat the false instrument as genuine, does something (or fails to do something) to his own or another's prejudice. The case presents no problems if D is charged with inducing Q to act to his own or another's prejudice in that D gains from Q a financial advantage otherwise than by way of remuneration.[9]

4) *The Offences*

1 Forgery

By s. 1 of the Act –

> "A person is guilty of forgery if he makes a false instrument, with the intention that he or another shall use it to induce somebody to accept it as genuine, and by reason of so accepting it to do or not to do some act to his own or any other person's prejudice."

By s. 6 the offence is triable either way; on summary conviction it is punishable by six months imprisonment and/or a fine of £1,000 and on trial on indictment by ten years imprisonment and/or a fine.[10]

Forgery is committed where D makes an instrument with the intention that somebody shall be induced to accept it as genuine. It is not enough, therefore, that D makes a copy of an instrument if his intention is to

---

6. Above, p. 652.

7. These are the facts of *Hurford* [1963] 2 QB 398, [1963] 2 All ER 254, CCA.

8. It may be that P is not prejudiced since he may be able to claim the whole of the price of the vehicle from Q.

9. Hence the Law Commission (Law Com. No. 55, para. 47) saw no need to reproduce the offence under s. 7 of the 1913 Act of demanding property under or by virtue of forged instruments.

10. The offence is finable on indictment by virtue of s. 30 of the Powers of Criminal Courts Act 1973.

represent it as a copy; were it otherwise the photo-copier would have made us a nation of forgers. Nor would it suffice, it is submitted, that, subsequently realising that the copy is good enough to pass as the original, D decides to pass it as the original. The definition requires that D *makes* the false instrument with the requisite intent.

2 Copying a False Instrument

By s. 2 of the Act –

"It is an offence for a person to make a copy of an instrument which is, and which he knows or believes to be, a false instrument, with the intention that he or another shall use it to induce somebody to accept it as a copy of a genuine instrument, and by reason of so accepting it to do or not to do some act to his own or any other person's prejudice."

The offence is triable and punishable in the same way as forgery under s. 1.

The commission of this offence requires (a) that the instrument that is copied is in fact a false instrument;[11] and (b) that D "knows or believes"[12] it to be false. In addition (c) the copy must be made with the intention of inducing someone to accept it as a copy of a genuine instrument.

It is not an offence simply to copy an instrument known or believed to be false if the copy is made to pass as a copy of a false instrument. At a trial for forgery copies of the allegedly false instrument may be photocopied for the convenience of judge and counsel and it can hardly be supposed that this falls within s. 2. The operation of the section may be illustrated by reference to the facts of *Harris*.[13] D, who owed money to P, had acquired a receipt to which P's signature had been forged. He told P that he had paid the debt and when P questioned this, D photocopied the forged receipt and sent the copy to P. Such conduct clearly falls within s. 2. Strictly it is arguable that a photocopy of a false instrument made with the intention of being passed *as a copy* of a false instrument does not tell a lie about itself and courts elsewhere[14] have been disposed to take this view. Only where the copy is made to pass as the original false instrument would the copy tell a lie about itself. The point is, however, no longer of importance in view of s. 2; the offence is committed if D intends to pass the photocopy as a copy of a genuine instrument. But if D intends to pass off his copy of the false instrument as the false instrument itself this is forgery under s. 1 and does not fall within s. 2.

3 Using False Instruments and Copies

By s. 3 –

"It is an offence for a person to use an instrument which is, and which he knows or believes to be, false, with the intention of inducing somebody to accept it as genuine, and by reason of so accepting it to do or not to do some act to his own or any other person's prejudice."

---

11. Just as for handling, above, p. 615, it must be proved that the goods are in fact stolen. If the instrument is not false but is believed by D to be false there may be an attempt, above, p. 304.
12. As to which see above, p. 632.
13. [1966] 1 QB 184, [1965] 3 All ER 206n.
14. *Chow Sik Wah and Quon Hong* [1964] 1 CCC 313 (Ontario Court of Appeal); *Tait* [1968] 2 NZLR 126 (New Zealand Court of Appeal).

And by s. 4 –

"It is an offence for a person to use a copy of an instrument which is, and which he knows or believes to be, a false instrument, with the intention of inducing somebody to accept it as a copy of a genuine instrument, and by reason of so accepting it to do or not to do some act to his own or any other person's prejudice."

Both offences are triable and punishable in the same way as forgery under s. 1.

The offence under s. 3 in substance replaces the former offence, under s. 6 of the Forgery Act 1913, of uttering. Under s. 6 a person who "uses, offers, publishes, delivers, disposes of, tenders in payment or exchange, exchanges, tenders in evidence or puts off" was guilty of uttering. This extravagance of language is now replaced by the single verb "uses" but this does not import any restriction on the ambit of the offence. The Law Commission was aware[15] that "uses" is the paramount verb, was so regarded by the courts,[16] and would do duty for the remaining expressions in the earlier legislation.

Any use of the false instrument will suffice. While the actual making of the false instrument can hardly be regarded as a use of it, its communication to another is clearly a use of it. No doubt it would be enough that it is left in a position where P will see it and it may be enough that it is sent to another.[17]

The use is not restricted to the maker of the false instrument. It is equally an offence for someone who did not make the false instrument to use it with the appropriate intent, whether or not there is any collaboration with the maker.

Whether making a copy of a false instrument, without any further steps taken to communicate it to another, constitutes a use of a false instrument[18] is no longer of importance in view of the fact that it would in any case be an offence under s. 2. Strictly, though, the case seems to fall within s. 3. While it can hardly be said that D in forging a document purporting to be made by P is "using" the very document he forges, there is no reason why E, who comes across D's forgery and photocopies it with the appropriate intent, should not be regarded as using D's forged instrument. In the ordinary use of language he has used the instrument which was forged by D. There may thus be a use of a false instrument though it is not communicated to another.

Little needs to be said about s. 4 which parallels s. 3 in relation to the use of a copy of the false instrument. It is submitted that copying a false instrument does not constitute a use *of the copy* within s. 4. As has just been indicated this may constitute a use of the false instrument within s. 3; at the stage of copying D may properly be said to have used the original forged instrument but he can hardly be said to be *using* the copy which he makes.

---

15. Law Com. No. 55, para. 49.
16. Cf. *Harris* [1966] 1 QB 184, [1965] 3 All ER 206n.
17. Cf. *Harris*, last note. There is clearly a use of a false witness statement when it is sent forward along with other documentation relating to the case. Cf. *A-G's Reference (No. 2 of 1980)* [1981] 1 All ER 493, [1981] 1 WLR 148, CA.
18. A point canvassed but left open in *Harris*, last note.

4 Possession Offences

By s. 5 of the Act –

"1) It is an offence for a person to have in his custody or under his control an instrument to which this section applies which is, and which he knows or believes to be, false, with the intention that he or another shall use it to induce somebody to accept it as genuine, and by reason of so accepting it to do or not to do some act to his own or any other person's prejudice.

2) It is an offence for a person to have in his custody or under his control, without lawful authority or excuse, an instrument to which this section applies which is, and which he knows or believes to be, false.

3) It is an offence for a person to make or to have in his custody or under his control a machine or implement, or paper or any other material, which to his knowledge is or has been specially designed or adapted for the making of an instrument to which this section applies, with the intention that he or another shall make an instrument to which this section applies which is false and that he or another shall use the instrument to induce somebody to accept it as genuine, and by reason of so accepting it to do or not to do some act to his own or any other person's prejudice.

4) It is an offence for a person to make or to have in his custody or under his control any such machine, implement, paper or material, without lawful authority or excuse.

5) The instruments to which this section applies are –
   a) money orders;
   b) postal orders;
   c) United Kingdom postage stamps;
   d) Inland Revenue stamps;
   e) share certificates;
   f) passports and documents which can be used instead of passports;
   g) cheques;
   h) travellers' cheques;
   j) cheque cards;
   k) credit cards;
   l) certified copies relating to an entry in a register of births, adoptions, marriages or deaths and issued by the Registrar General, the Registrar General for Northern Ireland, a registration officer or a person lawfully authorised to register marriages; and
   m) certificates relating to entries in such registers.

6) In subsection (5) (e) above 'share certificate' means an instrument entitling or evidencing the title of a person to a share or interest –
   a) in any public stock, annuity, fund or debt of any government or state, including a state which forms part of another state; or
   b) in any stock, fund or debt of a body (whether corporate or unincorporated) established in the United Kingdom or elsewhere."

The offences under s. 5 (1) and (3) are triable and punishable in the same way as forgery under s. 1. The offences under s. 5 (2) and (4) are also triable either way and are punishable on summary conviction with the same maxima of six months' imprisonment and/or fine of £1,000; on trial on indictment, however, these offences carry a maximum of two years imprisonment and/or a fine.

Section 5 penalises the possession of the instruments specified in s. 5 (5). The list is exhaustive so that it is not an offence under this section to possess a false instrument as such (say a false testimonial or will) unless it is one of the instruments specified.

Section 5(3) also penalises the possession of any "machine or implement, or paper or any other material, which to [D's] knowledge has been specially designed or adapted[19] for the making of an instrument" to which the section applies. It is accordingly not enough that D possesses implements with which he intends to make an instrument unless the implements are *specially* designed or adapted to make one of the *specified* implements. It is no offence to possess a pen though D's intention is to use it to make one of the specified instruments; nor is it an offence to possess a household cleanser in order to falsify one of the specified instruments[20] since neither the pen nor the cleanser are specially designed, nor need they be adapted, for the making of a false instrument. It is of course not possible to provide an exhaustive list of the machines, implements, paper or other materials which are specially designed or adapted for making instruments to which the section applies; it is for the prosecution to establish that the implement etc. is so designed or adapted and that D knew that. "Knowledge" in this sub-section is not coupled with "belief" as it is elsewhere in the section and generally in offences under the Act. Clearly "knowledge" is more restricted than "knowledge or belief" but the boundary between the two is somewhat speculative.[21]

It is only necessary to show that the implement etc. has been specially designed or adapted to make an instrument to which the section applies, not that the machine etc. has been designed or adapted to make *false* instruments. No doubt it will often be D's intention that he or another should so use it, but it suffices that the implement etc. is specially designed or adapted to produce any of the specified instruments. Very commonly cheque books are stolen and may be found in the custody or control of D; if D has one of the relevant states of mind he is guilty of an offence since the paper or other materials used are specially designed for the making of cheques and cheques are included in the specified instruments.

D must be proved to have "custody or control" of the false instrument or of the implement etc. which is specially designed or adapted for its making. The Law Commission, not entirely unreasonably, is reluctant to plump for "possession" because of the technicalities which have come to be associated with that concept.[1] The Commission prefers "custody or control" as it did

19. As to which see the discussion, above, p. 422.
20. Certain household cleansers can be used to remove the holder's signature from credit cards thus enabling D to sign the holder's signature in his own hand which can be easily reproduced by D.
21. See above, p. 634.
1. See above, p. 128.

with criminal damage and reference may be made to the discussion in that context.[2]

While s. 5 creates four offences, there are in essence two pairs of offences. All four offences have the common element of custody or control of instruments or implements. The offences under s. 5 (1) and (3) are more serious than those under s. 5 (2) and (4) in requiring proof that D has the instrument intending to induce another to accept it as genuine and thereby to do, or not to do, something to his own or another's prejudice, or has the implement with a view to its use to produce an instrument with like intent. This intent has already been discussed.[3] The offences under s. 5 (2) and (4) differ only, but differ markedly, in relation to the mental element that needs to be established. Under these provisions it is enough that D has custody or control of a specified instrument which he knows to be false, or a proscribed implement, "without lawful authority or excuse".

Lawful authority or excuse is not defined in the Act and its use in other contexts[4] affords no grounds for thinking that, so far as D is concerned, it will be generously interpreted. No doubt a police officer who in the course of his duty seizes false documents or implements has lawful authority for his custody, as does a private citizen who gains such custody with a view to delivering them to the police or other proper authority.[5] Lawful authority must extend not only to those authorised by law but also to those who plan to act in accordance with law. "Excuse" is more difficult to define. It must extend to cases other than those where D has available to him some general defence to crime (for example, insanity, infancy or duress) for otherwise its inclusion would be meaningless. What is capable of being an excuse must be a matter of law for the judge, but there is little in the decided cases by way of guidance[6] and the issue must turn on what the court believes is reasonable. It is thought unlikely that a court would consider it an excuse that a false instrument or an implement of forgery is kept as a curio.[7] Where D is charged under s. 5 with having control of an implement it would appear to be necessary to prove that D knows it to be specially designed or adapted. Knowledge of falsity is required for the offence under s. 5 (2) and knowledge that the implement is so designed or adapted is required for the offence under s. 5 (3); and by s. 5 (4) the custody of any *such* machine etc. is an offence.

The onus of proving lack of lawful authority or excuse lies on the prosecution. Once the prosecution has proved that D had custody of (a) an instrument he knew to be false, or (b) an implement specially designed or adapted, there would be an evidential burden on D to proffer an explanation. If D does adduce some evidence of lawful authority or excuse it will be

---

2. Below, p. 702.
3. Above, p. 655.
4. See above, p. 425.
5. Cf. *Wuyts* [1969] 2 QB 474, [1969] 2 All ER 799, CA.
6. Cf. *Dickins v Gill* [1896] 2 QB 310 where it was held in a case under the Post Office (Protection) Act 1884, s. 7 that the proprietor of a philatelist newspaper had no lawful authority or excuse for possessing a die which he made in order to produce black and white illustrations of a postage stamp in his newspaper.
7. See below, p. 673.

for the prosecution in the ordinary way to satisfy the jury that D has no authority or excuse.

2 Counterfeiting

Under the Treason Act 1351 the counterfeiting of the King's money or importing counterfeit money into the realm was made a treasonable offence, and to utter counterfeit coin was a cheat at common law. Beginning in 1742 a number of statutes have been passed for the purpose of protecting the coinage, and the various statutory provisions were brought together in the Coinage Offences Act 1936. The pattern is one which has heretofore been all too familiar in English legislation. To quote Lord Cross[8] –

"The code has grown up in haphazard fashion over the centuries and it cannot be said that it is an entirely logical structure either as regards what acts will or will not constitute offences or as to the scale of penalties."

Part II of the Forgery and Counterfeiting Act 1981 is intended to remedy the defects which Lord Cross noted and to provide a logical and comprehensive code.

1) *The Meaning of Counterfeiting*

The essence of counterfeiting, as it does of forgery, lies in the making of spurious currency notes or coins which may pass as the genuine articles. "Counterfeiting" is defined in s. 28 –

"1) For the purposes of this Part of this Act a thing is a counterfeit of a currency note or of a protected coin –

a) if it is not a currency note or a protected coin but resembles a currency note or protected coin (whether on one side only or on both) to such an extent that it is reasonably capable of passing for a currency note or protected coin of that description; or

b) if it is a currency note or protected coin which has been so altered that it is reasonably capable of passing for a currency note or protected coin of some other description.

2) For the purposes of this Part of this Act –

a) a thing consisting of one side only of a currency note, with or without the addition of other material, is a counterfeit of such a note;

b) a thing consisting –

i) of parts of two or more currency notes; or

ii) of parts of a currency note, or of parts of two or more currency notes, with the addition of other material,
is capable of being a counterfeit of a currency note.

---

8. *Selby v Director of Public Prosecutions* [1971] 3 All ER 810 at 821, HL.

3) References in this Part of this Act to passing or tendering a counterfeit of a currency note or a protected coin are not to be construed as confined to passing or tendering it as legal tender."

Counterfeiting extends only to a "currency note" or a "protected coin" as defined by s. 27 of the Act. A currency note includes any note lawfully issued as money either in this country or in any other country and which is customarily used as money. A protected coin includes any coin customarily used as money in any country. It is accordingly not an offence to counterfeit coins which are no longer used as currency. For purposes of historical research, and for reasons of security, electrolitic copies (to the ordinary eye indistinguishable from the originals) of early coins are frequently reproduced. Even if such copies were made with a view to passing as genuine and to be sold as such, the offences of counterfeiting do not apply to them.

To be counterfeit a note or coin must be "reasonably capable" of passing for the real thing. While an instrument may be forged, so long as D intends to pass it as genuine, though the falsification may be so inept as to be incapable of fooling anyone, a note or coin can be counterfeit only if it is reasonably capable of passing as genuine. Whether the note or coin is reasonably capable of so passing is to be objectively determined by the court or jury. It might be thought that whether counterfeit currency was reasonably capable of passing as genuine would depend on the circumstances. A counterfeit note which would not fool a judge and jury in the studied calm of a courtroom might easily fool a busy barman in a crowded bar.

The Law Commission noted that under the 1936 Act the offence of counterfeiting was complete though the note or coin was not in a fit state to be uttered but declined to continue an offence in these terms since[9] –

"a provision that the offence is committed if something that is not reasonably capable of passing is made provides no clear definition of the offence."

In the Commission's view a half completed note would, accordingly, not be reasonably capable of passing as a genuine note. It seems, then, that whether the counterfeit is reasonably capable of passing as genuine has to be decided by reference to the nature of the counterfeit and not by reference to the circumstances of its passing.[10]

By s. 28 (2) (a), however, a thing consisting of one side only of a currency note "is" counterfeit and in this case it would not be relevant to consider whether it was thought reasonably capable of so passing. Section 28 (2) (b) makes it clear that a thing consisting of parts of currency notes is "capable" of being counterfeit; whether it is in fact counterfeit presumably depends upon whether it is reasonably so capable.

Finally, s. 28 (3) makes it clear that counterfeiting is not restricted to passing currency as legal tender; notes and coins in use as currency are frequently sold or exchanged as collectors' items and it is entirely right that the law of counterfeiting should apply.

9. Law Com. No. 55, para. 86.
10. The incompetent counterfeiter is, of course, not beyond the reach of the criminal law. He may fall foul of ss. 16 and 17, below, p. 673, or be guilty of an attempt to counterfeit, and if he passes the item there is likely to be a deception offence.

2) *Mens Rea*

The offences of counterfeiting closely follow the pattern of the forgery offences and expressions defining the mental element in respect of counterfeiting offences ("intending that he or another shall pass or tender it as genuine", "without lawful authority or excuse", "knows or believes", "to his knowledge") are identical with those used in respect of forgery offences so that reference may be made to the discussion of these expressions in the first part of this chapter. So too the mental element required for "custody or control" is discussed elsewhere.[11] Little of further substance can be added.

One point that may be noted is that there is no requirement in respect of the counterfeiting offences that by reason of accepting the counterfeit as genuine the victim should be induced to act, or not act, to his own or another's prejudice. Such a requirement would be superfluous in that if someone is induced to accept counterfeit currency as genuine there is inevitably prejudice to him or others who may subsequently treat the counterfeit as genuine.

3) *Passing and Tendering*

Many of the offences of counterfeiting require an intent to pass or tender the counterfeit as genuine or a passing or tendering of the counterfeit as genuine. It follows that if the counterfeit is to be passed or tendered as counterfeit (as a copy) the conduct would not fall foul of these offences.[12] The point may well be illustrated by reference to *Selby v Director of Public Prosecutions*[13] where D had sold certain counterfeit sovereigns as counterfeit sovereigns, variously describing them as "snide" or "genuine reproductions". On such facts it is clear that D does not pass or tender the sovereigns as genuine since, as his argot makes clear, he is selling them as replicas of the genuine article.

Passing and tendering assume that D will at least proffer (or intend to proffer) to another the counterfeit as genuine. There is no requirement that the other should in the result accept it as genuine. A counterfeit note or coin may be passed or tendered as genuine by D to P though P is a police officer who is well aware that the currency is counterfeit. The Law Commission was of the view[14] that the offence ought not to extend to D who might display a number of counterfeit notes merely to impress P with his apparent affluence. This suggests that P must in some way accept (or be intended to accept) the counterfeit as genuine. "Tender" connotes the idea of an offer made with a view to acceptance by P and "pass" suggests the acceptance of that offer. In these senses D does not pass or tender the counterfeit as genuine where he merely exhibits the counterfeit with a view to making P believe that he is a man of substance. So D does not pass or

---

11. Above, p. 667 and below, p. 702.
12. Though there may be an offence under ss. 18 and 19, see below, p. 674.
13. [1972] AC 515, [1971] 3 All ER 810, HL.
14. Law Com. No. 55, para. 91.

tender counterfeit coins to P where he leaves them with P for safe custody,[15] nor where he uses a double-headed penny for the purposes of cheating at a game of pitch-and-toss;[16] in neither case does D pass or attempt to pass the coin to P as genuine.

4) *The Offences*

1 Counterfeiting

By s. 14 of the Act –

"1) It is an offence for a person to make a counterfeit of a currency note or of a protected coin, intending that he or another shall pass or tender it as genuine.

2) It is an offence for a person to make a counterfeit of a currency note or of a protected coin without lawful authority or excuse."[17]

The elements of the offence under s. 1 (1) have already been discussed. Section 1 (2) creates a less serious offence and is meant to provide for the case where no intent to pass the counterfeit as genuine can be established. It will deal with a case such as *Heron*[18] where D and others made coins resembling half sovereigns but it was not established that they intended to pass them as genuine. Quite what purposes they had in mind does not appear; if it was to pass them as reproductions or copies this would not constitute an excuse. There are real dangers in allowing counterfeit currency to circulate and these dangers are not diminished because D informs the initial purchaser that the coin is only a reproduction. Indeed it is difficult to envisage what would constitute an excuse[19] for the *making* of counterfeit currency. A possible case might be where D makes currency for a foreign country in pursuance of what appears to him, but which is not, a proper order from the authorities in that country.[20] But it is thought unlikely that the courts would regard it as an excuse that D makes the coins to demonstrate his skills as an engraver or even that he makes it for his own amusement.

2 Passing Counterfeit Currency

By s. 15 of the Act –

"1) It is an offence for a person –

a) to pass or tender as genuine any thing which is, and which he knows or believes to be, a counterfeit of a currency note or of a protected coin; or

b) to deliver to another any thing which is, and which he knows or believes to be, such a counterfeit, intending that the person to whom it is delivered or another shall pass or tender it as genuine.

15. Cf. *Shukard* (1811) Russ & Ry 200.
16. Cf. *McMahon* (1894) 15 NSWLR 131.
17. For the punishment of these and other offences of counterfeiting, see below, p. 676.
18. [1982] 1 All ER 993, [1982] 1 WLR 451, HL.
19. General defences, e.g. duress, would be available to D but "excuse" is presumably intended to refer to other circumstances of exculpation, see above, p. 425.
20. But note that by s. 21 the exportation of counterfeit currency without Treasury consent is prohibited.

2) It is an offence for a person to deliver to another without lawful authority or excuse, any thing which is, and which he knows or believes to be, a counterfeit of a currency note or of a protected coin."

This section creates offences which parallel those in s. 14 in relation to passing counterfeit currency whether or not D is the maker of the counterfeit. The offence under s. 15 (2) may be committed even though D delivers the currency to E as counterfeit currency and without any intent that E should pass it as genuine; if D gives E a counterfeit coin to keep as a curio an offence will be committed since this will not constitute a lawful authority or excuse for the delivery.

3 Possession of Counterfeit Currency

By s. 16 of the Act –

"1) It is an offence for a person to have in his custody or under his control anything which is, and which he knows or believes to be, a counterfeit of a currency note or of a protected coin, intending either to pass or tender it as genuine or to deliver it to another with the intention that he or another shall pass or tender it as genuine.

2) It is an offence for a person to have in his custody or under his control, without lawful authority or excuse, any thing which is, and which he knows or believes to be, a counterfeit of a currency note or of a protected coin.

3) It is immaterial for the purposes of subsections (1) and (2) above that a coin or note is not in a fit state to be passed or tendered or that the making or counterfeiting of a coin or note has not been finished or perfected."

The offences under this section parallel those under ss. 14 and 15 in relation to the custody or control of counterfeit currency. While the general definition of "counterfeit" in s. 28 (1) requires that the note or coin be reasonably capable of passing for a genuine note or coin, this requirement is excluded in relation to offences under this section. It is not enough that at the moment of detection D's notes or coins are incomplete and in their incomplete state are not reasonably capable of passing as genuine. But though it is not necessary to show that the making is completed it must be proved that it has commenced. If the making has not been commenced there may be an offence under the next section.

4 Possession of Counterfeiting Implements

By s. 17 of the Act –

"1) It is an offence for a person to make, or to have in his custody or under his control, any thing which he intends to use, or to permit any other person to use, for the purpose of making a counterfeit of a currency note or of a protected coin with the intention that it be passed or tendered as genuine.

2) It is an offence for a person without lawful authority or excuse –
   a) to make; or
   b) to have in his custody or under his control,

      any thing which, to his knowledge, is or has been specially designed or adapted for the making of a counterfeit of a currency note.

  2) Subject to subsection (4) below, it is an offence for a person to make, or to have in his custody or under his control, any implement which, to his knowledge, is capable of imparting to any thing a resemblance –

    a) to the whole or part of either side of a protected coin; or

    b) to the whole or part of the reverse of the image on either side of a protected coin.

  4) It shall be a defence for a person charged with an offence under subsection (3) above to show –

    a) that he made the implement or, as the case may be, had it in his custody or under his control, with the written consent of the Treasury; or

    b) that he had lawful authority otherwise than by virtue of paragraph (a) above, or a lawful excuse, for making it or having it in his custody or under his control."

This section creates offences in relation to the custody or control of "any thing" which may be used for the counterfeiting of notes or coins. It extends both to implements (a die or photographic equipment for example) and materials (the special paper on which currency is printed for example); it would extend to raw materials such as silver and copper if these were kept for counterfeiting.

    The section has much in common with its counterpart in s. 5 relating to the custody and control of implements of forgery.[1] It follows the usual pattern of creating a serious offence where the thing is intended to be used to make a counterfeit intending that it be passed as genuine, and less serious offences where materials or implements, known to be materials or implements designed for counterfeiting, are kept without lawful authority or excuse. It is rather odd that while for the offence under s. 17 (2) the onus is on the prosecution to show that D acted without authority or excuse,[2] under s. 17 (4) it is for D to establish (no doubt on the balance of probabilities) that he had authority or excuse.

5 Reproducing British Currency

By s. 18 of the Act –

  "1) It is an offence for any person, unless the relevant authority has previously consented in writing, to reproduce on any substance whatsoever, and whether or not on the correct scale, any British currency note or any part of a British currency note.

  2) In this section –

    'British currency note' means any note which –

    a) has been lawfully issued in England and Wales, Scotland or Northern Ireland; and

    b) is or has been customarily used as money in the country where it was issued; and

1. Above, p. 666.
2. As to which, see above, p. 668.

c) is payable on demand; and

'the relevant authority', in relation to a British currency note of any particular description, means the authority empowered by law to issue notes of that description."

And by s. 19 –

"1) It is an offence for a person –

a) to make an imitation British coin in connection with a scheme intended to promote the sale of any product or the making of contracts for the supply of any service; or

b) to sell or distribute imitation British coins in connection with any such scheme, or to have imitation British coins in his custody or under his control with a view to such sale or distribution,

unless the Treasury have previously consented in writing to the sale or distribution of such imitation British coins in connection with that scheme.

2) In this section –

'British coin' means any coin which is legal tender in any part of the United Kingdom; and

'imitation British coin' means any thing which resembles a British coin in shape, size and the substance of which it is made."

These provisions result from the concern that is felt about the dangers that may arise from allowing the reproduction of British notes and coins. "The dangers", said the Law Commission,[3]

"are two-fold. In the first place people may be tempted to use the vouchers or stage properties or even reproductions cut from magazines as genuine notes, and in the second place the existence of accurate plates for the making of the reproductions may tempt persons to print copies for their own dishonest use. There is also a danger in the reproductions of notes or parts of notes on a scale larger than an actual note that this may provide useful assistance to a counterfeiter in the preparation of plates or reproductions to the correct scale."

These dangers are met by making it an offence for any person, without the consent in writing of the relevant authority, to reproduce any British currency note or to make any imitation British coin where the note or coin is legal tender.

What has to be reproduced is a British currency note or part of it. Strictly it would be an offence for an editor without authority to publish copies of a proposed new currency note in his newspaper though his motive was no more sinister than that of acquainting his readers with the new design; it would not be an offence for him to publish a copy of a counterfeit note (since this is not a "currency" note) however good the counterfeit and however base the editor's motives.

The offence under s. 19 applies only to coins produced in connection with the promotion of the goods or products since it is only in such cases that the large scale manufacture of such coins or tokens may lead to real mischief.

3. Law Com. No. 55, para. 107.

6 Penalties

In relation to penalties Part II of the Act observes the same broad distinction as Part I; the more serious offences are those where there is an intention to make or pass the counterfeit as genuine, the less serious where the counterfeit is not so made.

All counterfeiting offences (other than offences under ss. 18 and 19 which are summary only and are punishable with a fine not exceeding the statutory maximum (presently £1,000) are triable either way. The more serious offences (under ss. 14 (1), 15 (1), 16 (1) and 17 (1)) are punishable on summary conviction by imprisonment for six months and/or a fine not exceeding the statutory maximum, and on indictment by imprisonment for ten years and/or a fine. The less serious offences (ss. 14 (2), 15 (2), 16 (2), 17 (2) and 17 (3)) are punishable on summary conviction in the same way, and on indictment by imprisonment for two years and/or a fine.

5) *Codification*

A feature of earlier legislation on forgery and counterfeiting is that it has never purported to be comprehensive and exhaustive. Thus the Forgery Act 1913, though it dealt in a substantial way with offences of forgery, did not in fact abolish common law forgery and was not considered any bar to the creation of particular offences of forgery in many subsequent statutes.

In a codified system the aim of course is that the whole of the law relating to particular crimes (theft, criminal damage, or forgery, for example) can be found within one instrument and is not to be garnered only by a painstaking search of the whole statute book. In accordance with this aim the Law Commission recommended, and the Act implements, a number of repeals of, or amendments to, Acts and provisions in Acts where the conduct is now provided for in the Forgery and Counterfeiting Act 1981. But the Law Commission had to recognise that there were offences analogous to forgery where the mental element needed to be defined in a different way which it was not possible to accommodate in the new scheme. Thus provisions of the Forgery Act 1861 (which include provisions penalising the defacement, destruction or concealment of registers of births, marriages and deaths) remain in force, as do provisions in the Customs and Excise Act 1952 when there were special reasons for having offences akin to forgery but with a different *mens rea*. The Act, however, now deals in a comprehensive way with offences of forgery and counterfeiting and within its field of operation is the authoritative source of law.

17 Offences of Damage to Property

The principal offences of damage to property are governed by the Criminal Damage Act 1971 which replaced the prolix and complicated provisions of the Malicious Damage Act 1861. Like the Theft Acts of 1968 and 1978 the Criminal Damage Act is an entirely new code, and it must be approached and interpreted in the same fashion.[1] The Criminal Damage Act is in the main the work of the Law Commission and reference to the papers of the Commission is helpful in understanding the underlying policies and in elucidating the provisions of the Act.[2]

One thing that is worth noting at the outset is that the Law Commission wished to keep the policies and concepts of the law of damage to property in line with the law of theft. Complete parity for theft and criminal damage is neither practicable nor desirable, but it is important that there should be no conflict of principle if the criminal code as a whole is to be consistent and harmonious. Thus, to take a simple example, while land cannot in general be stolen, there is no need for any similar limitation in relation to offences of criminal damage; on the other hand, it is clearly desirable that if it is not an offence to pick another's wild mushrooms, it should be no more an offence to destroy or damage them.

1 Destroying or Damaging Property of Another

By s. 1 (1) of the Criminal Damage Act 1971:
> "A person who without lawful excuse destroys or damages any property belonging to another intending to destroy or damage any such property or being reckless as to whether any such property would be destroyed or damaged shall be guilty of an offence."

And by s. 4 the offence is punishable by imprisonment for ten years.

1) *Destroy or Damage*

The expression "destroy or damage" was commonly used in the Malicious Damage Act 1861 and it would seem that previous decisions on the

---

1. See above, pp. 488–490.
2. See Law Com. No. 29, *Offences of Damage to Property* (1970). See also Law Commission Working Paper No. 23, *Malicious Damage*. As to Reports of the CLRC, see above, p. 63.

meaning of these words, though no longer binding, must retain a persuasive value.

What is contemplated by "destroy or damage" is actual destruction or damage; that is, some physical harm, impairment or deterioration which can be perceived by the senses. It was for this reason that intangible property was excluded from the definition of property.[3] It is not enough to show that what has been done amounts to a civil wrong, as for example a trespass to land or goods for neither requires proof of actual damage. It was held in *Eley v Lytle* (1885)[4] that D was guilty of no offence when, during a game of football, he ran over P's land and the only evidence of actual damage was that he had committed a trespass. It seems clear that the same result would follow under the Criminal Damage Act. Actual damage, however, need only be slight. Grass can be damaged by trampling it down,[5] and is easily and rapidly damaged by football, cricket, or even bowls.[6] And even sterner stuff is susceptible of damage, as where a stalagmite is broken away.[7]

A thing may be damaged though nothing is actually broken or deformed. A car is damaged just as much by uncoupling the brake cable as by cutting it with a pair of pliers. So a machine may be damaged by removing some integral part,[8] or by tampering with some part so that it will not work although no part is removed or broken,[9] or by running it in an improper fashion so that impairment will result.[10] These principles apply just as much to land as to chattels. To dump rubbish on another's land, even though there is no tangible hurt to the land beneath the rubbish, may be to damage the land if the owner is put to expense in removing the rubbish before the land can be put to his uses.[11] If property, whether real or personal, is rendered unfit for a use to which it might be put, it may sensibly be said to have been damaged. This is not to say that property is damaged merely by a denial of its use. It could not be said that a house or car is damaged by the theft of the keys to the front door or ignition keys even though the owner may be put to expense before he can put the house or car to their intended uses. On the other hand property may be damaged though there is no interference with its performance if it is rendered less valuable.[12] A car is damaged if the paintwork is scratched and food is damaged by spoiling as where milk is watered.[13]

---

3. See below, p. 680.
4. 50 JP 308.
5. *Gayford v Choulder* [1898] 1 QB 316.
6. Cf. *Laws v Eltringham* (1881) 8 QBD 283, below, p. 681, footnote 6.
7. See (1964) The Times, 12th September.
8. Cf. *Tacey* (1821) Russ & Ry 452.
9. Cf. *Fisher* (1865) LR 1 CCR 7; and see *Getty v Antrim County Council* [1950] NI 114 (dismantling). Though a machine or a structure may be damaged by the removal of a part or by dismantling, it does not necessarily follow that the *parts* are damaged by the removal or dismantling; if the parts are undamaged D can be charged only with damaging the whole: *Woolcock* [1977] Crim LR 104 and 161.
10. Cf. *Norris* (1840) 9 C & P 241.
11. *Henderson and Battley* (1984) unreported but extensively cited in *Cox v Riley* (1986) 83 Cr App Rep 54, [1986] Crim LR 460, CA.
12. Cf. *Foster* (1852) 6 Cox CC 25. Cf. *King v Lees* (1949) 65 TLR 21 (passenger urinating in taxi held to have caused injury for purposes of the London Hackney Carriage Act, s. 41).
13. Cf. *Roper v Knott* [1898] 1 QB 868.

But different things may be damaged in different ways. In *Samuels v Stubbs*,[14] Walters J said:

"It seems to me that it is difficult to lay down any very general and, at the same time, precise and absolute rule as to what constitutes 'damage'. One must be guided in a great degree by the circumstances of each case, the nature of the article and the mode in which it is affected or treated. . . . It is my view, however, that the word . . . is sufficiently wide in its meaning to embrace injury, mischief or harm done to property, and that in order to constitute 'damage' it is unnecessary to establish such definite or actual damage as renders the property useless, or prevents it from serving its normal function. . . ."

The learned judge then held that a "temporary functional derangement" of a policeman's cap resulting from its being jumped upon constituted damage though there was no evidence that the cap might not have been restored to its original state without any real cost or trouble to the owner.

The approach of Walters J was favoured in *Hardman v Chief Constable of Avon and Somerset Constabulary*[15] where it was held that pavement drawings in water soluble paint constituted damage to the pavement where the local authority was involved in expense in removing them with high-pressure water jets. This seems entirely right. No one would maintain that property which has been daubed by slogans or drawings was not damaged simply because the elements would eventually remove all trace of them or because the householder could remove them more quickly with soap and water. *Samuels v Stubbs* is, perhaps, a less clear case. If an article is accidentally trodden upon (and for the purpose of determining whether there has been damage it can make no difference that it is intentionally trodden upon) and the owner finds that it takes a matter of moments to press it back into shape, surely he would say that no harm had been done. In *"A" (a juvenile) v R*[16] it was held that spitting on a policeman's raincoat did not damage the raincoat where the spittle could be removed by a wipe with a damp cloth. No doubt it would have been otherwise had the material been capable of being stained by the spittle.[17]

While it may be difficult to lay down "any very general and, at the same time, precise and absolute rule as to what constitutes 'damage'", it is submitted that it goes too far, as some of the cases suggest,[18] to say that it is a matter of fact and degree to be determined by the trier of fact in a commonsense way. Once the facts have been determined and the degree of harm ascertained, it is submitted that it is then a question of law whether damage has been established. It is here pertinent to keep in mind, as did Walters J in *Samuels v Stubbs*,[19] the difference between fact and law. Counsel for the defendant argued that the finding "of fact" of the trial court ought not to be disturbed, only to be met with the withering reply

14. [1972] 4 SASR 200 at 203.
15. [1986] Crim LR 330 (Judge Llewellyn Jones & Justices).
16. [1978] Crim LR 689 (Judge Streeter & Justices).
17. But would the policeman have been unduly fastidious to insist that even a rainproofed material should be dry-cleaned after it had been spat upon?
18. *Roe v Kingerlee* [1986] Crim LR 735, DC; *Henderson and Battley*, unreported but approved in *Cox v Riley* (1986) 83 Cr App Rep 54, DC.
19. [1972] 4 SASR 200 at 201.

that not only was it the practice of Australian courts to distinguish between the determination of the evidence (a matter of fact) and the determination of the inferences to be drawn from those facts (a matter of law) but that this view was based on respected English authorities. In particular it had not escaped Lord Dunedin's notice that "there must be a discrimination as to what is the class of evidence being dealt with; whether the result arrived at depends on the view taken of conflicting testimony, or depends upon the inferences to be drawn from the fact as to which there [can be] no controversy."[20] This point is likely to be lost on English courts given their present predilection for regarding the interpretation of "ordinary" words (and "damage" is about as ordinary a word as is to be found) as a matter of fact. It is nevertheless firmly asserted here that it cannot be right for "damage" to be given one meaning in Berkeley Square and another meaning in Bermondsey.

How D regards his conduct is irrelevant if damage is caused in fact. P's painting may be damaged by D's additions though D regards them as improvements.[1]

"Destroy" clearly goes beyond damage and does not contemplate half measures. To destroy, of structures means to pull down or demolish, of crops or growing things to lay waste, of machines to break up, and of animals to deprive of life.[2]

2) *Property*

S. 10 (1) of the Criminal Damage Act provides:
"In this Act 'property' means property of a tangible nature, whether real or personal, including money and –
a) including wild creatures which have been tamed or are ordinarily kept in captivity, and any other wild creatures or their carcases if, but only if, they have been reduced into possession which has not been lost or abandoned or are in the course of being reduced into possession; but
b) not including mushrooms growing wild on any land or flowers, fruit or foliage of a plant growing wild on any land.
For the purposes of this subsection 'mushroom' includes any fungus and 'plant' includes any shrub or tree."

The exceptions in paragraphs (a) and (b) are of course to keep the law of damage to property in line with the law of theft.[3] But while there is a substantial measure of correspondence in the definitions of property for theft and damage, there are two significant differences.

In the first place land, which in general cannot be stolen, may be the subject of criminal damage. The policies which favour exempting land

---

20. *Dominion Trust Co v New York Life Insurance Co* [1919] AC 254 at 257.
   1. Nor is D's motive (e.g. painting fig leaves over parts he considers indelicate) relevant. Cp. *Fancy* [1980] Crim LR 171.
   2. Cf. *Barnet London Borough Council v Eastern Electricity Board* [1973] 2 All ER 319.
   3. But note that the destruction of, or damage to, wild animals and plants may be an offence under other legislation; see for example the Wildlife and Countryside Act 1981 and the Badgers Act 1973, as amended by the Wildlife and Countryside (Amendment) Act 1985.

from the offence of stealing[4] do not apply to the offences of damaging property. The distinction also has the support of history, for while land has always been excepted from definitions of stealing there has never been any such limitation in offences of damage to property. It is, then, still the law that while D cannot steal his neighbour's croquet lawn by annexing it, he may commit criminal damage by turning it over to vegetable marrows.

Secondly, while intangible property has now been brought within the subject matter of theft, it is still excluded from the definition of property for the purposes of criminal damage. "Offences of criminal damage to property," said the Law Commission,

"in the context of the present law connote physical damage in their commission, and for that reason we have not included intangible things in the class of property, damage to which should constitute an offence."[5]

Consequently such intangible property as easements and profits, patents and copyright, are excluded for the purposes of criminal damage.[6]

In *Cox v Riley*[7] it was held that D was guilty of criminal damage where he erased the programme from a plastic circuit card which operated a saw to cut wood to programmed designs. D's counsel "gallantly" argued that the programme was not "property of a tangible nature" within s. 10 (1) of the Act. In this he was no doubt right but his argument failed to take account of the fact that D was charged not with the erasure of the programme but with damaging the plastic card. The card had been rendered useless by the erasure of the signals it formerly contained. The court was of course aware of the increasing use of programmed discs, tapes and cards (not least the bank card used to withdraw money from a machine) but this was no mere policy decision. The disc had been fashioned to perform a certain function, as a key is fashioned to open a door or start an engine, and D had damaged the card by making it unfit for that use.[8]

3) *Belonging to Another*

The offence under s. 1 (1) may be committed only where D destroys or damages property "belonging to another". Here again the policy of the law of criminal damage, which must be to protect interests in addition to ownership, is very much the same as that for the law of theft. Consequently s. 5 of the Theft Act[9] has a substantially similar counterpart in s. 10 of the Criminal Damage Act which provides:

"2) Property shall be treated for the purposes of this Act as belonging to any person –

4. See above, p. 506.
5. Law Com. No. 29, para. 34.
6. Cf. *Laws v Eltringham* (1881) 8 QBD 283. D and others had been charged with damaging Newcastle Town Moor by playing bowls upon it. It was held that the property could not be laid in the freemen who had merely the (incorporeal) right of herbage; the property ought to have been laid in Newcastle Corporation as the freeholder.
7. (1986) 83 Cr App Rep 54, DC.
8. No doubt a battery would be damaged, destroyed rather, by exhausting its charge if it is an unrechargeable battery. The battery may look the same to the eye but it is of course clapped out.
9. See above, pp. 509–525.

      a) having the custody or control of it;

      b) having in it any proprietary right or interest (not being an equitable interest arising only from an agreement to transfer or grant an interest); or

      c) having a charge on it.

    3) Where property is subject to a trust, the person to whom it belongs shall be so treated as including any person having a right to enforce the trust.

    4) Property of a corporation sole shall be so treated as belonging to the corporation notwithstanding a vacancy in the corporation."

It is, then, enough that P has some proprietary interest in the property which D damages, and it does not have to be shown that P is the owner of the property; D may, for example, damage property of which P is the lessee or bailee. Further, D may commit an offence where the property belongs to him provided that P also has a proprietary interest in the property. In such cases it may be difficult to prove that D acted with *mens rea* or without lawful excuse,[10] but, given that, D may commit criminal damage though he both owns and possesses the property. Just as a co-owner of property may steal it by appropriating the other's share,[11] a co-owner may commit criminal damage by destroying or damaging the property.

But P must have some *proprietary* right or interest in the property.[12] Where property is insured the insurer acquires an interest in the property, but the interest is not a proprietary one.[13] If D destroys his own property which he has insured with P, he does not destroy property belonging to another even though he may have destroyed it with a view to making a dishonest claim against P.[14]

Property is also treated as belonging to a person who has a charge on it. This expression does not, in terms, appear in s. 5 of the Theft Act and was included in the Criminal Damage Act because the Law Commission thought

    "it should be made clear that a person who has a charge on property should be regarded as having a sufficient interest in the property to entitle him to the protection of the criminal law for damage done to it by the owner who subjected it to the charge."[15]

But it is not clear in what circumstances the creation of a charge, whether legal or equitable and whether on real or personal property, would not create a proprietary right or interest.

It will be noted that the definition of property belonging to another in the Criminal Damage Act, s. 10, contains no provision equivalent to s. 5 (4) of the Theft Act – property got by another's mistake. This distinction can be of no practical importance; the getting of property by another's mistake

---

10. See below, p. 687.
11. *Bonner* [1970] 2 All ER 97n, [1970] 1 WLR 838; above, p. 509.
12. See above pp. 509–525.
13. An insurer has an interest in the *safety* of the insured property but, without more, this does not constitute a proprietary interest. Cf. *Lucena v Crauford* (1806) 2 Bos & P NR 269, HL, per Lawrence J at 302.
14. Cf. *Denton* [1982] 1 All ER 65, [1981] 1 WLR 1446, CA, below, p. 689.
15. Law Com. No. 29, para. 39.

may well excite acquisitive instincts but it is unlikely to excite an outburst of vandalism.

Where D is the owner of property in which no other person has any proprietary right or interest, his destroying or damaging it cannot amount to an offence under s. 1 (1). Nor generally is it an offence to damage one's own property apart from the special case dealt with in s. 1 (2).[16] It is no offence for D to destroy a work of art which he owns, or to lay waste his plentiful stocks of food at a time of acute shortage. Such acts may be properly described as wanton but they are not criminal because there is at present no case for making them criminal. But where such a case does exist, and cruelty to animals provides an illustration, particular offences can be created which extend to harm by an owner to his own property.[17]

4) *Mens Rea*

Section 1 (1) requires that the destruction or damaging of the property should be intentional or reckless, and without lawful excuse.

1 Intention and Recklessness

"In the area of serious crime," said the Law Commission,

"the elements of intention, knowledge or recklessness have always been required as a basis of liability ... We consider, therefore, that the same elements as are required at present should be retained, but that they should be expressed with greater simplicity and clarity. In particular, we prefer to avoid the use of such a word as 'maliciously',[18] if only because it gives the impression that the mental element differs from that which is imposed in other offences requiring traditional *mens rea*. It is evident that from such cases as *R v Cunningham*[19] and *R v Mowatt*[20] that the word can give rise to difficulties of interpretation. Furthermore, the word 'maliciously' conveys the impression that some ill-will is required against the person whose property is damaged."[1]

By "traditional *mens rea*" it is clear that the Law Commission meant to convey that liability for damage was predicated upon conduct of D which was intended by D to cause the damage in question or was foreseen by D as creating a risk of causing that damage.

This view certainly governs *intentional* damage. It is not enough that D intended to do the act which caused the damage unless he intended to cause the damage; proof that D intended to throw a stone is not proof that he intended to break a window.[2] Nor is it enough that D intends to damage

---

16. Below, p. 696.
17. Protection of Animals Act 1911, s. 1.
18. "Maliciously" was the expression most commonly used in the Malicious Damage Act 1861 to describe *mens rea*.
19. [1957] 2 QB 396, [1957] 2 All ER 412; **SHC 63**, above, p. 62.
20. [1968] 1 QB 421, [1967] 3 All ER 47; **SHC 64**, above, p. 400.
  1. Law Com. No. 29, para. 44.
  2. Cf. *Pembliton* (1874) LR 2 CCR 119; **SHC 81**.

property if he does not intend to damage property *of another*. Since D commits no offence under s. 1 (1) of the Act in damaging or destroying his own property, it follows in principle that he ought to be guilty of no offence where he destroys P's property under the mistaken impression that it is his own. Whether D's mistake is one of fact or law he commits no crime for he lacks *mens rea*, and this view was firmly endorsed by the Court of Appeal in *Smith*.[3] Upon the termination of his tenancy of a flat D had caused £130 worth of damage in removing wiring which he had himself installed and boarded over. In law the landlord became the owner of the wiring and boarding as fixtures, and the trial judge directed the jury that D could have no lawful excuse since he had in law no right to do as he did. D's appeal against conviction was allowed. James LJ said on behalf of the court:[4]

> "Applying the ordinary principles of *mens rea*, the intention and reck-lessness and the absence of lawful excuse required to constitute the offence have reference to property belonging to another. It follows that in our judgment no offence is committed under this section if a person destroys or causes damage to property belonging to another if he does so in the honest though mistaken belief that the property is his own, and provided that the belief is honestly held it is irrelevant to consider whether or not it is a justifiable belief."

The mistake in *Smith* appears to have been a mistake as to the civil law; D knew all the facts and drew the wrong conclusion of law from them. The result is the same so far as criminal liability is concerned whether the mistake is one of fact or law so long as the mistake negatives *mens rea*.[5] Consequently D commits no offence in pulling down a house if he honestly believes the house is his whether his mistake is one of fact or law and however egregious his error may have been.[6]

Nor can it make any difference in destroying or damaging what is, or what he believes to be, his own property, that D's conduct might be described as wanton (as where he destroys a work of art) or that the property is destroyed for the purposes of a crime of fraud (as where property is destroyed to defraud insurers). If D does not intend to destroy or damage property of *another*, nothing can render him liable to a charge under s. 1 (1). In *Appleyard*[7] where D, the managing director of a company, set fire to the company's premises, it was argued that he could not be convicted of arson since he was "in effect" the owner of the premises. D's conviction for arson was upheld apparently on the basis that he was not the owner of the premises and knew that he was not. Had D believed that he owned the company's premises then he could not have been convicted whatever his motive (to defraud insurers or creditors, to inflict loss on the shareholders) may have been.

---

3. [1974] QB 354, [1974] 1 All ER 632; **SHC 534**.
4. [1974] 1 All ER 632 at 636.
5. See generally above, p. 207.
6. Cf. *Langford* (1842) Car & M 602.
7. (1985) 81 Cr App Rep 319, [1985] Crim LR 723 CA.

The Act extends liability not merely to damage which is caused intentionally but also damage which is caused recklessly. That recklessness in this context was meant to connote foresight of consequences is apparent from the Law Commission's Report. This is reinforced by the Law Commission's proposed definition of recklessness[8] which, as Lord Edmund Davies pointed out,[9] was surely in the draftsman's mind when he drafted the Criminal Damage Act.

But this was not the view taken in *Caldwell*.[10] There D had formed a grievance against P, the proprietor of a residential hotel, and, having got very drunk, decided to revenge himself by setting fire to the hotel though, fortunately, the fire was discovered and extinguished before serious harm was done.[11]

Caldwell establishes that D is reckless for the purposes of s. 1 (1) of the Act (damage to property) and for the purposes of s. 1 (2) of the Act (endangering life by damaging property)[12] if his conduct (1) creates an obvious and serious risk of damage to property (or of endangering life by damaging property); and (2) he either (a) gives no thought to the possibility of there being any such risk, or (b) recognising that there is such a risk (unjustifiably) goes on to take it.

For the purposes of establishing liability under 2 (a), the cases of *Elliott v C*[13] and *Stephen Malcolm*,[14] loyally following *Caldwell*, show that whether there is an obvious and serious risk of damaging property (or endangering life thereby) is to be determined by what a reasonable man would have appreciated; it matters not that D was incapable of appreciating the risk, and in applying the test of what is reasonably foreseeable the reasonable man is not to be notionally invested with characteristics of D, such as immaturity or exhaustion or mental incapacity, as might affect his ability to appreciate the risk. The test is thus entirely[15] objective.

Where D adverts to the issue of risk his liability is to be determined under 2 (b). Having adverted to the risk of damage to property it would seem that D might either (i) decide upon reflection that there is no risk; or (ii) decide to take the risk.

Case (ii) appears to present no problems. D has chosen to accept the risk and must take the consequences. Two points may, however, be made. The first is that in formulating the proposition contained in 2 (b) above, Lord Diplock omitted the bracketed word "unjustifiably". This seems to have been an oversight. It can hardly be supposed, for example, that a police officer pursuing escaping gunmen would be guilty of criminal damage to

---

8. "A person is reckless if, (a) knowing that there is a risk that an event may result from his conduct or that circumstances may exist, he takes that risk, and (b) it is unreasonable for him to take it, having regard to the degree and nature of the risk he knows to be present": Working Paper No. 31, *The Mental Element in Crime*. See now Law Com. No. 89, *Report on the Mental Element in Crime*.

9. *Caldwell* [1981] 1 All ER 961 at 969, HL.

10. [1981] 1 All ER 961; **SHC 68**.

11. The case is discussed extensively above, p. 61 et seq.

12. For the sake of completeness the same definition of recklessness applies to damage by fire (arson) under s. 1 (3). Cf. *Hardie* [1984] 3 All ER 848 at 851, CA.

13. [1983] 2 All ER 1005, [1983] 1 WLR 939 DC; **SHC 73**.

14. (1984) 79 Cr App Rep 334, CA; **SHC 76**.

15. Some possible exceptions are canvassed above, p. 64.

their car because he realised that in using his car to force them to a halt there was a risk of the collision which did in fact result.[16] The second is that D may be convicted if he realises that his conduct involves *a* risk of damage to property. Thus in *Chief Constable of Avon and Somerset Constabulary v Shimmen*[17] where D, while demonstrating his skills in Korean arts, put his foot through a shop window, it was held that his belief that he had eliminated as much risk as possible showed that he realised that there was still some risk and he could accordingly be convicted of criminal damage. No doubt the smallness of a risk may be a factor, along with others, in determining whether it is justifiable to take that risk; but, and in the absence of other factors, it is not acceptable to take *any* risk of breaking another's window.

Case (i) is more problematic. Literally it falls outside the propositions which Lord Diplock formulated in *Caldwell* and in *Shimmen* the court said it might well be arguable that a lacuna exists. If this is so then, assuming that the conduct of A and B creates the same obvious and serious risk of damaging property, A is liable if he gives no thought to there being any such risk, but B is not liable if, having adverted to the issue of risk, he decided there is none.[18]

A further issue that needs to be mentioned is the effect of intoxication in relation to offences of criminal damage. It appears that an allegation under subsection (1) or (2) of an intention to cause damage or, under subsection (2) of an intention to endanger life, is an allegation of a specific intent;[19] whereas, if intention *or* recklessness, or only recklessness,[20] is alleged under either subsection, the offence is one of basic intent.

The wide interpretation of recklessness reduces the significance of the distinction by diminishing the number of occasions on which intoxication may negative it; but it may still be important. D claims that, because he was drunk, he was firmly convinced that the property he damaged was his own, not P's. He is not *Caldwell*-reckless: but, if recklessness is alleged and is a basic intent, he is guilty.[1]

It needs to be stressed at this point perhaps that negligence which will ground civil liability will not suffice to support a charge of criminal damage. Where the charge is brought under s. 1 (1) the risk of damage must be "obvious". While it is clear that the defendant may be liable though it was

---

16. Nor could it make any difference that the officer gave no thought to there being any such risk though a reasonable person would have perceived the risk as serious and obvious. The justification for risk-taking is assessed independently of what D thought or did not think.
17. (1986) 84 Cr App Rep 7, [1986] Crim LR 800, DC.
18. See further above, p. 65.
19. Cf. *Caldwell* [1981] 1 All ER 961 at 967, per Lord Diplock. Lord Edmund-Davies's opinion (p. 972) was that all arson under subsection (2) is an offence of specific intent but he thought that the prediction of Professor Glanville Williams (TBCL, 431) "that *all* crimes of recklessness except murder will now be held to be crimes of basic intent ..." had been promptly fulfilled by the decision of the majority. And murder is no longer an exception.
20. Where the prosecution relies on intention and recklessness in the alternative, these should be embodied in different counts of the indictment: *Hardie* [1984] 3 All ER 848, [1985] 1 WLR 64, CA.
1. The same principles govern if the offences are charged as arson. The view expressed in *O'Driscoll* (1977) 65 Cr App Rep 50, CA, that the offence under s. 1 (2) was not a crime of basic intent must now be read subject to *Caldwell*.

not "obvious" to him, it is equally clear that a risk is not obvious merely because it is foreseeable and would result in civil liability.

It would appear that the doctrine of transferred malice[2] applies, so that if D intends, or is reckless as to, damage to property of A he may be liable where he in fact causes damage, neither intentionally nor recklessly caused by him, to property of B.

"The intention or the recklessness need not be related to the particular property damaged, provided that it is related to another's property. If, for example, a person throws a stone at a passing motor car intending to damage it, but misses and breaks a shop window, he will have the necessary intention in respect of the damage to the window as he intended to damage the property of another. But if in a fit of anger he throws a stone at his own car he will not have the requisite intention. In the latter case the question of whether he has committed an offence will depend upon whether he was reckless as to whether any property belonging to another would be destroyed or damaged."[3]

Williams suggests[4] that transferred malice would not apply where D, bent on damaging property other than by fire, accidentally starts a fire in circumstances where there is no obvious and serious risk of fire. This, with respect, seems an acceptable conclusion. Arson is a separate offence carrying a higher punishment than damage caused by other means and its *mens rea* requires not merely the intentional or reckless damaging of property but the intentional or reckless damaging of property *by fire*. A fortiori, D would not commit an offence of criminal damage where he throws a stone at P but misses him and breaks a window, unless of course D was reckless as to the risk of breaking the window.[5]

Obviously *mens rea* cannot be supplied by an afterthought. If D inadvertently breaks P's window he cannot become liable when, having learned that P is a tax inspector, he rejoices in the harm caused. On the other hand, if D inadvertently sets fire to P's property and subsequently becomes aware[6] that he has done so, he may be criminally liable if, intending or being reckless that *further* damage ensue to P's property, he lets the fire take its course when it lies within his power to prevent or minimise that further damage.[7]

2 Lawful Excuse

The Law Commission took the view that in most cases

"there is a clear distinction between the mental element and the element of unlawfulness, and in the absence of one or other element no offence will be committed, notwithstanding that damage may have been done to another's property. For example, a police officer who, in order to execute a warrant of arrest, has to force open a door of a house is acting with

2. See above, p. 73.
3. Law Com. No. 29, para. 45.
4. (1983) 42 CLJ 85, 86.
5. Cf. *Pembliton* (1874) LR 2 CCR 119.
6. It is not enough that D ought to have been aware, or was not aware because he gave no thought to it: *Miller*, next note.
7. *Miller* [1983] 2 AC 161, [1983] 1 All ER 978, HL. See above, p. 53.

lawful excuse although he intends to damage the door or the lock. On the other hand a person playing tennis on a properly fenced court who inadvertently hits a ball on to a greenhouse roof, breaking a pane of glass, acts without lawful excuse, but will escape liability because he has not the requisite intention."[8]

This distinction drawn by the Law Commission between the "mental element" and the element of "unlawfulness" may be a distinction of convenience but it is a distinction generally adopted in this work because it is convenient to consider separately, so far as the situation admits, the issue of intention or recklessness as to the damaging of the property, and the various grounds of exculpation or justification that may exist for damage deliberately done.

Under the former law it was not always clear in what circumstances it was justifiable to damage or destroy the property of another. Strictly the Criminal Damage Act 1971 is to be interpreted without reference to the earlier law, but it is of course impossible to legislate, as it were, in a vacuum; and there is always a risk that policies implicit in the earlier law will continue to flourish unless new policies are clearly articulated. Consequently s. 5 of the Act provides a partial definition of "lawful excuse" which contains the new policies and makes a clean break with the earlier law. The section in part provides –

"2) A person charged with an offence to which this section applies[9] shall, whether or not he would be treated for those purposes of this Act as having a lawful excuse apart from this subsection, be treated for those purposes as having a lawful excuse –

a) if at the time of the act or acts alleged to constitute the offence he believed that the person or persons whom he believed to be entitled to consent to the destruction of or damage to the property in question had so consented, or would have consented to it if he or they had known of the destruction or damage and its circumstances; or

b) if he destroyed or damaged or threatened to destroy or damage the property in question . . . in order to protect property belonging to himself or another or a right or interest in property which was or which he believed to be vested in himself or another, and at the time of the act or acts alleged to constitute the offence he believed –

i) that the property, right or interest was in immediate need of protection; and

ii) that the means of protection adopted or proposed to be adopted were or would be reasonable having regard to all the circumstances.

3) For the purpose of this section it is immaterial whether a belief is justified or not if it is honestly held.

4) For the purposes of subsection (2) above a right or interest in property includes any right or privilege in or over land, whether created by grant, licence or otherwise."

8. Law Com. No. 29, para. 49.
9. The section applies to an offence under s. 1 (1); as to other offences see below.

a) *Belief in consent.* Section 5 (2) (a) here very much follows the pattern of s. 2 (1) (b) of the Theft Act 1968,[10] and it is obviously right that it should since the parallel between theft and criminal damage is at this point exact. As appears to be the case with theft, D's belief is judged by the single criterion that it be honestly held; a point which, if it is not clear enough from the wording of s. 5 (2) (a), is put beyond doubt by s. 5 (3).

Most obviously this provision covers the case where D believes that the owner has consented to the destruction or damage, or would have consented if asked. So in *Denton*[11] it was held that D was not guilty of arson in setting fire to his employer's mill where D believed that his employer had encouraged him to do so in order to make a fraudulent claim against the insurers. The provision also covers the case where D believes that P is a person entitled to consent to the destruction or damage who has consented or would have consented if asked. Thus, for example, an employee destroying or damaging property belonging to the firm would commit no offence where he believed that some person in authority (say a foreman) was entitled to consent, and had consented or would have consented if asked.[12] The provision would also cover the case where D comes across an injured animal and, believing that the owner would have consented had he been able to contact him, D kills the animal to put it out of its misery.

b) *Defence of property.* A man is of course entitled to take measures to protect his own property, real or personal, from harm caused by, or by the use of, property belonging to another whether animate (such as trespassing cattle) or inanimate (such as a caravan). If, for example, P without permission erects a hut on D's lawn, D commits no offence in dismantling and removing the hut though some incidental damage is caused to the structure of the hut. But suppose that D, an unusually irascible owner, were to throw the hut into the sea.[13] On the face of it this is unreasonable but the Act makes it clear that D's criminal liability turns upon whether he believed his lawn was in need of immediate protection *and* whether he believed the means adopted were reasonable in the circumstances. Again the question is not whether D's beliefs were justifiable but whether they were honestly entertained by him.

Theoretically this means that D, given he is acting honestly, would incur no criminal liability in taking the most extravagant measures against the property of another in defence of his own. D might, for example, incur no criminal liability in laying waste an oil refinery because he believes that effluent from the refinery is damaging his geraniums. Cases where D can honestly claim to act so extravagantly will of course be extremely rare, but cases where D can honestly claim to act unreasonably can be expected to occur. In this connection it is important to note that D must honestly believe that the measures taken by him "were . . . reasonable having regard to all the circumstances". This does not mean that D's belief should have been reasonable as well as honest, still less does it mean that D's conduct

10. See above, p. 527.
11. [1982] 1 All ER 65, [1981] 1 WLR 1446, CA.
12. Cf. *James* (1837) 8 C & P 131.
13. Cf. *Clemens* [1898] 1 QB 556, DC.

must meet some objective requirement of reasonableness, but it does mean that D must have believed that it was reasonable for him to do as he did. It is not enough that D believed he was morally entitled to do as he did, or that he was honestly pursuing some political objective,[14] or that he did it in desperation, if he did not also believe that what he did was reasonable for the purpose of protecting his property.[15] It would surely be permissible to ask D whether he feels that other people similarly circumstanced would have reacted in the way that he did.[16]

While this defence may be available even where D acts extravagantly, it can only be available where D acts "in order to protect property". So where in *Hunt*[17] D, the deputy warden of a block of flats for old people, set fire to some bedding in order, as he claimed, to call attention to the defective state of the fire alarm, this defence was properly withdrawn from the jury. On his own admission D set fire to the bedding not to protect the alarm, nor to protect any other property, but merely to call attention to its defective state. Whether D acts to protect property involves ascertaining what his purpose is; it is not enough that property is in fact protected if D did not have it in mind to protect that property when he acted. D's purpose in this sense must be subjectively determined. But once his purpose is determined it is for the court to rule whether it constitutes a purpose of protecting property. This seems to have been the view taken in *Hunt*. There was no doubt what D's purpose was because he admitted what it was. It was then for the court to rule whether it would be a purpose of protecting property, and it was rightly ruled that it was not.

D must also believe that the property is in "immediate" need of protection. Again D commits no offence so long as he believes that immediate action is called for even though the sensible course would have been to defer action. Where P has without permission parked his car on D's premises and it is causing neither actual damage nor inconvenience, the sensible course may be to await P's return; but if D honestly believes its immediate removal is needed, he would commit no offence provided of course that he also believed that such damage as was caused in the removal was reasonable in the circumstances. Where the offending property, such as a parked car, is causing neither actual damage nor any inconvenience, this would be a factor in testing D's belief that immediate action was needed but it would not of itself deprive D of the benefit of the section.

A common case calling for action in protection of property is where a dog is worrying livestock; so common that, in relation to questions of *civil* liability, it is specifically dealt with in the Animals Act 1971. Clearly D would commit no offence in killing a dog which is worrying his sheep if he honestly believes that this is a reasonable measure in the circumstances.

14. Cf. *Phillips v Pringle* [1973] 1 NSWLR 275 (CCA of New South Wales), action pursuant to U.N. resolutions against racialism not a lawful excuse for damaging goal posts.
15. Cf. *Taylor v Mucklow* [1973] Crim LR 750, DC, when the court said, upholding D's conviction for having a firearm without reasonable excuse contrary to Firearms Act 1968, s. 19, "For anyone to argue nowadays that a loaded firearm was a suitable way of restraining the kind of bad temper exhibited by the builder [who was knocking down an extension built to D's house] was to show a lack of appreciation of modern trends and dangers."
16. Cf. the offence of blackmail, above, p. 590.
17. (1977) 66 Cr. App Rep 105, [1977] Crim LR 740, CA, and commentary.

The Animals Act, s. 9 (3) (a), provides that D incurs no civil liability in just this situation provided that D is a person entitled to act for the protection of the livestock and that he gives notice within 48 hours to the officer in charge of a police station of the killing or injury. But s. 9 (3) (b) then goes on to provide that D also incurs no civil liability for the killing of the dog where

"the dog *has been*[18] worrying livestock, has not left the vicinity and is not under the control of any person and there are no practicable means of ascertaining to whom it belongs."

In such a case D's sheep might not be strictly in "immediate" need of protection and the killing might be essentially a prophylactic measure. But it would be odd if D was criminally liable where he may be exempted from civil liability; it would involve D having to incriminate himself in order to take advantage of the civil defence. It is submitted that in these circumstances D would commit no criminal offence.[19]

D may not destroy or damage property of another because he honestly believes that harm may occur to his property at some time in the future. On the other hand it is not in general and as such unlawful for D to take defensive measures in relation to his own property.[20] It is an offence under s. 31 of the Offences against the Person Act 1861 to set traps so as to endanger life, and it is an offence under s. 1 (2) of the Criminal Damage Act 1971 to destroy or damage property in order to endanger life,[1] but it is not otherwise an offence merely to take defensive measures (to set broken glass on walls, erect spiked fences etc.) for the purpose of discouraging or preventing incursions by persons or their property. In such cases the question of criminal liability can arise only where some harm is caused to the person or property of another. So far as harm to another's property is concerned,[2] D will ordinarily have taken his defensive or protective measures at some stage before his property was in "immediate need of protection", and when the harm occurs D may be absent and unaware of it. It is submitted that where what D has done is a normal method of protecting property, say a barbed wire fence erected by a farmer, he would not be liable though a trespasser tears his best suit in climbing through the fence, and notwithstanding that D himself could not have justified ripping open the trespasser's suit as a use of reasonable force to eject him. But where D adopts unusual defensive measures, say traps calculated to maim animals, it would normally not be difficult to show that he did not honestly believe this was a reasonable way to protect his property.

A measure frequently adopted for the protection of property is the keeping of a guard dog. The Animals Act 1971 provides that a person is not civilly liable for damage caused if the animal is kept for the protection of persons or property and "keeping it there for that purpose was not unreasonable."[3] The Act also provides that no liability is incurred to any

---

18. Italics supplied.
19. See the discussion of *Workman v Cowper*, below, p. 695.
20. Above, p. 246.
1. Below, p. 696.
2. Harm to the person is dealt with above, pp. 240 and 382.
3. Section 5 (3) (b).

person who has "voluntarily accepted the risk thereof."[4] The Guard Dogs
Act 1975 now makes it a summary offence, punishable by a fine of £400, to
use or permit the use of a guard dog (i.e. a dog kept for the purpose of
protecting persons or property or a person guarding the same)[5] unless a
person capable of controlling the dog, the handler, is present and controlling it, except where the dog is secured and not at liberty to go about the
premises.[6] But it is further provided that the Act shall not be construed as
conferring any civil right of action, or as derogating from any remedy
(whether civil or criminal) in proceedings instituted otherwise than by
virtue of the Act.[7]

In *Cummings v Grainger*,[8] a civil action, it was held by the Court of
Appeal that it was not unreasonable for an owner to keep an unsecured
alsatian guard dog on enclosed business premises, and that he was not liable
to a trespasser who entered the premises at night having seen the notice
"Beware of the dog" on the gate. The attention of the court was drawn to
the provisions of the Guard Dogs Act but Lord Denning MR concluded
that they did not affect civil liability and so far as reasonableness was
concerned they had no application. If these facts were to recur the owner
would now commit an offence under the Guard Dogs Act in permitting the
use of an uncontrolled guard dog, but the question remains whether he
would be liable for an offence against the person or, if property is damaged,
under the Criminal Damage Act. So far as the latter is concerned the issue
is whether the owner believed that the keeping of an uncontrolled guard
dog was reasonable having regard to all the circumstances. In *Cummings v
Grainger* the Court of Appeal was firmly of the view that the keeping of an
uncontrolled guard dog was not, in the circumstances of that case,
unreasonable; and conduct is not necessarily unreasonable even though it
involves a breach of the criminal law.[9] No doubt in determining whether D
thought the measure was reasonable regard would be had to D's knowledge
of the risk of accidental as opposed to deliberate trespass, of the risk to
children not capable of looking properly to their own protection, of the
propensities of the particular dog and similar factors. What is important is
that at this point the civil and criminal laws should not set different
standards.

In most cases no doubt D will be the owner of the property which he
seeks to protect, but even if D is not the owner he will not incur criminal
liability if he honestly believes himself to be the owner and the other
circumstances exist. By s. 5 (4) property is expressly defined to include any
right or privilege in or over land. Consequently D may commit no crime
where, honestly but mistakenly believing he has a right of way across P's
land, he tears down a hut erected by P which, as D thinks, obstructs his
imagined right of way.

---

4. Section 5 (2).
5. Section 7.
6. Section 1. *Hobson v Gledhill* [1978] 1 All ER 945, [1978] 1 WLR 215, DC.
7. Section 5 (2).
8. [1977] QB 397, [1976] 1 All ER 104.
9. Cf. *Buckoke v Greater London Council* [1971] 1 Ch 655, [1971] 2 All ER 254; above, p. 225.

Moreover, D is in the same position though the right or interest which he believes himself to have in the property which he protects is not a right or interest which is recognised by law since, by s. 5 (3), it is immaterial whether a belief is justified or not so long as it is honestly held. Suppose, for example, that D has a right to kill and take game on O's land, and D kills P's dog which he sees chasing and destroying game. In such a case there is in law no right or interest in property to protect; until D himself reduces the game into his possession he has no proprietary interest in it whatever. But if D believes he has a right or interest in the game, he would incur no criminal liability in killing P's dog provided the other circumstances exist.[10] In such a case as this D's belief that he has a right in property to protect is understandable, but even if D's belief is absurd it is good for this purpose if honestly held.

The position is essentially the same where D claims no right or interest in the property which he protects, but acts to protect the property of another. An employee who caused damage to P's property in defending property belonging to his employer would commit no offence given his belief that the measures were reasonable and were immediately needed. But there need be no nexus whatever between the person intervening to protect the property and the owner of it. An officious bystander who chooses to intervene to protect the property of another will be free from criminal liability if he acts honestly in the same terms.

c) *Cases not falling within the Act.* By its terms s. 5 (2) recognises that there may be other circumstances which would constitute lawful excuse on a charge of criminal damage, and s. 5 (5) further provides:

"This section shall not be construed as casting any doubt on any defence recognised by law as a defence to criminal charges."

It is clear that certain general defences (such as infancy, insanity, duress) are available on a charge of criminal damage and these are discussed elsewhere in this work.[11] But some particular matters call for further discussion here.

d) *Self-defence and necessity.* So far as necessity is concerned the law relating to defence of property is a particular, and well defined, instance where necessity is recognised as a defence, as in the case with defence of the person. The question remains as to how far it is permissible to destroy or damage property on the grounds of necessity in circumstances not involving defence of property. As a starting point it must be obvious that just as harm to the person may be justified on the grounds of self defence of the person, so too the destruction of or damage to property may be justified in defence of the person.[12]

In so far as the attack involves the commission of a crime, as will be commonly the case, the situation would be covered by s. 3 of the Criminal

10. On the facts of *Gott v Measures* [1948] 1 KB 234, [1947] 2 All ER 609, DC, D would now be acquitted.
11. Ch. 9. As to drunkenness, see *O'Driscoll* (1977) 65 Cr App Rep 50, CA, above, p. 686, and *Caldwell* [1981] 1 All ER 961, HL.
12. So if D lawfully repelling an attack by E causes E to fall through F's window, D cannot be convicted of criminal damage to F's window: *Sears v Broome* [1986] Crim LR 461, DC.

Law Act 1967,[13] which provides that a person may use such force as is reasonable in the circumstances in the prevention of crime. If, then, P sets his dog to attack D, D would not commit an offence of criminal damage if in using reasonable force to defend himself he killed the dog. But s. 3 does appear to import an objective requirement of reasonableness,[14] and D could not rely upon this section where the force used is unreasonable even though D himself honestly believed it was reasonable. Thus there appears to be the odd situation that if D is defending his property it is enough that he honestly believed that the force used was reasonable, but if he is defending his person his honest belief will not save him unless the force used was in fact reasonable in the circumstances.[15]

Now suppose that P's dog, quite unknown to P, chances to attack D. Here s. 3 of the Criminal Law Act can have no application since D is not seeking to prevent the commission of any crime. If D kills the dog, is the test that he must have honestly believed this was reasonable or must it have been reasonable in the circumstances? Perhaps at this level of refinement the answer can be of relevance only to the academic, but the discussion shows, not only that there are loose ends as between the law relating to defence of the person and the law relating to defence of property, but there is a significant difference in that the former is mainly objective while the latter is largely subjective. The difference was seen by the Law Commission which observed:

"We appreciate that our extended definition of lawful excuse introduces a less stringently framed defence than that of self-defence, where the force used must be reasonable when looked at objectively. There may therefore be the anomaly that different tests will apply to self-defence against bodily injury, but we do not think that this is sufficient reason to dissuade us from the present recommendation in this context."[16]

Outside the particular context of defence of the person or property it is not easy to envisage realistic cases in which necessity might be raised as a defence to a charge of criminal damage. Traditionally it has been held that it is permissible to pull down a house in order to prevent the spread of fire but, should such necessity now arise,[17] the case would no doubt be treated as one of defence of property. *Hunt*[18] suggests a possible case. D might have been genuinely concerned with the risk to the old people in the event of a fire breaking out and his setting fire to the bedding in order to get the alarm repaired, though drastic, might not be seen as entirely unmeritorious. But since no necessity as yet existed D would remain liable and his good motive would not excuse. It would be different if a fire broke out and he damaged property to enable the occupants to escape, but in such a case there would

---

13. See above, p. 242.
14. See above, p. 242.
15. Perhaps, then, D should say that he feared for the safety of his trousers rather than his ankles.
16. Law Com. No. 29, para. 52.
17. In given circumstances drastic action could be justified, e.g. the destruction by bombing of a wrecked oil tanker lying within British waters where there is an imminent threat of damage by oil spillage; again a case of protecting property.
18. [1977] Crim LR 740. The facts are set out above, p. 690.

normally be a belief that the owner would have consented and the case is expressly covered by the Act.

e) *Claim of right*. It is clear that D cannot commit an offence under s. 1 (1) of the Act in destroying or damaging property which is, or which is believed to be, his own. The position would appear to be the same where D, though he does not believe he is the owner of the property which he destroys or damages, nevertheless acts under a claim of legal right. In *Twose*,[19] a case decided under the old law, where it appeared that persons living near a common had occasionally burnt the furze in order to improve the growth of the grass, it was accepted that D's belief in a right to burn the furze would be a good defence though there was no such right. Here D's belief was at least understandable, but in *Day*,[20] again under the old law, it was held that D was not guilty of an offence in maiming sheep belonging to P which he had distrained where he did so in the honest belief that he was entitled to do so upon P's refusal to pay compensation for damage done by the sheep. It would seem clear that cases such as these would be decided in the same way under the Criminal Damage Act where the clear emphasis is upon honest belief in right without any objective qualification.

In similar vein it is thought that a person who destroys or damages property found by him in circumstances where he believes the owner cannot be traced by taking reasonable steps can no more be convicted of criminal damage than he can be of theft by appropriating the property.

f) *Other cases*. While the foregoing discussion deals with the more obvious categories of lawful excuse for damage to property there are certainly other cases. Moreover "lawful excuse", like "lawful authority or reasonable excuse,"[1] may have an inbuilt elasticity which enables courts to stretch it to cover new situations so that it is never possible to close the categories that might constitute lawful excuse.

Clear cases arise where there is statutory authority for the destruction or damage.[2] The more general problem is set by the sort of facts that occurred in *Workman v Cowper*.[3] D had shot a foxhound, the owner of which was unknown at the time of the shooting, and which was running wild on common land. There was no evidence that the dog was attacking, or likely to attack, sheep, but it was the lambing season and D thought it best, attempts to catch the dog having failed, to shoot it. On such facts as these D might now bring himself within the terms of s. 5 if he honestly believed that the owner would have consented, or if he had honestly believed that his sheep were in need of immediate protection. But since owners of healthy

---

19. (1879) 14 Cox CC 327.
20. (1844) 8 JP 186.
   1. See above, p. 425.
   2. For example, statutory provisions for the destruction of dangerous, diseased or injured animals (Halsbury's Statutes, Vol. 2, *tit*. Animals); damage to property incidental to arrest, search and seizure (Police and Criminal Evidence Act 1984); where property is lawfully seized under statutory powers it would seem that in certain cases (firearms, offensive weapons, drugs) the police would have lawful excuse for destroying the property although the statute may not give an express power to destroy.
   3. [1961] 2 QB 143, [1961] 1 All ER 683, DC.

and expensive foxhounds do not readily consent to their destruction and there was no evidence that the dog was going to attack sheep, it may be assumed that D could not bring his conduct within s. 5. Nor was there anything to suggest that the dog had been abandoned so that D could claim that he did not intend to destroy property belonging to another. On the other hand, D could no doubt claim that he was acting honestly and that what he did was reasonable as a prophylactic measure – the dog, after all, might start attacking sheep. It is interesting to note that in the case itself the magistrates thought that D had acted reasonably and the Divisional Court had some sympathy for their conclusion. D was in fact convicted and it is thought that on similar facts he could still be convicted. Although there may be many who think that what D did was reasonable, even prudent, D was not acting in defence of property and it seems a necessary inference from s. 5 (2) (b) that unless his property is in immediate need of protection (or D honestly believes that it is) there can be no lawful excuse. But if D manages to catch the dog there is a procedure available authorising its destruction within seven days of capture if efforts to trace the owner fail.[4] There is, in effect, a loophole in lawful excuse through which an agile, friendly and healthy dog may avoid a premature death.

2 Destroying or Damaging Property with Intent to Endanger Life

S. 1 (2) of the Criminal Damage Act 1971 provides –
   "A person who without lawful excuse destroys or damages any property, whether belonging to himself or another –
   a) intending to destroy or damage any property or being reckless as to whether any property would be destroyed or damaged; and
   b) intending by the destruction or damage to endanger the life of another or being reckless as to whether the life of another would be thereby endangered.
   shall be guilty of an offence."
By s. 4 the offence is punishable by imprisonment for life.

This offence has no obviously traceable parents in the former law,[5] and it may be that it exhibits the hybrid features that are supposed to mark out those of doubtful stock. The Law Commission said of this new offence;
   "This proposed offence gives effect to our view that the policy of the criminal law is, and should continue to be, to select certain offences as attracting exceptionally high maximum penalties, because those offences are accompanied by aggravating factors. There are examples of this

---

4. Dogs Act 1906, s. 3.
   5. A possible ancestor is the offence of setting traps so as to endanger life under s. 31 of the Offences against the Person Act 1861, above, p. 691, but this need not and usually would not, involve damage to property. The Law Commission itself referred to s. 2 of the Explosives Substances Act 1883 (causing an explosion likely to endanger life or cause serious injury to property), and s. 16 of the Firearms Act 1968 (possession of firearm with intent to endanger life or cause serious injury to property); but damaging property is not the gist of either offence.

approach in section 8–10 of the Theft Act 1968 dealing with robbery, burglary and aggravated burglary, which may be regarded as theft accompanied by aggravating circumstances . . . We think that the proper criterion should be related to the endangering of life, a concept which appears in section 2 of the Explosive Substances Act 1883 and in section 16 of the Firearms Act 1968. It is not, therefore, a novel one likely to give rise to difficulties of interpretation, and we think that it correctly expresses the necessary seriousness. It is true that in adopting the criterion of endangering life there may still be some overlapping with offences against the person. It may be that when the Criminal Law Revision Committee completes its review of the law of offences against the person it will be necessary to look again at this matter."[6]

So the offence has features both of an offence against property and an offence against the person. In some circumstances (as where D severs the brake cable of P's car intending P to drive to his death) the offence will overlap with the offence of attempted murder, but it is wider than attempted murder in two respects. One is that it does not require the intent to kill which is necessary on a charge of attempted murder:[7] intention or recklessness as to the endangering of life will suffice. On facts such as those occurring in *Cunningham*,[8] for example, it could well be that when D severed the gas pipe he did not intend to asphyxiate P but was reckless whether her life would be endangered; he would not be guilty of attempted murder but he would be guilty of the offence under the Criminal Damage Act.[9] The other is that the offence under the Criminal Damage Act may be committed where the acts done by D are too remote to constitute an attempt[10] to murder. If, for example, D were to sever the brake cable of O's car intending thereafter to induce P to drive the car to his death, D's act of damaging the car might be too remote to support a charge of attempting to murder P but it would support a charge under the Act.

But even though the offence under s. 1 (2) of the Criminal Damage Act is in some respects wider than attempted murder it is difficult to see how, as a practical matter, these differences would amount to much. Moreover, attempted murder is in one respect wider than the offence under the Act in that it extends to all acts of attempt and it is not confined to acts involving damage to property.

Certain general features of the offence under s. 1 (2), (such as destruction or damage, property, intention and recklessness) are the same as for the offence under s. 1 (1) which has already been discussed. The following additional matters need to be discussed in relation to the offence under s. 1 (2).

---

6. Law Com. No. 29, paras. 21 and 27.
7. See above, p. 287.
8. [1957] 2 QB 396, [1957] 2 All ER 412, above, p. 62.
9. And also, of course, of the offence under s. 23 of the Offences against the Person Act 1861. It might be noted in passing that the toxic elements are now removed from gas used for domestic purposes and natural gas does not contain them; hence domestic gas can cause death only by asphyxiation, and even this risk is almost nil. But there remains a very high risk of explosion which is a serious danger to life.
10. See above, p. 291.

1 Intention and Recklessness

Intention and recklessness in relation to destroying or damaging property has been discussed above.[11] What is said there applies, *mutatis mutandis*, to intention and recklessness in relation to endangering the life of another,[12] and reference may also be made to the general discussion of intention and recklessness elsewhere in this book.[13] But in this particular it should be noted that there must be a causal connection between the destroying or damaging of the property and the endangering of life. If, to extend an example used above, D were to damage the lock in the process of entering P's garage in order to sever the brake cable of P's car, there would be no offence under s. 1 (2). D intends to damage the lock and he further intends to endanger P's life, but he does not intend "by the destruction or damage to endanger the life of" P. It is only when D damages the brake cable that he would commit the offence under s. 1 (2). So in *Steer*[14] it was held that the offence was not committed where D loosed off some shots at P and his wife as they stood at their bedroom window. While the shooting clearly endangered the lives of P and his wife and also caused damage by smashing the bedroom window, it was not *by* the damage to the window that their lives were endangered. On the other hand, it may be that if, having destroyed or damaged property belonging to P (e.g. having set fire to P's premises), D subsequently realises that P's life is in danger, D would commit the offence under s. 1 (2) if, provided it lies within D's power to prevent or minimise the further harm, he then intended that, or was reckless whether, P's life should be endangered.[15]

2 Lawful Excuse

Since the gist of the offence under s. 1 (2) lies in endangering life by destroying or damaging property, it is understandable that D may commit the offence whether he creates a risk to life by destroying or damaging the property of another or by destroying or damaging his own. The risk is just the same whether D severs the brake cable on P's car, or severs the brake cable on his own car before lending it to P to drive.

It is equally understandable that the partial definition of lawful excuse in s. 5 (2) should not be applicable to an offence of this nature, and s. 5 does not apply to offences under s. 1 (2). It can be appreciated that it ought not to be a defence to an offence of this nature that, say, D, with the assent of E, severed the brake cable on E's car before lending it to P to drive. Equally, D ought to have no lawful excuse in damaging property, although done for the purpose of protecting other property, where in so doing he knowingly creates a risk to life.

Clearly, then, the intention in framing the offence under s. 1 (2) was that certain matters (such as destruction by D of his own property, destruction

---

11. At p. 683.
12. *Hardie* [1984] 3 All ER 848, [1985] 1 WLR 64, CA.
13. Above, pp. 55–68.
14. [1987] 2 All ER 833, [1987] 3 WLR 205, HL.
15. *Miller* [1983] 1 All ER 978, HL, above, p. 53. Cf. *Fuller* [1974] Crim LR 134, CA. D pleaded guilty to damaging property being reckless whether life would be endangered though warned by his brother of danger arising from fractured gas pipe only after he had returned home. Appeal was against sentence only.

with owner's consent, destruction in defence of property) which constitute
lawful excuse where D is charged with an offence under s. 1 (1) do not
constitute lawful excuse where D is charged under s. 1 (2). This does not
mean that in no circumstances can there be a lawful excuse where D is
charged under s. 1 (2), because s. 1 (2) expressly states that the offence may
be committed only by one "who *without lawful excuse* destroys or damages
any property". It follows that there may be circumstances, presumably of
an exceptional character, where D would have lawful excuse for destroying
or damaging property even though he does it realising that he may
endanger life. An exceptional case of this character would be where D
damages property in self defence; if it is legitimate for D to kill in order to
prevent himself being killed, D would not commit an offence under s. 1 (2)
because he happened to use, and damage, property belonging to another in
killing his attacker.[16] Similarly, the police might have lawful excuse for
damaging property where this was done to prevent the commission of a
serious crime against the person, even though what was done might
endanger the life of the criminal. And if necessity is a defence where D
chooses to put one life at risk in order to save many others,[17] it would
extend to damaging property to do so.

3 Arson

The Law Commission took the view that there should be no separate
offence of arson, that is, of destroying or damaging property by fire,[18] and
simply provided in the Draft Bill that an offence committed under s. 1 (1)
by fire should be punishable on indictment by imprisonment for life. In so
far as arsonists may be frequently mentally unbalanced and in so far as fire-
raising creates extra hazardous risks, this seemed a sensible way to meet the
case and avoided complication of the substantive law. But this way of
meeting the case proved unacceptable to Parliament,[19] and s. 1 (3) of the
Act provides –

"An offence committed under this section by destroying or damaging
property by fire shall be charged as arson."

The provision is a mandatory one – "*shall* be charged as arson" – and where
D destroys or damages property by fire the proper course would appear to
be to charge him with an offence under s. 1 (1) and (3), or an offence under
s. 1 (2) and (3) as appropriate.[20]

The general features of arson are the same as for the offences under s. 1
(1) and s. 1 (2) except that the destruction or damage be by fire. For the

16. Cf. *Sears v Broome* [1986] Crim LR 461, DC, above, p. 693.
17. See above, p. 222.
18. Law Com. No. 29, paras. 28–33.
19. See H.C., Vol. 817, col. 1433 et seq. The reasons given for singling out damage by fire
would be equally applicable to singling out damage by explosives; that "arson" is such a
splendidly evocative term cannot have been unimportant in securing its retention.
20. Where D is charged under s. 1 (2) and (3) there should be separate counts of arson with
intent to endanger life and of arson being reckless that life is endangered so that in relation to
sentencing the court has the verdict of the jury: *Hoof* (1980) 72 Cr App Rep 126, CA.

offence to be complete some property must be destroyed or damaged by fire. The damage may of course be quite insignificant (it would be enough, for example, that wood is charred[1]) but there must be some damage by fire; it would not be enough that property is merely blackened by smoke though there might well be an attempt in such a case. Presumably D must intend, or be reckless as to, destruction or damage by fire; any other view would be out of keeping with the tenor of the offences under s. 1. D would not, therefore, be guilty of arson where he intends to destroy or damage property by explosion even though the explosion causes a conflagration and D ought reasonably to have foreseen that it would.

4 Threats to Destroy or Damage Property

Section 2 of the Criminal Damage Act 1971 provides –
   "A person who without lawful excuse makes to another a threat, intending that that other would fear it would be carried out –
   a) to destroy or damage any property belonging to that other or a third person; or
   b) to destroy or damage his own property in a way which he knows is likely to endanger the life of that other or a third person; shall be guilty of an offence."
The offence is punishable by ten years' imprisonment: s. 4 (2).

1 The Conduct Threatened

In order to constitute an offence under this section the conduct threatened must be conduct which would be an offence under s. 1 of the Act. D would commit the offence, therefore, where, without lawful excuse, he threatened to destroy or damage the property of another (whether property of the person threatened or of a third party), or where he threatened to destroy or damage his own property in a way which he knows is likely to endanger the life of another (whether the life of the person threatened or the life of a third party).

If D is charged under s. 2 (a) "lawful excuse" has the meaning ascribed to it by s. 5 so that D would not commit an offence where, for example, he threatens to shoot P's dog should he find it marauding his sheep.[2] But by s. 5 (1) the partial definition of lawful excuse in the section does not apply to an offence
   "involving a threat by the person charged to destroy or damage property in a way which he knows is likely to endanger the life of another. ...."
This does not mean that there cannot be a lawful excuse for an offence under s. 2 (b), merely that the partial definition of lawful excuse in s. 5 cannot apply.[3] Where D threatens to destroy property of another with intent to endanger life he would have to be charged under s. 2 (a), and

---

1. Cf. *Parker* (1839) 9 C & P 45.
2. See generally above, p. 690.
3. As to what may therefore constitute a lawful excuse, see above, p. 699.

cannot be charged under s. 2 (b). Curiously, it would seem that if D is in such a case charged under s. 2 (a) there would be a lawful excuse if it appeared that he believed the owner would have consented to the threatened destruction or damage (s. 5 (2) (a)), but if he is charged under s. 2 (b) it would not be a lawful excuse that he was threatening to destroy his own property. But the distinction can be of small practical importance; if D threatens to destroy P's property in order to endanger the life of Q then it would be difficult to show that D honestly believed that P would have consented to the threatened destruction "had [P] known of the destruction or damage *and its circumstances*".[4]

2 The Threat

The threat may take any form. The Law Commission said:

"There seems to be no good ground, for limiting threats to written threats, for a telephonic threat, particularly if repeated, can cause more alarm in the recipient than any written threat. If the law is to be extended to cover telephonic threats, then logically there is no reason why it should not be extended to all threats, however made. The only limitation that needs to be imposed is that the threats should be intended to create a fear that what is threatened will be carried out."[5]

This last limitation needs to be imposed because the gist of the offence is the threat and, given that D intends that P should believe that the threat will be carried out, there ought to be no requirement that D himself should have intended to carry his threat into effect. And if D intends that P would fear the threat would be carried out, D commits the offence notwithstanding that P knows the threat to be an idle one or is not intimidated by it. It would seem that the threat need not be a threat to do the damage immediately, but immediacy may be a relevant factor, along with other circumstances, in determining whether there is something that can be called a threat.

5 Possession Offences

By s. 3 of the Act –

"A person who has anything in his custody or under his control intending without lawful excuse to use it or cause or permit another to use it –
a) to destroy or damage any property belonging to some other person; or
b) to destroy or damage his own or the user's property in a way which he knows is likely to endanger the life of some other person;
shall be guilty of an offence."

The offence is punishable by imprisonment for ten years: s. 4 (2).

In line with the offence of threatening under s. 2, the possession of the thing must be for the purpose of committing an offence under s. 1 of the

4. Section 5 (2) (a), italics supplied.
5. Law Com. No. 29, para. 55.

Act. There is of course no need for the commission of an offence of destruction or damage, but there must be an intent to use the thing, or allow another to use it, for the purpose of committing what would be an offence under s. 1.[6] Accordingly the same provisions apply, mutatis mutandis, in relation to lawful excuse as apply to charges under s. 2.[7]

1 Custody or Control

Although it is convenient to talk of this offence as one of possession, the section speaks only of custody or control.

"Having regard to the difficulties inherent in the concept of possession, we prefer the idea of custody or control. These words are both to be found in the Statute Book, and together provide a better concept than 'possession', which is a technical term of some difficulty."[8]

It may well have been a wise decision to eschew the term "possession", but what really helps to simplify the situation is the clear requirement for *mens rea*.

As the Law Commission observe:

"Problems which may arise where a substance, such as a stick of gelignite, is slipped into a person's pocket without his knowledge will be wholly academic, because if that person has no knowledge of its presence he cannot have an intention to use it or permit or cause another to use it. If he has no intention to use it or permit or cause it to be used, he does not commit an offence. . . ."[9]

But there must be custody or control; a mere intention to use something to commit an offence of criminal damage will not suffice. D may be about to pick up stones from the highway to throw through a shop window, but since at this stage he does not have custody or control of the stones he commits no offence under this provision. D need not of course be the owner of the thing in order to have custody or control of it, but he must have the charge of it. Where D is charged with permitting E to use the thing D must be in a position where, as against E, he might properly have prevented E from using it.

2 The Things Used

The section imports no limitation on the things which may be possessed with intent to commit criminal damage – "anything" may do for the purpose.

"The essential feature of the proposed offence is to be found not so much in the nature of the thing – for almost any every-day article, from a box of matches to a hammer or nail, can be used to destroy or damage property – as in the intention with which it is held."

Clearly the nature of the thing may have significance in proving that D possessed the thing with intent to commit criminal damage (the possession of a box of matches may be one thing and the possession of a ton of

---

6. *Fancy* [1980] Crim LR 171.
7. Above, p. 687.
8. Law Com. No. 29, para. 59.
9. Ibid.

dynamite quite another) but given that the intent can be proved the nature of the thing is immaterial.

At this point it may be noted that under s. 6 of the Act a search warrant may be issued to a constable where it appears there is reasonable cause to believe that a person has anything in his control or custody or on his premises for the purpose of committing an offence under s. 1. This power of search was explained by the Law Commission[10] as being parallel to the power to search for stolen goods under s. 26 of the Theft Act 1968. On one view the power of search is a wide one since it extends to anything, but it is always limited by the requirement that there must be reasonable cause to believe that the thing has been used or is intended for use in committing an offence of criminal damage.

3 Mens Rea

The offence may be committed only where D intends to use, or cause or permit another to use, the thing to destroy or damage property. It is not enough that D realises that the thing may be so used: he must intend or permit such use. But it is not necessary that D should intend an immediate use of the thing; the offence is aimed at proscribing what is essentially a preparatory act and it is therefore enough that D possesses with the necessary intent even though he contemplates actual use of the thing at some time in the future. And it would also seem to be clear that a conditional intent (an intention to use the thing to cause damage should it prove necessary) will suffice.[11]

6 Kindred Offences

In keeping with the aim of codification[12] the Criminal Damage Act 1971 contains, as near as may be, the whole of the law relating to damage to property. The Act accordingly abolishes the common law offence of arson, repeals most of the provisions of the Malicious Damage Act 1861, repeals the Dockyards Protection Act 1772, and a large number of statutory provisions containing miscellaneous offences of damage to property.

But the Criminal Damage Act leaves untouched the Explosive Substances Act 1883. The Law Commission had at first planned to repeal s. 2 (causing an explosion likely to endanger life or to cause serious injury to property) and s. 3 (possessing explosives with intent to endanger life or cause serious injury to property, and doing any act to cause an explosion likely to endanger life or cause serious injury to property) since these might easily have been brought within the scheme of the Criminal Damage Act. But in the end the Law Commission did not do this because it was felt that the Explosive Substances Act belonged to the area of public order offences, and its replacement should be considered in the context of a review of

10. Law Com. No. 29, Appendix A, notes to clause 6.
11. *Buckingham* (1976) 63 Cr App Rep 159, CA; cf. *Bentham* [1973] QB 357, [1972] 3 All ER 271, CA.
12. See above, p. 677.

offences relating to public order. This means that on given facts there may be an offence both under the Criminal Damage Act and the Explosive Substances Act, and it should be noted that there are differences in relation to the *mens rea* that has to be established.

The Criminal Damage Act does not repeal the following provisions of the Malicious Damage Act 1861: s. 35 (placing wood etc. on rail lines or obstructing signals with intent to obstruct or overturn any engine); s. 36 (obstructing railway engines); s. 47 (exhibiting false signals with intent to endanger any ship); s. 48 (concealing or removing buoys provided for the guidance of shipping): and the retention of these offences has made necessary the further retention of general provisions of the Malicious Damage Act relating to malice (s. 58) and jurisdiction (s. 72). It will be seen that none of these offences would necessarily (or even ordinarily) involve damage to property, though the ultimate aim may be to cause damage to property. Frequently such acts might amount to an attempt to commit criminal damage, but in so far as the acts might be merely preparatory these provisions render the preparatory acts criminal.

Nor does the Act repeal offences of damage arising under other legislation where the liability for the damage may be grounded in negligence or where there is strict liability for the damage. In particular cases there may be thought valid policy reasons for imposing criminal liability for damage to property caused negligently,[13] or even for imposing strict liability for offences of damage to property.[14] These offences are perhaps best considered in relation to a review of criminal liability for negligence and a review of strict liability.

7 Miscellaneous Matters

While the maximum punishments provided by the Act for offences of damage tried on indictment (broadly, ten years for the simple offence, and life imprisonment for aggravated offences) may seem high, this was done merely to provide for the worst sort of case within each class and it was not intended in any way to alter present sentencing practice. The Act provides for summary trial of offences under s. 1 (1), s. 2 and s. 3, and in practice most offences will be so tried.[15] There used to be a complex rule relating to the ouster of the jurisdiction of magistrates in cases of damage involving title to real property, but this rule has now been abolished. In addition, all courts are empowered by s. 35 of the Powers of Criminal Courts Act 1973 (as amended by the Criminal Law 1977, s. 60) to make a compensation order (a magistrates' court may not award more than £1,000 on any one order) for loss of, or damage to, property.

13. E.g., s. 59 (c) of the Post Office Act 1953 punishes "carelessness, negligence or other misconduct" which may lead to injury to a postal packet.
14. An e.g. may be s. 60 of the Post Office Act 1953 – Placing dangerous substances against a letter box etc. "likely to injure the box".
15. As to summary trial of offences of damage when the value does not exceed £400, see above, p. 29. As to offences of damage triable either way see the Magistrates' Courts Act 1980, Sch 2.

18 Offences against Public Morals

1 Bigamy

Bigamy was originally only an ecclesiastical offence but it was declared to be a capital felony by statute in 1603.[1] Now, by s. 57 of the Offences against the Person Act 1861,[2] it is an offence triable either way[3] and punishable with seven years' imprisonment. The offence is committed by:

"Whosoever, being married, shall marry any other person during the life of the former husband or wife, whether the second marriage shall have taken place in England or Ireland or elsewhere ..."

The section goes on, however, to provide that it does not extend to:

1) "any second marriage contracted elsewhere than in England and Ireland by any other than a subject of Her Majesty"; or
2) "to any person marrying a second time, whose husband or wife shall have been continually absent from such person for the space of seven years then last past and shall not have been known by such person to be living within that time"; or
3) "any person who, at the time of such second marriage, shall have been divorced from the bond of the first marriage"; or
4) "any person whose former marriage shall have been declared void by the sentence of any court of competent jurisdiction."

1) *"Being Married"*

Obviously a person who is unmarried is incapable of committing bigamy[4] and the prosecution must prove that D was validly married at the time of the second ceremony. For most purposes a marriage may be presumed from evidence that the parties co-habited with the reputation of being husband and wife; but according to a dictum of Lord Mansfield in *Morris v Miller*,[5] a case of criminal conversation, this is not sufficient on a charge of bigamy:

"Perhaps there need not be strict proof from the register or by a person present, but strong evidence must be had of the fact: as by a person

1. 1 Jac. 1, c. 11.
2. Re-enacting, with minor modifications, s. 22 of the Offences against the Person Act 1828 which repealed the Act of 1603.
3. Criminal Law Act 1977, s. 16 and Sch. 3, para. 5 (i).
4. Cf. above, p. 132.
5. (1767) 1 Wm Bl 632.

present at the wedding dinner, if the register be burnt and the parson and clerk are dead."

There must be evidence of the celebration of the marriage and of the identity of the parties; but it is sufficient to call a witness who was present and can describe the ceremony and identify the parties, without any proof of the registration of the marriage or of any licence or publication of banns.[6] The formal validity of the marriage will be presumed, for omnia praesumuntur rite esse acta. Thus, where the building in which the marriage was celebrated has been habitually used for divine service, the prosecution need not prove that it was licensed unless D introduces credible evidence that it was not.[7]

Where there is cohabitation and repute, it is almost inevitable that D will have acknowledged that W is his wife;[8] and it has been held[9] that the production of a certificate of marriage coupled with an acknowledgment is sufficient evidence of the first marriage. Since 1914 the injured spouse has been a competent, but not compellable witness for the prosecution on a bigamy charge;[10] and, where she is willing to give evidence, the problem of proof of the first marriage is obviously greatly simplified.

If evidence is introduced suggesting that the first marriage is invalid, then the better view is that the onus is on the prosecution to establish its validity beyond any reasonable doubt.[11]

Evidence that one of the parties to the first marriage had, before that marriage, cohabited with a third party with the reputation of being husband and wife, is sufficient to establish a *defence*[12] on the ground of the invalidity of the first marriage.[13]

In the light of these principles the decision in *Naguib*[14] seems a harsh one. D, an Egyptian by birth, being charged with marrying C in the lifetime of B, gave evidence that, before "marrying" B, he had married A in Egypt according to the rites and ceremonies of that country. Where the prosecution relies on a foreign marriage, it must prove the requirements of the foreign law. The Court held that it followed that there was a similar onus on D with regard to his marriage with A. Although D may have described the ceremony, he had no expert knowledge of Egyptian law and there was no evidence that the ceremony was valid. It is, however, surely fallacious to equate the duties of the prosecution and defence in this respect. The prosecution must prove the first marriage alleged in the indictment beyond reasonable doubt. If the defence can establish a

6. *Allison and Wilkinson* (1806) Russ & Ry 109; *Manwaring* (1856) 7 Cox CC 192.
7. *Cresswell* (1876) 1 QBD 446, CCR.
8. The acknowledgment is admissible *against* D; but it was not, of course, admissible *in favour* of the plaintiff in an action for criminal conversation: East, 1 PC 471.
9. *Birtles* (1911) 6 Cr App Rep 177; cf. *Umanski* [1961] VLR 242.
10. Criminal Justice Administration Act 1914, s. 28 (3). See now PACE 1984, s. 80.
11. *Willshire* (1881) 6 QBD 366, CCR; *Morrison* [1938] 3 All ER 787, CCA and *Kay* (1887) 16 Cox CC 292. *Thomson* (1905) 70 JP 6 and *Kircaldy* (1929) 167 LT Jo 46 seem to go the other way. *Shaw* (1943) 60 TLR 344, CCA is inconclusive, as D introduced no evidence of invalidity. See *Naguib*, infra, Williams, CLGP, 906 and Cross, *Evidence* (5th ed.), 147, n. 1.
12. Contrast the case where the prosecution are relying on similar evidence; above, pp. 705–706.
13. *Wilson* (1862) 3 F & F 119.
14. [1917] 1 KB 359.

reasonable doubt whether there was a prior valid marriage, the prosecution case is not made out; and surely the description of the earlier ceremony should be evidence from which a jury might feel such a doubt. It is, of course, easy for a defendant who has lived abroad to go into the witness box and say he was married already and correspondingly difficult for the prosecution to rebut this; but that is not a good reason for upholding a conviction where there are real doubts about D's guilt.

1 Void and Voidable Marriages

A marriage which is defective is either void or voidable. The expression "a void marriage" is a contradiction in terms; but it is a convenient way of describing the situation where the parties have gone through a ceremony of marriage which is utterly ineffective in law, so that they have never acquired the status of husband and wife. In such a case, therefore, neither party is "married" for the purposes of s. 57 of the Offences against the Person Act 1861 and, without going through any formality, either may proceed to a second ceremony with impunity. The most obvious example of a void marriage is where, at the time of the marriage, one of the parties is already married to a third party. A marriage celebrated after July 31, 1971, may also be void on the ground (i) that the parties are within the prohibited degrees of relationship; (ii) that either party is under sixteen; (iii) that the parties have intermarried in disregard of certain requirements as to the formation of marriage; (iv) that the parties are not respectively male and female; or (v) that it was a polygamous marriage entered into abroad and when one of the parties was domiciled in England.[15] A marriage celebrated before August 1, 1971, might be void on any of the above grounds or on the further ground that there was a lack of true consent arising from a mistake of identity, or as to the nature of the ceremony, or from duress or unsoundness of mind. Such lack of consent now makes the marriage voidable.[16] In cases of this kind it is essential to determine whether the marriage took place before or after August 1, 1971.

A voidable marriage is entirely different. It is a valid marriage and the parties are husband and wife until a decree is pronounced by the court.[17]

The fact that a marriage is *voidable* is, therefore, irrelevant for the purposes of the law of bigamy[18] and the grounds on which a marriage may be voidable require no consideration here.[19] Where a voidable marriage has actually been *avoided* by a decree of nullity, however, an entirely different situation arises, which is considered below.

The first marriage need not have been celebrated in England.[20] Even before 1828, when it was probably necessary, even in the case of British subjects, that the second marriage should be within the jurisdiction, this was so; for it is the second marriage alone which constitutes the offence.[1]

---

15. Matrimonial Causes Act 1973, s. 11.
16. Ibid., s. 12.
17. *Algar* [1954] 1 QB 279, [1953] 2 All ER 1381 at 1384, per Lord Goddard CJ.
18. Co 3 Inst 88.
19. See Bromley, *Family Law* (7th ed.), 82 et seq.
20. Hale, 2 PC 692; East, 1 PC 465; *Topping* (1856) 7 Cox CC 103 (both marriages in Scotland).
1. East, loc. cit.

2 A Polygamous First Marriage

It seems now to be settled that "the marriage which is to be a foundation for bigamy must be a monogamous marriage."[2]

A marriage which is potentially polygamous when celebrated may change its character, for example, through legislation or through a change of domicile, and become monogamous.[3] In that event the formerly polygamous marriage becomes a foundation for bigamy. If D marries again, after the marriage has changed its character and while his wife is still alive, he commits bigamy. It was so held in *Sagoo*[4] where D, having contracted a potentially polygamous marriage while domiciled in Kenya, went through a ceremony of marriage in England after Kenyan legislation had converted his marriage into a monogamous one. A person domiciled in England lacks capacity to contract a polygamous marriage,[5] and a marriage contracted by a person domiciled elsewhere will be converted into a monogamous marriage if that person acquires an English domicile.[6] A person may, however, reside in England, though domiciled abroad and so continue to be a party to a potentially polygamous marriage. That marriage, so long as it subsists, invalidates any subsequent ceremony in England.[7] The effect seems to be that such a person may go through any number of ceremonies of marriage without committing bigamy.[8]

3 Subsistence of the First Marriage

It is necessary to prove not only that the first marriage was validly celebrated but that it was subsisting at the time of the second ceremony. In effect, this means that it must be proved that the wife was alive at that time, for the prosecution do not have to prove that there has been no decree of divorce or nullity unless some evidence of such a decree is first tendered by the defence.

If there is direct evidence that the first spouse was alive at the time of the second ceremony, there is no problem. Difficulty may arise where there is evidence only that she was alive at some time before the second ceremony. It is then a question of fact for the jury taking into account all the

2. *Sarwan Singh* [1962] 3 All ER 612 at 615 (T. R. Fitzwalter Butler), approved in *Sagoo* [1975] QB 885, [1975] 2 All ER 926 at 929, CA. See also *Harvey v Farnie* (1880) 6 PD 35 at 53, per Lush LJ (on appeal (1882) 8 App Cas 43); *Naguib* [1917] 1 KB 359 at 360, per Avory J. The Criminal Code Commissioners (Lord Blackburn and Barry, Lush and Stephen JJ), pointing out that in half a century no attempt had been made to apply the Act to such cases as that of a Hindu with two wives, presumed that the reason was that "'marriage' in these statutes means the union of one man with one woman to the exclusion of all others, as is well expressed by Lord Penzance in *Hyde v Hyde and Woodmansee*". While it is true that the attitude of English law to polygamous marriages has changed since *Hyde v Hyde*, it is legitimate to construe the 1861 Act in the light of the law as it was then believed to be.
3. Dicey and Morris, *Conflict of Laws* (11th ed.) 653–657.
4. Above, footnote 2.
5. Matrimonial Causes Act 1973, s. 11 (d).
6. Dicey and Morris, loc. cit.
7. *Baindail v Baindail* [1946] P 122, [1946] 1 All ER 342, CA.
8. Andrews, "A Licence for Bigamy" [1963] Crim LR 261; Polonsky, "Polygamous Marriage, A Bigamist's Charter", [1971] Crim LR 401. Dicey and Morris, 669, rely on *Naguib* (above, p. 706) for the proposition that D commits bigamy if he goes through two monogamous ceremonies in England. It is difficult to see how this can be so if the polygamous ceremony is proved (as it was not in *Naguib*) since it then invalidates the first monogamous ceremony.

circumstances of the case whether they are satisfied beyond reasonable doubt that she was alive at the crucial time.[9] There is no presumption of law that life continues for any time; but if the wife were proved to be alive and in good health only an hour, or a day beforehand, the jury could hardly fail to be so satisfied, in the absence of any evidence to the contrary. If she has not been heard of for say, two years, the result of the jury's assessment of the probabilities would be less predictable.

2) *The Second Ceremony*

The second "marriage" in bigamy is, in the nature of things, void; and it is immaterial that there are other grounds for voidness in addition to its bigamous nature:

> "It is the appearing to contract a second marriage and the going through the ceremony which constitutes the crime of bigamy, otherwise it could never exist in the ordinary cases."[10]

So where D, being married, went through a ceremony of marriage with his niece, he was guilty notwithstanding his lack of capacity to contract such a marriage.[11] The words, "shall marry another person", were taken to mean "shall go through the form and ceremony of marriage with another person"; but:

> ". . . in thus holding it is not at all necessary to say that forms of marriage unknown to the law, as was the case in *Burt v Burt*,[12] would suffice to bring a case within the operation of the statute. We must not be understood to mean that every fantastic form of marriage to which parties might think proper to resort,[13] or that a marriage ceremony performed by an unauthorised person, or in an unauthorised place would be a marrying within the meaning of the 57th section . . ."

It must be "a form of marriage known to and recognised by the law[14] as capable of producing a valid marriage." Thus, a polygamous form of marriage celebrated in England without a civil ceremony would appear to be insufficient.[15]

It is probably no defence that the law of D's domicile permits polygamy if, having married in England,[16] he goes through a second ceremony in

---

9. *Lumley* (1869) LR 1 CCR 196.

10. *Brawn* (1843) 1 Car & Kir 144, per Lord Denman (D "married" deceased sister's widower in lifetime of her own husband).

11. *Allen* (1872) LR 1 CCR 367, followed in *Robinson* [1938] 1 All ER 301.

12. (1860) 2 Sw & Tr 88; where D married a woman in Australia according to the form of the kirk of Scotland, but there was no proof that the form in question was recognised as legal by the local law.

13. Consider the pretended marriage ceremony in *Kemp and Else* [1964] 2 QB 341, [1964] 1 All ER 649; below, p. 718; and *Ali Mohammed* [1964] 2 QB 350 n, [1964] 1 All ER 653 n (2).

14. Presumably, the law of the place where it is celebrated: *Burt v Burt*, above, footnote 12.

15. Dicey and Morris, *Conflict of Laws* (11th ed.), 657 and Illustrations, p. 659. Cf. *Bham*, below, p. 718 and *A-G of Ceylon v Reid* [1965] AC 720, [1965] 1 All ER 812 where D, domiciled and resident in Ceylon, contracted a Christian marriage and later, having embraced the Muslim faith, went through a second Muslim ceremony. He was held not guilty of bigamy under the Ceylon Penal Code; the second marriage was valid by the law of Ceylon.

16. Or, presumably, anywhere else, provided that it is a valid monogamous marriage.

England in a form recognised by English law. Thus in *Naguib*,[17] D, an Egyptian by birth and a Mohammedan by religion, went through two ceremonies of marriage in England and was convicted, the court apparently not considering it relevant to inquire where he was domiciled.

Is a polygamous form of marriage a sufficient second ceremony if it is valid by the law of the place where it is celebrated and D's domicile? D, a British citizen, marries in England, returns to the colony where he is domiciled, and marries a second wife according to a polygamous form recognised by the law of the colony. If a polygamous form of marriage is enough, D is clearly guilty of bigamy; yet it seems that the English civil courts would recognise the second marriage as valid.[18] It would be preposterous that a marriage should be regarded as valid in one English court and an offence in another. On the other hand, if a polygamous ceremony will not found an indictment for bigamy, it must follow that D, domiciled in England, may marry there and then with impunity proceed to go through a polygamous ceremony in a country where that is recognised as a valid form of marriage. But why should this be regarded as criminal in England? A polygamous ceremony is not "the solemn ceremony" which it was the object of the legislators of 1603 and 1861 to protect from prostitution.[19]

It is submitted that the most convenient and consistent course would be to regard polygamous forms of marriage as irrelevant for the law of bigamy, wherever they be celebrated. This view seems to be supported both by that of the Criminal Code Commissioners[20] and by the general attitude of the law to polygamous ceremonies at the time of the enactment of the 1861 Act and its predecessors.[1]

1 Proviso (1): The Place of the Second Marriage

The second marriage, in the case of a British subject who is a British citizen,[2] may take place anywhere[3] in the world.[4] A British subject who is not a British citizen can only be guilty of bigamy if the second ceremony takes place in a part of the Commonwealth other than one of the independent countries mentioned in Schedule 3 of the British Nationality Act 1981. In the case of an alien, the second ceremony must have taken place in England or Northern Ireland.

---

17. [1917] 1 KB 359.
18. Dicey, op. cit., Rule 77 and authorities there cited.
19. Below, p. 716.
20. Above, p. 708.
  1. Bartholomew, "Polygamous Marriages and the English Criminal Law", (1954) 17 MLR 344, argues that a polygamous second ceremony in this country is indictable; but that the polygamous marriage abroad of a British subject whose personal law permits polygamy is not. Cf. *A-G of Ceylon v Reid* [1965] AC 720, [1965] 1 All ER 815.
  2. British Nationality Act 1948, s. 3 (1) and British Nationality Act 1981, s. 51(3)(a).
  3. The 1603 Act was limited to second marriages in England and Wales. This extension in respect of British subjects was made in the 1828 Act.
  4. In *Earl Russell*'s case [1901] AC 446, the argument that the words "or elsewhere" should be limited to "elsewhere within the King's dominions" was rejected.

In the case of a British citizen both marriages may take place outside the ordinary jurisdiction of the court. This was decided in *Topping*,[5] where both marriages were in Scotland.

2 Proviso (2): Continual Absence for Seven Years

The period of seven years was used in the original statute of 1603[6] and was subsequently adopted[7] by analogy to the common law rule that a person may be presumed dead when he has not been heard of for seven years by those who would be likely to hear of him if he were alive. But the statutory defence does not depend upon any presumption of death; indeed, D need not rely on the statutory defence unless the prosecution can prove that his wife was alive at the time of the second ceremony. Nor does the defence depend upon any belief by D that his wife was dead.[8] It is enough that he did not, at any period during the relevant seven years, know her to be alive.[9] If D did not know his wife to be alive during the seven years, it is irrelevant that he had the means of knowledge but did not take advantage of them.[10] Indeed, it would seem that if D hid himself in the Outer Hebrides for seven years for the purpose of not knowing his wife to be alive during that time, he would have a defence, for he comes within the plain words of the statute. It has been held[11] that the defence is available though the absence is due to D's own wilful desertion; and this result could hardly be altered by his motives in so absenting himself.

It is settled that, when seven years' absence is proved, the onus is on the Crown to prove beyond reasonable doubt that D knew his wife to be living during that time.[12] It is also settled that the burden of adducing evidence of seven years' absence is on D;[13] but whether he has to go further and *prove*, on a balance of probabilities, that the absence occurred is not so clear. The Australian cases suggest that he must;[14] but it is submitted that the principle of *Woolmington v Director of Public Prosecutions*[15] requires that, once D has introduced some evidence of seven years' absence, the onus should be on the Crown to prove beyond reasonable doubt either (a) that there was no such absence or (b) D knew his wife to be living during it.[16]

---

5. (1856) 7 Cox CC 103. D was usually resident in England at the time of both marriages, but this was irrelevant to his conviction – though it may be relevant in deciding whether to prosecute in England.

6. But under that Act it seems that D had a defence (i) if his spouse had been *beyond the seas* for seven years, even if D *knew* her to be alive; and (ii) if she were absent from him for seven years, but in England or Wales, and D did not know her to be alive.

7. See *Doe d Knight v Nepean* (1833) 5 B & Ad 86 at 94.

8. *Tolson* (1889) 23 QBD 168 at 183, per Cave J; **SHC 105**; *Gould* [1968] 1 All ER 849 at 853, per Diplock J; **SHC 107**.

9. *Cullen* (1840) 9 C & P 681.

10. *Briggs* (1856) Dears & B 98.

11. *Faulkes* (1903) 19 TLR 250.

12. *Curgerwen* (1865) LR 1 CCR 1; *Lund* (1921) 16 Cr App Rep 31.

13. *Jones* (1883) 11 QBD 118.

14. *Bonnor* [1957] VLR 227, where a full court of five judges of the Supreme Court of Victoria, by a majority of three to two rejected the contrary view of the majority (two to one) in *Broughton* [1953] VLR 572. But *Bonnor* was concerned with the onus of proof of a defence of mistaken belief in the dissolution of his first marriage, below, p. 716. See Norval Morris (1955) 18 MLR 452 and MacDougall (1958) 21 MLR 510.

15. [1935] AC 462; **SHC 39**; above, p. 31.

16. See Williams, CLGP, 909.

Proof of seven years' absence is only a defence to a criminal charge; it does not affect the validity of the first marriage.

The words in the proviso, "marrying a second time", refer to the second of the two "marriages" charged in the indictment and it is irrelevant that D has in fact gone through other ceremonies of marriage in the interval between the two referred to in the indictment. It is necessary to make this obvious point because the Court of Criminal Appeal had held in *Treanor*[17] that the defence was not available where the "second marriage" charged in the indictment was in fact the third ceremony he had gone through. Happily this decision was overruled in *Taylor*[18] where D was charged in two counts with "marrying" W4 in 1946 and W5 in 1948, both in the lifetime of his wife W1. He had not seen W1 since 1927, but did not raise the statutory defence because he had "married" W2 in 1927 and W3 in 1942 and thus the marriages charged were the fourth and fifth ceremonies. His convictions were quashed, for each of those marriages was the second marriage in the indictment in which it was charged.

3 Proviso (3): Divorce

The third proviso seems to be entirely unnecessary for a person who goes through a ceremony of marriage after being divorced does not do so "being married", if that expression is given its natural meaning as, so it has recently been held, it should.[19] The explanation[20] probably is that, in the original Act of 1603, the divorce referred to was a divorce a mensa et thoro pronounced by the Ecclesiastical Court which did not dissolve a marriage; and that the draftsman of the 1861 Act retained the proviso for the benefit of persons so divorced.[1]

In *Lolley*'s case,[2] D, being domiciled in England, obtained a divorce in Scotland and remarried in England. He was held guilty of bigamy. The grounds given by the court – that "no sentence or act of any foreign country or state could dissolve an English marriage" – were far too wide[3] but the decision (apart from the question of *mens rea*[4]) was correct. The Scottish divorce was invalid, not because the marriage was celebrated in England, but because D was domiciled in England. The position was similar in *Earl Russell*'s case,[5] where D, being a British subject domiciled in England, obtained a decree of divorce in Nevada, U.S.A., and there remarried. In neither case was the question of *mens rea* discussed.[6]

A case like *Lolley*'s would be decided differently today if the divorce were granted after December 31, 1971. Decrees of divorce granted after that date

---

17. [1939] 1 All ER 330.
18. [1950] 2 KB 368, [1950] 2 All ER 170.
19. *Gould* [1968] 1 All ER 849 at 852; **SHC 105.**
20. The courts sometimes say that they are bound to give meaning to every word in a statute if they can possibly do so: *Williams* [1953] 1 QB 660 at 666, [1953] 1 All ER 1068 at 1070.
1. Cf. the discussion by Williams, CLGP, 178–182.
2. (1812) Russ & Ry 237.
3. Cf. the rules stated in the preceding paragraph; and see *Bater v Bater* [1906] P 209 at 229–30 and 235, 236.
4. According to H. A. D. Philips (1885) 1 LQR at p. 475, Lolley was assured by several lawyers that his divorce was valid before he married again.
5. [1901] AC 446.
6. See footnote 4, above.

under the law of any part of the British Isles are now recognised in England.[7] A decree of divorce granted outside the British Isles will be a defence to a charge of bigamy if it would be recognised by English law as dissolving the marriage. For the circumstances in which such a divorce will be recognised, reference should be made to works on conflict of laws.[8] The law of the parties' domicile may allow the dissolution of marriage without judicial proceedings. Such a divorce obtained before January 1, 1974, is recognised as valid in England.[9] A non-judicial divorce effected after December 31, 1973, will not be recognised as dissolving a marriage if it takes place in the United Kingdom or (subject to certain exceptions[10]), both the parties have been habitually resident in the United Kingdom for one year immediately beforehand, where it takes place elsewhere.[11] A non-judicial divorce before January 1, 1974, or outside the United Kingdom of parties who have not been resident here for one year (or who fall within one of the exceptions) will be regarded as effective to dissolve the marriage and so must be a defence to a charge of bigamy.[12]

4 Proviso (4): Marriage declared Void

Where D's first "marriage" is void, as distinct from voidable, this proviso is unnecessary, for he has a defence whether he has obtained a decree absolute or not. Where the first marriage is voidable, however, D is liable unless he has obtained a decree absolute. If he has obtained a decree absolute before the second marriage, he need not rely on the proviso; he is not a person who, *being married*, marries. But this proviso is not, in terms, limited, as is the third one, to a decree obtained before the second marriage. It would seem, prima facie, to apply to a decree obtained at any time before the criminal case is brought. The explanation would seem to be that until the Nullity of Marriage Act 1971,[13] the annulment of a voidable marriage avoided it retrospectively and declared the parties never to have been married at all. If such a decree were made absolute after D had committed bigamy but before his trial, it was quite logical that he should have had a defence, for the decree established that there was no valid first marriage. The remarkable result apparently was that a person who had been guilty of bigamy became retrospectively innocent.[14] Any decree of nullity granted after August 1, 1971, however, operates only as respects any time after the decree has been made absolute. It would no longer be logical to allow D a defence where his voidable marriage has been annulled after he has married again and before trial. No amendment has been made to s. 57 of the

7. Recognition of Divorces and Legal Separations Act 1971, s. 1, as amended by the Domicile and Matrimonial Proceedings Act 1973, s. 15 (2).
8. See Dicey and Morris, rule 81.
9. *Qureshi v Qureshi* [1972] Fam 173, [1971] 1 All ER 325 (Simon P).
10. Proceedings recognised as valid by ss. 2–5 of the Recognition of Divorces and Legal Separations Act 1971.
11. Domicile and Matrimonial Proceedings Act 1973, s. 16.
12. The Act requires annulment to be by "a court of competent jurisdiction", but makes no such requirement in the case of divorce.
13. See now Matrimonial Causes Act 1973, s. 16.
14. *Wiggins v Wiggins* [1958] 2 All ER 555 (Judge Carr) decided that the second marriage was bigamous for civil purposes, notwithstanding the annulment of the first. But cf. *Mason v Mason* [1944] NI 134. The problem is now unlikely to arise, except in relation to parties domiciled in a jurisdiction when a decree is still retrospective.

Offences against the Person Act; but it is submitted the section should be read in the light of the law of marriage which prevailed when it was enacted so that "declared void" in Proviso (4) means "avoided ab initio." In that case, D's marriage has not been avoided ab initio and he cannot rely on the proviso.

The decree must have been granted by "a court of competent jurisdiction" if it is to afford a defence under the proviso. Reference should be made to works on the conflict of laws for elucidation of this phrase.[15]

What is the position if the marriage is annulled under the law of D's domicile otherwise than by the decree of a court? – as under the Turkish legal rule that if a Christian woman takes up the Mohammedan religion and marries a Moslem, her prior marriage is automatically annulled.[16] It is submitted that such a prior marriage would not thereafter be a valid first marriage so as to found an indictment for bigamy. Though the case is not within proviso (4), D did not "being married, marry".

3) *Mens Rea*

Section 57 of the Offences against the Person Act 1861 gives no indication of the requirement of *mens rea* and the question has caused a good deal of controversy and difficulty. In other sections of this Act[17] the word "maliciously" is found, and its absence from s. 57 has been used as an argument for the imposition of strict liability.[18] But this argument is weakened by the fact that the 1861 Act[19] was primarily a consolidating Act and simply brought together a number of crimes from other Acts. It is not surprising that the word is not to be found in the 1603 Act and no conclusion could properly be drawn from its omission from such an early statute.[20] Moreover, though it is now clear that "maliciously" has a technical meaning, it was not always so, and a legislator may well have jibbed, even in 1861, at the notion of "maliciously marrying"!

As a result of *Gould*,[1] and the acceptance by the House of Lords in *Morgan*[2] of the law as laid down in that case, the position is now clear. If D reasonably believes in the existence of facts which, if true, would preclude his conviction, he is not guilty, though his belief be mistaken; and no distinction is to be drawn

"... between facts the result of which would be that he was innocent because he did not come within the enacting words at all, and facts the result of which would be that he was excluded from the enacting words by the proviso."[3]

15. For example, Dicey and Morris, op. cit. 731–739.
16. Cf. *Kapigian v Der Minassian* (1962) 212 Mass 412; 99 NE 264.
17. See above, Ch 12.
18. *Tolson* (1889) 23 QBD 168 at 199, per Manisty J.
19. Like its predecessor of 1828.
20. Yet the preamble with its reference to "evil disposed persons" who "run out of one county into another or into places where they are not known" indicates that the statute was directed at persons with *mens rea*.
  1. [1968] 2 QB 65, [1968] 1 All ER 849.
  2. [1976] AC 182 at 192, [1975] 2 All ER 347.
  3. [1968] 2 QB at 76.

The position, as the law now stands, appears to be that, in the first instance, the prosecution need prove no more *mens rea* than that D intended to go through the second ceremony of marriage.[4] D may then establish a defence if he introduces evidence that, at the time of that marriage, he believed, on reasonable grounds (a) that his first wife was dead, or (b) that his first marriage had been dissolved, or (c) that his first marriage was void or had been annulled.

In *Tolson*,[5] the Court for Crown Cases Reserved, by a majority of nine to five, held that D was not guilty when she re-married, five years after being deserted by her husband, believing wrongly, but in good faith and on reasonable grounds, that he was dead. The majority rejected the argument that the seven-year rule in the proviso excluded by implication the defence raised. The argument would have been valid if the proviso had covered less ground, or the same ground, as the defence raised; but the proviso is, in one respect, of far wider application, not requiring an honest and reasonable belief in death;[6] and it would be "monstrous to say that seven years' separation should have a greater effect in excusing a bigamous marriage than positive evidence of death."[7] Indeed Lord Coleridge CJ,[8] who had at first been disposed to dissent, ultimately concurred with the majority precisely because of the presence of the proviso.

It was not strictly necessary in *Tolson* to decide that an *unreasonable* belief would not afford a defence for such a case was not before the court. But this point was directly in issue in *King*,[9] where D's defence, that he believed in good faith and on reasonable grounds that the first marriage alleged was void,[10] was rejected because the evidence showed no reasonable grounds for such a belief. It was accepted, however, that the defence would have been good if only there had been reasonable grounds for the belief.[11]

Between *Tolson*[12] and *King* was decided the unsatisfactory case of *Wheat*.[13] D, a man of little education, who had consulted solicitors about divorce proceedings, received from them a letter telling him they hoped to send him papers for signature in a day or two. He jumped to the erroneous conclusion that he was already divorced and married again. The jury, in answer to a question left to them by the judge, found that D believed in good faith and *on reasonable grounds* that he was divorced. The judge directed a verdict of guilty and D's conviction was upheld by the Court of Criminal Appeal, on the grounds (i) that there was no evidence to support

---

4. ". . . bigamy does not involve any intention except the intention to go through a marriage ceremony . . .", per Lord Fraser in *Morgan* [1975] 2 All ER 347 at 382.
5. (1889) 23 QBD 168; **SHC 105**; above, p. 208.
6. See, for example, per Cave J ibid., at 183.
7. Per Stephen J ibid., at 192.
8. Ibid., at 201.
9. [1964] 1 QB 285, [1963] 3 All ER 561. See notes at (1963) 27 MLR 222; (1964) 80 LQR 14.
10. Because, he said, he thought that an earlier marriage had not been dissolved at the time.
11. A number of earlier rulings at first instance are to the same effect: *Thomson* (1905) 70 JP 6; *Connatty* (1919) 83 JP 292; *Dolman* [1949] 1 All ER 813; and the Australian High Court so held in *Thomas v R* (1937) 59 CLR 279. *Kircaldy* (1929) 167 LT Jo 46 and *Johnston* (1940) 5 JCL 185, are to the opposite effect and must be considered wrong.
12. Supra.
13. [1921] 2 KB 119.

the jury's finding;[14] and (ii) that a belief in good faith and on reasonable grounds was no defence.

The decision was based on fallacious reasoning and a misinterpretation of the judgment in *Tolson*. It was widely criticised and has now been overruled by *Gould*.[15] This is a most welcome decision; and the only criticism to be advanced is of the courts' consistent insistence that the mistake must be a reasonable one.[16] The matter is still open to reconsideration in the House of Lords. It is submitted that the *mens rea* of bigamy ought to be, not an intention to go through a ceremony of marriage, which is a perfectly innocent intention, but an intention to go through a ceremony of marriage knowing that, or being reckless whether, one is married already. If that were accepted, it would follow that an honest mistake, even if unreasonable, would be a defence. The complications of the law of marriage and divorce are such, particularly in the case of immigrants, that it is all too easy for a person wrongly to suppose that he is not married, and it is wrong that he should be guilty, even theoretically, of a serious crime simply because he has made a mistake which he ought not to have made.

Where "mistake" is a defence, it is sufficient, it is submitted, if D introduces such evidence of it as might raise a reasonable doubt; and the onus is then on the Crown to establish *mens rea*. The Victorian case of *Bonnor*[17] is to the contrary, but this seems to be inconsistent with *Woolmington v Director of Public Prosecutions*.[18]

4) *The Rationale of Bigamy*[19]

The traditional rationale of bigamy is well stated by Cockburn CJ in *Allen*:[20]

"... it involves an outrage on public decency and morals, and creates a public scandal by the prostitution of a solemn ceremony, which the law allows to be applied only to a legitimate union, to a marriage at best but colourable and fictitious, and which may be made and too often is made, the means of the most cruel and wicked deception."

Bigamy clearly had its origin in religious concepts, being at first only an ecclesiastical offence. The Act of 1603 recited that men had been committing bigamy

"to the great dishonour of God, and utter undoing of divers honest men's children . . ."

Today the second marriage may, of course, take place in a registry office but this makes no difference to the gravity of the offence. To make the "prostitution" of this ceremony an offence punishable with seven years' imprisonment seems altogether out of proportion. The justification is hardly greater where the ceremony is performed in a church, for there are

14. The propriety of this ruling is questioned by Devlin J in *Trial by Jury*, 174, n. 35.
15. [1968] 2 QB 65, [1968] 1 All ER 849.
16. See above, p. 208. An insistence reiterated by Lord Diplock in *Sweet v Parsley*, above, p. 109 and by the House in *Morgan*, above, p. 86; but cf. *Gladstone Williams*, above, p. 88.
17. [1957] VR 227, criticised by MacDougall (1958) 21 MLR 516.
18. [1935] AC 462; **SHC 39**; above, p. 31.
19. See Williams (1945) 61 LQR at pp. 76–78.
20. (1872) LR 1 CCR 367 at 374–375; above, p. 709, footnote 11.

sound objections to the use of the criminal law to uphold religious beliefs. The bigamy which is likely to be severely punished today is that where the other party is innocent and is deceived into taking a highly detrimental course of action.[1] Such conduct should certainly be severely discouraged by the criminal law.[2] But where both parties know the facts and marry to make their co-habitation appear respectable the offence is a relatively minor one. It is right that it is now triable either way.

"The only anti-social consequences that are necessarily involved in the mere celebration of a bigamous marriage are (1) the falsification of the State records, and (2) the waste of time of the Minister of Religion or Registrar."[3]

Bigamy may still fulfil a useful purpose as a crime in the type of case with grave social consequences; but it cannot be regarded as satisfactory that a grave offence should extend so far beyond this to cases no longer regarded as really serious offences.

It might be answered that the law provides for extremely severe penalties for offences against the Marriage Acts;[4] but these, also, seem excessively severe.

2 Other Offences Relating to Marriage

1) *Offences Relating to Solemnisation of Marriages*[5]

By s. 75 (1) of the Marriage Act 1949, as amended by the Marriage Act 1983, it is an offence, punishable with fourteen years' imprisonment, knowingly and wilfully to solemnise a marriage,

1) at any time other than between 8 a.m. and 6 p.m. (subject to certain exceptions); or
2) according to the rites of the Church of England,
    a) where banns have not been duly published (except in the case of a special licence etc.); or
    b) in any place other than a church or other building in which banns may be published except a marriage by special licence, or the marriage of a house-bound or detained person under the Marriage Act 1983; or
    c) falsely pretending to be in Holy Orders.

By s. 75 (2) of the Act, it is an offence, punishable with five years' imprisonment, knowingly and wilfully to solemnise a marriage,

1) in a place other than those specified in the Act, as amended; or
2) in the absence of a registrar or "authorised person" (s. 43); or
3) within twenty-one days of, or after the expiration of three months from, the day on which the notice of marriage was entered in the marriage notice book.

1. Cf. *King* [1964] 1 QB 285, [1963] 3 All ER 561; above, p. 715.
2. If D is a man and intercourse takes place, he commits an offence under s. 3 (1) of the Sexual Offences Act 1956, above, p. 439.
3. Williams (1956) 72 LQR at pp. 77–78.
4. Infra.
5. See also, Marriage (Registrar General's Licence) Act 1970, s. 16.

By s. 75 (3) of the Act it is an offence, punishable with five years' imprisonment, if a superintendent registrar,

1) issues a certificate for marriage within twenty-one days of, or after the expiration of three months from, the day on which notice of marriage was entered in the marriage notice book;

2) issues a certificate where the issue has been forbidden under s. 30 of the Act by any person whose consent to the marriage is required under s. 3;

3) solemnises or permits to be solemnised in his office or, in the case of the marriage of a house-bound or detained person, in any other place, any marriage void under Part III of the Act.

1 A Marriage

It was held in *Bham*[6] that the Marriage Act 1949 is concerned only with marriage as known and permitted by English domestic law and has no application to a ceremony which does not purport to be a marriage of the kind allowed by that law. Accordingly D who performed a ceremony of nichan, a potentially polygamous marriage in accordance with the Islamic law, in a private house was not guilty of an offence under s. 75 (2) of the Act.

2 Knowingly and Wilfully

These words seem clearly to require that D shall know of the circumstances which make the solemnisation of the marriage an *actus reus* – that the time is not between 8 a.m. and 6 p.m., that the banns have not been duly published, that the place is not one in which banns may be published, and so on. In one instance at least, the requirements of *mens rea* go further. Where the charge is one of solemnising a marriage, falsely pretending to be in holy orders, it is not enough that D deliberately dressed up as if he were a clergyman, and officiated as a clergyman, reading out the words of the marriage service. He must also have intended to deceive. This seems to be the effect of *Kemp and Else*.[7] D1, who was married, wished to go through a ceremony of marriage with E. He persuaded D2, who was not and never had been in Holy Orders, to dress up as a clergyman and to officiate at a marriage ceremony according to the rites of the Church of England in a church. He told D2 that he was already married to E and that, as E and F knew, this was merely a re-enactment of the ceremony for the benefit of E's mother, F, who had been unable to be present at the real ceremony. E and F, however, believed, as D1 intended them to believe, that this was a genuine marriage ceremony. The Court of Criminal Appeal held[8] that D2 was not "knowingly and wilfully falsely pretending" to be in Holy Orders. "A pretender is one who claims to be what he is not." If D

"believes that he is only taking part in what everyone present knows to be a charade, the foundation of the offence must go."[9]

6. [1966] 1 QB 159, [1965] 3 All ER 124, CCA.
7. [1964] 2 QB 341, [1964] 1 All ER 649, [1964] Crim LR 312 and commentary.
8. Ibid.
9. D1's conviction was also quashed, apparently as a necessary consequence of the quashing of D2's. According to the view advanced above, p. 155, this was unnecessary. D2's conviction was quashed for lack of *mens rea*; but there was certainly an *actus reus* and D1 had abundant *mens rea*. The point does not seem to have been argued.

Though this decision might be confined to the crime charged because of the presence of the word "falsely" which does not appear in other parts of the section, it is thought more likely that it does apply to the other offences. D2's conduct was equated with that of one taking part in a play. If this analogy is accepted the defence would seem to be equally applicable to the other offences in the section – for example, it would not be an offence to enact a marriage ceremony in a play after 6 p.m.

2) *Offences Relating to the Registration of Marriages*

By the Marriage Act 1949, s. 76:

1) A registrar who knowingly and wilfully registers any marriage which is void under Part III of the Act commits an offence punishable with five years' imprisonment (s. 76 (3)).

2) Any person who refuses, or without reasonable cause omits, to register any marriage which he is required by the Act to register[10] is liable on summary conviction to a fine not exceeding level 3 on the standard scale (s. 76 (1)).

3) Any person who carelessly loses or injures or allows to be injured any marriage register book or certified copy of a marriage register book which is in his custody is liable on summary conviction to a fine not exceeding level 3 on the standard scale (s. 76 (1)).

4) A person who is required to make quarterly returns under s. 57 to the superintendent registrar commits an offence punishable summarily with a fine not exceeding level 1 on the standard scale if he fails to do so (s. 76 (2)).

3 Obscene Publications[11]

Obscenity was originally an ecclesiastical offence but it was held in *Curl*[12] that the publication of an obscene libel was a common law misdemeanour. The law is now to be found in the Obscene Publication Acts 1959 and 1964.

1) *What is Obscenity?*

The ordinary meaning of obscene is filthy, lewd, or disgusting. In law, the meaning is in some respects, narrower, in other respects possibly wider.

The 1959 Act, s. 1 (1), provides the test of obscenity:

10. See ss. 53 and 69.
11. N. St. John Stevas, *Obscenity and the Law* and [1954] Crim LR 817; C. H. Rolph, *The Trial of Lady Chatterley*; Street, *Freedom, the Individual and the Law*, Ch. 5; D. G. T. Williams, "The Control of Obscenity", [1965] Crim LR 471, 522.
12. (1727) 2 Stra 788; following *Sidley* (1663) 1 Sid 168; sub nom. *Sydlyes'* case. 1 Keb 620, a case of an indecent exhibition.

"For the purposes of this Act an article[13] shall be deemed to be obscene if its effect or (where the article comprises two or more distinct items) the effect of any one of its items is, if taken as a whole, such as to tend to deprave and corrupt persons who are likely, having regard to all relevant circumstances, to read, see or hear the matter contained or embodied in it."

This retains, in substantially the same form, the test at common law laid down by Cockburn CJ, in *Hicklin*:[14]

"... I think the test of obscenity is this, whether the tendency of the matter charged as obscenity is to deprave and corrupt those whose minds are open to such immoral influences, and into whose hands a publication of this sort may fall."

It has been said that the test was largely ignored at common law and that, if matter was found to be "obscene" in the ordinary meaning of the word, the tendency to deprave and corrupt was presumed; but, if that be so, the effect of the statutory enactment of the definition has been to require proof of an actual tendency to deprave and corrupt.[15] In *Anderson*[16] (the case of the "Oz School Kids' Issue") the conviction was quashed because the judge left the jury with the impression that "obscene" meant "repulsive," "filthy," "loathsome," or "lewd." An article might be all of these and yet not have a tendency to deprave and corrupt. Indeed its very "obscenity" (in the popular sense) may, paradoxically, prevent it from being "obscene" (in the legal sense). If the article were so revolting that it would put anyone off the kind of depraved activity depicted (the "aversion argument") then it would have no tendency to deprave.[17]

At the same time, it appears that the requirement that the article be "obscene" in the ordinary meaning of the word may have disappeared and that an article may be obscene within the statute if it has a tendency to deprave and corrupt, though it is not filthy, lewd or disgusting.

Until recently the law of obscenity was only invoked in relation to sexual depravity. The prosecutions invariably concerned publications of an erotic and pornographic kind. The words "deprave and corrupt" are clearly capable of bearing a wider meaning than this; and it has now been held that depravity and corruption is not confined to sexual depravity and corruption. In *Calder (John) Publications Ltd v Powell*[18] it was held that *Cain's Book* might properly be found obscene on the ground that it

"... highlighted, as it were, the favourable effects of drug-taking, and, so far from condemning it, advocated it, and that there was a real danger that those into whose hands the book came might be tempted at any rate to experiment with drugs and get the favourable sensations highlighted by the book."

13. For the definition of "article", see below, p. 734.
14. (1868) LR 3 QB 360 at 371. This was an appeal from a decision of a recorder quashing an order of the justices for the destruction of certain pamphlets under the Obscene Publications Act 1857; below, p. 732.
15. *Director of Public Prosecutions v Whyte* [1972] 3 All ER 12 at 18, HL, per Lord Wilberforce.
16. [1972] 1 QB 304, [1971] 3 All ER 1152. See Tony Palmer, *The Trials of OZ* (1971).
17. *Calder and Boyars Ltd* [1969] 1 QB 151, [1968] 3 All ER 644; *Anderson*, above.
18. [1965] 1 QB 509, [1965] 1 All ER 159.

The difficulty about extending the notion of obscenity beyond sexual morality is that it is not now apparent where the law is to stop. It seems obvious that an article with a tendency to induce violence is now obscene;[19] and, if taking drugs is depravity, why not drinking, or, if evidence of its harmful effects accumulates, smoking? Whether the conduct to which the article tends amounts to depravity would seem to depend on how violently the judge (in deciding whether there was evidence of obscenity) and the jury (in deciding whether the article was obscene) disapproved of the conduct in question. It is now clear that depravity may be a mental state, not resulting in external action of any kind. On the contrary, the protection of the minds of the people is the primary object of the law. In *Director of Public Prosecutions v Whyte*[20] it was found that the articles would enable their readers to engage in private fantasies of their own, not involving overt sexual activity of any kind. It was held that they were obscene. That case also settled that an article may be obscene although it is directed only to persons who are already depraved. It is enough that it maintains a state of corruption which might otherwise be escaped.

"The Act is not merely concerned with the once for all corruption of the wholly innocent, it equally protects the less innocent from further corruption, the addict from feeding or increasing his addiction."[1]

Expert evidence of the medical effects of cocaine and the various ways of taking it is admissible because this is a matter which is outside the experience of the ordinary juryman.[2] But whether those effects constitute depravity and corruption – i.e., whether the article, whatever it is, is obscene – is exclusively a question for the jury. Expert evidence is not admissible on that issue,[3] except apparently in the case of material directed at very young children, when experts in child psychiatry may be asked what the effect of certain material on the minds of children would be.[4] That case is to be regarded as "highly exceptional and confined to its own circumstances."[5] The theory seems to be that a juryman is as well able as an expert to judge the effect on an adult but not on a child. This does not mean that the jury should be left without guidance on the question. It would seem right that they should be reminded that "deprave and corrupt" are very strong words; that material which might lead morally astray is not necessarily corrupting;[6] and that they should keep in mind the current standards of ordinary decent people.[7] In the end, they have to make a judgment by what they believe to be the prevailing moral standard.

19. Cf. *Director of Public Prosecutions v A and BC Chewing Gum Ltd* [1968] 1 QB 159, [1967] 2 All ER 504; *Calder and Boyars Ltd* [1969] 1 QB 151 at 172.
20. Above, footnote 15.
1. At p. 19, per Lord Wilberforce.
2. *Skirving* [1985] QB 819, [1985] 2 All ER 705, CA, criticised by R. T. H. Stone, [1986] Crim LR 139 at 142.
3. *Calder and Boyars Ltd* [1969] 1 QB 151, [1968] 3 All ER 644; *Anderson* [1972] 1 QB 304, [1971] 3 All ER 1152; *Director of Public Prosecutions v Jordan* [1976] 3 All ER 775.
4. *Director of Public Prosecutions v A and BC Chewing Gum Ltd* [1968] 1 QB 159, [1967] 2 All ER 504.
5. *Anderson* [1972] 1 QB 304 at 313.
6. *Knuller (Publishing, Printing and Promotions Ltd) v Director of Public Prosecutions* [1972] 2 All ER 898 at 932, 936.
7. Ibid., at 904.

Nevertheless, much may depend on the tone of the judge's direction to the jury. In the case of *Martin Secker and Warburg*,[8] concerning the publication of *The Philanderer*, Stable J gave a direction to a jury which was acclaimed in the press for its enlightened attitude and was thought to be reassuring to those who fear that the criminal law as applied by the judges is out of touch with public opinion.[9] The learned judge told the jury:[10]

"... the charge is a charge that the tendency of the book is to corrupt and deprave. The charge is not that the tendency of the book is either to shock or to disgust. That is not a criminal offence. The charge is that the tendency of the book is to corrupt and deprave. Then you say: 'Well, corrupt and deprave whom?' to which the answer is: those whose minds are open to such immoral influences and into whose hands a publication of this sort may fall. What, exactly, does that mean? Are we to take our literary standards as being the level of something that is suitable for the decently brought up young female aged fourteen? Or do we go even further back than that and are we to be reduced to the sort of books that one reads as a child in the nursery? The answer to that is: Of course not. A mass of literature, great literature, from many angles, is wholly unsuitable for reading by the adolescent, but that does not mean that a publisher is guilty of a criminal offence for making those works available to the general public."

Dealing with the particular book, he said:[11]

"... the book does deal with candour or, if you prefer it, crudity with the realities of human love and of human intercourse. There is no getting away from that, and the Crown say: 'Well, that is sheer filth.' Is it? Is the act of sexual passion sheer filth? It may be an error of taste to write about it. It may be a matter in which, perhaps, old-fashioned people would mourn the reticence that was observed in these matters yesterday, but is it sheer filth? That is a matter which you have to consider and ultimately to decide."

Other directions to juries in recent times, however, have been a good deal less liberal and it has been suggested that Stable J's is not the typical judicial attitude.[12] Nor is it so clear that the law does not require us to take our standards from "the decently brought up young female aged fourteen". The article is obscene if it has a tendency to deprave "persons who are likely ... to read, see or hear the matter contained or embodied in it". Only if the number of readers likely to be corrupted is "so small as to be negligible" is the article not obscene.[13] It is certainly obscene if it has a tendency to deprave "a significant proportion" of those likely to read it.[14] It would not be obscene simply on the ground that it might tend to deprave "a minute lunatic fringe of readers".[15] If, however, a significant, though

8. [1954] 2 All ER 683, [1954] 1 WLR 1138.
9. See (1954) 17 MLR 571.
10. [1954] 2 All ER at 686.
11. Ibid., at 687, 688.
12. Street, op. cit., 122.
13. *Director of Public Prosecutions v Whyte* [1972] 3 All ER 12 at 21 and 25, per Lords Pearson and Cross.
14. *Calder and Boyars Ltd* [1969] 1 QB 151 at 168.
15. Ibid., at 984.

comparatively small, number of the likely readers were decently brought up fourteen-year-old-girls, then whether the book was obscene would turn on whether it was likely to deprave them.

The questions for the jury are of a highly speculative nature. How, for example, is the jury to say whether a significant proportion of the readers will be fourteen-year-old girls? The answer seems to depend on all kinds of matters of which the jury can, at best, have imperfect knowledge. The same article may or may not be obscene depending on the manner of publication. If it has a tendency to deprave fourteen-year-old girls, a bookseller who sells a copy to a club for fourteen-year-old girls is obviously publishing an obscene article; but if he sells the same book to the Conservative Club or a working men's club, this may not be so. The fact that the publisher (in the sense of the producer) of the book is acquitted of publishing an obscene libel, does not mean, then, that other subsequent "publishers" of the book do not commit an offence.

The actual intention of the author is irrelevant. If the article has a tendency to deprave a significant proportion of the readership, it does not matter how pure and noble the author's intent may have been,[16] the article is obscene. In *Martin Secker and Warburg* Stable J told the jury:[17]

> "You will have to consider whether the author was pursuing an honest purpose and an honest thread of thought, or whether that was all just a bit of camouflage ..."

This was too favourable to the defence, unless the jury were to take account of the author's intention, as it appeared in the book itself, as a factor which would have a bearing on whether people would be depraved.

It is now made perfectly clear by the Act that an "item" alleged to be obscene must be "taken as a whole" so that where an article consists of a single item, like a novel, the article must be judged as a whole. Where an article, like a magazine, comprises a number of distinct items, each item must be tested individually; and if one item is found to be obscene, the whole article is obscene.[18]

2) *Offences*

It is an offence if D:

1) publishes an obscene article whether for gain or not;[19] or
2) "has" an obscene article for publication for gain (whether gain to himself or gain to another).[20]

Making an obscene article is not an offence, as such; but those who participate in its manufacture may be liable as secondary parties to the publication, or the "having", which is a continuing offence.[1]

---

16. *Calder and Boyars Ltd* [1969] 1 QB 151 at 168–169. Cf. *Lemon*, below, p. 738.
17. [1954] 2 All ER 683 at 688.
18. *Anderson* [1972] 1 QB 304 at 312, above, p. 720.
19. Obscene Publications Act 1959, s. 2 (1).
20. Ibid., s. 2 (1) as amended by the 1964 Act, s. 1 (1).
1. *Barton* [1976] Crim LR 514, CA.

1 **Publication**

Section 1 (3) of the Obscene Publications Act 1959 provides:

"For the purposes of this Act a person publishes an article who –

a) distributes, circulates, sells, lets on hire, gives, or lends it, or who offers it for sale or for letting on hire; or

b) in the case of an article containing or embodying matter to be looked at or a record, shows, plays or projects it:

Provided that paragraph (b) of this subsection shall not apply to anything done in the course of television or sound broadcasting."

If the charge alleges publication to a named person, it must be proved that the article had a tendency to deprave and corrupt that person.[2] If the article does not have a tendency to deprave the person to whom it is published, it will be obscene only if either –

1) (a) there are "persons who are likely, having regard to all the relevant circumstances, to read, see or hear the matter contained or embodied in it" (whether they have done so or not) and (b) it will have a tendency to deprave and corrupt those persons;[3] or

2) it has in fact been published to a person whom it is likely to deprave and corrupt, and this publication could reasonably have been expected to follow from publication by D.[4]

If D is appropriately charged, he may then be convicted of publishing an obscene article to those persons.

In *Barker*,[5] where D published certain photographs to P and the judge told the jury that the fact that P kept them under lock and key was unimportant, the conviction was quashed. If the jury had been told that they were to consider the tendency of the article to deprave and corrupt only P, the direction would seem to be unobjectionable. If, however, they were directed or left to suppose that they should consider its tendency to deprave and corrupt others, then the direction was clearly wrong. The fact that P kept the articles under lock and key was not *conclusive*, for he may have intended to produce them at some future time; but it was certainly *relevant* to the answer to proposition 1 (a) above.

If the article has no tendency to deprave and corrupt the person to whom it is published and neither of the conditions specified above is satisfied, then D must be acquitted. So in *Clayton and Halsey*[6] where P was an experienced police officer who testified that he was not susceptible to depravity or corruption and there was no evidence of publication, or likelihood of publication, to a third party, the Court of Criminal Appeal held that the case should have been withdrawn from the jury.[7] Lord Parker CJ said:[8]

---

2. *Director of Public Prosecutions v Whyte* [1972] 3 All ER 12 at 29, per Lord Salmon.
3. Ibid., s. 1 (1).
4. Obscene Publications Act 1959, s. 2 (6).
5. [1962] 1 All ER 748, [1962] 1 WLR 349.
6. [1963] 1 QB 163, [1962] 3 All ER 500.
7. D, of course, did not know that he was dealing with an incorruptible police officer. He had *mens rea* and might now be guilty of an attempt under the Criminal Attempts Act 1981, above, p. 300.
8. [1963] 1 QB at 168, [1962] 3 All ER at 502.

". . . while it is no doubt theoretically possible that a jury could take the view that even a most experienced officer, despite his protestations, was susceptible to the influence of the article yet, bearing in mind the onus and degree of proof in a criminal case, it would, we think, be unsafe and therefore wrong to leave that question to the jury."

2 Having an Obscene Article for Publication for Gain

This second type of offence was introduced by amendments made by the 1964 Act and was intended to deal with the difficulties arising from *Clayton and Halsey*. In fact the accused in that case were convicted of *conspiracy* to publish the articles, because the buyers they had in view were not incorruptible police officers. But the implications of the case were serious; for, where there was no evidence that D had conspired with another, it made it virtually impossible to get a conviction on the evidence of a policeman that the articles had been sold to him. Under the amendment it is now possible to charge D with *having* the article for publication for gain; and the incorruptibility of the particular police officer who purchases it will be irrelevant. The jury is unlikely to suppose that D kept these articles solely for sale to police officers; and they need only be satisfied that, having regard to all the relevant circumstances, (i) D contemplated publication to such a person as the article would have a tendency to deprave and corrupt, or (ii) that he contemplated publication from which a further publication to susceptible persons could reasonably be expected to follow (whether D in fact contemplated that further publication or not). By s. 1 (3) (b) of the 1964 Act:

"the question whether the article is obscene shall be determined by reference to such publication for gain of the article as in the circumstances it may reasonably be inferred he had in contemplation and to any further publication that could reasonably be expected to follow from it, but not to any other publication."

The meaning of "having" an article is elucidated by s. 1 (2) of the 1964 Act:

". . . a person shall be deemed to have an article for publication for gain if with a view to such publication he has the article in his ownership, possession or control."

Thus the owner of the shop in which the article is stocked may be convicted as the owner of the article, as well as his servant who has possession or control of it. The van driver who takes it from wholesaler to retailer may also be thought to be in control of it for the purposes of gain.

This overcomes another difficulty which arose under the 1959 Act. It was held[9] that a person who displays an obscene article in a shop window is not guilty of publishing it. Of the various ways of publishing referred to in s. 1 (3), the only one which could conceivably have been applicable was "offering for sale"; and it was held that "offer" must be construed in accordance with the law of contract,[10] under which the display of goods in a

---

9. *Mella v Monahan* [1961] Crim LR 175, following *Fisher v Bell* [1961] 1 QB 394, [1960] 3 All ER 731.
10. For a criticism of this ruling, see [1961] Crim LR at 181; cf. *Partridge v Crittenden* [1968] 2 All ER 421, [1968] 1 WLR 1204.

shop window is an "invitation to treat" and not an offer.[11] This decision, of course, remains good law; but now a charge might successfully be brought of having the obscene article for publication for gain, whether it had been displayed or not.

The proviso to section 1 (3) (b) formerly extended to film exhibitions taking place otherwise than in a private house. The effect of the amendment to the proviso by section 53 of the Criminal Law Act 1977 is that the exhibition of a film anywhere is a publication for the purposes of the Obscene Publications Act; but no prosecution under section 2 may be brought without the consent of the Director of Public Prosecutions, where the article is a moving picture film not less than 16 mm. wide and publication of it took place or could reasonably be expected to take place only in the course of a film exhibition.[12]

"Film exhibition" in s. 2[13] means any exhibition of moving pictures which is produced otherwise than by the simultaneous reception and exhibition of television programmes broadcast by the BBC or ITA or programmes in a cable service which is, or does not require to be, licensed under s. 4 of the Cable and Broadcasting Act 1984.

If the film were such as to outrage public decency then its public showing was a common law offence. A local authority which, in performing its licensing duties, authorised the showing of an outrageously indecent film might have been guilty of aiding and abetting the offence.[14] A local authority has no duty to censor films, except in relation to children; but if it chooses to act, through its licensing powers, as a censor for adults, it must act in accordance with the law and not expressly permit the commission of an offence. Since the Criminal Law Act 1977, however, no proceedings may be brought for an offence at common law (including conspiracy) in respect of a film exhibition alleged to be obscene, indecent, offensive, disgusting or injurious to morality.[15] An indictment for statutory conspiracy, contrary to s. 1 of the Criminal Law Act 1977,[16] would lie in appropriate circumstances.

3) Defences

1 No Reasonable Cause to Believe Article Obscene

By s. 2 (5) of the 1959 Act and s. 1 (3) (a) of the 1964 Act, it is a defence for D to prove that he (i) had not examined the article and (ii) had no reasonable cause to suspect that it was such that his publication of it, or his having it, as the case may be, would make him liable to be convicted of an offence against s. 2. Both conditions must be satisfied; so if D has examined the article, his failure to appreciate its tendency to deprave and corrupt is no defence under these sections.

11. *Pharmaceutical Society of Great Britain v Boots Cash Chemists (Southern) Ltd* [1953] 1 QB 401, [1953] 1 All ER 482.
12. Obscene Publications Act 1959, s. 2 (3A).
13. As amended by the Cinemas Act 1985, Sch. 2.
14. *Greater London Council, ex parte Blackburn* [1976] 3 All ER 184.
15. Obscene Publications Act 1959, s. 2 (4A).
16. Above, p. 258.

2 Public Good

Section 4 of the 1959 Act (as amended by the Criminal Law Act 1977) provides a defence of "public good":

"1) Subject to subsection (1A) of this section a person shall not be convicted of an offence against section 2 of this Act . . . if it is proved that publication of the article in question is justified as being for the public good on the ground that it is in the interests of science, literature, art or learning, or of other objects of general concern.

2) It is hereby declared that the opinion of experts as to the literary, artistic, scientific or other merits of an article may be admitted in any proceedings under this Act either to establish or negative the said ground."

The defence becomes relevant only when the jury has decided that the book is obscene – that it has a tendency to deprave a significant proportion of those likely to read it. The Act assumes that this harm to a section of the community might be outweighed by the other considerations referred to in the section. The jury should be directed to consider first whether an article is obscene within s. 1. If not satisfied of that beyond reasonable doubt, they must acquit. If so satisfied, they should go on to consider whether, on a balance of probabilities, the publication of the article, though obscene, is for the public good.[17] The jury's task is then to

". . . consider, on the one hand, the number of readers they believe would tend to be depraved and corrupted by the book, the strength of the tendency to deprave and corrupt, and the nature of the depravity or corruption; on the other hand, they should assess the strength of the literary, sociological or ethical merit which they consider the book to possess. They should then weigh up all these factors and decide whether on balance the publication is proved to be justified as being for the public good."[18]

Expert evidence is not admissible in support of a defence under s. 4 to the effect that pornographic material is psychologically beneficial to persons who are sexually repressed, perverted or deviant, in that it relieves their sexual tensions and may divert them from anti-social activities. The House of Lords so held in *Director of Public Prosecutions v Jordan*.[19] The other "objects of general concern" must fall within the same area as those specifically mentioned. The effect on sexual behaviour and attitudes was a totally different area, covered in s. 1. The Court of Appeal[20] had reached the same conclusion on the ground that the same qualities relied on by the Crown to show that the article was obscene were being relied on by the defence to show that it was for the public good. To admit such evidence would be to allow every jury to decide for itself as a matter of public policy whether obscene material should be prohibited. Parliament has decided that it should – unless it possesses certain merits; and whatever doubt there

---

17. *Director of Public Prosecutions v Jordan* [1976] 3 All ER 775, HL. Cf. *Sumner* [1977] Crim LR 362 (Judge Davies).
18. *Calder and Boyars Ltd* [1969] 1 QB 151 at 172.
19. Above.
20. Sub nom. *Staniforth* [1976] 2 All ER 714, [1976] 2 WLR 849.

may be as to the range of those merits, they clearly cannot include obscenity itself. "Merits" must mean qualities which show that the publication of the article is for the public good in that it tends to the advancement of an object of general concern. In *Penguin Books* Byrne J said that merits from a sociological, an ethical and an educational point of view were included.[1] This must now be read in the light of *Jordan*. The "other objects of general concern" must not only be such as conduce to the public good but must also be of "concern" to members of the public in general. The Court of Appeal in *Jordan*[2] appears to have assumed judicial knowledge that the public generally are not "concerned" with, or about, the relief of the sexually repressed. It is not clear whether "concerned" is interpreted to mean "interest in" or "activity in". According to the court, "The disposal of sewage is no doubt for the public good but it is not a matter with which the generality of the public is concerned." The general public is certainly interested in the disposal of sewage, at least in the sense that if it were not efficiently done, they would have a great deal to say about it. On the other hand, it is difficult to suppose that the general public could ever be active in the disposal of sewage. It is submitted, however, that "concern" ought to be interpreted to mean "interest". The general public are not active in literature, art or science, but the Act assumes, rightly, it is submitted, that these are objects of public concern.

In *Reiter*,[3] the jury were asked to look at a large number of other books in order to decide whether the books which were the subject of the charge were obscene. The Court of Criminal Appeal held that this was wrong. It appears that it is still not permissible, under the Act, to prove that other books, which are just as obscene as the one in issue, are freely circulating;[4] but evidence relating to other books may now be admitted to establish the "climate of literature" in order to assess the literary merit of the book.[5]

In *Penguin Books*,[6] Crown counsel conceded in argument that the intention of the *author* in writing the book is relevant to the question of literary merit. If this is right, it must again[7] refer only to the intention as it appears in the book itself.

The onus of establishing the defence is on the accused and the standard of proof required is proof on a balance of probabilities.[8] The defence is not available on a charge of conspiracy to corrupt public morals; but Parliament has been assured that such a charge will not be brought so as to circumvent the defence.[9]

---

1. See *The Trial of Lady Chatterley* by C. H. Rolph, at 234; *Calder and Boyars Ltd* [1969] 1 QB 151 at 172; *John Calder (Publications) Ltd v Powell* [1965] 1 All ER 159 at 161.
2. [1976] 2 All ER 714 at 719, CA.
3. [1954] 2 QB 16, [1954] 1 All ER 741.
4. *Penguin Books* (1961) Rolph, op. cit., 127.
5. Ibid.
6. Rolph, op. cit., 87 and 123.
7. As with the question whether the book is obscene. Above, p. 723.
8. *Calder and Boyars Ltd*, supra, at 171.
9. "That should be known by all who are concerned with the operation of the criminal law", per Lord Morris in *Knuller v Director of Public Prosecutions* [1972] 2 All ER 898 at 912. See Lord Diplock's doubts as to the efficacy of the assurance (p. 924) and Lord Reid's opinion that it does not apply to conspiracy to outrage public decency (p. 906).

Subsection (1A) provides that subsection (1) does not apply where the article is a moving picture film or moving picture soundtrack.[10] In the case of these articles a similar defence of public good is provided except that the interests which may justify publication are those of drama, opera, ballet or any other art, or of literature or learning.[11]

4) *Mens Rea*

1 At Common Law

In *Hicklin*[12] it was held that it was not necessary to establish that D's motive was to deprave and corrupt; and that, if he knowingly published that which had a tendency to deprave and corrupt, it was no defence that he had an honest and laudable intention in publishing the work in question. D, a member of the Protestant Electoral Union, sold[13] copies of *The Confessional Unmasked*. He argued that he did so with the intention, not of prejudicing good morals, but of exposing what he deemed to be the errors of the Church of Rome and, particularly, the immorality of the confessional. To this Cockburn CJ answered:

"Be it so. The question then presents itself in this simple form: May you commit an offence against the law in order that thereby you may effect some ulterior object which you have in view, which may be an honest and even a laudable one? My answer is, emphatically, no."[14]

The case did not decide, as is sometimes supposed, that no *mens rea* is required. The argument was not that D did not know the nature of the thing published nor even that he did not know that its natural consequence was to tend to deprave and corrupt; but that the publication was justified by his predominant intention of exposing the errors of the Church of Rome. Cockburn CJ indeed assumed that D *did* know what the effect of the publication would be:

". . . it is impossible to suppose that the man who published it must not have known and seen that the effect upon the minds of many of those into whose hands it would come would be of a mischievous and demoralising character."[15]

A man who knows that a certain result will follow may properly be said to intend[16] it or, at the very least, to be reckless. Blackburn J relied particularly upon *Vantandillo*,[17] which lays down that it is a misdemeanour to carry a person with a contagious disease through the street, though no intent to infect anyone be alleged; but in that case the court insisted that D should have "full knowledge"[18] of the fact of the contagious disease.

---

10. "Moving picture soundtrack" means "any sound record designed for playing with a moving picture film, whether incorporated with the film or not", s. 4 (3).
11. Section 4 (1A). Cf. Theatres Act 1968, s. 3; below, p. 736.
12. (1868) LR 3 QB 360.
13. For the price he paid for them and not "for gain".
14. (1868) LR 3 QB at 371, 372.
15. Ibid., at 372. If the law requires knowledge, this is now clearly a question for the jury: Criminal Justice Act 1967, s. 8; above, p. 85.
16. Above, p. 55.
17. (1815) 4 M & S 73; below, p. 794.
18. Ibid., at 77.

Hicklin,[19] then, need not be taken to have decided more than that, if D publishes that which he knows will have a tendency to deprave and corrupt, it is no defence that he did so with the best of motives.

No case before the Act of 1959 decided anything to the contrary. In *Thomson*[20] the Common Serjeant admitted evidence of other books found on D's premises as tending to show that

"she sold this book with the intention alleged in the indictment [to corrupt morals], and not accidentally."

In *Barraclough*,[1] it was held unnecessary (but desirable) that the indictment should contain an allegation of intent, because the intent was implicit in the allegation of publishing obscenity.[2] In *De Montalk*,[3] D handed to a printer some poems he had written, intending to circulate about 100 copies, mostly to young people of both sexes ("literary people"). The printer sent the poems to the police and D was convicted. His appeal on the ground that there was no sufficient direction on intent was dismissed; but the headnote goes farther than the judgment in asserting that the jury should not be directed that they must find an intent to corrupt public morals. Crown counsel (later Byrne J) submitted merely that intention *was to be inferred* from the act of publication and that no affirmative evidence of intention need be given; and the court dismissed the appeal, saying that the law was accurately stated in *Barraclough*.[4] But in *Penguin Books*,[5] Byrne J held that, if D publishes an article which is obscene, the inference that he intends to deprave and corrupt is irrebuttable. Such an approach today would seem to be inconsistent with s. 8 of the Criminal Justice Act 1967;[6] but, though Byrne J used the language of proof, he was probably saying, in substance, that intent to deprave was not a constituent of the offence.[7] He conceded that the judgment in *De Montalk* was not very clear, but stated that the court came to the conclusion that there was nothing in the argument that the presumption was rebuttable, and that he was bound by that decision.

2 Under the Obscene Publications Act

In *Shaw v Director of Public Prosecutions*[8] D was charged with publishing an obscene article in the form of the *Ladies' Directory*. His appeal to the Court of Criminal Appeal[9] on the ground that the judge did not direct the jury to take into account D's "honesty of purpose" was dismissed. Ashworth J said:[10]

"If these proceedings had been brought before the passing of the Obscene Publications Act 1959, in the form of a prosecution at common

---

19. Above, p. 720.
20. (1900) 64 JP 456 at 457.
  1. [1906] 1 KB 201, CCR.
  2. "... intent ... is still part of the charge or the publication would not have been unlawful": per Darling J, ibid., at 212.
  3. (1932) 23 Cr App Rep 182.
  4. Supra.
  5. Above, p. 728.
  6. Above, p. 85.
  7. See the discussion of s. 8; above, pp. 85 and 328.
  8. [1962] AC 220, [1961] 2 All ER 446; **SHC 258**; above, p. 276.
  9. He was refused leave to appeal to the House of Lords on this count.
 10. [1962] AC at 227, [1961] 1 All ER at 333, CCA.

law for publishing an obscene libel, it would no doubt have been necessary to establish an intention to corrupt. But the Act of 1959 contains no such requirement and the test of obscenity laid down in s. 1 (1) of the Act is whether the effect of the article is such as to tend to deprave and corrupt persons who are likely to read it. In other words obscenity depends on the article and not on the author."[11]

This, of course, is inconsistent with the view of Byrne J who, in *Penguin Books*,[12] conceived that he was applying the common law rule. According to the Court of Criminal Appeal's view, he was wrong about the common law, but reached the right result by accident, the common law having been revised by the Act! As a matter of fact, it seems that this was not the intention of Parliament.[13]

It was not necessary to the decision to decide that no *mens rea* was required. To rule that "honesty of purpose" is irrelevant is one thing and no more than was done in *Hicklin*; to decide that no *mens rea* with reference to depravity and corruption is necessary, is another. D's motives of benevolence towards the prostitutes whom he was assisting to ply their trade may have been wholly admirable but if he knew (as he must have done!) that the inevitable result would be what the law regards[14] as depravity and corruption, he intended that result. Moreover, the test laid down in s. 1 (1) is not decisive, for this merely defines the *actus reus* and says nothing about *mens rea*. It is difficult, however, to dispute the conclusion of the Court of Criminal Appeal in the light of the defence provided by s. 2 (5).[15] If *mens rea* in the sense described above were required, this provision would be quite unnecessary. But the clear implication of s. 2 (5) is that D would be guilty (i) although he had examined the article and concluded that it had no tendency to deprave and corrupt if there were reasonable grounds on which he might have suspected that it would; (ii) although the jury thought it as likely as not that he did not suspect the article's tendency;[16] and (iii) although he had examined the article and failed to appreciate its tendency. Thus it appears likely that the Act, perhaps inadvertently, has restricted the requirement of *mens rea*. In *Anderson*,[17] the court thought it quite obvious that the jury had acquitted of conspiracy to corrupt public morals because they were not satisfied that there was the required intent to corrupt. But the court did not consider this fatal to the charge under the Obscene Publications Act and, indeed, considered whether they should uphold the conviction under s. 2 of the Criminal Appeal Act 1968 on the ground that no actual miscarriage of

---

11. The reference to the author is puzzling. Presumably "the publisher" is meant. They were one and the same in Shaw.
12. Supra.
13. Street, *Freedom, the Individual and the Law*, (3rd Ed.) 141.
14. Whether he knew the law so regarded it, is irrelevant. Cf. *Sancoff v Halford* [1973] Qd R 25.
15. Above, p. 726.
16. The onus of proof on a balance of probabilities is on D.
17. Above, p. 720.

justice had occurred[18] – something they could hardly have done if the jury had negatived the intent necessary for the crime.

5) *Forfeiture of Obscene Articles*

The Obscene Publications Act 1857 provided a summary procedure for the forfeiture of obscene articles. That Act is replaced by s. 3 of the Obscene Publications Act 1959. The procedure is that an information on oath must be laid before a magistrate that there is reasonable ground for suspecting that obscene articles are *kept* in any premises, stall or vehicle in the justice's area *for publication for gain*.[19] The justice may then issue a warrant authorising a constable to search for and seize any articles which he has reason to believe to be obscene and to be kept for publication for gain. Such a warrant authorises only a single entry and a second entry in reliance on the warrant will be unlawful; but, in the absence of evidence of "oppression", the court has no discretion to exclude any evidence unlawfully obtained.[20]

Any articles seized must be brought before a justice for the same area. If the justice, after looking at the articles, decides they are not obscene, then the matter drops and the articles[1] are, no doubt, returned.[2] But if he thinks they may be obscene (and he need not come to a decided opinion at this stage) he may issue a summons to the occupier of the premises, etc., to appear before the court and show cause why the articles should not be forfeited. If the court is satisfied[3] that the articles, at the time they were seized, were obscene articles kept for publication for gain, it must order the articles to be forfeited. The power does not apply to any article which is returned to the person from whom it was seized.[4] The section applies to material destined for publication abroad.[5] The magistrates may thus be required to form an opinion as to the likely effect of the material on foreigners with different attitudes and customs but, in practice, they are likely to rely on their knowledge of human nature and unlikely to hold an article to be obscene where it is destined for country X and not obscene where it is destined for country Y.

---

18. [1971] 3 All ER 1152 at 1161.
19. *Hicklin*'s case might thus now fall outside the Act. He sold the pamphlets for the price he paid for them and this was evidently considered not to be selling for gain: (1868) LR 3 QB at 368 and 374. But cf. p. 594, above.
20. *Adams* [1980] QB 575, [1980] 1 All ER 473, CA.
  1. It is not necessary for each justice to read all the material, provided the whole is discussed and considered by them: *Olympia Press Ltd v Hollis* [1974] 1 All ER 108. On an appeal to the Crown Court, the judge may take a number of articles at random to sample, showing them to the defence as an indication of the basis on which he has reached his decision: *R v Snaresbrook Crown Court*, ex *P Metropolitan Police Commissioner* (1984) 79 Cr App Rep 184, DC. Cf. R. T. H. Stone, [1986] Crim LR 139.
  2. *Thomson v Chain Libraries Ltd* [1954] 2 All ER 616, [1954] 1 WLR 999.
  3. In *Thomson v Chain Libraries* [1954] 2 All ER 616 at 618, Hilbery J said that the onus of proof is on the person who appears to show cause. *Sed quaere?* The magistrate must be *satisfied* that the article is obscene.
  4. Criminal Law Act 1977, Sch. 12.
  5. *Gold Star Publications Ltd v Director of Public Prosecutions* [1981] 2 All ER 257, HL.

The owner, author or maker of the articles, or any other person through whose hands they had passed before being seized, is entitled to appear and show cause why they should not be forfeited; and any person who appeared or was entitled to appear to show cause against the making of the order has a right of appeal to the Crown Court.

The defence of "public good" is available in proceedings for forfeiture;[6] but the decision is, of course, now in the hands of the justices and not in the hands of a jury. Thus, if proceedings for forfeiture are brought instead of an indictment, the author or publisher of a book can, in substance, be deprived of a right to jury trial.

There is not necessarily any uniformity of decision. One bench may pass a magazine or picture, while another condemns it.[7] In practice, it seems that the advice of the Director of Public Prosecutions is usually taken by the police before applying for a warrant. His advice is not *necessary* for it is thought undesirable that he should be in the position of a literary or moral censor.[8]

Where, however, the article is a moving picture film in respect of which a prosecution under section 2 of the 1959 Act could not be instituted without the consent of the Director,[9] no order for forfeiture may be made unless the warrant under which the article was seized was issued on an information laid by or on behalf of the Director.[10]

6) *The Common Law of Obscene Libel*

The 1959 Act did not, in terms, abolish the common law misdemeanour of obscene libel, but provided in s. 2 (4):

"A person publishing an article shall not be proceeded against for an offence at common law consisting of the publication of any matter contained or embodied in the article where it is of the essence of the offence that the matter is obscene."

It might be thought that the intention was that, in future, all proceedings in respect of obscene publications should be brought under the Act. The subsection has not been so interpreted. In *Shaw v Director of Public Prosecutions*[11] it was relied on by the defence in relation to the first count alleging a common law conspiracy to corrupt public morals by the publication of the *Ladies' Directory*; that is, as was held, the publication of an obscene article. The answer to this argument, accepted by the Court of Criminal Appeal[12] and the House of Lords,[13] was that the conspiracy did

6. Obscene Publications Act 1959, s. 4 (1).
7. The same thing could of course occur in relation to proceedings on indictment. If another publisher were to be prosecuted for publishing *Lady Chatterley*, the decision in *Penguin Books* (above, p. 728) would not be relevant in evidence, let alone an estoppel; and another jury, hearing different expert evidence, might well arrive at a different conclusion.
8. Under the Prosecution of Offences Regulations 1946, reg. 6 (2) (d), a chief officer of police must report to the Director any alleged commission of an *offence* of obscenity.
9. See above, p. 726.
10. Obscene Publications Act 1959, s. 3 (3A).
11. [1962] AC 220; **SHC 258**.
12. [1962] AC at 235, 236.
13. [1962] AC at 268, 269, 290, 291.

not "consist of the publication" of the booklet; it consisted in the agreement to corrupt public morals by publishing it.

It thus appears that it would still be possible to bring a prosecution for conspiracy to publish an obscene libel (and possibly an incitement or attempt to do so). Such a prosecution should not be brought to evade the statutory defence of public good.[14]

7) *What is an Article?*

The 1959 Act provides by s. 1 (2):

"In this Act 'article' means any description of article containing or embodying matter to be read or looked at or both, any sound record, and any film or other record of a picture or pictures."

This includes a video cassette.[15] In *Straker v Director of Public Prosecutions*[16] it was held that while a negative *might* be within this definition,[17] it was not kept for "publication" as described in s. 3 (1) since it was not to be shown, played or projected,[18] but to be used for making prints. It could not, therefore, be forfeited under s. 3. This gap is closed by s. 2 of the 1964 Act which provides

"1) The Obscene Publications Act 1959 (as amended by this Act) shall apply in relation to anything which is intended to be used, either alone or as one of a set, for the reproduction or manufacture therefrom of articles containing or embodying matter to be read, looked at or listened to, as if it were an article containing or embodying that matter so far as that matter is to be derived from it or from the set."

By s. 2 (2) of the 1964 Act an article is had or kept for publication

"if it is had or kept for the reproduction or manufacture therefrom of articles for publication".

The negatives in *Straker* clearly fall within this provision.

In *Conegate Ltd v Customs and Excise Comrs*[19] it was conceded that inflatable life-size dolls, though obscene, were not "articles". It has been suggested that the concession was wrong because the dolls, having faces painted on them, were to be "looked at". However the gist of the obscenity seems to lie in the use to which the dolls were intended to be put, rather than in their appearance.

8) *Posting Indecent or Obscene Matter*

It is an offence under the Post Office Act 1953, s. 11, punishable summarily by a fine of £1,000 and, on indictment, by imprisonment for twelve months, to

14. Above, p. 727.
15. *A-G's Reference (No. 5 of 1980)* [1980] 3 All ER 816, [1981] 1 WLR 88.
16. [1963] 1 QB 926, [1963] 1 All ER 697, DC.
17. Widgery LCJ had little doubt that this was so: *Derrick v Customs and Excise Commissioners* [1972] 2 WLR 359 at 361.
18. Section 1 (3) (b), above, p. 724.
19. [1987] QB 254, [1986] 2 All ER 688, [1986] Crim LR 562, DC.

". . . send or attempt to send or procure to be sent a postal packet which:

b) encloses any indecent or obscene print, painting, photograph, lithograph, engraving, cinematograph film, book, card or written communication, or any indecent or obscene article whether similar to the above or not . . ."

It was held in Stanley[20] that the words "indecent or obscene" in this section:

"convey one idea, namely offending against the recognised standards of propriety, indecent being at the lower end of the scale and obscene at the upper end of the scale . . .

. . . an indecent article is not necessarily obscene, whereas an obscene article must almost certainly be indecent."

Therefore the verdict of a jury holding that certain cinematograph films were not obscene (for the purposes of the Obscene Publications Act) but were indecent (for the purposes of the Post Office Act) was upheld.

If "indecent" comprehends everything which is obscene and more, the word "obscene" in the Act is redundant. "Obscene" here bears its ordinary meaning[1] and so may not extend to material simply because it advocates drug-taking or violence[2] which would not ordinarily be described as "indecent".[3] On the other hand, such articles might well be said to offend against "recognised standards of propriety"; and, for the purposes of other legislation, abusive language and shouts in church alleging hypocrisy against the reader of the lesson[4] have been held to be "indecent". It is possible therefore that "indecent" is not confined to sexual indecency, but extends to other improper matter.

The test of indecency is objective and the character of the addressee is immaterial.[5] Indeed, the object of the section, looked at as a whole, seems to be the protection of Post Office employees against dangerous, deleterious or indecent articles.[6] It is evidently not limited to employees, however, since it is only in rare cases that they will have access to matter "enclosed" as para. (b) requires. Evidence is not admissible by any person to say what the effect of the article was on him. The jury do not need assistance. They are themselves "the custodians of the standards for the time being."[7]

The improper use of telecommunication services is a summary offence under the Post Office Act 1969, s. 78; and sending unsolicited matter describing human sexual techniques, or unsolicited advertisement of such

---

20. [1965] 2 QB 327, [1965] 1 All ER 1035.
1. *Anderson* [1971] 3 All ER 1152 at 1162. The judge's direction (above, p. 720) was thus correct so far as the "Post Office count" was concerned. *Stamford* [1972] 2 QB 391, [1972] 2 All ER 427.
2. Above, p. 720.
3. *Lees v Parr* [1967] 3 All ER 181n (By-law).
4. *Abrahams v Cavey* [1968] 1 QB 479, [1967] 3 All ER 179 (Ecclesiastical Courts Jurisdiction Act 1860, s. 2); *Farrant* [1973] Crim LR 240.
5. *Straker* [1965] Crim LR 239, CCA; *Kosmos Publications Ltd v Director of Public Prosecutions* [1975] Crim LR 345.
6. *Stamford* [1972] 2 All ER 427 at 429.
7. Ibid., at p. 432.

matter, is an offence[8] under s. 4 of the Unsolicited Goods and Services Act 1971.

9) *Obscenity in the Theatre*

The Theatres Act 1968, which abolished censorship of the theatre, makes it an offence, punishable under s. 2, summarily with six months, and on indictment with three years' imprisonment, to present[9] or direct an obscene performance of a play. The definition of obscenity is the same as in s. 1 (1) of the Obscene Publications Act 1959,[10] except that attention is directed to the effect of the performance on the persons who are likely to *attend* it instead of "read, see or hear it". A defence of "public good" is provided by s. 3 which is the same as that under s. 4 of the 1959 Act,[11] except that the interests which may justify the performance are, as in the case of films, those of "drama, opera, ballet or any other art or of literature or learning".

A performance given "on a domestic occasion in a private dwelling" is excepted by s. 7 from the provisions of s. 2; and, by s. 8, proceedings may not be instituted except by or with the consent of the Attorney General.

If proceedings are to be brought in respect of the alleged obscenity of the performance of a play, they must be brought under the Act; for, by s. 2 (4), it precludes proceedings at common law (including conspiracy). A prosecution on indictment under s. 2 must be commenced within two years of the commission of the offence: s. 2 (3).

10) *Indecent Displays*

The Indecent Displays (Control) Act 1981 makes it an offence to make, cause or permit the public display of any indecent matter. Matter displayed in, or so as to be visible from, any public place is publicly displayed. A public place is one to which the public have or are permitted to have access, whether on payment or otherwise, except (a) where the payment is or includes payment for the display, or (b) the place is a shop or part of a shop to which the public can gain access only by passing an adequate warning notice, as specified in the Act. The Act is aimed at displays that people cannot avoid seeing as they go about their business – bookshop and sex shop window displays, cinema club posters, and so on. It does not apply to BBC or IBA television broadcasts, displays visible only from within an art gallery or museum, the performance of a play within the Theatres Act 1968 or a cinematograph exhibition as defined in the Cinematographic Act 1952. "Matter" is anything capable of being displayed except an actual human

---

8. *Director of Public Prosecutions v Beate Uhse (UK) Ltd* [1974] QB 158, [1974] 1 All ER 753.
9. Cf. *Grade v Director of Public Prosecutions* [1942] 2 All ER 118; above, p. 168.
10. Above, pp. 719–723.
11. Above, p. 727.

body or part of it. "Indecent" is not defined. Whether matter is indecent will no doubt be considered a matter of fact to be determined by applying the ordinary meaning of the word.[12]

11) *Other Statutes*

There are a number of other statutes under which summary proceedings may be, and are, instituted, where the safeguards of the Obscene Publications Acts do not apply. These include the Metropolitan Police Act 1839, s. 54, and the Children and Young Persons (Harmful Publications) Act 1955. No doubt there are also many local Acts and by-laws which may be invoked.[13]

4 Blasphemy[14]

1) *Actus Reus*

It is a common law misdemeanour to publish blasphemous matter whether orally or in writing. Matter is blasphemous if it denies the truth of the Christian religion[15] or of the Bible[16] or the Book of Common Prayer,[17] or the existence of God. The earlier cases required no more than this for, as Stephen says, they

"all proceed upon the plain principle that the public importance of the
Christian religion is so great that no one is allowed to deny its truth."[18]

The gist of the offence was said to be "a supposed tendency to shake the fabric of society generally."[19] Yet, while the law was stated in these broad terms, there is no recorded instance of a conviction for blasphemy where an element of contumely and ribaldry was absent.[20] In the course of the nineteenth century it came to be held that matter denying the truth of Christianity, etc., will not be held criminal if it is expressed in decent and temperate language and not in such terms as are likely to lead to a breach of the peace. "If the decencies of controversy are observed, even the fundamentals of religion may be attacked without the writer being guilty of blasphemy."[1]

12. Above, p. 735.
13. See, generally, Report of the Home Office Working Party on Vagrancy and Street Offences (1974).
14. G. D. Nokes, *History of the Crime of Blasphemy*. Stephen, 2 HCL 469–476. Street, *Freedom, the Individual and the Law*, 191–198.
15. *Taylor* (1676) 1 Vent 293.
16. *Hetherington* (1841) 4 State Tr NS 563.
17. According to Russell, 1519; Archbold (39th ed.) §3401.
18. 2 HCL 475.
19. Per Lord Sumner in *Bowman v Secular Society Ltd* [1917] AC 406 at 459.
20. This was common ground in *Bowman v Secular Society Ltd*, see, for example, per Lord Sumner [1917] AC 406 at 460. Stephen says that the placards held to be blasphemous in *Cowan v Milbourn* (1867), LR 2 Exch 230 "could hardly have been expressed in less offensive language": 2 HCL at 474; but that was a civil action, and Lord Sumner and the Court of Appeal thought the decision wrong: [1917] AC at 463.
   1. *Ramsay and Foote* (1883) 15 Cox CC 231 at 238, per Coleridge CJ.

Stephen found himself unable to accept this milder view of the law because of the weight of the earlier authorities;[2] but the milder view found favour with the House of Lords in *Bowman v Secular Society Ltd*.[3] In that case it was held that a company formed to promote the secularisation of the state was not unlawful although one of its objects was to deny Christianity. Blasphemous words are punishable

"for their manner, their violence, or ribaldry, or, more fully stated, for their tendency to endanger the peace then and there, to deprave public morality generally, to shake the fabric of society and to be a cause of civil strife."[4]

The application of this test would virtually abolish the crime because it is scarcely conceivable that any utterance regarding Christianity could seriously be expected to produce such drastic results today. In *Whitehouse v Gay News Ltd and Lemon*,[5] the first prosecution for over 60 years, the House of Lords applied a much less strict test. A publication is blasphemous if it is couched in indecent or offensive terms likely to shock and outrage the feelings of the general body of Christian believers in the community. There appears to be no need to prove any tendency to endanger the peace, still less "to shake the fabric of society". The publication in question, a poem and illustration vilifying Christ in his life and in his crucifixion, was, no doubt, extremely offensive to many people; but there was no indication that it had provoked or was likely to provoke violence and it would be ludicrous to suggest that it was likely to have any effect on the fabric of society.

Alderson B has held that it is only the Christian religion and, indeed, only the established church which is protected by the law of blasphemy.[6] The difference, it appears, is that the established church alone is part of the constitution of the country so that an attack on other religions was not thought to have the supposed tendency to shake the fabric of this society. This was characterised as "a strange *dictum*" by Lord Sumner who pointed out that

"After all, to insult a Jew's religion is not less likely to provoke a fight than to insult an episcopalian's . . ."[7]

It is perhaps conceivable, though not likely, that the protection of blasphemy could be extended to other branches of Christianity and non-Christian religions held by substantial numbers of people in this country.[8]

2) *Mens Rea*

In *Lemon and Gay News*[9] the majority of the House of Lords held that the only *mens rea* that need be proved is an intention to publish the offending

2. 2 HCL 474, 475 and *Digest* (4th ed.), Art. 161.
3. [1917] AC 406.
4. Per Lord Sumner, [1917] AC at 466.
5. [1979] AC 617, [1979] 1 All ER 898, [1979] Crim LR 311 and commentary.
6. *Gathercole* (1838) 2 Lew CC 237.
7. [1917] AC at 460.
8. Cf. Street, op. cit. 194.
9. [1979] AC 617, [1979] 1 All ER 898, [1979] Crim LR 311.

words. It is not necessary to prove that the defendant intended to attack Christianity or to shock and insult Christians or even that he knew that the words would or might have that effect. Lords Diplock and Edmund-Davies, dissenting, thought that the prosecution should be obliged to prove that D knew that this was the probable effect of the words. They considered that the decision of the majority turned the offence into one of strict liability, a charge which the majority denied. Presumably, however, it must be shown that D was aware of the presence and understood the meaning of the offending words. If they were in a foreign language and he believed they were a recipe for Christmas pudding, he would surely not be guilty.

3) *Reform of the Law*

Prosecutions for blasphemy have been extremely rare for over a hundred years[10] but several attempts to abolish the blasphemy laws have failed.[11] There is a strong case for their abolition. It is illogical that scurrilous publications relating to the Christian religion should be punishable because of their tendency to outrage the feelings of believers when similar publications relating to other religions are not. Christians are not alone in their susceptibility to outrage. On the other hand it would be wrong for the protection of the law to be extended to all religious beliefs, however weird. Events in Jonesville in Guyana in 1979 demonstrate that there may be religions which ought, in the public interest, to be vilified, however outraged their adherents might be. The rarity of prosecutions indicates that the Christian religion does not need the protection of the blasphemy laws. Other less strongly supported religions are well able to flourish in this country without it. The conclusion is that the law of blasphemy should be abolished. The Law Commission has indeed provisionally so recommended in a working paper.[12] They propose that it should be replaced by an offence of using threatening, abusive or insulting words or behaviour at any time in any place of worship of the Church of England, or in any other certified place of religious worship, in any churchyard or burial ground, with intent to wound or outrage the feelings of those using the premises concerned.[13]

10. *Pooley* (1857) 8 State Tr NS 1089; *Ramsay and Foote* (1883) 15 Cox CC 231; *Boulter* (1908) 72 JP 188; *Gott* (1922) 16 Cr App Rep 87 and *Lemon*, above.
11. R. S. W. Pollard, *Abolish the Blasphemy Laws*, 7.
12. Law Com. No. 79 (1981), discussed by J. R. Spencer in [1981] Crim LR 810.
13. Working Paper, §§13.13.

19 Offences relating to the Administration of Justice

1 Perjury

In the early days of the common law, the only false swearing which was punished was that of compurgators and jurymen. The jury originally fulfilled the function of the modern witness, for it was expected to know the facts. When witnesses in the modern sense began to be called, there was at first probably no offence of which they could be convicted for giving false evidence. Then a series of decisions in the Star Chamber[1] created the common law misdemeanour of perjury.[2]

At common law, perjury, strictly so-called, consisted in giving false evidence on oath in a material matter in a judicial proceeding. But it was also a misdemeanour to swear falsely outside a judicial proceeding where the statement was one required to be made by law, as, for example, for the purpose of obtaining a marriage licence.[3] A very large number of statutes also made criminal the making of false statements in a wide variety of circumstances.

The law is now to be found in the Perjury Act 1911[4] which codified and modified the common law and swept away the relevant sections of more than 130 statutes.[5]

Perjury is defined by s. 1 (1) of the Act:

"If any person lawfully sworn as a witness or as an interpreter in a judicial proceeding wilfully makes a statement material in that proceeding, which he knows to be false or does not believe to be true, he shall be guilty of perjury, and shall on conviction thereof on indictment, be liable to imprisonment for a term not exceeding seven years, or to a fine or to both such imprisonment and fine."

1 Lawfully Sworn as a Witness

Perjury originated as a spiritual offence and at common law the only oath recognised is one "calling Almighty God to witness that his testimony is

---

1. *Rowland ap Eliza* (1613) 3 Co Inst 164.
2. Stephen, 3 HCL 241.
3. *Foster* (1821) Russ & Ry 459; *De Beauvoir* (1835) 7 C & P 17.
4. For proposals for the reform of the law of perjury, see Law Commission Working Paper No. 33, "Perjury and Kindred Offences," (1970); a "Justice" Report, "False Witness" (1973) and D. W. Pollard, [1974] Crim LR 588.
5. See the Schedule to the Act.

true."[6] It is not necessary that the oath be in accordance with the Christian religion; it is sufficient that the witness believes in God by whom he swears in accordance with the particular religion he professes.[7] Since 1888 the common law has been modified by the Oaths Acts and the current Oaths Act 1978 allows any person who objects to being sworn to make a solemn affirmation instead of taking the oath. Where it is not reasonably practicable without inconvenience or delay to administer an oath in the manner appropriate to a witness's religious belief he may be permitted and, indeed, required, to affirm instead.[8] A solemn affirmation is of the same force and effect as an oath. A person who has affirmed is subject to the law of perjury as if he had taken the oath. The common law position, as modified by the Oaths Acts, is preserved by s. 15 of the Perjury Act which provides:

"1) For the purposes of this Act, the forms and ceremonies used in administering an oath are immaterial, if the court or person before whom the oath is taken has power to administer an oath for the purpose of verifying the statement in question, and if the oath has been administered in a form and with ceremonies which the person taking the oath has accepted without objection, or has declared to be binding on him.

2) In this Act –
      "The expression 'oath' in the case of persons for the time being allowed by law to affirm or declare instead of swearing, includes 'affirmation' and 'declaration', and the expression 'swear' in the like case includes 'affirm' and 'declare'. . . ."[9]

In a criminal case, a child of tender years who does not understand the nature of an oath but is of sufficient intelligence to justify the reception of his evidence and does understand the duty of speaking the truth, may be allowed to give unsworn evidence. Such a child, wilfully giving false evidence in such circumstances that it would be perjury if he had taken the oath is, if of the age of ten or above,[10] liable to punishment on summary conviction.[11]

A person who is not a competent witness but is sworn by mistake cannot be indicted for perjury. This was decided in *Clegg*[12] where D, the accused in a criminal case, tricked the court into receiving his evidence by pretending to be his own son, and was held not indictable for perjury. Since 1898, of course, an accused person is competent to give evidence for the defence at every stage of the proceedings and may be convicted of perjury even if the false evidence is given after verdict in mitigation of punishment but on oath.[13]

It is a defence to a charge of perjury that D was not lawfully sworn or affirmed. So in *Pritam Singh*[14] the case was withdrawn from the jury where D, a Sikh, had given evidence on affirmation although the taking of an oath

6. Co 3 Inst 165.
7. *Omychund v Barker* (1744) 1 Atk 21.
8. Oaths Act 1978, s. 5.
9. On declarations, see below, p. 750.
10. Above, p. 178.
11. Children and Young Persons Act 1933, s. 38.
12. (1868) 19 LT 47.
13. *Wheeler* [1917] 1 KB 283.
14. [1958] 1 All ER 199, [1958] 1 WLR 143.

was not contrary to his religious belief (as the law then required), because the copy of the holy book of the Sikhs was not available in the magistrates' court. If the same situation arose today, D, having been affirmed, would be "lawfully sworn" for the purpose of the perjury trial by virtue of the Oaths Act 1978.

An accused who gives evidence on oath may be guilty of perjury like any other witness. If he is acquitted of the offence charged because the jury believe his testimony, the Crown may prove at a subsequent trial for perjury that the testimony was false. Issue estoppel has no application in English criminal law.[15] If D is disbelieved and convicted of an offence, the court may not take the perjury into account in fixing the sentence; but D may be subsequently prosecuted and sentenced for it.[16] An accused who makes an unsworn statement from the dock commits no offence if he lies.

An exception to the rule that D must have been sworn is created by the Evidence (Proceedings in Other Jurisdictions) Act 1975.[17]

2 A Judicial Proceeding

By s. 1 (2) of the Perjury Act 1911:

"The expression 'judicial proceeding' includes a proceeding before any court, tribunal, or person having by law power to hear, receive, and examine evidence on oath."

Clearly, proceedings in all the ordinary courts of law, courts-martial and tribunals appointed under the Tribunals of Inquiry (Evidence) Act 1921 are judicial proceedings. Two Special Commissioners of Income Tax sitting to hear an appeal against an assessment to surtax constituted a judicial tribunal;[18] but where licensing justices held a special preliminary meeting, for which there was no statutory authority, they had no power to administer an oath, and thus the proceeding was not a judicial one.[19] Even though the oath be properly administered by the person having power to receive evidence on oath, there can be no perjury if that person should withdraw. This was decided in *Lloyd*,[20] where D was sworn in a bankruptcy proceeding before a county court registrar, but examined in another room in the absence of the registrar, no person having power to receive evidence on oath being present.

If the court before which the proceeding is brought lacks jurisdiction to deal with it, perjury is impossible. So where D gave false evidence against E on an information for furious *riding* contrary to the Highway Act 1835 his conviction for perjury was quashed, since only furious *driving* was an offence under the Act.[1] But D's conviction was affirmed where he swore

15. *Director of Public Prosecutions v Humphrys* [1977] 1 AC, [1976] 2 All ER 497, HL.
16. On the policy of prosecuting see (1973) 117 Sol Jo 654 commenting on *J. D. Williams v Director of Public Prosecutions* (ibid.).
17. Below, p. 743.
18. *Hood-Barrs* [1943] 1 KB 455, [1943] 1 All ER 665.
19. *Shaw* (1911) 6 Cr App Rep 103.
20. (1887) 19 QBD 213.
  1. *Bacon* (1870) 11 Cox CC 540; and see cases in 15 *English and Empire Digest* (Repl) 817–819. Presumably it is perjury to give false testimony in an inquiry by the court to ascertain whether it has jurisdiction, whatever the outcome of that inquiry.

falsely in an action brought by him in a fictitious name against defendants.[2] This was primarily because the Commissioners for Oaths Act 1889,[3] under which the prosecution was brought, extended to

"every case where, *if he had so sworn in a judicial proceeding* before a court of competent jurisdiction, he would be guilty of perjury;"

but the court also thought that the proceedings were judicial proceedings.

The statement need not have been made before the tribunal itself. It is enough that it is made for the purposes of the judicial proceedings before a person authorised to administer an oath and to record or authenticate the statement.[4] A statement so made in England for the purposes of a judicial proceeding anywhere abroad[5] is treated as a statement made in a judicial proceeding in England. Where an *unsworn* statement is made, either orally or in writing, under the Evidence (Proceedings in Other Jurisdictions) Act 1975, D commits an offence, under a new section 1A of the Perjury Act 1911,[6] punishable with two years' imprisonment if the statement is in fact false in a material particular and D knows or believes it to be false. Where a person is sworn outside England for the purposes of a judicial proceeding in England the statement is to be treated as if made in that proceeding, only if the person,

". . . . is lawfully sworn under an Act of Parliament –
a) in any other part of His Majesty's dominions; or
b) before a British tribunal or a British officer in a foreign country, or within the jurisdiction of the Admiralty of England."[7]

3 "A Statement Material in that Proceeding"

The doctrine that the statement must be material goes back to Coke:[8]

"For if it be not materiall, then though it be false, yet it is no perjury, because it concerneth not the point in suit, and therefore in effect it is extra-judiciall. Also this act[9] giveth remedy to the party grieved, and if the deposition be not materiall, he cannot be grieved thereby."

According to Stephen[10] the doctrine is based on a misunderstanding of Bracton but, however this may be, it became an established part of the common law, which is preserved by the Act. Settling a disputed point, the Act provides:[11]

"The question whether a statement on which perjury is assigned was material is a question of law to be determined by the court of trial."

The rule exempting immaterial statements from the sanctions of perjury has been very narrowly construed – so narrowly that clear illustrations of its operation are not very easy to find. In *Townsend*[12] a statement was held to be

---

2. *Castiglione and Porteous* (1912) 7 Cr App Rep 233.
3. Repealed by the Perjury Act 1911.
4. Perjury Act 1911, s. 1 (3).
5. This seems to be the effect of s. 1 (4).
6. See the 1975 Act, Schedule 1.
7. Perjury Act 1911, s. 1 (5); but see *O'Mealy v Newell* (1807) 8 East 364 at 372.
8. 3 Inst 167.
9. 5 Eliz 1, c. 9.
10. 3 HCL 248.
11. Section 1 (6).
12. (1866) 4 F & F 1089.

immaterial where it was made in the court of preliminary inquiry by magistrates into the truth of an alleged criminal libel, truth being irrelevant to such a charge at common law.[13] Similarly, in *Tate*,[14] D was acquitted of perjury where, at a trial for assault, he said that he had seen the defendant's wife committing adultery. The wife's adultery could affect neither the fact of the assault nor the defendant's liability for it and was therefore held immaterial.

The Court of Criminal Appeal has said[15] that it could not accept everything that Cockburn CJ said in *Tate*; but it may be that this refers to the fact that Cockburn CJ apparently considered that it made no difference that the adultery might have been relevant to the *punishment* of the defendant in the assault case, as affording provocation. It is now clear that evidence on oath directed solely to the issue of punishment – and even where given by the accused after conviction – is material.[16] But just as provocation might be relevant to punishment on a charge of assault, so might the truth of a statement in a charge of libel even if it were no defence in law. If this is an objection to *Tate*, it is equally an objection to *Townsend*.

A statement is obviously material if it bears directly on the result of the case. So D was guilty of perjury where he falsely swore that his Christian name was "Edward" and not, as was in fact the case, "Bernard Edward", with the result that the judge struck out the case because it had been brought against him in the latter name.[17]

Equally, circumstantial evidence is material, as where D, testifying to E's alibi, says not only (i) that E was in a certain house at the time of the crime (which is the matter directly in issue) but (ii) that he has lived there for two years and (iii) that he has never been absent during that time. All three statements are material,[18] for the second and third are circumstantial evidence supporting the first.

In *Phillpotts*[19] it was held that false testimony directed to procuring the admission of evidence which may be inadmissible on another ground is perjury. D swore falsely that he had examined a copy of a document with the original, with the object of having the copy admitted in evidence. It was held that he was guilty, notwithstanding that the copy would have been inadmissible even though it *had* been examined with the original. The argument to the contrary, said Campbell CJ,[20] had the effect of

> "making the offence of perjury to depend upon whether a judge were right or wrong in his direction on a question of law, and upon the decision of some nice point in a bill of exceptions, which might ultimately go to the House of Lords."

The evidence must be material "in that proceeding", not necessarily in the main issue which falls for decision. So it seems clear that an answer to a

---

13. Below, p. 824.
14. (1871) 12 Cox CC 7.
15. In *Hewitt* (1913) 9 Cr App Rep 192 at 195.
16. *Wheeler* [1917] 1 KB 283; above, p. 741.
17. *Mullany* (1865) Le & Ca 593. Erle CJ said that his inclination was to hold that any false swearing in a judicial proceeding with intent to mislead should be perjury whether it was material or not. But this was obviously not necessary to the decision and the Perjury Act settles the matter to the contrary.
18. *Tyson* (1867) LR 1 CCR 107.
19. (1851) 2 Den 302.
20. Ibid., at 309.

question going solely to the witness's credit and not at all to the question to be decided, is material.[1] In *Baker*[2] Lord Russell CJ held that

"the defendant's answers would affect his credit as a witness, and all false statements wilfully and corruptly made, as to matters which affect his credit, are material."

So in *Lavey*[3] D brought an action for goods sold and, in answer to a question put in cross-examination to test her credit, said that she had never been tried at the Old Bailey. This was untrue and Lord Campbell CJ told the jury that it was material if it might have influenced the County Court judge in believing or disbelieving her other statements.[4] In *Sweet-Escott*,[5] Lawton J held that a witness's false statement under cross-examination that he had no previous convictions was immaterial because the convictions were so old that a reasonable bench of magistrates could not have been led by them to take an adverse view of his credit. A fortiori, a false statement in civil proceedings as to a "spent" conviction under the Rehabilitation of Offenders Act 1974 is not material.

Where a matter is put to a witness in cross-examination which goes solely to his credit and he denies it, the general rule is that his answer is final and evidence is not admissible to rebut his denial. It was, no doubt, for this reason that the court held in *Murray*[6] that D was not indictable for false statements made when he was permitted to testify in rebuttal of a witness's denial under cross-examination. On similar facts, however, the opposite result was reached in *Gibbons*[7] where eleven judges (Martin B and Crompton J dubitantibus) held that D was guilty, apparently because his statement, though inadmissible in law, was logically relevant to the question to be decided – that is the witness's credibility. The court relied upon Hawkins:[8]

". . . though the evidence signify nothing to the merits of the cause and is immaterial, yet, if it has a direct tendency to corroborate the evidence concerning what is material, it is equally criminal in its own nature, and equally tends to abuse the administration of justice, and there does not seem to be any reason why it should not be equally punishable."

But what value is "tendency to corroborate", if the court is bound in law to ignore the evidence? The case goes farther than any other[9] and there is force in the objection of Martin B:[10]

"I cannot conceive how the error of the magistrates can make that evidence material in the sense in which it should be material to support an assignment of perjury upon it."

1. *Griepe* (1697) 1 Ld Raym 256 at 259, per Holt CJ; *Overton* (1842) 2 Mood CC 263 at 266, 267, per Lord Denman CJ *Worley* (1849) 3 Cox CC 535, seems to be an indulgent decision.
2. [1895] 1 QB 797 at 799.
3. (1850) 3 Car & Kir 26.
4. Today the question of materiality would be wholly for the judge; above, p. 743.
5. (1971) 55 Cr App Rep 316.
6. (1858) 1 F & F 80.
7. (1862) 9 Cox CC 105.
8. 1 PC, c. 69.
9. There was no question of the admissibility of the evidence turning on a nice point of law as in *Phillpotts*, above, p. 744.
10. 9 Cox CC at 109.

If *Gibbons* is correctly decided, this is another reason for doubting *Tate*,[11] though the decisions may be technically distinguishable – in *Gibbons* the evidence was directed to an issue which the magistrates were entitled to try – the veracity of the witness; in *Tate*, it was directed to an issue that was not before them at all.

Stephen thought that the interpretation of the law relating to materiality by Maule J in *Phillpotts*[12] "would practically get rid of the doctrine altogether."[13] Maule J said of the evidence in dispute:

". . . it is material to the judicial proceeding, and it is not necessary that it should have been relevant and material to the issue being tried."

This is substantially the doctrine adopted by the Perjury Act. As Stephen said:

"It is difficult to imagine a case in which a person would be under any temptation to introduce into his evidence a deliberate lie about a matter absolutely irrelevant to the matter before the court."[14]

Perhaps the statement is only immaterial where

"it is so irrelevant that it is no longer made by a person in the character of participant in the proceedings;"[15]

as if in answer to a question, "Were you at York on a certain day?", the witness were no reply, "Yes, and A.B. picked my pocket there", such statement having nothing whatever to do with the inquiry in hand. It was such a case that Holt CJ used as an example in *Griepe*:[16]

". . . if A being produced as a witness to prove that B was compos mentis when he made his will, swears that such a day he left his own house and went to C and lay there, and the next day lay at D, etc., if he swears falsely in these circumstances immaterial to the point of the issue, it will not be perjury."

4 The Statement may be True

It was no defence at common law that the statement was in fact true, if D believed it to be false, or was reckless whether it be true or false.[17] In *Rider*[18] the court said, "The wording of s. 1 (1), with its reference to a statement which the defendant 'does not believe to be true', appears to leave open the possibility that this is still the law." This understates the case. The words are difficult to explain on any other assumption.[19] But on that assumption, every material statement made on oath in a judicial proceeding is the *actus reus* of perjury; for, beyond the making of such a statement, nothing need

11. Above, p. 744.
12. (1851) 2 Den 302 at 306; above, p. 744.
13. 3 HCL 249.
14. Ibid. An example might be that of a woman who, out of motives of vanity, lies about her age when that is irrelevant to any issue before the court.
15. Street, *Torts*, 409, stating the rule under which a witness loses his privilege for the purposes of defamation. It would not be inappropriate that the extent of the privilege should be co-extensive with the liability to perjury.
16. (1697) 1 Ld Raym 256 at 259.
17. Co 3 Inst 160; Hawkins, 1 PC, c. 27, §§ 3, 6; *Ockley and Whitlesbye's* case (1622) Palm 294; *Allen v Westley* (1629) Het 97; Stephen, *Digest* (4th ed.), 95, 96.
18. (1986) 83 Cr App Rep 207 at 210, [1986] Crim LR 626. Cf. *Stokes* [1988] Crim LR 110 and commentaries.
19. But cf. *Haughton v Smith* [1973] 3 All ER 1109 at 1112, 1119 and 1124, holding that, under s. 22 of the Theft Act 1968, the goods must actually be "stolen", though the section says, "knowing or believing them to be stolen goods . . .".

be proved except that D made it with *mens rea*. This sits very strangely with s. 13 of the Act which requires more than one witness "as to the falsity of any statement alleged to be false". Section 13 appears to require corroboration of an immaterial fact. In *Rider*, the court thought there was "no true inconsistency" because s. 13 only applies where the statement is *alleged* to be false and, if an indictment will lie where the statement is in fact true (which the court found it unnecessary to decide), s. 13 does not apply. But, whether the section creates one offence or (improbably) two, it would seem to be open to the prosecution to avoid the corroboration requirement simply by withdrawing the allegation that the statement is false.

In practice, it seems that no one is ever prosecuted for making a statement which was true and the Law Commission has recommended that the law be brought into line with practice by re-defining perjury so as to penalise only the making of false statements.[20] It is not enough to prove that D has made inconsistent statements on oath on two occasions and that he must have known one of the statements to be false. He committed perjury on one occasion or the other but the onus is on the prosecution to prove that it was committed on a particular occasion. Practical difficulties have led both the Criminal Law Revision Committee and the Law Commission to recommend that no change should be made in the law.[1]

Where the prosecution relates to an unsworn statement under s. 1A, the Crown must prove that the statement was in fact false in a material particular.[2]

5 The Statement may be an Opinion

It is often said in the older authorities that it is not perjury unless the matter be stated "absolutely and directly".[3] Of course, the statement must be one which is sufficiently precise[4] to be capable of being proved false. If the statement is ambiguous, being true in one sense and false in the other, the Crown must prove that D used it in the false sense:[5] that is, that he intended it to be understood in the false sense. It is not clear that more than this is required. Thus it used to be said that an expression of opinion or belief was not enough but in *Schlesinger*[6] the Queen's Bench held that an expression of opinion, when that opinion is not genuinely held, is perjury.[7] The witness had stated that he "thought" a certain writing was not his, whereas in truth, he thought it was. The court recognised that this may be

---

20. Law Com. No. 96, 2.54–2.63.
   1. CLRC, Sixth Report (Cmnd. 2465, 1964), Law Com. No. 96 (1979). Cf. *Tsang Ping-nam* [1982] Crim LR 46 and commentary.
   2. Above, p. 743.
   3. Co 3 Inst 166; Hawkins, 1 PC, c. 27, §§ 7.
   4. In *Crespigny* (1795) 1 Esp 280, Lord Kenyon directed an acquittal apparently because the statement was as to the effect of a deed; but why should not this be perjury if D stated the effect to be other than he believed it to be? The true construction of the deed is immaterial. Supra.
   5. *Hayford* (1922) 62 DLR 90.
   6. (1867) 10 QB 670.
   7. The propositions to the contrary in Coke and Hawkins, above, must be considered wrong.

very difficult to prove; but that was not a good reason for holding it not to be perjury where it could be proved.

6 Mens Rea

The statement must be one which D "knows to be false or does not believe to be true". That is, either intention or recklessness will suffice. Negligence, of course, is not enough.

> "It seemeth that no one ought to be found guilty thereof without clear proof, that the false oath alleged against him was taken with some degree of deliberation; for if, upon the whole circumstances of the case, it shall appear probable, that it was owing rather to the weakness than perverseness of the party, as where it was occasioned by surprise, or inadvertency, or a mistake of the true state of the question, it cannot but be hard to make it amount to voluntary and corrupt perjury . . ."[8]

The presence of the word, "wilfully", emphasises that a degree of deliberation is required. Thus,

> "the attention of a witness ought to be called to the point upon which his answer is supposed to be erroneous before a charge for perjury can be founded upon it."[9]

If a man states that which he believes to be true, he is not guilty of perjury though he knows that the court may draw from his assertion a conclusion that he knows to be untrue, and though the statement is in fact false.[10]

The prosecution does not have to prove that D believed the statement to be material in the proceeding. Materiality is to be decided objectively by the judge.[11]

7 Subornation of Perjury

Section 7 of the Perjury Act provides:

> "1) Every person who aids, abets, counsels, procures, or suborns another person to commit an offence against this Act shall be liable to be proceeded against, indicted, tried and punished as if he were a principal offender."

This offence is now triable either way.[12] Subornation of perjury was an independent misdemeanour at common law. It consisted in procuring another to commit perjury. It was regarded as a separate offence apparently because the suborner was considered to be more blameworthy than the actual perjurer: "plus peccat author quam actor."[13] Subornation is no longer of any importance, and the reference to it in the section seems to be entirely unnecessary, as its meaning is comprehended in "procures". There can no longer be an attempt to suborn the commission of an offence.[14]

---

8. Hawkins, 1 PC, c. 27, § 2, p. 429.
9. *London* (1871) 24 LT 232 at 233, per Willes J; *Stolady* (1859) 1 F & F 518.
10. *Penn* [1966] Crim LR 681.
11. *Millward* [1985] QB 519. [1985] 1 All ER 859. [1985] Crim LR 321 and commentary, CA.
12. Criminal Law Act 1977, Sch. 2, para. 12.
13. Co 3 Inst 167.
14. Criminal Attempts Acts 1981, s. 1 (4) (b) and Schedule, Part 1.

2 Offences Akin to Perjury

1 Statements on Oath not in Judicial Proceedings and False Statements with reference to Marriage

By s. 2 of the Perjury Act 1911:

"If any person –

1) being required or authorised by law to make any statement on oath for any purpose, and being lawfully sworn (otherwise than in a judicial proceeding) wilfully makes a statement which is material for that purpose and which he knows to be false or does not believe to be true; or

2) wilfully uses any false affidavit for the purposes of the Bills of Sale Act 1878, as amended by any subsequent enactment,

he shall be guilty of [an offence triable either way], and, on conviction thereof on indictment shall be liable to imprisonment for a term not exceeding seven years."

By s. 3 (1) of the Perjury Act 1911:

"If any person –

a) for the purpose of procuring a marriage, or a certificate or licence for marriage, knowingly and wilfully makes a false oath, or makes or signs a false declaration, notice or certificate required under any Act of Parliament for the time being in force relating to marriage; or

b) knowingly and wilfully makes, or knowingly and wilfully causes to be made, for the purpose of being inserted in any register of marriage, a false statement as to any particular required by law to be known and registered relating to any marriage; or

c) forbids the issue of any certificate or licence for marriage by falsely representing himself to be a person whose consent to the marriage is required by law knowing such representation to be false,

he shall be guilty of a misdemeanour, and, on conviction thereof on indictment shall be liable to imprisonment for a term not exceeding seven years or to a fine or to both such imprisonment and fine."

It will be observed that a person who commits bigamy in England could hardly fail to be guilty of one of these offences. But where D, who had been divorced, described himself as "a bachelor", it was held that he committed no offence under s. 3 (1) (b); for "bachelor" means "an unmarried man" and D was then unmarried.[15]

If the statement is not required to be made by law, no offence can be committed under ss. 3 (1) (a) or 3 (1) (b). So the use of a forged document, purporting to be the parents' consent to D's marriage, was held to be no offence under s. 3 (1) (a).[16] The document was a form used for the convenience of superintendent registrars but there was no statutory authority for it.[17]

---

15. *Peters* [1955] Crim LR 712 (London QS).
16. *Frickey and Frickey* [1956] Crim LR 421 (Southampton QS).
17. But D was no doubt guilty of forgery. The comment in [1956] Crim LR 422 asserts that there was no intent to defraud, but see *Welham v Director of Public Prosecutions*, above, p. 271.

2 False Statements as to Births or Deaths

Section 4 (1) of the Perjury Act 1911 creates offences, punishable with seven years' imprisonment on conviction on indictment, or with a fine of £1,000 on summary conviction, of wilfully[18] making false statements, etc., relating to the registration of births and deaths or to the live birth of a child.

3 False Statutory Declarations and Other False Statements without Oath

By s. 5 of the Perjury Act 1911:

"If any person knowingly and wilfully makes (otherwise than on oath) a statement false in a material particular, and the statement is made –

a) in a statutory declaration; or

b) in an abstract, account, balance sheet, book, certificate, return, or other document which he is authorised or required to make, attest, or verify, by any public general Act of Parliament for the time being in force; or

c) in any oral declaration or oral answer which he is required to make by, under, or in pursuance of any public general Act of Parliament for the time being in force,

he shall be guilty of a misdemeanour and shall be liable on conviction thereof on indictment to imprisonment for any term not exceeding two years or to a fine or to both such imprisonment and fine.

d) with respect to a declaration made under section 16(1A) or 27B(2) of the Marriage Act 1949 –

i) enters a caveat under subsection (2) of the said section 16, or

ii) makes a statement mentioned in subsection (4) of the said section 27B,

which he knows to be false in a material particular."[19]

By s. 15 (2):

"The expression 'statutory declaration' means a declaration made by virtue of the Statutory Declarations Act 1835, or of any Act, Order in Council, rule or regulation applying or extending the provisions thereof;"

Before 1835, oaths were taken in a great number and wide variety of circumstances in the ordinary course of business. For example, an oath was required by the Bank of England of one who sought replacement of a mutilated banknote; of a churchwarden or sidesman on entering upon his office; and by the statutes regulating the business of pawnbrokers. The widespread use of the oath was not only very inconvenient, but also caused the oath to be regarded very lightly. The Act of 1835, therefore, provided that a "statutory declaration" in the form prescribed in the schedule to the Act should, or might, be substituted for an oath except in the case of an oath of allegiance and in the courts of justice. It will be noted that the false

---

18. Cf. the problem which may arise where a woman who has been artificially inseminated with the seed of a donor gives birth to a child. "If the informant does not believe that there is a real possibility that the husband may be the father, then we think the law is being broken. If, on the other hand, he is, rightly or wrongly, under the impression that there is genuinely such a possibility we cannot see how he can be found guilty of the offence of perjury": Report of the Departmental Committee on Artificial Insemination (Cmnd. 1105), para. 94.

19. Para. (d) was added by the Marriage (Prohibited Degrees of Relationship) Act 1986, s. 4.

statutory declaration is much less severely punishable than the false statement on oath.

Under s. 5 (b) the written statement must be one which D is "authorised or required" to make, whereas under 5 (c) the oral statement must be "required" and it is not enough that it is authorised.[20]

4 False Declarations to Obtain Registration for Carrying on a Vocation

Section 6 of the Perjury Act 1911 makes it an offence, triable either way and punishable on indictment with one year's imprisonment, to attempt to become registered on any statutory roll of persons qualified by law to practise any vocation or calling, by any written *or oral* representation known to be false or fraudulent.

3 Perverting the Course of Justice

1 The General Offence

It is a common law misdemeanour to do an act which has a tendency and is intended to pervert or obstruct the administration of public justice.[1] The Criminal Procedure Act 1851, s. 29, recognised the existence of an offence of conspiracy to obstruct, prevent, pervert, or defeat the course of public justice and modern cases have held that an indictment will lie for attempting[2] to pervert, or inciting[3] another to pervert, the course of justice. The charge always seems to have taken the form of an inchoate offence – incitement, conspiracy or attempt – even though justice has been manifestly defeated in fact – as in *Britton*[4] where D, by consuming alcohol, brought to summary end the course of justice under the provisions of s. 6 of the Road Traffic Act 1972.[5] Although it has been held that where an attempt is alleged the intention which must be proved is the same as for attempts generally,[6] the Court of Appeal has now said that the use of the word "attempt" in this context is misleading.[7] The charge is not one of an attempt to commit a substantive offence, but of the substantive offence itself. It follows that the authorities on proximity in the common law of attempts[8] are not directly in point. It does not follow that any act done with intent to pervert the course of justice will amount to the offence. The act

20. See *Mailey* [1957] Crim LR 328, and comment thereon.
 1. *Rowell* [1978] 1 All ER 665, 65 Cr App Rep 174 at 180, CA, approving Pollock B in *Vreones* [1891] 1 QB 360 at 369.
 2. *Grimes* [1968] 3 All ER 179 n (Kilner Brown J).
 3. *Andrews* [1973] QB 422, [1973] 1 All ER 857, CA, *Rowell*, supra.
 4. [1973] RTR 502.
 5. See now Transport Act 1981, Sch. 8.
 6. *Kellett* [1976] QB 372, [1975] 3 All ER 468 at 475.
 7. *Rowell* (1977) 65 Cr App Rep 174 at 180; *Machin* [1980] 3 All ER 151, [1980] 1 WLR 763, CA.
 8. Above, p. 291.

done must be one which has a *tendency* to pervert the course of justice. Suppose that D, a motorist, carries a hipflask for the purpose of defeating any process under s. 6 of the Road Traffic Act 1972. This preparatory act, it is submitted, does not have a sufficient tendency to obstruct justice.

The test of "tendency" may be very similar to that of proximity in attempts.[9] Indeed, in *Murray*[10] the court said that "there must be evidence that a man has done enough for there to be a risk, without further action by him, that injustice will result. In other words, there must be a possibility that what he has done, 'without more' might lead to injustice." This seems to be indistinguishable from the "last act" rule, the strictest test of proximity in attempts. In *Murray* D tampered with a blood sample which he had supplied under the Road Traffic Act 1972[11] and delivered it to his analyst. This was enough because it was a practical certainty that the fallacious information deduced from the sample would be communicated either to D's solicitor or to the prosecuting authority or, as happened, to the police. The court thought that mere tampering with the sample might have been enough,[12] but this is doubtful. D might lawfully have discarded the sample.[13] Is justice perverted where D omits to tender, or disables himself from tendering, evidence in his own defence?[14]

In *Bassi*[15] it was held that the offence was committed when D, who had been involved in an accident, offered not to give evidence, or to give evidence exonerating the other driver, in return for payment. A witness who deliberately absents himself in return for payment commits the offence, as the court made clear. But there is a difference between absenting oneself and offering or threatening to do so. The former will, without more, pervert the course of justice; the latter will not. *Bassi* is difficult to reconcile with the principle stated in *Murray*.

The offence is closely related to and overlaps with contempt of court, but the crimes are probably not coincident. The course of justice begins to run and may be perverted before proceedings are "active"[16] which is the first moment at which some types of contempt are possible. Conversely, when the proceedings are completed and justice irrevocably done, contempt, though not perversion, is still possible, by, for example, punishing a witness.

The offence may be committed by the fabrication of false evidence for the purpose of misleading a judicial tribunal;[17] by making false statements

---

9. *Andrews* [1973] QB 422, [1973] 1 All ER 857. D invited E to pay him to give evidence on E's behalf – an incitement to pervert.
10. [1982] 2 All ER 225 at 228, CA.
11. See now Transport Act 1981, Sch. 8.
12. [1982] 2 All ER at 229.
13. See commentary at [1982] Crim LR 372–373.
14. In *Vreones* [1891] 1 QB 360 Lord Coleridge CJ said he had no doubt that to manufacture false evidence for the purpose of misleading a court was an offence; but D had sent the false samples to the Corn Trade Association and, as Coleridge LCJ stressed, done all that he could to commit the offence.
15. [1985] Crim LR 671.
16. Below, p. 774.
17. *Vreones* [1891] 1 QB 360.

to the police;[18] by procuring another person to make such a false statement;[19] by stealing and destroying evidence;[20] by making improper threats against witnesses;[1] by attempting to influence a juryman;[2] by pleading guilty to an offence, in fact committed by another, so as to enable the other to escape liability;[3] by a police officer who aborts a prosecution, even for a worthy motive, knowing that he is acting outside his discretion.[4] The "course of justice" includes proceedings in any court, civil or criminal, or an arbitration. It is not necessary that proceedings should have been started or even that the tribunal should be in existence but, if procedings are not in being, they must be imminent, or an investigation which might bring about proceedings must be in progress.[5] This is not obviously reconcilable with the leading case of *Vreones*[6] where D falsified samples of wheat which had been taken from a cargo and sealed for use *in the event of a dispute*. No arbitrator had been appointed. However, the act about which the contemplated dispute might occur – the shipment of the cargo – had already taken place. In *Selvage*,[7] on the other hand, when D unlawfully attempted to use her position at the DVLC, Swansea, to remove endorsements from E's driving licence, she had in mind some future driving offence which E might commit; whereupon, if she were successful, he would be sentenced without his previous convictions being taken into account. It was held that there was no offence, as no course of justice had been embarked upon and no actual proceedings were within D's contemplation.

In *Britton*[8] D had been required to give a specimen of breath by a constable who suspected him of driving with an excess of alcohol in his blood.[9] D ran into his house and drank more alcohol, while his mother detained the constable, so as to vitiate any breath test. It was held that this was an attempt to pervert "the statutory course upon which justice had embarked" when the constable required the sample. The offence would not be committed, thought the court, by one who warned motorists in a public house that the police were waiting outside, or who warned motorists in a queue that the police further along the queue were using the breathalyser.[10] It is clearly not necessary for the prosecution to prove that the person

---

18. *Field* [1965] 1 QB 402, [1964] 3 All ER 269 (conspiracy to conceal identity by making false statement); *Rowell* (above, footnote 1) (False allegation of robbery by named person).
19. *Sharpe* [1938] 1 All ER 48.
20. *Welsh* [1974] RTR 478, CA.
1. *Kellett* [1976] QB 372, [1975] 3 All ER 468.
2. *Owen* [1976] 3 All ER 239, CA. D was convicted of embracery. The court thought embracery "obsolescent" and said that it ought to have been dealt with summarily as a contempt. They said that, if more than one person was involved, a conspiracy to pervert justice might be charged. This dictum, requiring two persons, appears to overlook the decisions that perversion of justice is a substantive offence.
3. *Devito and Devito* [1975] Crim LR 175, CA (conspiracy, D2 would have been liable on an additional charge (which would not lie against D1) if he had been prosecuted.)
4. *Coxhead* [1986] RTR 411.
5. *Selvage* [1982] QB 372, [1982] 1 All ER 96, CA.
6. [1891] 1 QB 360.
7. Supra.
8. [1973] RTR 502.
9. Above, p. 751.
10. Cf. the similar problem which has arisen under the statutory offence of obstructing the police: above pp. 392–393.

assisted to escape justice, or D himself where the obstructed proceedings would have been brought against him, was guilty of an offence.[11] It could not be proved that D was guilty of the Road Traffic offence in *Britton*. It appears to be enough that there were grounds for proceedings and that these proceedings were obstructed, etc., whatever their eventual outcome might have been. D perverts justice by tendering false evidence to prove that he has not committed adultery even though, in fact, he has not committed adultery.[12] The course of justice is perverted by false evidence or evidence given under improper pressures,[13] even though the evidence is directed to the establishment of truth. To persuade a witness to tell lies is obviously an attempt to pervert the course of justice – as well as an offence under s. 7 of the Perjury Act 1911.[14] To attempt to persuade a witness to tell the truth, or what D believes to be the truth is not, provided that the means of persuasion used are not "improper." There is nothing improper about reasoned argument nor, presumably, about pointing out to a witness who (it is believed) is proposing to lie, the immorality of his conduct. The use of threats, however, is unlawful – even if the threat is to do something which D may lawfully do. In *Kellett*[15] D threatened to sue P for slander unless P withdrew a statement he had made to solicitors in connection with divorce proceedings instituted against D by his wife. It was held that this was an offence though D believed P's statement to be false and though he intended to carry out his threat. Similarly, an offer of money to a witness to induce him to speak what the offeror believes to be the truth may be an offence.[16]

A man who seeks to establish only what he sincerely believes to be the truth might protest that his intention is to achieve justice, not to pervert it. The answer it would seem is that "justice" is the result at which the court would arrive on the evidence of witnesses free from improper pressures.

"Once legal proceedings have set the course of justice in motion, it is important that it should be allowed to flow unobstructed and undiverted, and that perjury should be exposed and truth ascertained only by examination and cross-examination of witnesses in open court and justice should be administered in the way which is ordinarily pursued."[17]

There is probably a distinction between litigants and witnesses. A party to litigation has no duty to proceed with it – he may "sell" his right to sue if he wishes. A witness has a duty to give evidence. He has nothing he can properly sell. It is lawful for one party to proposed civil litigation to offer the other money not to proceed. If the same money were offered to a witness not to give evidence this would be an offence. It would seem to be quite lawful for a defendant to pending litigation to threaten to bring a libel action unless the plaintiff dropped his claim, provided the defendant genuinely believed he had been libelled. The plaintiff's dropping the action

11. But see Williams [1975] Crim LR 432–433.
12. *Senat* (1968) 52 Cr App Rep 282, CA.
13. *Kellett* above.
14. Above, p. 748.
15. Above, p. 753.
16. Lanham, "Payments to Witnesses and Contempt of Court" [1975] Crim LR 144.
17. [1975] 3 All ER at 478, per Stephenson LJ.

would be a valid compromise of both claims. It is lawful for a third party to offer money to a litigant not to proceed in a civil court.[18] Threats by a third party may be more difficult to justify than promises, but in *Webster v Bakewell Rural District Council*[19] it was held lawful for a landlord to threaten to eject a tenant unless he dropped an action which she considered detrimental to her interest in the land.

An offer reasonably to compensate the victim of a crime if he will refrain from instituting criminal proceedings appears to be lawful.[20] Where the offence is an arrestable one and the sum offered is more than reasonable compensation, the person accepting or agreeing to accept it is guilty of an offence under the Criminal Law Act 1967, s. 5 (1), so the offeror is guilty as an inciter and, if his offer is accepted, an abettor of that offence. He may, in addition, be guilty of an attempt to defeat the course of justice.[1] When a victim of an alleged offence has made a statement to the police with a view to the provision of evidence in support of criminal proceedings, it is an attempt to pervert the course of justice to offer him an inducement to alter or withdraw that statement. It is immaterial that proceedings have not yet been instituted. In *Panayiotou*[2] P made a statement to the police alleging that she had been raped by E. D offered to find a flat for P on cheap terms if she would withdraw the allegation. It was held that P's role was now that of a witness and D was guilty of conspiracy to pervert the course of justice. The result would presumably have been different if the offer had been made before P, or anyone else, had gone (or was known to have gone) to the police, provided that the offer was no more than reasonable compensation. What if the offence had been reported to the police by a third party? It would appear that P, the victim, would again appear in the role of a witness, so an offer to her not to make a statement would be an offence.

Whether or not an attempt is charged, the intention which must be proved is the same as for attempts generally.[3] So it is enough that D knows that his act will inevitably cause a perversion of justice, even though that is not his purpose. The general principles of conspiracy and incitement are similarly applicable. Where the act amounts, as it commonly does, to the offence of contempt of court, there may be advantages for the prosecution in charging the latter offence, so avoiding the stricter *mens rea* requirements of inchoate offences.

The relationship between perverting justice and other common law misdemeanours is obscure. Thus it is sometimes said that there is a separate substantive offence of tampering with witnesses. In *Grimes* Kilner Brown J held that separate counts would lie for (i) using threats to dissuade

---

18. Acceptance of such an offer amounts to a binding contract: *Hirachand Punamchand v Temple* [1911] 2 KB 330, CA.
19. [1916] 1 Ch. 300, 304 (Neville J).
20. Cf. Criminal Law Act 1967, s. 5 (1), below, p. 764.
1. *Panayiotou* [1973] 3 All ER 112 at 116.
2. Above.
3. *Kellett* [1975] 3 All ER 468 at 475, CA, citing *Mohan*, above, p. 288. Cf. *Rowell* [1978] 1 All ER 665, 65 Cr App Rep 174, above, p. 751. *Selvage* [1982] QB 372, [1982] 1 All ER 96, above, p. 753.

a witness from giving evidence and (ii) attempting to defeat the course of justice by inducing the witness to make a false report. The law is untidy and vague and in need of reform.

2 Personating a Juryman

It is a misdemeanour at common law to personate a juryman even though D has no intention of perverting the course of justice or any dishonest intention other than of answering to the name of the juror summoned and taking his place on the jury. This was decided in *Clark*,[4] where D who took the place of his employer, "under a kind of blind obedience" to the employer's behests, was held guilty.

3 Disposal of corpse with Intent to Prevent an Inquest

If a person destroys or otherwise disposes of a dead body with intent to prevent an inquest being held, he is guilty of a common law misdemeanour, if the inquest intended to be held is one that might lawfully be held.[5] An inquest may lawfully be held if the coroner honestly believes information to be true which, if it were true, would make it his duty to hold an inquest.[6] It is not enough that the corpse has been concealed; the jury must be directed to convict only if satisfied of the intent.[7] According to Russell,[8] it is a common law misdemeanour to prevent the burial of a body and there is a recent case of conviction for conspiracy to do so.[9]

4 Embracery[10]

Embracery is an obsolescent[11] common law misdemeanour which consists in any attempt to influence a juror in the giving of a verdict otherwise than by evidence and arguments in open court. It is, of course, committed if a bribe is offered to a juror, but it is not necessary to prove that D went to these lengths. Conduct amounting to embracery is more appropriately dealt with today as a contempt of court.[12]

5 Prison Breaking, Escape and Rescue[13]

The offences of prison breaking and escape may be committed by one who is lawfully detained, whether in prison or not, in connection with a criminal offence, whether before or after trial, or a civil matter.[14] The onus of proof is on the prosecution to prove that the detention was lawful and they may not rely on the presumption of regularity, so as to require the defendant to

---

4. (1918) 82 JP 295 (Avory J).
5. *Stephenson* (1884) 13 QBD 331, CCR.
6. Ibid.
7. *Purcy* (1933) 149 LT 432.
8. *Crime* II, 1420.
9. *Hunter* [1972] Crim LR 369 (Crown Court).
10. Russell, 357; Archbold, § 24–18; Halsbury, Vol. 10, 622.
11. *Owen* [1976] 3 All ER 239; CA; above, p. 752, footnote 12.
12. Below, p. 767.
13. Russell, Chs. 19–21; Archbold, §§ 24–1 to 24–17; Halsbury, Vol. 10, 635–640.
14. *Allan* (1841) Car & M 295 (escape from imprisonment ordered by the Bankruptcy Court).

produce evidence of the unlawfulness of the detention.[15] If D is lawfully detained, it is immaterial that he has not been charged. Where, after a positive breath test, D escaped from custody while being taken to a police station for a further test, he was guilty of the offence of escape.[16]

1) Prison breaking is committed where D breaks out of the prison or other building in which he is confined. Unlike "breaking" under the common law of burglary,[17] an actual breaking must be proved and merely getting over the walls or passing through a door will not suffice.[18] An accidental breaking in the course of escape is enough. But if the breaking is effected by others without D's consent he does not commit the offence by escaping through the breach. If D is acquitted of the crime for which he was imprisoned he may not, thereafter, be convicted of prison breach.

2) Escape is committed where D escapes from confinement without any breaking as, for example, where the doors are left open by the consent or negligence of the gaoler, or where D escapes through a breach made by others without his consent or connivance. It is not necessary that D be confined in a building.[19]

The *mens rea* is an intention to escape from lawful custody and it must coincide with the act of withdrawing from lawful custody. One who withdraws from custody without intention to escape (because, for example, he has lost his memory) and thereafter deliberately remains at large does not commit the offence.[20]

3) It is a distinct offence for an officer of the law or a private person voluntarily to permit a prisoner, who is detained in a criminal (but not a civil[21]) matter, to escape. If the prisoner was guilty of treason, so too is the officer who permits him to escape.[1] If the escape is through the *negligence* of the officer or private person, a misdemeanour punishable by a fine is committed.

Escaping or attempting to escape from prison is also an offence under the Prison Rules 1949, rule 44. Since this is technically not a criminal offence and is dealt with by the Visiting Committee and not a court, the imposition of punishment under the Rules is no bar to a subsequent charge either of prison breach or escape.[2]

By the Prison Act 1952, s. 39, it is an offence punishable with five years' imprisonment to aid the escape or attempted escape of a prisoner, or, with intent to facilitate escape, to convey anything into or leave it outside a prison with a view to its coming into the possession of a prisoner. The escape must be from prison, so the offence is not committed where a

---

15. *Dillon* (1982) 74 Cr App Rep 274, [1982] Crim LR 438, PC, and commentary.
16. *Timmis* [1976] Crim LR 129 (Judge Mynett).
17. See the first edition of this book at p. 398; and above, p. 595.
18. *Burridge* (1735) 3 P Wms 439 at 484, per Lord Hardwicke CJ; Archbold, § 24–14; Russell, 332.
19. Russell, 339; *Hinds* (1957) 41 Cr App Rep 143, [1956] Crim LR 465 and commentary thereon.
20. *Scott* [1967] VR 276.
21. *Hawkins* 2 PC c. 19, s. 3.
 1. Hale, 1 PC 593.
 2. *Hogan and Tompkins* [1960] 2 QB 513, [1960] 3 All ER 149, [1960] Crim LR 775 and commentary thereon.

prisoner escapes from a magistrates' court to which he has been taken to be remanded in custody.[3]

Rescue is a common law misdemeanour consisting in forcibly liberating a prisoner from lawful custody. If the prisoner was gaoled for treason, the rescuer is also guilty of treason. The prisoner must be tried before the rescuer; and if the prisoner is acquitted, the rescuer can be convicted only of misdemeanour, whatever the nature of the charge against the prisoner.[4]

6 Wasteful Employment of Police

Section 5 (2) of the Criminal Law Act 1967 has created a new offence aimed at the kind of conduct which was the subject of prosecution as a "public mischief" in *Manley*.[5] The section provides:

"Where a person causes any wasteful employment of the police by knowingly making to any person a false report tending to show that an offence has been committed, or to give rise to apprehension for the safety of any persons or property, or tending to show that he has information material to any police inquiry, he shall be liable on summary conviction to imprisonment for not more than six months or to a fine of not more than two hundred pounds or to both."

The Criminal Law Revision Committee, when proposing this provision stated:[6]

"We considered including a provision that the conduct in question should not in future be prosecuted as a public mischief (if that offence exists) but only as a summary offence under the clause; but we decided that a provision was unnecessary because, having regard to the creation of the new offence and to the observations in *Newland*'s case, no prosecution for the public mischief offence would be likely to be instituted."

The new provision is, however, relatively narrow. Public servants other than the police may have their time wasted by false reports – for example, fire brigades, ambulance men and social workers and it is now clear that there is no offence of "public mischief". The consent of the Director of Public Prosecutions is required for a prosecution under s. 5 (2).

4 Impeding the Apprehension or Prosecution of Arrestable Offenders[8]

At common law anyone who gave to any party to a felony any assistance whatever, tending to and having the object of, enabling him to evade arrest,

---

3. *Moss and Harte* (1985) 82 Cr App Rep 116. Cf. *Nicoll v Catron* (1985) 81 Cr App Rep 339 (prisoner on remand escaping from police station yard does not escape "from prison" under Criminal Justice Act 1961, s. 22 (2)).

4. For other similar offences see Prisoners of War Escape Act 1812, s. 1; Mental Health Act 1959, ss. 129, 139.

5. [1933] 1 KB 529, CCA; overruled by *Director of Public Prosecutions v Withers* [1975] AC 842, [1974] 3 All ER 984, HL.

6. Cmnd. 2659, para. 45.

7. Williams, "Evading Justice" [1975] Crim LR 430.

trial or punishment, was guilty of the felony as accessory after the fact. The whole of the law relating to accessories after the fact is repealed by the Criminal Law Act 1967 and is replaced by s. 4 of that Act:

"1) Where a person has committed an arrestable offence, any other person who, knowing or believing him to be guilty of the offence or of some other arrestable offence, does without lawful authority or reasonable excuse any act with intent to impede his apprehension or prosecution shall be guilty of an offence [triable either way].

2) If on the trial of an indictment for an arrestable offence the jury are satisfied that the offence charged (or some other offence of which the accused might on that charge be found guilty) was committed, but find the accused not guilty of it, they may find him guilty of any offence under subsection (1) above of which they are satisfied that he is guilty in relation to the offence charged (or that other offence).

3) A person committing an offence under subsection (1) above with intent to impede another person's apprehension or prosecution shall on conviction on indictment be liable to imprisonment according to the gravity of the other person's offence, as follows:

a) if that offence is one for which the sentence is fixed by law, he shall be liable to imprisonment for not more than ten years;

b) if it is one for which a person (not previously convicted) may be sentenced to imprisonment for a term of fourteen years, he shall be liable to imprisonment for not more than seven years;

c) if it is not one included above but is one for which a person (not previously convicted) may be sentenced to imprisonment for a term of ten years, he shall be liable to imprisonment for not more than five years;

d) in any other case, he shall be liable to imprisonment for not more than three years."

The effect of *Courtie*[8] is that the section creates four offences, punishable with 10, 7, 5 and 3 years' imprisonment, respectively.

1) *The Actus Reus*

There are two elements in the *actus reus*: (i) an arrestable offence must have been committed by the person (O) whose apprehension or prosecution D is charged with impeding; and (ii) D must have done "any act" with the appropriate intent. No one may be convicted of an attempt to commit this offence.[9]

The arrestable offence alleged to have been committed by O must be specified in the indictment. If, however, it turns out that O was not guilty of the specified offence, D may still be convicted if O was guilty of another arrestable offence of which he might have been convicted on the indictment for the specified offence, under s. 6 (3) of the Criminal Law Act 1967.[10] If, for example, it is alleged that O committed murder and it transpires at D's

---

8. Above, p. 35.
9. Criminal Attempts Act 1981, s. 1 (4) (c).
10. *Morgan* [1972] 1 QB 436, [1972] 1 All ER 348. Quaere whether the same principle is applicable to other provisions allowing conviction of offences other than that charged?

trial that O was not guilty of murder but was guilty of manslaughter or attempted murder, D may be convicted. It is not necessary to direct the jury to find what offence D thought O had committed, though this may be a material factor in the imposition of sentence.[11] It is immaterial that O has been acquitted at an earlier trial if it can be proved at D's trial that O was guilty. Even where O and D are tried together, O's acquittal should not, in principle, be conclusive if it can be proved, as against D, that O committed the offence.[12] But O's conviction is presumptive evidence that he committed the offence: PACE, 1984, s. 74. Once the arrestable offence has been proved, the remaining element in the *actus reus* – any act – is almost unlimited. There must be an *act* – an omission will not suffice – but it need not be an act having a natural tendency to impede the apprehension or prosecution of an offender. Where the act does not have such a tendency, however, it will be difficult to prove the intent, in the absence of a confession. The common instances of the offence will undoubtedly correspond to the typical ways of becoming an accessory after the fact under the old law – by concealing the offender, providing him with a car, food or money to enable him to escape, or destroying evidence against him. According to the Criminal Law Revision Committee,[13] "The requirement that there should be an attempt to 'impede' a prosecution will exclude mere persuasion not to prosecute". Yet words are no doubt a sufficient act; so that the offence would be committed by intentionally misdirecting police who were pursuing an offender, or making a false statement to a detective.[14]

An act done through an agent would be sufficient. Indeed, the mere authorisation of the agent would be a sufficient act, when done with intent to impede, to constitute the offence, though the agent never acted on it.

2) *The Mens Rea*

There are two elements in the *mens rea*: (i) D must know or believe the offender to be guilty of the arrestable offence which he had actually committed, or some other arrestable offence; and (ii) D must intend to impede the apprehension or prosecution of the offender.

"Some other arrestable offence" must refer to an offence which O has not committed, for otherwise the words are redundant. If D thinks he has seen O commit a robbery and acts with intent to conceal this, he will be guilty, though O had in fact committed a murder and not a robbery. This is obviously as it should be, where, as in this example, D's belief relates to the transaction which constituted the actual offence. Suppose, however, that unknown to D, O committed murder last week. D believes, wrongly, that O committed bigamy two years ago. If D does an act with intent to impede O's prosecution for bigamy – such as burning O's letters – it would seem very odd indeed that he should be liable only because O committed murder last week – the murder has nothing to do with the case. This suggests that

11. Ibid.
12. Cf. *Shannon* [1975] AC 717, [1974] 2 All ER 1009, HL; above, p. 284 and commenting on *Donald* (1986) 83 Cr App Rep 49 [1986] Crim LR 535. Williams [1975] Crim LR at 432.
13. Cmnd. 2659, para. 28.
14. This would amount to other offences as well; see above, pp. 392–396.

the supposed offence must arise from the same transaction as the actual offence (and, undoubtedly, this will normally be the case) but so to hold would require the imposition of some limitation on the express words of the section.[15]

It is immaterial that D is unaware of O's identity.[16] What if he makes a mistake of identity? If D thinks he sees R committing an arrestable offence and acts, intending to impede his apprehension or prosecution, is he guilty under s. 4 if it was in fact O whom he observed? Perhaps the question should be answered by making a distinction. If D does an act which he intends to assist the person whom he in fact observed, his mistake of identity should be immaterial. For example, he sends a constable, who is pursuing the offender, in the wrong direction. Here D knows that the *person he is assisting* has committed an arrestable offence, and that person has in fact done so. Suppose, on the other hand, that D fabricates evidence the following day so as to provide an alibi for R and this evidence could not, and was of course not intended to assist O, of whom D has never heard. Here he does not intend to assist the person whom he in fact observed. An indictment charging D with doing an act, knowing O to be guilty of an arrestable offence and with intent to impede his prosecution is plainly bad. If R has never committed an arrestable offence, it would seem that D is not guilty under the section;[17] if R once did commit an arrestable offence, then D is guilty unless the limitation tentatively suggested in the previous paragraph be imposed.

D must *know or believe*. "... some other arrestable offence" must be governed only by "believing" since, *ex hypothesi*, the offence has not been committed and, therefore, D cannot "know" it has. "... the offence" – the arrestable offence which has actually been committed – is probably governed both by "knowing" and "believing", but, if "believing" is construed as in handling, it adds little to "knowing".[18] If the word "believing" had not been included "knowing" might well have been construed to include wilful blindness.[19] If D has a mere suspicion that O is an arrestable offender and, shutting his eyes to an obvious means of knowledge, assists him, he can hardly be said to "believe" in O's guilt. Thus recklessness may not be enough and, arguably, the subsection is unduly narrow in this respect.[20]

In order to know or believe that an arrestable offence has been committed, D need know no law. It will be enough that he believes in the existence of facts which, whether he knows it or not, amount in law to an arrestable offence.[1] His ignorance of the law cannot afford a defence.[2] The position is,

---

15. Cf. the discussion of s. 5, below, p. 764.
16. *Brindley* [1971] 2 QB 300, [1971] 2 All ER 698.
17. Nor could D be convicted of an attempt to commit the offence. See Criminal Attempts Act 1981, s. 1 (4) (c), above, p. 297.
18. *Ismail* [1977] Crim LR 557, CA; *Grainge* [1974] 1 All ER 928, CA; *Griffiths* (1974) 60 Cr App Rep 14; CA; above, p. 632.
19. Williams [1975] Crim LR at 435.
20. Above, p. 121.
1. Cf. *Sykes v Director of Public Prosecutions* [1962] AC 528 at 563, [1961] 3 All ER 33 at 42.
2. Above, p. 80.

perhaps, not quite so obvious where D has a positive mistaken belief. D knows that there is a duty not to conceal arrestable offenders, but, knowing what O has done, is wrongly informed that it does not constitute an arrestable offence. Arguably, he now has no *mens rea* on the ground that he has made a mistake of civil law,[3] whether there is a right to arrest being a civil and not a criminal matter.

The act must be done with intent to impede the arrestable offender's apprehension or prosecution. It seems that it must be proved that D's *purpose* was to impede, and that it is not enough that he knew his act would certainly impede if that was not his object or one of his objects; or, as it has been put above, that a "direct" and not merely an "oblique" intention is required.[4] At all events, this seems to be the Criminal Law Revision Committee's view of the clause which became s. 4. Discussing the case of harbouring, they wrote:

"If the harbouring is done with the object of impeding apprehension or prosecution . . . it will be within the offence; if it is done merely by way of providing or continuing to provide the criminal with accommodation in the ordinary way, it will not; and juries will be able to tell the difference."[5]

If this be the correct interpretation of the section, then, as under the old law of accessories after the fact, a handler of stolen goods will not be guilty of an offence under s. 4, even where he knows that his conduct has the effect of impeding the apprehension or prosecution of the thief, if that is not his object.[6] Nor is D guilty if, by acts done with the object of avoiding his own arrest or prosecution, he knowingly impedes the arrest or prosecution of another.[7] Where there is *prima facie* evidence of the necessary intent, it is for D to lay a foundation for a defence by introducing evidence that his sole purpose was of a different character. In the absence of such evidence, there is no duty to direct a jury to consider whether D might have had a different intent.[8] If D has the dual object of saving himself and the other from arrest or prosecution then, no doubt, he is guilty.

Under the old law, D was guilty as an accessory after the fact if he assisted a felon to evade his punishment by enabling him to escape or to remain at large. It is clearly not an offence under s. 4 to enable a convicted arrestable offender (as opposed to one awaiting trial) to escape from gaol; but this is not important as such acts will amount to other offences.[9] Whether it is an offence to assist such an arrestable offender who has escaped to remain at large depends on the interpretation of "apprehension". Does it extend beyond its obvious meaning of apprehension with a view to prosecution and include the re-arrest of the escaped convicted prisoner? There seems to be no reason why it should not be so interpreted.

---

3. Above, p. 83.
4. Above, p. 56.
5. *Andrews and Craig* [1962] 3 All ER 961n.
6. *Jones* [1949] 1 KB 194, [1948] 2 All ER 964.
7. Cmnd. 2659, para. 30.
8. *Brindley* [1971] 2 QB 300 at 304.
9. See above, p. 756.

Even though the act is done with intent to impede, it is not an offence if there is "lawful authority or reasonable excuse" for it. According to the Criminal Law Revision Committee:[10]

"The exception for 'lawful authority' will cover an executive decision against a prosecution, and that for 'reasonable excuse' will avoid extending the offence to acts such as destroying the evidence of an offence (for example a worthless cheque) in pursuance of a legitimate agreement to refrain from prosecuting in consideration of the making good of loss caused by that offence."

It is possible that the exception may have some application outside this situation.[11] As with the Prevention of Crime Act,[12] it enables the courts to afford a defence in circumstances in which they think it reasonable to do so.

3) The Sentence

Section 4 (3)[13] provides for a sliding scale of sentences which is related to the arrestable offence which has actually been committed. Where D believes that some other arrestable offence has been committed, the punishment to which he is liable is fixed according to the *actus reus*, not according to the *mens rea*. If D acts with intent to impede the apprehension of O whom he believes to have committed malicious wounding[14] (maximum, five years), he is liable to three years' imprisonment if his belief is correct; but if O has in fact committed murder, he is liable to ten years. This is another instance of the penalty being related to the harm, rather than the fault of the offender.[15]

It is clear that the arrestable offence which fixes the maximum under s. 4 must have been committed when the act of impeding takes place. D, rightly believing O to be guilty of malicious wounding, acts to impede his arrest. Subsequently, O's victim, P, dies, and O becomes guilty of murder. D is liable to only three and not ten years' imprisonment.

5 Compounding an Arrestable Offence[16]

The abolition of felonies by the Criminal Law Act 1967 eliminated two common law misdemeanours known respectively as compounding a felony and misprision of felony.[17] The former consisted in an agreement for consideration not to prosecute, or to impede a prosecution for, a felony.

10. Cmnd. 2659, para. 28.
11. Would a wife have a reasonable excuse for assisting her husband? See Pace, "'Impeding Arrest'. A Wife's Right as a Spouse?" [1978] Crim LR 82. According to *Lee Shek Ching v R.* Hong Kong, CA, 1985, No. 53, being O's wife is not, as such, a reasonable excuse.
12. Above, p. 425.
13. Above, p. 759.
14. Above, p. 397.
15. Above, p. 8.
16. Williams, "Evading Justice" [1975] Crim LR at 609.
17. See the first edition of this book, pp. 539–544.

The latter consisted simply in an omission to report a felony to the police. In place of these offences s. 5 (1) of the Criminal Law Act enacts an offence, triable either way, as follows:

"Where a person has committed an arrestable offence, any other person who, knowing or believing that the offence or some other arrestable offence has been committed, and that he has information which might be of material assistance in securing the prosecution or conviction of an offender for it, accepts or agrees to accept for not disclosing that information any consideration other than the making good of loss or injury caused by the offence, or the making of reasonable compensation for that loss or injury, shall be liable on conviction on indictment to imprisonment for not more than two years."

This provision is much less far-reaching than the previous law. It is narrower than misprision in that the offence is committed only if D accepts or agrees to accept a consideration for not disclosing the information relating to the arrestable offence. It is narrower than compounding in that it is not now criminal to accept or agree to accept consideration for not disclosing information relating to the arrestable offence, if the consideration is no more than the making good of loss or injury caused by the offence or the making of reasonable compensation for that loss or injury. No one may be convicted of attempting to commit an offence under s. 5 (1).[18]

1) *Actus Reus*

There are two elements in the *actus reus*: (i) an arrestable offence must actually have been committed; and (ii) D must accept or agree to accept consideration for not disclosing information which he knows or believes to be material.

The offence is committed only where D "accepts or agrees to accept" the consideration. The situation envisaged is that where an offer is made to D. If the offer comes from D, then he would seem to be guilty also of the much more serious offence of blackmail.[19] Consideration presumably bears much the same meaning as in the law of contract and extends to money, goods, services, or any act or forbearance.

The new offence is wider than misprision and compounding in that it extends to all arrestable offences which, of course, include some crimes which were not felonies; but it is provided by s. 5 (5):

"The compounding of an offence other than treason shall not be an offence otherwise than under this section."

It is thus clear that it is not an offence to agree to accept any consideration for not prosecuting a non-arrestable offence, though whether the resulting contract is enforceable is another matter.

18. Criminal Attempts Act 1981, s. 1 (4) (c), above, p. 297.
19. Above, p. 588.

The Act makes no provision for any privileged relationships (such as may have existed under the law of misprision) but proceedings may not be instituted without the consent of the Director of Public Prosecutions.[20]

2) *Mens Rea*

There are two elements in the *mens rea*. It must be proved that (i) D knew or believed that an arrestable offence had been committed and (ii) D intended to accept or to agree to accept consideration other than the making good of loss or the making of reasonable compensation.

Where D's knowledge or belief relates to the arrestable offence which has actually been committed, the application of the section seems quite straightforward. But D's belief may relate to some other arrestable offence which, *ex hypothesi*, has not been committed. Here D's acceptance, or agreement to accept consideration, must relate to the offence which he believes to have been committed and thus not to the offence which has actually been committed since they are different. Under this section D's belief need not – as, under s. 4, it probably must[1] – be that an arrestable offence has been committed by the same person who has in fact committed such an offence. If D wrongly supposes that he has seen an arrestable offence committed by R and accepts consideration for not disclosing what he saw, he will be guilty if in fact he saw O committing an arrestable offence.

The result is that the argument advanced in connection with s. 4, that D's belief must relate to the transaction which resulted in the actual offence, is much stronger in relation to s. 5. If D wrongly supposes that R has committed an arrestable offence and accepts consideration for not disclosing that fact, his guilt can hardly be established by proving that some time, somewhere, someone committed an arrestable offence – for example, that Dr Crippen committed murder. The offence which D supposes to have been committed must have something to do with the offence which has actually been committed. The most obvious point of connection is that the real and the supposed offence must both arise out of the same transaction. An alternative view might be that it is sufficient if either (a) the two offences arise out of the same transaction or (b) they both relate to the same person. Unknown to D, O committed murder last week. D believes, wrongly, that O committed bigamy two years ago. O offers money to D "to keep his mouth shut". D, believing that O is talking about the bigamy, accepts. According to the first view put above, D is not guilty; according to the alternative view, he is. It is submitted that the first view is better; according to the second, D's liability depends entirely on chance.

If D's acceptance of consideration relates to the transaction in question, then it seems that it will be immaterial that he is mistaken as to both (i) the nature of the arrestable offence and (ii) the identity of the perpetrator. He

20. Section 5 (3).
1. See above, p. 761.

supposes he saw R perpetrating a robbery. Actually, he saw O committing murder. If he accepts consideration for not disclosing what he saw he should be guilty.

The Criminal Law Revision Committee stated[2]

". . . the offence will not apply to a person who refrains from giving information because he does not think it right that the offender should be prosecuted or because of a promise of reparation by the offender. It would be difficult to justify making the offence apply to those cases."

It is difficult to see, however, how it can be a defence for D simply to say that he did not "think it right that the offender should be prosecuted", if he has accepted consideration for not disclosing information. Even if he convinces the court of his views as to the impropriety of the contemplated prosecution he still falls within the express words of the section. He could be acquitted only if the section were interpreted so as to require that D's object or motive be the acquisition of the consideration. As we have seen,[3] on a charge under s. 4, it is probable that a *purpose* of impeding must be proved, but this may be justified by giving a narrow meaning to the ulterior intent specified in that section. No ulterior intent is specified in s. 5 and, consequently, it is difficult to see how the section can be limited in the same way.

In the light of the new rules about compounding, it is perhaps a little surprising that the offence of advertising rewards for the return of goods stolen or lost has been retained.[4] Section 23 of the Theft Act provides:

"Where any public advertisement of a reward for the return of any goods which have been stolen or lost uses any words to the effect that no questions will be asked, or that the person producing the goods will be safe from apprehension or inquiry, or that any money paid for the purchase of the goods or advanced by way of loan on them will be repaid, the person advertising the reward and any person who prints or publishes the advertisement shall on summary conviction be liable to a fine not exceeding one hundred pounds."

In so far as an advertisement states that "no questions will be asked", it is only proposing what is perfectly lawful under s. 5 (1) of the Criminal Law Act.[5] It is not clear why this should be an offence because it is done through a public advertisement. Nor is it clear why it should be an offence to offer a reward for the return of stolen goods, even their return by the thief. The promise to pay the reward might be unenforceable for lack of consideration but, if it were actually paid, there would be nothing unlawful about that. Possibly the theory is that, if such advertisements were common, theft

---

2. Cmnd. 2659, para. 41.
3. Above, p. 762.
4. The section replaces s. 102 of the Larceny Act 1861 which provided for a penalty of £50 recoverable by a common informer. This was changed to a fine of £100 by the Common Informers Act 1951. The Criminal Law Revision Committee hesitantly recommended the retention of the provision "as advertisements of this kind may encourage dishonesty": Cmnd. 2977, para. 144.
5. Above, p. 764.

might be encouraged in that thieves would have an easy and safe way of disposing of the stolen goods for reward. This cannot apply to an advertisement addressed to the bona fide purchaser offering to recompense him if he will return the stolen goods; this seems quite a reasonable thing to do, especially since the bona fide purchaser commits no offence by retaining the goods for himself.[6]

The section creates a quasi-criminal offence, not requiring *mens rea*, so the advertising manager of a company was liable for the publication of an advertisement which he had not read.[7] "Stolen" bears the wide meaning given to that word by s. 24 (4) of the Theft Act so the bona fide purchaser may indeed have become the absolute owner of the goods where, for example, they have been obtained by deception and the property passed.

6 Refusal to Aid a Constable

It is a common law misdemeanour to refuse to go to the aid of a constable who, on seeing a breach of the peace, calls on D to assist him in restoring the peace. A ticket collector was held to be guilty of the offence when he failed to come to the assistance of a policewoman struggling with a thief. His defence that he had obeyed instructions not to leave his post was not accepted.[8] There must be a reasonable necessity for the constable to request assistance. It is no defence that D's aid would have been ineffective. So where a constable requested D to assist him in suppressing a breach of the peace among four or five hundred people at a prize fight, Alderson B directed that D's refusal was an offence.[9] It seems that it was no answer that he had his horses to take care of. Alderson B[10] recognised that physical impossibility or a lawful excuse would be an answer; but it is not clear what would constitute "lawful excuse". Is the citizen required to act where there would be a grave risk of death or serious injury?

7 Contempt of Court[11]

Contempts are of two kinds:
   1) Criminal contempt, which consists in acts tending to obstruct the due administration of justice.

6. Above, p. 503 and 630.
7. *Denham v Scott* (1983) 77 Cr App Rep 210, [1983] Crim LR 558, DC.
8. *Waugh* (1976) Times, 1st October (Knightsbridge Crown Court).
9. *Brown* (1841) Car & M 314. Cf. *Sherlock* (1866) LR 1 CCR 20.
10. In *Brown* above.
11. Arlidge and Eady, *The Law of Contempt* (1982); C. J. Miller, *Contempt of Court* (1975); Borrie and Lowe, *The Law of Contempt* (2nd ed., 1983); Fox, *Contempt of Court*; Street, *Freedom, the Individual and the Law*, Ch. 6; Fischer "Civil and Criminal Aspects of Contempt of Court" (1956) 34 Can Bar Rev 121; Beale, "Contempt of Court, Civil and Criminal" (1935) 48 Harv LR 161; Goodhart "Newspapers and Contempt of Court in English Law" (1935) 48 Harv LR 885; D. G. T. Williams [1961] Crim LR at 92 et seq. On the Contempt of Court Act 1981 see Miller, [1982] Crim LR 71, Bailey (1982) 45 MLR 301.

2) Civil contempt,[12] which consists in disobedience to the judgments, orders or other process of the superior courts.[13]

The distinction between the two types of contempt is not always by any means clear-cut and the practical importance of the distinction has diminished in modern times. The Phillimore Committee[14] noted that there were theoretical distinctions in respect of privilege, waiver of contempt, sanctions, execution and the Crown's prerogative of mercy, and recommended that in all these respects the civil law should be brought into line with the criminal.[15] That recommendation has not, however, been implemented.

Criminal contempt is a common law offence which might be dealt with on indictment in accordance with ordinary criminal procedure but in practice is invariably tried under the jurisdiction of the superior courts to punish contempt by summary process.[16] By s. 14 of the Contempt of Court Act 1981, in this section referred to as "the Act", committal must now be for a fixed term, but without prejudice to the power of the court to order earlier discharge and must not exceed two years in the case of a superior[17] court or one month in the case of an inferior court. As it is a criminal proceeding, the sentence may be remitted by the Crown.

Civil contempt, on the other hand, may be dealt with only by summary process and an indictment will not lie. The object of the proceedings is not punitive but coercive but a sentence for a definite term must now be imposed. D may be released by the court when he has purged his contempt; but the Crown never interferes.[18] Since the proceedings may result in imprisonment, certain of the rules of criminal trials are applied. The case must be proved beyond reasonable doubt,[19] and the defendant cannot be compelled to give evidence or to incriminate himself.[20] There must be conscious disobedience or wilful blindness.[1] Where D intentionally disobeys an order of the court, the proceedings may have the dual purpose (i) of enforcing the order for the benefit of the person in whose favour it was awarded and (ii) of punishing D for having "contumaciously set at naught" the order of the court.[2] In this case the proceeding is civil and it therefore

12. The distinction is criticised in *A-G v Newspaper Publishing plc* [1987] 3 All ER, 276 at 294, 306, CA.
13. The county court is an inferior court, even when exercising powers equivalent to those of the High Court in granting or enforcing injunctions, and does not have the powers of committal under the 1981 Act, s. 14 (1), of the High Court: *Peart v Stewart* [1983] 1 All ER 859, [1983] 2 WLR 451, HL, reversing *Whitter v Peters* [1982] 2 All ER 369, [1982] 1 WLR 389, DC. And see the Magistrates Courts Act 1980, s. 63 (3) and Contempt of Court Act 1981, s. 17.
14. Hereafter referred to as "Phillimore".
15. *Phillimore*, Cmnd. 5794, Ch. 8. See also Miller, *Contempt of Court* Ch. 2.
16. See Halsbury, Vol. 8, p. 30. The last case of trial by indictment seems to have been *Tibbits and Windust* [1902] 1 KB 77; D. G. T. Williams [1961] Crim LR at 93.
17. Defined in s. 19.
18. According to the Attorney General (Sir Charles Russell), arguendo, "... though the Crown could interfere, it would be unconstitutional to do so": *Re Special Reference from the Bahama Islands* [1893] AC 138 at 145, PC; *Seaward v Paterson* [1897] 1 Ch. 545 at 559, CA, per Rigby LJ.
19. *Re Bramblevale Ltd* [1970] Ch. 128, [1969] 3 All ER 1062, CA.
20. *Comet Productions UK Ltd v Hawkex Plastics Ltd* [1971] 2 QB 67, [1971] 1 All ER 1141, CA.
1. *Heaton's Transport (St Helens) Ltd v Transport and General Workers Union* [1972] 2 All ER 1214 at 1237, CA.
2. *Seaward v Paterson* [1897] 1 Ch. 545 at pp. 555, 556, CA, per Lindley LJ.

seems that if D2 aids and abets D1 in disobeying an order of the court made against D1 only, D2's contempt is criminal, whereas D1's is civil.[3]

While there has always been a right of appeal to the Court of Appeal from a committal for civil contempt,[4] no appeal lay from a committal[5] for criminal contempt until the Administration of Justice Act 1960.[6] By s. 13 of this Act, a right of appeal to the Court of Appeal is provided for all cases of contempt, both civil and criminal.

The summary procedure which applies in criminal contempt distinguishes it from all other crimes but, according to Lord Denning, the principles governing the offence itself are those applicable to criminal offences generally.[7] Thus, the general principles of participation in crime, incitement, conspiracy and attempt[8] probably apply and *mens rea* must be proved[9] except that, in one class of contempt,[10] strict liability exists, and has been recognised by Parliament to exist, at common law.

1) *The Actus Reus of Contempt*

The *actus reus* of contempt is any conduct which either (a) has a tendency or (b) is intended to obstruct or prejudice the course of justice in present or future legal proceedings.

For the purposes of the law of contempt, "court" means a court of judicature, a body established by law to exercise, either generally or subject to defined limits, the judicial power of the state.[11] Judicial power is to be contrasted with legislative and executive or administrative power.[12] There can be no contempt of a local valuation court because its functions are essentially administrative,[13] or a commission or committee of inquiry, even when presided over by a judge, in the absence of legislation extending the protection of the law of contempt to such a body.[14]

It has been stated in a modern case that the question is whether there was a "real risk" of prejudice or obstruction and that intention alone is not

---

3. Ibid. But Lord Atkinson thought there was an absurdity in holding that D2 was a criminal because he did what he was *not* prohibited from doing, yet D1 was not a criminal though he did the same thing, which he *was* prohibited from doing; *Scott v Scott* [1913] AC 417 at 456–460. And see *A-G v Newspaper Publishing plc* [1987] 3 All ER 276 at 306.
4. *Scott v Scott* [1912] P 241 at 285, per Fletcher Moulton LJ.
5. As distinct from a conviction on indictment where, of course, there was an appeal to the Court of Criminal Appeal.
6. See D. G. T. Williams [1960] Crim LR 87, at pp. 92–100.
7. *Balogh v St. Albans Crown Court* [1974] 3 All ER 283 at 289, CA.
8. But Stephenson LJ doubted whether an attempt to commit contempt is punishable as such: *Balogh*, above at p. 290. See also *Ingrams, ex parte. Goldsmith* [1977] Crim LR 40, DC.
9. *Re F (a minor)* [1977] Fam 58, [1977] 1 All ER 114, CA. *Re A-G's Application, A-G v Butterworth* [1963] 1 QB 696, CA, below, p. 782.
10. Below, p. 772.
11. In the Contempt of Court Act 1981, "'court' includes any tribunal or body exercising the judicial power of the State, and 'legal proceedings' shall be construed accordingly."
12. *A-G v British Broadcasting Corpn* [1981] AC 303, [1980] 3 All ER 161.
13. *Ibid.*
14. *Badry v Director of Public Prosecutions of Mauritius* [1983] 2 AC 297, [1982] 3 All ER 973, PC.

enough.[15] It seems, however, that this case is irreconcilable with long established law, that threats to, or attempted intimidation of, judges, parties, witnesses or jurors, or the offering of bribes to any of them, are contempt even though the person approached is impervious to threats and quite incorruptible.[16] To send a bribe to one of Her Majesty's judges would undoubtedly be a contempt, yet it can hardly be supposed that there is a "real risk" that he would allow it to influence his decision. There must be an *actus reus*[17] but it seems that any act done with intent thereby to obstruct the administration of justice would be enough. There is an *actus reus* where the court has made orders to preserve the subject matter of an action pending trial and D, a third party, knowing of those orders, destroys or seriously damages the subject matter.[17]

2) *Contempt in Court*

Contempt may take various forms. The most obvious is contempt "in the face of the court". This occurs when, for example, D makes a physical attack upon, or threats against, the judge,[18] counsel or a witness or potential witness[19] in the courtroom. The proceedings could not properly be carried on in the face of tumultuous and disorderly behaviour of this kind. Language which is insulting to the judge[20] or the jury[1] may amount to contempt. Whether it does so in the particular case depends on whether it interferes or tends to interfere with the course of justice. "No further definition need be attempted."[2] The court has an obligation to protect jurymen in the discharge of their duties against indignity and insult. Strong language will not be a contempt if used by counsel in the honest discharge of his duty for the purpose of vindicating the interests of his client;[3] but if he oversteps the bounds and refuses to withdraw when instructed by the judge, he will be in contempt.[4] An insult to counsel or the opposing litigant will, it seems, less readily be regarded as contempt though, if it is so outrageous and provocative as to be likely to lead to a brawl in court, then it will be.[5]

Section 12 of the Act gives magistrates' courts a power which county court judges already had under s. 157 of the County Courts Act 1959 to deal with any person who –

---

15. *Ingrams, ex parte Goldsmith* [1977] Crim LR 40, DC.
16. *Skipworth and de Castro's Case* (1873) LR 9 QB 230; *Re Ludlow Charities, Lechmere Charlton's Case* (1837) 2 My & Cr 316 at 319; Miller, op. cit. 159–160; Phillimore, para. 66.
17. *A-G v Newspaper Publishing plc* [1987] 3 All ER 276 at 303, CA.
18. *Re Cosgrave*, Seton's *Judgments and Orders* (7th ed.), 457, discussed in 38 LQR at 185 (throwing an egg at the judge). *Goult* (1982) 76 Cr App Rep 140, CA (threatening stare at jurors).
19. *Re B (JA) (an infant)* [1965] Ch. 1112, [1965] 2 All ER 168 at 174, per Cross J.
20. *Davison* (1821) 4 B & Ald 329.
 1. *Ex parte Pater* (1864) 5 B & S 299.
 2. *Parashuram Detaram Shamdasani v King-Emperor* [1945] AC 264.
 3. *Ex parte Pater* (1864) 5 B & S 299 at 301.
 4. Ibid.
 5. *Parashuram's case*, above.

(1)"(a) wilfully insults the justice or justices, any witness before or officer of the court or any solicitor or counsel having business in the court, during his or their sitting or attendance in court or in going to or returning from the court; or

    (b) wilfully interrupts the proceedings of the court or otherwise misbehaves in court."

Though the Act does not say so, this power presumably only applies or, at all events, should only be exercised, where the act has a tendency to interfere with the course of justice. Presumably the powers of the county and magistrates' courts to deal with contemptuous behaviour are no wider than those of the superior courts.

Defiance of the proper order of the court is a contempt, as where a person persists in the use of language or a line of conduct against the ruling of the judge; or a witness refuses to be sworn, or to answer,[6] or does not leave the court when told to do so.[7] The purpose of the proceedings is not to buttress the dignity of the judges and protect them from insult, but to protect the rights of the public by ensuring that the administration of justice is not obstructed.[8]

In *Balogh v St Albans Crown Court*[9] D planned to enliven the proceedings by injecting "laughing gas" into the courtroom. Had he carried out his plan, this would have been a contempt in the face of the court. Lord Denning thought that contempt may be "in the face of the court" although the act is not done in the sight of the judge or even in the courtroom and instanced a case[10] where a threat was made in a café to a girl who had just given her evidence and been released by the judge. This hardly seems consistent with his lordship's opinion that "in the face of the court" really means "contempt in the cognisance of the court" because the offending act was not in the cognisance of the court in that instance, until the judge was informed of it by a witness. Nothing of substance, however, seems to turn on any distinction between contempts in the face of the court and other contempts.

Contempt in the face of the court rarely presents problems of *mens rea*. The more blatant forms are so obviously aimed at interference with the course of the proceedings that the court will have no difficulty in holding that this was the D's purpose. In other cases it may be less clear. A person might interrupt the proceedings with the purpose of furthering rather than obstructing or perverting justice; but "the course of justice" probably means the established, orderly procedure of the court and it is probably enough that D intends to interrupt that. Section 12 of the Act requires that the interruption of a magistrates' court be "wilful" but it does not expressly require an intent to pervert justice.

---

6. *Ex parte Fernandez* (1861) 10 CBNS 3.
7. *Chandler v Horne* (1842) 2 Mood & R 423.
8. *Morris v Crown Office* [1970] 2 QB 114, [1970] 1 All ER 1079.
9. [1975] QB 73, [1974] 3 All ER 283, CA.
10. *Moore v Clerk of Assize, Bristol* [1972] 1 All ER 58, [1971] 1 WLR 1669.

3) *Contempt out of Court in relation to Particular Proceedings*

Contempt may be committed out of court by any conduct which has a tendency or is intended to interfere with the course of justice in a particular case. Threats to, or intimidation of, parties, witnesses or jurors or the offering of bribes to witnesses or jurors are contempt, even, as has been noted above, if the witness is incorruptible. Any private communication to a judge for the purpose of improperly influencing his decision is a contempt whether it is accompanied by a bribe or not.[11] Any published comment that an accused person is guilty of the offence charged,[12] or has confessed or has pleaded guilty to other charges,[13] and adverse comment on the character of a party to civil proceedings may constitute contempt if there is a risk that it will prejudice the jury or witnesses.[14] It may be contempt for a newspaper to carry out and publish the results of an independent investigation into a crime for which a man has been arrested;[15] or to publish the photograph of the accused where it is reasonably clear that a question of identity has arisen or may arise.[16] The publication of photographs and "identikit" pictures to assist in the apprehension of a suspect is presumably justifiable, even where it might cause prejudice, if the public interest in his apprehension outweighs that in the complete fairness of his trial. It is contempt to inhibit a suitor from availing himself of his constitutional right to have his legal rights and obligations ascertained and enforced by the courts; so the interception by a prison governor of a letter written by a prisoner to his solicitor so as to deny, even temporarily, the prisoner's right of access to the court, constitutes contempt.[17] Such conduct cannot be justified by reference to the Prison Rules.

1 Unintentional Interference

a) *The "strict liability" rule.* Contempt of this kind has been held to be an offence of strict liability.

In *Odhams Press Ltd, ex parte A-G*[18] D Ltd had published a newspaper article containing conspicuous allegations of crime against E. Unknown to D Ltd, E had not only been arrested and charged but had been committed for trial at the time of publication. D Ltd was held guilty of contempt. While the court was clearly disposed to think that D Ltd had in fact been negligent in not knowing of E's committal, the decision does not depend on that ground:

---

11. Per Cottenham LC, *Re Ludlow Charities, Lechmere Charlton's* case (1837) 2 My & Cr 316 at 319; *Re Dyce Sombre* (1849) 1 Mac & G 116 at 122. It would not, of course, be contemptuous to write to a judge drawing attention to relevant evidence or to an authority on a point of law involved in the case.
12. After a revolver had been dropped near the King's horse and a man was arrested, the publication in a cinema of a news film of the arrest with the caption, "Attempt on the King's Life", was a contempt: *Hutchinson, ex parte McMahon* [1936] 2 All ER 1514.
13. *Border Television Ltd, ex parte A-G* (1978) 68 Cr App Rep 375, [1978] Crim LR 221.
14. *Higgins v Richards* (1912) 28 TLR 202.
15. *Evening Standard, ex parte Director of Public Prosecutions* (1924) 40 TLR 833.
16. *Daily Mirror, ex parte Smith* [1927] 1 KB 845.
17. *Raymond v Honey* [1983] 1 AC 1, [1982] 1 All ER 756, HL.
18. [1957] 1 QB 73, [1956] 3 All ER 494.

"The test is whether the matter complained of is calculated to interfere with the course of justice, not whether the authors and printers intended that result, just as it is no defence for the person responsible for the publication of a libel to plead that he did not know that the matter was defamatory and had no intention to defame."[19]

The *Odhams* case was followed by the Divisional Court in *Griffiths ex parte A-G*.[20] D distributed in England an American magazine which contained prejudicial comments on a murder trial then proceeding in England. D was unaware of the existence of these comments. He was held to be guilty whether he was negligent or not. This time, the analogy of libel was rejected and the court held that the defence of innocent dissemination[1] was not available:

"Cases of contempt by the publication of matter tending to prejudice a fair trial stand in a class of their own and are not truly analagous to defamation."[2]

Section 1 (1) of the Contempt of Court Act 1981 adopts the common law rule:

"In this Act 'the strict liability rule' means the rule of law whereby conduct may be treated as a contempt of court as tending to interfere with the course of justice in particular legal proceedings regardless of intent to do so."

This restatement recognises some of the limits of the rule; it applies only to conduct prejudicing particular legal proceedings and not, for example, to scandalising the court or other conduct tending to prejudice or obstruct the course of justice in general.

Section 6 makes it clear that the common law rule of strict liability is in no way enlarged and that common law defences continue to apply.

Sub-sections (1), (2) and (3) of s. 2 impose three limitations on the scope of strict liability:

"1) The strict liability rule applies only in relation to publications, and for this purpose 'publication' includes any speech, writing, broadcast or other communication in whatever form, which is addressed to the public at large or any section of the public.

2) The strict liability rule applies only to a publication which creates a substantial risk that the course of justice in the proceedings in question will be seriously impeded or prejudiced.

3) The strict liability rule applies to a publication only if the proceedings in question are active within the meaning of this section at the time of publication."

A person might interfere with the course of justice by injuring or detaining a witness but, as this conduct is not a "publication", the Crown would have to prove "intent".[3] There is no strict liability then in respect of

---

19. [1957] 1 QB at 80, [1956] 3 All ER at 497, per Lord Goddard CJ. The court followed *Roach v Garvan* (1742) 2 Atk 469; and *Ex parte Jones* (1806) 13 Ves 237, and distinguished the more recent cases of *Metropolitan Music Hall Co. v Lake* (1889) 58 LJCh 513, and *Re Marquis Townshend* (1906) 22 TLR 341, as cases in which the court did not consider that the matter complained of was sufficiently serious to call for action.

20. [1957] 2 QB 192, [1957] 2 All ER 379.

1. *Emmens v Pottle* (1885) 16 QBD 354.

2. [1957] 2 QB at 204.

3. Below, p. 779.

a private communication which happens to create a risk of prejudice to the administration of justice. An offer to make a payment to a witness contingent on the outcome of a trial will be contempt only if it is "intended" to prejudice the outcome of the trial.[4]

The risk must be "substantial" and the threatened impediment "serious". A slight or trivial risk of serious prejudice is not enough nor is a substantial risk of slight prejudice.[5] An assertion that a man charged with, inter alia, burglary in Buckingham Palace was a "junkie" was too remote to create a "substantial" risk; but an assertion that he had admitted the offence could hardly fail to create a substantial risk of serious prejudice.[6] Where D was charged with a trivial common assault on P, an allegation that he had stabbed P in the neck was a contempt, either because it might lead the jury to think the prosecution were "pulling their punches",[7] or because the publication interfered with the defendant's freedom to conduct his defence as he thought best, by leading him to elect for trial on indictment when otherwise he would have consented to summary trial.[8] Phillimore[9] thought that any risk should be enough but the Act imposes a greater restriction and eliminates "technical contempts". The publication by a newspaper of material prejudicial to a trial in a place remote from the paper's area of circulation might not be "substantial". It is clearly no longer the law[10] that any "prejudgment" of the issues in a case is necessarily a contempt.[11]

Strict liability applies only while the proceedings are "active", a new term used in the Act to define the concept, *sub judice*, in precise terms. The Act distinguishes, as did the common law, between civil and criminal proceedings. In criminal cases at common law, the period began when proceedings were pending or "imminent", an unsatisfactorily vague term. Now, by Schedule 1 of the Act, criminal proceedings are active when there has been an arrest without warrant, the issue of a summons or warrant, the service of an indictment or an oral charge. Phillimore recommended that the period should begin only on charge or service of a summons, pointing out that the press might not know that a warrant for arrest had been issued or an arrest made. This is true, but the defence of innocent publication[12] is available to a person who can prove that, having taken all reasonable care, he did not know and had no reason to suspect that the proceedings were active.

Criminal proceedings are concluded by acquittal or sentence or any other verdict, finding order or decision which puts an end to the proceedings; or by discontinuance, or operation of law.[13]

---

4. Phillimore recommended an inquiry into the prevalence of this practice with a view to framing, if necessary, a separate criminal offence: para. 79. The practice caused concern at the trial of the "Moors Murders" in 1966 and of Jeremy Thorpe and others in 1979.
5. *A-G v Times Newspapers Ltd* (1983) *Times*, 12th Feb, DC, per Lord Lane CJ. See also *A-G v News Group Newspapers Ltd* [1987] QB 1, [1986] 2 All ER 833.
6. Ibid.
7. Per Lane LCJ.
8. Per Oliver LJ.
9. Para. 123.
10. *A-G v Times Newspapers Ltd* [1973] 3 All ER 54 at 65, 84; Phillimore, paras. 106–111.
11. Below, p. 779.
12. Section 3, below.
13. These matters are spelt out in some detail in the Schedule to the Act.

A problem arises where a warrant is issued for the arrest of a suspect who disappears for a long period, as in the case of Lord Lucan. To prevent comment being stifled indefinitely, the schedule provides that, in such a case, the proceedings cease to be active after the lapse of twelve months unless the suspect has been arrested, but become active again when he is arrested. This does not appear to apply in the case of a person who has been arrested but who escapes from custody before trial.[14]

Civil proceedings become active "when arrangements for the hearing are made or, if no such arrangements are previously made, from the time the hearing begins until the proceedings are disposed of, discontinued or withdrawn . . .". Civil proceedings were formerly "pending" from the issue of the writ, which made possible the "gagging writ", issued for the purpose of stifling discussion, perhaps without any intention of ever prosecuting the proceedings. Now, discussion will not be inhibited until the case is set down for trial.

The Act makes separate provision for appellate proceedings. These, whether civil or criminal, are active from the time when they are commenced by application for leave to appeal, notice of appeal or other originating process until disposed of or abandoned, discontinued or withdrawn.

The main risk of comment on active proceedings is that it will prejudice a jury. Judges should be immune from prejudice.[15] Arguably then, contempt, and particularly the strict liability rule, ought to have no application in civil cases where trial is to be by judge alone, or in appellate proceedings. There is, however, the possibility of some adverse effect upon the witnesses, the appellant or, in a civil case, the respondent.

b) *Innocent publication or distribution.* Section 3 of the Act, re-enacting s. 11 of the Administration of Justice Act 1960, provides:
   "1) A person is not guilty of contempt of court under the strict liability rule as the publisher of any matter to which that rule applies if at the time of publication (having taken all reasonable care) he does not know and has no reason to suspect that relevant proceedings are active.
   2) A person is not guilty of contempt of court under the strict liability rule as the distributor of a publication containing any such matter if at the time of distribution (having taken all reasonable care) he does not know that it contains such matter and has no reason to suspect that it is likely to do so.
   3) The burden of proof of any fact tending to establish a defence afforded by this section to any person lies upon that person."

Thus, if the facts of the *Odhams* case[16] were to recur, D would have a defence only if he were able to prove that he had taken all reasonable care to find out whether proceedings were pending or imminent. If the facts of the

Griffiths case[17] were to recur, D would have a defence only if he were able to prove that he had taken all reasonable care to find out whether the publication contained offensive matter.

It is no defence to either the editor or the proprietor that the editor has devised, "so far as humanly possible", a system to prevent the publication of prejudicial matter, if he knows, or has reason to suspect, that proceedings are pending.[18] Section 3 would have no effect on the decision in the *Evening Standard* case.[19] A reporter telephoned an inaccurate report of the evidence in a criminal trial and the defendant newspaper published it. The jury at the trial might thus have read of matters of which in fact no evidence had been given. It was held that the newspaper was liable for contempt. The responsible officers of the paper did not know, and had no reason to suspect, that the report was in any way inaccurate, but of course they knew that the proceedings were active, and they were not mere distributors of the paper.

The *Evening Standard* case is sometimes said to establish that contempt is also a crime of vicarious liability and, indeed, the court itself said that this was the law,[20] the editor and proprietors being liable for the act of the reporter. But surely the contempt was the *publication* and surely this was the act of the company, through its responsible officers.[1] The company is clearly a principal offender and the editor, because of the very special position of responsibility for the published matter which he occupies,[2] should perhaps be regarded as a joint principal. The journalist, however, committed no contempt of court in sending the material to his superiors. His liability, on a true analysis, was, if any, that of a counsellor or abettor. Yet the court did not believe "that the reporter for a moment deliberately or intentionally sent out false information". No doubt he was negligent, but negligence is not enough to found liability as a secondary party.[3] Thus it seems very doubtful whether the reporter was rightfully convicted.[4]

c) *Further limitations on the strict liability rule.* Sections 4 and 5 provide that contemporary reports of legal proceedings and discussion of public affairs, respectively, do not constitute contempt under the strict liability rule in the circumstances specified in the sections. Unlike s. 3,[5] these sections do not create "defences"[6] and the onus of proof is on the Crown. The sections provide that, in the specified circumstances, strict liability

---

17. Above, p. 773.
18. *Thomson Newspapers Ltd ex parte A-G* [1968] 1 All ER 268.
19. [1954] 1 QB 578, [1954] 1 All ER 1026.
20. [1954] 2 QB at 585, [1954] 1 All ER at 1029.
1. See above, p. 170.
2. See *Steiner v Toronto Star Ltd* (1956) 1 DLR (2d) 297; and cf. the peculiar position of the holder of a justices' licence who is a servant: *Goodfellow v Johnson* [1966] 1 QB 83, [1965] 1 All ER 941.
3. *Callow v Tillstone* (1900) 19 Cox CC 576; above, p. 143.
4. In *Griffiths, ex parte A-G* [1957] 2 QB 192 at 202, [1957] 2 All ER 379 at 382, Lord Goddard CJ said that it had never been held that the reporter who supplied the material was liable. This overlooks the *Evening Standard* case, above; but it seems that the reporter *ought* not to be convicted unless he has *mens rea*.
5. Above, p. 775.
6. *A-G v English* [1982] 2 All ER 903, [1982] 2 WLR 959, HL where s. 5 was in issue.

does not apply even though the publication in fact creates a substantial risk of serious prejudice. It is not necessary to rely on either section unless the Crown can prove that such a risk existed. By s. 4 (1):

"Subject to this section a person is not guilty of contempt of court under the strict liability rule in respect of a fair and accurate report of legal proceedings held in public,[7] published contemporaneously and in good faith."

This provision is in similar terms to s. 3 of the Law of Libel Amendment Act 1888[8] except that the requirement of "good faith" is additional.

Section 4 (2) gives the court a discretion to order the postponement of a report of proceedings where it appears to be necessary to avoid a substantial risk of prejudice to those or other proceedings, pending or imminent. Where such an order has been made, it seems that anyone who, knowing of the order, publishes a report in defiance of it, is guilty of an intentional contempt of court.[9] It is not necessary to show that the publication in fact caused a risk of prejudice to the administration of justice.[10] The contempt consists in the flouting of the order of the court. Where the publisher acts in ignorance of the order of the court, he could be liable, if at all, only under the strict liability rule and it would be necessary to show that the conditions of s. 2 (2)[11] were satisfied. The defence under s. 3 would not be applicable because D's ignorance is of the existence of the order, not of the fact that the proceedings are "active".

Section 4 (2) is applicable to committal proceedings and the prospective trial at the Crown Court is a "pending" proceeding although the committal proceedings may terminate with the discharge of the defendant.[12] If the court makes no order under s. 4 (2) it seems that it may now be lawful to publish matter although there is a substantial risk that it will seriously impair the administration of justice, as where evidence given in the absence of the jury is published. Formerly it would have been regarded as self-evident that such matter should not be published; but now it may be that the onus is on the court expressly to forbid it.[13] The rationale of the provision is to remove uncertainty and it does this by allowing the publication of anything that is not forbidden by the court. A possible answer to this view is that s. 4 (1) does not create any right to publish fair and accurate reports but merely provides a defence where strict liability is

7. This means proceedings in court and does not include an out-of-court arrest: *Rhuddlan JJ, ex p HTV Ltd* [1986] Crim LR 329.
8. Salmond, *Torts*; Winfield and Jolowicz, *Tort*.
9. *Horsham JJ, ex parte Farquharson* [1982] QB 762, [1982] 2 All ER 269, CA.
10. *Horsham JJ*, supra. Lord Denning MR, dissenting on this point, thought that s. 6 (b) requires the court to find that the publication would be punishable as a contempt apart from the provisions of the Act: [1982] 2 All ER at 284; but s. 6 (b) limits only the strict liability rule and not intentional contempts. Shaw LJ put his decision on the ground that publication known to be in contravention of the order could not be said to be made in good faith: [1982] 2 All ER 269 at 290. S. 4 (1) would be inapplicable and D would be subject to strict liability; but this seems, with respect, inconsistent with the rejection of the argument that the publication must be shown to have caused a substantial risk of serious prejudice – i.e. the strict liability rule. The better view is that of Ackner LJ, that the subsection creates a new head of contempt: [1982] 2 All ER at 295.
11. Above, p. 773.
12. *Horsham JJ*, supra.
13. [1982] 2 All ER at 286, per Lord Denning MR, and at 295 per Ackner LJ.

alleged; and that a publisher who knows that, or is reckless whether, his publication will prejudice the administration of justice commits a contempt quite independently of any rule of strict liability.

Section 5 provides that –

"A publication made as or as part of a discussion in good faith of public affairs or other matters of general public interest is not to be treated as a contempt of court under the strict liability rule if the risk of impediment or prejudice to particular legal proceedings is merely incidental to the discussion."

The section allows the discussion in the press of controversial matters of general public interest even though this will create a substantial risk of prejudice to the proceedings, provided that the discussion is "in good faith" and the risk is "merely incidental" to the discussion. The meaning of "good faith" is obscure. If the defendant intends to prejudice the proceedings, no doubt he lacks good faith; but then he would be liable apart from the strict liability rule, so the words have no real function in that situation. The risk may be "merely incidental" to the discussion (so that publication is not contempt) even though it could have been written as effectively without the passages which create the risk. The House of Lords has held that the test is whether the risk was no more than an incidental consequence of expounding its main theme.[14] A suggestion that D was a rootless, penniless neurotic having a liaison with a homosexual royal bodyguard created a substantial risk of serious prejudice to D's pending trial for burglary in Buckingham Palace, but was merely incidental to the main theme of an article discussing the protection of the Queen, a matter of great public interest, and, therefore, was not a contempt.[15]

In *A-G v English*[16] the defendants published an article in support of Mrs Carr, a "pro-life" candidate in a parliamentary by-election. It stated that handicapped babies were likely to be allowed by doctors to die, sometimes by starvation. In the same week began the trial of Dr Arthur[17] for the murder of a handicapped baby by allowing it to starve. The article did not refer to the doctor's trial and the publishers did not regard it as capable of being read by anyone as referring to it. The trial judge took a different view and referred the matter to the Attorney-General. The judges in the divisional court and the House of Lords all agreed that the article created a substantial risk of prejudice. The Crown relied on the strict liability rule and did not contend that the article was intended to be prejudicial. It was not disputed that the article discussed a matter of public interest. The question was whether the risk of prejudice was "merely incidental". The divisional court thought it was not; the matter complained of was "extraneous to the main intendment of the article" which could have been as effectively written without the reference to starving handicapped babies, which amounted to "accusations". The House of Lords disagreed. The article would have lost all its point, whether in relation to the parliamentary

---

14. *A-G v English* [1982] 2 All ER 903, at 920, HL, per Lord Diplock.
15. *A-G v Times Newspapers Ltd* (1983) *Times*, 12th February.
16. Supra.
17. See Helen Beynon, [1982] Crim LR 17.

election or as a contribution to the wider controversy, if it had eschewed all reference to what the author believed to be a common practice among doctors.

Lord Diplock thought the article in this case the antithesis of that in *A-G v Times Newspapers Ltd*[18] where the whole subject of the article was the impending civil actions arising out of the marketing of Thalidomide and its whole purpose was to put pressure on the defendants in the lawful conduct of their defence. The implication is that such an article continues to be contempt. This seems plainly right. Where the purpose of a publisher is to put pressure on a litigant, there is no need for the Crown to rely on the strict liability rule. In *A-G v English* there was no reference to, or intention to prejudice, Dr Arthur's trial, and to preclude discussion of the mercy-killing of babies would have prevented Mrs Carr publicising a main plank in her election programme. Lord Diplock said:

> "Such gagging of bona-fide public discussion in the press of contro-versial matters of general public interest, merely because there are in existence contemporaneous legal proceedings in which some particular instance of those controversial matters may be in issue, is what s. 5 of the Contempt of Court Act 1981 was in my view intended to prevent."

2 Intentional Interference

When D does an act which has a tendency to interfere with the course of justice in particular proceedings he may (i) be unaware of the tendency; (ii) be aware that there is a risk that his act might have such a tendency or (iii) wish to interfere, or know that his act is virtually certain to interfere, with the course of justice. If the act is a "publication", case (i) is an instance of strict liability and case (iii) is not. Under the Act, contempts which are not intentional are instances of strict liability. There is no intermediate category. The position of case (ii) therefore depends on the meaning of "intent" in s. 1 (1) of the Act. In *A-G v Newspaper Publishing Ltd*[19] it was held that "intent" in s. 1 (1) means "specific intent" and does not include recklessness; but "oblique" intent will suffice. It seems to follow that recklessness is to be equated with strict liability for this purpose and that case (ii) is therefore governed by the strict liability limitations.

Where D has an "intent" to interfere with the course of justice, he may be liable whatever form his conduct takes, whether or not there is a substantial risk that the course of justice will be impeded, or the impedi-ment serious, and whether or not proceedings are active. So a privately communicated threat to a person intended to deter him from taking legal proceedings may be a contempt, even though there is little or no chance that the threat will have the slightest effect on the particular litigant.[20]

---

18. [1974] AC 273, [1973] 3 All ER 54.
19. [1987] 3 All ER 276 at 304, 310, 313. The court referred to *Moloney* [1985] AC 905, which must be read in the light of *Hancock* [1986] AC 455, above, p. 56.
20. Above, p. 770. Cf. the law of blackmail and *Clear* [1968] 1 QB 670, [1968] 1 All ER 74, above, p. 590.

4) *Acts Tending to Interfere with the Course of Justice in General*

1 Scandalising the Court

Even though the proceedings have terminated it may be contempt to publish scurrilous personal abuse of a judge's conduct in them. In *Gray*[1] such an attack was published in a newspaper circulating in the town where the judge was still sitting. Lord Russell CJ said:

"Any act done or writing published calculated to bring a court or a judge of the Court into contempt or to lower his authority is a contempt of court. Further, any act done or writing published calculated to obstruct or interfere with the due course of justice or the lawful process of the Courts is a contempt of court."[2]

The former class of contempt, with which this section is concerned (but not the latter[3]), is subject to the qualification that:

"Judges and Courts are alike open to criticism, and if reasonable argument or expostulation is offered against any judicial act as contrary to law or the public good, no court could or would treat that as contempt of court."[4]

But scurrilous abuse is not "reasonable argument or expostulation" and D was convicted. On the other hand, the Privy Council allowed an appeal where the alleged contempt consisted of a reasoned argument about inequalities in sentencing, under the heading "The Human Element". Lord Atkin said:

"... provided that members of the public abstain from imputing improper motives to those taking part in the administration of justice, and are genuinely exercising a right of criticism, and not acting in malice or attempting to impair the administration of justice, they are immune."[5]

Applying these principles, the Divisional Court held[6] that the editor of the *New Statesman* was guilty of contempt in publishing a statement that

"... an individual owning to such views as those of Dr. Stopes [favouring birth-control] cannot apparently hope for a fair hearing in a court presided over by Mr. Justice Avory – and there are so many Avorys."

The court rejected the argument that this was permissible criticism, being intended only to convey that the subject of birth-control was so controversial that no one who held strong views on one side or the other could prevent his judgment from being unconsciously influenced by his personal views. Lord Hewart CJ[7] said:

"[The article] imputed unfairness and lack of impartiality to a Judge in the discharge of his judicial duties. The gravamen of the offence was that

---

1. [1900] 2 QB 36, DC. Lord Russell's observations were approved by the Privy Council in *Badry v Director of Public Prosecutions of Mauritius* [1982] 3 All ER 973 at 979.
2. Ibid., at 110.
3. Which is discussed above, pp. 772–779.
4. Ibid.
5. *Ambard v A-G for Trinidad and Tobago* [1936] AC 322 at 335, [1936] 1 All ER 704 at 708.
6. (1928) 44 TLR 301.
7. Ibid., at p. 303.

by lowering his authority it interfered with the performance of his judicial duties."

More recently, the Court of Appeal has held a vigorous and, in some respects, inaccurate criticism of itself not to amount to a contempt. Salmon LJ said:[8]

"... no criticism of a judgment, however vigorous, can amount to contempt of court, providing it keeps within the limits of reasonable courtesy and good faith. The criticism here complained of, however rumbustious, however wide of the mark, whether pressed in good taste or in bad taste, seems to me to be well within these limits."

It is contempt only when the judge is attacked in his capacity as such. The power of committal

"is not to be used for the vindication of the judge as a person. He must resort to action for libel or criminal information."[9]

So where a letter was published containing sarcastic allusions to the refusal by the Chief Justice of the Bahamas of a gift of pineapples, the Privy Council held that, while the letter might have been the subject of an action for libel, it was not a contempt because it was not calculated to obstruct or interfere with the course of justice or the due administration of the law.[10]

It must be proved that D intended to bring the judges in their judicial capacity into contempt or to cast suspicion on the administration of justice, or that he was reckless whether he did so. In *S v Van Niekerk*,[11] the South African case in which this principle was applied, it was held that a reasoned article by a lecturer in *The South African Law Journal*[12] might, objectively, be contemptuous, because it suggested that there was some racial bias in the imposition of the death penalty. D was acquitted only because he lacked *mens rea*. He ought to have foreseen the article's contemptuous effect, but the court was not satisfied he did so. This suggests that it is necessarily contemptuous to suggest judicial bias and it was so held by the Privy Council in *Badry v Director of Public Prosecutions of Mauritius*.[13] A finding that the appellant had alleged that the Supreme Court had unjustly dismissed a claim for damages because the other party happened to be a wealthy company led inevitably to the conclusion that his appeal must be dismissed. It is not inconceivable, however, that a judge might be biased. How is this to be revealed and the public interest vindicated if it is not permissible to say so?

2 Intimidation of a Juror or Witness

It is contempt to intimidate, threaten or punish a juror or witness with respect to his part in the proceedings, whether they are active[14] or terminated. It was so held in the case of a juryman in *Martin*.[15] D called on

---

8. *Metropolis Police Commissioner, ex parte Blackburn* (No 2) [1968] 2 QB 150 at 155, [1968] 2 All ER 319 at 321.
9. *McLeod v St. Aubyn* [1899] AC 549 at 561, per Lord Morris.
10. *Re Special Reference from Bahama Islands* [1893] AC 138.
11. 1970 3 SA 655 (T), criticised by Milton in (1969) 87 SALJ 424.
12. (1970) SALJ 424.
13. [1982] 3 All ER 973 at 979.
14. Above, p. 774.
15. (1848) 5 Cox CC 356.

the foreman of a jury which, the previous day, had convicted D's brother of a crime, and challenged him to mortal combat "for having bullied the jury". He was committed for contempt and Pigot CB said[16] that jurors must be protected:

"from all interference with them in the discharge of their duties, from all attempt to assail their characters or reputations, and from the imputation of motives other than those which should actuate men having such solemn and important duties to discharge: if it is necessary to guard their reputation how much more necessary is it to guard their persons from outrage, and the consequences of threats of outrage to their persons or their homes."

This rule was extended to witnesses by the Court of Appeal, reversing the Restrictive Practices Court, in the case of *A-G v Butterworth*.[17] D and others, members of a trade union, disapproving of evidence which E, another member, had given before the Restrictive Practices Court, censured him for his conduct and purported to relieve him of his position as branch treasurer. It was held that those of the defendants whose motives included that of punishing E for giving evidence in the way he did were guilty of contempt, whether this was their predominant motive or not. Defendants whose motives were not established were acquitted. While there was no precedent directly in point, there were a number of persuasive authorities, and the decision is supported by the general principles governing contempt cases.

"If this sort of thing could be done in a single case with impunity, the news of it would soon get round. Witnesses in other cases would be unwilling to come forward to give evidence, or, if they did come forward, they would hesitate to speak the truth for fear of the consequences."[18]

It was immaterial that the accused did not have any future proceedings in mind and had no intention to interfere with the course of justice. It seems that it is also immaterial that the revenge taken is unlikely to come to the knowledge of potential witnesses in future cases.[19]

The question of motive is crucial in such cases because it is only if the motive is to punish the witness, as such, that there is a tendency to obstruct the administration of justice; that is, if E had been removed from his position by the accused because, for example, he was inefficient or corrupt in his discharge of his duties, this could hardly have affected witnesses in future cases. Lord Denning MR was prepared to go further:[20]

"... contempt of court is a criminal offence, punishable summarily by the court itself, and, like all criminal offences, it requires in general, a guilty mind. I do not think that *Odhams Press Ltd, ex parte A-G* warrants the large proposition that has been drawn from it; and in any case it has

16. Ibid., at 359.
17. [1963] 1 QB 696, [1962] 3 All ER 326. See also *Wright* [1968] VR 164 (assault on witness after trial).
18. [1963] 1 QB at 719, [1962] 3 All ER at 329, per Lord Denning MR.
19. [1963] 1 QB at 726, [1962] 3 All ER at 333; *Chapman v Honig* [1963] 2 QB 502, [1963] 2 All ER 513; *Moore v Clerk of Assize Bristol* [1972] 1 All ER 58. See Miller, *Contempt of Court*, 201–203.
20. [1963] 1 QB at 722, [1962] 3 All ER at 331. Cf. *Re F (a minor)*, infra.

since been reversed by s. 11 (1) of the Administration of Justice Act 1960."

Donovan LJ on the other hand, did not appear disposed to question the correctness of the *Odhams* case and it was certainly not necessary to the decision to do so. It must be assumed that the propositions in *Odham*'s case remain good law.[1] Having been recognised by Parliament in the 1981 Act, they are unlikely to be questioned in the courts.

At a trial for blackmail the judge has jurisdiction to order that the name of the complainant shall not be disclosed. To publish the name is then contempt. Even where the judge has not expressly made an order, the fact that he has not allowed the complainant's name to be disclosed in court, requiring him to be referred to as "Mr. X", is sufficient.[2] Publication of the name defeats the purpose of the court.

3 Disclosure of Information in Breach of an Undertaking to the Court

Where the solicitor of a party to a civil action obtains possession of copies of documents belonging to the other party by way of discovery, the use of the documents for some collateral or ulterior purpose, not reasonably necessary for the proper conduct of the action, is contempt. In *Home Office v Harman*[3] the House of Lords (Lords Simon and Scarman dissenting) held that this was so even after the document had been read out in open court in the course of the litigation for which it had been produced. If it were otherwise, full and frank discovery of documents before trial would be discouraged and the proper administration of justice would be impeded by parties trying to ensure that documents were not read out in court.

4 Publication of Information relating to Court Sitting in Private

Section 12 (1) of the Administration of Justice Act 1960 provides: "The publication of information relating to proceedings before any court sitting in private shall not of itself be contempt of court except in the following cases." This suggests that in the cases which follow, the publication of such information, without more, is an offence. Section 12 (4) however provides that nothing in the section shall render any publication punishable as a contempt which would not have been punishable apart from the section. In *Re F (a minor)*[4] the Court of Appeal held that, where newspapers published information relating to wardship proceedings (one of the cases referred to in subsection (1)) it was necessary to consider whether such publication would have been an offence before the 1960 Act. They held that it would be contempt only if D intended to publish, or was reckless whether he published, material relating to proceedings held in private. Since D did not know that the information related to such proceedings, he was not guilty. Lord Denning again declared roundly that the offence of contempt requires guilty knowledge or intent; but Scarman LJ distinguished

---

1. Subject, of course, to the 1960 Act, re-enacted by s. 3 of the 1981 Act, above, p. 775.
2. *Socialist Workers Printers and Publishers, Ltd, ex parte A-G* [1975] QB 637, [1975] 1 All ER 142.
3. [1983] 1 AC 280, [1982] 2 All ER 532.
4. [1977] Fam 78, [1977] 1 All ER 114.

between contempt based on interference with the course of justice (where *mens rea* is not required) and other classes of contempt.

5 Confidentiality of Jury's Deliberations

By s. 8 of the Act it is a contempt of court to obtain, disclose or solicit any particulars of statements made, opinions expressed, arguments advanced or votes cast by members of a jury in the course of their deliberations in any legal proceedings. The object is to protect frankness in the jury room. The provision is very wide and apparently applies even to the most private communications. It applies to all juries, civil and criminal, including a coroner's jury.[5] Subsection (2) creates narrow exceptions where disclosure is made (a) to enable the jury to arrive at their verdict or in connection with it and (b) in evidence in subsequent proceedings for an offence alleged to have been committed in relation to the jury in the first proceedings. Proceedings may be instituted only by or with the consent of the Attorney-General or on the motion of a court.

6 Use of Tape Recorders

By s. 9 it is a contempt of court to use in court, or bring into court for use, a tape recorder, without leave; or to publish such a recording to any section of the public.

7 Obstructing an Officer of the Court

It is a contempt to obstruct an officer of the court when he is carrying out his duties, as by assaulting or threatening a process server,[6] a sheriff, a receiver, a bailiff, or a solicitor when leaving a judge's chambers after the hearing of an application:[7]

"The principle is that those who have duties to discharge in a court of justice are protected by the law and shielded on their way to the discharge of such duties, while discharging them, and on their return therefrom, in order that such persons may safely have resort to courts of justice."[8]

5. See the definition of "legal proceedings" in s. 19.
6. *Williams v Johns* (1773) 1 Mer 303 n (process server compelled to eat writ and beaten).
7. *Re Johnson* (1887) 20 QBD 68.
8. Ibid., at 74, per Bowen LJ and see below, p. 812.

20 Offences against Public Order

1 Offences under the Public Order Act 1986

The Public Order Act 1986 abolished the common law offences of riot, rout, unlawful assembly and affray and some statutory offences relating to public order[1] and replaced them with new offences. Three offences take the place of the four above-mentioned common law crimes. They are, in descending order of gravity, riot, violent disorder and affray. Riot requires the presence of 12 persons and violent disorder of 3, but affray may be committed where only the defendant is present. Riot is intended for exceptionally serious cases and no prosecution for it may be instituted except by or with the consent of the Director of Public Prosecutions. Notwithstanding the title of the Act, each offence may be committed in private as well as in public places and, though it is a constituent of each offence that the conduct (of the 12, or the 3, or the defendant, as the case may be) must be such as would cause a person of reasonable firmness present at the scene to fear for his personal safety, no person need actually be, or even be likely to be, at the scene.[2] Where no person is present, the court or jury has to answer a hypothetical question.

In riot and violent disorder the 12 or the 3 persons must be proved to have been present together, using or threatening unlawful violence. It must be proved that the accused intended to use violence or was aware that his conduct might be violent but it is unnecessary to prove any such mental element on the part of the remainder of the 12, or the 3, who are not charged.[3] It is sufficient to prove that their conduct was objectively unlawfully violent, or presented a threat of unlawful violence. In riot, however, a common purpose (which need not involve violence) must be proved in respect of 12 persons, though not all of them are charged.

It is probable that all three offences are continuing offences. It was held that a common law affray might continue for a considerable period of time and over a wide area. An indictment was not bad for duplicity where it

---

1. For the law before the 1986 Act, see the 5th edition of this work, Ch. 20; and for the background to the 1986 Act see the Home Office *Review of the Public Order Act and Related Legislation*, Cmnd. 7891 (1980) and Law Commission Working Paper No. 82 (1982) and Report, *Offences Relating to Public Disorder* (Law Com. No. 123, 1983). For detailed studies of the new law, see Richard Card, *Public Order. The New Law* (1987) and A. T. H. Smith, *Offences against Public Order* (1987).
2. Sections 1 (3) and (4), 2 (3) and (4) and 3 (3) and (4).
3. Section 6 (7); A. T. H. Smith, op. cit., 3–03.

alleged an affray on 31st August and 1st September "in divers streets".[4] It appeared in evidence that the accused were milling about, armed, uttering threats and fighting, from 8.30 p.m. to 12.30 a.m., over a radius of a quarter of a mile. This was held to be a single affray. Where the ingredients of the offence ceased to exist for a time, the affray was over; and, when those ingredients came into existence again, a second affray occurred. So, where the accused travelled in a coach to a number of sites where they created terror, there was an affray at each site. During the coach journeys there was no fighting and no one was put in fear.[5] It seems likely that the same principles will apply to the new statutory offence of affray and also to the offences of riot and violent disorder. Once the 12 or the 3, as the case may be, have used or threatened violence, the offence is constituted and will continue so long as they remain together (in the case of riot, for a common purpose) and at least one of them is continuing to use or threaten violence. One is enough, since it is provided that the persons present need not use or threaten violence simultaneously.

1) *Riot*

Riot is an indictable offence, punishable with ten years' imprisonment, or an unlimited fine, or both. It is defined by s. 1 of the Act as follows:

"1) Where 12 or more persons who are present together use or threaten unlawful violence for a common purpose and the conduct of them (taken together) is such as would cause a person of reasonable firmness present at the scene to fear for his personal safety, each of the persons using unlawful violence for the common purpose is guilty of riot.

2) It is immaterial whether or not the 12 or more use or threaten unlawful violence simultaneously.

3) The common purpose may be inferred from conduct."

If 12 or more persons with a common purpose threaten unlawful violence but only one actually uses it, there is a riot but only one principal rioter. Since they have a common purpose, the rest may be guilty as secondary parties but this is not necessarily so. Suppose that they have all agreed – "Threats, yes, but actual violence, no." If D, for the common purpose, then uses violence, D commits riot but the rest are not necessarily guilty and, if D has clearly gone beyond the scope of the concerted action,[6] as by producing a knife or gun which the rest did not know he had with him, they will certainly not be guilty.

The gravity of riot depends on the presence of large numbers. The number, 12, is arbitrary and it will not usually be necessary to offer evidence of a head-count, for the offence is unlikely to be used except in the case of a large crowd when well in excess of 12 are using or threatening violence.

By s. 8, in Part 1 of the Act:

4. *Woodrow* (1959) 43 Cr App Rep 105, CA.
5. *Jones* (1974) 59 Cr App Rep 120, CA.
6. Above, p. 148.

"violence" means any violent conduct, so that –

a) except in the context of affray, it includes violent conduct towards property as well as violent conduct towards persons, and

b) it is not restricted to conduct causing or intended to cause injury or damage but includes any other violent conduct (for example, throwing at or towards a person a missile of a kind capable of causing injury which does not hit or falls short).

Conduct which might well have caused injury or damage will clearly be capable of amounting to violence even though it was neither intended to, nor did, cause injury or damage. "Violent" movements of the body, where there is no possibility of any impact – as where D waves his fist at P who is across the street – are probably not "violence" but a threat of violence.

The common purpose need not be an unlawful one. It might be, for example, to persuade an employer to take back an employee who he has wrongfully dismissed. But the violence, whether used or threatened, must be unlawful. Force reasonably used or threatened in self-defence or for the prevention of crime cannot found a charge of riot. There is no requirement that the 12 or more should have come together in pursuance of any agreement. They may have assembled by chance, and one by one, so long as, at some point when violence is used, they are present together with a common purpose and using or threatening violence.

The mental element of riot includes the common purpose. It must be proved that a person charged with riot shared that common purpose and that he (but not the other 11 or more) intended to use violence or was aware that his conduct might be violent.[7] The Act wisely avoids the ambiguous word, "reckless", but, in effect adopts the *Cunningham*[8] meaning of recklessness, thus keeping the law of riot, violent disorder and affray in line with offences against the person generally. Because the meaning of violence itself is uncertain it is not entirely clear what the requirement of awareness will exclude. Possibly a person who was not aware that his conduct would cause any risk of injury or damage would be held to be unaware that his conduct might be violent when it did in fact cause a risk of, or actual, damage or injury.

Exceptionally, s. 6 (5) and (6) make special provision for the intoxicated defendant.

"5) For the purposes of this section a person whose awareness is impaired by intoxication shall be taken to be aware of that of which he would be aware if not intoxicated, unless he shows either that his intoxication was not self-induced or that it was caused solely by the taking or administration of a substance in the course of medical treatment.

6) In subsection (5) "intoxication" means any intoxication, whether caused by drink, drugs or other means, or by a combination of means."

In effect, this spells out the common law rule for offences "of basic intent"[9] but shifts the onus of proving that intoxication was involuntary to

7. Section 6 (1).
8. Above, p. 62.
9. Above, p. 211.

the defendant.[10] Yet if D denies that he had the alleged "purpose" because he was too drunk, s. 6 is inapplicable and the common law governs. If the indictment alleges only intent to use violence, that is presumably an allegation of a specific intent, so self-induced drunkenness would be an answer at common law; but D is still to be taken, apparently, to be aware of that of which he would be aware if not intoxicated; and, if the jury think he would have been aware that violence was a virtual certainty,[11] that is evidence on which they might find that he intended it. Thus intoxication might not be an answer even to an allegation of intentional violence.

The Riot (Damages) Act 1886

This Act provides that, where a house, shop or building in any police district, or property inside it, has been injured, stolen or destroyed "by any persons riotously and tumultuously assembled together", the owner shall be compensated out of the police rate. The word "riotously" is now to be construed in accordance with s. 1 of the Public Order Act 1986,[12] so the ambit of the 1886 Act is significantly reduced. No compensation is payable to a person whose property is damaged by a gang of eleven, tumultuously assembled. The assembly must be tumultuous as well as riotous. The word, "tumultuously", was added:

"... for the specific reason that it was intended to limit the liability of compensation to cases where the rioters were in such numbers and in such a state of agitated commotion, and were generally so acting, that the forces of law and order should have been well aware of the threat which existed, and, if they had done their duty, should have taken steps to prevent the rioters from causing damage."[13]

In fixing the amount of compensation regard must be had to the conduct of the claimant, in particular whether he took adequate precautions, or was a party to the riot, or offered any provocation. Where the claimant has received compensation from a third party, such as an insurance company, the sum payable under the 1886 Act is correspondingly reduced; but the third party is entitled to recover the sum so paid as if he had sustained the loss.

2) *Violent Disorder*

Violent disorder is an offence punishable on indictment with five years' imprisonment or an unlimited fine or both or, on summary conviction, with six months' imprisonment or the statutory maximum fine, or both. It is defined as follows by s. 2:

"1) Where 3 or more persons who are present together use or threaten unlawful violence and the conduct of them (taken together) is such as

10. Unless "shows", contrasted with "proves" elsewhere in the Act, implies a merely evidential burden.
11. Above, p. 56.
12. Above, p. 786. See s. 10 (1).
13. *J. W. Dwyer Ltd v Metropolitan Police District, Receiver* [1967] 2 QB 970, [1967] 2 All ER 1051 (Lyell J).

would cause a person of reasonable firmness present at the scene to fear for his personal safety, each of the persons using or threatening unlawful violence is guilty of violent disorder.

2) It is immaterial whether or not the 3 or more use or threaten unlawful violence simultaneously."

There need be no common purpose. Each of the three or more persons may have a different purpose or no purpose. At least three must be using or threatening *unlawful* violence,[14] so if one of only three persons present is acting in self-defence or the prevention of crime, no offence is committed.

It must be proved that D (but not the other two or more) intended to use or threaten violence or that he was aware that his conduct might be violent or threaten violence.[15] The intoxicated defendant is governed by s. 6 (5) and (6), considered above.[16]

This offence is intended to be the normal charge for serious outbreaks of public disorder, riot being reserved for exceptionally serious cases, but it clearly covers many relatively minor disturbances. Consequently, it is triable either way.

3) *Affray*

Affray is punishable on indictment with three years' imprisonment or an unlimited fine or both, or, on summary conviction, with six months' imprisonment or the statutory maximum fine or both. It is defined as follows by s. 3:

"1) A person is guilty of affray if he uses or threatens unlawful violence towards another and his conduct is such as would cause a person of reasonable firmness present at the scene to fear for his personal safety.

2) Where 2 or more persons use or threaten the unlawful violence, it is the conduct of them taken together that must be considered for the purposes of subsection (1).

3) For the purposes of this section a threat cannot be made by the use of words alone."

In this section, "violence" is limited to violence towards another person and does not include violence towards property.[17]

Only one person, the defendant, need be present; but subsection (2) makes it clear that, where two or more use or threaten the unlawful violence, it is the conduct of all of them which must be considered in deciding whether it would cause a person of reasonable firmness to fear for his personal safety.

The mental element is D's intention to use or threaten violence or his awareness that his conduct may be violent or threaten violence. Where reliance is placed by the prosecution on subsection (2), it will probably be necessary to show that D's awareness extended to the conduct of the other persons or persons using or threatening violence.

14. For the meaning of "violence", see above, pp. 786–787.
15. Section 6 (2).
16. P. 787.
17. Section 8, above, pp. 786–787.

The intoxicated defendant is governed by s. 6 (5) and (6), considered above.[18]

4) *Fear or Provocation of Violence*

It is an offence under s. 4, punishable on summary conviction with 6 months' imprisonment or a fine not exceeding level 5 on the standard scale, if a person:

a) uses towards another person threatening, abusive or insulting words or behaviour, or

b) distributes or displays to another person any writing, sign or other visible representation which is threatening, abusive or insulting

with intent to cause that person to believe that immediate unlawful violence will be used against him or another by any person, or to provoke the immediate use of unlawful violence by that person or another, or whereby that person is likely to believe that such violence will be used or it is likely that such violence will be provoked.

"Threatening, abusive or insulting". This is the first of eight offences under the Act of which "threatening, abusive or insulting" conduct is a principal constituent.[19] Whether conduct has this quality seems to be governed by an objective test. It has been noticed above[20] that a word describing the *actus reus* may imply a mental element. The Act, however, assumes that conduct or material may be threatening, abusive or insulting even though there is no evidence that the actor or author intended it to have, or was aware that it might have, that quality. When proof by the prosecution of such intention or awareness is required, the Act specifically so provides;[1] and, in other cases, it puts the burden on the defendant to prove that he did not suspect or have reason to suspect that it was threatening, abusive or insulting.[2]

The words, "threatening, abusive or insulting", which are taken from the repealed s. 5 of the Public Order Act 1936, are to be given their ordinary meaning. It has been said that it is not helpful to seek to explain them by the use of synonyms or dictionary definitions because "an ordinary sensible man knows an insult when he sees or hears it".[3] Whether particular conduct is "threatening", etc., is a question of fact. In *Brutus v Cozens*[4] D interrupted a tennis match to protest against apartheid and thereby angered the spectators. The House of Lords, reversing the Divisional Court, held that the finding of the magistrates that this was not "insulting" behaviour could not be disturbed because it was a not unreasonable finding of fact. If the magistrates had decided that the behaviour was insulting, it may be that their decision would have been equally beyond challenge.[5] Masturbation in

18. P. 787.
19. Sections 4 (1), 5 (1), 18 (1), 19 (1), 20 (1), 21 (1), 22 (1), 23 (1).
20. P. 32.
  1. Section 6 (3) and (4).
  2. Sections 19, 20, 21, 22, 23.
  3. *Brutus v Cozens* [1972] 2 All ER 1297 at 1300, per Lord Reid.
  4. Supra, note 3.
  5. Per Lord Kilbrandon at 1303. Lord Reid, obiter, agreed with the magistrates' finding; but it does not follow that he would have held a contrary finding to be unreasonable.

the sight of a stranger in a public lavatory is capable of being insulting behaviour because the stranger might be a heterosexual who would be insulted at being taken for a homosexual.[6] It is immaterial that the stranger is a policeman who is on the look out for this sort of thing, or a homosexual, who is not at all insulted. Words cannot be insulting (or, presumably, threatening or abusive) unless there is "a human target which they strike" and it seems that D must be aware of that "human target", though he need not intend the conduct to be "insulting": *Masterson v Holding*,[7] where intimate "cuddling" by two homosexual men in Oxford Street at 1.55 a.m. on a June morning, in the presence of two young men and two young women, was held capable of being insulting. It may be, however, that, for the purposes of s. 4 (though not for any other offence under the Act), the words "towards another" require that the words or behaviour be directed against that other.[8]

It must be proved that D:
- i) intended his words or behaviour towards P to be, or was aware that they might be, threatening, abusive or insulting;[9] and
- ii) either –
  - a) that he intended P to believe that immediate unlawful violence would be used against him or another; or
  - b) that he intended to provoke the immediate use of unlawful violence by P or another; or
  - c) that P was likely to believe that such violence would be used; or
  - d) that it was likely that such violence would be provoked.

Although the section creates only one offence,[10] alternatives (a) and (b) require proof of intention whereas in alternatives (c) and (d) the test is objective.

Where D's awareness that his conduct might be threatening, abusive or insulting is impaired by intoxication, s. 6 (5) and (6)[11] apply.

The offence may be committed in a public or a private place, except where D acts inside a dwelling[12] and P is also inside that, or another, dwelling.[13] Threatening gestures through the bedroom window to the neighbour in his bedroom window across the street do not amount to the offence. Where D is in a dwelling, it seems that, if the issue is raised, the prosecution must prove that D was aware that his conduct might be heard or seen by a person outside that or another dwelling.[14]

5) *Harassment, Alarm or Distress*

It is an offence under s. 5 (1), punishable on summary conviction with a fine not exceeding level 3 on the standard scale, if a person –

6. *Parkin v Norman* [1982] 2 All ER 583 at 588–589, DC.
7. [1986] 3 All ER 39, [1986] 1 WLR 1017.
8. Card, op. cit., 3. 11.
9. Section 6 (3).
10. S. 7 (2).
11. Above, pp. 787–788.
12. Defined in s. 8.
13. S. 4 (2).
14. Cf. s. 5 (3) (b), putting the onus of proof on D.

a) uses threatening, abusive or insulting words or behaviour, or disorderly behaviour, or

b) displays any writing, sign or other visible representation which is threatening, abusive or insulting,

within the hearing or sight of a person likely to be caused harassment, alarm or distress thereby.

This offence is wider than that under s. 4 in that it includes the further alternative of "disorderly" behaviour; and it extends beyond apprehension of violence to the causing of "harassment, alarm or distress". "Disorderly" is, no doubt, another ordinary word of the English language to be given its natural meaning and it will apply to acts of hooliganism likely to produce the specified effect. There is no requirement that the conduct be directed "towards another person"; but it must be proved that D intended his conduct to be threatening, abusive, or insulting or disorderly or was aware that it might be so.[15] Section 6 (5) and (6) apply to the intoxicated defendant.[16] The prosecution must prove that D's conduct took place within the hearing or sight of a person likely to be caused harassment, alarm or distress; but it is then for D to prove, if he can, that he had no reason to believe that there was any such person within hearing or sight. Once again, the offence may be committed in a public or a private place, except where D acts inside a dwelling and P is also inside that, or another, dwelling. It is a defence for D to prove that he was inside a dwelling and that he had no reason to believe that his conduct would be heard or seen outside that or another dwelling.[17]

6) *Acts Intended or Likely to Stir up Racial Hatred*

Offences of inciting racial hatred were first introduced into the law by the Race Relations Act 1965 which required proof of an intention to stir up such hatred. Because of the difficulty of proving intent, the law was amended by the Race Relations Act 1976 which replaced the requirement of intent with an objective test. It was enough that the defendant's conduct was likely to stir up racial hatred, whether he intended to do so or not. Part III of the Public Order Act 1986 replaces the old law with six new offences. They are all concerned with acts intended or likely to stir up racial hatred – the objective test is retained throughout – and, by s. 17:

"In this Part, 'racial hatred' means hatred against a group of persons in Great Britain defined by reference to colour, race, nationality (including citizenship) or ethnic or national origins."

It will be noted that the offences do not extend to stirring up hatred against religious groups as such but an attack on a particular religion, such as the Jewish religion, might be interpreted as an attack on Jews. Under the 1976 Act it was held that the term, "ethnic", was to be construed relatively widely and that the Sikhs, though originally a religious community, now

15. Section 6 (3).
16. Above, pp. 787–788.
17. Section 5 (3) (b).

constituted an ethnic group because they were a separate community with a long shared history and distinctive customs.[18]

Proceedings for an offence under Part III may not be instituted except by or with the consent of the Attorney General. Each offence is punishable on indictment with two years' imprisonment or an unlimited fine or both, or, on summary conviction with six months' imprisonment or a fine not exceeding the statutory maximum, or both.

The essence of each offence is that D does an act involving the use of threatening, abusive or insulting words, behaviour or material and either:

a) he intends thereby to stir up racial hatred, or

b) having regard to all the circumstances racial hatred is likely to be stirred up thereby.

The offences are:

s. 18 – using threatening, abusive or insulting words or behaviour or displaying any written material which is threatening, abusive or insulting;

s. 19 – publishing or distributing written material which is threatening, abusive or insulting;

s. 20 – presenting or directing the public performance of a play which involves the use of threatening, abusive or insulting words or behaviour;

s. 21 – distributing or showing or playing a recording of visual images or sounds which are threatening, abusive or insulting;

s. 22 – providing a broadcasting or cable programme service for, or producing, or directing, a programme involving threatening, abusive or insulting visual images or sounds, or using the offending words or behaviour therein;

s. 23 – possessing written material, or a recording of visual images or sounds, which is threatening, abusive or insulting, with a view to its being, displayed, published, etc.

7) *Mens Rea and Proof of "Threatening, Abusive or Insulting"*

This part of the Act provides a variety of requirements of *mens rea* and proof in relation to the "threatening, abusive or insulting" quality of the material in question. We have seen that for offences under ss. 4 and 5 the prosecution must prove that D intended his conduct to have, or was aware that it might have, that quality.[19] In Part III this requirement applies only to an offence under s. 18 where D is not shown to have intended to stir up racial hatred. Where he is shown to have such an intention it appears that the test for "threatening, abusive or insulting" is wholly objective. There is a variation in s. 22. Where D is not shown to have intended to stir up racial hatred, the prosecution must prove that he knew or *had reason to suspect* that the material was threatening, abusive or insulting. Where he is shown to have such an intention the test is purely objective.

18. *Mandla v Dowell Lee* [1983] 2 AC 548, [1983] 1 All ER 1062.
19. S. 6 (3) and (4), above, p. 790.

For offences under ss. 19, 20, 21 and 23, the prosecution need prove no intention or awareness with respect to "threatening, abusive or insulting", but it is a defence for a defendant, who is not shown to have intended to stir up racial hatred, to prove:

for s. 19, that he was not aware of the content of material and did not suspect or have reason to suspect that it was threatening, abusive or insulting;

for s. 20, that he did not know and had no reason to suspect that the offending words or behaviour were threatening, abusive or insulting;

for s. 21, that he was not aware of the content of the recording and did not suspect and had no reason to suspect that it was threatening, abusive or insulting; and

for s. 23 that he was not aware of the content of the written material or recording and did not suspect, and had no reason to suspect, that it was threatening, abusive or insulting.

2 Public Nuisance and Obstruction of the Highway

1) *Public Nuisance*[20]

Public nuisance is a misdemeanour at common law triable either way.[1] It consists in,

"... an act not warranted by law or an omission to discharge a legal duty, which act or omission obstructs or causes inconvenience or damage to the public in the exercise of rights common to all His Majesty's subjects."[2]

A person who has suffered particular damage as the result of a public nuisance can maintain an action for damages in tort;[3] and the major importance of public nuisance today is in the civil remedy which it affords.

1 Nature of Nuisance

The most common and important instance of a public nuisance is obstruction of the highway and this is more particularly considered below. But it also includes a wide variety of other interferences with the public; for example, the carrying on of an offensive trade which impregnates the air "with noisome offensive and stinking smoke" to the common nuisance of the public passing along the highway;[4] polluting a river with gas so as to destroy the fish and render the water unfit for drinking;[5] unnecessarily, and with full knowledge of the facts, exposing in a public highway a person infected with a contagious disease;[6] taking a horse into a public place

---

20. Brownlie, *Law of Public Order and National Security* (2nd ed. 1981), 75, 77.
1. Criminal Law Act 1977, s. 16 and Schedule 2.
2. Stephen, *Digest*, 184.
3. See Street, *Torts*, 313 et seq.
4. *White and Ward* (1757) 1 Burr 333. See also *Tysoe v Davis* [1983] Crim LR 684 (QBD).
5. *Medley* (1834) 6 C & P 292.
6. *Vantandillo* (1815) 4 M & S 73.

knowing that it has glanders and that that is an infectious disease;[7] sending food to market, knowing that it is to be sold for human consumption and that it is unfit for that purpose;[8] burning a dead body in such a place and such a manner as to be offensive to members of the public passing along a highway or other public place;[9] keeping a fierce and unruly bull in a field crossed by a public footway;[10] discharging oil into the sea in such circumstances that it is likely to be carried on to English shores and beaches;[11] by causing excessive noise and dust in the course of quarrying operations;[12] by giving false information as to the presence of explosives so as to cause actual danger or discomfort to the public;[13] and trespassing and sniffing glue in a school playground even in the absence of staff and pupils.[14]

A great many varieties of nuisance are now the subject of special legislation[15] and proceedings are unlikely to be brought at common law where there is a statutory remedy. But the common law may still be useful where no statute has intervened or where the penalty provided by statute is too slight.[16]

A public nuisance may be committed by omission, as by permitting a house near the highway to fall into a ruinous state[17] or by allowing one's land to accumulate filth, even though it is deposited there by others for whom D is not responsible.[18]

Whereas private nuisance always involves some degree of repetition or continuance,[19]

"an isolated act may amount to a public nuisance if it is done under such circumstances that the public right to condemn it should be vindicated."[20]

The interference with the public's rights must be substantial and unreasonable. Not every obstruction of the highway is a public nuisance:

"If an unreasonable time is occupied in the operation of delivering beer from a brewer's dray into the cellar of a publican, this is certainly a nuisance. A cart or wagon may be unloaded at a gateway; but this must be done with promptness. So as to the repairing of a house; – the public

---

7. *Henson* (1852) Dears CC 24.
8. *Stevenson* (1862) 3 F & F 106; otherwise if D did not intend it for human consumption: *Crawley* (1862) 3 F & F 109.
9. *Price* (1884) 12 QBD 247.
10. *Archbold*, §27–56.
11. *Southport Corporation v Esso Petroleum Co Ltd* [1954] 2 QB 182 at 197, [1954] 2 All ER 561 at 571, per Denning LJ (CA; reversed, [1956] AC 218, [1955] 3 All ER 894).
12. *A–G v PYA Quarries Ltd* [1957] 2 QB 169, [1957] 1 All ER 864.
13. *Madden* [1975] 3 All ER 155, CA. The court said "potential danger" to the public was not enough but that "actual risk" to the comfort of the public was. This is difficult to follow. Is not "potential" danger the same as risk? And should not risk be enough?
14. *Sykes v Holmes* [1985] Crim LR 791. DC (conduct capable of being a nuisance within s. 40 of the Local Government (Miscellaneous Provisions) Act 1982).
15. See, for example, *Archbold*, §§27–44 to 27–113.
16. Cf. obstruction of the highway, below, p. 798.
17. *Watts* (1703) 1 Salk 357.
18. *A–G v Tod Heatley* [1897] 1 Ch. 560.
19. Per Denning LJ [1957] 2 QB at 192.
20. Ibid. In *Mutters* (1864) Le & Ca 491, a conviction was upheld where the indictment alleged that D, on a particular day, caused an explosion which scattered pieces of rock on to neighbouring dwelling-houses and the highway; but the indictment did allege that D allowed the stones to remain on the highway for several hours.

must submit to the inconvenience occasioned necessarily in repairing the house; but if this inconvenience is prolonged for an unreasonable time, the public have a right to complain and the party can be indicted for a nuisance."[1]

The interference with the public's rights must be caused by some unnecessary and unreasonable act or omission by D. In *Dwyer v Mansfield*[2] it was held that, when queues formed outside D's shop because he was selling only 1 lb of potatoes per ration book in view of the wartime scarcity, he was not liable because he was carrying on his business in a normal and proper way without doing anything unreasonable or unnecessary. The nuisance, if there was one, had been created not by D's conduct, but by the short supply of potatoes.[3] The result would be different if D sold ice-cream through the window of a shop, causing a crowd to gather on the pavement, because this is not a normal and proper way of carrying on business.[4]

2 The Public

Blackstone says that a public nuisance must be an annoyance to all the King's subjects.[5] This is obviously too wide for, if it were so, no public nuisance could ever be established. Denning LJ declared that the test is,

". . . that a public nuisance is a nuisance which is so widespread in its range or so indiscriminate in its effect that it would not be reasonable to expect one person to take proceedings on his own responsibility to put a stop to it, but that it should be taken on the responsibility of the community at large."[6]

Whether an annoyance or injury is sufficiently widespread to amount to a public nuisance is a question of fact. In *Lloyd*,[7] where D's carrying on his trade caused annoyance to only three houses in Clifford's Inn, Lord Ellenborough said that this, if anything,[8] was a private nuisance, not being sufficiently general to support an indictment. But in the *PYA Quarries* case the nuisance was held to be sufficiently general where the inhabitants of about thirty houses and portions of two public highways were affected by dust and vibration. In *Madden* a telephone call stating that there was a bomb in a factory affected only eight security officers who could not be regarded as a class of the public.[9] If the call had stated that the bomb was in a public place, such as a highway, from which the public were consequently excluded, it would seem that there would have been a public nuisance, even

---

1. *Jones* (1812) 3 Camp 230, per Lord Ellenborough. And see *Cross* (1812) 3 Camp 224: "A stage-coach may set down or take up passengers in the street, this being necessary for the public convenience; but it must be done in a reasonable time": per Lord Ellenborough. For a similar statutory rule, see Public Service Vehicles Regulations 1936, reg. 7, and *Ellis v Smith* [1962] 3 All ER 954, [1962] 1 WLR 1486.
2. [1946] KB 437, [1946] 2 All ER 247.
3. *Sed quaere.* Would it be a defence to obstructing a pavement that D's strip-tease club was the only one in town?
4. *Fabbri v Morris* [1947] 1 All ER 315 (Highway Act 1835, s. 72).
5. *Commentaries*, iii, 216.
6. *A–G v PYA Quarries Ltd* [1957] 2 QB 169 at 191, [1957] 1 All ER 894 at 908.
7. (1802) 4 Esp 200.
8. The annoyance could be avoided by shutting the windows.
9. [1975] 3 All ER 155, CA. What if all the workers in the factory had been evacuated? See now, Criminal Law Act 1977, s. 51 (2); above, p. 427.

if few or no members of the public were in fact affected. Probably the same result should apply if the place were one to which the public have access on payment, such as a sports ground.

3 Mens Rea

It has been held that it is not necessary to establish that it was D's object to create a public nuisance. In *Moore*,[10] D was held liable where he organised pigeon-shooting on his land and, in consequence, great numbers of persons collected on the highway to shoot at pigeons as they escaped. Apparently this result (in 1832) was one which "the experience of mankind must lead anyone to expect."[11] Similarly the proprietor of a club[12] and of a theatre[13] have been held liable when the natural consequence of the nature of the entertainment provided within was to cause crowds or queues to gather outside and substantially to interfere with the public's use of the highway.

Although the authorities, on their face, suggest that D may be criminally liable in public nuisance for negligence, it would be dangerous to assume that this is necessarily and invariably so. References to "natural and probable consequences" are frequently ambiguous and may amount to no more than a finding of intention or recklessness. Modern civil cases on public nuisance certainly suggest that negligence is enough to establish civil liability. As the civil action involves establishing that the crime has been committed, this might be thought to settle the question. But it is not conclusive. While the plaintiff certainly has to establish the *actus reus* of public nuisance, it may well be that it is not necessary to prove the same degree of culpability as would be required in a criminal case. The rules in the civil action and the criminal prosecution are not necessarily the same. Thus Denning LJ tells us:

> "In an action for a public nuisance, once the nuisance is proved, and the defendant is shown to have caused it, the legal burden is shifted to the defendant to justify or excuse himself."[14]

But in a criminal prosecution the principle of *Woolmington v Director of Public Prosecutions*[15] surely requires that, at most, there is only an evidential burden on D who sets up justification or excuse.[16] Similarly, it may be that, in some types of nuisance at least, a higher degree of culpability – intention or recklessness – must be proved. It is true that Blackburn J has said that

> "the evidence which would maintain the action would also support the indictment";[17]

but that was a case where the proceedings were regarded as substantially civil in character.

---

10. (1832) 3 B & Ad 184.
11. Per Littledale J.
12. *Bellamy v Wells* (1890) 60 LJ Ch. 156.
13. *Lyons, Sons & Co. v Gulliver* [1914] 1 Ch. 631.
14. *Southport Corpn v Esso Petroleum Co Ltd* [1954] 2 QB 182 at 197, [1954] 2 All ER 561 at 571.
15. [1935] AC 462; **SHC 39**; above, p. 31.
16. Another obvious difference is that the civil case may be made out on a balance of probabilities, but the criminal case must be proved beyond reasonable doubt.
17. *Stephens* (1866) LR 1 QB 702 at 710; below.

Public nuisance covers a wide variety of different offences and it may be a mistake to assume that the same rules apply to all of them. In some of the cases, knowledge of the facts has been insisted upon.[18]

4 Vicarious Liability

In at least some types of public nuisance a master is liable for the acts of his servant, performed within the scope of employment, even though the mode of performance which creates the nuisance is contrary to the master's express orders. Thus in *Stephens*,[19] D was held liable for the obstruction by his servants of the navigation of a public river by depositing rubbish therein. The reason given was that the proceeding was, in substance, civil, the object being not to punish D but to prevent the continuation of the nuisance.[20] But Mellor and Shee JJ thought that there may be nuisances of such a character that this rule would not be applicable. Baty[1] criticises the ground of this decision and pertinently asks:

"who is to decide whether [the] prosecution is 'substantially civil' or tinged with criminology?"[2]

Certainly, prosecutions for obstructing the highway are by no means always civil in substance: frequently the object is the punishment of the offenders.[3] In *Chisholm v Doulton*[4] Field J said that *Stephens* "must be taken to stand upon its own facts";[5] and the court held that, on a charge under the Smoke Nuisance (Metropolis) Act 1853 D was not criminally liable for the negligence of his servant in creating a nuisance. In cases of statutory nuisance D is vicariously liable only if the words of the statute require it.[6]

The rule imposing vicarious liability for public nuisance may thus be neither so firmly established nor so all-embracing as is sometimes supposed.

2) *Obstruction of the Highway*[7]

1 By Public Nuisance

The highway can be used by members of the public for passing and re-passing and purposes reasonably incidental thereto.[8] It follows from this that there is a fundamental distinction between a public meeting on the highway and a public procession on the highway.[9] The public meeting is a

---

18. Above, pp. 794–795, footnotes 6, 7 and 8.
19. (1866) LR 1 QB 702; see also *Medley* (1834) 6 C & P 292.
20. Does this involve an inquiry into the motives of the prosecutor? Or does it reflect the courts' own view of what is the proper remedy for the wrong in question?
    1. *Vicarious Liability*, 204.
    2. In *Russell* (1854) 3 E & B 942, Lord Campbell thought that the obstruction of navigation by building a wall was "a grave offence".
    3. See below, p. 799.
    4. (1889) 22 QBD 736.
    5. Ibid., at 740.
    6. Cf. *Armitage Ltd v Nicholson* (1913) 23 Cox CC 416.
    7. Brownlie, Ch. 3.
    8. *Harrison v Duke of Rutland* [1893] 1 QB 142; *Hickman v Maisey* [1900] 1 QB 752.
    9. See Goodhart, "Public Meetings and Processions" (1937) 6 CLJ 161; E. C. S. Wade, "The Law of Public Meeting" (1939) 2 MLR 177; Ivamy, "The Right of Public Meeting" (1949) 2 CLP 183.

civil trespass against the person or body in whom the surface of the highway is vested. Not every trespass on the highway is necessarily a public nuisance; it is so only if it interferes in an appreciable way with the public's right of passage and an impediment may be too trifling to be properly called a nuisance.[10] So a coffee stall erected in the middle of the highway, but between a public convenience and a fountain, is not necessarily a nuisance.[11] This is the explanation of *Burden v Rigler*,[12] where it was held that a public meeting on the highway is not necessarily unlawful;[13] and that it does not follow that, simply because a public meeting is on the highway, it can be freely interrupted, notwithstanding the provisions of the Public Meeting Act 1908.[14] There was no evidence of any obstruction in that case and a small group of persons might – like the coffee-stall – be so placed on the highway as not to interfere appreciably with the public's right of passage. But any appreciable interference by a public meeting will amount to nuisance.

The procession, on the other hand, is prima facie lawful, even though it inevitably interferes to some extent with the rights of others to use the highway, for those taking part in it are using the highway for its proper purpose. The rights of any individual or group to use the highway, even for passage, must however be exercised reasonably. If they are exercised so as *unreasonably* to interfere with the rights of other members of the public, then the user ceases to be lawful and becomes a nuisance. A procession is a nuisance only if it is an unreasonable interference. Thus, a conviction will be quashed if the judge fails to direct the jury that the user must be unreasonable.[15]

2 Statutes relating to Obstruction of the Highway

There are many statutory rules relating to obstruction of the highway. The more important are briefly considered below.

By s. 137 of the Highways Act 1980,

"If a person without lawful authority or excuse, in any way wilfully obstruct the free passage along a highway he shall be guilty of an offence and liable in respect thereof to a fine not exceeding [level 1 on the standard scale]."

By s. 28 of the Town Police Clauses Act 1847,

"... every person who, by means of any cart, carriage, sledge, truck or barrow, or any animal or other means wilfully interrupts any public crossing, or wilfully causes any obstruction in any public footpath or other public thoroughfare ..."

is guilty of an offence punishable with a fine not exceeding level 3 on the standard scale.

---

10. *Ward* (1836) 4 Ad & El 384 at 387.
11. *Bartholomew* [1908] 1 KB 554.
12. [1911] 1 KB 337.
13. But it is prima facie a nuisance for a group of demonstrators to sit down in the highway: *Moule* [1964] Crim LR 303.
14. Which makes it an offence to act in a disorderly manner at any *lawful* public meeting for the purpose of preventing the transaction of business.
15. *Clark* (No. 2) [1964] 2 QB 315, [1963] 3 All ER 884 (incitement to public nuisance).

The essence of these offences is that the obstruction of the highway must be intentional and unreasonable. It is not enough to prove that D wilfully opened a car door which in fact obstructed the passage of a cyclist. Thus in *Eaton v Cobb*[16] D looked in his mirror and reasonably, but mistakenly, concluded that the opening of the door would obstruct no one. As under the common law relating to public nuisance, it is not every obstruction which will amount to an offence under these sections. There must be some unreasonable user of the highway.[17] A club tout who repeatedly stops small groups of pedestrians on the highway to attempt to persuade them to visit a nearby club makes such an unreasonable use of the highway as may amount to an obstruction of it, contrary to s. 137.[18] But an old lady pausing for breath, or a man waiting for a friend probably does not.[19] It appears to be irrelevant that no one was impeded in his usage of the highway.[20] Reasonableness is a question of fact, depending on all the relevant circumstances:[1] and whether there is a "lawful excuse" seems to depend simply on whether the obstruction is reasonable. In the absence of lawful authority, it seems that there can be no excuse for a permanent obstruction of the highway.[2]

Under the Highways Act it would seem that any unreasonable obstruction would suffice. So D was convicted where he made a speech in the highway causing a crowd to assemble;[3] but it may be that a narrower interpretation should be put upon the Town Police Clauses Act and "other means" be construed ejusdem generis with the preceding list, and therefore not to include obstruction by a crowd[4] or by walking four abreast on a pavement causing the public to step into the road.[5]

Persons who obstruct the highway with the purpose of compelling a pedestrian or vehicle to stop commit an offence even though they are acting in furtherance of a trade dispute.[6] The immunity conferred by statute[7] on peaceful picketing extends only to attendance for the purpose of peacefully communicating or obtaining information or peacefully persuading. There is no right to stop others whom the pickets may wish to speak to.

Obstruction by motor vehicles is likely to be dealt with under the Motor Vehicles (Construction and Use) Regulations 1978, reg. 122 which is punishable with a fine of £100:[8]

> "No person in charge of a motor vehicle or trailer shall cause or permit the motor vehicle or trailer to stand on a road so as to cause any unnecessary obstruction thereof."

16. [1950] 1 All ER 1016 (Highway Act 1835).
17. *Dunn v Holt* (1904) 73 LJKB 341; *Gill v Carson and Nield* [1917] 2 KB 674.
18. *Cooper v Metropolitan Police Commissioner* (1985) 82 Cr App Rep 238, DC.
19. *Bierton* [1983] Crim LR 392, Southwark Crown Court, and commentary.
20. *Gill v Carson*, supra (obiter); *Scarfe v Wood* [1969] Crim LR 265.
   1. *Absalom v Martin* [1974] RTR 145, DC.
   2. *Dixon v Atfield* [1975] 3 All ER 265, DC.
   3. *Horner v Cadman* (1886) 55 LJMC 110.
   4. *Ball v Ward* (1875) 33 LT 170.
   5. *Long* (1888) 59 LT 33; *Williams* (1891) 55 JP 406.
   6. *Broome v Director of Public Prosecutions* [1974] AC 587, [1974] 1 All ER 314, HL. Cf. *Kavanagh v Hiscock* [1974] QB 600, [1974] 2 All ER 177 DC.
   7. Now Trade Union and Labour Relations Act 1974, s. 15.
   8. SI 1978 No. 1017. Road Traffic Act 1972, s. 178. See *Langham v Crisp* [1975] Crim LR 652 and commentary.

Though the regulation uses the word "unnecessary", it has been held that what has to be proved is an unreasonable use[9] and –

"Whether or not the user amounting to an obstruction is or is not an unreasonable use of the highway is a question of fact. It depends on all the circumstances, including the length of time the obstruction continues, the place where it occurs, the purpose for which it is done, and, of course, whether it does in fact cause an actual obstruction as opposed to a potential obstruction."[10]

An honest and reasonable belief in a right to cause the obstruction would seem to amount to a "lawful excuse" if it arose from a mistake of fact, but not if it arose from a mistake of law, even if the mistake was induced by the police or a public authority.[11]

3 Offences of Entering and Remaining on Property[12]

At common law it was a misdemeanour unlawfully to enter upon, or keep possession of, land by menaces or force amounting to a breach of the peace. The common law offence was supplemented by the statutes of Forcible Entry 1381–1429 which created somewhat wider offences. The aim of the common law and statutory offences was the same: to prevent breaches of the peace so that even the lawful owner of land was required to resort to legal process in the courts if he could not recover possession without the use of force. The House of Lords decision in *Kamara v Director of Public Prosecutions*[13] took the matter a stage further by recognising, inter alia, that it was an offence to conspire to trespass on the land of another where the conspiracy involved, and was intended to involve, the infliction on the victim of something more than merely nominal damage, as by occupying his premises in order to exclude him from their enjoyment.

Following recommendations of the Law Commission[14] the former law has been replaced by Part II of the Criminal Law Act 1977.[15] What the Law Commission sought to do, and essentially their proposals were accepted by Parliament, was to preserve the peace by proscribing violent entry to premises; to extend the protection of the criminal law to a man deprived of his home by trespassers; to give special protection to embassies and

---

9. *Nelmes v Rhys Howells Transport Ltd* [1977] RTR 266, DC.
10. *Nagy v Weston* [1965] 1 All ER 78, per Lord Parker CJ; *Evans v Barker* [1971] RTR 453.
11. *Cambridgeshire and Isle of Ely County Council v Rust* [1972] 2 QB 426, [1972] 2 All ER 232, DC (pitching a stall on highway contrary to Highways Act 1959, s. 127); Law Commission Working Paper, No. 54.
12. Prichard, *Squatting* (1981), Part 3.
13. [1974] AC 104, [1973] 2 All ER 1242.
14. Law Com. No. 76, *Report on Conspiracy and Criminal Law Reform* (1976). See also Law Commission Working Paper No. 54, *Offences of Entering and Remaining on Property* (1974); Elliott, "Offences of Entering and Remaining on Property" [1974] Crim LR 501; Dashwood and Trice, "Offences of Entering and Remaining on Property" [1976] Crim LR 500; Prichard, "Squatting – the Law and the Mythology" (1976) 40 Conv (NS) 255; A. T. H. Smith, "Squatting and Sitting-in" [1977] Crim LR 139.
15. Part II was brought into force on 1st December 1977, the former law (as to which see the 3rd edn of this book at p. 626) applies to offences committed before this date.

consular premises because of our international obligations; and to provide for the obstruction of court officers executing the orders of the courts for recovery of possession of premises. In order to secure the prompt enforcement of these provisions a constable in uniform[16] may arrest without warrant anyone who is, or whom he with reasonable cause suspects to be, guilty of an offence.[17] For the purpose of effecting an arrest for one of these offences (other than in relation to an offence committed on diplomatic or consular premises) a constable in uniform may enter, if need be by force, and search any premises where the offender is or where he is reasonably suspected to be.[18]

1) *Entering Premises by Violence*

By s. 6 (1) of the Criminal Law Act 1977:
> "Subject to the following provisions of this section, any person who, without lawful authority, uses or threatens violence for the purpose of securing entry into any premises for himself or for any other person is guilty of an offence, provided that –
> a) there is someone present on those premises at the time who is opposed to the entry which the violence is intended to secure; and
> b) the person using or threatening the violence knows that that is the case."

The offence is summary only and is punishable by six months' imprisonment and/or a fine not exceeding level 5 on the standard scale (s. 6 (5)).

The law has always recognised the right of an occupier to use reasonable force to prevent entry by, or to eject, a trespasser. What is reasonable force depends on the circumstances,[19] and while it may now be assumed that it cannot be reasonable to kill in order to expel a trespasser,[20] it is clear that, if the circumstances warrant it, the occupier may use violence in defence of his property.[1] Violence may be returned with violence.[2] Obviously, therefore, an occupier commits no offence by *resisting an entry* by violence if the circumstances justify the means he employs. Nothing in the Act diminishes this right but s. 6 contains a general prohibition on *securing entry* by violence whether entry is sought by a trespasser or by one who is lawfully entitled to possession of the premises. Preserving the peace takes precedence over restoring proprietary rights.

1 The Entry
Commonly the purpose of the entrant will be to take possession of the premises but by s. 6 (4) (b) it is immaterial whether the entry is for the

---

16. Cf. *Wallwork v Giles* [1970] RTR 117, DC; *Cooper v Rowlands* [1971] RTR 291, DC.
17. Sections 6 (6), 9 (7) and 10 (5).
18. Police and Criminal Evidence Act 1984, ss. 17(1)(c) and 117.
19. See above, p. 242.
20. Cf. *Hussey* (1924) 18 Cr App Rep 160, CCA, above, p. 246.
 1. *Vaughan v McKenzie* [1968] 1 All ER 1154, DC – striking trespassing bailiff with bottle; *Broughton v Wilkerson* (1880) 44 JP 781, DC – striking trespasser in face and pulling out his whiskers; *Rossiter v Conway* (1893) 58 JP 350, DC – jamming trespasser's arm in door.
 2. *Green v Goddard* (1702) 2 Salk 641.

purpose of taking possession "or for any other purpose". Thus there is an entry where the purpose of the entrant is to gate-crash a party,[3] or to make a political protest, or take a short cut through another's yard. An actual entry is not required; the offence is complete as soon as violence is used or threatened for the purpose of securing entry which will usually occur before premises are entered.

2 Use or Threat of Violence

It is immaterial whether the violence used or threatened is directed against the person or property (s. 6 (4) (a)). The Law Commission deliberately preferred "violence" to "force" because –

"'Violence' will cover any application of force to the person, but it carries a somewhat restricted meaning in relation to property, which is not so in regard to the word 'force'. Forcing a yale-type lock with a piece of plastic, or a window catch with a thin piece of metal, would almost certainly amount to force, but not to violence,[4] and, on the basis that such conduct is unlikely of itself to cause a breach of the peace, we would not want it to be within the offence. On the other hand, splintering a door or window or its frame would be covered by the word 'violence' ... we feel that 'violence' carries the right flavour. ..."[5]

Any force amounting to an assault would suffice; it would be enough that entry is sought by pushing against a door held closed by the occupier, or even to lay hands on him unlawfully. Mere numbers cannot constitute a use or threat of violence otherwise many peaceable occupations of premises (as by workers of a factory, or by students of a college) would be criminal and it was never intended that this legislation should penalise peaceful occupations, however many might be involved.[6] And clearly an entry secured by a trick or strategem is not, as such, violent. No doubt there will be borderline situations but the Law Commission, aware of the current judicial practice of leaving the meaning of ordinary words to be determined as a question of fact,[7] felt that "it can safely be left to be decided as a question of fact whether or not there was violence within the ordinary meaning of the word." Yet the word has a special meaning, being different in its application to person and property. Since trial can only be by magistrates it may be assumed that they will be aware of the legal connotations of the word.

---

3. Cf. *Brittain* [1972] 1 QB 357, [1972] 1 All ER 353, CA.

4. But cf. *Re Calf and the Sun Insurance Office* [1920] 2 KB 366, CA, where it was held that to make an entry "by inserting a sharp instrument against the catch of the lock ... so sliding the catch back" was a "forcible and violent" entry for the purposes of an insurance policy. Atkin LJ expressed the view, at p. 383, that if a person uses a key there is force but not violence, but if he uses an instrument he uses force and violence. See also Bankes LJ at 378.

5. Law Com No. 76, para 2.61. The Law Commission's reasoning is, with respect, questionable. An offence can be committed only if someone (P) is present on the premises who is opposed to the entry. If P sees or hears D entering there is just as likely to be a breach of the peace whether D is entering by forcing the yale lock with a piece of plastic or by knocking down the door with a battering ram. It is the unwanted entry that is likely to cause the breach of the peace, not the manner of it.

6. But the jury is presumably entitled to take into account the numbers involved, along with other relevant circumstances, as evidence of an intent to use violence.

7. See above, p. 120.

3 The Premises

By s. 12 (1) (a)–

"'premises' means any building, any part of a building under separate occupation, any land ancillary to a building, the site comprising any building or buildings together with any land ancillary thereto . . ."

Suppose, then, that a block of flats stands in its own grounds. Assuming the other conditions are present, the offence may be committed when the grounds are entered, when the block is entered, or when an individual flat is entered. If violence is used to enter the flat it would be no defence to show that the grounds and the block were entered peaceably. But if the flat is entered peaceably, no offence is committed under s. 6 by using violence to enter any other part of the flat unless that part is in separate occupation. A part is in separate occupation if anyone, a sub-tenant or lodger for example, is in (or entitled to[8]) occupation of that part as distinct from the whole (s. 12 (2) (a)).

A building includes (a) any structure other than a movable one, and (b) any movable structure, vehicle or vessel designed or adapted for residential purposes.[9] As to (a) the use to which the structure is put is immaterial. It may be for housing man or beast or goods; it may be as large as an aircraft hangar or as small as a garden shed or even a telephone kiosk so long as it is not movable. Movable must mean more than that it can be moved, since practically any structure can be moved, and must refer to structures which are designed to be moved from place to place, such as the site huts used by builders. As to (b) the use to which the structure, vehicle or vessel is put is all-important. A site hut, being movable, cannot come within the section unless it is adapted for residential purposes. Structure is wider than building but in the context it suggests something in the nature of a building since it must be capable of occupation. It suggests something that is constructed which is intended to remain in one place with some degree of permanence. A tent would not be thought of as a structure in this sense.

Only such land as is "ancillary" to a building constitutes premises which means land adjacent to it and used or intended to be used in connection with the occupation of it (s. 12 (2) (b)). Anciently this might have been defined as land within the curtilage of the building, that is the land about the building, frequently but not necessarily enclosed, commonly used as part and parcel of the building. It would include a yard or a domestic garden but not the outlying fields of a farm.

4 Presence of Person Opposed to Entry

There must be present (that is physically present) on the premises a person who is opposed to the entry. That person need not be the occupier nor even someone authorised by the occupier to be there; that person may be a trespasser who has himself taken over the premises by violence. It is not necessary that this person should be prepared to oppose or resist entry for he may have decided that it would be safer to give up the premises without a struggle. It is only necessary that he is "opposed to" the entry, that he

---

8. But the offence under s. 6 (1) can be committed only if the sub-tenant or lodger is *in* occupation; it is not enough that he is entitled to occupation.

9. Section 12 (2). Cf. the discussion in connection with burglary, above, p. 602.

does not wish the entry to take place. There must be both presence and opposition in this sense; no offence is committed where the occupier, even though opposed to the entry, vacates the premises before violence is used or threatened.

5 Mens Rea

The *mens rea* involves (a) intentionally or recklessly using or threatening violence (b) in order to secure entry for oneself or another (c) knowing that there is a person on the premises who is opposed to the entry.

Where violence is used the offence may be committed though the owner is unaware of it. A burglar who gains entry by forcing a lock with a jemmy commits the offence though he intends not to disturb the sleeping occupant. Where violence is threatened[10] someone must know of the threat since a threat cannot exist without a victim.[11] Ordinarily the threat will be directed at the person on the premises opposed to the entry but the offence may be committed though the threat is directed at someone off the premises, for example a gatekeeper who is standing by the door outside the premises. The offence is committed only where violence is in fact used or threatened, but a conditional threat (a threat to use violence unless the occupier gives up possession) will suffice.

The violence must be used or threatened for the purpose of securing entry. It is not enough that D's use of violence enabled others to enter if it was not done by D for that purpose. D's conduct must be purposive so that an offence is not committed merely because D realised his use of violence might enable others to enter.

D must know of the presence of someone on the premises who is opposed to the entry. "This will ensure", said the Law Commission,[12]

"that in the rare type of case, where a person uses violence to enter premises to rescue another who is incapacitated or unaware of the danger, there will be no liability."

But it seems strange to say that D can claim he did not "know" of P's opposition merely because he believes that P would not have opposed the entry had he known the true purpose of it. Strictly D knows P is opposed and a more elegant solution would be to recognise this but to seek excuse for D's conduct on the grounds of necessity or defence of others.[13]

It is submitted that "knows" includes the case where D deliberately shuts his eyes to the obvious. This would accord with the general, though not universal, interpretation of "knows",[14] and seems the appropriate interpretation in this context. Would-be squatters may not *know* that there is someone on the premises who is opposed to their entry and may even hope to find them vacant, but if they shut their eyes to obvious signs of occupancy they should be held to know that the premises are occupied if that, unsurprisingly, turns out to be the case. It is not necessary that the

10. As to the requirements of a threat, see above, pp. 356 and 700.
11. But cf. *Treacy v Director of Public Prosecutions* [1971] AC 537, [1971] 1 All ER 110, HL, above, p. 589.
12. Law Com. 76, para. 2.65.
13. Cf. Prichard, *Squatting*, 11.
14. See above, p. 121.

occupier should know of the entry, only that D should know of his opposition to it. Since an occupier is ordinarily opposed to a trespassory entry, a fortiori where it is violent, the offence may be committed even though D succeeds in entering without the occupier being aware of it. In such a case, if D does not know of the occupier's opposition, he at least closes his eyes to the very obvious risk that he is opposed to entry.

6 Without Lawful Authority[15]

"It is necessary to qualify the entry by violence as being without lawful authority to allow, for example, the bailiffs and those acting under their authority to execute a court order, and the police to act within the scope of their authority under laws relating to search and arrest and the prevention of crime. The lawful authority which will take an entry by violence outside the ambit of the proposed offence must be an authority not merely to enter, but to enter by violence."[16]

But by s. 6 (2) –

"The fact that a person has any interest in or right to possession or occupation of any premises shall not ... constitute lawful authority for the use or threat of violence by him or anyone else for the purpose of securing his entry into those premises."

Since the reason for the offence lies in the need to preserve the peace, this sub-section makes it clear that (subject to an important exception in favour of a displaced residential occupier) even a person lawfully entitled to the premises may not use violence in order to re-enter them. What is meant by occupation in this context is no more and no less than physical presence. This means, for example, that if a shopkeeper returns from his lunch and finds his shop occupied by trespassers he cannot use violence to re-enter. Even if the shopkeeper is ejected from his shop by violence, he cannot use violence to re-enter for he now knows that there is someone (albeit a trespasser) who is present on the premises who is opposed to his entry. As a matter of civil law the shopkeeper remains the occupier and retains possession but he cannot assert his right of entry by the use or threat of violence.[17]

The owner is not rightless. Apart from his remedies under the civil law, he may re-enter his premises peaceably and, if he manages a peaceful re-entry, he may use reasonable force to expel the trespassers. Nor are any rights conferred on the trespassers though s. 6 indirectly affords them a measure of protection by proscribing violent entry.[18]

A lawful occupier who remains in physical occupation may authorise others to assist him in expelling trespassers. Suppose, however, that he authorises others who are not on the premises to come to his assistance. If the assistants have to use or threaten violence to enter they may commit the

---

15. See above, p. 425.
16. Law Com. 76, para. 2.66.
17. In *McPhail v Persons Unknown* [1973] Ch 447, [1973] 3 All ER 393, CA, it was accepted that an occupier kept out of his premises by squatters in whose possession he had not acquiesced, was entitled forcibly to turn them out. This right is now restricted (other than in relation to a displaced residential occupier) by s. 6. See generally, Prichard, 40 Conv (NS) 255.
18. The trespassers are presumably entitled to use reasonable force to prevent a violent entry by the lawful occupier on the grounds of prevention of crime!

offence because they know that there is someone (the trespasser) present on the premises who is opposed to their violent entry. The lawful occupier thus remains beleaguered.

7 The Displaced Residential Occupier

While the general rule is that a right to occupy premises does not excuse violent entry, an exception is made for the person who is kept out of his own living accommodation by trespassers. In his case there are reasons for condoning forcible self-help which outweigh the risk of a breach of the peace. Accordingly s. 6 (3) provides that it is a defence for D to prove –

"a) that at the time of the alleged offence he or any other person on whose behalf he was acting was a displaced residential occupier of the premises in question: or

b) that part of the premises in question constitutes premises of which he or any other person on whose behalf he was acting was a displaced residential occupier and that the part of the premises to which he was seeking to secure entry constitutes an access of which he or, as the case may be, that other person is also a displaced residential occupier."

A displaced residential occupier is defined by s. 12 (3) –

"... any person who was occupying any premises as a residence immediately before being excluded from occupation by anyone who entered those premises or any access to those premises, as a trespasser is a displaced residential occupier of the premises ... so long as he continues to be excluded from occupation of the premises by the original trespasser or by any subsequent trespasser."

Residence appears to mean a place where a man commonly sleeps, eats and drinks. Occasional use of premises for sleeping (as where a man sometimes sleeps at his shop or spends a night or two in an hotel) is not enough. It is of course a matter of degree and the test which suggests itself is whether P was living there (whether or not he was in physical occupation) immediately before[19] he was displaced. If he was then he commits no offence under s. 6 in using violence to regain possession of his premises though he may commit other offences if he uses more force than is reasonable in the circumstances.[20] He is not required to re-enter immediately since he remains a displaced residential occupier so long as he continues to be excluded by the trespasser. Nevertheless he should act with reasonable promptness because his delay may show acquiescence and confer possession on the trespasser.[1]

The trespasser himself (s. 12 (4)), or one who derives his occupation from him (s. 12 (6)), can never become a displaced residential occupier

---

19. "Immediately before" must mean "at the time when". If P has been living at premises which he vacates intending to make his residence elsewhere, he cannot be a displaced residential occupier if squatters move in some minutes later. P may have more than one residence (a town house and a weekend cottage) but he can be a displaced residential owner of either only if it can sensibly be said that he is living there at the time when he is displaced.
20. A T. H. Smith says (op. cit. at p. 145) this leaves the displaced residential occupier open to a range of offences and argues that a displaced residential occupier should commit no offence in using no more force than is reasonable in recovering his dwelling. But this appears to be the position.
1. See Prichard, 40 Conv (NS) at p. 274.

provided he *entered* as a trespasser. A tenant at sufferance (one who holds over at the end of a tenancy without the assent or dissent of his landlord) may become a trespasser but since he does not *enter* as a trespasser he qualifies as a displaced residential occupier.

The displaced residential occupier is entitled to use reasonable force not merely to regain his premises but also to gain access to them. It may be, for example, that while his flat is not occupied by the trespassers, they have taken over a staircase or passage that constitutes an ordinary, though not necessarily the sole, means of access. The effect of s. 6 (3) (b) and s. 12 (1) (b) is that he may use reasonable force to secure access to his living quarters.

The occupier is obviously displaced when he is denied entry or access to the whole of his premises. It is thought that he is also displaced if he is denied his use of any part of his living accommodation. The fact that he could use some part of the premises does not mean he is not displaced if he cannot use another part. He must be "excluded from occupation" but in the context exclusion from occupation of part should suffice so that he is excluded if he is kept out of occupation of the upstairs rooms even though he can use the ground floor. This interpretation derives support from the fact that he may use force to secure an access even if it is not the sole access (s. 12 (1) (b)). He may forcibly secure an access if it is an ordinary adjunct of the enjoyment of the premises; similarly he must be justified in securing entry to any part of the premises which is equally necessary for their enjoyment.[2]

The displaced residential occupier, or a person acting on his behalf, may use reasonable force to secure entry even though entry is sought for other than residential purposes. Nothing in the Act requires the displaced residential occupier to be entering solely for the purpose of taking up residence. Suppose, for example, that trespassers occupy D's house while he is in hospital during a protracted illness. It would be permissible for E, acting with D's authority, to enter the house by force in order to remove D's belongings and furniture.

8 Other Defences

Although s. 6 specifies a particular defence this is no reason for excluding other defences. Obviously defences of general application, such as infancy, insanity and duress, remain available. On principle mistake of fact would be a defence when D believes in facts which, if true, would render his conduct lawful. If, for example, D believes in facts which would constitute E the lawful occupier of residential premises, D would commit no offence in using reasonable force to help E regain possession. On the other hand if D knows of facts which constitute E a trespasser it will be of no avail to D to say that he believed E to be the lawful occupier since D's mistake is no longer one of fact but one of law.

---

2. Cf. Prichard, *Squatting*, 93.

2) *Adverse Occupation of Premises*

By s. 7 (1) of the Act –

"Subject to the following provisions of this section, any person who is on any premises as a trespasser after having entered as such is guilty of an offence if he fails to leave those premises on being required to do so by or on behalf of –

a) a displaced residential occupier of the premises; or

b) an individual who is a protected intending occupier of the premises . . ."

The offence is summary only and is punishable by six months' imprisonment and/or a fine not exceeding level 5 on the standard scale.

Although the displaced residential occupier has the right to use reasonable force to expel trespassers, it may not always be either practicable or prudent to do so. The creation of this offence enables him (and the protected intending occupier) to pray in aid the criminal law.

1 Entry as a Trespasser

It must be proved that D entered the premises[3] as a trespasser. It is not enough that D becomes a trespasser because, say, the occupier revokes a permission previously given. Nor does a tenant holding over at the end of his tenancy come within the offence for though he may become a trespasser he does not enter as one; entry in this case referring to the original entry into possession. D must know the facts which constitute him a trespasser but need not know that he is a trespasser in law.[4] D may be unaware of the facts constituting him a trespasser when he enters but become aware of them (as where he is informed of them by the displaced residential occupier) subsequent to entry. There would seem to be no difficulty in bringing this case within s. 7 (1) since D now knows that he entered as a trespasser.[5]

2 Requirement by Displaced Residential Occupier or by Protected Intending Occupier

The safest formula would be to use the words, "I require you etc." but any language making it clear that D is being directed to leave will suffice. A failure to leave does not require a refusal to leave; D fails to leave if he deliberately remains on premises after a reasonable time has elapsed for him to remove himself.[6]

The requirement must be by or on behalf of a displaced residential occupier or a protected intending occupier. The definition of the former is examined above.[7] The Law Commission proposed to confine the offence to the situation where a residential occupier was displaced but Parliament thought that an intending occupier ought also to be protected. He is either

---

3. The meaning of premises is discussed above, p. 804.
4. Cf. the discussion in connection with burglary, above, p. 597.
5. This is the view of the Law Commission, Law Com 76, para. 2.79, and cf. the discussion of burglary in relation to s. 9 (1) (b) of the Theft Act 1968, above, p. 602.
6. But D does not cease to be a trespasser by virtue of being given reasonable time in which to leave: s. 12 (7).
7. At p. 807.

(a) a person who has purchased a freehold interest, or a leasehold interest with not less than 21 years to run (s. 7 (2) (a)); or (b) a person authorised to occupy premises by certain authorities (s. 7 (4) (a)), for example by a local authority or a housing association.[8]

The person specified in (a) must also (i) require the premises for occupation as a residence; (ii) be excluded by a trespasser; and (iii) hold a written statement (signed by himself in the presence of a justice of the peace or a commissioner for oaths who must also sign as witness)[9] specifying his interest and stating that he requires the premises as a residence for himself (s. 7 (2)). The person specified in (b) must (i) be authorised to occupy the premises by a relevant authority; (ii) be excluded by a trespasser; and (iii) hold a certificate stating that he has been authorised by a relevant authority to occupy the premises as a residence.

The reason for the formal requirement in both cases is to help the police to identify the protected intending occupier, and accordingly to prevent misunderstanding and abuse. In the case of the displaced residential occupier identification must ordinarily be a simple matter because he will be known as such by his neighbours, hence there are no formal requirements in his case.

3 Defences

Since "there may be circumstances in which the defendant believes on reasonable grounds that the person requiring him to leave is not the displaced residential occupier"[10] (or the protected intending occupier) it is provided by s. 7 (6) that it is a defence for D to prove –

"... that he believed that the person requiring him to leave the premises was not a displaced residential occupier or protected intending occupier of the premises or a person acting on behalf of a displaced residential occupier or protected intending occupier."

While the Law Commission imported a requirement of reasonable grounds, it is thought that it would now accord with principle to require only that D's belief be honest[11] – the presence or absence of reasonable grounds bearing upon the genuineness of D's belief.

The protected intending occupier is not required to produce the certificate referred to above but a failure to produce it may afford some grounds for a claim by D that he did not believe P to be a protected intending occupier. And in addition s. 7 (8) provides that it is a defence for D to prove that he asked for the certificate and P failed to produce it. This is a defence even though D knows that P is a protected intending occupier.

As with the offence under s. 6, the provision of particular statutory defences cannot be taken to exclude the general defences available on a charge of crime.[12]

8. Section 7 (5). The effect is that by no means all persons who have an immediate right to possession of premises for residential purposes are protected. It was thought that to extend the offence more widely would place an undue burden on the police in relation to enforcement and might leave the law open to abuse by unscrupulous landlords.
9. Section 7 (3), which also makes it an offence knowingly or recklessly to make a false declaration.
10. Law Com. 76, para. 2.79.
11. See above, p. 87. And as to belief see further below, p. 813.
12. See above, p. 808.

3) *Trespassing with a Weapon of Offence*

By s. 8 (1) –

"A person who is on any premises as a trespasser after having entered as such, is guilty of an offence if, without lawful authority or reasonable excuse, he has with him on the premises any weapon of offence."

The offence is summary only and is punishable with three months' imprisonment and/or a fine not exceeding level 5 on the standard scale (s. 8 (3)).

Where trespassers resist lawful entry to the premises which they occupy they may commit various crimes, most obviously crimes of assault. But before this stage is reached the trespassers may have armed themselves in anticipation of eviction. S. 8 deals with this situation. It is modelled on s. 1 of the Prevention of Crime Act 1953 with the slightly modified definition of "weapon of offence" taken from s. 10 of the Theft Act 1968. The constituent elements of this offence are thus dealt with in other parts of this book.[13]

4) *Trespassing on Foreign Missions*

By s. 9 (1) a person who enters or is on any premises to which the section applies as a trespasser is guilty of a summary offence punishable by six months' imprisonment and a fine of £1,000 (s. 9 (5)). The premises specified in s. 9 (2) (amended by the Diplomatic and Consular Premises Act 1987) include not only diplomatic and consular premises but any premises in respect of which any organisation, body or individual is entitled to inviolability. A certificate from the Secretary of State certifying that the premises fall within the classes specified shall be conclusive proof that they do, and presumably a certificate will be obtained whenever any doubt about the issue is likely to arise.

Unlike the offences under ss. 6–8 this offence does not require, though it extends to, entry as a trespasser; and one who lawfully enters commits this offence on failing to leave within a reasonable time of a requirement to do so by the occupier or his agent.

The prosecution must prove that D was aware of the facts constituting him a trespasser[14] on the premises. Ordinarily the prosecution would have to prove also that D knew that the premises were diplomatic or consular, or was at least aware of the risk that they might be. But in this particular the onus is placed on D since by s. 9 (3) it is a defence for him to prove that he believed[15] the premises in question were not premises to which the section applies. The section does not presuppose any knowledge of law. If D knows of the facts, for example he knows that the house he enters is the private residence of a diplomat, it can be no defence that he was unaware that the section applies to private residences as well as official premises. No doubt the general defences available on a charge of crime are available on a charge under this section.

13. See above, pp. 416, 422 and 609.
14. As to which see above, p. 809.
15. As to belief see below, p. 812.

Otherwise D commits the offence although his purposes are entirely peaceable. The offence would be committed where D crosses an embassy garden as a short cut to a bus stop. Proceedings for the offence, however, may be commenced only by or with the consent of the Attorney General (s. 9 (6)).

5) *Obstructing Court Officers etc.*

By s. 10 (1) –

"... a person is guilty of an offence if he resists or intentionally obstructs any person who is in fact an officer of a court engaged in executing any process issued by the High Court or by any county court for the purpose of enforcing any judgment or order for the recovery of any premises or for the delivery of possession of any premises."

The offence is summary only and is punishable by imprisonment for six months and/or a fine not exceeding level 5 on the standard scale.

Since the Law Commission was concerned only with the particular problem of entering and remaining on property, s. 10 (2) limits the application of this offence to orders made, in effect, against persons who are squatters.[16]

Resistance and obstruction[17] are apt to cover both active and passive conduct, ranging from an assault to mere refusal to leave premises. Any conduct, such as boarding up doors and windows, which is done to impede the enforcement of a judgment or order will suffice. The obstruction need not be physical and it appears to be enough that D tells lies to an officer in order to delay or defeat enforcement.

The obstruction must be intentional. This invites comparison with wilful obstruction under s. 51 of the Police Act 1964.[18] It must at least be shown that the conduct causing the obstruction was deliberate and was meant to obstruct. It would not be enough that D realised his conduct might obstruct if it was not done with intent to obstruct. Once that is proved it seems clear from the wording of the section that the prosecution does not have to prove that D knew that P was (or even thought he might be) an officer of the court; it is enough that D obstructs a person "*who is in fact*" an officer of the court. But it is a defence by s. 10 (3) for D to prove –

"that he believed that the person he was resisting or obstructing was not an officer of a court."

The form of the defence is somewhat unusual. It requires D to prove that he believed that P was *not* an officer, just as under s. 7 (6) it is a defence for D to prove that he believed P was *not* a displaced residential occupier or protected intending occupier and under s. 9 (3) that D believed the

---

16. As to resistance to other court orders see Law Com 76, paras. 2.22–3.24.
17. Cf. the discussion in connection with resisting and obstructing constables, above, p. 392.
18. See above, p. 387.

premises in question were *not* premises to which the section applies. It seems clear that the defence is available so long as D's belief was honest, whether it was reasonable or not.[19] Whether D believes that P is not an officer of the court (or a displaced residential occupier etc.) is entirely subjective. Even if D considers the possibility that P may be an officer of the court he can still genuinely believe that he is not. A belief may be irrational and can be genuinely held even though the evidence is against it. On the other hand D cannot believe that P is not an officer of the court unless he has considered whether he might be or not and concluded that he is not. So if D obstructs P without giving any thought to P's status, he cannot prove that he believed that P was not an officer of the court. Somewhat paradoxically, therefore, D is entitled to an acquittal when he considered that P might be a court officer though he unreasonably believed that he was not; but must be convicted when it never occurred to him to consider what P's status might be because in such a case he cannot believe that P was not an officer of the court.[20]

"Resists", unlike "obstructs", is not qualified by "intentionally". It is not clear why this should be so except that it follows the substantially similar wording of s. 51 of the Police Act 1964. That might have led to the inference that knowledge that P was an officer of the court is irrelevant, but the statutory defence just discussed is available both in cases of resistance and obstruction. Presumably the only difference, so far as *mens rea* is concerned, is that resistance may be reckless as well as intentional.

The provision of a particular defence to a charge of resisting or obstructing court officers cannot be taken to imply that other general defences to crime are not available.

4 Criminal Eviction and Harassment

Section 1 (2) and (3) of the Protection from Eviction Act 1977[1] provides:
"2) If any person unlawfully deprives the residential occupier of any premises[2] of his occupation of the premises or any part thereof or attempts to do so he shall be guilty of an offence unless he proves that he believed, and had reasonable cause to believe, that the residential occupier had ceased to reside in the premises.
  3) If any person with intent to cause the residential occupier of any premises –
    a) to give up the occupation of the premises or any part thereof; or
    b) to refrain from exercising any right or pursuing any remedy in respect of the premises or part thereof;

---

19. In the Bill as originally presented to Parliament it was a defence for D to prove that "he believed, *and had reasonable cause to believe*" etc. The italicised words were deleted presumably to make it clear that the defence was available provided only the belief was genuine. Of course the reasonableness of the belief bears on whether it is genuinely held.
20. See the discussion above pp. 632–635, and below p. 849.
  1. Cf. Caravan Sites Act 1968, s. 3 and *Hooper v Eaglestone* [1978] Crim LR 161, DC.
  2. The tenancy of a single room is sufficient: *Thurrock Urban District Council v Shina* (1972) 23 P & CR 205, DC.

does acts[3] calculated to interfere with the peace or comfort of the residential occupier or members of his household, or persistently[4] withdraws or withholds services reasonably required for the occupation of the premises as a residence, he shall be guilty of an offence."

The offences are punishable with a fine of £1,000 or six months' imprisonment or both on summary conviction and by unlimited fine or imprisonment for two years or both, on indictment. It is not an offence under this section for a person who is entitled to possession of the premises in question to act in the manner described because s. 1 (1) defines "residential occupier" as –

". . . a person occupying the premises as a residence, whether under a contract or by virtue of any enactment or rule of law giving him the right to remain in occupation or restricting the right of any other person to recover possession of the premises."

It is not necessary to prove that force was used or threatened. Excluding the occupier by a trick or locking him out in his absence is enough. A contractual licensee or lodger living in a furnished room at his home is a residential occupier.[5] A person taking a room on a short visit, however, is not protected by the section. "Premises" include a caravan which D has allowed P to park on his land and to live in as his home.[6]

The deprivation under s. 1 (2) must be for a substantial period or, if only for a very short period, done with intent to exclude permanently.[7] The word "persistently" in s. 1 (3) governs "withholds" as well as "withdraws" so that it is not sufficient to allege that D, a landlord, withdrew the gas supply on a single day by failing to pay the gas bill with the result that the Gas Board cut off the supply.[8] Would it have been enough if it had been alleged that D "persisted" thereafter for some days in his refusal to pay? It is submitted that it would.[9]

Under subsection (2), the *mens rea* appears to be simply an intention to deprive the occupier of his occupation of the premises. The exception suggests that it would not be a defence that D believed that the eviction was lawful for some reason other than the cessation of residence by the occupier. Under subsection (3) there must be proof of an intention to cause a residential occupier to give up occupation of the premises, etc., so that if D believes P to be a squatter he is not guilty. According to dicta in *Phekoo*[10] the belief must be a reasonable belief. In the context, the word "calculated" probably means "likely" rather than "intended"; but this is not significant since proof of intent (a) or (b) is almost bound to involve proof that there

---

3. See *Ahmad* (1986) 84 Cr App Rep 64, CA and *Yuthiwattana* (1984) 80 Cr App Rep 55, above, p. 49. Cf. *Davidson-Acres* [1982] Crim LR 50 and commentary.
4. Cf. *Abrol* [1972] Crim LR 318, CA.
5. *Luganda v Service Hotels Ltd* [1969] 2 Ch 209, [1969] 2 All ER 692, CA.
6. *Norton v Knowles* [1969] 1 QB 572, [1967] 3 All ER 1061, DC.
7. *Costelloe v London Borough of Camden* [1986] Crim LR 249, DC and commentary.
8. *Westminster City Council v Peart* (1968) 66 LGR 561, DC.
9. In *Peart* (above) it was not necessary to decide whether a succession of acts was necessary to constitute persistence. Cf. *Dale v Smith* [1967] 2 All ER 1133, above, p. 476.
10. [1981] 3 All ER 84, [1981] 1 WLR 1117, CA, criticised above, p. 87.

was an intention to interfere, etc. It must be alleged and proved that the acts are in fact likely to interfere.[11]

The section does not give rise to any civil remedy in damages.[12]

5 Piracy and Hijacking[13]

A discussion of the law relating to piracy and hijacking involves some consideration of the rules relating to jurisdiction as well as consideration of the substantive law defining the offences. It is not the purpose of this book to deal with jurisdiction, but it will be at once appreciated that some mention of jurisdictional issues is inevitable in any consideration of the law relating to these offences.

1) *Piracy*

Piracy is an offence against the law of nations[14] and by international law all states may try and punish pirates. So far as English law is concerned it is doubtful whether international law is part of English law save in so far as it has been incorporated by statute or by judicial decision, but in this regard piracy jure gentium occupies a special position. English courts have traditionally exercised jurisdiction over persons who commit piracy *as defined by international law*. In such a case English courts exercise jurisdiction irrespective of the nationality of the defendant or the victim, or the nationality of the ships involved.[15] But from time to time statutes have been passed creating further offences of, or akin to, piracy; here, of course, the statute governs the definition of the offence and also governs questions of jurisdiction.

1 Piracy Jure Gentium

In *Re Piracy Jure Gentium*[16] the Privy Council was asked whether an actual robbery was an essential element in the crime of piracy jure gentium or whether piracy was not equally committed where an attempted robbery had been frustrated. Delivering the advice of the Board, Viscount Sankey LC recognised that what had to be determined was whether this was piracy

---

11. *Peart*, above.
12. *McCall v Abelesz* [1976] QB 585, [1976] 1 All ER 727, CA.
13. Oppenheim, *International Law*, Vol. 1, 8th ed, pp. 608–617 and passim; Colombos, *International Law of the Sea*, 6th ed, pp. 443–450 and passim; Brownlie, *Principles of Public International Law*, (3rd ed.), pp. 243–245; Greig, *International Law* (2nd ed), pp. 329–333.
14. Another view is that international law authorises universal jurisdiction only: Schwarzenberger, 3 CLP at 268–9.
15. "The king of England hath . . . an undoubted jurisdiction and power, in concurrency with other princes and states, for the punishment of all piracies and robberies at sea, in the most remote part of the world; so that if any person whatsoever, native or foreigner, Christian or Infidel, Turk or Pagan . . . shall be robbed or spoiled in . . . any . . . seas, it is piracy within . . . the cognizance of this court." *Dawson* (1699) 13 State Tr 451 at 455 per Sir Charles Hedges, judge of the High Court of Admiralty. Cf. *Re Piracy Jure Gentium* [1934] AC 586 at 589.
16. [1934] AC 586.

according to international law, and that there were considerable difficulties in determining what that law was. Having reviewed the extensive authorities he concluded that these showed that piracy was committed where the attempt was frustrated, but beyond that he said that their lordships would not themselves be prepared to hazard a comprehensive definition of the crime. Fortunately the problem of definition would now appear to be very much simpler because s. 4 of the Tokyo Convention Act 1967 provides that for the purposes of any proceedings in the United Kingdom in respect of piracy those provisions of the Convention on the High Seas which are included in the Schedule "shall be treated as constituting part of the law of nations". These provisions are set out in the schedule to the Act –

"Article 15. Piracy consists of any of the following acts:

1) Any illegal acts of violence, detention or any act of depredation, committed for private ends by the crew or the passengers of a private ship or a private aircraft, and directed:

a) On the high seas, against another ship or aircraft, or against persons or property on board such ship or aircraft;

b) Against a ship, aircraft, persons or property in a place outside the jurisdiction of any state:

2) Any act of voluntary participation in the operation of a ship or of an aircraft with knowledge of facts making it a pirate ship or aircraft;

3) Any act of inciting or of intentionally facilitating an act described in sub-paragraph (1) or sub-paragraph (2) of this article.

"Article 16. The acts of piracy as defined in article 15, committed by a warship, government ship or government aircraft whose crew had mutinied and taken control of the ship or aircraft are assimilated to acts committed by a private ship.

"Article 17. A ship or aircraft is considered a pirate ship or aircraft if it is intended by the persons in dominant control to be used for the purpose of committing one of the acts referred to in article 15. The same applies if the ship or aircraft has been used to commit any such act so long as it remains under the control of the persons guilty of that act."

While courts in the United Kingdom must treat Articles 15–17 of the Convention as authoritative, it does not follow that they must treat them as exhaustive. Section 4 of the Tokyo Convention Act states that these provisions "*shall* be treated as constituting *part of* the law of nations" and it is accordingly arguable that courts may resort to customary international law in so far as customary law may enlarge the definition of piracy. There is, for example, some authority for the view that insurgents[17] and even states[18] may commit piracy, but it seems clear that state action is excluded from the definition of piracy under the Convention and it is unlikely that

---

17. See Oppenheim, op. cit., at 612; Colombos, op. cit., at 451.

18. "Even an independent state may, in my opinion, be guilty of piratical acts. What were the Barbary pirates of olden times? What many of the African tribes at this moment? It is, I believe, notorious, that tribes now inhabiting the African coast of the Mediterranean will send out their boats and capture any ships becalmed upon their coasts. Are they not pirates, because, perhaps, their whole livelihood may not depend on piratical acts? I am well aware that it has been said that a state cannot be piratical; but I am not disposed to assent to such dictum as a universal proposition". *The Magellan Pirates* (1853) 1 Ecc & Ad 81 at 83 per Dr. Lushington.

the action of insurgents would normally be "for private ends" so as to bring it within the Conventional definition. It is submitted, however, that the definition in the Convention on the High Seas should be treated as exhaustive and as accurately stating the present customary law. In view of conflicting decisions and authorities on the definition of piracy, there was a real need for a re-definition. That re-definition was prepared by the International Law Commission[19] after consideration of existing authorities and current state practice. The wide measure of ratification[20] which the Convention has received strongly suggests that it is a comprehensive statement of the existing law, and it is thought that English courts would so treat it.

If this assumption is correct it follows that earlier decisions of English courts are no longer authoritative. The court is in this case applying international law and that necessarily involves[1] a reference to what the law is now, not what it may have been decades or even centuries ago. It would seem also to follow that the provisions of the Convention must be interpreted in its context as part of international law; this would allow reference to extraneous sources[2] and techniques of construction not normally incident to the interpretation of an Act of Parliament.[3]

a) *The elements of piracy.* The essential feature of piracy is that it is something done "for private ends". This would obviously exclude depredations, etc.[4] (even though they may be otherwise illegal under international law), authorised by a state, but it is also implicit in the Articles that piracy cannot be committed by a warship, or a government ship or aircraft, even if the act is unauthorised. Piracy may be committed only by private ships or aircraft, and the acts of government ships or aircraft are to be so regarded only where the crew has mutinied and taken control (Article 16). Where insurgents seize a ship and use it to commit depredations against other ships this will not be piracy if done as part of an attempt to overthrow the de jure authority within the state; such an act is not done for private ends. This would also seem to be the case though the insurgents have no hope of success and seize the other ship merely with a view to calling attention to real or imagined political grievances in their own state. From time to time in the past states have regarded depredations committed by insurgents as piratical,[5] but even if this view was generally held in earlier

19. See Yearbook of the ILC [1956] Vol. 2, 282.
20. The Convention has been ratified by 46 states, including most of the major maritime states. The view of H.M. Government appears to be that the Convention provides an internationally agreed definition of piracy: Parl Deb HL Vol. 284, col. 117. The Law Commission takes the same view: *Territorial and Extra-Territorial Extent of the Criminal Law*, Working Paper, Law Com No. 29, para. 76.
  1. Cf. *Trentex Trading Corpn Ltd v Central Bank of Nigeria* [1977] QB 529, [1977] 1 All ER 881, CA.
  2. Most obviously the deliberations of the International Law Commission.
  3. Cf. Vallat, *International Law and the Practitioner*, at 17, "I believe that the time has come when our Courts will do their best to give to treaties their true meaning under the law within which they normally operate – namely, international law – and will not defeat the real intention of applying strict methods of statutory construction."
  4. See definition, above, p. 816.
  5. Cf. the *Huascar* incident (1877): McNair, *International Law Opinions*, vol. 1, pp. 274–280. But it is not clear that the law officers necessarily regarded the actions of the *Huascar* (a Peruvian ship seized by insurgents) as piratical.

times, it has not survived the Convention. If the action is for private ends it is piracy where the intention is to commit any act of violence or detention as well as where the intention is to rob.

Piracy is ordinarily thought of as an act committed by persons on board one ship against another ship, and the Convention extends this to include acts committed by aircraft against aircraft, aircraft against ships and ships against aircraft. It seems clear enough from the wording of Article 15 (1) (a) that two vessels must be involved, and the International Law Commission said that:

"Acts committed on board a ship by the crew or passengers and directed against the ship itself, or against persons or property on the ship, cannot be regarded as acts of piracy. ... Even where the purpose of the mutineers is to seize the ship, their acts do not constitute piracy."[6]

Here again the view has been taken in the past that it is piracy for the crew or passengers to commandeer the vessel in which they sail,[7] but if the Convention contains an exhaustive definition of piracy then it follows that these older decisions no longer represent international law. Although hijacking (the seizure of a ship or aircraft by persons on board that ship or aircraft) is now a much more serious menace to international travel than attacks by other ships or aircraft, it is not piracy under the Convention.

This is the position under Article 15 (1) (a) where the acts take place on the high seas, but the position may be different under Article 15 (1) (b) where the acts are done in a place outside the jurisdiction of any state. Here the International Law Commission,

"had chiefly in mind acts committed by a ship or aircraft on an island constituting terra nullius or on the shore of an unoccupied territory. But the Commission did not wish to exclude acts committed by aircraft within a larger unoccupied territory, since it wished to prevent such acts committed on ownerless territories from escaping all penal jurisdiction."[8]

It would appear from the wording of Article 15 (1) (b) that though the depredation must be by a ship or aircraft it will be piracy if directed merely against persons or property in a place outside the jurisdiction of any state as well as where it is directed against a ship or aircraft. Paragraph (b) contains no requirement that the persons or property be on board a ship or aircraft. This interpretation would appear to be in line with the Commission's view, for if these acts against persons and property in places outside the jurisdiction of any state were not brought within the definition of piracy, there would be some risk that the wrongdoers would escape all penal jurisdiction.

---

6. Yearbook of the ILC, [1956] Vol. 2, 282.
7. In *A-G for the Colony of Hong Kong v Kwok-A-Sing* (1873) LR 5 PC 179, it was held that where a number of Chinese coolies, who were being taken from China to Peru in a French ship, killed the captain and took the ship back to China, they were guilty of piracy jure gentium. Cf. *Boniface* (No. 2) [1967] Crim LR 186, CA, where it was held that members of the crew of a trawler were guilty of piracy in assaulting the officers and taking possession of the ship, but it does not appear whether the defendants had been charged with piracy jure gentium or with statutory piracy.
8. Yearbook of the ILC, [1956] Vol. 2, 282.

b) *Mens rea*. Article 15 (2) contains an explicit requirement of *mens rea* for piracy by participation in the operation of a private ship or aircraft. Where the piracy consists in doing any of the acts set out in Article 15 (a) all such acts must be "illegal" and this was presumably intended to import a similar requirement for *mens rea*.

2 Piracy by Statute

From time to time statutes have created offences of piracy or offences ancillary to piracy. The interpretation and operation of these statutes is of course governed by English law and is unaffected by the Convention. Many of these statutory provisions wear an antique look[9] and are hardly appropriate to modern conditions,[10] but some provisions retain some importance. The hijacking of a ship by members of the crew, though probably not now piracy jure gentium,[11] is piracy under s. 8 of the Piracy Act 1698.[12] By the same section it is piracy to make a revolt on the ship, and it has been held to be piracy where the object of the revolt was to redress real or imagined grievances.[13] By s. 1 of the Piracy Act 1721 it is an offence of piracy to trade with pirates or to furnish them with ammunition, stores or provisions.[14]

Offences of piracy apart, the criminal law generally applies to British ships afloat[15] and in territorial waters,[16] so that persons (whether British nationals or not) who commit offences on board or within the territorial sea may be charged with offences under English law.[17] Consequently the statutory offences of piracy are for the most part unnecessary unless it is thought important to retain the label "piracy" for certain acts, or unless it is thought necessary to impose higher penalties for certain offences when committed at sea.

3 Punishment of Piracy

Provisions relating to the punishment of offences at sea are not free from obscurity but the position appears to be as follows. If the offence is committed on the high seas and is charged as murder, assault, theft etc. the offence attracts the same punishment as if committed "upon the shore":[18] Offences at Sea Act 1799, s. 1. Where a person commits an offence which

---

9. See Law Com Working Paper No. 29, *Territorial and Extra-Territorial Extent of the Criminal Law*, paras. 75–77, where the Law Commission expressed the view that all these provisions might be repealed subject to specific provision for the hijacking of ships and aircraft.

10. E.g. under s. 6 of the Piracy Act 1721 it is an offence for a seaman to utter words discouraging his fellows from defending the ship when attacked by pirates.

11. See above, p. 815.

12. Cf. *Cameron v HM Advocate* 1971 SLT 333. Five crew members taking over their ship in British territorial waters held to be guilty of piracy; it was agreed their conduct did not constitute piracy within the Convention, but it did constitute piracy within Scots law.

13. *Hastings and Meharq* (1825) 1 Mood CC 82; *McGregor and Lambert* (1844) 1 Car & Kir 429.

14. Cf. The Marine, &c. Broadcasting (Offences) Act 1967, s. 4 which makes it an offence to supply apparatus, goods or materials to "pirate" wireless stations operating outside the jurisdiction.

15. Law Com WP No. 29, para. 20.

16. Ibid. para. 16.

17. But the law relating to these matters is not free from difficulty and obscurity; see generally Law Com WP No. 29, paras. 9–29.

18. Which must mean within the territorial jurisdiction of English courts.

by statute amounts to piracy, the punishment is imprisonment for life: Piracy Act 1837, s. 3.

The punishment for piracy jure gentium is not provided by the Convention of the High Seas and is left to municipal law. Section 2 of the Piracy Act 1837 provides for the death penalty for "the crime of piracy" where at the time of commission, or immediately before or after, the pirate assaults with intent to murder or endangers the life of any person on board. It is not clear to what "crime of piracy" refers but it seems only to apply to piracy jure gentium since the following section is expressly applied to statutory piracy. Beyond this point it is not possible to go with any great confidence. Writers[19] appear to assume that s. 1 of the Offences at Sea Act 1799 applies; if this assumption is correct then in so far as the pirate commits robbery, theft, assault etc. the offence would attract the punishments normally incident to these offences.

2) *Hijacking and Related Offences*

By s. 92 (1) of the Civil Aviation Act 1982 –
"Any act or omission taking place on board a British controlled aircraft while in flight elsewhere than in or over the United Kingdom which if taking place in, or in a part of, the United Kingdom, would constitute an offence under the law in force in, or in that part of, the United Kingdom shall constitute that offence; but this subsection shall not apply to any act or omission which is expressly or impliedly authorised by or under that law when taking place outside the United Kingdom."

And for the purposes of conferring jurisdiction the offence is deemed to have been committed in any part of the United Kingdom where D is: s. 92 (3). So if, for example, D steals P's wallet on a British aircraft while the aircraft is in flight over France, D may be arrested when he lands in London and be tried under the Theft Act 1968. So too a person threatening to destroy or damage a British aircraft in flight would inevitably commit offences triable here. But conduct of this kind poses a general threat to the safety of international travel and, so far as law can contribute to its suppression, that law would be seriously defective if it restricted criminal jurisdiction to the state whose nationality the aircraft possesses. What is necessary where the crime affects the safety of travel by air, and piracy provides an apt analogy, is that any state which has secured the person of the defendant should be able to try and punish him irrespective of his nationality, or the nationality of the aircraft, or the place where the crime happens to be committed.

This is, in short, what the Hijacking Act 1971[20] did in respect of hijacking of aircraft and what the Protection of Aircraft Act 1973[1] did in

---

19. E.g. *Archbold*, para. 21–44, *Russell*, at 1539.
20. Implementing for the U.K. the Convention for the Suppression of the Unlawful Seizure of Aircraft, 1970, Cmnd. 4577.
  1. Implementing for the U.K. the Convention for the Suppression of Unlawful Acts against the Safety of Civil Aviation, Cmnd. 4822.

respect of acts likely to endanger the safety of aircraft. Both Acts are consolidated in the Aviation Security Act 1982.

1 Hijacking

Section 1 (1) of the Aviation Security Act 1982 provides –

"A person on board an aircraft in flight who unlawfully, by the use of force or by threats of any kind, seizes the aircraft or exercises control of it commits the offence of hijacking, whatever his nationality, whatever the state in which the aircraft is registered and whether the aircraft is in the United Kingdom or elsewhere, but subject to subsection (2)[2] below."

And by s. 1 (3) the offence is punishable by imprisonment for life. S. 6 (1) goes on to provide that if, in connection with an offence of hijacking, any person does acts which would amount to murder, manslaughter or specified offences under the Offences against the Person Act 1861 or the Explosive Substances Act 1883, he may be tried for that offence. Although hijacking itself carries life imprisonment this provision was thought necessary because in a given case the other crime (most obviously where it is murder) might be more serious than the hijacking itself and it would be unfortunate if the court was in the position of being able to deal with the hijacking but not the murder. Proceedings for an offence under the Act may not be instituted without the leave of the Attorney-General.

So far as offences under s. 6 (1) are concerned the relevant principles are discussed elsewhere in this book. So far as the offence of hijacking is concerned the requirement that the seizure be unlawful appears clearly to import *mens rea*.[3] To exercise control over the aircraft obviously D need do no more than issue commands or instructions to the pilot relating to the control of the aircraft which the pilot, by reason of the threat, is in no position to disregard. It is no defence that the commander of the aircraft collaborated willingly if force or threats were used against members of the crew.[4]

Endangering the Safety of Aircraft

Section 2 of the Aviation Security Act follows a similar jurisdictional pattern and creates the following offences:

1) Unlawfully and intentionally to destroy an aircraft in service, or to damage such aircraft to render it incapable of flight or as to be likely to endanger its safety in flight: s. 2 (1) (a).
2) Unlawfully and intentionally to commit on board an aircraft in flight any act of violence[5] which is likely to endanger the safety of the aircraft; s. 2 (1) (b).

---

2. This provides, in effect, that the offence cannot be committed by persons who are not British nationals in respect of foreign registered military, customs or police aircraft where the seizure takes place outside the U.K.; there is no such exemption for the offence of inducing or assisting in the U.K. an offence of hijacking outside the U.K.

3. Section 2 uses the formula "unlawfully *and intentionally*" but it is submitted that "unlawfully" in s. 1 should not be given a restricted meaning on that account.

4. *Moussa Membar* [1983] Crim LR 618, CA.

5. "Act of violence" means murder, attempted murder, manslaughter, assault and specified offences under the Offences against the Person Act 1861 and the Explosive Substances Act 1883; s. 1 (6).

3) Unlawfully and intentionally to place on any aircraft in service any device or substance which is likely to destroy the aircraft, or is likely so to damage it as to render it incapable of flight or as likely to endanger its safety in flight s. 2 (2).

4) Unlawfully and intentionally to destroy or damage any property used for the provision of air navigation (other than apparatus or equipment on board an aircraft) or to interfere with the operation of such property where the destruction, damage or interference is likely to endanger the safety of an aircraft in flight: s. 3.

5) Intentionally to communicate any information known to be false, or not believed to be true,[6] where the communication of the information endangers, or is likely to endanger, the safety of an aircraft in flight.

All these offences are punishable by life imprisonment.

The *mens rea* relating to these offences appears to have both subjective and objective connotations. While the act of destruction or damage (or the act of placing a substance on board or of communicating information as the case may be) must be intentional so that a negligent[7] act of destruction or damage would not suffice, it would seem unnecessary to show an intention to endanger, or foresight of endangering, the safety of the aircraft. The offences require an intentional act of damage etc. "as to be likely" or "which is likely" to endanger the safety of aircraft; these phrases appear to import an objective assessment and do not require that D himself should have foreseen that the endangering of the safety of the aircraft was likely.

6 Libel

1) *Actus Reus*

A libel is traditionally described as a writing[9] which tends to vilify a man and bring him into hatred, contempt and ridicule.[10] This definition has been thought to be inadequate in the law of tort where it is more likely that the test to be applied today would be that proposed by Lord Atkin:

"Would the words tend to lower the plaintiff in the estimation of right thinking members of society generally?"[11]

The traditional defintion has, however, been accepted as representing the law of criminal libel in recent cases.[12]

6. Cf. The offence of perjury, above, p. 740.

7. Curiously a reckless act of damage, etc. will not suffice even though D may have foreseen both the possibility of the damage and the possibility of endangering safety in flight. As to intention and recklessness see above, p. 55.

8. See J. R. Spencer [1977] Crim LR 383 and 465.

9. Defamatory words published in the course of the performance of a play amount to a criminal libel unless the performance is given on a domestic occasion in a private dwelling: Theatres Act 1968, ss. 4 and 6. It is uncertain whether broadcasting (except from a script) can constitute criminal libel. The Defamation Act 1952, ss. 1 and 6, does not apply to criminal proceedings. The Faulks Committee had recommended that it should so apply.

10. *Thorley v Lord Kerry* (1812) 4 Taunt 355.

11. *Sim v Stretch* [1936] 2 All ER 1237 at 1240.

12. *Goldsmith v Pressdram Ltd* [1977] QB 83 at 87, per Wien J; *Wells Street Stipendiary Magistrates' Court, ex parte Deakin* [1980] AC 477 at 487, [1979] 2 All ER 497 at 502, per Viscount Dilhorne.

The publication of a libel is a common law misdemeanour but by s. 5 of the Libel Act 1843, it is now punishable by no more than one year's imprisonment. It is also a tort[13] and the tortious aspect of libel is much more important. Criminal proceedings for libel are rare and are not encouraged by the courts. It was at one time thought that libel amounted to a criminal offence only if it was likely to result in a breach of the peace. It is now clear that this is not so except perhaps where the libel is published only to the person defamed,[14] or where the person defamed is dead. If criminal libel does require some additional constituent, it is that the libel must be "serious". If it is likely to provoke a breach of the peace or to disturb the peace of the community, then it is certainly serious; but it may be serious although it has no such tendency.[15] "Deliberate character assassination and the wild dissemination of defamatory matter by cranks" are – and, it is said, ought to be – offences, whether or not the person defamed, or anyone else is likely to resort to unlawful violence.[16] It seems that seriousness is now part of the definition of the offence.[17] An examining magistrate should not commit for trial unless he is satisfied that the alleged libel is so serious as to justify a prosecution in the public interest.[18] Evidence of the truth of statements complained of, or of the general bad reputation of P, is not relevant at this stage: *Gleaves v Deakin*,[19] where the House did not find it necessary to decide whether the examining magistrate had acted rightly in admitting evidence of P's convictions. As evidence of truth and general reputation were inadmissible, it seems that in principle convictions ought also to have been excluded. The House thought that the consent of the Attorney-General to the bringing of a prosecution should be required but there are at present no general restrictions. Where the prosecution is of any person responsible for the publication of a newspaper for any alleged libel therein, the leave of a judge is required by s. 8 of the Law of Libel Amendment Act 1888. The judge should not exercise his discretion in favour of an applicant unless he is satisfied that (i) there is a clear prima facie case, (ii) the libel is so serious that it is proper for the criminal law to be invoked and (iii) that the public interest *requires* the institution of criminal proceedings. Wien J found these conditions to be satisfied in a case where the applicant occupied important public positions, where his integrity had been impugned and a criminal offence alleged against him and where a campaign of vilification had been carried on for months.[20]

Libel is best studied as a branch of the law of tort but it is necessary here to note the differences which exist between the crime and the tort. In the first place, libel is the only form of defamation which is indictable. Slander

13. See Salmond, Ch 8, Street, Ch 24 and Winfield, Ch 12.
14. Adams (1888) 22 QBD 66, CCR; Law Com Working Paper No. 84, para. 38.
15. *Wicks* [1936] 1 All ER 384 at 386. *Gleaves v Deakin* [1979] 2 All ER 497, HJL.
16. J. R. Spencer in *Reshaping the Criminal Law*, 285, quoted by Lord Edmund-Davies, [1979] 2 All ER at 505.
17. See, however, somewhat ambiguous remarks of Lord Dilhorne at [1979] 2 All ER at 501. Cf. Law Com. Working Paper No. 84, paras. 3.6–3.7.
18. [1979] 2 All ER 502 and 505.
19. Supra, footnote 15.
20. *Goldsmith v Pressdram Ltd* [1977] QB 83, [1977] 2 All ER 557 (Wien J). Cf. *Desmond v Thorne* [1982] 3 All ER 268, [1983] 1 WLR 163 (Taylor J).

is not a crime.[1] The crime of libel is wider than the tort in at least two and possibly five respects.

1) Publication to the person defamed is sufficient in crime but not in tort.[2] In tort, the gist of the matter is the loss of the plaintiff's reputation and this only occurs through publication to a third party; but a principal reason why libel is indictable is the danger to the public peace[3] and this may obviously be even greater where the publication is to the prosecutor himself than where it is to another.

2) The truth of the defamatory statement affords a complete defence (justification) in tort but in crime the defendant must prove not only that the statement is true but that it is for the public benefit that it be published. This is the effect of s. 6 of the Libel Act 1843, modifying the common law under which it is probable that truth was not a defence to an indictment.

3) It is clear that the common law defence of privilege applies equally in crime as in tort[4] but it is not certain that the defence of fair comment on a matter of public interest is available. Wien J left the matter open in *Goldsmith v Pressdram Ltd*[5] and leading works say[6] that the defence may be relied on.[7]

4) A libel on a class of persons is not actionable unless the class is so small, like a body of trustees or directors, that it might be taken to refer to each member individually,[8] or it is otherwise so worded as to appear to refer to an individual. It is possible, however, that a libel intended to excite public hatred against a class, such as the clergy of Durham or the Justices of the Peace of Middlesex is indictable,[9] though no individual's reputation be harmed.

5) It is not actionable to defame a dead person, but according to Coke[10] it is indictable, again because of a tendency to cause strife. Later decisions, however, suggest that this is so only if the libel is designed to bring the surviving relations of the deceased person into hatred or contempt[11] – in which case it seems to be a libel on them – or was actually intended to provoke or annoy the surviving relatives.[12]

---

1. *Burford* (1669) 1 Vent 16; *Langley* (1704) 6 Mod Rep 124. But note that blasphemous or seditious spoken words, or words likely to cause a breach of the peace, are indictable.
2. *Adams* (1888) 22 QBD 66.
3. *Holbrook* (1878) 4 QBD 42 at 46; but cf. *Wicks*, supra.
4. *Perry* (1883) 15 Cox CC 169 and *Rule* [1937] 2 KB 375.
5. [1977] QB 83 at 90. In [1977] 2 All ER 557 he is reported to have said, without citation of authority, that the defence does not apply; but his (one assumes) second thoughts, being stated in the Law Report, must prevail.
6. 28 Halsbury's Laws of England (4th edn.), para. 285; Archbold, para 25–52; Russell, 803–805.
7. The Law Commission's provisional recommendation is that there should be no such defence in their proposed offence, which would require an intent to defame: Working Paper No. 84, 8–49.
8. *Knuppfer v London Express Newspapers Ltd* [1944] AC 116, [1944] 1 All ER 495.
9. *Williams* (1822) 5 B & Ald 595.
10. *De Libellis Famosis*, (1605) 5 Co Rep 125a.
11. *Topham* (1791) 4 Term Rep 126.
12. *Ensor* (1887) 3 TLR 366; and see Stephen, *Digest* (4th ed.), 208 n.

2) *Vicarious Liability*

In other respects, the crime is narrower than the tort. In accordance with general principle, a master is liable in tort for libels published by his servant in the course of his employment.[13] It may be that vicarious liability also extended at common law to a criminal charge against the proprietor of a newspaper in respect of libels published by his servant.[14] However that may be, by the Libel Act 1843, s. 7, it is a defence to prove that the publication was made without D's authority, consent or knowledge and that the publication did not arise from want of due care or caution on his part. It seems to follow from this provision that D is liable for the acts of his servants within the scope of their authority unless the statutory conditions are satisfied.

3) *Mens Rea*

The defendant must have intended to publish the words which are alleged to be libellous. It is not enough that he intentionally published a book or paper in which they were contained.[15] It is not certain what further mental element is required. In *Wicks*[16] Du Parcq J said that the crime was one of strict liability but this was obiter and not supported by the authority cited.[17] It is submitted that D must at least know of the existence, or the possibility of the existence, of the facts which render the statement defamatory.[18] Other authorities suggest that there must be an actual intention to defame.[19] As publication to the victim is sufficient, it is difficult to see how this can be so in that type of case since there is no evidence of an intention to injure the victim's reputation. Arguably, that is a special case. Analogy with blasphemous libel, as defined in *Lemon*,[20] would suggest that an intention to defame is not required.

As noted above, a person may be held vicariously liable for libel if he fails to prove that the publication did not arise from his negligence; but this is not inconsistent with the opinion expressed above. It is not unknown for vicarious liability to attach to offences requiring mens rea[1] and it may be that mens rea has to be proved in the agent.

---

13. Above, p. 99.
14. *Walter* (1799) 3 Esp 21; *Gutch, Fisher and Alexander* (1829) Mood & M 433. But cf. *Holbrook* (1877) 13 Cox CC 650.
15. *Munslow* [1895] 1 QB 758 at 765.
16. (1936) 25 Cr App Rep 168 at 173.
17. *Walter* (1799) 3 Esp 21.
18. So that there would be no criminal liability on the facts of *E. Hulton & Co v Jones* [1910] AC 20; *Cassidy v Daily Mirror Newspapers Ltd* [1929] 2 KB 331 or *Newstead v London Express Newspaper Ltd* [1940] 1 KB 377, [1939] 4 All ER 319.
19. *Abingdon* (1794) 1 Esp 226; *Creevey* (1813) 1 M & S 273; *Evans* (1821) 3 Stark 35; *Ensor* (1887) 3 TLR 366.
20. [1979] AC 67, [1979] 1 All ER 898.
 1. Above, p. 163.

4) *Publication of Libel Known to be False*

The publication of a libel *known to be false* is a misdemeanour under s. 4 of the Libel Act 1843 punishable with two years' imprisonment. If it is not proved that D knew the libel to be false, or if it is true, D may be convicted of the common law offence and sentenced to not more than one year's imprisonment.[2]

2. *Boaler v R* (1888) 21 QBD 284.

21 Offences against the Security of the State

1 Treason[1]

The law of treason, which is a capital offence, still stems from the Treason Act 1351. The Act was passed to clarify the uncertainty and arbitrariness of the common law which it supersedes. It declares that it is treason:

1) to "compass or imagine the death of our lord the King or our lady his Queen or of their eldest son and heir."
2) To "violate the King's companion [wife] or the King's eldest daughter unmarried or the wife [of] the King's eldest son and heir."
3) To "levy war against our lord the King in his realm".
4) To "be adherent to the King's enemies in his realm giving to them aid and comfort in the realm, or elsewhere".
5) To slay "the chancellor, treasurer, or the King's justices . . . being in their places, doing their offices."

In addition it is treason by the Treason Act 1702, s. 3:

6) By overt act to attempt to deprive or hinder the person next in succession to the Crown from succeeding.

The first, third and fourth of these forms of treason require some further consideration.

1 Compassing the King's Death

It is established that, despite the words of the Act, this requires more than a mental operation and that an overt act at least manifesting the intention, and perhaps intended to further it,[2] must be proved. Words used in conspiring or inciting to kill the sovereign are a sufficient overt act.[3] The Act was broadly construed by the judges to include conspiracies to imprison the King, to endanger his life and to depose him as well as actually to kill him. Certain of these "constructive treasons" are confirmed by the Treason Act 1795 which, by s. 1, provides that it is treason for any person to,

"within the realm or without, compass, imagine, invent, devise or intend death or destruction or any bodily harm tending to death or destruction,

---

1. For provisional proposals for the reform of the law relating to treason, sedition and allied offences, see Law Commission Working Paper No 72 (1977).
2. *Thistlewood* (1820) 33 State Tr. 681.
3. See the list of overt acts in Archbold, §§ 21–15 to 21–21.

maim or wounding, imprisonment or restraint, of the person of ... the King,"

such compassing, etc., being expressed by

"publishing any printing or writing or by any overt act or deed."

Other constructive treasons which were formerly in the 1795 Act were made felony by the Treason Felony Act 1848 and are now simply offences akin to treason.[4]

2 Levying War against the King in his Realm

The obvious form of treason under this head would be an insurrection against the authority of the sovereign. Enlisting and marching are sufficient overt acts without coming to an actual engagement. "War" has been interpreted in a wide sense and this type of treason was extended constructively to include forcible resistance to authority of the government in some public or general respect. So war is levied,

"when an insurrection is raised to reform some national grievance, to alter the established law of religion, to punish magistrates, to introduce innovations of a public concern, to obstruct the execution of some general law by an armed force, or for any other purpose which usurps the government in matters of a public and general nature."[5]

It is only in the generality of its object that this form of treason differs from an ordinary unlawful assembly or riot. Treason might consist in

"an assembling together for the purpose of destroying all meeting houses or all bawdy houses, under colour of reforming a public grievance; or an insurrection to reduce by force the general price of victuals, to inhance the common rate of wages, to level all inclosures, to expel all foreigners, to release all prisoners, or to reform by numbers or an armed force any real or imaginary grievance, of a public and general nature, in which the insurgents have no peculiar interest."[6]

If the object of the uprising is of a private or local nature, then it is not treason.[7]

"As if the rising be, only against a particular market or to destroy particular inclosures, to remove a local nuisance, to release a particular prisoner, unless imprisoned for high treason, or even to oppose the execution of an act of parliament, if it only affect the district of the insurgents; as in the case of a turnpike act."

Such an uprising would, of course, be a riot. The distinction is of no practical importance today, for such disturbances, amounting technically to treasons, would certainly be dealt with as riots.

3 Being Adherent to the King's Enemies

This is the most important form of treason, being that which is invoked to deal with acts of disloyalty in wartime. The Queen's enemies are foreign states in actual hostility against her, whether there has been a declaration of

4. Below, p. 832.
5. East, 1 PC 72.
6. Ibid., 73. *Dammaree* (1710) Fost 214.
7. Ibid.

war or not.[8] Whether there is war or not is a question of fact for a jury but a certificate from a Secretary of State is conclusive evidence.[9] To incite a foreign state to make war would not amount to adherence until the incitement was successful[10] as, until then, there would be no "enemy" to adhere to; but it might be "constructive" compassing of the Queen's death. Assisting rebels within the realm is not adhering to the Queen's enemies – though it may be levying war against the Queen in her realm.

The offence is *being adherent to* the King's enemies. The words "giving aid and comfort to the King's enemies" are to be read in apposition, to explain what is meant by being "adherent to." D is guilty if he adheres to the King's enemies in his realm – that is, gives them aid and comfort in his realm; or if he adheres to them elsewhere – that is, gives them aid and comfort elsewhere. The Court of Criminal Appeal so held in *Casement*,[11] rejecting the argument that the vital words "or elsewhere" govern only "giving aid and comfort" and not "being adherent". According to the rejected argument the person being adherent must be in the realm, though he may be giving aid and comfort in the realm or elsewhere. This is certainly a possible interpretation of the rather curious language of the statute; but the opinions of Coke, Hale, Hawkins and Stephen supported the wider view which found favour. The phrase, "the King's enemies *in his realm*", is not explained by the court. Pollock suggested that it excluded from the law of treason adherence to enemies of the King, not in his capacity as King of England, but as Lord (in the fourteenth century) of provinces abroad.[12]

The effect of the decision in *Casement* was that D could be convicted of treason, although all the overt acts alleged were committed in Germany.[13]

4 Who may Commit Treason

The common law rule is that anyone who owes allegiance to the Crown at the time of the act may commit treason. It follows that:

(1) British subjects who are British citizens who owe allegiance wherever they may be, may commit treason (under English law) in any part of the world.[14] A British subject cannot cast off his allegiance to the Crown in time of war by becoming a naturalised citizen of an enemy state. Indeed the act of becoming naturalised is itself an overt act of treason.[15]

(2) A British subject or a citizen of the Republic of Ireland who is not a British citizen may commit treason (under English law) only if the act be done in the United Kingdom or in any country of the Commonwealth

---

8. East 1 PC 77. As to the position of persons assisting enemies of a United Nations force, including British troops, see Bowett, *United Nations Forces*, pp. 53–54.
9. *Bottrill, ex parte Kuechenmeister* [1947] KB 41, [1946] 2 All ER 434.
10. East, 1 PC 78.
11. [1917] 1 KB 98.
12. (1917) 33 LQR 110. Serjeant Sullivan's rejected explanation, [1917] 1 KB at 101, 102 (see also *The Last Serjeant*, 269–270), was thought by Pollock "more ingenious than convincing."
13. The indictment is set out in full in Archbold (35th ed.), § 3029.
14. For an examination of the position in Rhodesia after the Unilateral Declaration of Independence, see [1966] Crim LR 5 and 68.
15. *Lynch* [1903] 1 KB 444.

which is not self-governing; unless he owes allegiance under the rules stated in 3 (b) and 3 (c), below. At common law, all British subjects were governed by the rule stated in paragraph 1, above; but now, by s. 3 of the British Nationality Act 1948, a British subject who is not a British citizen is not guilty of an offence against English law by reason of anything done or omitted in a foreign country, or in any self-governing country of the Commonwealth[16] unless the act or omission would be an offence against English law if he were an alien acting in a foreign country. Since aliens may not commit treason unless they either are on British territory at the time of the act, or owe allegiance under 3 (b) or 3 (c) below, the position appears now to be as stated at the beginning of this paragraph.

If the facts of *Casement*[17] were to recur today D, not being a citizen of the United Kingdom would not, prima facie, be guilty of treason because the acts done would not be an offence against English law if done by an alien in Germany. The position would be the same if the acts had been done, not in Germany, but in one of the independent countries of the Commonwealth, for example, Canada.

(3) An alien, even an alien enemy, may be guilty of treason if he has accepted the protection of the Crown, for this carries with it a correlative duty of allegiance. An alien is under the protection of the Crown:

(a) if he is voluntarily[18] on British territory (whether in one of the independent countries of the Commonwealth or not) at the time of the act, otherwise than as a foreign diplomatic representative or member of an invading or occupying force:[19] or

(b) if, having been within British territory, he leaves with a British passport which he still possesses at the time of the treasonable act.

Proposition (b) is the ratio decidendi of *Joyce v Director of Public Prosecutions*[20] where it was held immaterial that D obtained the passport by false pretences. The basis of the decision is that by possession of the passport, D was enabled to obtain in a foreign country the protection extended to British subjects; and, therefore, that he owed a corresponding duty of allegiance. It was immaterial that he had never availed himself, and had no intention of availing himself, of the protection of the Crown. If he had surrendered the passport or taken any overt step (other than the act of treason itself) to withdraw his allegiance, this would have been effective; but there was no evidence that he had done so.[1]

(c) Where an alien after residing in British territory, goes abroad without a British passport, but leaving behind a family and "effects", his duty of

---

16. As specified in Sch. 3 of the British Nationality Act 1981.
17. Above, p. 829.
18. It is assumed that a prisoner-of-war on British territory could not commit treason.
19. Such an alien's duty of allegiance does not cease merely because the protection of the Crown is temporarily withdrawn owing to the occupation by the enemy of the area in which the alien resides: *De Jager v A-G of Natal* [1907] AC 326.
20. [1946] AC 347, [1946] 1 All ER 186. And see *Re P. (G.E.) (an infant)* [1965] Ch. 568, [1964] 3 All ER 977.
   1. Lord Porter dissented on the ground that the jury had not been properly directed that they must be satisfied that the passport remained in Joyce's possession at the relevant date.

allegiance may continue so long as his family and effects remain under the protection of the Crown. According to Foster[2] it was so resolved by an assembly of all the judges in 1707, and he and other writers of authority[3] accept this as law. The resolution, being made extra-judicially, was in no sense a binding precedent,[4] but, having been emphatically approved by the House of Lords in *Joyce*, it must probably be accepted as law. But its extent is uncertain.

"Does 'family' mean wife or children or both?[5] Does the term include a wife living apart from her husband by judicial or voluntary separation? At what age, if any, do children cease to belong to the family?"[6]

The resolution seems to have been limited to the case where D had himself been in British territory and it could very reasonably be limited to that where D has his home in the realm at the time of the act.[7]

Joyce has been severely criticised.[8] Joyce had no *right* to protection while abroad; there was, at most, a possibility that he might have obtained protection through the passport. This makes the capital offence turn on the merest technicality.[9]

5 Procedure in Treason Trials

Certain special rules of procedure and evidence were enacted by Parliament for treason trials

"for the safeguard of the subject under the weight of a state prosecution and the popular odium of so detestable a charge."[10]

It was, for example, necessary, in the absence of an admission, for the prosecution to produce at least two witnesses swearing to the same overt act or one witness to one and a second witness to another overt act of the same treason.

These complexities were swept away by the Treason Act of 1800 for cases where the overt act was directed against the person of the King. They continued to be applicable, however, to all other cases of treason until the Treason Act 1945 which extended the operation of the Act of 1800 to all cases of treason and misprision of treason. Now, by the Criminal Law Act 1967, s. 12 (4):

". . . the procedure on trials for treason or misprision of treason shall be the same as the procedure as altered by this Act on trials for murder."

---

2. *Crown Law*, 185.
3. Hawkins, 1 PC, c. 2, § 5; East, 1 PC 52; Chitty on the *Prerogatives of the Crown*, 12, 13; Holdsworth in Halsbury (2nd ed.), Vol 6, 146 n (*t*).
4. *Entick v Carrington* (1765) 19 State Tr 1029 at 1071, per Lord Camden.
5. Lord Jowitt said he regarded parents or brothers or sisters as a family for this purpose: [1946] AC at 368.
6. Williams (1948) 10 CLJ at 62. See *Re P (GE) (an infant)* [1965] Ch 568, [1964] 3 All ER 977.
7. Cf. Pitt Cobbett's *Cases on International Law* (6th ed.), 199, 200.
8. Biggs, "Treason and the Trial of William Joyce" (1947), 7 Toronto LJ 162; Williams, "The Correlation of Allegiance and Protection" (1948), 10 CLJ 54; Pitt Cobbett, loc. cit.
9. On the position of British Protected Persons, see Williams, op. cit. and cf. *Re Mwenya* [1960] 1 QB 241, [1959] 3 All ER 525.
10. East, 1 PC 106.

2 Offences Akin to Treason

1 Under the Treason Felony Act 1848

The Statute of 1351 made it treason to compass the King's death and to levy war against the King: but it did not, in terms, make it treason to conspire to levy war. It was established doctrine, however, that a conspiracy to levy war might be given in evidence as an overt act of compassing the King's death. The notion of compassing death was broadened by judicial construction to include conspiracies to do acts whereby the King's life might be endangered and to depose or imprison him; for, as Foster says,

"experience hath shown that between the prisons and the graves of Princes the distance is very small."[11]

Other, perhaps less reasonable, constructions of the 1351 Act were adopted to extend its effect to conspiracies directed not at the royal person but at the overthrow of the government. This judicial extension of the 1351 Act led to the same kind of uncertainty as had brought about the enactment of the Statute itself; and in 1795 Parliament passed an "Act for the Safety and Preservation of His Majesty's Person and Government" which enacted that certain of these "constructive treasons" were indeed treason. The part of that Act which remains in force has been set out above;[12] but the remainder of its substantive provisions were repealed by the Treason Felony Act 1848[13] which enacted that certain constructive treasons were to be *felonies*, punishable with life imprisonment. The offence is committed by one who shall,

"within the United Kingdom or without, compass, imagine, invent, devise or intend",

any of the acts enumerated below:

1) "to deprive or depose ... the Queen, from the style, honour, or royal name of the imperial crown of the United Kingdom, or of any other of Her Majesty's dominions and countries,"

2) "to levy war against her Majesty within any part of the United Kingdom, in order by force or constraint to compel her to change her measures or counsels, or in order to put any force or constraint upon or in order to intimidate or overawe both Houses or either House of Parliament,"

3) "to move or stir any foreigner or stranger with force to invade the United Kingdom or any other of her Majesty's dominions or countries under the obeisance of her Majesty;"

and shall,

"express, utter or declare" [his compassing, etc.], "by publishing any printing or writing, or by open and advised speaking or by an overt act or deed,".

The Act specifically provides that

"nothing herein contained shall lessen the force of or in any manner affect any thing enacted by the Treason Act 1351"[14]

11. *Crown Law*, 196.
12. See p. 827.
13. See the explanation of this legislation by the Attorney-General in *Mitchel* (1848) 6 State Tr NS 599 at 636–639; and see *Mulcahy v R* (1868) LR 3 HL 306 at 317–321. See also Woodham-Smith, *The Great Hunger*, 340; and [1966] Crim LR 7.
14. Section 6.

and that an indictment for an offence under the Act is valid although the facts alleged and proved at the trial in law amount to treason.[15]

"The result is, that the judicial construction of the statutes of treason has been adopted by the legislature, making, however, many of the offences which they included felonies ... so that in cases of positive design to overthrow the Queen's government by armed force, there is, it seems a choice of remedies."[16]

That is, the same act may now be both treason punishable by death under the construction put upon the 1351 Act and an offence punishable by life imprisonment under the 1848 Act.

2 Misprision of Treason

Misprision of treason is a common law misdemeanour and is committed when any person who knows, or has reasonable cause to believe, that another has committed treason, omits to disclose this information or any material part of it to the proper authority within a reasonable time.[17]

Conviction entails forfeiture to the Crown of all the offender's goods and the profits of his lands during his life. Stephen thought that misprision of treason was overlooked when forfeiture for felonies was abolished.[18]

3 Seditious Words and Libels

Sedition is closely related to the form of treason consisting in "levying war" against the Queen in her realm and may be a preliminary step towards that crime. There is probably no offence properly described as "sedition" in English law,[19] but the oral or written publication of words with a seditious intention is a common law misdemeanour and an agreement to further a seditious intention by doing any act is a conspiracy. The question then is what is seditious intention? Stephen[20] defined it as:

"... an intention to bring into hatred or contempt, or to excite disaffection against the person of, Her Majesty, her heirs or successors, or the government and constitution of the United Kingdom, as by law established, or either House of Parliament, or the administration of justice, or to excite Her Majesty's subjects to attempt, otherwise than by lawful means, the alteration of any matter in Church or State by law established, or to raise discontent or disaffection amongst Her Majesty's subjects, or to promote feelings of ill-will and hostility between different classes of such subjects.

An intention to shew that Her Majesty has been misled or mistaken in her measures, or to point out errors or defects in the government or constitution as by law established, with a view to their reformation, or to

---

15. Section 7.
16. *Mulcahy v R* (1868) LR 3 HL 306 at 320, per Willes J delivering the opinion of the judges.
17. Cf. the discussion of Misprision of Felony in the first edition of this book at p. 539; Stephen, *Digest*, Art. 209 and p. 489.
18. *Digest*, p. 489.
19. Stephen, 2 HCL 298.
20. *Digest* (3rd ed.), Art 93. See now 9th ed., Art 114.

excite Her Majesty's subjects to attempt by lawful means the alteration of any matter in Church or State by law established,[1] or to point out, in order to their removal, matters which are producing, or have a tendency to produce, feelings of hatred and ill-will between classes of Her Majesty's subjects, is not a seditious intention."

This definition was approved by the criminal code Commissioners and followed by Cave J in his direction to the jury in *Burns*.[2]

a) *Real or presumed intention?* The most important and difficult question in the law of sedition is whether the "intention" which must be proved is a genuine intention or whether, as Stephen himself put it:[3]

"In determining whether the intention with which any words were spoken, any document was published, or any agreement was made, was or was not seditious, every person must be deemed to intend the consequences which would naturally follow from his conduct at the time and under the circumstances in which he so conducted himself."

There is some authority[4] in favour of this objective test, which would require no more *mens rea* than an intention to publish the words which were published. In the Scottish case of *Grant*,[5] five judges held that the use of the word "calculated" (that is, "likely") to produce disaffection, etc. was enough and that it was not necessary to prove an actual intention to produce that result. The court found support in the English authorities. But Lord Cockburn, who dissented, thought that there had been confusion between (a) the meaning of the libel and (b) the intention of the writer;[6] and that while the former is very cogent evidence of the latter, it is not the only evidence. Similar confusion has been found in other branches of the criminal law[7] and it would not be surprising that it should exist here also.

Lord Cockburn's view was that the true meaning of the English (as well as the Scottish) authorities was that either intention or recklessness as to the consequences must be proved. This would be in accordance with principle. One judge at least has gone even further and held that recklessness is not enough and that intention must be proved. In *Burns*,[8] Cave J told the jury that it was not enough that the natural consequence of the words used was disorder but:

". . . although it is a good working rule to say that a man must be taken to intend the natural consequences of his acts, and it is very proper to ask a jury to infer, if there is nothing to show the contrary, that he did intend

---

1. In the fourth and subsequent editions, Stephen inserted at this point ". . . or to incite any person to commit any crime in disturbance of the peace . . . ."
2. (1886) 16 Cox CC 355 at 360.
3. *Digest* (4th ed.) Art 94.
4. *Burdett* (1820) 1 State Tr NS 1; *Harvey and Chapman* (1823) 2 B & C 257; *Cobbett* (1804) 29 State Tr 1, as reported in Archbold (12th ed.), 607; see 7 State Tr NS at 621 n (a); *Lovett* (1839) 9 C & P 462.
5. (1848) 7 State Tr NS 507.
6. Where it is the writer who is charged. If it is not, his intention is irrelevant; below, p. 836.
7. Above, pp. 85, 208.
8. (1886) 16 Cox CC 355 at 364. See now Criminal Justice Act 1967, s. 8, above, p. 85.

the natural consequences of his acts, yet, if it is shown from other circumstances, that he did not actually intend them I do not see how you can ask a jury to act upon what has then become a legal fiction."

and that

"It is one thing to speak with the distinct intention to produce disturbances, and another thing to speak recklessly and violently of what is likely to produce disturbances."[9]

In so directing the jury, Cave J said he again had the authority of Stephen J. This is remarkable, since he had just read out Article 93 of the *Digest*, and in Article 94 Stephen says the opposite! But Cave J was at this point relying on the *History of the Criminal Law*[10] and this work does indeed support his direction. Stephen there appears to argue, in effect, that the law *was* as stated in his Article 94[11] before the Libel Act 1792 but that the Act enlarged the definition

"by the addition of a reference to the specific intention of the libeller – to the purpose for which he wrote."

Thus Stephen seems to have been inconsistent. Cave J's adoption of the view in the *History* in preference to that in the *Digest* can hardly have been accidental.

The ruling in *Burns* was, in effect, followed by Birkett J in *Caunt*,[12] where he expressly adopted the proposition in *Steane*,[13] under which nothing less than a *desire* to cause the disorder etc., would suffice.

One modern authority which is out of tune with these cases is *Aldred*,[14] where Coleridge J stated the test to be

"was the language used calculated, or was it not, to promote public disorder . . .";

and that the innocence of the motive with which it may have been published was no defence. The irrelevance of motive may be conceded – a man may conceivably have admirable motives for wishing to overthrow the government by violence – but Coleridge J's language seems also to exclude the necessity for proof of an intention to overthrow the government. It is submitted that the better view is that stated in *Burns*[15] and in *Caunt*.[16]

b) *Intention to cause violence.* There is a further qualification to be made to the rule as stated by Stephen. It is not sufficient that D used words with the intention of achieving one of the objects specified; he must have intended to achieve that object *by violence*. In *Collins*,[17] Littledale J according to Stephen,

"states the modern view of the law plainly and fully. . . . In one word nothing short of direct incitement to disorder and violence is a seditious libel."[18]

9. Ibid.
10. Vol. 2, 359.
11. 4th ed.
12. (1947) reported in *An Editor on Trial* (Morecambe Press, Ltd).
13. Above, p. 57.
14. (1909) 22 Cox CC 1.
15. Above, p. 834.
16. Supra. Consider the effect of s. 8 of the Criminal Justice Act 1967, above, p. 85.
17. (1839) 9 C & P 456 at 461.
18. 2 HCL 374, 375.

In *Burns*,[19] Cave J told the jury that the question was, did D incite the people whom he was addressing to redress their grievances *by violence*?[20] In *Aldred*, Coleridge J, though not requiring proof of intention, did require language calculated to incite others to

"public disorders, to wit, rebellions, insurrections, assassinations, outrages, or any physical force or violence of any kind."[1]

In *Caunt*,[2] Birkett J said:

"It is not enough to provoke hostility or ill-will ... sedition has always had implicit in the word public disorder, tumult, insurrections or matters of that kind."

c) *Actus reus*. It cannot be enough that the words are used with a seditious intention. There must also be an *actus reus*. That is, the words must have a tendency to incite public disorder. In deciding whether the words have this tendency, it is proper to look at all the relevant surrounding circumstances – the state of public feeling, the place, the mode of publication, and so on. Most important of all, the jury is entitled

". . . to look at the audience addressed, because language which would be innocuous practically speaking, if used to an assembly of professors or divines, might produce a different result if used before an excited audience of young and uneducated men."[3]

On the other hand if the tendency of the words is to incite ordinary people to violence, it is no defence that the audience addressed was unaffected by the incitement:

"A man cannot escape from the consequences of uttering words with intent to excite people to violence solely because the persons to whom they are addressed may be too wise or too temperate to be seduced into that violence."[4]

Thus words are seditious (i) if they are likely to incite ordinary men whether likely to incite the audience actually addressed or not; or (ii), if, though not likely to incite ordinary men, they are likely to incite the audience actually addressed.

D need not have himself written the libel. The crime may consist in the publication of the words of another with the appropriate intent. If the publisher has *mens rea* it is immaterial that the writer of the libel did not.[5]

Whether publication is necessary is not settled. In *Burdett*,[6] Holroyd J and Abbott CJ thought that the mere composition of the libel without

---

19. Above, p. 834.

20. In holding that an intention to cause violence was not a necessary ingredient of sedition under the Criminal Code of the Gold Coast, the Privy Council was concerned solely with the construction of the relevant section and cast no doubt on the authority of *Burns: Wallace-Johnson v R* [1940] AC 231 at 239, [1940] 1 All ER 241 at 243, 244.

1. (1909) 22 Cox CC at 4.

2. Supra.

3. *Aldred* (1909) 22 Cox CC 1 at 3, per Coleridge J.

4. *Burns* (1886) 16 Cox CC 355 at 365, per Cave J. In *Cohen* (1916) 34 WLR 210, it was held that, if the words were likely to be an incitement to an ordinary man, D was not entitled to the benefit of the steadfast loyalty of the person actually addressed.

5. (1789) 22 St Tr 300, per Eyre CB delivering the unanimous opinion of the judges.

6. (1820) 1 State Tr NS 1 at 122, 123 and 128, 139.

publishing it was an offence. Earlier cases[7] supported this view but their authority was forcefully attacked by Sir James Scarlett, afterwards Lord Abinger.[8]

d) *Sedition and freedom of speech.* It is common for the judge to stress the importance of freedom of speech and of the press. In *Burns*,[9] Cave J said

"You will recollect how valuable a blessing the liberty of the press is to all of us, and sure I am that that liberty will meet no injury – suffer no diminution at your hands."

and in *Caunt*,[10] Birkett J's last words to the jury were:

"Two matters would seem to emerge over all others in this case.

First of all it is in the highest degree essential that nothing should be done in this court to weaken the liberty of the press; and secondly, remember at all times that it is the duty of the prosecution to prove his case beyond all reasonable doubt."[11]

4 Incitement to Mutiny and Disaffection[12]

By the Incitement to Mutiny Act 1797 it is an offence punishable with life imprisonment "maliciously and advisedly" (a) to endeavour to seduce any member of the forces from his "duty *and* allegiance" to the Crown or (b) to incite to mutiny or (c) to make a mutinous assembly or (d) to commit "any traitorous or mutinous practice whatsoever ..."

By the Incitement to Disaffection Act 1934, s. 1, it is an offence punishable with two years' imprisonment "maliciously and advisedly" to endeavour to seduce any member of the forces from his "duty *or* allegiance" to the Crown. The 1934 Act is clearly very much wider in its scope since an endeavour to seduce from either "duty" or "allegiance" is enough, whereas under the 1797 Act the endeavour must be to seduce from both. A relatively trivial offence, such as persuading a soldier to overstay his leave is thus within the later Act, but not the earlier.[13] Notwithstanding the use of the disjunctive, "or", in the 1934 Act, it has been held that the section creates only one offence and a count alleging seduction from duty or allegiance is not bad for duplicity.[14]

It is not necessary to prove that the endeavour was directed against any named individuals; it may be addressed to the forces generally.[15]

It is clear that these offences require *mens rea*. The word "advisedly" appears to be equivalent to "knowingly"[16] and D cannot be convicted unless it is proved that he knew P to be a member of the forces. It has been said that maliciously bears its usual meaning[17] in criminal statutes: but in

---

7. They are cited in argument, ibid., at 57.
8. Ibid.
9. (1886) 16 Cox CC 355 at 362.
10. Above, p. 835.
11. See also Coleridge J in *Aldred* (1909) 22 Cox CC 1 at 4.
12. Street, *Freedom, the Individual and the Law*, 210–216.
13. See Street, op. cit., at 213.
14. *Arrowsmith* [1975] QB 678, [1975] 1 All ER 463 at 470; above, p. 81.
15. *Bowman* (1912) 76 JP 271.
16. *Fuller* (1797) 2 Leach 790.
17. See above, p. 122.

that case[18] the direction approved said that the unlawful act must be done "wilfully and intentionally". Since the offence is one of endeavouring, it appears to be in the nature of a statutory attempt, and possibly recklessness is not enough. It should also follow that if the soldier does not in fact owe allegiance, no offence is committed.[19]

It is also an offence under s. 2 of the 1934 Act to be in possession of a document, the dissemination of which would be an offence under s. 1, with intent to commit or to aid and abet or counsel the commission of such an offence.

By the Police Act 1964, s. 53, it is an offence punishable with two years' imprisonment if any person

"causes or attempts to cause or does any act calculated to cause disaffection"

among members of any police force, or does any act calculated to induce a policeman to withhold his services or commit breaches of discipline. It is by no means so clear that *mens rea* is necessary here: there are no such words as "maliciously and advisedly" and an "act calculated" may well mean no more than an act the probable consequence of which is disaffection, etc.

3 Official Secrets[20]

1 Spying and Sabotage

By s. 1 (1) of the Official Secrets Act 1911 it is an offence punishable with fourteen years' imprisonment,

"If any person for any purpose prejudicial to the safety or interests of the State –

a) approaches, inspects, passes over or is in the neighbourhood of, or enters any prohibited place within the meaning of this Act; or

b) makes any sketch, plan, model, or note which is calculated to be or might be or is intended to be directly or indirectly useful to an enemy; or

c) obtains, collects, records, or publishes or communicates to any other person any secret official code word or pass word or any sketch, plan, model, article, or note, or other document or information which is calculated to be or is intended to be directly or indirectly useful to an enemy; . . . ."

A "prohibited place" is defined by s. 3 and includes such places as naval, military and air force establishments, munitions factories and depots belonging to or occupied by the Crown, or used under contract with the

---

18. *Arrowsmith*, supra.
19. It is possible for aliens to be enlisted in the armed forces without taking the oath of allegiance but such an alien stationed in England owes allegiance at common law; *Joyce v Director of Public Prosecutions* [1946] AC 347, [1946] 1 All ER 186, HL; above, p. 830; *Arrowsmith*, above, at 81. An alien enlisted and stationed, for example, in Germany, might not owe allegiance.
20. D. G. T. Williams, *Not in the Public Interest*; "Offences against the State, 1964–73", [1974] Crim LR 634 at 639. Street, *Freedom, the Individual and the Law*, 216, et seq.

Crown; and any place belonging to or used by the Crown which a Secretary
of State may declare to be a prohibited place for the time being, on the
ground that information with respect to it, or damage to it, would be useful
to an enemy.

a) *Scope of the section.* The section is clearly directed against spying; and
the marginal note reads "Penalties for spying". But it has been held by the
House of Lords that the marginal note is no part of the Act and cannot be
used as an aid to construction.[1]

The literal meaning of the section extends beyond spying. A person may,
for example, approach an airfield or munitions factory with the object of
causing an explosion, so as to impede the defence of the realm against an
enemy. If this is a purpose prejudicial to the safety or interests of the State,
his conduct falls within the plain meaning of s. 1.

In *Chandler*,[2] the accused, members of an organisation supporting
nuclear disarmament, approached an airfield with the admitted object of
grounding all aircraft, immobilising the airfield and reclaiming it for
civilian purposes. The Court of Criminal Appeal and the House of Lords
held that this conduct was an offence against the Act. The interpretation
was fortified by the fact that the definition of "prohibited place" included
not only places where "information with respect thereto" would be useful
to an enemy, but also places where "damage thereto" or the "destruction or
obstruction thereof or interference with" would be useful to an enemy.
This suggests that

"The saboteur just as much as the spy in the ordinary sense is
contemplated as an offender under the Act."[3]

Apart from the rejected marginal note, there was nothing in the Act to
support the narrow construction which the defence sought to put upon it
and the decision on this point seems clearly correct, according to the
established rules of statutory interpretation. It has, however, been clearly
demonstrated[4] that the actual intention of Parliament was to legislate only
against spying. The restrictive rules of statutory interpretation allowed by
our law prevented the court from looking at the Parliamentary Debates on
the subject; but whether a prosecution should, in these circumstances, have
been brought on the facts of *Chandler* is a different matter. It has been
suggested[5] that it was

"indefensible on the part of the Attorney General to press arguments
upon the courts to give the section a wider meaning"

than, as he knew, or ought to have known, was intended by Parliament.

b) *Mens rea.* Clearly D must intend an *actus reus* as defined in s. 1 and he
must have a "purpose prejudicial to the safety or interests of the State".
The meaning of this latter element in the *mens rea* provided the most

1. *Chandler v Director of Public Prosecutions* [1964] AC 763, [1962] 3 All ER 142; **SHC 51**.
2. Above, footnote 1.
3. [1964] AC at 794, [1962] 3 All ER at 148, per Lord Radcliffe.
4. By D. Thompson, "The Committee of 100 and the Official Secrets Act 1911", [1963] *Public Law* 201.
5. Ibid.

difficult problem in *Chandler*. D argued unsuccessfully that his purpose was not prejudicial to the safety or interests of the State because he believed that it was in the interests of the State that these aircraft, which he believed to contain nuclear weapons, should be immobilised. It appears from the speeches of their Lordships:

   i) That the term "purpose" requires a subjective element. It must be proved at least that D, when he acts, knows that "certain objects will probably be achieved by the act whether he wants them or not."[6] This proposition perhaps understates the requirements of "purpose" and was wider than was necessary for the decision for, as Lord Reid said:

     "The accused both intended and desired that the base should be immobilised for a time, and I cannot construe purpose in any sense that does not include that state of mind."[7]

   ii) When it has been proved that D had certain objects for his purpose, the further question, whether those objects are prejudicial to the safety or interests of the State, is an objective one. D's opinion on this issue is irrelevant to his liability.[8] D's purpose was the immobilisation of the airfield. His opinion whether that was beneficial or prejudicial to the interests of the State was irrelevant. Of course, he knew that he was acting contrary to the policy of the State. The answer might be different if the accused was unaware that this was so.

   iii) The disposition of the armed forces of the Crown is within the exclusive discretion of the Crown.[9] Whether the policy of the Crown is right or wrong is not an issue capable of trial in a court of law and, accordingly, evidence is not admissible on it.[10]

It followed necessarily that D's intention to obstruct the operations of the armed forces of the Crown was a purpose prejudicial to the safety or interests of the State.

Though the decision has been vigorously criticised,[11] it is submitted that it arrived at the only sensible interpretation of the Act. If it were necessary to prove that D believed his object to be prejudicial to the interests of the State, a man would have had a defence if, during the world wars, he believed that it was in Britain's interests that Germany should win the war. Such an interpretation would obviously defeat the object of the Act. If the question were whether the policy of the Crown which D obstructed was in the interests of the state, the court would be presented with an issue which

---

6. [1964] AC at 805, [1962] 3 All ER at 155, per Lord Devlin.

7. [1964] AC at 790, [1963] 3 All ER at 146.

8. So in *Bettaney* [1985] Crim LR 104, CA, it was held that the trial judge rightly rejected a submission that D was entitled to argue that the quality of the information he had gathered during his employment in the security service was relevant in determining whether his purpose was prejudicial to the safety or interests of the state. What D's purpose is in collecting the information must be subjectively determined but once that has been determined it is for the judge to direct the jury as to whether that purpose is prejudicial.

9. "Those who are responsible for the national security must be the sole judges of what the national security requires", per Lord Parker of Waddington in *The Zamora* [1916] 2 AC 77 at 107, quoted with approval by Lord Parker CJ in the Court of Criminal Appeal and Lords Hodson and Devlin in the House of Lords in *Chandler*.

10. Lord Devlin differed from the remainder of the House in holding that, while it might be presumed that the immobilisation of the airfield was prejudicial to the interest of the state, the presumption was not irrebuttable.

11. By Thompson, op. cit.

it could not properly try; and, if the Act can reasonably be read so as to avoid raising such an issue, then it should be so read.[12]

The result, nevertheless, is that the Act appears to be uncomfortably far-reaching: Does it now follow, as defending counsel suggested in argument, that,

> "a workman on strike who approached a government establishment, for example Woolwich Arsenal, in order to induce workers there to come out on strike would be guilty under this Act . . . "?[13]

2 Wrongful Communication of Information

Section 2 of the Act of 1911 is designed to prevent the misuse of any sketch, plan, model, article, note, document or information to which the section applies. It is a misdemeanour for a person who has a sketch, etc., or information, within the meaning of the section –

1) To communicate it to any person except (a) a person to whom he is authorised to communicate it; (b) a person to whom it is, in the interest of the State, his duty to communicate it.[14]

2) To use it for the benefit of any foreign power or in any other manner prejudicial to the safety or interests of the State.

3) To retain it when he has no right to do so.

4) To fail to take reasonable care of it, or so to conduct himself as to endanger its safety.

A person who receives the article or information knowing or having reasonable cause to believe that it is given in contravention of the Act, is likewise guilty of an offence punishable by two years' imprisonment.[15]

The section is very far-reaching since it includes any of the specified articles or any information which D has obtained, "owing to his position as a person who holds or has held office under Her Majesty". The article or information need not be of a secret character or even confidential. In *Crisp and Homewood*[16] Avory J held that the section was applicable to the case of D, a clerk in the War Office, who handed to the director of a firm of tailors copies of documents containing particulars of contracts between the War Office and contractors for army officers' clothing. For the purpose of the section D may be employed "under" a person who holds office under Her Majesty though D is not employed *by* the office holder; it suffices that D works under the direction of the office holder.[17]

Under this section, no *mens rea* beyond an intention to cause the *actus reus* is required, and it is no defence that D did not intend to do anything to prejudice the safety or interests of the State.[18]

---

12. See Lord Reid [1964] AC at 791, [1962] 3 All ER at 147.
13. [1964] AC at 778.
14. Limb (b) assumes that D may, when it is in the interests of the state, lawfully communicate information to a person to whom under limb (a) he is not authorised to communicate it: see *Ponting* [1985] Crim LR 318 and commentary. It is possible to imagine circumstances (e.g. a plot to de-stabilise the Government of the day) where it must be in the interests of the state to communicate the information to, say, the Prime Minister. But (cf. *Chandler, Bettaney*, supra) it cannot be for D to say what is in the interests of the state.
15. Section 2 (2). See *Galvin* (1987) 88 Cr App Rep 85, [1987] Crim LR 700, CA.
16. (1919) 83 JP 121.
17. *Loat* [1985] Crim LR 154 (Judge Evans QC); *Loat v James* [1986] Crim LR 744, DC.
18. *Fell* [1963] Crim LR 207.

3 False Pretences to Gain Admission to Prohibited Places

By s. 1 of the Official Secrets Act 1920 it is an offence to practise various specified false pretences for the purpose of gaining admission to a prohibited place. These include using the uniform of a member of the forces, or one so nearly resembling it as to be calculated to deceive, forging a pass, personating one holding office under the Crown, using the die, seal or stamp of a government department, or one like it; and making a false statement or omission, orally or in writing in any declaration or application.

4 Obstruction of Guards in Prohibited Places

By s. 3 of the 1920 Act it is an offence for a person in the vicinity[19] of any prohibited place to "obstruct, knowingly mislead or otherwise interfere with or impede" any police officer or member of the forces who is "on guard, sentry, patrol or other similar duty" in relation to the prohibited place.

Offences under ss. 1 and 3 of the 1920 Act are punishable with two years' imprisonment.

5 Acts Preparatory, Incitement and Attempt

By s. 7 of the 1920 Act, to attempt to commit an offence under that Act or the Act of 1911, or to solicit or incite or endeavour to persuade another to commit such an offence; or to aid and abet or[20] to do any act preparatory to the commission of such an offence is an offence and is punishable as if the offence attempted, etc., had been committed. This provision goes further than the common law in that it includes "acts preparatory" which would not be offences at all at common law or under the Criminal Attempts Act 1981.

Thus, an act preparatory to the commission of an offence under s. 1 of the 1911 Act is an offence punishable with fourteen years' imprisonment. For example, D buys paper and pencils with a view to making a sketch of a military installation. In such a case it will, of course, be necessary to establish *mens rea* but this requires no more than that D has in mind the possibility that the commission of an offence might follow.[1]

4 Offences Connected with Terrorism[2]

Following a series of terrorist attacks in England which were themselves consequent upon the current political disturbances in Northern Ireland, Parliament passed the Prevention of Terrorism (Temporary Provisions)

---

19. It has been held that the words "in the vicinity of" means "*in, or* in the vicinity of"; so that D could be convicted where he obstructed a member of the RAF actually on an RAF Station: *Adler v George* [1964] 2 QB 7, [1964] 1 All ER 628.

20. The Act says "aids abets *and* does any act preparatory"; but it has been held that, in order to produce an intelligible result, the words quoted must be read as if "or" were substituted for "and": *Oakes* [1959] 2 QB 350, [1959] 2 All ER 92, CCA. See comment at [1959] Crim LR 457.

1. *Bingham* [1973] QB 870, [1973] 2 All ER 89, CA.

2. See Walker, *The Prevention of Terrorism in British Law* (1986); Greer, *Annotations to Current Law Statutes 1984.*

Act 1974 which was superseded by the Prevention of Terrorism (Temporary Provisions) Act 1976 which in turn has been re-enacted, with amendments, by the Prevention of Terrorism (Temporary Provisions) Act 1984.[3] The 1984 Act expires after twelve months unless continued by order made by the Home Secretary and approved by Parliament and cannot be continued in force for more than five years.[4] The 1984 Act retains the offences relating to membership of, and support for, proscribed organisations, and in respect of contributions to terrorism and failing to give information about acts of terrorism,[5] as well as the powers of the Home Secretary to make exclusion orders against persons concerned in terrorism and wide police powers of arrest and detention.

1) *Proscribed Organisations*

Section 1 (1) of the Prevention of Terrorism (Temporary Provisions) Act 1984 provides:

".. . if any person –

a) belongs or professes to belong to a proscribed organisation;
b) solicits or invites financial or other support for a proscribed organisation, or knowingly makes or receives any contribution in money or otherwise to the resources of a proscribed organisation; or
c) arranges or assists in the management of, or addresses, any meeting of three or more persons (whether or not it is a meeting to which the public are admitted) knowing that the meeting –
   i) is to support a proscribed organisation;
   ii) is to further the activities of such an organisation; or
   iii) is to be addressed by a person belonging or professing to belong to such an organisation,

he shall be guilty of an offence."

By s. 1 (2) a person committing an offence under s. 1 (1) is liable –

"i) on summary conviction to imprisonment for a term not exceeding six months or to a fine not exceeding the statutory maximum, or both, or
ii) on conviction on indictment to imprisonment for a term not exceeding five years or to a fine, or both."

3. These Acts were to some extent based on the Prevention of Violence (Temporary Provisions) Act 1939. The principal reason for replacing the 1974 Act by the 1976 Act rather than continuing the 1974 Act in force was to give Parliament the opportunity to review the working of the former and to make minor changes in the light of experience gained. In the result certain entirely new offences were introduced which were contained in sections 10 and 11 of the 1976 Act. The operation of anti-terrorist legislation was reviewed by Lord Shackleton (Cmnd. 7324, 1978) and by Lord Jellicoe (Cmnd. 8803, 1983). The outcome was the substantial re-enactment, with some revisions mainly emanating from the Jellicoe Report, in the 1984 Act of the 1974 Act. See Walker, op. cit., p. 25.
4. Section 17 and s. 14 (10) and (11). The Prevention of Violence (Temporary Provisions) Act 1939, though expressed to be for an initial period of 2 years, was continued in force for 15 years.
5. Proceedings for offences under the Act cannot be instituted without the consent of the Attorney-General: Sched 3, Part II.

In addition the court has power to order forfeiture of any money or property found in the possession of the defendant for the use or benefit of the proscribed organisations (s. 1 (10)).

By s. 1 (3) any organisation for the time being specified in Sch. 1 is a proscribed organisation (the Schedule specifies the Irish Republican Army and the Irish National Liberation Army) and in addition the Home Secretary may proscribe[6] any organisation that "appears to him" to be concerned with terrorism occurring in the United Kingdom which is connected with Northern Irish affairs.[7] Organisation is defined to include an "association or combination of persons"[8] so that even an unstructured body may be included.

1 Belonging or Professing to Belong

To belong to a proscribed organisation D must have been accepted as a member of it. Proof of D's formal enrolment is not required since admission to membership may be by entirely informal procedures.[9] Whether a member or not, D commits the offence if he professes membership. But what D must profess is membership: an expression of sympathy with, or even support for, the aims of the organisation would not suffice. An offence is not committed where D shows that he became a member before it was proscribed and that he has not since then taken part in any of its activities.[10]

2 Solicits or Invites

A person solicits (it is not clear that "invites" adds anything to "solicits") support where he asks or applies for it; and support is no less solicited where it is demanded or ordered even under threat. The solicitation may take any form and is complete upon communication to another[11] without proof that the recipient's mind was in any way affected by it. Support is no less solicited though it takes the form of a demand accompanied by threats.[12]

3 Support and Contributions

Section 1 (1) (b) creates offences of soliciting "financial or other support" for, and making or receiving "any contribution in money or otherwise to the resources" of, a proscribed organisation. The latter phrase is clearly apt

---

6. Sch.1. Any order made, whether to add or delete an organisation, requires the approval of Parliament before it takes effect but there is a procedure, in cases of urgency, under which the order takes immediate effect though it ceases to have effect after 40 days unless approved by Parliament before then s. 14 (10) and (11).

7. Section 1 (4) and Sch. 1. It suffices that the organisation is "promoting or encouraging" such terrorism; there is no need that the organisation should have been formed or be based in Northern Ireland.

8. Section 1 (6).

9. In view of Parliamentary opposition the Government withdrew a clause in the 1976 Bill that would have made the possession of certain documents emanating from a proscribed organisation evidence of belonging to that organisation. Such documents would, however, appear to be admissible in any event as constituting some evidence of membership.

10. Section 1 (7). The onus on D will be of proof on balance of probabilities.

11. Cf. *Krause* (1902) 66 JP 121, and see the discussion above p. 355. Without actual communication there may be an attempt.

12. See above, p. 252.

to cover contributions of any property but, in the particular context, is hardly apt to extend to the provision of services.[13] One who lends his car for the purposes of a proscribed organisation would not ordinarily be said to be making a *contribution* to the *resources* of the organisation. Walker, however, argues[14] that services rendered may constitute a contribution if they confer "a benefit of a permanent, assessable nature". On this view it would be an offence to repair guns for the organisation but not an offence to display posters supporting it.

But "other support" in the first part of s. 1 (1) (b) does not appear to be open to a restricted interpretation and would extend to the solicitation of services. The organisation is supported if it is helped in any manner to achieve its ends and a solicitation of such help appears to be an offence under the section.

These offences would also be committed notwithstanding that in soliciting support D offers consideration (for example, a broad-sheet or badge), or that in making or receiving a contribution D accepts or provides full value (for example, he is paid for the goods which he supplies). It can hardly be supposed that in these matters a distinction is to be drawn between one whose motivation is selfless and one whose motivation is selfish.[15]

4 Arranging Meetings

Under s. 1 (1) (c) D may commit an offence in arranging or managing a meeting of at least three persons; and D himself counts as one of the three if he attends (or proposes to attend) the meeting, as does any member or professed member of a proscribed organisation called on to address the meeting. The meeting may be entirely private (or secret) but must have been arranged. A casual meeting of three or more at which support for a proscribed organisation is expressed would not suffice; the meeting must be arranged or managed knowing that it is to further the activities of, or be addressed by a member of, such organisation. It was not the intention of Parliament to prohibit frank public or private discussion of contemporary political problems even though at such a meeting speakers might express support for a proscribed organisation.

The actual presence of three or more persons is required. To arrange a radio or television broadcast even to an audience of millions would not be an offence unless this involved the arrangement of a meeting in the studio of three or more persons for the proscribed objectives.

---

13. Cf. the offence under s. 10, below, p. 847, which creates similar offences relating to support for terrorism and which is expressly confined to "money or other property." This stands in obvious contrast to the less precise formulae in s. 1 (1) (b), but s. 10 was not part of the 1974 Act and was added only at the committee stage of the 1976 Act.

14. Walker, op. cit., at p. 37. In *Crumley* (1986) 7 NIJB 1, Hutton J declined to hold that the provision of a room for a single meeting of an IRA unit was a contribution to the "resources" of a proscribed organisation, distinguishing *Donnelly* (unreported) where it was held that making a room available as a "safe house" for meetings, messages and the storage of arms was a contribution to the resources of a proscribed organisation.

15. Again s. 10, below, p. 847, expressly makes the point clear by the inclusion of the expression "whether for consideration or not", but, see last note, this should not affect the ordinary interpretation of s. 1 (1) (b).

The offence is complete upon the arrangement of the meeting. An arrangement does not presuppose agreement and a meeting may be arranged (as by the selection of a venue and the issue of invitations) without the agreement of others.

5 Mens Rea

The offences under s. 1 (1) are concerned with membership of, and support for, proscribed organisations. On principle D must know[16] that he is joining or supporting the Irish Republican Army or the Irish National Liberation Army (the only organisations proscribed so far) but it does not have to be shown that he knows that the organisation is proscribed by law.

2) *Displaying Public Support for Proscribed Organisations*

Section 2 (1) of the Act provides:

"1) Any person who in a public place –
   a) wears any item of dress; or
   b) wears, carries or displays any article,
   in such a way or in such circumstances as to arouse reasonable apprehension that he is a member or supporter of a proscribed organisation, shall be guilty of an offence, and shall be liable on summary conviction –
       i) to imprisonment for a term not exceeding six months;
   or
       ii) to a fine of an amount not exceeding level 5 on the standard scale,
       or to both."

This offence is similar to the offence under s. 1 of the Public Order Act 1936, which prohibits the wearing in a public place[17] of a "uniform" signifying association with any political organisation. The offence under this section, which applies only in respect of proscribed organisations, is wider in applying to any item of dress or article which gives rise to a reasonable apprehension of membership of, or support for, the same. In *O'Moran*[18] it was held in a prosecution under the Public Order Act that the wearing of dark clothing, black berets and dark glasses constituted a uniform. Clearly, since the defendants in question were in fact showing support for the IRA, this would now also fall within the Prevention of Terrorism (Temporary Provisions) Act. In *O'Moran* it was said[19] that the wearing of a badge would not constitute a uniform but the wearing, carrying or display of any article (such as badge or flag or firearm) may fall within the Prevention of Terrorism (Temporary Provisions) Act. So long as the wearing etc. gives rise to a reasonable apprehension of membership

---

16. Wilful blindness would suffice. Cf. the offence under s. 10, below, p. 847, which uses the formula "knowing or suspecting".
17. "Public place" is defined by s. 2 (3) in the same terms as in s. 1 (4) of the Prevention of Crime Act 1953, see above, p. 426.
18. [1975] QB 864, [1975] 1 All ER 473, DC.
19. [1975] 1 All ER 473 at 480.

or support the offence is committed: there is no need to prove that D intended or foresaw that apprehension.

3) *Contributions to Terrorism*

By s. 10 of the Act:
"1) If any person –
  a) solicits or invites any other person to give, lend or otherwise make available, whether for consideration or not, any money or other property, or
  b) receives or accepts from any other person, whether for consideration or not, any money or other property, intending that it shall be applied or used for or in connection with the commission, preparation or instigation of acts of terrorism to which this Part of this Act applies, he shall be guilty of an offence.
  2) If any person gives, lends or otherwise makes available to any other person, whether for consideration or not, any money or other property, knowing or suspecting that it will or may be applied or used for or in connection with the commission, preparation or instigation of acts of terrorism to which this Part of this Act applies, he shall be guilty of an offence."

These offences are punishable on summary conviction by imprisonment for six months and a fine not exceeding the statutory maximum and on indictment by imprisonment for five years and fine;[20] and the court has power to order the forfeiture of money or other property found in the possession of the defendant and intended to be used by him in connection with terrorism.[1]

1 Actus Reus

The offences under this section are primarily aimed at fund-raising activities in this country and they overlap to some extent with the offences under s. 1 (1) (b) of the Act. Section 10 is wider in not being confined to support for proscribed organisations and extends to any contribution of money or other property to be used in connection with terrorism. "Terrorism" is defined in s. 14 (1) to mean:
"... the use of violence for political ends, and includes any use of violence for the purpose of putting the public or any section of the public in fear."

But in line with the policy of the Act the offence under s. 10 is limited to acts of terrorism occurring in the United Kingdom and connected with Northern Irish affairs.[2]

Terrorism is not as such an offence though it would be difficult to envisage an act of terrorism that did not involve the commission of a crime. The definition in s. 14 (1) is a broad one and would extend to such conduct

---

20. Section 10 (3).
1. Section 10 (4).
2. Section 10 (5).

as breaking up a political meeting by force; or by force compelling people to take part in a politically motivated strike – conduct which is in both cases illegal but which would not ordinarily be thought of as terrorism.

The offences under s. 10 are restricted to the provision of money or other property[3] and do not extend to the provision of services. The inclusion of "whether for consideration or not" makes it clear that the offence may be committed though some quid pro quo is exchanged for the contribution. Consequently a sale (such as the sale of materials which may be used in the manufacture of explosives) would fall within the offence.

2 Mens Rea

For an offence under s. 10 (1) the property must be sought or provided intending its use in connection with the commission, preparation or instigation of acts of terrorism. It need not be proved that D intended its use for any particular or identifiable act of terrorism, but the act of terrorism may be intended, even though it is not desired, if it is foreseen that the property will be inevitably applied in connection with terrorism.[4] The offence under s. 10 (2), on the other hand, extends to property given "knowing or suspecting" its use in connection with terrorism. This may be contrasted with the formula "knowing or believing" which is more commonplace in modern criminal statutes.[5] D may suspect that property may be used in connection with terrorism without believing it will be so used or without thinking it probable that it will be so used. A suspicion, however, involves more than fanciful conjecture. It would seem that D commits the offence where he suspects the property may be so used even though the recipient intends no such use.

4) *Disclosing Information about Terrorism*

Section 11 (1) of the Act provides:
"1) If a person who has information which he knows or believes might be of material assistance –
   a) in preventing the commission by any other person of an act of terrorism to which this Part of this Act applies; or
   b) in securing the apprehension, prosecution or conviction of any other person for an offence involving the commission, preparation or instigation of an act of terrorism to which this Part of this Act applies,
   fails without reasonable excuse to disclose that information as soon as reasonably practicable –
      i) in England and Wales, to a constable;
      ii) in Scotland, to a constable or the procurator fiscal; or
      iii) in Northern Ireland, to a constable or a member of Her Majesty's forces,
      he shall be guilty of an offence."

---

3. Section 10 (6).
4. See the general discussion, above, p. 55.
5. See above, pp. 120 and 632, and below, pp. 849–850.

The offence is punishable on summary conviction by imprisonment for six months and a fine not exceeding the statutory maximum, and on indictment by imprisonment for five years and fine.

This offence has features in common with the old offence of misprision of felony which was abolished by the Criminal Law Act 1967. Despite the arguments for the abolition of the offence which the Criminal Law Revision Committee found compelling,[6] Parliament has taken the view that an offence of this nature is justified in relation to terrorism. As with other offences under the Act its application is confined to terrorism occurring in the United Kingdom and connected with Northern Irish affairs.[7]

1 Actus Reus

Clearly the actus reus may consist in mere inactivity[8] since it lies in a failure to disclose information. The reference to "that information" in the section must refer to *all* the information possessed by D so that D may be convicted where he discloses some but not all of the information which he has.[9] The information must be of a kind which "might be of material assistance." Although some information (such as first hand knowledge of the identity of participants) is obviously material, quite what information may be material is difficult to assess. No doubt the information must be of such a kind that an ordinary citizen alive to his responsibilities would consider that it ought to be disclosed;[10] and information based on rumour or idle gossip would not be of such a kind.[11] The information must be disclosed "as soon as reasonably practicable." This is a question of fact and involves consideration of the means of communication available to D, the circumstances in which he was placed, and whether he passed on the information as soon as it was reasonable for him to have done so.[12]

2 Mens Rea

D must at least know or believe (i) that he has information which might be material; and (ii) that it relates to facts which in law constitute terrorism[13] or an offence involving terrorism. But it would seem that D need not appreciate that the facts constituted terrorism or an offence of terrorism for that is a question of law.[14] Hence D would commit an offence where he knows, but fails to disclose, that E had by force broken up a political meeting[15] though he did not appreciate that this conduct in law constituted terrorism. Knowledge, then, relates to knowledge of the facts, not the legal classification of those facts.

D can *know* that he has information which might prove material only if the information might in fact prove material. But D may *believe* that the

6. Seventh Report, *Felonies and Misdemeanours*, Cmnd. 2659.
7. Section 10 (5).
8. With one possible exception, see below, p. 851.
9. Cf. *Crimmins* [1959] VR 270, and see *Sykes v Director of Public Prosecution* [1962] AC 528 at 563, [1961] 3 All ER 33 at 42, per Lord Denning.
10. Cf. *Sykes v Director of Public Prosecutions* [1962] AC 528, [1961] 3 All ER 33.
11. D may, however, commit the offence if he *believes* it to be material, see below.
12. Note that s. 11 additionally provides for a defence of reasonable excuse, see below.
13. For the meaning of terrorism, see above, p. 847.
14. Cf. *Sykes v Director of Public Prosecutions* [1962] AC 528 at 563, [1961] 3 All ER 33 at 41, per Lord Denning.
15. See above, p. 847.

information *might* be material even though it may never be material in fact. The offence is so drafted that the prosecution does not have to prove that the information might have been material, only that D believed it to have been so. It would be difficult, however, to prove that D so believed unless the information was such as would have led a reasonable man to believe that it was material.

"Knows or believes" in s. 11 invites comparison with "knows or suspects" in s. 10.[16] "Suspects" is wider than "believes" in that D may suspect that something may be so without believing it to be so. Belief suggests complete conviction whereas suspicion leaves room for doubt.[17]

3 Reasonable Excuse

Section 11 provides for a defence of reasonable excuse,[18] and this would of course be in addition to the general defences available on a charge of crime. Most obviously in this context it would extend to a well founded fear of personal injury falling outside the narrow bounds of a defence of duress.[19] Under the former law of misprision it was suggested that non-disclosure of a felony might be justified on the grounds of a privileged relationship, such as lawyer and client or employer and employee.[20] There was little authority to support such a view but it might be argued in relation to the offence under s. 11 that the existence of some special relationship might constitute a reasonable excuse for the failure to communicate the information. However, where there is a possibility of loss of life or serious injury to property – which must ordinarily be the case with acts of terrorism – it is difficult to see how the existence of a special relationship could constitute a reasonable excuse.[1]

In this connection it should be noted that while s. 11 (1) (a) of the 1976 Act read "in preventing an act of terrorism", this provision in the 1984 Act is amended to read "in preventing *the commission by any other person* of an act of terrorism" – the italicised words being added to make it clear that D is not obliged to incriminate himself. But this does not mean that D cannot commit the offence whenever he is a party to an act of terrorism with others and his failure to inform on his confederates falls within the section. It may be, however, that D has a reasonable excuse for his mere failure to inform on his confederates if he could not do so without incriminating himself.[2] It would not be a reasonable excuse that D thought the matter was none of his

16. Above, p. 847. See also above pp. 632–635 and 813.
17. Suspicion is not enough where D is charged with receiving stolen goods knowing or believing them to be stolen, above, p. 632.
18. See generally above, p. 425.
19. Above, p. 229.
20. *Sykes v Director of Public Prosecutions* [1962] AC 528 at 564, [1961] 3 All ER 33 at 42, per Lord Denning.
 1. In *Sykes v Director of Public Prosecutions* [1962] AC 528 at 564, [1961] 3 All ER 33 at 42, Lord Denning did not think that close family or personal ties would suffice where the offence was of so serious a character that it ought to be reported. Lord Goddard was of the same mind: [1962] AC at 569, [1969] 3 All ER at 45.
 2. Cf. *King* [1965] 1 All ER 1053, CCA. But it was said that the felon might be guilty of misprision if he actively concealed the offence by telling lies to the police. Whatever the position may have been in relation to the offence of misprision it would seem under s. 11 that if D has reasonable excuse for his failure to disclose the information he does not become guilty of this offence (though he may be guilty of obstructing the police or causing wasteful employment) because he has no reasonable excuse for actively misleading the authorities.

business, still less that there was no gain or benefit to himself in his failure to disclose,[3] for it must be the concern of all to prevent terrorism.

5) *Exclusion Orders*

The Prevention of Terrorism (Temporary Provisions) Act 1984 confers upon the Home Secretary wide powers to serve exclusion orders on persons concerned in terrorism. Though detailed consideration of these powers is outside the scope of this work they need to be noted briefly in connection with the operation of the Act.

These powers are not subject to review by the courts. Exclusion orders, it has been said,[4] are concerned with national security and "There can be, therefore, no question of open proceedings or the public presentation of evidence."[5] The Home Secretary may exercise the powers in "such a way as appears to him to be expedient" to prevent acts of terrorism with respect to affairs in Northern Ireland.[6] Where the Home Secretary is satisfied that any person has been concerned in terrorism he may make an order excluding that person variously from Northern Ireland,[7] Great Britain,[8] or the United Kingdom,[9] but there are restrictions on making orders in respect of persons who are British nationals or who are ordinarily resident in Northern Ireland, Great Britain or the United Kingdom as the case may be. A person against whom an exclusion order is made has seven days in which to lodge an objection which, unless the Home Secretary considers that the grounds of the objection are frivolous, is referred for advice to one or more persons nominated by the Home Secretary for this purpose.[10] It is an offence to fail to comply with an exclusion order; and it is an offence knowingly to arrange for the entry or knowingly to harbour any person, knowing or having reasonable cause to believe that he is subject to an exclusion order.[11] These offences are punishable on summary conviction by imprisonment for six months and a fine not exceeding the statutory maximum, and on conviction on indicment by imprisonment for five years and fine.

6 *Arrest and Detention*

Section 12 of the Act confers exceptional powers of arrest and detention on constables. A constable may arrest without warrant any person whom he

3. Cf. *Sykes v Director of Public Prosecutions* [1962] AC 528, [1961] 3 All ER 33, where a suggestion that misprision required some benefit to D arising from the concealment was rejected.

4. By the Home Secretary, 882 H of C (5th Series) cols 637, 638.

5. For a criticism see Street, "The Prevention of Terrorism (Temporary Provisions) Act 1974" [1975] Crim LR 192.

6. Section 3. Street concludes that opportunities to challenge these powers in the courts are meagre; presumably challenge is possible only where the Home Secretary purports to exercise the powers not conferred at all by the Act.

7. Section 5.

8. Section 4. Great Britain means England, Wales and Scotland.

9. Section 6. The United Kingdom means the foregoing and Northern Ireland.

10. Section 7.

11. Section 9.

reasonably suspects to be (a) guilty of an offence under sections 1, 9, or 10 of the Act;[12] or (b) concerned in acts of terrorism;[13] or (c) subject to an exclusion order. The person arrested may not be detained in right of the arrest for more than 48 hours but the Home Secretary may extend this for a further period not exceeding 5 days.[14] Certain provisions which require the police to bring an arrested person before a court do not apply to a person detained in right of an arrest under this section.[15] Where a constable has a power of arrest under this section he may also stop and search that person to see whether he has in his possession any document or article which may constitute evidence that he is liable to arrest.[16]

7) *Suppression of Terrorism, etc.*

It remains to note the Internationally Protected Persons Act 1978,[17] and the Suppression of Terrorism Act 1978.[18] These Acts do not create any new substantive offences so that detailed discussion of them is outside the scope of this work. Both follow the jurisdictional pattern of the Aviation Security Act 1982[19] in embodying what has been called the principle of "prosecute or extradite."[20] They provide accordingly, as among convention states, for the prosecution of, or extradition in relation to, a wide range of offences committed against state officials or in connection with terrorism. It is anticipated that where the crime is committed outside the United Kingdom the offender will be normally extradited. The Suppression of Terrorism Act introduces an innovation by providing that the offences specified shall not be regarded as offences of a political character; but there is provision for refusing extradition where the request is made for the purpose of trying or punishing an offender on account of his race, religion, nationality or political opinions.

12. There is in s. 2 (2) a power of arrest for offences under that section (displaying support for proscribed organisations) but this does not attract the exceptional provisions of s. 12.
13. In this connection the power is not restricted to terrorism concerned with Northern Ireland.
14. Section 12 (4).
15. Section 12 (6).
16. Schedule 3, Pt. II, para. 6.
17. Which will implement the Convention on the Prevention and Punishment of Crimes against Internationally Protected Persons, Cmnd. 6176.
18. Which will implement the European Convention on the Suppression of Terrorism.
19. Above pp. 820–821.
20. By Lord Harris of Greenwich, HL Vol. 388, col. 927.

Index

Abetting. *See under* ACCOMPLICES

Abduction. *See also* KIDNAPPING
children, of, 415, 416
classification of offences, 452, 453
defective woman, of, 453
force, by, 453
girls, of—
  actus reus, analysis, 39
  generally, 452, 453
  mens rea, 72–73, 454
parent or guardian, from, 452, 453
property, for sake of, 453
taking—
  detaining, or, 453
  force unnecessary, 453
  parents, against will, 454
  permanent deprivation unnecessary, 454
  proof of, 454
women, of, 452–455

Abortion,
child capable of being born alive, as question of law, 364
child destruction overlapping, 364
common law rules, 366
conscientious objection, 373
defence—
  former, whether superseded, 372
  medical practitioners, certification of, 370
  necessity, of, desirable, 372
  pregnancy, termination necessary, whether, 370
  risk to life, of injury, etc., 369
  statutory provisions, 369, 370
duty to perform, whether, 372, 373
intent to procure, defence, 372
means used, 366–368
medical termination of pregnancy, 369, 370
miscarriage, attempt to procure, 366–368
modification of law, 369

Abortion—*continued*
poison or noxious thing—
  meaning, 367
  supplying or procuring—
    gap in legislation, 368
    knowingly, 368, 369
    statutory provision, 368
quickening of child, relevance, 366, 367
self-administration, distinction, 367, 368
statutory provision, 364, 365, 369–373
viable foetus, meaning of, 364
woman—
  committed by, 367
  conspiracy by, 367, 368

Abroad,
offences. *See* JURISDICTION

Abstracting Electricity,
offence of, 539

Abusive Words or Behaviour,
See under PUBLIC ORDER

Accessories. *See* ACCOMPLICES

Accomplices. *See also* IMPENDING APREHENSION; INCITEMENT
abetting—
  actus reus, of, 155, 156
  agreement, present in pursuance of, 136, 137
  assistance or encouragement, 135, 136
  attempt to commit offence, 150
  causation, 134, 135
  consensus, 134, 135
  conspiracy to commit offence, 150, 151
  definition of, 133–135
  incitement—
    commit offence, to, 150
    distinguished, 156
    not an offence, 255
  participation by inactivity, 137, 138

Accomplices—*continued*
abetting—*continued*
presence *prima facie* evidence, 136, 137
right of control, 137
suicide, attempt, 359
vicarious liability, whether, 169
withdrawal, effect, 156–158
abortion, 367, 368
accessory, secondary party distinguished, 131
aiding—
actual assistance, 135
causation, 134, 135
consensus, 134, 135
conspiracy to aid, 265, 266
incitement—
commit offence, to, 150, 151
distinguished, 131
not an offence, 255
intention to aid, 138–142
meaning, 133
participation by inactivity, 137
without a criminal motive—
advice sufficient, 138
seller and buyer, example, 140, 141
counselling—
actus reus, of, 155–156
attempt, 150
causation, 134, 135
consensus, 134, 135
conspiracy, 150, 151
definition, 133
incitement, 156, 157
distinguished, 131
withdrawal, effect of, 156, 157
degrees of participation, 130, 131
innocent agent—
doctrine of, 131, 132, 155
knowledge of—
circumstances, 142
substantial variation, 145, 146
type of crime, 143–148
principal offender lacking, 155
strict liability, cases of, 130, 142, 143
unforeseen consequences, liability for, 148–150
instigation for entrapment—
disapproval of practice, 160, 161
policeman, liability, extent, 160–162
joint principal and, distinction between, 132
liability of, 130
mens rea—
intention to aid, 138–142

Accomplices—*continued*
mens rea—*continued*
knowledge of—
circumstances, 142, 143
type of crime, 143–148
principal offender lacking, 155
strict liability, cases of, 130, 142, 143
unforeseen consequences, liability, 148–150
official secrets offences, 841
principal in the first degree, 130, 131
procuring—
causation, 134, 135
consensus, 134, 135
definition, 134
rape—
boys and women, 438
husband as secondary party, 431
secondary participation, 133, 134
secondary party—
abetting, *see* abetting, *supra.*
aiding, *see* aiding, *supra.*
causation, 134
consensus, 134
conviction—
principal acquitted, 151, 152
no principal, where—
accessory's offence, whether can rise higher than principal's, 153
actus reus, must be, 154–156
crime must be committed, 152
incapable of being principal, 155
two crimes, same *actus reus* but different *mens rea*, 152–154
counselling, *see* counselling, *supra.*
definition, 130
inchoate offences, 150, 151
liability as, types of activity founding, 130, 131
mens rea, 142–150, 152, 153
procuring, *see* procuring, *supra.*
time factor, 135–136
unforeseen consequences, liability—
abetting, 148–150
act outside agreement, 148, 149
counselling, 148
foresight, extent of, 147
grievous bodily harm, 148–150
joint enterprise, 148–150
murder, 148–150
substantial variation, 145, 146
transferred malice, 146, 147
withdrawal of consent, 146

Accomplices—*continued*
  secondary party—*continued*
    withdrawal, effect, 156–158
  suicide, in, 359, 360
    See also SUICIDE
  transferred malice, 146, 147
  victims of crime as—
    exclusion by implication, 158
    sexual offences, 159, 160
    tenants, 160
Accounts,
  false. *See* FALSE ACCOUNTING
Actus Reus. *See also* MENS REA
  abduction of girls, example, 39
  act—
    absence of, where, 33
    not merely, 33
    proof of, when required, 33
    surrounding circumstances, 39
    willed, must be, 39–40
  analysis of, 39
  attempt, 287, 291–295
  automatism, 40, 42–44
  causation—
    absence of, examples, 45
    foresight distinguished, 45
    proof of, necessity for, 45
  conduct must be willed, 39–44
  "conduct-crimes", 33, 34, 55
  constituent element of, absence
    unknown, 37
  continuous act, 53
  driving offence, epilepsy, 43
  excuse and, 35, 36
  involuntary acts, 40–44
  justification and, 35, 36
  lawful excuse, absence of, 39
  libel, 822–824
  mens rea, coincidence with, 32, 76
  nature of, 31, 33–36
  negative factors, 36, 52
  omission as—
    arson, in, 53, 54
    assault, whether, 49
    child, withholding food from, 49,
      50, 52
    commission and, where, 54, 55
    homicide, 49, 50
    medical cases, 51, 52
    person, protection of—
      general rule, 48
      special relationship, 48, 50, 51,
        52
      termination of duty, 52
    proof of, when required, 33
    railway crossing gate-keeper, 51
    statutory offences, 49
    See also OMISSION

Actus Reus—*continued*
  omission as—*continued*
    supervening fault, 53–55
    penalty provisions, effect of, in deter-
      mining *actus reus*, 35
    proof of, need for—
      defendant's belief, special rule, 36
      no offence without, 36–38
    "result-crimes", 33, 34, 55
    self-defence, 38
    state of affairs as—
      act, no need for, 33, 46
      aliens "being in U.K.", 46
      article for burglary, having, 46
      drunk in charge, 46
      possession, being in, 47
      strict liability, offences of, 41
    victim's state of mind, 34
    voluntariness, whether element of,
      41n
Adverse Occupation,
  premises, of, 809, 810
Advertising,
  return of stolen goods, for, 631, 766
Affray,
  continuing offence, 785, 786
  definition of, 789
  elements of, 789
  intoxicated defendant, 790
  one present, need only be, 785, 789
  penalties, 789
  public or private place, 785
  statutory provisions, 789
  violence, meaning of, 789
Aggravated Assaults. *See* ASSULTS
Aggravated Burglary. *See* BURGLARY
Aiding and Abetting. *See* ACCOM-
  PLICES
Aircraft,
  hijacking. *See* HIJACKING
  offences as to, 820–822
  piracy, 817, 818
  safety of, acts endangering—
    jurisdiction, 821
    mens rea, 822
    offences, 821, 822
  theft in, 820
Alarm,
  threatening, abusive of insulting
    words, behaviour or writing
    causing, 790, 791
Allowing,
  mens rea, whether importing, 124–
    126
Animals,
  wild, theft of, 508, 509
Appropriation. *See under* THEFT
Arrest. *See also* FALSE IMPRISONMENT

Arrest—*continued*
arrestable offences, 25, 26, 410, 411
conspiracy, 285, 286
false imprisonment. *See* FALSE IMPRI-
SONMENT
firearms, use to resist, 418
force, use of, to effect, 38, 241, 242,
243, 245, 246
general arrest conditions, under, 411,
412
homicide, defence to, 242
impeding. *See* IMPEDING APPREHEN-
SION
lawful—
killing in making, 242, 243
resisting—
grievous bodily harm, intent,
400, 401, 402, 403
wounding, intent, 400, 401, 402
powers of, 26, 285, 286, 409–412, 570,
802, 851, 852
reasonable suspicion, on, 410, 411
Arrestable Offences,
arrest for, 25, 26, 410, 411
compounding. *See* COMPOUNDING AN
ARRESTABLE OFFENCE
concept, introduction of, 25
impeding arrest. *See* IMPEDING
APPREHENSION
proper enforcement of law for, 26
Arson,
actus reus, omission as, 53, 54
common law offence, abolition, 703
destroying or damaging property,
699, 700
Art Collections,
articles, removal from, 578, 579
Assault. *See also* BATTERY
act required, 379
actual bodily harm, occasioning, 396,
397
actus reus, 376–379
aggravated, 375, 387
attempt, whether possible, 379
battery distinct, 375
boy, on, 375
buggery, with intent to commit, 473,
474
common, 375
constables, on—
breaches of peace, apprehension,
390
duty, in course of, 387, 388
mens rea, 391, 392
obstruction. *See* OBSTRUCTION
resistance and obstruction, 387–
396
statutory provision, 387

Assault—*continued*
defences—
consent—
duress negativing, 382
effect of, 382, 383
evil motives, 385
fraud, whether negativing, 382
limitations on, 383–386
physical harm, degree of, 383–
386
purpose of, 384, 385
sterilisation, legality of, 385
lawful correction, 386
self-defence. *See* SELF-DEFENCE
elements of, 376–379
female, on, 375
immediate violence, apprehension of,
378
indecent. *See* INDECENT ASSAULT
male child under fourteen, on, 375
meaning, 375, 376
mens rea, 379
mere words, whether can be, 377, 378
omission whether, 49, 379
threats, 376, 377
unloaded gun, knowledge, 377
unobserved act, 376
woman, on, 375
words negativing, 378
Attempt,
abetting or counselling of an, 150
abroad, to commit offence—
abroad, 299
England, in, 299
acts constituting—
common law rule, 291
preparation, acts of, distinguished,
291–295
statutory rule, 287, 292–294
acts of preparation and—
last act completed, 292, 293
preparatory act test, 291–295
proximity test, 292, 294
voluntary withdrawal, 299
actus reus, 287, 288, 291–295
aid or abet, to—
no offence, 297
suicide, 298, 359
assault, whether possible, 379
buggery, 473, 474
penalty, 475, 476
common law, at, abolition, 287
conspire, to, abolition, 254, 296
destroying or damaging property,
704
England, in, to commit offence
abroad, 298
failure essential, whether, 296, 297

Attempt—*continued*
impossibility and—
  common law, 301, 302
  conspiracy and attempt, examples
      where guilty of both, 303, 304
  future, in, 306
  incitement, 300, 301, 302
  intended result not a crime, 300
  intention to commit crime, must
      be, 303, 304, 305
  legal impossibility, 300
  prosecution, 305
  statutory law, 301, 302–305
  subject matter non-existent, 300,
      301
  theft, physical impossibility, 536
impossible, crimes where—
  compassing queen's death, 298
  examples, 297, 298
  manslaughter, 298
  omission, crimes of, 298
  state of affairs, *actus reus*, 298
  statutory exceptions, 297
incitement—
  commit an offence, to, 150
  whether an offence, 254, 297
indictable offence, 296
jurisdiction, 298, 299
mens rea, 287–291
  conditional intent, 289–291
  intent to commit offence, 287, 288,
      289
  murder, as to, 288
  rape, 289
merger, former doctrine of, 296, 297
miscarriage, to procure. *See* ABOR-
    TION
murder, 288, 291, 292, 297
offence completed, conviction where,
    296, 297
official secrets offences, 842
omission, by, 296
punishment of, 8
rape, 289
  boys under fourteen, 438
statutory offence, 287
successful, where, 296, 297
suicide, to aid and abet, 298, 359
summary offence, to commit, 298
vicarious liability, absence of, 169
withdrawal, effect, 299, 300
Attorney-General,
nolle prosequi, entry by, 18
Automatism,
actus reus, negativing, 42–44
burden of proof, 31, 42, 43, 196, 197
defence of, 41–44
diabetic, 216

Automatism—*continued*
drunkenness—
  causing, 40, 191, 211
  combined, with, 191
epilepsy, arising from, 42, 189, 480
"fault" of accused, induced by, 40
insanity and, 42, 188, 189, 190, 191
involuntariness not arising from, 44
non-insane, 189
reflex action and irresistible impulse
    distinguished, 43

Bailee,
theft—
  by, 538, 539
  from, 539
Battery. *See also* ASSAULT
actus reus, 379–381
assault distinct, 375
clothes, "person" includes, 381
defences—
  consent—
    duress negativing, 382
    effect of, 382, 383
    evil motives, 385
    fraud, whether negativing, 382
    limitations on, 383–386
    physical harm, degree of, 383–
        386
    prize fights, 383
    purpose of, 384, 385
    sterilisation, legality of, 385
  lawful correction, 386
detain without touching not, 380, 381
hostile, whether need be, 376
implied consent, 380
indecent, 450
  See also INDECENT ASSAULT
indirect, 381
meaning, 375
mens rea, 381
personal violence, infliction of, 379
touching, what is acceptable, 380, 381
violence, meaning of, 376
Betting,
winning by, obtaining by deception,
    as, 559, 560
Bigamy,
criticisms of law, 716, 717
defences, 714–716
divorce—
  foreign, effect of, 712
  formalities required, 712, 713
  honest beliefs as to, 714–716
  statutory defence, 712
first marriage—
  polygamous—
    contracted validly, 708

Bigamy—*continued*
first marriage—*continued*
polygamous—*continued*
effect of, 708
evasion of law, scope for, 708
spouse living, presumption, 708,
709
subsistence of, 708, 709
void, honest belief, 714, 715
limitations of offence, 705
marriage—
ceremony, proof of, 706
cohabitation and repute, 705, 706
invalidity of, 706, 707
previous, necessity for, 705
proof of, 705–707
void, declaration—
court of competent jurisdiction,
714
domicile, by law of, 714
retrospect effect, whether, 713
second ceremony, after, 713
voidable, void and, 707, 713
mens rea—
elements of, 714
honest, reasonable belief—
defence, as, 715
onus of proof, 716
reasonableness, 714–716
intention to go through ceremony,
716
mistake of law negativing, 83
mistake of law, 83
negligence, crime of, 93, 208
rationale of, 716, 717
second "marriage"—
ceremony, as meaning, 709
domicile, relevance of law, 709, 710
form recognised by law, 709
meaning, 712
place of, 710
polygamous ceremony, where, 709,
710
void, 709
seven years' absence—
other "marriages", relevance, 711,
712
proof, burden of, 711, 712
spouse alive, no knowledge, 711
statutory defence, as, 711
statutory provision, 705
Birth,
certificate, etc., forgery, 658, 666
concealment of. *See* CONCEALMENT OF
BIRTH
false statement as to, 358, 750
information, failure to give, 358
register, offences as to, 666, 676
what constitutes, 310

Blackmail,
demand—
belief in reasonable grounds for,
591
meaning, 588, 589
unwarranted, 590–592
gain or loss—
already taken place, where, 593
legal claim, where, 594
meaning, 592
remoteness of, relevance, 593
view to, need for, 592
intimidation supporting charge, 502,
503
menaces—
belief in, proper means, as, 591
earlier cases, relevance, 489
meaning, 589
origins of word, 588
statutory provision, 588
trial, non-disclosure of complainant's
name, 783
Blasphemy,
Christianity, as denial of, 737
established church, against, 738
manner, relevance, 737, 738
mens rea, 738, 739
modern test of, 738
reform of law, 73
strict liability, offence of, 100, 739
Bomb Hoax,
public nuisance, as, 796
statutory offence, 327, 328
Boys,
sexual offences by, 181, 438
Breach of Peace,
arrest, 411
peace officers, apprehending,
obstruction, 390
refusal to assist constable to suppress,
767
Broadcasts,
racial hatred, stirring up, 793
Brothels. *See* PROSTITUTION
Buggery,
actus reus, 35, 471
animal, with, 35, 471, 472
assault with attempt to commit, 473,
474
consent no defence, 471
consenting adults, between, 35, 471,
472
four distinct offences of, 471
merchant ships, on, 472
military law, under, 472
penalties for, 35, 471, 475, 476
person under fourteen, 472, 473
private, acts done in, 471
two offences, penalties where, 35

Buggery—*continued*
without consent, 35
woman, with, 471, 472
Building,
burglary, meaning in, 603, 604
entry by violence, 804
malicious damage to. *See* DESTROYING
OR DAMAGING PROPERTY
Burden of Proof,
abusive words or behaviour, 791, 793,
794
automatism, 31, 42, 43, 196, 197
bigamy, 706, 711, 712, 716
buggery, 472
counterfeiting, 674
duress, 31, 234
handling stolen goods, 628, 629
insanity, 31, 195–197
insulting words or behaviour, 791,
793, 794
manslaughter, 242, 243
murder, 242, 243
offensive weapons, 425
provocation, 31
public nuisance, 797
riot, 785, 787, 788
threatening words or behaviour, 791,
793, 794
unfitness to plead, 184
violent disorder, 785, 789
Burglary,
actus reus, 595–606
aggravated—
articles of aggravation, 609, 610
"at time of" offence, meaning, 610
firearms, 609, 610
"has with him", meaning, 610, 611
statutory provisions, 609
article for, having, 46
building—
extent of, 603, 604
meaning, 602, 603
part of, meaning, 604, 605
unlawful damage to, 607, 609
entry, meaning of, 595, 596
grievous bodily harm, to commit,
607, 608
housebreaking, articles for. *See*
HOUSEBREAKING, ARTICLES FOR
innocent agent, entry by, 597
intention—
trespasser, to enter as, 607
ulterior offence, as to, 70, 607–609
mens rea, 607–609
rape, to commit, 607, 608, 609
statutory provisions, 595
steal, intent to, 607, 608
trespasser—
consent to entry, 596, 598–601

Burglary—*continued*
trespasser—*continued*
entry as, 597–602
fraud, consent to entry by, 602
intention to enter as, 607
invitation, 596, 598–602
mens rea, 601
mistake, by, 597, 598
ulterior offences, 70, 607–609
vehicles, inhabited, of, 606
vessels, of, 606

Cable Programme Service,
racial hatred, stirring up, 793
Care Proceedings,
institution of, 180
Careless Driving. *See also* ROAD TRAF-
FIC OFFENCES
negligence as *mens rea*, 93, 480
Causation,
actus reus, as part of, 45
foresight and, distinct problems, 45
forgery, in, 662, 663
murder, in. *See under* MURDER
Causing,
mens rea, whether indicating, 126
Charity,
moneys, theft of, 516
Cheating. *See also* DECEPTION
common law offence, 568
public revenue, defrauding, 569
Cheque,
deception—
giving of, 545, 546, 551, 564, 573
use of cheque card, 546, 551–553,
573
forgery, 656
false signature, 648, 650, 653, 660
fictitious name, effect, 653, 660
indorsement, 660
instrument, as, 666
theft by using, 505
Cheque Card,
account overdrawn, use where, not
theft, 505
deception, use involving, 546, 551–
553, 573
forgery, 656, 666
Child. *See also* INFANCY
abduction, 415, 416
See also ABDUCTION
aggravated assault on, 375
alternative to criminal proceedings,
180
buggery, 472, 473
care proceedings, 180
chastisement by parents, 347, 348,
386
homicide by fright or shock, 325, 326

Child—*continued*
indecency with, 448–451
kidnapping, 413, 414
neglect as manslaughter, 350
provocation, 338
rape, 435, 438
Child Destruction. *See also* ABORTION
abortion—
cases, relevance, 364–366
overlapping with, 364
statutory defence as to, irrelevance,
364, 365
danger to life of mother, 364, 365, 366
murder, not constituting, 310, 311,
363, 365
necessity, defence of, 363–366
statutory provisions, 364
withholding food from child, 49, 50,
52
Claim of Right,
criminal damage, honest belief as
defence, 695
forgery, 656, 658–660
Coercion. *See also* DURESS; NECESSITY
duress distinguished, 230
proof, problem of, 239
unmarried couples, 240
wider than duress, whether, 239
wife—
defence available to, 238
presumption of, 238, 239
Coinage Offences. *See under* COUN-
TERFEITING
Commercial Exhibitions,
articles, removal from, 578–581
Common Informer,
penal action by, abolition, 21n.
Company Directors,
false statements by, 576, 577
Compensation,
destroyed or damaged property, 704
loss or damage to stolen property, 644
riot, damage caused by, 788
Compounding,
felony, abolition, 25, 26
treason, in, 26, 27
**Compounding an Arrestable
Offence,**
actus reus, 764, 765
consideration—
acceptance of, 765, 766
meaning, 765, 766
knowledge or belief as to offence, 765
mens rea, 765–767
offences replaced, 763, 764
privileged relationships, 765
scope of offence, 764
statutory provisions, 764

**Compounding an Arrestable
Offence**—*continued*
stolen goods, advertising reward for,
766, 767
Compulsion. *See* DURESS
Concealment of Birth,
death, must be after, 358
foetus, concealment of, 358
murder, formerly on acquittal of, 357
old rule, limitations, 357
origins of, 357
secret disposition, test of, 357, 358
statutory provision, 357
Connivance,
mens rea, whether importing, 121
Conspiracy,
abettor as principal, 132, 151
abortion, to procure, 367, 368
acquittal of other conspirators, 284,
285
agreement—
abroad, to commit offence in England, 269
actus reus, as, 257, 258, 278
aid and abet, to, 265
commit crime involving fraud, 258
crime complete on, 257
England, in, to commit offence
abroad, 268, 269
proof of, 279, 280
common design, 279, 280
difficulties, 279
direct communication unnecessary, 279
what constitutes, 279
arrest, powers of, 285, 286
attempt to conspire, abolition, 254,
296
common law—
corrupt public morals, to, 258
defraud, to, 256–258
mens rea—
conditional intention, 267
impossibility, 300
object of, 269–278
outrage public decency, to, 258
sentence, 285
statutory conspiracy and, relationship between, 257, 258
complete crime, effect of evidence of,
280, 281
corporations, liability for, 173
course of justice, to pervert, 271, 751,
755
definition, 256
defraud, to, 256, 257, 258, 269–276,
285, 286
mens rea, 271–274

Conspiracy—*continued*
handle stolen goods, 302
immunity of other parties, 282, 283
incitement to conspire, abolition, 254
Law Commission, 256, 267
mens rea, 258 *et seq.*
murder, to—
  jurisdictional point, 269
  sentence, 285
  statutory provision, 269
object of, 267 *et seq.*
  crime—
    abroad, to be committed, 268, 269
    commission in England, agreement abroad, 269
    fraud, 269–276
    law not yet in force, 268
    public decency, to outrage, 277, 278
    public morals, to corrupt, 276, 277
obscene libel, to publish, 733, 734
parties—
  acquittal of other, 284, 285
  child under ten, 282
  husband and wife, 282
  immunity of others, 282, 283
  mens rea, absence in other, 284
  mentally disordered person, 283, 284
  two or more, 281–284
  victim, 282
pervert course of justice, 271, 751, 755
public decency, to outrage, 256, 258, 277, 278, 726
public mischief, limitation on concept, 256, 276
public morals, to corrupt, 256, 257, 258, 276, 277, 472, 733, 734
  conduct no longer a crime, 277, 472
  public good, no defence of, 728, 734
rationale of, 286, 287
sentence, 285
statutory—
  agreement—
    carry out, intention to, 259, 260
    play some part in carrying out, intention to, 260
  arrest, powers of, 286
  commit offence, to, 257
  common law conspiracy and, relationship between, 257, 258
  corrupt public morals, to, 258
  course of conduct, 260–266

Conspiracy—*continued*
statutory—*continued*
  course of conduct—*continued*
    existence of unknown etc. circumstances, 263
    impossibility, effect, 301, 302–305
    inevitable consequences unforeseen, 264
    intended consequences, 261
    intention as to cirumstances, 261, 262
    interpretation of, 303
    knowledge of circumstances, 262
    meaning of, 260–262
    one party only with *mens rea*, 264
    secondary participation, agreement to do acts of, 265, 266
    strict liability offences, 262, 263
    unforeseen but inevitable consequences, 264
  definition, 260–262
  impossibility and—
    attempt and conspiracy, examples where guilty of both, 303, 304
    common law, 301, 302
    future in, 306
    prosecution, 305
    statutory law, 301, 302–305
  limitation period, 286
  mens rea, 258 *et seq.*
    conditional intention, 266, 267
    course of conduct, 260–266
    impossibility, 300
    recklessness, offence requiring, 262, 263
    strict liability, offences of, 262, 263
  object of, 267–269
  outrage public decency, to, 258
  sentence, 285
  two or more parties, 281
  steal, to, 270
  summary offence, to commit, 257, 267, 268
  triable on indictment, 256, 267, 268
  ulterior crime and, when counts for, 279n.
  unlawful object, *see* object of, *supra.*

Constables. *See* POLICE
Contempt of Court,
accused, suggesting guilt of, 772
actus reus, 769, 770
appeal, right of, 769
civil contempt, 768
  "active" proceedings, 775
court, in, 769–711

Contempt of Court—*continued*
criminal contempt, 767
disclosure of information in breach of
undertaking, 783
face of court, in, 770, 771
intentional interference, 779
judge—
prejudicing, 772
scurrilous abuse, 780
judicial bias, criticism of, 781
juror—
influence, attempt to, 756
intimidation, 770, 772, 781–783
motive, relevance, 782
jury—
deliberation, confidentiality, 784
prejudicing, 772
justices, insulting, etc., 770, 771, 772
kinds of, 767, 768
mens rea, 771, 782
obstructing officer of court, 784
particular proceedings, in, out of
court, 772
party, misrepresentations against,
772
perverting course of justice, 752,
755
prisoner's mail, interception, 772
publication—
fair and accurate report, 777
in good faith, 777, 778
innocent, 775, 776
matters of general public interest,
778
meaning, 773
proceedings *in camera*, of, 783
postponement, breach, 772
reasonable criticism, 780, 781
scandalising the court, 780, 781
strict liability rule—
active proceedings, 774
common law, at, 99, 769, 773
innocent publication or distribution, defence, 775, 776
limitations on, 773–779
publication—
applicable to, 773
fair and accurate report, 777
innocent, 775, 776
statutory provisions, 773
unintentional interference, 772–
779
tape recorders, use, 784
unintentional interference, 772–779
witness—
intimidation, 772, 781–783
motive, relevance, 782
refusal to be sworn, 771
vicarious liability, whether, 776

Contraceptive Advice,
girl under sixteen, to, 139
Conveyances,
driving or being carried in taken, 587
meaning, 582, 586
taking—
consent obtained by fraud, 584, 585
lawful authority for, 586
mens rea, 587, 588
own or another's use, for, 582–584
pedal cycles, 587
statutory provisions, 581, 582
use, nature of, 582–584
without consent or lawful authority, 584–586
Corporations,
non-vicarious liability of, 171–173
officers of, false statements by, 576,
577
property, offences against—
liability generally, 637
officers, liability, 638
theft of property of—
company involved, where, 523, 524
directors, appropriation by, 522,
523
partnership, where, 523
statutory provision, 522
vicarious liability—
difficulties, 170
employees, acts of, 171
exceptions, 171–173
extension of principle, 171–173
limitations on, 174, 175
nonfeasance and misfeasance, 171
officers, statutory liability, 175
personal appearance, 170
punishment, mode of, 174, 175
social purpose behind, 174
state of mind, 173, 174
statutory duty, failure to fulfil,
171
ultra vires doctrine, 170
unincorporated bodies, 176
wide principle, 170
Corpse,
cannot be stolen, 524
disposal of, 357, 358, 756
Corruptly,
mens rea, whether importing, 128
Counselling. *See under* ACCOMPLICES
Counterfeiting,
British currency, reproducing, 674,
675
burden of proof, 674
codification, 676
coin—
British, 674, 675
protected, 669, 670

Counterfeiting—*continued*
currency note—
British—
meaning, 674
reproducing, 674
counterfeit—
passing, 672, 673
possession, 673
meaning, 669
statutory provisions, 669, 672
former law, 645, 669
imitation British coins, 675
implements, possession, 673, 674
meaning, 669, 670
mens rea, 671
offences, 672–676
codification, 676
penalties, 676
passing, 671, 672
counterfeit currency, 672, 673
possession—
counterfeit currency, 673
counterfeiting implements, 673, 674
protected coin—
counterfeit—
passing, 672, 673
possession, 673
meaning, 669
statutory provisions, 669, 672
tendering, 671, 672
Court Officer,
obstruction—
contempt of court, 784
squatters, by, etc., 812, 813
Credit Card,
deception, use involving, 552, 553
forgery, 656, 666
Crime,
characteristics of—
moral wrong, 19
public wrong, 18
classification of—
arrestable offences, 25
felonies and misdemeanours, 25
indictable offences, 27
offences triable—
either way, 28–30
indictment, only on, 28
summarily only, 28
procedural significance, 27
summary offences, 27
treason, 25
"conduct-crimes", 33, 34, 55
criminal quality of act, 17 *et seq.*
definition of—
criminal proceedings—
civil proceedings distinguished, 21

Crime—*continued*
definition of—*continued*
criminal proceedings—*continued*
common informer, anomaly, 21n.
Crown, degree of control, 21, 22
difficulty of test, 21
procedural feature as test, 22
punishment inevitable, 22
difficulty, 17
King's Bench as *custos morum*, 20
legal classification as element in, 17
moral wrong—
controversy over, 19
test unhelpful, 19
necessity for, 17
practical test—
circularity of, 23, 24
condemnation and punishment, 23
courts, adopted by, 22, 23
public wrong—
Parliament or courts, endorsement by, 19
procedure, evidenced by, 18
society, threat to, 18, 19
elements of—
actus reus and *mens rea*. See ACTUS REUS; MENS REA
objective and mental, 31
involuntary, 39–44
modes of participation. See ACCOMPLICES; VICARIOUS LIABILITY
morals, as enforcement of, 19, 20
"result-crimes", 33, 34, 35
Criminal Damage. See DESTROYING OR DAMAGING PROPERTY
Criminal Law,
aims of, 3 *et seq.*
justice and equality—
locality as a factor, 11, 12
sentencing for similar cases, 11
moral blameworthiness basis of—
gradation, 5
maximum punishment, sentencing by reference to, 5
traditional attitude, 4, 5
offender, reform of—
courts, views of, 15, 16
judges, view rejected by, 15
public, protection of—
deterrent aspect, 12
exemplary sentences, 13
extended imprisonment, 14
"just" sentence, contradicting, 13
retribution—
degree of blameworthiness, 5–7
harm done, related to—
attempts, example of, 8

Criminal Law—*continued*
  retribution—*continued*
    harm done, related to—*continued*
      death, in case of, 8, 9
      moral guilt, related to, 6, 7
      public revulsion, related to, 6, 7
    vengeance, desire for, 7
Currency,
  counterfeiting. *See* COUNTERFEITING

Damage,
  definition, 677, 678
  property, to. *See* DESTROYING OR
    DAMAGING PROPERTY
Dangerous Driving. *See* ROAD TRAF-
  FIC OFFENCES
Dangerous Drugs. *See also* DRUGS;
  INTOXICATION
  intoxication by—
    affray, 790
    classed with alcohol, where, 209,
      210
    harassment, alarm or distress
      caused by, 792
    no defence as such, 210
    riot, 787, 788
    violent disorder, 789
    See also INTOXICATION
  management of premises, offences
    connected with, 106, 107, 109,
    110
  possession, *mens rea*—
    necessity for, 106–110
    onus of proof, 110
  strict liability for offences, 106–110
  talking as evidence of absence of *mens
    rea*, 209, 210, 212
  voluntary taking—
    medically prescribed, 190, 211
    non-specific intent crimes, 190,
      211–215
Dead Body,
  cannot be stolen, 524
  disposal or destruction, 357, 358, 756
Death,
  certificate, etc., forgery, 666
  false statement as to, 358, 750
  information, failure to give, 358
  reckless driving causing. *See under*
    ROAD TRAFFIC OFFENCES
  register, offences as to, 666, 676
  what constitutes, 311
Debtor,
  deception by, 564–568
  unlawful harassment of, 594, 595
Deception,
  appropriation by, 499–502
  cheque, giving of, 545, 546, 551, 564,
    573

Deception—*continued*
  cheque card, use of, 546, 551–553,
    573
  continuing representation of fact, 547
  corporations, offences by. *See* COR-
    PORATIONS
  credit card, use of, 552, 553
  debtor, by, 564–568
  definition of, 544, 559, 561
  deliberate or reckless, 545
  dishonesty, meaning, 555, 556, 573
  evasion of liability by, 544, 564–568
  fact or law, as to, 547–549
  false tokens, use of, 550
  husband and wife, liability of. *See*
    HUSBAND AND WIFE
  implied pretence, 553
  intention, statements of, 549
  liability—
    exemption or abatement, obtain-
      ing, 567
    legally enforceable, 568
    meaning, 564
    securing remission, 565, 566
  obtaining of services, by, 544, 561–
    564
    benefit, act conferring, 563
    services, nature of, 562
    understanding as to payment, 563
  offences involving, 543–558
  operative cause, as, 553
  opinion, statements of, 548, 549
  origin of goods supplied, relevance,
    553, 554
  payment—
    evasion of liability to make, 544,
      564–568
    inducing creditor to wait for or
      forgo, 566
  pecuniary advantage—
    betting, opportunity to win by, 560
    employment, opportunity to earn
      by, 560
    forms of, definition, 559
    insurance policies, 559, 560
    obtaining—
      deception must precede, 554
      mens rea, 558, 560, 561
      representations, true and false,
        554
      statutory provisions, 559
    overdrafts, 559, 560
  property—
    belonging to another, meaning, 557
    obtaining by—
      common law, no offence at, 543
      deception must precede, 554
      dishonesty, necessity for, 555,
        556

Deception—*continued*
property—*continued*
obtaining by—*continued*
effective cause of, 550, 554
false tokens, use of, 550
gullibility of victim, relevance, 555
intent, necessity for, 558
mens rea, 558, 560, 561
ownership—
possession or control, 557, 558
transfer of, 554
statutory provisions, 544
quality of goods, exaggerations as to, 548
representations, true and false, 548
restitution of goods. *See* RESTITUTION
theft and, relationship between, 520–522
words or conduct, 545–547
Defective,
abduction of woman, 453
procurement of, 443, 444
sexual intercouse with, 443
Demands,
menaces, with. *See* BLACKMAIL
Destroying or Damaging Property
"appropriation" for purposes of theft, whether, 497
arson, 699, 700
attempt, 704
belonging to another, meaning, 681, 682
compensation, 704
destroy or damage, meaning, 677–680
dogs, 690, 691, 692, 695, 696
explosives offences, 703, 704
fire, by, 699, 700
intent—
mens rea, 683–687, 698, 703
possessing anything with, 701, 702
to endanger life, with—
attempted murder, overlap with, 697
causal connection, 698
justifiable, 685, 686
lawful excuse, 698, 699
liability, 685
mens rea, 696–699
statutory provisions, 696
land, 678, 680, 681
lawful excuse—
claim of right, honest belief in, 695
consent, belief in, 215, 216, 689
defence of property, 689–693
general defences, 693
justifiable risk, 686
mistaken belief in ownership, 684, 695
necessity, 693–695

Destroying or Damaging Property—*continued*
lawful excuse—*continued*
self-defence, 693–695
statutory authority, 688
third party, in case of, 693
meaning, 677–680
mens rea—
intent to endanger life, in case of, 685, 696–700
intention, 683–687, 698
lawful excuse, 687–696
possession with intent, in case of, 703
recklessness, 683–687, 698
transferred malice, 687
miscellaneous offences, 703, 704
mistake, ownership, as to, 684, 695
own property, in case of, 682, 683, 684
penalties, 704
possessing anything with intent, 701–703
property, meaning, 680
statutory provision, 677
theft, consistency with law of, 677, 680
things used, 702, 703
threats, 700, 701
wild creatures, 680
Diabetic,
intoxication of, 216
Diminished Responsibility,
abnormality of mind, 203–205
burden of proof, 201
drunkenness and, 218
hospital orders, 182, 183, 206
insanity—
bordering on, 205
effect on plea of, 201, 202
introduction of—
effect of, 205, 206
statute, by, 201
irresistible impulse, 195, 204, 205
jury, function in determining, 203–205
meaning, duty of judge to direct on, 203
murder, confined to, 201
Scottish cases, 205
statutory provisions, 203
will-power, inability to exercise, 203–205
Directors,
false statements relating to, 575
property offences, liability for, 638
Disorderly House. *See* PROSTITUTION
Distress,
threatening, abusive or insulting

Distress—*continued*
threatening—*continued*
words, behaviour or writing causing, 790, 791
Document,
instrument, as, forgery, 646–649
See also FORGERY
suppression of, 577, 578
Dog,
destroying, lawful excuse, 690, 691, 695, 696
guard, protection of property by, 691, 692
Drink,
automatism arising from, 40, 211
drunkenness. *See* DRUNKENNESS; INTOXICATION
Driving Offences. *See* ROAD TRAFFIC OFFENCES
Drugs. *See also* INTOXICATION
dangerous. *See* DANGEROUS DRUGS
intent to injure by administration of, 404, 405
intoxication by—
absence of, 209, 210, 212
affray, 790
classification, 209, 210
harassment, alarm or distress caused by, 792
riot, 787, 788
valium, after taking, 217
violent disorder, 789
See also INTOXICATION
sexual offences, to facilitate, 404, 405, 440
Drunkenness. *See also* INTOXICATION
abnormality of mind, causing, 217, 218
affray caused by, 790
automatism—
arising from, 40, 190, 211
combined with, 191
"dangerous offences", proposals for reform, 220–222
diminished responsibility, and, 218
harassment, alarm or distress caused by, 792
induced with intent to commit crime, 219, 220
insanity—
causing, 190, 218
combined with, 191
involuntary, 211, 218, 787
Majewski's case, alternatives to, 220–222
mens rea—
criminal damage, 686
future act, 219
negativing, 89, 210, 218

Drunkenness—*continued*
mistake, as evidence of, 210
recklessness, 67, 787
riot caused by, 787, 788
specific intention and, 89, 211–215, 788
violent disorder caused by, 789
voluntary, crimes of non-specific intent, 40, 41, 211–216
Duress. *See also* COERCION; INTIMIDATION; NECESSITY
actual force, need to prove, 235
association voluntarily joined, by, 237, 238
burden of proof, 31, 238
circumstances of, 224–229
coercion distinguished, 230
death, threats of, 230, 231
defence, as, 224–229, 230–234
effect on other offences, 233, 234
murder, defence not available, 230, 232, 233
onus of proof, 238
procurement of woman by threats, 439, 444
proposals for reform, 238
rape, negativing consent, 433, 434
standard, subjective or objective test, 235–237
threat, sufficiency, 234–238
treason—
defence not available to some forms of, 230
fear of death, 231, 232
voluntariness and, 230, 231
war and peace, distinction, 231, 232

Electricity,
abstraction of, 539
appropriation, whether capable of, 505, 539
Embracery,
misdemeanour of, 753n, 756
Employment,
earning by, obtaining by deception, 560
Entering. *See* BURGLARY
Entry,
meaning, 595
property, on, and remaining—
obstructing court officers, 812, 813
offences replaced, 801
premises—
adverse occupation, 809
violent entry, 802–808
trespassing—
foreign missions, on, 811
weapon of offence, with, 811

Epilepsy,
defence, as, 186, 189
driving offences and, 43, 480
Escape,
offence of, 756–758
European Community,
law, non-compliance with, 251
Eviction,
criminal—
  mens rea, 814
  offence, 813–815
Evidence,
burden of proof. *See* BURDEN OF
  PROOF
false, fabrication of, 752
See also PERJURY
Excuse,
force, as to use of, 240
justification and, as defence, distinguished, 177, 178
Exhibitions,
articles, removal from, 578–581
Explosives,
offences involving, 703, 704

False Accounting,
actus reus, 575
elements of offence, 574, 575
gain and loss, meaning, 576
mens rea, 575, 576
statutory provision, 574, 575
False Declarations. *See* PERJURY
False Evidence. *See also* PERJURY
fabrication of, 752
False Imprisonment,
abduction of children, 415, 416
actus reus, 406
area of confinement, 407
arrest—
  arrestable offence, for, 410, 411
  breach of peace, 411, 412
  constable, by, 409–412
  general arrest conditions, under,
    411, 412
  private person, by, 410, 411
  statutory powers, 410–412
  unlawful unless information given,
    412
  valid warrant, under, 409
assault unnecessary, 406
consciousness of, relevance, 406, 407
crime and tort, as, 405
definition, 405
direction, free to go in other, 407
hostages, taking, 414
indirect means, 408
innoecent agent, 408
kidnapping as, 413, 414
meaning of imprisonment, 405

False Imprisonment—*continued*
omission, by, 408, 409
threat of force, 381
unlawful, must be, 409
False Instrument. *See* FORGERY
False Pretences,
obtaining by. *See* DECEPTION
procurement of women by. *See under*
  SEXUAL OFFENCES
prohibited place, to gain entry, 842
False Statements. *See also* PERJURY
making or using, 750, 751
Felony,
misdemeanours and, distinction abolished, 25, 26
Fire,
destroying or damaging property by,
  699, 700
Firearms. *See also* OFFENSIVE WEAPONS
aggravated burglary, 609
arrest, use to resist—
  additional offence, as, 418
  statutory provision, 418
  strict liability, 419
carrying with intent, 421, 422
imitation, 418, 419
meaning, 418
offensive weapons. *See* OFFENSIVE
  WEAPONS
possessing—
  intent, with, 420
  without licence for lawful object,
    247
prohibited weapons, 417
public place, having in, 421, 422
statutory definition, 417, 418, 420
statutory regulation, 416
trespassing with, 421
unlawful possession—
  offences, in relation to, 418
  other offence, commission neces-
    sary, 419, 420
  statutory provision, 418
  strict liability, whether, 419
Force, Use of,
arrest, to effect, 38, 241, 242,243, 245,
  246
attacker not criminally responsible,
  245
excessive—
  Australia, in, 248, 249
  known circumstances, in, 247–249
  murder charge, 247, 248
  no defence where, 247, 248
excuse for, 240
justification for—
  circumstances where, 88, 240–245
  excessive force, where, 248, 249
  unknown circumstances, 245, 246

Force, use of—*continued*
meaning of "force", 541
mens rea, 241, 245
prevent crime, to, 241, 242–249
property, for defence of, 246
public and private defence, in—
  answer to what offences, 246, 247
  effect arrest, to, 38, 241, 242, 243, 245, 246
  excessive in known circumstances 247–249
  general principle, 240–241
  killing—
    excessive force, following use of, 247–249
    whether justified, 242, 243, 244, 246, 247
    possessing firearm without licence, 247
    prevent crime, to, 241, 242–249
    right of private defence at common law, 243
    statutory provisions, 242
  reasonableness of, 88, 241, 242–249
  retreat, duty to, 244, 245
  self-defence, for—
    actus reus must be proved, 38
    defence not available, 244, 245
    justification for, 241, 242 *et seq.*
    mistake, 88
  steal, in order to, 540–543
  threat of, in order to steal, 540–543
Foreign Mission,
  trespass on, 811, 812
Forgery,
  authority, fictitious, 650
  cheque, 656
    false signature, 648, 650, 653, 660
    fictitious name, 653, 660
    indorsement, 660
    instrument, as, 666
  cheque card, 656, 666
  codification, 676
  common law offence, abolition, 645
  copies of false instrument, 664, 665
  copying false instrument, 664
  credit card, 656, 666
  document—
    false, making, 647, 648
    fictitious persons, in name of, 652, 653
    instrument, as, 646–649
  false instrument—
    accounts, false entries, 650, 651
    alteration, false, 650
    authorisation, false, 650
    copies, using, 664, 665
    copying, 664

Forgery—*continued*
  false instrument—*continued*
    falsity—
      generally, 650–652
      non-existing persons and, 652–654
    genuine, to be used as, 662
    jewellery valuations, 651, 652
    making, 646, 663
    meaning, 649, 650
    possession, 666–669
    statutory definition, 649, 650
    using, 664, 665
  former law, 645
  implements of, possession, 666–669
  instrument—
    copies, 664, 665
    currency note not, 646
    disc, tape, sound track, etc., 646, 649, 656, 661, 662
    document as, 646–649
    false, making, 646
    machines, information, responding to, 661, 662
    meaning, 646
    stamp as, 646, 666
    statutory definition, 646
  machines and, 646, 649, 656, 661, 662
    custody or control, having, 666
  mens rea, 655–663
  offences of, 663–669
    necessity for, 645
  omission, by, 654, 655
  possession offences, 666–669
    lawful authority or excuse, 668, 669
  prejudice, intent to—
    causation, 662, 663
    claim of right, 656, 658–660
    economic loss, 656, 657
    financial advantage, opportunity to gain, 656, 657
    honest belief, 659, 660
    loss, meaning, 656
    machines, forgery and, 656, 661, 662
    negativing, 659
    performance of duty, 656, 657, 658
    remuneration, opportunity to earn, 655
    statutory provisions, 655, 656
  signature—
    authorised, 660
    cheque, on, 648, 650, 653, 660
    alias, 653, 654
    indorsement, 660
    painting, on, 647
  strict liability, example, 98
  subject matter, 646

Forgery—*continued*
using of false instrument and copies, 664, 665
Fraud. *See also* BLACKMAIL; CHEATING; COMPANY DIRECTORS; DECEPTION; FALSE ACCOUNTING; FORGERY; FRAUDULENTLY; SUPPRESSION OF DOCUMENTS; THEFT
by whom committed, 274, 275
conspiracy to commit, 256, 257, 258, 269–276, 285, 286
jurisdiction over conspiracy to defraud, 275, 276
mens rea, 271–274
Fraudulently,
mens rea, whether importing, 127–128

Genocide,
offences, 374
penalties, 374
Girls,
sexual offences against. *See under* SEXUAL OFFENCES
Grievous Bodily Harm. *See also* WOUNDING
burglary, ulterior offence in, 607, 608
malice aforethought and, 328, 329
meaning, 328, 398
Gross Indecency,
men, between, 474, 475
penalities for, 476

Handling Stolen Goods,
actus reus, 615
advertising for return of, 631, 766
another person, for benefit of, 621, 629, 630
arranging to—
receive, 623
undertake or assist, 625, 626
assisting, 623–626
ceasing to be stolen, when, 617–620
conspiracy, 270
dishonesty, 635
forms of, 621–626
goods—
meaning, 615
original stolen goods, representing, 620, 621
impossibility, 302
innocent receipt, where, 630, 631
knowledge or belief, 632–635
land, 616
mens rea—
elements of, 632
proof of, 635, 636
proof, burden of, 628, 629

Handling Stolen Goods,—*continued*
receiving—
benefit of another, whether necessary, 621, 629, 630
innocent, subsequent retention, 630, 631
matters to be proved, 621, 622
possession or control, 622, 623
restitution, loss of right to, effect, 619
restoration to lawful custody, 618
retention, assist in, 625
statutory provisions, 615
stealing, otherwise than in course of, 626–629
stolen, meaning, 616, 617
theft distinguished, 626–629
thief—
by the, 631
guilt of, relevance, 617
things in action, 615, 616
undertaking, 623–625
whereabouts of stolen goods, knowledge of, 625, 626
Harassment,
debtor, of, 594, 595
residential occupier of premises, of—
mens rea, 814
offence, 813–815
threatening, abusive or insulting words, behaviour or writing causing, 790, 791
Highway,
obstruction of. *See under* OBSTRUCTION
Hijacking,
international law, 820
mens rea, 821
offences committed in process of, 821
piracy, as, 819
statutory provisions, 820
Homicide. *See* ABORTION; CHILD DESTRUCTION; GENOCIDE; INFANTICIDE; MANSLAUGHTER; MURDER; SUICIDE
Homosexual Acts. *See also* BUGGERY
consenting adults, between, 35, 471, 472
gross indecency, 474, 475, 476
insulting behaviour, 790, 791
penalties, 35, 471, 475, 476
procuring others to commit, 473, 476
Hospital Orders,
courts' powers to make, 182, 183, 206
Hostages,
taking of, 414
Housebreaking, Articles for. *See also* BURGLARY
meaning, 612

Housebreaking, *—continued*
  possession—
    actus reus, 612, 613
    mens rea, 613, 614
    offence, purpose of, 612, 613
    statutory provision, 611, 612
Husband and Wife,
  bigamy. *See* BIGAMY
  conspiracy, parties to, 282
  property, offences relating to—
    liability for each others, 637
    proceedings against the other,
      institution of, 636, 637
    statutory provisions, 636
  unlawful sexual intercourse, 430–432
  wife, coercion of. *See under* COERCION

Impeding Apprehension,
  actus reus, 759, 760
  arrestable offender, 758–760
  belief offence committed, 760–762
  intent, requirement of, 762
  knowing, meaning of, 761
  lawful authority, 763
  mens rea, 760–763
  mistake in identity of offender, 761
  reasonable excuse, 763
  sentence for, 763
  statutory provisions, 759
Impossibility,
  attempt and. *See* ATTEMPT
  default of defendant, due to, 251
  defence, whether, 250
  incitement, 300, 301, 302
Incest,
  incitement of girl under sixteen, 445,
    446
  offence of, consanguinity, 445, 446
Incitement,
  aiding and abetting—
    commit an offence, to, 150, 151
    distinguished, 156
    where an offence, 254
  attempts—
    commit an offence, to, 150
    impossibility, 300, 301, 302
    whether an offence, 254, 297, 298
  conspire, to, abolition, 254
  counselling—
    distinguished, 131
    not an offence, 255
  course of justice, to pervert, 751, 755
  crime incited, 254
  definition, 252
  disaffection, to, 837, 838
  impossibility of commission, 300,
    301, 302
  inchoate offence, of, 254
  incite, to, 254

Incitement—*continued*
  mens rea, 255
  misdemeanour, as, 252
  mutiny, to, 837, 838
  offences triable either way, of, 254
  offences triable on indictment, 254,
    255
  official secrets offences, 842
  racial hatred, to, 792, 793
  solicitation to murder, and, 355, 356
  successful, irrelevant whether, 252
  summary offences, of, 254
  victim incapable of, 252, 253
Indecency,
  assault. *See* INDECENT ASSAULT
  children, with, 447, 448–451
  exposure. *See* INDECENT EXPOSURE
  gross—
    men, between, 474, 475
    penalties for, 476
Indecent Assault,
  age, knowledge of, 447
  anomalies, 447
  assault, requirement of, 448, 449
  children, indecency with, 447, 448–
    451
  circumstances of indecency, 449–451
  consent, defence, as, 446, 447
  hostile act, 448, 449
  indecent battery and, distinguished,
    450
  invalid marriage, 447
  mens rea, 66, 67
  motive, indecent, 449
  physical contact unnecessary, 448
  recklessness in, 66, 67
  statutory offence, 446
  women, by, 451, 452
Indecent Battery. *See also* INDECENT
  ASSAULT
  indecent assault and, distinguished,
    450
Indecent Display,
  public, 736, 737
Indecent Exposure,
  act, number who must see, 469
  actus reus, 468, 469
  disgust, etc., proof unnecessary, 469
  female, intent to insult, 470
  mens rea, 469, 470
  "person", meaning, 470
  public, in, 468, 469, 470
  Vagrancy Act, under, 470
Indictable Offences,
  attempt, 296
  conduct crimes, potentially, 34
  conspiracy, 257
  crime, classification of, 27–30
  incitement to commit, 254

Infancy. *See also* CHILD
  buggery, and, 472, 473, 475, 476
  care proceedings, 179, 180
  criminal proceedings, 180
  fourteen years, over, 180, 181
  general defence, as, 178 *et seq.*
  homicide, provision as to, 180
  liability of infants generally, 178
  meaning, 178
  nine years, over, and under fourteen
      years, *see* ten to fourteen years,
      infra
  rape, and, 435
  sexual offences, boys, liability of, 181
  ten to fourteen years—
      care proceedings, 180
      mischievous discretion, proof of,
          179, 180
      serious wrong, knowledge of, 179,
          180
      test, whether out of date, 180
  ten years, under—
      care, etc., in need of, 179
      crime, incapable of, 178, 179
Infanticide,
  criticisms of, 362
  mother, only applicable to, 362
  onus of proof, 362
  origins of, 362
  statutory provision, 361, 362
Inflation,
  strict liability for offences, 105
Information,
  theft of, 506
Injuries. *See* WOUNDING
Inquest,
  corpse, disposal to prevent, 756
Insanity,
  automatism and, 42, 188, 189, 190,
      191
  burden of proof, 31, 42, 43, 195–197
  crime, at time of, 185 *et seq.*
  defect of reason, 191, 192
  defence of, as question of law, 186
  diminished responsibility. *See*
      DIMINISHED RESPONSIBILITY
  disease of the mind, 42, 186–191, 197
  drunkenness—
      causing, 190, 218
      combined with, 191
  external factors and internal factors
      distinguished, 189, 190
  fitness to plead—
      criteria of, 182, 183
      general issue, whether raised
          before, 184, 185
      onus of proof, 184
      raising issue of, 183
  hospital orders, 182, 183, 206

Insanity—*continued*
  infanticide, criticisms of, 361, 362
  insane delusions, 194, 195
  internal factors and external factors
      distinguished, 189, 190
  irresistible impulse—
      diminished responsibility, as, 195,
          204, 205
      law, not recognised by, 43, 195
      possibility of, 195
  jury, duty to determine issue of, 197,
      198
  M'Naghten Rules—
      diminished responsibility and, 200,
          201
      formulation of, 185, 186
      reform, proposals for, 198–200
  murder, confined to, in practice,
      201
  nature and quality of act—
      disease of the mind, 186, 192
      physical defects of brain, 187
      physical quality, 192
  presumption of sanity, 186
  prosecution, duty to allege, 201
  right and wrong knowledge—
      belief in moral rightness, 193
      law, act contrary to, 192
      moral and legal quality, 193
      particular act only, 192
  special verdict—
      appeal, right of, 197
      statutory reform, 192
  trial, relevance before, 182
Instrument,
  forgery. *See* FORGERY
Insulting Words or Behaviour. *See*
      under PUBLIC ORDER
Intention. *See also under* MENS REA
  statement of, as deception, 549
Intimidation. *See also* BLACKMAIL;
      COERCION; DURESS; THREATS;
      WRITTEN THREATS
  assault. *See* ASSAULT
  consent, negativing defence of—
      rape, 433, 434
      theft, in, 502, 503
  juror, of, 770, 772, 781–783
  procurement of women by threats,
      439, 440
  witness, of, 772, 781–783
Intoxication,
  affray caused by, 790
  alcohol, by. *See* DRUNKENNESS
  dangerous drugs, by. *See* DANGEROUS
      DRUGS
  diabetic, of, 216
  harassment, alarm or distress caused
      by, 792

Intoxication—*continued*
  intention to commit crime, induced
    with, 219
  involuntary, 211, 218, 787
  otherwise than by alcohol or danger-
    ous drugs, 216, 217
  riot—
    meaning of "intoxication", 787
    onus of proof, 787, 788
    specific intent, 788
    statutory provision, 787
  valium, after taking, 217
  violent disorder caused by, 789
Irresistible Impulse. *See under* IN-
  SANITY

Jewellery Valuation,
  false instrument, as, 651, 652
Jurisdiction,
  attempt to commit offence—
    abroad, 298, 299
    commission in England, attempt
      abroad, 298, 299
  conspiracy to commit crime—
    abroad, 268, 269
    commission in England, agreement
      abroad, 268, 269
  defraud, over conspiracy to, 275, 276
  hijacking, 820
  hostage taking, 414
  manslaughter, 309
  murder, 309
  piracy, 815
Juryman,
  embracery, 753n, 756
  impersonating, 756
  intimidation, 770, 772, 781–783
Justice,
  administration of, offences relating
    to—
    compounding   an   arrestable
      offence, 763–767
    contempt of court. *See* CONTEMPT
      OF COURT
    corpse, disposal of, 357, 358, 756
    embracery, 753n, 756
    escape, 756–758
    evidence, stealing and destroying,
      753
    false evidence, fabricating, 752
    false statements, 752, 753
    impeding apprehension of arres-
      table offenders. *See* IMPEDING
      APPREHENSION
    juryman—
      impersonating, 756
      influencing, 753, 756
    perjury. *See* PERJURY

Justice—*continued*
  administration of, offences relating
    to—*continued*
    pervert course of justice—
      act tending to, 752
      attempt, 751, 755
      compensation, offer of, whether,
        755
      conspiracy, 271, 751, 755
      contempt of court, 752, 755
      course of justice, meaning, 753
      incitement, 751, 755
      litigation,   compromise   dis-
        tinguished, 754, 755
      road traffic offences, 751, 752,
        753, 754
    police, wasteful employment of,
      428, 758
    prison breaking, 756–758
    rescue, 756–758
    witness, interfering with, 753, 754–
      756
Justification,
  excuse and, as defence, distinguished,
    177, 178
  force, for use of—
    circumstances where, 88, 240–245
    unknown circumstances of, 245, 246

Kerb-Crawling,
  offence of, 467, 468
Kidnapping. *See also* ABDUCTION
  false imprisonment, as, 413, 414
Knowingly,
  mens rea, whether importing, 103, 120

Land,
  criminal damage to, 678, 680, 681
  deception, obtaining by, 557
  stolen "goods", as, 615
  theft of, limitation on, 506, 507
Larceny. *See* THEFT
Liability,
  evasion by deception, 544, 564–568
Libel,
  actus reus, 822–824
  breach of peace, likelihood of,
    whether, 823
  crime and tort, differences, 823, 824
  dead person, of, whether indictable,
    824
  false, known to be, publication, 826
  meaning, 822
  mens rea, 825
  obscene, conspiracy to publish, 733,
    734
  penalty for, 823, 826
  reputation, serious injury, 822, 823

Libel—*continued*
seditious. *See* SEDITION
slander not criminal, 823, 824
vicarious liability, 825

Making Off,
payment, without, 569–574
goods, supplied or service done, for, 571, 572
mens rea, 573, 574
Malice,
transferred. *See under* MENS REA
Malicious Damage. *See* DESTROYING
OR DAMAGING PROPERTY
Malicious Wounding. *See* WOUNDING
Maliciously,
mens rea, whether importing, 122
Manslaughter. *See also* MURDER
abroad, triable in England, 309
attempt impossible, 298
bodily harm, unlawful—
act likely to cause, 346, 347, 348, 350–352
chastisement, 347
consent, absence of, 347
excessive force, meaning, 347n.
negligent act excluded, 350, 351
physical harm, battery causing, 350
boundaries, uncertainty of, 344
constructive, doctrine of—
act directed at another, 348, 349
child, neglect of, motive, 350
judges, reservations of, 345
meaning, 345
negligence not sufficient, 349
omission and commission distinguished, 350
risk of harm, 346, 347, 350, 351
unlawful act—
basis of doctrine, 345
bodily harm, *see* bodily harm, unlawful, *supra*.
directed at another, 348, 349
intention, importance of, 345–347
intoxication by drink or drugs, 348, 349
nature of, 347
negligence, not due to, 349, 350
defence—
arresting offenders, 242
conduct, reasonableness, 246
crime, force used in prevention of, 242, 243
duress, 231
lawful arrest, statutory provisions, 242
others, defence of, 243–245

Manslaughter—*continued*
defence—*continued*
property, defence of, 244, 246
self-defence—
attacker not committing crime, 245
force to prevent crime, same as, 243
retreat, whether duty to, 244, 245
diminished responsibility, 201, 203, 331
diverse crime, as, 331
driving offences, in, 485–487
force, excessive, use of. *See* FORCE, USE OF
frightening, killing by, 351
future act intended, where, 76
gross negligence—
elimination of, as sufficient fault for manslaughter recommended, 354
mistake no excuse, 241
reckless manslaughter and, 352–354
test, 353
hijacking, in process of, 821
infanticide as, 363
involuntary, 331, 344 *et seq.*
jurisdiction, 309
lawful arrest, killing in making, 242, 243
malice aforethought, and, 327, 344
mens rea, 213, 344 *et seq.*
mistake of fact—
excessive force, 247
provocation from, 342, 343
motor, 354
negligence—
gross, *see* gross negligence, *supra*
unlawfulness arising otherwise than through, 349, 350
omission, by, whether, 350
omission, by, 49, 50
provocation—
blow aimed at provoker, 333
burden of proof, 31, 332
common law rule, modification, 332
cooling time, 335, 336
deceased, act of, 333
defence to murder, 331, 332, 333
duty to direct jury on, 334, 338, 339, 340
Homicide Act, effect of, 332
jury—
duty to direct on, 334, 338, 339, 340

Manslaughter—*continued*
provocation—*continued*
jury—*continued*
function of, 332, 339, 340–342
withdrawal from, 332
lawful act, by, 344
loss of self-control, proof, 334–336
mistake of fact, arising from, 342, 343
mode of resentment, and, 340–342
objective condition, 332, 336–340
reasonable man, characteristics, 337–340
self-control, degree of, 338
reasonable man—
characteristics of, 337–340
Homicide Act, effect of, 332, 337, 338
introduction of concept, 336
jury, as question for, 337–340
physical defect, 337, 338
self-control, 337–340
words, effect of, 337–340
youthfulness, relevance of, 337
"reasonable relationship rule", 341
self-induced, 343, 344
subjective condition, 332, 334–336
temperament of accused, 334–336
things done or said by, 332, 333
third parties, acts involving, 333, 334
transferred malice, 333
weapon used, nature of, 340, 341
words, effect of 337–340
reasonableness, degree of force, mistake, 248
reckless—
Bateman test and, 353
compensation and negligence, 353
gross negligence and, 352–354
meaning of, 352
motor manslaughter, 354
reckless driving, 354, 485–487
See also ROAD TRAFFIC OFFENCES
recommendations, 355
suicide pacts, 331, 360, 361
unlawful act—
basis of doctrine, 345
bodily harm, *see* bodily harm, unlawful, *supra*.
direct harm, causing, 347, 351, 352
intention, importance of, 345–347
intoxication by drink or drugs, 348, 349
nature of, 347
unlawfulness, arising otherwise than through negligence, 349, 350

Manslaughter—*continued*
varieties of, 344
voluntary—
attempt, whether possible, 298
involuntary, and, 331
Marriage,
certificate, etc., forgery, 666
false statements as to, 749
offences relating to—
bigamy. *See* BIGAMY
registration of, 719
solemnisation of—
mens rea, 718
polygamous marriage, 718
statutory provisions, 717, 718
register, offences as to, 666, 676
Men,
indecency between, 474, 475
solicitation by, 476, 477
Menaces,
demanding with. *See* BLACKMAIL
Mens Rea. *See also* ACTUS REUS
abduction of women, 454
absence of claim of right, 84, 85
abusive words or behaviour, 793, 794
accomplices—
intention to aid, 138–142
knowledge—
circumstances, 142, 143
type of crime, 143–148
principal offender lacking, 155
strict liability, cases of, 130, 131, 142, 143
unforeseen consequences, liability for, 148–150
actus reus, coincidence with, 32, 76
assault, 381, 391, 392
attempts, in—
generally, 287–291
murder, 288
basic intent, concept of, 70
battery, 381
bigamy, 83, 714–716
blameless inadvertence, 69
See also STRICT LIABILITY
blasphemy, 738, 739
burglary, 607 *et seq.*
compounding arrestable offence, 765–767
conspiracy, 258 *et seq.*
constables—
assault and resistance to, 391
obstruction of, 394, 395
contempt of court, 771, 782
conveyances, taking, 587, 588
counterfeiting, 671
criminal eviction, 814

Mens Rea—*continued*

dangerous drugs—
offences, 106–110
taking—
as evidence of absence of, 209, 210, 212
intoxication by, 209–220
negativing, 89, 210–216
specific intention, crimes of, 89, 211–214
deception, obtaining—
pecuniary advantage, 558, 560, 561
property, 557, 558, 560
definition of, 55, 70
destroying or damaging property, offences as to, 683–696, 698, 702, 703
driving offences, 483
drunkenness—
deliberately induced, 219, 220
involuntary, 218
negativing, 89, 211–216, 218
recklessness and, 67, 787
specific intention, crimes of, 89, 211–214
entering premises by violence, 805
eviction, criminal, 814
excuse negativing, 35
exhibitions etc., taking articles from, 581
false imprisonment, 412
force, use of, 241, 245
forgery, 655–663
future act, 76, 219
girls, intercourse with, 441
handling stolen goods, 632–636
harassment, 814
historical development, 55
housebreaking, possession of articles for, 613
ignorance of law—
irrelevance, examples of, 80, 81
justification of rule, 81
mistake of fact compared, 81
moral responsibility and, 82
negativing—
bigamy, example of, 83
claim of right, belief in, 84, 85
legal concept in *actus reus*, 84
Scandinavia, different rule, 82
impeding apprehension, 760–763
incitement, 254
indecent exposure, 469, 470
insanity. *See* INSANITY
insulting words or behaviour, 793, 794
intention—
actual, must be proved, 85

Mens Rea—*continued*

intention—*continued*
aid, to, 138–142
attempts, in, 287–291
circumstances as well as consequences, with respect to, 60
consequences, failure to think about, 87
definition, generally, 55, 56
desire and, 57, 58, 59
destroying or damaging property, as to, 683–696, 698, 702, 703
"direct", 56, 71
dominant intention, relevance, 58, 729
drunkenness negativing, 89, 210–216, 218
force, use of, 88, 89
foresight—
belief, reasonableness of, 86, 87
excuse or justification, 88
extent of, 56, 57, 58, 59
highly probable result, 56, 57
proof of, 85
honourable purpose, 58
moral certainty, 57, 60
murder, in. *See under* MURDER
narrow interpretation, 58
"oblique", 56, 71
proof of—
circumstances, knowledge of, 86
difficulties of, 89, 90
presumption, abolition of, 85
statutory rule, 85
recklessness and, uncertain boundary between, 59
results—
conditions of achievement of purpose, 57–59
intended or virtually certain, 56, 57
virtually certain to accompany achievement of purpose, 59–61
seditious, 834–836
statutory rule as to proof of, 85
ulterior intent, 402, 403
intoxication, 218–220
See also dangerous drugs; drunkenness, *supra.*
libel, criminal, 825
malice aforethought. *See* MURDER
manslaughter, 344 *et seq.*
marriage, offences relating to solemnisation of, 719
meaning of, 55, 70
mental attitudes constituting, 55

Mens Rea—*continued*
mistake—
  fact, of, 86, 207
  law of, negativing—
    bigamy, example of, 83, 86, 87
    claim of right, belief in, 84, 85, 207
    defence, whether, 83, 86, 207
    legal concept in *actus reus*, 84, 207
    reasonableness, relevance of, 86–90, 208, 209
Morgan's case—
  defences and, 87–90
  significance, 86, 87
motive, irrelevance—
  consequence ulterior to crime, 79
  contrary view, criticism of, 78, 79
  exceptional cases, 79, 80
  general principle, 78
  murder, malice aforethought, 327
  obscene publications, 729
murder, 56, 59, 60, 327
mutiny, etc., incitement to, 837, 838
negligence, 68
  circumstances, as to, 68, 69
  See also NEGLIGENCE
obscene publications, 729, 730
offensive weapons, having, 427
perjury, 747, 748
piracy, 819
poison, administering, 404
possessing with intent to damage or destroy, 704
presumption of, 98, 102, 103
public nuisance, 797, 798
rape, 66, 67, 68, 69, 86–88, 207, 429, 430, 437, 438
reckless driving, 63, 65, 483
recklessness—
  Caldwell test, 63–69, 87, 214, 215, 289, 352
  circumstances, as to, 69
  Cunningham test, 61–63, 289
  destroying or damaging property, as to, 683–696, 698
  driving, in, 63, 65
  future of, 67, 68
  indecent assault, in, 66, 67
  indifference as element in, 68
  intention and, uncertain boundary between, 59
  intoxicated, of, 67, 787
  knowledge of risk, 61–68
  Lawrence test, 63, 64, 65, 66, 68, 352–354
  malice, in offences requiring, 67
  meaning, 61, 62, 63

Mens Rea—*continued*
recklessness—*continued*
  negligence, distinguished from, 68, 92
  rape, as to consent in, 66, 67, 68, 69, 87
  seditious intention, 834
  state of mind, proof of, 64–66
  unaware of obvious risk, 63, 64
reform, proposals for, 119
road traffic offences, 483
robbery, 543
secondary parties, of, *see* accomplices, *supra.*
seditious intention, 834, 835
self-defence, 88
spying and sabotage, 839–841
statutory offences, absence. *See* STRICT LIABILITY
strict liability, 41, 86, 100, 103
  accomplices, 130, 142, 143
  compromise between, and, 115–117
  not required, where, 86, 207
terrorism—
  contributions to, 848
  disclosure of information about, 849, 850
  proscribed organisation, membership, etc., 846
theft, 525 *et seq.*
threatening words or behaviour, 793, 794
transferred malice—
  application to accomplices, 146, 147
  destroying or damaging property, in case of, 687
  general principle, 73, 74
  limitations of doctrine, 74
  materiality of intended result, 75
  negligence, whether need for, 74
  provocation, 333
ulterior intent required—
  burglary, in, 70
  recklessness insufficient, 71
  specific intent distinguished, 71
varying requirements—
  abduction, belief as to age, 72, 73
  different crimes, 71, 72
  ideal rule, proposal for, 72
voluntariness, whether element of, 41n.
words, whether importing—
  allowing, 124–126
  causing, 126, 127
  connivance, 121
  corruptly, 128

Mens Rea—*continued*
words, whether importing—*continued*
fraudulently, 127, 128
knowingly, 103, 120, 121, 122
maliciously, 122
permitting, 124–126
possession, 128, 129
suffering, 124–126
wilfully, 122–124
wounding, 400–403
Mental Illness. *See* INSANITY
Mentally Disordered Patients,
sexual intercourse with, 444
Minor. *See* CHILD; INFANCY
Miscarriage,
attempt to procure. *See* ABORTION
Misdemeanours,
felonies and, distinction abolished, 25, 26
Misprision of Felony. *See also* COM-
POUNDING AN ARRESTABLE
OFFENCE
abolition of, 763
meaning, 25
non-disclosure, privilege, 850
Misprision of Treason,
common law misdemeanour, 26, 27, 833
Mistake,
defence, as, 93, 207–209
destroying or damaging property, defence in case of, 684, 695
drunkenness as evidence of, 210
fact, of—
generally, 86, 207
homicide, provocation, 342, 343
homicide, defence, conditions for, 245
law of—
mens rea, whether negativing, 83, 84, 86, 207
superior orders, obeying, 249
ownership, as to, 684, 695
property got by, 518–522
provocation arising from, 342, 343
rape, 86, 87, 207–209, 436, 437
reasonable—
defence, as, 86, 92, 93, 207–209
negligence, crime of, 92, 93, 207
strict liability, no defence where, 86, 207
reasonableness, relevance, 86–90, 207–209
M'Naghten Rules. *See* INSANITY
Motive. *See under* MENS REA
Motor Vehicle. *See also* ROAD TRAFFIC
OFFENCES
taking. *See* CONVEYANCES

Murder. *See also* MANSLAUGHTER
abroad, triable in England, 309
alive, whether victim still, 311
attempts to, 288, 291, 297
causation—
acceleration of death, 312, 313
but for principle, 314
child, withholding food from, 45, 50, 52
contributory causes, 314
culpability not cause, 315
deceased—
acts of, 315
negligence of, 315
fact and law, question of, 313, 314
frightening victim to take own life, 326, 327
intended consequences—
remoteness, 324
unconscious agent, 325
intervening cause—
examples, 318
human intervention, 318
natural consequences, 317, 318
original actor, act of, 320
substantial cause as, 317
unexpected consequences, 317–320
mental suffering and shock, 325, 326
neglect by injured person, 324
omission, 48, 49
operating cause, 317, 320, 323
others, acts of, 315
pain-saving drugs, 313, 316
perjury, killing by, 327
sine qua non of event, act must be, 314
sole cause, act need not be, 314, 315
substantial cause, 316, 317, 320, 323
treatment of injury—
competence of, 321
"not normal", 322, 323
present law, 323
substantial cause, 323
Coke's definition, 309
conspiracy, 269, 285
constructive malice—
abolition, 329
doctrine of, 345
felony, in course, etc., of, old rule, 329
grievous bodily harm, intent to cause, 329
Homicide Act, effect, 329
lawful arrest, resisting, 329

Murder—*continued*
  defence—
    arresting offenders, 242
    conduct reasonableness, 246
    crime, force used in prevention of,
      242, 243
    diminished responsibility. *See*
      DIMINISHED RESPONSIBILITY
    duress, whether, 230–234
    insanity. *See* INSANITY
    lawful arrest, statutory provisions,
      242
    necessity. *See* NECESSITY
    others, defence of, 243–245
    property, defence of, 244, 246
    provocation, 331, 332
      And see under MANSLAUGHTER
    self-defence—
      actus reus, whether, 38
      attacker not committing crime,
        245
      force to prevent crime, same as,
        243
      retreat, whether duty to, 244,
        245
  definition, 309
  degrees of, 330
  diminished responsibility. *See*
    DIMINISHED RESPONSIBILITY
  drunkenness, cases of, 219–222
  duress, whether, 230–234
  excessive force, death following use
    of, 247–249
  hijacking, in process of, 821
  Hyam's case—
    highly probable, 56, 59
    mens rea of murder, 56, 59, 328
  intention—
    foresight and, 55–61
    grievous bodily harm, to cause, 56,
      59, 60, 148–150, 328
    kill any person, to, 56, 328
    murder, to, 148–150
  joint enterprise, where, 148–150
  jurisdiction, 309
  malice aforethought—
    common law concept, 328, 329
    intention to cause grievous bodily
      harm, 328, 329
    manslaughter, distinguishing, 344
    meaning, 328
  mens rea, 56, 59, 60, 327–329
  murderer, who can be, 309
  offences ancillary to. *See* ATTEMPT;
    CONSPIRACY
  omission, by, 49, 50
  provocation as defence, 331, 332, 333
    See also under MANSLAUGHTER

Murder—*continued*
  Queen's peace, under, 311
  reasonable creature, 310
  reform, proposals for, 330, 331
  self-defence—
    defence, as, 243–245
    excessive force used in, 247–249
    reasonableness and, 240–242
  sentence for, 5, 330
  Smith's case—
    objective test of liability, 328
    whether overruled, 328
  threats to kill, 356, 357
  unborn child, of—
    pre-natal injury, 310, 311
    problem of, 310, 311
    separation from mother, 310
      See also CHILD DESTRUCTION
  victim, who can be, 310, 311
  who can commit, 309
  year and a day, death within, 312
Mushrooms,
  damaging or destroying, 677, 680
  theft of, 507
Mutiny and Disaffection,
  incitement to, 837, 838
  police force, causing, 838

Necessity. *See also* COERCION; DURESS
  abortion and child destruction, 366,
    369, 370, 372, 373
    See also ABORTION; CHILD DESTRUC-
      TION
  cases where justifiable, 222–226
  defence, as, 222 *et seq.*
  destroying or damaging property,
    defence in case of, 693–695
  difficulty of judging, 226, 227
  drawing of lots, 227, 228
  general doctrine, proposal for, 229
  innocent life, taking, not justified,
    228
  murder in shipwreck cases, 226–228
  physical compulsion distinguished,
    222
  possibility of unforeseen interven-
    tion, 227
  recognised defence, whether, 222
  squatting, no defence against, 224
  third party, to save, 228, 229
  uncertainty as to extent, 222
Negligence,
  bigamy as crime of, 93, 208
  constructive manslaughter, and, 349
  degrees of, in driving offences, 94
    See also under ROAD TRAFFIC
      OFFENCES
  gross. *See under* MANSLAUGHTER

Negligence—*continued*
liability, as basis of—
careless driving, 93, 480, 481
See also ROAD TRAFFIC OFFENCES
few crimes where, 92
justifiable, whether, 94–97
mistake, whether, 93, 207, 208
principal or subsidiary element, where, 92
manslaughter, as basis of, 92, 352, 353
mens rea and, 68, 69
objective standard, failure to comply with, 91
public nuisance, liability for, 797
punishment for, value of, 95
rationale, as basis of liability, 94–97
recklessness and, 68, 69
circumstances, as to, 69
transferred malice, where, 75
Nolle Prosequi,
Attorney-General, entry by, 18
Nuisance. *See* PUBLIC NUISANCE

Oath,
false statements on. *See* PERJURY
Obscene Libel,
conspiracy to publish, 733, 734
Obscene Publications,
articles—
publication, kept for, 733, 734
reproduction of matter from, 734
statutory definition, 734
background of offence, 719
defences—
no reasonable cause to believe, 726
public good—
author's intention, relevance, 728
merits, proof of, 727–729
objects of general concern, 727
onus of proof, 728
statutory provision, 727
forfeiture—
absence of uniformity, 733
procedure, 732
indecent displays, 736, 737
mens rea—
common law and statute, 729–732
honesty of purpose, 731
intention, what constitutes, 730
knowledge of effect, 729, 730
motive, relevance of, 729
obscene libel, conspiracy to publish, 733, 734
obscenity—
author, intention of, 723
common law test, 720

Obscene Publications—*continued*
obscenity—*continued*
courts, attitude of, 720, 721
depravity and corruption, 720 *et seq.*
persons likely to be depraved, 721–723
sexual depravity, not confined to, 720
statutory definition, 720
taken as a whole, 723
offences, 723–726
posting indecent etc. matter, 734–736
publication—
cinematograph exhibition, 726
forfeiture, order for, 733
corruption, persons liable to, 724
gain, for, having for—
elements of offence, 725, 726
having, meaning of, 725
obscenity, determination of, 725
meaning, 724
offering for sale, 725
persons likely to read, 724
statutory provision, 724
summary proceedings, statutes providing for, 737
test of, 719, 720
theatre, in, 736
Obscenity. *See* OBSCENE PUBLICATIONS
Obstruction,
constables, of—
act not unlawful in itself, 394
breach of peace, preventing, 390
duty, in course of, 387, 388
statutory provisions, 387
wilful, 392–396
liquor licensing offences, 392, 393
mens rea, 395, 396
road traffic offences, 392, 395, 753, 754
court officers, of, 784
squatters, etc., by, 812, 813
highway, of—
appreciable interference, 799
processions and meetings, 798, 799
public nuisance, 794, 798–801
See also PUBLIC NUISANCE
statutory provisions—
motor vehicles, 800
unreasonable, must be, 800, 801
wilful obstruction, 800
unreasonable user, 800
meaning, 392–395
mens rea, 395, 396
Official Secrets Act, guards in prohibited places, 842

Obstruction—*continued*
refusal to answer questions, 393, 394
warning as, 392–394
wilful, constable, of, 392–396
Obtaining,
deception, by. *See* DECEPTION
Occupier,
adverse occupation by trespasser,
809, 810
protected intending, 809, 810
residential. *See* RESIDENTIAL OCCUPIER
Offences Triable Either Way,
classification of offences, 27, 28, 29
incitement to commit, 254
Offensive Weapons,
aggravated burglary, 609
bomb hoaxes, 427–428
burden of proof, 425
injury—
carrying for purpose, 422–425
made or adapted for, 422–424
lawful—
authority, 425, 426
possession originally, 423, 424
meaning—
categories, 423
injury to person, for causing, 422
mens rea, 427
occasion, meaning, 425
poaching, night, 427
public place, 426, 427
reasonable excuse, 425, 426
smuggling, when, 427
statutory defence, 425
statutory provisions, 422
weapon of offence—
distinguished, 422, 423
trespassing on premises with, 811
Official Secrets,
attempt, 842
incitement, 842
information, communication of—
elements of offence, 841
far reaching scope, 841
mens rea, 841
person receiving, 841
preparatory acts, 842
prohibited place—
false pretences to gain entry, 842
guards, obstruction of, 842
meaning, 838, 839
spying and sabotage—
far reaching scope, 841
interpretation of provision, 838,
839
mens rea, 839–841
obstructing Crown forces, 840
purpose prejudicial to State, 838
scope beyond spying, 839

Official Secrets—*continued*
spying and sabotage—*continued*
statutory provision, 838
Omission,
actus reus, as element of. *See under*
ACTUS REUS
assault, whether, 379
attempt by, 296
false imprisonment by, 408, 409
forgery by, 608
manslaughter by, 350
obtaining services by, 562
public nuisance by, 795
rape by, 433
Overdrafts,
deception, obtaining by, 559, 560

Parents,
abduction of girls from, 452, 453
child—
abduction of, 415, 416
reasonable chastisement, 347, 348,
386
Parties,
accomplices. *See* ACCOMPLICES
conspiracy, in. *See* CONSPIRACY
principal in the first degree, 130, 131–
133
victims as, 158–160
Payment,
evasion of liability to make, deception, by, 544, 564–568
making off without, 569–574
Pecuniary Advantage,
deception, obtaining by. *See* DECEP-
TION
Pedal Cycles,
taking, 587
Penal Action,
common informer, by, abolished,
21n.
Perjury,
accused, by, 742
affirmation, 741
births or deaths, false statements,
358, 750
child, unsworn testimony, 741
common law offence, origins of, 740
conduct crime, as, 33
defence, not lawfully sworn, 741, 742
duress as defence, 235
false statements, and, 640
God, belief in, 740, 741
homicide by, 327
judicial proceeding—
jurisdiction, court lacking, 742, 743
power to receive evidence on oath,
742
statement made for, 743

Perjury—*continued*
  judicial proceeding—*continued*
    statutory definition, 742
  materiality, rule as to—
    admissibility, testimony, 744
    circumstantial evidence, 744
    common law, 743
    credit, testimony as to, 745
    narrow construction, 743
    Perjury Act, doctrine of, 746
    relevance to proceedings, 746
    result, evidence bearing on, 744
  mens rea, 747, 748
  mistake, witness sworn by, 741
  offences akin to—
    common law, at, 740
    false statements—
      births and deaths, as to, 750
      marriage, relating to, 749
      oath, on, 749
      statutory declarations, etc., 750
      vocation, registration for, 751
  opinion, statements of, 747, 748
  statutory definition, 740
  subornation of, 748
  true, statement may be, 746, 747
  witness lawfully sworn, 740–742
Permitting,
  mens rea, whether importing, 124–126
Personation,
  juryman, of, 756
Piracy,
  aircraft, extended to, 817, 818
  elements of, 817, 818
  hijacking as, 818
  international law, 815
  iure gentium, 815–819
  meaning, 816
  mens rea, 819
  places outside any jurisdiction, 818
  private nature of, 817
  punishment of, 819, 820
  robbery as element, 815
  statute, by, 819
  Tokyo Convention, provisions of, 816
Plants,
  theft of, 507, 508
Play,
  public performance of, to stir up racial hatred, 793
Poaching,
  night, by, offensive weapons, 427
Poison,
  administering—
    actus reus, 403, 404
    mens rea, 404
  marriage, to procure. *See under* ABORTION

Police,
  arrest, powers of, 409–412, 802, 851, 852
  constables—
    assault, etc. on. *See under* ASSAULT
    obstruction of. *See* OBSTRUCTION
    refusal to aid, 767
  detention of suspected terrorists, powers of, 852
  disaffection, causing, 838
  duty to co-operate with, 394, 395
  instigation of crimes, 160–162
  property in possession of, delivery up, 642, 643
  wasteful employment of, 428, 758
Pollution,
  strict liability for offence, 110, 111
Possession,
  actus reus, as an, 47, 48
  appropriation in theft and, 497–499
  counterfeit currency, 673
  counterfeiting implements, 673, 674
  dangerous drugs, of—
    defences, 108
    mens rea, 106–110
  forgery offences, 666–669
  mens rea, whether importing, 128, 129
  property, of, meaning, 681–683
  with intent to damage or destroy, 701, 702
Post,
  indecent etc., matter, sending by, 734–736
Premises,
  adverse occupation, 809, 810
  criminal eviction from, 813–815
  entry—
    remaining on, and, 801 *et seq.*
    violence, by—
      defences, other, 808
      displaced residential occupier, 807
      entry, 802, 803
      lawful authority, without, 806, 807
      mens rea, 805, 806
      premises, meaning, 804
      presence of person opposed, 804, 805
      statutory provisions, 802
      use or threat of violence, 803
  harassment of occupier, 813–815
  meaning, 804
  prostitution, use for. *See under* PROSTITUTION
  trespassing—
    foreign missions, on, 811, 812
    weapon of offence, with, 811

Premises—*continued*
unlawful sexual intercourse, use for, 444, 445
Principals. *See* ACCOMPLICES
Prison,
breaking from, 756–758
escape, without breaking, 757
Procuring,
abortion, poison, etc., for. *See under* ABORTION
women. *See under* SEXUAL OFFENCES
Property,
belonging to another, meaning, 681–683
deception, obtaining by. *See* DECEPTION
defence of, use of force for, 246
deprivation of. *See* TEMPORARY DEPRIVATION; THEFT
destroying or damaging. *See* DESTROYING OR DAMAGING PROPERTY
entering and remaining on, 801 *et seq.*
See also ENTRY; SQUATTERS
meaning, 680
Prostitution,
definition of, 455
earnings of, living on—
goods, services, etc., supply of—
advertisements, 461
inflated rent, 462, 463
price exorbitant, 462
reasonable limits, 463
referable to, 461
scope, two extremes, 461
statutory provisions, 460
usual arrangement, 460
women also liable for, 464
not criminal as such, 455
offences relating to, 455–468
premises, use for—
brothel—
keeping, statutory provisions, 457, 458
meaning, 458
disorderly house, keeping, 459
tenant permitting, 459, 460
procuring—
causing or encouraging, wide scope, 456, 457
girls, 456
other offences, overlapping, 457
statutory provision, 456
soliciting or loitering—
changes in law, 464
common prostitute, meaning, 465
kerb-crawling, 467, 468
loiter, meaning, 465
men soliciting women, 467, 468

Prostitution—*continued*
soliciting or loitering—*continued*
prostitute, aimed at, 464
public place, 466
solicit, meaning, 466
statutory provision, 464
street, meaning, 466
window, seen through, 466
woman exercising control, 464
Provocation. *See under* MANSLAUGHTER
Public,
places open to, removal of articles from, 578–581
Public Decency,
outrage on, 256, 257, 258, 277, 278
statutory offence, 258
Public Mischief,
concept of, rejected, 256, 276
Public Morals
conspiracy to corrupt—
concept, 256, 257, 258, 276, 277, 733
no defence of public good, 729, 733, 734
statutory offence, 258
Public Nuisance,
bomb hoax as, 796
burden of proof, 797
civil remedy, 794
community at large, affecting, 796
definition, 794
examples, 794, 795
isolated act, 795
mens rea, 797, 798
nature of, 794–796
natural consequences, knowledge of, 797
negligence, liability, 797
obstruction of highway, 794, 798–801
See also OBSTRUCTION
omission, by, 795
public, meaning of, 796
public rights, interference with, 794
queues outside shop, 796
statutory remedies, 794, 795
substantial and unreasonable, 795
unnecessary and unreasonable, 796
vicarious liability, 798
Public Order,
abusive words or behaviour, *see* threatening, abusive or insulting words or behaviour, *infra*
affray. *see* AFFRAY
alarm, element of offence of causing, 790, 791
distress, elements of offence of causing, 790, 791

Public Order—*continued*

entering and remaining on property, offences. *See* ENTRY

harassment, elements of offence of causing, 790, 791

insulting words or behaviour, *see* threatening, abusive or insulting words or behaviour, *infra*

libel. *See* LIBEL

obstruction of highway. *See under* OBSTRUCTION

public nuisance. *See* PUBLIC NUISANCE

racial hatred, stirring up, 792, 793

riot. *See* RIOT

seditious incitement, 835, 836

threatening, abusive or insulting words or behaviour—

   actus reus, 790

   harrassment, alarm or distress, causing, 791, 792

   homosexual acts, 790, 791

   meaning, 790, 791

   objective test, 790, 791, 793

   penalties, 790

   proof, burden of, 791, 793, 794

   public or private place, 791

   racial hatred, stirring up, 793

   statutory provision, 790

unlawful assembly, rout, riot, abolition of, 785

violence—

   fear or provocation of, 790, 791

   threats of unlawful, 786, 787, 789, 790, 791

violent disorder. *See* VIOLENT DISORDER

Public Place,

affray, 786

   See also AFFRAY

firearms, having in, 421, 422

definition, 426

indecent display, 736, 737

indecent exposure, 468, 469

offensive weapon, having in, 422, 426, 427

play to stir up racial hatred, public performance of, 793

proscribed terrorist organisation, displaying support for, in, 846, 847

prostitute, loitering, etc., in, 464–467

riot, 785

   See also RIOT

solicitation by man in, 476, 477

threatening, abusive, or insulting words or behaviour, 791, 793

violent disorder, 785

   See also VIOLENT DISORDER

Public Revenue,

cheating, 569

Publishing,

written material to stir up racial hatred, 793

Punishment,

attempt, 8

conspiracy, 285

degrees of—

   harm done, related to, 8–10

   moral guilt, related to, 4–7

equality in similar cases—

   locality as a factor, 11, 12

   policy of, 11

extended term of imprisonment, 14

fitting the crime, 10, 11

maximum, sentencing by reference to, 5

moral guilt, proportional to, 6

motive, importance of, 79, 80

"normal" sentence, 10

offender, reform of—

   courts, views of, 15, 16

   judges, view rejected by, 15

preventive detention, 14

public, protection of—

   deterrent aspect, 12

   exemplary sentences, 13

public revulsion, related to, 6, 7

retributive theory of, 4–7, 8

scale of, 5

severity, strict liability, where, 98

success of crime determining, 9, 10

vengeance, desire for, 7

Racial Hatred,

meaning of, 792

objective test, 792

religious groups, 792, 793

statutory provisions, 793

stirring up, elements of offence, 791, 792

Rape,

accomplices, boys and women, 438

actus reus, 430 *et seq.*

attempt, 289

boys under fourteen, 181, 438

burglary to commit, 607, 608, 609

consent, absence of—

   child, 435

   essential element, as, 433

   force not essential, 433, 434

   fraud—

      error induced by, 434, 435, 436

      mistake not arising from, 436, 437

   mistake, 86, 207–209, 436, 437

   recklessness as to, 66, 67, 68, 69, 87

Rape—*continued*
consent, absence of—*continued*
submission by duress, 433, 434
woman incapable of consenting, 433
definition, 429
mens rea, 66, 67, 68, 69, 86–88, 207, 429, 430, 437, 438
Morgan's case, 86–90, 207, 208
omission, by, 433
procuring by threats, and, 433, 434
sexual intercourse—
meaning, 432
unlawful—
husband—
secondary party, 431
wife, and, 430–432
statutory provision, 429
Receiving. *See* HANDLING STOLEN GOODS
Reckless Driving. *See* ROAD TRAFFIC OFFENCES
Recklessness. *See under* MENS REA
Recordings,
visual images, of, to stir up racial hatred, 793
Reflex Action,
automatism, 43
nature and effect of, 43, 44
Rescue,
offence of, 758
Residential Occupier,
criminal eviction, 813–815
displaced by trespassers—
requirement to leave by, 809
violent entry, defence, 807
harassment, 813–815
meaning, 807, 814
Restitution,
stolen goods, of—
compensation for loss or damage, 644
old procedure, differences, 642–644
Order—
circumstances in which made, 641
contents of, 641, 642
effect of, 642
purpose of provisions, 640
statutory provisions, 639, 640
Revenue,
defrauding, as cheat, 569
Reward,
stolen goods, for, advertising, 766, 767
Riot. *See also* PUBLIC ORDER
common purpose, 787

Riot—*continued*
compensation for damage caused by, 788
continuing offence, 785, 786
elements of offence of, 786
indictable offence, 786
intoxicated person—
meaning of "intoxication", 787
onus of proof, 787, 788
specific intent, 788
statutory provision, 787
numbers present, 785, 786
penalties, 786
proof, burden of, 785
prosecution, consent of DPP for, 785
public or private place, in, 785
Riot (Damages) Act, 788
statutory provisions, 786, 787
threat of unlawful violence, 786, 787
violence—
meaning, 786, 787
threat of unlawful, 786, 787
Road,
obstruction. *See* OBSTRUCTION, highway, of
Road Traffic Offences,
background and problems, 478
careless driving, 93, 479–482
dangerous driving—
abolition, 483
drunk etc., in charge, *actus reus*, 46
epilepsy, whether *actus reus*, 44, 448
inconsiderate driving, 479, 482
reckless driving—
causing death by—
cause, proof of, 487
manslaughter and, 354, 485–487
statutory provision, 485
verdict, 487
knowledge of dangerous factors, 484, 485
mens rea, 65, 483, 484
recklessness, meaning, 483, 484
statutory provision, 482
taking vehicles. *See* CONVEYANCES
Robbery,
any person, force used, etc., on, 541
definition of, 540
force—
immediately before or at the time of, 542, 543
purpose of, 542
use or threat of, 541
intent, scope of, 543
mens rea, 543
piracy, as element in, 815
statutory provision, 540

Sabotage. *See* OFFICIAL SECRETS
Secondary Party. *See* ACCOMPLICES
Sedition,
  actus reus, 836, 837
  freedom of speech, and, 837
  intention, seditious—
    definition, 834
    desire, whether necessary, 835
    objective test, whether, 834
    real or presumed, 834, 835
    recklessness, whether sufficient,
      834, 835
    violence, to cause, 835, 836
  oral or written words, publication,
    833
  public disorder, incitement, 836
  publication, whether necessary, 836,
    837
  words of another, publication, 836
Self-defence,
  defence, as—
    actus reus must be proved, 38
    burden of proof, 31
    destroying or damaging property,
      693–695
    justification for, 241, 242 *et seq.*
    mens rea, 88
    mistake, 88
    murder. *See under* MURDER
    not available, where, 244, 245
    See also FORCE, USE OF
Sentencing. *See* PUNISHMENT
Servant,
  master, liability. *See* VICARIOUS LIA-
    BILITY
Services,
  definition of, 562
  making off without payment for, 569–
    574
  obtaining by deception, 544, 561–564
Sexual Intercourse. *See also* RAPE;
  SEXUAL OFFENCES
  girl under sixteen, contraceptive ad-
    vice to, 139
  meaning, 432
Sexual Offences,
  abduction. *See* ABDUCTION
  boys under fourteen, 181, 438
  buggery. *See* BUGGERY
  children, indecency with. *See* IN-
    DECENT ASSAULT
  homosexual acts—
    consenting adults, between, 461,
      462
    gross indecency, 474–476
    insulting behaviour, 790, 791
    procuring others to commit, 473
    penalties for, 475, 476

Sexual Offences—*continued*
  indecent assault. *See* INDECENT
    ASSAULT
  indecent exposure. *See* INDECENT
    EXPOSURE
  intercourse, involving—
    defective—
      intercourse with, 442, 443
      procurement of—
        mens rea, 443
        persuasion, element of, 443,
          444
      procurer, intercourse with, 443
    drugs to facilitate, 404, 405, 440
    girls, against—
      marriage, foreign, 442
      mens rea, 441, 442
      procuration of, 442
      under sixteen, 441, 442
      under thirteen, 441
    incest, 445, 446
    mentally disordered patients, 444
    premises, permitting use for, 444,
      445
    procurement of women—
      false pretence, meaning, 440
      intercourse must take place,
        439
      procurer, for intercourse with,
        439
      prostitution, for, 456, 457
      See also PROSTITUTION
      statutory provisions, 439
      threats, by, 439, 440
    rape. *See* RAPE
  men, indecency between, 474, 475
  procuring to commit homosexual
    acts, 473
  prostitution, relating to. *See* PROSTI-
    TUTION
  rape. *See* RAPE
  sexual intercourse, meaning, 432,
    433
  solicitation by men—
    homosexuals, 476, 477
    kerb-crawling, 467, 468
    women, of, 467, 468
  unnatural offences, 471–477
  victims as accomplices, 159
Smuggling,
  offensive weapon, having, 427
Solicitation,
  men, by. *See* SEXUAL OFFENCES
  murder, to, 355, 356
  prostitutes, by. *See under* PROSTITU-
    TION
Spouses. *See* HUSBAND AND WIFE
Spying. *See* OFFICIAL SECRETS

Squatters. *See also* ENTRY; PREMISES
premises—
  adverse occupation, 809, 810
  entering—
    remaining on property, and, 801
    et seq.
    violence, by, 802–808
  obstructing court officers, 812, 813
  weapons of offence, having, on, 811
Sterilisation,
  legality of, 385
Stolen Goods,
  advertising reward for, 766, 767
  handling. *See* HANDLING STOLEN
    GOODS
  restitution of. *See* RESTITUTION
Street Offences,
  prostitution, loitering for. *See under*
    PROSTITUTION
Strict Liability. *See also* MENS REA
  absolute liability distinguished—
    actus reus only, 98, 111
    defences available, 111, 112
  absolute prohibition distinguished,
    98
  actus reus, proof in cases of, 41
  amendment, possibility of, 105
  arguments for and against, 112–117
  blasphemy, 99, 739
  common law offences, 99
  conspiracy to commit offences, 262,
    263
  contempt of court, 99, 772–775. *See
    also* CONTEMPT OF COURT
  courts, approach adopted by, 102
  dangerous drugs offences, 106–111
  defences available, 41, 42, 111, 112,
    117–119
  firearms, use to resist arrest, 419
  forged prescriptions, example, 98
  general prohibition, whether, 104,
    105
  inflation, 106
  justifiable, whether, 112–115
  management of premises, in connec-
    tion with, 106, 107, 109, 110
  mens rea, 41, 86, 100, 103
    accomplices, 130, 142, 143
    compromise with, 115–117
    not required where, 86, 207
  pollution, 110, 111
  possible developments, 115–117
  presumption of *mens rea*, 98, 102, 103
  punishment, severity of, 111
  real or quasi-crime, whether, 104
  reasonable precautions, when taken,
    115
  recognition of offences—
    courts, policy of, 102

Strict Liability—*continued*
  recognition of offences—*continued*
    "knowingly", relevance of word—
      dangerous drugs offences, 106–
      110
      general rule, absence of, 103
      mens rea, usually importing, 120–
      122
      pollution, 110, 111
      policeman, drink sold to, 103,
      104
    presumption of *mens rea*, 102, 103
    punishment, severity of, 111
  reform, proposals for, 119
  social danger of offence, 105
  special prohibition, whether, 104, 105
  statutory defences mitigating—
    burden on the accused, 117–119
    Food Act, under, 117–119
    limitations on effectiveness, 117,
    118
  statutory offences, examples—
    adulterated tobacco, selling, 100
    drink, selling to drunken person,
    101
    unsound meat, selling, 101
  vicarious liability—
    common law offences, 99
    distinguished, 162
  voluntariness essential, 43, 44
  words indicating whether—
    allowing, 124–126
    causing, 126, 127
    connivance, 121
    corruptly, 128
    fraudulently, 127, 128
    knowingly, 103, 120, 121, 122
    maliciously, 122
    permitting, 124–126
    possession, 128, 129
    suffering, 124–126
    wilfully, 122–124
Suffering,
  mens rea, whether importing, 124–126
Suicide,
  attempt to aid and abet, 360
  booklet giving advice, 360
  common law offence, 358
  complicity in another's, 359, 360, 361
  old rule—
    abolition, 360
    failure, effects of, 358, 359
    self-murder, as, 358
  pacts, complicity and manslaughter,
    331, 360, 361
Summary Offences,
  conspiracy to commit, 256, 267,
    268
  crime, classification of, 27–30

Summary Offences—*continued*
fines, standard scale, vi
incitement to commit, 254
Superior Orders,
defence of, 249, 250
Suppression of Documents,
offence of, 577, 578

Temporary Deprivation,
conveyances, taking. *See* CON-
VEYANCES
offences of, case for, 578
places open to the public—
articles, removal from—
elements of offence, 578–581
mens rea, 581
statutory provisions, 578, 579
meaning, 579
theft, excluded from, 578
Tenants,
fixtures, theft of, 506, 507
Terrorism,
arrest, powers of, 851, 852
contributions to—
actus reus, 847, 848
mens rea, 848
statutory provisions, 846
detention, powers of, 851, 852
disclosing information about—
actus reus, 849
mens rea, 849, 850
reasonable excuse, defence of, 850,
851
statutory provisions, 848
exclusion orders, 843, 851
meaning, 847
offences connected with, 842 *et seq.*
proscribed organisation—
arranging meetings, 845, 846
belonging to professing to belong,
844
contributions, 844, 845
displaying public support for, 846,
847
meaning, 843
mens rea, 846
organisation, meaning, 844
solicits or invites, 844
statutory provisions, 843
support, 844, 845
search, powers of, 852
state officials, offences against, 852
Theatres,
obscenity in, 736
Theft,
actus reus, 491–525
advertising for return of stolen goods,
631
aircraft, in, 820

Theft—*continued*
appropriation—
apparent possession, 497–499
bona fide purchasers, 503, 504
consent—
and appropriation, 499–503
deception, 499–502
continuing act as, 504, 542
conversion and, 496, 497
definition, 491–494, 496
intimidation and, 502, 503
keeping and dealing, by, 494, 495
owner, rights of, and, 495, 496
possession and, 497–499
property must be capable of, 505
supermarket frauds, 491–493
switching price tags, 491, 492, 496
theft, does not necessarily constitute, 491
trick, by, 494
unauthorised act, as, 491–494
bailee by or from, 510, 511, 539
bona fide purchasers, 503, 504
borrowing—
dishonest, whether, 530, 531
permanent deprivation, as, 537,
538
burglary, ulterior offence in, 607
charity moneys, 516
civil law concepts, relevance, 489
codification of law, 488
consent—
dishonesty and, 500, 501
intimidation, obtained by, 502, 503
conspiracy to steal, 270
corporations, offences by. *See* COR-
PORATIONS
corpse cannot be stolen, 524
debt, appropriation of, 505
deception and—
appropriation by deception, 499–
502
relationship between, 520–522
definition, 490
destroying as appropriation, 497
dishonesty—
awareness of circumstances, 531,
532
"borrowing" cases, 530, 531
consent and, 500, 501
jury, interpretation for, 529, 530
legal right, belief in, 526, 527
meaning, difficulties of, 525
moral claim of right, 529–532
old cases, relevance, 525
other's consent, belief in, 527
partial statutory definition, 526,
532
property lost, belief that, 527

Theft—*continued*
 dishonesty—*continued*
  scope of, 527
  view to gain or benefit, 528
  willingness to pay, 528
 earlier cases, relevance, 489
 electricity—
  abstracting, 539, 540
  whether capable of, 505, 539
 gain or benefit, relevance, 528
 handling distinguished, 626–629
 appropriation, when complete, 504
 husband and wife, liability. *See* HUS-
  BAND AND WIFE
 information, of, 506
 land, of—
  limitations on, 506, 507
  persons not in possession, by, 507
 legislation, interpretation of, 488–490
 mens rea, 525–539
 mistake, property got by, 518–522
 mushrooms, 507, 508
 new law, interpretation, 488–490
 obtaining by deception and, relationship between, 520–522
 ownerless property, 524, 525
 permanent deprivation—
  borrowing or lending, 537, 538
  conditional intention, 536, 537, 607
  disposal regardless of rights, 534–
   536
  intent, need for, 532, 535, 536
  no risk, where, 535, 536
  owner's interest, of, 539
  parting with condition as to return,
   538, 539
  physical impossibility and, 535,
   536
  statutory provision, 534
  "thing", significance of, 538
 plants, of, 507, 508
 property—
  belonging to another—
   apparent possession, another in,
    497–499
   charity, 516
   consent, and, 499–503
   contract of sale or return, 516,
    517
   difficulties of meaning, 509
   equitable interests, 513
   general rule, 510–513
   joint owners, where, 509, 523,
    682
   loan or advance, 514, 515
   mistake, got by, 518–522
   particular purpose, received for,
    513–518
   possession or control, 511, 512

Theft—*continued*
 property—*continued*
  belonging to another—*continued*
   proprietary right or interest, 512,
    513
   trust property, 513
  corporations, belonging to—
   company involved, where, 523,
    524
   directors, appropriation by, 522,
    523
   partnership, where, 523
   statutory provision, 522
  definition of, 504
  mistake got by—
   deception or theft, where, 520–
    522
   obligation to restore, 518, 519,
    520
   salary or wages overpaid, 518,
    519, 520
   statutory provision, 518
   too much change, 519
  punishment for, 490
  receiving as appropriation, 466
  restitution of goods. *See* RESTITUTION
  selling as appropriation, 497, 498
  sponsor money, 516
  stolen goods, handling. *See* HAND-
   LING STOLEN GOODS
  taking as appropriation, 497
  tenants, appropriation of fixtures by,
   506, 507
  things growing wild, 507, 508
  temporary deprivation. *See* TEMPOR-
   ARY DEPRIVATION
  trustees, appropriation by, 506, 507,
   513
  wild creatures, limitations on, 508,
   509
  willingness to pay, relevance, 528
Threats. *See also* BLACKMAIL; DURESS;
  INTIMIDATION
 assault, as, 376, 377
 force, of, in order to steal, 540–543
 kill, to, 356, 357
  written, 356
 procurement of woman, by, 439, 440
 property, to destroy or damage—
  form of threat, 701
  lawful excuse, 700
  offence, 700
 threatening, abusive or insulting
  words or behaviour. *See under*
  PUBLIC ORDER
 unlawful violence, 786, 787, 789, 790,
  791
 violence, of, entering premises with,
  802, 803

Torts,
fraud, conspiracy to commit, 256, 257, 269–276
mens rea, 271–274
vicarious liability in, 162, 163
Transferred Malice. *See under* MENS REA
Treason. *See also* MUTINY AND DISAFFECTION; OFFICIAL SECRETS; SEDITION
alien, by—
British passport, 830
British territory, voluntarily on, 830
family left in U.K., 830, 831
protection of Crown, 831
British subjects, 829, 830
classification of crime, as, 25
compassing king's death—
attempt impossible, 298
constructive treasons, 827
overt act required, 827, 828
duress, fear of death, 231, 232
escape and, 757
king's enemies, adherence to, 828
levying war, 828
misprision of, 26, 27, 833
offences akin to, 832 *et seq.*
overt acts committed abroad, 829
persons who may commit, 829–831
procedure at trials, 831
rescue and, 758
statutory provisions, 827
treason felony—
extension of 1351 Act, 832, 833
overlapping offences, 832, 833
statutory provisions, 832
Trespassing,
burglary, for purposes of, 597–602
firearms, with, 421, 422
premises, on—
foreign missions, of, 811, 812
weapon of offence, with, 811
trespasser, adverse occupation by—
defences, 810
displaced residential occupier, requirement by, 809, 810
entry as, 809
protected intending occupier, requirement by, 809, 810
statutory provisions, 809
violent entry on premises, 802 *et seq.*
See also PREMISES
Trustees,
land, theft of, 506, 507
trust property, theft of, 513

Unincorporated Bodies,
criminal liability, 176

Valium,
intoxication after taking, 217
Vehicles,
burglary from, 606
inhabited, violent entry of, 804
taking. *See* CONVEYANCES
Vessels,
burglary from, 606
inhabited, violent entry of, 755
taking. *See* CONVEYANCES
Vicarious Liability,
aiding and abetting, 169
attempt, 169
contempt of court, 776
corporations. *See* CORPORATIONS
delegation, principle of—
authority must be delegated, 164–166
café, prostitutes in, example, 164
co-licensees, example, 164
degree of delegation, 165, 166
doubts on, 166
partial or temporary, 165
statute, to give effect to, 164
libel, criminal, 825
master, liability of, 162, 163, 164
master's act in law—
examples of, 168
more extensive principle, 167, 168
"selling" cases, 167
participant, liability only as, 163
participation, mode of, 168, 169
principal—
in first degree, need to distinguish, 131
master only as, 168, 169
servant, cases where, 168, 169
public nuisance, for, 798
servant's liability, nature of, 168
statute, to give effect to, 164
strict liability—
common law offences, 99
distinguished, 163
tort, in, 162
unincorporated bodies, 176
Victims,
parties to crime, as, 158–160
Violence,
fear or provocation of—
offences of, 790, 791
penalties, 790
threatening, abusive or insulting words or behaviour. *See under* PUBLIC ORDER
threats of unlawful, 786, 787, 789, 790, 791

Violent disorder. *See also* PUBLIC ORDER

Violent disorder—*continued*
common purpose, no need for, 789
continuing offence, 785
definition of, 788, 789
indictable offence, 788
intoxicated person, 789
numbers present, 785, 788, 789
penalties, 788
proof, burden of, 785, 789
public or private place, 785
statutory provisions, 788, 789
triable either way, 789

Weapons. *See also* FIREARMS; OFFENSIVE
    WEAPONS
aggravated burglary, 609
offence, of—
    offensive weapons distinguished,
        422, 423
    trespassing on premises with, 811
offensive. *See* OFFENSIVE WEAPONS
Wife. *See* HUSBAND AND WIFE
Wild Creatures,
theft of, 508, 509
Wilfully,
mens rea, whether importing, 122–124
Witnesses,
contempt of court by, 771
interfering with, 753, 754–756
intimidation of, 772, 781–783
perjury. *See* PERJURY
Women,
abduction of. *See* ABDUCTION

Women—*continued*
procurement of. *See under* SEXUAL
    OFFENCES
Wounding,
grievous bodily harm—
    assault, whether inflict implies, 399
    burglary, ulterior offence in, 607,
        608
    causing and inflicting, 398, 399
    force, whether applied, 399
    meaning, 328
    threats causing, 376, 377
    ulterior intent, as, 402, 403, 608
malice—
    different offences, effect, 401
    foresight of consequences, 67, 401,
        402
    intention or recklessness, 67, 400
    resisting arrest, where, 400
meaning, 397, 398
mens rea, 67, 400
resisting arrest—
    malice, where, 400
    ulterior intent, 402
statutory provisions, 397
ulterior intent, 402
Written Threats. *See also under*
    BLACKMAIL; PUBLIC ORDER
harassment, alarm or distress, caus-
    ing, 792
murder, to, 356
property, to destroy or damage, 701
racial hatred, stirring up, 793